■ THE RESOURCE FOR THE INDEPENDENT TRAVELER

"The guides are aimed not only at young budget travelers but at the indepedent traveler; a sort of streetwise cookbook for traveling alone."

—**The New York Times**

"Unbeatable; good sight-seeing advice; up-to-date info on restaurants, hotels, and inns; a commitment to money-saving travel; and a wry style that brightens nearly every page."

—**The Washington Post**

"Lighthearted and sophisticated, informative and fun to read. [Let's Go] helps the novice traveler navigate like a knowledgeable old hand."

—*Atlanta Journal-Constitution*

"A world-wise traveling companion—always ready with friendly advice and helpful hints, all sprinkled with a bit of wit."

—*The Philadelphia Inquirer*

■ THE BEST TRAVEL BARGAINS IN YOUR PRICE RANGE

"All the dirt, dirt cheap."

—*People*

"Anything you need to know about budget traveling is detailed in this book."

—*The Chicago Sun-Times*

"Let's Go follows the creed that you don't have to toss your life's savings to the wind to travel—unless you want to."

—*The Salt Lake Tribune*

■ REAL ADVICE FOR REAL EXPERIENCES

"The writers seem to have experienced every rooster-packed bus and lunar-surfaced mattress about which they write."

—*The New York Times*

"A guide should tell you what to expect from a destination. Here Let's Go shines."

—*The Chicago Tribune*

LET'S GO PUBLICATIONS

TRAVEL GUIDES

Alaska & the Pacific Northwest 2003
Australia 2003
Austria & Switzerland 2003
Britain & Ireland 2003
California 2003
Central America 8th edition
Chile 1st edition **NEW TITLE**
China 4th edition
Costa Rica 1st edition **NEW TITLE**
Eastern Europe 2003
Egypt 2nd edition
Europe 2003
France 2003
Germany 2003
Greece 2003
Hawaii 2003 **NEW TITLE**
India & Nepal 7th edition
Ireland 2003
Israel 4th edition
Italy 2003
Mexico 19th edition
Middle East 4th edition
New Zealand 6th edition
Peru, Ecuador & Bolivia 3rd edition
South Africa 5th edition
Southeast Asia 8th edition
Southwest USA 2003
Spain & Portugal 2003
Thailand 1st edition **NEW TITLE**
Turkey 5th edition
USA 2003
Western Europe 2003

CITY GUIDES

Amsterdam 2003
Barcelona 2003
Boston 2003
London 2003
New York City 2003
Paris 2003
Rome 2003
San Francisco 2003
Washington, D.C. 2003

MAP GUIDES

Amsterdam
Berlin
Boston
Chicago
Dublin
Florence
Hong Kong
London
Los Angeles
Madrid
New Orleans
New York City
Paris
Prague
Rome
San Francisco
Seattle
Sydney
Venice
Washington, D.C.

NEW ZEALAND
INCLUDING FIJI

REBECCA BIENSTOCK EDITOR
MARK KIRBY ASSOCIATE EDITOR

RESEARCHER-WRITERS
DAN BARNES
KATE DAMON
MARK KIRBY
MARLY OHLSSON
TOM MERCER
TAMARA REICHBERG

ERIC GRAVES BROWN MAP EDITOR
CHRISTOPHER BLAZEJEWSKI MANAGING EDITOR
ALEXANDRA LEICHTMAN TYPESETTER

MACMILLAN

HELPING LET'S GO If you want to share your discoveries, suggestions, or corrections, please drop us a line. We read every piece of correspondence, whether a postcard, a 10-page email, or a coconut. Please note that mail receiveNew Zealand including Fiji after May 2003 may be too late for the 2004 book, but will be kept for future editions. **Address mail to:**

> Let's Go: New Zealand including Fiji
> 67 Mount Auburn Street
> Cambridge, MA 02138
> USA

Visit Let's Go at **http://www.letsgo.com,** or send email to:

> feedback@letsgo.com
> Subject: "Let's Go: New Zealand including Fiji"

In addition to the invaluable travel advice our readers share with us, many are kind enough to offer their services as researchers or editors. Unfortunately, our charter enables us to employ only currently enrolled Harvard students.

Published in Great Britain 2003 by Macmillan, an imprint of Pan Macmillan Ltd.
20 New Wharf Road, London N1 9RR
Basingstoke and Oxford
Associated companies throughout the world
www.panmacmillan.com

Maps by David Lindroth copyright © 2003 by St. Martin's Press.

Published in the United States of America by St. Martin's Press.

Let's Go: New Zealand including Fiji Copyright © 2003 by Let's Go, Inc. All rights reserved. Printed in the United States of America. No part of this book may be used or reproduced in any manner whatsoever without written permission except in the case of brief quotations embodied in critical articles or reviews. Let's Go is available for purchase in bulk by institutions and authorized resellers. For information, address St. Martin's Press, 175 Fifth Avenue, New York, NY 10010, USA.

ISBN: 1-4050-0076 7
First edition
10 9 8 7 6 5 4 3 2 1

Let's Go: New Zealand including Fiji is written by Let's Go Publications, 67 Mount Auburn Street, Cambridge, MA 02138, USA.

Let's Go® and the LG logo are trademarks of Let's Go, Inc.
Printed in the USA on recycled paper with soy ink.

ADVERTISING DISCLAIMER All advertisements appearing in Let's Go publications are sold by an independent agency not affiliated with the editorial production of the guides. Advertisers are never given preferential treatment, and the guides are researched, written, and published independent of advertising. Advertisements do not imply endorsement of products or services by Let's Go, and Let's Go does not vouch for the accuracy of information provided in advertisements.

If you are interested in purchasing advertising space in a Let's Go publication, contact: Let's Go Advertising Sales, 67 Mount Auburn St., Cambridge, MA 02138, USA.

HOW TO USE THIS BOOK

PRICE RANGES AND RANKINGS

Our researchers list establishments in order of value from best to worst, with absolute favorites receiving the Let's Go thumbs-up (👍). Since the best value does not always mean the cheapest price, we have incorporated a system of price ranges in the guide. The table below lists how prices fall within each bracket. The numbered icons are based on the lowest cost for one person, excluding special deals or prices. Read listings carefully, as accommodations listed as ❶ often offer higher-range lodging options as well.

NEW ZEALAND	❶	❷	❸	❹	❺
ACCOMMODATIONS	NZ$1-14	NZ$14-20	NZ$20-35	NZ$35-90	NZ$90-150
FOOD	NZ$1-6	NZ$6-12	NZ$12-18	NZ$18-24	NZ$24-40
FIJI	❶	❷	❸	❹	❺
ACCOMMODATIONS	FJ$1-12	FJ$12-23	FJ$23-45	FJ$45-65	FJ$65-150
FOOD	FJ$1-3	FJ$3-7	FJ$7-10	FJ$10-14	FJ$14-30

ORGANIZATION OF THIS BOOK

DISCOVER. **Discover New Zealand and Fiji** provides an overview of travel in both nations, including **suggested itineraries** on how to spend your time there.

ESSENTIALS. This section outlines the practical information you need for traveling in New Zealand and Fiji.

NEW ZEALAND AND FIJI. The **New Zealand** and **Fiji** chapters provide you with a general introduction to the history, culture, and flavor of these countries.

OUTDOOR NEW ZEALAND. A jam-packed resource for all things outdoor and adventure in New Zealand, including bungy jumping, kayaking, and tramping. The nine **Great Walks** and several other tramps are labeled throughout the book with a 🌿. If you're planning to hit the great outdoors, thumb through this chapter first.

COVERAGE. New Zealand is divided into 15 chapters, beginning with Auckland and moving roughly from north to south; Fiji is detailed in an additional two chapters. **Black tabs** in the margins will help you navigate chapters quickly.

APPENDIX. The appendix includes a **phrasebook** of handy Kiwi phrases and short Maori-English, Fijian-English, and Fijian Hindi-English dictionaries. It also has a climate chart and a table of holidays and festivals in New Zealand and Fiji.

PHONE CODES AND TELEPHONE NUMBERS

Area codes for each New Zealand city and town appear opposite the name of the region and are denoted by the ☎ icon. Phone numbers in text are also preceded by the ☎ icon. There are no phone codes in Fiji.

A NOTE TO OUR READERS The information for this book was gathered by Let's Go researchers from May through August of 2002. Each listing is based on one researcher's opinion, formed during his or her visit at a particular time. Those traveling at other times may have different experiences since prices, dates, hours, and conditions are always subject to change. You are urged to check the facts presented in this book beforehand to avoid inconvenience and surprises.

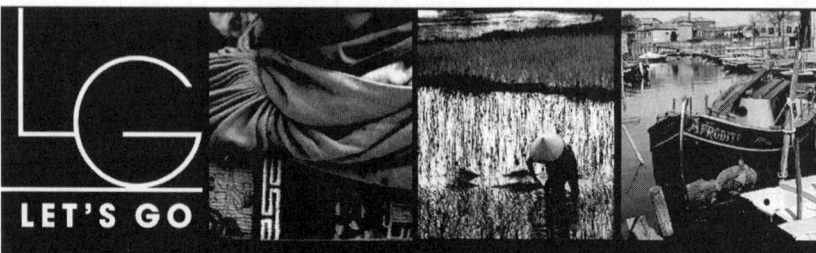

CONTENTS

**DISCOVER
NEW ZEALAND AND FIJI.......1**
When to Go 3
Things to Do 3
Suggested Itineraries 6

ESSENTIALS....................9
New Zealand Essentials 28
Fiji Essentials 41
Other Resources 44

**ALTERNATIVES
TO TOURISM....................46**
Studying Abroad 46
Working 47
Volunteering 49

**NEW ZEALAND
(AOTEAROA)...................50**

**OUTDOOR
NEW ZEALAND.................63**

AUCKLAND.....................76
HAURAKI GULF 99
Waiheke Island 99
Great Barrier Island 102

NORTHLAND.................105
Whangarei 105
BAY OF ISLANDS 109
Paihia 109
THE FAR NORTH 119
Kaitaia 119
Aupouri Peninsula and Cape Reinga 120
HOKIANGA REGION 122
Waipoua Forest Park 124
Dargaville 125

**COROMANDEL
PENINSULA...................127**
Thames 129
Coromandel 132
The Northern Tip 135

**THE WAIKATO
AND KING COUNTRY........142**
Hamilton 142
Raglan 149
Waitomo 154

BAY OF PLENTY.............160
Rotorua 161
Tauranga 170

**EAST COAST AND
HAWKE'S BAY...............179**
EAST COAST 179
Gisborne 179
THE EAST CAPE 184
Te Urewera National Park 186
HAWKE'S BAY 190
Napier 190

**TAUPO AND
TONGARIRO..................198**
Taupo 199
Tongariro National Park 207
Ohakune 214

**TARANAKI
AND WANGANUI.............218**
New Plymouth 219
The Taranaki Coast 222
Egmont National Park 223
Wanganui 229
Whanganui National Park 233

**WELLINGTON
AND AROUND................240**
WELLINGTON 240
KAPITI COAST 253
THE WAIRARAPA 257
Palmerston North 258

**MARLBOROUGH
AND NELSON.................262**
MARLBOROUGH 262
Picton 262
Marlborough Sounds 267
Kaikoura 273
NELSON 278
Nelson Lakes National Park 283
GOLDEN BAY 285
Abel Tasman National Park 285
Kahurangi National Park 296

CANTERBURY................302
CHRISTCHURCH 302
Akaroa and the Banks Peninsula 315
CANTERBURY SKIING 316
Arthur's Pass 321
SOUTH CANTERBURY 323
Tekapo 325
Aoraki/Mt. Cook National Park 327

THE WEST COAST..........330
Westport 330
Punakaiki 334
Greymouth 335
Hokitika 338
FRANZ JOSEF AND FOX GLACIERS 341
Franz Josef Glacier 341
Fox Glacier 346

OTAGO.......................348
Dunedin 349
Oamaru 358
THE SOUTHERN LAKES 361
Queenstown 361
Wanaka 378
Mt. Aspiring National Park 386

SOUTHLAND.................390
Invercargill 391
THE CATLINS 394
Owaka 396
STEWART ISLAND 400

FIORDLAND.................406
Te Anau 406
The Milford Road 414
Milford Sound 415
Manapouri 420
Southern Scenic Route 424

FIJI (VITI).....................429

VITI LEVU....................439
NADI 439

LAUTOKA 445
KINGS ROAD 449
Rakiraki 450
Nananu-i-ra 452
THE CORAL COAST 452
Sigatoka and Surrounds 452
Pacific Harbour 455
INTERIOR HIGHLANDS 456
Koroyanitu National Heritage Park 459
SUVA 460

OUTER ISLANDS...........468
THE MAMANUCA GROUP 468
Mana Island 469
THE YASAWA GROUP 471
Waya and Wayasewa (Waya Lailai) 471
Nacula Tikina 474
Tavewa 475
LOMAIVITI GROUP 476
Ovalau 476
Levuka 477
VANUA LEVU 481
Savusavu 482
Labasa 484
TAVEUNI 486
Around Somosomo, Naqara, and Waiyevo 488
Matei and Surrounds 490
Southern Taveuni 491
Eastern Taveuni 492
KADAVU 493

APPENDIX....................495
INDEX........................499

RESEARCHER-WRITERS

Dan Barnes — *Auckland, Bay of Plenty, East Coast, Northland, Taupo*

A Midwesterner with a scholarly appetite for the international scene, Dan deftly conquered Auckland's cosmopolitan sprawl, though his heart went most to small-town New Zealand. Experienced as the managing map editor for the *Let's Go 2002* series, we adored his choice cartography while Kiwi lasses swooned at his Renaissance talents: crafting haikus, hotwiring cars, and jumping out of planes.

Kate Damon — *New Zealand skiing, Viti Levu*

A former researcher for *Let's Go: Eastern Europe 2001*, Kate brought her anthropologically-trained eye to the South Pacific streets, churning out stellar interviews and perceptive copy. Fijian brothels, curious iguanas, and computer meltdowns were no match for this seasoned traveler. Halfway through, Kate traded sand for snow, showing off her ski skills while researching the Kiwi slopes.

Mark Kirby — *Fiordland, Otago, Southland, 67 Mt. Auburn St.*

Mark leapt from trekking the sands of Utah for *Let's Go: Southwest USA 2002* to bungy jumping off the bridges of Queenstown. Long days dodging sea lions and weathering backcountry storms would end with pints of hokey pokey ice cream and Monteith's ale. His editor's refreshments came in the form of his brilliant prose, his inspiring outdoors coverage, and his return to the office in Cambridge.

Marly Ohlsson — *Canterbury, Marlborough, Nelson, West Coast*

Marly faced down impertinent sheep, scaled glacial cliffs, and made challenging swimwear decisions with the determination of a lifetime athlete and outdoors woman. Hailing from the backwoods of Vancouver, her previous credentials include researching for *Let's Go: Europe 2000*, editing *Let's Go: Alaska and the Pacific Northwest 2001*, and serving as publicity manager for the *Let's Go 2002* series.

Tom Mercer — *Coromandel, Taranaki, Waikato, Wanganui, Wellington*

Texas-native and Nabokov-scholar, Tom departed Moscow to tame the New Zealand wilds. A researcher for *Let's Go: Alaska and the Pacific Northwest 2001* and editor of *Let's Go: Southwest USA 2002*, Tom carried with him a pen practiced at bringing nature to the page. Looking past dolphin-pestering eco-tourism and sleepy towns, he strode reverently through New Zealand's backcountry solitude.

Tamara Reichberg — *Fijian outer islands, Suva*

After tackling the rainforests of Costa Rica as a researcher for *Let's Go: Central America 2002*, Tamara journeyed to Fiji's outer isles, where she traded dengue fever remedies for kava root and hammocks for *bures*. Our history and literature major hopped from island to island, taking time to document sugarcane farms and backpacker resorts along the way. Her infectious smile endeared her to locals while her "sexy" prose captured Fiji's every curve.

CONTRIBUTING WRITERS

Amelia Lester is a a contributing writer for *Australian Vogue* and the Australian *Sun Herald*. Originally from Sydney, Australia, she now attends college in Cambridge, Massachusetts.

Steve Most was a researcher for *Let's Go: New Zealand 2002*. He recently earned his Ph.D. and is now a post-doctoral fellow in Nashville, Tennesee.

Ann Robinson was a researcher for *Let's Go: New Zealand 2000* and *2002* and an editor for the 2001 guide. A recipient of the Fulbright scholarship, she received her Masters in History at Victoria University in Wellington. She is now working as a consultant in Boston, Massachusetts.

ACKNOWLEDGMENTS

TEAM ENZED THANKS: The RWs—Dan, Marly, Tom, and the other guy for going it alone; Kate and Tamara for tackling Fiji with finesse. Chris for guidance and good times. Alex (NZ's greatest fan) for insightful suggestions and home-baked goodies. Eric for choice cartography and Rasta vibes. Dan for being the NZ map guru. The Commonwealth Pod for bleating sheep and colonial conviviality. Brian for '80s vocals. And final thanks to pavlova, penguins, and possum fur nipple warmers.

REBECCA THANKS: Mark, I can't imagine working with a more talented and easygoing person. Thank you for dedicating your year to NZ. David and Kathleen for Aero bars and laughter. Sonja and Teresa for tales from Wales. Candy, Anna, Ankur, and Angela for office fun. Chris for orange bowl cut memories. Erzulie for banana bread. Antoinette for style and spunk. Roger for trying sushi. Alex for unique perspectives. Andrew for always being there. Amber for four crazy years. Hillary, Nicole, Ingrid, Annie, Ari, Rebecca, Kimmie, and Kianja for growing up with me. Mom and Dad for love, support, and tropical travels.

MARK THANKS: Rebecca, for your devotion and drive, this book is yours. I'm honored to have contributed to your vision. To Mom & Dad for the freedom to get out there. To Paul & Pat; to JD for showing me what wild is; to the smilin' lass out west, groping with this country. To Hal, for teaching me writing and dreaming. To David, Kathleen, Sonja, and Teresa—'twas a jolly good craic. To Bry for being there as usual. To Sarah and Max for ice cream, shirtless crepes, and BBQs. Finally, to Michael P.

ERIC THANKS: Rebecca and Mark, it was a pleasure. Dan, you made my work easy. Thanks also to Bob and Pete for stirring it up, Asu for his desert, and K for her love of dogs.

Editor
Rebecca Bienstock
Associate Editor
Mark Kirby
Managing Editor
Christopher Blazejewski
Map Editor
Eric Graves Brown

Publishing Director
Matthew Gibson
Editor-in-Chief
Brian R. Walsh
Production Manager
C. Winslow Clayton
Cartography Manager
Julie Stephens
Design Manager
Amy Cain
Editorial Managers
Christopher Blazejewski, Abigail Burger, D. Cody Dydek, Harriett Green, Angela Mi Young Hur, Marla Kaplan, Celeste Ng
Financial Manager
Noah Askin
Marketing & Publicity Managers
Michelle Bowman, Adam M. Grant
New Media Managers
Jesse Tov, Kevin Yip
Online Manager
Amélie Cherlin
Personnel Managers
Alex Leichtman, Owen Robinson
Production Associates
Caleb Epps, David Muehlke
Network Administrators
Steven Aponte, Eduardo Montoya
Design Associate
Juice Fong
Financial Assistant
Suzanne Siu
Office Coordinators
Alex Ewing, Adam Kline, Efrat Kussel
Director of Advertising Sales
Erik Patton
Senior Advertising Associates
Patrick Donovan, Barbara Eghan, Fernanda Winthrop
Advertising Artwork Editor
Leif Holtzman
Cover Photo Research
Laura Wyss
President
Bradley J. Olson
General Manager
Robert B. Rombauer
Assistant General Manager
Anne E. Chisholm

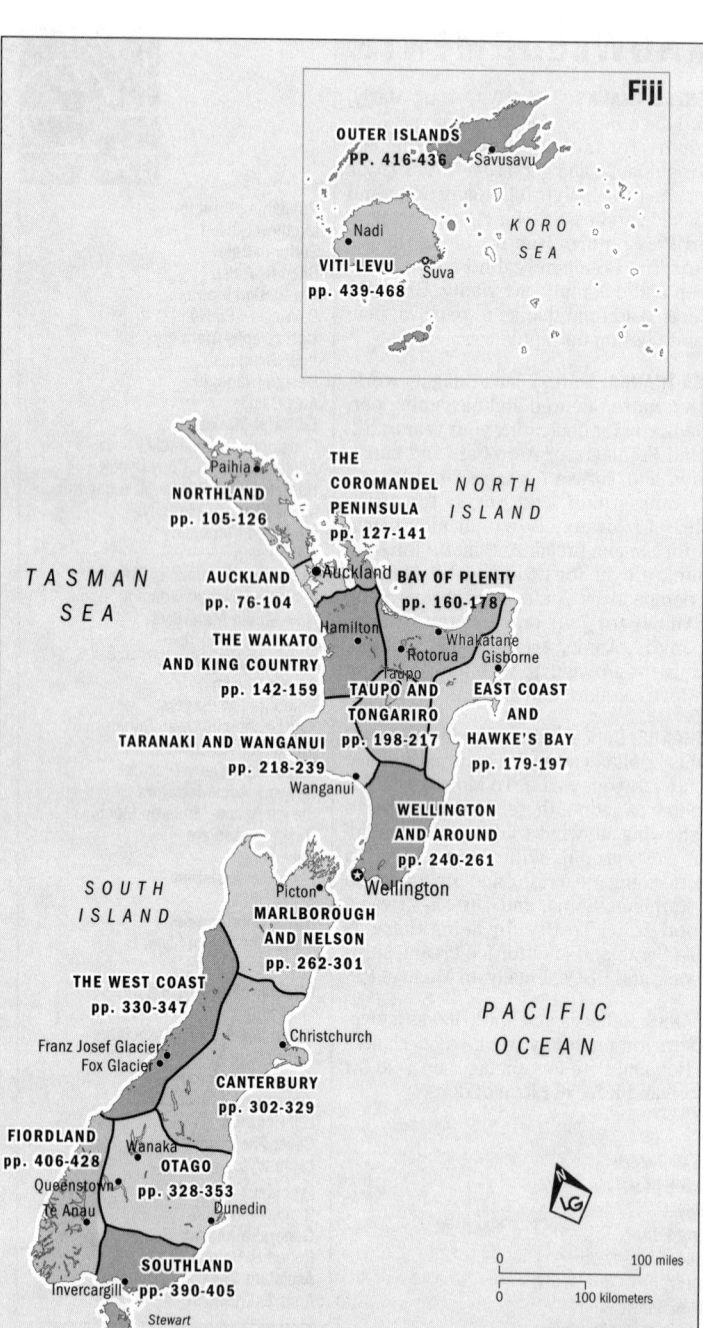

WHO WE ARE

A NEW LET'S GO FOR 2003
With a sleeker look and innovative new content, we have revamped the entire series to reflect more than ever the needs and interests of the independent traveler. Here are just some of the improvements you will notice when traveling with the new *Let's Go*.

MORE PRICE OPTIONS
Still the best resource for budget travelers, *Let's Go* recognizes that everyone needs the occassional indulgence. Our "Big Splurges" indicate establishments that are actually worth those extra pennies (pulas, pesos, or pounds), and price-level symbols (❶ ❷ ❸ ❹ ❺) allow you to quickly determine whether an accommodation or restaurant will break the bank. We may have diversified, but we'll never lose our budget focus—"Hidden Deals" reveal the best-kept travel secrets.

BEYOND THE TOURIST EXPERIENCE
Our Alternatives to Touism chapter offers ideas on immersing yourself in a new community through study, work, or volunteering.

AN INSIDER'S PERSPECTIVE
As always, every item is written and researched by our on-site writers. This year we have highlighted more viewpoints to help you gain an even more thorough understanding of the places you are visiting.

IN RECENT NEWS. *Let's Go* correspondents around the globe report back on current regional issues that may affect you as a traveler.

CONTRIBUTING WRITERS. Respected scholars and former *Let's Go* writers discuss topics on society and culture, going into greater depth than the usual guidebook summary.

THE LOCAL STORY. From the Parisian monk toting a cell phone to the Russian *babushka* confronting capitalism, *Let's Go* shares its revealing conversations with local personalities—a unique glimpse of what matters to real people.

FROM THE ROAD. Always helpful and sometimes downright hilarious, our researchers share useful insights on the typical (and atypical) travel experience.

SLIMMER SIZE
Don't be fooled by our new, smaller size. *Let's Go* is still packed with invaluable travel advice, but now it's easier to carry with a more compact design.

FORTY-THREE YEARS OF WISDOM
For over four decades *Let's Go* has provided the most up-to-date information on the hippest cafes, the most pristine beaches, and the best routes from border to border. It all started in 1960 when a few well-traveled students at Harvard University handed out a 20-page mimeographed pamphlet of their tips on budget travel to passengers on student charter flights to Europe. From humble beginnings, *Let's Go* has grown to cover six continents and *Let's Go: Europe* still reigns as the world's best-selling travel guide. This year we've beefed up our coverage of Latin America with *Let's Go: Costa Rica* and *Let's Go: Chile;* on the other side of the globe, we've added *Let's Go: Thailand* and *Let's Go: Hawaii*. Our new guides bring the total number of titles to 61, each infused with the spirit of adventure that travelers around the world have come to count on.

DISCOVER

NEW ZEALAND AND FIJI

Pristine wilderness, pure waters, majestic mountains, and exotic life forms—New Zealand's unique geology and biology make it a peerless exhibition of the wondrous natural world. Formed by the collision of continental plates and separated from the rest of the globe by immense stretches of ocean, this island nation is a living diorama of earlier times. The country's isolation evokes images of an exotic land—and so it should. New Zealand's startling landscapes are otherworldly: psychedelic lakes mirror volcanic peaks, Jurassic-era forests shelter rare birds, aqua-blue glowworms glitter in mysterious caverns, and twin glaciers creep toward a rugged shoreline. This diverse landscape is matched only by the tremendous number of ways to enjoy it. With a vast network of accessible hikes and the constant invention of new activities from bungy jumping to zorbing, New Zealand is the world's most stupendously scenic outdoor amusement park. Admission may require crossing oceans, perhaps even circumnavigating the globe; in return, New Zealanders will make the edge of the world both accessible and hospitable. With an abundance of outstanding hostels and an ever-growing tourism industry primed for exploration, relaxation, and adventure, a visit to New Zealand turns a fascinatingly foreign land into an inspiring and welcoming home.

Several thousand kilometers to the northeast, seductive sunshine and azure waters lure visitors into "Fiji time," a slowed-down chronology that sets island life to the perfect tempo for repose. Fiji possesses the fanciful splendor of a tropical paradise—cool misty waterfalls cascade through lush virgin rainforests, remote mountain villages offer immersion in cultural tradition, and world-class underwater reefs present incomparable diving opportunities. Whether a stop en route to another holiday or a vacation destination itself, Fiji's relaxed pace and golden beaches make it an excellent island getaway.

NEW ZEALAND FACTS	FIJI FACTS
CAPITAL: Wellington	**CAPITAL:** Suva
AGE OF THE INDEPENDENT NEW ZEALAND: 54 years	**AGE OF THE INDEPENDENT FIJI:** 32 years
AGE OF THE NEW ZEALAND RUGBY FOOTBALL UNION: 109 years	**NUMBER OF ISLANDS** Over 300
TALLEST MOUNTAIN: Mt. Cook, 3768m	**LENGTH OF COASTLINE:** 1129km
COMBINED LENGTH OF GREAT WALKS: 512.5km	**PERCENT OF POPULATION LIVING ON VITI LEVU:** 70%
SHEEP POPULATION AT LAMBING TIME: 130 million	**ANNUAL NUMBER OF VISITORS TO FIJI:** Over 400,000
RATIO OF SHEEP TO PEOPLE AT LAMBING TIME: 35:1	**YEAR OF FIRST TV BROADCAST IN FIJI:** 1991
AVERAGE AMOUNT OF SHEEPMEAT CONSUMED: 17kg per person annually	**LAST TIME HUMAN MEAT WAS CONSUMED:** late 1800s

WHEN TO GO

Most travelers to New Zealand visit during the sunny summer months (Nov.-Feb.), when temperatures are warmer, mountain-tops are snow-free, and the tourist infrastructure is in high gear. High-season visitors will have the greatest variety of options, but will also be surrounded by the largest crowds. The low-season occurs during the dead of winter (May-Sept.), when many tours and activities, with the exception of skiing and snowboarding, shut down. The best combination of weather, tour availability, and crowd size occurs during the shoulder seasons (Mar.-Apr. and Oct.-Nov.), although in some popular areas (such as Queenstown and Taupo), the crowds continue year-round. Travelers from the Northern Hemisphere should remember that seasons reverse after crossing the equator.

Fiji stays warm and tropical year-round. Kiwis and Aussies crowd the country's beaches during summer months (Nov.-Feb.), but cooler temperatures and less rain make a winter visit (May-Oct.) more enjoyable. Visibility for diving is best between April and November. For detailed charts on **climate** and **national holidays and festivals** in both New Zealand and Fiji, see the **Appendix**, p. 495.

THINGS TO DO

The sheer number of activities in New Zealand and Fiji can be overwhelming. No matter how long you stay, there's aways one more wave to surf, peak to summit, and cove to paddle. The information and itineraries below should help orient you to the endless possibilities and suggest how you might divide your time between them. For more specific regional attractions, see the **Highlights of the Region** box at the beginning of each chapter.

ADVENTURE

New Zealand's drug of choice is adrenaline...in high quantities. Kiwis have turned their natural surroundings into a true adventurer's wonderland—almost every New Zealand town has its own bungy jumping, skydiving, jetboating, white-water rafting, and kayaking operations. In the adventure capital **Queenstown** (p. 361), two bungy jump companies outdo each other with higher and more death-defying jumps while three jetboat operations compete for the most 360° spins. The North Island's energetic equivalent, **Taupo** (p. 199), lures budgeteers with one of the world's cheapest skydives. Meanwhile, in nearby **Rotorua** (p. 161), the Kiwi-conceived Zorb lets travelers live out their hamster dreams in clear giant balls.

However, not all of New Zealand's adventure activities involve rash action: swimming with dolphins in **Kaikoura** (p. 273), exploring the **Franz Josef and Fox Glaciers** (p. 341), contemplating glowworms in the caves of **Waitomo** (p. 154), sea-kayaking in the **Marlborough Sounds** (p. 267), and skiing and snowboarding down the sparkling peaks of the **Tongariro** (p. 210), **Canterbury** (p. 316), and **Southern Lakes** ski fields (p. 370 and p. 383) are but a handful of the hundreds of possibilities.

Both New Zealand and Fiji offer world-class **scuba diving**. In Fiji, Kadavu's **Astrolabe Reef** (p. 493), Viti Levu's **Beqa Lagoon,** and the **Rainbow Reef** between Vanua Levu and Taveuni teem with soft coral and tropical fish. In New Zealand, **Poor Knights Islands** (p. 109) were one of Jacques Cousteau's favorite dive sites. Choice breaks greet **surfers** on Fiji's **Coral Coast** (p. 452) and New Zealand's Manu Bay, near **Raglan** (p. 149).

THINGS TO DO

TRAMPING

Few places in the world combine spectacular scenery with a solid infrastructure for exploring it. With almost one-third of the country protected as wilderness areas and National Parks by the Department of Conservation (DOC), New Zealand leads the field. You don't have to be Sir Edmund Hillary, the first person to successfully scale Everest—and a Kiwi himself—to enjoy New Zealand's world-renowned walking tracks. The nine specially-designated **Great Walks** (3-5 days) cater to trampers of all experience levels. If an overnight seems too much, there are day hikes departing from virtually every town covered in this guide.

New Zealand has a greater concentration of diverse landforms than anywhere else in the world and many tramps to explore them all. The **Milford Track** ("the world's finest walk," p. 417), the **Kepler Track** (p. 411), and the **Routeburn Track** (p. 375) wander through the majestic fjords and ranges of **Fiordland National Park**. Golden shoreline scenery along the popular **Abel Tasman Coastal Track** (p. 288) unfolds to both sea-kayakers and trampers. On the North Island, the **Tongariro Northern Circuit** (p. 210) tip-toes between towering volcanoes, passing eerie geothermal scenery along the way.

Fiji's answer to New Zealand's tramps are hikes through untouched wilderness and hilltop villages. Trekkers pass through Viti Levu's interior highlands and Fiji's highest peak on **Koroyanitu National Park's Mt. Batilamu trek** (p. 459). Meanwhile, on the isle of **Taveuni, Bouma National Heritage Park** (p. 492) takes hikers through lush rainforests and cascading waterfalls.

CULTURAL DISCOVERIES

Before the arrival of gawking tourists or European settlers, the **Maori** people revered the sacred sublimity of the New Zealand landscape. Calling the islands *Aotearoa* ("the land of the long white cloud"), the Maori hunted ostrich-like moa birds, prospected for valuable *pounamu* (jade or greenstone), and imbued the landscape with ancestral spirits. Today, Maori art and culture remain a vibrant part of Kiwi life. Travelers take time to witness this cultural heritage by attending a *hangi* (feast) in **Rotorua** (p. 168), **Christchurch** (p. 312), or **Queenstown** (p. 361). Other opportunities to discover Maori tradition include a visit to the **Museum of New Zealand Te Papa Tongarewa** in Wellington (p. 250) and a night's stay at a Maori *marae* (meeting grounds) along the **Whanganui River Journey** (p. 235).

For a different "taste" of New Zealand culture, sample one of the many Kiwi **wines** and **beers**. Vintages from the **Hawke's Bay** (p. 190), **Blenheim** (p. 271), **Central Otago** (p. 372), and **Martinborough** (p. 257) regions have earned international renown. Beer-making in New Zealand is a strongly regional affair: **Monteith's** in **Greymouth** (p. 335), **Speight's** in **Dunedin** (p. 353), **DB** in **Timaru** (p. 324), and **Sunshine Brewing** in **Gisborne** (p. 184) are just some of the many Kiwi brewers who open their doors for **brewery tours**.

Though Fiji lacks vineyards, it makes up for it with **kava** (see **I Can't Feel My Lips,** p. 436). The Fijian national drink is traded, shared, and enjoyed just about everywhere in the islands. However, for a true cultural experience, "grog" should be sipped at traditional ceremony in Viti Levu's **Interior Highlands** (p. 456). Highland villages such **Navala** (p. 457), **Bukuya** (p. 458), and **Abaca** (p. 459) welcome travelers for overnight **village stays.** Be sure to read **Fijian Village Etiquette** (p. 433) before a visit.

OFF THE BEATEN PATH

The best way to discover off-the-beaten-path New Zealand is to rent or buy a car and get out there to find it. New Zealand has a glut of cheap cars for backpackers, and the popularity of buy-and-sell-back schemes is growing. With some advanced planning, many remote areas are also accessible by bus. New Zealand's small towns offer a wealth of nearby beaches, forests, and hillsides for casual exploration. In the **Marlborough Sounds** (p. 267), roaming travelers visit the homes of dolphins, seals, and penguins and find comfortable dwellings for themselves in the area's many outstanding accommodations. The **Coromandel Peninsula** (p. 132) has unsealed roads winding through uncut kauri forests and along relaxing coastal vistas. Small towns like **Papatowai** and **Curio Bay** in New Zealand's southernmost region, the **Catlins** (p. 394), delight with rugged, pastoral coasts and snug, welcoming hostels.

With over 300 islands, Fiji affords numerous virgin beaches, concealed coves, and pristine waters. East of Viti Levu, the isle of **Taveuni** (p. 486) is blanketed in green rainforests and surrounded by the world-renowned Rainbow Reef. On Ovalau, the former Fijian capital of **Levuka** (p. 477) is now a charming colonial town with historic walks.

LET'S GO PICKS

BEST PLACE TO BOOZE: You won't be alone atop the tables in **The Holy Cow** in Taupo (NZ; p. 202). On the other hand, if you prefer to get smashed, try the **Smash Palace** in Gisborne (NZ; p. 183). One of Fiji's oldest social clubs, the **Ovalau Club** in Levuka (F; p. 477) has a long history of intoxicating foreigners.

BEST PLACE TO TEMPT FATE: The skydive over **Taupo** (NZ; p. 204), or **Franz Josef** and **Fox Glaciers** (NZ; p. 341 and p. 346). Or, the world's most famous bungy jump in adrenaline-happy **Queenstown** (NZ; p. 361).

BEST AND WORST USE OF "PROTECTION": A.J. Hackett made his first commercial **bungy** (NZ; p. 368) with a latex rubber cord, making Queenstown the bungy capital of the world. **Te Urewera National Park** (NZ; p. 186), meaning "burnt penis," illustrates the perils of forgetting to make sure the fire is *out* before falling asleep.

BEST PLACE TO SEE THE KING: Elvis himself still lives on in **Hawera** (NZ; p. 228), thanks to one Kiwi's obsession with the rock 'n' roll legend.

BEST PLACE TO GET LOST: Entering the **Fiordland National Park** (NZ; p. 406) backcountry will leave you in delightfully wet and muddy solitude.

BEST PLACE TO SNOG: When you roll into **Whangarei** (NZ; p. 105) late at night, you'll find urban cowboys from Auckland whooping it up to DJ rhythms. In **Queenstown**, The World (NZ; p. 366) will keep you turning all night long. In **Ohakune** (NZ; p. 214), everyone knows each other by name by day, but forgets them by night.

BEST PLACE TO DIG YOUR OWN GRAVE AND LIE IN IT: You have to dig the thermal pools at **Hot Water Beach** (NZ; p. 139) yourself.

BEST PLACE TO MEET THE LOCALS: Stay with Fijian families in **Navala** (F; p. 457) and **Bukuya** (F; p. 458). Visit a *marae* and enjoy a *hangi* with Maori in **Rotorua** (NZ; p. 168).

BEST PLACE TO BE WASHED UP: Swimming with dolphins in **Kaikoura** (NZ; p. 273), surfing in **Raglan** (NZ; p. 149), soaking in the hot pools of **Hanmer Springs** (NZ; p. 277), and learning how to snowboard at **Cardrona** (NZ; p. 383).

BEST MEAT MARKET SINCE THE MISSIONARIES CONVERTED THE CANNIBALS: The throngs of twenty-something backpackers crowding the Mamanuca Group's **Beachcomber Island** (F; p. 470) are all pining for a piece of tanned flesh.

SUGGESTED ITINERARIES

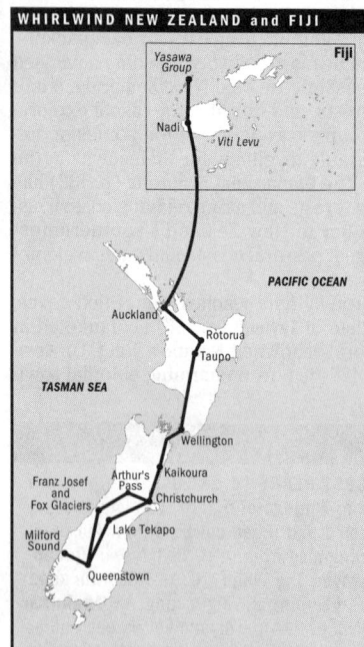

WHIRLWIND NEW ZEALAND AND FIJI (2 WEEKS) After flying into bustling **Nadi** (p. 439), the gateway to Fiji, take a deep breath and catch the first seaplane to Tavewa Island in the **Yasawas** (p. 471). After a couple days of indulgence in the brilliant waters of the Blue Lagoon, regretfully head back to Nadi and hop a flight to **Auckland** (p. 76). After a day in this metropolitan mecca's flavorful neighborhoods, and a throbbing night on the town, gather your pack and your throbbing head and immediately aim south for **Wellington** (p. 240), stopping at the hot spas and bubbling mud pools of **Rotorua** (p. 161) to rejuvenate, and at the adrenaline factory of **Taupo** (p. 199) on the way. After taking in Te Papa, Wellington's national museum in the capital city, make the ferry crossing to the **South Island** and head further south, stopping for the day in **Kaikoura** (p. 273) to swim with the dolphins. After refueling at the cafes of **Christchurch** (p. 302), take the spectacular train ride through **Arthur's Pass** (p. 321) to the rugged **West Coast**. Continue south to the enormous **Franz Josef** and **Fox Glaciers** (p. 341), where you can attack a behemoth of blue ice with only your ice axe and crampons to protect you. Take a deep breath before dashing to the madness of **Queenstown** (p. 361), where jumping off bridges and up onto bars to dance is all in a day's work. As much as your wallet may hurt at this point, a day trip to the awe-inspiring **Milford Sound** (p. 415) is worth the expense for a grand finale before a last breathtaking stop at **Lake Tekapo** (p. 325). Back in **Christchurch,** drop by the International Antarctic Centre (p. 312) on the way to the airport to become reacquainted with the cold, cruel world before you hop on your plane to rejoin it.

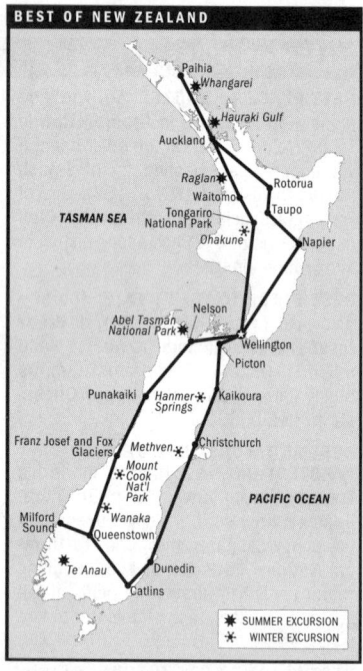

BEST OF NEW ZEALAND (5 WEEKS) Beginning in **Auckland** (p. 76), the trendy neighborhood of Ponsonby is pleasant for an afternoon's exploration and the nightclubs along K Rd. (p. 91) will keep you grooving until dawn. After Auckland, loop through Northland, up to the **Bay of Islands** (p. 109), a hot spot for watersports, and back down past the enormous trees of the

SUGGESTED ITINERARIES

Kauri Coast (p. 125). Next, **Rotorua's** (p. 161) geothermal wonders and Maori *hangi* will make a camera-happy tourist out of you. Farther south, **Taupo** (p. 199), set on New Zealand's largest lake, is the high-adrenaline capital of the North Island and the site of the country's cheapest skydive.

SUMMER SPOTS

Grab your togs and your shades and hit the surfer's safari to **Raglan** (p. 149), the "city kids on a rampage" nightlife of **Whangarei** (p. 105), the **Hauraki Gulf's** (p. 99) collection of seaside respites and sun worshipers, **Abel Tasman National Park** (p. 285), the playground of the tramped and tented, and **Te Anau** (p. 406), the walking capital of the world.

To calm your frayed nerves, the Art Deco town of **Napier** (p. 190) offers relaxation in liquid form—a day (or two) with a bottle (or two) of wine from one of the surrounding vineyards will leave you well prepared to catch the train to the nation's compact cosmopolitan capital. Absorb some culture at **Wellington's** Te Papa museum (p. 250) before crossing the Cook Strait to the beautiful and remote reaches of the **South Island**. Once you are back on dry land, the small gateway town of **Picton** (p. 262) and the nearby **Marlborough Sounds** (p. 267) encourage returning to the water, with stunning sanctuaries for seals, penguins, dolphins, and laid-back travelers. **Kaikoura** (p. 273) is the place to get all wet, swimming with playful dolphins in the stunning surf before moving on to **Christchurch** (p. 302), where New Zeaand shows its British colors.l

WINTER SPOTS

In frosty weather, you shouldn't miss the North Island slopes around **Ohakune** (p. 214), the South Island snowbunnies in **Methven** (p. 319) and **Wanaka** (p. 378), the majesty of **Mt. Cook National Park** (p. 327), or the revitalizing hot springs of **Hanmer Springs** (p. 277).

Christchurch is a great base for fantastic day trips to **Akaroa** and the **Banks Peninsula** (p. 315). From Christchurch, you can continue south to the university pub town of **Dunedin** (p. 349), where rugby, beer, and music represent the Father, Son, and Holy Ghost. From Dunedin, explore the rugged pastures, forests, and beaches of the **Catlins** (p. 394) before blitzkrieging **Queenstown** (p. 361), where all of New Zealand's heart-stopping adventure activities converge. In the middle of the Queenstown insanity (plan on spending NZ$100 per day in town), take a daytrip into the heart of the spectacular **Fiordland National Park** to the mystical **Milford Sound** (p. 415). Nearby **Wanaka** and **Glenorchy** are also worthwhile stops. As you head north, you'll pass the ice palaces of **Franz Josef and Fox Glaciers** (p. 341), several billion cubic meters of moving solid blue ice that you can, and should, explore in shorts. One of the most explosive West Coast highlights is the pancake rocks in **Punakaiki** (p. 334), which stupefy both tourists and scientists with their unique formations. Before heading back to the North Island, stay a day in **Nelson** (p. 262), one of its sunniest cities. The weekend flea market is an especially bright spot, and a great farewell to the South Island before you zip back through Picton to Wellington and northward to the volcanic moonscapes of Tongariro National Park for the **Tongariro Crossing** (p. 207), one of New Zealand's finest one-day tramps. Then, it's on to **Waitomo** (p. 154) for spelunking, glowworms, and rafting before tracing a weary but reluctant path back toward Auckland.

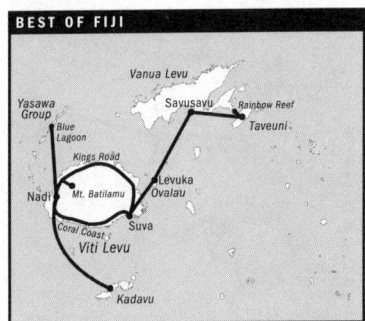
BEST OF FIJI

BEST OF FIJI (3 WEEKS) Sleep off your jetlag in **Nadi** (p. 439), taking a day to unwind and explore the lush Garden of the Sleeping Giant. Oil yourself up and grab your togs before catching the next seaplane to the **Yasawa Group** (p. 471). Revel in budget paradise as you island hop from beach to beach. Be sure to hit the **Blue Lagoon** before heading back to Nadi. After a quick walk through the city's bustling streets, it's up, up, and away to the remote isles of **Kadavu** (p. 493) to whet your scuba appetite on the world-renowned **Astrolabe Reef.** Fly back to Nadi, then head east along the **Kings Road** (p. 449) for a rough taste of rural Fiji or venture south along the Queens Road and the **Coral Coast** (p. 452) if surfing and resort glitz are up your alley. From both roads, treks to the **Interior Highlands** (p. 456) are a definite must to meet, greet, and eat the Fijian way. Take a day to hike over **Mt. Batilamu** (p. 459), the highest peak in Fiji. Regardless of your path, soak up some city sights in **Suva** (p. 460), Fiji's capital. Board a boat and go back in time to **Levuka** (p. 477), Fiji's first capital set on the island of **Ovalau** (p. 476). Stop by Lovoni Village before cruising back to Suva to catch a ride to **Savusavu** (p. 482) on **Vanua Levu** (p. 481). Enjoy the remote waters of this under-touristed island by kayak and catch a ferry to **Taveuni** (p. 486), the "Garden Island," where you'll have your pick of some of Fiji's best accommodations. Dive the scuba-friendly waters of **Rainbow Reef** (p. 489) before returning to Nadi's international airport.

FOLLOWING FRODO: A *LORD OF THE RINGS* TOUR OF NEW ZEALAND

National pride runs high over the tremendous success of Peter Jackson's *The Fellowship of the Ring*. This itinerary lists the filming locations of some of the cinematic trilogy's most spectacular scenes. Landing in **Auckland** (p. 76), spend a day acclimating yourself and finishing those last pages of *The Return of the King* at Ponsonby's hip cafes (p. 89). To reach the out-of-the-way filming locations, you'll want to either **rent** or **buy a car** while in town. Heading south along Rte. 24, the grassy hillocks of **Matamata** (near Cambridge, p. 147) appeared in *The Fellowship of the Ring* as **Hobbiton.** Pray the Ring Wraiths don't discover you as you enter the Vulcan landscape surrounding **Taupo** (p. 199) and plunge into the mythic realm of **Mordor.** Composite shots of the area's volcanoes appear in the film series as **Mt. Doom.** Northwest of Wellington, the forested scenery of the **Kapiti Coast** (p. 253) near **Otaki** became the **East Road** from Hobbiton and the elfin sanctuary of **Rivendell.** Crossing the Cook Strait, head west towards **Nelson** (featured as **Dimrill Dale;** p. 278) and **Takaka** (**Chetwood Forest;** p. 291) for more *Rings* locations. Further South, Peter Jackson found inspiration for the inhospitable peaks of **Misty Mountains** among the ruggedly majestic **Southern Alps** (p. 361). The placid waters of **Queenstown's Lake Wakatipu** (p. 361) appeared on film as **Lothlorien.** Jackson filmed extensively throughout the Southern Alps region and many locals can point to specific locations and boast of their part as an extra. Finally, the plains at Twizel, near New Zealand's highest peak, **Mt. Cook** (p. 327), hosted the dramatic battle of the **Pelenor Fields.**

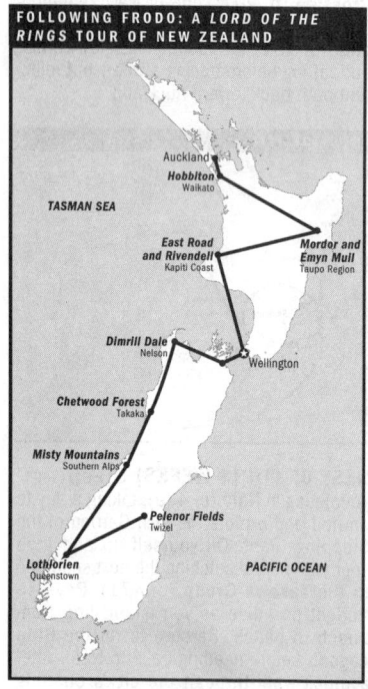

FOLLOWING FRODO: A *LORD OF THE RINGS* TOUR OF NEW ZEALAND

ESSENTIALS

ENTRANCE REQUIREMENTS
Passport (p. 11). Required for all visitors to New Zealand and Fiji.
Visa (p. 13). Not usually required unless you are planning to work or study. Contact an embassy or consulate for specific information.
Work Permit (p. 13). Required for all foreigners, except those from Australia, who plan to work in New Zealand and Fiji.
Driving Permit (p. 32). Required for all those planning to drive in New Zealand and Fiji.

EMBASSIES AND CONSULATES

CONSULAR SERVICES ABROAD

For listings of foreign embassies and consulates in New Zealand and Fiji, consult the country-specific **Essentials** sections (p. 28 and p. 41, respectively).

NEW ZEALAND

Australia: High Commission, Commonwealth Ave., Canberra ACT 2600 (☎02 6270 4211; fax 6273 3194; azhccba@austarmetro.com.au).

Canada: High Commission, 99 Bank St. (Ste. 727), Ottawa ON K1P 6G3 (☎613-238-5991; fax 238-5707; www.nzhcottawa.org). All visa queries ☎613-238-6097.

Fiji: Embassy and High Commission, Reserve Bank Building, Pratt St., P.O. Box 1378, Suva (☎311 1422; fax 300 0842; www.embassy.kcom.ne.jp/newzealand/).

Ireland: Consulate General, 37 Leeson Park, Dublin 6 (☎01 660 4233; fax 660 4228; nzconsul@indigo.ie).

Japan: Embassy, 20-44 Kamiyama-cho, Shibuya-ku, Tokyo 150 0047 (☎03 3467 2271; fax 3467 2278; www.nzembassy.com/japan).

South Africa: High Commission, Block C, 2nd fl., Hatfield Gardens, 1110 Arcadia St., Pretoria 0028 (☎012 342 8656; fax 342 8640; nzhc@global.co.za).

UK: High Commission, New Zealand House, 80 Haymarket, London SW1Y 4TQ (☎020 7930 8422; fax 839 4580; www.nzembassy.com/uk).

US: Embassy, 37 Observatory Circle NW, Washington, D.C. 20008 (☎202-328-4848; fax 667-5227; www.nzemb.org). Consulate-General, 12400 Wilshire Blvd., Ste. 1150, Los Angeles, CA 90025 (☎310-207-1605; fax 207-3605).

FIJI

Australia: Embassy, 9 Beagle St., Red Hill, Canberra ACT 2600; P.O. Box E159, Queen Victoria Tce. (☎06 239 6872; fax 295 3283).

Canada: Honorary Consul, 130 Slatter St., Ste. 750, Ottawa ON K1P 6E2 (☎613-233-9252; fax 594-8705).

Japan: Embassy, NOA Building, 3-5, 2 Chome Azabudai, Minato-ku, Tokyo 106 0047 (☎03 3587 2038; fax 3587 2063; fijiambrishi@hotmail.com).

New Zealand: High Commission, 31 Pipitea St., Thorndon, P.O. Box 3940, Wellington (☎04 473 5401; fax 499 1011; www.fiji.org.nz).

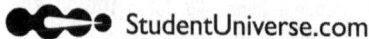

UK: Embassy and High Commission, 34 Hyde Park Gate, London SW7 5BN (☎ 020 7584 3661; fax 7584 2838; fijirepuk@compuserve.com).

US: Embassy and High Commission, 2233 Wisconsin Ave. NW, Ste. 240, Washington, D.C. 20007 (☎ 202-337-8320; fax 337-1966; fijiemb@earthlink.com).

TOURIST OFFICES ABROAD

NEW ZEALAND. The ever-helpful **New Zealand Tourism Board (NZTB)** offices can provide information galore about any aspect of the country. Their web page (www.purenz.com) is easy to use and enormously helpful.

   Australia: 35 Pitt St., Level 8, P.O. Box R1546, Sydney NSW 2000 (☎ 02 9247 5222; fax 9241 1136).

   Japan: World Trade Centre Building, 12th fl., 2-4-1 Hamamatsu-cho, Minato-ku, Tokyo 105-6112 (☎ 3 5400 1311; fax 3 5400 1312).

   South Africa: Holiday House, 158-160 Hendrik Verwoerd Dr., Randburg 2125 (☎ 011 289 8186; fax 289 8023).

   UK: New Zealand House, Haymarket, London SW1Y 4TQ (☎ 0171 930 1662; fax 839 8929; enquiries@nztb.govt.nz).

   US: 501 Santa Monica Blvd., Ste. 300, Santa Monica, CA 90401 (☎ 800-388-5494 or 310-395-7480; fax 310-395-5453). 780 3rd Ave., Ste. 1904, New York, NY 10071 (☎ 212-832-8482; fax 832-7602).

FIJI. The **Fiji Visitors Bureau (FVB)** staffs a number of extremely friendly and helpful tourist offices in Fiji and the rest of the world. Their impressive website (www.bulafiji.com) is a great starting point for planning your trip. Travelers should take note that the FVB is the *only* official tourist organization in Fiji.

   Australia: St. Martins Tower, 31 Market St., Level 12, Sydney 2000 (☎ 02 9264 3399; fax 9264 3060; www.bulafiji-au.com).

   Canada: 1275 West 6th Ave. Vancouver BC, V6HIA6 (☎ 800-932-3454; fax 310-670-2318; fiji@primenet.com)

   Japan: NOA Building, 14th fl., 3-5, 2 Chome Azabudai, Minato-ku, Tokyo 106 (☎ 03 3587 2038; fax 3587 2563; www.bulafiji-jp.com).

   New Zealand: 48 High St., 5th fl., P.O. Box 1179, Auckland (☎ 09 373 2133; fax 309 4720; www.bulafiji.co.nz).

   US: 5777 West Century Blvd., Ste. 220, Los Angeles, CA 90045 (☎ 310-568-1616; fax 670-2318; www.bulafiji-americas.com).

   UK: 34 Hyde Park Gate, London SW7 5BN (☎ 171 584 3661; fax 584 2838; fijirepuk@compuserve.com).

DOCUMENTS AND FORMALITIES

PASSPORTS

REQUIREMENTS. All visitors need valid passports to enter New Zealand or Fiji. Passports must be valid for at least three months beyond the time you intend to stay; returning home with an expired passport is illegal and may result in a fine.

NEW PASSPORTS. Citizens of Australia, Canada, Ireland, the United Kingdom, and the United States can apply for a passport at the nearest post office, passport office, or court of law. Citizens of South Africa can apply for a passport at the nearest office of Foreign Affairs. Any new passport or renewal applications must be filed well in advance of the departure date, although most passport offices offer rush services for a very steep fee.

PASSPORT MAINTENANCE. Be sure to photocopy the page of your passport with your photo and passport number, as well as any visas, travel insurance policies, plane tickets, and traveler's check serial numbers. Carry one set of copies in a safe place, apart from the originals, and leave another set at home.

If you lose your passport, immediately notify the local police and the nearest embassy or consulate of your home government. Any visas stamped in your old passport will be lost. In an emergency, ask for temporary traveling papers that will permit you to re-enter your home country. US Embassies and Consulates no longer issue American passports abroad. Consulates can only issue temporary passports, which cannot be extended. More detailed info regarding lost and stolen passports is available at http://www.usembassy.it/cons/acs/passport-lost.htm

VISAS AND WORK PERMITS

Citizens of the US, Canada, Japan, Ireland, South Africa, the UK, and most European nations do not need a visa to enter New Zealand or Fiji. For those travelers who need them, visas are available at most embassies and consulates and are usually valid for three months in New Zealand and four months in Fiji.

Upon arrival, travelers not requiring visas are granted **visitor permits.** To qualify for a visitor permit, you must display your passport and a valid airline ticket to a country to which you have the right of entry. In New Zealand, you may also need to display sufficient funds to support yourself during your stay (usually NZ$1000). Major credit cards and traveler's checks also constitute sufficient funds. The visitor permit allows you to visit New Zealand for three months (six months for UK citizens) and Fiji for four months; to extend your stay, you must reapply at an immigration office (fee NZ$60) before your current permit expires.

Be sure to double-check on entrance requirements at the nearest embassy or consulate for up-to-date info before departure. US citizens can also consult www.pueblo.gsa.gov/cic_text/travel/foreign/foreignentryreqs.html. Admission as a visitor to New Zealand or Fiji does not include the right to work, which is authorized only by a work permit. For information on **work permits,** see **Alternatives to Tourism,** p. 46.

IDENTIFICATION

When you travel, always carry two or more forms of identification on your person, including at least one photo ID; a passport combined with a driver's license or birth certificate is usually adequate. Many establishments, especially banks, may require several IDs to cash traveler's checks.

TEACHER, STUDENT AND YOUTH IDENTIFICATION. The **International Student Identity Card (ISIC),** the most widely accepted form of student ID, provides discounts on sights, accommodations, food, and transport. The ISIC is preferable to an institution-specific card (such as a university ID) because it is more likely to be honored abroad. All cardholders have access to a 24hr. emergency helpline for medical, legal, and financial emergencies (in North America call 877-370-ISIC, elsewhere call US collect +1 715-345-0505). Holders of US-issued cards are also eligible for insurance benefits (see **Insurance,** p. 21).

The **International Teacher Identity Card (ITIC)** offers teachers the same insurance coverage as well as similar but limited discounts. For travelers who are 25 years old or under but are not students, the **International Youth Travel Card (IYTC)** also offers many of the same benefits as the ISIC.

Each of these identity cards costs US$22 or equivalent. ISIC and ITIC cards are valid for roughly one and a half academic years; IYTC cards are valid for one year from the date of issue. Many student travel agencies (see p. 24) issue the cards. For a listing of issuing agencies, or for more information, contact the **International**

Student Travel Confederation (ISTC), Herengracht 479, 1017 BS Amsterdam, Netherlands. (☎ +31 20 421 28 00; fax 421 28 10; www.istc.org.)

CUSTOMS

As island nations, New Zealand and Fiji are free from many pests and crop blights, and they'd like to keep it that way. Before leaving for your travels, find out what you can bring home. Upon **entering** New Zealand or Fiji, you must declare all food, plant, and animal goods, dead or alive, so look out for the blue declaration of goods forms. Restricted goods may or may not be confiscated, but they must be declared. Camping equipment must also be declared. Customs officials will likely inspect your equipment and, in New Zealand, used equipment may be cleaned.

Upon **returning home,** you must declare all items you acquired abroad and pay a **duty** on the value of those articles that exceed the allowance set by your country's customs service. The Goods and Services Tax and Value Added Tax are not refundable upon leaving. Goods purchased at **duty-free** shops abroad are not exempt from duty or sales tax at your point of return.

NEW ZEALAND. Personal effects and goods up to a total combined value of NZ$700 are admitted free of duty or **Goods and Services Tax** (**GST**; see **Taxes,** p. 18). Anything beyond the allowance must be declared and is charged a duty in addition to the GST. Visitors over the age of 17 are also allowed to enter with the following concessions duty- and tax-free: 200 cigarettes, 50 cigars, 250g of tobacco, or a mixture of all three not weighing more than 250g; 4.5L of wine (six 750mL bottles) or 4.5L of beer; and one bottle containing not more than 1125mL of liquor. For more information on customs for New Zealand, go to www.quarantine.govt.nz.

FIJI. Personal effects and goods not intended for sale are admitted free of duty or **Value Added Tax** (**VAT**; see **Taxes,** p. 18). Dutiable goods (other than alcohol or tobacco) up to FJ$400 are admitted and charged accordingly. Visitors over 17 are also allowed to enter with the following concessions duty- and tax-free: 500 cigarettes or any combination of tobacco products not weighing more than 500g; 2L of liquor or 4L of wine/beer or any combination that does not exceed the prescribed limit for any one item.

MONEY

CURRENCY AND EXCHANGE

New Zealand's unit of currency is the **New Zealand Dollar (NZ$).** Coins come in denominations of 5, 10, 20, and 50 cents, $1, and $2; notes come in denominations of $5, $10, $20, $50, and $100. Fiji's unit of currency is the **Fiji Dollar (FJ$).** Coins come in denominations of 1, 2, 5, 10, 20, and 50 cents, and $1; notes come in denominations of $1, $2, $5, $10, $20, and $50. Carry considerably more small change in Fiji for transportation costs. **Unless otherwise specified, all prices in the text are either in New Zealand Dollars or Fiji Dollars (depending on region).** Typical bank hours in New Zealand are Monday through Friday from 9am to 4:30pm, and major banks include Bank of New Zealand (BNZ), Westpac Trust, Australia and New Zealand Banking Group (ANZ), and ASB Bank (ASB). Bank hours in Fiji are typically Monday through Thursday from 9:30am to 3pm, and 9:30am to 4pm on Fridays. Major banks in Fiji include ANZ, National Bank, Fiji Westpac, and Bank of Hawaii.

The currency charts below are based on August 2002 exchange rates. Check the currency converter on financial websites such as www.bloomberg.com and www.xe.com or a large newspaper for the latest exchange rates.

ESSENTIALS

NZ DOLLARS ($)		
AUS$1 = NZ$1.17		NZ$1 = AUS$0.85
CDN$1 = NZ$1.39		NZ$1 = CDN$0.72
FJ$1 = NZ$1.01		NZ$1 = FJ$0.99
IR£1 = NZ$2.69		NZ$1 = IR£0.37
ZAR1 = NZ$0.21		NZ$1 = SAR4.78
US$1 = NZ$2.18		NZ$1 = US$0.48
UK£ 1= NZ$3.33		NZ$1= UK£0.30
EUR€1 = NZ$2.12		NZ$1 = EUR€0.47

FIJIAN DOLLARS ($)		
AUS$1 = FJ$1.16		FJ$1 = AUS$0.86
CDN$1 = FJ$1.37		FJ$1 = CDN$0.73
IR£1 = FJ$2.66		FJ$1 = IR£0.38
NZ$1 = FJ$0.99		FJ$1 = NZ$1.01
ZAR1 = FJ$0.21		FJ$1 = ZAR4.83
US$1 = FJ$2.16		FJ$1 = US$0.46
UK£1 = FJ$3.29		FJ$1 = UK£0.30
EUR€1 = FJ$2.10		FJ$1 = EUR€0.48

As a general rule, it's cheaper to convert money in New Zealand or Fiji than at home. However, you should bring enough foreign currency to last for the first 24 to 72 hours of a trip to avoid being penniless should you arrive after bank hours or on a holiday. ATMs are widespread in New Zealand and are often the best and easiest way to acquire New Zealand currency. While not as common in Fiji, there are still readily accessible ATMs in many larger towns and cities.

Try to go only to banks that have at most a 5% margin between their buy and sell prices. Since you lose money with every transaction, **convert large sums** (unless the currency is depreciating rapidly), **but no more than you'll need.**

TRAVELER'S CHECKS

Traveler's checks are one of the safest and least troublesome means of carrying funds. Several agencies and banks sell them for a small commission. Each agency provides refunds if your checks are lost or stolen, and many provide additional services, such as toll-free refund hotlines abroad, emergency message services, and stolen credit card assistance.

   American Express: In Australia ☎ 800 251 902; in New Zealand ☎ 0800 441 068; in the UK ☎ 0800 521 313; in the US and Canada ☎ 800-221-7282; elsewhere US collect +1 801-964-6665; www.aexp.com. *Cheques for Two* can be signed by either of 2 people traveling together.

   Visa: Checks available (generally with commission) at banks worldwide. For the location of the nearest office, call Visa's service centers: in NZ ☎ 0508 600 300; in the US ☎ 800-227-6811; in the UK ☎ 0800 89 50 78; elsewhere UK collect ☎ +44 020 7937 8091; www.visa.com.

CREDIT, ATM, AND DEBIT CARDS

Credit cards are generally accepted in most New Zealand and urban Fijian establishments, and often offer superior exchange rates—up to 5% better than the retail rate used by banks and exchange services. Credit cards may additionally offer insurance or emergency help, and are sometimes required to reserve hotel rooms or rental cars. **MasterCard** and **Visa** are the most welcomed; **American Express** cards work at some ATMs and at AmEx offices and major airports.

   Cash cards—popularly called ATM cards—are widespread in New Zealand and urban Fiji. Depending on your bank's system, using an ATM card may be the best option for getting money while in New Zealand. ATMs get the same wholesale exchange rate as credit cards, but there is often a limit on the amount of money you can withdraw per day (around US$500) and there is typically also a fee of US$1-5 per withdrawal. To locate ATMs in New Zealand, call the two major international money networks, **Cirrus** (in the US ☎ 800-424-7787; www.mastercard.com; US$3-5 fee for overseas withdrawal) or **Visa/PLUS** (in the US ☎ 800-843-7587; www.visa.com). The back of your ATM card will have the symbol of networks with which it is compatible.

Debit cards are a relatively new form of purchasing power in which the money is withdrawn directly from the holder's checking account. Debit cards often also function as ATM cards and can be used to withdraw cash from associated banks and ATMs throughout New Zealand and Fiji.

GETTING MONEY FROM HOME

WESTERN UNION. Travelers from the US, Canada, and the UK can wire money abroad through Western Union's money transfer services. (In the US ☎ 800-325-6000, in Canada ☎ 800-235-0000, in the UK ☎ 0800 83 38 33, in Australia ☎ 800 501 500, in New Zealand ☎ 800 270 000, in South Africa ☎ 0860 100031, in Fiji ☎ 331 4812.) To locate the nearest Western Union, consult www.westernunion.com.

US STATE DEPARTMENT (US CITIZENS ONLY). In dire emergencies only, the US State Department will forward money within hours to the nearest consular office, which will then disburse it according to instructions for a US$15 fee. If you wish to use this service, you must contact the Overseas Citizens Service division of the US State Department (☎ 202-647-5225; nights, Sundays, and holidays ☎ 202-647-4000).

COSTS

If you stay in hostels, prepare your own food, and stick mostly to the free and low-budget natural attractions, you could probably get by on NZ$40-50 per day in New Zealand and FJ$35-45 in Fiji. The single biggest cost of your trip will probably be your round-trip **airfare** to New Zealand and/or Fiji (see **Airfares**, p. 23.) A bus pass (see **Buses**, p. 31 and p. 42), car rental (see **Cars**, p. 32 and p. 42), or island-hopping pass (see **By Plane**, p. 42) is another major pre-departure expense. You should keep handy larger amounts of cash when you are traveling into more rural areas. Also, don't forget to budget for emergency reserve funds (at least US$200).

STAYING ON A BUDGET. Considering that saving a few dollars a day over the course of your trip might pay for days or weeks of additional travel, the art of penny-pinching is worth learning. Learn to take advantage of freebies: in New Zealand and Fiji, nature is often the best attraction in town. Bring a **sleepsack** (a sheet folded in half and sewn together) to save on linen charges, and do your laundry in the sink (unless explicitly prohibited from doing so). You can split **accommodations** costs (in hotels and some hostels) with trustworthy fellow travelers; multi-bed rooms almost always work out cheaper per person than single rooms. Happy hours can provide both food and drink at reduced prices and going early to bars and clubs, especially in a big city, can often reduce or eliminate cover charges. You can also buy food in **supermarkets** or **local markets** instead of eating out.

TIPPING AND BARGAINING

Tipping is neither customary nor expected in New Zealand and Fijian establishments. In restaurants, gratuity is always included in the price of the meal. If the service provided is exceptional, you may consider offering a small tip, but it is by no means necessary or even common.

TAXES

NEW ZEALAND. A **departure tax** is levied at the airport. Prices depend on the airport but are generally NZ$20 for those over 12. The fee, sometimes included in your flight price, must be paid in New Zealand dollars. A 12.5% **Goods and Services Tax (GST)** is applied to all goods for sale and is usually included in display prices (see **Customs,** p. 15).

FIJI. A similar **departure tax** of FJ$20 is levied at the airport for those over 12. A uniform 10% **Value Added Tax (VAT)** is placed on goods for sale (see **Customs,** p. 15).

SAFETY AND SECURITY

The following section is intended as a general guide; refer to the **Essentials** sections of **New Zealand** (p. 29) and **Fiji** (p. 41) for more detailed information.

PERSONAL SAFETY

EXPLORING. While traveling in New Zealand and Fiji, try to blend in as much as possible. Respect local customs by dressing more conservatively. Familiarize yourself with your surroundings before setting out, and carry yourself with confidence; if you must check a map on the street, duck into a shop. If you are traveling alone, be sure that someone at home knows your itinerary.

When walking at night, stick to busy, well-lit streets and avoid dark alleyways. Do not attempt to cross through parks, parking lots, or other large, deserted areas. If you feel uncomfortable, leave as quickly and directly as you can, but don't allow fear of the unknown to turn you into a hermit.

When hiking, however, stick to marked and guide-posted paths. Do not venture beyond these boundaries. Always carry maps of the trail you are hiking. If you feel disoriented, immediately stop and check your map, or ask passersby for assistance. It is always best to venture into unfamiliar trails with company, and we do not recommend hiking in the dark or during inclement weather.

SELF DEFENSE. There is no sure-fire way to avoid all the threatening situations you might encounter when you travel, but a good self-defense course will give you confidence to combat unwanted advances. **Impact, Prepare, and Model Mugging** can refer you to local self-defense courses in the US (☎ 800-345-5425). Visit

TRAVEL ADVISORIES. The following government offices provide travel information and advisories by telephone, by fax, or via the web:

Australian Department of Foreign Affairs and Trade: ☎ 02 6261 1111; www.dfat.gov.au.

Canadian Department of Foreign Affairs and International Trade (DFAIT): in Canada ☎ 800-267-8376, elsewhere +1 613-944-4000; www.dfait-maeci.gc.ca. Call for their free booklet, *Bon Voyage...But.*

Fiji Ministry of Foreign Affairs: www.fiji.gov.fj.

New Zealand Ministry of Foreign Affairs: ☎ 04 494 8500; fax 494 8506; www.mft.govt.nz/trav.html.

United Kingdom Foreign and Commonwealth Office: ☎ 020 7008 0232; fax 7008 0155; www.fco.gov.uk.

US Department of State: ☎ 202-647-5225, automatic faxback 647-3000; http://travel.state.gov. For the free *A Safe Trip Abroad,* call 512-1800.

SAFETY AND SECURITY ■ 19

www.impactsafety.org for a list of nearby chapters. Workshops (2-3hr.) start at US$50; full courses run US$350-500.

DRIVING. Kiwis and Fijians drive on the left side of the road. For long drives in desolate areas, invest in a cellular phone and a roadside assistance program. Be sure to park your vehicle in a garage or well-traveled area, and use a steering wheel locking device in larger cities. **Sleeping in your car** is one of the most dangerous ways to get your rest. For info on the perils of **hitchhiking,** see p. 35.

TERRORISM. There are no known terrorist organizations or cells in New Zealand or Fiji. After the September 11 attacks on the United States, both countries have pledged themselves against terrorism. As of August 2002, the US Department of State has released no travel warnings for either country. Although there is low risk of any terrorist attacks or activity in New Zealand or Fiji, travelers should still stay alert for suspicious behavior throughout their stay, especially in crowded areas and on public transportation.

FINANCIAL SECURITY

PROTECTING YOUR VALUABLES. While traveling, *you* may be your worst enemy. Travelers often find within a few days of arrival they are so enamored of the friendly and mellow Kiwis and Fijians that their eternal vigilance begins to fade. Contrary to appearances, theft—while uncommon in New Zealand—does occur, and the number of reported thefts in Fiji has increased recently. There are a few steps you can take to minimize your risk. First, **bring as little with you as possible.** Leave expensive watches, jewelry, cameras, and electronic equipment at home. Second, buy a few combination **padlocks** to secure your belongings either in your pack—which you should **never leave unattended**—or in a hostel or train station locker. Third, **carry as little cash as possible;** instead carry traveler's checks and ATM/credit cards, keeping them in a **money belt** along with your passport and ID cards. Fourth, **keep a small cash reserve separate from your primary stash.** This should entail about US$50 sewn into or stored in the depths of your pack, along with your traveler's check numbers and important photocopies.

ACCOMMODATIONS AND TRANSPORTATION. Never leave your belongings unattended; crime occurs in even the most demure-looking hostel or hotel. Bring your own **padlock** for hostel lockers, and don't ever store valuables in any locker. In hostel shares, don't tempt your roommates by leaving a wallet or purse unattended. Be aware of the location of your belongings when traveling by bus or train. If traveling by **car,** don't leave valuables in it while you are away. If you do elect to hitchhike (see **Hitchhiking,** p. 35, for more on the dangers of doing so), always keep your belongings in the car with you.

DRUGS AND ALCOHOL

Remember that you are subject to the laws of the country in which you travel, not to those of your home country, and it is your responsibility to familiarize yourself with these laws before leaving. The legal **drinking age** in both New Zealand and Fiji is 18. First-time drunk-driving offenders in New Zealand can receive three months imprisonment, a NZ$4500 fine, and a six-month license suspension. Illegal drugs are, well, illegal. Possession of marijuana in New Zealand can result in a three-month imprisonment and a NZ$1000 fine; selling is punishable with a maximum sentence of eight years. Possession of harder drugs can result in a NZ$1000 fine and a six-month imprisonment; selling them can put you in jail for life. Fiji enforces similarly harsh drug laws, and in some situations penalties exceed those in New Zealand. If you carry **prescription drugs** while you travel, it is vital to have a copy of the prescriptions and a note from a doctor readily accessible at country borders.

HEALTH

In New Zealand and Fiji, common sense is the simplest prescription for good health. Travelers complain most often about their feet and their gut: drink lots of fluids to prevent dehydration, wear sturdy, broken-in shoes and clean socks, and use talcum powder to keep your feet dry.

BEFORE YOU GO

Preparation can help minimize the likelihood of becoming ill and maximize the chances of receiving effective health care in the event of an emergency. Although medical supplies are readily available in New Zealand, and most larger cities in Fiji have a pharmacy, it is often best to carry a few essential items from home. For tips on packing a basic **first-aid kit** and other health essentials, see **First-Aid Kit,** p. 23.

In your **passport,** write the names of any people you wish to be contacted in case of a medical emergency, and also list any allergies or medical conditions of which you would want doctors to be aware. Carry up-to-date, legible prescriptions or a statement from your doctor stating the medication's trade name, manufacturer, chemical name, and dosage. While traveling, be sure to keep all medication with you in your carry-on luggage.

Travel to New Zealand or Fiji does not require vaccination against infectious diseases. Travelers over two years old should be sure that the following vaccines are up to date: MMR (for measles, mumps, and rubella); DTaP or Td (for diptheria, tetanus, and pertussis); OPV (for polio); HbCV (for haemophilus influenza B); and HBV (for hepatitis B). Those with medical conditions (diabetes, allergies to antibiotics, epilepsy, heart conditions) may want to obtain a stainless-steel **Medic Alert** ID tag (first-year US$35, $20 annually thereafter), which identifies the condition and gives a 24-hour collect-call number. Contact the Medic Alert Foundation, 2323 Colorado Ave., Turlock, CA 95382 (☎ 888-633-4298, outside US 209-668-3333; www.medicalert.org).

ON THE ROAD

JET LAG. Many travelers to New Zealand and Fiji will arrive after a flight of over twelve hours and suffer from severe jet lag. While it may be tempting to sleep, it is best to force yourself to stay awake until early evening. Expect to spend a few days adjusting to the new time zone and plan your trip accordingly.

HOT AND COLD. The most dangerous safety hazards in countries like New Zealand and Fiji are often the most obvious ones. **Heat exhaustion,** characterized by **dehydration** and salt deficiency, can lead to fatigue, headaches, and wooziness. Avoid heat exhaustion by drinking plenty of clear fluids, eating salty foods, and avoiding diuretics such as alcohol or caffeinated beverages. Wear a hat, sunglasses, and a lightweight longsleeve shirt in the hot sun. Continuous heat stress can eventually lead to **heatstroke,** characterized by rising body temperature, severe headache, and cessation of sweating. Heatstroke is rare but serious, and victims must be cooled off with wet towels and taken to a doctor as soon as possible.

Depleted ozone levels and unpolluted air make New Zealand and Fiji high risk areas for **sunburn,** especially on the beach, water, or on the slopes. Apply sunscreen liberally. Protect your eyes with good sunglasses. If you become sunburned, drink more fluids than usual and apply Calamine or an aloe-based lotion.

In some areas of New Zealand during the winter, travelers are at risk for **hypothermia** and **frostbite.** A rapid drop in body temperature is the clearest warning sign of overexposure to cold. Victims may also shiver, feel exhausted, have poor coordination or slurred speech, hallucinate, or suffer amnesia. **Do not let hypothermia victims fall asleep** or their body temperature will continue to drop and they may die. To avoid hypothermia, keep dry, wear layers of synthetics or wool (no cotton!), and stay out of the wind. When the temperature is below freezing, watch for frostbite. If a region of skin turns white, waxy, and cold, **do not rub the area.** Drink warm beverages, get dry, and slowly warm the area with dry fabric or steady body contact, until a doctor can be found.

INSECT-BORNE DISEASES. Many diseases are transmitted by insects—mainly mosquitoes, fleas, and lice. For precautions against **mosquitoes,** see **Wilderness Safety,** p. 70. Both New Zealand and Fiji are virtually free from **ticks.**

FOOD- AND WATER-BORNE DISEASES. New Zealand and Fiji have few dangerous diseases that travelers should worry about. You can minimize the chances of becoming ill while traveling by taking a few precautionary measures. When spending time in the outdoors, never drink water from outdoor sources that you have not purified by boiling or treating with iodine tablets. Despite any reassurances from locals, **be very skeptical of most water sources in Fiji.** Although most visitors do not have problems with tap water in developed areas, bottled water is readily available and presents a much safer option.

Parasites (tapeworms, etc.) hide in unsafe water and food. **Giardia,** for example, is a major concern for outdoor enthusiasts, acquired by drinking untreated water. It can stay with you for years. General symptoms of parasitic infections include swollen glands or lymph nodes, fever, rashes or itchiness, digestive problems, eye problems, and anemia. Iodine may not be sufficient alone to treat water for giardia. As a general rule of thumb, boil your water, wear shoes, avoid bugs, and eat cooked food. **Amoebic Meningitis,** while rare, is a another serious infection, acquired by putting one's head under the hot, stagnant water in water holes. Symptoms include headaches, a stiff neck, extreme sensitivity to light, and a coma.

If you are concerned about disease in New Zealand and Fiji, or if you will be continuing your travels to other areas of the South Pacific, consult the **US Centers for Disease Control and Prevention (CDC;** ☎877-394-8747; toll free fax 888-232-3299; www.cdc.gov/travel), an excellent source of information for travelers.

AIDS, HIV, AND STDS

New Zealand and Fiji do not screen incoming travelers for the HIV virus; however, restrictions may apply to those staying longer to work or study in New Zealand (contact your nearest consulate). For detailed information on **Acquired Immune Deficiency Syndrome (AIDS)** in New Zealand and Fiji, call the **US Centers for Disease Control's** 24-hour hotline (US ☎ 800-342-2437), or contact the **Joint United Nations Programme on HIV/AIDS (UNAIDS),** 20 Ave. Appia, CH-1211 Geneva 27, Switzerland (☎ +41 22 791 3666; fax 22 791 4187). For more information once in New Zealand, you can contact the **AIDS National Hotline** (☎ 09 358 0099 or 0800 802 437), a 24hr. hotline that offers AIDS counseling and information. The hotline is sponsored by the **New Zealand AIDS Foundation,** P.O. Box 6663, Wellesley St., Auckland (☎ 09 303 3124; www.nzaf.org.nz). **Sexually transmitted diseases (STDs)** such as gonorrhea, herpes, and chlamydia can be just as deadly as HIV. Although condoms may protect you from some STDs, oral and even tactile contact can lead to transmission.

INSURANCE

Visitors who suffer personal injury by accident in New Zealand are covered by the local **Accident Compensation Corporation** (known locally as ACC), which entitles them to a claim, irrespective of fault. ACC does not cover illnesses and even accidents covered by ACC require that the traveler pay some of the cost of treatment.

For more information, or to request helpful ACC publications such as *Visitors to New Zealand*, visit the ACC website (www.acc.co.nz).

In spite of this free coverage, and for travelers to Fiji, it is a a good idea to have individual travel insurance as well. Such insurance generally covers four basic areas: medical/health problems, property loss, trip cancellation/interruption, and emergency evacuation. Although your regular insurance policies may well extend to travel-related accidents, you may consider purchasing travel insurance if the cost of potential trip cancellation/interruption is greater than you can absorb. Prices for travel insurance purchased separately generally run about US$50 per week for full coverage, while trip cancellation/interruption may be purchased separately at a rate of about US$5.50 per US$100 of coverage.

Medical insurance often covers costs incurred abroad; check with your provider. **US Medicare** does not cover foreign travel. **Canadians** are protected by their home province's health insurance plan for up to 90 days after leaving the country. **Australians** traveling in New Zealand are entitled to many of the services that they would receive at home as part of the Reciprocal Health Care Agreement. **Homeowners' insurance** (or your family's coverage) often covers theft during travel and loss of travel documents (passport, plane ticket, etc.) up to US$500.

ISIC and **ITIC** (see **Identification,** p. 13) provide basic insurance benefits to US citizens, including US$100 per day of in-hospital sickness for up to 60 days, US$3000 of accident-related medical reimbursement, and US$25,000 for emergency medical transport. Cardholders can access a toll-free 24hr. helpline for medical, legal, and financial emergencies overseas (US and Canada ☎ 800-626-2427, elsewhere US collect +1 713-267-2525). **American Express** cardholders, please note that American Express does not cover the required Collision and Damage Waiver in New Zealand, as it does automatically in most other countries.

INSURANCE PROVIDERS. Council and **STA** (see **Budget and Student Travel Agencies,** p. 24) offer a range of plans that can supplement your basic coverage. Other private insurance providers in the US and Canada include: **Access America** (☎ 800-284-8300; www.accessamerica.com); **Berkely Group/Carefree Travel Insurance** (☎ 800-323-3149; www.berkely.com); **Globalcare Travel Insurance** (☎ 800-821-2488; www.globalcarecocco.com); and **Travel Assistance International** (☎ 800-821-2828; www.travelassistance.com). Providers in the **UK** include **Campus Travel** (☎ 018 6525 8000) and **Columbus Travel Insurance** (☎ 020 7375 0011). In **Australia,** try **CIC Insurance** (☎ 9202 8000).

PACKING

PACK LIGHTLY. Lay out only what you absolutely need, then take half the clothes and twice the money. The less you have, the less you have to lose (or store and carry). Extra space will be useful for souvenirs or items you might pick up along the way. If you plan to hike a lot, also see **Camping and Tramping Equipment,** p. 69.

IMPORTANT DOCUMENTS. Don't forget your passport, traveler's checks, ATM and/or credit cards, and adequate ID (see **Identification,** p. 13). Also check that you have any of the following that might apply to you: a hostelling membership card (see **Hostelling International,** p. 37); driver's license (see **By Car,** p. 32 and **By Car,** p. 42); travel insurance forms; and/or bus pass (see **By Bus,** p. 31).

LUGGAGE. If you plan to cover most of your itinerary by foot, a sturdy **frame backpack** is unbeatable. While staying in one city, toting a **suitcase** or **trunk** is fine, but it is a very bad idea if you're going to be tramping the Great Walks or exploring multiple islands. For the basics on buying a pack, see **Pack,** p. 69.

In addition to your main vessel, a small backpack, rucksack, or courier bag may be useful as a **daypack** for sightseeing. Once abroad you can fill your luggage with purchases and keep your dirty clothes in a lightweight duffel.

CLOTHING. Due to New Zealand's unpredictable weather patterns and occasionally fierce winds, a rain jacket and heavy sweater are absolute necessities. Gore-Tex® is a miracle fabric that's both waterproof and breathable. No matter when you are traveling, it's a good idea to bring a **warm jacket,** sturdy shoes or **hiking boots,** and thick socks. Remember that wool will keep you warm even when soaked through, whereas wet cotton is colder than wearing nothing at all. **Flip-flops** or other waterproof sandals can also be used as shower shoes.

Travelers to Fiji will want lots of cool, breathable wear such as **shorts** and **T-shirts.** Keep in mind, however, that the weather can become slightly chilly in the higher interior mountain ranges, and always avoid skimpy outfits when visiting small villages so as not to offend locals. A **sulu** (sarong) is an appropriate and traditional outfit for both men and women at any time.

If you are planning on enjoying the nightlife in New Zealand or Fiji, you should add one outfit beyond the jeans and t-shirt uniform. While bars and pubs are often fairly casual, nightclubs and some bars require neat dress including **formal shoes** (not sneakers) and pants other than jeans.

CONVERTERS AND ADAPTERS. In both New Zealand and Fiji, electricity is 220/240 volts AC, enough to fry any 110V North American appliance. **Americans** and **Canadians** should buy an **adapter** (which changes the shape of the plug) and a **converter** (which changes the voltage; US$20). Don't make the mistake of using only an adapter (unless appliance instructions explicitly state otherwise). **South Africans** (who use 220V at home) won't need a converter but will need a set of adapters to use anything electrical.

TOILETRIES. Toothbrushes, towels, soap, deodorant, razors, tampons, and condoms are widely available in New Zealand and Fiji but slightly more expensive than those brought from home. **Contact lenses** may be difficult to find and costly, so bring enough extra pairs and solution for your entire trip. Also, bring your glasses and a copy of your prescription in case you need emergency replacements.

FIRST-AID KIT. For a basic first-aid kit, pack bandages, aspirin or other painkiller, antibiotic cream, a thermometer, a Swiss Army knife, tweezers, moleskin, waterproof tape, gauze, decongestant, motion-sickness remedy, diarrhea or upset-stomach medication (Pepto Bismol or Immodium), an antihistamine, insect repellent, and burn ointment.

FILM. Film and developing in New Zealand are reasonable (about NZ$6-10 to purchase a roll of 24 color exposures and an additional NZ$10 to have them developed) but are slightly more expensive in Fiji. Security X-rays *can* fog film, so buy a lead-lined pouch at a camera store or ask security to hand inspect it.

OTHER USEFUL ITEMS. For safety purposes, you should bring a **money belt** and small **padlock.** Basic **outdoors equipment** (plastic water bottle, iodine tablets, compass, waterproof matches, pocketknife, sunglasses, sunscreen, hat) may also prove useful. **Quick repairs** of torn garments can be done on the road with a needle and thread or electrical tape. Doing your **laundry** by hand (where it is allowed) is cheaper than doing it at a laundromat—bring detergent, a small rubber ball to stop up the sink, and string for a makeshift clothes line. **Other things** you're liable to forget: sealable **plastic bags** (for damp clothes, soap, food, shampoo, and other spillables); an **alarm clock;** safety pins; rubber bands; a flashlight; earplugs; garbage bags; and a small **calculator.**

GETTING TO NEW ZEALAND AND FIJI

BY PLANE

AIRFARE. When it comes to airfare, a little effort can save you a bundle. Tickets bought from consolidators and standby seating are good deals, but last-minute specials, airfare wars, and charter flights often beat these fares. Students, seniors, and those under 26 should never pay full price for a ticket.

Timing: Airfares to New Zealand and Fiji peak between Dec. and Feb.; holidays are also expensive. Midweek (M-Th morning) round-trip flights run US$40-50 cheaper than weekend flights, but they are generally more crowded and less likely to permit frequent-flier upgrades. Traveling with an "open return" ticket is usually not an option for the budget traveler; return-date flexibility is more economically achieved by fixing a return date when buying the ticket and paying later to change it. If planning to stop in Fiji en route to New Zealand or Australia, **Air Pacific** (a Fijian airline) allows for one free stopover in Honolulu or Fiji and **Air New Zealand** offers a free stopover in Fiji. You must book 3 weeks ahead and the stopover allows for a max. stay of 3 months.

Route: Round-trip flights are by far the cheapest; "open-jaw" (arriving in and departing from different cities, e.g. Los Angeles-Auckland and Christchurch-Los Angeles) tickets tend to be pricier. Patching one-way flights together is the most expensive way to travel.

Round-the-World (RTW): If New Zealand and/or Fiji are stops on a more extensive globe-hop, consider a RTW ticket. Tickets usually include at least 5 stops and are valid for about a year; prices range US$1200-5000. Try **Northwest Airlines/KLM** (US ☎800-447-4747; www.nwa.com) or **Star Alliance,** a consortium of 22 airlines including United Airlines and Air Canada (US ☎800-241-6522; www.star-alliance.com).

Gateway Cities: Flights between capitals or regional hubs will offer the cheapest fares. The cheapest gateway cities in New Zealand are typically Auckland and Christchurch, with very few international flights arriving into other cities. Almost all international flights to Fiji land in Nadi.

Fares: Approximate **airfares** from Los Angeles to Auckland range from US$900-1400, and from LA to Nadi US$850-1500, depending on the season.

BUDGET AND STUDENT TRAVEL AGENCIES. While knowledgeable agents specializing in flights to New Zealand and Fiji can make your life easy and help you save, they may not spend the time to find you the lowest possible fare—they get paid on commission. Travelers holding **ISIC** and **IYTC cards** (see **Identification,** p. 13) qualify for big discounts from student travel agencies.

Usit world (www.usitworld.com). Over 48 **usit campus** branches in the UK (www.usitcampus.co.uk), including 52 Grosvenor Gardens, London SW1W 0AG (☎087 0240 1010); Manchester (☎016 1273 1880); and Edinburgh (☎013 1668 3303). Nearly 20 **usit NOW** offices in Ireland, including 19-21 Aston Quay, O'Connell Bridge, Dublin 2 (☎01 602 1600; www.usitnow.ie), and Belfast (☎02 890 327 111; www.usitnow.com). Offices also in Athens, Brussels, Frankfurt, Johannesburg, Lisbon, Luxembourg, Madrid, Paris, Sofia, and Warsaw.

Council Travel (www.counciltravel.com). Countless US offices, including branches in Atlanta, Boston, Chicago, L.A., New York, San Francisco, Seattle, and Washington, D.C. Check the website or call ☎800-2-COUNCIL (226-8624) for the office nearest you.

CTS Travel, 44 Goodge St., London W1T 2AD (☎020 7636 0031; fax 7637 5328; ctsinfo@ctstravel.co.uk).

STA Travel, 7890 S. Hardy Dr., Ste. 110, Tempe AZ 85284 (24hr. reservations and info ☎800-777-0112; fax 480-592-0876; www.statravel.com). A travel organization with offices worldwide, including US offices in Boston, Chicago, L.A., New York, San Francisco, and Washington, D.C. In the UK, walk-in office 11 Goodge St., London W1T 2PF or call 087 0160 6070. In New Zealand, 2289 Queen St., Level 8, Auckland (☎09 309 9723). In Australia, 366 Lygon St., Melbourne, Vic 3053 (☎03 9349 4344).

StudentUniverse, 545 5th Ave., Ste. 640, New York, NY 10017 (☎800-272-9676, outside the US +1 212-986-8420; www.studentuniverse.com), is an online student travel service. Customer service line open M-F 9am-8pm and Sa noon-5pm EST.

Travel CUTS (Canadian Universities Travel Services Limited), 187 College St., Toronto, ON M5T 1P7 (☎416-979-2406; fax 979-8167; www.travelcuts.com). 60 offices across Canada. Also in the UK, 295-A Regent St., London W1R 7YA (☎020-7255-1944).

KEEPING IN TOUCH

SENDING MAIL TO NEW ZEALAND AND FIJI

Mark envelopes "air mail" or "par avion" to avoid having letters sent by sea. In addition to the standard postage system whose rates are listed below, **Federal Express** (Australia ☎ 132 610; US and Canada ☎ 800-247-4747; Ireland ☎ 1800 535 800; UK ☎ 0800 123 800; www.fedex.com) handles express mail services from most home countries to New Zealand and Fiji. For example, they can get a letter from New York to Auckland in two business days for US$33, and from London to Auckland in two business days for UK£32.

RECEIVING MAIL IN NEW ZEALAND AND FIJI

General Delivery: Mail can be sent via **Poste Restante** (General Delivery) to almost any city or town in New Zealand or Fiji with a post office. Address Poste Restante letters to New Zealand as in the following example: Mark BIENSTOCK, Poste Restante, CPO, City, NEW ZEALAND. For Fiji: Rebecca KIRBY, General Delivery, City, FIJI. No zip or area code is necessary. The mail will go to a special desk in the central post office, unless you specify a post office by street address or postal code. As a rule, it is best to use the largest post office in the area; this is especially true in Fiji. When possible, it is usually safer and quicker to send mail express or registered. When picking up mail, bring a form of photo ID, preferably a passport. Let's Go lists post offices in the **Practical Information** section for each city and most towns.

American Express: AmEx's travel offices throughout the world offer a free **Client Letter Service** (mail held up to 30 days and forwarding upon request) for cardholders who contact them in advance. Address the letter in the same way shown above. Let's Go lists AmEx office locations for most large cities in **Practical Information** sections; for a complete, free list, call US ☎ 800-528-4800.

BY TELEPHONE

PLACING INTERNATIONAL CALLS. To call New Zealand or Fiji from home or to call home from New Zealand or Fiji, dial:
1. The **international dialing prefix**. To dial out of **Australia**, dial 0011; **Canada** or the **US**, 011; the **Republic of Ireland, Fiji, New Zealand**, or the **UK**, 00; **Japan**, 001; **South Africa**, 09.
2. The **country code** of the country you want to call. To call **Australia**, dial 61; **Canada** or the **US**, 1; **Fiji**, 679; the **Republic of Ireland**, 353; **Japan**, 81; **New Zealand**, 64; **South Africa**, 27; the **UK**, 44.
3. The **city/area code**. Let's Go lists the city/area codes for cities and towns in New Zealand opposite the city or town name, next to a ☎. If the first digit is a zero (e.g., 09 for Auckland), omit the zero when calling from abroad (e.g., dial 011 64 9 from Canada to reach Auckland). There are **no area codes in Fiji.**
4. The **local number**.

CALLING HOME FROM NEW ZEALAND AND FIJI

A **calling card** is probably your cheapest bet. Calls are billed collect or to your account. You can frequently call collect without even possessing a company's calling card just by calling their access number and following the instructions. To **call** home with a calling card, contact the operator for your service provider in New Zealand or Fiji by dialing the appropriate toll-free access number (see inside back cover). *Let's Go* has recently joined with ekit.com to provide a calling card that offers a number of services, including email and voice messaging. For more information, visit www.letsgo.ekit.com

You can usually also make direct international calls from pay phones, but if you aren't using a calling card you may need to drop your coins as quickly as your words. Where available, prepaid phone cards and occasionally major credit cards can be used for direct international calls, but they are still less cost-efficient. Placing a **collect call** through an international operator is even more expensive, but may be necessary in case of emergency.

BY EMAIL AND INTERNET

It is best to set up a free, web-based email account before leaving home. There are a number of free providers, including Hotmail (www.hotmail.com) and Yahoo! Mail (www.yahoo.com). *Let's Go* lists internet access in **Practical Information** and **Accommodations** sections of cities and towns. To find cybercafes in New Zealand and Fiji, go to www.netcafeguide.com or www.cybercafes.com.

SPECIFIC CONCERNS

WOMEN TRAVELERS

Women exploring on their own inevitably face some additional safety concerns in Fiji, and even in a country as safe as New Zealand. As in most situations, it is best to trust your instincts and be more cautious than you think is necessary.

Stick to centrally located accommodations and avoid solitary late-night treks. When traveling, always carry extra money for a phone call, bus, or taxi. **Hitchhiking** is never safe for solo women, or even for two women traveling together. Look as if you know where you're going (even when you don't). Watch out for persistent, too-friendly locals, especially when hitting the pub scene. A self-defense course will not only prepare you for a potential attack, but will raise your level of awareness of your surroundings as well as your confidence (see **Self Defense**, p. 18). For more detailed information on female travelers in Fiji, see **Women Travelers**, p. 44.

TRAVELING ALONE

There are many benefits to traveling alone, among them greater independence and challenge. Traveling alone in New Zealand and Fiji is neither unwise nor uncommon. However, any solo traveler is a more vulnerable target of harassment and street theft. Lone travelers need to be well-organized and look confident at all times. If questioned, never admit that you are traveling alone.

For more tips, pick up *Traveling Solo* by Eleanor Berman (Globe Pequot, US$17) or subscribe to **Connecting: Solo Travel Network,** 689 Park Rd., Unit 6, Gibsons, BC V0N 1V7, Canada (☎604-886-9099; www.cstn.org; membership US$35), or the **Travel Companion Exchange,** P.O. Box 833, Amityville, NY 11701 (☎631-454-0880 or 800-392-1256; www.whytravelalone.com; US$48).

OLDER TRAVELERS

Many **senior citizens** discounts, especially on transport passes, only apply to local Kiwi and Fijian residents. If you don't see a senior citizen price listed, ask, and you may be delightfully surprised. The books *No Problem! Worldwise Tips for Mature Adventurers*, by Janice Kenyon (Orca Book Publishers; US$16) and *Unbelievably Good Deals and Great Adventures That You Absolutely Can't Get Unless You're Over 50*, by Joan Rattner Heilman (NTC/Contemporary Publishing; US$13) are both excellent resources. For information on organized tours for older travelers in New Zealand, see p. 26.

BISEXUAL, GAY, AND LESBIAN TRAVELERS

For country-specific information on bisexual, gay, and lesbian travelers, see the **Essentials** sections for **Fiji** (p. 44). **Out and About** (www.outandabout.com) offers a bi-weekly newsletter. Listed below are other helpful resources for general travel concerns.

Gay's the Word, 66 Marchmont St., London WC1N 1AB, UK (☎+44 20 7278 7654; www.gaystheword.co.uk). The largest gay and lesbian bookshop in the UK, with both fiction and non-fiction titles. Mail-order service available.

Giovanni's Room, 1145 Pine St., Philadelphia, PA 19107, USA (☎215-923-2960; www.queerbooks.com). An international gay bookstore with mail-order service.

International Lesbian and Gay Association (ILGA), 81 rue Marché-au-Charbon, B-1000 Brussels, Belgium (☎+32 2 502 2471; www.ilga.org). Provides political information, such as homosexuality laws of individual countries.

TRAVELERS WITH DISABILITIES

Below is a list of organizations for travelers with disabilities. For country-specific information, see the **Essentials** sections for **New Zealand** (p. 40) and **Fiji** (p. 44).

Mobility International USA (MIUSA), P.O. Box 10767, Eugene, OR 97440 (☎541-343-1284; www.miusa.org). Sells *A World of Options: A Guide to International Educational Exchange, Community Service, and Travel for Persons with Disabilities* (US$35).

Society for Accessible Travel and Hospitality (SATH), 347 Fifth Ave., #610, New York, NY 10016 (☎212-447-7284; www.sath.org). An advocacy group that publishes free online travel information for travelers with disabilities as well as the travel magazine *OPEN WORLD* (US$18, free for members). Annual membership US$45, students and seniors US$30.

MINORITY TRAVELERS

Asian tourism, particularly Japanese and Korean, is becoming increasingly common in New Zealand and Fiji; prejudice against Asians in some areas is also growing. However, such prejudice rarely leads to violence. Other minorities may find that they stand out in a New Zealand crowd, but are more likely to invite curious looks than harassment or violence. In Fiji, white travelers generally stand out much more than darker-skinned travelers.

TRAVELERS WITH CHILDREN

When deciding where to stay, call ahead to inquire about family rooms and to make sure they allow children. Be sure that your child carries a form of ID in case of an emergency or if he or she gets lost.

Have Kid, Will Travel: 101 Survival Strategies for Vacationing With Babies and Young Children, Claire and Lucille Tristram. Andrews McMeel Publishing (US$9).

Trouble Free Travel with Children, Vicki Lansky. Book Peddlers (US$9).

DIETARY CONCERNS

Despite the culinary prevalence of lamb and meat pies, **vegetarians** should have relatively little problem finding suitable cuisine in New Zealand. Most restaurants have vegetarian selections on their menus, and some cater specifically to vegetarians. Finding **vegan** fare will be a bit more challenging and will probably entail a good deal more self-catering. *Let's Go* often notes establishments with especially good vegetarian selections. Vegetarians and vegans traveling in Fiji will have no problem fulfilling their dietary needs, so long as they like curry.

The North American Vegetarian Society, P.O. Box 72, Dolgeville, NY 13329 (☎518-568-7970; www.navs-online.org), publishes information about vegetarian travel, including *Transformative Adventures: a Guide to Vacations and Retreats* (US$15). Since the Jewish populations in New Zealand and Fiji are considerably smaller than one half of one percent, travelers who keep **kosher** should be prepared to receive some blank stares when inquiring after acceptable restaurants. The best bet may be to contact the **Israel Information Office**, P.O. Box 4315, Auckland (☎09 309 9444; fax 373 2283).

NEW ZEALAND ESSENTIALS

The information in this section is designed to help travelers get their bearings once they are in New Zealand. For information about **general travel preparations** and **specific concerns** for New Zealand consult the **Essentials** section at the beginning of this chapter. For tips on working, volunteering, and studying in New Zealand, see **Alternatives to Tourism,** p. 46.

EMBASSIES AND CONSULATES

Australia: High Commission, 72-78 Hobson St., P.O. Box 4036, Wellington (☎04 473 6411; fax 498 7118; www.australia.org.nz). Consulate General, Union House, 7-8th fl., 132-138 Quay St., Private Bag 92023, Auckland (☎09 303 2429; fax 377 0798).

Canada: High Commission, 61 Molesworth St., 3rd fl., P.O. Box 12049, Wellington (☎04 473 9577; fax 471 2082; www.dfait-maeci.gc.ca/newzealand).

Fiji: High Commission, 31 Pipitea St., P.O. Box 3940, Wellington (☎04 473 5401; fax 499 1011; www.fiji.org.nz).

Ireland: Consulate General, 18 Shortland St., 6th fl., Auckland (☎09 977 2252; fax 977 2256; www.ireland.co.nz).

UK: High Commission, 44 Hill St., P.O. Box 1812, Wellington (☎04 924 2888; fax 473 4982; www.britain.org.nz). Consulate General, 151 Queen St., Private Bag 92014, Auckland (☎09 303 2973; fax 303 1836).

US: Consular Services, General Building, 29 Shortland St. (Private Bag 92022), Auckland (☎09 303 2724; fax 366 0870). American Embassy, 29 Fitzherbert Tce., Thorndon, Wellington (☎04 472 2068; fax 471 2380).

TOURIST SERVICES

VISITORS INFORMATION NETWORK (VIN). In most towns, all major cities, and many airports travelers should watch for the green "i" symbol denoting one of the 94 independently owned and operated **Visitors Information Network (VIN)** tourist offices throughout New Zealand. Coordinated by the New Zealand Tourism Board, these offices will help plan your travel, from booking hostels and hotels to transport to activities. Travelers can also tune into 88.2 FM, the 24hr. tourist radio station.

MONEY

EFTPOS. Providing an alternative to standard ATM and debit cards, **EFTPOS** (Electronic Funds Transfer at Point Of Sale; www.eftpos.co.nz) is an extremely common way for New Zealanders to pay for goods. ATM cards (from New Zealand banks only) swiped at the register work as debit cards, withdrawing money directly from your bank account. If you'll be in New Zealand for a couple of months or more, the convenience of this service may justify opening a New Zealand bank account. Two forms of identification are required; your home driver's license and your passport are the most sure-fire bets. Be sure to bring along home bank statements from the last three months; although you are allowed to open an account without them, they expedite the process significantly. You can also expect the bank to perform a routine check on your credit history. Accounts can be ready in as little as an hour if you provide bank statements from home.

SAFETY

With minimal crime, New Zealand enjoys its reputation as a warm and fuzzy tourist haven. As is true anywhere, however, tourists are probably more vulnerable to crime than most. Because the friendliness of New Zealanders is so infectious, you may be tempted to trust someone more quickly than usual, but it is always best to retain a certain measure of caution. If you are tramping alone, take advantage of the **intentions book** available at any Department of Conservation (DOC) office.

EMERGENCIES	The emergency number in all of **New Zealand** is ☎ 111.

DRIVING. The speed limit is 100kph (63mph) on major roads. Seat belts are mandatory. Almost all roads are sealed and in good condition, though they may be more narrow than foreign travelers are accustomed to. **Drunk driving** among New Zealanders is a major problem. As a result, police occasionally stop all traffic on certain roads in order to give each driver a quick Breathalyzer test. Speeding carries rather steep fines (up to NZ$630) and, in many cases, a suspension of license.

HEALTH

New Zealand offers a high standard of medical facilities, both public and private. However, these are not free; it is important to know that doctors often expect to be paid in cash right away for their services. A foreigner's office visit to most medical treatment centers costs about NZ$35. If your regular **insurance** policy does not cover travel abroad, you may wish to purchase additional coverage, although be sure you understand the coverage provided for New Zealand visitors by the **Accident Compensation Corporation (ACC;** see **Insurance,** p. 21). Except for Medicare, most American health insurance plans cover members' medical emergencies during trips abroad; check with your insurance carrier to be sure. It is common for pharmacies in a New Zealand town to take turns being the **late-night pharmacy;** call the local hospital to get the number.

TRANSPORTATION

Transport in New Zealand is remarkably easy for tourists, particularly in high season, when local shuttles and backpacker buses come out in full force to supplement the main bus lines. **Booking ahead** on buses and trains will often get you significant fare reductions as well as a guaranteed seat. **Discounts** for students and YHA cardholders can be tremendous so be sure to ask. Transportation can be booked by phone, at tourist offices and travel agencies, or at most backpackers.

BY PLANE

While domestic flying is fast, it deprives travelers of spectacular road-level scenery—arguably one of the best (and least anticipated) parts of traveling in New Zealand. The major domestic airline, **Air New Zealand** (NZ ☎ 0800 737 000; US ☎ 800- 262-2468; www.airnz.com) provides connections between major towns and cities. Air New Zealand covers the country comprehensively; a number of smaller companies are also grouped under Air New Zealand Link. "Flightseeing" is another option. Smaller local companies in each area provide beautiful views from the air for rates competitive to boat or ferry prices, starting at around NZ$90. See the **Sights and Activities** listings in each town for more details.

DISCOUNTED FARES. Air New Zealand's **Off Peak Saver fares** offer travelers extremely low prices during off-peak travel hours (Tuesday noon to Thursday noon as well as Saturday noon to Sunday noon). Book 21 days in advance and you will be able to stay at your destination over a Saturday night. These Off Peak fares are available for all 25 of Air New Zealand's domestic destinations. For travelers planning to visit Australia as well as New Zealand, it might be economical to explore multi-leg passes such as the **Boomerang Pass,** valid on Qantas, Ansett Australia, or Air Pacific. The Boomerang provides open one-way tickets among a number of destinations in New Zealand, Australia, and the South Pacific. Within New Zealand, trips are US$155; between New Zealand, Australia, and Fiji, segments run US$190 (minimum two, maximum ten segments). Travelers who plan on staying within New Zealand for the duration of their trip may wish to consider Qantas New Zealand's **Scenic Standby Airpass** (NZ$533 for ten days of unlimited standby travel, NZ$886 for 30 days). Even if just buying a ticket within New Zealand, ask about the special economy fares available. Some Air New Zealand flights feature fares discounted up to 50%, depending on the season (restrictions apply).

BY TRAIN OR FERRY

TranzRail (NZ ☎ 0800 802 802 daily 7am-9pm, elsewhere ☎ 04 498 3303; www.tranzrailtravel.co.nz) offers four different services and travel alternatives. Though some routes have been cut, the phenomenal **TranzScenic** (www.tranzscenic.co.nz) runs between major cities and towns, providing its passengers great views on the way. The **TransMetro** (www.transmetro.co.nz) is a convenient rail-service that criss-crosses the country for easy access to any town or city. The **Interislander** (www.interislander.co.nz) runs a ferry service between the North and South Island. Each run lasts three hours and includes an on-board meal and entertainment. If you are looking for a faster connection between New Zealand's two main islands, hop on the **Lynx** (www.interislandline.co.nz/thelynx) for a speedy ferry trip (135 minutes) across the Cook Strait. Both services carry vehicles. While train fares are generally more expensive than bus fares, TranzRail offers special discounted fares for children aged four to 14 (40% off), travelers over 60 (30%), VIP and YHA members (30%), ISIC cardholders (20%), and those taking day excursions (30%). Minimum fare is $14 (children $9). There are also a limited number of Economy (15%), Saver (30%), and Super Saver (50%) discounted seats on each train. Some trains have a "no-frills carriage" for backpackers with less luxurious seating, smaller windows, and cheaper fares. This is a great way to meet your fellow travelers. Economy fares are offered regularly for travel at certain times of day, as well. The **Best of New Zealand Pass** (www.bestpass.co.nz) uses a points system to encourage extended travel with discount fares. Each pass is valid for 180 days and, on average, an adult saves 28% on standard rail fares. Make sure to reserve all discounted fares well in advance, especially in peak season.

BY BUS

Many budget travelers, especially backpackers, choose the bus (or coach, as the Kiwis say) as their transport of choice, especially in more remote areas. Remember that bus schedules can be somewhat flexible, and many buses will leave if you are not at the stop when they arrive. Always reserve at least one day in advance (earlier to take advantage of aggressive discount schemes), show up 15 minutes early, and do not be alarmed if buses are 20 to 40 minutes late. Visitors centers will have the most up-to-date information about bus schedules and fares, and many offer discounts if fares are booked through them. **InterCity** (☎ 09 913 6100; fax 913 6121; www.intercitycoach.co.nz), the major bus line, recently combined service with **Newmans** to form **Coachnet**. This combination service covers both islands extensively. InterCity also offers a series of Coach Passes, valid for three months, that offer travel on scenic routes. Prices and tours range from the NZ$628 New Zealand Scenic Explorer, which covers extensive segments of the country, to local tours that cost less than NZ$100. All buses can be booked in advance by phone, at travel centers, or at most visitors centers. In addition, cyclists and snow bunnies will be happy to know that buses carry **bikes, skis,** or **snowboards** for a nominal fee.

DISCOUNTED FARES. BBH, VIP, and YHA membership along with possession of an ISIC card will get you 20% off fares for InterCity and Newmans. Children over 5 and under 16 travel for 60% off the full economy adult fare on major bus companies; travelers over 60 get 30% off. A limited number of Saver (30%) and Super Saver (50%) fares on each bus are also available by booking early (at least five days prior to travel for Saver and ten days for Super Saver, with tickets purchased no later than two days prior to travel). During school holidays and peak season, these discounts sell out fast. All discounts are valid only on fares over NZ$20.

BACKPACKER BUSES. Many backpackers, with too little time to explore New Zealand on their own, opt to join up with one of the ubiquitous **backpacker buses.** Keep in mind that experiences greatly vary, refunds are forbidden, and tickets cannot be sold to other travelers. These tours have planned itineraries (including brief stops at sights and activities along their route) and always stop for the night at pre-arranged destinations, which eliminates the spontaneity that so many backpackers treasure. But in return, you meet a bus load of starry-eyed young travelers and benefit from the knowledgeable tour guides. Trips range from whirlwind one week, one island loops to more leisurely whole country explorations. Accommodations are pre-booked by drivers with your input but are not included in the overall price; food is also at your own cost. Many backpacker buses also reserve spaces with various adventure companies, offering decent discounts on activities along the route. In addition to the New Zealand-based bus companies listed below, **Contiki Travel** (☎ 1-888-CONTIKI; www.contiki.com), offers comprehensive bus tour packages that include accommodations, transportation and some meals. In New Zealand, their 3 to 26-day tours start at $295.

Kiwi Experience, 170 Parnell Rd., Parnell, Auckland (☎ 09 366 9830; fax 366 1374; www.kiwiexperience.com), is the most conspicuous of the backpacker buses, with over 20 green giants rolling through the country. Popular with North Americans and Europeans, especially Brits, Kiwi Experience caters to the party backpacker. Whether you're riding with them or not, you'll notice the significant impact that the Kiwi Experience buses have on the tourism industry, filling up certain hostels and showing up en masse at a bar. Kiwi Experience is good for travelers in their late teens and early twenties. Kiwi Experience will soon be spreading to Fiji with the Feejee Experience backpacker bus. Trip prices range widely depending on discounts and location booked, from one island loops at US$150 and the whole country at US$475. VIP/YHA 5% discount.

Magic Travellers Network, Union House, 136-138 Quay St., Auckland (☎09 358 5600; fax 358 3471; www.magicbus.co.nz), provides a more subdued experience than the Kiwi bus, shuttling slightly older backpackers. Again, trip prices and routes vary, but Magic tends to be a bit cheaper than Kiwi, with trips ranging from about US$140-310. YHA 5% discount. Similarly, Magic has partnered with the New Zealand YHA to create **GoNZ** travel packages which include transport on the Magic bus as well as accommodation in YHA hostels (see www.yha.org.nz for more information).

Stray Bus, P.O. Box 14114, Enderley, Hamilton (☎07 824 3627; fax 824 3648; www.straytravel.co.nz). Started by one of the founders of Kiwi Experience, Stray Bus is the latest New Zealand backpacker bus line. With smaller buses, Stray caters to less party-hard travelers than its bright green counterpart. Each route has a personal moniker—"Pete" visits North Island hotspots such as Raglan, Taupo, and Wellington (NZ$209) while "Moe" does a whirlwind tour from Auckland to Christchurch (NZ$680).

SHUTTLE BUSES. Local shuttle buses often supplement the service of the major bus lines (and occasionally offer lower prices on mainstream runs). These services use vans, often collect travelers from their respective accommodations, and usually travel to small towns not serviced by the main coach lines. Companies include **Atomic, Fiordland Travel,** and **Westcoaster.** However, there is a high turnover in shuttle companies and they can be less reliable and comfortable. Local visitors centers will often have current info on prices and schedules and can do bookings. During winter and in more remote locations, make sure to call ahead.

BY CAR

INTERNATIONAL DRIVING PERMIT (IDP). As long as you have a current license from your own country, you probably won't need an IDP if you plan to drive a car while in New Zealand. However, a few car rental agencies do require the IDP, and it can serve as an additional piece of ID in a tough situation. Your IDP, valid for one year, must be issued in your own country before you depart; AAA affiliates

cannot issue IDPs valid in their own country. You must be 18 years old to receive an IDP. A valid driver's license from your home country must always accompany the IDP. An application usually needs to include one or two photos, a current local license, an additional form of identification, and a fee. Visit www.internationaldrivinglicense.com for more information.

CAR INSURANCE. Some credit cards cover standard insurance. If you rent, lease, or borrow a car, you will need the **"Green Card" (International Insurance Certificate)** to certify that you have liability insurance and that it applies abroad. Green Cards can be obtained at car rental agencies, car dealers, and some travel agents.

CAR RENTAL. **Avis** (NZ ☎ 09 526 2847 or 0800 655 111; www.avis.com), **Budget** (NZ ☎ 09 976 2222 or 0800 652 227; fax 976 2223; www.budget.com), and **Hertz** (NZ ☎ 03 358 6787; fax 358 6756; www.hertz.com) are the major car rental operators in New Zealand, and offer their services in all of the main cities and towns. Most agencies rent to those age 21 and over, although some agencies require drivers to be 25. Most cars in New Zealand are manual, so be sure to ask if you require an automatic. Rates vary according to season, as well as duration of rental and condition of car, and generally include unlimited mileage, loss damage waiver, and GST. (**American Express** cardholders, please note that American Express does not cover the required Collision and Damage Waiver in New Zealand, as it does automatically in most other countries.) Expect to pay at least NZ$40 (NZ$60 in high season) per day for a month's rental from one of these companies; for cars of better condition and make, the price may skyrocket to as high as NZ$130 per day. **Darn Cheap Rentals** (☎ 0800 800 327; www.darncheaprentals.co.nz) operates out of Auckland, Wellington, Christchurch, and Picton (from NZ$28 per day for seven days), though the cars are often very small. **Omega Rental Cars** (☎ 09 377 5573 or 0800 525 210; www.akldnz.co.nz) has budget cars from NZ$49 per day, and **Ace Rentals** operates out of Auckland, Wellington, Picton, and Christchurch (☎ 09 303 3112 or 0800 502 277; www.acerentals.co.nz) and rents from NZ$25 per day. Smaller operators often offer eye-poppingly low fares, but be cautious—look carefully into the reliability and reputation before committing.

Sometimes New Zealand rental companies also offer the opportunity of returning a rental car to its hub and only require you to pay for petrol. This arrangement allows travelers to cover long distances for minimal costs. Unfortunately, the opportunity is only found by searching bulletin boards in hostels. Oftentimes travelers look for others to join the trip and split the petrol costs. Check the boards in city YHAs or larger dorm style hostels.

BUY-BACKS

Buying a car, then selling it upon departure, may be a smart option for longer stays. Buy-back outlets, such as the **New Zealand Guaranteed Buy-Back Vehicle Associates,** 825 Dominion Rd., Mt. Roskill, Auckland (☎ 09 620 6587), sell cars specifically for this purpose. Prices range from NZ$3000-7000; you must keep the car for a minimum of a month. At the end of your stay, the buy-back outlet in Auckland buys back the vehicle minus the depreciation rate.

If you prefer to strike out on your own car-buying spree, Auckland is definitely a hot spot for the best car deals: check out one of its car auctions or the used car section of *The New Zealand Herald* (especially on Wednesdays). The *Trade and Exchange*, another good place to look, comes out Mondays and Thursdays.

A car must have a V.I.C. (vehicle inspection certificate, sometimes called a W.O.F.), which ensures that it is road safe. Make sure that your potential car has received one within the past month. They are good for six months and cost NZ$25. A car must be **registered** (six months around NZ$100, one year NZ$200).

Whenever there is a change of ownership, a **MR13A form** must be completed by the buyer and seller and turned in at a post shop. The buyer must also complete a **MR13B form** (NZ$9.20). Insurance is not necessary but highly recommended, as is membership in an Automobile Association (see **Rules of the Road,** below). The latter will get you emergency breakdown service, free service for simple problems, and free towing.

Before you buy your car, you should have it inspected. Vehicle inspection services can be found in the yellow pages under that heading and will do comprehensive pre-purchase checks for NZ$100. You may want to check out **car fairs** in Auckland; some are **Sell It Yourself,** 60 Wairau Rd., Glenfield (☎ 09 443 3800; open daily 7am-7pm); **Ellerslie Racecourse,** off the Greenlane roundabout (☎ 09 520 6329, open Sunday 9am-noon); and **Manukau City Park and Sell** (☎ 09 358 5000; open Sunday 9am-1pm), at the Manukau City Centre. **Car auctions** in Auckland are another option. **Turners Car Auctions** (☎ 09 525 1920; www.turners.co.nz), at the corner of Leonard and Penrose Rd., Penrose, sells budget cars Wednesday at noon and cars from $2000-8000 on Thursday at 6pm. **Hammer Auctions,** 830 Great South Rd., Penrose (☎ 09 579 2344; www.hammerauctions.co.nz), sells budget cars on weekdays at 6pm and at 10:30am on Saturday.

RULES OF THE ROAD

The Road Code of New Zealand (NZ$20), available at AA offices and bookstores, tells you all you need to know. First and foremost, Americans, join your Kiwi companions and drive on the left hand side of the road. Speed limits are strictly enforced; speed cameras are even set up at the traffic lights of many large towns to catch lead-footed offenders. Drunk driving laws are serious business in New Zealand and are strictly enforced. **Petrol** (gas) costs approximately NZ$1 per liter, although it is generally more expensive in smaller towns; when traveling, it can easily run NZ$15-20 per day. State highways are abbreviaed SH; SH2 is in the process of being renamed the Pacific Coast Highway. Members of worldwide Automobile Associations (see **IDP,** p. 32) can enjoy the reciprocal agreement with the

There's nowhere in the world like New Zealand. A Britz campervan can transport you into new adventures every day – at your own pace, in your own way.

- Includes living and sleeping equipment
- No extra driver fees
- Free road maps, campground and what to see and do information
- 24 hour on road assistance
- Large rental car fleet
- Variety of additional hire items

NEW ZEALAND
Freecall within NZ: 0800 831 900
(+64 9 275 9090)
Email: nzinfo@britz.com

AUSTRALIA
Freecall within Australia: 1800 331 454
(+61 3 8379 8890)
Email: ausinfo@britz.com

Website: www.britz.com

Branches located in Auckland, Christchurch and Queenstown, plus an outlet in Wellington

New Zealand Automobile Association (AA; ☎ 0800 500 543; www.aahost.co.nz) to obtain free maps and other services from AA offices in New Zealand. The AA **hotline** (☎ 0900 332 222) gives road reports for NZ$1 per minute.

BY THUMB

Some visitors to New Zealand, particularly backpackers, rely on hitchhiking as a primary mode of transport, and express satisfaction with its safety and convenience. Others, however, report that hitchhiking is much less safe than it used to be, especially for women traveling alone. A man and a woman are a safer combination; two men will have a harder time finding a ride. No matter how safe or friendly New Zealanders may be, you should always think seriously before trusting your life to a stranger, as you risk suffering an accident, theft, assault, or worse. Exercise caution if you elect to hitch: avoid getting into the back of a two-door car; when waiting for a ride, stand in a well-lit, public place; start early in the day; avoid hitchhiking at night; and avoid hitchhiking alone. Even at the risk of offending the driver, **do not put your backpack in the trunk;** you might not get it back. If you ever feel unsafe, don't hesitate to politely but firmly ask to be let off.

If you are planning on hitching, it is reported to be easiest just beyond the end of a town's residential area, but before the open highway. It is illegal on freeways. You can increase your chances of getting a ride if you choose a spot on the side of the road with ample space for a car to pull over. Walk backwards with the traffic with your thumb out and try to make eye contact with the driver. It is often easier to be picked up if you hold a sign indicating your desired destination; avoid accepting offers that will leave you in a small town, short of your ultimate goal.

 LET'S GO DOES NOT RECOMMEND HITCHHIKING. Let's Go strongly urges you to seriously consider the risks before you choose to hitchhike. Although we try to report accurately on the availability of hitching opportunities in each area, we do not recommend it as a safe means of transport, and none of the information printed here is intended to do so.

ACCOMMODATIONS

HOSTELS

For tight budgets and those lonesome traveling blues, hostels (or **backpackers** in New Zealand) can't be beat. Hostels are generally dorm-style accommodations with large co-ed or single-sex rooms with bunk beds, though some have private rooms for families and couples. They frequently offer bike rental, shuttle bus connections, a central lounge space, and storage areas; most have central kitchens and laundry facilities. Fees range from NZ$15-25 per night for a dorm bed.

Most backpackers offer **laundry** for a standard fee (NZ$1-4) but rarely have dryers. **Central heating** is also rare in New Zealand and is listed wherever found. In our listings, a **twin** contains two single beds; a **double** has one double bed. **Seasonal fares** are flexible, and some accommodations vary fares at their own discretion. **Booking ahead** is a must in summer and on major holidays.

> **Budget Backpacker Hostels (BBH):** Includes 290 of New Zealand's independent backpackers. Once a year, BBH surveys guests of all BBH backpackers and then compiles a free guide which lists its members and provides satisfaction ratings. The ubiquitous blue and green guide is helpful, reliable, and available in airports, Visitor Information

ACB
auckland central backpackers

Looking for the best accommodation in Auckland?

ACB is the travellers choice! Enjoy a warm welcome at Aucklands most central backpackers accommodation...at the right price.

- Unequalled Modern Facilities
- Open 24 hours
- Great Atmosphere
- Friendly Helpful Staff
- Luggage Storage
- Air-conditioned comfort
- Travel Centre
- Internet Café/Call Centre
- Globe Bar - Funky new basement bar

BRAND NEW!

Cnr Queen St & Darby St, 229 Queen St, Auckland, New Zealand.
Tel +64 9 358 4877 Fax +64 9 358 4872
email backpackers@acb.co.nz www.acb.co.nz

Backpacker Accommodation

For those free independent travelers who can get by without valets and bellhops, independent hostel accommodation in NZ represents unbelievable value. At around $US20 for a private double room, or $US 8 for a bed in a share room, you can afford to stay here forever. Or at least until your visa expires.

Full information on more than 290 customer graded BBH hostels is available free from
BBH NZ, 99 Titiraupenga St, Taupo, NZ.
Ph +64 7 377-1568
Fax +64 7 377-1548
email letsgo@backpack.co.nz
Or visit our internet site
www.backpack.co.nz.

Free and Independent

The New Zealand Way

What are you waiting for?

Network offices, participating backpackers, or online. In addition, you can purchase a BBH Club card for NZ$40 (including NZ$20 of pre-paid phone calls) good for guaranteed prices and various discounts on transport. Average overnight fee NZ$16-22. Reservations recommended, especially in peak season. Book directly to the backpackers. For more information, contact **Budget Backpackers Hostels NZ Ltd.**, c/o Rainbow Lodge, 99 Titiraupenga St., Taupo (☎07 377 1568; fax 377 1548; www.backpack.co.nz). Throughout the book, Let's Go indicates BBH accommodations.

Hostelling International-Youth Hostels Association of New Zealand (HI-YHANZ): National Office, Union House, 193 Cashel St., Level 3, P.O. Box 436, Christchurch (☎03 379 9970 or 0800 278 299; fax 365 4476; www.iyhf.org); **National Reservations Centre,** P.O. Box 436, Christchurch (☎03 379 9808; fax 379 4415; www.yha.org.nz). Because YHANZ is linked to the HI network, your **Hostelling International card** from home is recognized at all YHANZ backpackers. Or, you can purchase an annual membership card in New Zealand for NZ$40. Average overnight fee NZ$18-23. HI-YHA backpackers are inspected annually for quality and service standards; look in the HI-YHANZ Guide to see a hostel's quality rating. The privately owned YHA Associate hostels, on the other hand, meet YHA standards, but offer the same rates to all guests. Reservations can be made in advance at www.yha.org.nz. You must book at least 48 hours in advance and your reservations are accompanied by a NZ$1 booking fee. Most student travel agencies (see **Budget and Student Travel Agencies,** p. 24) sell HI cards. Throughout the book, Let's Go indicates YHA accommodations.

VIP Backpackers Resorts: Like HI-YHA cards, a VIP card obtains discounts at the 70 VIP backpackers in New Zealand. Annual membership fee NZ$35. Average overnight fee NZ$14-20. Book directly with backpackers (have credit card handy). VIP cards can be obtained from many visitors centers or VIP backpackers. In New Zealand, contact VIP Backpackers Resorts, P.O. Box 80021, Greenbay, Auckland (☎09 827 6016; fax 827 6013; www.vip.co.nz). Throughout the book, Let's Go indicates VIP accommodations.

NOMADS World: Though most NOMADS Hostels are in Australia, there are a few in New Zealand. For an annual fee of AUS$29, the NOMADS Card entitles the card-holder to discounts on accommodations, transport, attractions, and phone call deals. Contact NOMADS headquarters in Australia at NOMADS World Pty Ltd., 43 The Parade West, Kent Town, South Australia 5067 (☎08 8363 7633; fax 8363 7968; www.nomadsworld.com). Throughout the book, Let's Go indicates NOMADS accommodations.

MOTOR PARKS AND CAMPS

In New Zealand, camping facilities (known as **holiday parks**) vary in size from sprawling compounds to grassy plots, filling the niches occupied by both campgrounds and budget motels in the United States. Motor parks and camps usually feature tent sites (from NZ$10 per person) and caravan (RV or camper) sites (from NZ$20). Some also feature on-site caravans for rent. Most parks charge for tent and caravan sites per person. Many also offer cabins or flats with singles (from NZ$20), doubles (from NZ$30), modern tourist flats (from NZ$60) and bunk rooms (from NZ$15) with varying amenities (kitchens, linens, etc.). There are also 250 Department of Conservation (DOC) campsites located in the middle of nature. For more information on camping, see **Huts and Camping,** p. 68. Though frequently illegal, it is also possible to camp for free in New Zealand.

In New Zealand, renting a **campervan (RV)** will always be more expensive than camping or hostelling, but the costs compare favorably with the price of renting a car and staying in hotels. Rates vary widely by region, season (summer months are the most expensive), and type of campervan. A no-frills, two-berth campervan can cost as low as NZ$50 per day in low-season (NZ$100 in high-season), whereas a luxury six-berth camper will run closer to NZ$70 per day (NZ$150 in high-season). In New Zealand, caravan sites cost around $10 per person per night. To arrange a campervan rental, check with your local Automobile Association, contact a major international firm, such as Avis, Budget, or Hertz, or select one of the options below. In any case, it always pays to contact several different companies to compare vehicles, amenities, and prices. Those who plan on traveling by RV in New Zealand or doing a lot of camping may choose to join a network like the **Top 10 Holiday Parks** (www.topparks.co.nz; membership fee NZ$20 for two years) to reap consistent 10% discounts at member parks.

Auto Europe (NZ ☎ 0800 440 722; US ☎ 888-223-5555; UK ☎ 0800 899 893; www.autoeurope.com) rents campervans in New Zealand.

Maui Rentals: New Zealand, 36 Richard Pearse Dr., Mangere, **Auckland** (☎ 09 275 3013; fax 275 9690; www.maui-rentals.com) rents campervans in all shapes and sizes.

Newmans, P.O. Box 14069, **Christchurch** (☎ 03 358 1314; fax 353 5808; reservations@coachline.co.nz; www.newmans.com) rents a wide range of 2-6 berth vehicles.

BED AND BREAKFASTS

For a cozy alternative to impersonal New Zealand hotel rooms, B&Bs (private homes with rooms available to travelers) range from the acceptable to the sublime. Hosts will sometimes go out of their way to be accommodating by accepting travelers with pets, giving personalized tours, or offering home-cooked meals. On the other hand, many B&Bs do not provide phones, TVs, or private bathrooms and often discourage visits of children under 15. Rooms in B&Bs generally cost NZ$60 for a double. For more info on B&Bs, see **InnFinder,** 6200 Gisholt Dr. #100, Madison, WI 53713 (☎ 608-285-6600; fax 285-6601; www.inncrawler.com), or **InnSite** (www.innsite.com). For a further resource on B&Bs in New Zealand, J. J. Thomas' **New Zealand Bed and Breakfast Book** (US$18; www.bnb.co.nz) is an annually updated reference book and website including contact information, prices, illustrations of and directions to over 1500 businesses in New Zealand.

HOMESTAYS AND FARMSTAYS

An intensely memorable experience, homestays and farmstays involve staying on a real working farm or orchard, often alone or with a few other guests. These stays are usually arranged through the nearest town's tourist office, although some companies also specialize in booking homestays and farmstays. In New Zealand, prices start around NZ$100 per person and include participation in farm activities (more available in winter) and fresh, home-cooked meals; a few backpackers also provide some aspects of a "farmstay" experience, especially in more rural areas. **Rural Tours "Stay in a Country Home" Farmstays** books farmstays throughout New Zealand. Its central booking office is at 92 Victoria St., P.O Box 228, Cambridge (☎ 07 827 8055; fax 827 7154; www.ruraltours.co.nz). **American International Homestays,** P.O. Box 1754, Nederland, CO 80466 (US ☎ 800-876-2048 or 303-258-3234; fax 258-3264; www.aihtravel.com), also arranges lodgings with host families. For more information on farmstays, see **Alternatives to Tourism,** p. 46.

HOME EXCHANGES AND HOME RENTALS

Home exchange offers the traveler various types of homes, plus the opportunity to live like a native and to cut down on accommodation fees. For more information on home exchanges in New Zealand, contact **HomeExchange.Com** (P.O

Box 30085, Santa Barbara, CA 93130; US ☎800-877-8723; www.homeexchange.com), **Intervac International Home Exchange** (NZ ☎04 934 4258; www.intervac.com), or **The Invented City: International Home Exchange** (US ☎800-788-CITY, elsewhere call US +1 415-252-1141; www.invented-city.com) **Home rentals** are more expensive than exchanges, but they can be cheaper than comparably-serviced hotels. For information on home rentals in New Zealand, go to www.realenz.co.nz.

KEEPING IN TOUCH

SENDING MAIL HOME

Although post office hours vary somewhat with town size, most are open weekdays from about 9am to 5pm, and Saturdays from about 9am to noon. **Airmail** is the best way to send mail home from New Zealand. **Aerogrammes,** printed sheets that fold into envelopes and travel via airmail, are available at post offices. They cost NZ$1.50 to send anywhere in the world. It helps to mark "airmail." Most post offices charge exorbitant fees or simply won't send aerogrammes with enclosures. A 100g letter sent from NZ to the US through Airmail will cost you NZ$7. The same letter sent through Groundmail will cost you NZ$6.

Surface mail is by far the cheapest and slowest way to send mail. It takes 10-15 days for packages to reach Australia; to North America, 18-25 days; to the UK, Ireland, and most other international destinations, 25-45 days. This might be a good for items you won't need to see for a while, such as souvenirs or other articles you've acquired along the way that are weighing down your pack. For more information on New Zealand postal services, go to www.nzpost.co.nz.

CALLING WITHIN NEW ZEALAND

National directory assistance: ☎018.

National operator assistance: ☎010.

International directory assistance: ☎0172.

International operator assistance: ☎0170.

The **North Island** has several different area codes (see inside back cover). The **South Island** has a single area code of 03. Phone numbers that begin with 025, 027, or 021 are cellular phone numbers and cost more than a standard local call. Phone numbers that begin with 0800 or 0508 are toll-free freephone calls. Phone rates tend to be highest in the morning, lower in the evening, and lowest on Sunday and late at night. Local calls from pay phones start at NZ$0.20 per minute; non-local calls start at NZ$0.30 per minute; calls to mobile phones are considerably more expensive (from NZ$1.20); international calls start at NZ$3 per minute. Calls from private phones are substantially cheaper than those from New Zealand's pay phones.

The three kinds of public **pay phones** are color-coded: **card phones** are green, **credit card phones** yellow, and **coin phones** blue. Coin phones are gradually being phased out, however, so don't count on being able to access them everywhere. **Prepaid phone cards,** sold by Telecom New Zealand and operating using a computer chip, are widely available and can be purchased at tourist offices, backpackers, convenience stores and post offices.

If you will be staying in New Zealand for three months or more, it may be wise to get a mobile phone. The two main operators are **Vodafone** (www.vodafone.co.nz) and **Telecom** (www.telecom.co.nz), both of which offer **pre-paid phones.** Both companies sell phones for under NZ$100. It is also possible to rent mobile phones. Go to www.scotties.co.nz/cellphon.htm for more information.

EMAIL AND INTERNET

Cybercafes and other sources for internet access are proliferating in New Zealand, with fees normally between NZ$5-10 per hour. In addition to the traditional cybershops, sites everywhere from small backpackers to the ski slopes are increasingly being equipped with coin-operated internet stations (NZ$2 per 10min).

SPECIFIC CONCERNS

RESOURCES FOR WOMEN TRAVELERS

Wanderwomen, P.O. Box 68058, Newton, Auckland (☎09 360 7330; fax 360 7332; www.wanderwomen.co.nz), offers guided sea kayaking and other outdoor trips for both women-only and mixed groups.

New Zealand Family Planning Association, 6 Southmark House, 203-209 Willis St., Wellington (☎04 384 4349; fpanz@globe.co.nz), helps women considering abortions.

RESOURCES FOR OLDER TRAVELERS

ElderTreks, 597 Markham St., Toronto, ON M6G 2L7 (☎800-741-7956; fax 588-9839; www.eldertreks.com). Adventure travel programs for the 50+ traveler in New Zealand.

Elderhostel, 75 Federal St., Boston, MA 02110 (US ☎877-426-2166; www.elderhostel.org). Organizes 1- to 4-week adventures in New Zealand and Australia for those 55+.

The Mature Traveler, P.O. Box 15791, Sacramento, CA 95852 (☎800-460-6676). Deals, discounts, and travel packages for the 50+ traveler. Sends trips that cover the North and South Island. Subscription $30.

Walking the World, P.O. Box 1186, Fort Collins, CO 80522 (☎800-340-9255; www.walkingtheworld.com), organizes trips for 50+ travelers to New Zealand.

TRAVELERS WITH DISABILITIES

New Zealand is overall an accessible country for the disabled. Law requires that every new motel and hotel provides a certain number of fully accessible rooms. In addition, a number of **tramps** and **walks** are wheelchair-accessible; always check with the Department of Conservation (DOC). Main taxi companies in major cities and many towns have a **Total Mobility Taxi Service** offering transport for those with wheelchairs. With sufficient notice (2 weeks), some major car rental agencies will offer hand-controlled vehicles at select locations. **Accessible Tours** (www.tours-nz.com) provides resources and tours for wheelchair-bound travelers in New Zealand.

Those with disabilities should inform airlines and hotels of their disabilities when making arrangements for travel. **Guide dog owners** must apply for a **permit to import,** as well as provide appropriate documentation regarding the dog's health and qualifications. Applications for the permit should be made to the Chief Veterinary Officer, Ministry of Agriculture, P.O. Box 2526, Wellington. More information is provided at the Ministry of Agriculture and Forestry website (www.maf.govt.nz). Below is a list of organizations for travelers with disabilities in New Zealand.

Deaf Emergency Telephone Number, ☎0800 161 616.

Disability Resource Center, P.O. Box 24-042, Royal Oak, Auckland 3 (☎09 625 8069; fax 624 1633).

Disabled Persons Assembly (DPA), Tower Block, Wellington Trade Centre, 175 Victoria St., Level 4, Wellington (☎04 801 9100; fax 801 9565).

SPECIFIC CONCERNS ■ 41

Enable New Zealand, 60 Bennett St., Palmerston North (☎06 952 0011 or 0800 171 981; fax 952 0022; www.enable.co.nz). A wide variety of information, equipment, and referrals for the disabled and their families in New Zealand.

Taxi Companies for People with Disabilities: Cannons Total Mobility (☎09 836 4386); Co-op Taxis (☎09 300 3000); Independence Mobility (☎09 836 6761); North Harbor Taxis (☎09 443 1777); South Auckland Taxis (☎09 278 5678); Auckland Mobility (☎09 817 9442); United Taxis (☎09 298 1000).

Global Access (www.geocities.com/Paris/1502/disabilitylinks.html) has links for disabled travelers in New Zealand and details handicapped-accessible accommodations on the South Island.

FIJI ESSENTIALS

The information in this section is designed to help travelers get their bearings once they are in Fiji. For information about **general travel preparations** and **specific concerns** for Fiji consult the **Essentials** section at the beginning of this book. For tips on working, volunteering, and studying in Fiji, see **Alternatives to Tourism,** p. 46.

EMBASSIES AND CONSULATES

Australia: High Commission, 37 Princes Rd., P.O. Box 214, Suva (☎338 2211; fax 338 2065; austembassy@connect.com.fj).

Japan: Embassy, Dominion House, 2nd fl., P.O. Box 13045, Suva (☎330 2122; fax 330 1452).

New Zealand: High Commission, Reserve Bank Building, P.O. Box 1378, Suva (☎331 1422; fax 330 0842; nzhc@connect.com.fj).

UK: High Commission, Victoria House, Government Buildings, P.O. Box 1355, Suva (☎331 1033; fax 301 406; richard_emmerson@bhc.org.fj).

US: Embassy, 31 Loftus St., P.O. Box 218, Suva (☎331 4466; fax 330 0081; usemb-suva@connect.com.fj).

SAFETY

While Fiji is generally a safe country for foreign travelers, visitors should be aware of the concerns that arise in any developing nation. It is important to stay abreast of political developments while in Fiji, given the turmoil that has accompanied the failed 2000 coup (see **Political Upheaval,** p. 430). For the latest information on travel to Fiji, go to www.travel.state.gov/travel_warnings.html.

EMERGENCIES	The emergency number in all of **Fiji** is ☎911.

DRIVING. Driving in Fiji can be quite hazardous; loosely enforced regulations and speedy Fijian drivers combine to create numerous fatal accidents each year, with a large number occurring on the less well-maintained Kings Road.

HEALTH

The health care system in Fiji is often inadequate by Western standards. While the many state health centers and hospitals are generally fine for minor injuries, serious ailments should be dealt with at the **Suva Private Hospital** (☎330 3404; see **Suva: Practical Information,** p. 462), a first-rate 24hr. facility with well-trained doctors. If it is impossible or impractical to get to Suva, numerous **private clinics** (generally found only in more urban areas) are a better bet than state hospitals; usually staffed by just one or two professionals and only open during normal business hours, clinics accept cash and often traveler's insurance. If you are seriously injured anywhere in Fiji, **Island Hoppers** (☎672 0410) provides emergency **helicopter airlifts** to the Suva Private Hospital. In addition to the health concerns detailed on p. 20, travelers should watch out for the insect-born diseases, **dengue fever** and **filariasis**. Dengue fever is transmitted by mosquitoes and characterized by headache, severe joint pain, and a rash. Filariasis is a roundworm infestation transmitted by mosquitoes. Symptoms include fever, pain and swelling of the lymph glands, and enlargement of extremities.

TRANSPORTATION

Fiji has inexpensive and moderately reliable internal transportation. However, keep in mind that much of the country runs on **"Fiji Time"**—exact arrival and departure times can vary significantly.

BY PLANE

Domestic airlines are prevalent and reliable, often offering spectacular views. **Air Fiji** (☎ 331 3666; fax 330 0771; www.airfiji.net) and **Sun Air** (☎ 672 3555; fax 672 0085; www.fiji.to) provide service between major cities. Air Fiji features the 30-day Discover Fiji Pass, with several itineraries from FJ$472 (sold only with the purchase of international airfare; inquire when buying your ticket to Fiji). **Island Hoppers** (☎ 672 0410; fax 672 0172; www.helicopters.com.fj), **Turtle Airways** (☎ 672 1888; fax 672 0095; www.turtleairways.com), and **Pacific Island Seaplanes** (☎ 672 5644; fax 672 5641; www.fijiseaplanes.com) offer charter and scenic flights.

BY BUS

Most buses in Fiji are hot, noisy, and smoky, with tarpaulins pulled down to cover open windows during rain. Buses stop at stations in cities, but, in rural regions, it is necessary to hail the bus in order to board. When heading to rural areas be sure to check return times so you don't get stranded. **Pacific Transport Ltd.** (☎ 670 0044), **Sunbeam Transport Ltd.** (☎ 666 2822), **Sunset Express** (☎ 672 0266), and **United Touring Fiji** (☎ 672 2811) run regular and express services throughout Viti Levu. At press time, Kiwi Experience announced plans to launch a backpacker bus in Fiji called **Feejee Experience.** For more information, go to www.kiwiexperience.com.

BY CAR

Car rental in Fiji is expensive. Very few locals own cars; as a result there are many cheap public transportation options serving virtually all locations. However, some areas, especially the Kings Road on Viti Levu (p. 449), are best explored by rental car. **Avis** (☎ 672 2688; www.avis.com.fj), **Budget** (☎ 672 2735; www.budget.com.fj), and **Hertz** (☎ 330 2186; hertzfiji@connect.com.fj) are the major car rental outfits in Fiji. Third-party insurance is compulsory and most rental companies charge FJ$12-20 extra for collision damage waiver insurance. Check the **Transportation** sections for car rental information in specific areas. If you do rent a car, make sure to drive the Fijian way—on the left side of the road. For your first six months in Fiji, authorities will recognize your home driver's license. Standard Fijian speed limits are **80kph** (about 50mph) on highways and **50kph** (about 30mph) otherwise. For more information on driving safety, see **Personal Safety: Driving,** p. 19.

BY TAXI

The abundance of taxis in Fiji makes for some of the cheapest transport rates in the South Pacific. FJ$3 will usually be sufficient to get you anywhere in a town or city. Taxis often use a fixed rate system and the driver will name his/her price when you give your intended destination. It is always profitable to bargain with the driver for the price of long trips. The price will often be lowered if you allow the driver to pick up other passengers along the way. To save money, look for taxis making return trips. Often they will pick up passengers at bus stops and charge only the bus fare. Taxis can also be hired for a day or half-day, usually with prices equivalent to that of a rental car.

BY FERRY

A common way to travel between Fijian islands is by ferry; services range from the 42-passenger high-speed catamaran operated by **South Sea Cruises** (☎ 675 0500; southsea@connect.com.fj) to small open boats. **Patterson Brothers Shipping Company** (☎ 331 5644; fax 330 1652), **Consort Shipping Ltd.** (☎ 330 2877; fax 330 3389), and **Beachcomber Shipping** (☎ 330 7889; fax 330 7359) are the main ferry services between Viti Levu and the outer islands. Make sure that any boat has adequate safety equipment (life jackets, radio, etc.) before you get on board—**Let's Go does not recommend traveling in a boat without life jackets.**

BY THUMB

Let's Go does not recommend hitchhiking as a means of transport. However, locals frequently do hitch rides. If you decide to travel by thumb, it is customary to pay the driver the equivalent of the bus fare. For more information on hitchhiking and its dangers, see the New Zealand **Hitchhiking** section, p. 35.

ACCOMMODATIONS

HOSTELS, HOTELS, AND RESORTS

The quality of accommodations in Fiji varies greatly; some offer a slice of luxury while others barely scrape together the basics. Prices generally range from FJ$12-35. Many Fijian accommodations recognizable as hostels call themselves "hotels." In the outer islands, resorts with *bures* (traditional thatched-roof huts) are the norm. These generally have foam mats, cold water, gas lanterns, kitchens, and mosquito nets. Guests stay busy with resort-run activities (for a fee) and meals (usually included in the price).

CAMPING

Campgrounds can be found at some backpacker resorts in Fiji. Always get permission before setting up a tent because most land is owned by the indigenous population. If you are staying in a village, do not camp beside a Fijian's house as this will imply that you think his home is inadequate for a night's rest.

VILLAGE STAYS

Visitors can often arrange to sleep in a Fijian village. This provides an excellent escape from the touristy resorts and a way to learn more about the Fijian people. While village stays often require an acquaintance who lives in the village, many locations on Viti Levu including **Navala** (p. 457), **Bukuya** (p. 458), and **Abaca** (p. 459) have capitalized on the process as a means of generating income. For more information on the niceties of visiting a village, see **Fijian Village Etiquette**, p. 433.

KEEPING IN TOUCH

SENDING MAIL HOME

Post Fiji, the Fijian mail system, is occasionally unreliable. If you are sending something extremely important, you would do well to use **DHL** (available in most sizeable towns), **FedEx** (the national agent is **Carpenters Shipping** ☎ 672 2933; fax 672 0056), or some other international courier service. Allow from 1-2 weeks for regular airmail to North America, the UK, Ireland, Europe, and South Africa. Generally, postage for letters or postcards is under FJ$1. Airmail to New Zealand and Austra-

CALLING WITHIN FIJI

National directory assistance: ☎ 011.
National operator assistance: ☎ 010.
International directory assistance: ☎ 022.
International operator assistance: ☎ 012.

The Fijian phone system is quite small (one phone book covers the entire nation). In 2001, a seventh digit was added to the beginning of all Fiji numbers. All numbers beginning with 0800 are toll-free calls. While most of the areas covered in this book have regular phone service, some outlying islands and remote villages maintain contact through **radio phones.** Most payphones in Fiji operate on a card system and accept **Phonecard,** an automatic8 prepaid card. The few phones that don't accept Phonecards generally accept **Telecard,** a PIN-based prepaid service.

EMAIL AND INTERNET

All major cities in Fiji have cybercafes, although connection speeds can vary greatly as the number of local users fluctuates; late night and weekends are usually have the fast connections. Access averages FJ$6-10 per hr. Most of the outlying island groups and small to medium towns will have little to no Internet access.

SPECIFIC CONCERNS

WOMEN TRAVELERS. Women traditionally possess a subservient role in Fijian culture, and female travelers sometimes encounter unpleasant attitudes and actions. It is a good idea to follow the safety guidelines on p. 20. In **Suva,** the **Fiji Women's Crisis Centre,** 88 Gordon St., P.O. Box 12882, Suva (☎ 313 300; fax 313 650; www.fijiwomen.com), offers safety and counseling resources for women.

TRAVELERS WITH DISABILITIES. While Fiji openly embraces all visitors, extremely little infrastructure has been developed for disabled travelers. Though some upscale resorts may be wheelchair-accessible, most Fijian accommodations and local transportation do not yet cater to travelers with disabilities.

BISEXUAL, GAY, AND LESBIAN TRAVELERS. Although the 1998 Fiji constitution established official protection for homosexuals from discrimination, it was abrogated in the wake of the 2000 coup, and gay and lesbian cultures still remain very quiet segments of life. However, there are some bars in Suva and some resorts throughout Fiji that are explicitly gay-friendly.

MINORITY TRAVELERS. Fiji's population is mainly of Indian and native Fijian descent. Although there is social and economic tension between these two main groups, visitors of all backgrounds experience little of the conflict.

OTHER RESOURCES

TRAVEL PUBLISHERS AND BOOKSTORES

Rand McNally, 150 S. Wacker Dr., Chicago, IL 60606 (☎ 800-234-0679 or 312-332-2009; www.randmcnally.com). Publishes road atlases.

Adventurous Traveler Bookstore, 245 S. Champlain St., Burlington, VT 05401 (☎ 800-282-3963 or 802-860-6776; www.adventuroustraveler.com).

Bon Voyage!, 2069 W. Bullard Ave., Fresno, CA 93711 (☎800-995-9716, from abroad 559-447-8441; www.bon-voyage-travel.com). They specialize in Europe but have titles pertaining to New Zealand. Free catalog.

Travel Books & Language Center, Inc., 4437 Wisconsin Ave. NW, Washington, D.C. 20016 (☎800-220-2665; www.bookweb.org/bookstore/travelbks/.) Over 60,000 titles from around the world.

WORLD WIDE WEB

Almost every aspect of budget travel is accessible via the web. Listed here are some budget travel sites to start off your surfing. Because website turnover is high, use search engines (such as www.google.com or the Australia/New Zealand specific au.yahoo.com) to strike out on your own.

THE ART OF BUDGET TRAVEL

How to See the World: www.artoftravel.com. A compendium of great travel tips, from cheap flights to self defense to interacting with local culture.

Rec. Travel Library: www.travel-library.com. A fantastic set of links for general information and personal travelogues.

Lycos: http://travel.lycos.com. General introductions to New Zealand and Fiji, accompanied by links to applicable histories, news, and local tourism sites.

INFORMATION ON NEW ZEALAND

Pipers New Zealand Web Pages: www.piperpat.co.nz/nz. Links to (almost) all the New Zealand web sites you will ever want.

New Zealand on the Web: www.nz.com. The award-winning site has resources for and about New Zealand; includes a guidebook, virtual tours, and online marketplace.

New Zealand Tourism: www.purenz.com. The official site for New Zealand Tourism provides extensive support and resources for foreign and domestic travelers.

NZPages: www.nzpages.co.nz. A New Zealand website directory with links to government, tourism, and news sites.

TravelPage: www.travelpage.com. Links to official tourist office sites in New Zealand.

INFORMATION ON FIJI

Fiji Government Online: www.fiji.gov.fj. The official government website has extensive (and usually biased) recent news briefs.

Fiji Islands Backpackers Guide: www.fiji-backpacking.com. Provides information and colorful photos for Fiji-bound backpackers.

Fiji Visitors Bureau (FVB): www.bulafiji.com. Very slick and overly positive pages provide a great starting point for learning about Fiji.

Fijivillage.com: www.fijivillage.com. *Fiji Times* headlines, sports, and links to just about every Fiji site that exists.

US Embassy to Fiji: www.amembassy-fiji.gov. Online registration for US citizens traveling in Fiji, as well as links to latest consular travel advisories.

AND OUR PERSONAL FAVORITE...

 WWW.LETSGO.COM Our newly designed website now features the full online content of all of our guides. In addition, trial versions of all nine City Guides are available for download on Palm OS™ PDAs. Our website also contains our newsletter, links for photos and streaming video, online ordering of our titles, info about our books, and a travel forum buzzing with stories and tips.

ALTERNATIVES TO TOURISM

The joys of traveling stand alone, but this chapter focuses on other rewarding ways to see the world. If skydiving has left you broke, hostel-hopping has made you homesick, and tramping has exhausted your tired feet, it's time to consider alternatives to tourism. Both New Zealand and Fiji offer numerous opportunities to hop off the general backpacker circuit and enter the world of jobs, schools, and volunteering. Whether picking grapes on a Hawke's Bay orchard, building houses in Fijian highland villages, or studying at the University of Otago, choosing an alternative to pure tourism delivers a deeper taste of local life.

VISA INFORMATION
See the New Zealand Immigration service website (www.immigration.govt.nz) to apply for visa and work permit information. Australian citizens and residents with a current **Australian resident return visa** do not need a visa or permit to work in New Zealand. There are no working holiday permits for **Fiji,** though you can get a work permit if you are offered a job that cannot be filled locally. The following visas are required for temporary work and study in New Zealand.

Working Holiday Visa. For 18-30-year-old British, Canadian, and Japanese citizens. Valid for 12 months. Requirements include application and NZ$90-100 fee, valid passport, and proof of medical coverage and adequate funds.

Special Category Working Holiday Visa. For 18-30-year-old US citizens. Allows up to 4 months of temporary work with an approved exchange program. See p. 48 for eligible programs.

Student Visa. A student visa is required for those intending to study in New Zealand for more than 3 months. The visa can be obtained from any New Zealand Embassy or High Commission with an admission letter from a New Zealand educational institution or program. Visit www.nzemb.org/immigration/study.htm for more information.

STUDYING ABROAD

Study abroad programs range from high school cultural exchanges to college-level courses, often for credit. In deciding where to live, dorm life lets you mingle with fellow students, but gives you fewer opportunities lmto experience the local scene. If you live with a family, you might build lifelong friendships with residents and experience day-to-day life in more depth, but conditions can vary greatly from family to family. A good resource for finding programs that cater to your particular interests is www.studyabroad.com. The following is a list of organizations that can help place students in university programs abroad.

AMERICAN PROGRAMS

American Field Service (AFS), 310 SW 4th Ave., Ste. 630, Portland, OR 97204 (☎800-237-4636; fax 503-241-1653; www.afs.org/usa). AFS offers programs in New Zealand for US high school students and graduating high school seniors. Costs range from US$4395 (summer) to US$6995 (full-year).

Arcadia University for Education Abroad, 450 S. Easton Rd., Glenside, PA 19038 (☎866-927-2234; www.arcadia.edu/cea). Operates programs in New Zealand. Costs range from US$2200 (summer) to US$29,000 (full-year).

Association of Commonwealth Universities (ACU), John Foster House, 36 Gordon Sq., London WC1H OPF (☎020 7380 6700; www.acu.ac.uk). Publishes information about New Zealand universities.

Institute for Cultural Ecology, PO Box 991, Hilo, HI 96721 (☎808 933 1991; fax 808 733 7808; www.culturalecology.com). Organizes internships in New Zealand and Fiji. Programs range from 4-week national park apprenticeships to semester-long marine biology courses.

Institute for Study Abroad, Butler University (ISA), 1000 West 42nd St., Ste. 305, Indianapolis, IN 46208-3345 (☎800-858-0229 or 317-940-9336; www.ifsa-butler.org). Semester (from US$7,575) and full-year (from US$12,375) programs with the major universities of New Zealand. ISA takes care of applications to the universities, visas, housing, and provides personal guidance while abroad.

School for International Training, College Semester Abroad, Kipling Rd., P.O. Box 676, Brattleboro, VT 05302 (☎888-272-7881 or 802-257-7751; www.sit.edu). Semester-long programs in New Zealand cost US$13,850. Also runs the **Experiment in International Living** (☎800-345-2929; www.usexperiment.org), 5-week summer programs for high-school students in New Zealand that cost US$4600.

PROGRAMS IN NEW ZEALAND AND FIJI

NEW ZEALAND. New Zealand's eight state-funded universities all welcome international students. **New Zealand Education International,** P.O. Box 10 500, Wellington (☎04 472 0788; fax 04 471 2828; www.nzeil.co.nz), publishes a directory of universities, colleges of education and polytechnics, and secondary and English language institutions. American undergraduates can enroll in programs sponsored by US universities, though it may be cheaper to enroll in a local university directly. In New Zealand, the academic year begins in March and is divided into three terms. The long vacation is late November to early March, and there are three week breaks between terms in May and in August.

FIJI. Fiji's **University of the South Pacific** (p. 466) in Suva is the best university in the region, drawing students from hundreds of islands throughout the Pacific. While it is rare for international students to enroll at USP for an entire semester, it is possible to take more informal courses. Check the university's website (www.usp.ac.fj) or the *Fiji Times* diary page for listings.

WORKING

Working abroad will not only provide immersion into another culture but can also help finance the next leg of your journey. However, obtaining legal work permits in New Zealand can be difficult, especially for US citizens, and it is next to impossible to find jobs, legal or otherwise, in Fiji. In New Zealand, foreigners can only hold a job with a **work visa** or **permit** (see **Visa Information,** p. 46). To get these, you often need to be sponsored by an employer who can demonstrate that you have skills that locals lack—not the easiest of tasks. All visas must be obtained outside New Zealand, so if you think you meet these criteria, call the nearest New Zealand or Fijian consulate or embassy to get more information.

Throughout this book, look for **Work Opportunities** listings under the **Practical Information** heading. These listings will offer leads on job-hunting in the region or urban center, including what kind of work is generally available and how to contact local employment agencies.

Though most programs and employers hire travelers carrying a 12-month Working Holiday Visa, US citizens must obtain a Special Category Working Holiday Visa in order to work. The Special Category visa is valid for four months and only applies to the following organizations, which also accept Working Holiday Visas.

Bunac, P.O. Box 430, Southbury, CT 06488 (☎800-462-8622 or 203-264-0901; www.bunac.org), charges US$450 for organizing work permits, job placement, and travel through New Zealand. Americans 18-30 are eligible.

Council Exchanges, 52 Poland St., London W1F 7AB (☎44 020 7478 2000, US☎ 888-268-6245; www.ciee.org), charges a US$425 fee for arranging up to 6-month work permits as well as extensive information on different job opportunities in New Zealand. US college students, recent graduates, and young adults are eligible.

Work Experience Down Under, 2330 Marinship Way, Ste. 250, Sausalito, CA 94965 (☎800-999-2267 or 415-339-2728; www.ccusa.com). The US$365 cost includes visa processing, comprehensive work and travel insurance, 2-nights accommodation, arrival and city orientation, and access to a Job Search Centre.

LONG-TERM WORK

If you're planning on spending a substantial amount of time (more than three months) working in New Zealand, search for a job well in advance. Below is a list of resources for finding long-term work.

Monster: www.monster.co.nz. The New Zealand division of the well-known job network, Monster has listings as well as career advice.

New Zealand Herald: www.netclassifieds.nzherald.co.nz. This section of the popular newspaper has heaps of job listings.

NZ.jobs.co: www.nzjobs.co.nz. Lists thousands of employment opportunities in and around New Zealand cities.

SHORT-TERM WORK

Many travelers do odd jobs for a few weeks at a time to make some extra cash to fund their touring. To find out about work opportunities, ask around or peruse hostel bulletin boards. One of the best starting points is the bulletin board at **Auckland Central Backpackers** (see p. 85). The most popular short-term work options in New Zealand are **picking fruit** and working part-time in **hostels.** Orchard work is difficult and time-consuming but excellent for fitness and a tan. Fruit pickers are usually paid by the quantity gathered rather than an hourly wage. Expect to make around NZ$400 per week. Most work is usually available from January to May and is centered around the Hawke's Bay region. For information on fruit-picking jobs, go to www.seasonalwork.co.nz. Hostels offer more sedentary work-options. Many travelers will work as receptionists or housekeepers for around four hours a day in exchange for free room and board. Such work is normally arranged (under the table) through hostel owners or other locals.

Other options for short-term work can be found at bars, cafes, and restaurants in heavily-touristed destinations. Waitressing or bartending usually pays NZ$9-13 an hour with negligible tips. **Ski resorts** often hire people for the July to October season, usually in restaurant positions or as lift operators, but sometimes as instructors. Hourly pay may be supplemented by a lift pass or free food and drink. For example, the Mt. Ruapehu ski fields recruit 750 staff members every February.

VOLUNTEERING

Whether farming in New Zealand or building houses in Fiji, volunteering is an enriching and worthwhile experience. Many volunteer services charge you a fee to participate in the program and to do work. These fees can be surprisingly hefty (they frequently cover airfare and most, if not all, living expenses), but the rewards of community service make them worth the price. Throughout this book, look for **Volunteer Opportunities** listings under the **Practical Information** heading.

Earthwatch, 3 Clocktower Pl., Ste. 100, P.O. Box 75, Maynard, MA 01754 (☎800-776-0188 or 978-461-0081; www.earthwatch.org). Arranges 1- to 3-week programs in New Zealand to promote conservation of natural resources. Programs average US$1600.

Farm Helpers in New Zealand, 50 Bright St., Eketahuna, NZ (☎06 375 8955; www.fhinz.co.nz). Publishes a booklet (NZ$25) with information on farms and families looking for workers in exchange for free room and board.

Greenpeace, 113 Valley Rd., Mt. Eden, Auckland, NZ (☎09 630 6317; www.greenpeace.org.nz), or Old Town Hall, on Victoria Pde., Suva, Fiji (☎331 2861; www.greenpeace.org.au). Organizes environmental, social, and political volunteer work in New Zealand and Fiji.

Habitat for Humanity International, 121 Habitat St., Americus, GA 31709 (☎800-422-4828 or 229-924-6935 x2551; www.habitat.org). Offers opportunities to help build low-income housing in New Zealand and Fiji. Programs cost US$2400-3000, including airfare from Los Angeles.

Willing Workers on Organic Farms (WWOOF), P.O. Box 1172, Nelson, NZ (☎/fax 03 544 9890; www.wwoof.co.nz). Distributes a list of names of over 600 farmers who offer room and board in exchange for help on the farm. Membership fee is NZ$30 from within the country; from overseas, AUS$35, UK£12, or US$20. Couples' discounts available.

FOR FURTHER READING ON ALTERNATIVES TO TOURISM

Academic Year Abroad 2000/2001. Institute of International Education Books (US$45).

How to Live Your Dream of Volunteering Oversees, by Collins, DeZerega, and Heckscher. Penguin Books, 2002 (US$17).

International Directory of Voluntary Work, by Whetter and Pybus. Peterson's Guides and Vacation Work, 2000 (US$16).

International Jobs, by Kocher and Segal. Perseus Books, 1999 (US$18).

Overseas Summer Jobs 2002, by Collier and Woodworth. Peterson's Guides and Vacation Work, 2002 (US$18).

Peterson's Study Abroad 2002. Peterson's (US$30).

Vacation Study Abroad 2000/2001. Institute of International Education Books (US$45).

Work Abroad: The Complete Guide to Finding a Job Overseas, by Hubbs, Griffith, and Nolting. Transitions Abroad Publishing, 2000 ($16).

Work Your Way Around the World, by Susan Griffith. Worldview Publishing Services, 2001 (US$18).

NEW ZEALAND (AOTEAROA)

HISTORY AND CURRENT EVENTS

IMPORTANT EVENTS

c. AD 950-1300
Polynesian settlement

1642
Abel Tasman makes the first European discovery of New Zealand

1733
The first sheep brought ashore by Captain Cook

1769
Captain Cook circumnavigates New Zealand

1814
Missionary Samuel Marsden preaches the first Christian sermon in New Zealand

1820-35
Musket Wars: inter-tribal conflict among Maori

1835
Naturalist Charles Darwin, on his famed voyage of the *Beagle*, spends Christmas in the Bay of Islands

LEGENDARY PRE-HISTORY

According to Maori legend, at the beginning of time, Papa (the earth) and Rangi (the sky) clung together in darkness. To bring light into the world, their children (who were gods) schemed to separate the sky and the earth. The god Tane was finally able to drive a wedge between Papa and Rangi, and the world was flooded with light. Papa and Rangi cried because of their separation, and their tears form the rain, dew, and ever-present mist that blankets *Aotearoa* (New Zealand), the "land of the long white cloud."

Maori legend tells that New Zealand was created through the exploits of the irreverent and mischievous Maui, one of the most beloved demi-gods of Polynesian myth. One day, he stowed away on a fishing trip and cast a hook (made from his grandmother's jawbone) with his own blood as bait. Almost instantly he hooked a fish, which when brought to the surface extended in all directions. Magically making the fish lie still, Maui created *Te ika a Maui* (Maui's fish)—the North Island of New Zealand. Similarly, the South Island is known in legend as *Te waka a Maui* (Maui's canoe) and tiny Stewart Island is *Te punga o te waka a Maui* (Maui's anchor stone). A large rock with a hole in it lies offshore, at the tip of Ninety Mile Beach. The Maori believe that this is the eye of Maui's hook.

MAORI SETTLEMENT

Research indicates that the first settlers, the ancestors of the modern Maori, came to New Zealand from the eastern Polynesian Islands between 950-1300AD. While tribal life was highly communal, Maori were fiercely territorial, and intertribal warfare was both brutal and common. Tribes kept close watch over their hunting, fishing, and burial lands. This protective attitude toward their land was still in full force hundreds of years later, when they encountered the first Europeans.

THE EUROPEAN ARRIVAL

The first European to lay eyes on New Zealand was Dutch explorer **Abel Tasman**. In 1642, Tasman tried to land in what is now the South Island's Golden Bay but never set foot on the islands, as he was met at sea by a hostile Maori tribe that killed many of his men. Several years later, a cartographer used Tasman's account to put the country on a world map for the first time, naming it *Nova Zeelandia* after a Dutch province.

GET CARD. TRAVEL HARD.

There's only one way to max out your travel experience and make the most of your time on the road: **The International Student Identity Card.**

 Packed with travel discounts, benefits and services, this card will keep your travel days and your wallet full. Get it before you hit it!

Visit **ISICUS.com** to get the full story on the benefits of carrying the ISIC.

Call or visit STA Travel online to find the nearest issuing office and purchase your card today:
www.statravel.com   (800) 777-0112

90 minutes, wash & dry (one sock missing).
5 minutes to book online (Detroit to Mom's).

Save money & time on student and faculty travel at **StudentUniverse.com**

 StudentUniverse.com

Real Travel Deals

The first group of Europeans to actually tread upon the uncharted land did not arrive until 1769, on the *Endeavour*, a British ship captained by the legendary explorer **James Cook.** Because of the glowing reports of virtually untouched natural splendor brought back by Cook and others, European settlement in New Zealand exploded. **Sealers** and **whalers,** arriving in droves in the early 1800s, were among the first to respond to the promise of pristine wilderness. **Missionaries** also made an early appearance, but despite earnest efforts, Christianity did not spread quickly, as Maori did not believe that it was a suitable religion for warriors. Heralding the start of heavier European settlement, independent **traders** were the next to arrive, seeking flax and novelty items in exchange for firearms, metal tools, and other European goods.

This increase in interaction lead to cultural clashes. The arrival of Christianity had undermined the tribal authority of the Maori chiefs and religious authorities. Traders brought the fatal gift of European disease, which killed an estimated 25% of the Maori population, while Western weapons escalated Maori intertribal violence and drastically increased fatalities. The culmination of this devastating warfare came in the form of the **Musket Wars** of 1820-35.

THE TREATY OF WAITANGI

By the late 1830s, the tensions between Maori and Europeans over land, government, and law had reached a breaking point. In January 1840, the British Colonial Office sent **Captain William Hobson** to effect the transfer of sovereignty over the land and government from Maori chiefs to the British. With the help of British resident **James Busby** among others, Hobson wrote the **Treaty of Waitangi** and presented it to a gathering of more than two hundred Maori chiefs and leaders on February 5, 1840. The treaty called for a complete cession of sovereignty by each Maori chief to the Queen of England. In return, it promised the Maori full rights of British citizens and guaranteed them the use of their lands. More than forty Maori leaders signed the treaty parchment, after which Captain William Hobson shook each Maori's hand, proclaiming: *"He iwi tahi tatou"* ("Now we are one people").

By the start of September 1840, when the last signature was added to the Treaty, more than 500 signatures had been gathered, although the Treaty still lacked the support of a number of powerful and influential chiefs. Despite this lack of unanimous acceptance of British authority, in May of 1840, Hobson proclaimed full sovereignty over New Zealand.

CONFLICTS AND WARS

As European settlement increased after 1840, the relationship between Maori and settlers continued to deteriorate. Before long, the Maori began to suspect that they had given up more than they had intended by ceding some of their autonomy to the British and responded by rebelling against British authority. In 1844, **Hone Heke,** one of the first chiefs to sign the Treaty, cut

---

1839
First brewery established at Thames

1840
Maori chiefs sign the Treaty of Waitangi; British claim sovereignty over the whole of New Zealand

1856
Britain declares New Zealand a self-governing colony

1858
Potatau Te Wherowhero proclaimed first Maori king

1860s
New Zealand Wars: conflict between British and Maori

1861
Gold discovered in Queenstown, starting a South Island gold rush

1865
National capital moves from Auckland to Wellington

1867
Four Maori seats established in Parliament

1870
First rugby match played in New Zealand

1886
Mt. Tarawera explodes over Rotorua

1893
New Zealand becomes the first nation in the world to grant suffrage to women

1898
The first car imported, a Benz brought over from Paris, requiring an Act of Parliament before it could be driven

1907
New Zealand becomes a British dominion

1908
New Zealand native Sir Ernest Rutherford, the man who would split the atom, wins the Nobel Prize for Chemistry

1915
New Zealand troops land at Gallipoli to fight in the First World War

1930s
New Zealand pioneers universal social welfare programs

1933
Elizabeth McCombs becomes the first woman elected to the House of Representatives

1937
First commercial planting of Chinese gooseberries (better known as kiwifruit)

down the flagpole at Kororareka near Russell (see p. 116), which he saw as a symbol of British oppression of the Maori. The Russell incident marked the beginning of warfare between Heke's army and British-led forces, which lasted until 1846.

In 1852, the **Constitution Act** established a settler government with six provinces and a national parliament with a lower and an upper house. The Constitution Act also granted suffrage to men over 25 as long as they met a low property qualification. However, though the amount of property required was relatively low, Maori were almost entirely excluded because Maori land was often held under a communal, not individual, title.

As British governmental influence grew, the Maori became increasingly disturbed to see the body that denied them representation taking shape and gaining power. Maori tribal leaders urged tribes to unite under one common leader and began the Maori **King Movement.** Supporters of this policy sought to centralize Maori resources, naming Te Wherowhero of Waikato their king in 1858 (see p. 142). The British government refused to recognize the Maori king, whom they viewed as a barrier to further settlement. When violent conflict erupted once again in the Taranaki region in 1860, **Governor George Grey** blamed the King Movement instead of addressing the recurrent problem of land ownership. He decided to strike at Waikato, the movement's primary stronghold. The **New Zealand Wars** (also known as **The Maori Wars**) exploded across the North Island as a result, with British forces ultimately gaining victory around 1870.

REFORMS

With the end of the New Zealand Wars, a modicum of order was restored as land disputes were settled through the courts. In 1865, the first **Native Lands Act** established a court to investigate Maori land ownership and distribute official land titles. In 1873, the second Native Lands Act split up the title for a land block among its shared owners. In 1882, disillusioned with the colonial government, the Ngapuhi tribe sent the first delegation to England to petition Queen Victoria. Although they were never given audience, Maori continued to send representatives until the 1920s. By the end of the 19th century, an astounding 92% of New Zealand's land was out of Maori control. Even while Maori were struggling for their rights, the last decades of the 19th century were a period of dramatic **social reforms** for the non-Maori. Factory conditions improved, there were increasing conservation efforts, and in 1893, New Zealand women were the first women in the world to receive the right to vote.

PROSPERITY AND WARS

In the 20th century, New Zealand, still forging its national identity, had to navigate increasingly complicated global relationships, conflicts, and markets. In 1907, New Zealand became a dominion of the British Empire, allowing it to determine its own foreign policy. By virtue of their relationship with Britain, in 1915, the **Australia and New Zealand Army Corps (ANZAC)** were enlisted to join troops in World War I. Chosen to join the infamous Dardanelles campaign, ANZAC fought at Gallipoli on April 25, attacking Turkish forces entrenched in the Dardanelles strait. The battle was a huge military failure, leading to massive casualties for Australia and New Zealand but winning great respect for the soldiers' bravery.

Like most of the western world, New Zealand suffered immensely during the Great Depression of the 1920s. However, the following decades were characterized by increasing prosperity. In 1935, the victory of the liberal Labour Party spurred the creation of the world's first universal social welfare system, including free health care and low-rent public housing. By the 1940s, New Zealand's main industries were booming and the country maintained one of the highest standards of living in the world. This prosperity came just in time to be disrupted by **World War II;** this time, with widespread fighting in the South Pacific, the disturbance was much closer to home. Once again, when called to arms, New Zealand forces proved themselves to be tenacious and admirable soldiers. The **28th (Maori) Battalion,** in particular, won acclaim in battles fought from Crete to Africa and proved not only to be fierce in battle but creative and unorthodox in their tactics.

Negotiations between Maori and non-Maori continued into the early 20th century. In 1909, the third **Native Lands Act** set aside funds specifically for Maori land development in order to aid Maori farmers. In 1935, the first **Labour Party** came into government, touting official recognition of the Treaty of Waitangi as part of their platform.

POST-WWII

New Zealand was declared fully independent in 1947, but remained tied to a number of nations across the world. The war had demonstrated New Zealand's dependence for military protection, as US intervention protected New Zealand from possible Japanese hostilities. New Zealand aimed to secure its future by signing the **ANZUS Pact** (securing the mutual defense of Australia, New Zealand, and the US) and by independently harnessing its own energy resources. Maintaining strong ties to the greater community of nations, New Zealand became one of the member states of the United Nations in 1945.

Domestically, the government replicated its international spirit of cooperation, attempting to ease tensions with the Maori. Adherence to traditional beliefs among Maori declined dramatically, though the traditional tensions with the Pakeha (New Zealand residents of European descent) remained. In 1960, the **Waitangi Day Act** made February 6th a national "day of thanksgiving," in celebration of the bi-racial nature of the coalition created by the 1840 Treaty. Thirteen years later, it was declared an official public holiday. The 1975 **Treaty of Waitangi Act** set up the Waitangi Tribunal to hear Maori claims against the Crown.

In 1983, New Zealand and Australia established the **Closer Economic Relations Trade Agreement,** which allowed free and unrestricted trade between the two nations. With its foreign

1947
New Zealand becomes fully independent by adopting the Statute of Westminster

1953
Sir Edmund Hillary, New Zealand climbing god, and Sherpa Norgay Tenzing become the first men to summit Mount Everest

1960
First television broadcasts begin in New Zealand

1970
Nga Tamatoa forms, becoming one of the largest groups lobbying for Maori cultural identity and land claims

1975
Waitangi Tribunal established to investigate Maori claims against the government

1978
Kiwi Naomi Jones becomes the first woman to sail single-handedly around the world

1982
First licensed FM radio station in New Zealand goes on the air

1984
Labour Party wins election, leading to a new free-trade economy

1985
Greenpeace vessel *Rainbow Warrior* is sunk in Auckland Harbour (see p. 112)

1987
New Zealand declared a nuclear-free zone; New Zealand wins the inaugural rugby World Cup; inventor of bungy, A.J. Hackett, bungy jumps off the Eiffel Tower; and the Maori Language Act establishes Maori as an official language

1990
New Zealand hosts the Commonwealth Games and a visit from Queen Elizabeth II; mountaineers Gary Ball and Rob Hall summit the highest mountain on each of the 7 continents in 7 months, shattering the previous record by 2 years

1992
Shortland Street, New Zealand's emergency room soap opera, debuts

1995
New Zealand's *Black Magic* yachting squad wins the America's Cup

policy, New Zealand continued to retain its independent streak. In 1987, Labour Party Prime Minister David Lange committed New Zealand to the **anti-nuclear movement** by barring all nuclear-capable vessels from New Zealand harbors. His action was the culmination of a movement that was heightened by the 1985 bombing by French agents of the Greenpeace ship, *Rainbow Warrior*, while it was in Auckland harbor (see p. 112).

NEW ZEALAND TODAY

GOVERNMENT

New Zealand is a parliamentary government with a popularly elected single chamber legislature, although it lacks a written constitution. In 1993, the majority of New Zealanders voted to establish a **mixed-member proportional representation (MMP)** system of government. Under the system, a 120-seat Parliament was established, with a predetermined number of general electorate seats, party list seats (in which the elected party selects members), and Maori seats. New Zealand citizens are accorded two votes, one for the preferred ruling party and the second for a certain candidate to represent their electorate. Citizens of Maori descent may choose whether to register either on the general or Maori roll.

In recent years, New Zealand politics has been defined by behind-the-scenes maneuvering, fragile power-sharing arrangements, and allegations of corruption. In November 1997, **Jenny Shipley** of the **National Party** engineered a "coup" to seize party leadership. She was sworn in as New Zealand's first woman prime minister in December of that year. A primary focus of Shipley's government was to increase free-market competition and reduce government size. Shipley's term was thrown into disarray in August 1998. She inherited a fragile coalition between her own conservative National Party and the more liberal New Zealand First. During Shipley's tenure, she was often embroiled in controversy, a trait that may have led to her subsequent electoral loss.

In November 1999, parliamentary elections restored the center-left Labour Party, led by **Helen Clark,** to power after nine years in the opposition. Labour Party success was credited in part to its increased support from Maori citizens, following the erratic changes in the previously Maori-dominated **New Zealand First** party. As Prime Minister, Clark has allied with the left-wing Alliance Party in coalition but relies on support from the newly influential Green Party. In 2002, Clark began a push to replace Queen Elizabeth as the head of state and turn New Zealand into a republic.

MAORI ISSUES

The recognition of **Maori land rights** continues to be an issue of heated governmental debate. The **Office of Treaty Settlement** is the government organization responsible for mediating between Maori claims and the New Zealand Crown. In one recent large settlement in November 1997, the New Zealand Crown admitted in the **Ngai Tahu Deed of Settlement** that it had acted unfairly and in violation of the 1840 Treaty of Waitangi.

IN THE NEWS

ELECTION 2002. In June 2002, New Zealand Prime Minister Helen Clark announced an early election for July 27, 2002, almost three months before the government's three-year term was to expire. Clark and her Labour Party were able to win 41% of the vote by making concessions to the Progressive Coalition and conservative-leaning United Future parties. The election marks the end to a previous coalition between the Labour and the Green Party. Clark wants to end the moratorium on genetically engineered foods, and the Green Party failed to secure enough votes in the election to sustain the moratorium.

SPORTS. New Zealand is gearing up to defend the cup in **America's Cup 2003.** Russell Couts, the skipper who led Team New Zealand to its two previous America's Cup victories, quit after the 2000 campaign and will be leading Switzerland's Alinghi Team in 2003. American crew members have been studying the climactic records of the Hauraki Gulf for the past seven years, and with the recent announcement of the addition of Rob Waddell (2000 Olympic gold medalist in the single scull) to Team New Zealand as a grinder, the excitement continues to boil.

THE CULTURE

THE PEOPLE

The total population of New Zealand is about 3.9 million, with three-quarters of the population living in the North Island (half in Auckland). Most of the population is **caucasian. Maori,** the largest minority ethnic group, make up 15% of the population; other **Pacific Islanders** are the next largest group at 6%. **Asians** are also a fast-growing minority group, expected to nearly double in population between 1996 and 2016. In 2001, **Asians** comprised just under 5% of New Zealand's population.

Christianity is the predominant religion; Anglican, Presbyterian, and Catholic denominations are the most commonly practiced. Maori denominations of Christianity were first developed during the missionary era of the late-19th and early-20th centuries in an effort to synthesize traditional Maori beliefs with the precepts of Christianity.

MAORI ARTS AND CULTURE

New Zealand society is largely bicultural, comprised primarily of **Pakeha,** the Maori word for people of European descent, and those of Maori descent. The word *"maori"* has an interesting origin in itself, as it was originally used not to denote a common background but rather to distinguish the "ordinary people" from the extraordinary and strange European explorers. Similarly, **Maoritanga,** loosely translated as "the ways of the Maori," serves as an umbrella word for the communal, ceremonial, and cultural traditions and organization of Maori life. New Zealand has recently experienced a renaissance of *Maoritanga* as more Maori look to their rich heritage for security and identity.

1997
Jenny Shipley becomes Prime Minister and the first female leader in New Zealand history

1998
The Museum of New Zealand Te Papa Tongarewa opens (see p. 250); first edition of *Let's Go: New Zealand* goes to print

1999
New Zealand lowers the drinking age to 18

2000
Team New Zealand defends the America's Cup; US President Bill Clinton attends the APEC conference in Auckland

2001
DOC publishes goals and priorities for the environment; large oil fields discovered in Taranaki; World Champion Sculler, Rob Waddell joins Team New Zealand for the much anticipated America's Cup 2003. The first installment of the *Lord of the Rings* trilogy, filmed in New Zealand, opens in theaters

2002
PM Helen Clark opens New Zealand's 14th National Park on Stewart Island

BASIC CONCEPTS

The most fundamental idea of Maori custom is the notion of **tapu** and its lesser known counterpart **noa**. *Tapu* indicates the presence of supernatural power (whether good or evil) and commands respect and attention. *Noa* underscores the absence of such power and thus deserves no special caution. For example, a man has the *tapu* responsibility in a tribe to oversee ceremonial duties and give speeches at a *marae* (see **Marae,** below), but he cannot look respectable without the help of the female's *noa* duties of preparing food and singing songs.

Personal relationships within and between tribes also require an understanding of **mana**. Translated literally, the word means "prestige" or "respectability," but the true meaning is a supernatural essence that possesses and grants seniority to a worthy individual. Traditionally, the amount of *mana* in an individual depends on his ancestry, experience, and seniority in a tribe. Nowadays, *mana* is instead often influenced more by one's success and achievements.

Above all, Maori traditionally look for balance and fairness personally and in a tribal community. When someone is made to feel inferior, he becomes **whakama**—either ashamed due to undue criticism or actually guilty of a misdeed. Self-respect is just as crucial as the respect of others. One who is *whakaiti* (self-belittling) or *whakahihi* (arrogant) lacks the composure and humility—the *mana*—to be a leader in a tribe.

MAORI TRIBAL STRUCTURE

In New Zealand, association with a tribe is not an official designation; forty-two tribes are currently accorded the title of *iwi*. Within the *iwi* exist smaller regional communities called **hapu**. These communities were originally descent groups that owned land within the tribe. Today, each *hapu* seldom owns more land than a *marae* reserve (see **Marae,** below). For this reason, the *hapu* generally has more meaning to rural populations who live and work with other members of the same community; city-dwellers generally tend to identify less with their *hapu*.

THE MARAE

The *marae* is the sacred grounds around a Maori *whare tupuna* (ancestral meetinghouse) and the site of the **powhiri** (formal welcome) receiving visitors into the community. The ceremony consists of four basic components. Upon arriving at the *marae*, a warrior from the village will greet your group with a *haka* (see **Dance,** below), an elaborate set of prowling steps, body movements, and a tongue-protruding facial gesture (it's exceedingly uncouth to return such a gesture). The **wero** (challenge) ends when a **teka** (peace offering) is offered and accepted. After this step, a female elder will issue the **karanga**, a chant of welcome and mourning for the visitors' great ancestors. As your group crosses the *marae*, pause and bow in respect for the ancestors of the tribe before congregating in front of the *whare*. In his **whaikorero** (speech of welcoming), the chief of the tribe will welcome your group in Maori, and the designated chief of your group will deliver a brief speech in return (preferably in Maori as well, but protocol varies). To seal the bond of friendship, both chiefs press (but do not rub) noses together in the traditional greeting known as the **hongi**. After the *hongi*, the separate groups finally come together until called to dine in the *whare kai*. Shoes are not worn inside the *whare*, and pictures may not be permitted, depending on the tribe. After a **karakia** (prayer) is given, the dinner, **hangi**, is prepared by roasting sweet potatoes, meat, and other goodies in a pit of heated stones until they reach peak smoky delicacy.

SONG

Traditional Maori song and oratory are particularly important to ceremonial life. **Tau marae** orations are formal, stylized tributes to the dead performed at traditional funeral ceremonies for important chiefs. Another important type of oratory is **karakia** (chants), which were once strictly the property of **tohunga** (priests or specially learned men). *Karakia* imparted **mauri** (essence of its natural state) to objects, as in the Maori myth in which Tiki chants a *karakia* in order to bring his clay figurine to life. **Waiata** is the most common type of ceremonial song that is customarily performed at the conclusion of farewell speeches at **tangi** (funerals) and those of welcoming at *powhiri*. In modern times, the two kinds of *waiata* that have survived—the *waiata tangi*, songs of mourning (often composed by women), and the *waiata aroha*, love songs (solely composed by women)—often dwell upon unrequited love, obstacles in love, and delinquent lovers.

DANCE

Maori dance includes more than just fancy footwork; one's entire body, voice, and spirit are incorporated into what may be the most dramatic Maori art form. The vigorous arm-waving, chanting, foot-stomping **haka** is an all-male dance once performed by armed warriors before battle as an invocation to the god of war. To see a modern *haka*, head to a *marae* (see p. 56) or just check out the **All Blacks** (see p. 61) before every rugby match. **Taparahi,** on the other hand, are weaponless dances performed by both genders for a variety of reasons: to greet important guests, to honor the dead, or for sheer entertainment. In the **poi** (originally designed to increase suppleness and flexibility in the wrists of warriors), women twirl balls on strings in elegant synchronicity.

CARVING

An early Maori art form, carving is still practiced today. The most common materials are bone, wood, and greenstone *(pounamu)*. According to traditional Maori beliefs, it is the artist's responsibility to impart certain qualities such as fear, power, and authority to his or her pieces in order to transform them from mere material objects to **taonga** (highly treasured, even sacred objects). Each object also accumulates its own body of **korero** (stories) with each successive owner. A design particular to a tribe is passed down from generation to generation, distinguishing itself by its repetition of certain stylistic features and motifs, such as **tiki** (human forms), **manaia** (bird men), and **taniwha** (sea spirits). Carvers create items large and small, decorating both towering meeting houses and tiny *tiki* pendants.

MOKO (FACIAL TATTOOING)

Moko has been one of the most famous Maori art forms since the days when 19th-century Europe was transfixed by portraits and photographs of New Zealand "savages" with full facial tattoos. While most tribes reserved the practice for males, *moko* sometimes served as a rite of passage for both males and females, as well as a marker of achievements and status. Men's *moko* began with a simple design for youths; more spiral flourishes were added as the wearer won prestige in battle. Thus, only older, highly distinguished warriors could sport full facial tattoos. Women's *moko* were simpler, usually surrounding only the lips and the tip of the nose, although some stout-hearted women elected to have their thighs and breasts tattooed as well.

Traditionally, *moko* was only executed by *tohunga ta moko*, experts trained extensively in using the sharp wooden adze and mallet or birdbone chisel to etch the design into the skin, then in using a toothed chisel to fill in the ink dye (a mixture of burned kauri or totara resin and pigeon fat), all done in complete silence. While the tattoo was healing, the *tohunga ta moko* declared the recipient *tapu* (sacred), while leaves of the karaka tree were placed on the skin. During this time, sexual intimacy was prohibited and no one was permitted to view the *moko;* they believed it would fade if anyone saw it before it healed completely. Today, Maori continue to practice *moko*, though often using face paint to replicate this intricate art on occasions of ceremonial display.

VISUAL ARTS AND LITERATURE

A number of prominent and critically acclaimed artists have hailed from New Zealand in the last century. **Frances Hodgkins** (1869-1947) and **Colin McCahon** (1919-87) are two of the most famous 20th-century New Zealand painters. Hodgkins left New Zealand in 1913 for London, eventually becoming a leading figure in watercolor figurative painting, then in oils. McCahon retained his base in New Zealand and is considered one of the most important influences on modern art there.

New Zealand has its share of literary stars as well. **Katherine Mansfield** (1888-1923), a short story-writer, was another World War I expatriate to Britain. Her best-known short story collections are *The Garden Party* (1922) and before that *Bliss* (1920). Mansfield's childhood home in Wellington has been preserved as a museum (see p. 250). **Dame Ngaio Marsh** (1895-1982), most renowned for her mystery series featuring detective Roderick Alleyn, stayed firmly rooted in New Zealand as a member of the leading artistic group in Christchurch in the mid-1900s. Other notable New Zealand writers include poet **James K. Baxter** (1926-1972), renowned for his celebration of the New Zealand wilderness, and novelist **Janet Frame** (b. 1924), best known for *Owls Do Cry* (1957), *A State of Siege* (1966), and her autobiographical *An Angel at My Table* (1985), which was later adapted to film by Jane Campion.

Maori writers have surged onto the literary scene as well. For example, **Patricia Grace** (b. 1937), of Ngati Raukawa, Ngati Toa, and Te Ati Awa descent, is known for the bittersweet coming-of-age story *Mutuwhenua: The Moon Sleeps* (1978), about a young Maori girl's love for a Pakeha (non-Maori). **Witi Ihimaera** (b. 1944) is best-known for *Tangi* (1973), an exploration of father-son relationships. Ihimaera's later works focus on issues of gay identity in books like *Nights in the Gardens of Spain*. Perhaps the most well-known Maori author is **Keri Hulme** (b. 1947), a South Islander of Scottish, English, and Ngai Tahu descent, whose novel *The Bone People* won the 1985 Booker Prize. More recently, **Alan Duff** (b. 1950) made a big splash in the fiction world with his hit *Once Were Warriors* (1992) and its sequel *What Becomes of the Broken-Hearted* (1997) about the trials of a Maori family in the modern world (see p. 59).

MUSIC

Geographic isolation hasn't disconnected New Zealand from music trends of the past. Kiwis had **punk** in the 1970s too, a phase that continued throughout the decade with the influential Christchurch label **Flying Nun.** In the 1980s, **Split Enz** and its offshoot **Crowded House** enjoyed worldwide popularity as part of the **New Wave** movement. Alternative rock has also gained popularity, as with student band **Zed's** popular album *Silencer* and hits from **Th'Dudes'** like "Be Mine Tonight" and "That Look In Your Eyes." Today, electronic music reigns supreme in the nightclubs, in a range of genres from house to drum 'n' bass.

Check out *The Fix*, a free glossy mag, for info on the Auckland scene. Down in Wellington, **Mu** demonstrates his skills on the vinyl, while **Manuel Bundy** crisscrosses the country with rhythmically centered beats. Perhaps of more interest to Top 40 fans, **OMC** (Otara Millionaires Club) laid claim to the hip-hop and dance music scene with their hit "How Bizarre" before breaking up a few years ago. A recent addition to the New Zealand music scene is Chinese-Maori **Bic Runga**, known for her hit song "Sway."

New Zealand's premier professional orchestra, the New Zealand Symphony Orchestra enjoys an excellent reputation which merits its traveling over 20,000 kilometers a year to perform. Internationally renowned opera star and New Zealand native **Dame Kiri Te Kanawa** also performs for audiences worldwide.

FILM

New Zealand's own film industry was not fully established until the 1970s. One notable figure from the New Zealand film scene was **Len Lye** (1901-80), kinetic sculptor and modern filmmaker of the '60s. Lye pioneered the technique of "direct filmmaking," in which images are etched or painted directly onto the film itself. Born in Christchurch, Lye left New Zealand for London in the early 1900s, joining fellow expatriate Frances Hodgkins (see p. 58) in London's artsy elite of the '20s and '30s, then moving to New York in 1944. Today his work is shown at the Govett-Brewster Art Gallery in New Plymouth (see p. 222).

The early '70s saw works mainly by independent filmmakers. A significant event in New Zealand film during this time, as well as a landmark work in Maori representation on the silver screen, was the release of *Tangata Whenua: The People of the Land* (1974), a six-part documentary series by Maori filmmaker Barry Barclay.

In 1978, the government created the New Zealand Film Commission, which encourages and financially supports the film industry. Since then, recent films made in New Zealand have become both popular and critical hits. One-sixth of the country viewed *Goodbye Pork Pie* (1981), directed by Geoff Murphy. A film every Kiwi will tell you to see is *Once Were Warriors* (adapted from Alan Duff's 1992 book of the same name), from prominent director Lee Tamahori. The film was critically acclaimed for its stark, honest appraisal of the plight of urban Maori today. Jane Campion's *The Piano* (1993), filmed in New Zealand, broke box office records and won two Cannes Film Festival awards and a Best Supporting Actress Oscar for teen star **Anna Paquin**. Kiwis love to claim the rough, tough, and buff *Gladiator* **Russell Crowe** as a native; though born in Wellington, Crowe spent most of his life in nearby Australia. On the other hand, adoptive Kiwi **Sam Neill** wasn't born Down Under but did grow up on the South Island before landing coveted roles in *The Hunt for Red October* (1990), *Jurassic Park* (1993), *Event Horizon* (1997), *Jurassic Park III* (2001), and as a cat burglar on an episode of *The Simpsons*. Proving that Kiwis exist on the other side of the camera as well, writer-director and Wellingtonian **Peter Jackson** is perhaps most famous for *Heavenly Creatures* (1992), based on the true story of two unhappy teenagers' unstable friendship and their escape into a fantasy world. However, it is the *Lord of the Rings* trilogy (2001, 2002, 2003), all filmed in New Zealand, that has film critics and Tolkien fans across the world drooling in excitement. The first episode, *The Fellowship of the Ring*, was released in theatres in 2001. **Lucy Lawless,** formerly known as **Xena,** continues to be New Zealand's pride and joy, as she moves onto bigger and (debatably) better things *(The X-Files)*. You may still catch a glimpse of a rerun of *Xena, Warrior Princess* on late-night TV.

FOOD AND DRINK

"I myself prefer my New Zealand eggs for breakfast."
—Queen Elizabeth, after she was pelted with eggs on a New Zealand visit in 1968

In the tradition of the earliest inhabitants' dinners of roast moa and **kumara** (a sweet potato), New Zealanders still maintain a largely meat-and-potatoes diet. While **vegetarian** and vegan options are becoming increasingly trendy (**kosher** fare is still rare), traditional New Zealand food tends to run on the heavy, meaty side, with lamb, venison (called cervena when farm-raised), beef, and pork dominating the menus of traditional establishments. By far the national dish would have to be the hot **meat pies** loaded with lamb or beef and gravy in flaky pastry. Fresh **seafood** is always an abundant alternative; fresh fish, prawns (what Americans call jumbo shrimp), crayfish, shellfish, and more overrun coastal towns. Fruit-flavored **ice cream** loaded with chunks of real fruit is also consumed in vast quantities, although backpackers seem more likely to praise the **hokey pokey** variety (vanilla ice cream loaded with bits of toffee) and the **goody goody gumdrops** (mint ice cream filled with soft, jube candy). New Zealand proudly produces the most **ice cream per capita** in the world.

In small towns, the tendency toward the basic can be seen in the Main Street triumvirate of fish 'n' chips dives, cafes, and the ever-present Chinese restaurants, all serving fried and greasy goodies. Excellent foreign restaurants, such as Thai, Malaysian, and Indian, are no longer few and far between. Middle Eastern **kebab** joints, usually a good value, have proliferated recently. **BYO** (bring-your-own wine) restaurants without a license to sell liquor are widespread; some charge a corking fee. Keep in mind that ordering an **entree** will often get you an appetizer or starter in New Zealand; main courses are listed as **mains.**

With an average of 188 bottles per person annually, New Zealand ranks first in the world in **beer** drinking, consuming even more than their notorious guzzling neighbors, the Aussies. The Kiwis serve up a good brew, with various national lagers and draughts (such as Steinlager), regional beers (such as Speights and Tui), and specialty brews. The **wines** of the Marlborough and Hawke's Bay regions are world-famous, particularly the Sauvignon Blanc, Chardonnay, Riesling, Cabernet Sauvignon, and Pinot Noir varieties. New Zealand white wines are already challenging the French hold on the market, and red wines are improving yearly. Hard liquor is less popular because import taxes make it more expensive. For nonalcoholic refreshment, try **Lemon and Paeroa (L&P),** a popular carbonated lemon drink that is "world-famous in New Zealand," as the advertisements tell you with a wink. For a more refined thirst-quencher, you can enjoy a British-style **Devonshire tea.** The late afternoon snack traditionally plies you with tea, scones with Devonshire cream or jam, crumpets, and other delectables. A lighter Kiwi treat, often served for dessert, is the **pavlova,** a tribute to egg whites and kiwifruit. On a more nutritious note, New Zealand offers a range of exotic fruits and veggies, including feijoas, nashi, persimmons, and of course kiwifruit. In 2000, the newly-created golden kiwifruit, a yellower, sweeter version of the traditional kiwi, became popular around the world.

SPORTS

New Zealand is a sports-crazed nation; almost half the population belongs to the New Zealand Sports Assembly, which represents 150 national sporting associations. In addition to the multitude of outdoor sports, including skiing, rafting, swimming, hiking, and jetboating, New Zealanders also hit the grass in organized sports like rugby, cricket, golf, tennis, and field hockey.

New Zealand keeps certain sporting heroes at the center of national pride. **Sir Edmund Hillary,** the first to climb Mt. Everest in 1953, is perhaps the most famous and is also on the $5 bill. New Zealand has also seen the rise of many prominent Olympians, especially in track and field events. **Jack Lovelock** was a 1500m gold medalist in the 1936 Berlin Olympics. **Yvette Williams** was long jump champion in the 1952 Helsinki Olympics. And in the 1960 Rome Olympics, **Peter Snell** and **Murray Halberg** took home the gold in the 800m and 5000m respectively. Snell then went on to break records across five different events, including running a world record mile in 1962 and again in 1964. In recognition of his prodigious achievements, Peter Snell was celebrated throughout New Zealand in spring 2000 as the Alac "Sportsman of the Century."

THE CULTURE ■ 61

ALL BLACK ALL OVER From hostel walls to the TV, from the daily paper to bathroom stalls, New Zealand's national rugby team, the All Blacks, are there. Protected with a fierce pride against such abominations as the padded wimpiness of American gridiron, rugby is a source of national unity and honor. Each player must be strong on both offense and defense, quick and powerful, fit enough to last the full grueling 80min., and most of all, tough. In 1986, Buck Shelford gave new meaning to the phrase "he's got balls" when he almost lost his in a test (international match) against France, leaving the game to receive emergency surgery. Although they lost to South Africa in the 1995 World Cup final, the team has consistently been one of the world's best. An All Blacks loss is so unexpected that tears from devastated fans mix with beer in pubs across the country. The marketing power of the team is so strong that every other national team is spun from their yarn; New Zealand fields the female Black Ferns in rugby, the All Whites in soccer, the Tall Blacks in basketball, the Black Sox in softball, and the Black Caps in cricket. While it may take Kiwi blood to fully understand the intricacies and meaning of the game, you don't have to jump in the middle of a scrum to appreciate the athletic prowess of popular star Jonah Lomu, the intensity of the Maori *haka* (war dance) challenge offered to opponents before each game, or the delirious passion of fans at the scoring of a try. Rugby is not merely sport, it is love.

Though New Zealand's performance in the 2001 Sydney Olympics seemed less than stellar, **Rob Waddell** brought home a gold medal in the single scull. A two time world champion in the single, a world record holder for 2000m at 6:36.38, and well over 220 pounds, Waddell was and is a force to be reckoned with. Waddell is the only athlete who has ever been voted the "Sportsman of the Year" twice: 1998 and 1999. Though presently retired, Waddell's next hardware may come from defending the title for the America's Cup in 2003 for Team New Zealand.

RUGBY. This active country also likes to sit on the sidelines, especially to watch rugby. Kiwi pride swells enormously for the **All Blacks,** the national team whose season usually runs from late May to September. When a crucial match like the **Bledisloe Cup Championship** is being televised, forget about going out to eat, changing money, or shopping—all the locals will be glued to their TVs, not running businesses. If anything, this craze became even worse following the All Blacks' 1987 victory in the rugby World Cup. Despite the All Blacks' widespread popularity, however, the team has encountered controversial moments in its history. In 1960, for example, the All Blacks made a vehemently protested national tour of South Africa in which Maori players were excluded. Then, in 1981, the South African Springboks made a tour of New Zealand, prompting many to claim that New Zealand was tacitly supporting apartheid.

Most people in New Zealand are die-hard **Rugby Union** fans. Historically, the Rugby Union organized amateur competition among teams. As players gained fame and prominence, the Rugby Union eventually became a professional sport. **The Super 12** tournament is a popular rugby event with the best players from Australia, South Africa, and New Zealand organized into twelve national (and regional) teams. In 2000, defending champions Canterbury Crusaders barely defeated the Canberra Brumbies. The highlight of the year is the **Tri-Nations Games** that takes place among the New Zealand, Australia, and South Africa teams from July to August. This is the **All Blacks'** time to shine (see **All Black All Over,** above).

Be sure not to confuse Rugby Union with the less popular, but no less exciting, **Rugby League,** which features regional teams like the stalwart, ever-popular Auckland Warriors. The difference between the two can be confusing, but long ago the Rugby League split with Rugby Union over disagreement about the "purity" of professional rugby play. While Rugby League sanctioned professional play, Rugby Union insisted on remaining amateur until turning professional a few decades ago.

CRICKET. There are two basic types of cricket competition. The first is **test-match cricket,** which takes place between two teams in a 6hr. match each day for five days. The second method of competition is **one-day cricket,** typically played, as the name suggests, as a one-day series between pairs of teams or round-robin competitions between teams. A World Cup one-day competition is played between all the Test nations—the nine nations officially recognized by the International Cricket Council. New Zealand has always been one of the top competitors among the World Cup nations. But the **Black Caps** suffered a shocking defeat to India in 1999, marking their fifth semi-final defeat in seven World Cups. New Zealand is currently ranked fourth in the world leading into the 2003 World Cup in South Africa.

SAILING. In 1995 the Kiwi sailing team **Black Magic** swiped the America's Cup from the United States, marking only the second time in 144 years that the cup was not won by an American team. The cup's subsequent mauling at the hands and sledgehammer of a Maori activist drew international headlines. Fully restored, the cup made several countrywide tours.

In March 2000, **Team New Zealand**, determined to protect the Kiwi hold on the Cup, masterfully trounced their Italian opponent Prada Challenge with innovative racing techniques. With this decisive victory, New Zealand cemented its reputation as a top yachting nation, becoming the first country other than the US to successfully defend the Cup. For more on **America's Cup,** see **In the News,** p. 55.

OUTDOOR NEW ZEALAND

Outdoor-lovers, welcome to the playground of your dreams. Ringed by wild and frothy waters, site of a major tectonic plate collision, and home to thousands of endemic plant and animal species, New Zealand overflows with geological and biological wonders. Separating early from an ancient supercontinent, New Zealand's landmass charted an evolutionary course different from the rest of the world. Kiwis acknowledge, protect, and enjoy their nation's ecological uniqueness; even better, they love sharing it with visitors. Whether summitting a glacier-encrusted peak, skydiving above a pristine lake, or paddling a forgotten fiord, you're bound to bump into a few smiling Kiwis, grinning with pride over their beautiful backyard. This pride is certainly well-deserved, so strap on that pack, clip into a belay, and get yourself out there.

THE LAND AND ENVIRONMENT

BEFORE HUMAN ARRIVAL

The ancient supercontinent of **Gondwanaland** combined modern-day South America, Africa, peninsular India, Antarctica, and Australia. New Zealand split from the supercontinent roughly 80 million years ago, much earlier than the other present-day continents, making it an isolated biological time capsule. During the span of time before human arrival, the plants and animals on the islands evolved in ways different from creatures on the other continents. With the absence of predators, New Zealand's birds evolved to occupy the ecological niches that mammals assumed elsewhere in the world. They gained stronger legs, larger size, and occasionally lost use of their wings. Two excellent examples of these unique birds—the **Haast eagle** *(Hapagornis)* and the **moa**—are now extinct. The giant Haast eagle dominated the New Zealand food chain; the world's largest eagle, it's wings spanned more than three meters. The moa was New Zealand's chief grazing bird. All 11 species of moa were large, but some stood tall enough to look Big Bird in the eye. The smallest were the size of turkeys. The **kiwi**, a squat, thin-beaked bird—now a national emblem—also flourished on pre-human New Zealand.

PLANTS

Before 1800, 70% of the landscape was covered in forest; today, only 15% of the original lowland forest and only 10% of the original wetlands remain. Still, there are 2700 plants native to New Zealand (of which DOC reports that 80% are endemic). The most famous among these species are the towering **kauri**, whose forests are among the most ancient in the world and whose value to today's tourist industry in Northland is inestimable (see p. 105). Colonial loggers harvested ninety percent of the original kauri forests. The kauri are just one of a large family of **podocarps**, a class of conifers that includes other native trees such as **totara, rimu, miro, matai,** and **kahikatea**; such podocarps dominate many of New Zealand's forested regions. **Beech forests** are also common; the *Nothofagus* is the most famous genus and can trace its roots to the *Nothofagus* forests that blanketed Gondwanaland. There are 193 different species of fern in New Zealand, 88 of which are endemic. **Mamaku tree ferns** can grow up to 20m in height; the **ponga tree fern**, with its silver-undersided fronds, is the official national symbol.

The **pohutukawa**, often called "New Zealand's Christmas tree" for the bright crimson flowers that bloom in most varieties during late December, is another distinctive species found in the northern regions. Maori tradition holds that when these gnarled coastal trees bloom early there will be a long hot summer ahead. The **rata** begins life as a vine and slowly strangles its host tree to death. Similar to the pohutukawa, the rata adds a peachy-orangish cast to the landscape. Numerous other plant species are unique to the country including the world's largest buttercup, the Mt. Cook lily, and New Zealand's only native palm trees, the Nikau palms.

ANIMALS

Many animal families that evolved on the supercontinent never came into being in New Zealand. Most noticeably, New Zealand has no snakes and no native land mammals. Instead, the country has a preponderance of strange and exotic birds. Four different species of **kiwi** have slender and probing beaks with external nostrils to help in scrounging for food on the forest floor. These solitary birds are nocturnal, flightless, tail-less, and almost wingless. The **kea,** the world's only alpine parrot, is one of the few birds to reside in the peaks of the Southern Alps. Any visitor to the ski slopes or national parks of New Zealand will quickly realize that the kea is no ordinary polly but rather a clever, destructive, and bold menace (see **Peck and Destroy,** p. 332). The **kereru** is the native pigeon and the only bird able to disperse the larger seeds of some native plants. Fanciful names for New Zealand's amazing variety of birds abound: the **morepork** *(ruru,* the only native owl), the **muttonbird** *(titi),* and the **wrybill** *(ngutuparore,* with its slender and twisted beak) among others.

Unfortunately, many of New Zealand's beautiful birds are endangered today. A little over 250 turkey-sized, blue-green, and strong-beaked **takahe** remain. The **black stilt** *(kaki)* are down to 80. Only 62 nocturnal **kakapo,** the world's heaviest parrot (males can weigh in at 4kg), are still in existence; DOC states that the kakapo is perhaps "the slowest-breeding bird on earth." Intensive conservation efforts are underway for all three species, including the creation of predator-free sanctuaries on off-shore islands and in remote wilderness areas. Some of the most recognizable New Zealand bird species are its seven types of **penguins.** Among them, the blue, yellow-eyed, and Fiordland crested are the most common. These fascinating birds are popular with South Island tourists in Otago (see p. 348).

With over 1500 species of **land snails** (some of which are carnivorous), 11 species of the heaviest insect in the world (the ancient, mouse-sized, grasshopper-esque **weta**), teeming crayfish *(koura),* pesky sandflies *(te namu),* and the ethereal glowworms *(titiwai),* there is no shortage of diverse creepy-crawlies. New Zealand also has the coastal **katipo spider,** a relative of the black widow. Another ancient relic found in New Zealand is the **tuatara,** a lizard-like creature old enough to have roamed with the dinosaurs 200 million years ago. An interesting feature of this reptile is its third eye, which helps to regulate its exposure to the sun.

Bats are the only indigenous land mammals, but there are plenty of marine mammals hugging New Zealand's shores. Orca, seals, and sea lions can be found in the waters off the South Island. New Zealand also boasts almost half of the world's whale, porpoise, and dolphin populations. Marine mammals unique to New Zealand include **Hector's dolphins, beaked whales,** the **New Zealand fur seal,** and the **Hooker sea lion.** Marine mammal populations reached dramatic lows from the whaling and sealing trades earlier in the century; today, climate changes and water pollution threaten these animals.

INVASIONS

When the first settlers from Polynesia arrived over a thousand years ago with breeds of disease-carrying **dogs** *(kuri)* and **rats** *(kiore)*, an age of extinction began. The Maori and later the Europeans cleared forests for agriculture and hunted the moa to extinction. Man's presence on New Zealand brought the massive destruction of natural habitat and the introduction of invasive, non-indigenous species. Deer, goats, pigs, rabbits, and possums brought to make settlers comfortable in unfamiliar surroundings, out-competed native species. Stoats and weasels, brought to control the exploding population of introduced rabbits, started feeding on hapless native birds when the local rabbit and possum supply diminished. Millions of years of evolution left New Zealand's birds without any natural predator defense; even today, many bird species seem uncommonly friendly to tourists. Predation of native species continues to plague New Zealand; the kiwi is now vanishing at an annual rate of almost 6%. **Wasps** hidden in aircraft parts entered the ecosystem during World War II and since then have reached epidemic proportions, threatening the food sources of birds and endemic insects. In addition to losing 43% of the frog fauna and over 40% of the bird fauna since humans first arrived, New Zealand now has more than **600 endangered species.**

Non-native flora also disrupt the ecosystem by out-competing endemic flora for sunlight, space, and nutrients. These plants, accustomed to hardier weather, thrive in New Zealand's mild climate. Because these introduced plants lack native predators, and because introduced predators often feed on indigenous plant life, the addition of a single foreign plant species can destroy an ecosystem. Of the 20,000 non-native species introduced to the country, the Department of Conservation (DOC) reports that over 200 are now weeds.

CONSERVATION

New Zealand is hailed worldwide as a leader in conservation efforts, both on land and at sea. About one-third of the country is set aside as protected land, and a massive international whale sanctuary established in 1994 includes more than 11 million square miles. The country is covered with 14 national parks, plus numerous other forest parks, groves, and wildlife reserves. The first national park, **Tongariro National Park,** was created in 1887 as a result of the foresight and efforts of Te Heuheu Tukino IV, the high chief of the Ngati Tuwharetoa Maori tribe. He offered the area as a gift to the New Zealand government on the condition that it be kept *tapu* (sacred). The most recent national park, **Rakiura National Park,** was designated in 2002 to protect the largely untouched wilderness of Stewart Island.

The **Department of Conservation (DOC)** is involved in many projects to maintain the country's natural beauty. For more information, see www.doc.govt.nz/conservation. In addition to protecting 30% of the land and working with other specialized groups in conservation efforts, DOC currently oversees 13 marine reserves and regulates the dolphin and whale watching industries. It plays an active role in habitat protection, predator control programs, relocation of species, and conducting surveys and research on the current status of endangered wildlife. A new project involving six "mainland island habitats" allows DOC to restore endangered species' habitats by managing introduced pests.

66 ■ OUTDOOR NEW ZEALAND

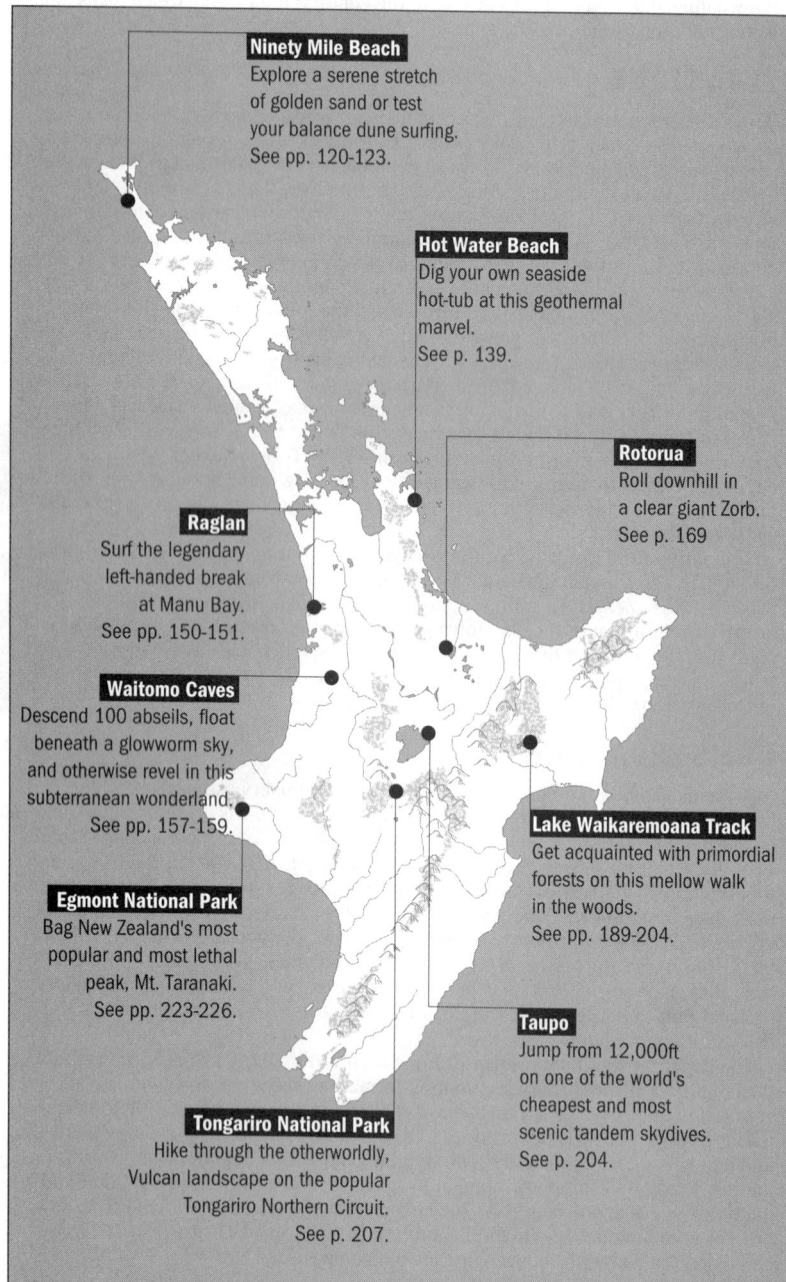

Ninety Mile Beach
Explore a serene stretch of golden sand or test your balance dune surfing. See pp. 120-123.

Hot Water Beach
Dig your own seaside hot-tub at this geothermal marvel. See p. 139.

Rotorua
Roll downhill in a clear giant Zorb. See p. 169

Raglan
Surf the legendary left-handed break at Manu Bay. See pp. 150-151.

Waitomo Caves
Descend 100 abseils, float beneath a glowworm sky, and otherwise revel in this subterranean wonderland. See pp. 157-159.

Egmont National Park
Bag New Zealand's most popular and most lethal peak, Mt. Taranaki. See pp. 223-226.

Lake Waikaremoana Track
Get acquainted with primordial forests on this mellow walk in the woods. See pp. 189-204.

Taupo
Jump from 12,000ft on one of the world's cheapest and most scenic tandem skydives. See p. 204.

Tongariro National Park
Hike through the otherworldly, Vulcan landscape on the popular Tongariro Northern Circuit. See p. 207.

Outdoor New Zealand: North Island

OUTDOOR NEW ZEALAND ■ 67

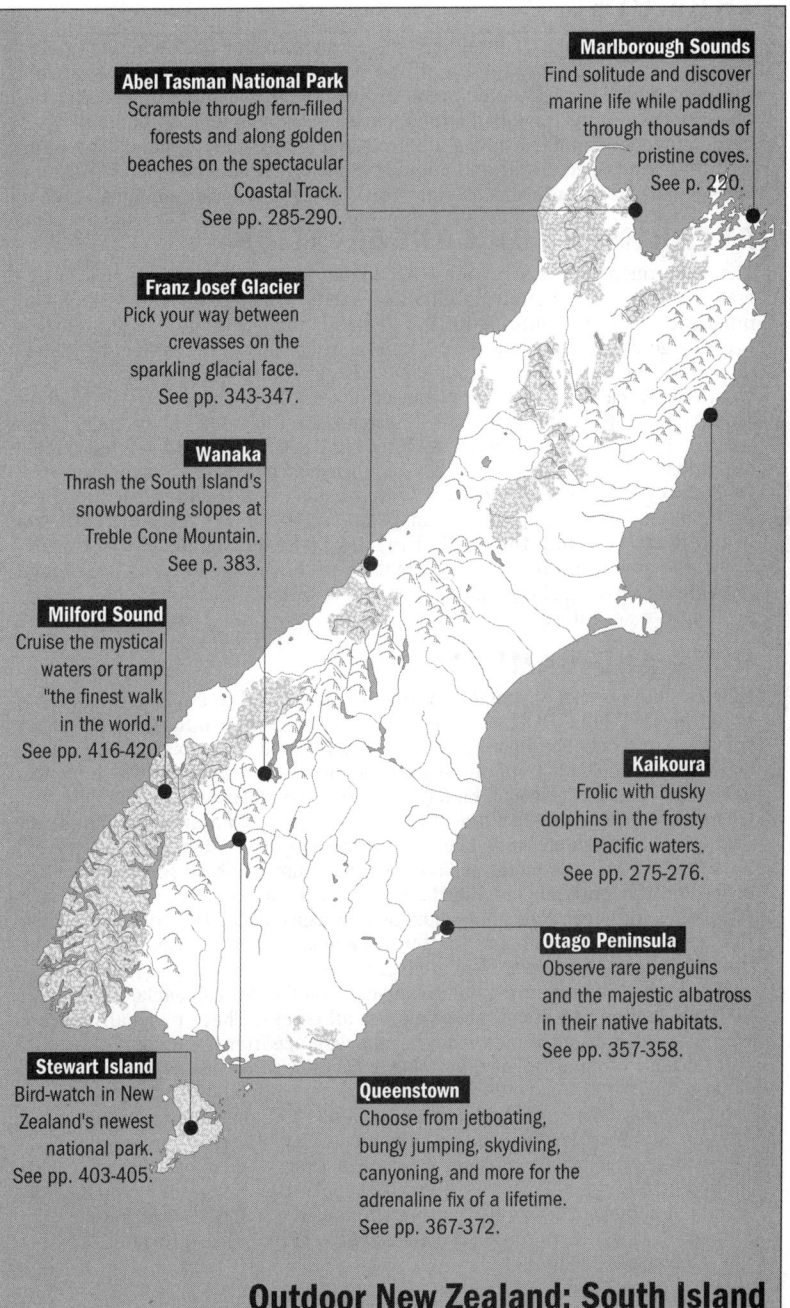

Outdoor New Zealand: South Island

TRAMPING

Backpacking, trekking, bushwalking—whatever you call it back home, it's called tramping in New Zealand. With all the national parks, forest parks, scenic reserves, and other protected areas in *Aotoearoa*, it is no surprise that the opportunities for overnight wilderness excursions are practically limitless. Hundreds of well-maintained tracks are scattered across New Zealand. The country's nine most spectacular and popular tramps (including one canoe trip) are classified as **Great Walks** and are run by DOC under a separate administration.

DEPARTMENT OF CONSERVATION

The Department of Conservation (DOC) is an unparalleled resource for information on the seasonal availability and safety of hikes, the regulations and practicalities for adventuring in New Zealand, maps, and more. Offices are in every large city, most small towns, and near virtually every protected wilderness area. The staff has information and advice on current track conditions and weather forecasts as well as an intentions book. Nearly every Great Walk requires trampers to provide their information in this book before starting the track, especially in winter months. Most city DOC offices will sell hut passes and assist with hut bookings, often only for nearby tracks. For most tracks, DOC also produces a $1 brochure with a basic but adequate map and track information. Detailed topographic maps are $11-13.50. The main DOC office is located at P.O. Box 10420, Wellington (☎ 04 471 0726; fax 471 1082; www.doc.govt.nz). For more information on hut passes, Great Walks, and bookings see below. Make a habit of checking with the local DOC office before any outdoor adventure.

HUTS AND CAMPING

New Zealand's tracks are home to a well-developed backcountry hut system with more than 960 huts. DOC builds huts for three reasons: to increase safety for trampers, to reduce the environmental damage caused by camping and hiking off-trail, and to provide the opportunity for meeting fellow trampers. There are **four categories** of huts. **Category 1** huts ($15+) are **Great Walks** huts and include mattresses, water, cooking facilities, fuel, and a warden. **Category 4** huts (free) are shelters with extremely limited facilities. **Category 2** ($10; 2 tickets) and **Category 3** huts ($5; 1 ticket) have intermediate facilities. Purchase **hut tickets** ($5) at DOC offices or from park rangers. Regular hut tickets cannot be used on Great Walks; hut passes for Great Walks huts must be purchased at the DOC office managing the track. Frequent trampers can buy an **Annual Hut Pass** for NZ$65. Children under 12 stay for free, ages 12-17 are half-price.

Those who prefer carrying their own accommodations can backcountry camp for free (in allowed areas) along almost all tracks. There is usually a small charge for camping near huts; camping at a distance from the track is often difficult because of dense foliage. **Camping is not allowed outside designated sites on Great Walks.** As with huts, there are categories of official **DOC campgrounds**: serviced, standard, and informal. Serviced grounds include flush toilets, tap water, kitchen, showers, laundry, and usually electricity. Standard grounds have toilets, water supply, and some type of vehicle access, while informal grounds have limited facilities, sometimes only a water supply. Prices depend on the facilities offered and range from $2-10. Informal grounds are free of charge. Fees are collected by camp wardens or the local agent. For more information, go to www.nzcamping.co.nz.

CAMPING AND TRAMPING EQUIPMENT

New Zealand has several renowned outdoor brands, including MacPac, Fairydown, and Kathmandu. Renting gear is a cost-cutting option when it's convenient to begin and end a tramp from a town with rental outlets. If you bring your own camping equipment with you into New Zealand, make sure it is clean, as customs officials will check and disinfect used equipment upon arrival. Below is a list of recommended equipment for tramping in New Zealand.

Sleeping Bag: Most sleeping bags are rated by season ("summer" means 30-40°F at night; "four-season" or "winter" often means below 0°F). Most summer-time trampers in New Zealand will be comfortable in a summer bag, but early and late season hiking may demand more warmth. Sleeping bags are made either of **down** (warmer and lighter, but more expensive, and miserable when wet) or of **synthetic** material (heavier, more durable, and functional when wet). Prices range US$80-210 for a summer synthetic to US$250-300 for a good down winter bag. Bring a **stuff sack** to store your bag and line it with a trash bag to keep it dry.

Pack: A poorly-fitted backpack can ruin a week in the woods; be sure to talk with an outdoor outfitter to ensure proper fit. **Internal-frame packs** mold to your back, keep a lower center of gravity, and flex to allow you to hike difficult trails. **External-frame packs** keep weight higher and distribute it more evenly. Any serious backpacking requires a pack of at least 4000 in^3 (16,000cc), plus 500 in^3 for sleeping bags in internal-frame packs. Sturdy backpacks cost anywhere from US$125-420. Either buy a **waterproof backpack cover** or several plastic bags to line your pack. Women should pack to concentrate weight near their hips; men should center their load at the lower back.

Boots and Socks: The terrain on most New Zealand trails is rough underfoot: be sure to wear hiking boots with good **ankle support.** They should fit snugly and comfortably over a pair of wool socks and a pair of thin liner socks. Break in boots over several weeks to spare yourself painful and debilitating blisters, and spray them with a waterproofing agent. Be sure to pack several extra pairs of socks (both wool socks and liners).

Tent: A tent is not necessary for tramping in New Zealand; the backcountry huts are excellent and there's little point in lugging several extra pounds around unless you're anti-social or a self-sufficiency purist. The best tents are free-standing (with their own frames and suspension systems) and set-up quickly. Good 2-person tents start at US$90, 4-person at US$300. Seal the seams of your tent with waterproofer, make sure it has a **rain fly,** and buy a **ground tarp** to prevent puddles from seeping in.

Sleeping Bag Pads: Foam pads (US$10-20), air mattresses (US$15-50), and Therm-A-Rest self-inflating pads (US$45-80) insulate from the heat-sapping ground. Self-inflating pads pack down easier but can loose their inflation in the middle of the night.

Base Layers: Pack several top and bottom pairs of synthetic base layers; fabrics like polypropylene will keep you warm even when wet. **Don't bring cotton into the backcountry.** Wool also insulates when damp, and several New Zealand companies now sell excellent **merino wool** layers that boast all the positive qualities of polypro without its stench-capturing tendency.

Backcountry Stove and Cookware: Great Walks huts contain gas stoves for cooking but lack cookware and matches. For other tramps, pack a lightweight camp stove (propane stoves are lighter and more compact, but run through fuel more quickly than liquid fuel stoves) and a spoon and pot (called a billy can in Kiwi-speak) for boiling water and preparing backcountry delectables.

Water Purification: One of the greatest joys of hiking in New Zealand is sipping straight from a mountain stream. Not all streams are safe, however, so carry either iodine tablets or a water purification system. Check with local DOC employees on water safety.

Personal Locator Beacon (PLB)/Mountain Radio: Most petrol stations rent PLBs for about $20 per week. These lightweight transceivers will alert rescuers to your location if disaster strikes. Mountain Radios are heavier and more expensive but they allow you to check weather forecasts and transmit information to DOC or outdoor outfitters.

Other Important Items: Good raingear (preferably Gore-Tex®), toilet paper, insect repellent and anti-itch lotion, pocket-knife or multi-tool, torch/flashlight/head lamp, quick-drying T-shirt and shorts, pile layers, camp shoes, maps and compass, candles, matches and/or lighters, plastic water bottles/water bladder, duct tape, sewing kit, bad weather items (cards or a novel), sunscreen, sunglasses, and a first-aid kit (see p. 23).

ENVIRONMENTALLY RESPONSIBLE TOURISM The idea behind responsible tourism is to leave no trace of human presence. A campstove is a safer (and more efficient) way to cook than using vegetation, but if you must make a fire, keep it small and use only dead branches or brush rather than cutting vegetation. Make sure your campsite is at least 150ft. (50m) from water supplies or bodies of water. If there are no toilet facilities, bury human waste (but not paper) at least four inches (10cm) deep and above the high-water line, and 150ft. or more from any water supplies and campsites. Always pack your trash in a plastic bag and carry it with you until you reach the next trash receptacle. For more information, contact one of the organizations listed below.

Earthwatch, 3 Clock Tower Place, Ste. 100, Box 75, Maynard, MA 01754 (US ☎ 800-776-0188; www.earthwatch.org).

Ecotourism Society, P.O. Box 668, Burlington, VT 05402 (US ☎ 802-651-9818; www.ecotourism.org).

National Audobon Society, 200 Trillium Ln., Albany, NY 12203 (US ☎ 518-869-9731; www.audobon.org).

Tourism Concern, Stapleton House, 277-281 Holloway Rd., London N7 8HN (UK ☎ 020 7753 3330; www.tourismconcern.org.uk).

WILDERNESS SAFETY

Stay warm, stay dry, and stay hydrated. Following this simple advice will prevent the vast majority of life-threatening wilderness situations. Be prepared by always packing raingear, a hat and mittens, a first-aid kit, a reflector, a whistle, high energy food, and extra water. Dress in wool or synthetic materials designed for the outdoors; never rely on cotton for warmth, as it is absolutely useless when wet. On any hike, however brief, you should pack enough equipment to keep you alive should a disaster occur. For backcountry trips, always fill out an **intentions form** at the nearest DOC office (and sign hut books along the way); also let someone know when and where you are tramping. The local DOC office will have the latest **weather forecasts.** Weather patterns change quickly all over New Zealand, especially in mountainous areas. A good guide to outdoor survival is *How to Stay Alive in the Woods,* by Bradford Angier (Macmillan, US$8).

A major hazard in the New Zealand wilderness is crossing swollen rivers. Weather systems skirting across the Tasman Sea mean that it's always raining somewhere in New Zealand. In the 19th century, colonials dubbed drowning in a river the "New Zealand death" because it happened so frequently. The safest bet is to wait it out; river levels generally fall as rapidly as they rise.

For info about outdoor ailments such as giardia and other food- and water-born diseases, see p. 21. **Mosquitoes** are most active in the summer; the ever-present and ever-annoying **sandflies** are especially populous in the southern parts of the South Island. To guard against both, wear long pants (tucked into socks) and long sleeves, buy a bed net for camping, and use insect repellent. Unlike mosquitoes, sandflies cannot bite through clothing, so even very light layers are an effective deterrent. Don't wait to apply repellent—just a few exposed minutes can make you miserable for a week. Calamine lotion or topical cortisones (like Cortaid) may stop insect bites from itching.

THE GREAT WALKS

DOC designates nine of New Zealand's grandest tramps as **Great Walks**. Ranging from the spectacular Milford Track through mystical Fiordland wilderness to the dazzling Abel Tasman Coastal Track along golden beaches and cerulean bays, the Great Walks serve up nine unique slices of New Zealand's diverse ecology. All nine walks are well-maintained, well-graded, and make excellent introduction-to-backpacking trips for those with little or no previous experience. Good maintenance, easy access, and superb facilities make for crowded summertime trails; hardened backpackers seeking a challenging and solitary wilderness trip may wish to explore less-trodden routes. Yet, despite crowding, the sheer richness and splendor of Great Walks scenery makes them irresistible to any nature-enthusiast.

Most walks require pre-purchased, time-limited, track-specific **Great Walks Passes,** except in winter when many revert to the backcountry hut pass system (huts become Category 2). The Great Walks Pass serves as proof of payment for accommodation in a hut or a designated campsite along the track; since camping is only allowed in certain areas, the pass is required to be on the track. Due to an increase in traffic, many walks necessitate booking in advance for the summer (Nov.-Apr.; bookings for the upcoming season begin on **July 1**), especially the **Abel Tasman, Milford,** and **Routeburn** tracks. This system restricts visitor numbers and guarantees an actual bunk in a hut, preventing a daily race of trampers eager to secure the next night's bed. Cancellations allow date-flexible couples and single trampers the chance to get onto the track. Placing your name on the waiting list will often secure you a last-minute spot. For comprehensive information on fees and bookings, visit www.doc.govt.nz or contact the DOC **Great Walks Booking Desk,** P.O. Box 29, Te Anau (☎ 03 249 8514; fax 249 8515), the **Abel Tasman Coastal Track Booking Desk,** c/o Motueka Information Centre, on Wallace St., Motueka (☎ 03 528 0005; fax 528 6563), or the regional office overseeing the other tracks.

- **Lake Waikaremoana Track** (Te Urewera National Park): 3-5 days, 48km. Moderately difficult. This track climbs towering bluffs topped with gnarled beech trees that trace the lakeshore. Advance reservations required. See p. 189.

- **Tongariro Northern Circuit** (Tongariro National Park): 3-4 days, 51.5km. More difficult. Winding around three great volcanoes, this track passes wild and spectacular lava flows, desolate moonscapes, and technicolor lakes. The **Tongariro Crossing,** "the finest one-day walk in New Zealand," is part of the circuit. See p. 210.

- **Whanganui River Journey** (Whanganui National Park): 3-5 days by canoe, 145km. More difficult. The only Great Walk that requires a paddle; canoeists and kayakers battle the small rapids beneath sheer backs and luxuriant greenery. Two Maori *marae* make the trip a cultural journey as well. See p. 235.

- **Abel Tasman Coastal Track** (Abel Tasman National Park): 3-5 days, 51km. Less difficult. The most popular of all Great Walks, this track boasts golden beaches and turqoise ocean vistas, framed by fern-filled forest. Advanced reservations required. See p. 288.

- **Heaphy Track** (Kahurangi National Park): 4-6 days, 82km. More difficult. Perhaps New Zealand's most ecologically diverse track: the Heaphy passes through lofty beech forests, alpine meadows, lowland podocarp forest, and wild beaches. See p. 296.

- **Routeburn Track** (Mt. Aspiring and Fiordland National Parks): 2-4 days, 32km. More difficult. Mostly traveling high above tree-line, the Routeburn skirts grand valleys and overlooks rugged mountain ranges. Advanced reservations required. See p. 375.

Kepler Track (Fiordland National Park): 3-4 days, 67km. More difficult. The most easily accessible of the Great Walks, the Kepler is an awe-inspiring ridge-walk, offering commanding views of Lake Te Anau and Fiordland. See **p. 411**.

Milford Track (Fiordland National Park): 4 days, 54km. Moderately difficult. Heralded as "the finest walk in the world," the Milford runs through two glacial valleys and over a spectacular mountain pass. Rock faces are watered by countless cascades, including Sutherland Falls, New Zealand's highest. Advanced reservations required. See p. 417.

Rakiura Track (Rakiura National Park): 2-3 days, 36km. Moderately difficult. This boardwalked track undulates through the primordial forest on Stewart Island. See p. 404.

JUST-AS-GREAT WALKS

Queen Charlotte Track (Marlborough Sounds): 3-5 days, 67km. Moderately difficult. This popular, mellow walk winds along the shimmering inlets of the Sounds. Pampered trampers can stay in trackside hostels and have packs transported by boat. See p. 269.

Wangapeka Track (Kahurangi National Park): 5-6 days, 60km. More difficult. Similar in scenery to its brother the Heapy, the Wangapeka offers a secluded taste of New Zealand's tremendous ecological diversity. See **p. 300**.

Greenstone and Caples Tracks (Wakatipu Recreational Hunting Area): 4-5 days, 50km. More difficult. Cattle graze in paradise, where green mountains overlook the golden meadows of the valley floor. See **p. 377**.

Rees-Dart Track (Mt. Aspiring National Park): 4-5 days, 72km. More difficult. The Rees and Dart River Valleys are crowned with glaciers galore. A daytrip up to the Cascade Saddle can afford one of the most mind-numbing views in New Zealand. See **p. 386**.

Dusky Track (Fiordland National Park): 8-10 days, 84km. Extremely difficult. New Zealand's most rugged track, the Dusky rewards the intrepid with alpine vistas, pristine forests and rivers, lots and lots of mud, and a satisfying challenge. Recommended only for groups of experienced trampers. See p. 422.

Hump Ridge Track: (Fiordland National Park): 4 days, 53km. More difficult. New Zealand's newest track, the Hump Ridge is run by a local trust and explores the rugged wilderness of southern Fiordland. Advanced bookings required. See p. 426.

OUTDOOR ACTIVITIES

BUNGY JUMPING

Bungy is big in New Zealand; the world's first commercial jump has been thrilling Queenstown visitors since 1988. A bungy jump taps exhilaratingly primal adrenaline stores—no matter how cool and collected you are when stepping over the edge, the rush of seeing the ground speeding towards you is inescapable. **Queenstown** remains the bungy capital of New Zealand (and the world) and boasts four different jump sites run by two fiercely competitive companies (see p. 368). If you think you can hack it, try the highest and most daring jump in New Zealand, AJ Hackett's **Nevis Highwire Bungy** in Queenstown (134m). Bungy jump sites also excite visitors in **Taupo** (see p. 204) and **Rotorua** (see p. 169).

CLIMBING AND CANYONING

New Zealand's turbulent geology has created plenty of rocky crags to scale and its abundant precipitation has sculpted dozens of dramatic canyons to descend. Major **rock climbing** areas in New Zealand include: the **Port Hills** near Christchurch (see p. 313), sport-climbing in **Wanaka** (see p. 378), limestone near **Golden Bay** (see p. 285), and some of the nation's best climbing at **Wharepapa South** (see p. 153). Alpine climbing in New Zealand centers on the mountainous South Island. Erosive and tectonic forces create marginal rock routes on flaky rock in the **Southern Alps,** but the high elevations and abundant moisture flows from the Tasman Sea make

OUTDOOR ACTIVITIES ■ 73

for excellent ice and snow climbing. **Mt. Cook National Park** (see p. 327) offers more mountaineering routes and guiding companies than anywhere else in New Zealand. For more information, visit www.climb.co.nz.

Canyoning challenges the bold with tricky abseils, treacherous leaps, and tons of icy water. Participants descend narrow gorges in wetsuits and helmets to protect them from frigid mountain flows and punishing rocks. Trips generally last several hours and offer plenty of opportunities to push your personal limits. Canyoning adventures are available in: **Queenstown** (see p. 369), **Auckland** (see p. 97), **Wanaka** (see p. 384), and **Wellington** (see p. 253).

CYCLING AND MOUNTAIN BIKING

With towns spread thinner than other popular cycling destinations, New Zealand's roads ensure long days in the saddle. The fabulous scenery along the way and the warm hospitality at the day's end make the effort more than worthwhile. The South Island contains more mountain passes but generally flatter terrain than the undulating North Island. Some cyclists claim that the wild ride from Haast Past up the **West Coast** is one of the world's best. Bike shops in **Christchurch** and **Auckland** have touring bike rental packages, but most dedicated cyclists bring their own. For more information on cycling, pick up a copy of the informative *Pedaller's Paradise* by Nigel Rushton at any New Zealand bike shop.

New Zealand mountain biking is growing in popularity. If you have the bucks, search the web for one of many companies that offer guided mountain biking tours. The **Southern Alps** region (**Queenstown, Twizel/Mt. Cook,** and **Wanaka**) boasts excellent single-track riding and several companies deliver heli-biking trips. Easy-access riding is available from **Wellington, Christchurch,** and **Dunedin**. The **Central Otago** region has recently become a mountain-biking hotspot; the **Central Otago Rail Trail** offers a multi-day mountain-bike touring trip that's well-graded and easy enough for beginners. For more information, visit www.mountainbiking.co.nz.

JETBOATING

A Kiwi original, **jetboats** have whisked tourists up and down New Zealand's scenic rivers since the 1960s. With specialized internal engines (no propeller), jetboats can travel rapidly over very shallow waters. Professional drivers thrill passengers with 360° spins and dangerously close passes to rocky bluffs. **Queenstown's** narrow gorges and scenic rivers make it a prime spot for jetboating (see p. 368), but companies run tours all over New Zealand. The steepest and wildest jetboating river is the **Wairaurahiri** in southern Fiordland (see Tuatapere, p. 425).

MARINE ENCOUNTERS

New Zealand's coastal waters offer the chance to frolic amidst pods of playful dolphins. The water can be chilly, but the thrill of coming face-to-face with the elegant creatures is unmatched. The waters off **Kaikoura** (p. 275) teem with dusky dolphins, **Akaroa** (p. 316), near Christchurch, abounds with rare Hector's dolphins, and the year-round warmth of **Paihia** (p. 113) assures temperate dolphin swims.

For a closer encounter with underwater life, New Zealand's waters are popular with scuba divers. **Poor Knights Islands** (p. 109), off the coast near Whangarei, was ranked as one of ten best dive sites in the world by Jacques Cousteau. The opaque water on **Milford Sound's** surface creates a unique diving environment (see p. 415); fooled by the lack of sunlight, deep sea creatures live closer to the surface in the sound.

RIVER AND PADDLE SPORTS

More than two dozen commercially-guided rivers greet rafting enthusiasts in New Zealand. Kiwi rivers offer a variety of difficulty levels (class 1-5) and some chances to drift through remote wilderness. Hotspots include the **Shotover River** in Queenstown (see p. 368), the **Buller River** outside Westport (see p. 333), the **Rangataiki River** near Rotorua (see p. 169), and the seasonal but spectacular, **Wairoa River** (see

THE LOCAL STORY

MAMAS, DON'T LET YOUR BABIES GROW UP TO BUNGY

Nigel Hobbs is a bungy jump master for AJ Hackett in Queenstown.

Q: What are the craziest bungy jumping variations you've ever seen?
A: We've had weddings. People say their vows and jump off. Some people jump with fire, which is a bit of a dodgy one! People go in crazy costumes. I've seen nine people jump off together, all attached, for a world record. I've seen lots of forward flips and back flips, and someone jumped in their kayak. Anything that you can think of, we can usually do.

Q: How often do jump masters themselves go bungy jumping?
A: Some people are crazy and may jump three times a week. In general, everyone jumps at least once every three months, just to keep you honest—so you know exactly what the customers are experiencing.

Q: Do you still get scared when you bungy jump?
A: Yeah! I still have that feeling of "What am I doing here?" No matter how many times you jump, the rush will still remain. You're taught as a child that you're not to jump off things, so you go through life remembering that. When you're doing it for the first time, you've got so much going through your head that your mind just runs overtime. That's the whole buzz of it.

Tauranga, p. 172). For more information, visit www.nz-rafting.co.nz. Whitewater **boogie-boarding** and **sledging** provide a more intimate encounter with raging rapids; outfitters operate from **Rotorua** (see p. 169) and **Wanaka** (see p. 384).

Experienced **kayakers** can paddle whitewater on many New Zealand rivers, but few opportunities exists for beginners. Some companies offer one-day intro courses but mastering whitewater kayaking requires time and money. With more stable boats and calmer waters, **sea-kayaking** is an excellent option for the less-experienced. Sea-kayakers have the freedom to explore golden bays and pristine sounds at their own pace, free from the droning hum of a tour boat. Prime sea-kayaking destinations include: **Doubtful Sound** (see p. 426), **Abel Tasman National Park** (see p. 285), and the **Marlborough Sounds** (see p. 267).

SKIING AND SNOWBOARDING

With the South Island's majestic mountain scenery and the North Island's symmetric volcano slopes, New Zealand has plenty of fantastic runs for skiers and snowboarders to enjoy. The nation's best **snowboarding** is at Treble Cone outside **Wanaka** (see p. 383) and popular ski fields surround **Queenstown** (see p. 370) and **Tongariro National Park** (see p. 210). Western **Canterbury** also hosts skiers and boarders at several popular resorts (see p. 317). On the North Island, the **Mt. Ruapehu Ski Area** (p. 210) is the largest and most developed ski area in the country. Experienced skiers can find excellent backcountry runs at one of the nation's many private ski fields; most are owned by local clubs and use rope tows instead of lifts.

SPELUNKING AND CAVE RAFTING

Tiny **Waitomo** (see p. 154) nearly monopolizes the New Zealand caving business. Its multitude of cave complexes hosts a wide variety of subterranean pursuits, from tame glowworm tours to full-day abseiling and rafting adventures. There's something magical about floating an underground river beneath a night's sky of bioluminescence. For other opportunities to descend into the bowels of the earth, visit **Westport** (p. 330) and **Greymouth** (p. 335) on the South Island's **West Coast.** Both serve as bases for caving adventures in the wild western range.

SKYDIVING AND PARAGLIDING

Skydiving is cheaper in New Zealand than in the US, UK, or Australia. As a result, nearly every major tourist town has its own skydiving operation eager to capture a chunk of the heavy tourist demand. Most companies offer tandem jumps from both 9000ft. and 12,000ft. Free-fall on the higher jump generally lasts 45 seconds and the prolonged rush is worth the extra $50. The cheapest skydive is in **Taupo** (see p. 204) but can feel like an out-of-the-plane conveyor belt. For a more scenic and personalized fall, try **Wanaka** (see p. 384) or **Franz Josef Glacier** (see p. 344).

Several companies offer travelers gentler falls from heights. Many **paragliding** outfitters provide both tandem rides and paragliding courses. The South Island's mountainous terrain makes leaping and gliding possible; **Queenstown** (see p. 369), **Wanaka** (see p. 384), and **Christchurch** (see p. 313) all have several operators.

SURFING

Tasman Sea swells crashing into the Kiwi coast inspired the surf-bum flick *The Endless Summer* in 1966. Today, New Zealand remains a popular surfing destination and attracts annual international competitions. Raglan's **Manu Bay** boasts the nation's greatest breaks (see p. 149), but the **Taranaki Coast** (see p. 222) and **Whangamata** on the Coromandel Peninsula (see p. 140) also deliver amazing waves. To indulge in surfer-culture and learn how to get up on a board yourself, consider spending a few summertime weeks in **Raglan.**

OTHER ZANY ADVENTURES

Kiwis never lack imagination when it comes to finding new ways to get a rush or have a laugh. If the standard adventure fare fails to entice, try one of these wacky activities. Enjoy a stomach-churning roll downhill in a giant, inflated balls by **Zorbing** in Rotorua (see p. 169) and Paihia (p. 114). **Dune surfing,** in Northland's Hokianga Region (see p. 122) or at Ninety-Mile Beach (see p. 120), is a sandier way to look hip atop a fiberglass board. One of New Zealand's wildest new thrills, **Fly By Wire** straps participants to a 60-horsepower aircraft engine and then sends them whipping around on a thick cable. Both **Queenstown** (see p. 369) and **Paekakariki** (outside of Wellington; see p. 255) have Fly By Wire sites.

FURTHER RESOURCES

Whether novice or expert, you can visit your nearest outdoors equipment store or bookstore to find publications and general info on camping and adventuring in New Zealand. Specific New Zealand titles, such as *101 Great Tramps in New Zealand,* by Pickering and Smith, or *Adventuring in New Zealand,* by Margaret Jefferies, provide good broad surveys of the New Zealand outdoors. Similarly, **GORP** (the Great Outdoor Recreation Pages; www.gorp.com) provides information on outdoor activities in New Zealand. For **topographical maps** of New Zealand, contact **Map and Chart Center,** 32 Goodshed Rd. (Private Bag 903), Upper Hutt, NZ (☎ 04 527 7019; fax 527 7246; mapcentre@terralink.co.nz). Once in New Zealand, you can buy topographical maps from local DOC offices.

Q: Do you actually have to push people off?
A: No, no. It's bungy jumping, not bungy pushing.

Q: What's the most rewarding or fun kind of customer for you?
A: Someone who's very scared and doesn't want to jump. You count them down from 5 to 1, and they're still there. To be able to spend time with them and talk them through the whole thing, and then actually talk them off the edge, that's a buzz.

Q: How about your most annoying kind of customer?
A: Some people really don't want to be there. If they know there's no way in hell they're going to jump, it can be frustrating that they weren't strong enough to say so earlier.

Q: How do people react to your job?
A: Well, when you sit around a table, you always hold the conversation. It seems that as soon as they know that you're involved with bungy jumping, the questions just pop out. My parents thinks it's pretty cool.

Q: Have you had any close calls?
A: No! Thank God! We have very strict procedures. No fatalities in 14 years of operation. Statistically, bungy jumping is safer than driving your car. It's probably one of the safest adventure activities you can do in Queenstown. Around the world, at all our sites, we've jumped more than a million people. All safely.

Q: What ages of people bungy?
A: We have people that are 10 years old (that's the minimum) and we've had a guy that was 93! He jumped twice in one day!

AUCKLAND ☎ 09

Squeezed onto a narrow isthmus between sparkling Waitemata and Manukau Harbours, the inhabitants of Auckland (pop. 1.18 million), New Zealand's largest and most cosmopolitan city, are never far from the sea. Home to the most boats per capita in the world, the metropolis clearly deserves its nickname, "City of Sails." Currently, Auckland's sleek waterfront landscape bubbles with excitement as the Kiwis prepare to defend their title in the America's Cup 2003 competition.

Auckland's massive urban sprawl creates a number of thriving neighborhoods, each with its own distinct flavor. In the heart of it all, Central Auckland's downtown streets throb with power suits, corporate logos, and buzzing cellphones. On the periphery, the surrounding areas of Ponsonby, Parnell, and Mt. Eden cater to a calmer cappuccino crowd. Tranquil ferry rides away, the islands of the Waitemata Harbour dazzle with their unique charm and beauty.

Originally settled by the Maori over 650 years ago, today Auckland is home to over one million Kiwis. Combining the largest Polynesian population in the world with 150 years of European settlement and a recent Asian immigration, the city is a multicultural mecca. A main arrival point for international visitors, Auckland is often viewed as a necessary stop before tackling the rest of New Zealand; those who linger enjoy Kiwi hospitality, hip cafes, and a vibrant nightlife.

AUCKLAND HIGHLIGHTS

2003 IS A GREAT YEAR for the Waterfront, as Kiwis gear up to defend their America's Cup 2000 title (see p. 94).

BUT ANYTIME IS A GOOD TIME on Auckland's K Rd. and High St. (p. 91), where the party lasts all night.

PICK YOUR URBAN POISON in Ponsonby, Parnell, or Mt. Eden, three character-laden neighborhoods with magnetic charm (see p. 95).

OR ESCAPE IT ALL on **Great Barrier Island,** a time warp to an isolated wilderness, or **Waiheke Island,** for wine tasting in paradise (see p. 102 and p. 99).

■ INTERCITY TRANSPORTATION

Flights: Auckland International Airport (AKL), a 40min. drive from Central Auckland, is the port of entry for about 80% of New Zealand's overseas visitors. **Super Shuttle** (freephone in the *Visitor Information* concourse upon exiting the International Terminal, ☎ 66 or 306 3960) may be the best option. **Airbus** runs every 20min. and makes many stops, including the YHA, Sky City bus station, and Downtown Airline Terminal. (☎ 0508 247 287. $13, return $22; children $6/$12; YHA/VIP $11/$18.) From the airport, a **taxi** downtown costs about $50. For international flights, **Air New Zealand** flies to Australian cities and Pacific Islands: **Brisbane** (3½hr., 3 per day, $474); **Fiji** (3hr., Tu-Su 1-2 per day, $794); **Melbourne** (4hr., 3 per day, $474); **Rarotonga** (3¾hr., 5 per week, $980); and **Sydney** (3½hr., 4 per day, $449), among others. For domestic flights, Air New Zealand (☎ 357 3000 or 0800 737 000) flies to: **Christchurch** (1¼hr., 1-2 per hr., from $390); **Queenstown** (direct 1½hr., or via **Christchurch** 3¾hr., 4-5 per day, from $595); **Rotorua** (45min., 5-11 per day, from $192); and **Wellington** (1hr., every hr., from $294). Backpackers and students receive discounts (see **By Plane,** p. 30).

Trains: TranzRail (☎ 0800 802 802; fax 0800 101 525; www.tranzrailtravel.co.nz) leaves from the **Auckland Railway Station** (☎ 270 5209), located just a bit inland off-

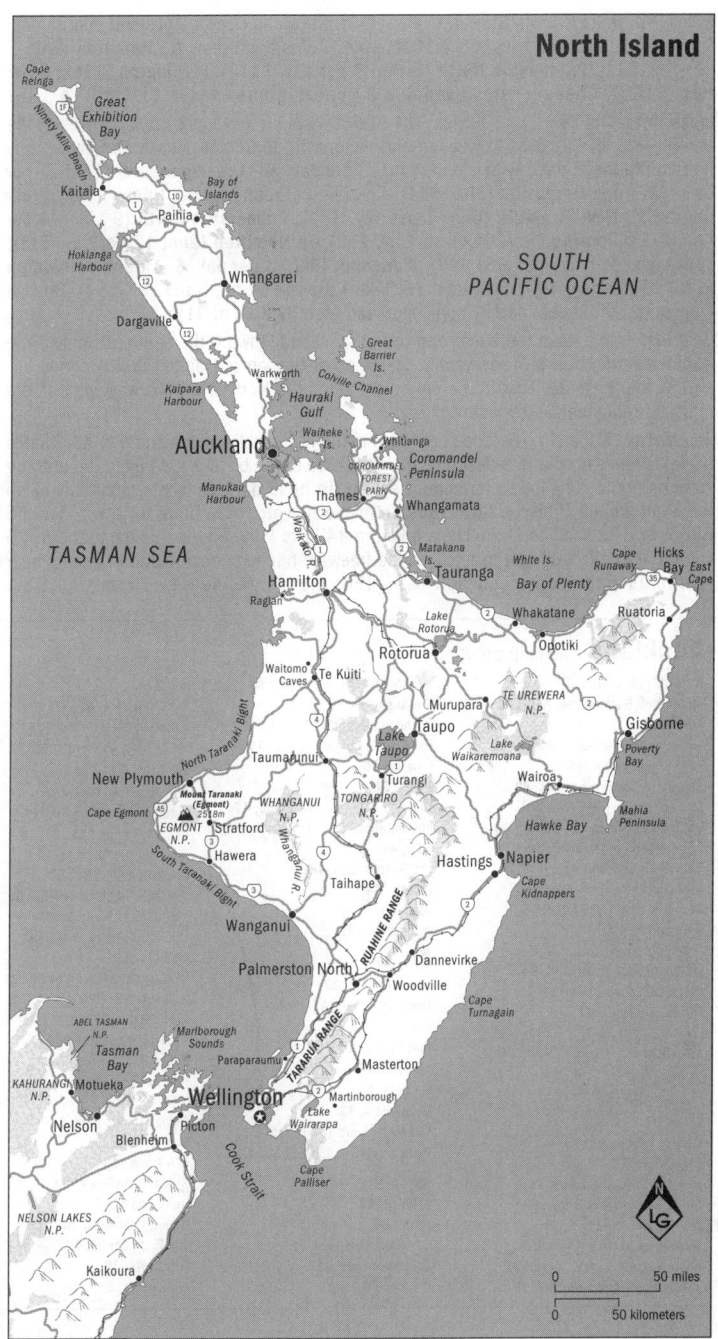

Beach Rd. (take Custom St. E past Anzac Ave.) between Central Auckland and Parnell. Open M-F 7:30am-6pm, Sa-Su 7:30am-1pm. Trains head daily to: **Hamilton** (2hr., 2 per day, $37); **Palmerston North** (8¾hr., 2 per day, $110); **Wellington** (11hr., 1 per day, $145). Cheaper fares available by booking ahead (see **By Train,** p. 30).

Buses: InterCity (☎913 6100; fax 914 0546; www.intercitycoach.co.nz) arrives at the travel center of **Sky City,** at Hobson and Victoria St. in Central Auckland. Service runs north to **Paihia** in the Bay of Islands (4hr., 3 per day, $44) via **Whangarei** (2¾hr., 3 per day, $32) and **Dargaville** (3hr., $41). Southbound runs include: **Napier** (7hr., 4 per day, $78); **New Plymouth** (6hr., 3 per day, $71); **Palmerston North** (9-10hr., 4 per day, $72); **Rotorua** (3½-5hr., 4 per day, $32) via **Hamilton** (2hr., 12 per day, $18); **Tauranga** (3½hr., 5 per day, $38); **Wanganui** (8hr., 3 per day, $71); and **Wellington** (11hr.; 3 per day; $97, night train $67) via **Taupo** (4½-5hr., 5 per day, $51). Special discounts can be obtained by booking ahead (see **By Bus,** p. 31).

Cars: SH1 is the main route into and out of Auckland. Toward the south, it's called the **Auckland-Hamilton Motorway,** with on-ramps at the top of Hobson St., Symonds St., and Khyber Pass Rd. Toward the north, it's called the **Northern Motorway,** with an on-ramp at Beaumont St. by Victoria Park.

Hitchhiking: While *Let's Go* does not recommend it, the collective wisdom of Auckland's backpackers says that the best hitchhiking can be found by taking a bus to the outlying suburbs and asking locals for current advice. To head north, hitchers reportedly catch the **Stagecoach** Hibiscus Coast Bus, from the downtown terminal to Orewa. (☎366 6400. $8.) To head south, hitchers take the #471 to Pahurere and switch to the #475 to Drury ($7). It is **illegal** to hitch on the freeway; hitchers recommend thumbing near on-ramps where cars can pull over. (For more info, see **By Thumb,** p. 35.)

Auckland see map pp. 80-81

🛏 ACCOMMODATIONS
Albert Park Backpackers (VIP), **31**
Albion, **32**
Auckland Central Backpackers (VIP), **9**
Auckland City YHA, **45**
Auckland International YHA, **43**
Bamber House (BBH), **62**
Central City Backpackers (VIP), **35**
City Garden Lodge (BBH), **82**
Downtown Constitution Hill
 Backpackers (VIP), **75**
The Fat Camel (NOMADS), **6**
Georgia Parkside
 Backpackers (BBH), **72**
Lantana Lodge (BBH/VIP), **84**
Oaklands Lodge (BBH), **65**
The Rocknasium, **64**

🍎 FOOD
The Bog, **80**
Circus Circus, **66**
Dhan, **67**
George Restaurant, **79**
Kebab Kid, **83**
Mexican Cafe Bar & Grill, **20**
Mt. Eden Bakery and Deli, **68**
The Occidental, **11**
Pizza Pizza, **37**
Rasoi Vegetarian Restaurant, **51**
Tanuki Sushi and Sake Bar, **39**

⭐ ENTERTAINMENT & CLUBS
The Angle, **58**
Cause Celebre/The Box, **24**
The Classic Comedy & Bar, **38**
Galatos, **60**
Jones, **57**
The Kiss Club and Bar/Bacio, **47**
Powerstation, **69**
SiLO, **41**
The Supper Club, **46**
Temple, **44**
Urge, **56**
Wunder Bar, **12**

🍺 BARS
Deschlers Bar, **22**
The Dog's Bollix, **61**
Khuja Lounge, **54**
Kiwi Tavern, **2**
Komodo, **76**
Leftfield, **1**
Margarita's, **33**
The Nag's Head Tavern, **85**
Papa Jack's Voodoo Lounge, **16**

☕ CAFES
Alleluya, **52**
Brazil, **59**
City Cake Company, **71**
Columbus Cafe, **25**
Frasers, **70**

Jolt, **27**
The Other Side, **81**
Strawberry Alarm Clock, **78**
Trinity Cafe, **77**

● SERVICES
Auckland Map Centre, **3**
Automobile Association, **29**
Beat Merchants, **18**
Cammell the Chemist, **14**
Cyber Culture, **53**
The Dead Poets Bookshop, **50**
e-xile Internet Lounge, **36**
The Flight Centre, **4** and **40**
high-net, **23**
Karangahape Road Community
 Constable, **49**
Maui Rentals, **63**
The National Bank, **30**
Netzone, **5**
New Zealand Motorcycle
 Rentals, **7**
Omega Rental Cars, **8**
Real Groovy, **42**
STA Travel, **15**
Student UNI Travel, **21**
Unity Books, **17**
Urgent Pharmacy, **74**
The Pride Centre, **48**
Travelcare, **10**
Whitcoull's, **26**

ORIENTATION ■ 79

ORIENTATION

Auckland and its environs stretch across a narrow isthmus that connects Northland to the main landmass of the North Island. **Waitemata Harbour** and the Pacific Ocean lie to the east of the city, while **Manukau Harbour** stretches southward with the Tasman Sea in the west. **SH1** (the Southern Motorway) pumps traffic up from the south, becoming the Northern Motorway north of the city and converging with **SH16**, which stretches west to the Waitakeres and north to Ninety Mile Beach.

Teeming with modern buildings, banks, and suits, **Central Auckland** is the commercial heart of the city. **Queen Street,** the main strip in Auckland, runs north-south toward the water where it meets **Queen Elizabeth II Square** (known as **QE II Square**). **Victoria Street,** another major thoroughfare, crosses Queen St. and goes east-west starting from Victoria Park (on the west side of town) to Albert Park (east side).

The **Waterfront** is at the bottom of Queen St. by Waitemata Harbour. The **American Express New Zealand Cup Village** sprawls around **Viaduct Basin** near Hobson Wharf along the waterfront. **Quay Street** also runs along the water, while **Customs Street** is parallel and one block inland. The **Ferry Building** is right off Quay St., across from **QE II Square.** Inland to the east, stands the **Railway Station** off Beach Rd. On the top of Queen St. past **Aotea Square** lies **Karangahape Road** (known as K Rd.),

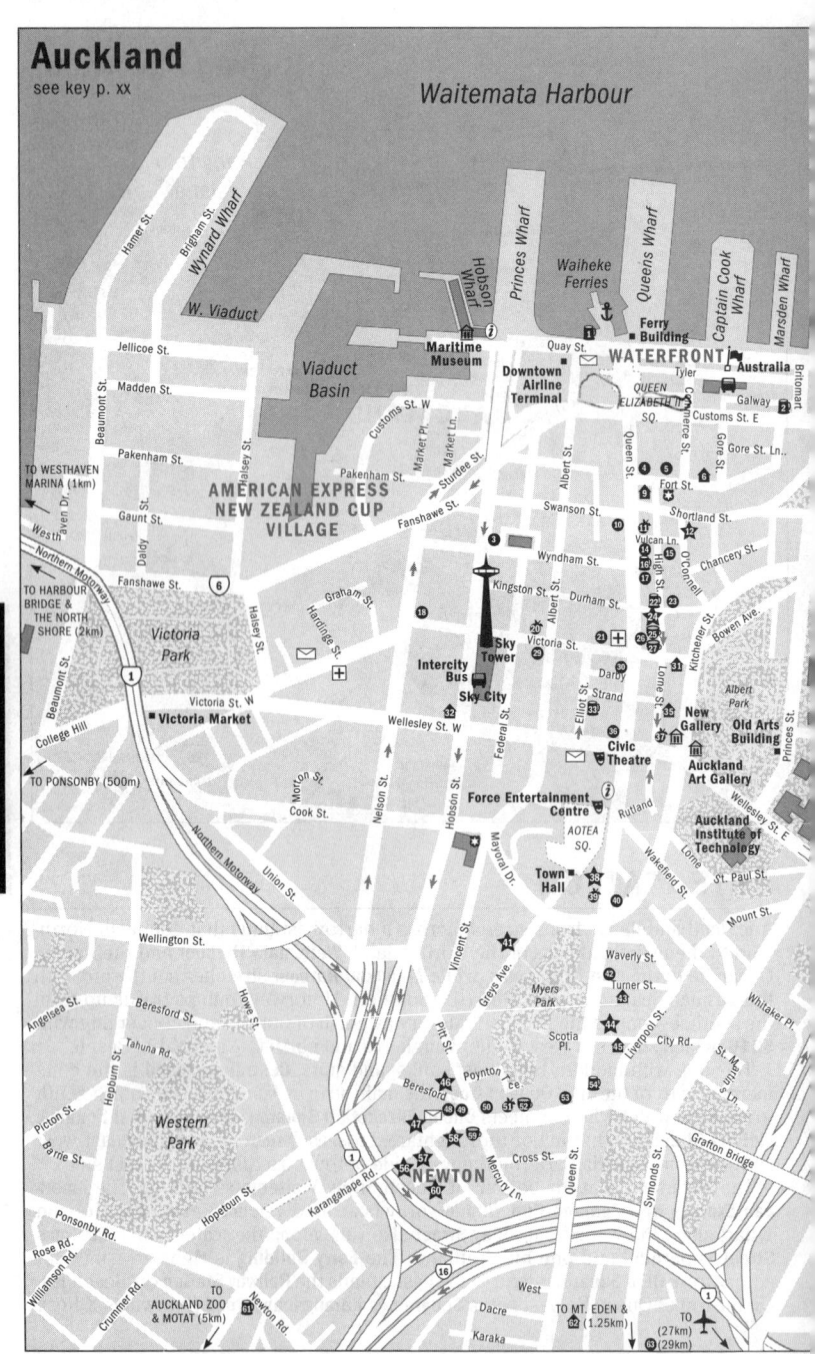

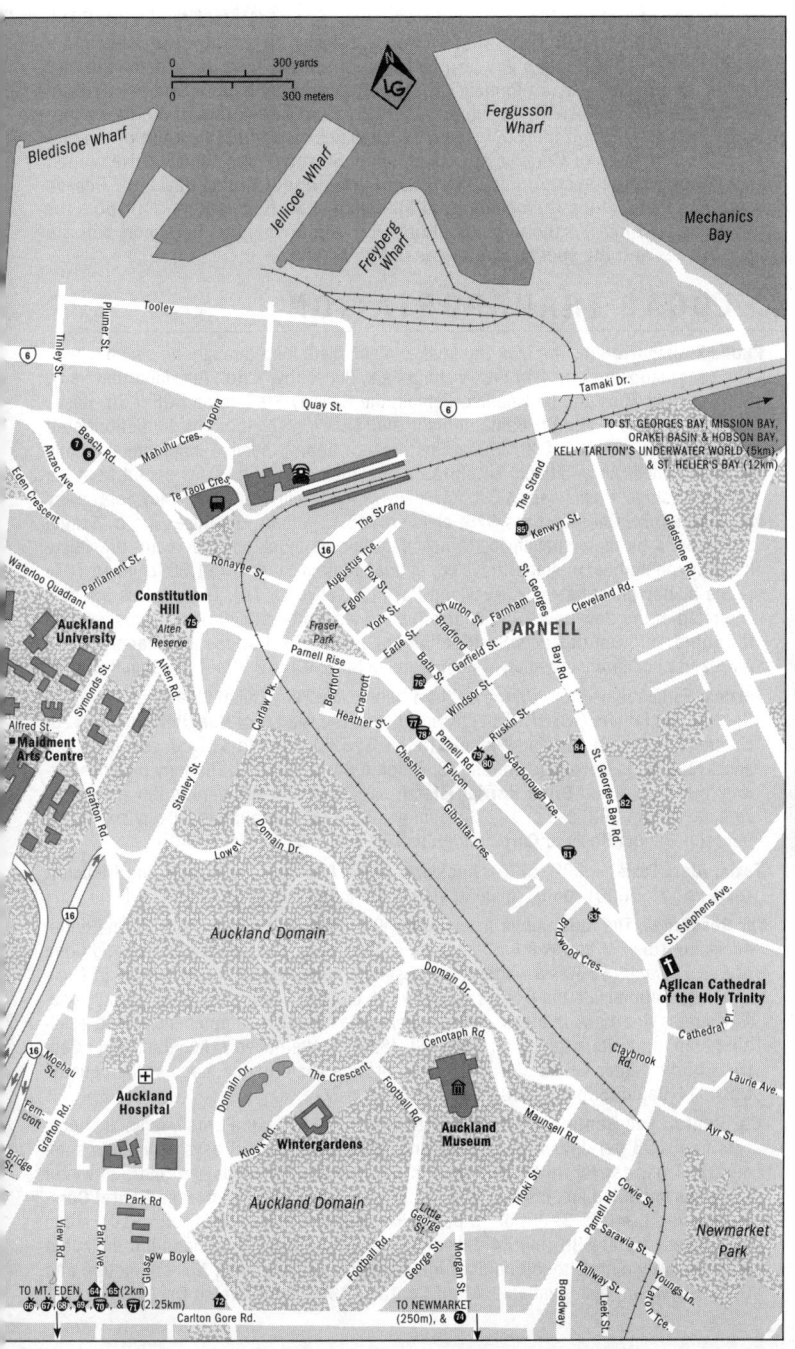

the gritty site of fashionable clubs and bars. Just west of Central Auckland, K Rd. leads to the trendy neighborhood of **Ponsonby,** filled with the hippest cafes and a substantial part of the city's gay and lesbian community. To the east of the city center is the upscale area of **Parnell,** the site of old-money estates and pricey boutiques. Just south of Parnell, Auckland residents go to **Newmarket** to do their shopping. Home to a large number of artists, **Mt. Eden** lies on a hill 2km south of the city center. Running east of Central Auckland, Quay St. turns into **Tamaki Drive,** which then swoops along the stunning coast. Take a look out at **Orakei Basin,** off **Hobson Bay, Bastion Point,** along the ocean, or at **Mission and St. Heliers Bays,** top spots for summer sunbathing. To the north, a short ferry ride away, lies **Devonport** with its many beaches and the spectacular vistas of **Mt. Victoria.**

LOCAL TRANSPORTATION

Public Transportation: The **Link Bus** makes a complete loop through the central city in 1hr. ($1). Stops include: Sky City, Victoria Park, Ponsonby, K Rd., Auckland University, the Auckland Museum, Newmarket, Parnell, the Railway Station, and QE II Sq. Buses leave M-Sa every 10min. 6am-midnight and Su every 20min. The tourist-oriented **Explorer Bus** (☎0800 439 756) offers hop-on, hop-off service connecting various Auckland sites. An additional **satellite bus** operates Oct.-Apr. Buses depart from the **Ferry Building.** (Buses depart Oct.-Apr. daily every 30min. 9am-4pm; May-Sept. every hr. 10am-4pm. One day pass $25, children $15.) Ordinary city buses run by **Stagecoach** are a bit more challenging to negotiate but are much cheaper. Fares are calculated by the number of stages traveled, and range from Stage 1 ($1.20, children 70¢) to the all-day unlimited-travel Auckland Pass ($8, children $5). These buses are concentrated at the **Downtown Bus Centre** (not a place to be at night), or across from **QE II Square,** both on Customs St. **Rideline** (☎366 6400) provides information on the Auckland public transportation system. Open M-Sa 6:30am-9:30pm, Su 8am-6:30pm.

Ferries: Ferries leave from **Prince's Wharf** behind the Ferry Building, across from QE II Sq.; contact **Fullers** (☎367 9111) for schedules. The islands of **Rangitoto** (return $20, children $10; see p. 99) and **Waiheke** (return $23.60, children $11.60; see p. 99) are accessible, as is **Devonport** (return $8, children $4; see p. 97). The ferry provides service to the unspoiled **Great Barrier Island,** departing from Mechanic's Bay during the summer (return $92; see p. 102). In summer, **Ship 'n' Shore** offers full-day excursions from the Viaduct Basin to **Coromandel.** (☎478 1462. $28. See p. 140.)

Taxis: Alert Taxis (☎309 2000), **Auckland Co-op Taxis** (☎300 3000), and **Discount Taxis** (☎529 1000) can be found at Victoria St. E and Queen St., and on K Rd.

Car Resources: The **Automobile Association,** 99 Albert St. (☎377 4660), is in Central Auckland. Open M and W-F 8:30am-5pm, Tu 9am-5pm, Sa 9am-1pm. *The Road Code of New Zealand* ($26) is a worthwhile investment for drivers. Similarly, drivers in Auckland might appreciate the *Driver's Guide,* which indicates all of Central Auckland's one-way streets and parking areas. The *Minimap* series is quite comprehensive and available from the Visitors Center on Queen St. ($3.25). Alternatively, **Auckland Map Centre,** 155 Wyndham St. (☎309 7725), can provide some handy maps of the country. Open M-F 9am-5:30pm, Sa 10am-4pm, Su 10am-2pm.

Car Rental: Ace Rentals, 39-43 The Strand (☎303 3112), in Parnell, rents economy cars from $55 per day up to 20 days and $34 per day for 20 days or more in summer; $34 per day for up to 20 days and $25 per day for 20 days or more in winter (includes unlimited km, insurance, 24hr. AA coverage, and tax). **Omega Rental Cars,** at the airport (☎275 3265) or 75 Beach Rd. (☎377 5573 or 0800 525 210), starts its budget cars at $39 (min. 4 days; includes insurance, AA service, and unlimited km). One-way rentals to joint offices in Wellington, Christchurch, Nelson, Picton, and Queenstown are also available. **Maui Rentals,** 36 Richard Pearse Dr. (☎0800 651

080), 2km from the airport, rents campers from $115 per day in summer and $59 per day in winter (with toilets and showers $229/$79). The worldwide chains **Avis** (☎ 526 2847 or 0800 655 111), **Budget** (☎ 375 2222 or 0800 652 227), and **Hertz** (☎ 0800 654 321) have offices at the airport.

Car Buying and Selling: If you'll be in New Zealand for an extended period of time, you may want to consider buying a car and will probably be inundated with ways to do it. Most **backpackers** have postings on bulletin boards, with the most extensive at **Auckland Central Backpackers** (see p. 85). **Car auctions** are one option; **Turners Car Auctions** (☎ 525 1920; www.turners.co.nz), at the corner of Leonard and Penrose Rd. in Penrose, sells budget cars; call for auction times. **Hammer Auctions,** 830 Great South Rd. (☎ 579 2344), also in Penrose, sells cars M-F at 6pm and Sa at 11am. **Car fairs** are another way to buy or sell a car; **Sell it Yourself,** 60 Wairau Rd., Glenfield (☎ 443 3800; open M-F 7am-7pm, Sa-Su 8am-6:30pm), and 1106 Great South Rd., Westfield (☎ 270 3666; open daily 8am-6pm), and **Manukau City Park and Sell** (☎ 358 5000; open Su 9am-1pm), at the Manukau City Centre, are two among many choices. Or, try **guarantee buy-back services** such as **Used Cars,** 825 Dominion Rd., Mt. Roskill (☎ 620 6587; open daily 8am-6pm). Alternatively, **Budget Car Sales** who will pick you up and take you to the warehouse to view and buy a car (☎ 379 4120; open daily 8am-7pm) For more information on short-term car purchase, see **Buy-backs,** p. 33.

Bike and Motorcycle Rental: Adventure Cycles, 4 Quay St., rents mountain bikes from $25 per day and $90 per week. Touring and racing bikes roll from $18 per day and $70 per week. (☎ 309 5566 or 0800 335 566. Open daily 7am-7pm.) **New Zealand Motorcycle Rentals,** 31 Beach Rd. (☎ 377 2005; fax 377 2006; www.nzbike.com), offers motorcycles and scooters with rentals from $39 per day, including unlimited km, insurance, and 24hr. service. Open M-Sa 9am-5:30pm, Su 10am-3pm.

PRACTICAL INFORMATION

TOURIST AND FINANCIAL SERVICES

Visitors Center: Auckland Visitor Centre, 287 Queen St. (☎ 366 6888; airport branch ☎ 256 8480; fax 366 6893; www.aucklandnz.com), in Central Auckland. The headquarters of New Zealand's extraordinary Visitor Information Network (VIN) offers a complete domestic booking system and every existing brochure and map about New Zealand. Open M-F 9am-6pm, Sa-Su 9am-5pm. Another option is the **New Zealand Visitor Centre** (☎ 979 7005; fax 979 7010), at the corner of Quay and Hobson St., in the American Express New Zealand Cup Village. Open daily 9:30am-5:30pm.

Department Of Conservation (DOC): (☎ 379 6476; fax 376 3609), on Quay St. in the Ferry Building. Open M-F 10am-1pm and 1:30-5:30pm, Sa 10am-3pm.

Budget Travel: STA Travel, 10 High St. (☎ 309 0458; www.statravel.co.nz), has 4 branches in Central Auckland. Open M-F 9am-5:30pm, Sa 10:30am-2pm. **Student UNI Travel,** 5 Victoria St. (☎ 0508 369 932 or 300 8266; www.sut.co.nz), is another option. Open M-F 8am-7pm, Sa 9am-6pm, Su 11am-6pm. Otherwise, try the in-house travel centers at **Auckland Central Backpackers** (☎ 358 4875) or the **Auckland City YHA** (☎ 309 2802)—both open to non-guests. The **Flight Centre** (☎ 0800 354 448) has offices throughout Auckland including: 350 Queen St. (☎ 358 4310) and 2 Fort St. (☎ 377 4655) in Central Auckland, and Broadway Plaza (☎ 529 2400) in Newmarket.

Consulates: Australia, 132-138 Quay St., 7th fl. (☎ 303 2429); **Canada,** all inquiries should be directed to the Wellington Office, 61 Molesworth St., 3rd fl. (☎ 309 8516 or 04 473 9577); **Ireland,** 18 Shortland St., Level 6 (☎ 302 2867); **UK,** NZI House, 151 Queen St., 17th fl. (☎ 303 2973); and **US,** General Building, 29 Shortland St., 4th fl. (☎ 303 2724). There is no **South Africa** consulate, but there is an honorary consulate (☎ 443 9700, ext. 9581) available at the Albany Campus of Massey University.

Banks and Currency Exchange: Interforex, 99 Quay St. (☎302 3066) in the Ferry Building. Open daily 8am-8pm. **The National Bank,** 205 Queen St. (☎359 9813), takes no commission on traveler's checks or foreign currency. Open M-F 9am-4:30pm. There are **banks** with **ATMs** all over Queen St., Ponsonby Rd., Parnell Rd., and Broadway.

LOCAL SERVICES

Luggage Storage: National Mini Storage LTD, 68 Cook St. (☎356 7020), stores luggage for $1 per piece per day. Open daily 8am-6pm.

Bookstores: Whitcoull's (☎356 5400), has 3 floors and a cafe. Open M-Th 8am-6pm, F 8am-9pm, Sa 9am-6pm, Su 10am-5pm. For pre-loved books, **The Dead Poets Bookshop,** 238 K Rd. (☎303 0555; open M-F 9am-6pm, Sa 9am-5:30pm, Su 10am-4pm), and **Unity Books,** 19 High St. (☎307 0731; open M-Th 8:30am-8pm, F 8:30am-9pm, Sa 9:30am-6pm, Su 11am-6pm), have a wide range of titles.

Women's Organizations: Auckland Women's Centre, 4 Warnock St. (☎376 3227), in Grey Lynn, offers counseling for women. Open M-F 9am-4pm. **Wanderwomen** (☎360 7330) coordinates trips for women. Weekend trips $260, 5-day $615.

Gay-Bi-Lesbian Organizations: The **Gay and Lesbian Line** (☎303 3584; aglw@xtra.co.nz) provides info, support, counseling, and referrals. Open M-F 10am-10pm, Sa-Su 5-10pm. **The Pride Centre,** 281 K Rd. (☎302 0590), gives away information, referrals, and an events calendar. Open M-F 10am-5pm, Sa 10am-3pm.

Ticket Agency: Ticketek (☎307 5000) sells tickets for music, theater, and sporting events; book over the phone or at the **Countrywide Bank box office** in the **Aotea Centre.** $6 surcharge for all advance tickets. Open daily 9am-5:30pm or later.

Weather Conditions: MetPhone (☎0900 999 09; $1.15 per min.).

Publications: The Auckland-based **New Zealand Herald** is the country's most comprehensive daily newspaper. **Metro** magazine has the pulse of Auckland's pop culture and politics, while **Express** is the gay and lesbian paper. **The Fix** and **Infusion** have the dope on Auckland's dance clubs, while **pulp** lists headliner events nation-wide.

EMERGENCY, MEDICAL, AND COMMUNICATIONS

Emergency: Dial ☎**111** throughout New Zealand.

Police: Auckland Central Police Station (☎379 4240), at the corner of Cook and Vincent St. The **Downtown Station** (☎379 4500) is at the corner of Jean Batten Pl. and Fort St. Other stations include **Airport International Terminal** (☎275 9046), the **Karangahape Road Community Constable,** 281 K Rd. (☎309 8177), and the **Devonport Community Constable,** 19 Anzac St. (☎489 4008), in Devonport.

Hotlines: Lifeline (☎522 2808 or 522 2999) provides counseling by appointment and support. The **Auckland Help Foundation** (☎623 1700) aids victims of sexual assault. For STD concerns, call the **AIDS Hotline** (☎0800 802 437). All hotlines **24hr.**

Medical Services: Urgent Pharmacy, 60 Broadway (☎520 6634), in Newmarket. Open M-F 6am-1am, Sa-Su 9am-1am. The **Auckland Hospital** (☎379 7440) sits on the edge of the Auckland Domain on Park St. in Grafton. For less dire cases, **Travelcare,** 87 Queen St., 5th fl. (☎373 4621), in Central Auckland, will immunize, vaccinate, heal, and soothe. Open daily 9am-5pm. **Ponsonby Accident and Medical Clinic,** 202 Ponsonby Rd. (☎376 5555), has its own **pharmacy** (☎378 6075). Clinic open daily 7:30am-10pm; pharmacy 8am-9:30pm. For pharmaceuticals in Central Auckland, **Cammell the Chemist,** 104 Queen St. (☎303 4253), has the best hours around. Open M-Th 8am-5:30pm, F 8am-6pm, Sa 10am-5pm, Su 11am-4pm.

Internet Access: There are Internet cafes all over the city; many also have cheap overseas phone rates. **Netzone,** 4 Fort St. (☎377 3906), has $5 per hr. connections. Open

M-Sa 8:30am-11pm. **e-xile Internet Lounge,** 327 Queen St. (☎309 2101), also charges $5 per hr. but throws in free coffee. Open M-Sa 9am-9pm. Possibly the cheapest, **high-net,** 48 High St. (☎379 7736), costs $3 per hr. Open daily 8am-7pm.

Post Office: Wellesley Street Post Shop (CPO), Bledisloe Building, 24 Wellesley St. (☎379 6710), holds Poste Restante. Open M-F 7:30am-5:30pm.

ACCOMMODATIONS

The accommodations in **Central Auckland** are all conveniently located in the heart of the metropolis. However, easy access to the city's offerings comes at the price of rowdy young crowds, urban fumes, and an impersonal feel. Older travelers, families, or those simply seeking a city location with a country feel should choose a neighborhood instead—the backpackers in **Ponsonby, Parnell,** and **Mt. Eden** are only a short bus ride away from the city center and are generally much nicer than the downtown hostels. **Key deposit** is $10, unless otherwise noted.

CENTRAL AUCKLAND

Albert Park Backpackers (VIP), 27-31 Victoria St. E (☎309 0336; fax 309 9474; bakpak@albertpark.co.nz). Brimming with 20-somethings, the kitchen and lounge area feature a pool table, a view of downtown, and premium television. Reception 7am-11pm; in winter 7am-10pm. Dorms $19-22; singles $45; doubles $53. ❷

Auckland International YHA, 1235 Turner St. (☎302 8200; fax 302 8205; yhaakint@yha.org.nz), just off Queen St. The long colorful hallways, huge kitchen, and downstairs lounges will dazzle you with their spotlessness. Internet. Key deposit $5. Dorms $26-27; twins and doubles $61, with bathroom $77. ❸

Auckland City YHA (☎309 2802; fax 373 5083; yhaauck@yha.org.nz), at the corner of City Rd. and Liverpool St., attracts an older crowd than the International YHA just down the hill. On-site **Tommy's Bistro** (open daily 7-11am and 4:30-7:30pm) has cheap eats. Internet. Reception 24hr. Dorms $24; singles $48; twins and doubles $51. ❸

The Fat Camel (NOMADS), 38 Fort St. (☎307 0181 or 0800 220 198, booking code 110; fax 307 0182). This hostel treats backpackers to shared apartment-like complexes, complete with telephone (incoming only), living room, TV, bathroom, and slick kitchenette. Free breakfasts M-F. Key and linen deposit $20. Dorms $20-21; singles $40; twins $45; doubles $45-55; studio apartments for 4-6 people $140. ❷

Central City Backpackers (VIP), 26 Lorne St. (☎358 5685; fax 358 4716; ccbnz@xtra.co.nz), caters to a lively crowd—with the noise, smoke, and constant craziness to prove it. Check out the bar **Embargo,** in the basement (☎309 1850; open daily 5pm-3am). Internet. Key deposit $20. Reception 24hr. Dorms $17-21, weekly $108-120; singles (winter only) $48; twins and doubles $55. ❷

Downtown Constitution Hill Backpackers (VIP), 6 Constitution Hill (☎303 4768 or 0800 366 1444). Hidden down on a hill on the other side of Albert Park and the Railway Station, this quiet cottage is refreshingly different from Auckland's large impersonal hostels. Internet. Dorms $16; doubles $36, with bath $42. Cash only. ❷

Auckland Central Backpackers (VIP), 9 Fort St. (☎358 4877; fax 358 4872; www.acb.co.nz). With a new location added at 229 Queen St. this hostel is huge—its 383 beds are more a place to dump your pack before heading upstairs to the **bar** (open daily 2pm-3am) than a spot to de-jetlag and unwind. Internet. Key deposit $20. On-premise travel agency. Reception 24hr. Reservations recommended. Dorms $20-22; singles $42; twins and doubles $55. ❷

Albion (☎379 4900), at the corner of Hobson and Wellesley St. Set in a refurbished Victorian building, Albion will calm your nerves after a trans-pacific flight. Sky TV in every room. Reception 24hr. Doubles $85; family rooms $120. Prices $10 lower in winter. ❹

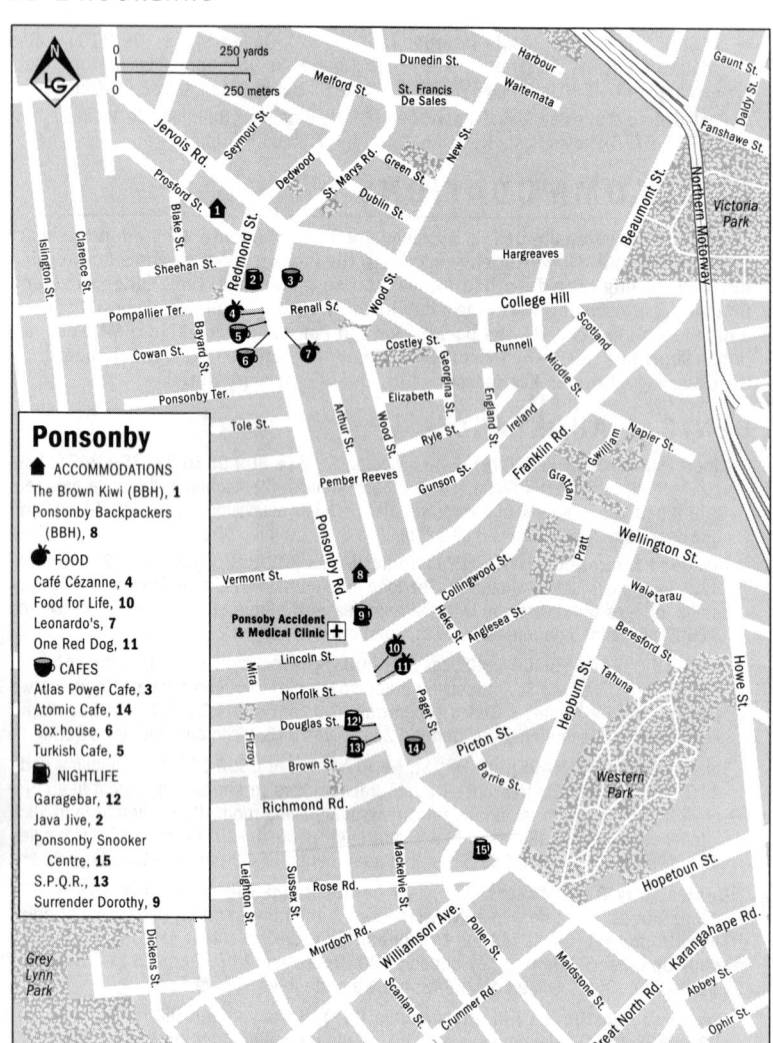

PONSONBY

The Brown Kiwi (BBH), 7 Prosford St. (☎/fax 378 0191). The Brown Kiwi puts you where you want to be—trendy Ponsonby. This 2-story home is a serene masterpiece, with an elegant garden and 2 Japanese-style fish ponds. They're even eco-conscious: "Save water, shower with a friend." Check out their new location at 217 Ponsonby Rd. Free local calls. Internet. Laundry. Gay-friendly. Dorms $19-20; doubles $48. ❷

Ponsonby Backpackers (BBH), 2 Franklin Rd. (☎360 1311 or 0800 476 676; fax 360 1365). Comfy couches and a fireplace warm the jumbled lounge. Internet. Reception 8am-8pm. Dorms $18; singles $25-30; doubles $46; tent sites $12. ❷

PARNELL

Lantana Lodge (BBH/VIP), 60 St. George's Bay Rd. (☎373 4546). This Victorian home charms with a gingerbread porch, flower garden and friendly staff. Small, simple, and compulsively clean, guests say this is one of the best hostels in Auckland. Free storage. Reception 8am-10pm. Dorms $18; twins and doubles from $44. ❷

City Garden Lodge (BBH), 25 St. George's Bay Rd. (☎302 0880, fax 309 8998; city.garden@compuweb.co.nz). Quiet and set on a ½-acre of land, this backpackers was once owned by the Queen of Tonga. Free storage. Internet. Key deposit $20. Reception 8am-noon and 3pm-late. Dorms $20-21; singles $40-42; twins $46; doubles $48. ❷

MT. EDEN

Bamber House (BBH), 22 View Rd. (☎/fax 623 4267; bamber@ihug.co.nz). This white-painted colonial home has a luxurious living room with a big screen TV. Take a dip in the outdoor pool or find your inner child in the backyard doll house. Internet. Laundry. Dorms from $22; singles $37; twins and doubles from $46. Family rooms available. ❸

Oaklands Lodge (BBH), 5a Oaklands Rd. (☎/fax 638 6545 or 0800 222 725), just off Mt. Eden Rd. This lodge relaxes even the most cramped of airplane muscles with sparkling clean, airy rooms and renovated bathrooms. Internet. Laundry. Reception 7:30am-8:30pm. Dorms $19-21; singles $40; doubles from $52. Family rooms available. ❷

BALMORAL AND GRAFTON

Rocknasium, 610 Dominion Rd. (☎630 5522; rocknasium@clear.net.nz), in **Balmoral**. Take Stagecoach bus #250-267 to the corner of Balmoral and Dominion Rd. or call for pick-up from the airport. Close to Mt. Eden, this brand new hostel is also the first indoor rock climbing facility in New Zealand. Key deposit $15. Reception 10am-10pm. Dorms $25 (includes full-day climbing pass). ❸

Georgia Parkside Backpackers (BBH), 189 Park Rd. (☎/fax 309 8999; bacpacgeorgia@xtra.co.nz), in **Grafton**. Close to Newmarket's shopping, Georgia is the only backpackers in the neighborhood. Internet. Reception M-F 7am-8pm, Sa-Su 9am-1pm and 5-7pm. Dorms $18-19; twins $40; doubles $42. Prices slightly lower in winter. ❷

FOOD

Auckland offers a mind-boggling selection of dining options, including ethnic foods from all corners of the globe. Takeaways and food courts dot the city center, but supermarkets tend to be concentrated in **Newmarket** and **Ponsonby**, the most central being **New World**, 2 College Hill, near Victoria Park; the Link Bus stops right outside. (☎307 8400. Open M-Sa 8am-10pm, Su 8am-6pm.) For good value in **Central Auckland**, it's best to venture to the top of Queen St. or along K Rd. The neighborhoods of Ponsonby and **Mt. Eden** feature restaurants with a funkier feel and affordable prices, while those in **Parnell** cater to an upmarket crowd. See the **Cafes** section (p. 89) for more dining options.

CENTRAL AUCKLAND

The Occidental, 6 Vulcan Ln. (☎300 6226). With oak-lined walls and an old-style bar, this is a popular spot for locals and tourists alike. Try the mussels ($11) or the pork loin with sauerkraut ($17.50). Live jazz Sa 9-11pm and Su 6-9pm. Open daily 7am-3am. ❸

Mexican Cafe Bar & Grill, 67 Victoria St. W (☎373 2311). Mexican mains satisfy burrito cravings ($15-20). While Happy Hour (5-7pm) means cheap starters, the bar tap sees the most action. Open daily 5pm-late; also M-F noon-2:30pm. ❸

Pizza Pizza, 57 Lorne St. (☎309 3333), tucked behind Queen St. to the East, on the second floor of an orange building. This funky, laid-back pizza pad gives students a 20% discount on smalls and larges. Free toppings and free delivery to Central Auckland (min. order $13). Open M-F 10:30am-10:30pm, Sa-Su 4:30-10:30pm. ❷

Tanuki Sushi and Sake Bar, 319 Queen St. (☎ 379 5353). Delectable Japanese mains ($5-16). Open Su-Th 5:30-11pm, F-Sa 5:30pm-midnight. In the darker depths below, **Tanuki's Cave** (☎379 5151) serves skewers of *yakitori* ($2-7.50) and over 35 different kinds of *sake*. Open Tu-Th and Sa-Su 6pm-midnight, F 5:30pm-1am. ❷

Rasoi Vegetarian Restaurant, 211 K Rd. (☎377 7780), is an all-veggie, all-the-time eatery. The Deluxe Thai platter, complete with rice and your choice of curry ($9.50), challenges even the hungriest. Open M-Sa 11am-9pm. Cash only. ❷

PONSONBY

One Red Dog, 151 Ponsonby Rd. (☎360 1068). This exotic pizzeria delights with such concoctions as the beef bernaise or sweet chili Thai pizza. Pastas $14.50. Bar downstairs. Open M-F 11am-1am, Sa-Su 10am-1am. ❸

Café Cézanne, 296 Ponsonby Rd. (☎376 3338). A colorful menu of big breakfasts (gigantic muffins $2.50), pastas, and salads ($8-12) feeds the equally colorful crowd. Open Su-Th 9am-midnight, F-Sa 8am-2am. ❷

Leonardo's, 263 Ponsonby Rd. (☎363 1556). A family-run, Italian restaurant where Leonardo himself greets diners. Enjoy the wide range of antipasto options or try the savory beef medallions ($27.50). Open Tu-Su 6pm-late; also F-Sa noon-3pm. ❺

Food for Life, 153 Ponsonby Rd. (☎376 5878). Vegetarians find nirvana in this world of organic nourishment. Soups $5-7.50, casseroles $12.50. The bar in the rear offers a great view over Auckland. Open daily 7am-10pm; bar open until 1am. ❸

PARNELL

The Bog, 196 Parnell Rd. (☎377 1510). The "Brendan behan" ($16.50) and kilo-of-mussels ($16) deliver more than Irish kitsch. Guinness and Kilkenny $6 a pint. Open daily 10:30am-late (usually 1am). ❸

Kebab Kid, 363 Parnell Rd. (☎373 4290). Middle Eastern fast food may seem foreign to most, but the Kid has your favorite kebab ($8.50) ready in a flash. Open M and Su 11am-10pm, Tu-Th and Sa noon-11pm, F noon-2am. ❷

George Restaurant, 144 Parnell Rd. (☎358-2600). Elegant place settings and impeccable service complement the sharp interior. Try the New York cut sirloin ($28) or the cajun tuna with artichokes ($26). Open daily noon-11pm. ❺

MT. EDEN

🔲 **Circus Circus,** 447 Mt. Eden Rd. (☎623 3833). Filled with vintage circus posters, assorted clown paraphernalia, and even a red tent for smokers, this eatery is a 3-ring utopia (sandwiches $2.50-7.50). "Show in progress daily" 7am-4:30pm. ❷

Mt. Eden Bakery and Deli, 464 Mt. Eden Rd. (☎630 1426). Travelers and hordes of locals simply can't resist the heavenly sandwiches, quiches, or cakes ($1-5), all brown-bagged at bargain-basement prices. Open M-F 7am-6:30pm, Sa-Su 7am-5:30pm. ❶

Dhan, 407 Mt. Eden Rd. (☎630 1143). The friendly staff of this Japanese restaurant will point out the best combination of sauces and sides. Lunch and dinner boxes ($10). Open daily 6-10pm; also Tu-Sa 11:30am-2pm. ❷

CAFES

Auckland's vibrant cafe scene is an integral part of its social fabric, coolly filtering out the espresso-ignorant. In **Central Auckland**, the narrow streets of High and Lorne as well as Vulcan Ln. and nearby K Rd. are brimming with coffee sippers; likewise, the main roads in **Parnell** and **Mt. Eden** feature a wide selection of java joints. However, stylish **Ponsonby** wins the caffeine crown for the highest concentration of great cafes. In addition to the universal love of coffee beans, most cafes serve light meals and alcohol, and some feature occasional live music.

CENTRAL AUCKLAND

Alleluya, 179-183 K Rd. (☎377 8424), in St. Kevin's Arcade. Situated on the oldest cafe site in Auckland, Alleluya is a spiritual caffeine-induced experience with an incredible view over Myer's Park and the Sky Tower. Salads and sandwiches around $10. Open M-Tu 9am-5pm, W-Sa 9am-midnight, Su 9am-4pm.

Jolt, 47 High St. (☎303 0066). This hole in the wall is a cross between Starbucks and your local mom and pop diner. With delicious bagel sandwiches and coffee to match, Jolt provides an automatic pick-me-up. Open M-F 7am-5pm.

Columbus Cafe, 43 High St. (☎309 5677). Step into the sleek, metal interior to order one of Columbus' gourmet espressos ($2.50-5.50). The outdoor patio is great for lounging. Open M-F 6:45am-5:30pm, Sa 9:30am-5:30pm, Su 10:30am-5:30pm.

Brazil, 256 K Rd. (☎302 2677). The fragrance of roasting beans wafts through the air as resident DJs spin and scratch. Breakfast around $11.3 Internet. Open M-Tu 8am-8pm, W-Th 8am-midnight, F 8am-1am, Sa 9am-1am, Su 9am-8pm; kitchen closes at 3pm.

PONSONBY

Atomic Cafe, 121 Ponsonby Rd. (☎376 4954). Readers of all ages search for deep meaning in the collection of Dr. Seuss books. Large breakfasts $7-13. Open M-W and F 7am-6pm, Th 7am-11pm, Sa 8am-5pm, Su 8am-4:30pm; kitchen closes M-F at 2:30pm, Sa-Su at 3pm.

Atlas Power Cafe, 285 Ponsonby Rd. (☎360 1295). Freshly roasted everyday, Atlas's coffee might not give you the strength of a Greek god, but it will certainly lift your spirits. Open daily 7am-6pm.

Turkish Cafe, 294 Ponsonby Rd. (☎360 0468). Turks-at-heart sip Turkicino ($5.50; a strong Turkish coffee) while listening to belly dance songs and eating falafel ($14.50). Open M-Th 11am-midnight, F-Sa 11am-2am.

Box.house, 286 Ponsonby Rd. (☎376 6538). The coffees ($2.50) and teas ($2.50) at this retro cafe will clear your mind late into the night. The restaurant serves mainly European/Chinese fare ($16.50-18.50). Open daily 7am-late (usually 2am).

PARNELL

Strawberry Alarm Clock, 119 Parnell Rd. (☎377 6959). Once a fruit and vegetable shop, today this colorful cafe mellows even the most stressed of suits. While you savor the serenity, take a hint from the writing on the wall— "No Smoking" is inscribed in every imaginable language! Open M-F 7:30am-5pm, Sa 8:30am-4:30pm, Su 9am-4pm.

Trinity Cafe, 107 Parnell Rd. (☎300 3042). This petite cafe serves fantastic, light fare (grilled chicken and avocado $10.50) as well as the requisite coffee and tea selection. Gay-friendly. Open M-F 7am-4pm.

The Other Side, 320 Parnell Rd. (☎366 4426), dares to be different with its location on the *other* side of the street. Try "The Works" breakfast ($10) with your joe for guaranteed full-day functionality. Open M-F 7am-10pm, Sa-Su 8am-10pm.

MT. EDEN

Frasers, 434 Mt. Eden Rd. (☎630 6825). Popular with locals, this corner cafe serves beverages and bites. Chat with a friend over the homemade quiche ($7) and a cappuccino ($2.50). Open M-F 7am-11pm, Sa-Su 8am-11pm.

City Cake Company, 426 Mt. Eden Rd. (☎638 6499). The wide array of sugar decadence will make any decision difficult, but the chocolate cake ($6) is a little slice of heaven. Open daily 9am-6pm.

ENTERTAINMENT

Not known for haute culture, Auckland tries to live up to its cosmopolitan status with a wide range of entertainment choices. From adult entertainment to the more classy opera, theatre, music, and dance options scattered along parts of K Rd., diversions abound. Check out *The New Zealand Herald* for entertainment info, or pick up the monthly *Real Groove* ($3.50).

MUSIC

Live music is a regular treat that livens up many local joints throughout the week (see also the **Cafes** and **Nightlife** sections). The intimate venue, **Temple,** 486 Queen St., features lives acts nightly. Monday is open mic jam night and Tuesday offers up jazz, poetry, or comedy. Their daily Happy Hour (5-8pm) serves two spirits or Kiwi beers for $5. (☎377 4866; www.temple.co.nz. Cover varies. Open daily 5pm-2am.) Filling more of a niche is **Java Jive,** at the corner of Ponsonby Rd. and Pompallier Tce. in Ponsonby. This subterranean blues/jazz/rock club has plenty of atmosphere and low-altitude attitude. (☎376 5870. Open Tu-Su 6pm-3am.)

When big bands pass through Auckland, they take the stage at **Powerstation,** 33 Mt. Eden Rd. (☎377 3488) or the **North Shore Event Centre** (☎443 8199). Check at **Real Groovy,** 438 Queen St., for schedule and ticket information. (☎302 3940. Open M-W and Sa-Su 9am-7pm, Th-F 9am-9pm.)

PERFORMING ARTS

The highbrow highlights of Auckland's entertainment scene cluster around the centrally-located Aotea (ow-TAY-ah) Square off Queen St.; known as the **Edge** (☎309 2677; www.the-edge.co.nz), the complex includes the Aotea Centre, the Civic, Auckland Town Hall, and the Force Entertainment Centre, all listed separately below. In the Aotea Centre, the 2256-seat **ASB Theatre** is the majestic home to the **New Zealand Royal Ballet,** the **New Zealand** and **Auckland Philharmonics,** and world-class productions for limited engagements; the 186-seat **Herald Theatre** and the **Ticketek** box office are also on site. Opposite Aotea Centre, classical music emanates from the **Auckland Town Hall Concert Chamber,** which is home to the **International Chamber Music Festival** (☎445 1863) in July. Just next door, the **Civic Theatre** (☎307 5700) hosts music and theater functions, including a range of classic films; the opulent interior is worth a peek. Theater, dance, and music performances are always on at the **Maidment Arts Centre,** 8 Alfred St., opposite the Auckland University Library. (☎308 2383. Tickets $15-45.) The **Auckland Theatre Company** (☎309 3395; tickets $18-41) does drama there, at the Herald, and at the Sky City Theatre; their **Second Unit** has up-and-coming playwrights and directors read their work once a month for free at the **Rydge Hotel.**

At the other end of the theater spectrum stands the **SiLO,** on Lower Greys Ave., behind Town Hall. Managed by art students, this underground experimental theater features a wide range of performances. (☎373 5151. Tickets $10-18.)

The **Classic Comedy & Bar,** 321 Queen St., serves up good laughs. Shows range from amateur open mic (M, $5) to the humorous musings of seasoned pros later in the week. Happy Hour is M-F 6:30-7:30pm. Live shows W-Sa start at 8pm. (☎373 4321. Cover varies. Open M-Th 6:30pm-midnight, F-Sa 6:30pm-2am.)

CINEMA AND SPORT

In mid-July, the **Auckland International Film Festival** captures the attention of movie buffs with two weeks of screenings from all over the world. (☎307 5000. Tickets $12.) Year-round, standard-issue Hollywood films are shown in the flashy new **Force Entertainment Centre,** 291-297 Queen St. (☎979 2405), a complex which houses the **IMAX** screen (☎979 2400; tickets $15, students $13, Tu $11), conventional cinemas, restaurants, bars, and video game parlors.

If you're feeling lucky, **Sky City** has casinos for both seasoned and beginning gamblers. (☎912 6000. Free gaming lessons available.) Across the street is the **Palace,** 73-75 Victoria St. (☎366 0200), the only bar in Auckland that stays open **24hr.**

For those who prefer games of skill to games of chance, the **Ponsonby Snooker Centre,** 106 Ponsonby Rd., is the classiest pool hall in Auckland, with three full-size snooker tables. (☎360 2356. $10 per hr., after 6pm $12 per hr. Open daily 11am-1am. Reservations necessary at night.)

NIGHTLIFE

BARS

Auckland's bars range from traditional Irish pubs to mellow lounges, but domestic beers are the drink of choice in almost every locale. Along the **Waterfront** colossal bars cater to huge crowds and provide excellent harbor views free of charge. The rest of **Central Auckland** is host to traditional pubs, funky lounges, and backpacker havens. The surrounding neighborhoods, best known as cafe spots, do have some choice bars, frequented predominantly as pre-clubbing spots. **Ponsonby** packs black-clad yuppies, **Parnell** is home to the old money crowd, and **Newmarket** has some relaxed watering holes. See the **Food** (p. 87) and **Cafes** (p. 89) sections for others places to enjoy a fine wine or an overflowing pint.

CENTRAL AUCKLAND

Khuja Lounge (☎377 3711), at the corner of K Rd. and Queen St. Lebanese for "melting pot," Khuja draws a multicultural crowd. DJs mix everything from soul to drum 'n' bass. W is *Brisa Luca* with samba and basa nova. Cover usually $5. Open W-Sa 8pm-late.

Margarita's, 18 Elliot St. (☎302 2764). Backpackers rush here for the cheap booze (M, Th, and Sa the first 100 patrons get 8 beers for $5) and the youthful vibe. Upstairs, **Chili Lounge** is swankier. Handles $3 daily 5-7pm and 9-10pm. Open daily 4pm-3am.

The Dog's Bollix (☎376 4600), at the corner of K and Newton Rd., proves Dublin is alive and well in Auckland. Su is locals' night with Irish dancing and spontaneous eruptions of folk in a free-for-all jam session (6:30pm). Live music Tu-Su. Open Tu-Th 4pm-late, F-Sa 11:30am-late, Su noon-late.

Papa Jack's Voodoo Lounge (☎358 4847), on Vulcan Ln. This 2nd-fl. lounge provides all the ingredients for a devilish evening—from the bats and scorpions embedded in the bar to potent potions like $6 shots of "dragon's blood." Auckland's main alternative venue, Jack's features live music Th 10pm. F cover $2. Open Tu-Sa 7pm-late.

Leftfield, Shed 19 Princes Wharf (☎307 9500). Built for the America's Cup 2000 and pumping ever since, this colossal sports bar features 3 bars, stadium seating, a lounge, a restaurant, and excellent views of the harbor. The TV show "Lion Red Sportscafe" tapes here live W at 8:30pm. Handles $5. Open daily 9:30am-late.

Deschlers Bar, 17 High St. (☎379 6811). Affectionately dubbed the "jazz version of Cheers," regulars return for the saxophone beer taps, posh dark surrounds, and live jazz 4 nights a week (M and F-Su). Open Su-Th noon-3am, F noon-late, Sa 3pm-late.

Kiwi Tavern, 3 Britomart Pl. (☎307 1717), east of QE II Sq. along Customs St. opposite the Oriental Markets. A backpackers' mainstay, this multi-level venue is packed with nightly discounts. Tu, 5 draft beers cost a mere $8. Downstairs, the **Kiwi Bar** complements with a creative, rustic aesthetic. Happy Hour daily 5-7pm (pints, wine $3). Tu DJ 8pm-late. Open Su-Th 11am-3am, F-Sa 11am-4am.

PONSONBY

Garagebar, 152 Ponsonby Rd. (☎378 8237). With oil cans for tips jars and a clear underground pit for a wine cellar, this garage-turned-bar sticks to its gasoline roots. House DJs Tu-Sa 9pm-2am. Open M-Sa 5pm-2am.

S.P.Q.R., 150 Ponsonby Rd. (☎360 1710). Lit by candles and glowing orbs, this spacious cafe and bar attracts a mixed crowd. The name refers to the liberal days of the Roman Republic; anything goes. Pizzas and pastas $15.50-19.50. Gay-friendly. Open M-F noon-2am, Sa-Su 10am-2am.

PARNELL

The Nag's Head Tavern, 117 St. George's Bay Rd. (☎309 3586), off the Strand. Down the hill from Parnell's hostel strip, a down-to-earth crowd packs in for the English pub feel and beer to match. Tu Happy Hour 5-6:30pm (pints $2.50). Open daily 11am-late.

Komodo, 106b Parnell Rd. (☎309 3161), entrance on Garfield St. A lush, winding walkway leads to a dark interior where DJs keep the crowd mesmerized with trance. "Big Wednesdays" offer $3 drink specials (spirits 2 for $5). Open W-Sa 5pm-2am.

NIGHTCLUBS

Although Auckland's surrounding neighborhoods light up with lively bars, **Central Auckland** dances til dawn. Up on **K Road,** style reigns supreme as clubbers don their favorite shade of black and join the queue. Adding color to the scene are drag queens, who come out at night and stay until the next day.

For the skinny on events, the free glossy mag *The Fix* can't be beat. Pick it up, as well as special events flyers, at **Beat Merchants,** 301 Victoria St. E, **CyberCulture,** 151 K Rd., and the mother of all record stores, **Real Groovy,** 438 K Rd.

The Kiss Club and Bar and **Bacio,** 309 K Rd. (☎303 2726), steal a huge percent of the K Rd. clubbers with their seductive interiors. A funk beat fills the dance floor while an eager line forms outside. Cover F-Sa $7. Open W-Sa 10pm-7am.

Cause Celebre and **The Box,** 33 High St. (☎303 1336). Auckland's longest running nightclub throbs with young dance machines who circulate through the 2 related venues. Weekends are a sweaty, drum 'n' bass and house-induced haze. Cover $10. Open W-Th 11pm-6am, F-Sa 5pm-10am.

Jones, 350 K Rd. (☎377 0033). This upstairs lounge offers plush booths and a large dance floor. Funky house, high energy, and trance keep the place pulsing all the time. DJs Th-Su from 11pm. Cover $10. Open Th 10pm-5am, F-Sa 10pm-7am, Su 9pm-4am.

The Angle, 258 K Rd. (☎307 0890). The seas of posh pool sharks here are a distraction when it comes to billiards; the real game, however, is angling for a date (and there's lots of fresh catch). Sa fire dancers and jugglers liven things up. Cover $5. Open F-Sa 9pm-late.

Galatos, 17 Galatos St. (☎303 1928), just behind K Rd. Attracting more mellow crowds than K Rd., Galatos lets aspiring DJs hire out the huge dance floor for the right to play their favorites (cover $5 and up). The upstairs lounge is free—if the bouncer thinks you're cool enough to get in. Open W-Th 9pm-3am, F-Sa 9pm-6am.

The Supper Club, 2 Beresford St. (☎300 5040), just behind K Rd. Once the home of Auckland's public toilets, this curiously-shaped club is now the destination of choice for pre- and post-clubbing partyers. Cover Sa $1-5. Open Tu-F 11am-late, Sa 4pm-late.

GAY AND LESBIAN NIGHTLIFE

Ironically, Queen St. is *not* the center of queer activity in Auckland—instead **Ponsonby** takes the cake. Many gay-run bars and brasseries line Ponsonby Rd., promising numerous opportunities for a fabulous night out. Gay nightlife is well-integrated into the Auckland scene, and **K Road** clubs are often gay-friendly. Downtown, **High Street** and **Vulcan Lane** also host some choice gay nightspots. Scope out the *express* newspaper ($2.50 at newsstands) for the most current listings.

Taking over Auckland for two weeks, the **HERO Gay and Lesbian Festival** (mid-February, 2003) is a carnivalesque celebration of theater performances, film screenings, and outdoor events including a parade and all-night dance party. Check *express* or the web at www.hero.org.nz for a peek at the schedule.

> **Surrender Dorothy,** 3/175 Ponsonby Rd. (☎376 4460), in Ponsonby. At the sign with the hairy legs and ruby slippers, you'll find an unpretentious and fun watering hole. Mixed but predominantly male couples. Drag queens strut their stuff Sa at 10pm. Open "for joy and fabulousity" Tu-Sa 5pm-12:30am.
>
> **Wunder Bar,** 5 O'Connell St. (☎377 9404), in the Administrator House. Red velvet and gold tassels, stiff drinks, and hard house all make for lush life and lavishness at this (very camp) club. Open daily 4pm-3am.
>
> **Urge,** 490 K Rd. (☎307 2155). The heavy black leather curtain at the entrance sets the tone for this dark and snug nightspot, where cruising is the norm for the mostly gay-male scene. F DJ party "Grind." Open Th-Su from 9pm.

SIGHTS

VANTAGE POINTS

Auckland offers many options for a higher perspective on its urban sprawl. Volcanic hills rise up around the city and provide keen lookouts, though man has made a fair attempt at offering concrete alternatives as well.

MT. EDEN AND ONE TREE HILL. The parks of Mt. Eden (Maungawhau) provide a bird's eye (or at least a giraffe's eye) view of Auckland. Look out for the herd of cows on your way up to the crater summit. Another fine lookout, One Tree Hill also houses the **Stardome Observatory** at its base, which features a planetarium show. After shows, you can take a peak at the cosmos through the EWB 50cm telescope. *(Mt. Eden: Take bus #274, 275, or 277 from Commerce St. near Fort St. Observatory: Take bus #30 or 31 from the corner of Victoria and Queen St. ☎624 1246. W-Su 2-6 shows per day. $10, children $5. Telescope $5, children $3; bookings essential.)*

SKY TOWER. Dominating the Auckland skyline, the 328m Sky Tower is 8m taller, and a lot brighter, than the Eiffel Tower (take that, France). The **observation deck** has a 360° view; the **Sky Deck** is 34m higher and offers almost the same views but without all the mayhem; you can even step onto the glass in the outer ring or eat at **Orbit**, its requisite rotating restaurant. The **Sky Jump** (see p. 96) was recently added for adrenaline junkies. *(In the middle of Hobson, Wellesley, Federal, and Victoria St. Open Su-Th 8:30am-11pm, F-Sa 8:30am-midnight; last elevator 30min. before closing. $15, children $7.50, seniors $13.50. Sky Deck $3 more. Discount tickets available at the Auckland Visitors Center.)*

CENTRAL AUCKLAND

ART GALLERIES. Next to Albert Park sits the prim white **Auckland Art Gallery.** Peruse the 19th century paintings of New Zealand landscape and history as well as the Maori portraits on the ground floor. Its sister gallery, the **New Gallery,** focuses on contemporary art; the steel and glass space houses traveling shows. *(Auckland Art Gallery: at the corner of Wellesley and Kitchener St. ☎307 7700. Open daily 10am-5pm. Standing collection admission free; exhibit admission varies. New Gallery: a block down on the corner of Wellesley and Lorne St. ☎307 4540. Open daily 10am-5pm. $4, students and seniors $2.)*

AUCKLAND MUSEUM. Auckland's largest museum displays Polynesian, European, and natural history exhibits. Upstairs, *Scars on the Heart* describes various New Zealand wars and may make you palpitate with patriotism; downstairs galleries feature *Aotearoa's* Maori heritage and house the **Hotuni whare,** a complete meetinghouse on loan from the Tainui tribe of the Thames area. The museum is also the venue for the **Pounamu Maori Performance Group.** *(Take the Link Bus to "Auckland Museum."* ☎ *309 0443. Shows daily 11am and 1:30pm. $10, students and seniors $5. Museum open daily 10am-5pm. $5 suggested donation.)*

AUCKLAND UNIVERSITY. As you traverse Albert Park, it is impossible to miss the handsome tower of the **Old Arts Building,** 22 Princes St. Built in 1926, the building is the symbol of **Auckland University,** the largest of New Zealand's eight public universities. The campus **library** is at the corner of Princes and Alfred St. *(University operator* ☎ *373 7599. Open to the general public M-Th 9am-9pm, F-Sa 9am-6pm, Su 10am-8pm.)*

PARKS. To escape from the city's chaos, **Victoria Park** to the west of Queen St. and **Albert Park** to the east is a welcome dose of nature. Across from Victoria Park, the aptly named **Victoria Park Market,** 210 Victoria St. W, bustles with crafts, clothes, cafes, and weekend flea markets. *(*☎ *309 6911. Open daily 9am-6pm.)*

THE WATERFRONT

The **Harbour Information Office,** a kiosk near the water, can answer most questions about the waterfront area. *(*☎ *357 6366. Open daily 9am-6:30pm; in winter 9am-6pm.)*

AMERICAN EXPRESS NEW ZEALAND CUP VILLAGE. Head to the bottom of Albert St. to find **Waitemata Harbour,** the site of the America's Cup regatta. Once there, turn left on Quay St. and continue to Viaduct Harbour to reach the American Express New Zealand Cup Village, home to numerous restaurants, bars, apartments, and hotels. *(Viaduct Harbour is just west of QE II Sq.)*

NEW ZEALAND NATIONAL MARITIME MUSEUM. This waterside museum has meticulously crafted exhibits on New Zealand's love-affair with the sea, all enhanced by true-to-life settings and sounds. *(At the base of Hobson Wharf.* ☎ *373 0800. Open daily 9am-6pm; in winter 9am-5pm. $12, students $6.)*

FERRY BUILDING. The beautiful 1912 Ferry Building is an important waterfront landmark and home of Fullers ferries, which has service to the islands of Waiheke (see p. 99), Rangitoto (see p. 99), and Great Barrier Island (see p. 102), as well as across to the North Shore community of Devonport (see p. 97). See **Auckland: Local Transportation,** p. 82, for schedules and prices. *(Ferry building, 99 Quay St. Fullers* ☎ *367 9111. Coffee Cruise 2hr.; 3 per day; $30, children $15.)*

COAST TO COAST WALK. The Coast to Coast Walk starts at the Ferry Building (see above) and travels through the city from Waitemata Harbor to Onehunga Beach, home to the first European settlements in Auckland. It passes the Auckland Domain, Mt. Eden Domain, and One Tree Hill on the way; the path is marked every kilometer by blue and yellow signs. *(One-way 16km., 4-6hr.)*

WESTHAVEN MARINA. A parking lot for Auckland's wealthy, Westhaven is the largest man-made marina in the Southern Hemisphere. Further down Westhaven Dr., along the Rolex-wearing arm of the Marina, are the upper-crust **yacht clubs,** where crews return from civilized competition to enjoy a civilized drink (or six). Back along Westhaven Dr. toward Central Auckland, the helpful staff at **Sea Tours** on **Pier Z** can answer questions about charter sailings. *(To reach Westhaven Marina, take Westhaven Dr. out of Auckland, along Gaunt St. from the American Express New Zealand Cup Village. Sea Tours* ☎ *378 9088; www.seatours.co.nz.)*

THE BAYS

Skirting subtropical waters and cream-colored sands, the Bays are a prime in-line skating, kayaking, and parading venue in the summer months. (Buses #765 and 769 run past both Mission Bay and St. Heliers Bay; call Rideline ☎ 366 6400.)

ACTIVITIES. If you have a car but want a different set of wheels, head to **Ferg's Kayaks** for **in-line skates.** Fit romantics might enjoy Ferg's **moonlight kayak trip** to Rangitoto Island. *(12 Tamaki Dr. ☎ 529 2230. Open daily 8am-6pm; in winter 8am-5pm. In-line skates 1hr. $10, $25 per day. Kayaks $9 per hr. Kayak trip $60. Bookings essential.)*

ORAKEI BASIN. The yacht-filled **Orakei Basin** is the sailing grounds for the rich of **Paritai Drive,** Auckland's wealthiest street in a gated community of million-dollar mansions. Take a longing look from Orakei Rd., which abuts **Hobson Bay** east of Central Auckland, for frequent rainbows, hundreds of pleasure yachts, and Auckland's most expensive real estate.

KELLY TARLTON'S UNDERWATER WORLD. Deep beneath Tamaki Dr. lurk stingrays, eels, and sharks in possibly the most ingenious use ever of converted sewage tanks. A dry-erase board at the entrance serves as a fishy tabloid of who's being fed, who's been born, and who's mating with whom. A moving walkway transports guests into the underwater world while a golf cart roller coaster takes passengers through the Antarctic Encounter, which features a colony of live King and Gentoo penguins. *(23 Tamaki Dr., 6km east of Central Auckland. ☎ 528 0603 or 0800 805 050; www.new-zealand.com/kellytarltons. Open Nov.-Feb. daily 9am-9pm, last entry 8pm; Mar.-Oct. 9am-6pm, last entry 5pm. $22, students and seniors $18, children $10.)*

MISSION AND ST. HELIERS BAY. Hiding around Bastion Point from the Orakei Marae of the Ngati Whatua tribe is **Mission Bay,** a sunbathing outpost with a stretch of lively bars and cafes. Nearby is the popular and accessible **St. Heliers Bay.** Quiet throughout the winter, Tamaki Dr. and St. Heliers Bay Rd. fill with hordes of people in the summer.

MICHAEL JOSEPH SAVAGE MEMORIAL GARDENS. This poppy-dotted park pays homage to New Zealand's first Labour Party Prime Minister. The view of Rangitoto and the Gulf is stunning. *(At the end of Hapimana just south of Bastion Point in Mission Bay. Contact City Parks Office with questions ☎ 379 2020.)*

INNER SUBURBS

PONSONBY. No visit to Auckland is complete without a jaunt to Ponsonby. While not exactly a historical district, the vibrant student and gay populations give the neighborhood a more welcom-

IN RECENT NEWS

SMOGGY NEW ZEALAND?

A recent report by the Auckland City Council suggests that when it comes to automotive emissions, New Zealand's clean green image may be a charade. The report, released in August 2002, claims that the carbon monoxide content of Auckland's air ranks second highest in the world. Only Tijuana, Mexico has more of the smog-forming gas.

Auckland lacks a mass-transit system and many residents travel the metropolitan area by car. Pollution caused by this heavy car use has not only increased the city's carbon monoxide levels but has proven fatal for Aucklanders. According to the City Council's report, car emissions were responsible for 253 deaths in 2001.

To combat this smog overload, the Auckland Regional Council is lobbying the Ministry of Transport for tougher emissions standards on imported cars. Currently, Kiwi regulations are lax: no emissions requirements govern the import of vehicles to New Zealand. Combined with lagging fuel quality standards, this polluter-friendly policy places New Zealand years behind Europe and the United States in controlling automotive emissions. The Council has also challenged the public to eliminate at least two car trips from their weekly routine by walking, cycling, or taking a bus.

In a nation of outdoor-lovers, it seems odd that so many could tolerate a polluted living environment. Smoggy New Zealand may sound oxymoronic, but the thick brown halo surrounding Auckland on a windless day suggests that the pollution isn't going to disappear on its own.

ing feel than Auckland's often sterile business district. Both sides of Ponsonby Rd. are lined with eateries, trendy cafes, and bars. Connecting Ponsonby to the top of the city, the bridge over the K Rd. motorway hosts an open-air market on Saturdays from 10am to 4pm.

AUCKLAND DOMAIN. To the east of Central Auckland lies the vast expanse of grass and trees that is the Auckland Domain. A duck pond laps ashore in the center, and a nearby gazebo often hosts free jazz concerts on summer weekends. Amid the various attractions in the Domain are the free Wintergardens, a collection of glass houses around a lily pond. *(The park is best accessed from the Grafton Bridge, which extends across the motorway just a block from the intersection of Queen St. and K Rd. Wintergardens open daily 9am-7:30pm; in winter 9am-4:30pm.)*

PARNELL AND NEWMARKET. On the far side of the Domain is the flashy, upscale neighborhood of Parnell, home to vast estates, historic buildings, and pricey shops. The most notable architecture is a group of Victorian homes-turned-boutiques, along the side of Parnell Rd., known as **Parnell Heritage Village** (look for the fleet of tour buses outside). At the top of the road on the opposite side sits Auckland's **Anglican Cathedral of the Holy Trinity**, which was moved completely intact in all of its 19th-century glory to make room for a larger church. The free and lovely **Parnell Rose Gardens** at the base of the hill bursts into bloom from November to March. Parnell Rd. leads straight into nearby Newmarket; take Carlton Gore Rd. when Parnell Rd. forks. A shopping mecca for Auckland residents, this tiny suburb bustles along Broadway St.

WESTERN SPRINGS

The residential suburb of Western Springs is home to two of Auckland's big name attractions: the **zoo** and **MOTAT**. To get to Western Springs, take the yellow bus #045 from Point Chevalier ($2.20), across from QE II Sq.

AUCKLAND ZOO. Auckland's zoo features impressive *Rainforest* and *Pridelands* sections. The kiwi and tuatara exhibits are worth a look, as are the red pandas and the Wallaby Walkabout. *(On Motion Rd. ☎ 360 3819; www.aucklandzoo.co.nz. Open daily 9:30am-5:30pm; last entry 4:15pm. $13, students $10, seniors $9, children $7.)*

MUSEUM OF TECHNOLOGY AND TRANSPORT (MOTAT). A classic streetcar connects the zoo to MOTAT, where science fans can get their hands on physics experiments or see steam engines and antique cars. The entrance fee includes **MOTAT II**, a collection of classic aircraft and seaplanes located 500m past the zoo on Motions Rd. *(805 Great North Rd. ☎ 846 7020. Open daily 10am-5pm, last entry 4:30pm. $10, children and seniors $5, families $20. Streetcar $2.)*

◪ OUTDOOR ACTIVITIES

I LIKE MY KNICKERS DRY

Bungy Bobbing: The **Sky Screamer** (☎ 0800 932 8649), at the corner of Victoria and Albert St., hurtles 2 or 3 passengers 160km in 1½min. and then lets them bob up and down for another 5min. ($35). Open daily 11am-10pm. For a thrill thrill, the **Sky Jump** (☎ 0800 759 5867; www.skyjump.co.nz) is a controlled 192m base jump off the top of the Sky Tower ($195). Open M-Th and Su 10:30am-7pm, F-Sa 10:30am-late.

Cycling: Auckland Adventures (☎ 379 4545 or 025 855 856) leads full-day area tours, some of which include several hours of mountain biking ($89, under 12 $44.50). **Adventure Cycles,** 1 Fort Ln. (☎ 649 309 5566 or 0800 335 566), rents mountain bikes ($25-35 per day) and touring bikes ($18-25 per day).

Motorbiking: 4 Track Adventures (☎ 420 8104 or 0800 487 225), 30min. north of the city ($20 pick-up available), guides 4-wheel motorbike "safaris" through Woodhill Forest and nearby beaches. 1hr. trip $95, 2hr. $155, 3hr. $195.

Rock Climbing: Rocknasium, 610 Dominion Rd. (☎630 5522), in Balmoral. Take bus #250-267 from Queen St. 11m high, this is the first indoor climbing center in New Zealand. $25 includes shoes, harness, chalk bag, and a night's rest in the hostel (see **Accommodations**, p. 87). Open daily 10am-10pm.

Skydiving: Mercer Skydiving Centre (☎373 5778 or 0800 865 867; www.skydivemercer.com), 35min. south of the city (return shuttle $20). Tandem jump from 12,000ft. $250. 10% student discount.

I'D PREFER THEM WET

Canyoning: AWOL Adventures (☎630 7100) runs 6hr. tours that involve an exploration of the canyons around Kitekite Falls ($125). **Canyonz** (☎0800 422 696 or 025 294 7724; www.canyonz.co.nz) runs full-day trips that include 3hr. in the Blue Canyons ($135, under 15 $105).

Kayaking: Auckland Wilderness (☎813 3399 or 025 582 409; www.nzkayak.co.nz) leads full-day trips to Rangitoto Island ($85) as well as 5hr. evening excursions ($75). **The Little Adventure Company** (☎0508 529 257 or 021 631 376; www.qualitykayaks.co.nz) also runs guided tours in the Auckland Harbor and Hauraki Gulf. Half-day $55, full-day $80.

Sailing: Designed to sail in the 1995 America's Cup (but not finished in time), the *NZL 40*, operated by **Viking Cruises** (☎0800 724 569), now makes several 2hr. outings daily ($75, under 14 $65). **LOGAN Ponsonby Sailing School** (☎376 0245; www.pcc.org.nz) conducts 20hr. dinghy-sailing courses, primarily on weekends ($250).

Swimming: The 60m salt-water pool at **Parnell Baths** (☎373 3561), on Judges Bay Rd. overlooking the harbor in Parnell, has the most pleasant location ($3.50, under 17 $3). Open Nov.-Mar. M-F 6am-8pm, Sa-Su 8am-8pm.

Swimming with Dolphins: Operating in conjunction with research projects, **Dolphin Explorer** (☎237 1466; www.dolphinexplorer.com) runs daily 4-5hr. trips through the Hauraki Gulf Maritime Park ($90, under 15 $45); if the boat doesn't encounter any dolphins or whales, you can take another trip for free.

Vineyard Touring: Aotearoa Van Coach Tours (☎834 5363 or 025 764 759) conducts half-day trips to 4 of the Auckland area wineries ($59). **Auckland Wine Trail Tours** (☎630 1540 or 025 227 4924; www.winetrailtours.co.nz) also does 4-vineyard trips ($65) as well as full-day tours that visit 6 ($95).

DAYTRIPS

NORTH SHORE

North of Auckland proper lies the North Shore, home to family beaches, suburban shopping centers, and vast numbers of commuters. The area was quickly populated after the completion of the Harbour Bridge in 1959. The bridge soon became so clogged with traffic that the city contracted a Japanese company to come and install extensions on either side of the bridge, expanding the meager four lanes to eight. Today, Devonport's Victorian charm and Takapuna's stunning natural beauty deserve a day's visit. North of Devonport, sprawling suburbs blend slowly into the natural beauty of the coast. To Takapuna and beyond, the coast is characterized by crescent sandy beaches separated into little bays by outcroppings of basaltic tuft. Some bays are protected environmental havens, and substantial fines (up to $5000) for pocketing shellfish are enforced; check the posted signs.

DEVONPORT. This small town with salty sea air and multi-colored Victorian rooftops feels miles away from urban Auckland, yet it's only a 12min. ferry ride away. Although Devonport is a wallet-friendly daytrip, accommodation prices are astronomical; backpackers should catch the last ferry back to Auckland. Most of Devonport's charming restaurants and cafes sit on Victoria Rd., the main street leading from the ferry wharf. Available to answer queries and direct the aimless, the chummy **Devonport Visitor Information Centre** is across from the harbor park. A jaunt to any of the three extinct volcanoes in town promises an unparalleled view; especially stunning 360° panoramas can be seen from **Mt. Victoria,** accessible by foot or car. *(Visitors Center: Victoria Rd., 1min. from the ferry, adjacent to the library.* ☎ *446 0677; fax 446 0581; actionline@nthshore.govt.nz. Open daily 9am-5pm. Devonport accessible by Fullers ferry* ☎ *367 9111. Departs daily 6:15am-11pm, F-Sa until 1am. $8, children $4.)*

BEACHES. The northern beaches all offer unspoiled views of Rangitoto and the Hauraki Gulf, without any hint of the city that lies just a few kilometers away. Just north of North Head, **Cheltenham Beach** (a protected area) and **Torpedo Bay** (closer to Devonport) are swimmer-friendly two hours before and after high tide. For a pleasant dip at any time, head to **Narrow Neck Beach,** around the Takapuna Head, or **Devonport Beach,** near the town. Narrow Neck Beach also harbors the recently restored **Fort Takapuna Historic Reserve,** home to a group of old military buildings and a beautiful park. Both Narrow Neck Beach and the summit of North Head provide million-dollar views of the **Hauraki Gulf** and the coastline. **St. Leonard's Beach,** which slides into **Takapuna Beach's** black sand, is an immense playground for all. A coastal walk from Takapuna north through **Thorne Bay** to **Milford Beach** features awesome **volcanic rock formations** and the manmade Algie's Castle with battlements from the 1920s. Nearby **Long Bay** is a regional park and marine reserve. Jutting off into the open seas from the top of Long Bay is the lofty **Whangaparaoa Peninsula,** where you can bask in the beautiful views of Gulf Harbour.

OTHER NORTH SHORE ACTIVITIES. Town tours in Devonport are popular, particularly the **Devonport Explorer Bus,** which provides a unique mode of transportation. You can also see Devonport for 45min. with **Tuk-Tuk Tours**—you'll know the Thai three-wheeler when you see it. Windsurfing is also popular on the North Shore, especially in the volcanic crater of **Lake Pupuke,** a clear blue lake with a reedy shoreline. *(Explorer:* ☎ *357 6366 or 0800 868 774. Departs from the wharf daily every hr. 10:25am-3:25pm. $22, including ferry return. Tuk-Tuk:* ☎ *0800 428 858. $15.)*

THE WAITAKERE RANGES

Beautiful yet undertouristed, the Waitakeres await those exhausted by Auckland's urban sprawl. Lying between **Manukau Harbour** and the **Tasman Sea,** the Waitakeres can be explored on over 250km of walking and tramping tracks. The **Arataki Visitor Centre,** on Scenic Dr. (Rte. 24) past Shaw Rd., can help you plan your route. Getting there without a car is difficult, although buses from the city go to Titirangi, 6km down the road. Hitchhiking in these parts is also a dim prospect. (☎ 817 8470; fax 817 5656. *Open daily 9am-5pm; Jul.-Aug. M-F 10am-4pm, Sa-Su 9am-5pm.)*

BEACHES. If you have a car, driving along the coastline offers access to some incredible beaches. **Karekare,** the setting for *The Piano* (see **Film,** p. 59), is the most scenic; a photogenic waterfall is accessible by a short walk from the carpark on the approach to the beach. Farther north, the black-sanded **Piha** has excellent surf but is usually more crowded. At the southern tip, right at the ocean entrance to Manukau Harbour, is **Whatipu,** which delights with rich fishing and exciting caves. Back along the harbor entrance with the sand bars lies **Cornwallis** and **Huia,** two beaches with calm waters for swimming and excellent picnic potential. **Muriwai Beach** and its famed gannet bird colony are another favorite (see below).

TOURS. Auckland Adventures guides treks and mountain bike tours to Muriwai Beach where 700 birds (including the rare **gannet** colony) reside. *(*☎ *379 4545 or 025 855 856. 5-8hr. treks $60-89. 8hr. mountain biking tours $89.)*

HAURAKI GULF

A sparkling antidote to urban exhaustion, the Hauraki Gulf has 57 islands of varying terrain and settlement. Volcanic Rangitoto makes for an educational daytrip and Waiheke harbors an artsy vacation community. Great Barrier Island lacks electricity, traffic, and crowds—even its stunning beaches lie empty. Another island worth a look is **Tiritiri Matangi,** an uninhabited bird and plant sanctuary that flaunts the many reasons the gulf has been protected as a marine park since February 2000. **Fullers** runs round-trip boats from Auckland that allow for a day on Tiritiri. (☎367 9102. 1¼hr.; departs from Auckland Th-Su 9am, leaves Tiritiri 3:30pm. $45, under 15 $23.) DOC administers a **bunkhouse** on the island, which is often booked months in advance. (☎476 0010. $20, under 15 $15.) **Fullers** tours the gulf with its "Coffee Cruise Harbour Explorer," which stops at Rangitoto Island and Devonport. (☎367 9102. 1¾hr. 3 per day. $30, under 15 $15.)

RANGITOTO ISLAND ☎09

Te Rangi i totongia a Tamatekapua ("The Day the Blood of Tamatekapua was Shed") proved too much of a tongue-twister for holiday-making colonials, so they shorted it to Rangitoto. Since 1854, when the Crown grudgingly shelled out £15 for what seemed a mere lump of rock, it's been a premier picnic spot for Auckland daytrippers. The island's most popular attraction is the **Summit Walk** (return 2hr.), which meanders through arboreal glens and lunar-like fields of volcanic rock. During the summer, walking the track is akin to hiking on charcoal briquettes, so be sure to wear solid shoes and a hat. At the top, you can take a peek into the perfectly inverted cone of the **crater.** The summit rewards with a stunning 360° view spanning Auckland, Great Barrier Island, and the Coromandel Peninsula. The **lava caves** are a side trail option (return 20min.); bring a flashlight and wear durable clothes if you plan to explore these jagged passageways. **Fullers** runs a **Volcanic Explorer Tour** for those who don't want to walk the whole track; the narrated 4WD tram ride drops passengers at the base of the 900m boardwalk that leads to the summit. (2hr.; 2-3 per day, departs when the ferries from Auckland come in; $49, under 15 $29, including return ferry.) Another worthwhile walk, the stroll down from the summit to **Islington Bay** leads to secluded swimming beaches. Be sure to check times for the last ferry (usually 4:20pm) so you're not stuck for the night. The Auckland **DOC office,** on Quay St. in the ferry building, has information on local tracks. (☎379 6476. Open M-F 10am-6pm, Sa 10am-3pm.)

Fit and ambitious folks can **kayak** to Rangitoto (see p. 96), but most take the ferry. **Fullers** runs to Rangitoto Wharf from Auckland's Pier 3. (☎367 9102. 45min.; 2-3 per day. Return $20, under 15 $10.) The area's only **campground** is located at Home Bay on adjacent Motutapu Island. Rudimentary facilities include toilets, running water, and barbecue sites ($5 per night, children $2.50; book with DOC).

WAIHEKE ISLAND ☎09

Waiheke's population of 6800 artists, retirees, and commuters more than quadruples during peak tourism seasons. With a stunning coastline, an internationally renowned Easter jazz festival, rolling hills (home to 26 top-notch vineyards), a jumping art scene, and a vital community spirit, Waiheke offers travelers an entertaining and relaxing corner of paradise.

TRANSPORTATION

Ferries: Fullers (☎367 9102) departs Auckland's Pier 2 or Waiheke's Matiatia Bay (35min.; 9-15 per day; return $23, under 15 $11); their **Link Ferry** travels between **Auckland's ferry building** and **Matiatia Bay** via **Devonport** (40min.; 2-4 per day; return $17). **Pacific Ferries** (☎303 1741) departs Pier 2 or Matiatia Bay (35min.; Nov.-Jan. daily every 2hr. 8am-9pm, Feb.-Oct. Sa-Su; return $17, under 15 $10).

Public Transportation: Fullers Waiheke Bus Co. (☎372 8823) meets all ferries and loops around the island. $1-3, all-day pass $7 or $5 with ferry ticket; under 15 half price. Fullers also offers an Island Explorer Tour, which includes return ferry, a 1½hr. island tour, and an all-day bus pass good on any island bus (daily 10am; $45, under 15 $21.50).

Taxis: Waiheke Taxi (☎372 8038) and **24hr. Dial-a-Cab** (☎372 9666).

Car and Scooter Rental: Waiheke Rental Cars (☎372 8635), at Matiatia Wharf carpark. Cars $45 per day plus 50¢ per km. Scooters $40 per day. Open daily 8am-5pm. **Waiheke Auto Rentals** (☎372 8998), also at the wharf carpark. Cars $45 per day plus 50¢ per km. Open daily 8am-5pm.

Bike Rental: Wharf Rats Bike Hire (☎372 7937), at Matiatia Wharf. Half-day $15, full-day $25. Open daily dawn-dusk. **Attitude Rentals** (☎372 8767 or 025 728 767) rents "motor-assisted" bikes. Half-day $35, full-day $40. Open daily dawn-dusk.

Hitchhiking: Although *Let's Go* does not recommend it, Waiheke islanders are a charitable bunch, though winding roads can make it hard to find a good spot to stop.

ORIENTATION AND PRACTICAL INFORMATION

The passenger ferry docks at **Matiatia Bay**. A 1km uphill walk (or a 5min. bus ride; see **Public Transportation**, above) takes you to **Oneroa**, the island's main town and the only one with an interesting strip of shops and cafes (along Ocean View Rd.). Other island centers include **Surfdale** and **Ostend** (both southeast of Oneroa, roughly 2km and 4km, respectively), **Onetangi** (7km directly east), and **Palm Beach** (4km northeast). All of these towns inhabit the western half of the 92 sq. km island; east of Onetangi, settlement drops off dramatically.

Visitors Center: Waiheke Island Visitor Information Centre, 2 Korora Rd. (☎372 9999; fax 372 9919; waiheke@iconz.co.nz), in the Artworks Centre in Oneroa. Island maps $1. Luggage storage $2 per bag. Open daily 9am-5pm.

Banks and Currency Exchange: BNZ, 110c Ocean View Rd. (☎372 1056), in Oneroa. **ATM.** Open M and Th-F 9am-4:30pm, Tu-W 9:30am-4:30pm.

Police: (☎372 8777), on Waikare Rd. in Oneroa. **Emergency** ☎ 111.

Medical Services: Centers in **Ostend** (☎372 5005) and **Oneroa** (☎372 8756).

Internet Access: Surfdale.com (☎372 5010), in the Surfdale Arcade on Miami Ave. in Surfdale. $7 per hr. Open M-Sa 9am-9pm. **The Lazy Lounge Cafe** (see **Food,** below) also has web access for $10 per hr.

ACCOMMODATIONS AND CAMPING

All accommodations are a long (40min.-2hr.), hilly walk from the ferry docks. Luckily, island bus service is cheap and comprehensive; ask bus drivers when to get off. **Campers** can head out to the little-visited **Whakanewha Regional Park** campground on the southeastern corner of the island. (Reservations required; call Parksline at ☎303 1530. $5 per person, under 18 $2.)

Hekerua Lodge (BBH), 11 Hekerua Rd. (☎/fax 372 8990; www.ki-wi.co.nz/hekerua.htm), in Little Oneroa. This cabin house is tucked into an acre of native bush, just

15min. from the beach. Its sleek decks and adjacent stone swimming pool define relaxation. Internet. Laundry. Linen $5. Spa $5 per 30min. Dorms $18; singles $30; doubles from $55; tent sites $15. Discounts on longer stays. ❷

Simkin Lodge, 54 Palm Rd. (☎372 8662), is so close to the water that guests can hear the surf break. Recently upgraded, it now has luxury suites and fewer dorms. Kayaks, boogie boards, and snorkeling gear for rent. Key deposit $10. Linen $5. Dorms $20; doubles $55; balcony units and apartments $135-180. ❷

Waiheke Island Hostel (VIP/YHA), on Seaview Rd. (☎/fax 372 8971; robb.meg@bigfoot.com), in Onetangi, a steep 4min. climb from the beach. Nothing can beat the view from the picnic tables. Mountain bikes. Dorms $20, weekly $115; doubles from $45. ❷

Kiwi Comfort, 4 Kuaka St. (☎372 2101; fax 372 2102; www.gotowaiheke.co.nz/kiwicomfort.htm), in Oneroa. In a semi-secluded spot, this comfortable B&B is a 10min. walk from the cafes and the beach. Oct.-Apr. $135 for 2; May-Sept. $110. ❺

FOOD

Ostend's **Woolworths** can take the sting out of Waiheke's pricey restaurant scene (☎372 2103; open daily 7am-9pm); there are also general stores in every town.

■ **The Lazy Lounge Cafe,** 139 Ocean View Rd. (☎372 5132), in Oneroa. Chill restaurant by day, Waiheke's only dance club by (weekend) night. Short but eclectic menu includes nachos ($12) and Thai chicken salad ($14). Internet. Open daily 8am-10pm or later. ❸

Oneroa Delicatessen, 153 Ocean View Rd. (☎372 7659), in Oneroa. This tiny street side spot serves a rotating menu of salads, sandwiches, soups, and pastas, all chock full of fresh vegetables ($6-12). Cakes $4.50. Open M-Sa 8am-5pm. ❷

Vino Vino, 3/153 Ocean View Rd. (☎372 9888), behind Oneroa Delicatessen in Oneroa. Sweeping views from the terrace and an open fire in winter lend an atmosphere worth the splurge. Mains $18-24. Open daily noon-9pm, until 11pm when busy. ❹

Waiheke Fish and Chips Shoppe, on Waikare Rd., just off Ocean View Rd. This no frills shop shells out battered fish, chips, and burgers ($2.40-7). Enjoy the vista from the outdoor picnic tables. Open M-Sa 11am-8:30pm, Su noon-7pm. ❶

SIGHTS AND ACTIVITIES

The **Waiheke Island Jazz Festival** (☎0800 529 933; www.waihekejazz.co.nz) shakes up the island every Easter weekend. Now in its 11th year, the festival features the best of Kiwi jazz as well as big names from Europe and New Orleans. With five days and 22 venues, it's usually possible to get tickets to something, though true aficionados may want to plan several months in advance to get tickets ($25-35) for the best shows, and more importantly, to book a bed. Less internationally renowned though no less popular on the island, the **Ostend Market** reappears every week at the corner of Ostend Rd. and Belgium St. in Ostend. Local vendors hawk pottery, organic foods, massages, books, and tarot card readings, with some of the proceeds going to the Waiheke Community Childcare Centre. (Open Sa 8am-1pm.)

BEACHES. Beaches surround Waiheke, but only the island's northern side has white sand. Just downhill from the town of the same name, **Oneroa Beach** is convenient; a bit farther east, Little Oneroa Beach is popular with families because of the adjoining playground. Between these two beaches lie two lovely **isolated coves,** beach-accessible at low tide (at high tide, follow the paths over the rocks). **Palm Beach** is another well-loved spot, although **Onetangi Beach,** the island's largest stretch of sand, draws the most sunbathers. Flout tan lines at the western (to the left if you're facing the water), "clothing optional" ends of both of these beaches.

THE ARTS. Waiheke's creative nerve lies at the **Artworks Centre,** 2 Korora Rd. in Oneroa, home to the Waiheke Community Art Gallery (☎ *372 9907; open daily 10am-4pm),* which displays varied works of New Zealand artists, and the Waiheke Community Theatre (☎ *372 2941),* which brings the best of the West End and Broadway to the Hauraki Gulf. *Art on Waiheke,* a free brochure available at the Visitors Center, includes a map of the island's two dozen other galleries. Aimed at true art buffs, **Ananda Tours** visits the sites of creation—the artist's studio. (☎ *372 7530 or 021 471 355. Tour 4hr. $50, includes a glass of Waiheke wine.)*

KAYAKING. Gulf Adventures has bred at least one champion (the owners' son is one of New Zealand's top two) and now offers guided trips and freedom rentals in single kayaks only. (☎ *372 7262 or 021 667 262. Rentals $45 per day, including all transport. 1-3hr. tours $35-55, depending on number of people. $5 backpacker discount.)* **Ross Adventures** runs guided tours at all hours. (☎ *372 5550. Half-day $60, full-day $110, 3hr. night trip $60.)*

HORSEBACK RIDING. Shepherd's Point Riding Centre conducts rides and lessons for all experience levels. (☎ *372 8104. 2hr. beach ride $60, full-day trip $100.)* **Club Waiheke** runs tours aimed at beginners—their $49 Scenic Circle Tour includes a lesson and a 1hr. ride. (☎ *372 6565 or 0800 800 6565.)*

WINE TASTINGS AND TOURS. There are 26 vineyards on Waiheke Island; several open regularly to the public for tours and tastings: **Camana Farm** (☎ *372 7257; tastings Dec.-Jan. W-Su 11am-4pm, Feb.-Nov. Sa-Su 11am-4pm; $5 for 2 wines);* **Stonyridge Vineyard** (☎ *372 8822; 45min. tours Sa-Su 11:30am; $10);* and **Te Whau Vineyard** (☎ *372 7191; tastings Nov.-Mar. M and W-Su 11am-5pm, Apr.-Sept. Sa-Su 11am-4:30pm; $3 per wine).* **Fullers' Vineyard Explorer tour** visits three vineyards. (☎ *367 9102. 3hr. Nov.-Mar. daily, Apr.-Oct. Sa-Su. $65, includes return ferry.)* **Waiheke Tours** visits two to four wineries in its half-day tours. (☎ *372 7262 or 021 667 262. $25-50, depending on number of people.)* **Jaguar Tours** swings by your choice of one, two, or three vineyards. (☎ *372 7312. 1 vineyard $18, 2 $24, 3 $34.)*

WALKS. Two free Visitors Center pamphlets outline walking routes on Waiheke; *Whakanewha Regional Park Visitors Guide* includes a map of 270 hectares in the southeastern part of the island, while *Waiheke Island Walkways* describes paths elsewhere on Waiheke. History buffs will appreciate the hike to **Stony Batter** (return 3hr.), a reserve at the remote northeast end of the island that served as a fortress during WWII.

GREAT BARRIER ISLAND ☎ 09

The largest and most remote of the Hauraki Gulf islands, Great Barrier (pop. 1200) maintains few connections with modernity. The island is an isolated world—it lacks electricity and banks and has unique weather patterns. It is also a a nature lover's dream, with deep forests and marshlands covering the terrain, silky white beaches breaking up the rocky coast, and blissful silence blanketing each night.

⌫ TRANSPORTATION

Flights: Great Barrier Airlines (☎ 275 9120 or 0800 900 600) from Claris Airport to: **Auckland** (30min.; 3-5 per day; return $189); **Whangarei** (30min.; F and Su 1 per day; return $189); **Whitianga** (30min.; F and Su 1 per day; return $189). **Great Barrier Xpress** (☎ 0800 222 123) flies to **Auckland** (35min.; at least 3 per day; return $169).

Ferries: Subritzky Line (☎ 373 4036) operates the *M.V. Sealink* between **Auckland's Wynyard Wharf** and **Tryphena** (3½hr.; M, W-F, and Su; return $75, students $45). **Fullers** (☎ 367 9102) runs between **Auckland's Pier 2** and **Tryphena, Whangaparapara,**

and/or **Port Fitzroy** (2½hr.; F, Su; return $99, under 15 $49.50). The Stray Possum Lodge (see **Accommodations and Camping,** p. 103) offers a number of fly-ferry-bus **combination passes** ($155-235), a good value for those also traveling to Northland or the Coromandel; all originate in Auckland and can be used in either direction.

Taxis and Shuttles: Bob's Island Tours (☎ 429 0988) offers a shuttle service that meets all ferries ($5 to Tryphena town, $15 to Claris) and a **24hr. taxi service** ($30 from Tryphena wharf to Claris, $100 from the wharf to Port Fitzroy). The Stray Possum Lodge's **Stray Bus Service** travels from Tryphena to Claris ($10) and back again 5-6 times per day; their Possum Pursuits Activities Passes allow for unlimited rides (1 day $25, 3 days $45).

Car Rental: Better Bargain Rentals (☎ 429 0092). $75 per day.

Bike Rental: Available as part of The Stray Possum Lodge's Activities Pass.

Hitchhiking: Although *Let's Go* does not recommend it, cars will often stop to pick up hitchers. However, there is little traffic on the island.

ORIENTATION AND PRACTICAL INFORMATION

Port Fitzroy in the north is the island's largest settlement, but most backpacker activity takes place on the southern half of the island, around **Claris** (home to the airfield) and, farther south, **Tryphena** (home to the ferry docks). Tryphena encompasses the sub-towns of Mulberry Grove and Pa Beach. Northwest of Claris, **Whangaparapara** is the island's other significant outpost. There is very little electricity (almost none after 10pm), so bring a **flashlight** or **candles.**

Visitors Centers: Great Barrier Island Visitor Centre (☎ 429 0033), near the Claris airfield. Open Sept.-Mar. M-F 9am-4pm, Sa-Su 9:30am-2pm; Apr.-Aug. M-F 10am-3pm, Sa 10am-noon. **Fullers Information Office** (☎ 429 0004), in Pa Beach. Open daily Christmas-Easter 8am-5pm. **DOC Field Centre** (☎ 429 0044), at Akapoua Bay in Port Fitzroy. Open M-F 9am-5pm.

Laundromat: Sunset Lodge (☎ 429 0051), in Mulberry Grove. Open Tu-Su 8am-2pm.

Police: (☎ 429 0343), on Kaitoki-Awana Rd. in Claris.

Pharmacy: Great Barrier Pharmacy (☎ 429 0006), just outside Claris. Open Nov.-Mar. M-Sa 9am-1pm; Apr.-Oct. M-F 9am-noon.

Medical Services: Community Health Centre (☎ 429 0356), in Claris by the airfield.

Internet Access: Email Internet Cafe, 59 Blackwell Dr. (☎ 429 0551), in Tryphena. $10 per hr. Open daily 9am-5pm.

Post Office: (☎ 429 0242), on Hector Sanderson Rd. in Claris. Open Nov.-Mar. daily 8:30am-4pm; Apr.-Oct. M-Sa 9am-1pm.

ACCOMMODATIONS AND CAMPING

Only December and January draw hostel-filling crowds. Accommodations can arrange transport from the ferry docks or airport. **DOC** maintains six **campsites** ($7, under 15 $3.50), a backcountry hut ($10, under 15 $5), and an eight-person **cottage** (Oct.-Apr. $50 for 2, May-Sept. $30; each extra person $10) near Port Fitzroy.

Pohutukawa Lodge (☎ 429 0211; PLodge@xtra.co.nz), in Pa Beach. Country-style rooms sit beside a sunny garden. For a free stay, (good) musicians can sing or play at the owner's Currach Irish Pub next door. Dorms $17; triples or quads with bath $95. ❷

The Stray Possum Lodge (VIP) (☎ 429 0109 or 0800 767 786; www.acb.co.nz/possum.html), in Tryphena. Free transfer from wharf. Its **Possum Pursuits Activities Pass,** also available to non-guests, includes bus transport around the island and use of bikes, boogie boards, and snorkeling gear. Reception 9am-2pm and 6-9pm. Bar open nightly 6-10:30pm. Dorms $19; doubles $55; private units $120; tent sites $12. ❷

The Crossroads Backpackers and Internet Cafe (☎ 429 0889; xroads@ihug.co.nz), in Claris. Food and hot springs are right near this dual-purpose hostel. The owners shuttle people to the beach. Free linen. Internet. Dorms $20; singles $30; twins $50. ❷

Medlands Beach Backpackers (☎ 429 0320; tim-mbb@ihug.co.nz), between Claris and Tryphena. Free boogie boards, bicycles, and Internet. Dorms $20; doubles $50; shared private rooms $60; cabins $150 for 6, tent sites $10. ❷

FOOD

There are small **grocery stores** in Mulberry Grove, Pa Beach, Claris, Whangaparapara, and Port Fitzroy; they cost significantly more than in Auckland.

Claris Texas Cafe (☎ 429 0811), in Claris. The island's most inventive fare. Dishes such as beef in black bean sauce with egg fried rice ($10) are hearty but not Texan. Open M-F 8am-5pm, Sa-Su 8am-9pm. ❷

The Currach Irish Pub (☎ 429 0221), in Pa Beach. A pub with an emphasis on food, Currach occupies one of the original homesteads in Tryphena. Th night jam sessions are a classic local event. Burgers $6.50-10.50. Mains $12-20. Open Tu-Su 4pm-late. ❷

The Cruisy Cafe (☎ 429 0997), in Pa Beach, serves standard bakery treats. Sausage roll $2. Vegetable sandwich $4. Small apple pie $3. Open Tu-Sa 9am-5pm. Closed July. ❶

SIGHTS AND ACTIVITIES

The Barrier's main draws are its gorgeous beaches and undisturbed nature—more than half the island's land belongs to DOC. The beaches on the east coast earn points with surfers. With its graceful dunes, sapphire sea, and blissful breezes, **Medlands Beach** is the island's most popular (which means 20 people at the height of summer). Other east coast beaches include: **Kaitoke, Awana, Haratonga,** and **Whangapoua Beaches,** all equally lovely and secluded. The west coast beaches are calmer and popular among yachts. Those in **Tryphena Harbour**—at Puriri Bay, Pa Beach, and Mulberry Grove—are good for snorkeling. **Aotea Kayak Adventures** runs a variety of guided kayak tours and freedom rentals. (☎ 429 0664. 2hr. trip $30; 4-5hr. trip with snorkeling $55; 6hr. trip with fishing $75; night trip $50; multi-day trip $85 per day. Rental $35 per day.) **GBI Adventure Horsetreks** leads riding trips. (☎ 429 0274. 1hr. farm ride $30; 2hr. beach ride $60.) Great Barrier's network of rugged roads also makes for superb **mountain biking;** the well-graded Forest Rd., which runs between Whangaparapara and Kaiarara and is closed to all non-DOC vehicles, is a favorite ride. For boot-bound travelers, the easy **Kaitoke Hot Springs Track** (return 1½hr.) leads to a set of bathing pools. The main one is formed by a dam at the junction of two rivers, while smaller pools of varying temperatures lie up the left-hand stream. The **Te Ahumata Track** (return 1½hr.), also known as the "White Cliffs Walk" for the quartz crystals in stream beds along the way, climbs gradually to a 398m summit that offers expansive views of the ocean, Mt. Hobson, and the Coromandel. Significantly more challenging, the **Kaiarara** and **Palmers Tracks** (return 5hr. in conjunction) ascend steeply through untouched subalpine forest to the island's highest point, the 621m **Mt. Hobson (Hirakimata).** The Visitors Center and DOC office can provide **directions,** as well as a listing of Barrier's tracks.

NORTHLAND

Northland is an enchanting, semi-subtropical world of verdant valleys, dramatic cliffs, and silky beaches. Home to the first landings of legendary explorers Kupe and Captain Cook, this area is rich with the history of New Zealand's Maori and European cultures. The sparkling Bay of Islands on the east coast is a collection of small towns and settlements admired by tourists and seasonal residents. The west coast shelters the quiet beauty of the Kaipara and Hokianga Harbours. At the very top, the hauntingly empty beaches of the Aupouri Peninsula and Cape Reinga provide a respite from the long-toothed trappings of predictability and convenience.

NORTHLAND HIGHLIGHTS

OVER the heads of tourists, ancient kauri tower in **Waipoua Forest Park** (see p. 124).

IN romantic **Russell**, pack a picnic and enjoy a quiet day on the bay (see p. 115).

AROUND the **Bay of Islands**, a marine paradise tempts visitors to swim with its dolphins, kayak among its mangroves, and sail between its isles (see p. 109).

TRANSPORTATION IN NORTHLAND

Rent a car if you have the means; it will give you the freedom to explore the **Twin Coast Discovery Highway** (SH1, SH10, and SH12) at your own pace, especially the Western and interior regions, which tend to be hard to access. Keep an eye on fuel levels, as **petrol pumps are rare** when away from tourist towns. If you travel by bus, strongly consider buying a pass that lets you travel at your discretion. Although *Let's Go* doesn't recommend thumbing, **hitchhikers** on the east coast north of the Bay of Islands encounter sparse traffic and, consequently, long waits. On the west coast, SH12 is the road less traveled, but the locals are more accommodating. Campers should note that annual hut passes do not apply in Northland; you must book in advance for all huts and lodges (though empty beds in winter make reservations less essential).

WHANGAREI ☎09

The journey to Whangarei, a three-hour drive north of Auckland, is a spectacular escape into lush hills. Loosely translated from Maori, Whangarei (FAHNG-a-ray) means "cherished harbor," a name honoring the local waters that have brought food, recreation, and profit to the region for years. Often neglected by backpackers eager to hit Paihia, Whangarei (pop. 47,000), the largest city in Northland, has a charm all its own. In addition to numerous parks, helpful local services, and world-class activities, the city has a nightlife that is lively without being debauched.

TRANSPORTATION

Buses: Coaches roll into the **bus stop** at **Northland Coach and Travel**, 11 Rose St. Open M-F 8am-5pm, Sa 8:30am-2:30pm, Su noon-6pm. **Northliner** (☎ 438 3206) and **InterCity** (☎ 439 2653) head to **Auckland** (2hr., 2-4 per day, $32) and **Kaitaia** (3½hr., $40) via **Paihia** (1hr., 4 per day, $19).

WHANGAREI ■ 107

Car Rental: Budget (☎ 438 7292) and **Hertz** (☎ 438 9790) have offices on Water St. **Rent-a-Cheepy**, 69 Otaika Rd. (☎ 438 7373), offers economy rentals from $35 per day.

Taxis: For a cab, call **Kiwi Carlton Cabs** (**24hr.** ☎ 438 2299).

Hitchhiking: Though *Let's Go* doesn't recommend it, hitching to Auckland is reputed to be easiest from the Visitors Center in Tarewa Park; those heading to the Bay of Islands often wait it on SH1 (Western Hills Rd.) before traffic picks up to 70kph.

ORIENTATION AND PRACTICAL INFORMATION

Whangarei wraps around **Whangarei Harbour**, 167km north of Auckland up **SH1** on the east coast. The main drag, **Bank Street**, intersects **Cameron Street** at a pedestrian mall that buzzes during business hours; the surrounding four blocks contain the majority of restaurants and bars. **Hatea Drive** stretches north from the Basin. Tourists and yachtees gravitate toward the **Town Basin** development by the harbor.

Visitors Center: Whangarei Visitors Bureau, 92 Otaika Rd. (☎ 438 1079; fax 438 2943; whangarei@clear.net.nz), in Tarewa Park, at the southern entrance to the city.

DOC: (☎/fax 430 2007), inside the Visitors Center. Open M-F 8:30am-5:30pm, Sa-Su 9:30am-5pm; Dec. 27 to Jan. 31 daily 8:30am-6:30pm.

Police: (☎ 430 4500), on Lower Cameron St.

Medical Services: White Cross Accident & Medical Clinic, 121 Bank St. (☎ 430 0046). Open daily 8am-10pm. **White Cross Pharmacy** (☎/fax 0800 438 7767) is in the same building. Open daily 9am-1:30pm and 2:30-9pm.

Internet Access: Cable Action (☎ 430 7477), Quayside, costs $5 per hr. Open M-F 7:30am-5pm, Sa 9am-5pm, Su 9am-4pm.

Post Office: (☎ 430 2761), on Robert St. Open M-F 8:30am-5pm, Sa 9am-1pm.

ACCOMMODATIONS AND CAMPING

Bunkdown Lodge (BBH), 23 Otaika Rd. (☎ 438 8886; fax 438 8826; bunkdown@ihug.co.nz). Friendly and hilarious owners cater to budget guests' every whim from diving to caving. Check out Pete's glowworm tour. Fancy mountain bikes. Free pick-up. Internet. Laundry. Two kitchens. Dorms $17; twins $40; doubles $45. ❷

Whangarei YHA Hostel, 52 Punga Grove Ave. (☎ 438 8954; fax 438 9525; yhawhang@yha.org.nz), off Riverside Dr. in a quiet residential area. Perched above the city, it's an arduous 20min. hike up the hill from the bus station. Large dorms and a spacious lounge. Internet. Off-street parking. Reception 8-11am and 5-7pm. Dorms $21; twins and doubles $48. MC/V. ❸

Central (Hatea) Backpackers (BBH), 67 Hatea Dr. (☎ 437 6174; fax 437 6141; www.backpackersnorthland.co.nz). A manageable 10min. walk up Hatea Dr. A tiny hostel with mini-kitchens in the cabins and a lovely garden view. Ask about the owner's caving tours. Duvet $1. Free pick-up. Kayak rental. Laundry. Dorms $18; singles $35-42; doubles $42; double cabins $47. Cash only. ❷

Whangarei Holiday Park, 24 Mair St. (☎ 437 6856; fax 437 5897; whangareiholiday@actrix.co.nz), a 25min. walk up Bank St. The sparkling clean cabins offer swell views of the surrounding scenic reserve. Dorms $15; cabins $30-36; tent sites $10. ❶

FOOD

The **Pak 'N Save**, at the Walton St. Plaza, is cheap and central, making self-catering easy. (☎ 438 1488. Open M-F 8:30am-8pm, Sa-Su 8:30am-7pm.)

Bogarts, 84 Cameron St. (☎ 438 3088). Small Uncle Scrooge gourmet pizza ($9) comes with tomato, cheese, and one topping. Open M-Tu 5-10pm, W-Su noon-3:30pm and 5pm-late. ❷

Killer Prawn, 28 Bank St. (☎ 430 3333 or 0800 661 555). This large restaurant and bar specializes in delicious seafood and impeccable presentation. Try their mussels or prawns ($25-32) along with a local beer. Open daily 11am-midnight. ❹

Rin Chin Chilla, 6 Vine St. (☎ 438 5882). Techno music and muralled walls set the tone. Super nachos for 2 ($9.50); lamb kebab ($6.50). Delivery $3.50. Open M-Th and Su noon-3:30pm and 5-9:30pm, F-Sa until 10:30pm. ❷

Taste Spud, 3 Water St. (☎ 438 1164). This simple joint hits the spot with cheap but filling stuffed potatoes and burritos ($5-6). Open M-Tu and F 10:30am-3:30pm, W-Th 10:30am-4:30pm. ❶

NIGHTLIFE

Although several restaurants and cafes have active bars and weekend dance floors (try **Bank Street**), **Powder Hound** and **Sound Factory** on Vine St. and **Spinners** at the corner of Bank and Cameron St. are full-time nightclubs.

Happy Daze, 21 Bank St. (☎ 430 0770). The *sub*-woofers at this red-walled club pump *sub*-par techno, making it more *sub*-urban than its city decor would suggest; youngbloods dance like there are no rules. Pints $4. Open M-Th noon-1am, F-Sa noon-3am.

Metro Bar, 31 Bank St. (☎ 430 0446). Munch a late-night snack (fries $3.50) to the tunes of your rock 'n' roll favorites. DJs enhance the scene F-Sa 9:30pm-1am. Open M 11:30am-7:30pm, Tu-Th 11:30am-late, F 11am-late, Sa 5:30pm-late.

Planet Earth B.C., 27 Bank St. (☎ 430 8000). Planet Earth is a good spot for couch lounging and some recreational boozing (pints $4). On weekend nights, this usually chill venue turns into a dancefest. Bar snacks $5-11. Happy Hour M-F 8-10pm. Occasional live acts. Pool $1. Open M-Th 11:30am-midnight, F-Sa 11:30am-3am.

SIGHTS AND ACTIVITIES

Whangarei's tourist zone is the waterfront area, lovingly known as the **Town Basin**, where eccentric museums and pricey cafes connect via paved walkways. The **Clapham Clock Museum**, begun in 1900, has become a 1600-piece tribute to timekeeping. (☎ 438 3993. Open daily 9am-5pm. $5.) A 10min. walk from Bank St. on Rust St. (which turns into Selwyn Ave.) leads to the **Craft Quarry**, a collection of open art studios. (☎ 438 4125. Quarry open daily 8:15am-5pm. Co-op store open daily 10am-5pm; in winter 10am-4pm.)

Leisure Craft Hire (☎ 437 2509), at the Town Basin, rents rollerblades ($10 per hr.), mountain bikes ($20 per half-day), and the "Orka Aqa Cykl," a self-propelled bike-boat ($15 per hr.) on summer weekends. The **Fernery**, at the end of First Ave., is an amazing collection of the world's most peculiar plants. (Open daily 10am-4pm. Free.) The pleasant landscaped grounds in **Cafler Park** and the **Rose Gardens**, next to the Fernery on Water St., make a good spot for picnicking or sunning. For more athletic exploration, numerous 1hr. **walking tracks** wind through the hills that embrace the town; it's best to leave from Mair Park, on Rurumoki St. off Hatea Dr. (pick up the great map from the Visitors Center). No visitor should miss the 26m **Whangarei Falls**, located only 5km from town off Kiripaka Rd. on the way to Tutukaka. Although *Let's Go* does not recommend initiation rituals, Maori youths have jumped off the dangerous cliff for hundreds of years as a rite of passage.

Those interested in spelunking should contact Central (Hatea) Backpackers (see p. 107). They can make affordable arrangements to explore the **Abbey Caves**. Or, for a thrilling (if more dear) combo, connect with the friendly folks at **The**

Bushwacka Experience for two tours of varying intensity. Both end at the **farm base,** where you can milk cows and shear sheep. (☎ 434 7839 or 025 578 240. 2hr. tour $55. Free pick-up with 1-day notice.) Those who want to venture farther (and have the wheels to take them) should explore the **Whangarei Heads** (a 30-40min. drive from Whangarei). **Ocean Beach** offers great surf and rocky coastline. Just south, the **Bream Head Scenic Reserve** challenges amblers with several walks. A manageable 90min. walk to **Peach Cove** departs from near Ocean Beach; **Mount Manaia,** a 1hr. summit hike, dishes out a 360° view, the five "figures" representing legendary Manaia and his family, including his unfaithful wife turning her head away in shame. Access from the **Early Settlers Memorial** just past McLeod's Bay.

POOR KNIGHTS ISLANDS ☎ 09

Eleven million years ago, eruptions off the coast of Northland gave birth to a string of islands, including the Poor Knight's Islands 24km off the east coast from Tutukaka. Although the Ngatiwai tribe had long inhabited these islands (calling them the Tawhiti Rahi and Aorangi Islands), a string of invasions and deaths in the early 1800s led the tribe to declare the islands *tapu* (forbidden). Today, landing on the islands without a permit is also *tapu*, but by decree of DOC, not the Maori. Thanks to a dearth of human interference, the islands are a haven for rare creatures, including prehistoric tuatara lizards and giant cat-sized weta grasshoppers.

Today, the biggest human draw is world-class **scuba diving;** Jacques Cousteau rated the island area one of the ten best sites in the world. Special mooring buoys off the coast serve as landing points for the scores of scuba, snorkel, and kayak trips run out of Whangarei and the coastal town of **Tutukaka** (30km and 30min. east of Whangarei). Sea caves both above and below water encourage the proliferation of marine life, making for awesome kayaking and snorkeling among moray eels, stingrays, and subtropical reef fish. There are also two newly sunk dive wrecks. **Dive! Tutukaka** runs three boats from the Marina Complex. Dive guides brief divers on the topography of each dive site and where the resident fish like to gather. Free shuttles to and from your accommodations in Whangarei leave at the crack of dawn; be sure to buy food for breakfast and lunch the day before. (☎ 0800 288 882; www.diving.co.nz. Guided dive $160; just tanks and weights $140. Free kayak use.)

BAY OF ISLANDS

Its temperate climate and beautiful coastline have long attracted summertime travelers to the Bay of Islands. The most celebrated visitor, Captain Cook, dropped anchor in 1769, befriended the local Maori, then sent word back to England to set the wheels in motion for permanent European settlement. Not particularly creative, he named the region after the 144 islands that now create little pockets of tranquility and keep local pocketbooks full from tourism. To best appreciate the Bay of Islands, follow Cook's lead—board a boat and discover the spectacular coast for yourself.

PAIHIA ☎ 09

Paihia, the center of commerce in the Bay of Islands, combines an inlet full of green isles with a strip full of packed motels. In summer, the low-season population of 3000 skyrockets to nearly 40,000, overwhelming the bay. Agents on every corner try to entice visitors to cruise, fish, sail, dive, and even zorb, while the friendly and relaxed locals patiently watch the annual feeding frenzy. Away from the crowd-covered wharf, miles of deserted coastline beckon the budget traveler.

110 ■ BAY OF ISLANDS

TRANSPORTATION

Buses: Buses arrive at the **Maritime Building**. Both **Northliner Coaches** (☎ 402 7857) and **InterCity** (☎ 357 8400) contract through **Westcoaster** and run daily to: **Auckland** (3¼hr., 2-3 per day, $44) via **Whangarei** (1¼hr., $19); **Auckland** via **Waipoua** (7hr., 3 per week, $69); and **Kaitaia** (2¼hr., 1 per day, $29) via **Kerikeri** (30min., $9).

Ferries: Fullers Passenger Ferry (☎ 402 7421) departs daily for **Russell** (15min., on the half hr., $5). Buy tickets on board or at the Fullers desk in the **Maritime Building**. The **vehicle ferry** departs from Opua (about 10km south of Paihia) for Okiato (about 8km south of Russell) every 20min. in summer and every 30min. in winter (5min.; 6:50am-10pm; cars $8, campervans $12, motorcycles $3.50).

Taxis: Haruru Cabs (☎ 402 6292) or **Paihia Taxis and Tours** (☎ 402 5064).

Hitchhiking: Although *Let's Go* doesn't recommend it, hitchhiking to Kerikeri or points north is reportedly best attempted near the rotary at the end of Marsden Rd. To head south, wait at Paihia Rd. at the edge of town.

ORIENTATION AND PRACTICAL INFORMATION

Marsden Road runs along the waterfront and is Paihia's main artery. **Paihia Wharf** is roughly in the middle of town beside the Maritime Building and opposite the commercial center of **Paihia Mall**. **Williams** and **Bayview Roads** border the mall, perpendicular to Marsden Rd.

Visitors Center: Information Bay of Islands (☎ 402 7345; fax 402 7314; visitorinfo@fndc.govt.nz), in the white octagonal pavilion to the left of Paihia Wharf. **Internet** $7 per hr. **24hr. ATM.** Open daily 8am-8pm; in winter 8am-5pm.

Banks: Banks with **ATMs** cluster around the Paihia Mall. Open M-F 9am-4:30pm.

Medical Services: Bay View Medical Centre, 7 Bay View Rd. (☎ 402 7132). Open by appointment M-F 9am-5pm. After-hours, call the on-duty doctor (☎ 404 0328). **Paihia Pharmacy**, 2 Williams Rd. (☎ 402 7034; fax 402 7342), is open M-F 8:30am-5pm, Sa 8:30am-1pm.

Post Office: 2 Williams Rd. (☎ 402 7800). Open M-F 9am-5pm.

ACCOMMODATIONS

The number of beds in Paihia has been steadily increasing as new backpackers spring up every summer. In peak season, however, reservations are essential. Most places lie mere yards apart on **Kings Road**, just minutes from the bus station.

Peppertree Lodge (BBH), 15 Kings Rd. (☎/fax 402 6122; www.peppertree.co.nz), has rooms so sanitary you would swear it was a hotel. Free use of owner's kayaks and tennis rackets (free courts across the street). Duvets $1. Internet. Laundry. Dorms $18-20; twins and doubles $57, in winter $55; studios $85/$75. ❷

Saltwater Lodge (BBH), 14 Kings Rd. (☎ 402 7075 or 0800 002 266; fax 402 7240; saltwater.lodge@xtra.co.nz). "The only 5-star hostel in New Zealand" is superbly clean with a large TV, gym, carpark, free kayaks, tennis racquets, and bikes. Internet. Laundry. Dorms $19-21; rooms with bunks and king size bed or 2 doubles $100 for 2, in winter $55; $110/$75 for 3; $130/$80 for 4. ❷

Mousetrap Backpackers (VIP), 11 Kings Rd. (☎/fax 402 8182; www.mousetrap.co.nz). An eclectic mix of maritime bric-a-brac and backpacker art decorates this funky abode. The ocean view transforms the porch into the soul of the hostel. Bike rental $10. Internet. Laundry. Reception 8am-9pm. Dorms $18; twins and doubles $44. Discounts in winter. ❷

Pipi Patch Lodge (VIP), 18 Kings Rd. (☎ 402 7111; fax 402 8300; www.acb.co.nz/pipi-patch). The giant green Kiwi Experience bus parks in front of this party hostel, complete with a well-equipped lounge, swimming pool, and free spa. Key deposit $20. Reception 7:30am-8pm, in winter 7:30am-7:30pm. Dorms $19; singles, twins, and doubles $45-55. Discounts in winter. ❷

Lodge Eleven YHA (☎/fax 402 7487; lodgeeleven@hotmail.com), at the corner of Kings and MacMurray Rd. Motel-style units are well-maintained by a friendly staff. Check-out 9:30am. Internet. Key deposit $10. Laundry. Reception 8am-7:30pm. Dorms $19-22; singles $52; twins and doubles $55, in winter from $40. ❷

Iona's, 29 Bayview Rd. (☎ 402 8072; ionas@xtra.co.nz), up the hill from the beach, has 2 beautiful suites each with their own kitchen. The front porch affords serene views of the bay. Reservations are essential. Studio $85, with porch $95. ❹

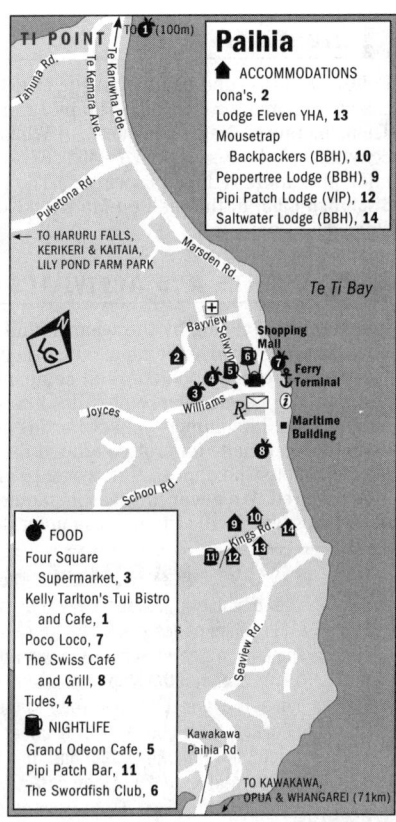

FOOD

Paihia's mall has dining choices around every corner. The **Four Square supermarket** is on Williams Rd. (☎ 402 8002. Open daily 7am-7pm.)

Kelly Tarlton's Tui Bistro and Cafe (☎ 402 7018), next to the Waitangi Rd. bridge. A converted 3-masted sailing ship houses Tarlton's collection of shipwreck artifacts. Dine on deck surrounded by beautiful bay views. Mains $16-35. Open daily 10am-10pm; dinner from 6pm. Museum $7 for non-diners, children $2.50. ❹

Poco Loco (☎ 402 8388), in the mall on Marsden Rd. across from the Wharf and only feet from the ocean. $8 blueberry pancakes and other breakfast treats all day. Splurge on the $18.50 Mexican chicken breast. Open daily 8am-midnight. ❷

The Swiss Café and Grille, 48 Marsden Rd. (☎ 402 6701), is known for excellent service and vegetarian options. Mains like Chicken Zürich have a Swiss flare ($16-24). Open daily 5:30-10pm; in winter closed Su. Closed mid-June to late July. ❸

Tides, (☎ 402 7557), on Williams Rd. Take care of all your nutritional needs with a menu ranging from french toast ($9) to Calamari salad and flounder ($18). Open daily 7:30am-2:30pm and 5:30-9pm. ❸

NIGHTLIFE

Follow the noise and plant yourself at the **Pipi Patch Bar** in the Kings Rd. hostel of the same name. (☎ 402 7111. Happy Hour 6:30-7:30pm. Open daily 3-11:30pm.) Then, migrate to **Grand Cafe Odeon,** 91 Williams Rd., for their Happy Hour or nightly cocktail and shooter special. (☎ 402 6677. DJs W-F. Open M-Sa 1pm-2am, Su 1pm-midnight; hours reduced in winter.) The cheapest beers ($2 specials) are at **The Swordfish Club,** in the mall on Marsden Rd. across from the wharf. (☎ 402 7773. Open daily 4pm-late.)

SIGHTS AND ACTIVITIES

The **Maritime Building** by the wharf is the meeting point for many trips and the booking agents who hock them. (Open daily 6:30am-9pm; in winter 7am-7pm.) The Visitors Center also books for all companies but sometimes at higher prices. In addition, the **Charter Pier** (☎ 402 7127) books most companies but specializes in fishing trips. In summer, expect hordes of fellow tourists—advance booking is essential, especially on cruises around the bay or to Cape Reinga. In winter, you may encounter the opposite—fewer trips and many activities with minimum numbers required. Whatever the season, inquire about backpackers' discounts. Many of the trips listed will also pick you up in Russell.

> **RAINBOW WARRIOR** The battered hull of Greenpeace's *Rainbow Warrior* rests offshore in Matauri Bay. After the French resumed nuclear testing in the South Pacific, Greenpeace dispatched the *Rainbow Warrior* to carry out a mission of protest. The French Secret Service got wind of the highly publicized endeavor and, on July 10, 1985, bombed the ship in Auckland Harbour. The event became instant international news. A bird reserve near Thames (see p. 129) was established in memory of Fernando Pereira, the on-board photographer who was killed, and the episode remains a sticking point in Kiwi-Franco relations. The sabotaged ship was moved to the Bay of Islands in 1987 and re-sunk in Matauri Bay, where it has become a playground for subtropical fish and world-class divers alike as part of an eco-friendly maritime park—an unexpected, but not altogether unfitting, end for the environmentalist vessel.

CRUISES. The **Hole in the Rock,** an island at the extreme end of the bay through which boats pass, is the one sight you are almost guaranteed to see. Aside from that, trips offered by different companies vary significantly; don't let price and duration be the sole criteria for your decision. **Fullers,** the ubiquitous ferry company, is the only operator to dock at **Urupukapuka Island,** which has hiking trails not overrun by mainland tourists. Hopping off the morning cruise (their Hole in the Rock tour) and back on the afternoon one provides enough time for a hike and a picnic. There is also a direct ferry service to Urupukapuka in the summer. (☎ 402 7421. Return 4hr. Sept.-May 2 per day, June-Aug. 1 per day. $60, children $30. Ferry service $35, children $18.) Fullers also offers a tame "undersea adventure" with the **Nautilus,** a semi-submersible boat that puts eye level below sea level. ($12, children $6.) The **Cream Trip Supercruise** meanders in and out of the smaller bays, delivering mail to the islands as part of the few official Royal Mail runs left in New Zealand. (6½hr. Sept.-May only. $75, children $38.) **Kings** offers a **Day in the Bay** cruise which includes the Hole in the Rock, an island stop, and a dolphin swim as well as a shorter trip that has a wharf-side *powhiri* (see p. 56) and a retelling of Maori myth. (☎ 402 8288 or 0800 222 979; www.kings-tours.co.nz. 6hr. $83, children $45. 3hr. $58/$28.) **Darryl's Mini Cruises** runs an entertaining evening cruise, with a scrumptious steak dinner included, although they don't make it to the Hole in the Rock. (☎ 402 7848 or 402 7730. 2½hr. $45.) The **Rock** Overnight Eco-Adventure Cruise is an all-in-one food, cruise, sleep, trek, swim, and play, with a 24hr. stay on the floating *Mothership*. (☎ 402 7796 or 0800 762 527. $90.)

ADVENTURE CRUISES. For those who seek the rush of shooting across the waves, several faster cruising options are available. The **Excitor** travels to the Hole in the Rock at up to 35 knots. (☎ 402 7020; www.excitor.co.nz. Return 1½hr. 4 per day 10:30am-6pm; in winter 2 per day. $60, children $30.) **Mack Attack** is an open air boat that hits up to 45 knots, making the individual seats with belts a necessity. (☎ 402 8180 or 0800 622 528. 1½hr. 4-5 per day, $60, children $30. ISIC, VIP, and YHA 10% discount.) **Dolphin Discoveries** runs the **Tornado**, which claims it is the fastest at over 50 knots and goes all the way out to Cape Brett. (☎ 402 8234. 1½hr. Up to 4 per day. $60.)

SWIMMING WITH DOLPHINS. Dolphin Discoveries, in the NZ Post Building at the corner of Marsden and Williams St., has been spotting dolphins since 1991 and has the highest success rate. (☎ 402 8234. $85, children $45.) **Awesome Adventures** also offers a possible swim with the friendly creatures. (☎ 402 6985. $95, children $48. VIP and YHA discounts.) Not wanting to miss out on any of the action, **Fullers** has a **Dolphin Adventures** trip. (☎ 402 7421. 4hr. $95, children $48.) **Kings** offers dolphin swimming as part of its **Day in the Bay** (see **Cruises**, above). For a more personal touch, **Carino** is a 40ft. catamaran and the only yacht licensed to swim with dolphins. Its trip is a steal, offering a full day of sailing, sunning, fishing, bushwalking, and swimming with dolphins. (☎ 402 8040 or 025 933 872; www.sailinganddolphin.co.nz. $69, children $35. $5 BBQ lunch and on-board bar.)

SAILING. She's A Lady Charters, which can take you on a day of sailing, snorkeling, and knee-boarding, is a bit of a misnomer, since it's run by the decidedly masculine Glen. (☎ 0800 724 584 or 025 964 010. 6½hr. $76, including lunch.) **Fullers** operates the **R. Tucker Thompson**, a majestic tall ship that replicates the Captain Cook experience, minus the hardtack and scurvy. (☎ 402 7421. 7hr. Nov.-Apr. $89, children $45; includes tea and BBQ lunch.) **Stray Cat Sailing** offers sailing trips with swimmingly and snorkeling stops on two islands. (☎ 402 6130. $72, children $45; includes lunch.)

FISHING. The good folks at **Charter Pier** are familiar with every fishing operator, handle all the bookings, and will match you with a boat and guide. Generally, trips are 4-6hr. long, and fish for snapper, marlin, shark, king fish, and hapuka. You can also hire self-drive boats. (*Halfway down the wharf on the left.* ☎ 402 7127. *Around $65 for small boats, $250 for game fishing.*)

KAYAKING. The oft-seen trademark logo of a woman drifting serenely through mangroves belongs to **Coastal Kayakers.** They offer independent kayak rentals, guided kayak tours, package tours, and hard-core wilderness expeditions. (☎ 402 8105; www.coastalkayakers.co.nz. Kayaks $10 per hr., half-day $28, full-day $40. Expeditions 2-3 days, Nov.-May, from $110.) **Bay Beach Hire** rents both individual and tandem kayaks. They also have catamarans, windsurfers, and fishing tackle. (*On Marsden Rd., opposite the Edgewater Motel.* ☎ 402 6078. Kayaks $10 per hr., half-day $25-35. Guided tours $45.) **Island Kayaks**, based out of Pipi Patch Lodge, features half-day tours topped off with an afternoon tea. (☎ 402 7111. 4hr., 1-2 per day, $55.) **New Zealand Sea Kayak Adventures** offers more remote kayaking along the northern shore. (☎ 402 8596; www.seakayakingadventuresnz.com. Half-day $40, full-day $60, multi-day $125 per day. Ask about backpacker specials.)

FLYING. Salt Air offers a 30min. flight around the Hole, a longer Bay Discovery tour, and a helicopter flight to the Hole. They also run a pricey tour to Cape Reinga, which catches the Cape before the lunchtime arrival of tour buses. (*Located in a kiosk just to the south of the Maritime Building.* ☎ 402 8338 or 0800 472 582; www.saltair.co.nz. Trips $95, $145, $150, and $285, respectively.) **Flying Kiwi Parasailing** floats the fearless high above the bay, attached to the back of a speedboat. The highlight of the trip is a simulated free-fall. (☎ 402 6078. Book with Bay Beach Rentals. 400m $50, 800m $60.)

SKYDIVING. SkyHi Tandem Skydive Ltd. gives you a rush for your money. Departing from Watea Airfield, they pick-up from accommodations and from wherever you land, too. (☎ 0800 927 593 or 021 756 758. 3000m $185, 4000m $235.)

DIVING. Paihia Dive, on Williams Rd., offers dives to the *Rainbow Warrior* as well as the Bay of Islands and Cape Brett reefs. (☎ 402 7551; www.divenz.com. 2 dives $150-160, includes full equipment; PADI certification $495.) **Dive North** also offers certification as well as fully guided tours with the aid of a high-speed boat. (☎ 402 7079. Guided dive $160; PADI certification $450.)

ON THE GROUND. Bay Beach Hire rents brand-spankin' new mountain bikes to explore the inland hills. (☎ 402 6078; www.baybeachhire.co.nz. Half-day $15, full-day $20.) For a unique Paihia experience, visit the **Lily Pond Farm Park.** Activities include horse and pony rides, feeding the animals, milking the cow at noon, a swimming hole, and a bush walk to a small waterfall. (On Puketona Rd. on the way to Kerikeri. ☎ 402 6099. Open daily 10am-4pm. Closed mid-July to mid-Sept. $6, children $4.) Less pastoral is **Zorb,** in which screaming loonies can roll down hills in a giant plastic ball. (On Puketona Rd. 1½km west of Paihia. ☎ 208 1319; www.zorb.com. $35.) For horse riding, try **Big Rock Springs Trail Rides,** which offers guided tours for all experience levels. (☎ 405 9999. Open Oct.-May. Full-day $70.)

TREKS. At the end of School Rd., 700m west of Pahia, the **Oromahoe Road Traverse** is a 2½hr. loop through regenerating forest to the **Opua Coastal Walk,** which returns to Paihia (another 2hr.). Alternatively, the **Opua Forest Lookout Track** starts at School Rd. and veers off to elevated forest and ocean views (one-way 30min.).

FESTIVALS. The **Bay of Islands Jazz & Blues Festival** (www.jazz-blues.co.nz) in August and the **Bay of Islands Country Rock Festival** (www.country-rock.co.nz) in May feature internationally acclaimed musicians as well as local talent.

WAITANGI ☎ 09

On February 6, 1840, more than 500 Maori, settlers, traders, dignitaries, and missionaries came ashore on the beach of Waitangi to witness the signing of the most important document in New Zealand's history—the **Treaty of Waitangi** (see p. 51). Today, the Treaty is the focal point of vigorously debated Maori land grievances.

The **Waitangi National Reserve** is a remarkably serene and verdant place. (☎ 402 7437. $9, children free. Open daily 8am-5pm.) To reach the reserve from Paihia, follow Marsden Rd. over the Waitangi Bridge, and then head up the rise. (30min.) Alternately, if you have a car, you can take the scenic route and check out **Haruru Falls** on Puketona Rd. on the way. The falls can also be reached via the **Waitangi National Trust Mangrove Walk,** a beautiful 2½hr. stroll from the Visitors Center. Take a lunch break at the **Waikokopu Cafe ❸,** on the Treaty Grounds; specials include the $13.50 Country Pumpkin Salad. (☎ 402 6275. Open daily 8am-5pm; in summer also evenings for dinner.) Waitangi's grounds include the **Treaty House,** one of the first architectural results of a British presence in New Zealand. From 1832 to 1844, it was home to watchdog "British Resident," **James Busby** (see p. 51); today, it is a museum. To the left of its lush lawn is the **Whare Runanga,** a Maori meeting house for all tribes, constructed in 1940 to celebrate the Treaty's centennial. The world's largest war canoe, *Ngatokimatawhaorua* (35m), is hauled out by 80 warriors and paddled around the bay every February 6th (Waitangi Day).

See the bits and pieces of less fortunate voyages at **Kelly Tarlton's Museum of Shipwrecks,** which floats at the mouth of the Waitangi River by the bridge. The assembly of over 1000 artifacts was salvaged from the watery graves of 20 wrecks (☎ 402 7018. Open 10am-10pm. $7, children $2.50.)

RUSSELL ☎ 09

On a sunny afternoon in Russell, it's hard to believe that the town was once known as the "Hell Hole of the Pacific" and was notorious for a thriving brothel industry, seedy sailor activity, and Maori-Pakeha clashes. Today, Russell's romantic, small-town charm is a welcome relief (and a short ferry ride) from the hubbub of Paihia.

TRANSPORTATION. Several companies provided identical **passenger ferry** service to Russell. **Fullers Passenger Ferry** is the largest and departs for **Paihia** daily on the hour. (☎ 402 7421. 15min.; 7am-7pm, in winter 9am-6pm; $5, children $2.50.) Buy tickets on board or at the Fullers' desk in the **Maritime Building** in Paihia. Rental cars are not allowed on the dirt road around the Bay to and from Paihia; the **vehicle ferry** departs from Okiato (about 8km south of Russell) for **Opua** (about 10km south of Paihia) every 20min. in summer and every 30min. in winter (5min.; 6:40am-9:50pm; cars $8, campervans $12, motorcycles $3.50, passengers $1).

ORIENTATION AND PRACTICAL INFORMATION. Matauwhi Rd. dumps cars into town on **York Street,** parallel to **the Strand,** which runs along the water from the **Russell Wharf.** All the shops are within two blocks of each other on these two streets, just east of a residential area, and south of **Long Beach Road,** which leads over a hill to (you guessed it) **Long Beach.** The privately run **Russell Information & Booking Centre** is in a kiosk on the wharf. (☎/fax 403 8020. Open daily 8am-6pm; in winter 8am-4pm.) The **Bay of Islands Maritime and Historic Park Visitor Centre,** on the Strand, one block south of the wharf, is also the main **DOC office** for the Bay of Islands. (☎ 403 7685; fax 403 764. Open daily 9am-5pm, in winter 10am-4:30pm.) Other services include: **BNZ,** on York St. (open M-F 10am-2pm), and **Westpac Bank,** on Cass St. near the Strand (open M-F 10am-1:45pm; extended hours in summer); **laundry** and **shower facilities** at **Little Fresh Fruit & Vegetables** (☎ 403 8021), on Matauwhi Rd.; **Russell Medical Services,** on Church St. north of the wharf (☎ 403 7690; open M-F 9am-4:30pm); **Russell Pharmacy,** 21 York St. (☎ 403 7835; open M-F 9am-5pm, Sa 9am-noon); **Internet access** at **Enterprise Russell,** in the Traders Mall on York St. (☎ 403 8843; $10 per hr.; open M-F 8am-5pm); and a **post shop,** in the Russell Bookshop (☎ 403 7674; open daily 8:30am-5:15pm), also in the Traders Mall.

ACCOMMODATIONS AND CAMPING. Run to the nearest phone and book one of only six beds at **The End of the Road (BBH) ❷,** 24 Brind Rd., at the top of Robertson Rd. and down the hill to the end of Brind. More of a homestay than a backpackers, Russell's best budget accommodation has amazing views of Matauwhi Bay and a lemon-tree-lined track to the water. (☎ 403 7632. Dorms $18, in winter $17; twins and doubles $40.) Just up the road, **Pukeko Cottage ❷,** 14 Brind Rd., can show you an amazing sunset from the dining room. (☎ 403 8498; barrymp@xtra.co.nz. Dorms $20, in winter $18; double in the cool converted caravan out back $35.) Flowering plants and trees abound at **Russell Holiday Park ❶,** at James St. and Long Beach Rd. A popular choice with families, this park has landscaped grounds with views of the bay. (☎ 403 7826; fax 403 7221; www.russelltop10.co.nz. Dorms usually only in winter $20; tent and powered sites $11-13; cabins, flats, and motel units $32-150.) Beachside luxury awaits at **The Duke of Marlborough Hotel ❺,** on the Strand. This 1920s-style hotel is complete with oak tables, plush furnishings, and friendly service. (☎ 403 7829; fax 403 7828; www.theduke.co.nz. Singles $95; doubles $125; waterfront suites $175-280.)

FOOD.

Waterfront Cafe ❷, on the Strand, one block south of the Wharf, has a beautiful beachfront view from the bar and an outdoor courtyard in back. Porridge ($6), huge vegetarian nachos ($8), and bottomless coffee ($2) are patrons' favorites. (☎ 403 7589. Open daily 7am-4:30pm; in winter Tu-Su 7:30am-4pm.) **The Gables ❷**, on the Strand near the Visitors Center, serves classics like eggs benedict ($9) with a touch of class. (☎ 403 7618. Open daily 7:30am-11pm.) **York St. Cafe ❶**, in the Traders Mall, doles out fresh, cheap food—an easy recipe for popularity. (☎ 403 7360. Open daily 10am-10pm.) The **General Store,** across from the Wharf, has groceries. (☎ 403 7819. Open daily 8am-7pm.)

SIGHTS AND ACTIVITIES.

The best collection of local historical treasures is housed at the **Russell Museum,** 2 York St. Displays range from the pertinent (a functional scaled replica of Cook's *Endeavour*) to the ridiculous (softball-sized cow hairballs and swordfish eye sockets). (☎ 403 7701. Open daily 10am-4pm; in Jan. until 5pm. $3, children 50¢.) The Anglican **Christ Church,** at the corner of Baker and Robertson Rd., is the oldest still standing in New Zealand. Illustrious worshippers have included Charles Darwin, who attended services here while the *HMS Beagle* was anchored in the bay. Not to be outdone by the Protestants, Bishop Pompallier arrived in 1838, and his Catholic missionaries soon followed suit. The 1841 **Pompallier,** on the esplanade at the end of the Strand, was the first Catholic mission in New Zealand and is the only mission building that remains. Now an award-winning *working* museum, it continues to tan leather and bind books in the Marist tradition. (☎ 403 9015. Open daily 10am-5pm; in winter for tours only 10:15, 11:15am, 1:15, 2:15, and 3:15pm. $5, students $2, children free.) To view New Zealand paintings and watercolors, head to **The Colonial Art Gallery,** 15 York St. (☎ 403 7268. Open daily 10am-6pm; in winter M-Sa 10am-5pm.)

On the opposite side of the Russell waterfront is **Flagstaff Hill.** A short walking track ascends to the site where **Hone Heke,** the man who felled the symbol of British rule (the flagpole) four times in 1844-45, displayed his axe-wielding skills (see p. 51). When the tide is out, the hill can be approached along the beach at the north end of the Strand; otherwise take the signposted route off Flagstaff Rd. Lovely **Long Beach** of Oneroa Bay lies just over the hill at the end of Wellington St. and offers plenty of opportunities to sun and swim. Rent kayaks and paddle boats in the summer outside the **DOC office** by the waterfront (from $25 per day).

Trekkers come from all over to walk the medium-grade **Cape Brett Lighthouse Track** (return 16hr.). The old lighthouse keeper's house has been turned into a hut with a gas cooker, running water, and toilets. ($8, children $4.) Book ahead at the DOC office in Russell, where you also pay the track fee ($8, children $4). The start of the track is a 1hr. drive from Russell and guides are usually available to introduce you to the history of the region (prices negotiable). One popular option is to be dropped off at the lighthouse by sea and then hike back, enjoying the coast and saving a day; contact DOC for more information. They can also tell you about the **campsite** ($6, children $3) on the island of **Urupukapuka,** right at the beach, which has running water and cold showers but no toilets; digging a hole is not allowed, meaning visitors must bring a chemical toilet, available for rent in Whangarei—ask the DOC in Whangarei for recommendations.

KERIKERI

☎ 09

Strategically placed at the head of an inlet, Kerikeri was home to the marauding Maori chief Hongi Hika and a group of English missionaries under his protection, making the town an economic center for Christians throughout the bay. Meaning "dig, dig," quiet Kerikeri is where the first English plow cut into New Zealand soil. Budget travelers now reap the fruit of colonial labors—literally. Temporary agri-

A SHEEPISH GLANCE AT NEW ZEALAND

With an estimated 14 sheep for every New Zealander, there's an endless supply of distasteful jokes implying intimate relations between Kiwis and their woolly neighbors. However, in the land of the long white cloud, the business of sheep is no laughing matter.

When British settlers introduced wide-scale sheep farming to New Zealand, they initiated the development of an efficient and self-reliant economy. Today, the economy continues to ride on ovine backs—industrious New Zealand sheep are responsible for 13% of the world's wool production, and lamb and mutton exports rank among the world's largest. After Australia, New Zealand is the world's largest sheep producer.

Why is it, then, that so many self-respecting sheep wouldn't dream of living anywhere else? A farm-friendly natural environment, including a mild climate and stable rainfall, has certainly helped to sustain huge sheep populations—at times the population has swelled to as many as 90 million. But New Zealand's sheep industry also shows a prime example of the benefits of scientific invention. When sheep were first introduced to New Zealand, huge sheep stations led to a dependence on volatile wool markets. The invention of refrigeration meant that it became possible to export lamb and mutton as food, and the first cargo shipping in 1882 ensured that New Zealand was no longer entirely at the mercy of fluctuating global wool prices. A flourishing trade in "Canterbury Lamb," named after the Canterbury plains of the South Island, cemented New Zealand's reputation as the world's premier lamb producer.

Sheep remain a predominant part of the landscape throughout New Zealand, with about half the nation's land used for farming purposes. With vast expanses of open land at their disposal, New Zealand sheep farms are very large by world standards, measuring an average of 536 acres or the area of 3000 tennis courts.

Despite cute and cuddly first impressions, when it comes to wool quality, not all New Zealand sheep are created equal. For example, the New Zealand Romney, the most common of the six main breeds, produces "cross-bred" wool, suitable for interior textile use. Meanwhile, the Merino, the first sheep breed introduced to New Zealand, produces fine wool used for clothing. To create woolly rugs and sweaters, teams of sheep shearers travel around the country, often shearing more than 200 sheep a day. Don't miss the opportunity to watch the shearers in action—their speed and dexterity are impressive.

Tourists should also be sure to take advantage of New Zealand's reasonably priced high quality wool products. Sheepskins are popular in all their manifestations—look for the "ugh boot," an aesthetically dubious but remarkably comfortable slipper crafted from the softest sheepskin. New Zealand farmers are also branching out into other sheep products. In recent years, lanolin from New Zealand merinos has been recognized for its extraordinary moisturizing properties.

The proverbial "cash cow" nature of New Zealand's sheep trade, however, does not come without a price of its own for the natural environment. Combined with the sizeable cattle population, New Zealand's sheep produce about 90% of the country's methane emissions and an estimated 43% of the country's greenhouse gases. In fact, it's estimated that the average New Zealand sheep produces the energy equivalent of an astonishing 100 liters of gasoline every year. The government plans to exempt its agricultural sector from any carbon taxes imposed by the Kyoto Treaty. In return, the agricultural sector must research ways to reduce emissions through biotechnology.

New Zealand has been increasingly recognized as an ideal petri dish for animal-related biotechnology experiments, since its animal population has never suffered from any major disease outbreaks. A Scottish company found the keys to cloning through New Zealand sheep. Such developments in biotechnology mean that New Zealand could once again be laughing all the way to the bank courtesy of the humble creatures.

Amelia Lester is a contributing writer for Australian Vogue *and the Australian* Sun Herald. *She is originally from Sydney, Australia.*

cultural employment attracts thin-walleted backpackers to Kerikeri year round, although the biggest wave hits in May at the start of the kiwifruit season.

TRANSPORTATION. InterCity (☎ 913 6100) buses run to **Kaitaia** (1½hr., 2 per day, $20) and **Paihia** (25min., 2 per day, $8). Never far from the tourists, **Fullers** tours Kerikeri from Paihia and hits history, horticulture, and shopping all in three hours. (☎ 407 7421. Daily 1:15pm; $45, children $25.)

ORIENTATION AND PRACTICAL INFORMATION. Kerikeri Road is the main street, leading 5km east from **SH10** through town to the water and Rewa's Village. Most of the services are clustered within the triangle it forms with **Hobson Avenue** and **Cobham Road** in the center of town. The **Visitors Center** in Paihia handles most Kerikeri queries, though information can be found in the office at Rewa's Village (☎ 407 6454) or at the **library** on Cobham Rd. in the center of town. (☎ 407 9297. Open M-F 9am-5pm, Sa 10am-noon.) The **DOC** office (☎ 407 8474) is on Landing Rd. north of Rewa's Village. **Work opportunities** abound in Kerikeri's fruit-picking industry. Farms or orchards in search of seasonal workers usually contact the hostels first, who then post the job listings. The best times to find work in the area are late March, early June, and late December.

Other services include: the **Kerikeri Medical Centre** (☎ 407 7777), on Homestead Rd.; **McFadziens Pharmacy,** at the corner of Homestead and Kerikeri Rd. (☎ 407 8003; fax 407 8016; open M-F 8:30am-5:30pm, Sa 9am-1pm); **ANZ**, on Kerikeri Rd.; **Internet access** at **Kerikeri Computers,** 88 Kerikeri Rd. (☎ 407 7941; $1 for 5min., 15¢ per additional min; open M, W, and F 9am-5pm, Tu and Th 9am-7:30pm, Sa 9am-1pm); and the **post office,** on Hobson Ave. (☎ 407 9721; open M-F 8:30am-5pm, Sa 9am-1pm).

ACCOMMODATIONS AND FOOD. Hostels in Kerikeri are geared toward working backpackers and offer good weekly rates. The closest hostel to town is the **Kerikeri YHA ❸**, 144 Kerikeri Rd., just past the edge of town toward the water. A rustic backpackers, it might remind you of summer camp. (☎ 407 9391; fax 407 9328; yhakeri@yha.org.nz. Internet. Dorms $21; twins and doubles $54; self-contained cottages $76 for 2, extra person $13.) To get to the **Hone Heke Lodge (BBH/VIP) ❷**, 65 Hone Heke Rd., turn off Kerikeri Rd. and then go left up the hill at the sign of the backpacking orange. This motel-style structure features a well-worn TV lounge and a recreation room with pool and ping-pong tables. (☎/fax 407 8170; www.kerikeri.net/honeheke. Free bike use. Free pick-up from bus stop. Laundry. Shuttle to orchards $1. Dorms $15, weekly $77; singles $27.50/$100, with bath $37.50/$150; doubles $36/$180, with bath $44/$200.) For a more spacious and private stay, stop at the **Kerikeri Homestead Motel ❹**, 17 Homestead Rd., and enjoy the views of the valley from your porch. (☎ 407 7063 or 0800 222 407. Doubles $85-115. Breakfast included.)

The **Fishbone Cafe ❷**, 88 Kerikeri Rd., smack in the center of town, has reasonably priced food and an impressive wine list in a trendy dark wood and chrome setting. (☎ 407 6065. Open M-Sa 8:30am-4pm; also Th-Sa 6-9pm; in winter closes Th at 4pm.) The award-winning **Rocket Cafe ❶**, on Kerikeri Rd. 500m from SH10, has a veggie-friendly menu with tasty $2.50 breakfast muffins. (☎ 407 3100. Open M-F 8:30am-5pm, Sa-Su 9am-4:30pm.) **Citrus Bar and Cafe ❸**, at the corner of Kerikeri and Cobham Rd., has an energy-packed brunch (salmon plate $10) as well as gourmet pizzas for $12-23. (☎ 407 1050. Happy Hour 5-6pm. Open daily 10am-late.) Seek staples at the **New World** supermarket, at Homestead Rd. and Fairway Dr. (☎ 407 7440. Open M-Tu and Sa-Su 8am-6pm, W-F 8am-8pm.)

SIGHTS AND ACTIVITIES. Kerikeri is rich in Maori and European history. Stroll to the **Kerikeri Basin,** a 20min. walk down Kerikeri Rd. toward the water, to view a trinity of Anglican missionary power: **St. James Church,** the graceful white **Kemp House** (which claims to be the oldest standing wooden European building in the country), and **Stone Store,** constructed in 1832-36 to house supplies for the Church Missionary Society. (☎ 407 9236. Open daily 10am-5pm; in winter 10am-4pm. Stone Store and Mission House $6, students and children $2.50.) Cross the footbridge over the **Kerikeri River,** and you will find yourself falling back in time at **Rewa's Village,** a replica pre-European Maori fishing village that provides a glimpse into the age of chiefs Hongi Hika and Rewa. (☎ 407 6454. Open daily 9am-5pm; in winter 9:30am-4:30pm. $3, children 50¢.)

The area near the SH10 rotary has kauri shops, ceramics, wineries, and a number of eccentric boutiques. Other (free) activities include swimming in the **Fairy Pools,** magical rock holes by the Kerikeri River. To reach the **Rainbow Falls,** start from the picnic area across the street from Rewa's Village and walk along the river 2km; alternatively, drive along Waipapa Rd. 2½km east of SH10. There are a number of walking tracks in the **Puketi and Omahuta Forests,** approximately 20km west of Kerikeri; access the park from Puketi (where there is DOC camping) off Puketotara Rd. or from Mangamuka off SH1; check with Kerikeri or Tarewa Park DOC for information.

THE FAR NORTH

KAITAIA
☎ 09

A mostly working-class population of 5000 inhabits this small, functional town in which gas stations and warehouse buildings hide the majestic hills and dairy farms of the surrounding landscape, the town is best used as a stop-off or transfer point to more beautiful destinations. The scenic walkways of Kaitaia and its ocean-facing neighbor **Ahipara** are windows into the kauri industry of yesteryear; the **Kaitaia Walkway** (45min.) is expandable into a 9km track suitable for experienced trampers. The Ahipara **Gumfields** spread over most of the peninsula out to **Tauroa Point,** southwest of Kaitaia, and are littered with remnants of 19th-century gum digging (trenches, dams, and an old gum diggers' shack).

Carless visitors to Kaitaia normally arrive on **InterCity** and leave the same way. Coaches head south daily to **Auckland** (7hr., 10:30am, $64) via **Paihia** (2hr., $28) and **Whangarei** (4hr., $38). For answers to all Cape queries, or $8 per hr. **Internet,** seek out the **Far North Information Centre,** in Jaycee Park on South Rd. (☎ 408 0879. Open daily 8:30am-5pm; in winter M-F 8:30am-5pm, Sa-Su 9am-1pm.) To overnight here, try **Main Street Backpackers (BBH/YHA) ❶,** 235 Commerce St., on the edge of town. This well-worn hostel is notable for its huge *Whare Wananga,* where visitors can learn to carve bone ($20) and other handicraft activities from local artisans. (☎ 408 1275 or 0508 624 678; www.tall-tale.co.nz/mainstreet. Key deposit $5. Laundry. Dorms $13-20; singles $39; twins and doubles $42; tent sites $13.) **The Bluehouse Cafe ❷,** 14 Commerce St., is a quiet, quality place, serving $6 paninis. (☎ 408 4935. Open M-F 8am-3:30pm, Sa-Su 8:30am-3:30pm.) For all day breakfasts, milkshakes, and delicious burgers, try **Cafe Blitz ❷,** on Commerce St. (☎ 408 0094. Open M-F 9am-3:30pm.) **Mussel Rock,** 75 Commerce St., is an intimate venue for drinking and dining. (☎ 408 0094. Beers $4-6. Open M-Th 10am-8pm, F-Sa 10am-midnight.) The **Pak 'N Save,** on Commerce St., stocks groceries. (☎ 408 6222. Open M-Tu and Su 8:30am-6pm, W-Sa 8:30am-7pm.)

AROUND KAITAIA

For more extensive trails, head to the **Karikari Peninsula,** 20km northeast of Kaitaia between **Rangaunu** and **Doubtless Bays.** The **Lake Ohia Gumholes** showcase the fossilized remains of a kauri forest amid rare ferns and orchids. The **Ancient Kauri**

Kingdom Ltd. (☎ 406 7172; www.ancientkauri.co.nz), on SH1 in Awanui, digs up kauri logs that were felled in the swamp 30,000-50,000 years ago, and carves the perfectly preserved wood into high-quality crafts and furniture. The massive spiral staircase in the center of the shop carved from a single log is masterful. Farther east along the base of the Karikari peninsula, **Coopers Beach** offers sunbathing and good surfcasting in Doubtless Bay. Farther north along the peninsula is a popular **DOC campground** at **Maitai Bay**. Facilities include cold showers, running water, and toilets. (Reserve through DOC in Kaitaia ☎ 408 6014. Tent sites $6, children $3.) Pushing farther east along SH10, halfway between Kaitaia and Kerikeri, is the fabulous ◨**Kahoe Farms Hostel (BBH)** ❷, a dazzling 114-year-old family farm that spreads from the roadside eastward for acres, eventually to the coast. The immaculate wood floors and antique furniture lend the restored kauri villa a simple beauty, while Stefan the Chef's gourmet pizzas (around $15) are simply *bella*. (☎ 405 1804; kahoefarms@xtra.co.nz. Internet. Free bike use. Kayak rental. Dorms $19; twins $47; tent sites $12. Reservations essential.)

Further southeast lies **Whangaroa Bay**, a narrow inlet with a snaking coastline. On the eastern shore is the town of **Whangaroa**, home to the **Sunseeker Lodge (BBH)** ❷, on Old Hospital Rd. A steep hill brings you to this small accommodation and its brilliant views of the bay. Call for free pick-up from the bus station in Kaeo. (☎ 405 0496; www.sunseekerlodge.co.nz. Internet. Kayak hire. Spa $5. Dorms $19; doubles $44; motel units $84-99 for 2.) **Northland Sea Kayaking** ❷, based 10km east of Whangaroa, does $60 per day kayak trips in Orua Bay, with accommodation available. (☎ 405 0381. Bring your own lunch. Private cabins $20 per person. Cash only.)

AUPOURI PENINSULA AND CAPE REINGA ☎ 09

The Aupouri Peninsula, a narrow finger of rolling land, extends up from the northern coast. The Maori believe spirits of the dead travel over the peninsula to Cape Reinga and dive into the ocean to return to the mythical homeland of Hawaiki.

> **DRIVING CAN BE HAZARDOUS TO YOUR HEALTH** Beware: the route along SH1 has some treacherous unsealed stretches frequented by top-speed tour buses. Resist the urge to keep pace with them—each season dozens of cars spin out on the curves and end up in the bush with a totaled car and a ruined holiday. Second, if you have a car, don't try to drive down the beach—although the beach is considered a road, you will get stuck. Guided trips pass the rusting automobiles of adventurous yet substantially less-skilled drivers who stopped on sandy Ninety Mile Beach. The buses parked along the sand are built for the terrain and helmed by drivers who have been navigating the changing sands for years. If you ignore this precaution, at least stay well away from the surf. Imagine you and a few chums (chumps?) watching helplessly as your car sinks out of sight. The Houhora Tavern (☎ 409 8501) runs a towing company that will remove cars for a steep price.

ORIENTATION AND PRACTICAL INFORMATION

The path to the afterlife is gilded on the west by the golden sands of **Ninety Mile Beach,** a name more poetic than "ninety-kilometer beach" or "fifty-six mile beach," both of which would be more accurate. Near the top of the beach, the sands are interrupted by the **Te Paki Stream,** which empties into the ocean. This is part of the **Te Paki Reserves,** administered by the **Te Paki DOC Field Centre** (☎ 409 7521), off SH1. With many walking tracks, the reserves offer a serenity punctured in the summer by the screams of thrill-seekers coasting on their boards down the 100m high sand dunes. Don't venture out to the very tip of the beach, which is sacred and protected Maori land. On the opposite side of the peninsula, boarders boogie in the ocean waters of **Tapotupotu** and **Spirits Bay,** while landlubbers lie on graceful curves of sand. Slightly south along the side of the peninsula is **Great Exhibition Bay,** which, despite the name, entertains more anglers than nude bathers. The Cape Reinga bluff is capped with a lighthouse that perches over the churning waters where the Pacific and the Tasman meet. **Cape Maria van Diemen** to the west and the **North Cape** to the east have equally breathtaking, if less celebrated, scenery.

ACCOMMODATIONS AND CAMPING

Travelers with the blessing of an automobile should steer toward **Pukenui** (pop. 1000), a tiny and charming coastal town with New Zealand's northernmost backpacker accommodations. One of Northland's best hostels, **North Wind Lodge Backpackers (BBH) ❷**, on Otaipango Rd., is 9km north of Pukenui in Henderson Bay. The beautiful and remote site offers a convivial cooking space, a comfy sleeping area, and breathtaking views of the ocean down a 400m path. Basic groceries and free boogie boards are available. (☎/fax 409 8515; northwindlodge@xtra.co.nz. Internet. Dorms $18; twins $36.) The **Pukenui Lodge (YHA) ❷**, at the corner of SH1 and Wharf Rd., has a welcoming backpacker cabin adjacent to its motel accommodations; both come with pool access and a mind-blowing view of the bay. (☎ 409 8837; pukenui@igrin.co.nz. Dorms $18; twins and doubles $45; motel singles $69-109.) A short walk down Lamb Rd., backpackers can camp next to trailers at the **Pukenui Holiday Park ❶**. Perks include a bountiful fruit garden in back and Internet access. (☎ 409 8803; fax 409 8802; pukenuiholidays@xtra.co.nz. Communal kitchen and bathrooms. Tent sites $10; basic cabins $35-60 for 2; tourist cabins with kitchen $50 for 2; flats with bathroom and kitchen $60 for 2.)

For more rustic accommodations, DOC maintains two **campsites** in the area of the Te Paki Reserve—they are only available in summer. One is **Tapotupotu Bay,** south of the Cape region, which has sheltered golden sands accessible by a posted turn-off 3km before the end of the road to the Cape. (Tent sites $6, children $3.) The other is at **Kapowairu,** along the east coast of Spirits Bay. (200 sites. $5, children $2.50.) Both are first-come, first-camped. DOC maintains a third campsite approximately in the middle of the Aupouri Peninsula at **Rarawa**. Sites can be found amid pine trees, a stone's throw from the white-sand beaches of Great Exhibition Bay. Follow the signs 1km north of Ngataki on SH1. (Open Labour Day-Easter. Sites $6, children $3.) All three feature DOC hallmarks of minimalism: cold showers, running water, and toilets. Call DOC at the Te Paki field center (☎ 409 7521) or in Kaitaia (☎ 408 6014).

SIGHTS AND ACTIVITIES

Most people elect to take a **guided day tour** in a specially designed sand-and-surf-worthy craft out of Paihia or Kaitaia. It makes for a long day, but it's a safer option for navigating the changing sands of an extremely remote region. Choose your tour carefully—many trips are designed with extreme thrill-seekers in mind.

Departing from Paihia, one good bet is **Northern Exposure Tours** (☎ 402 8644 or 0800 573 875), a "small bus with attitude" that makes a tree-hugging stop at the kauri in Puketi. Dig for *toheroa* on Ninety Mile Beach, get sandblasted tobogganing on the dunes at Te Paki, and get spiritual at Cape Reinga, all in an 11hr., $69 day. The **4x4 Dune Rider,** also of Paihia, runs a similar tour in a rugged, air-conditioned Mercedes Benz bus. (☎ 402 8681; www.dunerider.co.nz. Free pick-up daily from Paihia 7:30am and Kerikeri 8:15am. $86, children $50. Backpackers 15% and AA 10% discount.) For an even livelier experience, join the party-hard crowd onboard **Awesome Adventures**. Unlike most tours, lunch is not included. (☎ 402 6985; www.awesomeadventures.co.nz. Departs Paihia 7:30am. $80.) With larger buses and an older crowd, **Kings** (☎ 402 8288) and **Fullers** (☎ 402 7421) cater to a tamer crowd. (Tours $60-80.)

Some tours may stop at the **Wagener Museum** (☎ 409 8850), 40km north of Kaitaia on SH1 in Houhora, to check out the historic homestead ($3) or, better yet, the museum of natural and technological curiosities ($6).

HOKIANGA REGION ☎ 09

Every summer refugees from the commercialism of the Bay of Islands escape to the obscurity of the Hokianga region. In the constellation of tiny towns that sit on the Hokianga Harbour, adventure activities give way to bushwalking, fishing, swimming, and sand dune surfing. Hokianga is hailed as the last spot the great Maori navigator Kupe landed before departing home to Hawaiki. Long-standing Maori tradition holds that Kupe (as well as everyone else who pays a visit) will one day return to this area, known for its treacherous access to the Tasman Sea.

TRANSPORTATION IN HOKIANGA

Limited **bus service** among the Hokianga towns means that either a car or patience is necessary to explore the area. The **Northland Wanderer pass** ($80-85, children $54-57; available through InterCity) may be the best antidote for sporadic and expensive bus schedules. **Northliner** (☎ 438 3206, Auckland ☎ 307 5873) and **InterCity** (☎ 0800 401 500) contract out to **Westcoaster** in the region. Service is inconsistent at times, particularly in the winter, and runs on "Hokianga time"—reservations are necessary even if you have a pass. From Paihia, buses run to **Kaikohe** (30min.; in summer daily 9am; in winter M, W, F, and Su; $9) and through the **Hokianga region** (2hr., about $25), to the **Waipoua Forest** (3¼hr., $35) and eventually on to **Auckland** (8¼hr., $50). Buses from Auckland arrive in **Omapere** by 2pm. Although *Let's Go* does not recommend it, many **hitchhikers** bum a ride by standing on the straightaways or approaching drivers at markets and post offices; those heading north or south take the Rawene-Kohukohu ferry and find a ride from drivers on board.

PRACTICAL INFORMATION

The **Hokianga Visitor Information Centre**, by Omapere on SH12, 450m north of "town," has 1950s newsreels about town icon Opo the Dolphin in the "museum" upstairs. (☎ 405 8869; fax 405 8317; hokiangainfo@xtra.co.nz. Open daily 8:30am-5pm. Museum open daily 9:30am-4:30pm.) There are **no banks, ATMs, or cash advances** in the Hokianga, so bring EFTPOS or an adequate supply of cash. For medical assistance, **Hokianga Health** (☎ 405 7709) is located on SH12 just outside of Rawene; call before coming.

OMAPERE ☎ 09

Keeping watch over the dangerous waters at the mouth of the Hokianga Harbour, Omapere (pop. 1300) is a breathtaking spot to stop before heading south to Waipoua or eastward to Kaikohe and the Bay of Islands. A short drive from Omapere along Waiotemarama Gorge Rd. leads to the maze and quirky shop at **Labyrinth Woodworks**. (☎ 405 4581. Open daily 9am-6pm; maze open only in summer. $3.)

If you choose to stay in Omapere, **Globetrekkers (BBH) ❷**, off SH12, makes a good home. The backpackers cottage has a water view, comfortable beds, and a deck with picnic tables and rose bushes. (☎/fax 405 8183. Free pick-up from the Visitors Center. Laundry. Dorms $16; singles $25; doubles $40.) For a beautiful sleep right on the bay, try **Harbourside Bed and Breakfast ❹**, off SH12 just beyond Four Square. (☎ 405 8246. Singles $50; doubles $80.) **Panorama ❷**, just south of town on SH12, is bright with light pouring in its huge windows. The chicken burger ($4.50) and chargrilled catch ($17.50) are equally refreshing. (☎ 405 8708. Open daily 9am-around 10pm; in winter M and W-Su 9:30am-4pm.) The **Omapere Restaurant and Takeaway ❶**, on SH12, has simple fare (toasted sandwiches $4.50) and a super view. (☎ 405 8607. Open M-F 8am-4:30pm, Sa-Su 9am-4pm.) Next door, the **Four Square** has a **post shop** inside. (☎ 405 8892. Open daily 7:30am-6pm.)

OPONONI ☎ 09

In the 1950s, a friendly dolphin in the nearby waters, nicknamed Opo the Dolphin, captured the affection of the town and the attention of the region. In the four decades since Opo put it on the map, **Opononi** has progressed about four years. It is still a small fun-in-the-sun resort town with sand, sea, and simple food. **Kupe's monument,** an anchor stone and commemorative plaque, sits at the top of a hill on the harbor side of SH12 between Opononi and Rawene. The grave of **Opo the Dolphin** is located in front of the South Hokianga War Memorial. **Hokianga Express** offers water taxi service across the harbor to the dunes, which lure sand surfers keen on sliding down the dunes and into the water. They will even loan you boards and pick them up at the end of the day (☎ 405 8872; $18).

Opononi is a scant 3km up from Omapere on **SH12** and 23km from Rawene. Its wharf ties it to the harbor. If you're planning on spending the night, head up the hill from town to the epitome of Hokianga serenity, the **House of Harmony (BBH) ❷**. (☎/fax 405 8778; harmony@igrin.co.nz. Haircuts on site. Laundry. Dorms $18; twins and doubles $38; tent sites $12.) For accommodations right on the waterfront, bask in the faded luxury of the **Opononi Resort Hotel ❷**. In addition to the institutional, motel-style backpackers, the hotel features two bars. (☎ 405 8858. Laundry. Dorms $15; twins $40; doubles $35. Bars open 8am-midnight, or later. AmEx/MC/V.) For a quick bite, stop in at the **Opo Takeaway ❶** and try a dolphin-safe Opo Burger—fish, cheese, and tartar sauce for only $3.80. (☎ 405 8065. Open daily 10am-10pm; in winter 10am-8pm.) The **Four Square** has a **post shop** inside and **Internet** for $5 per 50min. (☎ 405 8838. Open daily 10am-9pm.)

RAWENE ☎ 09

Rawene's centrality made it vital to the kauri shipping industry of yore. Today ferries, rather than cargo ships, dominate the area, carrying passengers and vehicles to **Kohukohu** on the opposite shore. **Ferries** depart on the half-hour. (15min.; 7:30am-7:30pm; $2, cars $14 one-way or $19 return.) If all your travel has worn you out, Rawene has the perfect place for a sit (or a squat). Just past the service station on the waterfront are the much-celebrated **musical loos** of Hokianga. The fully automated, self-cleaning toilets play lovely piano music and feature mechanical toilet paper dispensers. Don't get too comfortable, though; the doors fly open after 10min. (Luckily there is a 1min. countdown).

The **Far North District Council,** on upper Parnell Rd. just up from the wharf, can answer travel queries. (☎ 405 7829. Open M-F 8am-4:30pm.) ◼**The Boat Shed Cafe,** on the water, up a bit from the ferry landing, makes a gorgeous espresso (flat white $2.50) to match its views and wood interior. The connected craft shop sells quality souvenirs without the kitsch. (☎ 405 7728. Open daily 8:30am-4:30pm.) Next door to the Boat Shed, **Hokianga Wholefoods** dispenses crunchy veggies and advice on the evils of genetically engineered foods. (☎ 405 7759. Open M-Sa 10:15am-5:15pm.) The **Four Square,** at the Waterfront, has a **post shop.** (☎ 405 7848. Open M-F 7:30am-5:30pm, Sa-Su 8:30am-4:30pm.)

KOHUKOHU ☎ 09

Most commonly known as the other end of the Hokianga ferry (which departs for Rawene daily at 7:45, 8:30, and 9am and then every hour on the hour until 8pm; $1.50), Kohukohu is renowned among budget travelers for its unique accommodations. ⬛**The Tree House (BBH) ❷,** 3km from town, is a sprawling wooden-planked network of decks and rooms in a 17-acre forest. Easily one of the best backpackers in the country, you'll find it hard to leave. A small shop at the front desk sells basic food and phone cards. Reservations are essential for everything (even tent sites). Call from Rawene for free pick-up from the ferry landing or from town if you arrive from points north. (☎ 405 5855; fax 405 5857; www.treehouse.co.nz. Duvets $2.50. Linen $2. Internet. Dorms $19; singles $30; twins $41; doubles $44; tent sites $12.) The **Bag End ❷,** on Yarborough St. up the hill from town, is a new hostel in a 12-year-old mud-brick house. (☎ 405 5806; bjcrooks@hotmail.com. Kayak rental. Dorms $18; twins $40; doubles $44.)

To explore farther upstream, you'll need the aid of **The Alma,** a 1902 kauri ship that swapped its twin masts for twin diesel motors and now tours up the harbor in the summer from Rawene. Meals, including fresh crayfish, are available ($5-15) if you book the day before. (☎ 405 7704 or 025 997 450. $25, children $12.50.)

WAIPOUA FOREST PARK

Waipoua (north of Dargaville on Northland's western coast) is New Zealand's least-logged and best example of primary kauri forest. Remoteness and inaccessibility protected the virgin woods of the Waipoua region from 19th-century axe blades. The 1940s demand for shipbuilding timber stirred up controversy that resulted in Waipoua's being declared a sanctuary by 1952.

Everyone who visits the forest wants to see "the big tree" in northern Waipoua, and most buses (including InterCity) stop for at least a snapshot. A brief trek from the carpark off SH12 leads through dense, dripping bush to the 2000 year-old, 52m high, 14m wide **Tane Mahuta.** Meaning "God of the Forest," it is the **world's largest living kauri** and **New Zealand's largest tree** of any kind. The boardwalk keeps admirers at a respectful distance to protect the Lord's shallow root system.

Waipoua's other "big trees" are accessible via walking tracks from the labeled carpark a few kilometers south of Tane Mahuta on SH12 ($2 security fee for carpark). A 20min. walk leads to the "diminutive" 30m **Te Matua Ngahere,** "Father of the Forest," the second largest living kauri; a 10min. walk takes you to the close-knit **Four Sisters,** four kauris side-by-side; a 30min. walk goes to the **Yakas Kauri,** the seventh largest kauri. Although the Maori began the tradition of naming individual trees, not all bear Maori monikers: witness **Darby and Joan,** flanking either side of the bridge on SH12 north of the Visitors Center. For those with time to explore, the 3hr. **Yakas Track** connects the campground and Visitors Center to Yakas Kauri Carpark, winding through all sorts of trees and fording the Waipoua River. The 6hr. **Waiotemarama Walk** begins off Waiotemarama Gorge Rd. near Omapere, reaching a spectacular waterfall within 15min. and ending at the base of Mountain Rd. At its steepest point, halfway through, the walk connects with the **Waima Main Range Route.** This is a serious 3-4 day tramp passing over the highest point in Northland (often through low-lying clouds) on a trail that is not regularly maintained; trampers should possess good wilderness skills and be well equipped for foul weather. A less taxing walk along mostly flat beach is the 2-3 day **Waipoua Coastal Walkway,** linking Hokianga Harbour to the **Kai Iwi Lakes** (see **Sights and Activities,** p. 126).

Along with the kauri giants, Waipoua is home to the **Waipoua Forest Visitor Centre,** several walking tracks, a swimming hole, and a **campground.** You can self-register at the communal kitchen/shower/toilet building. Obtain cabin keys from the Visitors Center or, after hours, check in with the caretaker. The closest grocery store is 23km away, so be sure to bring plenty of food. (Visitor Centre ☎ 439 3011; fax 439 3016. Open M-F 8:30am-5:30pm, Sa-Su 9am-5pm; in winter daily until 4:30pm. Tent sites $7, children $3.50; cabins $28 for 2, $40 for 4.)

DARGAVILLE ☎ 09

Dargaville (pop. 4600) is a good place to stock up on provisions—gas, food, and batteries. While a handful of amusements and proximity to the kauri forests beg travelers to linger, the absence of a seaside location make this riverside town more of a stopping point than a final destination.

TRANSPORTATION. As in the rest of Northland, **InterCity** contracts out to Westcoaster to reach **Auckland** (3½hr.; M and Th-F 8:30am; $42) and **Paihia** (4¼hr.; in summer daily, in winter 3 per week; $35) via the **Waipoua Forest Park** (1¼hr., $15). They also service the Hokianga towns of **Omapere, Opononi,** and **Rawene** (2½-3hr., $17-25). Although *Let's Go* does not recommend thumbing, **hitchhikers** find that traffic along the Waipoua Forest Rd. in either direction is fairly regular and tend to wait at the edge of town past the Mangawhare Bridge.

ORIENTATION AND PRACTICAL INFORMATION. Dargaville borders the **Northern Wairoa River,** 187km north of Auckland on the west coast. **Normanby Street** is the main road by which **SH12** traffic passes through town. One street over toward the river is **Victoria Street,** home to most of the shops. For information, try the **Kauri Coast Information Centre,** corner of Poto and Normanby St., where there is also **Internet access** for $7 per hr. (☎ 439 8360; fax 439 8365; www.kauricoast.co.nz. Open daily 8:30am-6pm; in winter M-F 8:30am-5pm, Sa-Su 9:30am-4:30pm.) If you do nothing else in town, get plenty of money here, as there are no banks farther north in the Hokianga; **banks** with **ATMs** line Victoria St. Other services include: the **police,** on Portland St. (☎ 439 3400); the **Kaipara Unichem Pharmacy,** at the corner of Hokianga Rd. and Parenga St. (☎ 439 8349; open M-F 8am-6pm, Sa 9am-1pm, Su 9:30am-12:30pm); the **Dargaville Medical Centre,** in the hospital complex on Awakino St. (☎ 439 6015, after hours ☎ 439 8079; open M-F 8am-5pm, Sa 9am-noon); and the **post office,** 80 Victoria St., in the Terartz Stationary Shop (☎ 430 6051; open M-Tu and Th 8am-5pm, W and F 8am-6pm, Sa 8am-7pm).

ACCOMMODATIONS AND CAMPING. Just 33km north of town beyond Kaihu on SH12 is the **Kaihu Farm Backpackers (BBH)** ❷, a motel-clean hostel with at-home style. The owner drops off visitors at nearby lakes and forest walks for a small fee, and prepares home-made meals for dinner. (☎ 439 4004. Bike rental. Dorms $18; twins and doubles $40; tent sites $12.) The **Northern Wairoa Hotel** ❷, at the corner of Hokianga Rd. and Victoria St., offers shocking value in the form of clean, well-kept single rooms. The rollicking pub downstairs features bands and karaoke on Thursday and Friday, with occasional "win-a-keg" competitions. (☎ 439 8923; fax 439 8925; northern-wairoahotel@win.co.nz. Singles with plush linen and wash basin $20, with bath $40; doubles with bath $60; triples with bath $90.) **The Greenhouse (BBH)** ❷, 13 Portland St., has a dorm room—a large, spotless, mural-decorated sleeping hangar—with beds separated by privacy-enhancing, shoulder-high dividers. (☎ 439 6342; fax 439 0222. Laundry. Dorms $16; singles $25; twins and doubles $38; negotiable weekly rates.) The **Baylys Beach Motor Camp** ❶, 22 Seaview Rd., provides adorable cabins on a *pohutukawa*-edged green, which positively teem with families when the weather warms. (☎/fax 439 6349. Tent and powered sites $10; basic double cabins $20, extra person

$10; double cabins with bath $33/$12.) Another camping option, the **Kai Iwi Lakes Camp ❷**, is on Kai Iwi Lakes Rd. Divided into two parts, the larger **Pine Beach Camping Ground**, on Lake Taharoa, accommodates up to 500 campers with rudimentary blocks of showers, toilets, and basins, no electricity, and coin operated gas BBQs. The second site, **Promenade Point** (100 sites), has only drop-toilets and basins. (☎ 439 8360. Water taps. No power for caravans. Both sites $8, children $4.)

FOOD. Blah Blah Blah Cafe & Bar ❷, 101 Victoria St., has an eclectic cafe menu that changes every six weeks, though the prices are fairly stable (lunch $8.50, dinner from $12). (☎ 439 6300. Open M-Th 9am-midnight, F-Sa 9am-late, Su 9am-4pm. VIP and YHA 10% discount.) The **Country Flair Cafe ❶** 75 Victoria St., is a local's lunchtime favorite, with fresh muffins ($1.20) and sandwich bagels ($3.30). (☎ 439 0393. Open M-F 7:15am-5pm, Sa 8am-3pm.) **Cuppa 'N A Cake ❷**, 37 Victoria St., is the place to go for all-day-brekkies as well as the usual lunch and dinner fare. (☎ 439 1081. Open M-F 8am-4pm, Sa 10am-1pm, Su 11am-2pm.) **Woolworth's** grocery is on Victoria St. at Gladstone St. (☎ 439 3035. Open daily 7am-10pm.)

SIGHTS AND ACTIVITIES. The **Kai Iwi Lakes** are rimmed with pure white silica sand and are a summertime mecca for water enthusiasts of all sorts. **Lake Taharoa** is the largest of the three and the best bet for swimming. Waterskiing is the sport of choice on **Lake Waikere**. The smallest and most serene is **Lake Kai Iwi** itself, trafficked solely by sails and dinghies and offering excellent fishing. **Buses** make it to the turn-off on Omamari Rd., 24km north of Dargaville on SH12, but you'll have to be resourceful to cover the remaining 11km to the first of the lakes. Though *Let's Go* doesn't recommend it, most travelers hitchhike. Closer waters lap the expanse of **Baylys Beach** (also known as Dargaville Ocean Beach or Ripiro Beach), which, at 100km, is New Zealand's longest. Astonishing in breadth as well as length, its vanishing point is often obscured by mist, as are the tops of nearby cliffs. Perhaps more remarkably, the beach is officially a public highway. Road rules apply; it's best to have a 4WD vehicle and a knowledge of conditions (see **Driving can be Hazardous to your Health,** p. 120).

A more sedate pursuit, the **Kauri Museum**, on SH12 45km south of Dargaville in Matakohe, has exhibits about the mighty tree, but the gum display downstairs is the real star. An InterCity shuttle runs past the museum from Dargaville to Auckland Monday through Saturday, leaving town at 9am and 2pm; prebook to return at 11am and 4:05pm (return $16), otherwise the bus won't stop. (☎ 431 7417. Open Nov.-Apr. daily 8:30am-5:30pm; May-Oct. 9am-5pm. $9, children $2.50.)

Quad Safari can transfer passengers by boat or bus to the Pouto sand dunes for an individual 4WD adventure. (☎ 439 6554. From $50.) For an excellent trek, the volcano **TokaToka** offers panoramic views of the region from its summit, 17km south of Dargaville. The track's steep 30min. ascent begins behind the TokaToka Tavern, a 15min. drive south along SH12. In town, and intended to "keep the kids off the streets" more than to entertain tourists, is the **The Multiplex** on Logan St., an all-in-one indoor recreation center, with $2 rollerblade and skateboard rentals, skateboard ramps, table tennis, pool tables, indoor cricket, netball, and other juvenile diversions. (☎ 439 6093. Open W-F 3-6pm, Sa-Su noon-6pm, though hours change frequently. $2.) For a throwback, go see the Monday **animal auctions** at the corner of Kings Court and River Rd., just south of Victoria St., at 1pm.

COROMANDEL PENINSULA

Isolated, if not entirely removed from the tourist loop, this charming peninsula harbors untouched natural beauty. Coromandel towns first arose out of the dust of 19th-century gold mining and kauri logging, and since the 1960s, when potters and hippies moved here in search of communal bliss and artistic inspiration, things seem to have changed little. From the transport gateway of Thames, the Firth gently curves up to the artisan town of Coromandel. The coastal road continues to the wild, breathtaking Coromandel Walkway, but the main road (marked as the Pacific Coast Highway) cuts inland. Occasionally turning to gravel, the rough road passes several tramping trailheads before reaching the beach town of Whitianga. At Hot Water Beach, Hahei, and Opoutere, life is even simpler; it is here that Coromandel time seems to stand still. While the peninsula is packed with Aucklanders and other Kiwis during holidays (avoid it altogether right after Christmas), there are no tour buses, crowds, or worries for most of the year.

COROMANDEL PENINSULA HIGHLIGHTS

UNDER-APPRECIATED AND OVERHEATED The beaches around Hahei are well-known, but it's easy to find your own plot of sand. And where else but **Hot Water Beach** can you gleefully dig a grave and lie in it (see p. 139)?

UNDER-TOURISTED Often passed over by the typical tourist loop, **Coromandel town** offers tranquility and unique local crafts (see p. 132).

REMOTE Way off the beaten path, the **Northern Tip** and its Coromandel Walkway present unadulterated natural beauty (see p. 135).

TRANSPORTATION IN THE COROMANDEL

Flights: Air Coromandel (☎0800 900 600) flies from **Whitianga** to **Auckland** (daily, $99) and **Great Barrier Island** (3 per week; $99, return $189).

Buses: Bus transport on the Coromandel's narrow roads can be infrequent, especially in winter. Consider buying a **Coromandel Busplan** from **InterCity,** which allows travel from **Auckland** to **Thames** and a circuit of the peninsula in a clockwise direction (Thames to Coromandel town to Whitianga to Thames) and a final leg to either **Auckland** or **Rotorua** ($89). **The Loop Pass** ($49), an abbreviated version, begins and ends in Thames. The **Pacific Coast Highway Traveler Pass** covers **Auckland,** the **Coromandel loop, Tauranga, Rotorua, Whakatane, Gisborne,** and **Napier,** and continues to **Palmerston North** and **Wellington.** Contrary to the name, the pass conveniently skips 8hr. of East Cape coastline and sets you back $149. (Loop runs Oct.-Apr. daily; May-Sept. Su-F. Book each leg the day before.) For direct service from **Coromandel town** to **Thames,** InterCity contracts out to **Turley Murphy Buses** (1hr., M-F 7:30am, $12).

Shuttles: Go Kiwi Shuttles (☎07 866 0336, 0800 446 549, or 025 220 1598; fax 866 0337) services the eastern peninsula to and from **Auckland city** and **airport.** The Auckland service ($45-70 depending on pick-up and drop-off locations) leaves **Whitianga** at 7:45am and **Thames** at 9:30am, arriving in downtown **Auckland** at 11:45am. The return begins in **Auckland** at 1-1:30pm (depending on your pick-up point). The

128 ■ COROMANDEL PENINSULA

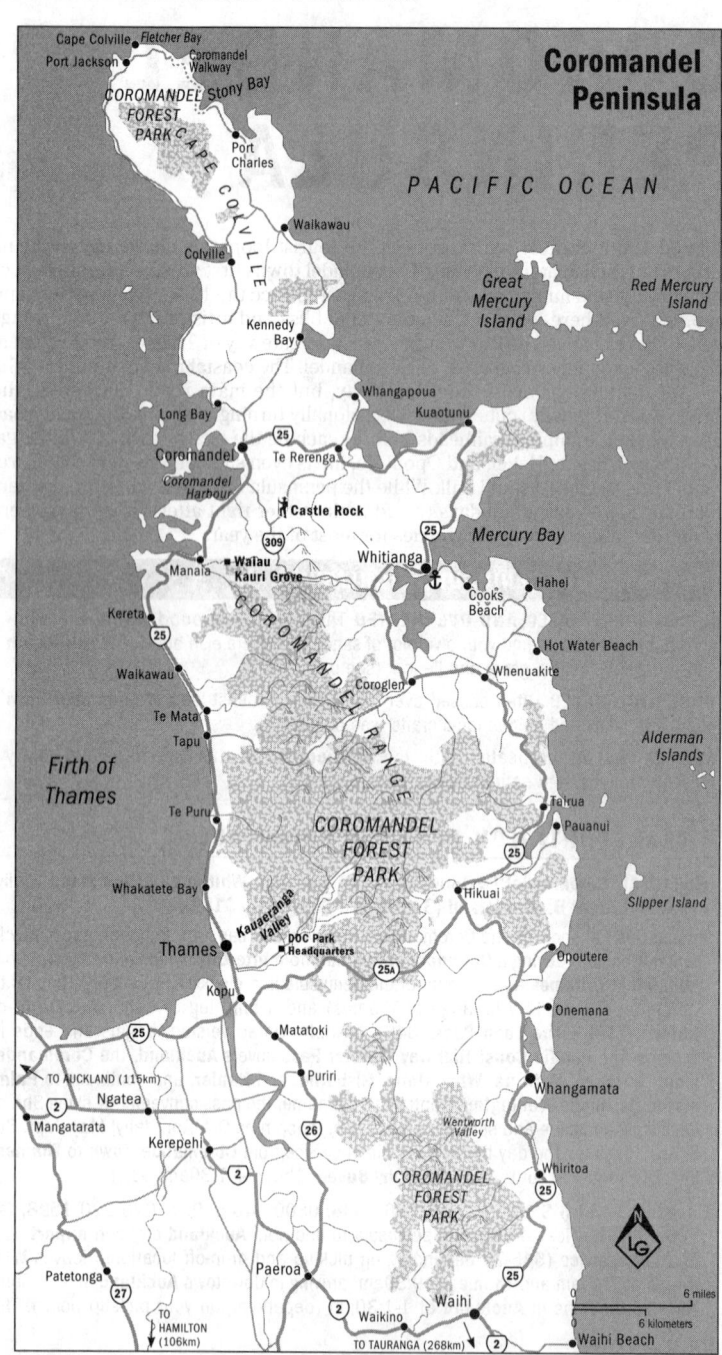

Pacific Coast Pass ($79), also with Go Kiwi, covers 30 days of one-way transportation through **Auckland, Whitianga, Thames,** and **Tauranga. Coromandel Bus Service** (☎ 866 8598), based in Coromandel town, crosses to **Whitianga** ($15-20). **Turley Murphy Buses** run between **Hot Water Beach** and **Hahei** among other destinations. **Driver Rob** (☎ 0800 454 678) gives tours to some of the best spots in the peninsula, including Waiau Falls and Hot Water Beach (departs Thames M-Sa 10:15am, in winter M, T, and Th-Sa; return $69).

Cars and Car Rental: The Coromandel begs to be explored by car. Most roads are sealed and in good repair but have harrowingly narrow shoulders, steep drop-offs, and hairpin turns. **Unsealed roads** up the Kauaeranga Valley, north to Fletcher Bay, and across the peninsula require caution and patience. Be sure to check your **rental agreement** carefully for restrictions on driving in the Coromandel. The only **petrol** north of Coromandel town flows in **Colville.** In Thames, **Rent-a-Dent,** 733 Pollen St. (☎ 868 8556 or 0800 736 822), at Wiseman's Auto Workshop, starts at $40 per day plus 20¢ per km. Three years of driving experience required.

Biking: Bike touring is popular, if you've got the legs—many roads are hilly, unsealed, and winding, with especially narrow shoulders. The ride to Coromandel town from Thames is a solid 4-5hr. with additional 2-3hr. segments up to Colville and Fletcher Bay. The pedalling past Colville is tough and remote. Instead of doubling back, cyclists with appropriate tires should consider riding single-track to Stony Bay and continuing down the east coast. The entire peninsula loop requires 3-5 days. **Price and Richards,** 430 Pollen St. (☎ 868 6157), in Thames, rents 21-speed bikes with all necessary gear and advice. $20 per day. Other bike rental outfitters are listed by town.

Hitchhiking: Although *Let's Go* does not recommend it, hitching between the major towns is reportedly fairly easy. Posting notices and making acquaintances in hostels boosts chances of a ride to Fletcher Bay or into Coromandel Forest Park. Thumbers report long waits from some of the smaller towns (Hahei, Opoutere); arranging a ride back is advisable.

THAMES ☎ 07

Arriving in this small, sunny town (pop. 6500), you'd never guess that it was briefly the country's largest city. In the 1870s, more than 100 hotels and bars poured whiskey for over 18,000 inhabitants, among them streams of hopeful gold miners. No longer shaken by pounding stamper batteries and the miners' drunken revelry, today the town is known as the gateway to (and last shopping outpost of) the peninsula. While in Thames, visitors should dig up some cash of their own; ATMs are scarce on the peninsula.

TRANSPORTATION

InterCity departs the Visitors Center for: **Auckland** (2hr., 2 per day, $22); **Coromandel town** (1¼hr., M-F 3:50pm, $16); **Tauranga** (2hr., 2 per day, $26); and **Whitianga** on a non-loop run (1¾hr., 3:35pm, $35). **Thames Gold Cabs** (☎ 868 6037) runs M-Th 8am-late, F-Sa 8am-even later. Although *Let's Go* does not recommend it, thumbers report that it's possible to get to Coromandel town on Pollen or Queen St. For bike and car rental, see **Transportation in the Coromandel,** above.

ORIENTATION AND PRACTICAL INFORMATION

From Auckland, **SH25 (the Pacific Coast Highway)** wraps around the east coast of the **Firth of Thames** before heading around the tip. Thames itself lies flat between the Firth and the upsweep of the Coromandel Range. Most of Thames' shops stretch along **Pollen Street.** Parallel is **Queen Street,** the local stretch of SH25.

Visitors Center: Thames Information Centre, 206 Pollen St. (☎868 7284; fax 868 7584; thames@ihug.co.nz). Open M-F 8:30am-5pm, Sa-Su 9am-4pm. **Kauaeranga Valley Visitors Centre (DOC),** 13km from town (☎867 9080; see **Coromandel Forest Park,** p. 132). Open daily 8am-4pm.

Banks: BNZ (☎868 5811), at the corner of Sealey and Pollen St. Open M and Th-F 9am-4:30pm, Tu-W 9:30am-4:30pm.

Police: 402 Queen St. (☎868 6040), across from Goldfields Mall.

Medical Services: A **pharmacy** (☎868 9095) is in the Mall. Open M-Th 8:30am-5:30pm, F 8:30am-8pm, Sa-Su 9am-4:30pm. **Thames Medical Centre** (☎868 9444) is on Rolleston St., just down from the hospital's side entrance. Open M-F 8:30am-5pm. The **Thames Hospital** (☎868 6550) is on MacKay St., parallel to Pollen St.

Internet: United Video (☎868 8999), on Pollen St., charges $3 per 15min., $9 per hr. Open Su-Th 9am-9pm, F-Sa 9am-late. The **Visitors Center** also has web access.

Post Office: 517 Pollen St. (☎868 7850). Open M-F 8:30am-5pm, Sa 9am-12:30pm.

ACCOMMODATIONS AND CAMPING

Several motor camps lie along the coastal road between Thames and Coromandel, and DOC runs eight **campgrounds** in the Kauaeranga Valley (see **Coromandel Forest Park,** p. 132). On summer weekends, dorms fill fast; make sure to book ahead. Contact the Visitors Center to investigate numerous B&B options.

Huia Lodge B&B, 589 Kauaeranga Valley Rd. (☎/fax 868 6557; huia.lodge@xtra.co.nz), 8km up the road toward Coromandel Forest Park from Thames. The forbidding driveway may repel the faint of heart, but the brave will be rewarded with killer views of the rugged valley and distant peaks. Occasional pick-up from town, but this out-of-the-way joint is best-suited to car- or bike-born travelers. Dinner $20. Singles $40; doubles $75. ❹

Sunkist Lodge (BBH/VIP), 506 Brown St. (☎868 8808; sunkist@xtra.co.nz). About 4 blocks north of the Mall, 1 block west of Queen St. This former gold-rush hotel comes with fabulously airy communal spaces, a sun-kissed 2nd-floor deck, and its own muddy-footprint-tracking ghost. Internet. Dorms $17-19; twins and doubles $40. ❷

Adventure Backpackers Coromandel, 476 Pollen St. (☎/fax 868 6200). Formerly the Imperial Hotel, this hostel offers institutional-feeling rooms in the middle of town. Free laundry. Dorms $14; singles $24; doubles with bath and TV $44. ❶

Dickson Holiday Park YHA (☎868 7308; fax 868 7319; www.dicksonpark.co.nz), on Victoria St. 3km south of town off SH25. The peaceful, wooded setting makes up for a minor case of camper park sprawl. Game room, solar-heated pool, and kitchen. Metered showers (20¢ per 5min.). Dorms $16; tourist cabins and on-site caravans with kitchenette $38-41 for 2; bush hut $34; tent sites $11. ❶

FOOD

Pinch pennies at the **Pak 'N Save,** in the Goldfields Mall. (☎868 9565. Open daily 8am-8pm.) Takeaways and cafes line **Pollen Street.**

Sealey Cafe, 109 Sealey St. (☎868 8641), has filling and inventive portions (mains from $15). Jazz photos on the brick and plaster walls add class; chill tunes fix the rhythm. Espresso drinks $3-4. Open daily 11am-late. ❸

Food for Thought/Second Thought, 574-576 Pollen St. (☎868 6065), stocks healthy vegetarian fare. Fresh breakfast and lunch options forgive a spare, cafeteria-tray ambience. Small veggie pizza $3, sandwiches $3-5. Open M-F 6:30am-4pm; Second Thought also open Sa 6:30am-2pm. ❶

The Udder Bar and Cafe/The Krazy Kow Bar, 476 Pollen St. (☎868 6200), both downstairs from Adventure Backpackers. Townspeople and backpackers gather at the Udder to suck down burgers ($9), salads ($8-12), and seafood specials. At the Krazy Kow, rowdy crowds dance on tables under the spell of cheap beer ($3.20 handles). Udder open daily noon-2:30pm and 6-9pm; Kow F-Sa 9pm-2am. ❷

SIGHTS AND ACTIVITIES

An impressive memorial to the 19th-century gold industry, the **Gold Mine and Stamper Battery,** on SH25 at the north end of town, hosts rock-crushing and sifting demos that will leave you with a pounding headache and no illusions about the glamour of gold mining. (☎868 8514. Open daily 10am-4pm. $10, children $5.) Illuminated at night, the **WWI Peace Memorial,** up Monument Rd. from Waiotahi Rd. at the north end of town, gives a wide view of both the town and the Firth. The **Karaka Bird Hide,** built with French compensation funds for the bombing of the *Rainbow Warrior* (see p. 112), stands just past Goldfields Mall.

The best walk around town is **Rocky's Goldmine Trail** (return 3hr.), which starts and ends at the Dickson Holiday Park. Beware that the area is riddled with old and dangerous mine shafts; stay on the path, as some are hidden. Ask at the Dickson office for the status of Tararu Creek Rd., which leads to the 3m **Black Hole Waterfall;** the road was washed out by flooding and is impassable until further notice. Also at the Holiday Park is the **Butterfly & Orchid Garden,** with 400 colorful insects fluttering around a climate-controlled greenhouse. (☎868 8080. Open daily 10am-4pm; in winter 10am-3pm. $8, children $4. 25% discount for Holiday Park guests.

The winding 55km scenic drive to Coromandel town, with rocky inlets and bays shifting from the muddy brown of Thames to the jewel blue of the northern peninsula, is arguably the loveliest drive on the North Island. When the road turns inland, the views over **Coromandel Harbour** will undoubtedly bowl you over (at which point you should pull over). Along the way, the **Waiomu Kauri Grove,** one of the finest oldgrowth stands, contains ancient, stout kauri. Turn right off of SH25 at the sign for Waiomu Bay Holiday Park and walk 1hr. through farmland and bush from the end of Waiomu Creek Rd., 15km from Thames. About 5km farther is the turn-off for the **Tapu-Coroglen Road,** which cuts across the peninsula. Follow it for about 8.5km and look for the sign marking a steep 10min. walk through native bush to the 1200-year-old "square kauri tree." It's worth the quick detour.)

FALLEN GIANTS As stunningly scenic as it may be, the Coromandel is in many ways a case study in human greed—its very name is taken from a Royal Navy vessel that collected massive kauri logs from the peninsula in 1820. The knot-free wood and huge, straight trunks of these noble trees were coveted for ship masts and buildings. By the 1870s, the logging moved into the area's mountainous ridges, where elaborate innovations were used in tree removal. Logs were dragged, trammed, or rolled into streambeds behind dams. As water built up, loggers tripped the dams, releasing floods of trees that crashed down the valleys in a wasteful process that damaged the logs and gouged out the stream bed. Between logging and burning the land for farming, less than 1% of the region's forest survived the short-sighted exploitation. Although today you can see more of the original kauri wood in San Francisco and Auckland buildings than in the forest, much of the irreparably altered (but regenerating) landscape on the peninsula is now part of the Coromandel Forest Park.

COROMANDEL FOREST PARK ☎ 07

The hills of the 72,000-hectare Coromandel Forest Park are tangled with regenerating bush, crawling with creepers, and drained by high waterfalls and small, fern-lined creeks. Deep within the hills that stretch up the peninsula's volcanic backbone, old kauri dams and mine shafts are interspersed with the few remaining patches of original forest. Active replanting efforts of native species are underway, as are rigorous pest management techniques (especially in the north, where possums have not fully infiltrated).

Getting to Kauaeranga Valley without your own transportation is a hassle, especially at non-peak times. **The Sunkist Lodge** (see **Accommodations and Camping,** p. 130) occasionally runs a shuttle service (return $20, but negotiable). Although *Let's Go* does not recommend hitchhiking, the road to Kauaeranga is fairly hitchable on weekends (daily in summer), but finding a ride at other times is risky. Most thumbers arrange a return ride or run the risk of getting stuck. The **Kauaeranga Visitors Centre (DOC)** is 13km straight up Kauaeranga Valley Rd., a winding half-paved road that branches off at the BP station at the south end of Thames. Stop in before heading to the trails to fill out intentions forms. (☎ 867 9080. Open daily 8am-4pm.) **DOC campgrounds** are liberally scattered throughout the valley, with eight off the road and three accessed by trails from the road's end; the sites are cheap and basic ($7, children $2). The only hut in the area is the **Pinnacles Hut,** a rugged Ritz with views, a year-round warden, wood stove, gas cooking (bring your own utensils), 80 mattresses with fitted sheets, solar lighting, and toilets. It's about a 1hr. climb from the gravel's terminus. ($15, children $7.50. Book in advance at the Visitors Center; hut passes not applicable.)

The **Kauaeranga Valley** is one of the most hiked spots on the peninsula, with a wide variety of walks leading off the road. A 5min. hop from the Visitors Center leads to an old yet intact kauri dam and the bludgeoned stream bed it helped carve out. A trip to two of the Valley's only surviving large **kauri** departs from the **Wainora campground** (return 2-3hr.). The **Kauaeranga Kauri Trail** heads up to Pinnacles Hut and the sheer jagged bluffs of the **Pinnacles** themselves, arching like fins out of emerald water. It's well worth the swing bridges and the thousand-step staircase through fern-laden bush, but scrambling towards the end gets challenging. Atop the Pinnacles, 1hr. from the hut (3-4hr. return from the road), the views across the peninsula will strip you of any breath that is left. The **Kauaeranga River,** running along the road up the valley, sports tons of swimming holes. Find your own, or check out **Hoffman's Pool,** a 2min. walk beginning just beyond the DOC office.

COROMANDEL ☎ 07

The peaceful town of Coromandel (pop. 2000) unites artisans, individualists, and country bumpkins in a common love of the mesmerizingly blue waters of Coromandel Harbour, and the deep greens of the sweeping hills above town. Ambitious visitors undertake long treks along the north coast or into the interior; the road-weary retreat to the town's remarkable accommodations and lazily bask in its fresh spirit. Whatever you do, leaving Coromandel won't be easy.

▐ TRANSPORTATION

As in most of the peninsula, transport services change rapidly and vary considerably by season—check with the Visitors Center for up-to-date schedules. The **InterCity Coromandel Busplan** passes through to **Whitianga** (1hr.; daily 11:05am; in winter M-F and Su), continuing to **Thames** (3hr.). You can go directly to **Thames** with **Turley Murphy** (1hr.; M-F 7:30am; $12-16) or via **Whitianga** for the same price on the same day. Rod Carter's **Coromandel Bus Service** (☎ 866 8045) goes to **Fletcher's Bay** and the **Coromandel Walkway** (pick-up after walk at Stony Bay) daily in the summer and on the weekends in winter (numbers permitting, 4 people min.; departs 9am, returns about 5:30pm; $65). **Biking** is another good option; Whitianga is a 2½hr. ride, Colville is a 3hr. pedal, and Fletcher Bay is 7hr. away. Bike rentals are available at the Tui Lodge (see below; $10 per day) or through Mark Bradshaw at **Expedition,** on Wharf Rd. Mark will also offer outdoor equipment for sale and rent, and some well-measured advice for free. (☎ 866 8189. Bikes $30 per day, $20 per half-day.) Although *Let's Go* does not recommend it, **hitchhiking** to Thames is reportedly easy, and only slightly more difficult to Whitianga. The SH25 road that turns off just past the fire station on Tiki Rd. sees much more traffic than the 309 Rd. Hitching northward in winter is difficult.

PRACTICAL INFORMATION

The **Coromandel Information Centre** lies on Kapanga Rd. across the creek. (☎ 866 8598; fax 866 7285; coroinfo@ihug.co.nz. Open daily 9am-5pm; in winter 10am-4pm.) The **DOC office** is in the same building, although you should obtain all necessary permits in Thames or Hamilton because this branch does not issue any. **Internet access** is available at the **Visitors Center** for $10 per hr. Other services include: **BNZ,** at Tiki and Kapanga Rd., with **ATM** (open M-F 10am-3pm); the **police** (☎ 866 8777), next to the Visitors Center; and the **post office,** 190 Kapanga Rd. (☎ 866 8865; open M-F 8:30am-5pm).

ACCOMMODATIONS AND CAMPING

Bring cash; few of the hostels have credit card capabilities. Homestays spring up in the holiday season. If you decide to camp in peak months, be prepared to deal with crowds. Book far ahead for the summer, when every bed in town is filled.

- **The Lion's Den (BBH),** 126 Te Tiki St. (☎/fax 866 8157). This laid-back backpackers beats its competition by a country kilometer with friendly hosts and the feel of a communal experiment gone wonderfully right. Free vegetables from the organic garden. Excellent home-cooked meals on request ($5-10). Dorms $16; doubles $32; tent sites $12. Cash only. ❷

- **Tui Lodge,** 60 Whangapoua Rd. (☎ 866 8237). From Kapanga/Wharf Rd., turn onto Tiki Rd. by the BNZ, and left onto Whangapoua Rd. The lodge is 500m on the right, down a gravel drive. With sheep grazing in the front pasture and an orchard in back, adjustment to

THE BIG SPLURGE

AN (ALMOST) PRESIDENTIAL HOLIDAY AT THE CELADON MOTEL

One lush kilometer from Coromandel town, Celadon Motel is a relaxing and entertaining North Island retreat. Entering the rainforest, travelers are greeted by giant Kiwi ferns, musical tui birds, and a friendly note, "Am around. Please toot. Ray."

After a few toots, Ray Morley, the man in charge, emerges from the forest, bringing warm hospitality and tales of American royalty. In August 2000, Celadon's forested grounds hosted the family of US Presidential hopeful, Al Gore. As Ray eagerly tells guests, Tipper, Sarah, Kristin, and their bodyguards were all "wonderful people." After the visit, the humble motel appeared in national and international newspapers.

Though current guests may not sleep alongside foreign dignitaries, they can indulge in individually-named, self-contained cottages. Hidden in thick foliage, the "Tipper Gore" suite is a favorite with honeymooners. This spotless abode has luxurious showers and glorious views of Coromandel town and harbor. Next door, the "Bodyguard's Cottage" features original artwork and sumptuous beds.

Days are spent brushing up on American politics, gathering fresh herbs in the garden, or sculpting clay with Mr. Morley ($15 per hr.).

Up a steep hill on Alfred St., off Rings Rd., 1km from Coromandel town. ☎/fax 866 8058; wilsonmc@wave.co.nz. Cottages and B&B rooms $70-120 for 2, extra person $10. $5 off with Let's Go.

Coromandel time is made easy. Bike rental, free laundry, in-season fruit, Internet, trampoline. Dorms $16; twins and doubles $34; tent sites $8. ❷

Tidewater Tourist Park (YHA), 270 Tiki Rd. (☎866 8888; fax 866 7231; tidewatr@world-net.co.nz). Explore on a mountain bike ($10 per day) or kick back and enjoy the bay. Private sauna $5 for 30min. Kayak rental $5 per hr. Compact shares $24; twins and doubles $41-43; tent sites $9. ❸

Long Bay Motor Camp (☎866 8720), 3km from town on Wharf/Long Bay Rd., features beautiful views of the water. Take your tent to remote, on-property Tucks Bay sites to escape the motoring masses. Kayaks $5 per hr. Metered showers. 2-person units $30; tent sites $10, powered $11. ❶

🍴 FOOD

For veggie options and the town's best, most affordable dinners, head to ⭐**The Success Cafe** ❷, 104 Kapanga Rd. A hefty plate of steamers is $9—we don't know their secret, but we like their style. (☎866 7100. Open daily 10am-late.) The **Umu** ❷, across from BNZ, offers several specialty pizzas ($10-18), vegetarian options, and all organic produce. (☎866 8618. Open daily noon-3:30pm and 6pm-late.) **The Pepper Tree Restaurant and Bar** ❹, on Kapanga Rd. in the town center, specializes in fresh seafood. You'll have to shell out a few clams, but the food is memorable. (☎866 8211. Open daily 8am-1am; in winter 11am-9pm.) **Driving Creek Cafe** ❷, 3km out of town just short of the Railway, is the perfect place for a weary soul to put up his soles. Sandwiches $6-8. (☎866-8760. Internet. Open W-Su 10am-4pm.) **Price Cutter,** on Kapanga Rd. just before the bridge, is a convenient place to pick up groceries. (☎866 8669. Open M-Sa 7:30am-6pm, Su 8am-6pm.)

👁 🥾 SIGHTS AND ACTIVITIES

The artistic community of Coromandel draws much of its inspiration from the area's natural endowments. Upon arrival, visitors should soak up the views and then head into the bush to see nature in its raw form. The **309 Road,** branching off 4km south of the town of Coromandel and ending in Whitianga, may be the explorers' best avenue. Although the road is unsealed, winding, and narrow at times, it's quite passable for any car; just go slow around the bends and keep to your side of the road. The most eccentric attraction in the peninsula is the **Waiau Waterworks,** 9km from Coromandel town. This collection of whimsically and brilliantly engineered kinetic sculptures is powered by—you guessed it—water. (☎866 7191; www.waiauwaterworks.co.nz. Open Sept.-June daily 9am-5pm, $8.) One hundred meters past Waiau Waterworks, the **Castle Rock Trail** (return 2hr.), the best and steepest tramp in town, yields 360° views of the peninsula. Driving down 309 Rd. to the trailhead is best, but a rigorous 2hr. bike trip (much of it uphill) will also get you there if you can survive the workout. The **Waiau Falls,** set in a bush glade just off the road 7.3km from Coromandel, is a good place to cool off after a dusty ride. Be sure to make it all the way up to the **Waiau Kauri Grove** about 15km from Coromandel. Walk for 10min. to join other astonished visitors in the cathedral of soaring trees that once covered the peninsula.

Coromandel exudes artistic spirit from nearly every corner, and the pottery, weaving, sculpture, and woodwork of local artisans dot the town and landscape. The **Weta Design Studio,** on Kapanga Rd., is the best of these local shops, offering quality over quantity with reasonably-priced local and national art, crafts, and sculpture in the delightful outdoor courtyard. (☎866 8823. Open daily 10am-5pm.) Besides crafts, Coromandel town's biggest attraction is probably the **Driving Creek Railway,** 3km north of town. Begun as a pet project in 1975 to extract clay and kiln fuel from the hills, the narrow-gauge railroad has become the 20yr. passion of owner and potter Barry Brickell. The ever-growing track snakes through glowing forest and tunnels, around spirals, and over bridges. (☎ 866 8703. $15, children $7.) Also just north of the town, visitors can pan for their own gold at the **Coromandel Gold Stamper Battery** while learning about the gold-mining industry that was once the pillar of the peninsula. (☎ 866 8758 or 021 257 8942. Open daily 10am-4pm. $6, children $3.) Owner Ashley also provides guided geological tours of the area. (3hr. tours $30, children $15.)

THE NORTHERN TIP ☎ 07

North of Coromandel, travelers are on their own. Comfy lodgings are few and far between, and the only cafe is a hole-in-the-wall in Colville. Jumbled green hills, deserted crescent bays, twisting trees that would make Van Gogh proud, and a wild coastline of cliffs and rocky beaches are broken up only by placidly grazing sheep. The spectacular **Coromandel Walkway**, between Fletcher Bay and Stony Bay, is worth any effort it takes to get there.

TRANSPORTATION. The quality of roads in the region is inversely proportional to the "gasp" factor—if the scenery is beautiful, the drive is probably harrowing. The narrow gravel roads do add charm and a pleasant sense of isolation, although they have a tendency to flood out in rain. One road winds up the west side to **Fletcher Bay** at the top of the Tip; another branches off just past **Colville** (28km north of Coromandel) and finds its way to Stony Bay. The well-stocked **Colville General Store** is the northernmost opportunity to fill up on **petrol** (and groceries) on the Tip. (☎ 866 6805. Open M-Th and Sa-Su 8:30am-5pm, F 8:30am-6pm.) Before heading out in your rental car, check your rental agreement about this area. Public transportation is non-existent. Mountain biking is a great, but strenuous, way to circuit the Tip along the track connecting Fletcher and Stony Bay. *Let's Go* does not recommend **hitchhiking**, which is all but impossible up north in winter. However, some succeed in summer (once past Colville thumbers usually only accept rides going all the way). Prospective hitchers should keep in mind that it's easy to get stuck out on the road and should prepare accordingly.

ACCOMMODATIONS AND FOOD. Colville Farm Backpackers (BBH) ❷ offers good, clean, rural fun (horses, glowworms, cow milking) and tidy accommodations. Many cyclists spend two nights and ditch their saddlebags here during the day to lighten their load for the trip around the Tip. (☎/fax 866 6820. Dorms $15-17; singles $17-19; self-contained huts $50-65 or $14 per person; self-contained houses $70-75 for 2; tent sites $5-9.) Just down the road is the restaurant **Colville Caff ❷**, the best place in Colville to briefly mellow out before hitting the road ahead. (☎ 866 6912. Open daily 9am-9pm; in winter M-Th 9am-4pm, F-Su 9am-9pm. Cash only.) **Fletcher Bay Backpackers ❶**, next to the Coromandel Walkway trailhead, is a base for tramps into the bush or along the coast. Owned by DOC, Fletcher's has just 16 beds, making bookings essential. (☎ 866 6712; js.lourie@xtra.co.nz. Dorms $13.) In addition, DOC manages five basic **campgrounds** in the northern region.

ACTIVITIES. The peninsula's crowning track, the 10.7km **Coromandel Walkway** (one-way 3hr.), explores lonely bays and coves, dips into inlets and bushy valleys, and overlooks turquoise waters from high bluffs along the coast between Fletcher and Stony Bay. Other than a few short and steep climbs, it's not difficult, although it can be a bit hairy in winter before it's cleared for the summer season (it quickly becomes overgrown and can be quite muddy). **Carter Tours** will do drop-offs and pick-ups in summer. (☎ 866 8045 or 025 937 259. $65, min. 3 people.) If you have to return to a parked car but don't want to hike for 6hr., start from the eastern Stony Bay side, walk for 1-2hr. and turn around; many regard this half, with its thick forests and cascading streams, as the best part of the hike. Another great tramp goes up the peninsula's tallest mountain, the 892m **Mt. Moehau**. As the top is private Maori land, you're requested to turn back just as you get tantalizingly close. Approachable from several points, the peak is perhaps most accessible from **Te Hope Stream,** 12km north of Colville (return 5hr.). The more strenuous **Stony Bay** route follows an exposed ridge (taking most of a day).

WHITIANGA ☎ 07

Moving east across the peninsula, the coastline softens from mud and rocks into sandy beach. Among the dunes, Whitianga (fit-ee-ANG-guh; pop. 3700) has become the Coromandel's main resort town. Whitianga loses a bit of its relaxed vibe during the summer, when it seems like every frenzied angler, boater, and sun fiend from Auckland descends to plumb the deep-sea fishing waters, explore the nearby marine reserve, or hit one of the many surrounding beaches.

TRANSPORTATION. The **InterCity Coromandel Busplan** buses leave the Visitors Center for **Auckland** (1½hr., 2 per day, $57) with a connection to **Thames** via **Whenuakite, Tairua,** and **Hikuai** ($24). To get to **Whangamata**, take the bus to Hikuai and arrange to be picked up by InterCity affiliate **Whangamata Tours.** (☎ 866 4397. 1½hr., daily 2:15pm, $29.) **Guthreys Express** leaves for **Tauranga** and **Mt. Maunganui** at 12:40pm ($30). **Mercury Bay Taxis** (☎ 866 5643) will also do a run to **Coromandel** for about $50 per van (fits 10). Book bus transport at the **Visitors Center** (see below) or through **United Travel/Travel Options.** (☎ 866 4397. Open M-F 9am-5pm, Sa 10am-noon.) **The Rental Car Centre**, 32 Campbell St., offers basic economy cars at a decent rate. (☎ 866 5901. Cars from $55 per day, 150km free per day.) **Whitianga Water Transport** sends shuttles across the harbor to Ferry Landing. (☎ 866-5472. 5-10min. Runs daily 7:30am-10:30pm. Return $2.)

The Visitors Center also rents out **bicycles** ($25 per day, $15 per half-day). To ride around the other side of Whitianga Harbour, call on **Chris Axeby,** whose bike shop is right at Ferry Landing. (☎ 866 5241. $20 per day.)

ORIENTATION AND PRACTICAL INFORMATION. Whitianga sits where **Mercury Bay's** beach meets **Whitianga Harbour.** The route to **Hahei** and **Hot Water Beach** is a lengthy detour around the harbor. **SH25** runs along the beach as **Buffalo Beach Road** and turns south to become **Albert Street,** the main drag. The **Whitianga Information Centre,** 66 Albert St., is run under the umbrella of the Business Association—be sure to ask the staff about *all* of your accommodation options, because the brochures only list members of the Association. The Visitors Center also offers **Internet access** for $3 per 15min. (☎ 866 5555; fax 866 2205; whitvin@ihug.co.nz. Open Dec.-Mar. daily 8am-6pm; Apr.-Nov. M-F 9am-5pm, Sa-Su 9am-4pm.) The **Westpac Trust Bank,** on Albert St. by Monk St., has an **ATM.** (☎ 866 4532. Open M-Tu and Th-F 9am-4:30pm, W 9:30am-4:30pm.) Other services include: the **police** (☎ 866 4000), on Campbell St.; **Mercury Bay Medical Centre** (☎ 866 5911), at Albert and Owen St.; and the **post office** (☎ 866 4006; open M-F 8:30am-5pm).

ACCOMMODATIONS AND CAMPING. In a stout converted motel about 1km from downtown, the ◙**On the Beach Backpacker's Lodge (BBH/YHA)** ❷, 46 Buffalo Beach Rd., is just that—on the beach. The enthusiastic owners joke with guests and provide a courtesy van as well as free kayaks, boogie boards, fishing rods, and shovels for Hot Water Beach. (☎/fax 866 5380; corobkpk@wave.co.nz. Bikes available. Internet. Dorms $18; twins and doubles $44.) Near the town center lies **The Cat's Pyjamas Backpackers Lodge ❷**, 4 Monk St., off Albert St. Ask Buster, the affable owner, about scenic flights in his Cessna. After a long day's work (or flight), the patio is a great place to sit, unwind, and have a tasty beverage. (☎/fax 866 4663; catspjs@ihug.co.nz. Flights $22 per person. Dorms $18; twins and doubles $40; tent sites $12.) Though **Bay Watch Backpackers ❷**, 22 Esplanade, along the bay beyond where Buffalo Beach Rd. turns into Albert St., conspicuously lacks the red bathing suits and contrived plot lines you might expect, even David Hasselhoff would laud the perfect location. (☎ 866 5481; fax 866 5489; kristorb@ihug.co.nz. Bikes available. Dorms $20; doubles $60; motel units with bath $75-150.) **The Mercury Bay Motor Camp ❶**, 121 Albert St., is 500m south of town center with standard motor park amenities. (☎ 866 5579; fax 866 4891. Tourist flat singles $40; doubles $60, in peak season $120; tent and caravan sites $10-13.) Those wishing to escape the bustle of the summer season in Whitianga may wish to try the **309 River Lodge ❷**, on the 309 Rd., 12km from town. Occupying an old schoolhouse, the lodge has bush walks, a swimming hole, organic produce, and farm animals that craft a country feel. (☎ 866 5151; fax 866 5137; colin.megan@paradise.net.nz. Free pick-up for groups. Dorms $17; doubles $35; tent sites $10-14. Call far ahead Jan.-Feb.)

◨◧ FOOD AND NIGHTLIFE. As a resort town, the price of food in Whitianga tends to outstrip its quality. To be safe, visit **Four Square**, on Albert St. by the Visitors Center, for groceries. (☎ 866 5777. Open M-Sa 7am-7pm; in winter M-F 7am-6pm, Sa 8am-6pm.) A diamond in the rough, **Cafe Nina ❷** is on Victoria St. at the back side of the park. The muffins melt in your mouth and the lunch menu ($6-9) has some veggie options. (☎ 866 5440. Open daily 8am-5:30pm; winter hours vary.) **The Fire Place ❸**, 9 Esplanade, across from the wharf, is the place to splurge for dinner. The food is of consistently high quality; brick-oven pizzas ($17.50) are especially savory. (☎ 866-4828. Open M-F 4pm-late, Sa-Su 10am-late.) At **Smitty's Bar and Grille ❷**, 37 Albert St., burgers and a double-decker BLT are under $10. Smitty's also happens to be the pinnacle of the town's nightlife (handles $3.20) and a happening place during televised rugby games. (☎ 866 4647. M-Sa 11am-1am, Su 5pm-1am.)

◨◧ SIGHTS AND ACTIVITIES. The greatest joys in Whitianga are outdoors. Cross the river on the ferry and take the path to the small **Scenic Reserve** on the right. Follow the water's edge up to the 24m bluff of **Whitianga Rock**, an old Maori *pa*, from which stone for the old ferry landing wharf was taken. The walk from **Ferry Landing** up to the **Shakespeare Lookout**, named for a resemblance to the Bard, is worth the hour (you can also drive). The walk jaunts along **Front Beach** to the crescent of **Flaxmill Bay** and climbs steeply from the sign on the pohutukawa at the far end. The expansive view from the top includes a clear peep at **Lonely Bay** below—the only legal nude beach on the Coromandel (bring your binoculars). Isolated from unsightly buildings and roads, the cove's golden sands and turquoise surf are accessible only by boat or by the steep footpath down from Shakespeare Lookout. The next beach over is **Cooks Beach**, a shallow 3km stretch of swimming area. **Buffalo Beach**, directly on the shores of Whitianga, is named for the HMS *Buffalo*, which wrecked in 1840 while collecting kauri for England. In order to fully explore the area on the other side of the harbor, rent a bike either in town or at Ferry Landing and make a loop all the way out to Hahei and Hot Water Beach.

It's that blue water that draws most people to the **Mercury Bay** area. With **Cathedral Cove Marine Reserve** nearby and the Mercury Bay Islands off the coast, every kind of water activity from snorkeling to banana boating can be found here. Whitianga has some of New Zealand's best big-game **fishing** from December to March.

Exercise your artistic fingers at **Bay Carving**, on the Esplanade opposite the wharf beside the museum. The metamorphosis from paper to polished pendant in

3hr. is amazingly satisfying. (☎866 4021. Designs and tutelage from $35. Hours variable due to demand and the Kiwi Experience. Call ahead.) Next door, the **Mercury Bay District Museum** details Maori history starting with Kupe's landing and displays shipwreck artifacts. (☎866 0730. Open daily 10am-4pm; in winter Tu, Th, and Su 11am-2pm. $2.) **Twin Oaks**, 9km north of town on the road to Kuaotunu, takes horseback riders of any skill through farmland and to dramatic views of the peninsula. Transport is possible if you call ahead. (☎866 5388. 2hr. $30.)

HAHEI ☎07

The name Hahei (HA-hey) stems from Chief Hei of the Arawa canoe that docked somewhere off the coast around AD 1350. A tiny town, most visitors come for the pristine water of stunning Cathedral Cove Marine Reserve or the sandy hot pools percolating up at nearby Hot Water Beach.

TRANSPORTATION. Guthreys Express departs for **Auckland** via **Thames** daily at 12:45pm ($30). **Hot Water Beach Connections** has great service to and through the area, making a circuit between **Ferry Landing, Hahei, Hot Water Beach**, and **Cooks Beach.** (☎866 2478. In summer 2-3 per day, 7:30am-5:30pm.) Connections also meets the **InterCity** bus from **Whitianga** to **Thames** into **Hahei** or **Hot Water Beach** (return $14). The **Explorer Bus Pass** ($35) lets you on and off all day, or you can travel each segment independently (ferry to Hahei $10).

ACCOMMODATIONS AND FOOD. ☒Tatahi Lodge (BBH) ❷, on Grange Rd., is reason enough to consider a stay in Hahei instead of Whitianga. Its lovely wood lodge, lounge, and window seats are perfect for post-beach bliss. (☎866 3992; fax 866 3993; tatahi_lodge@xtra.co.nz. Bike rental. Internet. Book far ahead in summer. Dorms $20; twins and doubles $50. Motel units also available.) Not quite as spiffy are **Hahei Holiday Resort** and the accompanying **Cathedral Cove Backpackers Lodge (VIP) ❷**, at the end of Harsant Ave. off the town's main road. Located just over the dune from the beach, the sliding Japanese screens at this resort duo lend scant privacy from the corridor. (☎866 3889; fax 866 3098; info@haheiholidays.co.nz. Dorms $16; twins and doubles $38; tent sites $10; powered and campervan sites $11; tourist flats $49 for 2; studio rooms with bath and TV $120 for 2. Prices for non-backpacker units jump in the high season.)

The **Hahei Store**, on Beach Rd., sells groceries and snacks. (☎866 3855. Open daily 8:30am-7pm; in winter 8:30am-6pm.) **Luna Cafe ❸**, around the corner from the Hahei Store and next to the Tatahi Lodge, has a rotating menu with salads and light meals under $15. (☎866 3016. Open 9am "until we've closed.")

ACTIVITIES. Hahei's **beach**, sheltered by offshore islands, is a perfect calm for swimmers. Many surfers head instead to **Hot Water Beach** (see p. 139) where the breaks are higher. To the south of Hahei rises the dramatic bluff of **Hereheretaura Point,** an ideal spot for an old Maori *pa;* cross the creek at the beach's end and follow the path (return 1hr.) for 360° views. To the north, around a green hill, gaze out at the small islands speckling the ocean and amble down to the Coromandel's poster child (literally): the **Cathedral Cove Marine Reserve (Te Whanganui-a-Hei).** To reach the majestic rock formations over the cove, you can either walk from the beach or turn left past the general store to reach the 1hr. track to the cove (45min. from the carpark atop the hill). One of the most visited in New Zealand, the path snakes through pastures and descends hundreds of steps. The white sands and lapping turquoise waters of **Gemstone Bay** and **Stingray Bay** (though they beg you to go for a wade or snorkel) are merely preludes to neighboring **Mare's Leg Cove** and the famous ☒**Cathedral Cove.** With a pristine, white, sandy beach and arching rocks, this idyllic expanse of subtropical water is only accessible through a stone archway carved out by the sea (which can fill to the waist at high tide). To enjoy the Cove's many splendors, swim out to the warped stone formations, standing like forgotten sculptures in the shallows, or sample the freshwater falls trickling over the white cliffs.

For another perspective of Cathedral Cove, take a guided kayak trip with **Cathedral Cove Sea Kayaking.** For Whitianga-based folk, the trip includes pick-up from Ferry Landing. (☎ 866 3877; www.seakayaktours.co.nz. Half-day trips $55.) Nigel and his **Hahei Explorer** provide motorized scenic trips at any time of year to explore the local islands, hidden caves and archways, and a spectacular 30m blowhole. (☎ 866 3910. 1hr. $40.) He also rents snorkel gear with wetsuits ($35 per day).

On the wetter side of things (depending on your perspective and drinking habits), the **Purangi Winery** is favorably situated on the main road between Ferry Landing and the Hahei and Hot Water Beach area. The organic winery makes 23 varieties of fruit wines, ports, and liqueurs that you can taste in succession. (☎ 866 3724. Open daily 9am-9pm; in winter 9am-5pm.)

HOT WATER BEACH ☎ 07

Imagine a beach where you can take a shovel, dig a little hole, and watch the hot water fill in to create your own ocean-side thermal pool. Well, fantasize no longer. Proving once again that Mother Nature can outdo the resort industry, the 30-50m golden crescent of steaming sands is a free spa, percolating with water as hot as 65°C. Rent a cheap shovel from the beachfront store (open daily 9am-5pm; shovel $4 per 2hr. plus $20 deposit). For 2hr. on either side of low tide you can soak in your own hollowed series of pools while watching dolphins or surfers offshore. The pools don't always work; locals say the nature gods cooperate only 60-70% of the year. Chances are better in summer, though you probably won't have the only set of legs poking out of the sand; the Kiwi Experience Bus stops here, and on occasion up to 1500 people simultaneously try to dig pools in the limited space. The beach is beautiful, but the rips, reefs, and sandbars that bring good surfing breaks also make for treacherous swimming.

Hot Water Beach Connections (☎ 866 2478) runs past the beach several times daily on its circuit (Explorer pass $35), and also picks up from the holiday park to meet **InterCity** at Dalmeny Corner (1-2 per day, return $14) on its way to **Thames.** While aboard, you may as well rent a $2 shovel. Call dibs on the best plots at the beachfront at **Hot Water Beach Holiday Park ❶**, a small, tree-lined park that can cram up to 400 people in its tent, caravan, and campervan sites. (☎ 866 3735. Free showers. Tent, caravan, and campervan sites $12; in winter $8-10.)

OPOUTERE ☎ 07

Linger by the tides for a day or two to experience the sounds of silence, punctuated only by the shrieks of shorebirds, the chortles of tui and bellbirds, and the wash of surf along one of the last undeveloped beaches in Coromandel. Lying on a harbor estuary at the mouth of the Wharekawa River, Opoutere (oh-POH-tury) isn't a town—it's just a place, home to an idyllic hostel, motorcamp, and little else but 5km of perfect, lonesome beach.

To reach this magical nowhere, a mere 15min. drive north of Whangamata, **Whangamata Tours** runs through to connect with the InterCity bus. (☎ 863 8627 or 025 727 708. Nov.-Mar. daily; Apr.-Oct. 3 per week. Bookings can and should be made ahead of time through InterCity.) Capitalizing on this oasis from civilization is the appropriately peaceful 🌿**Opoutere YHA Hostel ❷,** 4km from the Opoutere turn-off from SH25 (follow the light of the glowworms). Housed in a group of school buildings, this backpackers is a communal oasis, a vacation from a vacation. The office sells basic groceries and ambrosial homemade yogurt. (☎ 865 9072; fax 865 6172; yhaopout@yha.org.nz. Dorms $18-20; twins and doubles $46; tent sites $15.) About 1km down the road at the far end of the estuary is the **Opoutere Park Beach Resort ❶.** Tent sites are afforded privacy by pine plantings; tourist flats and chalets rest near massive old pohutukawas just 200m from the beach. The office has few groceries; stock up before you come. (☎ 865 9152. Open Sept.-May. Tent and caravan sites about $10; tourist flats about $50; chalets about $66.)

The **Wharekawa Harbour Sandspit Wildlife Reserve** is one of New Zealand's few remaining nesting places for the scarce Variable Oystercatcher, a large black bird with shockingly pink extremities, and for the similarly threatened New Zealand Dotterel. During the nesting season (Oct.-Feb.), DOC tries to fence off and guard the exposed sand where these claustrophobic birds nest (they require an almost 360° view of their surroundings.) At low tide you can cross the sand bar and head up the shelly beach to watch kingfishers dart above herons stalking their prey and the oystercatchers digging for pockets of clam-like pipis. At high tide, the sandbar floods and birdwatchers must take the bridge and footpath to the nesting site (10min.). **Ocean Beach,** on the opposite side of the sandspit from the estuary, is a great spot to study the incoming waves and the jagged outline of the **Alderman Islands** far offshore. Diving into the bush will scare up flighty fantails (small sparrow-like birds that the Maori believed brought death when they entered a home) and numerous other native birds that constantly clamor around. Opoutere on their way to the summit of **Maungaruawahine pa.** The summit itself towers over the hostel and is easily accessible via trail from the hostel grounds (return 1hr.).

WHANGAMATA ☎ 07

Whangamata's (Fahn-ga-mah-TAH's) 4km of white sand cradling an island-studded bay is known as one of the North Island's top surf spots. Outside the summer crunch of surfers and vacationers, small Whangamata (pop. 4000) is sleepily residential and full of easy-going locals mingling among the main drag's surf shops, cafes, and takeaways. You're always within a board's length of the beach and a short ride from the bush.

☞ TRANSPORTATION. No major bus lines come directly to Whangamata; local shuttles carry passengers out to meet them. Make arrangements with **Whangamata Travel and Services,** 640 Port St. (☎ 865 8776. Open M-F 9am-4:30pm, Sa 10am-1pm.) **Whangamata Tours** offers a shuttle to **Waihi** for InterCity connections to **Tauranga.** (☎ 863 8627 or 025 727 708. 30min.; 2-3 per day; $18, students and seniors $15.) For the same price, they also run out to the bump in the road that is **Hikuai** to meet the **InterCity** bus running from **Whitianga** to **Thames.** (30min., leaves at 1:35pm to meet 2:15pm bus.) **Whangamata Taxi** (☎ 865 8294) makes the same run to Hikuai to meet the **Go Kiwi** shuttle that continues on to **Thames** and the **Auckland Airport** (leaves from town at 8:15am; $60-70). All shuttles swing by **Opoutere.** To get to **Whitianga,** you must wait two hours at Hikuai for the 4:05pm InterCity bus from Thames. Make a reservation because Whangamata Tours and the taxi service might not make the run if there is no demand, especially in winter.

■ ⁊ ORIENTATION AND PRACTICAL INFORMATION. Snug against the beach at the mouth of **Whangamata Harbour,** the town is a maze of residential streets. Action centers on **Port Road,** the main street that runs into SH25 at either end. **Whangamata Information Centre,** 616 Port St., is a low-key, largely volunteer establishment. (☎/fax 865 8340; info-whangamata@xtra.co.nz. Open M-Sa 9am-5pm, Su 10am-4pm; in winter M-Sa 9am-5pm, Su 10am-2pm.) Other services include: **Westpac Trust Bank,** on Port Rd. (☎ 865 9771; open M-Tu and Th-F 9am-5pm, W 9:30am-5pm); **Whangamata Medical Centre,** 103 Lincoln Rd. (☎ 865 8032); **Internet access** at

WHANGAMATA ■ 141

Bartley Internet & Graphics, 706 Port Rd. (☎ 865 8832; open M-F 9am-6pm, Sa 10am-4pm; $3 per 15min., $10 per hr.); and a **post shop,** on Port Rd. (☎ 865 8230; open M-F 9am-5pm, Sa 9am-noon).

ACCOMMODATIONS AND CAMPING. Dude, holiday surfers often bunk in their car (price: free), or even someone else's (price: depends on the surfer). For more traditional accommodations, prices skyrocket in the summer and beds are scarce. The rooms at the **Garden Lodge (BBH/VIP)** ❷, 500m south of the town center on Port Rd., are clean, comfortable, and quite expensive in the summer—borrow a free bodyboard to feel better. (☎/fax 865 9580; www.gardenlodge.whangamata.co.nz. Dorms $18-23; doubles $45-50; motel units from $80. Prices flexible in winter.) To get to **Whangamata Backpackers Hostel (BBH)** ❷, 227 Beverly Tce., turn off of Port Rd. onto Ocean Rd. heading southeast. Then, turn left onto Short Rd. and right onto Beverly. Don't be afraid to toss a wetsuit over the mismatched chairs in this house across the street from the ocean. (☎/fax 865 8323. Dorms $15-17; doubles $30-35.) Park your tent by the sheep and enjoy basic facilities and a pool at the **Pinefield Holiday Park** ❶, a little less than 1km south on Port Rd. (☎/fax 865 8791; pinefield@xtra.co.nz. Caravan and tent sites $12; basic cabin shares $18; cabins with kitchen from $55 for 2; chalet doubles from $75.)

FOOD. With the summer influx of Aucklanders, Whangamata's dining scene is hopping. However, by the end of January, things simmer down, and restaurant schedules become quite erratic. **Vibes Cafe** ❷, in the center of town, spreads good vibes with great espresso, cheap vegetarian melts, and $10 lunch combos. (☎ 865 7121. Open daily 9am-5pm.) For live music, check out **Cafe 101** ❷, on Casement Rd., where owner Gary occasionally tickles the ivories during the evening. (☎ 865 6301. Open Dec.-Jan. M-F 10am-late, Sa-Su 9am-late.) Late at night and at odd hours, try **La Hacienda** ❷, set back from Port Rd. on the beach side right near the center. This place doles out cheap burgers ($6-8) and burritos ($6-7) to surfers. (☎ 865 8351. Open Dec.-Feb. Su-Tu and Th 11am-8pm, F-Sa 11am-late; Mar.-Nov. closed Tu-W.) Get fresh food at **Quarry Orchards,** next to the post office. (☎ 865 8282. Open M-F 7am-5:30pm, Sa 7am-4:30pm.)

ACTIVITIES. Most come to Whangamata to marinate in the sun and surf or take low-tide wades out to **Hauturu Island.** Surfers say the best waves are near the harbor mouth. **Whangamata Surf Shop,** 634 Port Rd., is owned by a long-time surfer who rents surfing accessories at fair prices. (☎ 865 8252. Half-day board rental $18, full-day $25. Boogie boards also available. Open daily 9am-5pm.) **Windsurfing Whangamata** has been teaching people to windsurf since 1982. (☎ 865 8186 or 025 264 9463. Board hire $20 per hr., with lesson $30. Open 3hr. either side of high tide during summer school holidays.)

Good hiking and biking trails abound in 11,500-hectare **Tairua Forest,** north of town. **Wentworth Valley,** on the turn-off 3km south of town on SH25, is the center for outdoor activities in Whangamata. The river valley's walks are strewn with mine shafts and relics from turn-of-the-century days. A 1hr. walk leaves the campground (tent sites $5) and heads up to **Wentworth Falls.** At low tide, the sea tunnel at **Pokohino Beach** leads to a rocky cove with isolated white sand. A short, steep walk goes to the beach from a carpark at the end of Pokohino Rd., a forest road that branches off Onemana Rd. 6km north of Whangamata on SH25. The Tairua Forest is owned by the Carter Holt Harvey logging company, and while hiking on their land is free, biking requires a $10 monthly permit, available at the Visitors Center. **Whangamata Mowers and Cycles,** on Port Rd., can provide mountain bikes. (☎ 865 8096. $7.50 per hr., $25 per half-day, $100 deposit.)

THE WAIKATO AND KING COUNTRY

Today, tranquility settles over the lush pastureland and lazy streams of the Waikato and King Country, but living in these parts has not always been so easy. In the 1840s and '50s, the Maori tribes of the Waikato banded together to resist the encroaching European settlement, proclaiming Potatau Te Wherowhero the first Maori king in 1858. The king's signature white top hat was passed on to his son, King Tawhiao, who used it during the Waikato War (1863-64) to make a legendary gesture of defiance, casting his "crown" onto a map of the North Island and proclaiming grandly, "There, I rule!" As a result, his people called the region *Rohe Potae*, "the brim of the hat." To the European settlers, however, it was simply "King Country," in grudging deference to the Maori dominance that lasted until the 1880s. Modern times brought a different kind of power to the region: the Waikato River, the longest river in New Zealand, churns out 50% of the North Island's electricity.

◪ WAIKATO HIGHLIGHTS

UNDERGROUND CAVES in **Waitomo** allow curious spelunkers and adventuresome adrenaline-philes to explore New Zealand's mysterious underworld (see p. 154).

UNDERGROUND CULTURE of a different color defines the world-class surfing outpost of **Raglan** (see p. 149).

HAMILTON ☎ 07

As the home of Waikato University, Hamilton has a reputation as a lively town; the extraordinary number of bars are testament to its youthful exuberance. Due in part to all of these youngsters, Hamilton is the fifth-largest city overall (pop. 117,000) in New Zealand. Other than the scenic Waikato River and many pea-soup-thick foggy nights, Hamilton has few astounding geographical or climatological features. It does, however, have a central location—half of the North Island and its wonders are a few hours' drive away. Weekends are when the town really jumps, so if you're planning a layover here, shoot for a Friday or Saturday night.

▰ TRANSPORTATION

Trains: TranzScenic (☎ 0800 802 802) heads daily to: **Auckland** (2hr., 2 per day, $20-40); **Rotorua** (2hr., 10:20am, $43); **Tauranga** (1½hr., 10:27am, $35); **Wellington** (9hr., 3 per day, $80) via **Palmerston North** (6½hr., $79-89).

Buses: InterCity and **Newmans** head daily to: **Auckland** (2hr., 20 per day, $18-20); **Gisborne** (7hr., noon, $50); **Rotorua** (2hr., 7 per day, $25); **Palmerston North** (9hr., 10am, $59); **Wellington** (9hr., 4 per day, $80). **Guthreys** (☎ 0800 759 999) runs to **Auckland** (2hr., 5 per day, $20) and **Rotorua** (1½hr., 4 per day, $20). **Dalroy Express** (☎ 06 755 009 or 0508 46 56 22) runs to **Auckland** (2hr., 2 per day, $18) and **Hawera** (5hr., 2 per day, $55), with stops along the way. **Pavlovich buses** (☎ 847 5545) depart from the Transport Centre for **Raglan** (1hr., M-F 3 per day, $5.50).

Public Transportation: From the transportation depot next to the Visitors Center, **Hamilton City Buses** (☎ 846 1975) makes stops around the city, including the University, the gardens, and various suburban areas.

Taxis: Red Cabs (☎839 0500) and **Hamilton Taxis** (☎847 7477) are abundant, especially at the corner of Victoria and Collingwood St. during evening hours.

Car Rental: Rent-a-Dent, 383 Anglesea St. (☎839 1049 or 0800 736 822). Cars with unlimited mileage from $55 per day.

Hitchhiking: Although *Let's Go* does not recommend it, hitching to Raglan is reportedly easiest along SH23. North to Auckland, many try from SH1 past the junction of Te Rapa St. and Avalon Dr., though it's reported that chances are better taking a city bus to the outskirts of town and hitching from there.

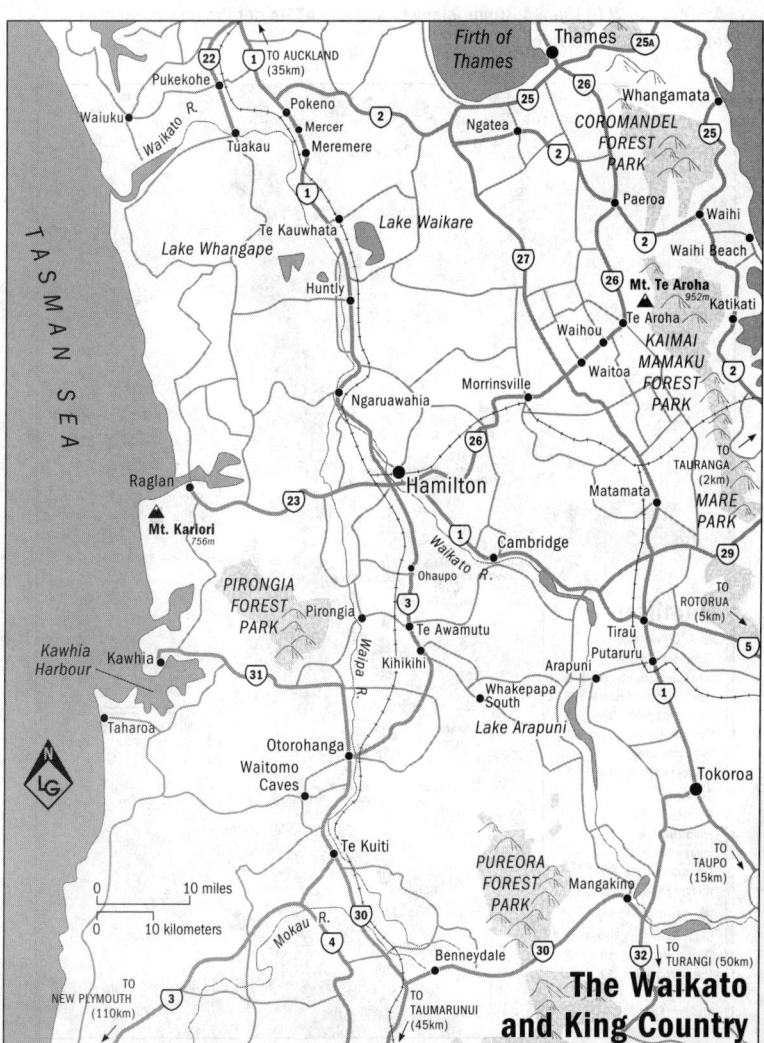

144 ■ THE WAIKATO AND KING COUNTRY

ORIENTATION AND PRACTICAL INFORMATION

Hamilton lies northeast of **SH1** and is bisected by the **Waikato River**. Most commercial activity and nightlife is on the river's west bank. **Victoria Street** is the main drag, with the stretch between **Ward** and **Hood Streets** prime for daytime shopping and nighttime carousing. **East Hamilton** houses **Waikato University** and many cafes.

Visitors Center: Visitor Information Centre (☎839 3580; fax 839 3127; www.hamilt-oncity.co.nz), in the Transport Centre at Bryce and Anglesea St. Open M-F 8:30am-5pm, Sa 9am-4pm, Su 10am-4pm.

Banks: BNZ (☎824 8607), across Victoria St. from Garden Pl. Open M and Th-F 9am-4:30pm, Tu-W 9:30am-4:30pm. Many banks and **ATMs** dot the downtown area.

Police: (☎858 6200), on Bridge St.

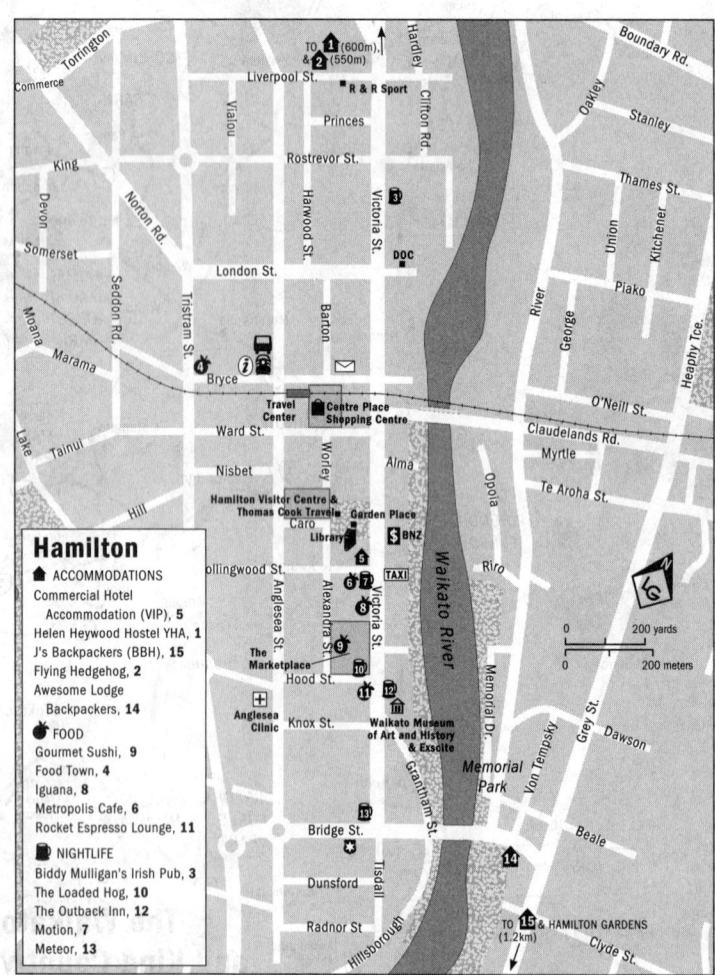

Hamilton

▲ ACCOMMODATIONS
Commercial Hotel Accommodation (VIP), **5**
Helen Heywood Hostel YHA, **1**
J's Backpackers (BBH), **15**
Flying Hedgehog, **2**
Awesome Lodge Backpackers, **14**

🍴 FOOD
Gourmet Sushi, **9**
Food Town, **4**
Iguana, **8**
Metropolis Cafe, **6**
Rocket Espresso Lounge, **11**

🍺 NIGHTLIFE
Biddy Mulligan's Irish Pub, **3**
The Loaded Hog, **10**
The Outback Inn, **12**
Motion, **7**
Meteor, **13**

HAMILTON ■ 145

Medical Services: Hamilton Pharmacy, 750 Victoria St. (☎834 3444). Open daily 8am-10pm. **Anglesea Clinic** (☎858 0800), at the corner of Thackeray and Anglesea St. Open 24hr. **Waikato Hospital** (☎839 8899), on Pembroke St.
Internet Access: The **library** (☎838 6826) has connections: $6 for the first 30min., $4 each additional 30min. Open M-F 9am-8:30pm, Sa 9am-4pm, Su noon-3:30pm. The **Visitors Center** charges $2 per 15min., $3 per 30min., $5 per hr.
Post Office: 36 Bryce St. (☎838 2233). Open M-F 8:30am-5pm.

ACCOMMODATIONS

Hamilton's hostels lack flashy incentives to lure guests and they are spread out over town, so call ahead and arrange a ride. During National Fieldays in June (see **Sights and Activities,** p. 146), prior bookings are essential.

Helen Heywood YHA Hostel, 1190 Victoria St. (☎838 0009; fax 838 0837; yhahamil@yha.org.nz). Heading north on Victoria St., it's on the right. Quiet and reserved, this utilitarian 24-bed YHA rests riverside with a deck to enjoy the quiet. Internet. Laundry. Reception 8-10am and 4-8pm. Dorms $21; singles $30; twins and doubles $50. ❸

J's Backpackers (BBH), 8 Grey St. (☎856 8934; www.jsbackpackers.co.nz), in residential East Hamilton, only 2 houses north of SH1 on the east side of the street, more than 1km from downtown. A petite house with a sunken kitchen/lounge and impeccable restrooms. Free bike use with 2-night stay, otherwise $5. Internet. Laundry. Linen $2. Free pick-up. Dorms $17-19; twins $40. ❷

Awesome Lodge Backpackers/Parklands City Hotel (VIP), 24 Bridge St. (☎838 2461; fax 834 3342; awesome_lodge@hotmail.com), across the bridge from Victoria St.; it's just a 5min. stumble from the nightlife. Free pick-up. Laundry. Overpriced but convenient breakfast $5-15. Dorms $20; singles $30; twins $55; motel options $70-100. ❷

Flying Hedgehog, 1157 Victoria St. (☎839 2800; fax 834 0098; flyinghedgehog@xtra.co.nz), just south of the YHA and across the street. The draw of the peppy rodent logo is questionable, but the no-frills rooms are comfortable. Dorms $20; motel suites $25 per person, $80 per unit. Ask about long-term rates. ❷

Commercial Hotel Accommodation (VIP), 287 Victoria St. (☎839 4993; fax 834 2389; commercial.hotel@clear.net.nz). This renovated vintage hotel has private rooms along a long, dim corridor, 2 neighborhood bars/clubs, and a restaurant. Lounge has Sky TV. Laundry. Singles $45-50; doubles $60-70. ❹

FOOD

Universities mean students, and students mean cheap food. Droves of ethnic restaurants run along Victoria St., mostly between Hood St. and Garden Pl. **Food Town,** at the corner of Bryce and Tristram St., is the most central market. (☎838 2739. Open M-W and Sa-Su 7:30am-8pm, Th-F 7:30am-9pm.)

Iguana, 203 Victoria St. (☎834 2280). One of Hamilton's hippest, most creative cuisiniers. The pizzas ($17-23) and salads ($10-16) come in heaping portions. Open M-F 10am-late, Sa-Su 9am-late. No reservations; very busy F-Sa around 7:30pm. ❸

Metropolis Cafe, 211 Victoria St. (☎834 2081). Recently voted the country's best cafe, "Metro" serves mostly wine and coffee but delivers items like steamed mussels in lime, Riesling, and butter broth ($9). High ceilings and metal-edged interior borders craft a sleek urban feel. Open M-F 10am-midnight, Sa-Su 9:30am-midnight. ❷

Gourmet Sushi (☎838 3500), in the Marketplace on Hood St., has fresh fish to go. Vegetarian rolls under $1; inventive tofu-wrapped rice pieces or a small selection of fish rolls and sashimi $1.50-2. Open M-Sa 10:30am-4:30pm. ❶

IN RECENT NEWS

MAIZE MATTERS

Although it may seem like any other crop, the experimental corn growing in some Waitomo fields contributed to the outcome of New Zealand's 2002 election. Host to test-crops of genetically engineered (GE) maize, Waitomo is one of the few New Zealand sites permitted to grow the modified seeds. Legislation passed by Parliament in 2001 created a moratorium that prohibits the commercial release of GE crops until Fall 2003.

The GE debate may be more prominent in New Zealand than anywhere else in the world. The nation's Green Party has continuously voiced its strong opposition to the release of GE crops, declaring that it would boycott any government coalition that supported lifting the ban. The popular Labour party, Green's traditional ally, has advocated lifting the ban, citing the economic advantages of GE crops. Proponents of GE argue that a GE boycott would make New Zealand a nation of Luddites, out of pace with the rest of the technological world.

In the 2002 election, the Greens did not receive enough votes to uphold the GE ban. As a result, Labour has allied with more conservatively-minded parties, making the introduction of commercial GE crops to New Zealand appear inevitable. Recent scientific studies indicate that GE crops could overrun all other varieties, rendering impossible the Green ambition to make New Zealand 100% Organic by 2020. As much as New Zealand desires to preserve its natural image, the economic benefits appear to outweigh environmental concern.

Rocket Espresso Lounge (☎839 6422), at the corner of Victoria and Hood St. Potent espresso ($3) provides inertia, heavenly muffins ($2.50) set you in orbit, and delicious panini ($6) complete your mission. Open daily 7:30am-4pm. ❶

ENTERTAINMENT AND NIGHTLIFE

With live music venues, university bars, Irish pubs, and two movie theaters from which to choose, there's plenty to do at night in Hamilton. Hamilton is home to numerous live theaters, many affiliated with Waikato University. The most dynamic and impressive is the **Meteor**, 1 Victoria St. (☎834 2472), a versatile space for performances, raves, and other community events. The **Riverlea Theatre** (☎856 5450 or 0800 800 192) has a more continuous theatrical schedule. When in doubt, tap into the scene with *City Happenings*, available at the Visitors Center.

Motion, 270 Victoria St. (☎834 0230), across from the Commercial Hotel Accommodation, tucked away in an alley. Enter through the right-hand door and descend into the basement. Black lighting with red highlights sets a mood for house, drum 'n' bass, and trance on weekends. Th Hip hop. Cover F-Sa $2. Open W-Sa 10pm-3am or later.

The Outback Inn, 141 Victoria St. (☎839 6354). Waikato U's students try to memorize all 102 shooters ($5.50 each). Vegetarians beware: on weekends, this is a beefy meat market where sawdust floors are more for sanitation than ambience. Open M 5-11pm, Tu-Sa noon-3am, Su noon-11pm.

The Loaded Hog, 27 Hood St. (☎839 2727). DJs' Top 40 tunes spill out into the street from this hog heaven. Torches out front contribute to an "alcohol *Survivor*" feel, as do $2.50 handles (W-Th). Open M-Tu 10:30am-10:30pm, W 10:30am-1am, Th-Sa 10:30am-3am, Su 11am-2am.

Biddy Mulligan's Irish Pub, 742 Victoria St. (☎839 0306). Somewhat removed from the University and packed with older locals on weeknights. Th DJs play '60s-'80s hits. Irish music F-Sa. Open Tu and Su 11am-11pm, W 11am-midnight, Th-Sa 11am-2am.

SIGHTS AND ACTIVITIES

A walk through the **Hamilton Gardens** is a highlight of the many cerebral diversions in town. Its historically-themed gardens are more than green; the enlightening and enlivening Japanese tea garden has a pleasant picnic pavilion, and, in the Modernist Garden, Marilyn Monroe's shining visage looks down upon strollers. (☎856 3200; www.hamiltongardens.co.nz.

Grounds open 7:30am-sunset.) At the **Waikato Museum of Art and History,** at the corner of Victoria and Grantham St., you can admire towering Maori carvings, an epic kauri wood canoe, and rotating exhibits. (☎ 838 6606; www.waikatomuseum.org.nz. Open daily 10am-4:30pm. Admission by donation.) Next door, the Waikato Society of Arts showcases a variety of exhibits at **Artspost,** 120 Victoria St. (☎ 839 3857. Open M-Sa 10am-4:30pm, Su 11am-4:30pm.)

Not surprisingly, much of the recreation in Hamilton happens around the river. Paths on either side are ideal for joggers and cyclists. The paddle-wheel replica, **M.V. Waipa Delta,** launches three trips per day, Thursday to Sunday. The luncheon cruise (12:30-2pm, $35) and afternoon tea trip (3-4pm, $20) are cheaper, although the dinner trip (7-10pm, $49) features live entertainment. (☎ 854 7813 or 0800 472 3353; www.waipadelta.co.nz. Book ahead on weekends.)

From June 11-14, 2003, 120,000 people will descend on tiny Mystery Creek (situated between Hamilton and Cambridge) for the ⊠**National Fieldays,** the Southern Hemisphere's largest A&P (agricultural and pastoral) show. With chainsaw demonstrations, head-to-head tractor pulls, and a fashion show of recycled farm material clothing, stereotypes of the simple farmer will be shaken. (☎ 843 4497. $12, children $6. Book hostels at least 1 month in advance.) **Balloons Over Waikato,** an awe-inspiring hot-air festival, takes place in early April (☎ 839 6677; www.balloonnz.co.nz). For information on this and other events in the area, contact **Events Hamilton** (☎ 838 6945; www.hamiltonevents.co.nz).

CAMBRIDGE ☎ 07

Nestled in the middle of thoroughbred country, Cambridge (pop. 13,000) is the genteel country-neighbor of Hamilton and Raglan, displaying the polished civility (and old money) of its English ancestry. Priding itself upon its reputation as the "town of trees," Cambridge roots itself firmly by the banks of the Waikato River and branches out to farm plots that speckle the surrounding volcanic hills.

🚍 **TRANSPORTATION. InterCity** runs daily to: **Auckland** (2½hr., 16 per day, $32) via **Hamilton** (30min., $10); **Rotorua** (1hr., 7 per day, $23); **Taupo** (2½hr., 8 per day, $40); and **Wellington** (8½hr., 3 per day, $80). **Guthreys** (☎ 0800 759 999) runs to: **Rotorua** (2hr., 8 per day, $20); **Auckland** (2½hr., 4 per day, $27); and **Taupo** (2hr., 12:55pm, $35). **Cambridge Taxis** operate **24hr.** (☎ 827 5999). **Four Seasons Mowers and Cycles,** 42 Victoria St. (☎/fax 827 6763), rents bikes for $40 per day. Although *Let's Go* doesn't recommend it, many **hitchhikers** headed to Hamilton walk along Hamilton Rd. (which becomes SH1) and stick their thumbs out before the 50kph sign.

🛈 **ORIENTATION AND PRACTICAL INFORMATION.** Cambridge is 24km east of Hamilton on **SH1.** The **Waikato River** runs through town, and sunken **Te Kouto Lake** is a short walk from the **village green.** The **bus station** is on Lake St., behind the **Visitors Center.** The **Cambridge Information Centre** is at the corner of Victoria and Queen St. (☎ 823 3456. M-F 9am-5pm, Sa-Su 10am-4pm.) Other services include: **BNZ,** 51-53 Victoria St. (open M-F 9am-4:30pm); the **police,** 18 Dick St. (☎ 827 5531), across from the town square; **Clayton's Pharmacy,** down Victoria St. from the town center (☎ 827 7358; open M-Th 8:30am-5:30pm, F 8:30am-6pm, Sa 9am-noon); **Waikato Hospital** (☎ 839 8899), on Pembroke St; **Leamington Health and Medical Centre,** 127 Shakespeare St. (☎ 827 5959), with a forwarding service to the **24hr.** on-call doctor; **Internet access** at the **library,** 23 Wilson St. (☎ 827 5403; open M and Th 9am-5pm, Tu 9:30am-5pm, W and F 9am-8pm, Sa 9:30am-noon; $10 per hr.) and at the **Cambridge Country Store** (see **Sights and Activities,** below) for $3 per 15min. or $5 per 30min.; and the **post office,** 43 Victoria St. (open M-F 9am-5pm, Sa 9am-noon).

148 ■ THE WAIKATO AND KING COUNTRY

ACCOMMODATIONS. You can taste rural life in the middle of the five-acre hobby farm at the **Cambridge Country Lodge (VIP) ❷**, 20 Peake Rd., 2km north of Cambridge on SH1. The lodge is a series of adjacent units converted from stables into rooms with comfy beds. (☎/fax 827 8373. Free linen. Free pick-up and drop-off. 2- to 4-bed dorms $18; twins and doubles $38; self-contained units $60 for 2, extra person $15.) The other cheap option in town, the **National Hotel ❸**, at the corner of Lake and Alpha St., is around the block from the bus station. Pressed tin ceilings and intricate woodwork accent the 14 rooms; some have balconies overlooking Victoria St. The hotel has a bar and casino. (☎ 827 6731; fax 827 3450. Singles $30; twins and doubles $60.)

FOOD AND NIGHTLIFE. None of the dining options in Cambridge compare with a picnic on the shores of Lake Te Koutu. **Countdown Foods,** at the corner of Kirkwood and Lake St., is the place to stock up on groceries. (☎ 827 7606. Open daily 8am-8pm.) **Fran's Cafe ❶**, 62c Victoria St., has antique tea pots and country crafts on display. In the amorous confines of the back courtyard, you might fall in love with Fran's vegetarian lasagna ($4) or the sumptuous desserts. (☎ 827 3946. Open M-F 7am-5pm, Sa 7am-3pm.) **Prince Albert English Pub ❷**, 75 Victoria St., in the Victoria Plaza, has more substantial fare. In the evenings, those who come out to play in Cambridge play here. (☎ 827 7900. Pints $4.50. Open M-W 11am-10pm, Th-F 11am-2am, Sa 10am-2am, Su 10am-10pm. Bar meals daily 11am-2pm and 5-9pm.)

SIGHTS AND ACTIVITIES. Cambridge is well-known for being a stud area. Hold your horses, folks: "stud area" means it's a district for thoroughbred horse breeding. Add the antiquing and artisanship, and it's not surprising that this area has a reputation for being on its high horse; such pastimes regularly attract the moneyed elite of Auckland for weekends of indulgence.

Equine activities lie a bit afield; a walk or bike ride down **Racecourse Road** in Cambridge will take you past many stud, deer, and other hobby farms. Those 18 and over can slap money down on the pony of their choice at the renowned **Cambridge Raceway,** 47 Taylor St., about a 6min. drive from town. (☎ 827 5506; www.cambridgeraceway.co.nz. Contact the raceway for schedules. Closed in July. Basic stand ticket $4.) **Cambridge Thoroughbred Lodge,** on SH1 6km south of Cambridge, offers special horse shows that encourage audience participation. Many famous New Zealand race and show horses are quartered here. (☎ 827 8118; www.cambridgethoroughbredlodge.co.nz. Open daily 10:30am-4pm for casual tours. Show runs Tu-Su 10:30am. $12, children $5, families $25.) To ogle the studs working out, head to **Matamata Raceway** (☎ 888 8898), 35min. by car from town, New Zealand's largest thoroughbred training center. Eat breakfast (5-7:30am) while watching jockeys train the horses.

Closer to town, the **Cambridge Country Store,** 92 Victoria St., flags down passing tourists and vends a selection of Kiwi souvenirs inside its 1898 church frame. (☎ 827 8715. Open daily 8:30am-5:30pm; in winter M-Sa 8:30am-5pm, Su 9am-5pm.) More interesting and well worth a look is **Tribal Art Collectors & Traders,** 89 Victoria St., which feels museum-like with its amazing tribal masks, but everything is for sale. (☎ 827 8848. Open M-F 10am-5pm, Sa 10am-1pm.) Saturday afternoons from October to May, **cricket matches** often cover the lawn in the town square.

The nickname "Town of Trees" pays homage to the arboreal splendor cultivated by locals since Cambridge's founding. The **Cambridge Tree Trust** maintains the many "Tree Trails" around Lake Te Koutu. **Walking tracks,** accessible from the Victoria St. bridge, dart between riverbank and residential road on both sides of the water. To observe the green canopy from above, climb to the top of **Sanitarium Hill.** Even wetter than Te Koutu, the larger **Lake Karapiro** lies 15km out of town towards Rotorua. **Flatout Watersports,** at the lake, offers various float trips, mainly down the Waikato River just beyond the dam, as well as a nighttime glowworm trip. (☎ 827 8286; www.flatoutkayaks.co.nz. Glowworm trip in summer 7-11:30pm. $45.)

RAGLAN ☎ 07

The inhabitants of the small coastal town of Raglan (pop. 3500) take relaxation and a "no worries" lifestyle seriously. The left-handed break at Manu Bay is considered one of the world's finest, and short of experiencing it first-hand (which is very dangerous for all but experts), it is best appreciated in its full splendor in the classic 1966 film *The Endless Summer*. Kick back with the locals or join the stampede of surfers from around the world that cruise here each summer.

TRANSPORTATION

The only **public transport** service to Raglan are the **Pavlovich buses,** with a departure schedule designed for those who live on the coast but work or study in Hamilton. Buses head to **Hamilton** from West Raglan, pausing right in front of the Visitors Center about 10min. later. There is no weekend service, but a weekend in Raglan might be just what you need if you're *that* concerned about keeping to a schedule. (☎ 856 4579. M-F 3-4 per day, $5.50.) Although *Let's Go* does not recommend it, **hitchhiking** is practiced regularly along SH23, at the edge of town before the traffic picks up to 100kph. The favorite spots are the top end of Bow St. by the water tower (look for the giant surfing mural) and at the Te Uku outpost dairy. Out towards Whale Bay, many show the thumb at the Stewart St. church.

ORIENTATION AND PRACTICAL INFORMATION

Forty-eight kilometers of mountain road **(SH23)** winding around extinct volcanoes separate Raglan from Hamilton. The town rests in the harbor, 6km from the coastline and the good surfing points. The **Raglan Visitor Information Centre,** 4 Wallis St., lies near the intersection with Bow St. Call for weather and road conditions, as well as high tide information. (☎ 825 0556; fax 825 0557. Open M-F 10am-5pm, Sa-Su 10am-4pm. Go next door to the council office if no one is there.) **Volunteer opportunities** can be found at the **Whaingaroa Environment Centre** (☎ 825 7382), on Bow St. across from the bank. Come here to plant trees and improve trails with organizations like **Friends of Wainui Reserve, Whaingaroa Harbour Care,** and **DOC.**

Exchange currency or use the **ATM** at **WestPac Trust Bank,** at the top of Bow St. (☎ 825 8579. Open daily 9 or 9:30am-4:30pm.) The **Raglan Surf Co.,** 3 Wainui Rd., rents surfboards for $35 per day and wetsuits for $20 per day. (☎ 825 8988. Open daily 9:30am-5pm.) **Gag Surf Shop,** behind the video store, also hires gear. (☎ 825 8702. Boards $30 per day, $45 per 24hr.; wetsuits $10 per day. Open daily 10am-6pm.) For **daily surf conditions,** call Raglan Surf Co. or listen to "The Rock" 93 FM.

Other services include: the **police** (☎ 825 8200), in a little clapboard house on Nero St.; **Raglan Pharmacy and Lotto,** for medicine or a chance at millions of dollars (☎ 825 8164; open M-F 9am-5pm, Sa 9am-7pm); **After-Hours Doctors** (☎ 825 0007); **Raglan Medical Centre,** 2 Wallis St. (☎ 825 8822); **West Coast Health** (☎ 825 0114); **Internet access** at **Raglan Video,** 9a Bow St. (☎ 825 0008; $5 per 30min.; open daily 10am-8:30pm) or the **library,** across from the Visitors Center ($5 per 45min.; open M-F 9am-5pm, Sa 9am-12:30pm); and the **post office,** 39 Bow St., next to the town hall (☎ 825 8007; open M-F 9am-5pm).

ACCOMMODATIONS AND CAMPING

Raglan's wee population increases by 50% during the summer. In the winter, expect to find a number of visitors who came for a weekend and stayed for the season, as the surf is good year-round. Surfers are known for sleeping in their cars in the parking lots at the beaches and Manu Bay.

Raglan Backpackers and Waterfront Lodge, 6 Nero St. (☎825 0515). Sharp rooms open onto an airy inner courtyard with hammock, flowers, and surfers lazing in the sun. Free kayak and bike use. Surfboards $10 per day. Surf lessons $25. Drop-off to beaches and walking tracks. Dorms $16; twins and doubles $38. Cash only. ❷

Raglan Wagon Cabins (☎825 8268), on Wainui Rd. 6km from the city center. With the raging surf of Manu Bay only 2km away, this is a favorite with surfers. The brightly-painted retired railway cars offer great views of the bay and of Raglan. Linen $10. Dorms $20; self-contained cottages $80 for 2; tent sites $10. ❷

Sleeping Lady Accommodations (VIP) (☎/fax 825 7873; www.raglansurfing-school.co.nz), up Wainui Rd. just past the Whale Bay roundabout on the left. This converted youth camp is run by Raglan Surfing School (see **Sun, Surf, and Sand, p. 150**) and offers a range of accommodation, when not booked ahead by large groups (call ahead). Excellent location and outdoor activity options. Free pick-up in town for surfing patrons. Laundry. Dorms $21-22; motel-style suites up to $120; tent sites $10. ❸

The Raglan Kopua Holiday Park (☎825 8283; fax 825 8284), over the footbridge on Marine Pde., next to the Aerodrome and airstrip. The vast area can accommodate 2000 travelers and fills up during the Christmas holidays. Tent sites $8, in winter $7; powered sites $9/$8; chalets $24/$20 for 2. ❶

FOOD AND NIGHTLIFE

Molasses ❷, on Bow St., is a prime brunch spot, offering Green Eggs and Ham ($12) for your inner child and a Hangover Cure (priceless) for your remorseful adult. Occasional concerts by local and regional bands. (☎825 7229. Open daily 8am-late.) Farmers and surfers chow down at the **Tongue and Groove ❸**, at the corner of Bow St. and Wainui Rd. The veggie-friendly menu includes breakfast until 2pm ($5-10) and dinner mains beginning at 6pm ($15). On weekend nights, the Tongue occasionally grooves to live music or DJs. (☎825 0027. Open daily 8:30am-late; kitchen closes at 9pm.) In 1847, scores of prefab kauri wood cottages were deposited in Raglan in anticipation of a crush of immigrants. One of the only units remaining is now **Vinnie's ❷**, 7 Wainui Rd., having progressed from church, to school, to town hall, to pizza pad and smoothie bar. Now the menu covers all manner of tastes (venison burger with apricot sauce $6.50; fruit smoothies $4-5). (☎825 7273. Open M-F 10:30am-8:30pm, Sa-Su 8am-8:30pm; in winter W-Su only.) Helpings of fresh fish for eat-in or takeaway can be found at **Seagull's Seafoods ❶**, around the corner from the Visitors Center, where live jazz charms the house every other Sunday. (☎825 8022. Open daily 8am-late.) Raglan's only bar, **The Harborview Hotel,** adjacent to the hotel of the same name in the center of town, is a popular local hangout. (☎825 8010. Open daily 7pm-1am; closes earlier on slow nights.) **Petchells Four Square,** 16-18 Bow St., is a market, auto supply, and sundry shop all in one. (☎825 8300. Open M-F 7:30am-5pm, Sa-Su 7:30am-4pm.)

SUN, SURF, AND SAND

Whether you're seeking an "endless summer" or the dead quiet of winter, Raglan's black-sand beaches are worth the trip. Catching a ride to the coast is easy with one of the many beach-bound vehicles in town. If you have a car, make sure you lock it while you are at the beach; **theft** has been a problem in recent years.

Of the many choices for beach fun, **Te Kopua Beach** is the most accessible, reached via the footbridge at the base of Bow St. Accessibility has its price, though, as the beach is overrun with families and their screaming children in the summer. Te Kopua also occupies a perfect harbor location for windsurfing. The less crowded **Cox's Bay** and **Puriri Park (Aro Aro Bay),** to the east of the town center,

RAGLAN ■ 151

are ideal for children and picnics. Walk along Wallis St. away from the Visitors Center to reach them. Find an open shoreline with surfing and swimming at **Ocean Beach (Ngaranui Beach);** the strong gusts also allow good windsurfing. Watch out for powerful undertows; only the west end of the beach is patrolled by lifeguards.

Beginning surfers should start at **Ocean Beach,** where the surf is a bit less challenging and the sand bottoms are much more forgiving. Only experts head to **Manu Bay (Waireke)** for world-class breaks. Farther down the coast is **Whale Bay (Whaanga),** where green surf and rocky shore are accessible by a walking path from the cul-de-sac at the end of Calvert Rd. The surfing here is awesome in autumn, and there are often professional surfing competitions in April and May. Farther down the coast, **Ruapuke Beach** offers rugged coastline, good surfcasting, and the chance to beat the crowds, even in summer. Of course, your car (or someone else's) will have to endure 18km of winding, unsealed roads to find solitude.

For first-time surfers, instruction on both technique and water safety is extraordinarily important. Perfect for the determined and patient beginner, Jeremy, owner of **Raglan Backpackers** (see p. 150), offers lessons to his guests ($25) as well as a fiberglass board rental. For those more interested in organized group learning, **Raglan Surfing School** gives 2hr. surfing lessons for $70 (equipment provided; 10am and 2:30pm). They also rent out surfboards, boogie boards, swimming flippers, and wet suits by the hour. (☎ 825 7873. Open 10am-6pm daily.)

If you're in search of a holy grail (or a red herring), wander between Manu Bay and Ocean Beach in hopes of discovering the elusive **Tattooed Rocks.** Years ago, an unknown artist chiseled his way to local fame by sculpting two large rocks on the beach. They are only accessible at low tide, and some locals have searched for years without success. If it rains, rent *The Endless Summer* and wallow in self-pity, or call the **Raglan Museum** on Wainui Rd. to see the photographic chronicle of the town's surfing legacy. (☎ 825 8129. Open 1-3:30pm or by appointment. Free.)

OTHER OUTDOOR ACTIVITIES

Although surfers might lead you to believe otherwise, Raglan has more to offer than the ocean. If you can't catch a wave, capture a spot on the slower (in fact, totally inactive) volcanoes of **Mt. Karioi** and **Mt. Pirongia** in **Pirongia Forest Park.** One glance at Mt. Karioi's feminine silhouette and it's no wonder that in Maori legend it is referred to as "the sleeping lady" (look SW from town in order to see her). With curves in all of the right places, Mt. Karioi's **Whaanga Road** wraps around the mountain's coastal side, making for terrific mountain biking and interesting driving. Refrain from careening around curves during the week—the one-lane road carries a considerable amount of traffic, and vehicles seem to be perpetually flying over the edge. To find the walk to the top of Mt. Karioi, follow the Whaanga Rd. all the way to **Te Toto Gorge.** Park in the first available lot on the beach side just across from the signs, and begin the walk from that side of the gorge. With some hairy spots of steep muddy climbing and ladder stretches, this climb to and from the peak (return 6hr.; return 4hr. to "the lookout," a false summit on the mountain) requires good footwear, is quite scenic, and not often traveled.

Freshwater wonders also await. The locals are mighty proud of **Bridal Veil Falls** and the fact that it is higher than its Niagara counterpart. Thirteen kilometers off the main road between Hamilton and Raglan, its thin, delicate spray is best photographed from the lookout, a 20min. walk from the carpark on Kawhia Rd. The hike to the base is a steep one, but the pool is swimmable. Soak out many of life's aches and pains at the **Waingaro Hot Springs,** north of Raglan on SH22. (☎ 825 4761. Open F-Su 9am-9pm. $6.) With the proper DOC permits, you can also hunt wild pigs or fly-fish for rainbow trout in the **Kaniwhaniwha Stream.**

OTOROHANGA ☎ 07

The literal meaning of the town's name, "food multiplied for the long journey," originates with the legend of a great Maori chief who paused here to multiply his meager supplies, with a few magical incantations, into enough to sustain his continued trek. Today, Otorohanga (pop. 2600) is known for its first-rate bird house (and Wiki, the town's giant kiwi) and a feisty town spirit.

TRANSPORTATION. The **train station** is on Wahanui Crescent. **TranzScenic** goes to: **Auckland** (2½hr., 2 per day, $40-45) via **Hamilton** (1hr., $19-21); and **Wellington** (8hr., 2 per day, $95-106) via **Palmerston North** (6hr., $68-77). **InterCity** heads to: **Auckland** (3hr., 2-3 per day, $42) via **Hamilton** (1hr., $19) and **Wellington** (8hr., M-F and Su 12:05pm, $91) via **Wanganui** (5hr., $46). **Dalroy Express** runs service to **Auckland** (2½hr., 1 per day, $33), and to **Hawera** (3½hr., 1 per day, $45). To get to **Waitomo**, take Bill Millar's **Waitomo Shuttle** from the Visitors Center or any accommodation. Informative history of the area is given on request and is free of charge during the 15min. ride. (☎ 0800 808 279. 5 per day, $8.) Bill also operates **Otorohanga Taxis** for your other local transport needs. (☎ 0800 808 279. Runs M-Th and Su 8am-11pm, F-Sa 8am-1am.) Although *Let's Go* does not recommend it, **hitchhiking** is said to be best from the bypass road, Huiputea Dr., north of town.

ORIENTATION AND PRACTICAL INFORMATION. Maniapoto Street is the central road in town where most business takes place. The **bus station** is at Wahanui Crescent and Maniapoto St., right next to the Visitors Center. While at the **Visitor Information Centre,** 57 Maniapoto St., keep an eye out for Wiki, the giant kiwi who greets visitors. (☎ 873 8951; fax 873 6132; www.otorohanga.co.nz. Open M-F 9am-5:30pm, Sa-Su 10am-4pm.) **WestPac Trust Bank,** on Maniapoto St., has one of the town's **ATMs.** Fill up at one of the **petrol stations** in town, as there is no petrol station in Waitomo. Other services include: the **police,** 4 Ballance St. (☎ 873 7399); the **doctor on call** (☎ 873 8399), who can be reached all day; **Internet access** at the **Visitors Center** ($2.50 for 15min.) and the **public library,** set back in the middle of Maniapoto St. across from the ANZ bank. (☎ 873 7175; $10 per hr; open M-Th 10am-5pm, F 10am-6pm, Sa 10am-noon); and the **post office,** inside King's Paper Plus, on Maniapoto St. (☎ 873 8816; open M-F 8:30am-5pm, Sa 9am-2pm.)

ACCOMMODATIONS AND FOOD. At the **Oto-Kiwi Lodge (BBH) ❷,** 1 Sangro Crescent, the energetic hosts welcome "backpackers, globetrotters, and musicians" to their compound at the end of the cul-de-sac. Signs point the way from the north end of Maniapoto St. (☎ 873 6022; fax 873 6066; otokiwi@xtra.co.nz. Internet. Laundry. Dorms $17-18; doubles $40-42; beds in recording studio $12; tent sites $8.50.) For hotel lodgings, try the adequate brown units in the **Royal Hotel ❹,** at the corner of Turongo and Te Kanawa St. Check in at the bar and pick up some cheap grub. (☎ 873 8129; fax 873 8744. Free laundry. Singles $43; doubles $56.) On the bypass road east of town lies **Otorohanga Holiday Park ❶,** 12 Huiputea Dr., a well-groomed facility just across the railroad tracks. With a nice lawn, ensuite cabin options, and a well-equipped fitness center ($6 for guests), this place suits a wider crowd than just holiday park regulars. (☎ 873 7253; fax 873 7256; www.kiwiholidaypark.co.nz. Caravans and tent sites $10; simple cabin $30 for 2; self-contained unit $57 for 2, extra person $10-15.)

Most days in Otorohanga, finding a good feed is difficult. However, locals take pride in their town's newest establishment, a **Woolworth's,** at the southern end of Maniapoto St. (☎ 873 7378. Open daily 7am-10pm.) During the day, stop at **Toni's ❶,** 13 Maniapoto St., for tempting homemade goodies to top off your tasty $3 sandwich. (☎ 873 6611. Open M-F 8:30am-4pm, Sa 9am-3pm.) **Regent Cafe & Bar ❶,** across the street from and slightly north of the Visitors Center, caters to stopping tour buses and offers a large sampling of cafeteria-quality sandwiches, pies, and coffee. (☎873 7370. Open daily 6:30am-5pm; light meals F-Sa 5-9pm, Su 6-9pm.)

◎ SIGHTS. Let no one tell you otherwise—Otorohanga is for the birds, but that's not necessarily a bad thing. No stop in Otorohanga is complete without a visit to the **Otorohanga Kiwi House and Native Bird Park**, on Alex Telfer Dr. Although the birds are only awake in the day for 4hr., a sighting in the "moonlit" kiwi house is guaranteed; kiwis stay awake in shifts throughout the day. New Zealand's original walk-through aviary also houses tuataras, geckos, and cave wetas. Don't look up. (☎873 7391; www.kiwihouse.org.nz. Open daily Sept.-May 9am-5pm; June-Aug. 9am-4pm. Last entry 30min. before closing. $9, BBH/YHA $8, children $3. Kiwi feeding daily 1:30 and 3pm.) The Kiwi House operates a nightly **Kiwi Watch** where off-duty kiwis rest. Bookings before 4pm are essential and group size is restricted. (In summer around 8:45pm; in winter 7:45pm. 1½-2hr. Group size 2-6 people. $15.)

The Visitors Center hopes to sell Otorohanga as the **"Kiwiana capital"** of New Zealand; posted explanations of bits of Kiwi culture appear in every third shop window along Maniapoto St. These informational posters explain such cultural staples as pavlova, "Ches 'n' Dale," gumboots, and the multifaceted word, "kiwi." In the middle of town, in front of the library and next to Regent's, stand pairs of **wooden poles,** carved to depict the history of the Maori people.

WHAREPAPA SOUTH ☎07

As you drive towards the crossroads of Wharepapa South (pop. Y-O-U) and its four or five buildings that pass for a "place on the map," pat yourself on the back for venturing so far afield. Out of the idyllic pastorals tower some incredible ignimbrite (volcanic tuff) crags. These were shipped airmail all the way from Taupo, New Zealand's original post shop, which distributed petrified parcels all over Australasia about two millennia ago. Thanks to this volcanic special delivery, half of the North Island's sport climbing and bouldering lie nearby.

📞🛈 TRANSPORTATION AND PRACTICAL INFORMATION. To reach town and the crags, leave SH3 in Kihikihi and go east on Whitmore Rd. After 9km, turn right on Owairaka Valley Rd., which leads 14km to an intersection with Wharepapa South Rd. This intersection serves as a town center with a store and a cafe. Believe it or not, the **Waitomo Wanderer** (☎349 2509) will make stops here twice daily for pre-booked reservations on its way between **Rotorua** and **Waitomo** (about 8am to Waitomo, 5pm to Rotorua; 1hr.; $20). *Let's Go* does not recommend **hitchhiking,** which can be very difficult because of the area's thin traffic.

As far as services, information, and accommodations go, there are only two hubs in town. A sure-fire way to learn more about climbing in the area is to pay a visit to Bryce at his **Wharepapa Outdoor Centre,** 1424 Owairaka Valley Rd. (☎872 2533; wharerock@xtra.co.nz). With some advance notice, he matches amateurs with professional guides and informs experienced climbers of their equipment needs and route options. There are **no petrol, ATM, police,** or **medical services** in this area. The closest proper municipality is **Te Awamutu,** about 18km away.

🏠🍴 ACCOMMODATIONS AND FOOD. The **Castle Rock Adventure Lodge (BBH/YHA) ❷,** 1250 Owairaka Valley Rd., 2km before the crossroads, caters to outdoor enthusiasts with access to Froggatt Edge, Wharepapa Crags, and two established biking tracks. The sumptuous new lodge boasts luxury amenities and a beautiful deck overlooking the rocks. (☎872 2509 or 0800 225 462; fax 872 2519; jeffrock@ihug.co.nz. Free local calls. Internet. Pool. Dorms $17-21; singles $45; doubles $50; tent sites $6.) Bryce at the **Wharepapa Outdoor Centre** ❷ lets well-maintained rooms to weary climbers. (Dorms $15; private rooms $20 per person.) Also at the center is **Bryce's Cafe** ❶, which offers the best coffee ($3) for kilometers and is the only food service in "town." (☎872 2533. Open daily 9am-4pm.)

♫ CLIMBING. The unique volcanic rock around Wharepapa South can be tricky even for expert climbers, but bolted routes in the most popular areas allow climbers to get accustomed quickly. Most climbing lies on privately owned farmland and climbers need permission from the owner before ascending. Two of the major climbing areas, Wharepapa and Froggatt Edge, are owned by **Castle Rock Adventure Lodge**, whose management charges a $6 fee for access. Castle Rock also offers full-day climbing lessons ($100-120) and bike and equipment hire. In poor weather, bouldering wall in the **Wharepapa Outdoor Centre** is available to the public ($5) and free of charge for guests staying there.

WAITOMO ☎ 07

Back in 1887, Maori chief Tane Tinorau and European surveyor Fred Mace chose to ignore Maori legend and explore the depths of the local river cave. Although no gods were found that day, the two spelunkers were treated to an otherworldly display of bioluminescent blue, courtesy of thousands of glow-worms. Within a year, Tinorau opened the cave for a few visitors to experience the ethereal wonder. One hundred years later, the glowworm population remains stable, but the number of tourists has soared to nearly 500,000, putting this miniscule hamlet (pop. 250) squarely on the map. Every morning, over 50 tour buses roll into town and after a few hours—and several million glow-worms—they cruise right on out again. While most visitors come for the "light show," the unique adventure-caving industry attracts its own crowd to trips at varying degrees of difficulty, low degrees of water temperature, and high degrees of pleasure.

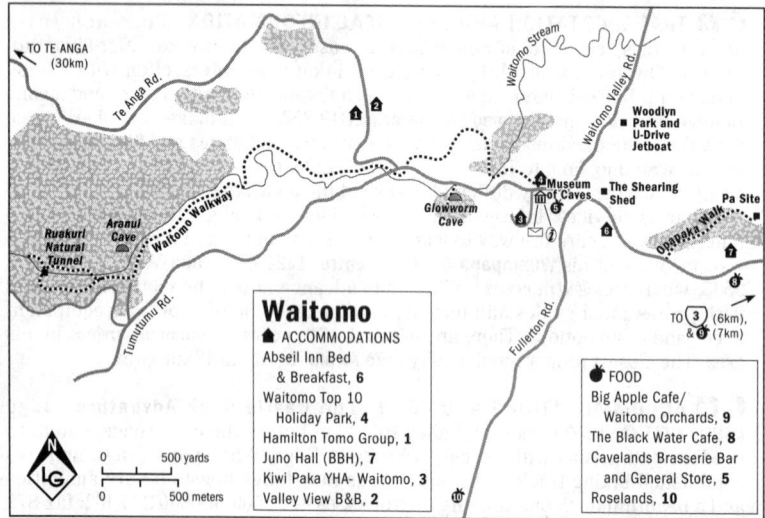

WAITOMO ■ 155

⎕ TRANSPORTATION

Nearly 70% of visitors to the caves arrive by coach, and most transportation schedules accommodate same-day arrival and departure. **InterCity** runs daytrips from **Auckland** (4hr., 9am, $48) and **Rotorua** (4hr., 9am, $40); both returning buses leave at 2pm. **Guthreys** runs to: **Auckland** (4 hr., 1 per day, $38); **Rotorua** (2½hr., 1 per day, $38); and **Wellington** (8hr., 11:15am, $99). The **Waitomo Wanderer** offers service between **Rotorua** (departs 7:15am) and **Waitomo** (departs 4pm), with a possible pre-arranged stop at **Wharepapa South**. (☎349 2509. 2hr.; $30, return $55.) The **Waitomo Shuttle** is the best option for those making **InterCity** or **TranzScenic** connections in Otorohanga. Pick-up from any Waitomo hostel is included. (☎0800 808 279; fax 873 8214. 15min.; 5 per day; $8, by arrangement $18.) Although *Let's Go* does not recommend it, **hitchhiking** from Waitomo is reportedly best accomplished by standing at the junction of Waitomo Caves Rd. and SH3.

⎕ PRACTICAL INFORMATION

The Museum of Caves Information Centre is inside the entrance to the **Museum of Caves** in Waitomo village. Aside from booking any cave-related activity you desire, the helpful staff will also give detailed firsthand accounts of exactly how wet you'll get and how many glowworms you'll see. The **post office** and a shop offering the village's lowest prices on **groceries** and **souvenirs** are inside the Museum, and the town's **ATM** lies just outside, along with **card phones** and **public toilets**. (☎878 7640; fax 878 6184; waitomomuseum@xtra.co.nz. Open daily 8:15am-5pm; Jan.-Feb. 8am-8pm.) For medical help, call the **Otorohanga on-call doctor** (☎873 8399). There is **Internet access** at the **Museum** ($1.50 for 15min., $6 per hr.) and the **Black Water Cafe** (see **Food**, below; $5 per hr.).

⎕⎕ ACCOMMODATIONS AND CAMPING

Despite Waitomo's popularity as a daytrip, accommodations fill rapidly in the summer. Bookings are essential if you plan on spending the night during peak season.

Hamilton Tomo Group (☎878 7442), 2km past the village up Te Anga Rd. Run by a local spelunking club, this is undeniably the coolest place to stay in Waitomo. If you show interest, you may be able to tag along on other guests' spelunking trips. Free laundry. Dorms $12 for 1st night, $10 thereafter. Tent sites available. ❶

Kiwi Paka YHA - Waitomo (☎878 3395; fax 878 3396; waitomo@kiwipaka-yha.co.nz), directly behind Waitomo Caves Tavern. This red-and-gray corrugated metal tank is the most recent (and most gigantic) hostel in town. Internet. On-site cafe. Dorms $20; twins and doubles $50, with bath $60. ❷

Juno Hall (BBH) (☎/fax 878 7649), on Waitomo Caves Rd. 1km from the Visitors Center across from the Black Water Rafting headquarters. Perched on a hill just outside the village proper, Juno feels more isolated than it really is. Free pick-up and drop-off. Laundry. Dorms $18; doubles $44; suites with TV and bath $54; tent sites $10. ❷

Abseil Inn Bed & Breakfast, 709 Waitomo Caves Rd. (☎878 7815; abseilinn@xtra.co.nz), sits atop a hill that requires low gear and some positive thinking to surmount. Hosts Kimba and Brett work as adventure tour guides for the local caves, so ask all the questions you want. Twins $90; doubles $100 for 2, $80 for 1. ❺

Valley View B&B (☎/fax 878 7063; valley123@xtra.co.nz), just up the hill and across the road from Hamilton Tomo Group on Te Anga Rd., 2 km out of town. The comfy beds in this large semi-self-contained unit hold up to 5 easily, and the private lounge (with Sky TV) gives everyone their own space. No full breakfast, but hot drinks, toast, and cereal provided. Singles $45; doubles $70; extra person $20. ❹

Waitomo Top 10 Holiday Park (☎/fax 878 7639; www.waitomopark.co.nz), across the street from the Museum of Caves. Discount vouchers for Waitomo Caves. Laundry. Full linen and towel $5. Budget beds $16; cabins for 2 $35, extra person $10; self-contained units $70 for 2, extra person $12; tent and powered sites $10-11. ❶

FOOD

Grocers in the village overprice their wares; stock up at the markets of Otorohanga, Hamilton, or Rotorua, or at least at the visitors shop. The best meals lie outside of the village proper. If you're stuck in the village hungry, **Cavelands Brasserie and Bar and General Store** ❷, next to the museum, serves breakfast and lunch (☎ 878 7700; open daily 7am-8:30pm; shorter hours in winter).

Roselands (☎ 878 7611). Ironically, the best lunch in town is 5km out of it, up Fullerton Rd. east of the village. The bountiful barbecue buffet ($22) is more than enough for you and a few tour buses. Salad bar prices are negotiable ($12-15). Come after 1:30pm for the best bargains and lightest crowds. Open daily 11:30am-2pm. ❹

Black Water Cafe (☎ 878 7361), 1km east of the village inside Black Water Rafting, has the best prepared food nearby, from large breakfasts ($5-13.50) to fresh lunch items ($3-6). Internet ($5 per hr.) available; hurry out of your wetsuit or face the queue. Open June-Aug. daily 8:30am-4pm; Sept.-May daily 7:30am-5:30pm. ❸

The Big Apple Cafe and **Waitomo Orchards** (☎ 873 8753) are next to each other on SH3, 1 km north of the intersection with Waitomo Caves Rd. Besides free coffee for drivers, cheap produce, and venison burgers ($9), the cafe has a freakish hollow apple structure that visitors can climb for views of the countryside. Cafe open daily 8am-8pm; fruit stand open daily 8:30am-6pm. ❷

SIGHTS

The holes dotting the green pastures around Waitomo are gateways to a mystical world where neither time nor temperature seem to exist—centuries are measured by centimeters of change, and the caves stay dark and cool regardless of conditions outside. New adventure trips are constantly springing up to satisfy growing demand, and some advertise only in Waitomo. Given the labyrinthine array of caving possibilities (climbing, canoeing, strolling, and glowworm watching), it is best to book ahead and to check with the Visitors Center for the latest and greatest.

WAITOMO CAVES. If you are curious to see where all of those tour buses are headed and eager to empty your wallet, visit the cave everyone talks about. Stroll along the stage-like boardwalk beside dramatically lit formations for a theatrical experience. **"The Cathedral"** has served as a venue for the likes of Kenny Rogers, the Vienna Boys' Choir, and Kiwi opera diva Dame Kiri Te Kanawa (see p. 59). The Disney-esque boat ride at the end is breathtaking and probably the only time you'll find silence anywhere in the tourist-filled cave. Hear only the drip of water as the boat slips under a mantle of glowing stars. Midday trips bulge with large coach tours. *(On Waitomo Caves Rd., 500m around the bend west of Waitomo village. Tours every 30min. 9am-5:30pm; in winter 9am-5pm. $24, children $12.)*

WAITOMO ■ 157

ARANUI CAVE. This cave holds a treasure trove of rock formations, and you don't even have to get your feet wet to see them. *(Tours run daily every hr. 10-11am and 1-3pm. $24, children $11. Combination trip with the Waitomo Caves $35, children $10.)*

MUSEUM OF CAVES. Any visit to Waitomo should include a trip to this revamped shrine to all things subterranean. Inside, learn about how the caves were formed, contemplate resident wildlife, and take in a multimedia spelunking experience. Black Water Rafting provides a complimentary museum pass as part of their adventure, and Waitomo Down Under and Long Tomo Rafting will provide one on request. *(☎ 878 7640. Open daily 8:30am-5pm. $5, under 18 free.)*

ADVENTURE CAVING AND SUBTERRANEAN RAFTING

Always go caving with a guide; **never cave solo,** even if you consider yourself an experienced spelunker. Virtually all caves are privately owned, and trespassing can be risky. Before you suit up, you may want to consider testing yourself for claustrophobia—head to the Museum of Caves and try the cave "crawl-through."

OPERATORS

Waitomo Adventures (☎ 878 7788 or 0800 924 866; www.waitomo.co.nz), next door to the Visitors Center, has the greatest variety of adventure caving trips ($70-300). Booking through Auckland Central Backpackers (see p. 85) confers substantial discounts.

Black Water Rafting (☎ 878 6219 or 0800 228 464; fax 878 5190; www.blackwater-rafting.co.nz). Founded in 1987, BWR is the oldest operator. Experienced guides are sometimes called away from tours to perform cave rescues all over New Zealand.

Waitomo Down Under (☎ 878 6577 or 0800 102 605; wdu@xtra.co.nz). WDU offers 4 tours, frequently guided by direct descendants of Tane Tinorau. Trips depart from the WDU building next to the museum. Students and VIP/YHA members 10% discount.

Waitomo Wilderness Tours (☎ 878 7640 or 0800 228 372), an independent operator that runs **Long Tomo Rafting,** offers a less commercial approach and is the best value for limited budgets. Small group size (max. 6) allows trips to be tailored to the individual. Tours daily 11am and 3pm; in winter 9am and 2pm.

TRIPS

Adventure tours in Waitomo cater to all levels of experience and enthusiasm. Standard protocol for caving involves shelling out some bucks and then slapping on a wetsuit and some coveralls (or just the coveralls if it's a "dry" trip), a hard hat with a head lamp, and gumboots. Check to see if you need to bring swimwear, a towel, and shower supplies. Trips that emphasize tubing or rafting are generally tamer than their spelunking brethren.

I AM SCARED OF MY OWN SHADOW

These trips are, first and foremost, beautiful. While you will undoubtedly gasp, it will be from amazement and not from lack of oxygen.

BLACK WATER I. The progenitor of all underwater tubing tours in Waitomo, this trip involves a gentle float and the obligatory glowworm sighting. *(BWR. 3hr., includes ritualistic dressing procedure and post-rafting snack; 5-10 per day; $69.)*

TUMU TUMU TOOBING. Generally only available in the dry summer months, this trip features more caving and is the most adventurous of the gentle trips. Optional jumps and small rapids spice up the float. *(Waitomo Adventures. 4hr., 4 per day, $70.)*

158 ■ THE WAIKATO AND KING COUNTRY

> **STARRY NIGHT** Over the eons, humans have looked heavenward in search of inspiration and answers. Standing inside a glowworm cave, however, the answers might not be what you'd expect. The glowworm (*Arachnocampa luminosa*; in Maori *titiwai*) is actually not a worm at all, but the larva of a fly. After hatching, the baby flies secrete sticky threads (sometimes as many as 70, 1-50cm long) each with a drop of shiny stuff—the worm's waste product, lit up by the light of the bioluminescent larva itself (with the brightness of one-billionth of a watt). After months of trolling with poo, the glowworm undergoes metamorphosis and becomes a fly. Unfortunately, evolution was so busy figuring out how to make the glowworm's stool shine that it forgot to develop its mouth. After only a day or two of adult life—flying, mating, and laying eggs—the fly dies of starvation (or from being oversexed). The next time you gaze up in awe at the bluish stars in the nighttime sky of a cave's ceiling, remember that the speck of light is a maggot fishing for lunch with a glob of excrement. Ain't nature grand?

ADVENTURE I. This trip does provide the standard glowworm float, but a number of artificial structures (ladders, walkways, and a water slide) mar the natural beauty of the cave. *(WDU. Book at least one day in advance. 3hr., about 5 per day, $75.)*

I AM ALLERGIC TO WATER

If you hear someone calling these trips "dry," rest assured they are not talking about their excitement level. More akin to true spelunking, perhaps, than rafting, these trips are a compromise between cave walks and full-on adrenaline.

ADVENTURE II. Abseiling 50m into an absolutely stunning cave known as the "Baby Grand" gives real adventurers a little extra bang for their buck—you can choose to lock off your ropes and then swing, flip, and dangle in mid-air. Don't wear jeans or tight clothes. *(WDU. 2hr., about 4-5 per day, $75.)*

NIGHT ECOTOUR. Basically, it's Adventure II under the cover of darkness. Once you reach the free hang, the lights are turned out for a space walk in a galaxy of glowworms. Again, no jeans or tight clothes. *(WDU. 2hr.; 1 per day upon demand, start time depends on daylight hours; $85.)*

ADVENTURE III. A spelunking extravaganza where guests squeeze, climb, and get grubby with a smile. Bring a towel and soap. *(WDU. 2hr.; $35.)*

BLACK WATER DRY. A family-friendly tour bringing visitors on a rafting journey beneath a canopy of glowworms. *(BWR. 2½ hr.; 3 per day; $35, children $25.)*

I AM A BAD ASS

The next level of cave tours is a cross between being Indiana Jones and being flushed down the loo on a string. These trips all require basic fitness and comfort with tight spaces.

HAGGAS HONKING HOLES. Not for the faint of heart, this the closest you'll get to genuine caving with a commercial operation. "The Honk" lets participants explore caves on Farmer Haggas' property. The action includes three waterfall abseils, plenty of climbing and squeezing, and admirable formations all at a tearing clip. Prepare to get wet, dirty, and exhilarated. *(Waitomo Adventures. Bring swimwear and shower supplies. 4hr., about 2hr. underground; 2 per day; $135.)*

BLACK WATER II. In October 1999, while Daddy was attending the APEX conference in Auckland, Chelsea Clinton and her buddy for the day, the daughter of New

Zealand's Prime Minister, slapped on wetsuits to conquer abseils, waterfalls, rock climbs, and a flying fox. BWII spends 2-3hr. underground, but quite a bit of that is in view of artificial structures. *(BWR. 5hr., 2-3 per day, $140.)*

LONG TOMO RAFTING. This trip is arguably the best value for the money. With a dry abseil, tubing, and glowworming in a natural cave, the comparably low pricetag can't be beat. *(Waitomo Wilderness Tours. 5hr., 2-4 per day, $65.)*

LOST WORLD TRIPS. To say the Lost World Cave is just another cave is like saying that Notre Dame is just another church. In 1906, an awestruck reporter from the *King Country Chronicle* dubbed it "a fairyland without the fairies." **The Lost World Four Hour** is a 100m freehanging abseil into an ethereal world of mist and miniature ferns. Don't wear jeans or tight pants—100m is a long time to endure a wedgie. The most daunting part of the trip is the 30m ladder climb back to civilization. *(Waitomo Adventures. 4hr., 2 per day, $195.)* If you've got the cash, spend it on the **Lost World All Day Epic Adventure.** The 7hr. odyssey begins with the epic abseil, but skips the ladder in favor of swimming, wading, and walking a few kilometers upstream, passing spectacular formations along the way. *(Waitomo Adventures. 7hr.; 1 per day; $300, includes lunch and dinner.)*

AGRICULTURAL AND OTHER ACTIVITIES

THE SHEARING SHED. It's actually not what you think. Each day visitors are treated to a free and unique experience—a shearing show that involves not sheep, but Angora rabbits, native to the Pyrenees but now only surviving in captivity and servility. The fuzzy bunnies are buzzed right before your eyes, but don't feel too sorry for them—they would overheat and die without the regular haircut. *(On Waitomo Caves Rd. ☎ 878 8371. 12:45pm. Free.)*

WOODLYN PARK AND U-DRIVE JETBOAT. Farmer, historian, and globe-trotting sheepshearer Barry Woods puts on an entertaining and authentic **Pioneer Show,** detailing Waitomo's colonial history. Expect animal antics, audience participation, and general agricultural hijinks. *(Turn-off along Waitomo Caves Rd. toward Waitomo village. ☎ 878 6666. Daily 1:30pm; in winter book ahead. $13, children $7, families $38.)* Although travelers inexperienced at piloting a **jetboat** might rename this activity "U-Crash," safety equipment is in place, and the sloping walls of the water course are lined with tires. *(Also at Woodlyn Park. ☎ 878 6666. Open daily 9am-5pm; in summer also 6:30-8pm. Runs available continuously except during the pioneer show. 8 laps $42. Book ahead.)*

BAY OF PLENTY

At the junction of natural wonders, cultural spectacles, and flowing dollars, the Bay of Plenty is one of the North Island's most touristed regions. Land of lakes, geysers, and hot springs, the inland town of Rotorua captivates visitors with its pungent sulfuric smell and its wealth of Maori culture. Along the coast Mt. Maunganui rests on sun-warmed beaches while neighboring Tauranga pulses with nightlife. At the eastern end of the bay, the rough-edged Opotiki opens onto the remote, uncompromising natural beauty of the East Cape.

🕮 BAY OF PLENTY HIGHLIGHTS

FOR SKIN CARE geysers spray, ponds glow, and thermal spas and gurgling mud pools relax, reinvigorate, and exfoliate in **Rotorua's** thermal wonders (see p. 164).

FOR SUSTENANCE a **Maori** *hangi* is a tasty cultural experience (see p. 168).

FOR SANCTUARY White Island, hidden in a perpetual cloud, is an eerie escape from the mainland (see p. 176).

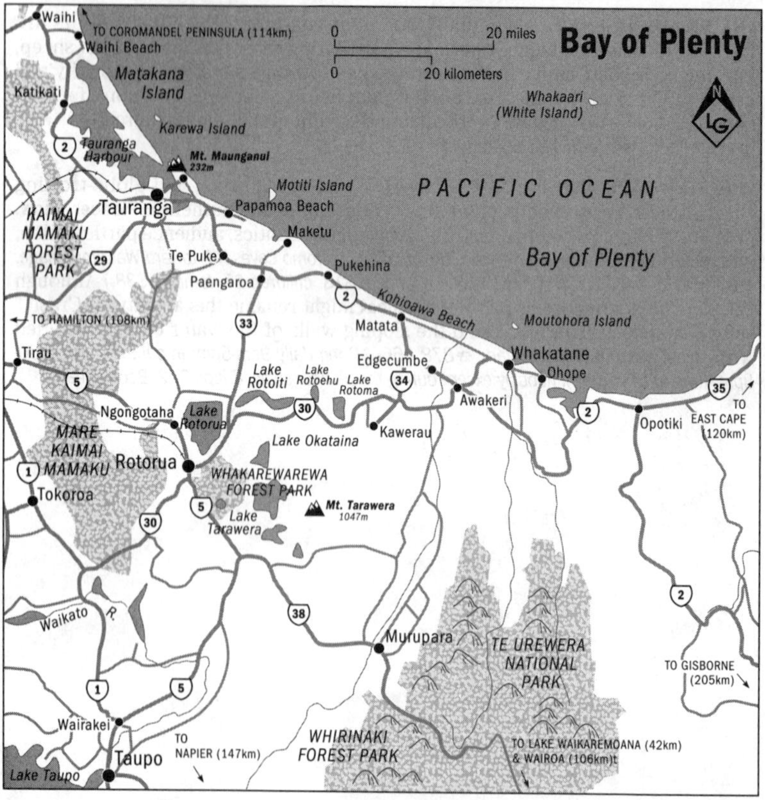

ROTORUA ☎ 07

You'll know when you've hit Rotorua. The smell of sulfur wafting through the air, the threads of steam rising from the pavement, and the constant hum of tour buses will awaken your senses. Named Roto- (lake) rua (two) upon the Maori discovery of the second (of 15) lakes in the region, the town is the North Island's most popular destination. Rotorua's energetic thermal activity and enlightening Maori offerings attract nearly a million visitors annually. Although tourism here is most definitely an industry, you'll undoubtedly find that the beauty justifies the hype.

TRANSPORTATION

Flights: The **Rotorua Airport** is off SH30, around the east side of Lake Rotorua. **Air New Zealand**, 1103 Hinemoa St. (☎343 1100) has 3-4 flights per day to: **Auckland** (45min., $97-225); **Christchurch** (1¼hr., $214-393); **Queenstown** (2½hr., $369-669); and **Wellington** (1hr., $138-256). **Super Shuttle** (☎349 3444. $10, 2 for $12) runs an airport shuttle to town.

Buses: All buses come and go from the Visitors Center. **Newmans** and **InterCity**, both accessible at the **bus depot** (☎349 0590), depart daily for: **Auckland** (4hr., 4-7 per day, $33-36) via **Hamilton** (1½hr., $19-24); **Napier** (4½hr., 3 per day, $50-53); and **Wellington** (7¼hr., 4 per day, $60-78) via **Taupo** (1hr., $18-25). **Waitomo Wanderer**

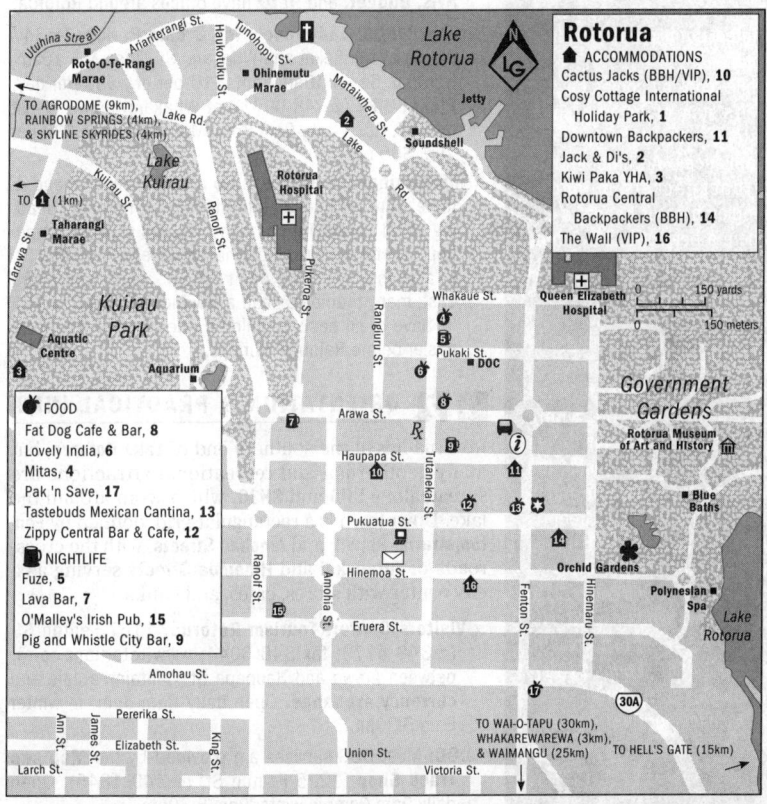

THE HIDDEN DEAL

FUNKY GREEN VOYAGER

With a dash of spunk, a patch of lawn, and a sprinkling of Rotorua-bound travelers, this stellar hostel lives up to its memorable name. The Funky Green experience begins at the door—a no-shoes policy keeps the floors shiny and geothermal-mud-free. Inside, sparkling rooms and an environmentally-conscious staff let you unwind from a day of soaking in hot springs or Zorbing down hills. Home-style accommodations range from well-appointed dorm rooms to plush ensuite doubles.

Meanwhile, cooking comes easy in Funky Green's state-of-the-art kitchen, which glistens with white tiles and modern appliances. An independent crowd of backpackers munches instant noodles here or heads to the lounge, where a bevy of board games provides ample amusement. Rounds of Scrabble, Monopoly, and cards bring the guests and staff together for wholesome fun and an adjoining sunroom lets you catch afternoon rays on puffy couches. Perhaps the funkiest feature of all is in the loo, where industrially-inspired designer toilets encase jagged barbed wire inside the clear plastic seats. A Rotorua must-sleep, it's no wonder Funky Green is one of the highest rated BBH backpackers in New Zealand.

4 Union St. Walk down Fenton St. to Victoria St. and turn right; Union St. is 2 blocks down. ☎346 1754; fax 350 1100. Key deposit $10. Dorms $16-17; twins and doubles $39; doubles with bath $43. Discounts for BBH members. Cash only.

(☎349 2509) goes to **Waitomo** (2hr., 7:15am, $30), with pick-up and drop-off. **Guthrey's** (☎0800 759 999) departs 4 times daily for **Auckland International Airport** (4¼hr., $50) via **Hamilton** (1½hr., $23), and **Auckland** proper (4hr., $38).

Public Transportation: Ritchie's Buses (☎349 2994, ext. 2902) are cheap and run M-F 7am-5:15pm, Sa 8am-5pm. Routes are divided into sections; 1 section costs $1.60, 2 cost $2.20. The main stop is Pukuatua St. between Tutanekai and Amohia St. The green Ngongataha route goes to Rainbow Springs, the blue to Whakarewarewa.

Taxis: Fastaxis (☎348 2444) and **Rotorua Taxis** (☎348 1111) operate **24hr.**

Car Rental: Link Rentals, 1222 Fenton St. (☎349 1629), has "super saver" cars for $25 per day plus 18¢ per km. Open M-F 8am-5pm, Sa-Su 8am-noon. **Rent-A-Dent**, 14 Ti St. (☎349 3993), off Fenton St. past Big Fresh, has $49 per day rentals with 100km free. Open daily 7am-5:30pm. The worldwide chains **Avis, Budget,** and **Hertz** have offices around Rotorua.

Bike Rental: Lady Jane's Ice Cream Parlour (☎347 9340) at Tutanekai and Whakaue St. Open M-F 10am-6:30pm, Sa-Su 10am-8pm. $10 per hr., $30 per day. **Planet Bike** (☎348 9971), at Whakarewarewa Forest off SH5. Open daily 9am-6pm. Mountain bikes $30 per 2hr., $50 per day.

Hitchhiking: Although *Let's Go* does not recommend it, there's always hitchable traffic leaving Rotorua. Heading south toward Taupo, many hitchers start past Amohau St. and work toward Whakarewarewa. Amohau St. is also the branching point for SH5 north and SH30 east; many thumbers head a few blocks away from Pak 'N Save to go east. Catching a ride north is reportedly easier before Rainbow Springs.

ORIENTATION & PRACTICAL INFO

Rotorua lies at the southern end of **Lake Rotorua**, but many geothermal and recreational attractions are spread along **SH5** and **SH30**, which wrap around the lake. Downtown is a rectangular grid, defined by **Fenton, Arawa, Ranolf,** and **Amohau Streets**, with the crossroads of **Tutanekai** and **Hinemoa Streets** serving as a city center with stores, cafes, and banks.

Visitors Center: Tourism Rotorua, 1167 Fenton St. (☎348 5179; fax 348 6044; www.rotoruanz.com), between Arawa and Haupapa St. Contains a cafe and **currency exchange.** Open daily 8am-6pm; in winter 8am-5:30pm.

DOC: Most DOC services are provided by the **Map and Track Shop**, 1225 Fenton St. (☎349 1845). Open daily 9am-6pm; in winter 9am-5:30pm.

Banks and Currency Exchange: Banks with **ATMs** line Hinemoa St. Open M-F 9 or 9:30am-4:30pm.

American Express: Galaxy Travel, 1315 Tutanekai St. (☎347 9444), won't cash checks but will hold mail for AmEx members. Open M-F 8:30am-5pm.

Medical Services: Lakes Care Pharmacy (☎348 4385), under the big turquoise sign at the corner of Arawa and Tutanekai St. Open daily 8:30am-9:30pm. **Lakeland Health Centre** (☎348 1199), Rotorua's public hospital, is on Pukeroa St. off Arawa St. at the northeast corner of the city center. **Lakes PrimeCare** (☎348 1000), next to the Lakes Care Pharmacy, has a doctor on call **24hr.** Open daily 8am-11pm.

Police: Diagonally across Fenton St. from the Visitors Center (☎348 0099).

Internet Access: There are places everywhere but one of the cheaper sites is **Cybershed,** 1176 Pukuatua St. (☎349 4965), for $6 per hr. Open daily 9am-11pm.

Post Office: 1189 Hinemoa St. (☎349 2397), near Tutanekai St. Open M-F 7:30am-5:30pm, Sa 8:30am-4pm, Su 9am-3pm.

ACCOMMODATIONS AND CAMPING

Rotorua has no shortage of beds, though it may feel that way if you neglect to call ahead. Some good budget places line **Ranolf Street,** while the strip of motels along **SH5,** both at **Fenton Street** and the northeast side of town, give Rotorua its nickname: "Roto-Vegas." If you're desperate for a room contact the Visitors Center.

Kiwi Paka YHA, 60 Tarewa Rd. (☎347 0931; fax 346 3167; www.kiwipaka-yha.co.nz), 1km from town center. Walk west on Pukuatua St. past Kuirau Park and turn right on Tarewa Rd. An upbeat spirit reigns in this quasi-resort YHA, complete with a kidney-shaped thermal pool and an in-house cafe. Free shuttle service to bus stop and hitchhikers' points. Key deposit $10. Dorms $20; singles $27; twins and doubles $46, with bath $54; triples and quads with bath $70-92; tent sites $9, powered $10.50. ❷

Rotorua Central Backpackers (BBH), 1076 Pukuatua St. (☎/fax 349 3285; rotorua.central.bp@clear.net.nz). From the bus station, turn right down Fenton St. and left on Pukuatua St. Central offers a bunk-bed rest, 2 lounges, and an indoor spa. Internet. Key deposit $20. Dorms $17-18; twins and doubles $40. ❷

Cactus Jacks (BBH/VIP), 1210 Haupapa St. (☎/fax 348 3121 or 0800 122 228; isabella.pavlova@xtra.co.nz). For a Kiwi-inspired wild-west experience, head to this themed hostel. Small bedrooms surround the "town" courtyard. Bike rental. Spa. Internet. Key deposit $10. Dorms $15.50; singles $33-35; twins $38; doubles $43. ❷

Downtown Backpackers, 1193 Fenton St. (☎/fax 346 2831; downtown-rotorua@xtra.co.nz), next to the Visitors Center. This large, ultra-central hostel has a quiet atmosphere for older travelers. Internet. Dorms $17-18; twins and doubles $42, in winter $40. ❷

The Wall (VIP), 1140 Hinemoa St. (☎350 2040 or 0800 843 392; fax 350 2020; www.thewall.co.nz). New to Rotorua, the Wall has 3 floors of clean rooms and common areas overlooking an indoor climbing wall. Game room. Internet. Key deposit $20. Dorms $20-22; twins and doubles $48, with bath $65. ❷

Cosy Cottage International Holiday Park, 67 Whittaker Rd. (☎348 3793; fax 347 9634; www.cosycottage.co.nz), 2km from town, off Lake Rd. Thermally-heated sites and a private sand beach make up for the tired feel of communal facilities. Bike rental. Double flats with kitchenette $48, extra person $11; cabins for 2 with kitchenettes $44, extra person $11; tourist flats $65; tent sites $10, powered $11. ❶

Jack & Di's, 21 Lake Rd. (☎346 8482 or 0800 522 534; fax 346 6486; www.jdbedbreakfast.co.nz). Antique furnishings, marble floors, and sweeping views of the lake make this bed and breakfast the ideal splurge. Twins and doubles $85-120; self-contained units for 4-6 people $150-160. ❺

FOOD

A unique alternative to the droves of standard restaurants is the delicious and entertaining Maori *hangi*. Although the meals (which include a cultural show and/or concert) exceed the normal backpacker allowance, they shouldn't be missed (see **A Maori Evening**, p. 168). If you must self-cater in order to save up, **Pak 'N Save** is located at the corner of Fenton and Amohau St. (☎347 8440. Open daily 8am-9pm.)

- **Zippy Central Bar and Cafe,** 1153 Pukuatua St. (☎348 8288). Neon green walls and kitschy decor infuse this cafe with a happy dose of funk. With an ever-changing menu, the tuna melt bagels ($6.50) are one of the tasty constants. For a few bucks more, dinner mains share the tables with candles. Open Su-Th 9am-9:30pm, F-Sa 9am-11pm. ❷

- **Fat Dog Cafe and Bar,** 1161 Arawa St. (☎347 7586). Paying homage to its roly-poly namesake, this cafe shines with a playful atmosphere and colorful decor. $6 lunches and $9 dinners will surely coax a smile. Open M-F 8:30am-late, Sa-Su 8am-late. ❷

- **Tastebuds Mexican Cantina,** 1213 Fenton St. (☎349 0591), under a "Mexican Food" sign. The cantina is always full of patrons bumping elbows to dig into plates of burritos, enchiladas, and tacos (all $5-9; choice of mild, hot, extra hot, or super hot salsa). Open M-W 10am-9pm, Th-Su 10am-10pm; in winter M-Sa 10am-9pm, Su 11am-8pm. ❷

- **Mitas,** 1114 Tutanekai St. (☎349 6482). Large portions of delicacies like steak mandarin ($32) and king prawns in coconut sauce ($28.50) provide the finishing touches to this classy establishment. Reservations essential. Open Tu-Su 5:30-9:15pm. ❺

- **Lovely India,** 1123 Tutanekai St. (☎348 4088). A friendly staff brings a fresh slice of India (on a bed of basmati rice) to hungry locals. $13 lunch and dinner specials M-W. Open daily 5:30pm-late; also Tu-Su 11:30am-2:30pm. ❸

NIGHTLIFE

Rowdy tourists feed a lively Rotorua nightlife scene. Even after a long day of mud and *marae*, travelers manage to hit the bars and beers with gusto.

- **Pig and Whistle City Bar** (☎347 3025), at the corner of Tutanekai and Haupapa St. Hog a bar stool at this former police station. Patrons nowadays are less degenerate, although weekend nights with live bands still get downright felonious. Cover F-Sa $2. Handles $4.50. Pub food until 9:30pm. Open daily 11:30am-late.

- **Lava Bar,** 1286 Arawa St. (☎348 8618). Green-bused backpackers crowd this mixer nightly, grinding to Top 40 dance music and pounding Lava's special shooters ($3). Happy Hour daily 4:30-6pm. Open daily 4:30pm-late.

- **O'Malley's Irish Pub** (☎347 6410), on Eruera St. by Ranolf St. The round pool table and live bands (F) at this shamrock-green pub attract a sprightly crowd. Happy Hour F 5-7pm. Open M-W 11am-midnight, Th-Sa 11am-2am, Su 11am-10pm.

- **Fuze,** 1122 Tutanekai St. (☎349 6306). With a marble bar and modernist metal stools, Fuze infuses Rotorua with a dose of sleek style. Crowds fill the dance floor on weekends. Open Tu-Su 3pm-late.

SIGHTS

GEOTHERMAL WONDERS

Rotorua's thermal activity is caused by a volcanic fault line running from White Island (see p. 176), 50km offshore from Whakatane, to Mt. Ruapehu in Tongariro National Park (see p. 207). Colliding tectonic plates created the spectacular mountains, the bizarre landscape of the major geothermal parks, and innumerable steaming pools, craters, and vents—a veritable magmatic buffet.

WAI-O-TAPU. This unbelievably beautiful "Thermal Wonderland" is the most colorful (and probably the finest) geothermal spot in the nation. Leased from DOC by private operators, the reserve is explored by self-guided tour, weaving among boiling mud, an expansive silicate terrace, brilliantly hued pools, craters, and (you are in Rotorua) crowds of tourists. While frustratingly veiled in steam all too often, the stunning ochre and turquoise colors of the bubbling **Champagne Pool** make the celebratory beverage pale in comparison. Erupting up to 21m each day at precisely 10:15am, **Lady Knox Geyser** is another Wai-O-Tapu attraction. Mother Nature isn't really that regular—the geyser gets a liberal dose of soap every morning to relieve surface tension and allow the upper level of water to erupt. Prisoners discovered this handy trick in 1896 while washing clothes. *(30km south of Rotorua on SH5. ☎ 366 6333; www.geyserland.co.nz. Open daily 8:30am-5pm. $14, children $4.)*

THE NEW ZEALAND MAORI ARTS AND CRAFTS INSTITUTE. Containing the Te Whakarewarewa Thermal Reserve and Maori Cultural Centre, this attraction, commonly called **Whaka**, is the source of a billowing cloud of steam, boiling mud pools, a kiwi house, and demonstrations on carving, weaving, and crafts. Along the reserve's walking tour, New Zealand's largest and most famous geyser, **Pohutu**, spurts daily up to 30m. *(3km south of town, accessible by Sala St. off Fenton St. ☎ 348 9047; www.nzmaori.co.nz. Open daily 8am-6pm; in winter 8am-5pm. Free guided tours every hr. 9am-4pm. 30-min. cultural performance daily 12:15pm. $18.)*

WAIMANGU VOLCANIC VALLEY. This southern end of the rift created by Tarawera's 1886 eruption hosts several hot geothermal phenomena. Along its trail, the **Echo Crater** is home to the world's largest hot springs, where dancing steam creates fanciful patterns on the gleaming water. The ice-blue and extremely acidic **Inferno Crater Lake** is actually a geyser, living on a 38-day cycle. The path also passes the site of **Waimangu**, once the world's largest geyser; the white cross nearby marks the site where four overzealous tourists were killed in 1903. Exercise your powers of imagination on a 1hr. guided boat cruise to the former sites of the **Pink and White Terraces** and the steaming cliffs. *(23km from Rotorua off the Taupo Hwy. ☎ 366 6137; www.waimangu.co.nz. Open daily 8:30am-5pm. Valley $16, with boat ride $36; boat ride alone $20.)*

HELL'S GATE. In addition to admiring 10 hectares of seething mud, pools, and the largest steaming hot waterfall in the Southern Hemisphere, you can pretend to be a Maori warrior salving his battle wounds in New Zealand's only "mud bath" complex. *(15km west of Rotorua on SH30. ☎ 345 3151; www.hellsgaterotorua.co.nz. Open daily 9am-8pm. Park entry $12, children $6; spa $10/$6; mud bath $25.)*

PROPHET OF DOOM The events of May 31, 1886 were troubling to the Maori living under Mt. Tarawera. Sophia Hinerangi witnessed a vision: a spectral war canoe, its warrior paddlers wearing ominous symbols on their heads, emerged from a bend in the lake and then disappeared. Consulted for interpretation, the old priest Tuhoto said these natural and supernatural signs foretold something cataclysmic. He had warned his people in Te Wairoa that their departure from the ancestral ways—their gradual adoption of the white man's greed—would lead to punishment by his ancestor, the spirit Tamahoi, buried within the mountain. The night of terror came on June 10, 1886, when the three domes on the now flat-topped volcano blew and rent the mountain asunder, ripping a 17km wound of red, white, and black scoria-lined craters. The largest eruption in 500 years, it blasted away the bed of Lake Rotomahana, burying Te Wairoa and other nearby villages in mud, rock, and ash; roars were heard as far as Christchurch and Auckland. When the search parties finally uncovered Tuhoto's house, days later, they found the old man still alive. Tamahoi had protected his prophet. The Rotorua Museum of Art and History (see **Other Sights,** p. 167) screens a great dramatized version of this story.

TOURS

THERMAL AND CULTURAL SHUTTLE. These friendly and informed drivers make runs to Wai-O-Tapu, Waimangu, Tamaki Maori Village, and Waikite Hot Pools from the Visitors Center and most accommodations. (☎ *0800 287 2968. Operates daily 7:55am-4:15pm. Day pass including entry to Wai-O-Tapu $25.*)

CAREY'S SIGHTSEEING TOURS. This operation offers a wide array of half-, three-quarter, and full-day tours including pick-up and in-coach commentary. A full-day tour covers the geothermal wonders of Wai-O-Tapu, Waimangu, and Whakarewarewa as well as Rainbow Trout Springs and Farm Show. (*1108 Haupapa St.* ☎ *347 1197 or 0800 222 739. $65-145, children $33-80.*)

TE KIRI TREK. As advertised—rough, tough, wet, and wild. After a traditional Maori welcome, a walk through Wai-O-Tapu and a thermal river swim, 4WDer Roger—sporting his daily uniform of gumboots, camouflage jacket, and buzzcut—takes you up to Tarawera Falls and down through Rotoiti Forest, with an all-you-can-eat lunch along the way. (☎ *345 5016 or 025 391 288. Pick-up 8:30am, drop-off around 6:30pm. $120.*)

MT. TARAWERA. The volcanic Mt. Tarawera (1111m), the cause of the 1886 commotion, towers over all Rotorua backpackers. While getting up Tarawera

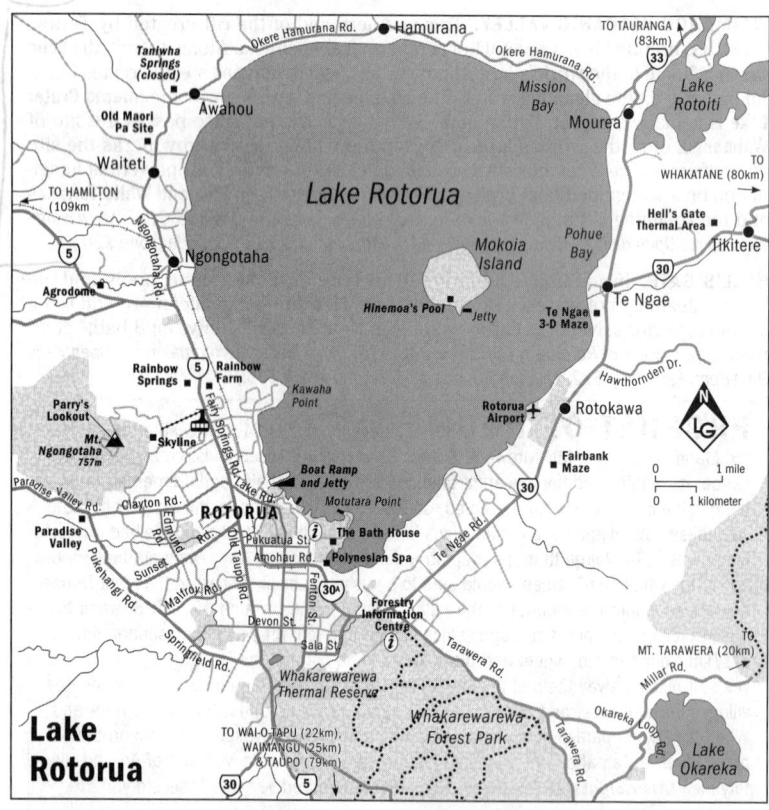

Lake Rotorua

ROTORUA ■ **167**

by foot is possible, the access point from Ash Pit Rd. near Lake Rerewhakaaitu south of town is nearly impossible to reach without your own transport. **Mt. Tarawera NZ** issues day passes ($23) and runs a 4WD shuttle service ($80) for getting up the mountain. They also lead half-day 4WD tours, which include a guided walk around the crater, and helicopter trips with a landing on Mt. Tarawera. (☎ 349 3714; www.mt-tarawera.co.nz. 4WD tours depart 8am and 1pm, $110. Flight time approx. 45min., $299.) **Volcanic Air Safaris** also flies over Mt. Tarawera and the Crater Lakes District. (☎ 0800 800 049. Tarawera: floatplane $165, helicopter $275. Crater Lakes: $115/$165.)

AGRICULTURAL DIVERSIONS

AGRODOME. Entertaining bus loads of tourists daily, the Agrodome's resident "farmer" shears 19 breeds of sheep, performs a mock auction, leads sheepdog trials, and coaxes the camera-happy crowd to milk cows and pet baby lambs. You can also tour the actual working farm. (10km north of town on SH5. ☎ 357 1050 or 0800 339 400; www.agrodome.co.nz. Both activities 3 times per day. $15 each, $27 for both.)

RAINBOW SPRINGS. For an agricultural experience almost identical to the aforementioned Agrodome (but with only 15 breeds of sheep), the **Rainbow Farm Show** gives visitors five chances a day to see its ovine extravaganza. A 40min. walk among animals and hot springs included with ticket. (On SH5, 5km north of town, opposite the Skyline Gondola. ☎ 347 9301; www.rainbownz.co.nz. $19.50.)

MAORITANGA

OHINEMUTU. A visit to this lakefront Maori village of the Ngati Whakaue tribe rewards visitors with a patient introduction to Maori culture. Of the compound's buildings, the **Tamatekapua Meeting House** is the most symbolically important. The interior is closed to the public, except for nightly concerts (see **A Maori Evening,** p. 168), and showcases a smattering of paua shells and rich, red carvings. (Off Lake Rd., down Tutanekai St. ☎ 349 3949.)

ST. FAITH'S ANGLICAN CHURCH. Across from Ohinemutu, this church has an incongruous combination of Tudor exterior and Maori interior. The pulpit is supported by carved figures of five Maori ancestors, while an etched window shows Christ clad in the cloak of a Maori chief—from a certain angle, he appears to be walking on Lake Rotorua. A potent focus of cultural history, the church still holds services (the original St. Faith's held Rotorua's first Christian service in 1831).

OTHER SIGHTS

ROTORUA MUSEUM OF ART AND HISTORY/TE WHARE TAONGA O TE ARAWA. To gain a greater appreciation for just about everything in Rotorua, give yourself 1½hr. in this outstanding locale. A former luxury spa, it houses permanent exhibitions on the eruption of 1886, the Te Arawa people, area geology, and the former spa itself. The various films featuring Rotorua stories are must-sees. (In the neo-Tudor Bath House, to the right of the public Government Gardens at the end of Hinemaru St. ☎ 349 4350. Open daily 9:30am-6pm; in winter 9:30am-5pm. $9, students $7.50.)

THE BLUE BATHS. Begun as the first unisex pool in the country, today the original site houses a museum devoted to the history of the baths, an elegant outdoor hot pool, and a charming tearoom that serves tiered cakes on antique trolleys. (Next to the Rotorua Museum. ☎ 350 2119. Museum open daily 10am-5pm; in winter 10am-4pm. $9. Pools open daily 10am-8pm; in winter 10am-6pm. $7.)

ACTIVITIES

A MAORI EVENING: THE HANGI

The best way to learn about Maori culture is through participation in a Maori *hangi*, or feast. Some emphasize learning about Maori history and traditions, while others consist solely of song and dance. Some *hangi* are held on real *marae*, some in specifically built commercial locations, and others in plush motel restaurants; be prepared, many evening commercial packages tread a delicate line between education and exoticization. The package you choose, and the attitude the sponsoring company displays, can significantly alter your *hangi* experience. Although the camera flashing can be disconcerting, this may be your best chance to move beyond postcard images of tongue-protruding tattooed Maori warriors to get a glimpse of the beauty, power, and richness of the Maori tradition. The *hangi* is also a damn good meal. Full evening tours by several Maori-owned operators usually include an introductory communication protocol, challenge and welcome ceremony, concert, and *hangi*—all with transport from any accommodation.

TAMAKI TOURS. Rotorua's most popular and polished Maori experience begins by choosing a chief from each of the several bus loads of spectators who will represent his canoe (tour bus) for the remainder of the evening. After the welcome, groups walk through a model *pa* built to showcase age-old customs performed by Maori. Then there is an engrossing group concert and festive *hangi*. (☎ 346 2823; www.maoriculture.co.nz. $70, children $35; advance bookings essential.)

MAI ORA. At a pre-European village overlooking the **Whakarewarewa Thermal Reserve,** this *hangi* is prepared by the underground heat of the water. Whakarewarewa also offers daytime concerts. (☎ 348 9047. $65, children $35. Summer only.)

ROTOITI TOURS. Run by the Ngati Rongamai tribe, Rotoiti Tours stages more authentic evenings in the Rakeiao *marae*, on the shores of scenic Lake Rotoiti. Groups average 80-100 people on summer evenings. Winter groups may be under 20, but performances are sporadic, so call. Overnights are also possible, but mainly for groups of more than 10. (☎ 348 8969. $55, under 12 $27.50. Overnights in summer from $60, based on group size. Includes bedding, kitchen, and breakfast.)

WATER ACTIVITIES

POLYNESIAN SPA. Where else can you don your swimsuit, soak in ecstasy, and comfortably chat with travelers from around the globe? The **Radium** and **Priest Springs** ($10), filled with acidic water that reaches 33-43°C, are famed for their supposed healing powers. The luxurious **Lake Spa,** a landscaped terrace of caves and waterfalls, has a steep $25 price tag, commensurate with its stunning scenery. (At the Government Gardens end of Hinemoa St. ☎ 348 1328; www.polynesianspa.co.nz. Open daily 6:30am-11pm; last ticket sales at 10:15pm. $10.)

FISHING. With all its lakes (and purportedly more trout per capita than even Lake Taupo), Rotorua is an angler's paradise. Lakes Rotorua and Okareka are open year-round; other fishable lakes are open October through June. (Fly guides begin at $70 per hr.; contact the Visitors Center for a listing of operators and to get a $13 1-day license.)

KAYAKING. Adventure Kayaking provides the transport to travel the azure lakes that gave Rotorua its name. Conditions are especially good on Lake Tarawera and Lake Rotoiti. (☎ 348 9451. Kayaks $40 per day, tandem $80 per day. Full-day guided trip $80, half-day $65. Twilight paddles $65.)

ADVENTURE ACTIVITIES

AGRODOME ADVENTURE CENTRE. With four original attractions immune to the "been there, done that" brag, this adrenaline mecca draws the bold. You can **bungy jump** off a 43m tower, zip around a small rubber-banked pond in a tiny 450-horsepower jetboat, the **Agrojet**, or roll down a hill in a **Zorb**. The **Swoop** raises one, two, or three people linked in padded sleeping-bag-like-sacs to a height of 40m, and then lets you pull a rip-cord and fall at 130kph. (☎ 357 4747; www.agrodome.co.nz. Bungy $80; Agrojet $35, children $25; wet or dry Zorb $40; Swoop $35-45. All of the adventure rides operate daily 9am-6:30pm; in winter 9am-5pm.)

SKYDIVING. One of the cheaper options for skydiving in New Zealand, **Tandem Skydiving Rotorua** offers a drop over spectacular Lake District scenery. (☎ 345 7520. 9500ft. $190; 12,000ft. $225. Book ahead.)

SKYLINE SKYRIDES. Rotorua is the semi-official luge capital of the country (not that there was much competition) thanks to **Skyline**. After ascending in a scenic gondola ride ($13.50), the luge hurls you back down on a three-wheeled plastic cart. Other attractions at the top include a sidewinder toboggan, a shooting gallery, a skyline ride, and mountain biking. (4-5km from the city center, next to Rainbow Springs on SH5. ☎ 347 0027; www.skylineskyrides.co.nz. Open M-Th and Su 9am-5pm, F-Sa 9am-9pm. Luge rides $5, 5-pass $18.)

WHITEWATER RAFTING. Adrenaline junkies twitching for their next fix will rush to the short but sweet Kaituna River, with 7m Okere Falls spilling onto Lake Rotoiti. Trips to other area rivers, including the Rangitaiki, Wairoa, and Tongariro, are offered by many companies, but are contingent on good weather and safe water levels. The original company, with strong local endorsement, is **Kaituna Cascades**. (☎ 357 5032 or 0800 524 8862; www.kaitunacascades.co.nz. 50min. $75.)

SLEDGING. Sledging is a unique form of insanity for a generation jaded with rafting or kayaking white water. **Kaitiaki Adventures** will lead you down chutes and rapids in a buoyant plastic sled. For the more traditional, the experienced guides also run rafting trips. (☎ 0800 338 736; www.kaitiaki.co.nz. Sledging $115. Rafting $80.)

WHAKAREWAREWA FOREST PARK. It may not be native bush, but the 5667-hectacre exotic pine plantation draws visitors with awesome mountain biking trails and lake-skirting walks. For walking or riding, get maps and permits from **Fletcher Challenge Forest Visitor Centre**. (On Long Mile Rd., a short drive or bike from the city center off the road to the airport. ☎ 346 2082. Open M-F 8:30am-6pm, Sa-Su 10am-4pm; in winter M-F 8:30am-5pm, Sa-Su 10am-4pm.)

THE LOCAL STORY

THE TRUTH ABOUT ZORB

Keith Kolver has been the manager of Zorb in Rotorua for three years.

Q: Where does "Zorb" come from?
A: The word Zorb came from the word "orb" with the "Z" added for New Zealand because it's a New Zealand invention. There's a whole Zorb culture that's come from that. People who go in the Zorbs are called Zorbonauts. People who play with Zorbs everyday are called Zorbrangers. We've had a lot of fun with it during the five years it's been operating.

Q: Is it true that if you go Zorbing naked it's free?
A: It used to be up until about a month ago. Then we had to stop because of the sheer numbers of naked people going. There were just too many people who turned up and said, "We've heard you can do it naked and for free." We were doing up to 20 naked Zorbers a day. It was just getting a bit much. We were giving all these free rides and people were getting embarrassed watching. At heart, we're really just conservative Kiwis down here *(said with a chuckle).*

Q: Are there are any other funny stories of people Zorbing?
A: There are funny things happening all the time. We've got dishwashing liquid that we put in to make it super slippery. You've got to watch how much you put in otherwise it foams right up over the heads of the people inside. Every now and then, you get some very soap-suddy-looking people who slip out with a big smile on their face. We're always having fun here.

TAURANGA ☎ 07

Tauranga's warm weather and commercial conveniences have made it one of New Zealand's fastest growing cities (pop. 53,000). The sprawling town has some attractions—the kiwifruit orchards in nearby Te Puke, the surrounding beaches, and the peaked Mt. Maunganui. However, most travelers simply view Tauranga as a quick breath of sea air before sulfurous Rotorua.

TRANSPORTATION

Buses: Station at the Visitors Center. **InterCity/Newmans** heads daily to: **Auckland** (4hr., 1:20pm, $29); **Hamilton** (2hr., 4:15pm, $25); and **Rotorua** (1hr., 4 per day, $22-24). Transfers from Rotorua for **Whakatane** and points in **East Cape**. **Guthreys** (☎0800 759 999) runs to **Auckland** via the **Coromandel Peninsula** (3½hr., 3 per day, $30). **Supa Travel** (☎571 0583) runs additional service to **Auckland** ($26-36).

Ferries: (☎578 5381) from **Coronation Pier** to Mt. Maunganui (in summer daily 9am-5pm; 1 per hr.; $6, children $3).

Public Transportation: Bayline Coaches (☎578 3113) runs local buses between Tauranga and Mt. Maunganui ($2.50) and to some of the suburbs.

Taxis: Tauranga Taxis (☎578 6086), **Bay City Cabs** (☎577 0999), and **Coastline Taxis** (☎571 8333) are all available **24hr.**

Hitchhiking: Although Let's Go does not recommend it, hitchhikers heading to Auckland or the Coromandel suggest trying Waihi Road (SH2), past Jonathon St., about 500m beyond the Otumoetai Rd. roundabout. Thumbers to Whakatane or Rotorua often start on Dive Crescent before the bridge and head east via Mt. Maunganui.

ORIENTATION AND PRACTICAL INFORMATION

Downtown Tauranga is located on a narrow northern peninsula in **Tauranga Harbour.** With the most attractions on **The Strand,** a strip of cafes and clubs along the eastern coast of Waipu Bay, the commercial area spreads west to **Cameron Street** and south to **Elizabeth Street.** Cross-streets south of Elizabeth St. are numbered in a southward ascending order. **15th Avenue** is the continuation of SH2. The bridge to Mt. Maunganui begins at the northeastern tip of the city-peninsula, while the bridge to Otumoetai starts at the northwestern tip on Chapel St.

Visitors Center: Visitor and Information Centre, 95 Willow St. (☎578 8103; fax 578 7020; trqvin@tauranga-dc.govt.nz). Open M-F 7am-5:30pm, Sa-Su 8am-4pm.

DOC: 253 Chadwick Rd. (☎/fax 578 7677), in West Greerton, 7km south of the city center. Take Cameron Rd. south to the 2nd roundabout in West Greerton, then turn right. DOC is on the right, just across from the police station. Open M-F 8am-4:30pm.

Work Opportunities: Fruit-picking opportunities abound Apr.-June. The **Baypak orchard** (☎573 3400) is a good place to start your search. Also, many **accommodations** have info on available jobs; **Just the Duck's Nuts** (see below) and the **Pacific Coast Lodge** in Mt. Maunganui (see p. 174) are well-connected to the fruit industry.

Banks: BNZ (☎578 8009), on Willow St., and **ANZ** (☎578 2049), at the corner of Spring and Grey St., are both open M-F 9am-4:30pm.

Police: (☎577 4300), at the corner of Willow and Monmouth St.

Medical Services: John's Photo Pharmacy (☎578 3566), at the corner of Cameron Rd. and 2nd Ave., operates evenings. Open daily 8am-9pm. For after hours only, try **Baycare Medical Services** (☎578 8111), on 10th St. and Edgecumbe Rd. Open daily 5pm-8am. The **hospital** (☎579 8000) is on Cameron Rd. between 17th and 18th Ave.

TAURANGA ■ 171

BAY OF PLENTY

Internet: Cybersurf (☎ 578 0140), in the Picadilly Arcade between Devonport Rd. and Grey St. 20¢ per min., $9.60 per hr. Open M-F 9am-6pm, Sa 10am-4pm, Su 11am-4pm. Also at **Fish Crazee** (see **Food**, below) for $6 per hr.

Post Office: 17 Grey St. (☎ 577 9911), inside Books & More. Open M-F 8:30am-5pm, Sa 9am-noon.

ACCOMMODATIONS

While those without vehicles stay downtown, more mobile visitors will find an array of motorparks and motels along **Waihi Road** (coming from Auckland) or **Turret Road/15th Avenue.**

Just the Duck's Nuts (BBH/VIP), 6 Vale St. (☎ 576 1366; fax 570 1226; www.justtheducksnuts.co.nz), in Otumoetai. Take Chapel St. from Tauranga. Suburban hostel with a glassed-in conservatory, fireplace, and 2 lounges. Free bike use. Free pick-up. Dorms $20; twins and doubles $40; tent sites $12. Weekly singles from $90. ❷

Tauranga YHA, 171 Elizabeth St. (☎ 578 5064; fax 578 5040; yha-taur@yha.org), a convenient 10min. walk from The Strand. Employment help and discounts for area activities. Internet. Reception 8-10am and 5-10:30pm; in winter 5-8:30pm. Dorms $20; doubles $44; tent sites $10. ❷

Bell Lodge (BBH), 39 Bell St. (☎ 578 6344; fax 578 6342; www.bell-lodge.co.nz), 4km south of town, near the Otumoetai Rd. roundabout off Waihi Rd. (or SH2). Bell offers a range of modern rooms overlooking a patio. Free shuttle into town and to hitching points. Internet. Reception 8am-9pm. Dorms $19; twins and doubles $44; tent sites $10. ❷

FOOD

Shiraz Cafe, 12 Wharf St. (☎ 577 0059). The cream of Tauranga's cafe crop, Shiraz offers Middle Eastern cuisine (hummus $6, filled pitas $9) and outdoor seating. Open M-Sa 11am-2:30pm and 5-10pm (closing time varies). ❷

Fish Crazee, 85 The Strand (☎ 577 9375). A friendly cafe-cum-fish 'n' chipper with bronze fish on display and fried fish (under $5) on the plates. Have your crazee delivered for $3.50 extra. Internet. Open M-Tu 4-9pm, W-F 4pm-late, Sa-Su 10am-late. ❶

The Sunrise Natural Cafe, 10 Wharf St. (☎ 578 9302). Vegetarian sandwiches and an intimidating dessert selection (all $2-4) offer a respite from deep-fried fare. Shares seating with Shiraz. Open M-F 8am-4pm, Sa 9am-2pm. ❶

NIGHTLIFE

Bahama Hut, 19 Wharf St. (☎571 0839). 2 pool tables, a big-screen projection TV, surfboards, and glowing torches complete the party picture. A young crowd dances to a pop/techno mix. Th Gimmick night. Cover varies on weekends. Open M-Sa 4pm-3am.

Roma, 65 The Strand (☎578 3100). The hippest, most sophisticated club in town with the best DJs on weekends. House, trance, and drum 'n' bass thump in the club's dark, stark environs. Open W-Th 5pm-3am, F-Sa 5pm-5am.

The Crown & Badger, 91 The Strand (☎571 3038), at the corner of Wharf St. Ample space and live music on weekends. Caters more to the adult bar set, but is perfect for a sit-down-and-talk beer (pints $4). Snacks $3-8. Meals served noon-2:30pm and 6-9:30pm ($8.50-14.50). Open daily 10am-2am.

SIGHTS

If the line at the **Bungee Rocket** (see **Activities,** below) is too long, visit **Te Awanui,** an intricately carved replica Maori canoe at the end of The Strand. The small greenhouse and rose gardens of **Robbins Park** provide a great picnic site, with a view of the harbor and the less-than-picturesque shipping industry. Up Cliff Rd. and left on Mission St., the beautiful territory of the **Elms Mission Station** was established in 1835 as Tauranga's first mission. Walk the small path through the tranquil grounds where ripe kiwifruit and tangerines hang down by the chapel in late fall. A bit farther off the beaten track is the Mission's cemetery on a mound, just to the right of Dive Crescent's intersection with Marsh St. (☎578 4011. Building open Su 2-4pm. Grounds open anytime.) The **Mills Reef Winery,** 143 Moffat Rd., off Waihi Rd. on the way out of town, has free tastings of traditional grape and a kiwifruit wine. (☎576 8800; www.millsreef.co.nz. Open daily 10am-5pm.)

ACTIVITIES

Tauranga's outfitters make the most of the town's few natural endowments. A full-day excursion with shaggy-bearded Butler and the **Tauranga Dolphin Company** will take you onto the open seas to swim with Flipper's kin and explore off-shore islands and seal colonies. (☎578 3197 or 0800 836 574; www.swimwithdolphins.co.nz. Tours leave at 9:30am. $90, gear provided.) For those who don't have a whole day to burn, the Mt. Maunganui-based company, **Dolphin Safaris,** offers a marine adventure packed into a busy morning. (☎ 575 4620 or 0800 326 8747; www.nzdolphin.com. Tours depart 7:45am. $100.)

Tauranga is not far from the **Wairoa River** and its gut-wrenching Class V rapids. However, the river is only raftable 26 days a year from Sept.-May, mainly on Sundays, when the dam on its upper reaches is opened. On those rare days, **Wet 'n' Wild Adventure** runs 1hr. jaunts down the Wairoa. They also offer trips on other area rivers. (☎348 3191 or 0800 462 7238; www.wetnwildrafting.co.nz. Wairoa run $80, double run $130.) Whether it's deep-sea fishing or reefer-game, most trips are booked at, and leave from, the **Fishing and Boat Charters office,** on Coronation Pier (☎577 9100).

For those with an aversion to water, there are other fish in the proverbial sea of activities. You can act out your death wish in a 4000m fall with **Tandem Skydiving.** (☎576 7990. $190.) Slightly less precipitous for both body and budget, the **Tauranga Gliding Club** offers varying height levels of flights on weekends. (☎575 6768. From $80.) For the still restless and sufficiently reckless, there is the **Bungee Rocket,** a bizarre manifestation of the Kiwi obsession with all things bungy. Situated on The Strand right on the waterfront, the rocket shoots its hapless passenger 50m into the air at speeds of up to 160kph. (☎ 578 3057; www.bungeerocket.co.nz. Open M-Th and Su 10am-8pm, F-Sa 10am-1am. $35, YHA $20.) **Papamoa Adventure Park** in Papamoa off Welcome Bay Rd., provides horse-trekking, grass-skiing, target shooting, and 160 acres of pastoral land with superb vistas for picnics. (☎ 542 0972. Park entry $5, luge $15.)

DAYTRIPS AND WALKS

Thirty-five kilometers offshore lies **Mayor Island,** an isolated and undeveloped volcanic protrusion under Maori ownership. Snorkeling and diving areas abound but the island has no amenities beyond a rugged campground and huts with a few backpacker beds (dorms $10; tent sites $5). Good supplies and gear are necessary for any trip, as bad weather might strand you there for longer than you anticipate. **Blue Ocean Charters,** at the pier, makes runs to the island depending on demand, weather, and season. (☎ 578-9685. In summer departs Tauranga 7:30am, departs Mayor Island 3pm. Daytrip $75, children $45.) Go down to **Coronation Pier** and ask for other transport options. Even fewer people make it out to the 24km of beaches at nearby **Matakana Island.** However, stretching across the entrance to Tauranga Harbour and absorbing the blows of the Pacific, the island makes for one of the Bay of Plenty's best surf spots.

The **McLaren Falls Park Track,** beginning a 15min. drive down SH29 toward Hamilton, is a pleasantly pastoral area hike. For more mobile travelers, the **Kaimai Mamaku Forest Park,** extending to the west of town, provides 37,140 hectares of forests and rivers laced with trails. With a connecting web of north-south trails, ambitious and experienced trampers can trek the entire spine of the range. The park, with its volcanic origins and andesite plugs, is essentially an extension of the **Coromandel Forest Park,** but harbors fewer crowds.

From **Waihi Beach,** 1hr. north of Tauranga, a web of coastline tracks explores the less-developed coastlines and harbors to the north. From the north end of Waihi Beach, the trail leads 2.4km to **Orokawa Bay** (one-way 45min.) and 8.2km to **Homunga Bay** (one-way 2½hr.). If you stick around the city, you'll have to duke it out with joggers on the boardwalks around the popular **Waikareao Estuary.**

MT. MAUNGANUI ☎ 07

An extinct volcanic cone visible from kilometers away, Mt. Maunganui rises from the otherwise flat shoreline of Tauranga Harbour. Formerly a Maori stronghold, the mountain now reigns over the seasonal town (pop. 16,250) that bears its name. Attracting cruise ships and tourists with its white beaches, "the Mount" bustles with activity in the summer.

TRANSPORTATION. Local buses, **InterCity,** and **Newmans** (☎ 571 3211) run daily to **Tauranga** (15min.), with stops at the Hot Pools, the Visitors Center, near the Pacific Coast Lodge, and the Bayfair Shopping Centre (3km from town). Depending on the bus you catch, service may continue to **Thames, Auckland, Hamilton,** or **Hastings. Guthreys** (☎ 0800 759 999) also runs service to **Auckland** via **Tauranga** three times a day. Taking the local bus will save you some dough (see **Tauranga: Transportation,** p. 170). In the summer, take the **ferry** to **Tauranga** from Salisbury Wharf. (Every hr. 9am-5pm, $6.)

ORIENTATION AND PRACTICAL INFORMATION. The town's main drag is **Maunganui Road,** and the center of town is almost directly below the Mount. **Marine Parade/Ocean Beach Road** runs along the ocean and toward the fine sands of **Papamoa Beach Reserve. The Mall** runs on the harbor side of downtown. The

Information Centre is on Salisbury Ave. west of Maunganui Rd. (☎575 5099; fax 578 7020. Open M-F 9am-5pm, Sa-Su 9am-4pm.) Other services include: **banks** on Maunganui Rd.; **Internet access** at **Mount Internet**, which doubles as Mount Backpackers. (see **Accommodations**, below; $10 per hr.; open daily 9am-8pm); and the **Post Shop and Copy Centre**, 155 Maunganui Rd. (☎575 8180. Open M-F 9am-5pm, Sa 9:30am-noon.)

ACCOMMODATIONS AND FOOD. Bright blue **Pacific Coast Lodge (VIP) ❷**, 432 Maunganui Rd., 2km from the town center, has plenty of space filled with comfy mattresses, educational murals, an ambitious recycling program, and good employment resources. (☎/fax 574 9601 or 0800 666 622; www.pacific-coastlodge.co.nz. Key deposit $10. Dorms $16-18; singles $35; twins and doubles $40-50.) **Mount Backpackers (BBH) ❷**, 87 Maunganui Rd., in the town center, attracts long-term residents. Space is tight but the hosts are helpful and it's a stone's throw from the beach. (☎/fax 575 0860; mountinternet@xtra.co.nz. Dorms $16-18, weekly in winter $95; doubles $45.) At the base of the mountain is **Maunganui Domain Motor Camp ❷**, 1 Adams Ave., with 274 powered tent or caravan sites stretching from the harborside to the beachfront. (☎575 4471; fax 575 4476; domaincamp@xtra.co.nz. $15 deposit per night. Tent sites, vehicles, and caravans $20-22 for 2.)

Food in the Mount is overpriced to fleece the Kiwi vacationers and cruise-ship tourists. However, before you run for the fast food, there are a couple of decent options. The laid-back **Two Small Fish ❹**, 107 Maunganui Rd., serves the funkiest, freshest grub in town. Generous portions of vegetarian and seafood fare are proportional to the inflated price. (☎575 0096. Open daily 9am-10pm, closes early M.) For the most chow for your buck, **Kwang Chow ❷**, 241 Maunganui Rd., next to the cinema, offers an all-you-can-eat smorgasbord of bountiful Chinese food (lunch $11, dinner $14-17). (☎575 5063. Open 11:30am-late. Reservations suggested F-Sa.) **Bombay Brasserie ❸**, at the corner of Pacific Ave. and Maunganui Rd., deals in tasty Tandoor cuisine (mains $15-17), suitable for sit-down meals and sunset takeaways. (☎575 2539. Open daily 6pm-late.) Across the street, **Downtown Food Mart** has beach snacks. (Open M-Sa 7:30am-6pm, Su 8am-6pm.)

SIGHTS AND ACTIVITIES. It doesn't take a rocket scientist or a geologist to find the attraction in the Mount—it sticks out like an **extinct volcano** rising 232m out of the sea. Follow Adams Ave. or The Mall to where they peter out into a paved lot (which may very well be full) and a well-maintained track around the base of the volcano. The track is an easy and dramatic 45min. walk with fantastically warped rocks and crashing surf on one side and grazing sheep and tangled forest on the other. Routes go up the mountain at several spots off the base track, each offering a strenuous 40min. ascent and a knee-knocking 25min. descent. There's also a short jaunt out onto the oddly peninsular **Moturiki Island** that juts into the main beach, and the nearby **Blow Hole**.

The Mount's other major draw (beaches notwithstanding) is the **hot saltwater pools**, located at the base of the mountain. A tepid (read: not quite "hot") lap pool, private pools, storage lockers, and multi-trip passes are all available. (☎575 0868. Open M-Sa 6am-10pm, Su 8am-10pm. $2.50, children $1.50. Private pools $3.50 per 30min.) The prime surfing **beach** is next to the mountain, but white sand stretches for miles to the east, and sheltered waters wait across the peninsula in **Pilot Bay**. **Ocean Sports**, 96 Maunganui Rd., rents surfboards, bodyboards, and wet suits. (☎575 9133. Surfboards $30 per day; wet-suits $10 per day; lessons $25 per hr; kayaks $45 per day. Open daily 9am-5pm.)

WHAKATANE ■ 175

WHAKATANE ☎ 07

The town of Whakatane (FAH-ka-tah-nee; pop. 14,400) struggles to best the wealth of its natural surroundings. Visitors come mainly for the beaches, the climate, and White Island, the ominously smoking volcano 50km offshore.

▣ TRANSPORTATION. **InterCity** departs from the Whakatane Information Centre (☎ 308 6058), on Boon St., for: **Gisborne** (3hr., 1 per day, $26) via **Opotiki** (45min., $15); **Tauranga** (5¾hr., 1 per day, $25) via **Rotorua** (1¾hr., $18); and **Auckland** (6hr., 1-2 per day, $39-71). For **Wellington,** catch the InterCity bus to Rotorua and connect from there. For **taxis,** call **Dial-a-Cab** (☎ 0800 342 522). Local transport options are limited; it's a good idea to **rent a car** to see surrounding attractions. **Hertz,** 105 Commerce St. (☎ 308 6155), is downtown. Although *Let's Go* doesn't recommend it, **hitchhikers** often head immediately across the Whakatane River Bridge. The roundabout where Gorge Rd. branches off Commerce St. towards Ohope is considered to be the best spot for those going east.

▣⑰ ORIENTATION AND PRACTICAL INFORMATION. Whakatane lies on drained wetlands between high bluffs and the final bend of the Whakatane River. The commercial center is pushed up against the bluffs along **The Strand,** with **Boon** and **Richardson Streets** branching off. **Landing/Domain Road,** the western entrance of SH2, and **Commerce Street** against the bluffs are the main routes in and out of town. The **Whakatane Information Centre** is at the corner of Kakahoroa and Quay St. (☎ 308 6058; fax 308 6020; whakataneinfo@xtra.co.nz. Open M-F 8am-5:30pm, Sa-Su 9am-4pm.) Other services include: **WestpacTrust** with **ATM,** on The Strand between Boon and Commerce St. (☎ 308 5129; open M-Tu and Th-F 9am-4:30pm, W 9:30am-4:30pm); the **police** (☎ 308 5255); the **hospital** (☎ 307 8999), west on Domain Rd., left on King St., and right on Stewart St; **Internet access** at Friends Cafe (see **Accommodations and Food,** below; $10 per hr.); and a **post office,** on Commerce St. at The Strand (☎ 307 1155; open M-F 8:30am-5pm, Sa 9am-noon).

▣▣ ACCOMMODATIONS AND FOOD. For beachfront views at comparable prices, those with transport should head 7km over the hill to the **campground** or motels at Ohope Beach (see p. 177). In town, **Karibu Backpackers (BBH) ❷,** 13 Landing Rd., near the corner of King St., is a good bet with new facilities and free transfers to and from the bus stop. Ask about trips to the Whakatane Observatory. (☎/fax 307 8276. Free bike use. Dorms $17; twins and doubles $42; tent sites $12.) **The Whakatane Hotel (VIP) ❷,** 79 The Strand, is clean and centrally located with a kitchen and lounge area. (☎ 307 1670; fax 307 1679; whakatanehotel@xtra.co.nz. Dorms $16; singles $30; twins and doubles $55.) The **Whakatane Motor Camp and Caravan Park ❶** pulls no punches. Follow Beach Rd. to the end of McGarvey Rd. 1km from the town center to find typical facilities with a game room. (☎ 308 8694; fax 308 2070. Tent sites, caravans, and vehicles $10; austere cabins $30; tourist cabins with TV, kitchen, and fridge $40; extra person $10.) For weary travelers seeking added comfort, **Sisam House ❹,** on The Strand near the wharf, pleases with spacious and spotless rooms. (☎ 307 2190. Rooms $70-90.)

Enter the small screen at **Friends Cafe ❷,** on The Strand across from Cinema 5, where you can sample one of "Joey's sandwiches" ($8) or "Ross's coffees" ($3). (☎ 307 8008. Open daily 7am-10pm.) For a waterfront meal, try **The Wharf Shed ❸,** in the Main Wharf beyond The Strand. Seafood specials (lunch $10-16, dinner $23-32) satisfy in an all-wood interior. (☎ 308 5698. Open daily 10:30am-midnight.)

OUTDOOR ACTIVITIES. The two biggest attractions in the area are trips to **White Island** (see below) and dolphin swimming with **Dolphins Down Under,** on the wharf at the end of The Strand. They provide equipment, instruction, refreshments, and even hot showers for the 3-4hr. trip. Depending on the tides and weather, there can be as many as three trips per day during the summer. They also offer a combination cruise every other day which includes a trip to White Island. (☎ 0800 354 7737; www.dolphinswim.co.nz. Direct booking $100, under 12 about $75.) For a more predatory interaction with Whakatane marine life, join **M.V. Charmaine** on a fishing trip. (☎ 308 6871. $30.)

There are three **scenic reserves** in the small area around Whakatane, providing a number of fine bush walks: **Kohi Point,** atop the hill over Whakatane, has panoramic views; **Ohope Scenic Reserve** is home to one of New Zealand's largest remaining pohutukawa forests; and **Mokorua Bush Scenic Reserve** is a recovering pasture land. The walk around the hill between Whakatane and nearby Ohope Beach is breathtaking without leaving you gasping for air. The walk to the **Tauwhare Pa** (1hr.), built several hundred years ago, and the **Mt. Tarawera Crater Walk** (2hr.), a difficult but rewarding walk up a dormant volcano (see **Geothermal Wonders,** p. 164), are also worth a try. Access may be restricted during the summer due to the danger of fires. A long walk, the **Nga Tapuwae o Toi** (the Footprints of Toi) connects the three reserves; while the 20km trail can be covered in one day, it may be more enjoyable to split it into three shorter segments. The Visitors Center in Whakatane has more information including departure points.

WHITE ISLAND ☎ 07

Fifty kilometers off the coast of the Bay of Plenty, Whakaari, "that which can be made visible, uplifted to view," and its vapor sheath are visible from Whakatane on most sunny days. Captain Cook, in his circuit around New Zealand, called it White Island because of the steam cloud perpetually hanging above its volcanic peaks. Composed of three distinct cones, of which two are now extinct, White Island is a landscape of lunar quality, with craters and steaming vents, boiling sulfuric acid pools, and sinuous flows of solid rock. The still living volcano occasionally becomes more active, spewing out ashes that are carried by wind as far as Whakatane, giving the town a thin white coating. Even in such an inhospitable environment, ever-resourceful humans attempted to eke out profit with a sulfur mine that operated intermittently throughout the late 1800s and early 1900s. This evidently did not please the gods; a violent explosion and landslide killed ten men in 1914. Today, mining for gold in tourists' purses has become the popular way to exploit White Island. For a price, anyone can strap on a gas mask, brave the noxious sulfur fumes, and make their own offering to the volcano.

The most affordable approach is by boat. **PeeJay Charters** was named "guardian" of White Island—perhaps the reason behind their slightly higher prices. (☎ 308 9588 or 0800 733 529; www.whiteisland.co.nz. 5-6hr. trip $110, including lunch and morning tea. Weather and tide dependent.) **Blue Sky Tours** runs daily trips in the summer and weekend trips in the winter. (☎ 323 7829 or 025 988 748. $95, including lunch.) To view the volcano from the air, **Scott Air** (☎ 308 9558) and **East Bay Flight Centre** (☎ 308 8446) offer trips over White Island. (Return 50min., $135.) For a touch-down on the cratered surface and a fly-over, a trip with **Vulcan Helicopters** (☎ 0800 804 354; www.vulcanheli.co.nz) costs $375 per person. Both planes and helicopters depart from the airport on Aerodrome Rd., about a 10min. drive from Whakatane town center.

OHOPE BEACH
☎07

Ohope Beach is 11km of unbroken strand blessed with rolling blue waves and views of the rugged East Cape. Visitors come to marinate in sun and surf or to tramp around Mokorua, the hill between Ohope and Whakatane. A 2hr. journey by sand allows travelers to traverse the length of Ohope's narrow strip of land, from the steep bluffs of Mokorua, where surfers struggle to ride small waves, to the entrance of Ohiwa Harbour, a historically rich shellfishery and current resting place for wayward golf balls from the Ohope Beach Golf Course.

The ever-changing main road, branching off at the end of the highway, is West End Rd., becoming Pohutukawa Rd. as you move east, which morphs to Harbour Rd. The **Whakatane Information Centre** staffs a beachfront hut off West End Rd. (Dec.-Feb.). **Buses** on the way to Opotiki stop across from the Mobil Station on Pohutukawa Rd., 300m down from the West End turn-off (daily around 3:45pm; book in Whakatane). Although *Let's Go* doesn't recommend it, thumbers who head to Ohope Beach report that **hitchhiking** prospects are fairly good. The **Ohope Beach Holiday Park ❶**, at the east side of the beach, offers spectacular views. (☎/fax 312 4460; ohopebeach@xtra.co.nz. Tent and powered sites $11-15; tourist flats and cabins from $42 for 2.) Right next door on Harbour Rd. is **Surf & Sand Holiday Park ❷**. Showers, toilet, kitchen, TV room, and laundry are all free. (☎312 4884. Open mid-Dec. to early Feb. Powered sites $15, children $7.50; beachfront apartments for up to 8 people $100.)

OPOTIKI
☎07

A day in Opotiki (o-PO-tah-kee) often brings the sensation of isolation and wilderness, even within the town limits—but it's precisely that wildness and independence that draws most visitors. It is the last town of any size (pop. 4153) before the rugged beauty and remote Maori settlements of the East Coast.

🚍🛈 TRANSPORTATION AND PRACTICAL INFORMATION. InterCity leaves from the **bus depot,** next to the Caltex station at the corner of Church and Bridge St. 1km from the Visitors Center for **Gisborne** (2hr., 1 per day, $18) and **Rotorua** (2hr., 1 per day, $18) via **Whakatane** (1hr., $16). Book tickets at the **Whakatane Information Centre** (☎308 6058).

The **Information Centre** is at St. John and Elliott St. (☎/fax 315 8484; infocentre@odc.govt.nz. Open daily 8am-5pm; in winter M-F.) Pick up the very helpful *Opotiki and the East Cape* brochure. The **DOC** office is in the same building but closes at 4:30pm. The **ANZ**, on Church St., has a **24hr. ATM.** (☎315 1185. Open M-F 9am-4:30pm.) The **post office** is on Church St. in Paper Plus. (Open M and W-F 8:30am-5pm, Tu 9:30am-5pm, Sa 9:30am-noon.)

🛏🍴 ACCOMMODATIONS AND FOOD. You can almost skip a rock across the surf from the porch of the **Opotiki Beach House Backpackers (BBH) ❷**, on Appleton Rd. at Waiotohi Beach 5km west of town on SH2. Sit on the deck (an informal cafe in summer) and watch White Island smoke, or borrow a free surf kayak or surfboard and hit the beach. (☎315 5117; slowry@paradise.net.nz. Free bike use. Dorms $16; doubles $37; tent sites $11. Cash only.) The inside of **Central Oasis Backpackers (BBH) ❶**, 30 King St., endears itself with a homey kitchen and relaxing lounge. (☎315 5165; centraloasis@hotmail.com. Dorms $14; twins and doubles $30; triple $42; tent sites $8.) The **Masonic Hotel ❸**, at Elliott and Church St., has small rooms and a popular restaurant below (mains $15-21; open daily 6pm-late). Stay for the outdated, but historic, 19th-century feel. (☎315 6115. Singles $25; twins and doubles $45.)

If you have seen Church St., you have seen your **food** options. However, the **Flying Pig Cafe ❶**, 95 Church St., breathes some life into the area. Try their hearty breakfasts ($4-12) or the $5.50 BLT. (☎315 7618. Open M 8am-3:30pm, Tu-Th 8am-4pm, F 8am-4:30pm, Sa 9am-2pm.)

◉ SIGHTS. There's not much to see in Opotiki beyond the beach. On rainy days, head to the **Opotiki Heritage and Agricultural Society Museum,** 123 Church St. (Open M-Sa 10am-3:30pm, Su 1:30-4pm. $2, children 50¢.) Across the street, **Hiona St. Stephen's Anglican Church** is the site of the brutal 1865 murder of Rev. Karl Volkner, a casualty of a Maori-Pakeha conflict (ask at the museum for a key). A popular attraction 7km from town is **Hukutaia Domain,** an 11-acre park with a great collection of New Zealand's native plant species. It's worth going, if only for the **Taketakerau,** a huge hollow puriri tree that was sacred to the local Whakatorea tribe.

EAST COAST AND HAWKE'S BAY

The East Coast and Hawke's Bay are blessed with the boundless optimism of those first to see the sun. Gisborne's Mt. Hikurangi is the self-proclaimed home of the world's first dawn while Napier beams with flamboyant Art Deco. These sundrenched locales give rise to orchards and fields overrun with luscious produce and grapes, ripening the "Fruit Bowl of New Zealand." The area also offers visions of primordial New Zealand with the remote East Cape, the dense wilds of Te Urewera National Park, and the North Island's largest remaining tract of native forest.

EAST COAST AND HAWKE'S BAY HIGHLIGHTS

NATURAL SPLENDOR abounds among the waterfalls and tramps of the virtually tourist-free **East Cape** (see p. 184).

NATURAL DIVERSITY flourishes in the isolation of the **Whirinaki Forest Park,** which supports a wide range of New Zealand's flora and fauna (see p. 190).

UNNATURAL ARCHITECTURE brightens the streets of **Napier** in joyfully garish Art Deco fashion (see p. 190).

EAST COAST

GISBORNE ☎ 06

The site of Captain Cook's first landing in 1769, Gisborne (pop. 30,000) has a deep history it won't let you forget, no matter how hard you may *Endeavour*. The city's 50% Maori population and Polytech art classes also make it New Zealand's largest center for contemporary Maori art. Outside the urban limits, stellar beaches offer surfing and swimming, surrounding bluffs give stunning vistas across the sea, and the mild, sunny climate makes ideal farmland.

TRANSPORTATION

Flights: The **airport** is west of the city, at the end of Chalmers Rd. off Gladstone Rd. **Air New Zealand Link** (☎ 867 1608) has many daily flights to **Auckland** (1hr., $235) and **Wellington** (1hr., $250). Book direct or use the **ANZ** office, 37 Bright St. (☎ 868 2700; fax 868 2701). Taxis to the airport run about $10.

Buses: The **bus station** (☎ 868 6139) is at the Visitors Center. **InterCity** leaves daily for: **Auckland** (9hr., 8am, $78); **Napier** (4hr., 9am, $34); and **Rotorua** (4hr., 1 per day, $61) via **Whakatane** (3hr., $45). For transportation in the **East Cape,** see p. 184.

Taxis: Gisborne Taxis (☎ 867 2222) and **Sun City Taxis** (☎ 867 6767) run **24hr.**

Car Rental: Scottie's, 265 Grey St. (☎ 867 7947), next to the Visitors Center and part of Ray Scragg Motors, offers the cheapest rates. Standard economy vehicle from $35 per day, 19¢ per km, or $55 per day, unlimited mileage. Open daily M-F 7am-5pm. For weekend service, use **Budget** (☎ 0800 650 700) at the airport.

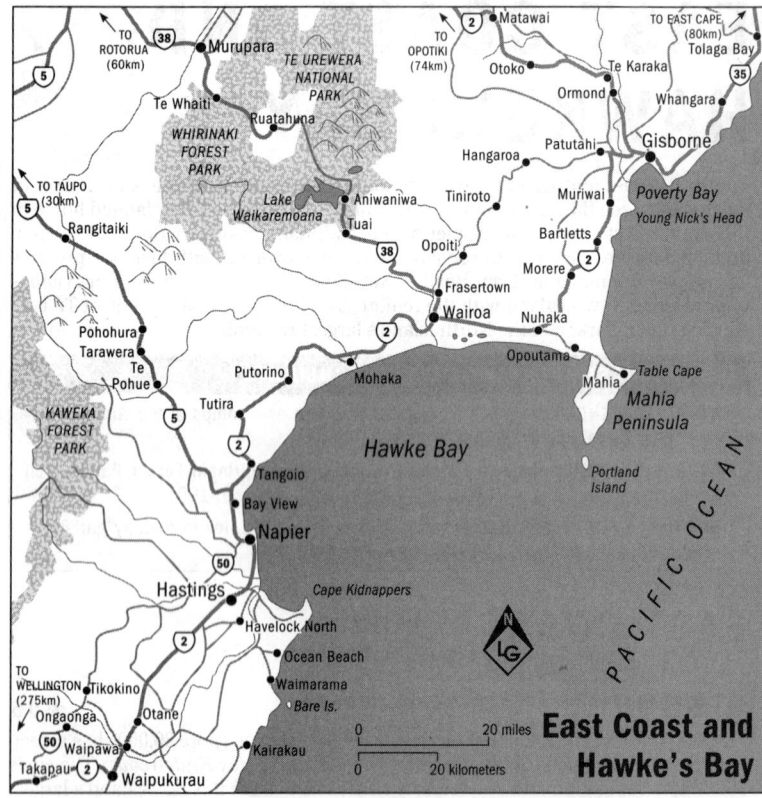

Bike/Surf Rental: Maintrax Cycle (☎867 4571), at the corner of Roebuck and Gladstone St., has bikes ($10 per day, deposit $50). **Sungate,** 55 Salisbury Rd. (☎868 1673), rents surfboards ($30 per day), body boards ($20), and kayaks ($35).

Hitchhiking: To head to the surf beaches at Wainui or Makorori, many hitchhikers start out along Wainui Rd. Hitchers going southwest toward Wairoa or north to Opotiki head to the end of SH35/Gladstone Rd. at Makaraka Rd., where the highway branches off to its respective destinations. *Let's Go* doesn't recommend hitchhiking.

ORIENTATION AND PRACTICAL INFORMATION

Gisborne is located where the **Taruheru** and the **Waimata Rivers** join to form the **Turanganui River** (one of the world's shortest rivers at 1200m). **Gladstone Road** (**SH35,** which turns into **Wainui Road** over the Turanganui Bridge) is the main drag; orient yourself by the **clock tower** at Gladstone and Grey St., alongside the mock-up of Captain Cook's *Endeavour*. The **Esplanade** runs along the Wainui Rd. side of the river, while **Awapuni** and **Salisbury Roads** run parallel to the main beaches.

Visitors Center: Gisborne Information Centre, 209 Grey St. (☎868 6139; fax 868 6138; www.gisbornenz.com), has East Cape tourism info. Open M-F 7:30am-5:30pm, Sa-Su 10am-5pm.

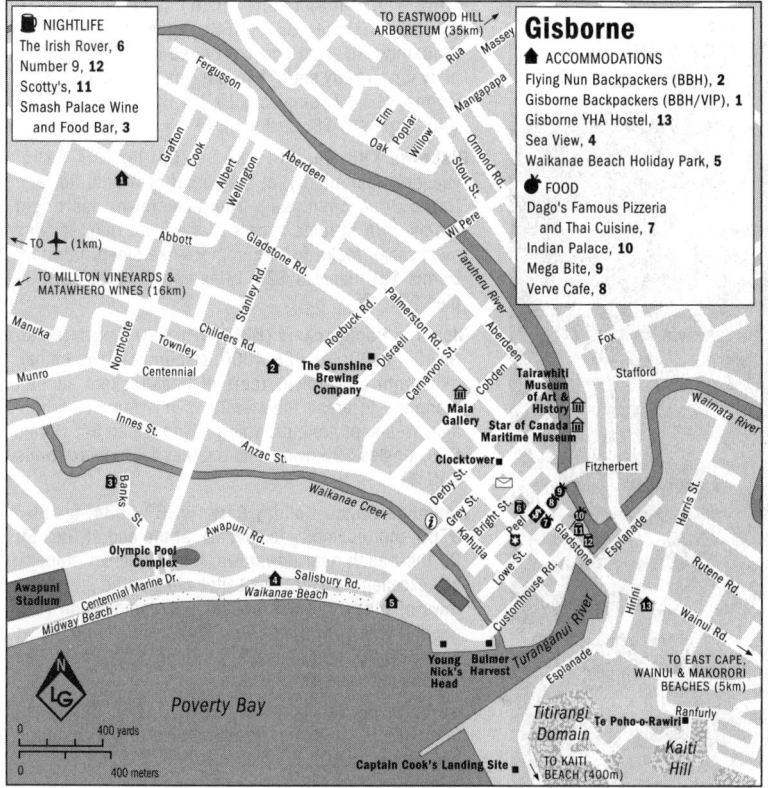

DOC: 63 Carnarvon St. (☎ 867 8531; fax 867 8015). Open M-F 8am-4:30pm.

Banks: Westpac (☎ 867 1359 or 0800 400 600), at the corner of Gladstone Rd. and Peel St. Open M-Tu and Th-F 9am-4:30pm, W 9:30am-4:30pm.

Police: (☎ 867 9059), at the corner of Peel St. and Gladstone Rd.

Medical Services: Kaiti Road Medical Centre (☎ 867 7411), at the corner of Turenne and De Lautour Rd., off Wainui Rd. Open M-F 8am-8pm, Sa-Su 9am-6pm. For **urgent care** only, look to the **hospital** (☎ 867 9099), on Ormond Rd.

Internet Access: Cyber-zone, 83 Gladstone Rd. (☎ 868 7138). $12 per hr. Open M-Sa 10am-8pm, Su noon-6pm; in winter M-Sa 10am-5pm.

Post Office: The Gisborne Post Shop, 166 Gladstone Rd. (☎ 867 8220), inside Books & More. Open M-F 8:30am-5:30pm, Sa 9am-4pm, Su 10am-3pm.

ACCOMMODATIONS AND CAMPING

Beachfront accommodations often charge $10-20 more than those just across the street. In the off-season, hostels attract permanent boarders who rent out rooms for months at a time, creating a very different atmosphere from the summer.

IN RECENT NEWS

SACRED LANDS AND TOURIST DOLLARS

Young Nick's Head, named for Captain Cook's cabin-boy who spotted the site, has recently become the site of controversy. When John Griffin, an American financier, announced his plan to buy the historic landmark in 2002, the local Ngai Tamanuhiri tribe responded with protest. The Maori group, who identify Young Nick's Head as the landing place of the first members of their tribe over 1000 years ago, wanted the coastal stretch to stay in Kiwi hands. After occupying Young Nick's Head, protesters marched from Gisborne to Wellington and camped on Parliament grounds for two days, forcing the government to include the group in negotiations.

New York-bred Griffin fell in love with New Zealand on a visit and decided to purchase a chunk of the splendor for himself—even if that chunk came at a $3.3 million price tag. After extensive discussions with the Maori, the wealthy businessman agreed to donate the cliffs, a *pa* site, and the headland's peak to public ownership. In addition, he guaranteed that the site will remain undeveloped and that he will create a fund to recognize the tribe's cultural and spiritual values in the property.

Griffin intends to live on the land during the American winter. His purchase may demonstrate a prevailing trend in New Zealand land use. The Maori first landed at Young Nick's Head, then the British, and now, foreign tourists have a firm grasp on New Zealand land use. The next wave of colonization may well be by wealthy holiday-makers.

Flying Nun Backpackers (BBH), 147 Roebuck St. (☎868 0461; fax 867 0463; yager@xtra.co.nz), off Gladstone Rd. This convent-turned-hostel has traded piety for a rowdy set of backpackers. Key deposit $10. Dorms $15-17; singles $25-27; twins and doubles $40; tent sites $8. Cash only. ❷

Gisborne YHA Hostel (☎867 3269; fax 867 3296; yha.gis@clear.net.nz), at the corner of Wainui Rd. and Harris St. A 5min. walk from downtown, this bright orange YHA attracts people of all ages. Thin, sagging mattresses make for a hammock-like sleep. Internet. Dorms $16; singles $26; twins and doubles $38; triples $57. ❷

Gisborne Backpackers (BBH/VIP), 690 Gladstone Rd. (☎868 1000; fax 868 4000; gisbornebp@xtra.co.nz), 2km from downtown. Years of backpackers haven't managed to erase the sterility of this former orphanage. Well-kept grounds. Free pick-up. Linen $4. Dorms $16; singles $25; twins and doubles $40; deluxe twins $50. ❷

Waikanae Beach Holiday Park (☎867 5634; fax 867 9765; motorcamp@gdc.govt.nz), at the end of Grey St. On the beach near downtown, this municipal property has excellent facilities. Tent sites are granted privacy by rows of pines. "Ranch house" accommodation (1-2 people) with vinyl mattresses $28; self-catering tourist flats $55-60; tent sites $9, powered $10. Prices rise $2-5 in summer. ❶

Sea View, 68 Salisbury Rd. (☎867 3879). This waterfront B&B is an attractive alternative to the Gisborne backpacker scene. Doubles with bath $90. ❹

FOOD

Gisborne's nicer downtown cafes and restaurants, most on **Gladstone Road,** offer a respite from the usual artery-clogging budget cuisine. And there's always **Pak 'N Save,** 274 Gladstone Rd. (☎868 9029. Open daily 8am-8pm.)

Dago's Famous Pizzeria and Thai Cuisine, 50 Gladstone Rd. (☎868 7666 or 867 0543), cooks up some of Gisborne's tastiest and most creative takeaway dishes. Read National Geographic while waiting for mini pizzas ($6), Thai mains ($12-15), sushi ($6), and pasta ($12). Delivery $4. Open daily 9:30am-9:30pm. ❷

Mega Bite (☎867 5787), on Peel St. by Palmerston Rd. Backpackers from across the globe find home-cooking sanctuary here; just read the personal testimonies written on the walls. Grab a pen to share the ingredients of your $3 self-made sandwich. Open daily 6:30am-5pm; later in summer. ❶

Indian Palace, 55 Gladstone Rd. (☎863 0901). Mouth-melting butter chicken curry ($15) and other Indian platters satisfy in this enticing eatery. Open daily 5:30pm-late; also Tu-Su 11:30am-2:30pm. ❸

Verve Cafe, 121 Gladstone Rd. (☎868 9095). The airy Verve has local artwork on the walls, couches in the back, and limited Internet access. Grilled sandwiches ($8) and filling fish dishes ($13) round out the menu. Open daily 8:30am-10pm. ❷

NIGHTLIFE

Smash Palace Wine and Food Bar, 24 Banks St. (☎867 7769). Take Awapuni Rd. west into the industrial district. A surreal post-industrial trove of junk decor crashes into the walls, from the antique cars suspended in mid-air to the old DC-3 flying into the roof. Consume local $3.50 brews like Gisborne Gold. Open daily noon-late; in winter M-Tu and Su 3pm-late, W-Sa 1pm-late.

The Irish Rover (☎867 1112), on Peel St. Snag a Guinness ($5.50) in this popular barn-style pub. Weeknights are low-key, but weekends often feature live music (cover $3). Handles on tap $3.50. Open M-F 11am-3am, Sa 3pm-3am, Su 10am-10pm.

Number 9, 9 Gladstone Rd. (☎867 3199). This funkadelic pub is No. 1 with surfers. Collecting residual sand on F-Sa nights, the wooden floorboards resound with live music. Open W-F 11:30am-3pm; also Th-Sa 4:30pm-3am.

Scotty's, 33 Gladstone Rd. (☎867 8173). The oldest bar in Gisborne offers a laid-back atmosphere. Enjoy one of the 13 beers on tap ($4) in the back garden. Happy Hour 5-7pm. Open daily 7am-3am.

SIGHTS

Titirangi Domain, also known as **Kaiti Hill,** is a good starting place for seeing Gisborne's sights. Once across the river, follow the signs from Hirini Rd. At the base of the hill sits **Te Poho-o-Rawiri,** the largest traditional *marae* built from modern materials in New Zealand. It is cavernous and stunningly crafted, with painted roof rafters, woven tukutuku reed panels, and intricately carved dark wood panels with iridescent paua shell eyes. Large *pou pou* (panels) chronicle Maori genealogy; each figure represents a specific ancestor. Ask permission at the office first and remove your shoes before entering. Nearby sits **Toko Toru Tapu,** a Maori church nestled on the hillside.

Continue up the hill—a steep one popular with masochistic joggers—for a series of phenomenal views across the city and Poverty Bay to the white cliffs of **Young Nick's Head,** named after Captain Cook's cabin boy Nicholas Young, who first sighted New Zealand from the *Endeavour*. Kaiti Hill can also be tackled via a path winding up from the base of the Cook Landing Site (accessible from the Esplanade along the river).

The **Tairawhiti Museum of Art and History** (☎867 3832), on Stout St., features rotating art galleries and displays on natural and cultural history. Just behind the Art and History museum on the riverbank sits the **Star of Canada Maritime Museum,** the transplanted bridgehouse of a British steamer that grounded on Kaiti Beach in 1912. (Both museums open M-F 10am-4pm, Sa-Su 1:30-4pm; Jan. daily 10am-4pm. Free.) For contemporary art-in-progress, head to the **Maia Gallery,** on Cobden St. between Gladstone Rd. and Palmerston St. This airy showroom and workshop is a studio for students in the *Toihoukura* (Maori Visual Arts) course at the local Tairawhiti Polytechnic. (☎868 8068. Open M-F 8am-5pm. Free.)

The **Eastwoodhill Arboretum** is a popular attraction 35km northwest of the city on the Ngatapa-Rere Rd. Laid out by a meticulous collector, its 64 hectares grow some of the finest flora from the Southern Hemisphere. (☎863 9800; www.eastwoodhill.org.nz. Open daily 9am-5pm. $5, children free.)

ACTIVITIES

For the area's safest and most convenient waters, try **Waikanae Beach,** stretching from the end of Grey St.; it gets a bit crowded at peak times. The shore becomes **Midway Beach** a little farther along Poverty Bay, with soft sand and a prime surf spot at its western end. While the bay beaches have their golden wave moments, many surfers with more experience head north of the city to the coastal beaches at **Wainui,** about 6km out on SH35, and **Makorori,** another 4km along. These beaches are used for swimming as well but occasionally have riptides. With plenty of open land between the road and the beaches, the area is popular with campers. **Kaiti Beach,** at the base of Kaiti Hill, is rocky and unpatroled, but the exposed location provides strong gusts for windsurfing. Or, head one block inland from Waikanae Beach to the **Gisborne Olympic Pool Complex,** on Centennial Marine Dr. (☎867 6220. Open daily 6am-8pm. $2.50, children $1.50.) **Waimoana Horse Trekking,** based on Mysnar St. off Wainui Rd., offers an unforgettable trek over sheep-dotted bush and surf-crashing beach; all levels welcome. (☎868 8218. 1hr. $35; 2hr. $45.)

Stop by the organic **Millton Vineyard** (☎862 8680), in Manutuke on Papatu Rd. off SH2 towards Wairoa, or the **Matawhero Wines** (☎868 8366), on Riverpoint Rd., to sample the area's finest vintages. For touring and tasting of a different spirit, clear your palate for the cider, scrumpy, and schnapper of **Bulmer Harvest,** on Customhouse St. by the water. (☎868 8300. Open daily 9am-5pm; in winter M-F.) **The Sunshine Brewing Co.,** 109 Disraeli St., off Gladstone St., makes Gisborne Gold, Sundowner, Moonshine, and other naturally brewed beers. (☎867 7777. Open M-Sa 9am-6pm. Call ahead for free tour.) If you're around in October, partake of the **Gisborne Wine and Food Festival;** ask the Visitors Center for information.

THE EAST CAPE ☎07/06

New Zealand's final frontier of tourism, the East Cape's stunning craggy coastline draws travelers in search of the increasingly-elusive "untouched New Zealand." From Gisborne to Opotiki, the Pacific Coast Highway (SH35) passes scores of sleepy seaside towns on its way around the rugged Raukumara Mountains. The vast majority of the people living here are Maori, and intricate traditional carvings adorn the many churches and *marae*.

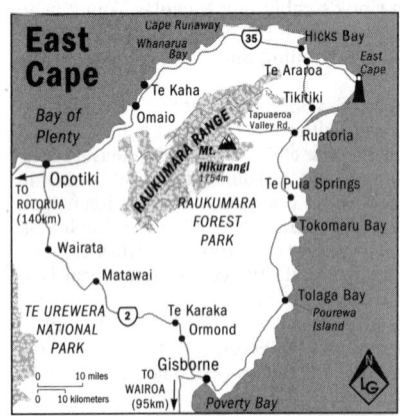

TRANSPORTATION

Buses: Slim's East Cape Escape (☎07 345 6645) is the only bus that circumscribes the region. In partnership with Kiwi Experience, Slim runs a 3-day circuit letting passengers on and off as they like. Buses depart **Rotorua** M and W-F (in winter M, W, and F), spend 1 night on the **East Cape,** 1 in **Te Urewera National Park,** and then loop back to Rotorua. $220, not including meals or accommodations, which Slim's can arrange.

Courier Transport: These mini-vans deliver parcels and supplies from **Opotiki** and **Gisborne** to the various settlements and farms around the Cape,

THE EAST CAPE ■ 185

allowing passengers to see much that would be missed from the main highway. **Polly's Passenger Courier Service** (☎ 020 702 9621) runs between Whakatane and Hicks Bay (3½hr.; M-F departs Whakatane noon, Hicks Bay 7:30am; $30, between Opotiki and Hicks Bay $25) and between Hicks Bay and Gisborne (3½hr.; M-F departs Hicks Bay 6:30am, Gisborne 1pm; $30). **Dick Cook Courier Service** (☎ 025 371 364) travels between Hicks Bay and Gisborne (4½hr.; M-Sa departs Hicks Bay 7:30am, Gisborne 2pm; $25) and can transport between Whakatane and Hicks Bay with a related courier (4½hr.; M-F departs Whakatane 1pm, Hicks Bay 6:30am; $30, between Opotiki and Hicks Bay $25).

Hitchhiking: Hitchhikers find friendly rides around the cape in summertime; late afternoon is peak traffic time as people return from Gisborne or Opotiki. In winter, increased rain and reduced traffic make hitching a more dubious prospect, particularly on the less populated northern coast. Let's Go does not recommend hitchhiking.

ORIENTATION AND PRACTICAL INFORMATION

Well maintained and fully paved, **SH35** runs the Cape's 334km perimeter. Most towns along the way have at least one store, takeaway, gas station, and postal service, sometimes all in one.

Visitors Center: The visitors centers in **Opotiki, Gisborne,** and the **Te Puia Springs Service Centre** (☎ 06 864 6853) are the best bet for questions regarding the southern coast. Open M-F 8am-4:30pm. The comprehensive and free *Opotiki and East Cape*, available at all of the above, lists most travelers' resources, kilometer by kilometer.

Banks: Westpac (☎ 06 864 8443), in Ruatoria, is the only bank in the East Cape. Open M-Tu and Th-F 9am-4:30pm, W 9:30am-4:30pm. There are **no ATMs.**

Telephone Codes: ☎ 07 from Opotiki to Hicks Bay; ☎ 06 from Hicks Bay to Gisborne.

ACCOMMODATIONS AND CAMPING

The coastline between Gisborne and Hicks Bay contains several designated spots for **free camping** (between Labour Day and Easter), usually recognizable by a morass of caravans. Try **Pouawa Beach** (17km north of Gisborne), **Loisel's Beach** at Waihau Bay (50km), **Tokomaru Bay** (90km), **Waipiro Bay** (106km), or **Hicks Bay** (180km). The East Cape's northern shore tends to restrict camping. As for **food,** the East Cape lacks restaurants and supermarkets. Departing from ordinary *Let's Go* format, the following accommodations are listed in **geographical order** (following SH35 from Opotiki to Gisborne) rather than in order of researcher preference.

Te Kaha Holiday Park and Motel (☎ 07 325 2894), at the northern end of **Te Kaha.** "Luxury" backpacker facilities (reading lamps, TV, in-room kitchen). Dorms $15; tent sites $9, powered $10. ❷

Robyn's Place (☎ 07 325 2904), in **Whanarua Bay.** A house complete with a lounge deck, an ocean view, excellent music, and a batik thrown over the couch. Free laundry and linen. Dorms $17; doubles $40; tent sites $9. ❷

Rendezvous on the Coast Holiday Park (☎ 07 325 2899), in **Whanarua Bay.** A well kept campground with a pool, skateboard half-pipe, and a mini-golf course. Half-day kayak rental $20. Internet. Dorms $15; tent sites $8, powered $10. ❶

Maraehako Bay Retreat (BBH) (☎ 07 325 2648; thumbloon@paradise.net.nz), in **Whanarua Bay** 50m past Rendezvous on the Coast. Tucked into a rocky cove, this handcrafted retreat with super friendly owners is a stone's throw from the ocean. Dorms $18; singles $25; doubles $50; tent sites $13. ❷

Hicks Bay Backpackers Lodge (VIP) (☎/fax 06 864 4731), on Onepoto Beach Rd. in **Hicks Bay.** Plain and simple, this lodge is adjacent to a good swimming and surfing beach. Free use of videos, boogie boards, and kayaks. Dorms $15; doubles $50. ❷

186 ■ THE EAST CAPE

SunRise Lodge and Beachcamp (☎ 06 864 4854), in **Te Araroa**. This windswept patch of land and its home-style accommodations are as peaceful as it gets. Dorms $17; doubles $40; B&B twins and doubles $80; tent sites $8. ❷

Brian's Place (BBH) (☎ 06 864 5870), up the hill from Potae St. in **Tokomaru Bay**. Cool lofts, premium views, and a porch studded with Central American hammocks define this tiny backpackers. Dorms $16; 1 double $38; tent sites $8. ❷

SIGHTS AND ACTIVITIES

From Opotiki to Hicks Bay, the highway skirts the green lush coast and reveals the Cape's spectacular views, especially in December when the pohutukawa trees explode with red flowers. In **Whanarua Bay,** the road across from the macadamia nut farm leads down to a stunning and undeveloped section of rocky beach full of tidal pools. After Hicks Bay, the road moves inland. En route to Te Araroa it passes the Te Araroa Holiday Park, home to the **world's easternmost cinema.** (☎ 06 864 4873. $5, children $3.) Just down the road, the beachfront schoolyard in **Te Araroa** holds the **world's largest pohutukawa tree**. Te Araroa is also the gateway to the lonely **East Cape Lighthouse,** at the easternmost point in mainland New Zealand. **East Cape 4WD Sunrise Tours** does a morning run along the 20km road to the lighthouse. (☎ 06 864 4775. $25, min. 2 people.)

Tikitiki lies 27km south of Te Araroa. Its **St. Mary's Memorial Church** perches on a hill overlooking SH35. One of the most impressive Maori buildings in the region, the church's exterior hides an ornately carved inner sanctuary. A turn-off from the main highway near **Ruatoria** leads to Pakihiroa Station, the trailhead for the track up **Mount Hikurangi** (1754m). Access to the peak is restricted, but eager hikers can usually obtain permission to stay in a hut 10km up the mountain ($5 per night) at the **Te Runanga o Ngati Porou** office (☎ 06 867 9960).

Brian of Brian's Place (see **Accommodations and Camping**, p. 186) runs **horse treks** out of **Tokomaru Bay** (2hr. $30, full-day $70, overnight $130; longer trips available on demand). Another 36km toward Gisborne, **Tolaga Bay** harbors the longest wharf in the Southern Hemisphere, a deteriorating 600m testament to the days before highways, resting at the end of Wharf Rd., 1.5km off SH35. Nearby is the **Cooks Cove Walkway,** an easy trip to the site of one of Captain Cook's first landings in *Aotearoa* (5.8km, return 2½hr.; closed Aug.-Oct. for lambing).

TE UREWERA NATIONAL PARK ☎ 06

The misty ridges and untamed valleys of Te Urewera National Park shelter a mesmerizing blend of cultural and natural history. The region's isolated bush has long been home to the Tuhoe (TOO-hoy) Maori, who resisted European intrusion with greater force and success than most other tribes. The beech and podocarp now stand in the largest national park on the North Island—and the only one in New Zealand named for a camping accident ("urewera" means "burnt penis," the ailment of a rather unfortunate Maori chief who rolled onto his fire one night). Today, the floor of Lake Waikaremoana and several adjoining parcels of land remain under Maori ownership.

WHEN TO GO The park is best enjoyed in the summer (mid-Oct. to Mar.) since the winter weather can be wet and cold; the walks are open year-round with the right equipment. Always be prepared for all weather conditions.

TE UREWERA NATIONAL PARK ■ 187

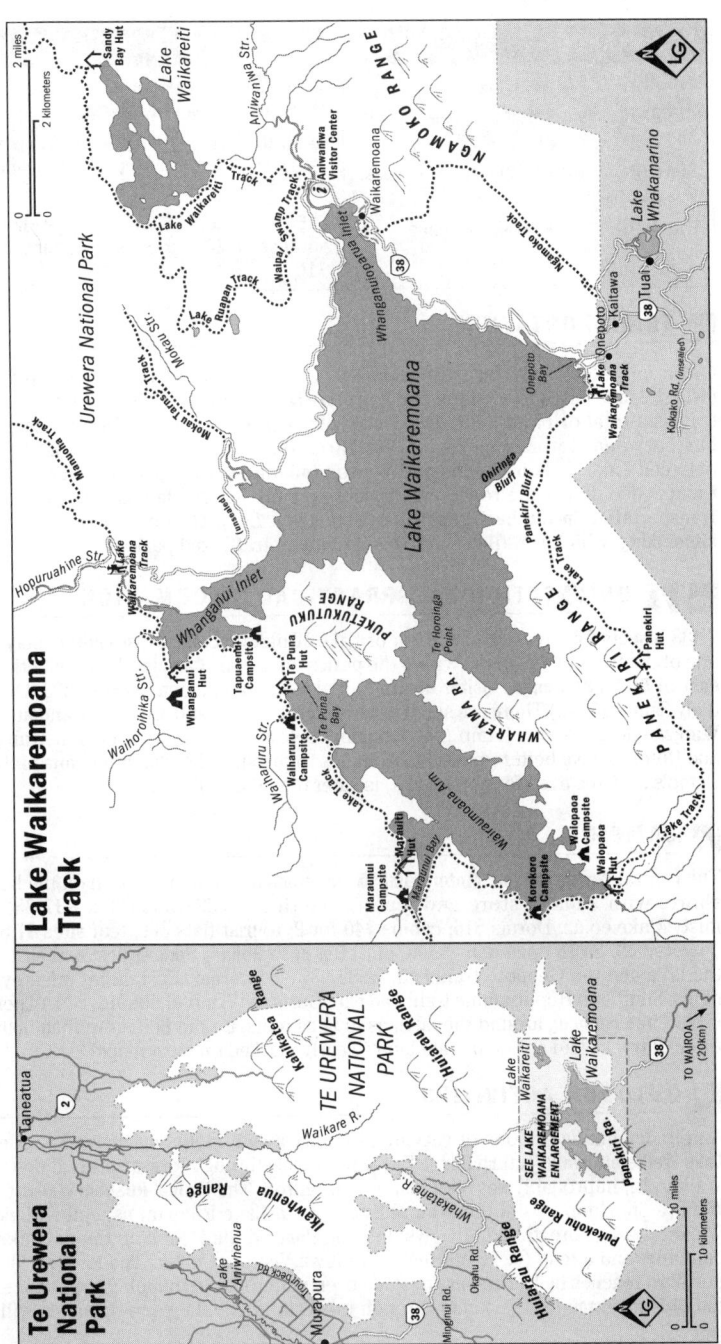

188 ■ THE EAST CAPE

AT A GLANCE	
AREA: 212,672 hectares.	**GATEWAYS:** Whakatane, Taneatua, Murupara, Ruatahuna, Wairoa.
CLIMATE: Warm weather Oct.-Mar. Cold and boggy in winter.	**CAMPING:** Fully serviced motor camp at Lake. Unserviced campsites. Backcountry huts.
FEATURES: Largest forested wilderness. Hunting, fishing.	
HIGHLIGHTS: Lake Waikaremoana.	**FEES & RESERVATIONS:** Book well in advance in summer. Huts $14, camping $10.

TRANSPORTATION

Often unsealed, **SH38** cuts through the park on its way from Wairoa to SH5 (which leads north to Rotorua and south to Taupo). From Wairoa to Rotorua, it travels a total of 170km. **Big Bush Holiday Park** (see **Camping**, p. 188) operates a **bus** between Rotorua and Lake Waikaremoana (3½hr., M and F, $65) and between Lake Waikaremoana and Wairoa (45min., daily, $25). **Slim's East Cape Escape** also drives the road's length as part of a several-day shuttle tour (see **Transportation in the East Cape: Buses**, p. 184). *Let's Go* doesn't recommend **hitchhiking**, which is difficult in the relatively untrafficked park.

ORIENTATION AND PRACTICAL INFORMATION

SH38 bisects Te Urewera just north of Lake Waikaremoana. Most visitors stay at one of the two holiday parks within the park's limits (see **Camping**, below); both lie east of **DOC's Aniwaniwa Visitor Centre** on Lake Waikaremoana. (☎837 3803. Open daily 8am-4:45pm.) There are small **general stores** in Tuai and Murupara, and at the Waikaremoana Motor Camp (see **Camping**, below), but supermarkets in Wairoa and Rotorua have better prices and **ATMs**. As for parking, the Waikaremoana Motor Camp's lot (free even for non-guests) is safer than the trailheads.

CAMPING

The central **Waikaremoana Motor Camp** ❶ occupies a gem of a location on the lake shore, with a small store and a petrol station. (☎837 3826; fax 837 3825; misty@lake.co.nz. Dorms $16; cabins $40 for 2; tourist flats $60; tent sites $7.50, powered $9. Store open daily 8am-5pm.) **Big Bush Holiday Park** ❷ lies 3km east of the lake and the Onepoto trailhead. (☎837 3777. Internet. Restaurant open evenings. Shuttle to Hopuruahine trailhead $25. Dorms $17; motel doubles $70.) There is also **free camping** around the lake, as long as tents are pitched more than 500m from all tracks and not on private land (clearly marked on most maps).

OUTDOOR ACTIVITIES

Ample day-hiking options of varying difficulty await, including the well-graded **Lake Waikareiti Walk** (return 2hr.). The walk travels through forest to island-dotted Waikareiti, improbably set on a lush green hilltop. The **Waipai-Ruapani-Waikareiti Walk** (a 6hr. loop) visits the Waipai Swamp and Lake Ruapani as well as Lake Waikareiti. For breathtaking views, hike up **Panekiri Bluff.** Pick up the day hikes pamphlet and a map ($2) from the Aniwaniwa Visitors Center. The less-traveled northern reaches of Te Urewera provide even more remote tramping experiences; the **Six Foot Track** (3 days) cuts through the Tauranga Valley and demands solid navigational skills, while the nearby **Whakatane Loop Track** (4-5 days) makes a full circuit through the Whakatane Valley.

Since all of the desirable fish and game in the park are introduced species, DOC smiles upon their slaughter. **Fishing licenses** are available at **Waikaremoana Motor Camp** ($28 per week, $13.50 per day), which also rents and sells gear (1-day rod rental $5). Noel Himona of **Waikaremoana Guided Tours** leads hunting trips and fishing forays. He also rents **kayaks** and **canoes.** (☎ 837 3729. Fishing and hunting $250 per day for 1 person, $300 for 2; kayaks $30-35 per day; canoes $45 per day.) Additionally, DOC rents rowboats ($30 per day).

LAKE WAIKAREMOANA TRACK

With its vast tangles of native trees and the sounds of kiwis crying throughout the night, the Lake Waikaremoana (WIE-kah-ray-moe-AH-nah) Track affords an ideal opportunity to experience New Zealand's bizarre biology. Hulking bluffs conceal azure inlets, hooting birds fly alongside humming insects, and dense bush gives way to sweeping panoramas. With both challenging ascents and mellow stretches, the track appeals to a range of tramping abilities.

Length: 48km, 3-5 days.

Trailheads: Trampers can begin at either **Onepoto** (which tackles the toughest climb right off the bat), a 20min. drive south of the Visitors Center and 500m off SH38, or **Hopuruahine** (which leaves Panekiri Bluff for when one's pack is lighter), 1km off SH38 a 30min. drive north of the Visitors Center.

Transportation: Waikaremoana Guided Tours (☎ 837 3729) shuttles trampers between the Waikaremoana Motor Camp and **Onepoto** ($15), **Hopuruahine Landing** ($25), **Waiopaoa Hut** ($80), **Korokoro Campsite** ($80), **Marauiti Hut** ($70), and **Waiharuru Hut** ($70). Though *Let's Go* does not recommend it, **hitchhiking** to and from the trailheads is a cheaper but far more time-consuming endeavor.

Seasonality: It's possible to complete the track year-round, but it gets awfully boggy and cold in winter. The best weather generally lasts from mid-Oct. to Mar.

Huts and Campsites: There are 5 huts and 5 campsites. **Booking system** operates year-round. The **Aniwaniwa Visitor Centre,** SH38, Private Bag 2213, Wairoa (☎ 837 3803; fax 837 3722), handles reservations. Huts $14, under 18 $7; camping $10/$5. Huts have untreated water, wood or gas heating stoves, and toilets.

Storage: Free at the Waikaremoana Motor Camp store.

ONEPOTO TRAILHEAD TO PANEKIRI HUT. *8.8km, 5hr.* The track starts on the small trail beside the DOC sign in the grassy field just off SH38. After passing a small shelter, the trail briefly follows a wide grassy track until it reaches a fork for **Lake Kiriopukae** (return 20min.). From the fork, the track makes a calf-burning 600m ascent to **Panekiri Bluff.** A gauntlet of roots leads through wind-wracked forest, which occasionally parts to reveal a fresh vista of the lake waters below. The steepest section comes within the first hour, after which the incline mellows some as it winds up the ridge of the Panekiri Range. There is **no water** along this section of the trail. The highest bunch of beds on the track, tall-ceilinged **Panekiri Hut** (1180m; 36 bunks) perches on a ridge with a two-way view: the lake lies to the north, while the Hawke's Bay region's cleaved hills roll into the southern horizon.

PANEKIRI HUT TO WAIOPAOA HUT AND CAMPSITE. *7.6km, 3½hr.* From Panekiri Hut, the track drops steadily, often steeply, passing plenty of tree ferns, tea trees (kanuka), and mossy rock walls and eventually reaches the shore of Lake Waikaremoana. Snug **Waiopaoa Hut** (21 bunks) sits at the base of the bluff; nearby

Waiopaoa Campsite lies by a frog-filled inlet. As with all of the track's lakefront campsites, sandflies pester this otherwise lovely spot.

WAIOPAOA HUT AND CAMPSITE TO MARAUITI HUT. *12.1km, 4½hr.* A flat stretch of lakeside track leads to the turn-off for stunning **Korokoro Falls** (return 1hr.), where hundreds of rivulets gush down a vertical stone slab. **Korokoro Campsite** lies on a lagoon shortly past the turn-off for the falls (head right after the bridge). From the campsite, the track rolls above the shoreline. Past a private hut and the DOC warden's quarters sits **Maranui Campsite,** with a choice inlet view and surrounding bluffs. **Marauiti Hut** (22 bunks) waits on the other side of a peninsular hill, on the edge of a cove perfect for fishing or swimming.

MARAUITI HUT TO WAIHARURU HUT AND CAMPSITE. *6.2km, 2hr.* Beyond Marauiti, the track continues to undulate, as does its surface—this is the muddiest part of the tramp. Posh **Waiharuru Hut** (40 bunks) features separate kitchen and bunkroom buildings, a gas heater, washrooms, and wide porches overlooking the lake. Adjacent **Waiharuru Campsite** borders what could almost be called a beach.

WAIHARURU HUT AND CAMPSITE TO HOPURUAHINE TRAILHEAD. *10.5km, 3½hr.* A kilometer past the Waiharuru complex, the track runs a steep 100m over the **Puketukutuku peninsula.** Keep your ears perked for the sounds of kiwi birds. On the other side of the hill, sites at the **Tapuaenui campsite** are well segregated by shrubbery. Largely flat hiking along some of Waikaremoana's most striking inlets leads to **Whanganui Hut** (18 bunks), which rests next to a creek but has minimal lake access. The remaining walk to **Hopuruahine Landing** (where Waikaremoana Guided Tours picks up its passengers) is brisk and undaunting, as are the last kilometers through grassy fields and up a river valley to the **Hopuruahine Trailhead.**

WHIRINAKI FOREST PARK ☎ 07

Although not as dramatic as the neighboring Te Urewera National Park, 55,000-hectare Whirinaki Forest Park contains magnificent lowland rainforest. Soaring podocarp and tawa canopy shelter tree ferns and native birds like the tui and the kiwi. Although Whirinaki is accessible year-round (if somewhat drizzly in the winter), relatively few visitors make it this far into the sticks. The **Rangitaiki Area DOC Office,** on SH38 in Murupara 60km southeast of Rotorua, distributes information on park walks and weather conditions. (☎ 366 5641. Open M-F 8am-5pm.)

HAWKE'S BAY

In February 1931, a massive earthquake (7.9 on the Richter scale) rattled much of Hawke's Bay into rubble. Though the history of the region didn't begin with the big bang, it certainly seemed to freeze there. Napier and Hastings were rebuilt in the flamboyant Art Deco and Spanish Mission styles popular at the time. Today, the main attractions of the region are the anachronistic buildings and scenic wineries. Most tourists zip past Hawke's Bay, leaving the region uncrowded and relaxed.

NAPIER ☎ 06

You know you've hit Napier when cafes outnumber takeaways, and even the McDonald's is McDeco. The city is an Art Deco overload of zigzags, bubbling geometric fountains, and neon-lit clock towers, all in riots of confectionery colors. But the surreal sensibility isn't limited to the Deco; Napier has the highest per capita rate of oddball attractions in New Zealand. A furry opossum mortuary selling

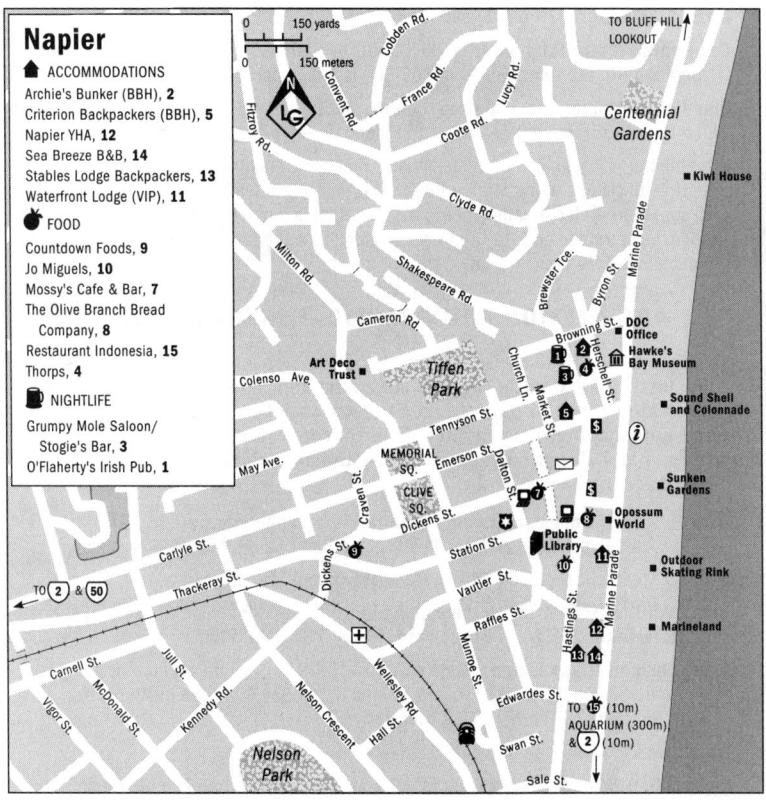

souvenirs is just down the road from a sanctuary for disabled penguins and overweight sea lions. A major stopping point for fruit-picking travelers, the town is packed from November to April.

TRANSPORTATION

Flights: The **Hawke's Bay Airport** (☎835 1130) is north of Napier on SH2. The **ANZ Travel Centre** (☎833 5400), at the corner of Hastings and Station St., books flights to **Auckland** (7 per day, around $243) and **Wellington** (5 per day, around $218). Open M-F 9am-5pm, Sa 9am-noon. The **Supershuttle** (☎844 7333) offers service to the **airport** ($9) and **Hastings** ($25 for min. 2 people). A taxi to the airport costs about $9.

Buses: Coaches leave from the Napier Travel Centre (☎834 2720), at the train station on Munroe St. **Intercity/Newmans** departs for: **Wellington** (6hr., 2-3 per day, $60) via **Palmerston North** (3hr., $38); **Auckland** (7hr., 3 per day, $78) via **Rotorua** (3hr., $55) and **Taupo** (2hr., $35); and **Gisborne** (4hr., 1 per day, $34) via **Wairoa** (2hr., $21). **Nimbus** (☎877 8133) runs M-F every hr. 7am-5:30pm to **Hastings** (45min., $5) and **Havelock North** (1hr., $5). Nimbus departs from the bus terminal on Dalton St. near Dickens St. To get to Hastings on weekends, catch an InterCity or Newmans bus heading south ($11).

Taxis: StarTaxis (☎ 835 5511) and **Napier Taxis** (☎ 835 7777 or 0800 627 437).

Car Rental: Metro Rent-A-Car (☎ 835 0590 or 0508 350 590), on Corunna Bay off Hyderabad Rd. Economy cars from $69 per day; min. age 21.

Bike Rental: Napier Kart and Cycle Centre, at the corner of Tennyson St. and Clive Sq. W (☎ 835 9528), rents Oct.-Apr. for $25 per day with helmet and lock.

Hitchhiking: Although *Let's Go* doesn't recommend it, hitchhikers heading south recommend getting rides along Marine Pde.; a bit past the Aquarium, it becomes SH2 and picks up more traffic. Heading north, the best spot is reputed to be across Pandora Rd. Bridge. Most traffic heads to Taupo; those going to Wairoa or Gisborne should ask to be let out where SH5 branches off.

ORIENTATION AND PRACTICAL INFORMATION

Marine Parade and **Hastings Street** run parallel to one another, stretching southward along the bay. Central Napier's streets lie up against the bluffs. Be careful when walking through palm-lined **Emerson Street**—despite the misleading bricked landscaping, it's a main traffic thoroughfare. **Tennyson** and **Dickens Streets** run parallel to it on each side; the gardens of **Clive Square** mark the edge of the town center.

Visitors Center: Napier Information Centre, 100 Marine Pde. (☎ 834 1911; fax 835 7219; info@napiervic.co.nz). Open M-F 8:30am-5pm, Sa-Su 9-5pm; later in summer.

DOC: 59 Marine Pde. (☎ 834 3111). Open M-F 9am-4:15pm.

Banks: ASB (☎ 834 3128), at the corner of Hastings and Emerson St. **BNZ,** 126 Hastings St. (☎ 0800 275 269). Both open M-F 9 or 9:30am-4:30pm.

Bi-Gay-Lesbian Organizations: Gayline (☎ 843 3087) has info on current goings-on. Dances are hosted the third Sa of each month at the **Bay City Club** on Milton Rd., partway up Bluff Hill, off Tennyson St. Cover $5.

Police: (☎ 835 4688), on Station St.

Medical Services: The Doctors, 30 Munroe St., (☎ 835 4696), has a **pharmacy.** Open daily 8am-9pm. **Napier Health Centre** is on Wellesley Rd. (☎ 878 8109).

Internet Access: Cybers, 98 Dickens St. Open M-F 8:30am-midnight, Sa-Su 9am-midnight. **Cybershed,** 177 Hastings St. (☎ 834 3055), at the corner of Station St. Open M-Th 9am-10:30pm, F-Su 9am-midnight. Both charge $8 per hr.

Post Office: 57 Dickens St. (☎ 835 9800). Open M-F 8am-5pm, Sa 9am-noon.

ACCOMMODATIONS

Napier has been blessed with a number of high-quality accommodations, many right in the center of town. Be aware that during the fruit-picking season (Nov.-Apr.), the hostels fill up with eager backpackers seeking work.

Archie's Bunker (BBH), 14 Herschell St. (☎ 833 7990; fax 833 7995; archiesbunker@xtra.co.nz), opposite Hawke's Bay Museum. It's all in the family at this hostel with spotless facilities and an enormous upstairs lounge. Bike rental. Internet. Free pick-up and drop-off. Dorms $18; singles $24; twins $38; doubles $44, with TV $52. ❷

Stables Lodge Backpackers (BBH), 370 Hastings St. (☎/fax 835 6242; http://homepages.ihug.co.nz/~stables). With the lovable dog Max making the rounds, goodwill abounds at this environmentally-aware hostel. Comfy bunks, lockable storage plus free tea, blankets, and use of bikes. Internet. Dorms $15; twins and doubles $36. ❷

Criterion Backpackers (BBH), 48 Emerson St. (☎835 2059; fax 835 2370; cribacpac@yahoo.com). Enjoy a bunk-free sleep at this Spanish Mission-style misfit in the land of Art Deco. The carpet is liable to spark psychedelic flashbacks. Bike rental. Key deposit $10. Dorms $16; singles $22; twins and doubles $38, with bath $50. ❷

Napier YHA, 277 Marine Pde. (☎/fax 835 7039; yhanapr@yha.org.nz), at the corner of Vaultier St. Winding hallways and colorful walls give this YHA more character than most. Some rooms have an ocean view. Bike rental. Reception 8-10am and 5-8pm. Dorms $21; singles $28; twins and doubles $45. ❸

Waterfront Lodge (VIP), 217 Marine Pde. (☎/fax 835 3429; waterfrontlodge@xtra.co.nz). Sip free tea or coffee in the inner courtyard or catch some Zs in the comfortable beds. Bike rental. Free pick-up and drop-off. Reception 8am-9pm. Dorms $17; singles $25; twins and doubles $40-55; family rooms $75; tent sites $10. ❷

Sea Breeze B&B, 281 Marine Pde. (☎835 8067; fax 835 0512). Turkish- and Indian-themed rooms give this stellar B&B an exotic feel. Kick back on the greenhouse porch overlooking the water. Singles $70; doubles $85-95. ❹

FOOD

Countdown Foods, at the corner of Dickens and Station St. near Thackeray St., is one of many supermarkets. (☎835 2496. Open M-F 8am-9pm, Sa-Su 8am-8pm.)

Thorps, 40 Hastings St. (☎835 6699), by Tennyson St. With 7 breads, 7 meats (including salmon), and over 10 dressings, only the indecisive should dodge this coffee shop. Open M-F 7:30am-4:30pm, Sa 7:30am-2pm. ❶

Mossy's Cafe & Bar, 88 Dickens St. (☎835 6696), dishes out hearty breakfasts and lunches ($5-15) amidst hanging vines and colorful walls. For dinner, Mossy's pulls out all the stops with $21 lamb roast. Open daily 8am-late. ❸

Restaurant Indonesia, 409 Marine Pde. (☎835 8303). The signature 15-dish "Rijsttafel" (Dutch-Indonesian banquet; $27-35) has made this restaurant one of the hottest spots in town. The less adventurous can try more traditional dishes like chicken satay. Open daily 5-10pm. Reservations essential. ❸

The Olive Branch Bread Company (☎835 8375), on Hastings St. by Albion St., has ready-made sandwiches ($4.50) and sweets, but the real deals are the filling freshly-baked breads ($2-5). Open M-F 8am-3pm, Sa 8am-2pm. ❶

Jo Miguels, 193 Hastings St. (☎835 8477). Bringing a bite of Spain to New Zealand, Jo serves large tapas ($2.50-7) and gourmet pizzas ($14). Live music (often flamenco) Th-Su. Open Tu-Th 11:30am-late, F-Sa 11:30am-1:30am, Su 1-10pm. ❷

NIGHTLIFE

With a dozen bars in a 200m radius, Napier offers one of the easiest pub crawls in the country. Start your stumble at the intersection of **Hastings** and **Tennyson Streets.**

O'Flaherty's Irish Pub, 37 Hastings St. (☎834 1235), by Tennyson St., is an authentic tavern for both novice and veteran drinkers. Pints $2 during the 5-7pm Happy Hour. Live music every weekend and fresh homemade pies. Open daily 11am-late.

Grumpy Mole Saloon and **Stogies Bar** (☎835 5545), at the corner of Hastings and Tennyson St. The club/saloon, attractive 20-somethings, and American West decor are an odd but popular combo for those who pass the "no-scruffiness" door test. Stogies, in the same building and connected through a door, is a jazzy lounge bar serving Cuban cigars, late night coffee, and single malt whiskeys. Open Tu-Sa 4pm-3am.

SIGHTS AND ACTIVITIES

TOURS

Tours in Napier come in two varieties: local architectural tours that pay tribute to Deco-dent architecture, and winery tours that travel farther afield in pursuit of that perfect vintage.

ART DECO NAPIER. The color-laden symmetry of the buildings is perhaps itself the main sight in Napier—even the manhole covers can't escape the craze. Tennyson St. has a row of classic structures; admire the Maori Deco of the **Antique Centre**, the Shamrock Deco of the **Munster Chambers**, and the Deco-overload of the **Daily Telegraph building**. Market St. has terrific glass windows; the peach and green **Countrywide Bank** building on Dalton and Emerson St. is impressive. And don't forget to check out the Greco Deco of the **Colonnade** and the **Sound Shell**. The **Tom Parker Fountain** in the gardens along Marine Pde. gets **technicolor** light treatment from dusk until midnight. The most famous of all is **Rothmans Building** (built in 1933), at the corner of Bridge and Ossian St., combining elements of Art Deco, Art Nouveau, and the Chicago School architect Louis Sullivan. **The Art Deco Trust** runs a 1.5km guided walking tour of Napier's Deco. *(163 Tennyson St.* ☎ *835 0022. Oct.-June 2 per day; July-Sept. W and Sa-Su. Departs 10am from the Visitors Center, 2pm from the Art Deco Trust. $8.)* The Trust's brochures (available at the Trust or the Visitors Center, $4) enable self-guided walks.

GRAPIER NAPIER. Napier sits on the edge of the vineyard-studded Hawke's Bay plains, one of New Zealand's major wine-producing regions. Though we couldn't possibly list all the best estates in this region, there are a couple which stand out for both the wines and the setting. Pick up the guide to Hawke's Bay's wineries at the Visitors Center. Originally set up by priests for religious wine, **Mission Estate Winery** is New Zealand's oldest winery. *(*☎ *844 2259. Open M-Sa 8:30am-5:30pm, Su 11am-4pm. Tours M-Sa 10:30am and 2pm. Free tastings.)* **Ngatarawa Wines** is a small winery in a restored stable on lovely grounds. *(*☎ *879 7603; www.ngatarawa.com. Tastings daily 11am-5pm.)* Several tour operators offer short guided tours and tastings. **Vicky's Wine Tours** *(*☎ *843 9991)*, **Bay Tours and Charters** *(*☎ *843 6953)*, **Vince's Vineyard Tours** *(*☎ *836 6705)*, and **Toast of the Bay** *(*☎ *844 2375)* run 3½-5hr. tours ranging $35-50 per person with free pick-up.

FESTIVALS

Napier shakes, rattles, and rocks in February with festivals. Dust off your zoot suit for the glam **Art Deco Weekend** and its series of stylish events from balls and cafe crawls to champagne breakfasts and country house tours. (☎ 835 1191; www.hb.co.nz/artdeco/weekend; 3rd weekend of February.) If you're short on cash, check out the museum exhibitions, free jazz, and Sunday's **Great Gatsby Picnic** on the beach. There's also the **Harvest Hawke's Bay Wine and Food Festival** (1st weekend of February), a weekend of similarly upscale revelry, with evening outdoor concerts. The **International Mission Estate Concert** from January to March at the Mission Estate Winery is a big regional deal in a gorgeous setting. If in Napier outside of these dates, don't despair; at any time of year, there are impromptu jazz concerts at the wineries or other entertainment in the soundshell.

MUSEUMS AND AQUARIUMS

If you've begun to overdose on Deco, head to Marine Pde. Interspersed among manicured gardens, burbling fountains, and statues like Pania of the Reef (a distinctively toothy mermaid), there are some quirky sideshows.

HAWKE'S BAY MUSEUM. In addition to its garish and impossible-to-miss large colored cylinders, this museum has exhibits on the earthquake, the East Coast Ngati Kahungunu Maori, Hawke's Bay dinosaur fossils, and, of course, Art Deco. A video display on the lower level has some fascinating first-hand accounts from survivors of the earthquake. *(65 Marine Pde. ☎ 835 7781. Open Dec.-Mar. 9am-6pm; Apr.-Nov. 10am-4:30pm. $5, children free.)*

MARINELAND. Two of the largest and oldest attractions at this mecca of undersea activities are Shona and Kelly, the two aged dolphins. To get a better look, Marineland offers a daily swim-with-the-dolphins program with advance booking. Those not keen on swimming can get a sensory behind-the-scenes tour of Marineland, petting and feeding the dolphins. *(☎ 834 4027; www.marineland.co.nz. Dolphin shows daily 10:30am and 2pm. $9, children $4.50. Dolphin swim $40, gear hire $10. Book at least a month ahead in summer. Behind-the-scenes tour daily 9am. $15, children $7.50. Book at least a day in advance. No sandals. Penguin workshops daily 1-1:45pm. Arrive 15min. early. Advance booking required. $15.)*

NATIONAL AQUARIUM. Recently opened, this marine wonderland includes a walk-through bush exhibit and frequent shark feedings. Qualified divers can call a day in advance to tempt sharks and fate itself during feeding time. *(☎ 834 1404; www.nationalaquarium.co.nz. $12, children $6. Open M-F 9am-5pm, Sa-Su 8:30am-6pm.)*

ODDBALL ANIMAL ATTRACTIONS

OPOSSUM WORLD. This bizarre shrine to all things rodent features a static display on opossum trapping and a boutique tannery that borders on fetish fascination. Odd, but can you really pass up a stuffed kiwi made of the hide of its predator? Now there's irony for you. *(157 Marine Pde. ☎ 835 7697. Free.)*

CLASSIC SHEEPSKINS. Gain insight into what really happens to 80,000 of those cute fluffy herbivores each year—a violent and painful, but profitable, death. The tour passes massive vats curing the hides on the way to a field of sheepskins drying in the sun. At the retail shop, don't miss the bins of "seconds" skins, available for as little as $21. *(22 Thames St., off Pandora Rd./SH2 North. A courtesy van picks up from the Visitors Center. ☎ 835 9662; www.classicsheepskins.co.nz. Shop hours M-F 7:30am-5pm, Sa-Su 9am-4pm. Free tours daily 11am and 2pm.)*

IN FLIGHT AND ON HOOVES

Though not known for its adventurous pursuits, Napier has its fair share of adrenaline fun. To experience the full force of gravity, try **Napier Skydive,** 22 Marine Pde. (☎ 0800 835 5184. 12,000ft. $225.) For a calmer jaunt through the air, **Airplay Paragliding** offers tandem flights and various training programs. (☎ 025 512 886. Tandem $120.) Alternately, **Balloon Adventures** embarks on 1hr. hot-air balloon rides over the bay. (☎ 858 8480. $240, children $150.) If you prefer to keep your feet on the ground (or at least much closer), try **Riverlands** for horse treks along scenic routes. (☎ 834 9756. 1hr. $25, 4hr. $50.)

HASTINGS ☎ 06

Hastings may be known as Napier's twin city, but the resemblance is strictly fraternal. Only 12km away, it fell victim to the same quake as Napier but was partially rebuilt in Spanish Mission style. The architecture never reached the same gaudy heights as Napier, and little effort has been put into promoting the style further. Though Hastings may lie in Napier's shadow, the nearby kiwifruit orchards draw hordes of fruit pickers during the annual harvest season.

196 ■ HAWKE'S BAY

TRANSPORTATION. Napier and Hastings are about 30min. apart by bus or train. **InterCity, Newmans,** and **Bay Express** leave from the Hastings Travel Centre, at the beginning of Caroline Rd. (☎878 0213. Bookings M-F 7:45am-4pm.) Fares are generally $2-3 less for southbound routes and more for northbound routes than those from Napier (see **Transportation,** p. 191). **The Nimbus** leaves from Eastbourne St. near the Russell St. corner. (☎877 8133. Runs every hr. M-F 7am-5:30pm.) **Car rental** is available from **Metro Rent-A-Car** (☎835 0590) in Napier. Although *Let's Go* does not recommend it, hitchhikers going south often head out just past the 30kph zone beyond the racecourse; those going to Napier usually hitch from Karamu Rd. N, while those heading to Taupo, Wairoa, or Gisborne take the route that bypasses central Napier by getting rides from Pakowhai Rd.

ORIENTATION AND PRACTICAL INFORMATION. Flat and orderly Hastings is perturbed only by the railway track slicing through the heart of the city center. **Heretaunga Street,** the main road, turns pedestrian for a block on either side of the railway (a herd of ceramic sheep flock at the Market St. end of this stretch). Streets are tagged west to one side of the railway and east to the other; south and north designations split at Heretaunga St. The **Visitors Information Centre** is at the corner of Heretaunga and Russell St. (☎873 5526; fax 873 5529; vic@hastingstourism.co.nz. Open daily 8:30am-5pm.) From November to April, there are numerous **work opportunities** for fruit-picking around Hastings. Other services include: **BNZ,** on Heretaunga St. (open M and Th-F 9am-4:30pm, Tu-W 9:30-4:30pm); the **police** (24hr. ☎878 0870), on Railway Rd.; a **pharmacy** at **The Doctors,** 110 Russell St. (☎876 8445; open daily 8am-9pm); **Internet access** at **Internet World,** 102 Queen St. E, for $12 per 1hr. (☎876 4876; open M-F 8:30am-6:30pm, Sa 9am-4pm, Su 10am-4pm); and the **post office** (☎878 9425), on Russell St. in The Plaza with K-Mart.

ACCOMMODATIONS AND CAMPING. Most backpackers accommodations will help arrange work for fruit-picking travelers. **AJ's Backpackers (BBH) ❷,** 405 Southland Rd., just off Southhampton St., is a home away from home. The hospitable owners Jackie and Alan make time to take care of weary backpackers along with their two small daughters and friendly dogs. (☎878 2302; ajslodge@xtra.co.nz. Free pick-up. Internet. Dorms $15, weekly $90 if you're employed locally.) At **Hastings Backpackers (BBH) ❶,** 505 Lyndon Rd. E, between Hastings St. and Willow Park Rd., you can pick fruit at an orchard or kick back in the flower-filled patio. (☎876 5888; www.medcasa.co.nz. Dorms $14, weekly $85; doubles $28; tent sites $12.) Summer BBQs fill the courtyard at **Travellers Lodge (BBH) ❷,** 606-608 St. Aubyn St. W. Turn right from the train station and follow signs. Spacious rooms complement a sizeable TV lounge, foosball table, and sauna. (☎878 7108; fax 878 7228; travellers.lodge@clear.net.nz. Free pick-up and bike use. Internet. Key deposit $10. Dorms $16, weekly $90; singles $24; doubles $36.) The **Hastings Holiday Park ❶,** 25min. from town by Splash Planet on Windsor Ave., has lots of green space, large trees, and a duck-filled creek. (☎878 6692; fax 878 6267; holidaypark@hastingstourism.co.nz. 3-bed cabins $40 per room; tourist doubles $65; motel doubles $80; tent and powered sites $10-11.)

FOOD AND NIGHTLIFE. The best eats in Hastings are the rich scoops at **Rush Munroe's Ice Cream Gardens ❶,** 704 Heretaunga St. W. With 74 years in the business, they have perfected loads of luscious fruity flavors. (☎878 9634. Open daily 10am-9pm; in winter 10am-5:30pm.) The **Corn Exchange ❷,** 118 Maraekakaho Rd., has an a-maize-ingly chic central fireplace. The menu features gamey cuts of venison and bison, as well as wood-fired pizzas for $14-16. (☎870 8333. Open M-Th 11:30am-11pm, F-Sa 10:30am-1am or later, Su 10:30am-11pm.) **Robert Harris Cafe ❶,**

104 Russell St. S, is in the town center. A franchisee in a coffee shop chain fixing to become the Starbucks of New Zealand, this cafe offers fresh sandwiches for under $4. (☎ 878 2931. Open M-F 8am-5pm, Sa-Su 8am-3pm.) For groceries, **Countdown Foods** is on Queen St. N. (☎ 878 5091. Open M-F 8am-9pm, Sa-Su 8am-8pm.) Nightlife in Hastings usually includes a pint of Steiny or cider under the beer-towel-lined pine beams at the **Cat and Fiddle Ale House,** 502 Karamu Rd. N. (☎ 878 4111. Open M-W and Sa-Su 11am-midnight, Th-F 11am-2am.) **Friends Bar & Cafe,** 131 Heretaunga St., at the corner of Karamu Rd., crafts a mellow feel with picnic and pool tables. (☎ 878 6701. Open M-Sa 11am-3am, Su noon-10pm.)

◐ ◪ SIGHTS AND ACTIVITIES. Hastings shares many of its attractions with Napier (see p. 190), such as **wineries, Cape Kidnappers,** and killer surfing beaches like **Ocean Beach** on the south side of the Cape and **Waimarama** farther south. However, there are a few attractions in Hastings worthy of special attention. Amusement-seekers will enjoy **Splash Planet,** New Zealand's only water theme park that offers both year-round (heated indoor pools, jeeps, mini-golf course, etc.) and summer attractions (water slides, etc.). The 6½-hectare park is a 25min. walk from downtown Hastings. (☎ 876 9856; www.splashplanet.co.nz. Open Sept.-Apr. daily 10am-6pm; May-Aug. Sa-Su and school holidays 10am-5pm. $22, children $16; in winter $11/$8.) Or one can sample over 85 different varieties of pitted fruits (in season) at **Pernel Fruitworld,** on Pakowhai Rd., about a 5min. drive northwest of Hastings. (☎ 878 3383. Tours every hr. 9am-4pm. $8, children $4.) The **Hawke's Bay Exhibition Centre,** 201 Eastbourne St. E, has local and national art and scientific displays. (☎ 876 2077. Open M-F 10am-4:30pm, Sa-Su 11am-4pm. Free.)

CAPE KIDNAPPERS

From September to March, the remote cliffs of Cape Kidnappers are home to the world's largest mainland nesting grounds of the **Australasian gannet.** Fifteen thousand of the large tawny-headed, white-and-black birds arrive en masse in early September and set up their nests in quasi-orderly rows at the 13-hectare Cape Kidnappers Gannet Reserve. Chicks hatch in early November and mature through the summer before flying the coop on their ambitious maiden air voyage of 2800km across the Tasman Sea to Australia. In the meantime, it's a scene straight from Alfred Hitchcock: male gannets bearing down like 747s toward the teeming colony then stopping on a dime to drop nesting material to their Mrs. Gannet below.

The area is closed to the public between July and October, when the birds are in the early nesting stage. At other times, you are free to visit the gannets (and gannet, ahem, residue). It's a stunning walk at any time of year, even in winter when the birds are gone. Check with the Napier Visitors Center for local tour operators and hiking trails. (Trips usually 4hr., $20-38.)

TAUPO AND TONGARIRO

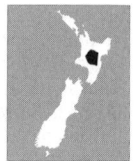

With fire and brimstone beneath its surface and snow-capped peaks towering at its center, the Taupo and Tongariro region uneasily awaits further volcanic tantrums. Lake Taupo, the largest freshwater lake in the Southern Hemisphere, fills a crater formed by a monumental explosion 26,000 years ago. If you can find a patch of surface undimpled by jet skis, kayaks, or sailboats, the shimmering lake reflects an impressive scene: fishermen cruise the waters in search of their next trout while beaming backpackers float downwards on morning skydives. In the background tower the mighty trio of Mounts Ruapehu, Ngauruhoe, and Tongariro, home to the famed Tongariro Northern Circuit tramp (located in Tongariro National Park) and the popular Whakapapa and Turoa ski fields. Enjoy this striking natural scene before the underground rumbling upheaves the landscape yet again.

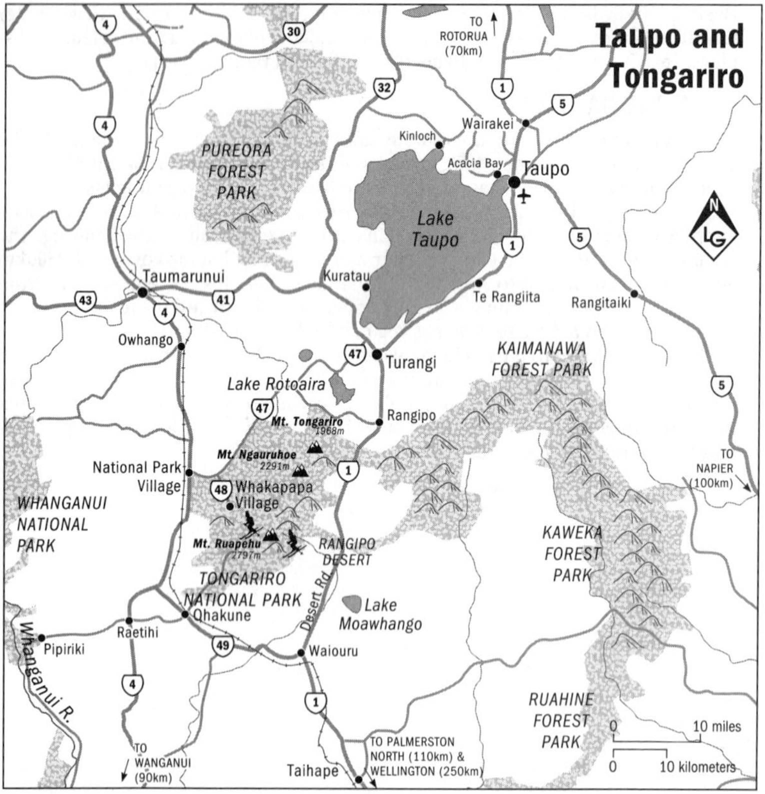

TAUPO AND TONGARIRO HIGHLIGHTS

TRAMP the rugged volcanic terrain and steaming turquoise pools of the splendid **Tongariro Crossing**, often called the best day hike in New Zealand (see p. 210).

TRAP the trout in **Lake Taupo**, which, averaging 10lbs. each, have bent the rods of fishermen from around the world (see p. 205).

TRAIL the steady stream of backpackers who finally take the **skydiving** plunge in Taupo, one of the cheapest dives in the world (see p. 204).

TAUPO ☎ 07

Maybe it's something in the water. Possibly, it's the relief after surviving a morning skydive and bungy jump combo. Or, it might be the happy-go-lucky vibes from the residents of this sunny community (pop. 21,257) who preside over the largest lake in New Zealand (616 sq. km) and its population of fat trout. Whatever it is, smiling comes easy in Taupo. The town lies at the origin of the Waikato River and rides the same belt of smoking geothermal activity that powers Rotorua, harboring natural attractions that rival even its thrilling, and ubiquitous, adrenaline offerings.

TRANSPORTATION

Flights: Air New Zealand (Taupo airport ☎ 378 5428), 7km south on SH1, flies daily to: **Auckland** (55min., 3 per day, $196); **Wellington** (1hr., 3 per day, $230); **Christchurch** (2¼hr., 3 per day, $349); **Queenstown** (5hr., 2 per day, $558); and **Nelson** (2hr., 3 per day, $294). Taxis run from the airport (10min., door-to-door, $9).

Buses: InterCity/Newmans leave from Taupo Travel Centre (☎ 378 9032), on Gascoigne St., to: **Auckland** (5hr., 4 per day, $39-53); **Hamilton** (3hr., 4 per day, $24-34); **Napier** (2hr., 3 per day, $18-37); **Rotorua** (1hr., 4 per day, $16-25); and **Wellington** (6hr., 4 per day, $34-71). InterCity connects daily with **Turangi's Alpine Scenic Tours** (☎ 378 7412 or 025 937 281) to reach **National Park** and **Whakapapa Villages** (2hr., 2:30pm, $29). During ski season, **Tongariro Expeditions** (☎ 377 0435 or 0800 828 763) runs daily from Pointons Ski Shop to the **Whakapapa ski field** (7:30am, return $30) and to/from **Tongariro Crossing** and **Northern Circuit** (departs Taupo 5:45am, Ketetahi Hut 3:30pm; return $25-35).

Taxis: TOP Cabs (☎ 378 9250) and **Taupo Taxis** (☎ 378 5100) have **24hr.** service.

Rentals: Rent-a-Bike (☎ 025 322 729) rents bikes (half-day $20, full-day $25) and front shock bikes (half-day $30, full-day $40) and delivers them right to your door. On Tongariro St., near the Lake Tce. Cross, **Pointons Ski Shop** (☎ 377 0087) has a ski, boot, and pole package for $25 or a snowboard and boots combo for $40. Open daily 7am-7pm. For fishing gear, **Taupo Rodin' Tackle,** 7 Tongariro St. (☎ 378 5337), rents fly-fishing outfit (half-day $20, full-day $35) and spin-fishing outfit (half-day $10, full-day $20). Open daily 8am-5:30pm; in winter closed Su.

Hitchhiking: Taupo is at the crossroads of the North Island; rides are easy, but getting far enough out of town (especially to go south on SH1) may not be. To head north on SH1, many thumbers cross the Waikato to the intersection of Norman Smith St. Note that *Let's Go* does not recommend hitchhiking.

ORIENTATION AND PRACTICAL INFORMATION

Tucked into a corner created by the **Waikato River** as it gushes from the northeast bulge of **Lake Taupo,** the city radiates out from the lake and river. **SH1** and **SH5** barrel through town as **Tongariro Street,** home to the Visitors Center and the Boat Harbour, and bend south along the lakeshore as **Lake Terrace. Spa Road** travels east along the south bank of the Waikato.

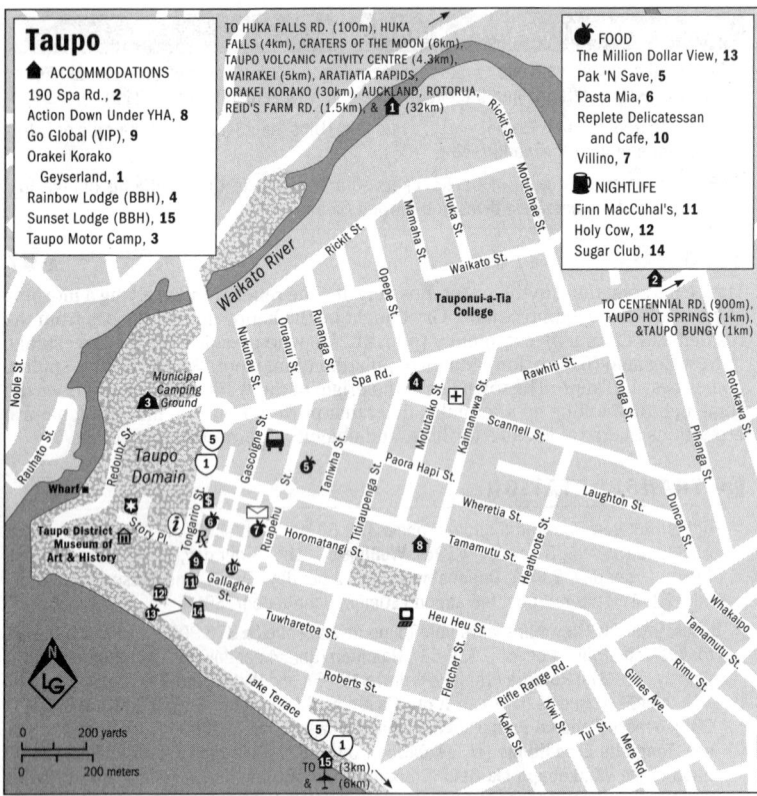

Visitors Center: Taupo Visitor Centre, 30 Tongariro St. (☎376 0027; fax 378 9003; www.laketauponz.com). Open daily 8:30am-5pm.

DOC: 115 Centennial Dr. (☎378 3885), off Spa Rd. Open M-F 8am-4:30pm.

Banks and Currency Exchange: Banks line Tongariro St. with **ASB Bank** (☎376 0063), at Tongariro and Horomatangi St. Open M-F 9am-4:30pm.

Police: (24hr. ☎378 6060), behind the Visitors Center in Story Pl.

Medical Services: Main St. Pharmacy (☎/fax 378 2636), at the corner of Tongariro and Heu Heu St. Open daily 9am-8:30pm. The **Taupo Health Centre**, 117 Heu Heu St. (☎378 7060). Open M-F 8:30am-5pm. The **hospital** (☎378 8100) is on Kotare St.

Internet Access: Central Plateau Reap (☎378 8106), at the corner of Heu Heu and Kaimanawa St., is the cheapest at $5 per hr. Open M-Th 9am-4:30pm, F 9am-3pm.

Post Office: At Horomatangi and Ruapehu St. Open M-F 8:30am-5:30pm, Sa 9am-noon.

ACCOMMODATIONS AND CAMPING

Older, cheaper places are clustered along the streets a few blocks east of the town center. Otherwise, the least expensive riverfront bed in town is the free camping on Reid's Farm Rd., a bit south of the Falls along Huka Falls Rd. (2km north of town off SH1). As always, never leave any of your possessions unattended here.

■ **Action Down Under YHA** (☎ 378 3311; fax 378 9612; yhataupo@xtra.co.nz), at the corner of Tamamutu and Kaimanawa St. Enjoy speckless rooms and beautiful views of snow-capped peaks at this top-notch YHA. Bike rental, central heating in winter, heated spa, Internet. Disabled rooms available. Dorms $15-17; singles $30; twins and doubles $40, with bath $45; family rooms with bath $70; tent sites $10. ❷

■ **Rainbow Lodge (BBH)**, 99 Titiraupenga Rd. (☎378 5754; fax 377 1548; rainbow@clear.net.nz), just off Spa Rd. Follow the rainbow mailbox to Taupo's own pot of gold. The spacious kitchen and outdoor patio are great for socializing. Free coffee. Mountain bike and fishing rod rental. Sauna. Key deposit $10. Dorms $18-21; singles $33; twins $41; doubles $44, with bath $47. ❷

Burkes Lodge and Backpackers, 69 Spa Rd. (☎378 9292; fax 378 9092; burkesbp@ezysurf.co.nz). Hidden among car dealerships, this renovated motel has private bathrooms and a pleasant central courtyard. Bike rental. Spa. Internet. Key deposit $10. Dorms $17; doubles $38, with bath $40. Family rooms available. ❷

Go Global (VIP), at the corner of Tongariro and Tuwharetoa St. (☎377 0044; fax 377 0059; www.go-global.co.nz). With a popular Irish pub downstairs, this large and centrally located backpackers clears a well-worn path for a lively young crowd. Internet. Key deposit $20. Dorms $20; twins and doubles $45, with bath $50. ❷

Sunset Lodge (BBH), 5 Tremaine Ave. (☎378 5962; sunset@reap.org.nz), 3km from town. Turn off Lake Tce. onto Hawai St. Don't let the free bikes and shuttles to Craters of the Moon distract you from the homemade banana bread. Internet. Key deposit $10. Dorms $15-18; twins and doubles $36. ❷

190 Spa Rd., 190 Spa Rd. (☎377 0665; orbiii@reap.org.nz). Perched above the Waikato River, you can contemplate Taupo's adrenaline offerings at this hospitable homestay—the bungy jump site is right nearby. Singles $55; doubles $75-80. ❹

Taupo Motor Camp, 15 Redoubt St. (☎/fax 377 3080; tpocamp@voyager.co.nz). Go up Tongariro St. about 100m past the Visitors Center, then turn left. So central it needn't be fancy. Dorms $18, in winter $15; cinderblock cabin singles $40/$25; doubles $44; tent sites $11. ❶

■ **Orakei Korako Geyserland** (☎378 3131; fax 378 0371; www.orakeikorako.co.nz), 35km from Taupo. If you've got your own transport, this hidden lakeside lodge across the water from Taupo's best geothermal site is unbeatably scenic and peaceful. Bring bedding and food. Rustic communal lodge and bunks that were once trees $20; tourist flats with kitchenettes $80, extra person (up to 7) $20. ❷

🍴 FOOD

For the true Taupo experience, delight in some trout. While it can't be sold over the counter, many places around town will prepare your catch (for a fee). For groceries, head to **Pak 'N Save**, at the corner of Ruapehu and Tamamutu St. (☎377 1155. Open M-F 8am-8:30pm, Sa-Su 8am-8pm.)

Replete Delicatessen and Cafe, 45 Heu Heu St. (☎378 0606). This terracotta-toned cafe is replete with inventive and well-presented dishes. With most items under $7, it's no wonder that lunchtime reels in the crowds. Open M-Tu and Th-F 8:45am-4:30pm, Sa-Su 8:45am-3:30pm. ❶

Pasta Mia, 5 Horomatangi St. (☎377 2930). Enjoy delicious single servings of pasta for $8.50 (double $15.50). For around $13, you can transport enough uncooked pasta and sauce back to your hostel to feed you and a few friends. Open M and F-Su 11am-10:30pm, Tu-Th 11am-5:30pm; in winter daily 11am-5:30pm. ❷

The Million Dollar View, 5 Tongariro St. (☎378 8539). The name says it all; the view through the large lakefront windows can't be beat. Excellent catch of the day ($16-26) and burgers ($12-13). Open daily 5:30pm-late; also open in summer 11am-2pm. ❸

Villino, 45 Horomatangi St. (☎377 4470). The calming decor compliments the superb dishes. Feast on confit of duck ($28.50) or seared venison ($29.50). Open daily 11:30am-4pm and 6pm-late. ❺

NIGHTLIFE

Holy Cow, 11 Tongariro St. (☎378 0040). Every backpacker, her uncle, and the guy they hitched in with head to *the* bar of Taupo. Tables are mounted fairly early in this rump-shaking 2nd-floor mixing bowl; it can get racy here! Belching DJs mix commercial hits nightly. Handles $3.50. Happy Hour 7-9pm (handles $2.50). Open daily 7pm-3am.

Sugar Club (☎377 4466), at the corner of Tongariro and Tuwharetoa St. This large bar draws a lively crowd downing beer (handles $4) and grooving to the beats of the live DJ (Th-Sa). Th 10pm-midnight beer and spirits are half price; F 5-7pm everything is $1 off. Open M-W and Su noon-midnight, Th-Sa noon-3am; closed M and Su in July-Aug.

Finn MacCuhal's (☎378 6165, ext. 3), at the corner of Tongariro and Tuwharetoa St., right below Go Global. With M quiz nights and live music 4 nights a week (W and F-Su), a rollicking crowd keeps the Guiness flowing. $10 meals include free ale or wine. Happy Hour 4:30-7pm. Handles $3-4. Open daily 11am-3am.

SIGHTS

GEOTHERMAL WONDERS

CRATERS OF THE MOON. A 1954 explosion, resulting from the drilling of a geothermal bore, created a steaming pockmarked landscape of craters and boiling mud pools so unique it is now managed by DOC. As small vents collapse and become blocked, minor eruptions can occur at any time. Whirling steam adds a ghostly otherworldly feel. *(A few kilometers north of town on SH1. Free.)*

ORAKEI KORAKO GEYSERLAND AND CAVE. Although it is far away (and inaccessible to those without transport), this dramatic and undeveloped private geothermal reserve is well worth the trip. A shuttle boat crosses the idyllic lake during the day to reach a range of steamy wonders. On the far side lie pockets of glistening silica terraces, spurting geysers (including a fascinating horizontal geyser), colorful mineral crusts, and deep, scalding hot cyan pools. Don't miss the spectacular fern-lined amphitheater of Aladdin's Cave with its warm mineral pool. Reportedly, the pool's chemical cocktail shines jewelry in a flash while visitors gaze at the postcard view from the cave's mouth. *(Reached via a sign-posted road that winds through hills and deer farms off SH1 about 25min. north of Taupo. ☎ 378 3131. Open daily 8am-4:30pm; in winter 8am-4pm. Entrance and boat ride $17.)*

TAUPO VOLCANIC ACTIVITY CENTRE. The public side of the adjacent IGNS (Institute of Geological and Nuclear Sciences), the Centre has a crack team of researchers who monitor the Taupo volcanic zone. This attraction recently became more interactive with the introduction of a model geyser, a small earthquake simulator, and even a glass-encased tornado machine. Check out the seismograph readings of Ruapehu and recent eruption film footage. *(Take the Huka Falls Rd. turn-off from SH1. ☎ 374 3875. Open M-F 9am-5pm, Sa-Su 10am-4pm. $5, children $2.50.)*

TAUPO HOT SPRINGS. After a long day of touring, you may want to pay a visit to one of Taupo's bubbling pools of tranquility. Both public and private indoor or outdoor pools are available. *(On the Taupo/Napier Hwy., only 5min. from town. ☎ 377 6502. Open daily 7:30am-9:30pm; last entry 9pm. Pools $9-10.)*

TOURS

You can approach the lake scenery with your own rented boat or with relatively cheap narrated cruises. The western shores of **Acacia Bay** end at cliff and bush, with an undulating edge of rocky inlets and bays. Along part of the uninhabited coastline, a set of impressive (if not ancient) Maori carvings have been chiseled into the rock faces at **Mine Bay**, on private land accessible by boat only. Many cruises include the **carvings,** the **Western Bays, Hot Water Beach,** and much of the lake itself; contact the **Charter Office** (☎ 378 3444) at the harbor to book.

SUPERJET. The only way to see all the sights in a relatively short amount of time is on this speedy jetboat, which does a 2hr. comprehensive loop at up to 50 knots. Informative commentary, windsuits, and life jackets are provided. *(☎ 377 4855 or 0800 278 737; www.superjet.co.nz. 1hr. $29, children $15; 2hr. $59/$29.)*

BARBARY. For a more active experience, this sexy 1920s sailing yacht, once owned by none other than **Errol Flynn,** is now captained by colorful Bill Dawson, who teaches you how to sail it yourself. You won't even have to rob the rich to pay your fare. *(☎ 378 3444. 2½hr.; 2-3 per day; $25, children $10.)*

REPLICA STEAMBOAT CRUISES. Board a 1920s steamboat replica for informative and affordable one- and two-hour scenic tours to Hot Water Beach, the Maori rock carvings, Jerusalem Bay, Acacia Bay, and Two Mile Bay. *(☎ 378 3444. Written commentary also in French, German, Japanese, Chinese, Dutch, and Korean; book ahead. Hot Water: $22, under 15 $11. Two Mile: Oct.-Apr. $11/$6.)*

OTHER SIGHTS

WAIRAKEI PARK. The park combines a slightly bizarre amalgamation of sights, recreational activities, a geothermal power station, a geothermally heated prawn farm, shops, and lodgings. At its north end sits the world's first geothermal power station, the **Wairakei Geothermal Power Development** (built 1959-64), right near the Huka Jet. From the **Bore Lookout,** at the end of the road turn-off, a post-apocalyptic terrain of massive, steaming, stainless-steel tubes worm along the ground to feed Taupo's energy needs. *(Across the Waikato Bridge on SH1, less than 8km from town.)*

IT'S A BIRD, IT'S A PLANE, IT'S... Your one-stop potty shop, the **SuperLoo,** located on Tongariro St. next to the Visitors Center, was voted "the best loo in New Zealand" by Keep New Zealand Beautiful. The country is full of automated public toilets, but nothing compares to SuperLoo. Inside the stalls, exclamations of "this really *is* a super loo" can be heard. Kids heading into the toilets spread their arms out and, while swooping inside like an airplane, yell "SUUU-UUUPER LOOOO. Here I come to save the day!"

Envisioning a new standard of sanitation in New Zealand, the makers of the Super-Loo set a lofty goal; some said it couldn't be done. But in October of 1993, when the SuperLoo first opened its lids, Taupo knew it had something special. The opening celebration was said to have been epic with toilet paper streamers and bobbing for apples in the fresh toilet water. Especially enthusiastic attendees vowed never to wipe again. Today, after ten years of operation, the SuperLoo hasn't lost its sheen. (Toilets 20¢. 4min. shower $1; towel hire $1, soap 30¢, shampoo 50¢. Lockers $1 per day. Open daily 7:30am-9pm; in winter M-Th 7:30am-5:30pm, F-Su 7:30am-6:30pm.)

HUKA FALLS. Maori for "long white water," the Falls are a popular place to watch nature fight reason—bus loads of camera toters flock each day to witness the 100m-wide, 4m-deep Waikato River force itself into a 15m-wide, 3m-deep rock chute. Spurting out of the bottleneck, the water rushes breathlessly below a footbridge over the channel and ejects finally into a pool below, dumping enough water to fill two olympic pools every second. The cheapest and most aerobic way to capture the falls on your roll of film is via the **Huka Falls Track.** *(Leaves from Spa Thermal Park, off Spa Rd. Return 1hr.)*

ACTIVITIES

PLUMMETING OUT OF THE SKY

If you've been resisting peer pressure or sudden impulses, Taupo is the place to throw both caution and your body to the wind from an airplane at 12,000ft. Or, you and your fears can plummet toward water attached only to an elastic cord. For a deal on three charged activities (bungy, skydiving, and Huka jetboating), complete the **MaxBuzz Challenge** (www.maxbuzz.co.nz). To promote the area's adrenaline boosters, MaxBuzz offers **a free beer** at the **Holy Cow** (see **Nightlife**, p. 202) for each activity completed and a free T-shirt once you conquer all four activities ($370; trip to Holy Cow included). Call ahead for all activities.

TAUPO TANDEM SKYDIVE. A tandem jump here is **cheaper** than anywhere else in the world (doubtless because of the factory-like number of jumps—over 50,000), and the views on a clear day are spectacular, stretching from Ruapehu to Taranaki to Tarawera. This ultra-professional organization has been sending people up (and "escorting" them back down) since 1990. *(☎ 377 0428 or 0800 275 934; fax 378 0468; www.skydive.net.nz. 12,000 ft. $199, 15,000ft. $299. 100kg weight limit.)*

TAUPO BUNGY. Since 1991, more than 130,500 have ventured off the cantilever platform 47m above the hauntingly crystalline Waikato River. For $99, you can hook up and ponder the sheer cliffs, the impending water, or the pickup raft below. Or, you can just close your eyes and take the plunge. Touching water is an option. *(202 Spa Rd. ☎ 377 1135 or 0800 888 408; fax 377 1136; www.taupobungy.co.nz. Free shuttle within Taupo. Open daily 9am-7pm; in winter 9am-5pm.)*

ROCK 'N ROPES. This grown-up playground has a variety of ropes and adventure exotica including the Chicken Walk, Criss Crotch, Floating Log, Vertical Playpen, and Giant Swing. Great value for money and a surefire confidence builder; many find these challenging highwires even scarier than the bungy or skydive. *(Located at Crazy Catz Adventure Park, off Hwy. 5 just north of Wairekei. ☎ 374 8111 or 0800 244 508; fax 378 1351; www.rocknropes.co.nz. Free transport available. Swing $15; high beam, giant trapeze, and swing combo $35; half-day $59.)*

GRAVITY HILL. A daredevil cross between skateboarding, snowboarding, and surfing, mountainboarding at Gravity Hill will test the abilities of experienced and novice riders alike. Strapped to the board, you can jump, turn, and cruise on 12 acres of grass and dirt courses. *(Rakanui Rd., off Centennial Rd. ☎ 0800 472 8489; www.gravityhill.co.nz. $29.)*

ON THE WATER

Lake Taupo's blue waters fill the crater of the volcano responsible for some of the most violent eruptions the world has ever witnessed. Its final blast, 1809 years ago, ejected ash and pumice meters-thick over much of the North Island—the resulting blood-red skies were recorded in ancient Chinese and Roman literature.

FISHING. The world-famous Taupo trout, both brown and rainbow, were introduced from California in the late 1800s and continue to draw novice and experienced anglers from across the world. Regulations appear on the **fishing license** you must purchase for any line you drop. The apex of the fish phenomenon is ANZAC Day (April 25, 2003), when the ECNZ International Trout Fishing Tournament takes over town with 500 anglers eager to take the biggest, prettiest, and feistiest trout of the lake. *(Charters $50-130 per hr. Spinning and fly-fishing permitted in Lake Taupo year-round; on rivers, only fly-fishing is allowed. 12 fish per day license $12.50; 26 per week license $27. Available from the Visitors Center, sports shops, or the offices at the harbor.)*

KAYAKING. Kayaking Kiwi offers half-day paddles to the carvings and other sights. *(☎/fax 378 5901 or 025 288 1137; www.kayaking-kiwi.co.nz. $54.)* **Zig Zag Fun Co.** runs kayaking trips past the Orakei Korako thermal park and then farther up the Waikato than other kayaking companies. *(☎377 0688 or 025 755 294. Free pick-up. Half-day $50, full-day $80.)* **Kiwi River Safaris** takes adrenaline junkies and first-time adventurers on white-water-rafting and kayaking trips. *(45min. north of Taupo. ☎0800 723 8577; www.krs.co.nz. 1-day rafting $85, 2-day $275; kayaking $40.)*

HUKA JET. Take this heart-racing jetboat blast down the Waikato, performing 360° turns for the Kodak-heavy crowds at **Huka Falls**. *(6km north of Taupo off SH1. ☎374 8572 or 0800 485 2538; www.hukajet.co.nz. Boats run every 30min. Free shuttle from the Visitors Center. 30min. ride $69, children $39. Reservations essential.)*

TURANGI ☎07

The self-proclaimed "Trout Fishing Capital of the World," Turangi (pop. 3800) has made a fishy name for itself in the tourism market. Waters teem with anglers, but there is plenty of space, tackle, and catch to go around. Alternatively, fit, fish-fearing folk can find foot-borne fun on the much-hyped Tongariro Crossing and other hikes in Tongariro National Park.

TRANSPORTATION. InterCity/Newmans stops at the **Travel Centre** (☎386 8918), right across from Extreme Backpackers, and heads daily to: **Auckland** (5½hr., 3-4 per day, $62) via **Taupo** (45min., $17-18) and **Hamilton** (3½hr., $42); and **Wellington** (5½hr., 3 per day, $62) via **Palmerston North** (3hr.). InterCity's **Starlighter** overnight service heads to **Auckland** daily at 1:10am and to **Wellington** daily at 1:45am. The laid-back folks of **Alpine Scenic Tours** (☎386 8918 or 025 937 281), also at the Travel Centre, run daily shuttles to **National Park Village** (1hr., 1-2 per day, return $20) and **Whakapapa Village** or straight to **Whakapapa** (45min., 2-3 per day, return $20). In summer, Alpine also travels to the endpoints of the **Tongariro Crossing** (return $25). Other summer shuttle services to Tongariro endpoints include **The Bellbird Lodge** (☎386 8281; departs 6:30 and 7:15am; return $20-25) and **Tongariro Expeditions** (☎377 0435 or 0800 828 763; departs 6:30 and 7:15am; $20-25). On all of the hiking shuttles, the 6:30am "early-bird" service is for those who want to try (in futility) to beat the crowd and will generally cost $5 more than regular service. Although one should always consider the risks involved, **hitchhiking** to Taupo is reportedly not too difficult; those heading north on SH1 wait at the corner of Pihanga Rd. near the Visitors Center or near the Shell station. Traffic is lighter going south.

ORIENTATION AND PRACTICAL INFORMATION. Some 4km from Lake Taupo on **SH1**, Turangi has no lakefront view. SH1 continues both north around the lake to Taupo and south where it's known as the **Desert Road. Ohuanga Road** is the main road through town, and virtually all essential shops and services are in the **Town Centre** complex, a short diagonal walk from the bus stop. The **Turangi Visitor Centre** is just across from the Town Centre. Check here in winter to make sure

206 ■ TAUPO AND TONGARIRO

the Desert Rd. is open before heading south. (☎386 8999; fax 386 0074; turangivc@laketauponz.com. Open daily 8:30am-5pm.) For more park information and before attempting any serious Tongariro walks, stop by the **DOC** office in Turanga Pl., at the south edge of town. (☎386 8607. Open M-F 8am-5pm.) Other services, all located in the Town Centre unless noted, include: a **bank** (open M-F 9am-4:30pm); the **police** (☎386 7709), at Ohuanga and Tautahanga Rd.; **Turangi Pharmacy** (☎386 8565; open M-F 8:30am-5:30pm, Sa 9:30am-1:30pm, Su 11am-12:30pm); **Dr. Liaw** (☎386 8898) and **Dr. Leigh** (☎386 0680), Turangi's main general practitioners; **Internet access** at the **Visitors Center** ($2 per 15min.) or **Civic Video**, in the Lotto shop next to the BP (☎386 8811; open M-Sa 8:30am-8pm, Su 10am-8pm; $2.50 per 15min.); and the **post office** (☎386 7769; open M-F 9am-5pm), at Naylor's Bookshop.

ACCOMMODATIONS AND CAMPING. Turangi's accommodations will set you up with shuttles and discounts for affiliated area outfitters and may provide reason enough to use Turangi as a base for Tongariro's trails. With a serene courtyard, state-of-the-art kitchen, and open log fire in the Sky TV lounge, **Extreme Backpackers (BBH) ❷**, 26 Ngawaka Pl., around the corner from the bus depot, is better than home. (☎386 8949; fax 386 8946; ebpcltd@xtra.co.nz. Internet. Linen $3. Key deposit $5. 4-bed dorms $17; doubles with linen $40, with bath $48; family rooms $55; tent sites $10.) Quiet reigns in the four houses of the **Bellbird Lodge (BBH) ❷**, at Ohuanga and Rangipoia Rd. in the residential north end of town. Friendly owners bring free cake around nightly. Call for pick-up. (☎386 8281; fax 386 8283; www.bellbird.co.nz. Mountain bike rental. Dorms $16-18; twins and doubles $36-40; tent sites $10-12.) The coolest thing about institutional **Club Habitat (VIP/YHA) ❷**, 25 Ohuanga Rd., is the backpacker-oriented bar with home-brewed beer. (☎386 7492; fax 386 0106; habitat@voyager.co.nz. Internet. Key deposit $10. Sauna, spa, restaurant, and bar. Shuttle services. Dorms $16; singles $23; twins and doubles $40, with bath $64; tent sites $8.) Swankier digs are delivered with a smile at **Del's Place ❹**, 44 Ohuanga Rd., south of town past Club Habitat. The spic 'n' span bedroom cleanses the mind and the palate for the full breakfast service. (☎386 5925; fax 386 5926. Singles $45; doubles $65; extra person $10.) Former bunkhouse of the Tongariro Power Scheme workers, the **Turangi Cabins and Holiday Park ❶**, off of Ohuanga Rd., west of the town center, still has a blue-collar feel. (☎386 8754; fax 386 7162; cabinsgalore@xtra.co.nz. Cabins and chalets $16 per person; on-site caravans $40 for 2; tent sites $9.)

FOOD. The fishing near Turangi can deliver the traveler from a culinary Hades; just catch your own dinner and avoid town restaurants. The best bet for good-value food and a brew is the **Brewhaus Bar and Restaurant ❸**, at Club Habitat, just south of town, where backpackers simmer over a $4 handle of homebrew and a $15-20 filling main. (☎386 7294. Open daily 7-9:30am and 6-9pm.) The **Grand Central Fry ❶**, 8 Ohuanga Rd., is a cut above the typical takeaway, with excellent burgers and fish 'n' chips, most under $7. (☎386 5344. Phone ahead to avoid the wait. Open daily 11:30am-9pm; reduced hours in winter.) **Baks Brasserie & Bar ❹**, at the corner of Pihanga and Ohuanga Rd., serves up good brunch fare and also operates as a bar with frequent karaoke nights. Summers feature an outdoor beer garden. (☎386 6340. Open Tu-Su 11am-3:30pm and 5-9:30pm.) A gift for insomniacs, the **Turangi Truck Stop ❶**, 1km west of the town center, on Atirau Rd., stays open 24hr. (☎386 8760. Grub $1.50-8.) For groceries, head to the **New World**, in the Town Centre. (☎386 8780. Open M-F 8:30am-6pm, Sa-Su 9am-5pm.)

SIGHTS AND ACTIVITIES. The **Tongariro River** is ideal for three things: fishing, kayaking/rafting, and walking around. Knowing, perhaps, that they are Turangi's premier attraction, husky 1½-2kg **trout** are a sure-fire bite. Fishing guides for the river and lake range from about $50 per hr. That cost does not include licenses, which start at $12 per day and are available at the Visitors Center as well as several sports and fishing tackle shops. Licenses are cheaper for multiple days. Several operators raft down the Class III upper section, over 60-odd rapids closed in by walls of bush. **Rock 'n' River** will take you rafting, let you jump off a hidden waterfall, and soak you in a hot pool at the end of the day. (☎386 0352 or 0800 865 226. $85.) The **Tokaanu Thermal Pools** are off the main road of tiny Tokaanu Village down SH41 from Turangi. Immerse yourself in small, covered private pools ($6 per 20min., includes public pool) or in the slightly cooler, less expensive $4 public pool. (☎386 8575. Open daily 10am-9pm.)

Turangi's other big attractions are tracks, such as the nearby **Tongariro Crossing** (see p. 210), often hailed as the finest one-day trek in the world, and paths in the rugged hills east of Tongariro that constitute part of the **Kaimanawa Forest Park**. Kaimanawa, primarily used for multi-day hunting and tramping trips, is huge (77,348 hectares), hard to access, and not developed for visitors. Only one hut (Waipakihi) lies on the west side of the park, and access via the Kaimanawa Rd. requires a hut ticket ($5) from the Visitors Center. Plan your trip carefully and consult DOC or the Visitors Center to find out whether you will need permission to cross private land. The **Lake Rotopounamu walk**, which leaves from a sign-post 11km up SH47, does an easy 5km loop through native fern forest around the small lake hidden at the base of **Pihanga** (the 1325m extinct volcano towering over Turangi). Pihanga's summit is only accessible by bushwhacking (not recommended by *Let's Go*), but **Mt. Tihia**, also near town, can be summitted (return 4hr.) from Te Pananga Saddle, 7km up SH47.

TONGARIRO NATIONAL PARK

Three larger-than-life volcanic peaks tower over the roof of the North Island: massive, blocky Ruapehu (rue-uh-PIE-oo; 2797m), conical Ngauruhoe (nair-uh-HO-ee; 2291m), and sprawling Tongariro (1967m). These volcanoes—all still active—were once considered so sacred that all but the highest-born Maori shielded their eyes against their grandeur. An eerie, wind-scoured land, the park encloses New Zealand's only "desert" (the desolate Rangipo), native forests of beech, hardy alpine shrublands, and famous gem-like crater lakes set against colorful volcanic scoria.

AT A GLANCE	
AREA: 78, 651 hectares.	**GATEWAYS:** Turangi, National Park, Ohakune. Whakapapa is in the park.
CLIMATE: Mild climate in summer, extreme conditions in winter.	**CAMPING:** Accommodations and camping in Whakapapa. Backcountry huts along tramping routes.
FEATURES: Craters, active volcanoes, ski fields, tussock, semi-arid desert.	
HIGHLIGHTS: Emerald Lakes, Tongariro Crossing, circuit tracks.	**FEES & RESERVATIONS:** Camping $10-12, summertime hut pass $14-18 for the Great Walk. In winter, huts revert to backcountry system.

TRANSPORTATION

Highways encircle Tongariro National Park. To the east, **SH1**, also called the **Desert Road**, streaks through the **Rangipo Desert;** ice occasionally closes this road in winter. To the south, **SH49** splits off from SH1 at the army base town of

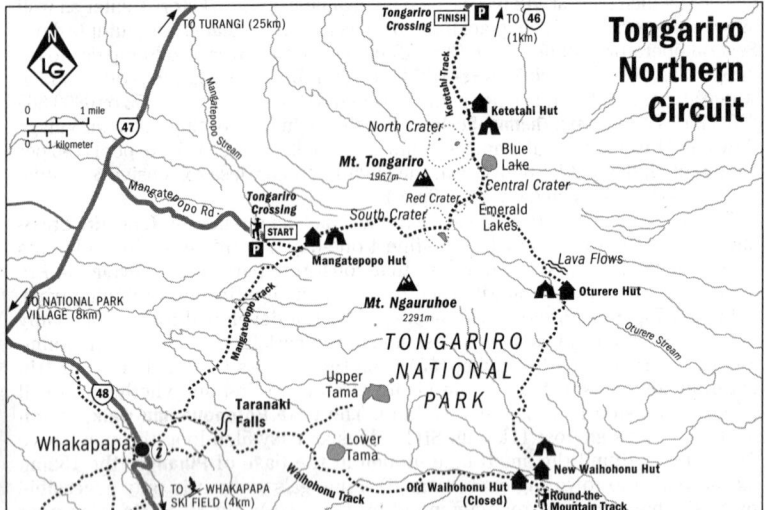

Tongariro Northern Circuit

Waiouru and then runs west until it hits **SH4**, which flanks the park's western side. **SH47** traces the park's northern edge between SH4 and SH1. **SH48** (also called Bruce Rd.) and **SH46** branch south from SH47 to Whakapapa and the Mangatepopo road end, respectively. **Hitchhiking** along any of these roads can be a slow process, but traffic is particularly sparse along SH48. Those determined to get past Whakapapa Village start early to catch ski field employees and never wait until dark to try their luck going down. The same is true for those hitching along Ohakune Mountain Rd., which heads north from SH49 to the base of Ruapehu and Turoa Ski Field. Most visitors to the park stay in **Turangi** (see p. 205), **National Park Village** (see p. 212), **Whakapapa Village** (see p. 214), or **Ohakune** (see p. 214). Whakapapa Village is the most convenient for the **Tongariro Northern Circuit** and the **Whakapapa ski fields,** while Ohakune provides the easiest access to the **Turoa ski fields.** Operators shuttle walkers to the **Tongariro Crossing** trailheads from Turangi, National Park Village, Whakapapa Village, and Ohakune.

>
> **WHEN TO GO.** Though the Tongariro National Park can be visited year round, extreme weather conditions and avalanches make winter tramping dangerous. Trampers must be experienced and have appropriate gear, including crampons, an ice axe, and appropriate clothing. Skiers should also dress warmly and are advised to keep an eye on Ruapehu and Ngauruhoe, which could end a ski season at any moment.

ORIENTATION AND PRACTICAL INFORMATION

Tongariro National Park lies just southwest of Lake Taupo. Start your exploration at **DOC's Whakapapa Visitor Centre,** which presents two high-tech audiovisual shows ($3, children $1, discount for 2-show package) and a treasure trove of biological, cultural, and geological displays. (☎07 892 3729; fax 892 3814. Open daily 8am-6pm; in winter 8am-5pm.) Its **Tongariro Summer Programme** (late

Dec.-early Jan.) features ranger-led activities from backcountry heli-hikes ($110) to free evening talks. There are also smaller **DOC offices** in Turangi (☎07 386 8607; open M-F 8am-5pm) and Ohakune (☎06 385 0010; open M-F 9am-3pm). Turangi and Ohakune harbor **supermarkets** and have **ATMs**. **Secure parking** is available at the DOC lot beside the Whakapapa Visitors Center; vandalism and theft run rampant in many other area lots, particularly those at trailheads. The **telephone codes** for this region are 06 in Ohakune and 07 in all points further north.

OUTDOOR ACTIVITIES

For information on the **Tongariro Northern Circuit** or the **Tongariro Crossing**, see p. 210. Less-crowded than the park's namesake walks, the **Round-the-Mountain Track** (4-5 days; huts $10, camping $5) runs around the mountain (Mt. Ruapehu), traversing windswept slopes, crossing a deep gorge, and passing along the edge of the forsaken Rangipo Desert. The track intersects the Northern Circuit at both Whakapapa Village and Waihohonu Hut; people often walk the two in conjunction—storing food for the second half of the journey in Whakapapa means a 10min. detour off the hike, but much less pack weight in the initial days. Many **daywalks** start right from Whakapapa Village. The relatively easy **Tama Lakes Walk** (return 5hr.), which follows an undulating, tussocked landscape past Taranaki Falls to the incongruous blue of Tama Lakes, is one of the best of these. The unmarked climb to the active **Ruapehu Crater**, on the other hand, is the most difficult (official) dayhike in the park. Ice, snow, and volcanic activity can make the trip a risky one, and several unprepared people have died doing it. Most begin the trek from the top of Bruce Rd. (SH48) near the base of the Whakapapa ski lifts (return 7hr.); others ride the lifts to their terminus (open daily 9am-4:30pm; return $15) and start from there (return 5hr.). Staff from the **Mt. Ruapehu Ski Area** conduct **guided walks** along this route. (☎07 892 3738. Dec.-Apr. daily 9:30am. $45, under 16 $20.)

Experienced, alpine-savvy rock climbers will find a challenging 120m route on Pukekaikore called the **Bomb Arete** off the track near Mangatetopo Hut (mere mortals need not apply). Also nearby, the walls of **Mangatetopo Valley** provide a more reasonable challenge for casual climbers, who might be interested in climbing on the park's unique volcanic rock.

THE LOCAL STORY

OF HALF-PIPES AND HOSPITALITY

Jess Mortimer is New Zealand's #2 ranked snowboarder.

Q: What's your favorite part about competition?
A: I loo-ove the half-pipe. Bring it on!

Q: How does the snowboarding future look for New Zealand?
A: The level of snowboarding in New Zealand is going to go through the roof now that half-pipes are appearing everywhere. Also, fads tend to catch on quite well here. People just love adventure and sport. So now we've got snowsuits. They're like a skateboard, but you've got a little ski underneath. You can ollie kick-flip them, you can ride rainbow rails. Yeah, you can basically skateboard on the snow.

Q: How does New Zealand snowboarding compare with the rest of the world?
A: As far as snow quality and the workmanship of the jumps, it's best in the northern hemisphere, but here we have a little bit of everything. So, even though the runs are shorter, you can go off-piste really easily and you can do really nice open bowls, or you can go to undulating little relievers where you can ollie off and just land in the powder.

Q: Do you think you'll always come back to New Zealand?
A: Definitely! The friendliness of the people and smaller size of the towns means you know everyone. A lot of us that snowboard around the world, doing seasons back to back, we always come back to New Zealand.

SKIING AND SNOWBOARDING

Tongariro National Park draws nearly half of its visitors in the winter months, thanks to the commercial ski slopes hugging Ruapehu's slopes. The **Mt. Ruapehu Ski Area** is the largest and most developed ski area in New Zealand. One pass provides access to lifts on both sides of the mountain (Whakapapa and Turoa) and to a traverse between the two for intermediate and advanced skiers only that is in the works. The mountain was a sacred gift from a Maori chief in 1887 and the ski area still respects the sanctity of the crown—no lifts or groomers touch the top, which welcomes powder-hungry skiers and boarders. Although Ruapehu attracts bad weather like a 2797m magnet (gale-force winds and storms often close the fields), the management offers a weather guarantee that allows refunds or credits if lifts have to close or you're unhappy with the conditions. Even so, volcano skiing is, by nature, unpredictable. Lack of sufficient snow can severely limit the mountain's operations. More dramatically, the recent Ruapehu eruptions cut both the 1995 and 1996 seasons short, reminding everyone that the mountain yields to no one. (☎07 892 3738, snowphone ☎0900 99 333; www.mtruapehu.com. Open July-Oct.; lifts open daily 9am-4pm. Ski, boot, and pole rental $31, under 16 $19. Snowboard and boot rental $43. Lift pass $56, under 16 $28; half-day $31, under 16 $16; deals available on multi-day and beginners' equipment and lift passes.) Nearby **Mt. Ngauruhoe** beckons experienced and adventuresome skiers. With no lifts or grooming, there's excellent above-tree-line powder skiing in the spring. Check with DOC for specific weather conditions, avalanche status, and hiking recommendations.

WHAKAPAPA. The Whakapapa side of the mountain has killer views of Mt. Taranaki on clear days. The ski field includes six chairlifts, eight T-bars or platters, six rope tows, a beginner's area, plenty of groomed, patrolled trails, open terrain, and lots of easily accessible "backcountry" extreme areas. Snowboarders are welcome, but most seem to prefer Turoa. *(At the top of Bruce Rd. from Whakapapa Village.)*

TUROA. With the country's longest vertical drop (720m) and 400 hectares of patrolled snow, Turoa is known for open terrain and long runs (the longest is 4km). The trails slope down from four chairlifts, three T-bars, four platter lifts (two in the beginners' area), and one rope tow. Turoa also has some off-trail skiing; it's even possible to haul gear up to Crater Lake and ski down (always check with the Ski Patrol first). Another culture altogether, snowboarders love Turoa for the natural half-pipes in its gulleys and the lack of any major flats. At any time, almost half of the slope is covered with bleached-blonde, styled-out boarders. There is also a terrain park with rails, snow jumps, and a groomed half-pipe. *(Accessible via Ohakune Mountain Rd.)*

TONGARIRO NORTHERN CIRCUIT

Winding around the park's trinity of volcanoes, the Tongariro Northern Circuit is one of the country's most breathtaking tracks. The otherworldly terrain is pocked with steaming vents, technicolor lakes, and bizarre rock formations, not to mention the three volcanoes: Mt. Ngauruhoe's perfect cone, Mt. Tongariro's jumbled mass, and Mt. Ruapehu's slumbering snow-capped hothead. The **Tongariro Crossing**, a head-spinning highlight-reel track, is acclaimed as the best one-day walk in the country. While it shares almost the whole length of the Crossing, the Northern Circuit's highlights are not exclusive to that stretch. Beyond where the two part ways, the Circuit leads to a field of angular, naturally-sculpted lava flows, a few tranquil (if mystifyingly isolated) patches of native forest, the Tama Lakes, the Taranaki Falls, and views of the volcanoes from nearly every angle.

TONGARIRO NATIONAL PARK ■ 211

Length: 51.5km, 3-4 days.

Trailheads: Start from **Whakapapa Village**, the **Mangatepopo** road-end (6km off SH47), the **Ketetahi** road-end (1km off SH46), or **SH1**, across from Rangipo Intake Rd. Most begin and end in Whakapapa Village. To **avoid the crowds on the Crossing**, spend the night before at Mangatepopo Hut or hit the trail mid-morning—most day trampers arrive between 7:30 and 8:30am. The majority of trampers walk clockwise so as to avoid fighting the flow of the Crossing mobs.

Transportation: Alpine Scenic Tours (☎ 07 386 8918 or 025 937 281) shuttle between the **trailheads, Turangi, National Park Village,** and **Whakapapa Village** (1-3 per day, return $20). **Tongariro Track Transport** (☎ 07 892 3716 or 021 256 3109) runs Oct.-Apr. daily from **National Park Village** (departs 7:45am) and **Whakapapa Village** (departs 8am) to **Mangatepopo** (return $15, under 16 or over 65 $10), and picks up at **Ketetahi** (4:30 and 6pm). Some area hostels also run on-demand shuttles in the summer. **Hitchhiking** to any of the trailheads is usually difficult, and *Let's Go* does not recommend it. Leaving a **car** unattended is a bad idea—the Mangatepopo and Ketetahi carparks are among the country's most unsafe.

Seasonality: Harsh conditions due to high altitudes and extreme exposure are possible in any season. A winter circuit is a technical tramp necessitating equipment and experience. Dec.-Mar are safest; Feb. has the most stable weather patterns.

Huts and Campsites: Four 26-bunk **huts**. From late Oct.-early June, the huts have on-site wardens, gas cookers, toilet facilities, rainwater supply (sometimes scarce during drought), and require a **hut pass** ($14-18). There is no booking system, so a bunk is never guaranteed during the busy season. Each hut has an adjacent cluster of **tent sites** ($10-12). From late June-early Sept., fees revert to the backcountry ticket system (huts $10, tent sites $5) and huts have fewer amenities.

Storage: Whakapapa Visitor Centre ($3 per bag); most accommodations store for free.

WHAKAPAPA VILLAGE TO MANGATEPOPO HUT. *8.5km, 2½hr.* The section of track from Whakapapa Village to **Mangatepopo Hut** crosses several streams and affords memorable views of solitary Pukeonake and the jumble of volcanoes next to it—an enticing teaser of what's to come. The downside: it is extremely rutted and can get very muddy in adverse weather, leading some folks to skip this section by starting at the Tongariro Crossing Trailhead on Mangatepopo Rd. The hut itself, 25min. from the Mangatepopo road-end, faces Mt. Tongariro, Mt. Ngauruhoe, and the saddle between them.

MANGATEPOPO HUT TO EMERALD LAKES. *7.7km, 3½hr.* From the hut, the trail follows Mangatepopo Stream up the valley to its origin, **Soda Springs**, which is a short 10min. marked spur from the main trail. The water from the springs and the stream is not drinkable, even when treated, due to high mineral content. From there, the track up to the saddle is quite steep, but the climb ends in less than an hour. At the top, strong winds blow across **South Crater**, a Mars-like world almost entirely devoid of plant life. A demanding side trip leads up the great **Mt. Ngauruhoe** (2291m; ascent 2hr., descent 45min.). Much of the climb is unmarked, but if you stay left along the rocky outcrop on the way up and find the scree chute on the way down, you shouldn't lose your bearings. The main track continues across South Crater's flat expanse, then ascends another steep slope to the rim of steaming **Red Crater**. From here, a well-marked spur route leads very gradually to the peak of **Mt. Tongariro** (1967m; return 1½hr.). Meanwhile, the main track skirts Red Crater's edge and climbs to the track's highest point (1886m), where first views of the limpid Emerald Lakes reward the effort. It's just a quick, steep scree-run down to their scenic and (we have to say it) smelly shores.

EMERALD LAKES TO KETETAHI HUT OR OTURERE HUT. *9.3km, 3½hr. or 3.3km, 2hr.* At the **Emerald Lakes Junction,** just beyond those amazing green pools, trampers completing the Northern Circuit have a choice. They can head north to Ketetahi Hut or veer southeast to Oturere Hut. One-and-a-half hours off the main circuit via a trail that skirts the steep eastern slope of North Crater, ridge-top **Ketetahi Hut** offers thrilling views of Lakes Rotoaira and Taupo, but the Crossing crosses its front porch—literally—so the place turns into a major thoroughfare on pleasant afternoons. The nearby Ketetahi Hot Springs are on private land and off-limits. Past the hut, the track drops rather steeply, the surrounding vegetation changes from tussock to podocarp forest, and eventually the Ketetahi road-end appears (2hr.). Heading toward Oturere from the junction, the track drops steeply into a valley strewn with chunks of lava that have hardened into jagged shapes and pinnacles. The Circuit cuts a relatively flat path across the valley floor, at the end of which, on a ledge overlooking a waterfall and stream, sits **Oturere Hut,** generally the quietest hut—and the best from which to catch a stunning sunrise.

OTURERE HUT TO NEW WAIHOHONU HUT. *8.5km, 3hr.* Beyond Oturere, the track winds down into sandy washes and over a series of gravel hills studded with the occasional wind-whipped treelet. After about two hours, the path crosses a river to enter honest-to-gosh forest, ascends through cool beeches to a scenic ridge, and descends again through forest to **New Waihohonu Hut,** which stares Mt. Ruapehu straight in the face. Those who reach the hut with energy to spare can drop their pack and head a bit farther along the track straight through a junction, following signposts to the pond-like **Ohinepango Springs** (return 40min.), where exquisitely tasty (and freezing cold) water gushes straight out of the ground.

NEW WAIHOHONU HUT TO WHAKAPAPA VILLAGE. *15.5km, 5hr.* Just a bit beyond New Waihohonu a spur trail leads past century-old **Old Waihohonu Hut** (return 6min.), which is unlivable and filled with decades of tramper graffiti. Stick by the stream here to follow the main track, which rises and falls only slightly (but repeatedly) as it continues through stream-furrowed tussockland to the pass between Ngauruhoe and Ruapehu. If you have time, make the sidetrip to the Tama Lakes: **Lower Tama** (return 20min.), a shining blue pool couched in an explosion crater, and crescent-shaped **Upper Tama** (return 1½hr.), which lies steeply uphill amid wind-buffeted vistas. The final stretch forks about an hour short of Whakapapa Village; an upper route travels through more rutted tussock terrain, while the equidistant, forested lower route starts by passing the brilliant 20m **Taranaki Falls.**

NATIONAL PARK VILLAGE ☎ 07

National Park Village is little more than a cluster of accommodations at the junction of SH4 and SH47, but the Tongariro Crossing, Whakapapa ski fields, and Whanganui River Journey are all nearby.

TRANSPORTATION. The **train station** is on Railway Rd., at the end of Carroll St.; **buses** depart from the dairy near Carroll and Ward St. at the huge "Ski Hire" sign. **TranzScenic** has daily service to: **Auckland** (5½hr., $67-76); **Hamilton** (3½hr., $39-44); **Palmerston North** (3½hr., $42-46); and **Wellington** (5½hr., $66-74). **InterCity** heads daily north to: **Auckland** (5½hr., $39-49) via **Hamilton** (3½hr., $26-32); and south to **Wellington** (5½hr., $44-55) via **Ohakune** (30min., $11) and **Wanganui** (2½hr., $27). **Ski Haus** and **Howard's Lodge** (see below) handle bookings. **Howard's Lodge** runs a shuttle to the Tongariro Crossing trailheads in summer and to the ski fields in winter ($10, return $16). **Alpine Scenic Tours** (☎ 386 8918 or 025 937 281) runs to **Whakapapa Village** ($6, return $10) and **Turangi** (2-3 per day, $15).

NATIONAL PARK VILLAGE ■ 213

PRACTICAL INFORMATION. National Park Village lacks both a **Visitors Center** and an **ATM**. The small **police station** (☎ 892 2869) is on Buddo St., parallel to SH4. The **BP station** at the highway junction stocks basic groceries and serves as a **post office**. (☎ 892 2897. Open daily 7:30am-7pm.) The nearest hospital is in Taumarunui (☎ 896 0020). **Internet access** is available at most accommodations but is free at **Pukenui Lodge**. Most accommodations rent a range of **gear** for all seasons. For **ski and snowboard rental**, head to **Roy Turner Ski & Board Shop** (☎ 892 2757 or 0800 766 9963; www.snowzone.co.nz) or **Ski Biz** (☎ 892 2717). Both charge $25-30 for ski, boot, and pole rental and $40 for snowboard and boot rental.

ACCOMMODATIONS AND CAMPING. The quality lodges of National Park Village are absolutely stuffed with skiers in winter and the summer traffic of trampers is swelling. At the corner of Findlay and SH4, **National Park Backpackers and Climbing Hall (BBH)** ❷ has a two-story rock climbing wall ($9 for entire stay) surrounded by immaculate dorm rooms. Other perks include a spacious kitchen, central heating, and a hot tub. (☎/fax 892 2870; nat.park.backpackers@xtra.co.nz. Internet. Dorms $18-20; singles $30; twins and doubles $60; tent sites $10. Lower prices in summer.) **Howard's Lodge (BBH)** ❷, down Carroll St., pleases travelers with its extensive shuttle services. Clean and hospitable, the free spa and ski clothing for guests are added bonuses. Winter weekends demand bookings up to three weeks in advance. (☎/fax 892 2827; www.howardslodge.co.nz. Internet. Mountain bike rental $20 per 2hr. Reception 7am-9pm. Dorms $18; twins and doubles $70, in summer $50; rooms with bath $100/$70.) At **Pukenui Lodge (BBH/VIP)** ❺, at the corner of SH4 and Millar St., summer backpackers enjoy the serenity of the spacious lounge and free Internet. In winter, skiers scramble for space and fully catered meals. (☎ 892 2882 or 0800 785 168; fax 892 2900; www.tongariro.cc. In summer dorms from $16; twins and doubles from $44; in winter package rates from $95 for 2 including meals.) For summer visitors who require minimal amenities, the **DOC Mangahuia Campsite** ❶, 4km from National Park Village on SH47, has a nice streamside location with pit toilets (tent and caravan sites $4).

FOOD. The best bet for grub is stocking up on **groceries** before reaching this isolated outpost. The only remaining non-lodge dining venue in town is the **Schnapps Hotel** ❸, at Findlay St. and SH4. This unassuming spot rocks the ski season with bands every Saturday night (cover $5) and a bizarre grab-bag of drinking games. Unwind with one of the mains ($12-18) and a cold beer. (☎ 892 2788. Open daily 11am-2am; in summer noon-2am, closes earlier when slow.) Otherwise, the **National Park Hotel** ❷, up Carroll St. close to the rails, is a basic pub food possibility. (☎ 892 2805. Open daily 11am-late; hours vary greatly in summer.)

ACTIVITIES. The **Tongariro Forest Conservation Area,** just north of town, is home to the **42nd Traverse,** one of the country's most satisfying mountain bike trails. The organ-jiggling 4-5hr. ride follows well-maintained old logging trails, with a stream crossing and a 570m descent. Howard's Lodge (see **Accommodations,** above) runs an on-demand shuttle service to the starting and ending points ($20 per person for 2 people). For a warm-up, on bike or foot, follow the **Fisher's Track** from the end of Carroll St. on the other side of the tracks. The wooded path leads to a bushy summit 4km from town with views of Taranaki. The opposite side's descent makes a great roll, but bikers should keep the return climb in mind.

WHAKAPAPA VILLAGE ☎ 07

This tiny clutch of establishments, the most prominent of which being the non-budget Grand Chateau, is the foundation of ski operations in Tongariro National Park and is the most immediate base for skiing on the north side of Ruapehu.

TRANSPORTATION. Alpine Scenic Tours (☎ 386 8918 or 025 937 281) leaves Whakapapa Village for **National Park Village** (2-3 per day, $10), the Tongariro Crossing endpoints at the **Ketetahi** and **Mangatepopo carparks** (on request), and **Turangi** ($15). Service can be flexible to accommodate tight travel schedules, but it must be booked in advance. **Whakapapa Shuttle** (☎ 892 3716 or 021 256 3109) provides winter service from the village up to the **ski field** ($7, return $12); in summer, the shuttle becomes **Tongariro Track Transport,** which runs a daily shuttle on demand to Mangatepopo and from Ketetahi ($10, return $15). Many travelers reportedly **hitchhike** to the ski fields.

PRACTICAL INFORMATION. The **Whakapapa Visitor Centre** doubles as the **DOC** office (see **Tongariro National Park,** p. 208). They have several excellent free displays about the area and two audio visual shows about the land and the volcano ($3, children $1). There are **no banks or ATMs. Internet access** ($8 per hr.) and the **post office** are in **Fergusson's Cafe** (see **Food,** below).

ACCOMMODATIONS AND CAMPING. Grand Chateau, Grand Schmateau. The perky **Skotel (VIP)** ❹ has, hands down, the finest view of any budget accommodation on the North Island. To get to this spot, follow the road between the Grand Chateau and the Visitors Center for 200m. Bask in all the ski-lodge amenities—Internet, spa, sauna, games, drying room, cushy mattresses, and a small communal kitchen. (☎ 892 3719 or 0800 756 835; fax 892 3777; www.skotel.co.nz. Dorms $60, in summer $20; motel units from $105-110. Reservations recommended.) Set beside a stream and just across the road from the Visitors Center, the **Whakapapa Holiday Park** ❶ offers small but private sites carved out of the native bush and good kitchen facilities. Spartan bunks populate the backpackers lodge. (☎ 892 3897; fax 892 3026; whakapapaholpark@xtra.co.nz. Key deposit $5. Dorms $16.50; cabins $35 for 2, extra person $10; tourist flats $55 for 2; tent sites $8; caravan sites $10.)

FOOD. Refined, historic, and decidedly non-budget, the **Grand Chateau** hotel dominates the village both in size and in cuisine. Aside from the in-house bar and restaurant at the Skotel, all of the town's food establishments run under the capable hands of the Chateau. The lodge-like **Fergusson's Cafe** ❶ does a brisk business of soups, hot quiches, sandwiches, and coffee. (☎ 892 3809, ext. 8435. Internet. Open daily 7:30am-3pm.) Across the road, the elegant interior of **Pihanga Cafe** ❸ has surprisingly affordable mains, usually $14-20. (☎ 892 3809, ext. 8560. Open daily 11:30am-late; kitchen closes at 9pm.) **Whakapapa Holiday Park** (see **Accommodations and Camping,** above) stocks only the most basic groceries, but it beats gnawing on your hiking partner's forearms. (Open daily 7am-7pm.)

OHAKUNE ☎ 06

At one end of Ohakune (pop. 1500) stands Mt. Ruapehu, a massive snow-covered time-bomb that triples the town's population in winter. At the other end lies Ohakune's symbolic alter-ego—a giant statue of a carrot, symbolizing the importance of post-ski-season farming. When the snow melts and the scarfed visitors trickle out of town, Ohakune produces world-class carrots, sprouts, and potatoes from the area's rich volcanic soils.

OHAKUNE ■ 215

TRANSPORTATION

Trains: TranzScenic (☎ 0800 802 802) runs daily to: **Auckland** (6hr., 2 per day, $70-81) via **National Park** (30min, $14-16); and **Wellington** (5hr., 2 per day, $61-68), via **Palmerston North** (3hr., 2 per day, $29-41).

Buses: InterCity runs M-F and Su to **Auckland** (6hr., 1 per day, $56) and **Wellington** (5hr., 1 per day, $51). To get to **Taupo**, either take the train to Waiouru and catch a bus just north of the public toilets—check at the Visitors Center for variable schedules.

Ski Shuttles: The **Snowliner Shuttles** (☎ 385 8573) run on demand to the ski-fields of **Turoa** ($9, return $16). **Snow Express** also runs on demand to **Turoa** (☎ 385 9280; $9, return $15). In the summer, **Tongariro National Park Shuttle Transport** (☎ 0800 825 825) picks up in town and delivers to **Turoa** (return $15), **Whakapapa** (return $20), and the **Tongariro Crossing** (return $25).

Hitchhiking: Although *Let's Go* does not recommend it, hitchhiking is reportedly not too hard between Ohakune and National Park or Waiouru. Hitching up the mountain is said to be easier in the morning, but success depends on your amount of gear. Catching a ride is significantly more difficult in the summer.

ORIENTATION AND PRACTICAL INFORMATION

The south end of town, where **SH49** merges along the main drag **(Clyde Street)**, has most services and is active year-round. The north end, known as the **Junction**, lies 3km north by the railroad tracks and comes alive during the winter with seasonal chalets and a jumping nightlife. It also marks the start of the **Ohakune Mountain Road**, leading up past the trailheads to several scenic tramps and the ski lifts of Turoa. Goldfinch Street/Mangawhero Terrace (the road changes names) runs between Clyde St. and Ohakune Mountain Rd. (20-25min. by foot).

Visitors Center: Ohakune Visitor Centre, 54 Clyde St. (☎/fax 385 8427; www.ohakune.info), has a relief map of Tongariro National Park. Open M-F 9am-5pm, Sa-Su 9am-3:30pm.

DOC: (☎ 385 0010; fax 385 0011), beyond the railroad tracks on Ohakune Mountain Rd. One of Tongariro's 2 field centers. Open M-F 9am-12:30pm and 1-3pm; during school holidays daily 9am-4pm.

Work Opportunities: The seasonal gig (mainly Feb.-Mar.) in Ohakune relates to local agricultural pursuits: carrot and potato sorting and packing. If you're looking for your roots, ring Steve at **Mountain Carrots** (☎ 385 9490). Pay is about $9-10 per hr. There's also plenty of work options on Mt. Ruapehu's ski fields (see p. 210).

Ski and Snowboard Rental: Ski & Board Shop (☎ 385 8888), at the bottom of Mountain Rd., has the cheapest prices and 15% student discounts. Ski, boot, and pole rental $35; snowboard, boot, and wrist guard rental $43. Open M-Th and Sa-Su 7:30am-5:30 or 6pm, F 7:30am-midnight. There's also a dense string of rental companies near the Junction. Clothing rental available at all shops.

Banks: Several banks line **Goldfinch Street**, including **Westpac Trust** (☎ 385 8154), next to New World. Open M-F 9 or 9:30am-4:30pm.

Medical Services: Dr. Perera (☎ 385 8356), on Goldfinch St. just past the fire station, is the town's one-man medical service. **Ohakune Photo Pharmacy** (☎ 385 8304) is open M-F 9am-5pm; in winter also Sa 9am-noon.

Police: 17 Rata St. (☎ 385 0100).

Internet Access: Snowbird Copy Centre, 92 Clyde St. (☎ 385 8756), charges $7.50 per hr. Open M-F 9am-5pm, Sa-Su 9:30am-5pm. **The Video Shop** (☎ 385 8295), across the street from the Visitors Center, costs $10 per hr. Open M and Th 10:30am-8pm, Tu-W and Su 11am-8pm, F 10:30am-9pm, Sa 10:30am-8:30pm.

Post Office: 5 Goldfinch St. (☎385 8645), in Broadbents Bookshop. Open ski season M-F 6:30am-6pm, Sa 6:30am-7pm, Su 8:30am-4pm; off-season M-F 6:30am-5pm, Sa 6:30am-4:30pm.

ACCOMMODATIONS AND CAMPING

As one big bedroom for Turoa, Ohakune has an impressive number of accommodations. For travelers not requiring amenities, the DOC-run **Mangawhero Campsite**, about 1.5km up Ohakune Mountain Rd., is ideal. (Toilets but no water. $4.)

Rimu Park Lodge and Chalets (VIP), 27 Rimu St. (☎385 9023; fax 385 9121; www.go.to/ohakune). Close to the nightlife, Rimu has an open fire, free pick-up and breakfast in winter, and 30min. free Internet with 2-night stay. Dorms from $23 midweek, weekends $30, summer $16; twins and doubles $70/$60/$36. ❸

Matai Lodge (BBH) (☎385 9169; fax 385 9196; matai.lodge@xtra.co.nz), at the corner of Clyde and Rata St. A clean, spacious, and stark lodge complete with central heating, local phone access, a game room, and Internet. Dorms M-Th and Su $21, F-Sa $23; in summer $16. ❸

Ohakune YHA, 15 Clyde St. (☎/fax 385 8724; yhaohak@yha.org.nz). A laid-back atmosphere and an open kitchen foster easy conversation among guests. Dorms $16-18; twins $44; doubles with bath $52; family room $66. ❷

The Hobbit Motel Lodge (☎385 8248 or 0800 843 462; fax 385 8515), at the corner of Goldfinch and Wye St., 1km north of town. Once a used bookstore, this Hobbit predates the latest *Lord of the Rings*-induced craze. No kitchen. Laundry. Spa. Dorms $30-35, in summer $20; double studio units $120-150/$85-95. ❸

Ohakune Top 10 Holiday Park, 5 Moore St. (☎/fax 385 8561; www.ohakune.net.nz), off Clyde St. Tent and caravan sites $10; backpacker cabins $18, extra person $12; doubles $50; prices 20-40% higher in winter. ❶

FOOD AND NIGHTLIFE

Utopia ❸, 47 Clyde St., serves up tasty nibbles (read: nachos, paninis) and full-out dinner mains on the weekends (fresh fish dishes, creative salads) in a hip locale. During the ski season, Thursday nights feature $15 curries. (☎385 9120. Open M-W and Su 9am-3pm, Th-Sa 6pm-late; in summer M-W and Su 9am-2pm, Th-Sa 6-10pm.) Just a few doors down, **Mountain Kebabs Cafe** ❷, 29 Clyde St., has filling meat and vegetarian kebabs (medium $7-7.50) in a newly renovated setting. (☎385 9047. Open daily 10am-10pm; frequently closed in summer.) Up at the junction end of town, near the corner of Rimu and Thames St., **Margarita's** ❸ serves heaping Mexican mains (from $14.50) and a chill nightlife. Sundays are super with $10 specials served around the huge open fire. (☎385 9222. Open in ski season daily 4pm-3am. Closed Nov. to mid-Apr.) **La Pizzeria** ❸, 6 Thames St., next to the Turoa Ski Lodge, offers terrific $14 gourmet pizzas. (☎385 8558. Open in ski season daily 6pm-late; in the off season F-Sa 6pm-late.) Stock up for your own virtuoso cooking at **New World,** 12 Goldfinch St. (☎385 8587. Open M-Sa 8am-6pm, Su 8:30am-5pm.) At the corner of Ohakune Mountain Rd. and Thames St., the polished wood of the **Powderkeg Bar** explodes on weekends with DJ and drink specials providing the spark. (☎385 8888. Open daily 7am-3am; hours vary in summer.)

 OUTDOOR ACTIVITIES

Most people come to Ohakune to ski the fine slopes of **Turoa** (see p. 210), but the area does have summer activities. The sealed 18km **Ohakune Mountain Road** makes for exhilarating and scenic **biking** when ski traffic is gone. Ron Rutherford's **Ride the Mountain** operation rents bikes and runs to the top. (☎385 8257. $30.) The **Powderhorn Shop and Ski Hire,** in the Grand Chalet, rents bikes (half-day $25, full-day $35) and tramping equipment. (☎385 8888. Open daily 7:30am-6pm; in summer 9am-5pm.) Trampers will revel in the **Round-the-Mountain Track** (see p. 209), which comes through the Ohakune side of Ruapehu, following Ohakune Mountain Rd. for about 3km before diving back into wilderness on the west side of the mountain. Other good walks depart from the upper reaches of the road, including a short jaunt over to **Waitonga Falls** (return 1hr.) from a trailhead 11km up the road. More strenuous and exposed is the unmarked full-day track up Mt. Ruapehu to **Crater Lake** from the Turoa ski field. From October to April, Ohakune is a point of departure for **canoe trips** on the Whanganui River, a tranquil ride running through the heart of the wilderness. Many rental and guide companies either operate in town or offer pick-up service here (see p. 233). Before you leave town, make sure to check out the giant **carrot** on SH49.

TARANAKI AND WANGANUI

The pinnacle of Mt. Taranaki (Mt. Egmont) is the focal point of the North Island's westernmost peninsula. Maori legend speaks of Taranaki as a restless, sorrowful place, a reputation commensurate with its volcanic heart. Yet the rugged green slopes surrounding the peak nourish one of the richest dairylands in the world, defying geological instability with pastoral charm. Year-round relaxation is afforded by this rural setting and the region's balmy summers and gentle, wintry moods. The mild climate pleases travelers and, more importantly, dairy cows, earning Taranaki its reputation as the "Udder of New Zealand."

TARANAKI AND WANGANUI HIGHLIGHTS

ONE IF BY LAND The prominent and diverse **Egmont National Park** has excellent opportunities for tramping and skiing (see p. 223).

TWO IF BY SEA The **Whanganui River Journey** is the only Great Walk where you float to the finish line (see p. 233).

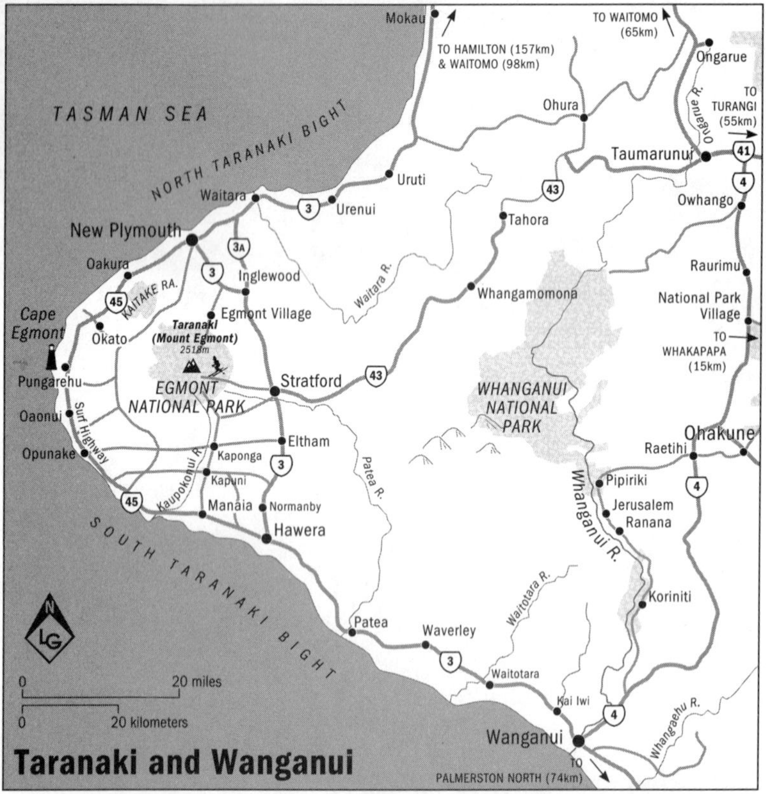

Taranaki and Wanganui

NEW PLYMOUTH

☎ 06

Residents of New Plymouth (pop. 49,200) love to point out that surfing the Tasman and skiing the slopes of Taranaki are both within an hour's drive. While this is indeed an enticing proposition for sports enthusiasts, the city itself gets lost in the excitement. Regardless, Taranaki's only urban center manages to make waves of its own. Featuring renowned parks and numerous walks, New Plymouth might capture your attention as more than just a waystation between snow and surf.

TRANSPORTATION

Buses: Depart from the **Travel Centre,** at the corner of King and Queen St. **InterCity** (☎ 759 9039) departs for: **Auckland** (6¼hr., 2 per day, $53) via **Hamilton** (4hr., $33); and **Wellington** (6¾hr., 2-3 per day, $61) via **Stratford** (30min., $14), **Hawera** (1¼hr., $19), **Wanganui** (2½hr., $30), and **Palmerston North** (4hr., $41). **Dalroy Express** (☎ 755 0009) runs to **Auckland** (5hr., 1 per day, $55) via **Hamilton** (3½hr., $35) and **Hawera** (1hr., $13). **White Star** (☎ 758 3338) also runs to **Wellington** (6¼hr., 1-2 per day, $48) via **Wanganui** (2½hr., $24) and **Palmerston North** (4hr., $32).

Taxis: New Plymouth Taxis (☎ 757 5665), **Egmont City Cabs** (☎ 754 8801), and **Energy City Cabs** (☎ 757 5580) queue at the corner of Brougham and Devon St.

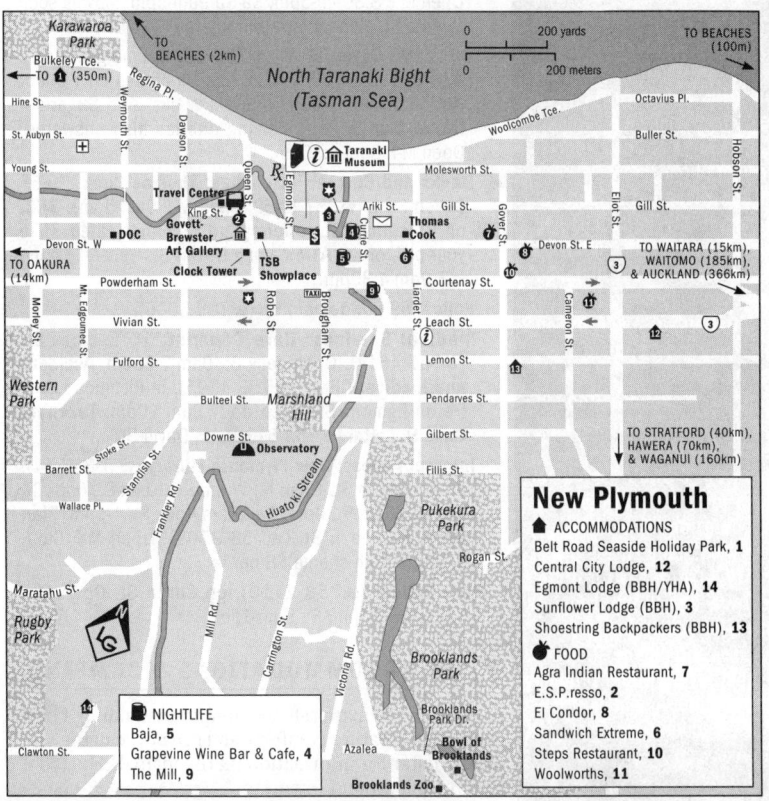

New Plymouth

ACCOMMODATIONS
Belt Road Seaside Holiday Park, 1
Central City Lodge, 12
Egmont Lodge (BBH/YHA), 14
Sunflower Lodge (BBH), 3
Shoestring Backpackers (BBH), 13

FOOD
Agra Indian Restaurant, 7
E.S.P.resso, 2
El Condor, 8
Sandwich Extreme, 6
Steps Restaurant, 10
Woolworths, 11

NIGHTLIFE
Baja, 5
Grapevine Wine Bar & Cafe, 4
The Mill, 9

FROM THE ROAD

SO FAIR AND SO FOUL

It was a perfect day for climbing Mt. Taranaki. The stillness and sunshine were uncharacteristic for a mountain usually shrouded in mist and battered by winds. Notorious for its perilously fickle climate, sixty-two people have perished on Taranaki, mostly the unprepared victims of suddenly foul weather.

When the weather's fair, however, bevies of trampers from all over Taranaki congregate at the peak. The sudden influx often creates a crowded, urban feel. When I reached the busy summit on this cloudless day, a handful of jubilants took advantage of the "excellent reception" to report their feats to lower elevations by cellular phone.

The trip down featured all sorts of late-embarking folk. While descending the firm rock ridge near the summit, I ran across a group of 15-20 students, many of whom appeared to be without any equipment at all. After an entertaining scree run, I spotted a fellow ascending the "Puffer" in sneakers and jeans. It seemed as though everyone thought they were walking the streets of Auckland.

To escape the crowds, I tried to imagine what the peak and its rocky haunches would look like in heavy rain or a big wind storm. These unexpected "city streets" would be reclaimed by a deadly solitude. I thought of my pack full of Gore-Tex, polypropylene, and fleece, hoping that those thin layers would protect me from the wrathful mountain if the weather took a sudden turn.

—Tom Mercer

Car Rental: Rental Car Centre, 281 Devon St. W (☎ 757 5362). Daily rates from $45.

Bike Rental: Raceway Cycles and Mowers, 207 Coronation Ave. (☎ 759 0391). Mountain bikes from $30 per day.

Hitchhiking: Although *Let's Go* doesn't recommend it, hitchhiking toward Wanganui around the east side of Egmont is reportedly easiest near the outskirts of town on SH3, close to the race course.

ORIENTATION & PRACTICAL INFO

New Plymouth is located at the junction of **SH3** and **SH45.** The main thoroughfare is **Devon Street,** which runs east-west through town. **Pukekura Park** sits in the southeast corner of the city while the **Tasman Sea** makes waves to the north.

Visitors Center: New Plymouth Information Centre (☎ 759 6080; fax 759 6073; www.newplymouthnz.com), at the corner of Leach and Liardet St. Open M-F 8:30am-5pm, Sa-Su 9am-5pm. Moving soon to Ariki St. along the waterfront.

DOC: 220 Devon St. W (☎ 759 0350, emergency 025 438 956; fax 759 0351), has brochures on Egmont National Park, North Taranaki Walks, and Sugarloaf Island Marine Park. Fishing queries also answered. Open M-F 8am-4:30pm.

Banks and Currency Exchange: Thomas Cook, 55-57 Devon St. E (☎ 757 5459; open M-F 9am-5pm). **BNZ,** on Brougham St., offers good exchange rates. Take your pick of the **ATMs** along Devon St. Generally open M-F 9am-4:30pm.

Police: 89 Powderham St. (☎ 759 5500).

Medical Services: Care Chemist, 10 Egmont St. (☎ 757 4614). Open daily 8:30am-9:30pm. **Accident and Medical Clinic** (☎ 759 4295), in Richmond Centre on Egmont St. Open daily 8am-10pm. **Taranaki Base Hospital** (☎ 753 6139), on David St.

Internet Access: New Plymouth Library (☎ 758 4544), on Brougham St. Open M, W, and F 10am-8:30pm, Tu and Th 10am-5:30pm, Sa 10am-4pm, Su 1-5pm. **Plan Copy,** 53 Leach St. (☎ 758 3709). Open M-F 8am-5:15pm. Both charge $8 per hr.

Post Office: (☎ 758 2110), on Currie St. Open M-F 7:30am-5:30pm, Sa 9am-1pm.

ACCOMMODATIONS & CAMPING

Hostels in town are reliable, if not outstanding. For a step up in creature comforts and privacy, call the Visitors Center for information on the many B&Bs ($35-150) in and around town.

Shoestring Backpackers (BBH), 48 Lemon St. (☎/fax 758 0404), a 5min. walk from the town center. Get to know potential mates at the large dining table or, better yet, in the sauna ($4). Free transport to bus station and hitchhikers' spots. Internet. Laundry. Dorms $16; singles $23; doubles $36, with TV $40. Motel units available. ❷

Egmont Lodge (BBH/YHA), 12 Clawton St. (☎ 753 5720; fax 753 5782; egmontlodge@taranaki-bakpak.co.nz). Take Frankley Rd. at the Dawson St. fork and follow the signs, or call for a ride. Nightly servings of mountain-shaped "Egmont Cake" and the TV-free lounge encourage conversation. Key deposit $10. Reception 8-10:30am and 5-9pm. Dorms $19; doubles $46; tent sites $12. ❷

Sunflower Lodge (BBH), 25 Ariki St. (☎ 759 0050; fax 759 0051; jrsanders@xtra.co.nz), right in town. The ascetic lounge doesn't promote socializing, so strike up a conversation about the curious mural. Internet. Laundry. Reception 7:30am-9pm. Dorms $15-17; singles $30-32; twins and doubles $45-50. Cash only. ❷

Central City Lodge, 104 Leach St. (☎ 758 0473; fax 758 6559; centralcity@xtra.co.nz), can accommodate everyone from the solo backpackers to traveling rugby teams. Heated indoor pool and spa $2. Key deposit $5. Reception 7am-10pm. Dorms $15; singles $30; doubles $40; B&B singles $40, doubles $60; motel ensuites $74. ❷

Belt Road Seaside Holiday Park, 2 Belt Rd. (☎/fax 758 0228 or 0800 804 204; www.beltroad.co.nz). The 25min. walk from town yields sweet rewards: an exquisite view of the sea and proximity to the beach. Backpackers cabins $18, $25 for 2; cabins with bath $30-55; tent and powered sites $9. ❶

FOOD

New Plymouth's **Devon Street** is sprinkled with an assortment of takeaways. Gorge here or head to **Woolworths,** at the corner of Leach and Cameron St. (☎ 759 7481. Open 24hr.)

E.S.P.resso (☎ 759 9399), adjacent to the Govett-Brewster Art Gallery. The food may not heighten your 6th sense but it will satiate your tastebuds. Hearty lunches go for about $8. Open daily 8am-4pm. ❷

El Condor, 170 Devon St. (☎ 757 5436). Renowned for its Argentinian cuisine, El Condor draws flocks of voracious diners nightly. Pasta dishes (mains $14.50) and gourmet pizzas ($10.50-24) soar to voluminous heights. Open Tu-Sa 5-10pm. ❸

Agra Indian Restaurant, 151 Devon St. E (☎ 758 0030). An open kitchen lets diners watch the chefs prepare tasty, filling dishes (mains mostly $12-15). Open M-Su 5:30pm-late. ❸

Steps Restaurant, 37 Gover St. (☎ 758 3393). Step up to gourmet Mediterranean cuisine that's worth the price tag. The rotating menu features painstakingly-prepared mains ($20-30). Reservations necessary. Open Tu-F 11:45am-2pm and 6-10pm; also Sa 6-10pm.❺

Sandwich Extreme, 52 Devon St. E (☎ 759 6999), caters to caffeine addicts and frugal, hurried lunch-munchers with subtly-flavored sandwiches ($4-6). Wash it down with one of the extreme espresso drinks ($2-3). Open M-F 8am-3pm, Sa 9am-1:30pm. ❶

NIGHTLIFE

The Mill, 2 Courtenay St. (☎ 758 1935), impossible to miss at the south end of Currie St. Once a functioning flour mill, today the grinding at this local bar involves bodies, not wheat stalks. Music pumps in the basement dance area dubbed **Underground** (open F-Sa 10pm-3am). Open M-Sa 11am-late.

Baja, 17-19 Devon St. W (☎ 757 8217). This pseudo-Mexican cafe-bar serves tasty meals ($7-17) and assorted drinks (margaritas $3.50). **The Beaten Path** (open W-Sa 6pm-3am), at the back, hosts DJs nightly. Open M-W 11am-11pm, Th 11am-1am, F 11am-3am, Sa 10am-4am, Su 10am-10pm.

Grapevine Wine Bar & Cafe, 38c Currie St. (☎ 757 9355). Catering to a slightly more sophisticated set, this bar and cafe serves up more vintages than an antique show. Live music Th-Sa, with jazz Th. Open Tu-Sa 5pm-late.

SIGHTS AND ACTIVITIES

For a firsthand look at New Plymouth's municipal splendors, head to the contained nature of **Pukekura Park** at the top of Liardet St., reportedly the most stunning park in New Zealand. If the weather cooperates, visit the calla lilies in **Stainton Dell** or the green grandeur of **King Fern Gully.** Rain or shine, the **Fernery** warmly awaits hushed footfalls on a carpet of cedar chips. (Fernery open daily 8:30am-4pm. Gates to Pukekura Park open daily 8:30am-6pm.) Adjacent to Pukekura Park is the **Brooklands,** which includes a **children's zoo.** (Open daily 8:30am-5pm. Free.) If you are in town anytime from the week before Christmas 2002 until February 6, 2003 (Waitangi Day), see the park in a different light as it will be illuminated for the annual **Festival of Lights.**

Once you've had your fill of man-made parks, point your hiking boots toward one of New Plymouth's many scenic walkways. Detailed guides are available at the Visitors Center. The **Te Henui Walkway** (return 4½hr.) is one of the best, following the Te Henui Stream through 5.9km of natural splendor down to the sea. The **Coastal Walkway** offers dramatic views of the sea crashing against the rocky coastline (return 4-5hr.). Follow the path south past industrial areas and arrive at **Paritutu,** an old volcanic plug that juts up prominently at the edge of the shore. Epic views of the coast and, on a clear day, the mountain are the reward for those brave souls who take the very steep, scrambling 154m-vertical trip.

With its proximity to the Tasman Sea, New Plymouth also offers a variety of aquatic options. Surfers and windsurfers can get their adrenaline fix year-round at **Fitzroy** and **East End** beaches. For those who prefer watching the surf to being immersed in it, let Dave Chadfield of **Happy Chaddy's Charters** take you for a cruise around the Sugar Loaf Islands, where you can enjoy a visit to the seal colony. (☎ 758 9133. $20, children $10; fishing trips $10 per hr.)

On rainy days (and there may be a fair share), head to the town center to see why New Plymouth is the only real roost for Taranaki's culture mavens. A stroll down **Devon Street** reveals the city's 19th-century heritage, evidenced by artful moldings and dates embossed on the upper levels of the downtown shops. A few blocks away, the sleek exterior of the **Govett-Brewster Art Gallery,** at the corner of King and Queen St., gives way to a collection of contemporary work of artists from New Zealand and abroad. The permanent collection (when it's not touring) features the work of **Len Lye** (see p. 59). (☎ 758 5149; www.govettb.org.nz. Open daily 10:30am-5pm. Free.)

THE TARANAKI COAST ☎ 06

Excellent for catching rays on handsome beaches and catching waves on year-round surf, the Taranaki coast from New Plymouth to Hawera is a surprisingly under-appreciated and underdeveloped destination. Generally, it's best to rent a car or, possibly, a bike. You can circumnavigate Mt. Taranaki (Egmont) and travel along the coast in two ways. For a scenic journey (1½hr.) with easy access to various bush walks and the best views of the Taranaki Bights and the Tasman Sea, take Carrington Rd. from New Plymouth to Okahu Rd. and then circle around. The coastal route (3½hr.) is best done on SH45, but unless you stop and walk to the shore, expect only glimpses of the ocean (much of the view on this route is obscured by either hedges, great distance, or both). Hitchhikers find sporadic rides at best; in winter frequent rains make the experience even more unpleasant.

OAKURA ☎ 06

A wee town (pop. 1300) with an awesome beach that is wide, flat, and family-filled in summer, the town of Oakura is representative of the population "centers" that dot the coast along "Surf Highway 45." The town itself provides little diversion to those looking for something other than waves and rays. In summer people pitch tents down by the beach, but **Oakura Beach Camp ❶**, 2 Jans Tce., offers less tenuous oceanside tracts. (☎ 752 7861; fax 752 7286; oakurabeachcamp@internet.co.nz. Tent sites $7.50, powered $8.50; on-site caravans $40 for 2.) For anyone who requires them, the **Oakura Boardriders Club** provides free toilets, showers, and changing rooms just off the beach, near the corner of Wairau Rd. and Tasman Pde. The point at the end of **Ahu Ahu Road** boasts amazing surf and the **Wavehaven Hostel (VIP) ❷**, just east of the corner of Ahu Ahu Rd. and SH45. Surfboard and kayak rentals (half-day $10, full-day $15) with wetsuits are available, and surfing lessons for novices can be arranged. There is also a climbing wall and volleyball court. (☎ 752 7800; fax 782 7363; wave.haven@taranaki.ac.nz. Laundry. Dorms $15, weekly $75; singles $25; doubles $30.) Those not staying at the hostel can hire a board in town at **Vertigo Total Surf.** (☎ 752 7363. Board with wet suit $30 per day.) Oakura is also home to **Deelush ❸**, on Main South Rd., where a gourmet pizza ($25) will feed you and three of your closest friends. (☎ 752 7303. Open Tu-Su 10am-late; in winter 6pm-late, with F-Su brunch from 10am.) Just next door, **Butler's Bar and Cafe ❷** offers pub food and $3.40 handles. (☎ 752 7765. Open 11:30am-late.)

OPUNAKE ☎ 06

The closest to a bustling metropolis on the coast, Opunake (pop. 2091) harbors both the dramatic cliffs of Middleton's Bay and the pleasantly swimmable **Opunake Beach,** with its teeming campground. (☎ 761 7525. Tent sites $9.) A coastal walkway and easy access to other beaches round out the town's main attractions. For a good night's sleep and quintessential Taranaki views (mountain in the background and cattle in the foreground), head to the **Opunake Motel and Backpackers ❷**, 36 Heaphy Rd., an oft-deserted but comfortable accommodation. (☎ 761 8330; fax 761 7022; opunakemotel@xtra.co.nz. Dorms $15; cottages $20 per person; motel units $55, for 2 $70, extra person $13.) Snag supplies at **Beau's Supermarket,** 77-79 Tasman St. (☎ 761 8668. Open M-Th 7:30am-6pm, F-Sa 7:30am-8pm, Su 7:30am-5pm.)

EGMONT NATIONAL PARK ☎ 06

Rolling hills bow like green-robed disciples to their master and maker, majestic Mt. Taranaki (Egmont). In 1881, everything within a 10km radius of the nearly symmetrical volcano was declared part of New Zealand's second national park, thankfully restraining the vigorous logging boom of the day. With more than 300km of prime tracks ranging from well-maintained to backcountry adventure, Egmont remains the country's most accessible national park.

TRANSPORTATION

Although there are no public buses to Egmont National Park, **Cruise New Zealand Tours** shuttles trampers. (☎ 758 3222. Daily from New Plymouth at 7:30am, returns 4:15pm. $35 return.) **Withers Coachlines** runs a competing service. (☎ 751 1777. Daily at 7:30am. $30 return.) Both companies pick up at New Plymouth accommodations. Guided trips offer transportation as well (see **Outdoor Activities,** p. 225).

224 ■ TARANAKI AND WANGANUI

AT A GLANCE	
AREA: 33,534 hectares. **CLIMATE:** Dictated by the mountain, which attracts foul and unpredictable weather, especially dangerous in winter. **FEATURES:** Mt. Taranaki. **HIGHLIGHTS:** Round-the-Mountain Track and the Taranaki Summit (see p. 225).	**GATEWAYS:** New Plymouth, Stratford, and Opunake. **CAMPING:** Permitted except at the summit. Backcountry huts and lodges managed by DOC and private alpine clubs. **FEES & RESERVATIONS:** DOC Hut pass $5.

 WHEN TO GO Fall snows bring North Island skiers to Manganui for an early start to the winter season. Tramping is popular from late November to early April, but winter conditions in the alpine zone are extremely dangerous.

ORIENTATION AND PRACTICAL INFORMATION

Three paved roads enter the park but do not intersect: **Egmont Road,** from New Plymouth to the **North Egmont Visitor Centre; Pembroke Road,** from Stratford to the **Stratford Mountain House** and the **Manganui Ski Field;** and **Manaia Road,** from the Manaia/Hawera area to the **Dawson Falls Visitor Centre.** A fourth road, **Carrington Road,** bisects the northern arm of the park between the Pouakai and Kaitake Ranges. The **North Egmont Visitors Centre,** about 16km from Egmont Village, is the port of entry for most of the park's visitors. Here, DOC officers point trampers in the right direction with the aid of color-coded maps. Watch a 20min. audio/visual presentation ($1) on the park's natural and cultural history. (☎756 0990; fax 756 0991; nevc@doc.govt.nz. Open daily 8am-4:30pm.) About 8km from the park entrance along the southern Manaia Rd., the **Dawson Falls Visitor Centre** has easy access to ski fields and dozens of bush walks. (☎025 430 248; fax 08 326 1844; bthurston@doc.govt.nz. Open daily 8am-4:30pm; in winter W-Su 8:30am-4:30pm.)

ACCOMMODATIONS AND CAMPING

NORTHERN EGMONT. Just outside the park and east of New Plymouth on Egmont Rd., hop over to **Missing Leg Backpackers (BBH) ❶,** 1082 Junction Rd. The name comes not from a horrific tramping incident, but from the three-legged pooch that used to reside here. (☎/fax 752 2570; jo.thompson@xtra.co.nz. Inquire at the New Plymouth Information Centre or call ☎756 6193 about the $4 weekday shuttle from New Plymouth to Inglewood. Free bike use. Dorms $14; doubles $35; tent sites $8.) Only 3km from the National Park boundary, the **◙Eco Inn (BBH) ❸,** 671 Kent Rd., is both a rustic farm hostel and a cutting-edge energy venture. To reach this outpost, leave SH3 halfway between Inglewood and New Plymouth; go southwest on Kent Rd. for 5-6km. A waterwheel, wind turbines, and solar paneling collect power for home use and the electric car, which runs free pick-ups in New Plymouth. The small farm operation yields fresh, tasty treats, and there's even a treehouse offering airy arboreal accommodation. (☎752 2765; ecoinn@xtra.co.nz. Singles $22; twins and doubles $40; tent sites and treehouse $10.)

DOC has reopened the **Camp House,** a spare, budget accommodation only 50m from the North Egmont Visitors Center. ($15, children $7.50. Book at Visitors Center.) There are also three private huts on the mountain—the Tahurangi Lodge, the Manganui Lodge, and the Kapuni Lodge—each run by one of the three regional mountain clubs. The **Tahurangi Lodge,** owned and run by the Taranaki Alpine Club, offers kitchen facilities and a great location at 1520m ($15 per night). Prior booking is essential; inquire at the Visitors Center or call Terry Baldwin (☎ 758 6310).

SOUTHERN AND EASTERN EGMONT AND DAWSON FALLS. For a night's rest at the base of the ski area, try the **Manganui Lodge,** a private hut run by the Stratford Mountain Club. Advance booking is required; contact the club officer, Deborah Robson (☎ 758 1095). Right near the Dawson Falls Visitor Center, DOC runs the somewhat bare **Konini Lodge,** complete with a large kitchen and common rooms. (☎ 025 430 248. $15 per person, children $7.50. Prior booking is required.) Up the mountain from Dawson Falls and just short of Fanthams Peak is the **Kapuni Lodge,** which rounds out the trio of private huts on the mountain. Maintained by the Mt. Egmont Alpine Club of Hawera, the club offers gas cooking, running water, and 18 bunk beds ($10); book ahead of time with Jan Fleming (☎ 278 9928) to arrange picking up a hut key in Hawera.

 CLIMBING TARANAKI. Summitting Mt. Taranaki (Egmont) is far more than a leisurely walk in the park. The mountain has already claimed the lives of 62 people, making it the most dangerous peak in New Zealand. The upper slopes are prone to dramatic and sudden weather changes, and chilling rain can fall at any elevation at any time of the year. Even during the summer months and when weather conditions are favorable, only physically fit people with a good level of outdoor experience and proper clothing and supplies should hike without a guide. In winter, even the most hardened mountaineers are strongly advised to take a guide. DOC urges that trekkers leave their plans with a family member or friend before the hike and to sign the North Egmont center's intentions book. It is also imperative that climbers assemble proper gear and check the mountain forecast before setting out. If these requirements seem daunting, various services offer guides to assist in the ascent of Mt. Taranaki.

OUTDOOR ACTIVITIES

TRAMPING IN EGMONT. There are *endless* trail options in the park; visit the DOC office at Northern Egmont or Dawson Falls and make your own hiking plans. While camping is permitted in Egmont National Park, it is strongly discouraged on the summit out of respect for both the Maori and the environment. **Syme Hut** on Fanthams Peak (1966m) is arguably the best place to watch the sun rise or set; however, the hut's prime location also means that it is exposed to wind and ice. The **Mt. Taranaki Round-the-Mountain Circuit** *(3-5 days, 55km)* traverses the upper slopes of the volcano, affording excellent views of the surrounding farmland and coast. It can begin from any of the several main entrances to the park. During the summer and in appropriate conditions, the trail can be shortened substantially by taking short-cuts at higher altitudes. In the spring and sporadically during other seasons, water runoff from the mountain and rains cause rivers and streams to rise, making it difficult to cross. In the interest of safety, hikers should wait for levels to subside, as the flows are fast and deceptively deep. Take heart, however—stream levels tend to fall quickly.

Chris Prudden's **Mountain Guides Mt. Egmont** *(☎ 758 8261 or 025 474 510),* out of New Plymouth, will guide one person for $300 and groups of two to four for $300-400. **MacAlpine Guides** provides similar service for $150-200 per person (max. 2 in winter, 5 in summer) and also leads tramping tours in Egmont National Park. (☎ 751 3542 or 0800 866 486; www.macalpineguides.com.)

NORTHERN EGMONT. Well-prepared trampers might make the full-day trek to the **Ahukawaka Swamp,** home to lichen, mosses, and microbes. For the less hardy, briefer day hikes abound. One short-but-sweet walk, the **Connet Loop Track** *(return 30min.),* departs from the base of the North Egmont carpark and winds its way through the "Mountain Forest." For a 1½hr. bush experience, hit the **Veronica Loop Track. Bells Falls,** best reached from **Holly Hut,** is also worth checking out. The safest route to the **summit of Taranaki** leads from North Egmont, following "The Puffer" up to a transistor tower. Then, the track passes Tahurangi Lodge, leads through a gully, up a long scree-ridden ridge, and to the rock-scrambling summit block. The trip *(return 8-10hr.)* should not be attempted or even considered in winter or in otherwise questionable weather. The north side of the volcano offers great views of New Plymouth and beyond.

SOUTHERN AND EASTERN EGMONT AND DAWSON FALLS. Roughly 15% of park visitors enter the perimeter from the east, by way of Stratford and the **Stratford Mountain House,** with access to the Manganui ski fields in winter and several trails in other seasons. Direct trips to the summit can also be attempted from this side, but the route is longer *(return 1 day),* less defined, and more technically demanding. The official northern route up **Taranaki** is accessible from the ski fields by following the Round-the-Mountain Track north to the Tahurangi Lodge and connecting with the summit climb there.

From the Dawson Falls Visitor Centre, you can hike to the **Wilkies Pools** *(return 3hr.),* a series of plunge pools spilling into each other—remember that the water is ice-cold. The sidekick summit of **Fanthams Peak** is also climbable from this side *(return 5-6hr.)* for those who want to reach a high point.

LITTLE-KNOWN EGMONT. To the north and west of the main peak lie the gentler slopes of the **Kaitake** and **Pouakai Ranges.** These old peaks are the volcanic ancestors of Taranaki, which once also spewed lava and ash before being cut off from their magmatic source. The Pouakais are accessible via Carrington Rd. from New Plymouth and the Kaitakes from Lucy's Gully and other trailheads off SH45.

STRATFORD ☎ 06

Would a town by any other name smell as sweet? Perhaps, but in this small hamlet (pop. 5700), the moniker is half the character. One of 13 towns in the world christened after Shakespeare's birthplace, Stratford has taken this connection to heart by naming most of its streets after the Bard's characters and erecting a Glockenspiel (New Zealand's only) that thrice daily recites lines from *Romeo and Juliet.* The other half of Stratford's claim to fame, and the reason most visitors pass through, is its proximity to Mt. Taranaki.

TRANSPORTATION. InterCity buses depart from the Visitors Center and head to: **Auckland** (7hr., 1-2 per day, $58) via **New Plymouth** (35min., $10-15); and **Wellington** (5½hr., 2 per day, $54) via **Hawera** (20min., $13), **Wanganui** (1½hr., $25), and **Palmerston North** (3hr., $37). **Dalroy Express** (☎ 755 0009 or 0508 465 622) heads to **Auckland** (6hr., 1 per day, $58) and **Hawera** (30min., 1 per day, $6). **Central Cabs** (☎ 765 8395) and **Stratford Cabs** (☎ 765 5651) are available for local transportation needs. The **Stratford Leisure Centre,** 311 Broadway, rents nice mountain bikes for $15 per day. (☎ 765 7580. Open M-F 9am-4:30pm, Sa 9am-12:30pm.) Although *Let's Go* does not recommend it, **hitchhikers** report that getting rides to New Plymouth and Wellington is easier the farther along SH3 you get from the center of town.

ORIENTATION AND PRACTICAL INFORMATION. Broadway (SH3) is the main drag. **Pembroke Road** departs from the north of town and runs to the National

Park and the ski area. The **Information Centre** is on Prospero Pl., opposite the Glockenspiel (☎/fax 765 6708; stratford@info.stratford.govt.nz. Open M-F 8:30am-5pm, Sa-Su 10am-3pm; in winter closed Su). The **DOC office,** 10km from town on Pembroke Rd., RD 21, provides only basic info on Egmont National Park (☎ 765 5144; fax 765 6102. Open M-F 8am-4:30pm). Other local services include: **BNZ,** on Broadway (☎ 765 7134; open M-F 9am-4:30pm); the **police,** on Miranda St. (☎ 765 7145); **Stratford Medical Centre,** on Miranda St. S (☎ 765 7189; open M-W and F 8:30am-5pm, Th 8:30am-6pm); a **24hr. on-call doctor** (☎ 765 5300); the **post office,** 49 Miranda St. (☎ 765 6009; open M-F 8:30am-5pm); and **Internet access** at the Visitors Center ($10 per hr.) and the **library,** across the street from the post office on Miranda St. (☎ 765 5403; open M-F 9:30am-5:30pm, Sa 9:30am-noon).

ACCOMMODATIONS AND CAMPING.

You certainly won't feel claustrophobic at the **Taranaki Accommodation Lodge (BBH) ❷,** 7 Romeo St., but you might not feel at home, either. Renovated from a nurse's home, this lodge lets 42 rooms (the others belong to permanent residents) and offers free use of the tennis courts. (☎/fax 765 5444; mttaranakilodge@hotmail.com. Communal kitchen, showers, and toilets. Internet. Linen $5. Singles $16-18; doubles $18-20. Cash only.) The **Stratford Top 10 Holiday Park ❶,** 10 Page St., offers a wide variety of accommodations. After exploring the area on bike ($5 per hr., $20 per day), visitors can soak in the $3 spa. (☎/fax 765 6440; stratfordholpark@hotmail.com. Internet. Key deposit $10. Laundry. Linen $5. Reception 7am-10pm. Dorms from $16; cabins from $35 for 2, extra person $12; tent sites $9, powered $10.) **Pretty Croft B&B ❹,** 193 Regan St., 1km south of town on the road to Taumarunui, achieves a higher standard of comfort and hospitality than the strictly budget accommodations in town. (☎ 765 6820; fax 765 8092; davidandedna@xtra.co.nz. Internet. Laundry. Singles $45; doubles $70.)

FOOD AND NIGHTLIFE.

Those camping or graced with kitchens may want to head to **New World,** at the corner of Orlando and Regan St. (☎ 765 6422. Open daily 8am-8pm.) The little red-walled bistro, the ✪**Backstage Cafe ❷,** on Miranda St., is the exception to Stratford's general culinary mediocrity. Enter stage left (or, if heading north, stage right) for food that is right on cue. The inexpensive lunch options ($8-12) definitely merit applause. (☎ 765 7003. Open Tu-F 10am-late, Sa 10am-2pm and 6pm-late, Su 10am-2pm.) The **Axeman's Inn ❷,** 305 Broadway, pays tribute to the prolific logging industry in an appropriately rugged setting. Wash down standard pub food ($8-20) with a $3.30 handle of ale. (☎ 765 5707. Live music Th. Open daily 11am-3am.) When the weekend rolls around, **Hotshotz,** 295 Broadway, is the place to be. The only (and therefore best) dance club in Stratford features a DJ and plenty of room to groove. (☎ 765 6525. Open F-Sa 5pm-3am.)

SIGHTS AND ACTIVITIES.

With **Mt. Egmont** looming in the background, it's little wonder that skiing is a major activity in the area. Unpredictable snow falls mean that the season can range from a few weeks to a few months. The **Manganui Ski Field** is the sole field on the mountain and is generally open June through October. One T-bar and three rope tows offer access to several expert runs and two half-pipes for snowboarders. (Ski conditions ☎ 765 7669; www.snow.co.nz/manganui. Lift ticket $30, students $20, children $15, over 60 free; half-day rates available.) For rentals, call the **Mountain House Motor Lodge.** (☎ 765 6100. Skis, boots, and poles around $30 per day.) Outdoor excitement continues with **Off the Beaten Track Adventures.** Adventurers Paddy and Margaret Gooch will help you put together a choose-your-own-adventure day. Activities include hunting, canoeing, bushwalking, and 4WD trips. (☎/fax 762 7885. $25 per hr.; half-day $50; full-day $85, lunch provided.) For a stroll through Stratford's past, head to the **Taranaki Pio-**

neer Village, just outside town on SH3. The 50 fully-restored, turn-of-the-century buildings help celebrate Taranaki's pioneer history in an amazingly undeveloped, un-Disney-fied setting. (☎ 765 5399. Open daily 10am-4pm. $7, children $3.).

HAWERA
☎ 06

Since its founding in 1884, Hawera (pop. 11,500), which means "the burned place" in Maori, has suffered four major fires. However, it is the heifer, not the phoenix, that has risen from the ashes. Today, Hawera's tourism industry suckles at the teat of the dairy industry's herd, offering farmstays and informative displays at Dairyland for travelers eager to take a cold, frothy sip of Taranaki's rural life.

TRANSPORTATION. The **bus station** is at the base of the water tower and is the point of departure for **InterCity,** which leaves daily for: **New Plymouth** (1hr., 3-4 per day, $18); and **Wanganui** (1hr., 3-5 per day, $20), with continuing service to **Palmerston North** (3hr., $30) or **Wellington** (5½hr., $48). **Dalroy Express** (☎ 755 0009 or 0508 46 56 22) heads to **Auckland** (6½ hr., 1 per day, $70) via **New Plymouth** (1hr., $13) and **Hamilton** (5hr., $50). The **White Star** (☎ 758 3338) goes to **New Plymouth** ($15) and **Wellington** ($35). **Hawera Taxis** (24hr. ☎ 0800 278 7171) has a stand on Victoria St. near High St. Rent a used bicycle for $15 per day from **Seaver Cycles,** 18 Regent St. (☎ 278 6046. Open M-F 8am-5pm.) **Hitchhikers** often find a ride on High St. between Argyle and Albion St. or at the junction of SH3 and SH45 (South and Waihi Rd.). Most cars head to New Plymouth or Wanganui via SH3; hitchhiking to the coastal beach communities of western Taranaki along SH45 can be more difficult.

ORIENTATION AND PRACTICAL INFORMATION. The main drag through town is **High Street.** At the west end of High St., **Waihi Road** (SH3) is the primary northern route. **South Road** becomes the coastal route to New Plymouth (SH45) in one direction and to Wanganui (SH3) in the other. The **South Taranaki Visitor Information Centre,** 55 High St., is located at the base of the water tower and sells **DOC hut tickets** for area tracks. (☎ 278 8599; fax 278 6599; visitorinfo@stdc.govt.nz. Open Nov.-Feb. M-F 8:30am-5pm, Sa-Su 10am-3pm; Mar.-Oct. M-F 8:30am-5pm.) Other services include: **ATMs** and **banks** along High St.; the **hospital,** on Hunter St. (☎ 278 7109); the **police,** on Princes St. (☎ 278 0260); the **post office,** in Books & More, 92 High St. (☎ 278 5921; open M-F 8am-6pm, Sa 8am-7pm, Su 10am-4pm); and cheap **Internet access** at Hawera Library, 46 High St. ($4 per hr.; open M-Th 9 or 9:30am-5:30pm, F 9am-6pm, Sa 9am-noon), or **Bitworks,** 155 High St. (☎ 278 4927; $8 per hr.; open M-F 8:30am-5pm).

ACCOMMODATIONS AND CAMPING. Wheatly Downs Farmstay (BBH) ❷, 7km out of town on Ararata Rd., offers free pick-up with advance notice. Fifth-generation farmer and entrepreneur Gary Ogle gives backpackers hands-on experience riding horses, herding cattle, and shearing sheep. Enjoy views of Mt. Taranaki from the front lawn or fly around the mountain ($50 for a 40min. flight) in a plane that picks you up in front of the farmhouse. (☎ 278 6523; fax 278 6541; wheatlydowns@taranaki-bakpak.co.nz. Free laundry. Dorms $16; singles $25; doubles $36. Cash only. Book in advance.) For those not quite ready for an udder encounter, **King Edward Park Motor Camp ❶,** 70 Waihi Rd., reigns over a kingdom of communal showers, kitchens, and toilets. (☎/fax 278 8544; nikida@xtra.co.nz. Cabins for 4-5 and onsite caravans $28 for 2, extra person $10; tent sites $8, powered $9.) For basic rooms with shared facilities, try the bars/hotels on Princes St.

FOOD AND NIGHTLIFE. If you don't mind eating off the floor, **Morrieson's Cafe and Bar ❸**, 60 Victoria St., just might be the place for you. The tables here are floorboards from the demolished home of the late, local novelist Ronald Hugh Morrieson (1922-68). The menu features a medley of delectable mains ($12-20) and traditional brews. (☎278 5647. Open M-Sa 11am-1am, Su 11am-10:30pm.) Though the name may conjure images of a smoky dive, **Rough Habits Sports Bar and Cafe ❸**, 79-81 Regent St., has a well-groomed look. Try one of the less deep-fried mains ($17-20) and wash it down with a $3.30 handle. (☎278 7333. Open M-Sa 11am-late, Su 11am-11pm; kitchen closes around 9:30pm.) For a "kwik" bite, **Kreative Kebabs ❶**, 135 High St., offers tasty kebabs ($5-9) and burgers. (☎278 5552. Open M-F 11am-2:30pm and 4:30-8:30pm, Sa 4:30-9pm.) Fill your grocery needs at **Price Chopper**, at the corner of Union and Nelson St. (☎278 0026. Open daily 6am-midnight.)

SIGHTS AND ACTIVITIES. The **water tower**, a response to Hawera's frequent fires and the most prominent landmark in town, is temporarily closed to visitors as work is done to shore up structural instabilities. Nigel Ogle's **Tawhiti Museum**, near the corner of Ohangi and Tawhiti Rd., has been acclaimed as the best private museum in New Zealand, and it's easy to see why. With a subtle sense of humor and the skill to craft stunningly realistic fiberglass figures, the former art teacher brings regional history to dioramic life. (☎278 6837. Open M and F-Su 10am-4pm; Jan. daily; in winter Su only. $6.50.) Afterwards, stop at the adjoining **Mr. Badger's Cafe**, where visitors dine among *Wind in the Willows* dioramas, and dinner guests enjoy fireside readings of the book. For a taste of Maori history, **Turuturu Mokai**, a few kilometers out of town (up Turuturu Rd.), displays the scant remains of a 400-year old Maori fortress. Today, only the large man-made mounds and a carved post remain at was once the setting of a bloody battle. Pick up a brochure on the site at the Visitors Center before setting out. Fans of the King will rejoice at Kevin D. Wasley's garage-turned-**Elvis Presley Memorial Record Room**, 51 Argyle St. Although you won't see the King himself, you can feast your eyes on a collection of rare recordings, assorted memorabilia, and even Wasley's own **Elvis-esque haircut**. (☎278 7624 or 025 982 942; www.digitalus.co.nz/elvis. Visits by appointment only. Donation requested.)

The staple of dairy county, **Dairyland**, at the corner of SH3 and Whareroa Rd., offers a million-and-one ways to get your calcium fix. Acting as the Visitors Center for **New Zealand Milk Products** (known on the shelf as "Tararua"), the largest milk processing plant in the world, Dairyland features a kid-friendly exhibit and a revolving cafe. Moo-ve on in to learn about the multiple uses of milk, watch live footage from the dairy, and experience the vibrating pleasure of a **simulated milk tanker.** (☎278 4537. Exhibit and cafe open daily 9am-5pm; cafe open for dinner W-Su 6pm-late. $3.) If less pastoral thrills appeal, try **Dam Dropping**. Darren Parata guides you as you plunge head-first on a boogie board over an 8m dam, followed by 3hr. of "white-water sledding." (☎021 461 110. $80, 1hr. $40.)

WANGANUI ☎06

Home to an art school, an opera house, and a regional museum, Wanganui (pop. 45,000) merges bohemian mentality with historic sensibility to create the most funky and cosmopolitan spirit in the region. Despite its welcoming charm, vestiges of colonial animosity linger passively in the background. Slight tensions between Maori and European cultures are exhibited in the grassroots movement among locals to restore the "h" to the town's name—"accidentally" Anglicized in the early 20th century. Regardless, Wanganui remains a pleasant stop for a stroll down picturesque main street or some coffee by the Whanganui River.

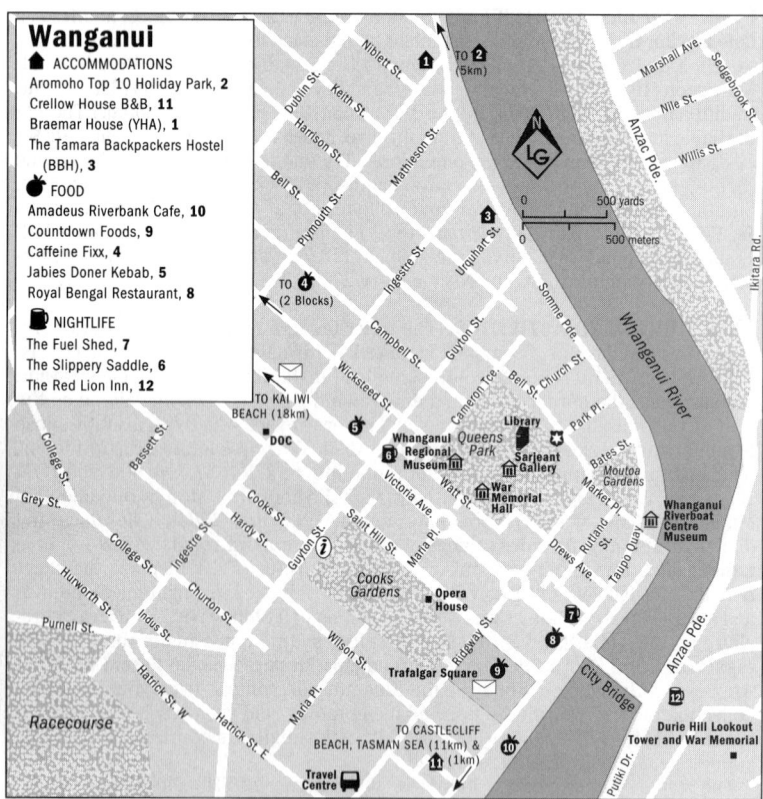

TRANSPORTATION

Buses: InterCity stops at the **Wanganui Travel Centre,** 156 Ridgway St. (☎345 4433). Open M-F 8:15am-5:15pm. Buses leave for: **Auckland** (8hr., 1-3 per day, $71) via **Hamilton** (6hr., $52); **New Plymouth** (2½hr., 3-5 per day, $31); **Palmerston North** (1½hr., M-F 3-4 per day, $18); and **Wellington** (4hr., 2-3 per day, $36). **White Star Buses** operates from Budget Rent-a-Car, 161 Ingestre St. (☎347-6677) to **New Plymouth** (2½hr., 1 per day, $22-25) and **Wellington** (4hr., 1 per day, $27).

Public Transportation: Tranzit CityLink (☎345 5566) handles bus transport to **Castlecliff Beach** and the suburbs. All buses depart from Maria Pl. between Victoria Ave. and Saint Hill St. and run until early evening ($2).

Taxis: River City Cabs (☎345 3333) and **Wanganui Taxis** (☎0800 500 000).

Car Rental: Rent-A-Dent, 26 Churton St. (☎345 1505). $38 per day plus 100km free. Open M-F 7am-5:30pm, Sa 7:30am-5pm. **Affordable Rentals** (☎343 9288), at Anzac Pde. and Jones St. From $50 per day, plus 30¢ per km. Open daily 6am-10pm.

Hitchhiking: Though Let's Go doesn't recommend it, thumbers head to the outskirts of town. People going toward Taranaki do so by way of Great North Rd., toward Ruapehu

WANGANUI ■ 231

by way of Anzac Pde., and toward Wellington by way of Main South Rd. Be sure to stay clear of Cobham Bridge, which is not legally traveled by pedestrians or cyclists.

ORIENTATION AND PRACTICAL INFORMATION

Wanganui is located at the junction of **SH3** and **SH4**; the latter is called **Anzac Parade** within the city and runs alongside the east bank of the **Whanganui River** (**Taupo Quay** and **Somme Parade** follow a similar course on the west bank). They meet at **Victoria Avenue**, which runs perpendicular to the river and is the main street in town.

Visitors Center: Wanganui Visitor Information Centre (☎ 349 0508; fax 349 0509; info@wanganui.govt.nz), near the corner of Guyton and Saint Hill St. next to the District Council. Open M-F 8:30am-5pm, Sa-Su 10am-3pm. Extended hours in summer.

DOC: (☎ 345 2402; fax 345 8712), at the corner of Saint Hill and Ingestre St. Heaps of information on Whanganui National Park. Open M-F 8am-5pm.

Banks: Money ebbs and flows along Victoria Ave. at **BNZ, ANZ, Westpac Trust,** and **National Bank** (all with **ATMs**). Most open M-F 9am-4:30pm.

Police: 10 Bell St. (☎ 349 0600).

Medical Services: Esquilant Unichem Pharmacy, 145 Victoria Ave. (☎ 345 7529). Open M-F 8:30am-5pm, Sa 9am-2pm, Su 10am-2pm. After-hours service through **Wanganui City Doctors,** 163 Wicksteed St. (☎ 348 8333). The **Wanganui Hospital** (☎ 348 1234) is on Heads Rd.

Post Office: Main Branch, 226 Victoria Ave. (☎ 345 4103). Open M-F 8:30am-5pm.

Internet Access: Available at the **library,** in Queens Park (☎ 345 8195; open M-F 9am-8pm, Sa 9am-4:30pm), and the **Visitors Center** for $6 per hr.

ACCOMMODATIONS AND CAMPING

Most of Wanganui's backpackers and campgrounds are rooted on the riverbanks beside English oak trees.

The Tamara Backpackers Hostel (BBH), 24 Somme Pde. (☎ 347 6300; fax 345 8488; www.tamaralodge.com), 5min. from the center of town. Amiable hostel with heated rooms, river views, and lounges. A guitar, piano, pool table, and dartboard provide amusement. Free pick-up. Internet. Key deposit $10. Laundry. Linen $1. Reception 8am-9pm. Dorms $17; singles $27; twins and doubles $38, with bath $48. ❷

Braemar House (YHA), 2 Plymouth St. (☎/fax 347 2529), 5-10min. from the center of town. The intensity of the pink exterior has faded over the years, but the B&B vibes of this century-old Victorian house still spill over into the backpackers units. Laundry. Dorms $16; doubles $36; B&B singles $50; B&B doubles $70; tent sites $10. ❷

Aramoho Top 10 Holiday Park, 460 Somme Pde. (☎/fax 343 8402 or 0800 272 664; aramoho.holidaypark@xtra.co.nz), 5km from town center. "Aramoho" bus stops at the gate. Sidle up to the river in this tranquil setting. Internet. Spa $5 per 30min. Kayaks $5 per hr., $10 per half-day. Cabins $30 for 2; tourist flats $55 for 2; motel units $70 for 2, powered $10. ❶

Crellow House B&B, 274 Taupo Quay (☎ 345 0740), 1½km southwest of the town center. The 3 rooms here share a bathroom, but the riverside location and impressive international cheese dish collection make communal rituals a pleasure. Free laundry. Rooms $40 for 1, $60 for 2. ❹

FOOD

Eateries cluster around **Victoria Avenue** and its side streets from the river to **Guyton Street**. Whip up your own dish after a stop at **Countdown Foods**, at Taupo Quay and Saint Hill St. (☎ 345 8720. Open daily 8am-9pm.) At the other end of Victoria Ave., **Woolworths** is open 24hr. (☎ 348 9470).

> **Amadeus Riverbank Cafe,** 69 Taupo Quay (☎ 345 1538). Delicious burgers and sandwiches ($6.50-12.50) supply savory satiety. Sweets from the Calorie Gallery ($3-5.50) and occasional live music top it all off. Open M-Th 8:30am-4pm, F 8:30am-7pm, Sa-Su 10am-5pm; no evening hours in summer. ❷
>
> **Royal Bengal Restaurant,** 7 Victoria Ave. (☎ 348 7041). Across the street from the city cinema, the bright blue interior lends a cheerful atmosphere to the Indian cuisine. Curry dishes are $12-13, but $10 M-Tu or anytime with copy of *Let's Go*. Open daily 5:30-10:30pm; also W-Sa 11am-2pm. ❸
>
> **Caffeine Fixx,** 71 Liverpool St. (☎ 345 7557), between Victoria Ave. and Wickstead St. Suits mix with students amid edgy pastels and original art. Get a light meal and coffee buzz while surfing the web. Open M-F 8:30am-6:30pm, Sa-Su 9:30am-4:30pm. ❶
>
> **Jabies Doner Kebab,** 168 Victoria Ave. (☎ 347 2800), just northwest of Guyton St. A good, cheap filling meal. King-size kebabs $9-10. Open M-W and Su 11am-9pm, Th-Sa 11am-10pm. ❷

NIGHTLIFE

> **The Fuel Shed** (☎ 345 7278), at the corner of Victoria Ave. and Taupo Quay. Guzzle a $2.50 handle or fill your tank with gourmet pizza ($13.95). DJs mix it up F-Sa. Open M-Th 3:30pm-late, F-Su 11am-3am.
>
> **The Slippery Saddle,** 146 Victoria Ave. (☎ 348 5599). On weeknights, there may be more action in the rodeo murals than on the dance floor, but this cowboy-themed spot sees life once the weekend moseys around. Have a saddle burger ($8.50) at a giant cactus table. DJ F-Sa. Open M-Tu 11am-9pm, W-Th 11am-midnight, F-Sa 11am-3am.
>
> **The Red Lion Inn,** 45 Anzac Pde. (☎ 345 3831). Across the river from downtown, 2 separate rooms house different scenes. On the right, locals bet on horses while "skulling" handles of the namesake brew ($3.70). On the left, the more clean-cut crowd in "Burton's Cafe" gazes at the river over glasses of wine ($4-6). Open daily 11am-late.

SIGHTS AND ACTIVITIES

Before heading out into the wilderness, get your bearings and survey the land from the top of the **Durie Hill Lookout Tower.** The journey begins from Anzac Pde. at the base of Victoria Ave. where a long tunnel takes you 205m into the hill. Then an elevator whisks you 66m up *through* the hill, depositing you at the top. (Elevator runs M-F 7:30am-6pm, Sa 10am-6pm, Su 11am-5pm. One-way $1.) But why stop there? Climb the nearby 33.5m **Durie Hill Memorial Tower** for the ultimate view. If the silty waters of the Whanganui beckon, the **PS Waimarie** is at your service. Built in 1899, the restored paddle steamer (the last in New Zealand) chugs from the Whanganui Riverboat Centre 16km up the river. (☎ 347 1863; www.riverboat.co.nz. Return 2hr. $25, seniors $20.) The narrow and winding 79km **River Road** (see p. 237) also heads upriver and makes a good daytrip.

Get your fill of culture in **Queens Park,** just a block away from Victoria Ave. toward the river. Overlooking the green hills is the stunning white-domed exterior of **Sarjeant Gallery,** most notable for its collection of contemporary regional and national art. (☎349 0506; www.sargeant.org.nz. Open M-F 10:30am-4:30pm, Sa-Su 1-4:30pm. Donations appreciated.) Just steps away, modernity gives way to Maori history at the **Whanganui Regional Museum**. Its "Te Atihaunui A Paparangi" gallery (a place for all peoples to "anchor their canoes") houses the largest surviving *waka taua* (war canoe) in the region. New Zealand's first barrel organ plays your hymnal favorites on the first Sunday of each month. (☎345 7443; www.wanganuimuseum.org.nz. Open M-Sa 10am-4:30pm, Su 1-4:30pm. $2.) If your cultural appetite is still not sated, try further stops on the city's **Arts and Cultural Trail** (pamphlets with maps available at the Visitors Center).

Sports enthusiasts should circle **Cooks Gardens**, on Maria Pl., home to a rugby pitch, New Zealand's wooden cycling velodrome, and a running track that was the site of Peter Snell's world-record mile (see p. 60). For recreational water action, head to one of the local beaches for killer waves. **Castlecliff Beach**, where the river meets the sea, is notable for black sand and good surf. To get there, take Quay St. West to Heads Rd. and continue another 9km. Alternatively, head for Maria Pl. in town and catch the #3 or 4 taxi bus. Farther up the coast, **Kai Iwi Beach** also has good swells and attracts locals who wish to avoid the crowds, but is not accessible by public transport. **Mountain bikers** in the area get their kicks on a host of singletrack trails built by the Wanganui Mountain Bike Club up the river at Hylton Park in Aramoho. Another popular spot is the heavily-logged Lismore Forest, 17km from town up SH4, which is only open for recreation on Sundays.

The **Blooming Artz Festival**, a celebration of visual arts, occurs in the September of odd-numbered years, whereas the **Wanganui Arts Festival** features performing arts and occurs at the end of February in even-numbered years. Every Boxing Day, accommodations fill to the brim, and the town is rattled to its bones by the grave-rumbling **Cemetery Circuit Motorcycle Race**.

WHANGANUI NATIONAL PARK ☎06/07

According to legend, the great mountains Tongariro and Taranaki fought over a lovely summit named Pihanga. Defeated and angry, Taranaki gouged a furrow in the earth on his way westward, a cleft that his wise rival filled with life-bestowing water. As a result, lush greenery surrounds the Whanganui (fang-gah-NEW-ee) River as it flows from the slopes of Tongariro down to the Tasman Sea—the longest navigable course (234km) in New Zealand. Maori *pa* (fortified villages) topped these high ponga-lined bluffs before European missionaries and farmers, steamboats, and logging operations changed the river life during the 19th century. In recent years, however, local Maori families have re-established *marae* along the river, bringing vital community spirit to those who journey downstream.

AT A GLANCE

AREA: 74,231 hectares.	**GATEWAYS:** Whanganui, Ohakune, National Park Village, and Taumarunui.
CLIMATE: Mild summers. Changeable weather year-round.	**CAMPING:** Tents permitted. Backcountry huts available.
FEATURES: Hills and valleys through lowland forests, mudstone cliffs.	**FEES & RESERVATIONS:** Hut passes $5 each, more in summer.
HIGHLIGHTS: Whanganui River, the longest navigable river in New Zealand.	

TRANSPORTATION

Few roads penetrate the park's boundaries. The **River Road** (see p. 237) dips into the southern limits, while a road from Owhango heads to **Whakahoro Hut** (see p. 236). People who have **hitched**, report that flexibility is necessary; however, *Let's Go* does not recommend hitchhiking. Most people planning a Whanganui excursion stay in **Taumarunui** (see p. 238), **National Park Village** (see p. 212), or **Ohakune** (see p. 214) and arrange transport with the operators who rent equipment for the River Journey (see **Gear Rental**, p. 236). Trampers who require river transport to return to their point of departure can call **Bridge to Nowhere Lodge** (☎ 06 348 7122) for a ride that will cost quite a sum, depending on the endpoints.

> **WHEN TO GO** The park is better enjoyed in the summer since its greatest attraction is the Whanganui River, but the river can be run year-round. Be sure to bring warm clothing and waterproof gear for unpredictable weather.

ORIENTATION AND PRACTICAL INFORMATION

The Whanganui National Park boundaries encompass various pockets west of SH4. Between the towns of Taumarunui and Wanganui, the biggest swaths of bush enclose the middle reaches of the Whanganui River. Despite its name, the city of **Wanganui** is not the best base for exploring the Whanganui River, though it does contain the park's main **DOC office** (☎ 06 345 2402. Open M-F 8am-5pm). There are also sporadically open **DOC field centers** in Taumarunui (☎ 07 895 8201) and Pipiriki (☎ 06 385 5022). In Taumarunui, you'll find a **supermarket** and **ATMs**; in Pipiriki, you won't find much of anything. Most gear outfitters (see **Gear Rental**, p. 236) can provide secure **parking**, however there are no places to stay directly adjacent to the park. The **telephone codes** for Taumarunui, National Park Village, and points in between is 07; Ohakune and points farther south use 06.

TRAMPING

The **Mangapurua** and **Kaiwhakauka Tracks** combine to form a 40km (3-4 day) trip. Mangapurua takes off from **Mangapurua Landing** (see p. 237) on the river, then heads over the **Bridge to Nowhere,** through the Mangapurua Valley, and past vast sections of former farmland. The track climbs to the **Mangapurua Trig**, which offers clear-day panoramic views of Mt. Tongariro, Mt. Taranaki, and the junction with the Kaiwhakuaka Track. Then it's down through farms and bush to the Kaiwhakuaka Valley and the **Whakahoro Hut** ($10; see p. 236). This is the only hut along the whole track, though flat campsites are plentiful.

The park's other major trail is the **Matemateaonga Track,** which tempts diehard hikers with 42km (3-4 days) of serpentine trail following an old Maori route into the bush. The path leads from the **Kohi Saddle** on Upper Mangaehu Rd. east of **Stratford** (see p. 226) and across to **Tieke Marae** (see p. 237) on the Whanganui River. There are three huts ($10 each) on the track, which is flatter than the Mangapurua/Kaiwhakauka. **Wades Landing Outdoors** (☎ 07 895 5995 or 025 797 238) and **Bridge to Nowhere Lodge** (☎ 06 348 7122 or 025 480 308) do jet-boat river pick-ups and drop-offs for trampers. Prices depend on numbers and times; call well ahead to arrange a trip. A significantly shorter option, the **Atene Skyline Track** (6-8hr.) leads to a lookout with views of Mt. Ruapehu, Mt. Taranaki, and the Tasman Sea, almost forming a complete loop. The Skyline makes a good daytrip from Wanganui, as the trailhead is only 36km north of town on the River Rd.

WHANGANUI RIVER JOURNEY

Not only is the Whanganui River Journey the only **Great Walk** over water, but it also provides an outdoor experience unique to New Zealand. Those who paddle between the river's steep banks will meet rapids, an endless number of worried-looking goats, and hundreds of waterfalls. Moreover, the journey passes numerous reminders of its long human history, from the Lombardy poplars planted by missionaries to the iron moorings used by steamers headed upstream. The tramp also has a living legacy in its two *marae*, Tieke and Mangapapapa, both of which welcome overnight guests.

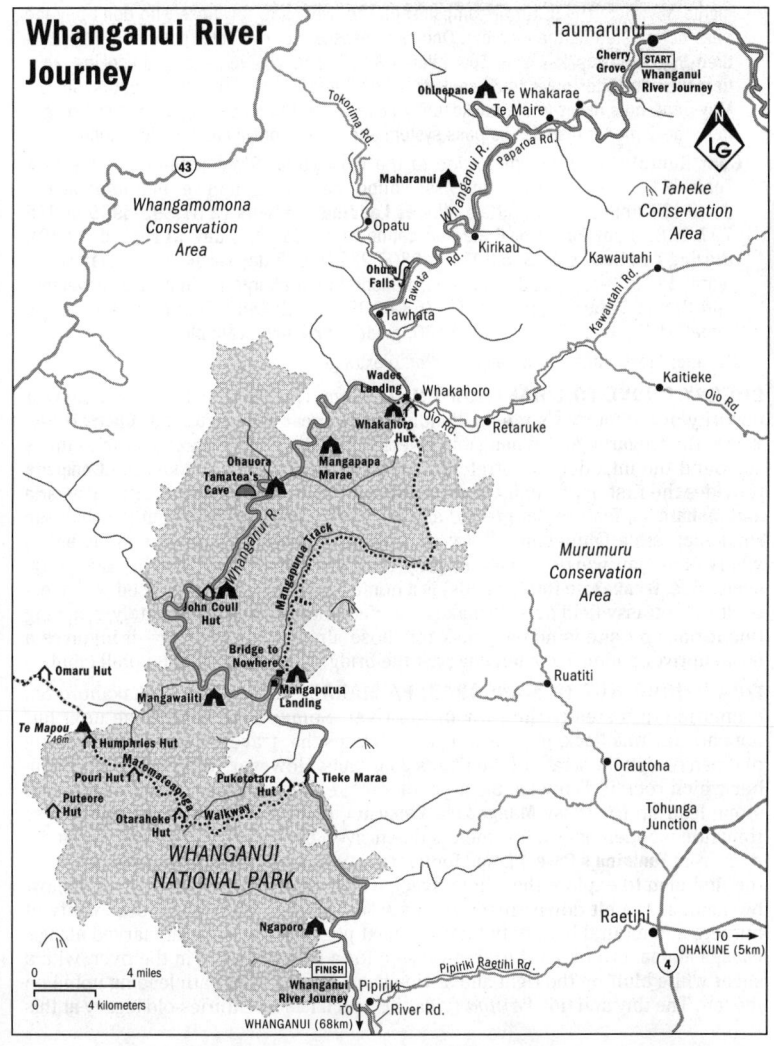

Length: 145km, 3-5 days, by canoe.

Trailheads: Heads downstream from Cherry Grove, near Taumarunui, to Pipiriki landing. Other put-ins between the two include Whakahoro and Ohinepane.

Transportation: Land-lubber **shuttle service** to the put-in and take-out points is included in the kayak and canoe rental packages (see **Gear Rental,** below). On-river transport, **Bridge to Nowhere Jets** runs trampers upriver from Pipiriki to its namesake. (☎ 06 385 4128. Return 4hr. $70, children $35.)

Seasonality: Dec. to Feb. and weekends are most busy. The water gets cold and the weather gets rainier June-Sept., making crowds a non-issue and experience a must.

Huts and Campsites: Oct.-Apr. DOC charges a flat fee of $25 for paddlers spending 2-6 nights anywhere (be it hut or campsite) on the river ($35 for those who don't buy the pass before starting the journey). One-night passes are available (jetboaters $10, children $5; canoeists/kayakers $6, children $3.) The huts have water and cooking facilities; the campsites have small cooking shelters and usually have water, but no stoves. May-Sept. huts revert to the backcountry ticket system ($10 per night), and camping is free. The 2 *marae* dispute the pass system and receive only voluntary donations.

Gear Rental: Check out the *Guide to the Whanganui River* compiled by the New Zealand Recreational Canoeing Association, describing the river and its rapids in detail ($8 from DOC). Outfitters: **Wades Landing Outdoors** (☎ 07 895 5995 or 025 797 238; 5-day kayak or Canadian canoe rental $130, 3-day $115, 2-day $70); **Blazing Paddles** (☎ 07 895 8074 or 0800 252 946; 5-day kayak or Canadian canoe rental $130, 3-day $120; additional transportation charge for individual travelers); and **Canoe Safaries** (☎ 06 385 8758 or 0800 272 3353; 5-day kayak or canoe rental $145, 4-day $135, 3-day $120; guided trips also available).

Storage: Most outfitters can also hold onto extra gear.

CHERRY GROVE TO WHAKAHORO HUT. *57km.* This two-day leg covers the vast majority of the journey's rapids. Paddlers begin near Taumarunui at **Cherry Grove,** where the Ongarue and Whanganui rivers meet. Roads and grazing farm animals surround the introductory stretch of river. Large, lawn-like **Ohinepane Campsite** provides the first opportunity to stop and camp. The next two campsites, **Poukaria** and **Maharanui,** feature flat ground and lush bush and tend to be quieter than the road-accessible Ohinepane. Between these rise the imposing carved **niu poles,** where Hau Hau warriors used to pray before embarking for battle. Also road-accessible, **Whakahoro Hut** (16 beds) is a homey old schoolhouse blessed with electricity; the grassy field outside makes a perfect tent pitch. Unfortunately, reaching this former *pa* site is no easy task for those already on the river—it involves a 600m upriver paddle (to a landing past the bridge) and then a 500m uphill climb.

WHAKAHORO HUT TO MANGAPAPAPA MARAE. *10.5km.* From Whakahoro on, dramatic cliffs steady the flow of the river. Somewhere before the next hut hunches **Taniwha Rock,** on which legend dictates that travelers must place a sprig of green or risk the wrath of the river's guardians. However, as few people remember which rock is Taniwha, most paddlers take their chances. Stairs of rounded stone lead up to grassy **Mangapapa Campsite,** but it's easier to land by the less romantic wooden ones a few meters down river. **Ohauora Campsite** lies across the river from **Tamatea's Cave,** named for a former temporary inhabitant (who was also the first man to explore the whole river), which exhibits a small glowworm show by night. Just a bit downstream, roomy **John Coull Hut** (30 beds) sports plenty of burners and natural history tidbits. The next possible rest stop, unmarked **Mangapapapa Marae,** is a bit hard to find—watch for a leftward bend in the river, with a sheer white bluff on the right and a wide beach with a faint path leading uphill on the left. The tiny and tidy *kainga* (village), which has a centuries-old legacy at this site, was reestablished in 1996. The elders here place an emphasis on spiritual learning, and encourage visitors to participate in communal cooking and cultural exchange. Tenting is available outside, though all guests are welcome to sleep indoors. If you're planning to stay at Mangapapapa, leave advance notice with Patrick (☎ 06 385 8258), who will radio ahead for you.

MANGAPAPAPA MARAE TO TIEKE MARAE. *46km.* At **Mangawaiiti Campsite,** marked "CAMP-SITE," a long staircase leads above the river to some beautiful plots, all set about with ponga trees. **Mangapurua Campsite** rests on the river's right bank across the water from **Mangapurua Landing.** From the landing, an easy 30-40min. walk leads deep into the bush, opening onto an astounding view of the ponga canopy, with a tannin-stained stream far below, and in the middle of it all, a perfectly ordinary concrete bridge. This **Bridge to Nowhere** is the last remnant of an isolated WWI rehabilitation settlement, which officially failed in 1942. Back on the water, the river leads to the well-marked **Tieke** (TEE-ehh-kee) **Marae,** a hospitable settlement hosting a rotating roster of caretakers who urge guests to make themselves at home in the kitchen, on the mattresses in the bunk room, or atop the beautiful lawn. Reestablished in 1993, Tieke functions primarily as a community center for Whanganui Maori families, though recently it has been working with DOC to create a new sleeping house and kitchen for passing paddlers. Across the river, the unrelated, privately owned **Bridge to Nowhere Lodge** charges $5 per person for camping, $10 for cabins. There are also B&B units available.

TIEKE MARAE TO PIPIRIKI LANDING. *21.5km.* This final stretch holds several of the journey's largest rapids. Set between two rather choppy sections, **Ngaporo Campsite** makes for nice, well-perched tenting, framed by sheer gray rock faces. By the time **Pipiriki Landing** appears at journey's end, the native forest has again yielded to cleared sheep fields.

THE RIVER ROAD ☎ 06

After a 30-year construction fraught with floods and mudslides, 1934 saw the opening of the aptly named **River Road.** Dancing a *pas de deux* with the bushy banks of the Whanganui River, the road affords the only automobile access to settlements upstream from Wanganui. Defined by natural beauty and enriched by the Maori and Pakeha cultures that have called this land home, the River Rd. seems to be a time and place apart, allowing those visitors who linger to gain new appreciation for fluvial life. The River Rd. parallels SH4 some 15km to the east, connecting Wanganui and **Pipiriki.** From Pipiriki, the road turns east and out of Whanganui National Park to meet up with SH4 at **Raetihi** (27km), less than 15km from the ski town of **Ohakune** (see p. 214). The northern extremes of the park can be reached from **Whakahoro** via roads from **Owhango** (south of Taumarunui, below) or **Raurimu** (just north of National Park Village, p. 212), both from SH4. If you don't have your own car, riding along with **Rivercity Tours** (a.k.a. "the mail run") is a great way to get into the heart of the river valley and meet locals at the same time. The run returns to Wanganui around 1:30-2:30pm, or you can ask to be dropped off anywhere along the way and be picked up the next day. (☎ 344 2554 or 025 443 421; www.rivercitytours.co.nz. Pick-up 7:15am from Wanganui with advance reservation; otherwise, show up early behind the post office, 60 Ridgway St. $30). Most river outfitters also offer a canoe or kayak rental package with transportation for a day or overnight (generally $55 per person; see **Gear Rental,** p. 236).

Travelers heading up the road from Wanganui soon see the **Oyster Cliffs,** which take a large white bite out of the river—a reminder of a time when oceans enveloped this valley. A bit farther up, there's riverside camping at the **Otumaire Campsite** (toilets and water). Continuing upstream, the accommodations get plusher. At

Omaka Farm and Homestay ❶, 35km north of Wanganui, a thick, comfy mattress in an "authentic" (smell included for ambience) sheep-shearing shed proves a popular alternative to tenting along this beautiful stretch of river. For non-rustic souls, a proper bed awaits in their welcoming B&B just up the road. (☎ 342 5595; omakaholiday@xtra.co.nz. Tent sites $8; shed $12 per mattress; B&B $55 per person.) Those who venture further arrive at one of the most jaw-dropping homestays in New Zealand, ⚑**The Flying Fox ❹**, 44km up the River Rd. from Wanganui. Truly off the beaten track, this edenic place is accessible only by boating down the river or via an aerial zipline—a "flying fox" in Kiwispeak—suspended 20m above the river. Self-proclaimed hippie proprietors Annette and John may feel personally insulted if you don't gulp down a homemade beer made entirely from ingredients grown organically on site. Due to access limitations, only booked guests are invited to use the cableway. (☎/fax 342 8160; www.theflyingfox.co.nz. Canoes $35 per day. Free laundry. Cabins $80-90 for 2, with full meal catering $80-85 per person; single rates negotiable; tent sites $8. Advance booking absolutely required.)

A trio of Maori villages stand farther upstream; visitors should only enter the *marae* upon prior invitation. **Koriniti** (Corinth) features the Opeiriki *pa* (never once taken in battle), a lovely *marae*, and the first Anglican church on the river (est. 1840). **Ranana** (London) is one of the bigger villages on the river and retains traces of its past as a traditional center of agriculture. **Kauika Campsite ❶** is pleasantly set by a river with shower, toilet, and kitchen facilities. (☎ 342 8061. Tent sites $6 plus $5 per person; caravans $10 plus $5 per person.)

Hiruharama (Jerusalem) was home to a French Marist Mission and guards the grave of the poet James K. Baxter. A **convent ❶** built in the 1890s now resides here and welcomes the occasional backpacker. (☎ 342 8190. Dorms $10. No linen. Advanced booking recommended.) Just before Hiruharama is **Moutoa Island** from which Maori followers of Hauhauism (a xenophobic religious sect) launched ritualized battles against the tribes of the lower river. Continuing upstream, find the cascading beauty of **Omorehu Waterfall**. A bookend of a town, **Pipiriki** is at the end of the River Rd. and is also the beginning for many jetboat rides and walking tracks. Once well-guarded but now just "well-graded," the **Pukehinau Walk** loops 1km to the Pukehinau crest, once a Hauhau outpost with strategic (and gorgeous) views of the river valley.

TAUMARUNUI ☎ 07

When Chief Pikikotaku fell ill here about two centuries ago and commanded his minions to construct a cover over his bed, the town of Taumarunui ("big overhanging shelter") was christened. If only travelers could command the same attention as they wander the underdeveloped town looking for suitable accommodation. Despite its shortcomings, Taumaranui (pop. 5800), situated at the confluence of the Ongarue and Whanganui Rivers and the junction of SH4 and SH43, does afford proximity to Tongariro National Park and the Whanganui River Journey begins just south of the municipality.

🚆 TRANSPORTATION. TranzScenic heads to **Auckland** (4½hr., 2 per day, $64) and **Wellington** (6½hr., 2 per day, $72-84). **InterCity** also runs to **Auckland** (4¾hr., M-F and Su, $49) and **Wellington** (6hr., M-F and Su, $74). **Pioneer Jet Boat Tours Ltd.** (☎ 895 8528) buses to **Hamilton** (M-F 8am, $28). Toward National Park, most **hitchhikers** (*Let's Go* does not recommend it) try the area by the Hakiaha St. railyards, past the former Main Trunk Cafe. Toward Te Kuiti, thumbers go from Ongarue River Rd. (SH4). **Silver Cabs** (☎ 895 5444) will help you get around town.

TAUMARUNUI ■ 239

ORIENTATION AND PRACTICAL INFORMATION. Taumarunui sits along the **Main Trunk Railway** at the junction of **SH43** and **SH4** (called Hakiaha St. within the town limits). The **Visitor Information Centre** is located in the railway station on Hakiaha St. (☎895 7494; fax 895 6117. Open M-F 9am-4:30pm, Sa-Su 10am-4pm.) Take a nature walk through Cherry Grove to get to the **DOC Field Centre.** (☎895 8201 or 025 946 650. Open M-F 8am-5pm.) Other services include: **banks** with **ATMs** on Hakiaha St. (open M-F 9am-4:30pm); the **hospital** (☎896 0020), on Kururau Rd.; the **police** (☎895 8119), on Hakiaha St.; **Internet access** at the public **library** in the center of town (☎895 7538; $3 per 15min., $5 per 30min.; open M-F 10am-5pm, Sa 9am-noon); and the **post office,** 47-49 Miriama St. (☎895 8149; open M-F 9am-5pm).

ACCOMMODATIONS AND CAMPING. Taumarunui's glaring lack of budget accommodations will have you yearning for anything with four walls and a ceiling. The only establishment in town that knows backpackers exist is **Calvert's Spa Motel ❸,** 6 Marae St. When the spa is temporarily out of order, Calvert simply offers shares with Sky TV and breakfast service. (☎895 8501 or 0800 378 501; fax 895 8502; calvertsmotel@xtra.co.nz. Shares $40; motel units $65-70.) **Taumarunui Holiday Park ❶,** 4km south of town on the Whanganui River, has free pick-up. Activities include fishing, swimming, and kayaking. (☎895 9345; fax 895 6345; taumarunui-holiday-park@xtra.co.nz. Tent sites $8, powered $9; cabins $29 for 2; self-contained tourist flats $45, extra person $12.)

FOOD. Though quality dining establishments are scarce in Taumarunui, the **Rivers II Cafe ❷,** 43 Hakiaha St., stands out. The French toast with banana ($9) and hearty lunch specials ($6) deserve special praise. (☎895 5822. Open M-Th and Sa-Su 8am-5pm, F 8am-10:30pm.) **Ruddie's Place ❹,** 93 Hakiaha St., opens on the weekends to serve sit-down dinners (mains $17-22) a notch above the town's pervasive fried fare. (☎896 7442. Cafe open M-W 10am-3:30pm, Th-F 9am-5pm; restaurant open Th-Sa 5:30-9:30pm.) Your best bet in town is feeding yourself at **New World,** at the northern end of Hakiaha St. (☎896 0070. Open daily 8am-7pm.)

SIGHTS AND ACTIVITIES. Most people who visit Taumarunui use the town as a stopover before their trip down the **Whanganui River** (p. 233). Otherwise, Taumarunui's sights might not be worth a prolonged stay. The town's biggest draw is the serpentine **Raurimu Spiral.** A mighty feat of engineering, this 1908 section of railway track loops and twists and at one point doubles back on itself as it climbs onto the central plateau. The best way to experience the stomach-churning glory of the spiral is to take a **scenic train ride,** which departs Taumarunui daily at 1pm, returning at 3pm ($28). Or just spy upon its loopiness from the lookout 37km south on SH4 at Raurimu. The Visitors Center also has a 3-dimensional model of the spiral on display. The **Manu Ariki Marae,** on Okahukura Back Rd., 12km north of Taumarunui on SH4, offers tours of the *marae* ($10) and a miniature train ride ($5) on a 5km track. (☎896 6971. Open M-Sa 9am-5pm, Su 9am-noon. Call ahead.) Drivers can also ride the **Taumarunui-Stratford Heritage Trail,** a 150km stretch of SH43 established in 1990 to introduce travelers to the region's history. Teal and yellow signs along the road mark lookout points and historic sites.

WELLINGTON AND AROUND

WELLINGTON ☎04

Although it lies directly on a major earthquake fault and is one of the windiest cities on earth, the compact capital city of Wellington (pop. 157,000) is a better place for catching your breath than losing it. Looking out on scenic Wellington Harbour near the North Island's southern tip, New Zealand's second-largest city is a cultural mecca with an impressive series of festivals, some of the country's best theater and dance, and the renowned Museum of New Zealand Te Papa Tongarewa. In 2002, extensive *Lord of the Rings* footage featured the telegenic scenery around Wellington. Before passing through, take a refreshing dip into the cuisine, caffeine, and character of the cosmopolitan Kiwi capital.

WELLINGTON AND AROUND HIGHLIGHTS

EAT a snack on **Cuba Street** in Wellington, where the highest density of **cafes** in the Southern Hemisphere turns it up at night (see p. 247).

DRINK the fine wines of the nearby Wairarapa (see p. 257).

AND BE MERRY at the Kiwi cultural epicenter of **Te Papa Museum,** Wellington's pride and joy (see p. 250).

■ INTERCITY TRANSPORTATION

Flights: The **Wellington International Airport** (☎385 5123) stretches across the Miramar Peninsula in the city's southeastern suburbs. The only international flights here are those from **Sydney, Brisbane,** and **Melbourne** on **Qantas** or **Air New Zealand (ANZ). ANZ** has an office at the corner of Lambton Quay and Grey St. and covers most domestic destinations (☎474 8950 or 0800 737 000). **Freedom Air** (☎0800 600 500), a subsidiary of ANZ, is a "value-based" airline that flies to **Auckland** and **Christchurch.** Frequent flights to **Auckland** start from $100 one-way (1hr., 1-2 per hr.); flights to **Christchurch** are slightly cheaper (45min., around 1 per hr., one-way from $80). **Soundsair** (☎388 2594 or 0800 505 005) flies to **Picton** (25min.; 6-8 per day; $79, backpackers $61, return $139), while **Origin Pacific** (☎0800 302 302) heads to **Nelson** (40min., 4-7 per day, $79-149). The **Stagecoach Flyer** (☎801 7000) runs service every 30min. between the airport, downtown Wellington, and Lower Hutt ($4.50 between the airport and downtown). **Co-op Shuttle** (☎387 8787) runs one-way from the Railway Station to the **airport** (every hr. 9am-4pm, every 30min. 7:30-9am and 4-6pm; $5) and does pre-booked door-to-door service ($10).

Trains: The **Railway Station,** on Bunny St. at Waterloo/Customhouse Quay, houses the train and bus depots. A **Travel Centre** there books for TranzScenic and InterCity (open M-F 7:15am-5:30pm, Sa-Su 7:15am-12:15pm). **TranzScenic** (☎0800 802 802) provides daily service to: **Auckland** (11hr.; day train 8:45am, overnight train 7:50pm; $90-102) via **Palmerston North** (2hr., $21-23), **National Park** (5½hr., $46-52), and **Hamilton** (9hr., $74-81). A taxi between the Railway Station and downtown costs $8-

12. **TranzMetro** (☎ 498 3000, ext. 44933), a regional commuter line, leaves from the Railway Station. There are 4 regular lines including routes up **Hutt Valley,** the **Kapiti Coast,** and the **Wairarapa.** Limited service to **Palmerston North** is offered by **Capital Connection** (1½hr., M-F 5:17pm, $18).

Buses: InterCity/Newmans (☎ 472 5111) departs daily from the rail station to: **Auckland** (11hr., 3-6 per day, $67-99) via **Hamilton** (9hr., $67-80); **Napier** (5hr., 2-3 per day, $60); **New Plymouth** (6hr., 3-4 per day, $61) via **Wanganui** (4hr., $36); **Palmerston North** (2hr., 1-6 per day, $27); and **Rotorua** (7½hr., 4 per day, $78) via **Taupo** (6hr., $69). Just across Thorndon Quay, **Freeman's Lotto & Cafe,** 23 Lambton Quay, sells tickets for **White Star Coach Services** (☎ 478 4734), which runs up along the

Wellington and Around

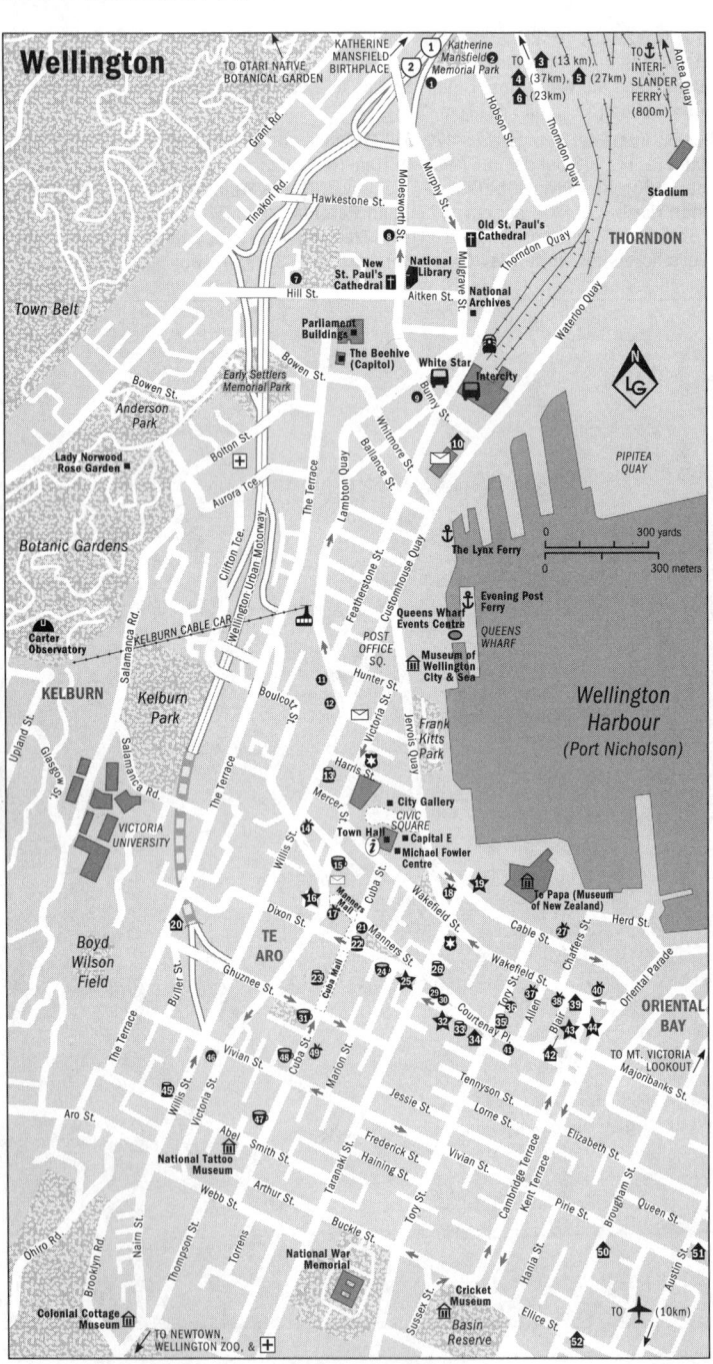

Wellington

♠ ACCOMMODATIONS
Beethoven's (BBH), **50**
Booklovers B&B, **51**
The Cambridge Hotel (BBH), **42**
Downtown Backpackers (VIP), **10**
Top 10 Hutt Park
  Holiday Park, **3**
Maple Lodge (BBH), **52**
Moana Lodge (BBH), **5**
Paekakariki Backpackers (BBH), **4**
Stillwater Lodge, **6**
Wellington City YHA, **39**
World Wide Backpackers (BBH), **20**
Wildlife House (BBH), **34**

♦ FOOD
Big Thumb, **37**
Daawat, **17**
Kopi, **14**
Mr. Chan's, **27**
New World, **40**
One Red Dog, **38**
The Vegetarian Cafe, **49**
Wellington Market
  Food Court, **18**

🍺 BARS
£, **22**
Bar Bodega, **45**
The Grand, **33**
The Malthouse, **13**
Matterhorn, **23**
Molly Malones, **26**
Wellington Sports Cafe, **35**

★ ENTERTAINMENT & CLUBS
BATS Theatre, **44**
Circa Theatre, **19**
Downstage Theatre, **43**
StudioNine, **16**
Phoenix, **25**
The WestPac Trust St. James
  Theatre, **32**

☕ CAFES
Ed's Juice Bar, **15**
Eva Dixon's Place, **24**
Fidel's, **47**
The Krazy Lounge, **31**
Midnight Espresso, **48**

● SERVICES
Australian High Commission, **2**
Automobile Association, **12**
Canadian High Commission, **8**
DOC, **9**
The Map Shop, **46**
Out! Bookshop, **36**
Penny Farthing Cycles, **30**
Pharmacy, **21**
STA Travel, **29**
Thomas Cook, **11**
UK High Commission, **7**
United Video (Internet), **41**
US Embassy, **1**

west coast to **New Plymouth** (6¼hr., 1-2 per day, $48) via **Palmerston North** (4hr., $32) and **Wanganui** (2½hr., $24).

Ferries: The Interislander ferry terminal is inconveniently located on **Aotea Quay,** north of town on SH1. There's a free shuttle from Platform 9 of the Railway Station 40min. before each scheduled departure and back to the station upon ferry arrival. The **Interislander** (☎ 0800 802 802) runs daily to **Picton,** on the South Island (3hr.; 4-5 per day; $36-52, cars $129-179). The **Lynx,** a high-tech, high-speed catamaran, plays the hare to the Interislander's tortoise and departs from Waterloo Quay in downtown Wellington (2¼hr.; 2 per day; $47-68, cars $149-199). Advance bookings are essential; fares drop with significant lead time. Ask about 1-day or 3-night excursion fares.

Hitchhiking: Although *Let's Go* does not recommend it, hitchhikers report that riding from Wellington can be difficult, but a few pick-up spots are worth a try. If Aotea Quay or the Railway Station aren't working, the old main road (where SH1 and SH2 branch a few kilometers north of the ferry station on Hutt Rd.) is known to be a successful spot. This branchpoint is a nasty 3-4km walk from downtown, so some hitchers try their luck where the cars roll right off the boat at the ferry terminal. Many believe it's best to take the train to Paraparaumu (on SH1) or Masterton (on SH2) and catch a ride from there.

▣ ORIENTATION

Central Wellington is remarkably compact, though its suburbs stretch around the harbor into nearby valleys and out onto the **Miramar Peninsula.** Its main downtown zone sits between the **Railway Station, Cambridge,** and **Kent Terraces** at the base of **Mt. Victoria** and can be explored in the course of a day. **Lambton Quay,** home to hordes of suits, big shopping centers, and pricey restaurants, is the main artery. **Courtenay Place,** between Cambridge Tce. and **Taranaki Street,** hops with nightlife, while **Cuba Street** between **Abel Smith** and **Manners Streets** cultivates a more bohemian air. Locals say that the intersection of Cuba and **Vivian Streets** is the "red-light district." The **Civic Square** is both a conceptual and spatial bridge between downtown and the harbor, leading to the waterfront with its public parks, **Queens Wharf, Te Papa,** and **Oriental Bay's** flashy cafes, and beach. In the northern part of the city is the historic area of **Thorndon,** home to old wooden houses, the **Railway Station,** and government buildings such as the **Beehive** of Parliament. The little wooden houses, quiet residential streets, and backpackers of the **Mt. Victoria** area form the southern edge of downtown.

LOCAL TRANSPORTATION

Public Transportation: The **Ridewell Service Centre** can answer questions about public transportation in Wellington. (☎801 7000 or 0800 801 700. Open M-Sa 7:30am-8:30pm, Su 9am-3pm.) **Stagecoach** (☎387 8700) services the main city and most surrounding suburbs. Main line buses run daily 6:30am-11pm. Most backpackers use the line between the Railway Station and the Cambridge Tce. end of Courtenay Pl. ($1). The #1 and 2 buses run between these points every 10-15min. during the day and every 30-45min. during evenings and weekends. Most other buses cover this route: all but #7, 8, 10, and 11—just check with the drivers. The **City Circular** (☎387 8700) runs every 10min. from all the major city sights ($1). Alternatively, there is a $5 Daytripper pass available that allows for unlimited downtown travel (M-F 7:30am-6pm, Sa 9am-6pm, Su 10am-6pm). **Cityline Hutt Valley** (☎569 2933) runs the #81 and 83 buses between Courtenay Pl. and the Railway Station and around the bay to Petone and Eastbourne every hr. during the day (more in peak times, fewer in evenings).

Taxis: Taxis frequent **Lambton Quay** and **Courtney Place**. If you need to call one, try **Wellington Combined Taxis** (☎384 4444) or **Wellington City Cabs** (☎388 8000).

Car Rental: Avis (☎0800 374 832), **Budget** (☎0800 652 227), and **Hertz** (☎0800 654 321) are at the airport. You can often arrange to get the car at the ferry terminal. **Omega Rentals,** 96 Hutt Rd. (☎472 8465), has free pick-up and 24hr. AA breakdown help. Four-day unlimited mileage in a budget car is $39 per day. **AA,** 342-352 Lambton Quay (☎470 9999), has a Travel Centre. Open M-F 8:30am-5pm, Sa 9am-1pm.

Bike Rental: Penny Farthing Cycles, 89 Courtenay Pl. (☎385 2279), rents bikes for $35 per day, $120 per week. Open M-F 8am-6pm, Sa 9:30am-4pm, Su 10am-4pm.

PRACTICAL INFORMATION

TOURIST AND FINANCIAL SERVICES

Visitors Center: The Wellington Information Centre, 101 Wakefield St. (☎802 4860; fax 802 4863; www.wellingtonnz.com), at the Civic Centre. Luggage storage $4 per day. Internet $6 per hr. Open M-F 8:30am-5:30pm, Sa-Su 9:30am-4:30pm. **Airport branch** (☎385 5123) meets incoming flights. Open daily 7am-7pm.

DOC: (☎472 7356; fax 471 2075), in the Old Government Building across Lambton Quay from the Beehive. They sell backcountry hut passes and permits for Kapiti Island. Open M-F 9am-4:30pm, Sa 10am-3pm.

Budget Travel: STA Travel, 100 Courtenay Pl. (☎472 8510). Open M-F 9am-5:30pm, Sa 10am-5pm. There is also a profusion of discounted ticket consolidators and agents along Lambton Quay and in the Willis St. vicinity.

Consulates: Australia, 72-78 Hobson St. (☎473 6411), in Thorndon, north of the Railway Station. **Canada,** 61 Molesworth St., 3rd fl. (☎473 9577; fax 471 2082). **UK,** 44 Hill St. (☎924 2888; fax 471 1974). **US,** 29 Fitzherbert Tce. (☎472 2068; fax 471 2380), in Thorndon.

Banks and Currency Exchange: In the main downtown areas, you're never more than a mad dash from an **ATM. Thomas Cook,** 358 Lambton Quay (☎472 2848), near Willis St., has long hours. Open M-F 9am-5:30pm, Sa 9:30am-1pm.

LOCAL SERVICES

Tramping Gear: Mainly Tramping, 39 Mercer St. (☎473 5353), provides 10% YHA and student discounts. Open M-Th 9am-5:30pm, F 9am-7pm, Sa 10am-4pm, Su 11am-3pm. Several other shops grace the corner of Mercer and Willis St.

Maps: The Map Shop (☎385 1462), at Vivian and Victoria St., sells a complete set of New Zealand park, city, and topographical maps. Open M-F 8:30am-5:30pm.

Bi-Gay-Lesbian Organizations: Gay Switchboard (☎473 7878) runs a hotline daily 7:30-10pm and provides support and info on the Wellington scene. It's also a contact point for other area groups like **Icebreakers**, a young gay/bi support group. **Out! Bookshop**, 15 Tory St. (☎385 4400), has a wide array of gay-oriented magazines and other items. Open M-Sa noon-11pm, Su noon-9pm. The *Express* paper, available at the nightclub £ or at the Wellington YHA, has info on Wellington's gay scene.

EMERGENCY & COMMUNICATIONS

Emergency: Dial ☎ 111 throughout New Zealand.

Police: (☎381 2000), at the corner of Victoria and Harris St.

Hotlines: AIDS hotline (24hr. ☎0800 802 437). **Rape and Sexual Abuse Support Hotline** (24hr. ☎801 8178), run by the Help Foundation.

Medical Services: James Smith Life Pharmacy (☎499 1466), at the corner of Cuba and Manners St. Open M-Th 8:30am-6pm, F 8:30am-9pm, Sa 9:30am-6pm, Su 10am-6pm. **Wellington Accident and Urgent Medical Centre,** 17 Adelaide Rd. (☎384 4944), in Newtown by the Basin Reserve, has a doctor on duty **24hr.**, and a **pharmacy** (☎385 8810), next door. Open M-F 5-11pm, Sa-Su 9am-11pm. The **hospital** (☎385 5999) is in Newtown on Riddiford St.

Internet Access: United Video, 31 Courtenay Pl. (☎385 1470), charges $4 per hr. Open M-Th and Su 8am-1am, F-Sa 24hr. Other Internet stops abound on Courtenay Pl.

Post Offices: Scattered throughout the city. Only the **Post Shop**, 43 Manners St. (☎473 5922), holds Poste Restante. Open M-F 8am-5:30pm, Sa 10am-1:30pm.

ACCOMMODATIONS

Central Wellington has several satisfactory backpackers, most south of Civic Square with a few along quiet, tree-lined **Brougham Street**. Consider heading a bit north along the coast for some truly outstanding seaside sleeps. Book your bed in advance during the summer and on weekends.

Wellington City YHA (☎801 7280; fax 801 7278; yhawgtn@yha.org.nz), at the corner of Cambridge Tce. and Wakefield St. Centrally located, this 6-story behemoth has 219 beds, 2 kitchens, and big lounges. Internet. Laundry. 6-bed dorms $23; 4-bed dorms with bath $28; twins and doubles $58; family rooms from $73. ❸

THE HIDDEN DEAL

A COASTAL ESCAPE: PAEKAKARIKI BACKPACKERS

A blazing orange sun sets softly on the horizon. In its wake, stripes of pink streak the sky and supremely-sculpted waves lap against the Tasman shore. Sitting on a well-placed chaise lounge, you watch, you listen, and you sigh. Wellington's bustling streets, jostling suits, and jittery caffeine-addicts seem more than an hour's drive away. The lazy lawn of Paekakariki Backpackers, perched high on the carefree Kapiti Coast, is a tranquil sanctuary.

Upon arrival, laid-back hosts Peter and Denise greet guests with complimentary coffee by the small pond. Their impressive array of pets—4 cats, a yellow dog, an axolott, and a cockateel—remind visitors how lucky they are to have escaped the urban zoo.

When night falls, safari-style dorms and private rooms await with country quilts, antique furniture, and hanging veils. Doze off to the buzz of crickets and sounds of the sea.

One block from the Paekakariki train station, a steep brick path leads to this quiet wooden cottage and its breathtaking views of wind-swept hills. More of a restful retreat than a stop-along-the-highway, Paekak regularly converts one-night travelers into month-long residents, so come prepared to linger.

11 Wellington Rd., in Paekakariki, 40min. from Wellington on the Kapiti Coast. ☎902 5967; fax 902 5969; paekakbp@voyager.co.nz. Dorms $18; twins and doubles $44, with bath $49; tent sites $10. Call ahead.

World Wide Backpackers (BBH), 291 The Tce. (☎ 802 5590 or 0508 888 555; fax 802 5591; worldwide@paradise.co.nz). From town, go up Ghuznee St. and turn right. A homier hostel with board games, complimentary breakfast (7:45-9am), free local calls, free Internet (5-9pm), and free pick-up. Key deposit $10. Reception 7:45am-noon and 4:30-10pm. Dorms $22, weekly $120; singles $39; twins and doubles $51. ❸

The Cambridge Hotel (BBH), 28 Cambridge Tce. (☎385 8829; fax 385 2503; www.cambridgehotel.co.nz), delivers hotel facilities to backpackers. Free linen. 8-bed dorms $20; singles $46; doubles $70-80. ❷

Maple Lodge (BBH), 52 Ellice St. (☎385 3771), around the corner from Brougham St., feels close to home and far from the bustle of the city. Reception 8:30am-noon and 5-10pm. Dorms $20; singles $26; twins $41; doubles $44. ❷

Wildlife House (BBH), 58 Tory St. (☎381 3899 or 0508 005 858; www.wildlifehouse.co.nz). This zoo recognizes your animal desires with free condoms at reception. Free pick-up. Internet. Laundry. Linen $5. Key deposit $20. Reception 8am-10pm. Dorms $19-20; twins and doubles $45, with bath $55. ❷

Beethoven's (BBH), 89 Brougham St. (☎939 4678). With an eccentric owner, bizarre signs all over the house, and a classical music wake-up call before the 8am complimentary breakfast, this place isn't for everyone. Internet. Dorms $18, weekly $108; doubles $44. Cash only. ❷

Booklovers B&B, 123 Pirie St. (☎384 2714; booklovers@xtra.co.nz), in Mt. Victoria. A published author welcomes guests to peruse her own works or to partake in the upstairs book exchange. Breakfast included; dinner can be arranged. Singles from $75; doubles from $100, with bath from $120. ❹

Downtown Backpackers (VIP), 1 Bunny St. (☎473 8482; fax 471 1073; www.downtownbackpackers.co.nz), across from the Railway Station. While close to transport terminals, Wellington's largest, most institutional hostel is far from the city's bars and restaurants. Free pick-up from ferry. Internet. Key deposit $20. Reception 24hr. Dorms $21; singles $46; twins $46; doubles with bath $55, with Sky TV $60. ❸

Top 10 Hutt Park Holiday Park, 95 Hutt Park Rd. (☎568 5913 or 0800 488 872; fax 568 5914; www.huttpark.co.nz), in Lower Hutt some 13km from Wellington, is the closest holiday park. Tent and powered sites $11.50. Cabins $35 for 2; tourist cabins $50 for 2; extra person $8-11. ❶

NEARBY SEASIDE BACKPACKERS

Moana Lodge (BBH), 49 Moana Rd. (☎233 2010; fax 233 9465; moanalodge@clear.net.nz), in Plimmerton, 20min. north of Wellington. With an idyllic seaside location, a well-equipped kitchen, and plush rooms, this is definitely one of the best backpackers in New Zealand. Make the trip to enjoy John and Helen's warm hospitality and choice freebies—kayaks, mountain bikes, tea, and coffee. Call for pick-up. Internet. Laundry. Singles $25; twins and doubles $40-44. Call ahead. ❸

Stillwater Lodge, 34 Mana Esplanade (☎233 6628), in Mana, 15min. north of Wellington, a 10min. walk from the Mana train station and the InterCity stop. This beautiful home-turned-backpackers is a few steps from the "still waters" of Pauatahanui Inlet. Laundry. Dorms $19; twins and doubles $44, with bath $50. ❷

🍴 FOOD

Lambton Quay and **Willis Street** are full of lunch spots, but are rather dead at night. The fashionable length of **Courtenay Place** and its side streets are where Lambton Quay's young and chic migrate on evenings and weekends, while **Cuba Street** is populated by smaller ethnic restaurants and cafes. A surprising mixture of food types reside at the **Wellington Market Food Court,** at Wakefield and Taranaki St.

(open F-Sa 10am-6pm). The well-regarded Thai purveyor **Aranya's House** keeps later hours (☎ 384 8666; open Tu-Sa noon-9pm, Su noon-7pm). You can find groceries at **New World,** 279 Wakefield St. (☎ 384 8054; open daily 7am-midnight), and fresh fruit and veggies nearby at **Mr. Chan's,** 100 Cable St. (☎ 384 6622; open M-W and Sa 8:30am-7:30pm, Th-F 8:30am-9pm, Su 8:30am-6pm). See the **Cafes** section for more dining options.

Daawat, 88 Manners Mall (☎ 472 0060). *The* place in Wellington for curry fulfills the trinity of backpacker desires: low prices, great quality, and heaping portions. Wash down a divine *Dal makhani* ($9; black lentils in spicy tomato puree) with a creamy mango *lassi* ($3). Open daily 5:30pm-late; also M-F 11:30am-2pm. ❷

Kopi, 103 Willis St. (☎ 499 5570), has a strong local following among those who know good food. Enjoy award-winning Malaysian dishes like the tender lamb *korma* ($15.50) in the intimate 2-story setting. Be early or be prepared to wait. Open daily 10am-late. ❸

The Vegetarian Cafe, 179 Cuba St. (☎ 384 2713). A sarong-clad staff happily feeds diners wearing everything from suits to tongue studs. Massive bowls filled with vegetarian concoctions ($6-12) are enough to sate even the staunchest carnivore. Open M-Sa 9am-9pm, Su 9am-4pm. ❷

One Red Dog, 9-11 Blair St. (☎ 384 9777), off Courtenay Pl. There's never a dull bite into these thick pizzas with trendy toppings (med. $16.50, large $24.90). The ridiculously overstuffed calzones, however, are a true steal ($14). Open M-Th and Su 10am-11:30pm, F-Sa 10am-1:30am. ❸

Big Thumb, 9 Allen St. (☎ 384 4878), off Courtenay Pl. A swollen neon digit flags the entrance to this spacious Chinese eatery. Scan the long menu for items like the smoked beef with red chili ($14). Open daily 11am-2:30pm and 5-11pm. ❸

CAFES

With the highest number of cafes per capita in the Southern Hemisphere and yet only three Starbucks, Wellington is certainly doing something right. **Courtenay Place** is lined with standard cafes, while funkier finds dot the bohemian stretch of **Cuba Street.** Most cafes serve food and many extend the party with liquor licenses and late hours.

Fidel's, 234 Cuba St. (☎ 801 6868). The tight inside passages, patio military netting, and revolutionary memorabilia place you firmly in the trenches. A delicious blackboard menu and caffeine buzz ($3-4) take you higher. Live jazz every Th at 8pm. Licensed. Open M-F 7:30am-midnight, Sa-Su 9am-midnight.

Midnight Espresso, 178 Cuba St. (☎ 384 7014). Despite its Y2K compliance, the clock struck twelve and froze here, coaxed by the good music, laid-back patrons, and plaster monsters. Fill up on coffee ($3-4) and fresh juices from Lucky's Juice Joint ($2.50) so you don't miss the black-lit, trippy trip to the loo. Salads $3-5. Open daily 8am-3am.

The Krazy Lounge (☎ 801 6652), at the corner of Cuba and Ghuznee St., under the joker's cap. Krazy lures a sizeable crowd, who nod to the beat of soft ambient rhythms over a frothy mug. Licensed. Open Su-Th 8am-1am, F-Sa 8am-3am.

Eva Dixon's Place, 35 Dixon St. (☎ 384 1000). Entrance through alley, on the 2nd fl. at the corner of Eva and Dixon St. If you can find this delightful, anti-trendy cafe, you'll be rewarded with wrap-around windows, comfy turquoise seats, and an all-day "brekkie" menu ($3-14). Open M-F 7am-7pm, Sa 8:30am-7pm, Su 9am-7pm.

Ed's Juice Bar, 95 Victoria St. (☎ 478 1769). Savor an irresistible smoothie ($2-7) or a steaming soup ($5). Great selection of vegetarian and vegan food. If you can stand it after a long night on the piss, ask Ed for "Big Detox," a veggie-blended anti-oxidant boost for your liver. Open M-Sa 7am-6:30pm.

🎭 ENTERTAINMENT

With a wide variety of diversions, from high art to sport, Wellington has something for everyone. The Visitors Center has schedules and information about rush tickets. **Ticketek** (☎384 3840), on Wakefield St., sells seats for most events, though rugby tickets are sold through **Red Tickets** (☎0800 000 575) or at any **Post Shop**.

MUSIC AND PERFORMING ARTS

Downstage (☎801 6946; www.downstage.co.nz), at the corner of Courtenay Pl. and Cambridge Tce. Wellington's oldest professional theater puts on a wide range of productions from classic drama to cabaret and comedy. Tickets $20-35, student rush $15.

Circa, 1 Taranaki St. (☎801 7992; www.circa.co.nz), next to Te Papa. Mainstage plays (tickets $30, students $24) and a studio with smaller, more experimental shows and cheaper seats (tickets around $25, students $19).

BATS, 1 Kent Tce. (☎802 4175; www.bats.co.nz), is the most experimental, on-the-fringe venue, putting on exclusively New Zealand productions—you won't stumble into any of the classics here. Tickets $15-20, students or unwaged $8-14.

The WestpacTrust St. James Theatre, 77 Courtenay Pl. (☎802 4060). Restored Edwardian lyric theater, home to the Royal Ballet, opera, and musicals. Prices often $45-55.

The Opera House, 111-113 Manners St. (☎384 3840), managed by the St. James, is refurbished and ready to welcome community events and some touring productions.

Wellington Convention Centre (☎801 4242; www.wellingtonconventioncentre.com) stages lectures as well as classical and chamber music concerts (including the New Zealand Symphony Orchestra), mainly at the Michael Fowler Centre and Wellington Town Hall. Book through **Ticketek** (see above).

CINEMA AND SPORT

Cinema: Paramount, 25 Courtenay Pl. (☎384 4080), dishes out arthouse cinema fare, as does **Rialto** (☎385 1864), at the corner of Cable St. and Jervois Quay. For a dose of Hollywood, check out the new **Reading Cinemas 10** (☎801 4600), in Courtenay Central Mall; **Embassy,** 10 Kent Tce. (☎384 7657); **Hoyt 5** (☎472 5182), at Manners Mall; or **Midcity** (☎384 3567), on Manners St. Showings change each Th.

WestpacTrust Stadium (☎473 3881), on Waterloo Quay. The 3-year-old, $128 million stadium is jokingly called "The Cake Tin" for its metallic outer shell. But don't let that fool you—Wellington is mighty proud of its stadium can which hosts events like rugby, cricket, soccer, and concerts. Prices vary, but rugby tickets usually cost $35-45.

Queens Wharf Events Centre (☎470 0190), at Queens Wharf, is the main venue for indoor sporting events like international basketball and netball, popular music concerts, and various weekend festivals and exhibitions. Prices vary.

Basin Reserve (☎384 5227), on Kent Tce., a 20min. walk from downtown, has been home to Wellington cricket for more than 125 years and enjoys National Heritage status. Most matches Nov.-Mar., with 1 or 2 international series every year. Tickets usually $10-20.

FESTIVALS

Kicking the year off right is the **Summer City Festival** (☎801 3777; www.feelinggreat.co.nz; Dec. 31-late Feb. 2003), a brilliant parade of concerts, celebrations, and events like Sunday night jazz in the Botanic Gardens, mass walks up Mt. Victoria, and a Pacific Island festival. The biennial **New Zealand Festival** (☎309 9241; www.nzfestival.telecom.co.nz; Feb. 27-Mar. 21, 2004), the country's biggest celebration, brings artists and performers from across the globe. Another marathon event, the **Fringe Festival** (☎495 8015; www.fringe.org.nz; Feb. 14-Mar. 9, 2003), takes Wellington to the cutting edge, celebrating alternative and experimental theater, music, dance, and spoken word. May plays the fool with the **TV2 International Laugh! Festival** (☎ 385 0162; May 1-19, 2002), showcasing comedians from inside and outside New Zealand. July rolls out the red carpet for the Kings and Queens of the Silver Screen in the annual **New Zealand International Film Festival** (☎ 385 0162; www.enzedff.co.nz; July 20-Aug. 5, 2003), a regular stop on the post-Cannes film festival circuit. Echoing the sweet sounds of spring, the **Wellington Jazz Festival** (☎ 385 0162; www.jazzfestival.co.nz; late Oct. 2003) takes to the streets and the waterfront during the last two weeks of October.

◪ NIGHTLIFE

Wellington nightlife comes in flavors ranging from business chic to skater cool; the trick is finding your vibe. The **Courtenay Place** stretch is clogged with stylishly slick bars frequented by after-work suits and black-clad students; most are indistinguishable from one another. For those who aren't fond of rock remixes, the pubs on **Cuba Street** and the nearby blocks tend to be just as crowded but more relaxed. Be sure to carry appropriate identification as many bars will card patrons. For the latest happenings, grab the free weekly *The Package, Capital Times,* or *City Voice* from newsstands or check cafes for fliers. Scope out *Express* for gay nightlife listings.

BARS

◪ **Matterhorn,** 106 Cuba Mall (☎ 384 3359). Walk down a long dark hallway to enter the realm of Matterhorn. Mellow vibes permeate the intimate lounge bar with $5 beers, $3.50 coffees, and a selection of munchies from $4. Late-night DJs (Th-Su) get a funky crowd grooving in the rear courtyard. Jazz W. Open M-Sa 11am-3am, Su noon-2am.

◪ **The Malthouse,** 47 Willis St. (☎ 499 4355), on the 2nd fl. While the post-work crowd often overwhelms the bar, the sun porch is a bright, toasty place to unwind. Like any great pub, The Malthouse takes its beer seriously—a separate menu describes in loving detail each of their 30 draught beers. Open M-Sa 11am-late.

Molly Malones (☎ 384 2896), at the corner of Courtenay Pl. and Taranaki St. Every hour is Happy Hour at this Wellington staple with live Irish and cover bands every night. No cover. Open daily 11am-late.

Bar Bodega (☎ 384 8212), at the corner of Willis and Abel Smith St. This small space with sparse seating attracts an eclectic crowd and some of the best live music in town. Live bands Tu-Sa 10pm. Cover from $5. Handles $4.50. Open daily 4pm-3am.

BARS WITH DANCE FLOORS

The Grand, 69 Courtenay Pl. (☎ 801 7800). Get done up and cruise past the bouncers to join the gyrating scene upstairs. Mostly top pop, the music keeps an all-ages crowd hopping until the wee hours. Drinks $5-7. Open daily 11am-late; F-Sa 11am-3 or 4am.

Wellington Sports Cafe (☎ 801 5115), at the corner of Courtenay Pl. and Tory St. Part sports bar, part grind-fest. After the game of the moment ends, the tables are pushed aside and open season is declared on one of the wildest dance floors in town. Lines often form late. Handles $4-5. Live music W-Th. DJs F-Sa. Open daily 11am-5am.

£ (☎ 384 6024), at Dixon St. on the 2nd fl. of the Oaks Complex. The mainstay of Wellington's gay nightlife scene draws a subdued after-work crowd with $4.50 pints. After dark, migrate to the dance floor next door where DJs spin house and techno (W-Sa) and a drag show takes the stage (F-Sa). Free pool and Happy Hour on Su. Open W-Th and Su 5pm-3am, F 5pm-5am, Sa 8pm-5am.

NIGHTCLUBS

StudioNine, 9 Edward St. (☎384 9976), on the 2nd fl. above **Curve Bar** and **Sub Nine.** A large club complex, the underground masses gather here for trance, drum 'n' bass, progressive house, and the big-time DJs who spin the tracks. Cover from $5. StudioNine open F-Sa 11pm-9am; Curve Bar open W-Su 7pm-3am.

Phoenix, 13 Dixon St. (☎384 5148), with the stairwell behind "The Club" at the intersection with Taranaki St. The rough-edged club in town spins hard house and trance with a big Sa night. Cover up to $25. Open F-Sa 10pm-6:30am.

SIGHTS

MUSEUMS

MUSEUM OF NEW ZEALAND TE PAPA TONGAREWA. Like a massive father figure encouraging your first stumbling steps as a tourist in Wellington, this enormous collection of ambitious, informative, and entertaining exhibits seems to bellow, "Come Te Papa." The giant is deservedly Wellington's pride and joy; the free admission is an added bonus. Standing exhibits explore New Zealand's land, history, culture, and art. Upstairs, *Te Marae* offers a contemporary interpretation of Maori iconography. Or, for a fee ($2-9), try the interactive exhibits including a virtual bungy jump, virtual sheep-shearing (complete with virtual blood if you do a bad job), a virtual ride into prehistoric moa-laden New Zealand, and more. *(On the waterfront, just at the end of Taranaki St. on Cable St. ☎381 7000; www.tepapa.govt.nz. Open daily 10am-6pm, Th 10am-9pm. Free.)*

THE MUSEUM OF WELLINGTON CITY AND SEA. Constructed in 1892, this museum explores the unique relationship between Wellington residents and the sea. This is probably not a comforting trip before heading to the South Island, as one gallery features a video on the 1968 sinking of the *Wahine* interisland ferry. *(At the corner of Queens Wharf and Jervois Quay. ☎472 8904; www.bondstore.co.nz. Open daily 10am-6pm; in winter M-F 10am-5pm, Sa-Su 10am-5:30pm. $5, children $2.50.)*

KATHERINE MANSFIELD BIRTHPLACE. Home to the beloved short story writer for the first six years of her life, this painstakingly restored house is a haven for literature lovers. A narrated display explores Mansfield's early life as it influenced her work and an elaborate dollhouse depicts one of her most famous stories; strong debate apparently raged over what shade "oily spinach green" should be. *(25 Tinakori Rd., in Thorndon. Go up Murphy St. past the Motorway or take the #10 bus to Park St. and walk through the park. ☎473 7268; www.tinakorilodge.co.nz/kmb. Open daily 10am-4pm. $5, students $4, children $2. Call ahead to book a guided tour.)*

OTHER MUSEUMS. The **Dowse Art Museum** usually features off-beat, contemporary object artists, with a New Zealand hip-hop exhibit coming in February 2003. *(35 Laings Rd., in Lower Hutt. Catch the #83 Eastbourne bus to Queensgate from Courtenay Pl. ☎570 6500. Open M-F 10am-4pm, Sa-Su 11am-5pm. Free.)* If you miss the thwack of the national pastime, the **National Cricket Museum** has more old bats than a bingo game in Boca. *(In the Basin Reserve grandstand. ☎385 6602; www.nationalcricketmuseum.co.nz. Open daily 10:30am-3:30pm; in winter Sa-Su. $3, children $1.)* The **National Tattoo Museum** mainly features pictures and designs of Maori *moko*, while the preserved skin sample in back is a bit overdone. A tattoo parlor, **Underground Arts,** lies next door for the inspired. *(42 Abel Smith St. ☎385 6444; www.mokomuseum.co.nz. Open Tu-Th 10am-6pm, F 10am-8pm, Sa-Su noon-6pm. Admission by donation.)*

CITY SIGHTS

PARLIAMENT. The most prominent visual attractions in Wellington—the capital city since the government moved from Auckland in 1865—have prime national significance. The distinctive **Beehive**, a monstrosity of '70s architecture, houses the offices of the Prime Minister and other bigwigs, but the interior is closed to the public. Next door, the Neoclassical **Parliament House** is home to the **Visitors Center** on the ground floor. From here, free hourly tours give a peek at parts of the buildings that would otherwise be off-limits. See the carefully designed Maori Affairs Select Committee Room and the huge art installation representing New Zealand's cultural traditions. The ornate Victorian Gothic **Parliamentary Library**, restored from a 1992 fire, is part of the tour as well. To see the House in action, get a schedule in advance. *(Molesworth St., a few blocks from the Railway Station. ☎ 471 9503. Tours leave on the hour; groups of 10 or more call ahead. Open M-F 10am-4pm, Sa 10am-3pm, Su noon-3pm.)*

CIVIC SQUARE. The public buildings in Wellington's bricked **Civic Square** are the perfect place to people-watch on sunny weekends. At one side sits the elegant **City Gallery**, which hosts contemporary exhibitions by top caliber New Zealand and international artists, the Gay and Lesbian Festival, and short film showings. *(101 Wakefield St. ☎ 801 3021; www.city-gallery.org.nz. Open daily 10am-5pm. NZ exhibits free; international exhibits up to $10.)* In the far corner of Civic Square is the circular **Michael Fowler Centre** *(☎ 801 4242)*, an events and conference center which is home to the New Zealand Symphony Orchestra. Inside are the two towering modern Maori pillars, *Te Pou O Wi Tako* and *Te Pou o Taviwi*, dedicated to the people of the land and to visitors, respectively. Just under the base of the bridge sits **Capital E**, a children's center with a hands-on toy store, constantly changing exhibitions, and a theater for kids. *(☎ 384 8502; www.capitale.org.nz. Open daily 9:30am-5:30pm. Exhibitions range from free to $8. Theater $10.)* Cross the bridge to the waterfront and the green public space of **Frank Kitts Park**.

VANTAGE POINTS. Rising from the city's south end, **Mt. Victoria** can elevate you to new heights of long-range vision. If you're not up for the 30min. hike, you can drive or ride. *(M-F take bus #20.)* Some locals say that the view from the **ECNZ wind turbine** is even better. *(Take bus #7 from the Railway Station or Willis St. up to the shops on Brooklyn St.; there are signposts from there. Beware: it's a steep climb.)*

LIBRARIES AND CATHEDRALS

NATIONAL LIBRARY. The library is home to over 1.8 million books, including the **Cartoon Archives**, the **Gay and Lesbian Archives**, and the **Alexander Turnbull Library**, which shelves a collection of early printed materials and photographic archives. *(58 Molesworth St. ☎ 474 3000; www.natlib.govt.nz. Open M-F 9am-5pm, Sa 9am-1pm. Research and Gallery only Su 1-4pm. Free. Archives are available for viewing by arrangement.)*

NATIONAL ARCHIVES. A dimly lit vault toward the back of the archives building displays New Zealand's most important documents, including the original copy of the 1840 Treaty of Waitangi, the Statute of Westminster, and the petition for women's suffrage. *(10 Mulgrave St. ☎ 499 5595. Open M-F 9am-5pm, Sa 9am-1pm. Free.)*

OLD ST. PAUL'S CATHEDRAL. Erected in 1866 from native timber, this small Anglican church might look simple from the outside, but the colonial Gothic interior has warm, rich color and superb stained-glass windows. The contrast between this charming cathedral and salmon-colored **New St. Paul's** *(next to Parliament on Molesworth St.)* is almost comical. *(On Mulgrave St., one block past the Archives. ☎ 473 6722. Open daily 10am-5pm. Free.)*

GARDENS AND TOURS

BOTANIC GARDENS. A trip to the gardens may call to mind similarities between Wellington and San Francisco, especially if you ride the Wellington Cable Car 610m up to the Kelburn Terminal. (☎472 2199. *Departs every 10min. from 280 Lambton Quay, Cable Car Ln. Open M-F 7am-10pm, Sa-Su 9am-10pm. $1.50, students and children $1.*) Relax in the 26-hectare public **Botanic Gardens** and follow one of the many paths snaking from the herb garden to the **Carter Observatory** with canopied views of the city and hills in the distance. The observatory features planetarium shows and telescope viewings. (☎472 8167; www.carterobs.ac.nz. *Open M-F 10am-5pm, Sa-Su 12:15-5pm; also Tu, Th, and Sa 6:30-9pm.*) One of the most spectacular spots in the gardens is the **Lady Norwood Rose Garden**, with hundreds of different kinds of roses blossoming out from a central fountain. After you explore, walk down the lush gardens and follow Bolton St. out to the Terrace and downtown. (☎801 3073. *Always open, though best visited during the day. Roses Nov.-May only. Free.*) Anyone with a botanical bent should also visit the 90-hectare **Otari Native Botanic Garden**, which is dedicated solely to native plants. (*160 Wilton Rd. Take the #14 Wilton bus.* ☎475 3245. *Free.*)

WELLINGTON ZOO. New Zealand's oldest zoo and a world leader in breeding programs for some of the country's most famous species, the Wellington Zoo is a wild escape located just 10min. from the city. Rare and exotic animals such as the Sumatran Tiger and the Malayan Sun Bear sit near such New Zealand favorites as the Brown Kiwi and the Giant Weta. (*On Daniel St. in Newtown. Take the #10 or 23 Stagecoach bus to Newtown Park.* ☎381 6750. *Open daily 9:30am-5pm. $9.*)

KARORI WILDLIFE SANCTUARY. Situated on a fault-line valley well above the city and surrounded by a 2m impenetrable fence used to keep away introduced pests, this sanctuary uses its 252-hectare reserve to recreate a native habitat for endangered species. The lush 35km of hiking tracks represent an eden for bush-starved denizens. Evening tours showcase nocturnal species like the kiwi, weka, and morepork. (*Through the Karori Tunnel and at the end of Waiapu Rd. Take buses #12, 17, 18, 21, and 22, marked Karori, from downtown.* ☎920 9200; www.sanctuary.org.nz. *Open Nov.-Mar. daily 10am-5pm; Apr.-Oct. 10am-4pm. Nocturnal tours start 30min. before sunset. Daylight entrance $6, children $3; nocturnal tours $15. Call ahead for guided or evening tours.*)

ALL THINGS "RINGS". Though none of the sets remain and many of the landscapes were altered by computer graphics, some die-hard J.R.R. Tolkien or Peter Jackson fans might want to make a quick car tour of the area, catching several shooting sights. The **Otaki Gorge Road** winds by the woods and roads of **Hobbiton**, as seen at the beginning of the first film (though the actual streets and village of Hobbiton were filmed outside of Matamata, east of Cambridge). **Rivendell**, the elven spot home to the first gathering of the fellowship, was filmed at Kaitoke Regional Park, outside of Upper Hutt. **Queen Elizabeth Park**, near Paekakariki, hosted filming for the rumbling battle of Pelennor Fields. Finally, **Bree**, the first stop on Frodo & Co.'s journey after a squealing equestrian chase scene, finds its real home in Seatoun, at **Fort Dorset**. For more info, go to the Visitors Center.

ACTIVITIES

WALKS AND RIDES. The **Northern, Southern,** and **Eastern Walkways**, detailed in leaflets from the Visitors Center or DOC office, are tame and accessible walks through the city's greenbelt and coastline. Alternately, rent a bike from town and ride along the spectacular coast all the way from Oriental Bay out around the Miramar Peninsula and to the end of the pavement. From there, the **Red Rocks Coastal Walk**, a terrific 8km return trip along the jagged southern shore, winds past the pillow lava formation of Red Rocks. The walk continues out to the crashing surf of **Sinclair Head,** where a colony of fat fur seals is sure to be lazing around in winter. A 4WD ride from **Red Rocks Seal Tour** travels to the colony along rugged and otherwise inaccessible tracks. (☎ *0800 732 5277. 2½hr. trip $50.)*

ADVENTURE ACTIVITIES. For more cardiovascular pursuits, **Fergs Rock 'n' Kayaks** has **rock climbing** trips and hires **sea kayaks, inline skates,** and **scooters.** *(At Queens Wharf.* ☎ *499 8898; www.fergskayaks.co.nz. Rock climbing from $12; kayaks $12-15 per hr.; inline skates $10-15 per hr.; scooters $10 per hr.)* **HangDog** and **Top Adventures** specialize in caving, rafting, canyoning, and rock climbing in Titahi Bay. *(453 Hutt Rd., in Lower Hutt.* ☎ *589 9181; www.topadventures.co.nz. Trips from $55.)* Up in Karori's suburban expanses, **Mud Cycles** rents bikes for use at the adjacent Makara Park. *(1 Allington Rd.* ☎ *476 4961; www.mudcycles.co.nz. Open daily 8am-6:30pm. Bike rental $40 per day.)*

BEACHES AND HARBOR

Within walking distance from downtown, **Oriental Bay,** while popular with city dwellers, is less a beach than a grassy promenade overlooked by trendy cafes. Locals like **Lyall Bay,** which has a patrolled swimming stretch and relatively consistent breaks at the airport end. If you have the time, Plimmerton and the Kapiti Coast provide consistently better swimming and sunning. Wellington's **surfing** is rather wind-dependent: winter southerlies cause stronger waves, but breaks are more consistent east of the Wairarapa towns of Martinborough and Masterton. Windsurfing is popular but intense and for professionals only.

The **Evening Post Ferry** is one cheap way to get out onto the harbor. Full of Wellingtonians escaping the city, it leaves from Queens Wharf and crosses to the little cafe-and-antique-shop community of **Day's Bay,** with its small but popular swimming beach. Past Day's Bay is the village of **Eastbourne,** similarly bedecked with cafes, blue penguins, and a pebbly beach. (☎ *499 1282. M-F 9 sailings per day, Sa-Su 5 per day; return $15.)* Some ferries also stop at **Matiu/Somes Island.** For a good 3hr. getaway, bring a picnic lunch, wander the revegetating bush, and admire the great views of Wellington. *(Sailings daily 10am, noon, and 2:15pm; return $16.50.)*

KAPITI COAST

Arcing 32km up the west coast, the Kapiti Coast is Wellington's scenic weekend getaway, a 40min. drive from the city. Stretching from Paekakariki to Otaki, small wildlife sanctuaries, stunning coastline, and wild, bird-filled Kapiti Island draw visitors to the region. While nearly every town has a public beach, Waikanae Beach is the region's finest, with a long stretch of often uncrowded sand. Though Porirua's suburban strips and sheltered inlets are not technically within the boundaries of Kapiti's shore, a couple of stellar hostels and a few diversions make it a comfortable stop along SH1.

KAPITI COAST TRANSPORTATION

TranzMetro (☎ 498 3000, ext. 44933) stops hourly at **Plimmerton** (30min., $4.40), **Paekakariki** (45min., $6), and **Paraparaumu** (1hr., $7.50) on its way north from Wellington. An unlimited day pass will get you anywhere for only $10 (travel must begin after 9am weekdays). Trains run weekdays from 6am to midnight and sporadically through the night on weekends; prices are 25% lower between 9am and 3pm and 20% off for a 10-trip pass. **InterCity/Newmans** buses stop along the **Kapiti Coast** as well, but booking is required. (☎ 472 5111. 9 per day, from $11.) **Mana**

Coach Services (☎ 0800 801 700) operate a number of buses within the Kapiti Coast and Porirua ($1.40-2). There's also a fair amount of regional traffic all the way from Otaki to Paekakariki north of where the Motorway ends. Although one should always consider the risks, **hitchhikers** reportedly have a good chance of bumming a ride on the outskirts of each town.

KAPITI ISLAND ☎ 04

Once the stronghold of Te Rauparaha and an anchorage for whalers, Kapiti Island has been cleansed of introduced mammals as part of a stunning experiment in floral and avian regeneration. A true bird-lover's paradise, Kapiti Island is one of the only wild and accessible places in New Zealand where you're practically guaranteed to see takahe and kaka, whole flocks of melodious tui, and perhaps one of the last saddlebacks or kokako.

Kapiti Island lies about 5km offshore from Paraparaumu Beach; the nature reserve contains toilets, a shelter, three tracks (two to the island's summit and one along the coastline), and no other amenities. **DOC** limits access to the island to 50 people per day and requires a permit ($9, children $4.50); book with the **Wellington Office** (☎ 472 7356; fax 471 2075). Spaces fill up far in advance from December to February, especially during the weekend slots, but there's often last-minute availability on weekdays; in winter, there can be too *few* visitors for the boats to run, and rough seas can bring trips to a halt. **Kapiti Marine Charter** (☎ 297 2585 or 0800 433779; www.kapitimarinecharter.co.nz) and **Kapiti Tours** (☎ 237 7965 or 0800 527 484; www.kapititours.co.nz) both run daily from Paraparaumu Beach to the island (15-20min., 9am and 9:30am, return $30). From Wellington, only the 6:55am **TranzMetro** ($7.50) reaches Paraparaumu in time to catch the 7:55am **Mana Coach** (☎ 0800 801 700; 20min., $1.70) from the railroad station, which is the latest to arrive at Paraparaumu Beach before the 9am boats leave. It's more convenient to spend the previous night on the coast. Visitors are given a nature talk upon arrival and must catch the boats back around 3pm.

PORIRUA AREA AND MANA ISLAND ☎ 04

Splitting the distance between the upper Kapiti Coast and Wellington, Porirua City is centered on a fresh blossom of strip-mall-ification on the edge of Wellington's suburbia proper. The area is saved by its smaller communities and the coast of inlets and bays punctuated by spits and reefs, which harbor Mana Island and the **Pauatahanui Inlet**. The inlet tempers stiff breezes for beginning and intermediate **windsurfers**. **Wildwinds** (☎ 384 1010), near the most inland point of the inlet, offers board rental ($35 per hr.) and 2hr. beginner lessons ($60, including board). Wellington's adventure operators use the inlet for windsurfing and **Titahi Bay** for rock climbing. Among the worthwhile walks in the area is the climb up **Colonial Knob** (return 5-6hr.), which summits the sizeable hill for amazing views from Wellington to the South Island to Taranaki (on a clear day). The **Wairaka Walkway** (one-way 4-5hr.) leaves from the end of Moana Rd. in Plimmerton and follows an oceanside route all the way to Pukerua Bay, where you can catch a train back to the start. The very early Saturday morning **Porirua market** (5-9am) offers everything Polynesian at dirt-cheap prices. Take the TranzMetro to Porirua, and you'll see it by the McDonald's. More information about Porirua can be mined at the **Visitors Center,** under the white canvas mountains at the Cobham Court strip mall. (☎ 237 8088; fax 237 9997; visinfo@pcc.govt.nz. Open M-F 9am-5pm, Sa 7am-4pm, Su 11am-3pm.)

Only 4km offshore from Titahi Bay lies **Mana Island.** Once an integral part of Te Rauparaha and his nephew Te Rangihaeata's domain as well as the site of the first sheep farm in New Zealand, the island is experiencing ecological rebirth through a massive DOC regeneration program. **The Dive Spot** (☎ 233 8238) operates transport to the island (return $25). **Friends of Mana Island** (☎ 292 8582) provides info on the scientific reserve. **Moana Lodge** (see p. 246), in Plimmerton, makes a perfect jump-off point to Mana Island.

PAEKAKARIKI ☎ 04

Meaning "resting place of the green parakeet," Paekakariki has outgrown its name in more ways than one. First, its colorful namesake birds were driven out by European colonization, and, more recently, locals have informally shortened the town's unwieldy name to the more user-friendly "Paekak." Paekakariki's location at the southern point of the Kapiti Coast makes for breathtaking coastal views; if you have your own transport, take **Paekakariki Hill Road,** off SH1, up through a blindingly green valley before turning the corner to a drop-dead view of the Tasman Sea and the entire curve of Kapiti Coast. **Kapiti Island** and the **Marlborough Sounds** float in the distance. A higher-speed craze in Paekakariki is yet another invention in the country's endless search for an adrenaline rush: the **Fly By Wire,** a patented, 12min. thrill ride in an open-air, rocket-like contraption. (☎ 0800 359 299 or 025 300 366; www.flybywire.co.nz. Park at the BP station and walk up a steep dirt path. $99, including video. Open M-F 10:30am-4:30pm, Sa-Su 9:30am-5pm.) Off SH1 at Queen Elizabeth Park is the **Wellington Tramway Museum,** where you can take an old-school ride to the beach on one of Wellington's 19th-century tramcars. (☎ 292 8361. Open Dec.-Jan. Sa-Su 11am-4:30pm. $4, children $2.) A pleasant night or several can be had at Paekak's well-perched **Paekakiriki Backpackers** (see p. 245).

PARAPARAUMU ☎ 04

After the financial, meteorological, and promotional disaster of 2002's New Zealand Open, Paraparaumu (locals say "Paraperam" or "Pram") is saddled with the bill and second thoughts of what could have been. But despondent Paraparaumuans need not look far for ingestive therapy solutions. The #4 Mana Coach delivers passengers to the sweet smells of the **Nyco Chocolate Factory & Shop,** at the corner of SH1 and Raumati Rd. Short tours are a prelude to the free tastings and unlimited shopping and eating. (☎ 299 8098. Tours M-F 10:30am and 2:30pm; $1. Store open M-Sa 9am-5pm, Su 10am-4:30pm.) The **Lindale Centre** serves up free samples of frozen happiness (a.k.a. homemade ice cream) and various Kapiti cheeses. If that doesn't put a cherry on top of your day, then sheep shearing, cow milking, and animal feeding will appeal to your inner farmer. (☎ 297 0916. Ask for free samples. Show and farm walk $10, farm walk only $5. Open daily 9am-5pm.) Just down the road, the **Southward Car Museum** has a collection of vintage autos and motorcycles. You can peek into Marlene Dietrich's custom-made Cadillac or check out the bullet holes in the gangster car. (☎ 297 1221; www.southward.org.nz. Open daily 9am-4:30pm. $5, children $2.) Both Southward and Lindale are on the #75, 76, and 77 local **Mana Coach** routes that continue to Waikanae; #71-74 run from Paraparaumu Centre to its beach. The beach itself is a nice, sheltered stretch of sand.

The **Coastlands** shopping complex, just across from the railroad station, contains a **post office, supermarket,** and **pharmacy.** The **Paraparaumu Information Centre** is an island in the sea of concrete. (☎/fax 298 8195; alison.lowes@clear.net.nz. Open M-Sa 9am-4pm, Su 10am-4pm.) Motels stretch along Kapiti Rd. and down the beachfront. **Barnacles Seaside Inn (BBH) ❸,** 3 Marine Pde., is seaside and relatively cheap. (☎ 902 5856; fax 902 5857; lin&lois@xtra.co.nz. Singles $28, with linen $33; twins and doubles $40/$44.)

TEACHING TRADITION TO TOTS:
New Zealand's *Kohanga Reo* Schools and the Revitalization of *Maori* Language and Culture

It isn't unusual to meet a Kiwi bloke and fail to understand half the words that come out of his mouth. While partly the accent and the unique Kiwi vocabulary, this confusion is often compounded by Maori words that have slipped into everyday New Zealand speech. Newscasters open broadcasts with *kia ora* (hello), students return home to visit their *whanau* (family), and teenagers invite their crushes out for some *kai* (food). The prevalence of Maori language on signs, in publications, and on television makes it hard to believe that in 1960, *te reo Maori* (the Maori language) was pronounced a "relic of ancient Maori life"—a language that was going the way of Latin and Aramaic. Predictions were dire. Maori was "dying."

In the 1960s and 1970s, *te reo* was spoken primarily by the elders within Maori communities. English was becoming the language of choice for young Maori, especially in urban areas. Fewer children and young adults were truly bilingual and speakers of *te reo* were aging. Maori communities were concerned that, within the space of a few generations, knowledge of *te reo* would disappear. Out of this fear, the *kohanga reo* were born.

Kohanga reo, literally "language nests," are community nursery schools, staffed primarily by Maori elders. Their most striking feature is that English is banned at the door. Everything from instruction to playtime to art and music is conducted entirely in *te reo*. The culture, values, and context of the *kohanga reo* mirror modern Maori life—contemporary, but mindful of the culture's traditional roots. Within the centers, *te reo* is used to explore traditional Maori concepts like *mana* (prestige, power) and *aroha* (love) and also to discuss popular culture essentials like the Internet, the X-Box, and Eminem.

Founded in 1981 by the Department of Maori Affairs, the *kohanga reo* program has expanded considerably in recent years. There are now more than 700 *kohanga reo* centers nationwide enrolling more than 13,000 children. Recent government estimates indicate that 9% of students receiving early childhood education are receiving it through a local *kohanga reo*. The ramifications for *te reo* and Maori culture have been profound. In fact, the program has so successfully reintroduced and revitalized the language and its ties to culture and community that it now serves as an exemplar for populations with fading languages across the world, from the Welsh to the Navajo.

In recent years, *kohanga reo* have broadened their mission beyond early childhood education and have become truly inter-generational educational centers. As more and more children became proficient in *te reo*, parents were frustrated by their own lack of fluency. Now night-time, weekend, and longer immersion classes in *te reo* for parents and other adult members of the *tanga whenua* (community) are gathering large audiences. Such classes encourage inter-generational interaction and the speaking of *te reo* on the *marae* (community meeting place) and in the home.

A visit to a *kohanga reo* is a fascinating and rewarding Kiwi experience. The vibrancy of the atmosphere coupled with the children's facility in *te reo* testifies to this unique educational system's efficacy. Most *kohanga reo* are affiliated with local *marae* and trips can often be arranged—be sure to ask before visiting and to observe the proper protocol (if in doubt, just ask). While speaking in English is not appropriate during your visit, one way to engage is to learn a *waiata* (song) to share with the children, or just brush up on a few key phrases and expect gestures to take you the rest of the way. And do expect some incredulous stares—the children often cannot comprehend your inability to converse in *te reo*. During your visit, you may wish to consider a traditional Maori proverb: *Toku reo toku ohooho*—my language, my awakening.

Ann Robinson has made many contributions to Let's Go: New Zealand. She was a researcher-writer for the 2000 and 2002 guides and an editor for the 2001 guide. A recipient of the Fulbright scholarship, she received her Masters in History at Victoria University in Wellington, focusing on comparative US-New Zealand history. Currently, she works as a consultant in Boston.

THE WAIRARAPA ☎ 06

In summer, the Wairarapa buzzes with daytrippers and weekenders from Wellington seeking the solace of its pastoral landscapes and award-winning wines. The vineyard-checkered plains and accompanying yuppies are newcomers to a region of natural austerity. The blocky Tararua Mountains form the North Island's blustery tailbone, while Pacific swells rage and retreat along dramatic, isolated coastal stretches from mighty Castle Rock down to Cape Palliser's prominent lighthouse. Regional transportation is a little pricey, since cars or tour buses are needed to access the coast and wine valley from towns along SH2, but once you're there, attractions are easy on the wallet if not on the liver.

MASTERTON ☎ 06

Hub of the Wairarapa and gateway to the Tararuas, Masterton (pop. 19,800) has outgrown its agricultural roots, but has yet to develop sufficient facilities and accommodations for travelers. One sight that visitors and locals can share is the 32-hectare **Queen Elizabeth Park** on Dixon St. Its suspension bridge, rose gardens, and pedal-boat pond exude tranquility. The recently added skate park does not. On the last weekend in February things become a tad more frenzied as the park is transformed by the **Masterton Wine and Food Festival,** which celebrates the growing fame of the area's vineyards. A bit farther afield, 30km north of Masterton on SH2, the **Mt. Bruce National Wildlife Centre** lets you see a kiwi and a tuatara in the same day, a feat you may not be able to accomplish in the wild. (☎375 8754; www.mtbruce.doc.govt.nz. Open daily 9:30am-4pm; Jan.-Mar. 9am-4:30pm. $8.) Closer to home, the gleaming **Aratoi Museum,** at the corner of Bruce and Dixon St., hosts rotating local exhibits. (☎370 0001. Open daily 10am-4:30pm. Free.) World-class sheep shearers gather and lay everything bare during the **Golden Shears competition** (www.goldenshears.co.nz) held at the end of February.

TranzMetro (☎04 498 3000, ext. 44933) is the only service that runs to **Wellington** (1½hr., 2-5 per day, $11.50). **Tranzit Coachlines** (☎377 1227) goes from the Queen St. terminal to: **Palmerston North** (2hr., 1-2 per day, $17) via **Mt. Bruce Wildlife Centre** (25min., $8); and **Featherston** (40min., $3.50).

Queen Street, which runs parallel to **Chapel Street** (SH2), is home to most of Masterton's cafes, stores, and restaurants. The **Tourism Wairarapa Office,** 5 Dixon St., is at the intersection with Bruce Rd. in front of the park. (☎378 7373; fax 378 7042; tourwai@xtra.co.nz. Open M-F 9am-5pm, Sa-Su 10am-4pm.) Banks with **ATMs** (open M-F 9 or 9:30am-4:30pm) and a **post shop** (in Books & More; open M-F 8am-5pm, Sa 9am-1pm) are located on the upper end of Queen St. The **Empire Lodge ❷,** 94 Queen St., has a central location with rooms that are sunny and cheaper than you'll find at area motels. (☎377 1902; fax 377 2298. Free laundry. Dorms $20-25; singles $55; doubles $70.) On the second floor of the same building, the **Slug and Lettuce ❷** serves an $8 fish platter that contains neither of the restaurant's namesakes. (☎377 3087. Open daily 11:30am-10:30pm.) Alternatively, Queen St. teems with cafes, takeaways, and other small cafeteria-style eateries—**Food for Thought ❶** is one of the best. Sandwiches and fresh muffins go for $2-5. (☎377 5195. Open M-F 7am-5pm, Sa 8am-3pm.) **Woolworth's** supermarket, near the end of Queen St., deals in foodstuffs. (☎377 0050. Open daily 7am-10pm.)

MARTINBOROUGH ☎ 06

Turn up your nose, practice your inquisitive tasting face, and stroll into Martinborough, the major wine village of the Wairarapa. Staged pretensions may find some company here, but the wine culture is not nearly as refined as the wines themselves (including some fine Pinot Noirs). High sunshine and low autumnal rainfall are key elements in cultivating choice vintages from the more than 25 area wineries. The weather also cultivates choice afternoons for visitors, who wander the diagonals of Martinborough's charming square, laid-out by the town's loyal founder in the shape of a Union Jack.

Before embarking on the wine trail, head to the **Martinborough Information Centre,** on Kitchener St. (☎306 9043; fax 306 8033; open daily 10am-4pm), and the **Tourism Wairarapa Office** in Masterton; they provide maps and information for your drinking pleasure. Some well-respected, year-round wineries are the **Palliser Estate,** on Kitchener St. (☎306 9019; open daily 10:30am-4pm), **Martinborough Vineyard,** on Princess St. (☎306 9955; tastings daily 11am-5pm), and **Te Kairanga Vineyard,** on Martins Rd. (☎306 9122; tours Sa-Su 2pm). The **Martinborough Country Fair** draws huge Wellington crowds (1st Sa of Feb. and Mar.), while **Toast Martinborough** (☎306 9183; www.toastmartinborough.co.nz; 3rd Su in Nov.) sells you the proverbial bottomless glass, providing a "staggering" opportunity to sample the region's best. If you are short on time or transport, the **Martinborough Wine Centre,** 6 Kitchener St. (☎306 9040; www.martinboroughwinecentre.co.nz), assembles the best regional vintages in one central location.

To get to Martinborough, **Wairarapa Coach Lines** (☎378 2961 or 0800 666 355) connects to Masterton and meets most commuter trains in Featherston. Prior booking is essential. **Tranzit Coachlines** also connects with **TranzMetro's** weekend service to offer wine tour shuttles and packages (☎0800 843 596; return from $30). For a bed, try Featherston, where the **Leeway Motel ❷,** 8 Fitzherbert St., near the train station, gives you some of its namesake with flexible, well-maintained rooms. (☎308 9811 or 0800 533 929; stop@leeway-complex.co.nz. 2-bed dorms $20; motel units from $68; tent sites $10.) A huge, battered-looking building, the **Fareham House ❸,** 1km from town up Wakefield St., serves a full breakfast to guests, who sleep in named rooms. The large dorm room is a plain, partitioned old schoolhouse for the intrepid only. (☎308 9074. Rooms $30-35 per person; "bunkroom" $15.)

TARARUA FOREST PARK ☎06

There are some great hikes off the tourist radar in Tararua Forest Park, though severe wind and mist have made this region famous for capricious weather. Covering 117,225 hectares and 75% of the Tararua Range, it was the first forest park established in New Zealand. Marked tracks meander through beech forests, alpine grasslands, and even leatherwood shrublands. The popular **Mt. Holdsworth-Jumbo Tramp** (24km, 2-3 days) begins at **Mt. Holdsworth Lodge,** 20min. west of Masterton, and climbs up through bush to an exposed alpine ridge before winding back to the lodge (huts $8; tent sites $4). The Class 2 **Waiohine River** runs though the Waiohine Gorge in the southeastern part of the Tararuas. A large swing bridge crosses the river by the carpark for the camping and recreation areas nearby, surrounded by rimu, beech, rata, and kahikatea trees. From there, the **Loop Track** (return 1½hr.) crosses through regenerating bush, while the **Cone Hut Track** (return 6hr.) climbs to a terrace of the **Tauherenikau River.** Though the **Holdsworth Road,** off SH2 just south of Masterton, and the **Waiohine Gorge Road,** just south of Carterton, are the park's main eastern access points, **Kiriwhakapapa Road,** just south of Mt. Bruce, and **Otaki Gorge Road,** on the east side, also lead to trailheads. Get **hut tickets** from the local **DOC** in Masterton on South Rd. across from the Aerodrome (☎377 0700; open M-F 8am-5pm), the Holdsworth ranger (☎377 0022), or local visitors centers.

PALMERSTON NORTH ☎06

Around 40% of Palmerston North's 75,000 residents are involved in higher education, giving credence to its nickname, "Knowledge City." Home to Massey University, New Zealand's second-largest university, and a host of other schools, "Palmy" is more of a transport hub than a top destination.

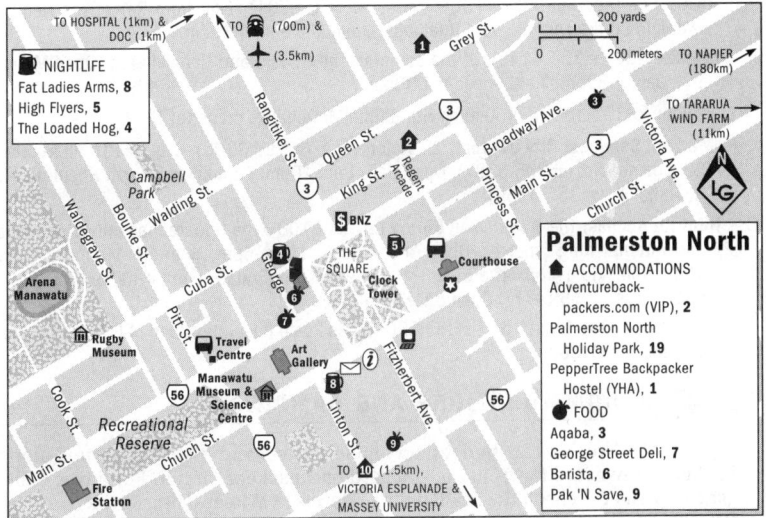

TRANSPORTATION

Trains: TranzScenic (☎0800 802 802) leaves from the Railway Station on Matthews Ave. off Tremaine Ave., a 20min. walk from The Square. Trains leave daily for: **Auckland** (8½hr.; 10:57am and 10:09pm; $104-116) via **National Park** ($42-46) and **Hamilton** ($79-89); **Napier** (3hr., 10:14am, $47); and **Wellington** (2hr., 3 per day, $30-33). **TranzMetro** (☎04 801 7000) runs to **Wellington** M-F via the **Kapiti Coast**.

Buses: Buses leave from the **Travel Centre** at Pitt and Main St. (☎355 5633). **InterCity/Newman's** goes to: **New Plymouth** (4hr., 2-3 per day, $42) via **Wanganui** (1½hr., $18); **Wellington** (2hr., 2-3 per day, $27); **Auckland** (8-10hr., 2-4 per day, $72); **Masterton** (1¾hr., 1-2 per day, $17); and **Rotorua** (5hr., 2 per day, $57) via **Taupo** (4hr., $44). **Guthreys** (☎0800 759 999) runs to **Auckland, Rotorua, Napier, Taupo,** and **Wellington** at comparable prices. **White Star** (☎358 8777) leaves from the courthouse on Main St. and runs to: **Wellington** (2hr., 1-2 per day, $18); and **New Plymouth** (4hr., 1-2 per day, $32) via **Wanganui** (1hr., $13) and **Stratford** (3¼hr., $26).

Taxis: Palmerston North Taxis (☎355 5333) and **Gold & Black** (☎355 5059).

Hitchhiking: Thumbers report finding rides along any of the main roads. Rangitikei St. joins SH1 at Bulls, heading toward the volcanic heartland and Auckland. Napier Rd./SH3 (Main St. E) heads to Napier. Pioneer Highway (further along Main St. W) and Fitzherbert St. both head to Wellington.

ORIENTATION AND PRACTICAL INFORMATION

Downtown is centered around **The Square,** Palmerston North's well-kept green space. **Rangitikei Street** heads north, while **Fitzherbert Avenue** leads south toward the Manawatu River. **Main** and **Church Streets** head east and west from The Square.

Visitors Center: Destination Manawatu Visitor Centre, Square Edge Building, The Square (☎354 6593; fax 356 9841; manawatu.visitor-info@xtra.co.nz). Open M-F 9am-5pm, Sa-Su 10am-3pm.

DOC: 717 Tremaine Ave. (☎350 9700; fax 350 9701), 1km from Rangitikei. Helpful with info on the Tararuas and Ruahines. Open M-F 8am-4:30pm.

Banks: BNZ (☎358 4149), at the corner of The Square and Rangitikei St. Open M and Th-F 9am-4:30pm, Tu-W 9:30am-4:30pm.

Police: (☎351 3600), on Church St., off the McDonald's corner of The Square.

Medical Services: City Doctors, 22 Victoria Ave. (☎355 3300). **City Health Pharmacy,** 22 Victoria Ave. (☎355 5287). Open daily 8am-10pm. **Palmerston North Hospital,** 50 Ruahine St. (☎356 9169).

Internet Access: The $13 million **library** (☎351 4100), The Square, has **public showers** and Internet for $5 per hr. Open M-Tu and Th 10am-6pm, W and F 10am-8pm, Sa 10am-4pm, Su 1-4pm. **iCafe** (☎353 7889), at The Square and Fitzherbert Ave., has fast access for $5 per hr. Open daily 9am-11pm.

Post Office: 338 Church St. (☎353 6900), has Poste Restante. Open M-F 7:30am-6pm, Sa 9:30am-12:30pm.

ACCOMMODATIONS AND CAMPING

Palmerston North's few budget accommodations and plentiful motels along Fitzherbert Ave. are far from the standard backpackers' circuit. For a true collegiate experience, check the availability of dorms at **Massey University.** (☎350 5056; fax 350 5675; k.l.macey@massey.ac.nz. Singles from $30.)

PepperTree Backpacker Hostel (YHA), 121 Grey St. (☎355 4054; fax 355 4063; peppertreehostel@clear.net.nz), at the corner of Princess and Grey St. Host Cherie holds a standard of excellence that makes PepperTree the best and busiest in town. Free bike use. Dorms $17; singles $30; twins and doubles $40; tent sites $8. ❷

Palmerston North Holiday Park, 133 Dittmer Dr. (☎/fax 358 0349). From Fitzherbert Ave.; take Park Rd. towards the Esplanade, turn left on Ruha St., and go into the park. Suburban with clean facilities. Tent and powered sites $10; cabins $28-55 for 2. ❶

Adventurebackpackers.com (VIP), 95 King St. (☎/fax 358 9595). The spaces in this recently renovated hostel are plain and dark, but the location is right and the friendly host might help you get a discounted rafting or canyoning trip. Free pick-up from town, $4 from airport. Internet. Linen $3. 14-bed dorms $15; singles $25; twins and doubles $35-40. ❷

FOOD

Knowledge City needs food for thought, and food it has. **George Street,** home to funky cafes with long hours and affordable eats, is worth a wander. Stock up on groceries at **Pak 'N Save,** 335 Ferguson St. (☎356 4043. Open daily 8am-midnight).

Barista, 77 George St. (☎357 2614). A gem on George St.'s stretch of cool cafes. Start the day right with Barista's superb coffee ($2.50) and the "heart stopper" ($15), a smorgasbord of all your favorite breakfast goodies. Open daily 6:30am-midnight. ❷

George Street Deli (☎357 6663), at the corner of George and Main St. More of a cafe than a deli, squeeze between the colorful walls to witness a stream of hungry folks devouring quality eats ($4-10). Open M-F 6am-5pm, Sa-Su 6am-4pm. ❶

Aqaba, 186 Broadway Ave. (☎357 8922). Don't let the decor fool you; the menu holds no national allegiance. Suits, students, and families enjoy affordable dishes (most $11-20) in the airy environs. Open M-F 7:30am-late, Sa-Su 9am-late. ❸

NIGHTLIFE

Palmerston North nightlife can get lively during the school year, although "nightlife" is a loosely defined—on rugby Saturdays, drinking starts at 3pm or earlier.

High Flyers (☎ 357 5155), at the corner of Main St. E and The Square, "where everybody is somebody." A fashion-savvy crowd boogies down to DJs Th-Sa. Dress code enforced. Open daily 11am-3am.

Fat Ladies Arms (☎ 358 8888), at the corner of Church and Linton St. Despite the rather unpleasant image the name inspires, Fat Ladies throbs with a lively university crowd who can't resist the W-Sa DJs or $3 Th drinks. Open Tu-F 4pm-3am, Sa 2pm-3am.

The Loaded Hog (☎ 356 5417), at the corner of George St. and Coleman Pl. You can dance, drink, or enjoy $5 breakfasts (Sa-Su 10am-noon) and $5 lunches (M-F 11am-noon). Open M-F 11am-late, Sa-Su 10am-late; kitchen closes at 10pm.

SIGHTS AND ACTIVITIES

Paying homage to the pinnacle of sport, one block north and several west of The Square, is the **New Zealand Rugby Museum**, 87 Cuba St. Quite the shrine for die-hard fanatics of The Game, this two-room gallery is plastered with uniform displays, trophies, and memorabilia, including one of the world's oldest remaining jerseys. (☎ 358 6947; www.rugbymuseum.co.nz. Open daily 1-4:30pm; also M-Sa 10am-noon. $4.) On Saturdays in winter, you can watch the real thing at the outdoor **Arena Manawatu** next door. The beautiful **Victoria Esplanade** (walk down Fitzherbert Ave. and turn right on Manawaroa St.) is a horticultural pleasure, with a conservatory, rose garden, miniature railway ($1), and paddling pool. (☎ 356 8199. Open daily 8am-9pm; in winter 8am-6pm.)

For more traditional cultural pursuits, disregard the oversized bronze beetles creeping over the roof of the **Manawatu Art Gallery**, 398 Main St. W, and venture inside to view contemporary works by New Zealand artists. (☎ 358 8188. Free.) The gallery is part of the **Te Manawa** complex, which includes the **Manawatu Museum** and **Science Centre**, with rotating exhibits and interactive science displays. (☎ 355 5000. All open 10am-5pm. Free except Science Centre $6, students $4.) **City Rock Adventures**, 217 Featherston St., has indoor **rock climbing** and will organize trips to go caving, canyoning, kayaking, and even bridge-swinging. (☎ 357 4552. Climbing $11; other activities from $15. Open M-F 3:30-10pm, Sa-Su 10am-10pm.) **Manawatu Gorge Adventures** is one of several outfitters that show visitors the region's wetter side, either by jetboat or kayak. (☎ 0800 746 888. From $55.)

MARLBOROUGH AND NELSON

Stretching from the tip of Farewell Spit to the tranquil Marlborough Sounds and from the marine paradise of Kaikoura to the secluded Nelson Lakes, the "top of the South" provides an incredible variety of natural gems and endless ways to appreciate them. Popular yet pristine, the region offers travelers a choice between taking full advantage of the well-developed tourism infrastructure or escaping it all in the majestic seclusion of the Sounds. Whether it's soaking in a hot spring, tasting award-winning wine, swimming with playful dolphins, or hiking through fern-filled forests, Marlborough will inspire a love of nature and the fruits of its vines.

■ MARLBOROUGH AND NELSON HIGHLIGHTS

IT'S ALL WET in **Kaikoura,** where visitors can swim with dolphins, frolic with seals, and search for surfacing whales (see p. 273).

IT'S ALL AFLOAT in the **Marlborough Sounds,** with many of the best hostels and lodges accessible only by water-taxi (see p. 267).

IT'S ALL ON YOUR BACK... along the **Abel Tasman Coastal Track,** with terrain ranging from verdant rain forest to golden beaches (see p. 288).

OR NOT... along the **Queen Charlotte Track,** where you can have all your bags carried for you (see p. 269).

MARLBOROUGH

PICTON ☎ 03

In Picton, sea-wearied European sheep first stepped on Kiwi soil nearly 150 years ago. Today, starry-eyed travelers, arriving from Wellington on the Interislander ferry, tread their first path on the South Island. Sitting at the head of the dramatic Queen Charlotte Sound, Picton is often a way-station for travelers switching islands or switching gears between traveling and tramping.

▐▀ TRANSPORTATION

Flights: The **Koromiko airstrip** is about 9km away. **Sounds Air** (☎ 520 3080 or 0800 505 005) has daily flights to **Wellington** (25min., up to 8 per day 8:40am-7:10pm, $49-79) and a free shuttle to and from the airstrip in Picton.

Trains: TranzScenic (☎ 573 8649 or 0800 802 802) offers service to **Christchurch** (5hr., 1 per day, $54-77) via **Kaikoura** (2½hr., $29-42).

Buses: InterCity (☎ 573 7025) leaves from the ferry terminal for **Christchurch** (5½hr., 2 per day, $30-44) via **Blenheim** (30min., $10) and **Kaikoura** (2¼hr., $35); and **Nelson** (2½hr., 4 per day, $15-22).

Ferries: Interislander Ferry (☎ 04 498 3302 or 0800 802 802) leaves from the **Foreshore** for **Wellington** (3hr., 3-5 per day, $36-52). **The Lynx** takes just over 2hr. (2-4 per day, $47-68).

Taxis: Colin's Picton Taxis Ltd. (☎ 573 8993).

Car Rental: Rent a car from any of the many companies located at the ferry terminal.

264 ■ MARLBOROUGH

ORIENTATION AND PRACTICAL INFORMATION

Home to the ferry terminal and other crucial transport links, the whole area lining the harbor is known as the **Foreshore**. **Auckland Street** is the hub of transport in Picton, while **High Street** is home to **Mariner's Mall** and many of the town's shops and cafes. Residential neighborhoods stretch up into the hills.

Visitors Center: Picton Visitor Information Centre (☎ 573 8857; fax 573 8858; pictonvin@xtra.co.nz), inside the railway station on Auckland St. near the Foreshore. Open

Jan.-Feb. daily 8:30am-8pm; Mar.-Apr. and Oct.-Dec. 8:30am-6pm; May-Sept. 8:30am-5pm. The **DOC office** (☎ 520 3007) is also inside. Open M-F 8:30am-4:30pm.

Banks and Currency Exchange: BNZ, 56-8 High St., has an **ATM.** Open M, Th, and F 9am-4:30pm, Tu-W 9:30am-4:30pm. **Four Square supermarket,** 49 High St. (☎ 573 6443), will change money after hours. Open daily 7:30am-9pm.

Police: 36 Broadway St. (☎ 573 6439).

Pharmacy: Rob Roy's Pharmacy, 6 High St. (☎ 573 6420). Open M-F 9am-6pm, Sa 9am-2pm; extended hours in summer.

Medical Services: Picton Medical Centre, 71 High St. (☎ 573 6092, after hours 577 1941). Open M-F 8:30am-5:30pm, Sa 9am-noon.

Internet Access: United Video, 61 High St. (☎ 573 7466; open daily 9am-8:30pm), for $6 per hr. The **library,** 67 High St. (☎ 520 3200; open M-Th 8am-5pm, F 8am-5:30pm, Sa 10am-noon), charges $2 per 15min.

Post Office: (☎ 573 6900), Mariner's Mall on High St. Open Oct.-Apr. M-F 8:30am-5pm, Sa 9:30am-12:30pm; May-Sept. M-F 8:30am-5pm, Sa 10am-noon.

ACCOMMODATIONS AND CAMPING

The Villa Backpackers Lodge (BBH), 34 Auckland St. (☎/fax 573 6598; www.thevilla.co.nz). Unexpected bonuses raise this restored villa from standard to stellar—free pick-up, free breakfast, free apple crumble with ice cream in the winter, and free use of bicycles and fishing gear. All you can eat veggie soup during the winter $2. Internet. Spa $2. Book in advance. Dorms $20-21; twins and doubles $49. ❷

Sequoia Lodge, 3a Nelson Sq. (☎/fax 573 8399 or 0800 222 257; stay@sequoia-lodge.co.nz). This comfortable and eye-catching hostel relieves stomach grumblings with nightly servings of fresh bread. Large homey common room. Free pick-up and drop-off. Dorms $18; twins and doubles $48. ❷

The Jugglers' Rest Backpackers (BBH), 8 Canterbury St. (☎/fax 573 5570; jugglers-rest@xtra.co.nz). The owners (3 professional jugglers) give free daily juggling workshops as well as fire-eating lessons by request. Free pick-up and drop-off, tea and coffee, and use of bikes. Dorms $18, in winter $16; twins and doubles with linen $45/$40. Juggle 4 balls and get a $1 discount, 5 balls for $2, 6 balls for $3.... ❷

Bayview Backpackers and Lodge (BBH), 318 Waikawa Rd. (☎/fax 573 7668; www.truenz.co.nz/bayviewbackpackers). A 4km trek from Picton, you won't find better views anywhere in town. Free pick-up and drop-off, kayaks, rowboat, fishing gear, and bread in winter. Dorms $15-18; singles $25; twins and doubles $38. ❷

The Wedgewood House (YHA), 10 Dublin St. (☎ 573 7797; fax 573 6426; wedgewood-house@xtra.co.nz). This sterile lodge has a large wooden porch and a minuscule kitchen. Free in-room lockers and duvets. Reception 8-10am, 1-2pm, 5-6:30pm, and 8-10pm. Dorms $17; twins $20. ❷

Picton Lodge (VIP), 9 Auckland St. (☎ 573 7788 or 0800 223 367; fax 573 8418; www.pictonlodge.co.nz). The closest hostel to the ferry, crash here before heading north or south. Bikes. Internet. Dorms $17; singles $31; twins and doubles $44. ❷

Blue Anchor Top 10 Holiday Park, 78 Waikawa Rd. (☎/fax 573 7212 or 0800 277 299; 2stay@blueanchor.co.nz). Clean and modern cabins offer privacy and comfort. Standard cabins $35 for 2, with kitchen $48; units $60 for 2, extra adult $15; powered sites $11 per person ($15 for 1); tent village $10 per adult, $6 per child. ❶

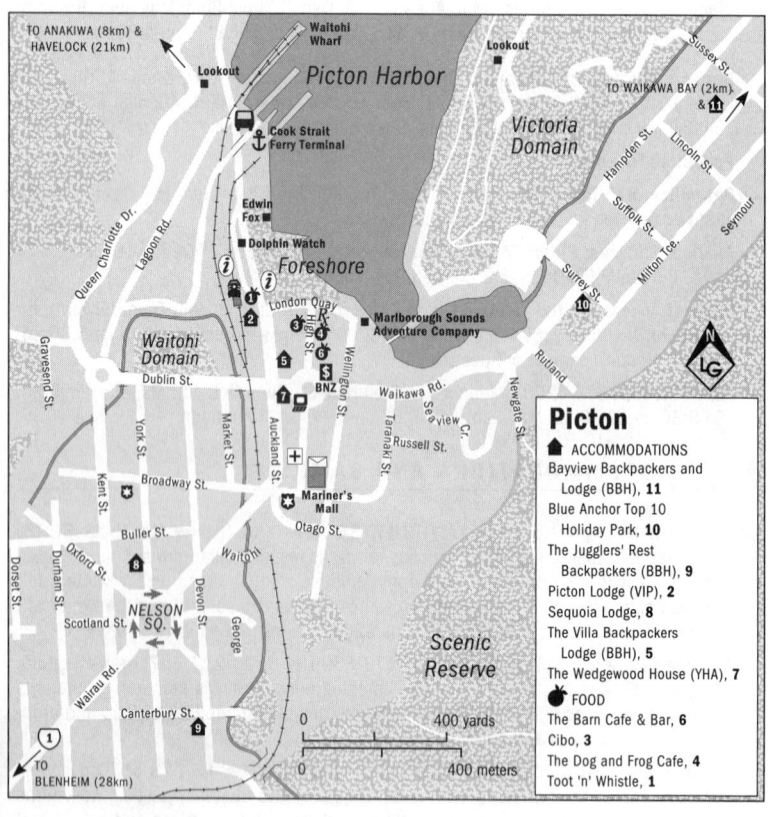

FOOD

Picton is small enough to wander, with **High Street** acting as home to a variety of restaurants. **Supervalue,** in the **Mariner's Mall** is chock full of groceries. (☎573 0463. Open M-W 8am-6pm, Th 8am-7:30pm, F 8am-8:30pm, Sa 8am-7pm, Su 9am-5pm.)

Cibo, 33 High St. (☎573 7171). Sit at the funky carved table and enjoy a rotating menu, which includes tapas ($3.50-12), veggie options, and tasty deserts. Mains ($12-20). Open daily 9am-8:30pm. ❸

The Barn Cafe & Bar, (☎573 7440), on High St. Country music completes the feel. Veggie options ($9.50-16). Open daily 4:30-10pm. ❷

The Dog and Frog Cafe, 22 High St. (☎573 5650), contains a scattering of amphibious statues and canine pictures to complement the all-day breakfast ($10.50), sweet treats ($5.50), and fish 'n' chips ($11). Open daily 8am-late. ❷

Toot 'n' Whistle, 7 Auckland St. (☎573 6086), near the Visitors Center. A smoky diner and bar with a friendly, laid-back atmosphere and a broad menu. All-day breakfast. Meals from $8. Open daily 7am-late; in winter from 9am. ❷

SIGHTS AND ACTIVITIES

Many visitors to Picton come to tramp the 71km **Queen Charlotte Track** (see p. 269). The trailheads are inaccessible from town by foot, but several transportation services cater to those wishing to approach by boat. (See **Marlborough Sounds: Transportation,** p. 267.) Picton also has some great day hikes which look out over the harbor, Pine Bay, and Waikawa Bay. Cross the parking lot and the footbridge to get to the walks from Wellington St. The **Victoria Domain** (return 3hr.) leads up to the lookout over the Scenic Reserve and continues out to "The Snout" and the **Queen Charlotte Lookout** (return 4hr.).

Picton retains vestiges of its dignified history all about town. The **Edwin Fox,** the oldest wooden merchant ship in the world, greets arrivals at the Foreshore. Built in 1853 in Calcutta, it transported tea to London, British immigrants to New Zealand, convicts to Australia, and troops to Europe during the Crimean War. Claiming a brief but well-deserved rest in dry dock, it is now an informative exhibit at the **Edwin Fox Maritime Centre,** which chronicles the ship's history and details plans for its eventual restoration. (☎573 6868. Open daily 8:45am-5pm. $5.) Wine connoisseurs can explore the Marlborough region's famous **wineries** by bus through **De Luxe Travel Lines** (☎0800 500 511; $49) or **The Sounds Connection** (☎573 8843 or 0800 742 866; $45 half-day, $55 full-day). **Marlborough Sounds Adventure Company,** at the Waterfront, rents mountain bikes and kayaks (☎0800 283 283).

MARLBOROUGH SOUNDS ☎03

A grand maze of waterways at the South Island's northeastern extremity, the Marlborough Sounds harbor ample sea life and green peaks amid thousands of beautiful coves. Day activities run from Picton, but the multi-day **Queen Charlotte Track** (see p. 269) is the most well-known and well-tramped attraction. Whether you actually backpack, or just laze around one of the lovely and secluded backpackers, you will not leave the Marlborough Sounds disappointed.

TRANSPORTATION. All transport departs from the **Foreshore** in Picton, between Wellington St. and the footbridge. **Ferry** services provide the most transport around the sounds. **The Cougar Line** (☎573 7925 or 0800 504 090) goes to various points along the Queen Charlotte Track (3 per day, $48); they also arrange full return transport for the entire track ($58-65). **Endeavour Express** (☎579 8465) offers transport to stops along the track ($45) as well as round-trip transport with 3 free pack transfers ($50). **West Bay Water Transport** (☎/fax 573 5597) runs four times daily to: **Torea Wharf** ($15); **Lochmara Lodge** ($15); **Te Mahia Resort** ($15); and **Anakiwa** ($20). **Beachcomber Cruises** (☎573 6175 or 0800 624 526) drops people off for day walks at **Ship Cove, Torea Wharf,** and **Mistletoe Bay** ($30-45); they also offer a return ticket for overnight trampers ($50).

Some areas in the Sounds are also road-accessible; the scenic and sealed 35km **Queen Charlotte Drive** connects Picton and Havelock. While there are always risks involved, **hitchhikers** report that the drive attracts a fair amount of through-traffic, though the same cannot be said of the north-bound routes.

ACCOMMODATIONS AND CAMPING. Accommodations are scattered throughout the Sounds; many are outstanding, but two in particular combine a laid-back, uncommercial aura with a load of free activities and low rates. **The Chill Inn (BBH) ❷,** 770 Queen Charlotte Dr., 8km toward Picton from Havelock, embodies relaxation. The hammock-speckled balcony affords outstanding views over Kenepuru Sound (a 5min. walk away), while the sunny lounge amuses with

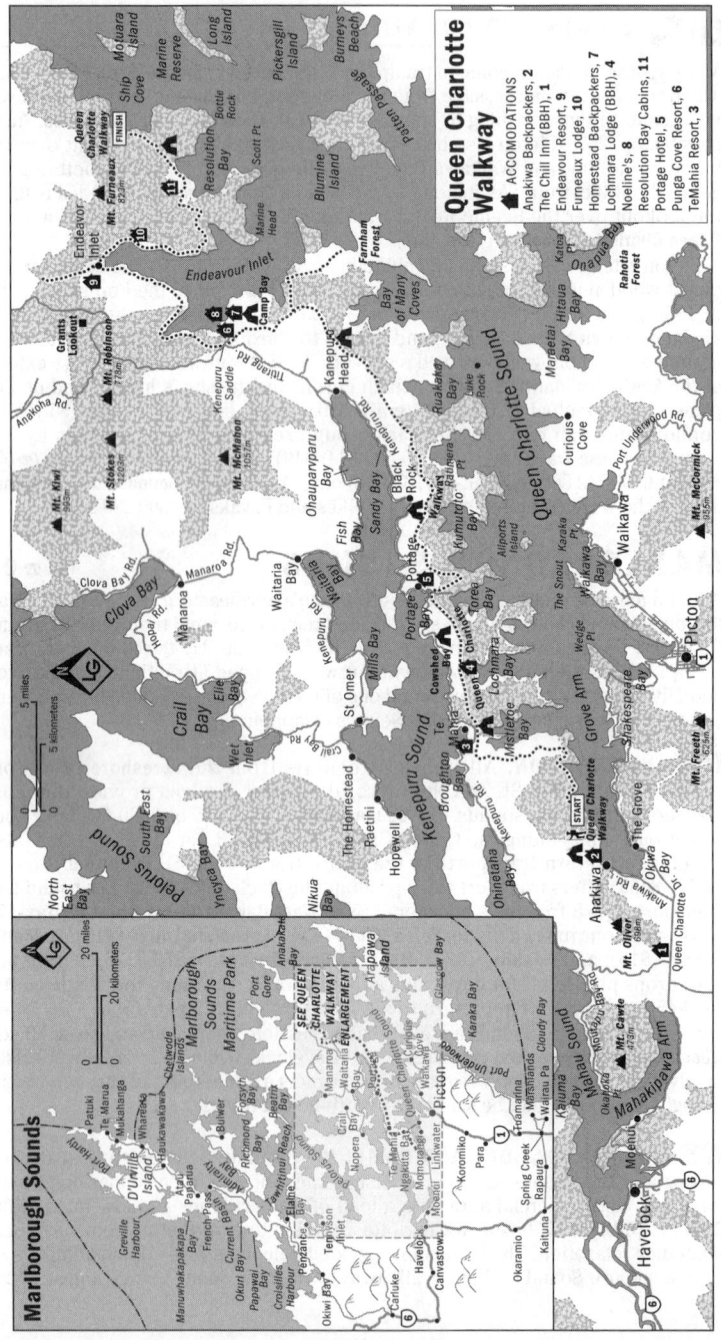

games and guitars. Car-less travelers should come prepared with food. (☎ 574 1299 or 025 606 2684; thechillinn@hotmail.com. Free breakfast. Free shuttle from Havelock or Anakiwa. Internet. Spa. Bikes. Kayaks. Closed July-Aug. Dorms $20; doubles $52.) **Lochmara Lodge (BBH)** ❸ sits on more than 10 acres of native bush, with hammocks and tree carvings scattered throughout. Free use of sea kayaks, windsurfer, rowboat, and snorkeling gear, and a rope swing over the water make for fun-filled days; a guitar, spa ($2), and resident glowworms take care of the nights. (☎/fax 573 4554; www.lochmaralodge.co.nz. Tiny shop. Closed June-Sept. Call ahead to arrange transport. Return water taxi from Picton $30. Dorms $22; doubles with bath $60-80; self-contained cabins $120 for 2, extra person $20.)

DOC maintains 40 **campsites** ($5 per person, under 14 $2.50) throughout the Sounds. Some are near roads and tend to get crowded, while others are accessible only by boat and feel as though they're at the end of the earth. All have toilets and untreated water supplies. *The Marlborough Sounds: A Guide to Conservation Areas* pamphlet ($1), available at area DOC offices, contains a complete listing.

OUTDOOR ACTIVITIES. Sea kayaking allows the freedom to explore the curving coastline, tranquil inlets, and hidden accommodations, while **mountain biking** lets you zoom through the Queen Charlotte Track or access backcountry trails. **Marlborough Sounds Adventure Company** (☎ 573 6078 or 0800 283 283; www.marlboroughsounds.co.nz), on the waterfront in Picton, rents single and double kayaks to a minimum of two people (1-day $50 per person, multi-day $35-40 per day per person) and mountain bikes ($40 per day). Their guided kayak trips range from one-day tours ($85, includes lunch) to all-inclusive three-night expeditions ($475). **Sea Kayaking Adventure Tours** (☎ 574 2765; www.marlborough.co.nz/sea-kayak), based in Anakiwa, also rents kayaks ($40 per day, $35 per day after 3 days) and mountain bikes ($40 per day), and runs guided kayak trips (1-day $65, 3-day $280). **Sea Kayaking Wilderness Co.** (☎ 574 2610; www.soundswild.com), based in Havelock, rents kayaks (1-day $50; 4 days $150) and conducts guided tours (1-day with lunch $75; multi-day self-catering $95 per day, catered $140 per day).

Diver's World (☎ 573 7323), across London Quay from the Visitors Center, organizes shore dives into the Queen Charlotte Sound. (Shore dive to 1 wreck with equipment $59, boat dive to 2 wrecks with equipment $145. Open Water certification Course $399.) **Dolphin Watch Marlborough,** next to the Visitors Center in Picton, runs eco-tours to bird life sanctuary **Motuara Island** and historic **Ship Cove,** encountering penguins and dolphins along the way. (☎ 573 8040; www.dolphinwatchmarlborough.co.nz. $65, under 18 $35.) If you've ever dreamed of being a postman, **Beachcomber Cruises** (see **Transportation,** p. 267) takes travelers on the **mail runs** to Queen Charlotte (4-5hr.; M-Sa 1:30pm; $58, under 15 free) or Pelorus Sound (6+hr.; Tu and Th-F mid-morning; $90, under 15 free).

QUEEN CHARLOTTE TRACK

Trumpeted for its green-and-blue beauty, the **Queen Charlotte Track** is a pleasant outdoor experience, if not a rugged wilderness adventure. Along its vista-filled path above the Queen Charlotte and Kenepuru Sounds, signs of development abound—sheep graze on either side, boats buzz through the waters below, and a string of private accommodations welcomes weary travelers. Thanks in large part to this proximity to civilization, the Queen Charlotte is the only track in New Zealand where even trampers on a budget can have their gear transported for them. While a die-hard survivalist may be disappointed, outdoor enthusiasts will welcome the baggage transport as an opportunity to **run** or **mountain bike** the trail.

Length: 67km, 3-5 days.

Trailheads: The track runs between **Ship Cove** in the east and **Anakiwa** in the west; water taxis and luggage transport encourage traveling from east to west.

Transportation: A variety of ferry companies based in Picton will deliver you out to Ship Cove, transport your bag down the track, and pick you up in Anakiwa (see **Transportation,** p. 267). To access Anakiwa from Havelock, the **Havelock Outdoors Center** (☎574 2114) will transport up to 8 people for $40. They will also do pick-ups from Anakiwa.

Seasonality: Year-round. The section between Ship Cove and Kenepuru Saddle **closes to mountain bikes Dec.-Feb.,** the busiest walking season. **Droughts** can present the largest obstacle to traveling the trail.

Campsites & Accommodations: 7 **DOC campsites** vary widely in amenities and seclusion ($5 per night). No huts. For those less bent on tents, numerous **private seaside establishments** provide a variety of dorms and double rooms.

Gear Rental: If you need to hire gear or a mountain bike, contact **Marlborough Sounds Adventure Company** (see **Outdoor Activities,** p. 269). 2-person tent $10 per night, bed roll $1 per night, stove with fuel $5 per day, plates and cutlery $4 per day, day-packs $5 per day, sleeping bags $3 per night, camp set for 2 (tent, bed rolls, stove, cutlery) $15 per night.

Storage: Most accommodations in Picton store for free; the Visitors Center charges $4 per bag per night.

SHIP COVE TO RESOLUTION BAY CABINS. *4.5km, 1½hr.* Ship Cove's **Captain Cook Monument** commemorates the many weeks the great navigator spent anchored here on five separate visits, harvesting scurvy-fighting grass for his crew and flogging those who refused it. As the track climbs steeply over a small saddle, it passes through the walkway's finest primary forest. Five minutes off the track, **School House Bay Campsite** has spare and sloping sites on Resolution Bay. Farther downhill, life flows slowly at the rambling bungalows of **Resolution Bay Cabins ❶**, where the shop is always open but better stocked in the summer. (☎579 9411. Free use of kayaks. Linen $5. No electricity. Basic bunks $25 for the 1st night, $20 each additional night; cottages $70-110; tent sites $10.)

RESOLUTION BAY CABINS TO ENDEAVOUR INLET. *10.5km, 2¼hr.* Past Resolution Bay, the track undulates along to **Furneaux Lodge ❶**, where tidy lawns slope down to the sound. (☎579 8259. Restaurant. Kayaks $15-18 per hr. Rowboat $10 per hr. Dorms $18; doubles $50; tent sites $10.) Just past the lodge turn-off, the **Waterfall Walk** (return 1hr.) leads through a tall rimu-filled forest to a small cascade. The area's other accommodation option is **Endeavour Resort ❷**, where stunning gardens liven the small basic cabins. (☎579 8381. Free use of canoes. Dorms $20; double cabins $70.)

ENDEAVOUR INLET TO CAMP BAY CAMPSITE. *13km, 3-3½hr.* At the head of Endeavor Inlet, a steep spur trail climbs into the bush to great views by the long-unused **antimony mines** (return 3½hr.). As the main track rounds **Big Bay,** its surroundings alternate between towering tree ferns and developed grazing land. After arriving in **Camp Bay,** a DOC campsite, a side trail leads to two excellent accommodations; both are road-accessible. **Punga Cove Resort ❸** offers family-style luxury, with a pool, spa, and beach-side trampoline. (☎579 8561. Restaurant. Kayaks $15 per hr. Dorms with linen $35.) Funky **Homestead Backpackers ❷** (☎579 8373) occupies a great 1908 beachside building, with sunny deck dorms ($18), gypsy-themed caravans ($17 per person, no power), romantic doubles ($45-50), and a fire-warmed outdoor bathtub. Up a little hill, **Noeline's ❷** is a fresh and intimate place with six beds (four in the winter) and wide views. Charming world-traveler Noeline and Penny, the possum-catching lapdog, disarm guests with beaming hospitality and grandmotherly care. (☎579 8375. Linen $5. 2-bed dorms $18.)

CAMP BAY CAMPSITE TO PORTAGE HOTEL AND COWSHED BAY CAMPSITE.

20.5km, 6hr. Trampers can reach **Kenepuru Saddle** via a 15min. scramble from Camp Bay Campsite or a slightly longer track up an unsealed road from Homestead Backpackers. From the saddle, the track travels through scrubby vegetation before reaching the steep spur to **Eatwells Lookout** (15min.), a nearly 360° panorama. A half hour of rolling track later, the **Bay of Many Coves Campsite** has lofty sea views and bumpy, kanuka-sheltered plots. Boat companies will not be able to deliver packs here until Kiwi ingenuity perfects a high-precision baggage cannon.

From here, the track encounters some of its beautiful trademark vistas, which encompass both Queen Charlotte and Kenepuru Sounds. **Black Rock Campsite**, another boat-inaccessible spot, has small, grassy sites, plus a handsome cooking gazebo that overlooks Kumutoto Bay and Picton.

Although it continues to roll, the trail slowly descends to **Torea Saddle.** A 10min. walk down the road north of the saddle sits the snazzy **Portage Hotel ❸**, with its restaurant, swimming pool, and flashy rooms. (☎ 573 4309. Dorms $25, with linen $35.) Nearby, **Cowshed Bay Campsite** is a bayside but caravan-heavy complex with major road access. Water-taxis don't deliver gear to the campsite or the hotel, since they sit on the Kenepuru (rather than Queen Charlotte) Sound; the hotel picks up luggage from Torea Wharf and brings it over the Saddle (return $4 per bag).

COWSHED BAY CAMPSITE TO MISTLETOE BAY RESERVE.

7.5km, 2½hr. Prepare yourself for a long ascent as you truck from sea level back up onto the saddle. Once you've regained the ridgeline, the track traverses many switchbacked ups and downs and passes the steep turn-off to **Lochmara Lodge** (one-way 40min.; see **Accommodations and Camping,** p. 267). A side-trip to **Hilltop Lookout** (return 40min.), which showcases great views over Kenepuru Sound, begins 30min. farther along the main trail. Another relatively steep sidetrack descends past fungus-blackened beeches to the **Mistletoe Bay Reserve** (one-way 20min.), a DOC campsite on a small and quiet bay. In addition to a grassy flat for tents, the reserve maintains three ramshackle cottages with full kitchens ($10 per person; contact the **Picton DOC office**, p. 264, for reservations). Several short trails explore the forest from here.

MISTLETOE BAY RESERVE TO ANAKIWA.

12.5km, 3hr. Beyond the trail junction for Mistletoe Bay, the track follows the road. Down a side road, the tropical-themed **TeMahia Resort ❸** has a backpacker room with its own piano. (☎/fax 573 4089. Dorms $25, tent sites $12.50.) Meanwhile the main track follows Mistletoe Bay's lovely length before descending to **Davies Bay Campsite**, situated on an estuary. About 45min. of relatively level walking later, teeny **Anakiwa** marks the finish line; the small, domestic **Anakiwa Backpackers ❷** sits right by the end of the track. (☎ 574 2334. Closed Apr.-Nov. Dorms $15.)

BLENHEIM ☎ 03

Most tourists who flock to Blenheim come to indulge in the region's award-winning wines. Many vineyards are open to the public and offer tastings in addition to exquisite food. More frugal travelers in need of work see these same wineries as a gold mine, seeking vines in need of pruning and grapes in need of plucking.

TRANSPORTATION. The **railway station,** which also serves as a **bus station,** is located across the river at the end of Alfred St. Some buses also leave from the Visitors Center. **TranzScenic** (☎ 0800 802 802) goes to **Christchurch** (5hr., 1 per day, $30-77); and **Picton** (30min., 1 per day, $15). **InterCity** (☎ 577 2890) heads daily to: **Christchurch** (5hr., 2 per day, $26-55) via **Kaikoura** (2¾hr., $15-30); **Nelson** (1¾hr., 1 per day, $15-22); and **Picton** (30min., 2 per day, $8-10). **Kiwilink** (☎ 0800 802 300) and **Knightline** (☎ 547 4733) go to **Nelson** (1¾hr., 3 per day, $17); and **Picton** (30min., 3 per day, $7). **Blenheim Taxis** (☎ 578 0225) provides in-town transport.

272 ■ MARLBOROUGH

🛈 PRACTICAL INFORMATION. The **Blenheim Information Centre,** 2 High St., can whet visitors' parched lips with a $2 map of the Marlborough wine region. (☎578 9904; fax 578 6084; blm_info@clear.net.nz. Open daily 9am-6pm; in winter M-F 9am-5:30pm, Sa-Su 9am-12:30pm.) The **DOC field center** is on Gee St. in nearby Renwick. (☎572 9100. Open M-F 8am-4:30pm.) Blenheim offers many **work opportunities** in the area's busy fruit industry. To find employment, talk to hostel owners or look in local newspapers. Other services include: the **medical center,** 24 George St. (☎578 2174); the **police,** 8 Main St. (☎578 5279); **Internet access** at **Internet Direct,** 15 High St., across from the Visitors Center (☎578 1100. $2 per 15min.; open M-F 8:15am-5pm.); and the **post shop,** at the corner of Main and Scott St. (578 3904. Open M-F 8:30am-5:15pm, Sa 9:30am-12:30pm.)

🛏️ ACCOMMODATIONS AND CAMPING. Fresh paint, comfy beds, plentiful videos, and a friendly resident group of fruit pickers make **Koanui Backpackers (BBH) ❷,** 33 Main St., a welcoming stop on your travels. (☎/fax 578 7487; www.koanui.co.nz. Free pick-up and bike use. Reception 7:30am-9:30pm. Dorms $18, $100 per week; singles $37; twins and doubles $44.) To get to **The Grapevine Backpackers (BBH) ❷,** 29 Park Tce., follow Main St. and take a left onto Park Tce. Paddle the free canoes in the adjacent river, or ride a free bicycle to the local vineyards. A house across the street offers less cramped accommodations for long-term fruit pickers. (☎578 6062; rob.diana@xtra.co.nz. Free pick-up and laundry. Internet. Dorms $15; twins and doubles $32-36; tent sites in summer $10.) When the four-legged namesake at **Jack's Backpackers (BBH) ❷,** 144 High St., gives you his loud barking welcome you'll know you're home. (☎578 7375 or 0800 864 382; hjscott@xtra.co.nz. Dorms $20-22, weekly $129; doubles $44.) **Blenheim Bridge Top Ten Holiday Park ❶,** 78 Grove Rd., has a range of choices for all budgets. (☎/fax 578 3667; grove.bridge@xtra.co.nz. Self-contained tourist flats $68 for 2; cabins without bath $40-50 for 2; tent sites $10, powered $22 for 2. Lower rates in winter.)

🍴 FOOD. If paid employment and frugality are the order of the day, Blenheim is a great place to cut back on eating out. **New World,** on Main St., will fulfill your grocery fantasies. (☎578 5112. Open daily 8am-8:30pm.) **The Elbow Room ❸,** at the convergence of Main, Maxwell, and Arthur St., dishes up pizza pies ($14) in a minimalist interior. (579 4777. Open Su-Tu 9:30am-10:30pm, W-Th 9:30am-11pm, F-Sa 9:30am-midnight.) While the totem pole, scattered cacti, and faux adobe walls are intended to conjure up images of the American Southwest, the menu at **Bar Navajo ❸,** at the corner of Maxwell and Queen St., is decidedly Kiwi. All mains, including rib-eye steak, hotpot, and local specialty Marlborough mussels, are under $15. (☎577 7555. Open M-Th 11am-late, F-Sa 11am-2am.)

🍷 GETTING SLOSHED. The Wairau valley is the largest wine-producing region in New Zealand, making Blenheim a great spot to visit a vineyard, to learn about winemaking and, more importantly, to savor Marlborough in all of its red, white, and rosé splendor. **Wineries** abound, as do different tour and tasting options; the Visitors Center can help make concrete plans. **Cloudy Bay** (☎520 9140) and **Cairnbrae** (☎572 8018), up Jackson Rd., are two excellent nearby wineries; be sure to taste the award-winning Sauvignon Blanc of Cloudy Bay and the noble Riesling of Cairnbrae. For an organized coach trip, contact **De Luxe Travel Line** (☎0800 500 511; www.deluxetravel.co.nz. $45). For those who can hold their liquor, **Wine Tours by Bike** offers a unique two-wheeled perspective on the wine region. (☎577 6954; www.winetoursbybike.co.nz. $35 for half-day bike rental, $50 for full-day; $25 per hr. for guide.)

KAIKOURA

☎ 03

Kaikoura's brilliant blue bay and snowcapped peaks are the dramatic setting for a a fully interactive ecological wonderland. Kaikoura (pop. 3300) means "to eat crayfish" in Maori, and while these crunchy crustaceans can be found paddling beneath the waves, the offshore waters are also replete with fur seals, albatross, dusky dolphins, and whales. The local tourism industry has worked out every way short of being swallowed by a whale to experience this unique environment.

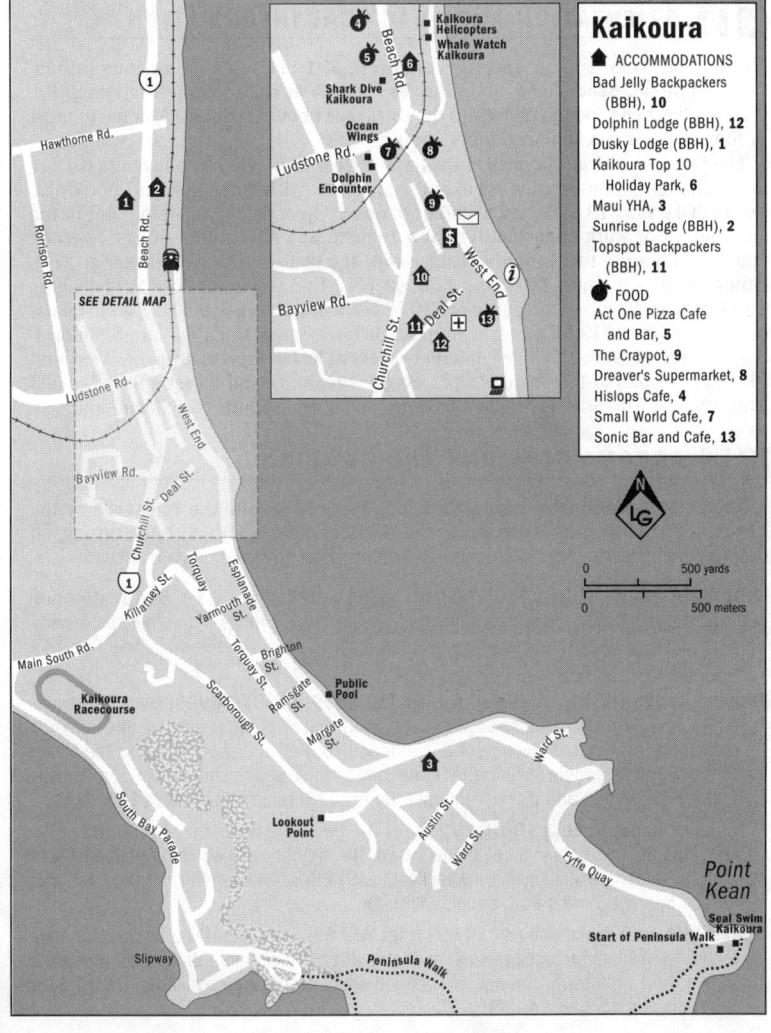

Kaikoura

■ ACCOMMODATIONS
Bad Jelly Backpackers (BBH), **10**
Dolphin Lodge (BBH), **12**
Dusky Lodge (BBH), **1**
Kaikoura Top 10 Holiday Park, **6**
Maui YHA, **3**
Sunrise Lodge (BBH), **2**
Topspot Backpackers (BBH), **11**

● FOOD
Act One Pizza Cafe and Bar, **5**
The Craypot, **9**
Dreaver's Supermarket, **8**
Hislops Cafe, **4**
Small World Cafe, **7**
Sonic Bar and Cafe, **13**

TRANSPORTATION

TranzCoastal (☎0800 802 802) has train service to **Christchurch** (3hr., 1 per day, $19-44) and **Picton** (2½hr., 1 per day, $18-42). Kaikoura handles all transport bookings at the **Visitors Center**. **InterCity** runs to: **Christchurch** (2½hr., 2-6 per day, from $15); **Picton** (2hr., 2-3 per day, from $15); and **Nelson** (5hr., 1 per day, from $43). At least four bus and shuttle companies run daily to **Christchurch** (2½hr., $15-20) and **Picton** (2hr., $15-20). **Hanmer Connection** (☎0800 377 378) also heads to **Hanmer Springs** (2hr.; 3 per week; $30). For taxi service, call **Kaikoura Taxi** (☎319 6214).

ORIENTATION AND PRACTICAL INFORMATION

Midway between Picton and Christchurch, **SH1** becomes, at various points, **Churchill Street, Beach Road,** and **Athelney Road.** Bear right just before Beach Rd. onto the **West End** (which turns into the **Esplanade** about 1km south), home to most of Kaikoura's shops and accommodations.

The **Kaikoura Visitor Information Centre,** on West End, will store luggage ($1 per day), change money on the weekends, and help with transport and bookings. (☎319 5641; fax 319 6819; www.kaikoura.co.nz. Open daily 9am-4pm; later in the summer.) For **work opportunities, New Zealand Sea Adventures** offers 12-week courses in marine tourism, dive leadership, and scuba certification (see p. 275). Other services include: **BNZ,** with **ATM,** 42 West End (open M, Th-F 9am-4:30pm, Tu-W 9:30am-4:30pm); the **police** (☎319 5038); a **hospital** (☎319 5040); a **pharmacy,** on West End (☎319 5035, after hours 319 7067; open M-Th 8:30am-5:30pm, F 8:30am-6pm, Sa 9am-12:30pm); **Internet access** at **Kodak Express shop,** on West End ($6 per hr.; open M-F 8:30am-6:30pm, Sa-Su 9am-5pm); and a **post office,** 41 West End (open M-Tu and Th-F 8:30am-5:30pm, W 8:30am-6:30pm, Sa 8:30am-7pm.)

ACCOMMODATIONS AND CAMPING

Most accommodations lie along **West End, Beach Road,** and the **Esplanade** by the beach, while a few others are on the hill overlooking the bay. With the throngs of dolphin-seeking tourists, make sure to book well in advance of your arrival.

Dolphin Lodge (BBH), 15 Deal St. (☎319 5842; fax 319 6148; dolphinlodge@xtra.co.nz). A lodge with a quiet and peaceful air. Lounge in the free spa or hammock while gazing at the incredible sea and mountain views. Book exchange. Free bike use. Internet. Dorms $17; doubles $40, with bath $45. ❷

Dusky Lodge (BBH), 67 Beach Rd. (☎319 5959; fax 319 6929; duskyjack@hotmail.com). With hot pools, a swimming pool, and a tropical garden, the recently revamped Dusky's has become the granddaddy of Kaikoura backpackers. The owner Jack often hires people in return for a free bed (min. 1 week commitment). Free bikes, breakfast in winter, and pick-up. Internet. Dorms $18; twins and doubles $45. ❷

Topspot Backpackers (BBH), 22 Deal St. (☎319 5540; fax 319 6587; topspot@xtra.co.nz) packs in a boisterous crowd. The loft brings TV-watching to new heights and the garden beckons with backpacker-friendly BBQs. Free apple crumble in the winter and Internet. Dorms $18; doubles $50. ❷

Maui YHA, 270 Esplanade (☎319 5931; fax 319 6921; yhakaikr@yha.org.nz). The pastel, motel-like interior, ocean views, and intriguing manager more than make up for the 20min. hike from town. Storage lockers and small hostel shop available. Dorms $18-20; twins and doubles $44. ❷

Sunrise Lodge (BBH), 74 Beach Rd. (☎319 7444; fax 319 7445). This sunny, pint-sized hostel (only 14 beds) is a quiet alternative to some of the rowdier Kaikoura sleeps. Closed June-July. Free bikes. Dorms $18; doubles $45. ❷

Bad Jelly Backpackers (BBH), 11 Churchill St. (☎319 5538; fax 319 5539). This homey backpackers offers multi-colored rooms plus a garden and spa out back. Twins and doubles $45. ❹

Kaikoura Top 10 Holiday Park, 34 Beach Rd. (☎/fax 319 5362 or 0800 363 638; kaikouratop10@clear.net.nz), provides award-winning camping facilities. Follow Beach Rd. away from the town center and cross under the railway overpass. Dorms $15; standard cabins $35 for 2, deluxe $45, extra person $12; tourist cabins $45-85 for 2; tent sites $10, powered $11. ❶

FOOD

The **Small World Cafe** ❷, on West End seats patrons on swiveling iron chairs in its purple interior. Delight in the chicken, lamb, or falafel souvlakis ($5.50-9). The bread and bagels ($3-6) come fresh out of the oven. (☎319 7070. Open daily 9am-late; in winter 10am-5pm.) **Act One Pizza Cafe and Bar** ❷, 25 Beach Rd., has rehearsed its creative, gourmet pizzas ($11-30) to perfection. (☎319 6760. Open daily 5pm-late.) In the true spirit of Kiwi environmentalism, **Hislops Cafe** ❹, 33 Beach Rd., prides itself on using only organic produce. The award-winning mains ($21-31) are worth the extra coins. (☎319 6971. Open daily 10am-10pm; in winter Th-M 10am-8:30pm.) With a giant fish seemingly poised to cough Jonah up onto the patrons, **Sonic Bar and Cafe** ❸, 93 West End, caters to backpackers. Enjoy pizzas ($13-18) amidst urban bric-a-brac and occasional live music. (☎319 6414. Open daily 11am-late.) **The Craypot** ❹, 70 West End, is perfect for people-ogling or an afternoon tea ($3). After a couple years of fruit-picking, the seafood platter ($125) just might be within monetary reach. (☎319 6027. Open daily 9am-late.) **Dreaver's Supermarket**, 31 West End, has all your grocery needs. (☎319 5333. Open daily M-F 8am-7pm, Sa-Su 8am-6:30pm.)

SIGHTS AND ACTIVITIES

DOLPHINS. Weather permitting, ■**Dolphin Encounter** gets you into a wetsuit and plops you in the ocean, smack in the middle of a friendly and playful pod of dusky dolphins. The water can be chilly and the frolics exhausting, but the thrill of being circled and investigated by a posse of sleek dolphins is unmatched. Bring a towel and warm, wind-resistant clothes. *(58 West End. ☎319 6777 or 0800 733 365; www.dolphin.co.nz. $95, spectators $48. Book well in advance; waits can be as long as 2-4 weeks in the high season.)*

SEALS. A highlight of Kaikoura is the **Point Kean seal colony**, where visitors can literally walk among the seals. The reef off the coast is a major breeding site for fur seals and is busiest during the breeding season (Nov.-Feb.), although the furry critters are present year-round. The seals are relatively accustomed to humans, so stay at least five meters from them. After strolling among the seals, there is no better way to view the entirety of the colony and the beauty of the bay than the **Peninsula Walkway**, which explains the history of the peninsula along the way. If you elect to follow the cliff route, prepare for hurdling turnstiles and getting chummy with the local livestock (the route crosses private farmlands at times). If you want to travel the shoreline route, which allows you to see more seals and explore local tide pools on the limestone (be careful; the rocks are slippery), check the Visitors Center first; the walk is best enjoyed within 2hr. of low tide. *(Colony 1hr. walk down the Esplanade from the Visitors Center.)* If you just can't get enough of the stinky creatures, **Ohau Point** is the main breeding site on the Kaikoura Coast. DOC has set up a viewing platform overlooking the scores of sunning fur seals. *(24km north of Kaikoura off the main highway.)* **Seal Swim Kaikoura** operates land-based seal snorkeling from November to April. *(☎ 319 6182 or 027 886 235. 2½ hr., $40.)* **New Zealand Sea Adventures** runs a similar trip by boat from September to May as well as scuba diving excursions and certification courses. *(85 West End. ☎ 319 6622 or 0800 728 223; www.scubadive.co.nz. Snorkeling trips $60, viewing $30. First scuba dive $95, each additional dive $60. PADI beginner's certification course $475.)* Other seal snorkeling tours include **Topspot Backpackers** (see p. 274) and guided, up-close kayak encounters through **Seal Kayak Kaikoura** *(Topspot: 2hr., daily Nov.-Apr., $50. Seal Kayak: ☎ 319 5540. Half-day trips $55. Departs year-round from the Visitors Center.)*

SHARKS. If coming face to face with ocean life sounds like sissy stuff, try to catch a glimpse of a shark with **Shark Dive Kaikoura**. There's nothing like being dropped in shark territory with only a special bite-proof cage between you and Jaws' brother. *(☎ 319 6888 or 0800 225 297. 5hr., daily Dec.-Apr.; $120, with all equipment provided. No scuba experience necessary.)*

WHALES. Whale Watch Kaikoura conducts tours of waters filled with whales, seals, royal albatross, and gulls. They offer a refund of up to 80% if no whales are seen during the trip. In June and July, keep an eye out for sperm whales; in summer, look for orca instead. *(At the old "whaleway" station. ☎ 319 6767 or 0800 655 121; www.whalewatch.co.nz. 3½hr. $100, ages 3-15 $60. Book 1-2 weeks ahead in summer, 3-4 days in winter.)* **Wings Over Whales** operates aerial whale-watching tours with a short lesson on the magnificent sperm whales before takeoff. The flight also provides a beautiful view of the coastline and mountains. *(☎ 319 6580 or 0800 226 629; www.whales.co.nz. 30min. flights $135, children $75. Transport to airfield $5.)* If you'd rather hover over the whales (which may make photo-opportunities easier), **Kaikoura Helicopters** will help you do just that *(☎ 319 6609 or 0800 674 181; www.worldofwhales.co.nz. 30-50min. trips $165-$275.)*

SEABIRDS. Albatross Encounters combines with **Ocean Wings** to run a 2½hr. boat trip to view Kaikoura's pelagic (ocean-going) bird life. Feathers unruffled by the presence of humans, small seabirds and giant albatross flock, squawk, and tustle within arm's reach over pieces of fish liver tossed overboard. More than 15 different species of bird, as well as dolphins and seals are sighted. *(☎ 319 6777 or 0800 733 365; www.oceanwings.co.nz. $60, children $30. Book at Dolphin Encounter.)*

KAYAKING. Paddle away with **Sea Kayak Kaikoura** to float into sheltered bays. Even when the rest of Kaikoura is overcast, you'll enjoy nearly 100% visibility. *(☎ 025 201 3298. Half-day $50, children $40.)*

WALKS. The circular **Hinau Track** and **Fyffe-Palmer Track** are steep but manageable; you may see a black-eyed gecko or the world's heaviest insect, the giant weta. *(Hinau starts 15km from town, return 45min. Fyffe-Palmer starts 6km from town, return 2hr.)* The **Peninsula Walkway** (see *Seals*, p. 275) will take you to the fur seal colony. For more ambitious trampers or mountain bikers, the privately-owned **Kaikoura Coast Track** takes three days by foot and two days by bike. *(☎ 319 2715; www.kaikouratrack.co.nz. Starts 45min. out of town. By bike $60, by foot $120; both include accommodations.)* Artistically-minded walkers should consider a self-guided tour of Kaikoura's galleries. Pick up a copy of the *Kaikoura Art Trail* at the Visitors Center.

HORSE TREKS. If you prefer land-based mammals to sea-going creatures, take a ride up through the foothills and over some farmland with **Fyffe View Horse Treks.** In the summer they offer spectacular sunset rides. *(☎ 319 5069 or 025 353 904. 2hr. $40.)* **Lake View Horse Treks** *(☎ 319 5997)* and **Ludley Horse Treks** *(☎ 319 5978)* run similar excursions.

SKIING. For ski addicts, **Mt. Lyford** is a mere 60km from Kaikoura. Graham from Seal Swim can provide transportation to the ski fields (☎ 319 6182). For a day excursion from Kaikoura including ski hire, field pass, and transport, inquire at the Visitors Center. (☎ 315 6178. Open June–Sept. Day pass $40, university students $35, high school students $20. Ski hire $15-25, snowboard hire $40.)

HANMER SPRINGS ☎ 03

The rare combination of converging faultlines and connected underground fractures brings Hanmer Springs (pop. 700) to geothermal life. Frown lines melt away in the thermal springs at the center of this small resort town, where shivering skiers from the nearby slopes and bone-weary jetboaters flock to unwind in the steaming waters. After drying off, the relaxation therapy can continue with soothing walks through the gentle surrounding hills and shadowy peaks. Or, try one of the many nearby adventure activities to recharge your adrenaline.

TRANSPORTATION. Some coach transport does not enter Hanmer proper, but instead deposits riders at the **Hanmer Turnoff** (10km from the village); inquire before booking. Both **Hanmer Connection** (☎ 315 7575 or 0800 377 378) and **Lazerline** (☎ 0800 220 001) drive into the main town. Coming by the **Southern Link** (☎ 358 8355) bus from the West Coast via Lewis Pass, you will probably be dropped off at the **Hanmer Turnoff;** arrange for a $5 pick-up on M, W, F, and Su from **Hanmer Connection.** To get out of town, **Hanmer Connection** runs to **Christchurch** (2hr.; 2 per day; $25) and **Kaikoura** (2hr.; 3 per week; $30) from their station on Amuri Ave. **Lazerline** runs to **Christchurch** ($22) and **Nelson** ($35) upon request.

ORIENTATION AND PRACTICAL INFORMATION. Hanmer Springs is about 10km off SH7 and 136km north of Christchurch. The **Hurunui Visitor Information Centre,** 42 Amuri Ave., sits to the side of the thermal pools. (☎ 315 7128 or 0800 442 663; www.hurunui.com. Open daily 10am-5pm.) Other local services include: **BNZ** in the Visitors Center (☎ 314 7220; open M-F 10am-2pm); an **ATM,** in the exit from the thermal pools (open daily 9am-9pm); the **Four Square supermarket,** in the Conical Hill Rd. shopping center, containing a small **post office** (☎ 315 7190; open M-F 8:30am-6pm, Sa 9am-5pm, Su 10am-4pm); the **Hanmer Springs Medical Centre** (☎ 315 7503; 24hr.); and the **ambulance** (☎ 0800 222 600).

ACCOMMODATIONS AND FOOD. Only a couple of budget accommodations are within walking distance of the pools. The lodge-like **Hanmer Backpackers (BBH) ❷,** 41 Conical Hill Rd., a 5min. walk past the thermal reserve on the right, houses guests in a loft and an insulated aluminum house out back. The lounge and kitchen area are happily co-habitated by both the backpackers and the owners. (☎ 315 7196; fax 315 7521; hanmerbackpackers@hotmail.com. Dorms $17; doubles $42.) **Kakapo Backpackers ❷,** 14 Amuri Ave., just underwent a major expansion and now has a plentiful offering of clean, cookie-cutter rooms. (☎/fax 315 7472; stay-kakapo@xtra.co.nz. Dorms $16; twins and doubles $40.) Away from the center of town, **Hanmer Springs Scenic Views Motel ❺,** 10 Amuri Ave., offers modern self-contained rooms overlooking the mountain vista. (☎ 315 7419; scenic.views@xtra.co.nz. Doubles $99; family rooms $139.) **Mountain View Top 10 Holiday Park ❶,** at the corner of Bath St. and Hanmer Springs Rd., is the most conveniently located motor camp, about an 8min. walk out of town. (☎ 315 7113; fax 315 7118; mtview.hanmer@clear.net.nz. Cabins with communal kitchen $36, extra person $12; kitchen cabins $46 for 2; tourist flats $60; tent sites $9, powered $11.) The best food options cluster around the small shopping center in town. **Jollie Jack's Cafe & Bar ❸** is the standout among them, offering flavorful meals for $13.50-23. (☎ 315 7388. Open daily 11am-late.)

OUTDOOR ACTIVITIES.

Hanmer's main attraction is never hard to find; if the smell of sulfur isn't enough, follow the plumes of steam to the **Hanmer Springs Thermal Reserve**, on Amuri Ave. Prove your superhuman powers of endurance in the 42°C pool, or pull a Goldilocks and try each of the seven different public pools until you find one that's just right; Baby Bear never had it this good. (☎315 7511; www.hotfun.co.nz. Open daily 10am-9pm. $8, return entry $11; waterslide $5 extra.) The **Hanmer Springs Health, Body, and Mind** center next to the pools provides the icing on the cake with indulgent package deals for facials, manicures, or massages. (☎315 7567 or 0800 873 529. $30-95. Open 11am-7:30pm.)

Thrillseekers Adventure Centre (☎315 7046; www.thrillseeker.co.nz), at the Historic Ferry Bridge, takes advantage of the Waiau River's natural splendor by offering bungy jumping above it ($99), jetboat rides down it (30min., $69), and rafting through its steep-sided gorge ($69). Book directly by phone or at their office outside the town shops. Transport will be arranged. **Hanmer Springs Adventure Centre** (☎315 7233), just up the road from the Visitors Center, picks up right where Thrillseekers leaves off, covering almost all overland pursuits. For only $65, their **Twin Pass** gets you a mountain bike with suspension, a drink, a ride out of town to a sweet trail, and for your return, a pass to the hot springs. (☎315 7233. Open daily 9am-5pm. Bikes 1hr. $14-18, 6hr. $28-45. Scooter 1hr. $28, each additional hr. $12. Rollerblades 1hr. $12. Fishing rod $25 per day.)

Short walks, day-hikes, and serious tramps run directly out of, or near, Hanmer Springs. The **Woodland Walk** (45min.), **Forest Walk** (1hr.), **Conical Hill Walk** (1hr.), and **Waterfall Track** (3hr.) are the most popular; many treks can be combined for longer excursions. Hikers should check in with the Visitors Center for track conditions and maps.

In winter, hit the slopes at the **Hanmer Springs Ski Area**, a 40min. drive (with $10 toll) from town. (☎315 7233 or 0800 733 426; snow phone ☎366 7766, ext. 5. Tow fees $34, students $23, under 18 $17. Ski hire $20-30, snowboard and boots $45.) Call **Hanmer Springs Adventure Centre** (see above) for a shuttle out to the field. (Departs 9am. Return $22.)

NELSON ☎03

Home to the country's first game of rugby, the first eight-hour working day in the world, and the oldest New Zealand railway, Nelson (pop. 55,000) is the geographic center of the country and a popular domestic holiday destination. "Sunny Nelson" is surprisingly on top of modern social trends for a city its size, with a stylish movie theater, bustling coffee houses, and a wide range of dining, shopping, and activities. The clay in the area is particularly suited for pottery (traded throughout the South Pacific), making Nelson a haven for sculptors. Nelson's art scene reaches its zenith with the **Wearable Art Awards** every September, but the scores of artisan dens and studios maintain the creative spirit year-round.

TRANSPORTATION

Flights: The **airport** is located past the Tahunanui Beach area. **Air New Zealand Link** (☎0800 767 767) flies daily to **Christchurch** (50min., 2-5 per day) and **Wellington** (35min., 8-12 per day). **Origin Pacific** (☎0800 302 302) covers the same routes and often has cheaper one-way fares.

Buses: All buses leave from the Visitors Center. Inquire about hostel pick-ups when booking. **InterCity** (☎548 1539) heads daily to **Fox Glacier** (10½hr., 1 per day, $77) via **Westport** (4½hr., $38), and to **Picton** (2hr., 2 per day, $22) via **Blenheim** (1½hr., $18). You can also take the bus to Blenheim and transfer to a **Christchurch** bus (4½hr., $25-44). **Lazerline** (☎0800 220 001) and **White Star/Southern Link** (☎546

8687) also go daily to **Christchurch** (7½hr., 1-2 per day, $30) via **Springs Junction** (3½hr., $23). White Star makes it possible to transfer at Springs Junction for **Westport** (6hr., $35). **Atomic Shuttles** (☎322 8883) also goes to **Westport** (1 per day, $30). **Wadsworth Motors** (☎522 4248) is significantly cheaper but runs less frequently to **St. Arnaud** (3½hr.; 3 per week, $12) than Atomic Shuttles (3½hr., 1 per day, $20). To get to **Abel Tasman National Park** or the **Kahurangi National Park,** call **Abel Tasman Coachlines** (☎548 0285) or **Kahurangi Bus Service** (☎525 9434). Prices and times vary according to destination (1½-4hr., 3 per day, $9-44).

Taxis: Nelson City Taxis (☎548 8225 or 0800 108 855) and **Sun City Taxis** (☎548 2666 or 0800 422 666) run **24hr.**

Car Rental: Pegasus Rental Cars Nelson, 83 Haven Rd. (☎548 0884 or 0800 803 580). Cars average $30-40 per day.

Bicycle Rental: Stewarts Cycle City, 114 Hardy St. (☎548 1666). Half-day $15, full-day $20. Open M-F 9am-6pm, Sa 9am-1pm.

ORIENTATION AND PRACTICAL INFORMATION

While the Nelson suburbs reach far into the hills, Nelson proper is very compact. **Christ Church Cathedral,** on Trafalgar St., dominates central Nelson and stands tall above its surrounding gardens. **Trafalgar, Bridge,** and **Hardy Streets** comprise the main shopping district and enclose a plethora of shops, accommodations, and restaurants. From the bus depot, take a left onto Bridge St. and you'll hit Trafalgar St.

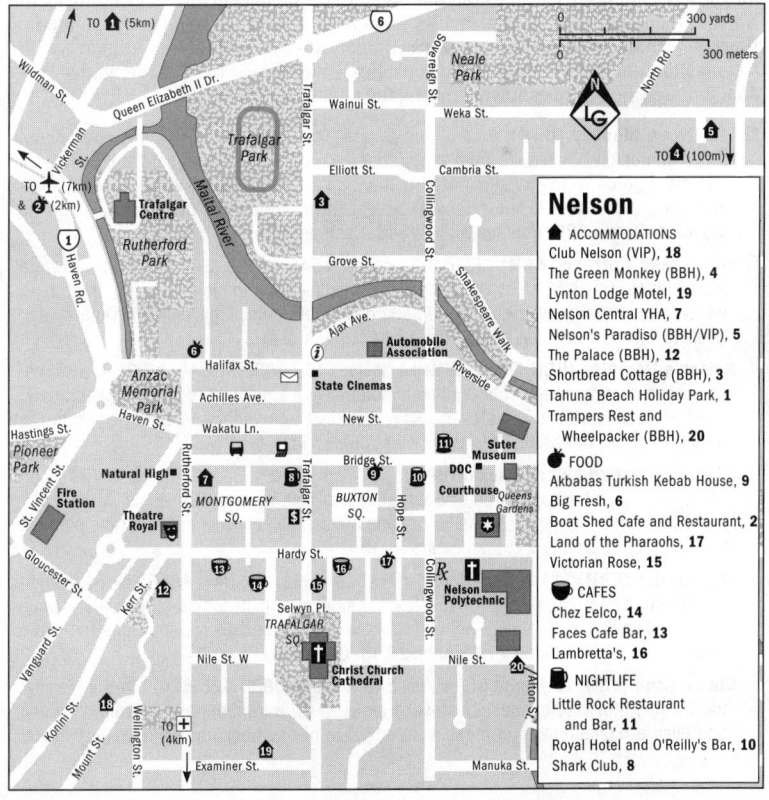

Nelson

ACCOMMODATIONS
Club Nelson (VIP), 18
The Green Monkey (BBH), 4
Lynton Lodge Motel, 19
Nelson Central YHA, 7
Nelson's Paradiso (BBH/VIP), 5
The Palace (BBH), 12
Shortbread Cottage (BBH), 3
Tahuna Beach Holiday Park, 1
Trampers Rest and
  Wheelpacker (BBH), 20

FOOD
Akbabas Turkish Kebab House, 9
Big Fresh, 6
Boat Shed Cafe and Restaurant, 2
Land of the Pharaohs, 17
Victorian Rose, 15

CAFES
Chez Eelco, 14
Faces Cafe Bar, 13
Lambretta's, 16

NIGHTLIFE
Little Rock Restaurant
  and Bar, 11
Royal Hotel and O'Reilly's Bar, 10
Shark Club, 8

Visitors Center: Nelson Visitor Centre (☎ 548 2304; fax 546 7393; www.nelson.co.nz), at the corner of Trafalgar and Halifax St., a 10min. walk on Trafalgar St. from the cathedral steps. Open daily 8:30am-5:30pm; in winter M-F 8:30am-5pm, Sa-Su 9am-5pm.

DOC: 186 Bridge St. (☎ 546 9335), in the Monro State Building. In the summer, DOC provides information at the Visitors Center. Open M-F 8am-4:30pm.

Banks: All major banks with **ATMs** on Trafalgar St. Open M-F 9am-4:30pm.

American Express: 153 Trafalgar St. (☎ 548 9079).

Tramping Gear: Rollo's BBQ and Camping Centre, 12 Bridge St. (☎ 548 1975). Open M-F 8:30am-5:30pm, Sa 9am-2pm.

Police: (☎ 546 3840), on St. John St. in central Nelson.

Medical Services: Prices Pharmacy, 296 Hardy St. (☎ 548 3897), at Collingwood St. Open M-F 8:30am-8pm. **Nelson Hospital** (☎ 546 1800), on Tipahi St. **City Care,** 202 Rutherford St. (☎ 546 8881), has a doctor on duty until late.

Internet Access: Boots Off, 53 Bridge St. (☎ 546 8789), near the bus terminal, has a slew of terminals. $6 per hr. Open daily 9am-10pm; reduced hours in winter.

Post Office: 108 Trafalgar St. Open M-F 7:45am-5pm, Sa 9:30am-12:30pm.

ACCOMMODATIONS AND CAMPING

Maybe it's something in the water, but outstanding hostels just keep popping up in Nelson. As a general rule, the smaller hostels are lovely home-style accommodations, whereas the larger backpackers compensate for their lack of intimacy with freebies and facilities. Some of Nelson's hostels close for part of the winter season, but are filled to overflowing during the summer.

The Green Monkey (BBH), 129 Milton St. (☎/fax 545 7421; www.skywebbiz.com/thegreenmonkey). A respite from the craziness, warm colors permeate the bedrooms and the 2 gardens beg for summer BBQ. Thoughtful extras like individual reading lights in dorm rooms attest to the extensive budget travel experience of the owners. Linens provided. Dorms $20; doubles with TV $48. Cash only. ❷

Shortbread Cottage (BBH), 33 Trafalgar St. (☎ 546 6681). Surrounded by a white picket fence, this bright cottage is the most inviting nook in Nelson. Fresh shortbread baked almost daily sweetens the already delectable deal. Free pick-up. Dorms $18; doubles with TV $45. Call ahead—the 12 beds fill fast. ❷

Nelson's Paradiso (BBH/VIP), 42 Weka St. (☎ 546 6703; fax 546 7533). If a sauna, spa, swimming pool, and volleyball court sound like a smashing recipe for a good time, call the Paradiso for a free pick-up. Free breakfast and vegetable soup served in the winter. Internet. Dorms $20-22; twins and doubles $50. ❷

Trampers Rest and Wheelpacker (BBH), 31 Alton St. (☎ 545 7477; fax 548 7897), on one of Nelson's heritage streets. Book ahead to reserve one of 6 spots in this calm oasis. The Rest offers fresh herbs for tea and a grand selection of music for the piano in the living room. Dorms $18; doubles $46. ❷

The Palace (BBH), 114 Rutherford St. (☎ 548 4691; fax 548 4658; thepalacenelson@hotmail.com). The Palace occupies a magnificent hilltop historic home and waylays travelers with its friendly vibe, city views, and 24hr. spa. Reception 8am-9pm. Free breakfast. Internet. Dorms $19; doubles $48. Cash only. ❷

Club Nelson (VIP), 18 Mount St. (☎/fax 548 3466 or 0800 425 826), up the Wellington St. hill. Multiple lounges, clusters of citrus trees, a swimming pool, tennis courts, and even a basketball court make wonderful use of this backpackers' 4-acre grounds.

Reception 8-11am and 2-8pm. Dorms $18-20; singles $38; twins and doubles $48; tent sites $12. Inquire about weekly rates. ❷

Nelson Central YHA, 59 Rutherford St. (☎545 9988; fax 545 9989; yhanels@yha.org.nz). Spotless rooms, an eco-friendly staff, and a location ideal for exploring Nelson's nightlife. Internet. Reception 8-10am and 3-9:30pm. Dorms $23; singles $38; twins and doubles $56, with bath $76. ❸

Lynton Lodge Motel, 25 Examiner St. (☎/fax 548 7112), just behind the Cathedral. This 100-year-old home lets spacious, self-contained units, some with city-sweeping views. Doubles $75-85. ❹

Tahuna Beach Holiday Park, 70 Beach Rd., (☎548 5159 or 0800 500 501; fax 548 5294; www.tahunabeachholidaypark.co.nz), in Tahunanui, 5km from Nelson. With its own store, function center, mini-golf course, and highway system, all this 54-acre facility is missing is its own government. Hundreds of tent sites ($19-20) and an incredible variety of cabins and motels ($28-80). Reception 8am-9pm. ❷

FOOD

Many of Nelson's restaurants, cafes, and takeaways are located on **Trafalgar, Bridge,** and **Hardy Streets.** Several seafood restaurants on Wakefield Quay, along the oceanfront, can be reached by bus ($2), taxi ($5), or car. Your best bet for groceries is **Big Fresh,** at the corner of Paru Rd. and Halifax St. (☎546 6466. Open daily 7am-10pm.)

Land of Pharaohs, 270 Hardy St. (☎548 8404). Behind Egyptian hieroglyphics and cartouches, a Middle Eastern menu is dished up hot and fast. Mains $15-18.50. Open M-Sa 11:30am until around 9pm. ❸

Victorian Rose, 281 Trafalgar St. (☎548 7631). Probably the most recognized joint in town, many pub meals can be had for $9-13. The Sunday roast ($13) is an all-you-can-eat affair with soup and dessert included (from 5:30pm). Look for a coupon granting 10% off all meals. Kitchen open daily 11am-9:30pm. ❷

Akbabas Turkish Kebab House, 130 Bridge St. (☎548 8825). A small restaurant and takeaway with low tables and floor pillows. Spicy chicken kebab in a pita $6.50-8.50; falafels $5-6.50. Open daily 11am-9pm. ❶

Boat Shed Cafe and Restaurant, 350 Wakefield Quay (☎546 9783), on the oceanfront (a taxi ride away). Highly recommended by locals, this converted boat shed practically sits on the ocean. Known for fresh seafood with a great view on the side, this is definitely the place to splurge (mains from $25). Open daily 9am-10pm. ❺

CAFES

Chez Eelco, 296 Trafalgar St. (☎548 7595). A mellow vibe spills out of this earthy cafe and onto its sunny patio. Coffee $3-4; light snacks $5-8. Internet. Open daily 7am-7pm; in winter until 3pm.

Lambretta's, 204 Hardy St. (☎545 8555). Paying homage to the famous scooter, this cafe buzzes with the chatter of all ages. The menu is a mix of light counter meals and reasonably-priced mains (small pizza $10.50). Open M-Sa 9am-late, Su 5pm-late.

Faces Cafe Bar, 136 Hardy St. (☎548 8755). Stylish interpretive art adorns the walls while the floor is dominated by two lampposts. A classier late-night venue for drinks or specialty coffees. Open M-F 11am-late, Sa 11am-2pm and 5pm-late.

ENTERTAINMENT AND NIGHTLIFE

A definite party, every September the **Montana New Zealand Wearable Art Awards,** in Nelson's Trafalgar Centre, churn out human spectacles. For judges, gawkers, and their own entertainment, contestants design themselves as everything from wispy, gauze dragonfly beauties and surreal spiked cyberpunks to jellyfish swathed in gyrating colors. Tickets sell out as early as six months in advance. Call **Everyman Records,** 249 Hardy St. (☎548 3083), to reserve yourself a slot.

If sobriety is the order of the day (or night), Nelson also offers a four-screen cinematic experience at the **State Cinemas** (☎548 8123), at the corner of Trafalgar and Halifax St., across from the Visitors Center. Tickets are $8 before 5pm (and all day Tuesday) and $11 in the evenings; student discounts on weeknight shows ($8.50).

Victorian Rose, 281 Trafalgar St. (☎548 7631). This popular restaurant (see **Food,** p. 281) also attracts a sizeable bunch to its bar. Don't let the delicate English name fool you, crowds frequently gather to celebrate (or mourn) the outcome of the most recent rugby game. Open daily 11am-late.

Little Rock Restaurant and Bar, 165 Bridge St. (☎546 8800). The high roof, open-beamed rafters, and metal sculptures create the perfect venue for wining, dining, and listening to live music acts. Open M-Sa 4pm-late.

Shark Club, 132-136 Bridge St. (☎546 6630). If you are looking to hustle in Nelson, this mammoth pool club with a sleek interior will present you with plenty of opponents. Free pool daily 5-7pm. Backpacker drink deals and specials. Open M-Sa 3pm-late.

Royal Hotel and O'Reilly's Bar, 152 Bridge St. (☎546 9279). So Irish, this pub even has green lighting. Irish jam nights are not to be missed (Tu 8pm). Handles $3-4. Open M-Th and Su 11am-midnight, F-Sa 11am-3am.

SIGHTS AND ACTIVITIES

The best way to groove with the many faces of Nelson is to wander among them at Nelson's weekly **flea market.** Held Saturday and Sunday mornings (9am-1pm) in the Montgomery Sq. carpark, the market offers local crafts, art, fresh produce, and food vendors as well as a selection of the trendiest local activists.

ADVENTURE ACTIVITIES. Most backpackers to Nelson only have eyes for one thing—**Abel Tasman National Park** (see p. 285). In fact, it is quite easy to use the city as a base from which to take a variety of trips. If you came to sea kayak, both **Abel Tasman Kayaks** (☎0800 527 802) and **Ocean River** (☎527 8266 or 0800 732 529) provide pick-up in Nelson for guided trips. Additionally, transport from Nelson to various trailheads along the Coastal Track can be arranged.

Several different adventure options provide a look at Nelson's wild side without venturing so far north. **Stonehurst Farm Horse Treks** (☎542 4121; www.stonehurst-farm.co.nz) offers a variety of 1-4hr. adventures, including the Rambler Trail through scenic farmland (1hr., $30) and the longer River Ride, complete with an afternoon tea (half-day, $79). The recently-opened **Skywire ride** (☎545 0304), a zipline, which sends you and three of your nearest and dearest hurtling down the longest 1.6km of your life. Call for prices. **Happy Valley 4x4 Motorbike Adventures** (☎545 0304; www.happyvalleyadventures.co.nz) runs four-wheel motorbike excursions, such as the Farm Forest (1hr., $55) and the Bay View Circuit (2½hr., $85), both of which see Matai trees that are 40m tall and over 2000 years old.

"Adrenaline dealers" **Natural High** rent mountain bikes, guide bike tours, run kayak trips to Abel Tasman, and rent tramping gear. *(52 Rutherford St. ☎ 546 6936; www.cyclenewzealand.com. Bikes half-day from $15, tours from $40. Guided multi-day sea kayaking trips from $225.)* See the scenery from the sky with **Nelson Paragliding.** *(☎ 544 1182. Tandem flight $110.)* **Tandem Skydive Nelson** provides a more daring option, often taking the plunge over the Abel Tasman. *(☎ 528 4091 or 0800 422 899; www.skydive.co.nz. From 3000m $210; from 4000m $260.)*

TOURS. To get up close and personal with Nelson's various creators and producers, head out of town by car or tour bus. **JJ's Wine Tours** offers the full booze tour, hitting several local wineries, breweries, and distilleries. *(☎ 544 7081. Half-day $55.)* **Nelson Day Tours** covers a range of local highlights, including the city district and several wineries and craft centers. *(☎ 548 4224. 3hr., $45.)* They also run trips to Golden Bay (from $90) and Lake Rotoiti (from $65) on demand. Stop by **McCashin's Brewery.** *(660 Main Rd., in Stoke, about 15min. outside Nelson. ☎ 547 0526. Tours $5.)* Their product, **Mac's Beer,** is a local favorite, made at the brewery without chemicals or preservatives. Continuing on SH6, look for the signposts just before Richmond that mark the way to the **Craft Habitat** *(☎ 544 7481).* Watch the artisans at work, as some weave rich wool while others perfect their jewelry or pottery. From SH6, turn right on Queen St. in Richmond, then left on Lansdowne Rd. to get to the **Höglund Art Glassblowing Studio,** where two galleries display glass. *(☎ 544 6500. Open daily 9am-5pm. Free.)*

OTHER SIGHTS AND ACTIVITIES. If you have a hankering for a fowl-free picnic, head to **Anzac Memorial Park,** off Rutherford St., or to the **Miyazu Japanese Garden,** on Atawhai Dr. near the water. Otherwise, the Victorian **Queens Gardens** has plenty of bold birds guarding entrances on Hardy and Bridge St. **Suter Art Gallery,** next to Queens Gardens, on Bridge St., is a public art museum with a strong collection of New Zealand and local art, as well as a craft shop, cinema, and restaurant. *(☎ 548 4699. Open daily 10:30am-4:30pm. $2, students 50¢.)* A mixture of industrial and Gothic architecture, **Christ Church Cathedral** sits atop Church Hill on Trafalgar St.

The best guide to Nelson's natural history is *Walk Nelson,* a brochure which outlines 30 local walks ($4); the pamphlet is available from the Nelson City Council office. *(110 Trafalgar St. Open M-F 8am-4:30pm.)* The steep **Centre of New Zealand Walk** will get you close to the center of *Aotearoa.* (Return 40min.; begins in the Botanic Gardens.) The **Maitai River Walkway** (return 4hr.) will take you along the river, past a wishing well, and into the countryside. The fine sands of **Tahunanui Beach** ("shifting sands") make it a popular holiday destination; it's accessible by bike down Wakefield Quay, which turns into Rocks Rd. (20-30min.).

NELSON LAKES NATIONAL PARK ☎ 03

Pristine byways pass through evergreen beech forests, craggy mountains, and tussock grasslands on the banks of Lake Rotoiti and Lake Rotoroa. In winter, nearby slopes are a haven for skiers while tramping options allure travelers in the summer. The forests shelter abundant birdlife and recent efforts by DOC to create predator-free zones promise the re-introduction of even more native species. The gateway to the park is the lakeshore village of **St. Arnaud,** which sits on the moraine of the glacier that originally formed Lake Rotoiti.

TRANSPORTATION. Atomic Shuttles (☎ 322 8883) runs to **Nelson** (1 per day, $20). **Wadsworth Motors** (☎ 522 4248) makes the trip as part of a lengthy mail run (2½hr., 3 per week, $12). Both buses depart from the **Nelson Lakes Village Centre.**

WHEN TO GO. Nelson Lakes National Park can get very cold in winter—be sure to bring adequate clothing and equipment if you plan on doing winter hiking. While the Park is gorgeous in summer, huts can become overcrowded.

PRACTICAL INFORMATION. The **DOC headquarters** in **St. Arnaud**, on View Rd. off SH63, also serves as the **Nelson Lakes National Park Visitors Centre**. (☎ 521 1806; fax 521 1896. Open daily 8am-4:30pm; extended hours in summer.) The **petrol station, post office,** and **general store** are all at the **Nelson Lakes Village Centre**. (☎ 521 1854. Open M-Th and Su 7:30am-6:30pm, F-Sa 7:30am-7pm.)

ACCOMMODATIONS AND CAMPING. Sleeping options are slim in St. Arnaud. The bright **Yellow House (YHA)** ❸, 150m from the petrol station, is a good bet with a park-savvy staff. Warm, clean rooms make for a relaxing stay. (☎ 521 1887; fax 521 1882. Camping and hiking gear available. Internet. Spa pool. Dorms $21; twins and doubles $50.) The **Alpine Chalet** ❷, part of the Alpine Lodge, across the street from the petrol station, has tight budget accommodations. No one mans the chalet so visit the lodge to get your questions and concerns answered. (☎/fax 521 1869 or 0800 367 777. Shower $1. Dorms $16; doubles $45.) Lake Rotoiti has two **DOC campgrounds,** one at **Kerr Bay** and another at **West Bay.** Both have tent sites, though West Bay is closed in winter. ($8; powered sites $9.)

OUTDOOR ACTIVITIES. The most well-known trail is the **Travers-Sabine Circuit,** a strenuous, 4-7 day hike that crosses the 1787m Travers Saddle. The huts in the Travers Valley are first-come, first-served, and often fill in summer; tickets can be purchased at DOC ($10 per night). Hikes begin in the Kerr Bay carpark and range in duration from 30min.-9hr. depending on your ambition; a pamphlet is available at the Visitors Center, or just follow the well-marked signs. Those crunched for time can do the **Honeydew Walk** (return 45min.), with a beautiful view of Kerr Bay and the daunting mountains behind Lake Rotoiti. If you don't have your own gear, the **Rotoiti Outdoor Education Centre** (☎ 521 1820) rents tramping clothing year-round.

The glaciers that carved out the Travers Valley were also responsible for creating **Lake Rotoiti**—8km long, 80m at its deepest point, and jumping with brown trout. You can fish, canoe, jetboat, or waterski on the lake where Maori once fished for eels and mussels. **Rotoiti Water Taxis** can take you to the head of the lake, among other spots. They also hire kayaks and canoes. (☎ 521 1894 or 021 702 278. $60 per hr.) Lake Rotoiti's big sister, **Lake Rotoroa** (off SH6), was carved out by two glaciers that formed the Sabine and D'Urville Valleys. Jetboating and waterskiing are prohibited on Rotoroa, but fishermen and birdwatchers can contact **Rotoroa Water Taxi** for a ride to the lakehead. (☎ 523 9199. $25 per person; min. 3 people.)

Wintertime revelers use **Mt. Arnaud** as a skiing and snowboarding base. The 350-hectare **Rainbow Ski Area** offers slopes for all levels of ability. They also hire ski and snowboarding equipment and run a shuttle to and from the ski field for $10 return. (☎ 521 1861, snowphone ☎ 0900 47 669; www.skirainbow.co.nz. 99¢ per min. Day lift pass $49, students $37; afternoon pass $39/$27. Skis, boots, and poles $35 per day; snowboard and boots $47 per day.) **Mt. Robert Ski Club** is a private club, but nonmembers are still welcome. Huts are available on the mountain for $15 per night but be sure to book ahead. Helicopter transport up the mountain is available for $40 per person; gear is not available for hire on the mountain. Bring warm clothes and sturdy boots as a 2hr. hike may be necessary to leave the mountain, depending on weather conditions. (☎ 548 8336. Pass $20, students $15; cash only.)

GOLDEN BAY

Golden Bay is where Abel Tasman first saw Aotearoa and Captain Cook bid it farewell; it was the setting for New Zealand's first gold rush and its first gold rush collapse a few years later. Today, Golden Bay is a seductive half-moon where international hippies sprout roots and a community of organic farmers and artists rave through the New Year (www.gathering.co.nz). Artsy Takaka and tiny Collingwood lie at the core of the region, the beaches of Abel Tasman National Park and the wide wilderness of Kahurangi National Park sprawl on either side, and the shifting sands of Farewell Spit crown the area known as the North of the South.

ABEL TASMAN NATIONAL PARK ☎03

In 1941, conservationist Pérrine Moncrieff was struggling to convince the New Zealand government that a gorgeous swath of coastal forest was worth protecting from the timber industry. Then, according to Moncrieff, came the "super-fly to tempt the Authority-fish," the 300-year anniversary of Abel Tasman's 1642 visit to these shores. What better way to celebrate than with a brand-new park? The MPs took the bait, and Abel Tasman National Park was founded. With subtropical weather, turquoise waters, golden sands, and bizarre rock formations, New Zealand's smallest national park draws 200,000 kayakers and trampers each year.

AT A GLANCE	
AREA: 22,530 hectares.	**GATEWAYS:** Marahau and Totaranui.
CLIMATE: Mild and sunny.	**CAMPING:** Abel Tasman Track has 4 huts. Inland Track has 4 huts and free camping.
FEATURES: Coastal and inland tracks, world class kayaking.	
HIGHLIGHTS: Golden beaches along turquoise water.	**FEES & RESERVATIONS:** Great Walks Pass required ($7-9). Coastal huts $14, inland $5. Reserve in summer.

TRANSPORTATION. Just outside the park borders, at the southern end of the Coast Track, **Marahau** is the main water transport base for the park and the primary point of land access from the south. **Abel Tasman Coachlines** (☎548 0285) runs between **Motueka** and **Marahau** (30min., 2-3 per day; $7) and between **Takaka** and **Wainui carpark** (30min., Oct. 15-Apr. 1 per day; $7); **Kahurangi Bus Services** (☎525 9434) does the same: Motueka-Marahau (1-4 per day; $7, in winter $10), Takaka-Wainui (1 per day; $8, in winter $15). Although *Let's Go* does not recommend it, **hitchhikers** report plenty of traffic in summer. It is reportedly easier to hitchhike to or from Marahau than from Wainui carpark.

ORIENTATION AND PRACTICAL INFORMATION. Abel Tasman National Park lies east of SH60, on the peninsula that separates Golden Bay from Tasman Bay. **Sandy Bay Road** breaks off from SH60 between Motueka and Takaka Hill and terminates at **Marahau** (18km north of Motueka), the tiny tourist village at the southern end of the park. **Abel Tasman Drive** heads east from Takaka to **Wainui carpark** (21km east of Takaka), **Totaranui campground** (32km east of Takaka), and **Awaroa Inlet** (31km east of Takaka), all near the park's northern end. The **Motueka DOC office** (☎528 1810; open M-F 8am-4:30pm) on High St. and the **Takaka DOC office,** 62 Commercial St. (☎525 8026; open M-F 8am-4pm) are the main contact centers for the park. The **Motueka Visitors Centre,** on Wallace St., also handles bookings and issues hut passes for area walks, including the Abel Tasman Coastal Track. (☎/fax 528 6543; mzpvin@xtra.co.nz. Open Nov.-Feb. daily 8am-7pm; Mar.-

286 ■ GOLDEN BAY

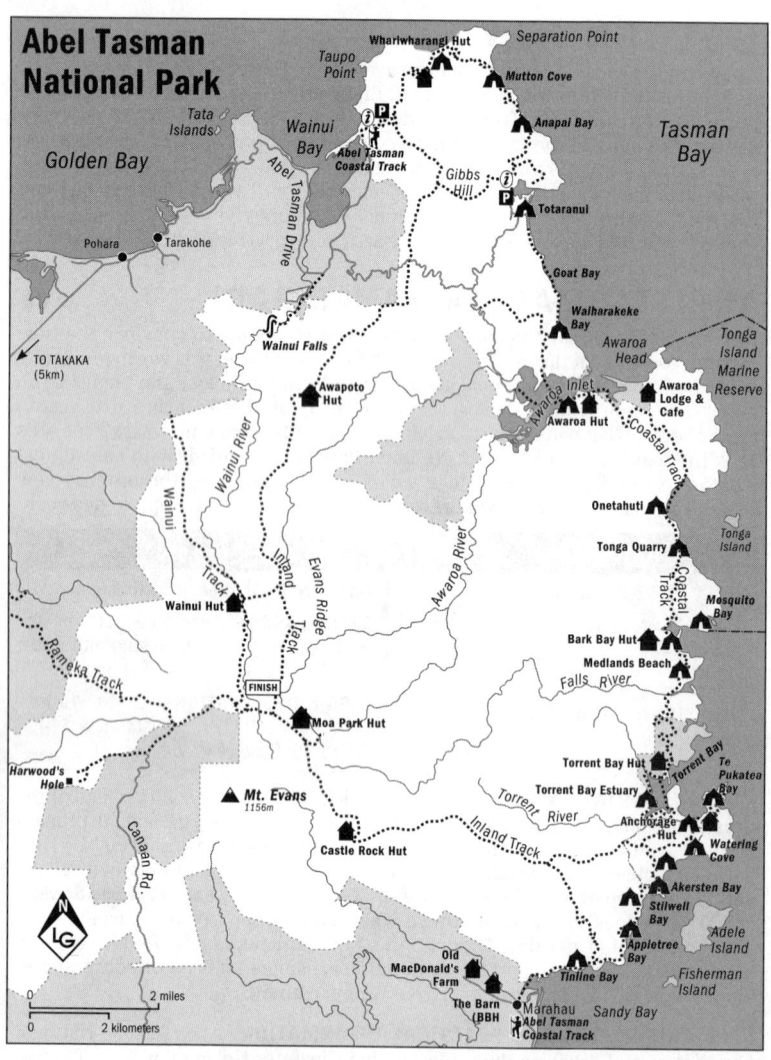

Oct. 8am-5pm.) The nearest **supermarkets** and **ATMs** are in Motueka and Takaka. The best bet for **secure parking** is in backpackers' carparks; in Marahau, Old Macdonald's Farm (see **Accommodations and Food,** below) employs a guard dog to watch its cars ($3 per night for non-guests).

ACCOMMODATIONS AND FOOD. Just a stone's throw from the Coast Track's Marahau trailhead, **The Barn (BBH)** ❷ offers a tranquil and cheerful range of accommodations—some with sea views, many in a refurbished barn. (☎527 8043. Free bike use. Small shop. Dorms $16; doubles in a truck or teepee $40; tent sites $9.) Just up the road, surrounded by the same lush hillside, the 100-acre **Old**

Macdonald's Farm ❶ has a bustling caravan park, some tired indoor rooms, and a clothing-optional swimming hole. (☎527 8288; oldmacs@xtra.co.nz. Camping gear for hire: stove $3.50 per day, 2-person tent $10 per day. Internet. Restaurant open Nov.-Mar. Small shop. Dorms from $15; doubles $40; tent sites $10, powered $12.) Marahau's sole proper restaurant, **The Park Cafe ❷** serves burgers ($10), bagel sandwiches ($9), and other middle-of-nowhere gourmet fare. (☎527 8270. Open daily 8am-9pm. Closed May-Sept.) The DOC-run **Totaranui Campsite,** home to a harem of caravans and tents, lies along a gorgeous beach but is also road-accessible. (☎528 8083. Small shop. Dec. 20-Jan. 31 bookings must be made by July 1-5. Tent sites $8, children $4; $2 penalty if you don't check in on arrival.)

🔲 OUTDOOR ACTIVITIES. For information on the **Abel Tasman Coastal Track,** see p. 288. The less-traversed **Inland Track** (3-5 days) also connects Marahau and Wainui but is considerably more challenging than the Coastal Track. Added to the park in the 1970s, it passes a variety of mixed forests, sub-alpine vegetation, and strange marble formations. The Inland Track has four huts ($5); camping is free. It is also possible to access the track at its midpoint via the 11km **Canaan Road,** which branches off SH60 midway between Takaka and Motueka. The end of Canaan Rd. is also the starting point for the walk to the stone splendor of **Harwood's Hole's** 183m vertical drop (return 1½hr.); numerous other **day hikes** begin from Totaranui campground and Wainui carpark.

Of course, many visitors bypass Abel Tasman's land-based activities in favor of wetter sports. Established in 1993, the **Tonga Island Marine Reserve** stretches one nautical mile into the sea between Awaroa and Bark Bay and confers full protection to all the creatures that dwell there. Make sure to stay at least 10m away from the shore so you don't disturb the seals. **Abel Tasman Seal Swim and Water Taxi** gets visitors in the water with Tonga Island's sea lions without coercing or feeding the animals. (☎0800 527 8136. Nov.-Apr. daily 8:45am and 1pm. $65, children and spectators $55, with day at beach $83.) **Windrider Sea Adventures,** near Kaiteriteri Beach, offers the chance to cruise Tasman Bay in your own kayak-cum-sailboat trimaran. (☎526 8749 or 0508 732 238. 1-day trips $90-115, half-day $65.)

🔲 KAYAKING. The park's clear waters, trackless beaches, and fine weather have inspired a sea kayaking explosion in recent years. Sea kayakers can visit beaches such as **Mosquito Bay** and **Observation** that the Coast Track doesn't reach, as well as numerous off-shore islands. The profusion of companies can be overwhelming at first, but most offer similar guided excursions, independent rentals (2-person min.), kayak/tramp options, and kayak pick-up ($25-35) for paddlers who don't want to double back; all provide extensive instruction before sending anyone out. The trips and rentals listed below give an idea of each company's prices but do not by any means cover all the offerings.

Abel Tasman Kayaks (☎527 8022 or 0800 527 802; www.kayaktours.co.nz), in Marahau. Free transport from Nelson or Motueka. 1-day rental $60, $35-40 per subsequent day, 5th day free. 1-day guided $99-130. 3-day guided $295 (BYO food) or $385 (including food).

Ocean River (☎527 8266 or 0800 732 529; www.seakayaking.co.nz), in Marahau. 2-day rental $99, $40 per subsequent day, 5th day free. No 1-day rental. 1-day guided $99-129. 3-day guided $495 (including food). Fancier lodge-based trips also available.

Marahau Beach Camp (☎527 8176 or 0800 808 018), in Marahau. 1-day rental $55. Multi-day rental $55 1st day, $40 per subsequent day, 5th day free.

Kaiteriteri Kayaks (☎527 8383 or 0800 252 925), near Kaiteriteri Beach. Half-day rental $40. 2-day rental $95. No 1-day rental. Half-day guided $55. 1-day guided $85-125. 3½hr. guided sunset trip $50.

Golden Bay Kayaks (☎525 9095; www.seakayakingnz.com), in Pohara. The only operator by the northern side of the park. Operates Nov.-May only. Rental $40 per day. Half-day guided $50. **Windsurfers** $40 per day. **Snorkeling gear** $5 per day.

ABEL TASMAN COASTAL TRACK

One of New Zealand's best-loved and most-walked tramps, the easygoing Abel Tasman Coastal Track promises a stunning and colorful outdoor scene: emerald forests give glimpses of turquoise through the trees and eventually open onto azure bays surrounding the park's famous golden beaches. Although the Coast Track's lingering pockets of private enterprise and occasionally maddening crowds may not please wilderness-hungry trampers, its scenery remains scintillating and accessible.

Length: 51km, 3-5 days.

Trailheads: Marahau in the south and **Wainui carpark** in the north. An intermediate point at **Totaranui** is also car-accessible, and **water taxis** (see **Transportation**, below) can make any point a start or finish.

Transportation: For information on getting to the trailheads, see **Transportation**, p. 285. Inside the park, many **water-taxis** service the track's various coastal sections, heading north from **Marahau** to: **Torrent Bay** (30min.-1hr., $18-19), **Bark Bay** (40min.-1½hr., $22), **Onetahuti Beach/Tonga Bay** (45min.-1¾hr., $24-25), **Awaroa Bay** (1½-2¼hr., $27-30), and **Totaranui** (1¼-3hr., $30), then looping back. On calm days, some travel beyond Totaranui on demand (usually min. 2 people). The following run daily from Marahau: **Abel Tasman Aqua Taxi** (☎527 8083 or 0800 278 282; departs Oct.-Apr. 4 per day, May-Sept. 2 per day) has the fastest boats; **Abel Tasman Enterprises** (☎528 7801 or 0800 223 582; departs Oct.-Apr. 4 per day, May-Sept. 1 per day); **Marahau Beach Camp** (☎527 8176 or 0800 808 018; departs Oct.-Apr. 4 per day, May-Sept. 2 per day); **Abel Tasman Water Taxis** (☎528 7497 or 0800 423 397; departs Oct.-Apr. 5 per day, May-Sept. on demand); and **Abel Tasman Seal Swim and Water Taxi** (☎0800 527 8136; departs Nov.-Apr. 2 per day).

Tides: The tides can affect one's timing on the track, since **Awaroa Inlet** can only be crossed on foot within 2hr. on either side of low tide (though Awaroa Lodge runs a launch across M-F 1hr. before high tide; $5). If you are off on the tides, there is also a walkable inland track. **Onetahuti Beach** has a river best crossed within 3hr. on either side of low tide. **Tide tables** are posted at area visitors centers and in each hut.

Seasonality: Year-round. Christmas and Easter are the busiest.

Huts and Campsites: 4 **huts** on a **booking system**, Oct.-Apr. (hut pass $14 per night). DOC accepts bookings starting July 1 for the following season. From May-Sept. (pass $10 per night), it is not necessary to book a spot in advance. The track's 21 **campsites** require permits year-round ($7 per night). All huts and most campsites have toilets and taps.

Storage: Most accommodations store for free. **Kahurangi Bus Services** charges $5 per bag for transport between Motueka and Takaka.

MARAHAU TRAILHEAD TO ANCHORAGE HUT AND CAMPSITE. *11.5km, 3hr.* Beginning at the southern end of the park, the track proceeds past the unremarkable trailside grass that marks **Tinline Creek Campsite** (15 sites), down to the long and lovely beach at **Appletree Bay Campsite** (15 sites). **Stilwell Bay Campsite** (3 sites) is on a nice beach, but high tide can create an access problem. Shortly thereafter, a switchback descent to **Akersten Bay Campsite** (5 sites) offers terraced sites among trees next to a small beach. From here, the track rises to a ridge, giving some stunning sea views of **Anchorage Bay.** A steep side trip down the other side of the ridge leads to the excellent sites of **Watering Cove Campsite** (10 sites), right on the beach. The main track descends more gradually to a wide, golden, and often rather busy arc of sand, with the modest **Anchorage Hut** (24 bunks) nearby. The wide field next door is **Anchorage Campsite** (50 sites), a veritable tent town with drying lines and heaps of taps. Both Anchorage Hut and Campsite have taps that dispense **filtered drinking water** from October to April.

About a 10min. walk from Anchorage Campsite is the secluded **Te Pukatea Bay Campsite** (10 sites), on a perfect golden crescent hemmed by lush headlands. There's no water on-site, but the sublime sunrise makes up for any inconvenience. It was here and at nearby **Pitt Head** that Te Rauparaha's forces slaughtered the local Ngati Apa in 1828, taking few prisoners and burying no bodies.

ANCHORAGE HUT TO BARK BAY HUT. *9.5km, 2½-3hr.* To continue toward Bark Bay from Anchorage without doubling back up the ridge, go all the way to the western edge of the beach to where a signpost points to the high-tide route (1hr.) and low-tide route (20min.) to Torrent Bay Estuary. A side trip off the high tide route, **Cleopatra's Pool** (return 20min.) sees water spill down a rocky chute into a magnificent pebble-bottomed swimming hole.

Neither **Torrent Bay Estuary Campsite** (6 sites) nor nearby **Torrent Bay Campsite** (10 sites) is terribly ideal—the former overlooks a mudflat half the time, while the latter is in a grove of pines. Near Torrent Bay Campsite, a path leads to the densely forested upstream portion of the **Falls River** (return 3hr.). Tiny **Torrent Bay Township** is most notable for its **public telephone** with free local calls. Back in the wilderness, **Medlands Beach Campsite** (6 sites) offers sandy plots framed by a gorgeous combination of estuary and surf. **Bark Bay Campsite** (40 sites) is a crowded, kanuka-filled monster, though the bay is big and beautiful. Just before the spacious rooms and freshwater shower of the inland **Bark Bay Hut** (25 bunks), the miniscule **Bark Bay Hut Campsite** (5 sites) is hidden, yet only paces off the track. Both Bark Bay Hut and Bark Bay Beach Campsite have **filtered drinking water** from October to April.

BARK BAY HUT TO AWAROA HUT. *11.5km, 3-4hr.* The track crosses Bark Bay Estuary (an alternative high-tide route goes around the inlet) and then winds steadily up and over a small peninsula before hitting **Tonga Quarry Campsite** (20 sites), which features a stream, a nice white stretch of sand, and some big blocks of stone from the old quarry days. Another brief up-and-over breaks onto the huge, golden arc of **Onetahuti Beach,** host to the ample **Onetahuti Campsite** (20 sites) and, all too often, scores of buzzing water taxis. The track runs the length of the beach until, after about 20min., it crosses a river at the northern end that can rise chest-high at high tide (see **Tides,** p. 288).

Heading back inland, the track climbs gently toward the **Awaroa Lodge ❺,** a swank resort and restaurant that runs a **barge** across Awaroa Inlet for those anxious to continue their tramping, no matter what the tide. (☎ 528 8758. Barge M-F 1hr. before high tide; $5. Restaurant open daily 7:30-10am, 11:30am-2:30pm, and 5:30-8:30pm. Soup $12. Free toilets and drinking water. Hot shower $165, sauna $10.) Even those not interested in the barge can pass through this posh slice of civilization en route to **Awaroa Inlet;** the route takes an hour less than the main track, though at high tide it navigates a waist-deep stream. Simple **Awaroa Hut** (25 bunks) and the hard-packed dirt of neighboring **Awaroa Campsite** (18 sites) sit beside the inlet, which becomes a pebbly and crossable mudflat within two hours on either side of low tide.

AWAROA HUT TO TOTARANUI CAMPGROUND. *5.5km, 1½hr.* After the inlet, the track turns inland again before it comes to the grassy plots and long nearby beach of **Waiharakeke Campsite** (10 sites). The track then passes a couple of huge beech trees and stunning Goat Beach before emerging into the caravan sprawl of **Totaranui Campsite** (see **Accommodations and Food,** p. 286).

TOTARANUI CAMPGROUND TO WAINUI CARPARK. *13km, 3¾hr.* Comprised of hillier terrain than other parts of the track, lined with majestic beaches, and featuring superior overnight options, this section is arguably the Coastal Track's most beautiful. It also attracts fewer day-trippers, since the water taxis rarely venture north of Totaranui. **Anapai Bay Campsite** (4 sites) lies next to a beach fringed by fluted rock faces, its sites concealed inside a dense canopy of windswept kanuka. **Mutton Cove Campsite** (20 sites) also sits alongside an elegant beach, though unsightly felled pines mar its plots. From Mutton Cove the track forks for an extra loop around **Separation Point** (return 1hr.), a walk through kanuka-clad hillsides that leads to a lighthouse with misty vantages of Farewell Spit, the North Island, and the occasional fur seal. The main track descends gradually to **Whariwharangi Hut** (20 bunks), an old two-storey farmhouse with freshwater showers and the fields of **Whariwharangi Campsite** (20 sites) outside. The rugged beach nearby may have seen the first brutal Maori-Pakeha encounter upon Abel Tasman's arrival to New Zealand (see p. 50). Only one very large (but very scenic and gradually graded) hill stands between Whariwharangi and the Wainui carpark.

MOTUEKA ☎ 03

Motueka (pop. 10,000) sits at the mouth of the Motueka River on SH60. The entire area was once under water; today the land is unusually fertile, making it a choice location for fruit growing—the apple, pear, and kiwifruit orchards attract legions of fruit pickers each summer. Motueka's ample services and budget digs make it a comfortable place to start trips into Abel Tasman National Park and the rest of Golden Bay.

TRANSPORTATION. Abel Tasman Coachlines (☎528 0285) runs to: **Marahau** (30min., 2-3 per day, $7) via **Kaiteriteri Beach** (15min., $7); **Nelson** (50min., 1-3 per day, $9); and **Takaka** (1hr., 1-2 per day, $15). **Kahurangi Bus Services** (☎525 9434) runs to: **Marahau** (30min., Nov.-Apr. only, 3-4 per day, $7) via **Kaiteriteri Beach** (15min., $7); **Nelson** (1hr., 1-4 per day, $9); and **Takaka** (1½hr., 1-2 per day, $15). **Mountain bike rental** is available at **Hollidays Cycle Centre,** 277 High St. (☎528 9379. Open Dec.-Jan. daily 8:30am-5:30pm, Feb.-Nov. M-F 8:30am-5:30pm, Sa 9am-12:30pm. $25 per day.)

ORIENTATION AND PRACTICAL INFORMATION. SH60 becomes **High Street** as it cuts through town. All shops and most backpackers lie on or just off High St.; building numbers increase as one heads south (toward Nelson). Buses drop-off at the **Motueka Visitors Centre,** on Wallace St. (☎528 6543. Open Nov.-Feb. daily 8am-7pm; Mar.-Oct. 8am-5pm.) The **DOC office,** on High St. at King Edward St., is 2km toward Nelson from the Visitors Center. (☎528 1810. Open M-F 8am-4:30pm.) Motueka has many **work opportunities** for fruit-pickers. **Coppins Great Outdoor Centre,** 225 High St., stocks and hires tramping gear. (☎528 7296. Open Oct.-Mar. M-Tu 8am-6:30pm, W-Th 8am-7pm, F 8am-9pm, Sa 8:30am-6:30pm, Su 9am-5:30pm; Apr.-Sept. M-Th 8:30am-6pm, F 8:30am-7pm, Sa 9am-4pm, Su 10am-4pm.) Other services include: **banks** with **ATMs** along High St. (most open M-F 9am-4:30pm); the **police,** 68 High St. (☎528 1220); **Healthcare Pharmacy,** 125 High St. (☎528 9080; open M 9am-5:30, T-Th 8:30am-5:30pm, F 8:30am-6pm, Sa 9am-1pm); the **Motueka Emergency Duty Doctor Number** (☎528 8770); **Internet access** at **Cyberworld,** 15 Wallace St., for $6 per hr. (☎025 627 0419; open M-F 9am-9pm, Sa 10am-9pm, Su 10:30am-8pm); and the **post office,** 207 High St. (☎528 6600; open M-F 8am-5:30pm, Sa-Su 9am-5pm).

ACCOMMODATIONS AND CAMPING. The **White Elephant ❷,** 55 Whakarewa St., lies less than 1km off High St. From the Visitors Center, take a left onto High St., turn right at KFC, and continue down Whakarewa; the hostel is on the left. This sunny Victorian house should be your first choice; cushy common spaces and soft beds are the most inviting in town. Rent tramping equipment for a fee; bikes are free. (☎528 6208; fax 528 0110; white.elephant@clear.net.nz. Dorms $18; twins and doubles $44; tent sites $10.) The facilities at the large **Bakers Lodge (BBH/YHA) ❷**, 4 Poole St., are so shiny and antiseptic that the place still feels new. From the Visitors Center, take a right onto High St.; the hostel is two long blocks down on the right. (☎528 0102; bakers@motueka.co.nz. Internet. Dorms $17-18; twins and doubles $40-50.) A snug affair run by Aussie and German expats, **Twin Oaks Cottage (BBH) ❷**, 25 Parker St., has a kitchen full of friendly faces. They also hire tramping gear. (☎/fax 528 7882; twinoakscottage@xtra.co.nz. Dorms $17; doubles $44-52. Inquire about longer stays.) **Fearon's Bush Camp ❶**, 10 Fearon St., just off High St., allows tenters to pitch anywhere in its shady fields. (☎528 7189. Tent sites $10, under 15 $5; double cabins $35.)

❐ **FOOD.** Brightly muralled walls support the astronomical ceiling at ☒**Hot Mama's Cafe ❸**, 105 High St. Lunch ($4-12) in the mellow garden or sup (mains $14.50-19) at the indoor, Jackson Pollock-inspired tables. (☎528 7039. Occasional live music. Open daily 8:30am-late, usually closed July-Oct.) **Bake House ❸**, on Wallace St., across from the Visitors Center, serves delicious pizzas ($13-34) and pastas ($17-20) in a room curiously dotted with fish tanks and pictures of Rome. (☎528 6111. Open daily 9am-9pm; in winter M-W 9am-3pm, Th-Su 9am-8:30pm.) **The Swinging Sultan ❷**, 172 High St., serves juicy beef, chicken, and vegetarian kebabs ($6-9) to take away. (☎528 8909. Open daily 10am-8pm.) Self-caterers can head to **Supervalue**, 108 High St. (☎528 7180. Open daily 8am-8pm.)

❐❐ **SIGHTS AND ACTIVITIES.** Relatively quiet **Kaiteriteri Beach** is just a 15min. drive (13km) north from town; buses stop en route to **Marahau** (see **Transportation**, p. 285). **Takaka Hill** (791m), 20km from town, serves as a starting point for a multitude of short walks, including the **Takaka Hill Walk** (return 15min.) at the very top. Also at the top of Takaka Hill, the **Ngarua Caves** showcase moa bones and illuminated stalactites. (☎528 8093. Open Sept.-May daily 10am-4pm. $11, under 8 $4.) Back in town, the **Motueka District Museum**, 140 High St., has an assortment of Maori artifacts and an exhibit on the history of the area. (☎528 7660. Open M-F 10am-3pm; in winter closed M. $2, children 50¢.)

TAKAKA ☎03

Dredlocked types inhale deeply and repeatedly in Takaka (pop. 1500), the main town of Golden Bay. A convenient access point for the Kahurangi and Abel Tasman National Parks, the earth-friendly community of Takaka also has its own attractions. Visitors are mesmerized by the famously clear Pupu Springs, the tame (but hungry) Anatoki eels, and the limestone Rawhiti Caves.

❐ **TRANSPORTATION.** Takaka is 58km north of Motueka, 8km west of Pohara, and 27km east of Collingwood. **Abel Tasman Coachlines** (☎548 0285) travels from mid-October to April to **Nelson** (2½hr., 1 per day, $22) via **Motueka** (1hr., $15); and **Totaranui** (1hr., 1 per day, $11) via the **Wainui carpark** (30min., $7). From mid-October to mid-April, **Bickley Motors** (☎525 8352) heads to the **Heaphy Track** (1¼hr., 1 per day, $20) via **Collingwood** (30min., $14). **Kahurangi Bus Services** (☎525 9434) runs to: **Nelson** (2hr.; in summer 1 per day, in winter 4 per week; $25) via **Motueka** (1hr., $18); **Totaranui** (1hr., 1 per day Oct.-Apr. only, $11) via the **Wainui carpark** (30min., $8); and the **Heaphy Track** (1¼hr., 1 per day, $20) via **Collingwood** (30min., $12). For **bike rental**, head to the **Quiet Revolution Cycle Shop**, 7 Commercial St. (☎/fax 525 9555. Half-day rental $15, full-day $25. Open M-F 9am-5pm, Sa 9:30am-12:30pm.)

292 ■ GOLDEN BAY

ORIENTATION & PRACTICAL INFORMATION. Takaka's main (some might say only) drag is **Commercial Street,** which becomes Willow St. at its southern (Motueka-bound) extremity. **Motupipi Street** branches northeast where Commercial St. becomes Willow St. Buses arrive and depart from the **Golden Bay Visitor Information Centre,** on Willow St. (☎525 9136. Open daily 9am-5pm.) Trampers head to the **Golden Bay Area DOC Office,** 62 Commercial St. (☎525 8026. Open M-F 8am-4pm.) Takaka offers many **work opportunities** for WWOOFers. Other services on Commercial St. include: **Westpac Trust Bank** (☎525 8094; open M and Th-F 9am-4:30pm, Tu-W 9:30am-4:30pm), with an **ATM;** the **police** (☎525 9211); the **Golden Bay Pharmacy** (☎525 9490; open M-Th 8:30am-5:30pm, F 8:30am-6pm, Sa 9:30am-noon); the **Golden Bay Medical Centre** (☎525 9911); **Internet access** at Baylink Communications for $7.50 per hr. (☎525 8863; open M-F 9am-5pm, Sa 9:30am-noon); and the **post office** (☎525 9916; open M-F 8:30am-5:30pm, Sa 9:30am-12:30pm).

ACCOMMODATIONS AND FOOD. Annie's Backpackers (BBH) ❷, 25 Motupipi St., provides soft, fully made-up beds, a garden common room, and a typically Takakan old-hippy atmosphere. (☎525 8766 or 0800 266 937; fax 525 8758; anniesbackpackers@xtra.co.nz. Free bike use. Dorms $20; doubles $45.) **The Nook (BBH) ❷,** an 8min. drive away in nearby Pohara (turn right down Abel Tasman Dr. from Motupipi St.), is set up in impeccable white adobe-style buildings with terracotta-tiled floors. (☎525 8501; nook@clearnet.net.nz. Free pick-up from Visitors Center. Closed June 15-Aug. Dorms $20; twins and doubles $50; tent sites $11.) In Takaka, **Golden Bay Barefoot Backpackers (BBH) ❷,** 114 Commercial St., beds its guests in clean pastel rooms. It also offers complimentary fruit, milk, fresh bread, use of bikes, Visitors Center pick-up, and transport to Pupu Springs. (☎525 7005 or 0508 525 700; goldenbaybackpackers@clear.net.nz. Dorms $17; 1 tiny double $36.) **Kiwiana (BBH) ❷,** 73 Motupipi St., is the new face on the Takaka streets. Guests park it in the garage-turned-lounge or soak up steam in the free spa. (☎0800 805 494; fax 525 7636. Dorms $17-18; doubles $42.) **The Wholemeal Cafe ❸,** on Commercial St., is a Golden Bay cultural mecca, drawing in art exhibits, live music, and the community at large. The rotating menu often includes curries ($12.50-16) and fresh pastas ($10-15). Their notice board is a good place to find WWOOFing opportunities. (☎525 9426. Open daily 9am-9pm.) **Golden Bay Organics,** 47 Commercial St., peddles all organic produce. (☎525 8677. Open M-Th 9am-5:30pm, F 9am-6pm, Sa 9:30am-2pm.) **Supervalue,** on Commercial St., is the place to buy groceries. (☎525 9383. Open M-Th 8am-6pm, F 8am-6:30pm, Sa 9am-1pm.)

SIGHTS AND ACTIVITIES. The bubbling **Te Waikoropupu Springs** ("Pupu Springs" for short), 7km northwest of Takaka, is New Zealand's largest freshwater springs system. Ages ago, underground streams carved out chambers and passages in the marble, which eventually filled with the rushing waters of a full-on subterranean river. Now among the clearest in the world, these crystalline depths have an underwater visibility of more than 70m. **River Inn** (☎525 9425 or 0800 222 572) in Takaka organizes **"float and swim"** excursions that include transport to the springs, snorkeling gear, and wet suits. The **Rawhiti Caves,** a one-million-year-old hole (with a 60m-wide entrance) filled with thousands of naturally colorful stalactites, remains pristine and untainted by artificial lighting. Lying a 45min. bush walk from the nearest road, the caves are best visited with John Croxford of **Kahurangi Guided Walks** (☎525 7177), who runs informative 3hr. trips ($25).

Tasman Tandems gets visitors involved (and aloft) in one of Golden Bay's pet pastimes: paragliding off Takaka Hill. (☎528 9283 or 021 544 800. 10-15min. flight $110, discounts for groups. Will pick-up in Takaka.) Climbers should touch base with **Hang Dog Camp** (☎525 9043; hangdog.camp@paradise.net.nz) for the scoop on climbing the region's limestone faces.

The highlight of a trip to the **Bencarri Farm and Cafe,** on McCallum's Rd. 5km south of Takaka, is feeding the hungry but harmless native eels. Cool your hand in the river before touching their heat-sensitive skin, then put your trust in the adage about biting the hand that feeds you. (☎ 525 8261. Open Sept.-Apr. Th-M 10am-5:30pm; in winter on demand, usually 1:30pm. $10, children $5.) With its antiques, tools, geological specimens, and handful of Powellipanta shells, the **Golden Bay Museum,** in the old post office on Commercial St., represents the best of the small town collections that try to explain the history of the Abel Tasman. (☎ 525 9990. Open daily 10am-4pm; in winter closed Su. $2.)

COLLINGWOOD AND FAREWELL SPIT ☎ 03

In 1856, New Zealand's first big gold rush made a boom town of Collingwood, where 4000 residents clamored to name it the capital city. Three major fires and one depleted gold supply later, modern-day Collingwood (pop. 300) may be a shadow of its former self, but that doesn't affect its prime location. Full of swamp, scrub, mudflats, and 18m sand dunes, the country's largest sandspit (33km at low tide) can change from just 1km wide at high tide to 7km wide when the tide goes out. The most interesting time to visit is from September to mid-March, when flocks of up to 90 different species of birds swoop in from as far away as Siberia.

TRANSPORTATION. **Bickley Motors** runs to Takaka from October to April. (☎ 525 8352. 30min., 1 per day, $20.) **Kahurangi Bus Services** does the same for less. (☎ 525 9434. $12.) **There is no bus to Collingwood May to September.** Although one should always consider the risks, **hitchhiking** in Golden Bay is reportedly common.

ORIENTATION AND PRACTICAL INFORMATION. Collingwood lies at the terminus of **SH60,** 27km north of Takaka and 23km south of **Puponga,** the settlement at the base of Farewell Spit. As SH60 enters Collingwood from the west, the first street on the left is **Tasman Street,** the town's one-block-long main thoroughfare. One block farther east, **Beach Road** runs parallel to Tasman St. alongside the ocean. **Farewell Spit Cafe and Visitor Centre** in Puponga is the only info outlet in the area. The cafe has spectacular views of the spit. (☎ 524 8454. Lunch $10. Open Jan.-Feb. daily 9am-6pm; Mar.-June and Sept.-Dec. 10am-4:30pm. Closed mid-June to Aug.) The area has **no ATMs.** Correspondence services include **Internet access** at Farewell Spit Nature Tours on Tasman St. (☎ 524 8188; $10 per hr.) and the **post office** on Tasman St. (☎ 524 8916; open M-F 8:30am-5:30pm, Sa 9am-noon).

ACCOMMODATIONS AND FOOD. The best places to stay in the area are outside town but easily reached by car. **The Innlet (BBH) ❷,** 11km from Collingwood toward Farewell Spit, is a lovely and eco-friendly spot with several kilometers of marked bush walks. Their doubles are beautiful cottages set in the woods. Two creek-side, cast-iron hot tubs are the ultimate luxury. (☎ 524 8040; www.goldenbayindex.co.nz/theinnlet.htm. Bike rental. Guided kayaking $75. Freedom hire $45. Internet. Dorms $18.50; twins and doubles $44-55; self-contained cottages $110; tent sites $15. Prior bookings only July-Aug.) Serene, environmentally conscious **Shambhala Guesthouse (BBH) ❷,** 9km out of Collingwood toward Takaka, takes hippie vibes to new levels. Guests enjoy private beach access, rooms with water views, and rides on Pedro the resident horse. Call for pick-up from the Mussel Inn. (☎ 525 8463. Bike rental. Dorms from $17; twins and doubles $38. Closed June-Nov.) **Skara Brae ❹,** at the corner of Elizabeth and Tasman St., offers up peachy pastel motel and B&B accommodations just 2min. from the beach. (☎ 524 8464; fax 524 8474; skarabrae@xtra.co.nz. Self-contained motel units $85; B&B rooms $100-110.) **Collingwood Motor Camp ❶,** at the far end of Tasman St., has tent sites overlooking the water. (☎ 524 8149. Canoes $5 per hr. Dorms $18; cabins $50 for 2; deluxe cabins $100 for 2, extra person $7-10; tent sites $9, under 14 $5.)

Great grub awaits at the ◪**Mussel Inn ❸**, on SH60, 200m toward Collingwood from the turn-off to Shambhala Guesthouse. Bohemian offerings include strangely named local brews and a mean veggie lasagna ($13). Live music and an outdoor bonfire bring out the Golden Bay community in full force—you'll be hard pressed to find a more welcoming crowd in all of New Zealand. (☎ 525 9241. Open daily 11am-late; in winter Tu-Su 5pm-late.) ◪**Rosy Glow Chocolates ❶**, on Beach Rd., produces treats so sweet that they're already the stuff of local legend. From the beginning of Tasman St., head a block down Elizabeth St. and take a right on Beach; Rosy's is a 5min. walk on the right. (☎ 524 8348. Chocolates $3-3.50 per piece. Open M-Th and Sa-Su 10am-5pm.) **The Courthouse Inn and Cafe ❸**, at the corner where SH60 turns into Tasman St., serves tempting gourmet lunches ($6-12) and dinners ($19-25). They also let small dorm rooms. (☎ 524 8572. Dorms Dec.-Mar. only; $15. Cafe open daily 7:30am-late. Reduced hours in winter.) For less hedonic needs, stock up at the **Collingwood General Store.** (☎ 524 8221. Open M-Th 8am-5:30pm, F 8am-6pm, Sa-Su 9am-1pm.)

◨◩ **SIGHTS AND ACTIVITIES.** There are two ways for visitors to explore Farewell Spit. They can walk 4km out onto the sand peninsula, stopping first at the Visitors Center for directions, or take a tour with one of two companies licensed to drive the Spit all the way to the lighthouse near the tip. Most of the east coast belongs strictly to the birds, so tours travel along the west coast. Tour structure and departure times change with the tides but run daily most of the year. **Farewell Spit Tours** has been running 4WD trips along the Spit since the mid-1940s. (☎ 524 8257 or 0800 808 257; www.farewellspit.co.nz. 5½hr. trip $58. 6½hr. trip to a gannet colony $65. 10hr. trip to experience high tide on the Spit $250.) **Farewell Spit Nature Tours** has cushy vehicles and usually makes a stop in Puponga Farm Park before or after exploring the Spit. (☎ 524 8188 or 0800 250 500; www.farewell-spit.co.nz. 6½hr. $75, including lunch.)

At the Spit's base, **Puponga Farm Park** serves as an environmental buffer for the unique sand habitat. Thirty kilometers of walking trails allow visitors to roam through a patchwork of native plants and bleating livestock. The park's undertouristed **Wharariki Beach** is also definitely worth a visit. Low tide reveals fascinating caves and arches that beg exploration. The nearest carpark lies at the end of Wharariki Rd., 6km west of Puponga town; from there, it's a 20min. walk through sand dunes to the beach. **Cape Farewell Horse Treks** leads trips through the area for riders of all levels. (☎ 524 8031; www.horsetreksnz.com. 3½hr. ride on Wharariki Beach $65. Also runs multi-day expeditions. Pick-up from Collingwood $10.) Meanwhile, many locals consider the **Te Anaroa Caves**, 9km southeast of Collingwood in Rockville, to be the Golden Bay's most stunning cave system. (☎ 524 8131. Jan. 4 tours per day; Feb.-Dec. by appointment. $15, under 15 $6.)

KARAMEA ☎ 03

Karamea is a small town in the shadow of the big wilderness, and should serve as a gateway rather than a destination in and of itself. Best known as the endpoint of the **Heaphy Track** (see p. 296), the village also the nearby **Oparara Basin**, famous for its huge limestone arches and delicate Honeycomb Cave system. From the carpark on Oparara Rd. (a well-marked 1hr. drive north of town), the **Oparara (Big) Arch trail** (return 45min.) leads to the 43m-high, 219m-long arch, while the **Moria Gate trail** (return 1½hr.) heads to Little Arch. **Last Resort** (see below) offers **transport** (return $30) as well as **tours** through the area; their 5½hr. Honeycomb Cave tour ($60) takes in several caves and Big Arch and is a worthwhile option for would-be spelunkers, as **it is not possible to visit the Honeycomb Caves except as part of a tour.**

The **Fenian Track** (return 5hr.) gives trampers a taste of the rainforest. The walk to **Scott's Beach** (return 1½hr.) begins at the Heaphy Track trailhead. There are numerous other short hikes near town as well, though most require a drive—**hitchhikers** say locals are receptive to outstretched thumbs, but even in summer there's little traffic; *Let's Go* does not recommend hitching.

Karamea sits at the northern end of SH67. **Cunningham's Motors** (☎ 789 7177) and **Karamea Express** (☎ 782 6617) run to **Westport** (1½hr.; M-F 8:20am, Karamea Express also Oct.-Apr. Sa 8:10am; $15). The **Karamea Information and Resource Centre**, on Bridge St., has information on Kahurangi and sells hut passes. (☎ 782 6652. Open daily 9am-5pm; in winter M-F 9am-5pm, Sa 9am-1pm.) Other local services include: a **Four Square** (☎ 782 6701; open M-Th 8:30am-6pm, F 8:30am-7pm, Sa-Su 9am-noon; in summer Sa until 5pm); **petrol stations**, at Market Cross near the Visitors Center; the **police** (☎ 782 6801), on Wharf St.; **Karamea Medical Centre** (☎ 782 6737); **Internet access** at the Visitors Center ($2.50 per 15min.); and **postal facilities** at the Karamea Hardware Store (☎ 782 6700; open M-F 8am-6pm, Sa-Su 9am-noon). There is **no bank or ATM** in Karamea. For accommodations, your first resort should be the **Last Resort ❷**, 71 Waverley St., a 7min. walk west from the center of town. It has two restaurants and reading lights in the airy dorms but does not provide kitchen access. (☎ 782 6617 or 0800 505 042; fax 782 6820; www.lastresort.co.nz. Internet. Dorms $20; twins and doubles $50-60; doubles with bath $75-140.) **Punga Lodge (BBH) ❷**, 130 Waverley St., greets with psychedelic murals, continuous music, and thrift-store furniture. They will pick you up from the end of the Heaphy track for free. (☎/fax 782 6667. Dorms $15; doubles $38.)

KAHURANGI NATIONAL PARK ☎ 03

The vast wilderness that dominates the northwest corner of the South Island forms the 452,002-hectare Kahurangi National Park. The country's youngest and second-largest national park, Kahurangi accommodates snow-capped peaks, rolling tussock, verdant valleys, and palm-lined coasts. This biodiversity supports an astounding array of natural fauna; over half of New Zealand's native plant species grow here (67 of them live nowhere else in the world). While experienced kayakers can brave the Class 5 Karamea River, Kahurangi is most accessible through a network of challenging tramping tracks.

AT A GLANCE	
AREA: 452,002 hectares.	**GATEWAYS:** Motueka, Takaka, Karamea, Murchison.
CLIMATE: Temperate forest.	**CAMPING:** Backcountry huts.
FEATURES: Rivers, high plateaus, coastal forest, alpine herb fields.	**FEES & RESERVATIONS:** Inform DOC of any plans and for possible hut passes.
HIGHLIGHTS: Trout fishing and over 570km of walking track.	**TRAMPS:** Heaphy, Wangapeka.

▸ TRANSPORTATION. Aorere Valley Road and **Karamea-Kohaihai Road** head southwest from Collingwood and north from Karamea, respectively, to the Heaphy Track's two trailheads. See **Heaphy Track: Transportation,** p. 296, for information on bus transport to these points. Additionally, **Cobb Valley Road** heads 27km from Upper Takaka to the Cobb Reservoir.

WHEN TO GO. Kahurangi is beautiful year-round. Most visitors come between December and February; March and April are drier and chillier.

296 ■ GOLDEN BAY

ORIENTATION AND PRACTICAL INFORMATION. Kahurangi stretches from the west coast east to SH60 and from the base of Farewell Spit south to SH6. The park's sprawl leads to highly decentralized information and access. The **DOC offices** in Nelson (see p. 278), Motueka (see p. 285), Takaka (see. p. 291), Karamea (see p. 294), and Westport (see p. 330) all sell hut passes and have information on the park. There are **supermarkets** and **ATMs** in Takaka and Westport; Collingwood and Karamea have smaller food shops. Although most of the trailhead carparks don't have troubled histories, it's still safer to **park** in a hostel lot in one of the nearby towns.

ACCOMMODATIONS. Almost all convenient accommodations are in the outlying towns. **Heaphy Backpackers ❷,** 3km toward Collingwood from the Heaphy Track's northern trailhead, is a notable exception. This hostel has incredible views of the Aorere River valley; its Swiss-artist owner provides free transport to and from the trailhead. (☎524 8252. Closed in winter. Dorms $16; doubles $40.)

OUTDOOR ACTIVITIES. There are many sub-alpine dayhikes around **Mt. Arthur** and the **Cobb Valley.** A steep and narrow track to the incredible viewpoint of **Parapara Peak** (1249m; return 9hr.) begins just 2km off SH60 between Takaka and Collingwood at the end of Ward-Holmes Rd. An intensive tramping option is the **Leslie-Karamea Track** (6-9 days), which connects with the **Wangapeka Track** (p. 300).
Ultimate Descents runs **rafting** trips on the **Karamea River** and can organize **kayak** rental. (☎523 9899 or 0800 748 377; www.rivers.co.nz. 5-day hike in, raft out journey $795. 3-day heli-journey $895. 1-day heli-journey $295. Kayaks $45 per day.) **Buller Adventure Tours** conducts heli-rafting trips. (☎789 7286 or 0800 697 286; www.adventuretours.co.nz. Full-day $259). Karamea's **Last Resort** (see p. 294) runs rafting and canoe trips on mellower parts of the river (2½hr., $30).

HEAPHY TRACK

The longest of the overland Great Walks, the Heaphy Track is also the most diverse, traversing no fewer than four completely different ecosystems. From east to west, trampers pass through mountain beech forests, flat and tussock-tufted expanses, primary podocarp forests, and the palm-intensive beachgasm at journey's end. For the past century, environmentalists have managed to keep the proposed road that would connect Collingwood and Karamea in the planning stages. Though the issue has returned to the table in recent years, for now the Heaphy provides a glimpse of Kahurangi's still largely untainted natural richness.

Length: 82km, 4-6 days.

Trailheads: Brown Hut, 28km southeast of **Collingwood** (see p. 293) and **Kohaihai carpark,** 16km north of **Karamea** (see p. 294); most start at Brown Hut.

Transportation: Transportation is somewhat complicated. If possible, try to move all the way to the other coast in one go; this will probably require sending stuff with the tourist office (see **Storage and Baggage Transport,** below). **Bickley Motors** (☎525 8352) runs Oct.-Apr. daily from Takaka to the trailhead (1¼hr., 10am, $20) via Collingwood; the bus departs the trailhead at 12:15pm. **Kahurangi Bus Services** (☎525 9434) does the same (departs Motueka 8am, Takaka 9:30am, trailhead 11:15am; $20). **Farewell Spit Tours** (☎524 8257) runs on demand between Brown Hut and Collingwood ($15). **Karamea Express** (☎782 6916, after hours 782 6617) runs Oct.-Apr. daily between Karamea and Kohaihai carpark (departs Karamea 1:45pm, departs Kohaihai 2pm; $5) and on demand year-round ($25 up to 5 people, $5 each additional person). **Karamea Taxis** (☎782 6757 or 0800 505 042) runs any time on demand ($25 up to 4 people, $6 each additional person). If you have a **car,** it will require a fair

KAHURANGI NATIONAL PARK ■ 297

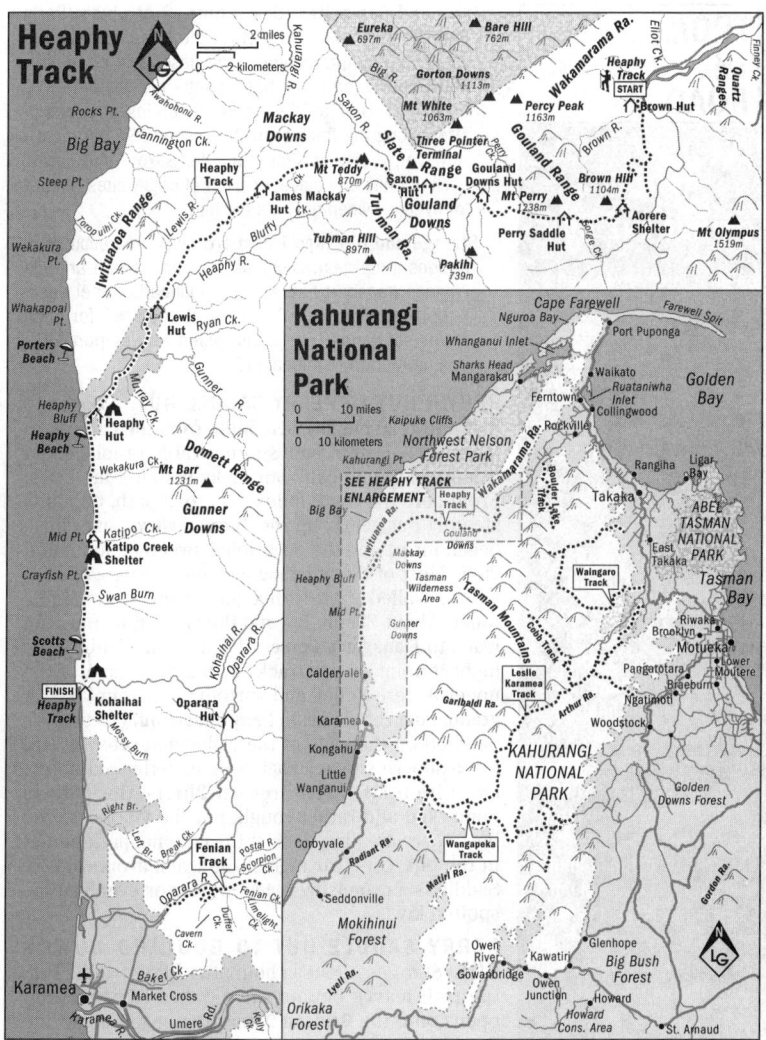

amount of backtracking to pick up your vehicle; your best bet is to leave it in Motueka. If you are driving up the Aorere Rd. to leave your car at Brown Hut (only advisable if you are doing a loop so that you finish your hike there), beware that the drive entails fording 3 streams. Although *Let's Go* doesn't recommend it, **hitchhiking** to either trailhead can be difficult, as there is no through traffic; Kohaihai reportedly sees more cars.

Seasonality: Oct.-Apr. is the peak season for the track; it's most crowded in the middle of summer. Winter hiking (May-Sept.) is inadvisable. Although rain is never far off, the track is best enjoyed in dry weather; the rain cause the rivers to flood and brings out the mud.

FROM THE ROAD

RACE AGAINST THE SUN

I had been on a late-season tramp in Kahurangi National Park for four days, during which my emotional state had alternated between utter loneliness and extreme elation. Now, nearing the end of my hike, I arrived at the much-anticipated climb, 1000 meters to the saddle. The path was smooth but it climbed stubbornly—jumping in fits and spurts yet always managing to gain.

I kept my eye out for Splugen's Hut, the climb's halfway point. I had promised myself that if I didn't reach it before 3:30pm, I would have to spend the night there. I'd read *Into Thin Air* and I knew you need to be firm about your deadlines. I hated the thought of spending a cold, dark, and exposed night in the wild forest. However, when I reached Splugen's Hut at 3:10pm, I decided I had to hike on to Salisbury Lodge—there was absolutely no way I could wake up in the morning and face the second half of the climb.

I found a second walking stick and began to practically drag myself up. The climb got steeper, my knees got shaky, my quads began to feel weak. I kept drinking and eating. As I rose, the sun started to set. I realized it was good that I was gaining elevation, because down in the valleys it was already getting dark. I was still basking in the sun. I began to feel like I was racing the sun. I was so intent on beating it that I didn't notice a crowd of deer until I'd scared them off the path and could only see their white tails bouncing away. Nearing the top, I turned around and beheld the valley behind me.

Huts and Campsites: Seven **huts**, 5 of which (Perry Saddle, Saxon, Mackay, Lewis, and Heaphy) have gas cookers. Oct.-Apr. requires a hut pass ($14 per night). May-Sept. reverts to a backcountry hut system ($10 per night). DOC officially permits tenting at 3 **campsites** along the track's coastal section ($7 per night). However, except for Perry Saddle, Saxon, and Lewis, each hut has an adjacent cluster of boggy sites (meant for overflow when the huts are full).

Storage and Baggage Transport: Most area accommodations store gear. Local visitors centers can arrange luggage transport between the trailheads (label destination prominently). Generally, it costs $5 for each change-of-hands (e.g. Collingwood to Westport $10; Collingwood to Karamea $15).

BROWN HUT TO PERRY SADDLE HUT. *17km, 5hr.* **Brown Hut** (20 bunks), just 5min. from the carpark at the track's eastern end, sports a large fireplace and free local phone calls but lacks cooking facilities. From here the track follows a broad path, climbing steadily but gently up the **Aorere Valley**, past dense beech forest and the occasional sweeping mountain view. Most of the climbing is done by **Aorere Shelter**, a three-walled affair with a grand view, water, and a toilet. About 25min. beyond the shelter, a spur trail leads to **Flanagan's Corner** (910m, return 7min.), the highest point on the track, with a panorama of the upper Aorere Valley and surrounding mountains. A gradual descent leads to **Perry Saddle Hut** (26 bunks), perched on the edge of the valley and offering still more superb views. From here, experienced hikers can climb **Mt. Perry** (return 2hr.)—the trail is unmarked and rather rough, but the vistas are the best; there are directions in the national park binder in the hut. On clear nights, the track around Perry Saddle is a promising place to hear or even see the spotted kiwi.

PERRY SADDLE HUT TO GOULAND DOWNS HUT. *8km, 2hr.* About an hour after Perry Saddle Hut, the trail leaves behind the patches of beech and opens onto the **Gouland Downs**, the beginning of the track's most exposed section. Wind-swept grass stretches to the horizon, broken only by tiny carnivorous sundews or the odd shoe tree. **Gouland Downs Hut** (10 bunks) is the smallest and most bare on the track, with a warm stone hearth but no gas burners. The tent sites are unremarkable, but they're the grassiest you'll find between Aorere Shelter and Lewis Hut. Just a few hundred meters farther awaits a Tolkien-esque forest, full of bizarre moss-shrouded rock formations, caves, and arches. Several beautiful streams wind through and around the limestone.

GOULAND DOWNS HUT TO SAXON HUT. *5km, 1½hr.* The track traverses the western end of Gouland Downs, gradually reentering beech forest; **Saxon Hut** (16 bunks) sits amid decent scenery, offering one cozy room with gas cookers and a fireplace. The campsites here can get extremely muddy.

SAXON HUT TO MACKAY HUT. *14km, 3hr.* The track winds gradually uphill, in and out of forest and the **Mackay Downs.** This area can flood quite seriously during heavy rain, and the inconsistent boardwalking means wet feet during any degree of downpour. Past variegated mosses, **Mackay Hut** (26 bunks) features flush toilets and views down to the Tasman.

MACKAY HUT TO LEWIS HUT. *13.5km, 3½hr.* From Mackay it's all downhill to the sea. As the elevation decreases, the forest changes from beech to rimu and tree fern. By the time **Lewis Hut** (20 bunks) comes into view, the bush has thickened and diversified, the beautiful nikau palm has appeared, and rata lace the hillsides with red (in summer). Lewis Hut sits at the junction of the Heaphy and Lewis Rivers and offers flush toilets. Be warned: **sandflies** begin to appear here.

LEWIS HUT TO HEAPHY HUT. *8km, 2½hr.* After Lewis, the vegetation grows more extreme. Epiphytes (plants that grow from another tree's branches) drip from giant rata, the tree ferns grow taller and taller, and after traversing four long swing bridges the track finally reaches the sea. Cheery **Heaphy Hut** (20 bunks) holds court by the mouth of the Heaphy River; highlights include a large fireplace, flush toilets, and stellar views on all sides. Its adjacent campsite is excellent: wide and grassy with a well-kept shelter. Out front, there's a beach littered with driftwood, an ideal spot to watch high tide's waves surge upstream the otherwise lazy Heaphy, or the sun set over the angry Tasman Sea.

HEAPHY HUT TO KOHAIHAI CARPARK. *16.5km, 4½hr.* This palm-filled stretch of track runs entirely along the coast and is almost totally flat. The Tasman surf is ferocious; riptides make the water too dangerous for swimming. **Katipo Creek Campsite** has a small number of tent sites, an aging shelter, and a toilet, but no water. Shortly after, the shelter **Crayfish Point** floods frequently—use the cliff-side path except within two hours on either side of low tide. There are tide tables posted at Kohaihai and Heaphy Hut. The longest stretch of sand before Kohaihai is **Scotts Beach;** those on an excursion from the carpark need go no farther to enjoy the track's sublime coast. Flax and nikau palms ring **Scotts Beach Campsite,** which

I had come up a terrific distance and the view was spectacular—all the jagged peaks crowded around me, many below my lofty height. With regret and determination, I turned my back on the view and faced the sun. Half my heart hoped the sun would postpone its imminent setting while the other half willed my legs to keep moving.

The track was steep, and it got to the point where a lower grade felt like a flat. Time passed and I played games to keep moving. Then, suddenly, I burst out of the trees onto the tussocks. Plains opened around me and I knew that I had made it onto the Tablelands; there couldn't be much more ground to gain. A quick drink and granola bar fueled me for the final push. I ducked briefly into the trees, came back into the tussock, and finally arrived at a sign that said it was only 2km to Salisbury Lodge.

As I was reading the post, the sun finally slipped behind a mountain. I made a mental thank-you to the orange sphere for hanging with me this long and quickly set off for the last 30 minutes to the hut, now racing against the quickly plummeting temperature. When I made it to the hut, a group of Kiwis welcomed me with open arms. Once I dropped my bag, I felt my feet and realized that I could hardly walk. The day had ripped several layers of skin off my feet, my ankles and knees were swollen, and I was all-around licked. But I had made it, and the athlete inside me and my competitive spirit danced together to a victory song of, "I've still got it, I've still got it..."

—Marly Ohlsson

lies within earshot of the waves. From here, the track does its only real coastal climbing as it skirts **Kohaihai Bluff** before reaching the carpark. At Kohaihai, there waits a shelter, a phone for ringing a ride, and a free campground (it's not part of the Great Walk system), with water, toilets, and a great view of the bluff. The Karamea shuttle picks up trampers here at 2pm, so plan your day accordingly.

WANGAPEKA TRACK

Situated in the southern portion of Kahurangi National Park, the Wangapeka travels up deep river-cut gorges, through beech forest, along trout-filled waters, and over two alpine saddles. A rugged and untouched tramp, it offers more seclusion and challenge than its Great Walk neighbor, the Heaphy.

Length: 60km, 5-6hr.

Trailheads: The eastern end of the track is **Rolling Junction Shelter,** 31km from Tapawera and best accessed from Motueka or Nelson. **Little Wanganui,** 25km south of Karamea, is the trailhead on the western end of the tack. If you plan to hike the Wangapeka as a loop in conjunction with the Heaphy, you need to arrange transport north to the Heaphy trailhead. Both trailheads have telephones.

Transportation: Several small charter bus companies head to the Rolling Junction Shelter on demand. Rory, from **Trek Express** (☎0800 128 735; rorymoore@xtra.co.nz), runs from Nelson or Motueka to Rolling Junction for $80-120 ($9 per person with full van of 9 people). Hewill also do pick-ups from the West Coast trailhead for $290. **Tasman Taxis** (☎528 1031) takes trampers from Motueka to Rolling Junction (1-3 people $130, 4-6 people $175). **Jilly's Excellent Adventures** (☎528 9461) runs from Nelson to Rolling Junction ($42.50 per person, min. $170) or Motueka to Rolling Junction ($35 per person, min. $120). She also leads guided tours. **Wadsworth Motors** (☎522 4248) runs from Nelson to Tapawera (1½hr.; M, W, and F 10:30am; $8) and back (1hr., 6pm). They offer an on-demand taxi service from Tapawera out to Rolling Junction or Flora carpark ($60, max. 7 people). To connect from the Little Wanganui carpark to the Heaphy trailhead, contact Karamea Express or Karamea Taxis (see **Heaphy Track: Transportation,** p. 296).

Seasonality: See **Heaphy Track: Seasonality,** p. 297.

Huts: Backcountry tickets or an annual hut pass are required to stay in the huts. All are Category 1 ($10) except for the Rolling Junction Shelter, which is Category 3 ($5), and the Cecil Kings Hut and Stag Flat, which are free. The huts have pot belly stoves or fireplaces, but no gas cookers. There are no campsites.

Storage: Most area accommodations will store for free.

ROLLING JUNCTION SHELTER TO KINGS CREEK HUT. *9.5km, 3½-4½hr.* After crossing a swing bridge across the Rolling River, the path wanders down through grassy floodplains alongside the Wangapeka River. The view up the gorge is spectacular, particularly when the clouds are rolling up from the West Coast. Entering the woods, the track rolls gently but never sways from its course alongside the river. Signs mark the turnoffs for Gibbs Route and up Kiwi Stream into an area full of gold mining relics. The track first passes spacious and modern **Kings Creek Hut** (30 bunks), but your first choice should be the **Cecil Kings Huts** (4 bunks), another 5min. down the trail. Originally built in 1935, this hut was occupied by the prospector Cecil King during many summers until his death in 1982.

KINGS CREEK HUT TO STONE HUT. *6.5km, 2½-3½hr.* Leaving Kings Creek Hut, the track comes to the confluence of the North and South branches of the Wangapeka and follows the North Branch while steadily climbing. Swing bridges span

Luna Stream and the North Branch en route to **Stone Hut** (12 bunks), a cozy affair on a grassy field.

STONE HUT TO HELICOPTER FLAT HUT. *8km, 3-4½hr.* Departing the hut, the track emerges into a rash of boulders tossed about by the 1929 Murchison earthquake. Traversing a long gravel stretch peppered with barren tree trunks and reentering the forest, the track begins to climb in earnest, grinding up switchbacks to the **Wangapeka Saddle** (1009m). Fantastic views require dropping your pack and climbing for another hour; well-marked routes show the way. After the saddle, the track levels and begins descending, crossing the Karamea River several times before the modern **Helicopter Flat Hut** (12 bunks).

HELICOPTER FLAT HUT TO TAIPO HUT. *8km, 3½-4½hr.* The trail continues in a quiet mossy forest with scattered fern stands and eventually leaves Karamea Gorge. Atop Brough's Tabernacle Lookout, there's a gorgeous view of the valley below. In 1898, while surveying the original track, Jonathan Brough set up an A-frame here. Today, only a few tools, a commemorative plaque, and the enduring vista remain. After the lookout, a side track darts off to the Luna Hut or the Trevor Carter Hut, both on the Leslie-Karamea Track. Those finishing the Leslie-Karamea Track to the east join the Wangapeka Track here. After crossing the Taipo River, the trail splits again, offering another route to the Trevor Carter Hut. From here, it's a 2½hr. gradual climb to **Taipo Hut** (18 bunks).

TAIPO HUT TO LITTLE WANGANUI HUT. *9km, 6-7hr.* After crossing the Pannikin Creek, the track pushes upwards to **Stag Flat** (4 bunks), situated in a boggy mess. This shelter serves as a contingency for poor weather on the Little Wanganui Saddle. An intense climb summits the saddle at 1110m, the tramp's highest point. Skirting Saddle Lakes, the trail begins an abrupt drop down to the Little Wanganui River. Passing through Tangent and McHarrie Creeks, the climbing begins anew, following the Little Wanganui Gorge and returning to the river atop the bridge to **Little Wanganui Hut** (20 bunks).

LITTLE WANGANUI HUT TO THE CARPARK. *10km, 3-4hr.* When weather obliges, the remaining 8km of the tramp is a cruisey promenade. At a junction between the foul and fair weather tracks lies Drain Creek. The fair route winds back and forth across the Little Wanganui River, eventually joining up with an old logging road. In piss-poor weather, take the higher alternate route, which circumvents several river crossings and joins up to the same logging road. Beware: the end of the track is slip prone. Be sure to check on its condition before setting out.

CANTERBURY

A spacious farmland nurtured among the shadows of the majestic Southern Alps, Canterbury quenches the thirst of all types of travelers. Serious skiers flock to the treeless heights of the slopes, while summer visitors seek out the charms of the Banks Peninsula and nearby beaches. Beneath the borrowed sensibilities of its British heritage, Christchurch itself offers the best of Kiwi culture and ethnic dining. The city extends in orderly blocks from its central cathedral, gradually giving way to orchards and vineyards. Situated in the agricultural heartland of the South Island, Canterbury draws equally from its urbane and pastoral roots.

■ CANTERBURY HIGHLIGHTS

SLOPE down the **Southern Alps** to hit some of the nation's finest skiing (see p. 316).

SCOPE the scene in vibrant **Christchurch**, from Gothic architecture to botanic gardens to eclectic street performers (see below).

STARE at some of the most breathtaking scenery in the world on the famed train ride through **Arthur's Pass**—getting there is *all* the fun (see p. 321).

DARE to ascend formidable **Mt. Cook National Park**, which challenges thrill-seekers with its dramatic peaks, demanding walks, and majestic glaciers ().

CHRISTCHURCH ☎ 03

Although this Garden City (pop. 350,000) remains closely bound to its English heritage, it has a flamboyant tilt that could only be Kiwi. Named after Oxford's Christ Church College, the stone Gothic Revival churches and meeting houses that front the willowed banks of the Avon River hearken to Great Britain. Christchurch itself is more bohemian, nurturing a vibrant community of artists who instill a proud cultural spirit. Foreigners flock to Christchurch's countless seasonal festivals, when street entertainers, ethnic food stalls, and even a wizard (see p. 310) clog Cathedral Square and the nearby Arts Centre.

■ INTERCITY TRANSPORTATION

Flights: The **Christchurch Airport** is 9km from the city on Memorial Ave. and is served by **Air New Zealand, Qantas,** and many Asian and South Pacific carriers (☎ 374 7100). **Air New Zealand,** 549 Colombo St. (☎ 363 0600 or 0800 737 767) flies daily to **Auckland** (1½hr., 1-2 per hr., $198-340) and **Wellington** (45min., 1 per hr., $130-592). Open M-W and F 9am-5pm, Th 9:30am-5pm, Sa 9:30am-1pm. The Airport "A" bus ($4) departs from the airport and Cathedral Sq. twice an hr. during the day, and once every hr. in the evening. **Super Shuttles** (☎ 357 9950) to downtown cost about $12; a taxi is $20-25.

Trains: To reach the **train station,** located 3km from Cathedral Sq., head away from town on Riccarton Ave., turn left on Deans Ave., right onto Blenheim Rd., then left onto Foster St., and left again onto Clarence St. Taxis to town cost about $12, though several hostels offer a free shuttle from the station. No public buses run directly from the station into the city. **TranzAlpine** goes to **Greymouth** (4½hr., 9am, $57-81) via **Arthur's Pass** (2½hr., $40-57). **TranzScenic** (☎ 0800 802 802) runs daily to **Picton** (5½hr., 7:30am, $31-77) via **Kaikoura** (3hr., $19-44).

INTERCITY TRANSPORTATION ■ 303

Buses: InterCity and **Newmans**, 123 Worcester St. (☎379 9020 or 0800 686 862) run to: **Dunedin** (6hr., 4 per day, $26-32); **Kaikoura** (2¾hr., 4:45pm, $15); **Nelson** (8hr., 7:15am, $55-69); and **Queenstown** (7hr., 7:45am, $50). **Atomic Shuttles** (☎322 8883) often has the best bargain rates for South Island service. **Alpine Coaches** (☎0800 274 888) and **Coast to Coast** (☎0800 800 847) traverse the South Island to **Greymouth** (4hr.; $35, return $60) via **Arthur's Pass** (1½hr., $25). **Great Sights** (☎0800 808 226), **Southern Link Shuttle** (☎358 8355), **South Island Connections** (☎366 6633), and **East Coast Express** (☎0508 830 900) also run shuttles around the South Island.

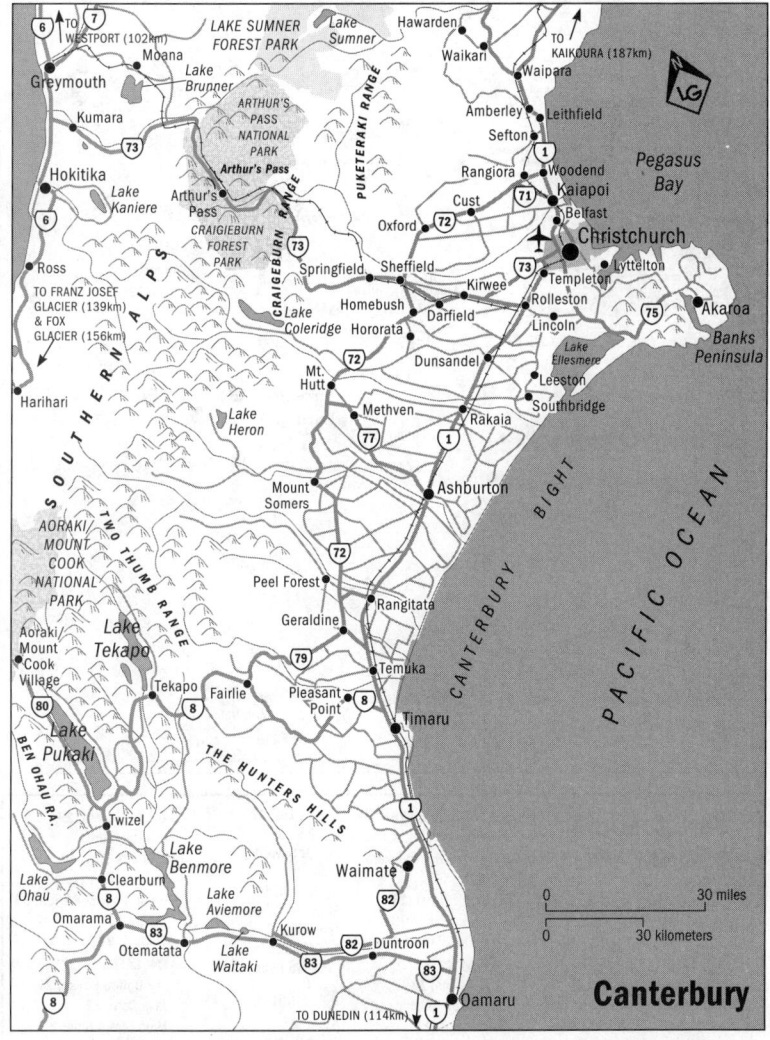

Canterbury

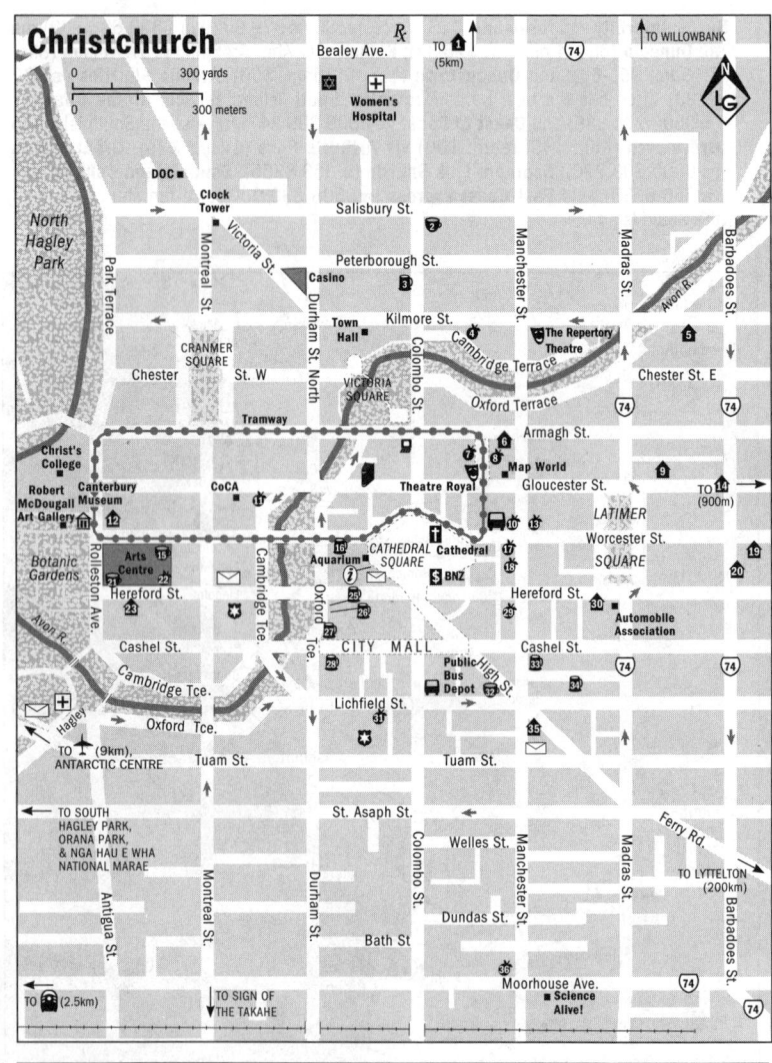

Christchurch

ACCOMMODATIONS
Christchurch City Central (YHA), **6**
Frauenreisehaus: The Homestead (BBH), **20**
Foley Towers (BBH), **5**
New Excelsior Backpackers (NOMADS), **35**
Occidental Backpackers, **30**
The Old Country House (BBH), **14**
Rolleston House YHA, **12**
Stonehurst (VIP), **9**
Vagabond Backpackers (BBH), **19**
Thomas's Hotel, **23**
Meadow Park Top 10 Holiday Park, **1**

FOOD
Alva Rados, **13**
Blue Jean Cuisine, **18**
Carnivores, **17**
Death by Chocolate, **4**
Dux de Lux, **22**
Il Felice, **31**
Pak 'N Save, **36**
Pronto Nachos Cafe, **8**
Raj Mahal, **10**
Santorini Greek Ouzeri, **11**
Thai Tasty, **7**
Topkapi Turkish Kebab House, **29**

NIGHTLIFE
Azure, **27**
The Bog, **28**
The Boulevard, **25**
The Holy Grail Sports Bar, **16**
The Loaded Hog, **33**
Sammy's Jazz Review, **34**
Stogies, **3**
Viaduct, **26**

CAFES
The Coffee House, **21**
Java Cafe, **32**
Main Street Cafe, **2**
Le Café, **15**

Hitchhiking: Though one should always consider the risks, thumbers report finding rides from the city outskirts, where urban traffic is steady. Those heading north toward Kaikoura often take the **Rangiora** bus and ask the driver to be dropped off on Hwy. 74, while those heading south towards Dunedin take the **Templeton #5** bus. Hitching west toward Arthur's Pass is possible by taking the **Hornby #84** bus to the Yaldhurst Roundabout. The best bet for hitching to Akaroa is the **Halswell #7** bus.

ORIENTATION

Christchurch's flat grid of streets stretches in every direction from **Cathedral Square**, the city's heart, where food stalls and artisans congregate beneath the bell tower of **Christchurch Cathedral**. From there, cobblestoned **Worcester Boulevard** continues east through **Latimer Square** and west, over the **Avon River**, to the gothic **Arts Centre** buildings, the **Canterbury Museum**, and the extensive **botanic gardens.** The city's central thoroughfare, **Colombo Street**, is lined with wool and jewelry souvenir shops and runs north-south through the square. Arcades and plazas extend out from the **City Mall**, the pedestrian walkway one block south from the Cathedral where Cashel St. would be. North of the Cathedral, **Victoria Square** fronts both the town hall and the domineering Park Royal Hotel. The shallow **Avon River** runs through the square, and is followed along much of its route by **Oxford** and **Cambridge Terraces**. Central Christchurch is bordered to the west by the gigantic **Hagley Park**, to the north and east by residential suburbs, and to the south by **Moorhouse Avenue**, the boundary of the industrial area.

LOCAL TRANSPORTATION

Public Transportation: The **Bus Crossing at the Exchange** (☎366 8855), at the corner of Colombo and Lichfield St., serves as the brand new depot and information center. (Open M-F 7:30am-5:40pm, Sa 9am-5pm, Su 10:30am-4:50pm.) Buses depart roughly every 30min. 6am-11:30pm, depending on time of day and route. Fares are calculated by zone (there are 6), and tickets ($2-6.30) are purchased on board. If you are going to more than 1 sight, a **Big Red Bus Pass**, good for a full day of travel on Red Buses, is quite economical. ($5, families $10. Available at the Visitors Center or on board.) **The Shuttle** is a **free** service that sends out a fleet of bright yellow buses each day to circle the city center every 10min. Get a route map at the Visitors Center.

Taxis: Choose from **First Direct** (☎377 5555 or 0800 505 550), **Gold Band** (☎379 5795), and **Blue Star** (☎379 9799) for **24hr.** service.

Car Rental: The major car-rental companies are all in town, but for cheaper deals, try **Atomic Rentals** (☎322 8883), which rents from about $25-35 per day with unlimited mileage; the $750 credit bond is standard ($1000 if under 25). **Pegasus,** 127 Peterborough St. (☎365 1100; fax 365 1104); **Rent-a-Dent,** 132 Kilmore St. (☎365 2509 or 0800 736 823); **Ace Rentals,** 237 Lichfield St. (☎366 3222 or 0800 202 029; fax 377 4610); and **Shoestring Rentals** (☎385 3647; fax 385 3694) offer comparable rates. Prices vary by season, duration of rental, and model of car. Most companies require a min. age of 20. The **AA office,** 210 Hereford St. (☎379 1280 or 0800 500 222), sells excellent road maps and dispenses sage traveling advice. Breakdown service available to members. Open M-F 8:30am-5pm.

Bike Rental: Trailblazers (☎366 6033), at the corner of Oxford Tce. and Armagh St., has standard mountain bikes. $6 per hr., half-day $18, full-day $26. Hours are variable, but generally open M-F 9am-6pm, Sa-Su 10am-5pm. **Cyclone Cycles,** 245 Colombo St. (☎332 9588), has bikes with suspension. Half-day $30, full-day $40. **City Cycle Hire** (☎0800 343 848) is open daily and offers half-day hires for $20 and full days for $30. **Free bicycle storage** (bring your own lock) is available in the Lichfield St. carpark, at **City Self Storage,** between Oxford Tce. and Colombo St. Open M-Th 7:30am-7:15pm, F 7:30am-11:45pm, Sa 9am-5:30pm, Su 10am-4:30pm.

306 ■ CHRISTCHURCH

🛈 PRACTICAL INFORMATION

Visitors Center: Christchurch & Canterbury Visitor Centre (☎379 9629; fax 377 2424; www.christchurchnz.net) is in the Old Chief Post Office Bldg. in Cathedral Sq. Open M-F 8:30am-6pm, Sa-Su 8:30am-5pm; in winter M-F 8:30am-5pm, Sa-Su 8:30am-4:30pm. Other information offices (☎353 7774) are located in the domestic and international terminals of the airport. Open daily 7:30am-8pm.

DOC: 133 Victoria St. (☎379 9758). Open M-F 8:30am-5pm.

Budget Travel: STA Travel, 90 Cashel St. (☎379 9098), in City Mall. Open M-F 9am-5:30pm, Sa 11am-2pm. **Budget Travel,** 683A Colombo St. (☎366 6032). Open M-Th and F 8:30am-5:00pm, Sa 10am-1pm.

Maps: Mapworld (☎374 5399 or 0800 627 967), at the corner of Manchester and Gloucester St. Open M-Th 8am-6pm, F 8am-8pm, Sa-Su 9am-4pm.

Banks: BNZ (☎353 2532), in the glass and steel building in Cathedral Sq., provides MC/V cash advances and exchanges money. Open M-F 9am-4:30pm.

Work Opportunities: Kelly Services (☎0800 453 559; www.kellyservices.co.nz) and **Adecco** (☎379 9060) are good temp agencies.

Bi-Gay-Lesbian Organizations: Gay Information Line (24hr. ☎379 3990); **Gay Information Collective** (☎/fax 379 3990).

Emergency: ☎111.

Police: Cathedral Square Kiosk (☎379 0123). Open Su-W 8am-midnight, Th-Sa 8am-2am. **Main branch** (☎379 3999), at the corner of Hereford St. and Cambridge Tce.

Hotlines: Lifeline (☎366 6743) offers 24hr. counseling; **Victim Support** (☎379 6767); **AIDS Hotline** (☎0800 802 437); **New Zealand AIDS Foundation** (☎379 1953); **Disability Info,** 314 Worcester St. (☎366 6189). Open M-Th 9am-4:30pm, F 9am-4pm.

Medical Services: After Hours Surgery (☎365 7777), at the corner of Bealey Ave. and Colombo St. Open 24hr. Also houses **Urgent Pharmacy** (☎366 4439). Open M-Th 6-11pm, F-Su 9-11pm; also Sa-Su 9-11am. **Christchurch Public Hospital** (☎364 0640), on the corner of Oxford Tce. and Riccarton Ave.

Internet Access: E-Caf (☎365 6480), in the Arts Centre. $3 per hr., free 15min. with purchase of coffee. Open daily 8am-11pm. **E-Caf@Farmers** (☎366 3186), in the Farmer's Food Court, at the corner of Armagh and Colombo St. $3 per hr. Open M-Th 9:30am-6pm, F 9:30am-9pm, Sa 9:30am-6pm, Su noon-5pm.

Post Office: (☎353 1899). Entrances at Hereford St. and Cathedral Sq. Poste Restante. Open M-F 8am-6pm, Sa 10am-4pm.

🏠 ACCOMMODATIONS

While Christchurch has few of the charmingly quirky gems found in the smaller towns of the South Island, there are plenty of stately Victorian houses throughout the city that have been converted into hostels, B&Bs, and hotels. Try to **book ahead** for all Christchurch accommodations, although last minute bargains at high-end hotels are occasionally available; inquire at the Visitors Center.

WORCESTER STREET AND SOUTH

🏠 Vagabond Backpackers (BBH), 232 Worcester St. (☎379 9677), 5 blocks east of the Cathedral. An extremely popular house with a clean, well-maintained interior, lovely garden, friendly hosts, and quiet location. Good selection of free videos. Dorms $17-19; singles $30; twins and doubles $44. ❷

Frauenreisehaus: The Homestead (BBH), 272 Barbadoes St. (☎366 2585; fax 366 2589). From the Cathedral, head east on Worcester Blvd. and hang a right on Barbadoes St. Women are fortunate to have this **female-only** backpackers to themselves. An excellent collection of videos and music, free use of bikes, fresh mint in the garden, and free laundry. Internet. Reception 8am-10pm. Dorms $17; singles $27; twins $42. ❷

New Excelsior Backpackers (NOMADS), 120 Manchester St. (☎366 7570; fax 366 7629; newexcel@ihug.co.nz), at the corner of High St. Bev and Warren run a tight ship, complete with roof-top deck above and classy pub below. Internet. Key deposit $20. Reception 7am-8pm. Dorms $15-20; singles $35; twins $40; doubles $45, with bath $55. $1 *Let's Go* discount. ❷

Thomas's Hotel, 36 Hereford St. (☎379 9536; fax 379 9556; www.thomashotel.co.nz), across from the Arts Centre. Newly opened, rooms are airy and tasteful. Enjoy their BBQ, lounge, sparkling kitchen, and central location. Dorms $17-20; singles $40-85; doubles $55-95; triples $75-95. ❷

Rolleston House YHA, 5 Worcester Blvd. (☎366 6564; fax 365 5589; yhachrl@yha.org.nz), at the corner of Worcester Blvd. and Rolleston Ave. You can hardly get closer to the city's cultural heart, with the Arts Centre, cafes, and museums right outside your door. Reception 8-10am and 3-10pm. Dorms $20-23; twins $52. ❷

Occidental Backpackers (BBH), 208 Hereford St. (☎357 0005 or 0800 847 467; fax 379 9284; www.occidental.co.nz). Closest hostel to the Sq., the Occidental is warm, welcoming, and boisterous. Jumping downstairs bar. Free breakfast. Reception 7am-midnight. Internet. Laundry. Dorms $16; singles $30; twins and doubles $45. ❷

NORTH OF WORCESTER STREET

The Old Country House (BBH), 437 Gloucester St. (☎381 5504), at the corner of Stanmore Rd. You can't help but feel at ease in this farm-style house. Herb garden out back, and frequent home-baked goodies. Free pick-up from Cathedral Sq. Reception 8am-8pm. Internet. Dorms $17-19; twins and doubles $42. ❷

Stonehurst (VIP), 241 Gloucester St. (☎379 4620 or 0508 786 633; fax 379 4647; accom@stonehurst.co.nz). Their swimming pool hits the spot after a long day tramping around the city. Stylish new rooms have a hotel feel. Internet. Reception 24hr. Dorms $19; singles $40; doubles $50-60; tourist flats for 2-6 people $100. ❷

Christchurch City Central (YHA), 273 Manchester St. (☎379 9535; fax 379 9537; yhachch@yha.org.nz), near Armagh St. Classic YHA ambience: central, modern, and ultra-clean with tremendously helpful staff. Reception 7am-10pm. Pool table. Internet. Dorms $25; singles $40; twins and doubles $50, with bath $64. ❸

Foley Towers (BBH), 208 Kilmore St. (☎366 9720; fax 379 3014; foley.towers@back pack.co.nz). Take Worcester Blvd. east to Madras St., go left, and then right on Kilmore St. Rooms line the extensive garden. Most rooms have sinks, but a quick duck outside is necessary to reach the loo. Internet. Linen charge $2 for whole stay. Key deposit $10. Reception 9am-9:30pm. Dorms $17-19; twins and doubles $44, with bath $50. ❷

Meadow Park Top 10 Holiday Park, 529 Cranford St. (☎352 9176; fax 352 1272; meadowpark@xtra.co.nz). Drive north 10min. from the city center on Sherborne St., which becomes Hwy. 74, then Cranford St. A sprawling complex with swimming pool, trampoline, and spa. Reception 8am-10pm. Cabins $36 for 2, extra person $10; tourist flats from $70 for 2, extra person $15; tent and powered sites from $11; funky hexagonal "kozy kiwi cottages" $60 for 2, extra person $15. ❶

◘ FOOD

Many restaurants are concentrated on **Colombo Street,** north of Kilmore St., and on **Manchester Street,** south of Gloucester St. Vendors in **Cathedral Square** sell a range of kebabs and stir-frys around lunchtime; on weekends they take over a corner of the Arts Centre. Throughout the city center, Thai, Indian, and sushi joints offer backpacker-friendly lunch specials. The **Pak 'N Save,** at the corner of Moorehouse Ave. and Manchester St., is the cheapest of the several megamarkets clustered a few blocks from Cathedral Sq. (Open daily 8am-10pm.) See the **Cafes** and **Nightlife** sections for more food options.

WORCESTER STREET AND SOUTH

Dux de Lux, 41 Hereford St. (☎366 6919), at the Arts Centre. Serves only vegetarian and seafood dishes ($15-22) meant to be washed down with 1 of 7 house brews. Internet. Open daily 11:30am-late. ❸

Alva Rados (☎365 1644), at the corner of Worcester and Manchester St. Sangria pitchers, mega-nachos, and multicolored blankets put a Latin spin on the refined wood and iron decor. Mains $12.50-20. Open Tu-Su 6-9pm. ❷

Il Felice, 56 Lichfield St. (☎366 7535), serves Italian cuisine in an upscale, though boisterous, setting. Large portions of freshly made pastas ($17) and mains ($26-28) are worth a splurge. Reservations recommended. Open M-Sa 6pm-late. ❹

Blue Jean Cuisine, 205 Manchester St. (☎365 4130). The noise level loudly confirms Blue Jean's popularity. So hip, your bill comes in a CD case. Filling lunches ($6.50-17.50) and dinners ($16-23). Open M-F 11am-late, Sa-Su 5:30pm-late. ❸

Topkapi Turkish Kebab House, 185a Manchester St. (☎379 4447). In this tiny piece of Turkey, kebabs and falafels are prepared windowside ($5-10). Open M-Tu 11:30am-10pm, W-Th 11:30am-10:30pm, F 11:30am-late, Sa 3pm-late. ❷

Carnivores, 207 Manchester St. (☎365 0371). Meat. Lots of meat. Between bread. Tasty. The line out the door attests to this lunch spot's popularity. Sandwiches $5-6. Open M-Th 10:30am-2:30pm, F 10:30am-3:30pm. ❶

NORTH OF WORCESTER STREET

Raj Mahal (☎366 0521), at the corner of Manchester and Worcester St. Terrible puns aside, authentic Indian music wafts through this colorful dining room. Choose from several tandoori ($15-20) and vegetarian ($14.50-16) dishes. Takeaways $9-13. Open M-Sa 5:30pm-10pm, Su 5:30pm-9:30; takeaway from 4:30pm. ❸

Death by Chocolate, 209 Cambridge Tce. (☎365 7323). Walk north on Colombo St. and turn right onto Cambridge Tce. As the name implies, you may have to be carried out. The namesake dessert ($16) could fill 2, and the "Multitude of Sins" ($24 for 2) is enough to inspire a gastronomic orgasm. Open Tu-Su from noon-late. ❸

Santorini Greek Ouzeri (☎379 6975), at the corner of Gloucester St. and Cambridge Tce. A fun-loving family restaurant with big Greek dinners ($22). Patrons are encouraged to dance on wine casks. The conga lines have even been known to invade the kitchen. Open Tu-Sa 6pm-late. ❹

Pronto Nachos Cafe, 8 New Regent St. (☎366 4676). Enormous nachos ($3.20-8.80) and tasty chicken burritos ($9) are served with fresh, homemade guacamole. Open M-Sa 11am-9pm. ❷

Thai Tasty, 10/129 Gloucester St. (☎379 7540), tucked inside the Gloucester Arcade. You won't find it much cheaper, friendlier, faster, or Thai-tastier than this, with meals running $5-9. Open daily M-Sa 11am-3:30pm and 5-9pm. ❷

CAFES

Fly in the face of tradition in Christchurch (home to the custom of tea) by opting for an alternative caffeine kick. Reasonably priced, and with consistently good food, Christchurch's cafes are good for breakfast, lunch, or late-night lounging.

- **The Coffee House,** 290 Montreal St. (☎365 6066), near the Arts Centre. Shelves and shelves of tea and coffee tins ($2.50-4.50) provide pleasant torture for the indecisive. Open M-F 7:30am-late, Sa-Su 8:30am-late.
- **Java Cafe** (☎366 0195), at the corner of High and Lichfield St., where the rebellious call home. Hot chocolate served in jam jars ($3), and the best breakfast in town make Java a necessary stop in Christchurch. Open M-W and Su 7am-late, Th-Sa 24hr.
- **Main Street Cafe,** 840 Colombo St. (☎365 0421). An earthy crowd sprawls amidst dim lighting and comfy couches in this mellow bar/cafe/restaurant. Many inventive vegetarian and dairy-free options. Lunch $9, dinners $17. Open daily 10am-late.
- **Le Café** (☎366 7722), on Worcester St. in the Arts Centre, is always busy, always lively, and almost always open. The iced chocolate drink ($4) will make you tremble with delight (or a sugar high). Dinners $10-15, breakfast $8-13. Open daily 7am-midnight.

ENTERTAINMENT

Christchurch has several excellent art cinemas and a professional theater company; check the back page of *The Press* for a full current listing. The **Court Theatre** at the Arts Centre has two theaters running some of New Zealand's best professional repertory productions. (☎963 0870. Adults generally $27, students generally $20.) The **Theatre Royal,** 145 Gloucester St. (☎366 6326), is the forum for touring musicals and ballet companies. The **Repertory Theatre,** 146 Kilmore St., is a community theater running five plays a year. (☎3798 8866. Tickets about $15.)

The **Academy Cinema Cloisters,** in the Arts Centre, shows art and foreign flicks. (☎366 0167; www.artfilms.co.nz. Open 11am-9pm. $8, after 5pm $10.) For your Hollywood fix, hit up **Regent On Worcester,** 94 Worcester St. (☎366 0140.)

Gamblers can try their luck at the 24hr. **Christchurch Casino,** at Victoria and Durham St. While it may resemble an overgrown parking garage from the outside, the gaming room and cafes feature tasteful balconies and chandeliers. (☎365 9999. Free nightly transportation. No jeans or sneakers. Must be 20 to gamble.)

FESTIVALS. Christchurch hosts an amazing number of festivals for a city its size. Check out www.bethere.org.nz for a comprehensive listing of festivals in Christchurch and elsewhere in New Zealand. In November, **Showtime Canterbury** hits the city with its concerts, fireworks, and parades. Since 1983, **Summertimes** has been one of the most popular festivals in Canterbury, bringing a series of concerts and theater performances to the city throughout the summer, as well as a huge "teddy bear picnic" (www.summertimes.org.nz). The **International Buskers Festival** (Jan. 16-26, 2003) brings nutty street entertainers from around the world to the city in one of the wackiest outdoor festivals in the world. The **Festival of Flowers** blooms every February, bedecking Cathedral Sq. with a floral carpet (www.festivalofflowers.co.nz, Feb. 14-23, 2003). It includes garden competitions, street decorations, and visits to private gardens. The **Wine and Food Festival** intoxicates in May, and the two-week **Adventure Canterbury** in April celebrates Canterbury's adrenaline activities. The **Christchurch Arts Festival** runs at the end of July in odd years, with multimedia performing arts and exhibitions (www.artsfestival.co.nz; July 16-Aug. 3, 2003). During the first week of every August, the **Montana Christchurch Winter Carnival** (www.wintercarnival.org.nz) celebrates the ski season with imported snow (part of Cathedral Sq. is even covered with makeshift drifts and huge snow sculptures).

NIGHTLIFE

On weekends, a university crowd crams the clubs, bars, and saloons until midmorning. If bars packed with twenty-somethings looking to pound some beers are your bag, **Manchester Street** is the stretch to roam. **The Strip,** along Oxford Tce., is the place to see and be seen. True dance aficionados should head to **Lichfield Street,** home to Christchurch's major nightclubs. The **After Midnight Express** gets post-revelry partyers home safely, running through the central city and to selected suburbs. (☎0800 733 287. Runs Sa and Su mornings every hour midnight-4am. $4.)

The Loaded Hog (☎366 6674), on Manchester St. at Cashel St. The lines are long at this homebrew chain where bartenders pour an excellent lager. Live jazz Tu from 8pm. DJs Th from 8pm, F-Sa from 9pm. Open M-F 11am-late, Sa 10am-3am, Su 10am-late.

The Holy Grail Sports Bar, 99 Worcester St. (☎365 9816). Once a movie theater, All-Black games and live videos of the gyrating crowd now fill the screens. Live DJ Th-Sa. Open daily 11am-late.

The Bog, 82 Cashel Mall (☎379 7141). This ain't your grandpappy's Irish pub. Live music (W-Sa from 9:30pm) and DJs get a young crowd going on the dance floor until the wee morn. Open daily 10am-late.

Sammy's Jazz Review, 14 Bedford Rd. (☎377 8618), a block east of Manchester St., has a classy interior and a lavish brick courtyard. Live jazz nightly. Open M-Sa 5pm-late, F-Sa 7:30pm-1am.

Dux de Lux, 41 Hereford St. (☎366 6919), by the Arts Centre. Droves of students pack this enormous old house for its 3 separate bars and 7 freshly brewed beers. Live jazz Tu. Punk, funk, rock, or reggae W-Sa. Open daily 11am-late.

Stogies, 817 Colombo St. (☎379 1200). Cigars aside, this swanky bar attracts an older clientele. Sit back in the leather couch and puff your own Cuban. Open Tu-Sa 6pm-late, Su 5pm-late.

Viaduct, 136 Oxford Tce. (☎377 9968), on the Avon. Well-dressed 20-somethings pack into this dimly lit bar. Open daily 10:30am-late.

The Boulevard (☎374 6676), at the corner of Oxford Tce. and Hereford St., is a cafe by day, but come the late evening hours, the floor swells with dancing throngs. Open Su-Th 8am-late, F-Sa 8am-5am-ish.

Azure, 128 Oxford Tce. (☎365 6088). Brave the dance floor and shake it to cutting-edge house funk, or watch from one of the arching alcoves. Open daily 11am-late.

PAY NO ATTENTION TO THE LITTLE MAN BEHIND THE CURTAIN

King of Christchurch's motley array of eccentrics, **The Wizard** makes his presence known daily in summer, around noon in Cathedral Sq. Dubbed the official wizard of Christchurch by the local government, the outspoken linguistic Merlin will do everything in his power to rile up the crowd. You may flee disgusted, which means that the pointed cap- and cape-bearing Wizard has won the day. Still, he's a strikingly intelligent orator and entertainer, and has created trademark upside-down maps proclaiming an enlightened understanding of the world. The Wizard even flees the nation during census time to escape political oppression from the forces of the government. In and out of season, you can find The Wizard on the web (www.wizard.gen.nz).

SIGHTS

OUTDOOR SIGHTS

CHRIST CHURCH CATHEDRAL. This looming 1865 Gothic Revival Cathedral, a centerpiece of Christchurch, is an exercise in juxtaposition, combining stones quarried and hewn in Canterbury with hulking natural roots from native matai and totara. Inside, ornate stained-glass windows imported from England abut Maori *kai kai* (flax) weavings. You can even climb the 134 steps of the Cathedral's tower for a view of the city. (☎ 366 0046. Admission free. Tours M-F 11am and 2pm, Sa 11am, Su 11:30am. $3, children $1. Tower climb $4, children $1.50. Camera permit $2.50.)

AVON RIVER. Walk west down Worcester Blvd. and you'll cross the lovely river Avon, which meanders through the city under willows and arched bridges. Boating on the Avon is an enchanting experience. **Punting on the Avon** and **Punting in the Park** run regular tours from Worcester Blvd. (Avon: ☎ 379 9629. $18 per 30min., $12 per 20min. Park: ☎ 366 0337. 30min. $12.50, children $5.)

BOTANIC GARDENS. These free public gardens feature one of the country's best arrays of indigenous tree and plant life, with 10,000 different species sharing 30 hectares of land. The 450-acre **Hagley Park,** with jogging tracks and rugby fields, surrounds the gardens on three sides. (Gardens open daily from 7am.)

ARCHITECTURAL TOURS. Benjamin Mountfort conceived many of the Gothic Revival stone and brick structures in the 1860s and 1870s that lend the city its distinctive architectural character. At the Visitors Center, pick up a copy of the *Christchurch City Centre Walks* pamphlet, which details three walks past churches, government houses, and statues along the banks of the Avon. The bright paint, arched wooden ceilings, magnificent stained-glass windows, and long neo-Gothic hallways of the **Provincial Council Buildings**, at Gloucester St. and Cambridge Tce., have yet to be noticed by most tourists or even by many locals. (Open M-Sa 10:30am-3:30pm; Oct.-May also Su 2-4pm.) For more comprehensive commentary, contact the **Personal Guiding Service, Private Garden Tours,** or **Heritage Homes Tours** through the Visitors Center.

MUSEUMS

CANTERBURY MUSEUM. One of the best regional museums in the country, exhibits catalogue the natural history of Canterbury. Subjects include a panoramic ode to the moa, Maori artifacts, and a history of Antarctic exploration. (Beyond the Arts Centre on Rolleston Ave. ☎ 366 5000. Open daily 9am-5:30pm; in winter 9am-5pm. Free.)

ROBERT MCDOUGALL ART GALLERY. Specializing in New Zealand and British painting, in April 2003 these galleries will move into a sparkling new art museum on the corner of Worcester and Montreal St. With strong modern lines, the new space has raised some controversy over whether the architecture is too bold. (Before April 2003: Around the other side of the Canterbury Museum. ☎ 365 0915. Open daily 10am-5:30pm; in winter 10am-4:30pm. Free, with guided tours 11am-3pm.)

CENTRE OF CONTEMPORARY ART (COCA). This tribute to Kiwi modernity is an independently supported gallery of innovative modern works with both rotating and permanent exhibitions. (66 Gloucester St., near the Arts Centre. ☎ 366 7261. Open Tu-F 11am-5pm, Sa-Su noon-4pm. Free.)

SCIENCE ALIVE! This hands-on science experience includes a climbing wall, a human gyroscope, and New Zealand's highest vertical slide. (On Moorhouse Ave., near Manchester St. ☎ 365 5199; www.sciencealive.co.nz. Open M-F 9am-5pm, Sa-Su 10am-6pm. $7, children $5.)

OTHER DOWNTOWN SIGHTS

ARTS CENTRE. Formerly the University of Canterbury, the Gothic Revival complex now houses cafes, galleries, art studios, shops, the Court Theatre, and two cinemas. Some of the university remains, however, and visitors can walk into **Ernest Rutherford's Den** for a biographical multi-media presentation set in the lab where he first experimented with high-frequency magnetization of iron. On weekends craftsmen and clothiers practice the science of persuasion, selling goods in the outdoor market, while ethnic food stalls crowd the back courtyard. Sweettooths will love the 1hr. guided tour (with free samples) at the **Fudge Cottage Kitchen,** also in the Arts Centre. *(Bordering the Botanic Gardens on the east and stretching over an entire city block toward the city. ☎ 363 2836, www.artscentre.org.nz. Guided tours depart from the Arts Centre Information Centre, near the end of Worcester Blvd. every 30min. starting at 10am. Free. Fudge Kitchen: ☎ 363 2836; tours M-F 2pm, $5, bookings recommended; Arts Centre open daily 10am-5pm.)*

SOUTHERN ENCOUNTER AQUARIUM. The plastic-wrought walls of this underwater attraction (designed by the same firm that created rockwork for *Xena*) evoke local rock formations and unique South Island sea creatures. The eels are fed at 11am, the salmon and trout at 1pm, and the marine fish at 3pm. *(Right in Cathedral Sq.; enter via the Visitors Center. ☎ 377 3474. Open daily 9am-5:30pm; last admission at 4:30pm. $10, students $8, children $5.)*

OUTLYING SIGHTS

Some of the area's most worthwhile attractions lie just outside the downtown area; most are accessible by a short bus ride from the city center. The **Black Double Decker** (☎ 366 5643) and **City Circuit Bus** (☎ 332 6012) visit various sights.

NGA HAU E WHA NATIONAL MARAE. The "Marae of the Four Winds," this national *marae* provides an excellent window into Maori culture and history. The building itself represents the body of Maui, who fished the North Island out of the sea using his grandmother's jawbone (see p. 50). Symbolic flax ornamentation and painted carvings of ancestors decorate the marae. An outstanding guided tour plus an evening concert is available, as is a complete *hangi* (see p. 56), tour, and concert. *(250 Pages Rd., east of Christchurch; take bus #5 from Cathedral Sq. ☎ 0800 456 898. Guided tour $30, children $19; hangi, tour, and concert $65/36.)*

INTERNATIONAL ANTARCTIC CENTRE. This is as close as you'll probably ever get to the coldest, driest, windiest continent on earth. Educate yourself with interactive exhibits that include a "snow and ice experience" room, kept at -5°C and stocked with snow to simulate an Antarctic spring. Or take a behind-the-scenes tour of the international center in a genuine Antarctic Hagglund. *(Take the A bus; or drive to the airport, head north around Hagley Park, and follow the signs. ☎ 358 9896; www.iceberg.co.nz. Open daily 9am-8pm; in winter 9am-5:30pm. $18, children $9, families $39. Antarctic Hagglund tour $10.)*

WILDLIFE RESERVES. Willowbank maintains extensive walk-through aviaries and a nocturnal kiwi house. The curious kea will attack any unattended baggage and the gibbons keep up an almost constant cacophony. *(North of the city off Gardiners Rd., accessible by car or one of the tour buses. ☎ 359 6226. Open daily 10am-10pm. $15, students $13, children $7.)* **Orana Park** is a complete African plains park with lions, zebras, rhinos, a variety of savannah animals, native birds, and the ageless tuatara. *(18km from the city, north off Johns Rd. City Circuit departs daily from the Visitors Center for $15 return. ☎ 359 7109. Open daily 10am-5pm. $12, children $5.)*

OUTDOOR ACTIVITIES

ON THE GROUND. In good weather, catch the Black Double Decker bus (see above) out to **Port Hills** and the **Mt. Cavendish Gondola**. (☎ 384 0700.) Take the gondola or walk up the steep bridle path (about 1hr.) to the top for a view encompassing Christchurch, the distant Southern Alps, and Lyttelton Harbour. *(Return $16, students $15, children $7.)* Once at the summit, you can choose from numerous **walking tracks**, some excellent sport-climbing crags, or hurtle down on a mountain bike that **The Mountain Bike Adventure Company** will bring to you at the top of the gondola. *(☎ 0800 424 534. $40 including gondola ride. Book at the Visitors Center.)*

FARTHER AFIELD. If you've got a car or bike, continue along the summit road to reach **Godley Head**, a rugged promontory of grassy paths and sheer cliffs overlooking the austere Pacific. In the other direction along Summit Rd., down Dyers Pass Rd., is the **Sign of the Takahe**, one of three Gothic mansions built as a stopping point for travelers decades ago. The Takahe offers a magnificent view of the lights of Christchurch and the Canterbury Plains. *(Take the #2 Cashmere bus (runs during the day only) into the hills. ☎ 332 4052.)*

HOT AIR BALLOONING. Hot air balloon enthusiasts flock to the vast flatness of the Canterbury plains. Join **Up Up and Away** or **Aoraki Balloon Safaris** for a leisurely float. Aoraki often leads higher-flying trips from Methven that afford better mountain views. *(Up Up and Away: ☎ 358 9859. $200, with champagne. Aoraki: ☎ 0800 256 837. $275 with champagne breakfast; call a week ahead for discount standby rate of $245.)*

OTHER AIRBORNE PURSUITS. Christchurch Parachute School, at Wigram Aerodome, offers tandem skydiving. Or, paraglide from the Gondola down to Sumner with **Phoenix Paragliding, Tandem Paragliding**, or **Nimbus Paragliding**. *(Christchurch: ☎ 025 321 135. $245. Phoenix: ☎ 326 7634. $120. 1-day class $165. Tandem: ☎ 385 4739. $125. Nimbus: ☎ 326 7922. $110.)*

HORSE TREKS. Equestrians have many options for exploring the Canterbury countryside; some of the best trips are run by **Longspur Lodge**, on the road to Akaroa. *(☎ 329 0005. 1hr. $30, 1½hr. $40, 2hr. $50; return transport $20.)*

ON THE WATER. ■**Rangitata Rafts** offers full-day trips over Class 4 and 5 rapids from September through May. **Jet Thrills** leads fast-paced river jet boating adventures, while **Waimak Alpine Jet** runs longer trips into the Waimakariri Canyon. **Canterbury Fishing Adventures** takes you out on nearby rivers for some good angling. *(Rangitata: ☎ 0800 251 251. $130 includes lunch, dinner, and pick-up. Jet Thrills: ☎ 025 387 485. $55, children $36; free pick-up. Waimak: ☎ 318 4881 or 0800 263 626; waimakalpine-jet.co.nz. $55, children $28. Canterbury: ☎ 0800 484 485. Half-day $140, full-day $210.)*

DAYTRIPS

LYTTELTON. Clinging to the hills bordering the industrialized Lyttelton Harbour, suburban Lyttelton (pop. 4000) is Canterbury's major port and a pleasant escape from Christchurch. Just 12km from the city via the Tunnel Rd. (bus #28, $2), the port shelters a melange of far-flung sailors and bohemian types, blending seamlessly amid small cottages, oddball curiosity shops, and cafes lining the main strips of London St. and Norwich Quay. The best way to enjoy Lyttelton's picturesque setting is by getting out and **walking** it. Grab a map from the Visitors Center ($1) and head up the Bridle Path to the Mount Cavendish Gondola (return 1-2hr., steep). Alternately, take the Major Hornbrook Track or the Chalmers Track to the

CHRISTCHURCH

Crater Rim Walkway (full-day). Many people choose to drive to a point along Summit Rd., which runs alongside much of the walkway, and take a short daytramp. On a clear day at Crater Rim, you can look onto the Canterbury Plains and see as far as the Southern Alps and Kaikoura.

The **Lyttelton Timeball Station** once communicated Greenwich Mean Time to the boats in the harbor so they could accurately gauge their longitude. Today, it is one of just five in the world that still works. (☎328 7311. Usually open daily 10am-5pm; in winter W-Su. $2.50, children free.) **Christchurch Wildlife Cruises** take dolphin- and shag-lovers on a 2hr. journey from 17 Norwich Quay into the harbor, where travelers often encounter Hector's Dolphins and other forms of marine life. (☎328 9078 or 0800 436 574; www.blackcat.co.nz. $39. Bookings essential.) **Sea Cruises Ltd.** (☎328 7720) runs a similar service at a comparable price. If you want to see the dolphins while simultaneously learning to sail a 1903 Gaff Yawl, check out **Jack Tar Sailing Co.** (☎389 9259 or 0800 253 2663.)

The **Visitors Centre**, 20 Oxford St., between London St. and Norwich Quay, has self-guided walking tours as well as Internet access for $2 per 15min. (☎328 9093. Open daily 9am-5pm.) With two stellar accommodations, Lyttelton tempts travelers as more than just a daytrip. **Tunnel Vision Backpackers (BBH) ❷**, 44 London St., has polished wooden floors and a sunny deck. (☎328 7576; www.tunnelvision.co.nz. Closed June-Aug. Key deposit $10. Laundry. Dorms $16-18; twins $40; doubles $44.) **Dockside Accommodation ❹**, 22 Sumner Rd., is a self-proclaimed "boutique motel." Immaculate suites overlook the harbor and a pleasant garden. (☎328 7344; kathyg@nhf.org.nz. Doubles $60-80. Book well in advance.) An upscale bistro, **Satchmo ❸**, 8 London St., pleases with tasty platters ($12.50-24.50) and a lush garden. (☎328 8348. Open W-F 10am-8pm, Sa-Su 9:30am-7pm.) Next to the grocery-haven, **Supervalue**, on London St. (☎328 7038; open daily 8am-9pm), bright signs lead the way to **Wunderbar**. Follow them down the stairs, through the parking lot, and up the ramp—it's worth the walk. Illuminated mannequins in lingerie and neckties cast light on the velvet seats along the bar, as music from scratchy vinyl LPs wafts overhead. In back, the aptly named **Backroom Bar**, a shimmering cabaret stage complete with a Saturn-shaped disco ball, opens Thursday to Saturday for dancing, live music, and cabaret shows. (☎328 8818. Open M-F 5pm-3am, Sa-Su 3pm-3am.)

SUMNER. Surfers and sun worshippers flock to Sumner (accessible by bus #30, 31, or 32; $2), Christchurch's summer beach-resort town. Those seeking more seclusion continue on to **Taylor's Mistake**, a beach on the other side of the town popular with surfers. **Cave Rock**, near town, is a natural grotto accessible at low tide; beware of sudden surges if you choose to venture inside. If you'd rather view the Pacific Ocean from stunning heights, call **Phoenix Paragliding**, based in town. (☎/fax 326 7634; www.paragliding.co.nz. Tandem flights $120, lessons $165 per day.)

You can feel stylish, enjoy a great view, and score a tasty meal, all at one place—**Cafe Rock ❸**, 22a Esplanade, opposite the Cave Rock. Bask in the sun on the patio as you sample one of the creative pastas ($17) or salads ($6-17). Live music gets going on Thursdays after 8pm. (☎326 5358. Open Su-W 9am-9pm, Th-Sa 9am-10pm.) Restart your motor after a beachside stroll with a cuppa from the bright yellow **Coffee Culture**, along the main street. (☎326 5900. Open M-F 7:30am-late, Sa-Su 8:30am-late.) Those lacking big resort dollars can finally move into Sumner thanks to **The Marine Backpackers (BBH) ❷**, 26 Nayland St. You can almost smell the fresh paint at this brand new hostel. The lounge beckons with a giant world map and cushy throw pillows. (☎326 6609; info@themarine.co.nz. Key deposit $20. Dorms $18; singles $25; twins $50; doubles $44, with bath $54.)

AKAROA AND THE BANKS PENINSULA ☎ 03

The French explorers who sailed to Akaroa (pop. 1000) in 1840 may not have succeeded in loosening the British stronghold on New Zealand, but they did leave some indelible cultural imprints—particularly the French monikers sprinkled throughout the town. Today, the historic *maisons*, craft shops, and fishing harbor of the Banks seem worlds away from the Anglicized and urbanized Christchurch. Cyclists, hikers, and food connoisseurs gravitate to Akaroa and the relatively untrafficked Banks Peninsula for a serene getaway.

TRANSPORTATION. The **Akaroa Shuttle** travels between the Akaroa and Christchurch Visitors Centers daily, offering commentary and a stop at the cheese factory along the way. (☎ 0800 500 929. 1½hr. Nov.-Apr. 3 per day; May-Oct. 1 per day. $17, return $30.) The **French Connection** departs from the Christchurch Visitors Center daily at 8:45am (less frequently in winter) and leaves Akaroa at 11am and 3:30pm. (☎ 0800 800 575. $15, return $20.) Hop on the **mail run** to see the most remote reaches of the peninsula; inquire at the Visitors Center. (☎ 304 7207 or 025 355 249. Departs M-Sa 8:20am, returns 1:30pm. $20.) Although *Let's Go* does not recommend it, **hitchhiking** is possible to and from Christchurch, as most traffic goes all the way to Akaroa; most thumbers take the #7 Halswell bus from Cathedral Sq. Hitchers heading back to Christchurch have the best luck just outside the township, at the bottom of Old Coach Rd.

ORIENTATION AND PRACTICAL INFORMATION. Running past **Lake Ellesmere** and through several tiny towns, **SH75** winds southeast for 80min. from Christchurch, up over the lip of the now-extinct Akaroa volcano, and back down to the harbor of Akaroa. The town itself, with most of the food and accommodations, sits on **Rue Lavaud** and **Beach Road** along the water. The end of town that visitors enter is known as the French side; when Rue Lavaud becomes Beach Rd., you have crossed over to the English side.

The **Akaroa Information Centre**, 80 Rue Lavaud, has information on Akaroa and can help arrange forays into the greater peninsula. (☎/fax 304 8600; www.akaroa.com. Open Oct.-Apr. daily 9:30am-5pm; May-Sept. 10am-4pm.) Other local services include: the **post office**, next door to the Visitors Center (☎ 304 7701; open M-F 8:30am-5pm); **BNZ**, opposite the Visitors Center, which changes money (☎ 304 1024; open M and Th-F 9am-4:30pm, Tu-W 9:30am-4:30pm); the **police** (☎ 304 1030); the **hospital** (☎ 304 7023); a **pharmacy** (☎ 304 7002; open M-Th and Sa 9am-6pm, F 9am-7pm, Su 11am-5pm); and the **library**, 141 Rue Jolie, which provides **Internet access** (☎ 304 8782; $8 per hr.; open M-F 10am-4pm, Sa 10am-1pm).

ACCOMMODATIONS AND FOOD. Built by a Spaniard in 1860, **Chez La Mer Backpackers (BBH) ❷**, 50 Rue Lavaud, still exudes Old World charm with its herb garden, complete with fish pond and gazebo, and free muesli. (☎/fax 304 7024; chez_la_mer@clear.net.nz. Reception 8am-9pm. Dorms $18; singles $27; twins and doubles $44, with bath $49.) June, the cheerful owner of **Bon Accord Backpackers (BBH) ❷**, 57 Rue Lavaud, welcomes all to stay and use the fully-equipped communal kitchen, den, and small porch. (☎ 304 7782; bon-accord@xtra.co.nz. Dorms $18; doubles $44-50.) A tempting alternative to the backpackers is **Akaroa Top 10 Holiday Park ❶**, on Morgans Rd., off Old Coach Rd., on the northern outskirts of town. The clean, heated cabins offer beautiful views of the harbor, the hills, and the town all at once. (☎/fax 304 7471; akaroa.holidaypark@xtra.co.nz. Standard units with kitchen from $46, with a view from $48; self-contained units from $60; on-site caravans from $36; tent sites $9, powered $10.)

While Akaroa may be a small town, its cuisine presents big city flair. In the French end of town, **Le Jardin ❸**, 43 Rue Lavaud, beckons with all-day breakfast (eggs benedict $13) served fireside, on the porch, or in the garden by the bocce balls. (☎304 7447. Open Tu-Su 8am-5pm.) **Cafe Eiffel ❷**, 37 Rue Lavaud, gives new meaning to takeaway with its delicious picnic lunches ($6.50-14), complete with a loaned blanket. They rent their two scooters for $35 a day and $22 for a half-day. (☎304 7717. Open M-Tu and Th-Sa 8am-10pm, Su 8am-5pm.) On the harbor, **Dolphin Cafe & Bar ❸**, 6 Rue Balguerie, is cheerfully decorated with fishing and boating artifacts. The TV is housed in a window from the sunken Greenpeace vessel, the *Rainbow Warrior*. (☎304 7658. Open daily 11am-9:30pm.) **Four Square**, on Rue Lavaud across from the museum, has groceries. (☎304 7054. Open daily 9am-6pm.)

SIGHTS AND ACTIVITIES. There are numerous ways to get up-close and personal with area wildlife. **Dolphin Experience** takes you swimming with rare Hector's dolphins. (☎304 7726 or 0508 365 744. 3hr. $75, children and spectators $50.) **Akaroa Harbour Cruises**, on the main wharf, showcases much of the harbor, including the seal and cormorant colonies. (☎304 7641 or 0800 436 574. 2hr. $33, children $15.) **Akaroa Seal Colony Safari** takes you in a 4WD over the crater and down the outer slopes to the Pacific Ocean, where fur seals await. (☎304 7255 or 025 942 070. 2½hr. $50, children $30. Max. 6 people.) **Bluefin Charters** will take you fishing outside the bay or on a 2hr. harbor tour. (☎304 7866. Half-day fishing $500, full-day $750; max. 8 people. Harbor tour $35.) For the do-it-yourself adventurer, inquire about kayak hires from **Akaroa Boat Hire**. (☎304 8758. $35 per day.) **Mount Vernon Lodge** (☎304 7180) can arrange **Horse Treks** from $15 per 30min. **Mountain bikers** can rent bikes at **Akaroa Village Inn** (☎304 7421; $12 per hr., $30 per day) or at **Chez La Mer** ($15 per day; free to guests).

The **Akaroa Museum**, at the corner of Rue Lavaud and Rue Balguerie, has informative exhibits detailing the cultural history of the region. In particular, the 20min. video *The Long Harbour* enlightens viewers on the convergence of Maori, British, and French culture. (☎304 1013. Open daily 10:30am-4:30pm; in winter 10:30am-4pm.) **Barry's Bay Cheese** (☎304 5809) shows visitors the wheys of cheese-making on alternate days from October to April. Outdoor enthusiasts, take heart: numerous tracks depart from Akaroa. The 2- to 4-day coastal **Banks Peninsula Track** requires fees, as the path traverses private property. For day-hikers, there are other trails of varying difficulty levels through bush and up the volcano. Inquire at the Visitors Center for details and maps.

CANTERBURY SKIING ☎03

The ski fields in the Southern Alps get downright crazy in winter, with ski fever breaking out just as surely as kids busting out of school for summer. The slopes of Canterbury offer great runs, less glitz, and in some cases cheaper rates than the tourist-heavy Southern Lakes and are much more likely to attract a Kiwi rather than international following. In addition to traditional commercial fields, several club fields open their slopes to the public. For detailed information on ski fields, check out www.nzski.com, www.snow.co.nz, or pick up the annual *Brown Bear* guide ($2) at the beginning of July (www.brownbear.co.nz).

SKI TRANSPORTATION

Several companies, including some inevitable mid-season newcomers, shuttle the 90min. drive from Christchurch; check at the Christchurch Visitors Center for cur-

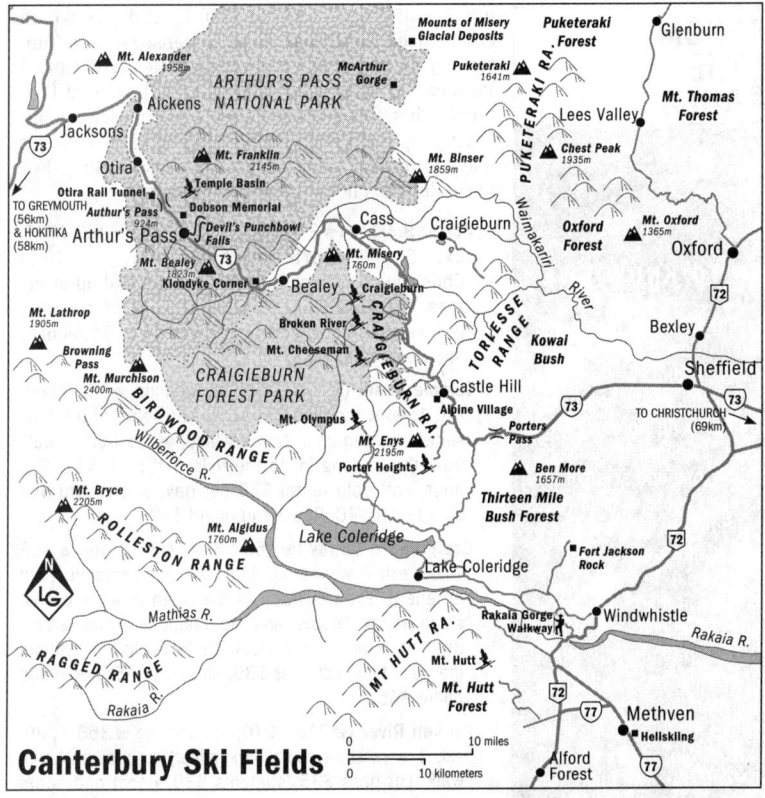

Canterbury Ski Fields

rent departures. As a jumping-off point, **The Ski Shuttle** runs regularly from Christchurch to **Mt. Hutt** and to **Porter Heights** on demand. (☎ 324 3641. Return $40, students $32.) **Ski Bus** does the same. (☎ 332 5000. Return $35, students $30.) Similarly, **Snowline Tours** runs from your door to **Mt. Hutt, Broken River, Porter Heights, Mt. Cheeseman, Mt. Olympus,** and **Craigieburn Valley.** (☎ 0800 766 954. Return $42-45, students $38; no special student rate to Mt. Olympus.) Bring snow chains if you're driving; in some cases expect a walk from the parking lot.

SKI FIELDS

While none of these smaller mountains and their clubs is as popular as nearby Mt. Hutt (see below), each has its own character and loyal following. Most club fields offer overnight accommodations practically atop the runs, and all but Mt. Hutt are only 30min. from the comfortable backpackers in Arthur's Pass (see p. 321). Each of these clubs offers lessons and packages, but they do not hire equipment unless noted. If you plan on skiing for a number of days or in a number of locations, you may want to consider the **NZ Superpass** or the **Chill 5 Pass.** The Superpass (☎ 372 1494; www.nzsuperpass.com) allows you to purchase a

FROM THE ROAD

GETTING TO KNOW EWE

After traveling for over a month in a country populated by 35 times as many sheep as people, I was ready to befriend one of the woolly creatures. Since sheep are both domesticated and abundant, I figured it would be easy to get up close and scratch one behind the ears. I could wrap my arm around its shoulders, hold a camera out in front of us, and snap a photo of me and my ovine pal.

When I arrived in the farming town of Methven, I stopped by a paddock filled with four particularly fluffy sheep. As they munched away on the grass inside, I stood patiently, exuding an aura of calm friendliness. Usually, sheep tend to run in a flock as soon as they catch you staring at them. This may be a defense mechanism evolved from one too many encounters with shears. However, as I stood beside the paddock, one sheep's head jerked up and her eyes met mine. I had expected her to bolt with her friends in tow, but she trotted straight toward me and then stopped ten feet away. I had clearly made a breakthrough in sheep communications. The sheep stared at me with unwavering eyes. After about ten seconds of intense eye-contact, she shifted, almost imperceptibly, and began to urinate. As she peed, her eyes remained locked on mine. When she was done, she shook herself briefly, and with a haughty turn, marched back to her comrades. Bizarre.

number of coupons (from $130 for 2 days), which can be used for lift passes on Queenstown and Canterbury ski fields or on other activities. The Chill 5 Pass (☎318 3288; www.chillout.co.nz), valid at Porter Heights, Craigieburn Valley, Mt. Cheeseman, Mt. Olympus, and Broken River, is perfect for longer stays (from $175 for 7 days; full season $495). For more details, check out www.nzski.com.

Porter Heights (☎318 4002; snowphone ☎366 7766, ext. 6; www.porterheights.co.nz), 1hr. from Christchurch, claims the longest vertical drop in the area. Lift pass $47, students $35; M 2-for-1 adult passes. Ski, boot, and pole rental $29. Snowboard and boot rental $40.

Temple Basin (☎377 7788; snowphone ☎366 7766, ext. 1; www.templebasin.co.nz) has some of the best snowboard terrain in New Zealand, with a 50min. walk from the parking lot to the field. Lift pass $34. Ski, boot, and pole rental $30 per day. Snowboard and boot rental $40. Room and board $42.

Craigieburn Valley (☎365 2514; snowphone ☎366 7766, ext. 7; www.craigieburn.co.nz) is demanding but excellent. Experts flock to the open powder bowls, steep narrow shoots, and the infamous 600m vertical descent in the middle basin—it's like heliskiing without the hefty fees. Lift pass $39, students $25. Room and board $45.

Broken River (☎318 7270; snowphone ☎366 7766, ext. 3; www.snow.co.nz/brokenriver) requires a 25min. walk. Lift pass $35, students $30. Room and board from $40.

Mt. Olympus (☎0800 686 596; snowphone ☎366 7766, ext. 4; bookings ☎318 5840; www.mtolympus.co.nz) is known for light powder, cool mornings, and night skiing under the lights. Lift pass $35, students $25. Bottom hut $20; top hut $40 including breakfast and dinner.

Mt. Lyford (☎315 6178; www.mtlyford.co.nz) is known for its natural pipe and good board-learning terrain. Lift pass $40, university students $35, high school students $25. Ski, boot, and pole rental $15-25; snowboard and boot rental $40.

Mt. Cheeseman (☎379 5315; snowphone ☎366 7766, ext. 02; www.mtcheeseman.com) has a reputation for being family-friendly, and features a quarter pipe. Lift pass $42, students $35, M 2-for-1 adult passes. Lift pass, room, and board $120; students $106. Ski, boot, and pole rental $29, students $24. Snowboard and boot rental $40/$35.

METHVEN AND MT. HUTT ☎ 03

The modest farming town of Methven (pop. 1350) swells every winter with skiers and snowboarders coming to indulge in the longest ski season in New Zealand. The salmon-rich Rakaia and Rangitata Rivers frame the countryside, irrigating a landscape for sheep grazing, stud farming, and cropping. In 2000, the town played host to the *Lord of the Rings* technical and construction crew, who were filming at nearby Mt. Potts.

TRANSPORTATION. Most transport in Methven either arrives from or departs for Christchurch. As a concession to the ski beast, the **InterCity/Newmans** team (☎379 9020) runs from Christchurch and connects to a shuttle that deposits you in front of the **Methven** Visitors Center (1½hr., 1 per day, $20). Book at least a day in advance. Other similar options include **Methven Travel** (☎0800 684 888), which drops by the **Christchurch airport** on the way, and Southern Link's **Ski Link** (☎358 8355). InterCity/Newmans also runs to **Queenstown** via **Aoraki/Mt. Cook** (9hr.; 1 per day; $60, express $40). The **Leopard SkiBus** runs to **Mt. Hutt** from Methven. (☎302 8707. Departs from several downtown locations at 8, 10am, and noon. Hostel pick-up can be arranged. Return $22, students $18.) **Mt. Hutt Tours** runs a door-to-door shuttle. (☎302 8106. Departs town at 8, 9, and 10am. Return $21, children $15.)

ORIENTATION AND PRACTICAL INFORMATION. SH77 becomes **Main Street** in town and makes a crossroads with **Forest Drive/Methven Chertsey Road.** Most services and accommodations lie within a 5min. walk of the **Visitors Information Centre,** south of the crossroads on Main St., which doubles as a booking agent for transport, accommodations, and activities. (☎302 8955 or 0800 764 444; fax 302 9367; www.methven.net.nz. Internet. Open daily 7:30am-6pm; in summer M-F 9am-5pm, Sa-Su 10am-4:30pm.) **Big Al's,** at the crossroads, is the one-stop adventure shop, renting a variety of clothing and accessories. (☎302 8003; www.bigals.co.nz. Ski hire $28; snowboard $39; mountain bike $28 per day; fishing gear $8 per day. Open in winter daily 7:30am-7:30pm.) **Wombat's Ski Shop** also rents snow gear and can book accommodations. (☎302 8084 or 0800 804 747. Ski hire $20; snowboard $45. Open in winter daily 7:30am-7pm.) The **Boarding House,** on Forest Dr. near the center of town, specializes in snowboards, and also has an indoor skateboard park. (☎302 9661; www.boardinghouse.co.nz. Snowboard hire $35. Open in winter daily 7:30am-7pm.) **Ski and board shops at the mountain are slightly more expensive.** Other

---

Fifteen minutes later, I walked past the same sheep paddock. After a couple of seconds of waiting, the same sheep snapped up and ran to me, stopping at the same, predetermined ten-foot mark. The stare-off began again, in earnest. And again, she proceeded to urinate without blinking an eye. My mouth fell open but I didn't avert my gaze. I felt as though we were engaged in a power struggle, but I was disadvantaged because I could hardly drop my pants and pee by the side of the road. Again, the sheep shook. But this time she stayed and kept staring. We sat for another 30 seconds. But then her coat began to twitch, indicating that something was about to happen.

I waited eagerly. And then, all of a sudden, she began to defecate. I couldn't believe this. She continued to stare, right into my eyes, insulting me. Finally, trying to figure out what I had just witnessed, I broke our gaze and turned to walk away. Her eyes bore into my back and, ten steps later when I turned around to look, she was still staring at me. Promptly, as if this signaled my defeat, she turned her tail and pranced back to her admiring sheep friends.

I had the strangest sense of having just lost, of having been put in my place, of having been shown that I was not welcome, and nor would I ever be. These sheep were not cuddly; they were mean and disgusting. I walked away knowing I would never attempt to befriend haughty farm animals again.
—Marly Ohlsson

services include: the **BNZ**, on Main St. (open M and Th-F 9am-4:30pm, Tu-W 9:30am-4:30pm); the **police** (☎302 8200); the **Methven Medical Centre**, opposite the Visitors Center (☎302 8105; open M-F 9am-5:30pm; weekend clinics June-Oct.); the **Methven Pharmacy**, next to the Visitors Center. (☎302 8103. Open M-F 8:30am-6pm, Sa-Su 4-6pm; in summer M-F 8:30am-5pm); **Internet access** at the **Email Shop** (☎302 8700; $3 for 15min., $8 per hr.; open in winter daily 2-9pm); and the **post office**, in Gifts Galore on Main St. (☎302 8463; open M-F 8am-6pm, Sa-Su 10am-noon and 3-6pm; in summer M-F 8am-5pm).

⛰ ACCOMMODATIONS. Lodges line the streets of Methven, though many accommodations close in the summer. All have the bare essentials: waxing racks and somewhere to put your skis. The ■**Alpenhorn Chalet ❸**, 44 Allen St., the third left past the pubs on Main St. from Forest Dr./Methven Chertsey Rd., stands out from the rest. This chalet has a glowing rimu kitchen, central heating, and a glass-enclosed solarium with spa and view of Mt. Hutt. (☎302 8779; fax 302 8789. Free laundry. Dorms $22; doubles $50. In summer $15 per person.) ■**Snow Denn Lodge (YHA) ❸**, at the corner of McMillan and Bank St., features fully made-up beds, free continental breakfast, a spa, and spacious lounges. (☎302 8999; fax 302 8997; www.methvenaccommodation.co.nz. Dorms $30-35; singles $35-40; twins and doubles from $43. Lower rates in summer.) The cozy **Mt. Hutt Accommodation Limited: Bedpost ❷**, 177 Main St., occupies a small complex of brick houses near the center of town. (☎/fax 302 8508; www.aboutmethven.co.nz/mthuttbeds/bedpost.htm. Free laundry. Dorms $15-19; twins and doubles $15-23.) **Skiwi House (BBH) ❷**, 30 Chapman St., is a half-block up Chapman St., which begins behind the Visitors Center and runs parallel to Forest Dr. A brightly painted suite of bungalows and a narrow lounge compose this lively backpackers. (☎302 8772; fax 302 9972; www.skiwihouse.com. Dorms $19, in summer $17; doubles $46/$40.) Turn right down Main St. from the Visitors Center, right again onto South Belt, and left onto Wayne Pl. to reach **Ski Hut/Redwood Lodge (BBH) ❷**, 5 Wayne Pl. Cabins have a rustic feel and log fires. (☎/fax 302 8964; www.snowboardnz.com. Reception 24hr. Dorms $18-23; twins and doubles $46. Rates lower in summer.) For a more private stay, **Abisko Lodge ❸**, 74 Main St., offers visitors a hotel-style lounge, bar, and restaurant. (☎302 8875; fax 302 8795; www.abisko.co.nz. Internet. Spa and sauna. Doubles $105, in summer $80; extra person $15.)

❒ FOOD. Many bars in town serve hearty pub fare during daylight hours (see **Nightlife**, below). The urban **Cafe 131 ❷**, 131 Main St., is plushly appointed. Servers churn out $12 sandwiches for the snow-bound crowd. (☎302 9131. Open daily 8am-4:30pm; in summer 9am-4pm.) The elegant **Steelworx Restaurant ❹**, a block down Forest Dr., sits behind the rowdy Steelworx Bar. Complement a culinary feat (mains $22-28) with a fine wine by the hearth. (☎302 9900. Open mid-Mar. to Dec. Tu-Su 6-10pm; bar open daily 5pm-3am.) Set in the old post office, **Last Post Saloon ❹**, across from the Visitors Center, serves up American Southwest classics (Texas ribs $23.50) amidst buffalo memorabilia. (☎302 8259. Open in winter daily 5pm-late.) **Lisah's ❸**, in the Value Tours Building on Main St., is an upscale spot with fine wines and creative cuisine ("penne Lisah" $15). At night, Lisah's morphs into a buzzing bar. (☎302 8070. Mains $14-22.50. Open M-Sa 5:30pm-late; in summer W-Sa 5:30pm-late. Reservations recommended.) If your ski-legs have energy for the walk, luxury and charm await at **Ski Time ❸**, down Racecourse Rd. Tasty mains run $13-26. (☎302 8398. Open daily 5pm-late.) **Four Square Discounter**, on McMillan St. (☎302 8114; open daily 7am-9pm), and **Supervalue**, across the rotary (☎302 8050; open daily 7am-8pm; in summer 8am-7pm), are the two supermarkets in town.

NIGHTLIFE. Many of the restaurants become lively bars at night (see **Food,** above). Color-coded for easy recall, the **Blue Pub** (☎302 8046; open daily 11am-2am) announces its azure self at the crossroads. The **Canterbury Hotel/Brown Pub** (☎302 8045; open daily 11am-3am) lies just across the road. In broad terms, Blue is for skier and Brown is for local, but visitors to both enjoy the reasonable pub fare ($9-15). The nightly $10 roast at the Brown Pub deserves special kudos. When the ski bums get raucous, they head to **Fusion,** on Ashburton Rd., where a live band, pool tables, and a hilarious mountain video (bi-weekly) provide ample amusement. (☎302 8252. Open daily 7pm-3am; in summer Th-Sa.)

ACTIVITIES. With the longest ski season in Australasia and the best snow-cover in New Zealand, **Mt. Hutt** is the main reason that crowds flock to Methven. The 2075m summit looks down upon 365 hectares of beautiful powder, 42 hectares of snow-making, and views reaching into the heart of the Southern Alps. The varied terrain is suitable for all abilities. Two sweet half-pipes beckon boarders and terrain parks attract tricksters. (☎302 8811; snowphone ☎308 5074 or 0900 99 766. Lift passes $68, students $50. Usually open June-Oct.) If your plan includes several days of skiing, you should consider the **NZ Superpass** (see p. 317). **Mt. Hutt Heliskiing** runs professionally guided heliskiing trips throughout the Southern Alps. (☎302 8401 or 0800 443 5475; www.mthuttheli.com. North Peak $130; powder ski hire $10 per day.) At the Mt. Hutt Ski Area Car Park, the cleverly marketed **Mt. Hutt Bungy** claims to have "New Zealand's highest bungy" only because the jump is the highest above sea-level. (☎302 9969; www.mthuttbungy.com. $99; all-day unlimited jumping $150; ski/snowboard jump $129.)

Those seeking immersion in nature will find no shortage of **scenic walks** in the Methven area. If you are in for a longer haul, head for the 1687m **Mt. Somers Summit** (return 7hr.) or the geologically intriguing **Rakaia Gorge Walkway** (return 3-4hr.), which passes through forest and shrub and allows inspection of several coal mine shafts. The **Scotts Saddle Track** (return 5hr.) leaves from the carpark in the Awa Awa Reserve, at the end of McLennan's Bush Rd., and climbs 1000m to views of Mt. Hutt. **Planet Argo** (☎302 8464 or 0800 2746 386) takes adventurers on a half-day excursion on six- and eight-wheel ATVs ($60). The company also has a small paintball court ($25 per person) and has been known to combine the two activities.

ARTHUR'S PASS   ☎03

Snaking through the towering Southern Alps, Arthur's Pass (pop. 60) is a haven for skiers and trampers; several major ski areas rise to glory within 30 minutes of each other. The tramping in the 230,000 alpine and sub-alpine hectares of Arthur's Pass National Park and nearby Craigieburn Forest Park is beautiful, challenging, and uncrowded year-round. In winter, the road through the pass (SH73) is occasionally closed due to snow, but the TranzAlpine rail trip, considered one of the world's best, is reliable. Amenities are scarce; it is best to bring groceries.

TRANSPORTATION. The aptly named **TranzAlpine** line, run by **TranzScenic** (☎0800 802 802), bridges Canterbury and Westland with Arthur's Pass at its center. The line travels over gorges, river valleys, and alpine fields to **Christchurch** (2hr., 1 per day, $57) or **Greymouth** (2hr., 1 per day, $36). Departing from the Tearooms, **Coast-to-Coast** (☎0800 800 847) runs daily bus service to: **Christchurch** (2½-3hr., 1 per day, $25); **Greymouth** (2hr., 1 per day, $15); and **Hokitika** (2hr., 1 per day, $15). **Alpine Coach** (☎0800 274 888) and **Atomic Shuttles** (☎322 8883) run the same service at comparable prices.

ORIENTATION AND PRACTICAL INFORMATION.

SH73 runs through Arthur's Pass Village parallel to the railroad tracks. When exiting the underpass below the tracks, turn right and walk 100m north along the railway to reach the **Arthur's Pass DOC Visitor Information Centre** (☎318 9211; fax 318 9210; mlimpus@doc.govt.nz. Open daily 8am-5pm.) The **police** (☎318 9212) are on the main road, across Rough Creek, south of town. A tiny **post office** sits just past Oscar's Haus Cafe (open M-F 9:30-10am). For local **breakdown service**, call ☎318 9266.

ACCOMMODATIONS AND CAMPING.

Mountain House Backpackers (BBH) ❷, on the main drag near the Visitors Center, has a great view of the pass from the comfortable lounge. A true tramper's rest, there are ice-axes, crampons, sleeping mats, and more for hire as well as a taxi service to the trailheads for $10-55 per carload. (☎318 9258; fax 318 9058; www.trampers.co.nz. Reception 8:30am-8pm; sign-in booking otherwise. Dorms $18; twins and doubles $49; tent sites in summer $12.) The **Sir Arthur Dudley Dobson Memorial YHA ❷**, across the street, commemorates the first man to survey Arthur's Pass in 1864 with a handsome mural in the lounge. (☎318 9230. Internet. Reception 8-11am and 5-10pm; sign-in booking otherwise. Dorms $20; doubles $46.) **Alpine Motels ❹**, south of town towards the police station, is a string of self-contained bungalows. (☎/fax 318 9233; alpine.motels@xtra.co.nz. Doubles $75; twins $80; extra person $15.) There are simple **DOC tent sites** and a day shelter opposite the Visitors Center. (Toilets year-round; treated water in summer. $4.) Five **free** roadside camping facilities are in the surrounding area, all with pit toilets and untreated water. On SH73 towards Christchurch, **Greyney's Shelter** is 6km from town and **Klondyke Corner** is 8km from town. On SH73 towards Greymouth, **Kelly Shelter** is 17km from town. On Mt. White Rd, **Hawdon Shelter** and **Andrew's Shelter** are 27 and 28km from town, respectively.

FOOD.

Oscar's Haus Cafe ❷ serves sandwiches from $4 and vegetable-packed mains from $9. (☎318 9234. Open daily 9am-5pm; in winter 11am-4pm.) Behind the gasoline pumps, **Arthur's Pass Tearooms ❶** concocts pastries and packaged sandwiches and sells groceries, petrol, and booze. (☎318 9235. Open daily 7:30am-7pm; in summer 7am-9:30pm.) Amid the alpine decor and tourist crowd at **The Chalet Restaurant and Bar ❸**, on the right a few minutes past the hostels, patrons can decide between the bar and dining room. Light meals by the hearth run $5-14, while more elegant mains ($18-28) are served on polished wooden tables. (☎318 9236. Open daily 11am-late.)

OUTDOOR ACTIVITIES.

Arthur's Pass National Park and the adjacent **Craigieburn Forest Park** enjoy a diverse terrain, from gorges to ascents and from alpine meadows to riverbeds, allowing for both easy walks and demanding year-round tramps. Overnight trampers in either area should be aware that local weather can be volatile and rivers can rise swiftly. Since there are no bridges in the parks, and overnight huts cannot be reserved, trampers should check with the Arthur's Pass Visitors Center for **hut** ticket purchase (Category 1 through 3), weather reports, and track conditions before leaving. Whatever your destination, emergency overnight gear is essential—and don't feed the keas!

Pick up a brochure ($1) for a self-guided historic walk of the consistently peaceful village (1½hr.), which includes directions to original tunnelers' huts on the main road. Tramps in this area are steep, ungroomed, and strenuous. The **Devil's Punchbowl Waterfall Trail** (return 1hr.) begins just past the **Chalet Restaurant** and leads to an arresting view of the falls. A beautiful spot near the start of the trail rewards early birds with a view of the sunrise over the mountains. A number of great day hikes cluster around the **Craigieburn Environmental Centre** (2km off of SH73, about a 30min. drive east of Arthur's Pass village), where travelers can find picnic sites, campsites, and shelter. The **Cass-Lagoon Saddle** (return 2-3 days) is a popular summertime tramp (beware of avalanches in winter) and one of the easier overnight hikes.

Farther east, dayhikers can explore the limestone formations of the **Castle Hill** basin, though local Maori request that climbers stay off the rocks to respect their *tapu* (sacred) status. A few minutes closer to Arthur's Pass, the **Cave Stream Scenic Reserve** awaits cautious amateur spelunkers bearing polypropylene and torches; expect to get wet in the flowing cave-water that can reach waist height. Both are located off of SH73, a 45min. drive east of Arthur's Pass and 7km past the turn-off to Craigieburn headquarters.

SOUTH CANTERBURY ☎03

Speckled with small agricultural outposts, the Canterbury Plains are an area of serene, rural beauty. To the east lie the coastal climes of Timaru while, to the west, Mackenzie Country accounts for a large percent of New Zealand's sheep population. The mighty Aoraki/Mt. Cook lies in majestic repose at the northern end of Lake Pukaki, and in the heart of the Southern Alps, mountains everywhere are reflected in Tekapo, the basin's most famous lake. Covered with tussock grassland and dotted with brilliant lakes, southern Canterbury is ruggedly pastoral.

TIMARU ☎03

Home to a cheery downtown and beautiful ocean vistas, Timaru (pop. 26,000) beckons with an honest charm. First named Te Maru, meaning "place of shelter," Timaru once provided water and rest for Maori hunters. Today, an artificial harbor built in 1877 protects the international fishing fleet and rigs full of sheep bound for Asia. The wharves also shelter Caroline Bay from rough seas, making it popular with summer beachgoers.

TRANSPORTATION. Buses run by **Atomic Shuttle** (☎322 8883) leave daily from the Visitors Center for **Christchurch** (2½hr., $20) and **Oamaru** (1¼hr., $10). More expensive but more frequent, **InterCity** buses leave from the train station for Christchurch (2½hr., 2-3 per day, $22-28) and Dunedin (3hr., 2-3 per day, $32) via Oamaru (1¼hr., $20). For taxi service, try **Timaru Taxis** (☎800 846 829) or **Budget Taxis** (☎688 8779). **Hitchhikers** report that the base of the highway up to Aoraki/Mt. Cook is a common place to catch a ride in the mountains. Otherwise, SH1 north or south of town is considered the easiest place to grab a ride.

ORIENTATION AND PRACTICAL INFORMATION. Midway between Christchurch and Dunedin, Timaru slopes down from the foothills of the Central Alps to the sea. **SH1** snakes through the town's rolling hills as **Craige, Theodosia, and Evans Streets** and meets **SH8** to Tekapo and Mt. Cook just north of town. The scenic **Caroline Bay** is a 15min. walk from the Visitor Centre along **Stafford Street**, Timaru's main commercial avenue.

Just off Stafford St., the **Visitor Information Centre**, 2 George St., in the old lava-built Landing Service Building, is where you'll find free maps, local bus schedules, self-guided walking tours, and information on regional events. Also available from the Visitor Centre are **DOC** information, various **shuttle** schedules, and other bookings. (☎688 6163; fax 684 0202. Open M-F 8:30am-5pm, Sa-Su 10am-3pm.) Other services include: **ATMs** along Stafford St.; the **police** station (☎688 4199), at North and Barnard St.; **pharmacies** along Stafford St.; the **hospital** (☎684 4000), on High and Queen St.; **Internet access** for $4 per 30min. and free with hot breakfast ($8.50) at the hip **Purple Lizard Cafe**, 332 Stafford St. (☎688 8890; open M-F 7:30am-5pm, Sa-Su 10am-5pm); and the **post office**, 19 Strathallan St., (☎686 6040; open M-Th 8am-5:30pm, F 8am-6pm, Sa 9am-1pm).

ACCOMMODATIONS AND FOOD. The clean and comfortable **Timaru Backpackers (YHA)** ❷, 42 Evans St. has a kitchen and lounge area with TV. Call the owner for pick-up, as the uphill walk from the train station is tough. (☎684 5067; fax 684 5706. Internet. Dorms $17; singles $25; twins and doubles $40; self-contained units $40 for 2.) For a location nearer to Timaru's shops and sights, try the restored **Dominion Backpackers** ❷, 334 Stafford St., (☎684 4729. Dorms $18; singles $30; doubles $45-50.) At **Timaru Selwyn Top 10 Holiday Park** ❷, an extensive camp facility 2km outside of town on Selwyn St., the 100 powered sites sit by a gently burbling creek. You can't beat the video games, TV lounge, sparkling kitchen, immaculate shower blocks, and free access to the neighboring golf club. (☎684 7690; fax 688 1004; www.timaruholidaypark.co.nz. Tent and powered sites $20-21 for 2; cabins and flats $35-58 for 2; motel units $70 for 2; extra adult $10-13.)

For stellar coffee and food at non-astronomical prices zip off to **Red Rocket** ❸, 4a Elizabeth St., adjacent to Chalmers Church off Sophia St. Red is the color of the day for the space-aged decor, and pizzas ($12-17) with names like "astronomic gastronomic apricot chicken." (☎688 8313. Open M-W 10am-10pm, Th 10am-11pm, F-Sa 10am-midnight, Su 11:30am-10pm.) Roosters watch from their stained-glass perches in the windows of **The Coq and Pullet** ❶, 209 Stafford St. The mammoth berry muffins ($2.50) are a good start to any day. (☎688 6616. Open M-F 7am-4pm, Sa 10am-1pm, Su 11:30am-1:30pm.) Near the hostels, **South of the Border** ❷, 88 Evans St. serves heaping helpings of Timaru's only take on Mexican fare. Bring your appetite for the massive $10-15 enchilada plates (☎688 5189. Open daily 11am-late.) **The Loaded Hog** ❷, 2 George St., in the Landing Service Building by the Visitors Center, is a trendy microbrew chain that serves as the late-night hot spot for a young professional crowd. Bite into the $5 lunch specials (noon-2pm) and wash them down with a $4.50 pint of Hog's Head Dark. (☎684 9999. Open Su-Th 11am-1am, F-Sa 11am-3am.)

SIGHTS AND ACTIVITIES. A major fixture of the South Islander's diet, Timaru's own beer is produced in massive vessels at **DB Brewery**, Sheffield St., using their patented continuous fermentation method. If you can, sample just one of the 55 million liters produced here. (☎688 2059. Tours M-F at 10:30am. Free, but call for reservations. No sandals.) Housed in a 1908 historic home overlooking Timaru's rooftops and the Caroline Bay, **Aigantighe Art Gallery**, 49 Wai-iti Rd., features a collection of paintings dating from early colonial New Zealand to the present. The manicured back lawn houses sculptures from an international Stone Carving Symposium. (☎688 4424. Open Tu-F 10am-4pm, Sa-Su noon-4pm. Free.) From Boxing Day (December 26) until mid-January, the bay area hosts a grand **Christmas/New Year Carnival**.

The **Timaru Botanic Gardens**, a 20min. walk south along Stafford St. (which becomes King St.), include rare plant species, ponds flitting with ducks, and grassy knolls fit for a picnic. Tennis courts and an education center (offering botany classes Wednesday and Sunday afternoons) augment the botanic delights. **Caroline Bay** and its shallow sweep of sand bustle in the summer months—the reclaimed park contains an **aviary** swarming with technicolor parakeets, an open stage, miniature golf during the summer, and a host of other activities. The **Benvenue Cliffs** on the far side of the beach are the best place for a view of the harbor. Today, memorial plaques nailed to a post commemorate lost ships.

TEKAPO ☎ 03

Busy SH8 and tranquil Lake Tekapo are the body and soul of tiny Tekapo village (pop. 300). Bus traffic traveling between Christchurch and Queenstown sustains the disproportionate density of souvenir shops, accommodations, and restaurants while Lake Tekapo's soft blue waters soothe the restless traveler. The simple Church of the Good S.hepherd, perched on the lake's shore, is a lucid proclamation of the mystical wonder of the place, as much a work of art itself as the scenery which it celebrates.

TRANSPORTATION. InterCity (☎ 0800 777 707), **Southern Link Shuttles** (☎ 358 8355), and **Atomic Shuttles** (☎ 322 8883) all run buses daily to **Christchurch** (4hr., $25-30) and **Queenstown** (5½hr., $25-30). **InterCity** also runs to **Mt. Cook** (1½hr., $21), as does **The Cook Connection** (☎ 025 583 211; Tu, Th, and Sa; $25, return $40). Book InterCity shuttles at **High Country Crafts** (☎ 680 6905) and Southern Link and Atomic Shuttles at **Kiwi Treasures** (☎ 680 6686). Buses also depart from the **Godley Inn** (☎ 680 6848), next to the dam.

ORIENTATION AND PRACTICAL INFORMATION. All services, souvenir shops, and food options in Tekapo lie along **SH8,** cultivating a true waystation feel. **Kiwi Treasures** in the village functions as the official **Visitors Center** and can book accommodations, activities, and some transport. (☎/fax 680 6686. Open daily 8am-8pm; in winter 8am-6pm.) In emergencies, call the **police** (☎ 680 6855). There are **no banks** in Tekapo, although the Shell Station has an **ATM** and the Visitors Center has EFTPOS and exchanges credit card checks. The **Godley Inn** (☎ 680 6848) changes money but takes a 5% commission. Stock up on **groceries** and fuel at the **Shell Station** (☎ 680 6809). The **post shop** is next to the Visitors Center. (☎ 680 6861. Open M-Sa 8:30am-5:30pm, Su 9am-5pm.)

ACCOMMODATIONS AND CAMPING. The **Tekapo YHA ❷** is on Simpson Ln., past the pub on the west side of town. The lounge has massive windows, providing a soulful panorama of the lake. (☎ 680 6857; fax 680 6664; yhatekpo@yha.org.nz. Bike and fishing rod rental. Internet. Laundry. Reception 8-10am, 5-6:30pm, and 8-9:30pm. Dorms $20; twins and doubles $48; tent sites $12.) Formerly housing for dam-workers, **Tailor-made Tekapo Backpackers (BBH) ❷**, 9-11 Aorangi Crescent, is a collection of three spacious buildings, with access to the community tennis courts and two stone BBQs. (☎ 680 6700; tailor-made-backpackers@xtra.co.nz. Internet. Linen $2. Dorms $18; twins and doubles $44,with bath $52; triples and quads $20 per person.) **The B&B at Studio 25 ❹**, 25 Murray Pl., combines the quirkiness of an artist's gallery with a lakeview deck, a manicured yard, and a cuddly pile of teddy bears. (☎ 680 6514. Breakfast included. Doubles $85.) Cyclists are fortunate to have the **Pedallers Paradise ❶**, 1 Aorangi Crescent (the first house on the left), as an inexpensive and informative stop along the way. The owner wrote a comprehensive book on cycling New Zealand (also called *Pedallers Paradise*) and has plenty of advice on routes. (No bookings—go to the Visitors Center or just show up. Closed May-Sept. Dorms $14; tent sites $10. Cash only.) To get to the **Lake Tekapo Motels and Motor Park ❶**, follow signs for the Tekapo Domain. Practically floating in the lake, rooms are in varying states of newness. (☎ 680 6825 or 0800 853 853; fax 680 6824; www.laketekapo-accommodation.co.nz. Cabins $38; tourist flats $65; motel doubles $90-98; tent sites $10, powered $11.)

FOOD AND NIGHTLIFE. Restaurants and takeaways cluster around the Shell Station on SH8. **Reflections ❷**, at the western end of the village, has won cuisine awards; if you're game, choose from delectable beef, lamb, and venison mains (lunch $9-14, dinner $13-28) while enjoying sunset hues on the mist-enshrouded

THE HIDDEN DEAL

SUSHI'S PROMISED LAND: KOHAN RESTAURANT

The fresh-fish faithful travel from far and wide to eat sushi at Kohan Restaurant in Lake Tekapo. Besides doing big business with the Asian tour-bus crowd, Kohan also attracts epicures from Christchurch and Dunedin willing to make a four-hour journey for a plate of salmon sashimi. The salmon farm is just down the road toward Mt. Cook—you'd have to snag it, scale it, and slice it yourself to find fish any fresher. Plenty of non-raw Japanese standards round out the menu for the sushi neophyte; mains start at $10.

When making your pilgrimage, don't be put off by Kohan's seeming lack of ambience. Sure, you'll have to wander through a tourist-trap shop filled with paper-weights and possum mittens to reach the restaurant from SH8. And, yes, the newly-refurbished interior barely has the character of a hospital ward. These are but trials for the faithful. Persevere. Once you're seated and gazing at Lake Tekapo over your lunch, these aesthetic indignities will fade. The views of the lake from Kohan's tables will dazzle with an enchanting blue that rivals even the colorful slices of fish on your plate. Lift chopsticks. Pinch fish. Dip in soy sauce and wasabe. Insert in mouth. Smile. You've reached the South Island's sushi promised-land.

Find Kohan by entering through the Observatory Cafe on SH8 and winding past the souvenir shop. ☎ 680 6688. *Open daily 11am-2pm; also M-Sa 6-9pm.*

mountains. Cheaper bar food is available at the adjoining Lake Tekapo Tavern. (☎ 680 6808. Open daily 7am-9pm; bar open 11am-late.) Everyone's raving about **Pepe's Pizza and Pasta Co. ❸**, east of the Shell Station on SH8, the newest addition to Tekapo's culinary scene. Gourmet pizzas ($15.50-24.50) and heaping pasta dishes ($13) are delightful. The bar at Pepe's also doubles as one of Tekapo's few nightlife options. (☎ 680 6677. Open daily 11am-late.) **Robin's Cafe & Bar ❷**, next to the Visitors Center, provides stunning views, meaty mains (from $11), and budget-friendly takeaways. (☎ 680 6998. Open daily 8am-8pm.) The **Bread Crumb Bakery ❶**, on the main road, sells huge loaves of pizza bread ($4.50) as well as pies and baked goods. (☎ 680 6655. Open daily 7am-9pm; in winter 8am-5pm.)

SIGHTS AND ACTIVITIES. If you're just passing through Tekapo, make sure to cross the bridge to the **Church of the Good Shepherd,** a tiny interdenominational church of wood and stone constructed in 1935. The interior windows afford beautiful views of the lake and surrounding countryside. Longer walks in the area include the popular 2½hr. circuit up **Mt. John,** through pine forest and up to the observatory (it begins past the motor park, near the ice-skating rink along the lake's western side). A circuit track to **Cowan's Lookout** leaves from the far side of the bridge and reveals lake views comparable to those from Mt. John in about an hour less. Follow the green and yellow stakes through the fields and over to the rocky shore and the church. If you become truly fascinated with Mt. John, it may be worthwhile to return at night for an entirely different look at Tekapo. **Star Watching** takes visitors on a trip through the universe in which constellations, galaxies, and planets are pointed out through the massive telescope on Mt. John. Most tours are in Japanese, but some are in English. (☎ 680 6565; www.stargazing.co.nz. 1¾hr. $35; min. 4 people.)

The **MacKenzie Alpine Trekking Co.** (☎ 680 6760 or 0800 628 269) guides 30min. horseback rides through the forest ($25) as well as longer trips up Mt. John (1hr. $45, 2hr. $80). Located on SH8, **Kiwi Express,** a satellite activities desk of the Godley Inn, rents kayaks (1hr. $10, each additional hour $5), golf clubs ($15; green fees at the nearby club under $10), and mountain bikes (half-day $10, full-day $15). (☎ 680 6224. Open in summer daily 9am-dusk; in winter see the Godley Inn reception desk.) **Kineski Adventures** (☎ 680 6966) rents kayaks (single $15 per hr., double $25 per hr.) and front suspension mountain bikes (half-day $25, full-day $40) and runs guided kayak tours ($50-95, including lunch).

Small, family-operated **Mt. Dobson** in Fairlie devotes one-third of its mountain to beginning **skiers**, while the rest of the mountain is streaked with intermediate and some black diamond runs. (☎685 8039; www.dobson.co.nz. Lift tickets $30-44, students $24-30; rentals $24.) Another ski field in Tekapo is **Roundhill Ski Area**, providing gently undulating slopes that are perfect for beginners. (☎680 6977; www.roundhill.co.nz. Lift tickets $30-40, beginners $20-25, students $18-30, children $8-14; ski rental $22-28, children $12-15.) Many **scenic flight** companies serving the Aoraki/Mt. Cook area can depart from the Tekapo airport; see **Mt. Cook Village: Air Adventures**, p. 329).

AORAKI/MT. COOK NATIONAL PARK ☎03

With one-third of its area permanently snow-covered, Aoraki/Mt. Cook National Park and its jagged peaks have an austere and spectacular profile. To many Maori, the park represents the most sacred of ancestors, and a recent agreement with the national government has placed restrictions on Aoraki/Mt. Cook's use. Climbers must turn back before reaching the summit, and all references to the mountain must place the Maori name before the English one. Notoriously capricious weather and frequent avalanches make this one of the most dangerous regions in New Zealand and a favorite playground for world-class alpinists. Dark lateral moraines and milky blue glaciers give an otherworldly flavor to the desolate landscape: a silence interrupted only by the screeching calls of the world's only mountain parrot, the kea. With the highest mountain in New Zealand (Aoraki/Mt. Cook), the longest glacier in Australasia (Tasman), plus 25 peaks over 3000m and a few hundred over 2000m, Aoraki/Mt. Cook National Park is near the top of the bottom of the world.

AT A GLANCE	
AREA: 70,696 hectares.	**GATEWAYS:** Aoraki/Mt. Cook Village is located within the park; Twizel and Tekapo are outside.
CLIMATE: Severe weather patterns; especially dangerous in winter.	
FEATURES: Highest mountains, largest glacier coverage (40%). No forest, but alpine plants and wildlife.	**CAMPING:** Indoor accommodations only in the village; campsites at Glentanner and White Horse Hill Campground.
HIGHLIGHTS: Aoraki/Mt. Cook, the tallest mountain in New Zealand.	**FEES & RESERVATIONS:** Inform DOC of plans and check for necessary hut passes.

AORAKI/MT. COOK VILLAGE ☎03

At the end of SH80, a 45min. drive from Twizel along the shores of Lake Pukaki, the buildings of tiny Aoraki/Mt. Cook Village (pop. 120, in summer 300) are nestled in the heart of Aoraki/Mt. Cook National Park. Not just anyone can live here; residents must be employed by DOC or one of the local accommodations. The village itself doesn't have much to offer the budget traveler outside of scenery: accommodations and food tend to be pricey. Come here to embark on day walks and alpine climbs or to contemplate the sublime mountains and powerful glaciers.

TRANSPORTATION

You can book **bus** transport with **InterCity** (☎0800 777 707); the schedule is flexible. Buses depart daily from the Hermitage and the YHA for **Christchurch** (5½hr.; 12:45pm;

$75, YHA $63) and **Queenstown** (4hr.; 2:45pm; $63, YHA $53) via **Twizel**. **Great Sights** (☎ 358 9029) and **Grey Line** (☎ 0800 800 904) also run through Aoraki/Mt. Cook on their way between Christchurch and Queenstown. Both depart for **Queenstown** at 2:20pm and for **Christchurch** at 2pm; Great Sights (with full commentary) is $58, while Grey Line (no commentary) is $40. **High Country Shuttles & Tours** (☎ 0800 435 050) runs between **Twizel** and Aoraki/Mt. Cook. (Departs Twizel 7am and 12:30pm; departs Aoraki/Mt. Cook 9:30am and 4:30pm; in winter runs only on demand. $15, return $25.) **The Cook Connection** (☎ 025 583 211; Oct.-Apr.) shuttles passengers at 8:30am to **Timaru** (3hr.; M, W, and F; $45, return $80) and **Oamaru** (3hr.; Tu, Th, and Sa; $45, return $80).

PRACTICAL INFORMATION

The map for Aoraki/Mt. Cook is on p. 342. The **Aoraki/Mt. Cook Visitor Centre,** near the Hermitage, is the place to book activities, check track conditions, and check in and out for all trips in the park. If the weather doesn't allow a good glimpse of the mountains, you are assured of one through the Centre's $3 audio-visual presentation. (☎ 435 1186; fax 435 1080. Open daily 8:30am-6pm; in winter 8:30am-5pm.) The nearest doctor and pharmacy are located in Twizel. Head to the **Hermitage** (☎ 435 1809) for the **post office, grocery store, Internet** ($10 per hr.), and **currency exchange** (24hr.). There is a self-serve **petrol** pump that accepts EFTPOS but no international credit cards. Pick up the phone at the pump to reach a Hermitage staff member, who will help you purchase with cash or international credit card. Consider bringing enough food and gas to avoid the high prices in Aoraki/Mt. Cook altogether.

ACCOMMODATIONS AND FOOD

With comfy couches, pine-planked walls, a sauna, and a great video collection, the **Mt. Cook YHA ❸** blends into its alpine surroundings. What's more, it's the only budget place to stay in the village proper, so be sure to book far in advance. (☎ 435 1820; fax 435 1821; yhamtck@yha.org.nz. Internet, some groceries, and lockers available. Reception 8:30am-8:30pm; in winter 8-10am, 5-6:30pm, and 8-9pm. Dorms $25; twins $64; doubles $68.) The **Hermitage ❺** monopolizes the rest of the accommodations in the park. (☎ 435 1809 or 0800 686 800; fax 435 1879; www.mount-cook.com. Reception 24hr. Doubles from $130 with TV/kitchenette; hotel suites from $400.) Less expensive options are available 23km from the Mt. Cook Village at the **Glentanner Park Centre ❶**. Also owned by the Hermitage, this motor park has a variety of rooms and an on-site restaurant. (☎ 435 1855 or 0800 453 682; fax 435 1854; www.glentanner.co.nz. Shuttles to Mt. Cook $5-10. Dorms $15; cabins $40-50; tourist flats $70; tent sites $9.) At the end of the Hooker Valley Rd. is the **White Horse Hill Camping Area ❶** with on-your-honor tent sites ($5).

Food options in town are extremely limited. The **Chamois Bar ❸**, in the Glencoe wing of the Hermitage, offers bar meals and drinks. (Open M-W and Su 5pm-midnight, Th-Sa 5pm-1am; kitchen closes at 10:30pm.) In the main area of the Hermitage, the **Hermitage Coffee Shop ❶** serves quality java. (Open daily 7:30am-5:30pm; in winter 10am-5pm.)

OUTDOOR ACTIVITIES

WALKS. The peaks, glaciers, and ice cliffs of Aoraki/Mt. Cook National Park draw visitors from all over the world. Those traveling on a shoestring rather than a belay rope can taste glacial terrain with the many short day walks in the area. The most popular walk is the **Hooker Valley** *(return 4hr. from the village)* with a beautiful viewpoint and two swing bridges. The strenuous uphill climb to **Red Tarns** *(return 2hr.)* rewards exertion with exhilarating views down into the Hooker Valley and up into the cloud-piercing Alps. Slightly milder, the **Kea Point Walk** *(return 2hr.)* leads

AORAKI/MT. COOK VILLAGE ■ 329

through scraggly gorse to a lookout over the Mueller Glacier, with Mt. Sefton's azure ice falls in the background. The only feasible overnight tramping options are the popular and strenuous 3-4hr. route to **Mueller Hut** ($18) and the 3-4hr. scramble along Tasman glacier moraine to the **Ball Shelter Hut** ($8). The walk to the Mueller Hut traverses higher terrain and offers more alpine scenery, while the Ball Shelter walk provides closer views of the glacier and the chance to sleep in the shadow of Aoraki/Mt. Cook. The rest of the huts in the park ($8-18) are accessible only to experienced climbers and serve as bases for technical ascents.

MOUNTAINEERING. The crags and crevasses surrounding the Cook Range's peaks have trained some of the world's great mountaineers, including Sir Edmund Hillary of Everest fame; they've also killed or severely injured many climbers, both novices and experts. Several reputable companies offer guided ascents and multi-day, wallet-slimming courses in mountaineering. **Alpine Guides** (☎ 435 1834; www.alpineguides.co.nz) runs a variety of guided ascents and technical courses, with prices beginning around $2000 for week-long courses (includes aircraft access to mountains, food, and technical equipment). Alpine Guides also rents alpine equipment, including ice axes ($10 per day), crampons ($10 per day), and avalanche transceivers ($8 per day). **Alpine Recreation** runs a series of shorter, cheaper courses aimed at teaching mountaineering basics. (☎ 680 6736; www.alpinerecreation.co.nz. 4-day intro courses from $880.) Travelers with basic mountaineering skills seeking a non-guided option can traverse the **Ball Pass Crossing**, a popular and challenging route. Alpine Recreation also runs guided trips over the pass (3 days, $650). Always check in with DOC if you are planning a trip.

ADVENTURE ACTIVITIES. The Hermitage and the YHA have information on (and also book) several tours. In the summer, **Glacier Explorers** runs a boat tour of the Tasman Glacier that glides past the icy blue cliffs jutting over the lake. (☎ 435 1077; www.glacierexplorers.com. 2½hr. $75, YHA $65, children $55.) **Alan's 4WD Tours** travels over rough terrestrial terrain to the Tasman Glacier. (☎ 435 1809. $80, YHA $75, children $55.) **Glacier Sea-Kayaking** runs one-of-a-kind sea kayaking trips to the Tasman Glacier. (☎ 435 1890 or 025 342 277; www.mtcook.com. $70, children $50; YHA 10% discount.) To explore the headlands of Lake Pukaki via equine legs rather than your own, call **Glentanner Horse Trekking.** (☎ 435 1855. Summer only. 30min. rides from $30.)

AIR ADVENTURES. Heli-biking and heli-hiking adventures are available through **Heli-Bike** (☎ 435 0626 or 0800 435 424; www.helibike.com. Heli-biking from $135, heli-hiking from $75.) The **Helicopter Line** has a 20min. flight with a snow landing as well as several longer—and more expensive—options. (☎ 435 1801 or 0800 650 651; www.new-zealand.com/thl. 20min. flight $165, YHA $150.) **Air Safaris** flies a scenic tour called the "Grand Traverse," guaranteeing a window seat and good commentary along the way. (☎ 680 6880 or 0800 806 880; www.airsafaris.co.nz. 50min. $230, children $150; YHA 10% discount.) **Mt. Cook Ski Planes** runs the popular Flight Spa 1, with gorgeous views of Murchison and Tasman Glacier and a glacier landing in-between. If you are lucky, your pilot may do some plane skiing as he takes off from the hangar. (☎ 435 1026 or 0800 800 702; www.new-zealand.com/skiplanes. 40min. $250; YHA $20 discount.)

SKIING. The small family ski field of **Ohau**, between Twizel and Omarama, is not far off. The field has some beginner runs and a good number of intermediate and advanced slopes as well. Budget accommodation including a bed, dinner, and breakfast runs $55. (☎ 438 9885. Lift passes $45, students $30; rental $25, children, $15.) **Alpine Guides** runs **heliskiing** trips during the winter, whisking skiers to remote terrain. (☎ 435 1834. From $65.)

THE WEST COAST

When UNESCO declared the West Coast a World Heritage site in 1990, the region graciously assumed its place in a hall of fame that included the likes of the Grand Canyon, the Great Barrier Reef, and Mount Everest. Of course, the Kiwis already knew they had a sweet thing—along the coast, the towering Southern Alps bound the region to the east and form a geological wall a mere 40 to 50km from the Tasman Sea. With snow-capped peaks, lush tropical rainforests, and pounding waves, it's no wonder that 80% of the West Coast is government-owned, set aside in national parks, forests, and scenic reserves.

WEST COAST HIGHLIGHTS

CHIP AWAY with ice-axe in hand on **Fox** or **Franz Josef Glacier** (see p. 341).

GET BLOWN AWAY by the pancake rocks and blowholes of **Punakaiki** (see p. 334).

THROW YOUR CARES AWAY in the tiny, seaside outpost of **Okarito**, where worries neither enter nor leave (see p. 340).

TRANSPORTATION ON THE WEST COAST

West Coast travelers should keep in mind that there are **no banks** or **supermarkets** on the long stretch between Hokitika and Wanaka, and petrol stations are often few and far between. Daily **buses** provide a dependable way to travel. While *Let's Go* doesn't recommend **hitchhiking** through the West Coast, those with patience (and good rain gear) report success.

WESTPORT ☎ 03

Westport's lifeblood has always been its river, its gold, and its coal. A 19th-century gold-rush town, the original Westport washed away in a flood in 1872. Gold fever subsided, but the town soon bounced back to boomtown size thanks to the coal mining, shipping, and fishing that took its place. Today, Westport has learned to tame and utilize its two beaches and the tempestuous Buller River, which lures visitors with whitebait fishing and thrilling rafting.

TRANSPORTATION

InterCity (☎ 379 9020) heads daily from Craddock's Energy Centre/Caltex Garage, 197 Palmerston St., to: **Fox Glacier** (7hr., 11:05am, $64) via **Punakaiki** (1hr., $19), **Greymouth** (2hr., $24), and **Franz Josef Glacier** (6hr., $59); and **Nelson** (3¾hr., 4pm, $47). **East West** (☎ 789 6251 or 0800 142 622) runs daily from Craddock's to **Christchurch** (4½hr., 8am, $44). The following buses depart from the Visitors Center. **Karamea Express** (☎ 782 6617) runs to **Karamea** (1½hr.; Oct.-Apr. M-Sa 11:30am, May-Sept. M-F; $15). **Cunningham's Motors**, 179 Palmerston St. (☎ 789 7177), heads to **Karamea** (2½hr., M-F 3pm, $15), stopping to drop off mail at various points along the way. **Southern Link Shuttles** (☎ 546 8687) goes to **Christchurch** (6hr., M-F and Su 10am, $35) and **Nelson** (6hr., M-F and Su 10am, $35). **Atomic Shuttles** (☎ 768 5101) departs daily for **Greymouth** (2hr., 3:30pm, $20) and **Nelson** (5½hr., 9:40am, $30) and continues all the way to Picton. For a lift in town, call **Buller Taxis** (☎ 789 6900).

WESTPORT 331

The West Coast

FROM THE ROAD

PECK AND DESTROY

The world's only alpine parrot, the kea is often called a "cheeky" fellow. Based on my experience, I can only assume that "cheeky" is Kiwi-speak for "two-faced, cost-inducing, destructive little bugger."

Sure, keas are cute—that's what I thought when I pulled over to the side of the road along the West Coast. It was the next to last day of my New Zealand trip, and I was relieved that after two months of traveling, I had managed to keep my rental car unscathed. A mini-van of fellow travelers had pulled over ahead of me, and its occupants were busy snapping close-ups of three stocky, gray-green birds. The birds looked back at them with no intention of smiling for the camera. They seemed to be considering which of the photographers' clothes/body parts would make good nest accessories. I should have known to leave while I could, but the cool, crisp winter air had gone to my head, and I decided to explore a nearby hiking trail for a few hundred yards. I heard the mini-van zoom away, and I was alone on the mountain.

Suddenly, I froze. A cracking sound echoed off the cliffs above me, sounding very much like the beginnings of a rockslide. Then, there was another crack. And another. Visions of tomorrow's headlines flashed through my head—"Travel Writer, Crushed Under Falling Rubble"—and I high-tailed it back to the car. Coming around the bend, I again froze in my tracks. I had left my driver's side window open. I had thought, "Heck, there's nobody around for miles."

ORIENTATION & PRACTICAL INFO

The **Buller River** marks Westport's western border. Two blocks east lies the main drag **Palmerston Street**, which intersects **Brougham Street** near the center of town. The **Westport Visitor Information Centre**, 1 Brougham St., answers queries. (☎789 6658; fax 789 6668; westport.info@xtra.co.nz. Open M-F 9am-7pm, Sa-Su 9am-6pm; in winter M-F 9am-5pm, Sa-Su 9am-4pm.) Other services include: **banks** on Palmerston St. (generally open M-F 9am-4:30pm); **bike rental** at **Becker's Sportsworld**, 204 Palmerston St. (☎788 8002; $15 per day; open M-F 8:30am-5pm, Sa 9:30am-12:30pm); the **police** (☎788 8310), on Wakefield St.; **Buller Pharmacy**, 160-162 Palmerston St. (☎789 7629, after hours 789 8379; open M-Th 8:30am-5:30pm, F 8:30am-6pm, Sa 9:30am-12:30pm, Su at noon for emergencies); **Buller Medical Centre**, 45 Derby St. (☎789 8230); **Internet access** at **The Web Shed**, 208 Palmerston St., for $6 per hr. (☎789 5131; open M-F 10am-6pm, Sa 10am-1pm); and the **post office**, at Palmerston and Brougham St. (☎789 7799; open M-F 8am-5pm, Sa 10am-12:30pm).

ACCOMMODATIONS & CAMPING

Bazil's Hostel (VIP), 54 Russell St. (☎789 6410; fax 789 6240; bazils.backpackers@xtra.co.nz). With your back to the Visitors Center, head left, then take a left on Russell. The toasty lounge and intimate setting mean it's often full—Kiwi Experience stays here almost every night. Dorms $17; twins and doubles $40; tent sites $10. ❷

Robyn's Nest (BBH), 42 Romilly St. (☎789 6565; robyns.nest@xtra.co.nz). Head left from the Visitors Center and take a left at the first intersection; after 3 blocks, take a right on Pakington St. for 3 blocks. Robyn and her tots welcome guests to this charming Victorian house and garden. Bikes. Internet. Dorms $16; doubles $35; tent sites $8. ❷

The Happy Wanderer (BBH/YHA), 56 Russell St. (☎789 8627; fax 789 8396; happywanderer@xtra.co.nz), next to Bazil's. Every 2 dorms have their own kitchen and common room. Bikes. Internet. Dorms $18, in winter $16; twins and doubles $45/$38; tent sites $8, powered $18 for 2. ❷

Bella Vista Motel, 314 Palmerston St. (☎789 7800 or 0800 493 787; fax 789 8110; www.bellavistamotels.co.nz). Colorful quilts and homemade cookies will lull you into relaxation. Internet. Laundry. Doubles $75, with kitchen $90-105; extra person $15. ❹

Westport Holiday Park, 37 Domett St. (☎789 7043; fax 789 7199; westportholidaypark@xtra.co.nz). With your back to the Visitors Center, head left for 7 blocks, then take a left onto Domett St. Friendlier and better kept than most holiday parks. Dorms $13.50; tent sites $9, powered $10; cabins $32 for 2, with bath $44. ❶

FOOD

An oasis in the surrounding deep-fried culinary desert, **Percy's ❸**, 198 Palmerston St., attracts an eclectic crowd with hot drinks, fresh beats, and an affordable menu. (☎789 6648. Open daily 7:30am-late; in winter 7:30am-2:30pm and 6-8:30pm.) **Bailie's Bar and Restaurant ❷**, 187 Palmerston St., is nothing flashy, but nightly backpacker meals (burger and beer $10) can be tough to turn down. (☎789 7289. Internet. Open M-Th and Su 11am-late, F-Sa 11am-very late.) Or, just hit **New World,** 244 Palmerston St., for groceries. (Open M-F 8am-8pm, Sa-Su 9am-6pm.)

SIGHTS AND ACTIVITIES

The famed West Coast limestone **cave formations** are truly a regional highlight. **Norwest Adventures** offers trips through Westport's share of these wonders. Their "Underworld Rafting" adventure lets you float in inner tubes through the stalactites and stalagmites in the **Metro Cave** system's river. (☎789 6686 or 0800 116 686; www.caverafting.com. 4-5hr. $105. Min. age 10.)

The **Buller River,** the third largest in New Zealand, provides plenty of **rafting** excitement, from mellow floats to raging whitewater expeditions. **Ultimate Descents,** based in nearby Murchison, navigates the river by raft, by kayak, and by sledge. (☎523 9899 or 0800 748 377; www.rivers.co.nz. 2hr. $95, full-day $145.) **Buller Adventure Tours** (☎789 7286 or 0800 697 286; www.adventuretours.co.nz) also works out of Murchison and operates tours on the Buller's rougher waters (half-day $85, full-day $120). **Burning Mine Adventures** (☎789 7277 or 0800 343 337; www.burning-mine.co.nz) conducts mountain bike trips (4hr., $75) and tours of the Stockton Opencast Mine (4hr., $65). **Kekeno Tours,** in Tauranga Bay, offers land yachting and surf rafting. (☎789 8156 or 0800 553 5366. Land yachting $12.50 per 15min., $35 per hr. Surf rafting $45.)

The Westport area also harbors several beaches with swimming areas; **Carters Beach,** 6km from town, extends from Cape Foulwind to the mouth of the Buller River, and **North Beach,** 4km from town, stretches along Craddock Dr. to the north end of the Buller. Just 16km out of town, **Tauranga Bay** is famous

Apparently, I was wrong—one of the keas was perched inside my car, making short work of the vinyl interior. With each pluck of the kea's beak, a resounding crack echoed against the mountains.

"Get away from there!" I shouted, and I ran to my injured vehicle. The driver's door was completely ruined, in tatters, with stuffing billowing from its wounds. The kea looked at me nonchalantly, walked across the car roof, and went to work on the rubber molding around the window.

"Nooo!" I screamed, and I ran around to the other side, thoroughly failing to agitate the kea, who simply crossed the roof toward one of the back windows. Finally, I opened the car door and got in. Rubber molding fell on my shoulders as the kea peered at me through the windshield. The "cheeky" creature fell off as I sped away.

At a scenic overlook, I stopped to survey the extensive damage. As I gazed morosely at the surrounding scenery, my eyes fell on an information plaque. On it was a picture of a kea chewing up a leather boot, accompanied by a warning not to leave one's car windows open. Whoops. Cheeky birds.

—Steven Most was a researcher for Let's Go: New Zealand 2002. He recently earned his Ph.D. and is now a post-doctoral fellow in Nashville, Tennessee.

for some of the best **surfing** in New Zealand and the **seal colony** that makes its home here. The **Cape Foulwind Walk** (return 3hr.) lets you see the seal colony from above. Try your luck **fishing** for whitebait around the Buller River (Sept. 1-Nov. 15; no license needed).

Finally, head to **Coaltown**, a museum and replica coalmine, south on Queen St. across the railway tracks. (☎789 8204. Open daily 9am-4:30pm. $6, students $4, children $3.) A drive along the 120km **Buller Coalfields Heritage Trail** hits other highlights of Westport's coal mining history; pick up a pamphlet at the Visitors Center. The **Miner's Brewery**, 10 Lyndhurst St., lets you guzzle a beer made from a 16th-century recipe. (☎789 6201. Tours M-Sa 11:30am and 1:30pm. $5.)

PUNAKAIKI ☎03

Waves crash with thunderous claps against the layered rocks, drenching the expectant sightseers clustered in their bright, crayon-colored raincoats. At last the waves strike just right, the blowholes spray high into the air, and the cameras click away in a fury of photographic zeal. Sharing smiles, the tourists congratulate each other on capturing that once-in-a-lifetime (or at least once-in-an-hour) shot of Punakaiki. Between Greymouth and Westport on SH6, the incredibly popular "pancake rocks" and blowholes are the highlights of the water-carved landscape of **Paparoa National Park**.

TRANSPORTATION. InterCity (☎768 7080) passes through Punakaiki daily en route to **Greymouth** (45min., 12:50pm, $9) and to **Nelson** (4¾hr., 3pm, $56-61) via **Westport** (1hr., $18), pausing long enough to allow riders to witness the explosive blowhole action. **Atomic Shuttles** (☎768 5101; return $20) and **Greymouth Taxis** (☎768 7078; return $25, min. 3 people) also run from Greymouth.

PRACTICAL INFORMATION. The **Punakaiki Visitor Centre**, on SH6 across from the blowholes, has park info. (☎731 1895; fax 731 1896; punakaikivc@doc.govt.nz. Open daily 9am-6pm; in winter 9am-4:30pm.) The nearest **petrol** stations are 35-60km away, but the **Wild Coast Cafe**, beside the Visitors Center, keeps a small emergency supply. The **police** can be reached at ☎768 1600. The cheapest **Internet access** in town is at the Punakaiki Beach Hostel (see below; $6 per hr.).

ACCOMMODATIONS AND FOOD. Punakaiki's accommodations are scattered along SH6. If you're coming by bus, ask the driver to drop you off at your destination. The **Te Nikau Retreat (BBH) ❷**, on Hartmount Pl., is a 30min. walk north of the Visitors Center; call for free pick-up. Several wooden buildings connect through the lush rainforest. (☎731 1111; fax 731 1154. Internet. Dorms $16-18; doubles $40, with bath $45; motel units $50-60; tent sites $12.50.) The **Punakaiki Beach Hostel (BBH) ❷**, at the corner of Webb St. and Dickenson Pde., is a 15min. walk from the Visitors Center with the ocean on your left; call for free pick-up. Somewhat crowded but comfortable rooms open onto a magnificent beach. (☎731 1852 or 0800 726 225; fax 731 1152; www.punakaikibeachhostel.co.nz. Internet. Dorms $19; twins and doubles $42-46.) Next door, **Punakaiki Beach Camp ❶** has a range of pleasant cabins and tent sites. (☎731 1894. Cabins $26-33 for 2; tent sites $8.50, powered $10.) For limited groceries and takeaway, stop by **Wild Coast Cafe ❶**, near the Visitors Center. (☎731 1873. Open daily 8am-7:30pm; in winter 8am-6pm.) **Punakaiki Tavern ❸**, on SH6 at the turn-off for the Beach Hostel, is usually packed with pubgoers. (☎731 1188. Open daily 8:30am-late.)

◎ ☒ **SIGHTS AND ACTIVITIES.** The **Punakaiki blowholes** and mysterious 350-million-year-old **pancake rocks** are at the end of the **Dolomite Point Walk** across from the Visitors Center (return 20min.; wheelchair accessible). If possible, check the tide schedule before planning your visit—the blowholes are practically nonexistent at low tide. The ☒**Trumans Track** (15min.), off SH6 3km north of the Visitors Center, heads out to a dramatic viewpoint at the ocean's edge. At low tide the beach and rocks can be explored; keep your eyes peeled for starfish. Grab a flashlight to explore the **Punakaiki Cavern**, 500m north of Punakaiki, to the right of SH6. The **Punakaiki Pororari Loop** (return 3hr.) winds through the stretch of rainforest from the Punakaiki River to the Pororari River (check in advance to see if the rivers can be crossed). More rugged trekkers can explore the **Inland Pack Track** (27km, 2-3 days), which began as a safe alternative to the pitfalls of coastal travel during the 1860s gold rushes. Check in and get full trail information at the Visitors Center before you go; stay on the track, as there are numerous sinkholes. There are **no huts** along the track. **Punakaiki Canoe Hire,** 1km north of the Visitors Center beside the tavern, has guides and rents canoes for paddling in the Pororari Gorge. (☎731 1870; www.riverkayaking.co.nz. 1hr. $20, half-day $40, full-day $50.) **Coast and Mountain Adventures** will guide you through the wilderness or set you up to scale high Paparoa limestone. (☎731 1853. 2-3 hr. nature walk $35, rock-climbing $55, overnight trek $135.) Call **Paparoa Horse Treks** to view the pancake rocks from horseback, or take a longer trip through the Punakaiki River Valley. (☎731 1839. 1hr. $40, 2½hr. $70. Closed in winter.)

GREYMOUTH ☎03

After the gold rush of the late 1800s, Greymouth's timber, coal, and fishing resources facilitated its growth into the biggest town on the West Coast. Besides being in the heart of extraordinary tramping, caving, and rafting terrain, Greymouth is the western end of the TranzAlpine railroad, one of the most breathtaking routes in the world. Those voyaging through Westland should pause here to stock up on groceries, cash, and gear.

☐ TRANSPORTATION

Trains: The **TranzAlpine** (☎0800 802 802) leaves daily for **Christchurch** (4hr.; 2:25pm; $89, students $70) via **Arthur's Pass** (2hr.; $39, students $31).

Buses: InterCity (☎768 7080) heads from the railroad station daily to: **Fox Glacier** (4hr., 1:50pm, $37) via **Hokitika** (30min., $11) and **Franz Josef Glacier** (3½hr., $37); and **Nelson** (6hr., 1:50pm, $67) via **Punakaiki** (40min., $8) and **Westport** (2hr., $20). **Atomic Shuttles** (☎768 5101) is usually cheaper and runs south daily to **Queenstown** (10½hr., 7:30am, $80) via **Hokitika** (30min. $10), **Franz Josef Glacier** (3hr., $30), and **Fox Glacier** (3½hr., $30). **Coast-to-Coast** (☎0800 800 847) runs to **Christchurch** (4hr., 1pm, $35) via **Arthur's Pass** (2hr., $20). **Alpine Coaches** (☎0800 274 888) goes daily to: **Christchurch** (4hr., 8:30am, $35) via **Moana** (30min., $14); and **Arthur's Pass** (2hr.; $18, daytrips $30).

Taxis: Greymouth Taxis (☎768 7078) runs to **Shantytown** (one-way $23, min. 2 persons), **Hokitika** (one-way $63), and **Punakaiki** (return $75, min. 3 persons).

Car Rental: Budget (☎768 4343) is at the train station. **Half Price Rental,** 170 Tainui St. (☎768 0379), and **Hertz,** 92 Tainui St. (☎768 7379), are in town.

Bike Rental: Mann Security and Cycles, 37 Mackay St. (☎768 0255; half-day $10, full-day $20), and **Cole's Sports World,** 53 Mackay St. (☎768 4060; half-day $20, full-day $30).

336 ■ THE WEST COAST

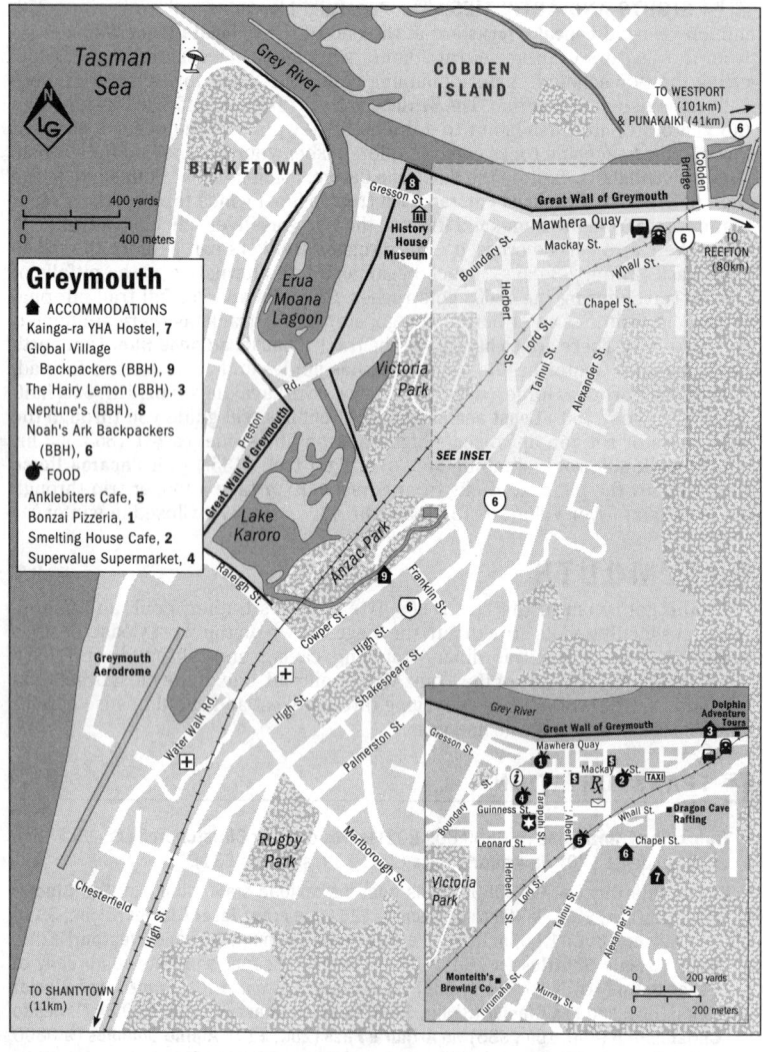

Greymouth

ACCOMMODATIONS
Kainga-ra YHA Hostel, **7**
Global Village
 Backpackers (BBH), **9**
The Hairy Lemon (BBH), **3**
Neptune's (BBH), **8**
Noah's Ark Backpackers
 (BBH), **6**

FOOD
Anklebiters Cafe, **5**
Bonzai Pizzeria, **1**
Smelting House Cafe, **2**
Supervalue Supermarket, **4**

ORIENTATION AND PRACTICAL INFORMATION

From the steps of the **Greymouth Railway Station,** the main drag, **Mackay Street,** runs left to the town center and right to the Grey River behind the massive "Great Wall" down **Mawhera Quay.** The city bustle lies at **Mackay** and **Guinness Streets.**

Visitors Center: Promote native flora by purchasing seeds at the **Greymouth Information Centre** (☎ 768 5101; fax 768 0317; www.westcoastbookings.co.nz), at the corner of Herbert and Mackay St. Open daily 8:30am-7pm; in winter 8:30am-6pm.

GREYMOUTH ■ 337

Banks: Banks cluster around the intersection of Tainui and Mackay St. and are generally open M-F 9am-4:30pm. Almost all have **ATMs**.
Police: 47 Guinness St. (☎ 768 1600), at the corner of Tarapuhi St.
Medical Services: Check with **Mason's Pharmacy**, 34 Tainui St., for the number of the on-duty doctor. (☎ 768 7470. Open M-Th 8:30am-5pm, F 8:30am-6pm.) **Greymouth Hospital** (☎ 768 0499) is on High St., 1km south of the town center.
Internet Access: Available at the **Visitors Center** for $2 per 7min. **DP-1 Cafe**, 108 Mawhera Quay (☎ 768 4005), charges $8 per hr. Open M-Sa 9:30am-7pm.
Post Office: (☎ 768 0123), on Tainui St. Open M-F 8:30am-5pm, Sa 10am-12:30pm.

ACCOMMODATIONS

Global Village Backpackers (BBH), 42-54 Cowper St. (☎ 768 7272 or 0800 542 636; fax 768 7276; globalvillage@minidata.co.nz). Walk down Tainui St. away from town, bear right onto High St., take a right on Franklin St. then a left on Cowper St. Rooms are inviting with international decor. Free hot drinks, kayaks, bikes, and fishing rods. Free pick-up. Linen $2. Dorms $16; twins $40, in winter $25; doubles $42. ❷

The Hairy Lemon (BBH), 128-130 Mawhera Quay (☎ 768 4022 or 0800 769 251; fax 768 4022; hairylemon@xtra.co.nz). Bizarre name aside, this friendly new kid in town offers good rates on recently renovated rooms. Popular downstairs bar. Dorms $15; singles $20; twins and doubles $40. ❷

Neptune's (BBH), 43 Gresson St. (☎/fax 768 4425), along the Greymouth Great Wall by the old rail tracks. This former fishermen's pub and motel has been refitted into a deep-sea wonderland. Free spa. Dorms $18; singles $30; twins and doubles $44. ❷

Kainga-ra YHA Hostel, 15 Alexander St. (☎ 768 4951; fax 768 4941; yhagymth@yha.org.nz). Turn left off Mackay St. onto Tainui, then left on Chapel St., and right on Alexander St. The hillside manor, formerly a residence for men of the cloth, commands an impressive view of the coast. Dorms $19-21; twins and doubles $45. ❷

Noah's Ark Backpackers (BBH), 16 Chapel St. (☎/fax 768 4868 or 0800 662 472). See directions for Kainga-ra. The friendly owners, pets, and resident tour bus crowd conspire to keep things lively. Dorms $17; twins and doubles $45; tent sites $10. ❷

FOOD

The **Supervalue Supermarket** is at the corner of Guinness and Herbert St. (☎ 768 7545. Open M-F 8am-8pm, Sa 8am-7pm, Su 8am-5pm.)

Smelting House Cafe, 102 Mackay St. (☎ 768 0012). Creative, mouth-watering hot meal selections ($6-9) and sandwiches ($3-4) rotate daily. Open daily 8am-5pm. ❶

Anklebiters Cafe, 33 Albert St. (☎ 768 5026). Munch on basic eats in the energetic blue interior or sip tea by the trickling fountain in the back patio. Open M-F 7am-5pm, Sa 8am-4pm. ❶

Bonzai Pizzeria, 31 Mackay St. (☎ 768 4170). International newspapers cover the walls of this busy joint. Small pies from $11.50, large from $17.50. Ample breakfast and non-pizza menu. Open M-Sa 7:30am-late, Su 3pm-late. ❷

SIGHTS

Founded to quench the thirsts (and empty the pockets) of gold rushers, ■**Monteith's Brewing Company**, at the corner of Herbert and Murray St. (off Tainui St. about 10min. from town), produces between 30,000 and 60,000 liters of beer each day. Their informative tour gives visitors a 30min. chance to taste the rainbow (from Black to Original Gold to Celtic Red) that has Kiwis raving. (☎768 4149; www.monteiths.co.nz. Tours M-F 10, 11:30am, and 2pm. Book ahead. $5.)

For a more traditional approach to settler history, visit **Shantytown**, 11km south of Greymouth on SH6. Re-creating an 1880s gold rush town, Shantytown has its own post office, sawmill, working steam train, horse and cart rides, and gold mine. (☎762 6634; www.shantytown.co.nz. Open daily 8:30am-5pm. $10.50, with panning $13.50.) To get to Shantytown, **Kea West Coast Tours** will pick you up from your digs and liven up the ride with running commentary on regional history. (☎768 9292 or 0800 532 868. 3hr., daily 10am and 2pm, $34.) **Greymouth Taxis** also runs with less talk for less dough. (☎768 7078. 10:15am, 12:15, and 2:15pm. $23; min. 2 people.) Locals highly recommend a self-guided tour of the **Brunner Mine Site** (1hr.), just north of town on Rte. 11 past Taylorville, and the **Woods Creek Track** (45min.), with gold mining and flora infoboards (bring a flashlight to explore the glowworm-inhabited tunnels), south of town near Shantytown. Pick up a brochure at the Visitors Center ($1). To wander farther, Kea West Coast runs tours to **Punakaiki** (4hr., 9am and 2pm, $45 return) and to **Lake Matheson** (full-day; 8:30am, $130-185).

ACTIVITIES

Dragon's Cave Rafting, operated by **Wild West Adventures,** runs a caving trip in the **Taniwha Caves.** The half-day excursion includes a beautiful 30min. rainforest hike, a slick water slide, and a dip in the hot spa back at headquarters. (☎768 6649 or 0800 223 456; www.browserbuys.co.nz/everest. $105.) **Eco-Rafting Adventures,** run out of the DP-1 Cafe, plans custom trips for kayaks or rafts on low-grade to Class V rapids, including extreme heli-rafting adventures. (☎768 4005; www.ecorafting.co.nz. Half-day $70, full-day $120, heli-rafting from $210 per hr.) For a tamer float down the river, try **Jungle Boat Rafting,** 8 Whall St. (☎0508 474 837. $89.)

Dolphin Watch, run by **Dolphin Adventure Tours,** brings you by kayak or boat to the dolphin areas and shag nesting sites off the coast of **Point Elizabeth.** (☎768 9770 or 0800 929 991; www.dolphintours.co.nz. Grey River trips $67, trips with sea kayaking or dolphin swimming $87.) For land lubbers, **On Yer Bike!** runs 4WD farm bike tours through the bush on demand. (☎762 7438 or 0800 669 373; www.onyerbike.co.nz. 1hr. $60, 2hr. $95.) The nikau palms on the coast can be seen along the **Point Elizabeth Walkway** (return 3hr., tide dependent). To walk, go past the rail station inland, across the bridge, turn left down Bright St., and turn right along the coast on Domett Esplanade toward the trailhead (return 2hr.).

About 30min. east of Greymouth lies the trout fishing of **Lake Brunner** and the avian attractions of **Moana.** (**Alpine Coaches** stops at Moana; see **Buses,** p. 335.) Swim, kayak, or canoe among the white herons *(kotuku)* on the lake. In Moana, the **Moana Hotel ❷**, 34 Ahau St., rents rooms. (☎738 0083. Dorms $18.) There's also a campground at the Moana end of the lake. **Lake Brunner Boat Hire** will set you up with aquatic gear. (☎738 0291. Kayaks $15 per hr., half-day $25; dinghies half-day $25.)

HOKITIKA ☎03

Once the largest port in New Zealand, Hokitika (ho-kuh-TEEK-uh) is no longer a bustling center of activity. Today it is famous for its abundance of crafts; virtually all of New Zealand's jade is quarried within a 20km radius of the town. If you spend more than an afternoon in Hokitika, meander along the beach to enjoy a magnificent sunset over the Tasman Sea.

TRANSPORTATION. InterCity drops off at **Hokitika Travel Centre**, 60 Tancred St. (☎755 8557), and heads daily to: **Nelson** (7hr., 12:45pm, $62) via **Greymouth** (45min.,

$11) and **Westport** (3¼hr., $27); and **Fox Glacier** (3hr., 3:05pm, $33) via **Franz Josef Glacier** (2¼hr., $33). **Coast-to-Coast** (☎0800 800 847) goes to **Christchurch** (4½hr., 1:05pm, $35) via **Arthur's Pass** (2hr., $20). **Atomic Shuttles** (☎768 5101) runs daily to: **Greymouth** (45min., 10:45am and 5:15pm, $10); and **Queenstown** (10hr., 8am, $65) via **Franz Josef Glacier** (2½hr., $25) and **Fox Glacier** (3hr., $30).

🛈 PRACTICAL INFORMATION. The **Westland Visitor Information Centre** is in the Carnegie Building at the corner of Tancred and Hamilton St. (☎755 6166. Open daily 8:30am-6pm; in winter M-F 9am-5pm, Sa-Su 10am-3:30pm.) The local **DOC** is on Sewell St. near the river. (☎755 8301. Open M-F 8am-4:30pm.) Other services include: **banks** with **ATMs**, near the corner of Weld and Revell St. (generally open M-F 9:30am-4:30pm); the **police,** 50 Sewell St. (☎755 8088); **Westland Medical Centre,** 54 Sewell St. (24hr. ☎755 8180); **Westland Pharmacy,** 10 Weld St. (☎755 7612; open M-F 8:30am-5:15pm, Sa 9:30am-12:30pm); **Internet access** at **Cybergate,** 26b Weld St., for $7 per hr. (☎755 6930; open daily 9am-9pm, in winter 9:30am-8pm); and the **post office,** on Revell St. (☎756 8034; open M-F 8:30am-5pm, Sa 10am-12:15pm).

🛏🛏 ACCOMMODATIONS AND CAMPING. If you decide to stay in Hokitika overnight, try the **▨Blue Spur Lodge (BBH) ❷,** 5km out of the city on Hampden Rd. turning to Hau Hau Rd. Overlooking Mt. Cook and the Southern Alps, the welcoming wood lodge is as private as backpackers get. The 100-acre property offers a 1hr. bushwalk and an open gold mine tunnel where guests can pan for treasure using the lodge's free equipment. Kayak trips are also available, with free transport to and from Lakes Kaniere and Mahinapua. (☎/fax 755 8445; bluespur@xtra.co.nz. Free bike use. Dorms $17; doubles $42, with bath $50. Self-contained cottage for up to 4 $110; less in winter.) Or stay with the "Mad Kiwi" (his real name is Gordon) at **The Jade Experience Backpackers ❷ (BBH),** 197 Revell St. Right on the beach, the house only holds 8 people. Staying a night might get you a discount on a jade carving lesson. (☎755 7612; madkiwi@xtra.co.nz. Dorms $15; doubles $35.) A short walk from the center of town, **Beach House Backpackers (BBH) ❷,** 137 Revell St., has a beachfront location, a tidy atmosphere, and friendly owners. (☎755 6859 or 0800 755 6859. Free Internet. Dorms $17; twins and doubles $42; tent sites $9. Discounts for longer stays.) **Stumpers ❸,** 2 Weld St., has pulled out all the stops in renovating this old hotel. The result is a pleasant upbeat atmosphere with a downstairs bar and cafe. (☎755 6154; fax 755 6137; www.stumpers.co.nz. Dorms $22; singles $35; twins $50; doubles $45, with bath $55.) Lake Kaniere, 23km from town, has **DOC campgrounds** with water and toilets ($4 donation). Lake Mahinapua, 10km south of town, also has campgrounds with water, toilets, and fireplaces ($4 donation).

🍴 FOOD. Savor tea and hot meals at **PR's Cafe and Restaurant ❷,** on Tancred St., home to the largest collection of tea cups in New Zealand. (☎755 8379. Open daily 8am-4pm.) **Café de Paris ❷,** a few doors down, exudes a dash of class. (☎755 8933. Lunch $7-15. Open daily 6:30am-11:30pm; in winter 9am-8:30pm.) The **Filling Station Cafe ❷,** 111 Revell St., is popular for its cheap lunch ($5.50-9.50) and all-day breakfast. (☎755 8344. Open M-Th and Su 7:15am-9pm, F-Sa 7:30am-9:30pm; in winter closed Su.) A heaping helping of Chinese at **Wong's Wok Chinese Restaurant ❷,** 41 Weld St., downstairs from Mountain Jade Backpackers, is easy on the wallet but hard on the biceps. The soup, entree, and main special is just $17.50. (☎755 6444. Open daily 9:30am-late.) Stock up on groceries at **New World,** 116 Revell St. This is the last supermarket north of Wanaka and has the best prices you will find before then. (☎755 8390. Open M-W 8am-6:30pm, Th 8am-8pm, F 8am-7pm, Sa 8:30am-7pm, Su 9am-6pm.)

◐ ◪ SIGHTS AND ACTIVITIES. Hokitika is renowned for the expertise of its greenstone, woodworking, and glass-blowing artisans. In spite of the touristy kitsch that accompanies the sale of crafts, finely worked and reasonably priced pieces can be found in Hokitika, and, if nothing else, the demonstrations showcase considerable skill. **Westland Greenstone,** 34 Tancred St., has jade pendants, pins, and paperweights for sale. (☎ 755 8713. Open daily 8am-5pm.) Across the street, **Quades House of Wood** displays a large, expensive wooden turtle with a removable shell. (☎ 755 6061. Open daily 9am-5pm.) The **Hokitika Glass Studio,** 28 Tancred St., exhibits glass artistry ranging from a whimsical penguin chess set to elephants and dainty flowers. (☎ 755 7775. Open daily 9am-5pm.) All three shops allow visitors to view the artisans at work. To become the glass maker yourself, ring Gordon (☎ 755 7612) at Jade Experience Backpackers for a **carving lesson** and piece of jade. Carvings begin at $80 and usually take all day.

The **Glowworm Dell,** a 30min. walk north of Hokitika on SH6 by the right side of the road, displays phosphorescent larvae separated from curious hands by a chain link fence. **Lake Mahinapua** is rife with walking tracks and picnic areas, and **Lake Kaniere** draws nature lovers to its stands of rimu, tussock grassland, and subalpine scrub. There is no public transport from Hokitika to the lakes, but **Hokitika Cycles and Sports,** 33 Tancred St., rents bikes for $20 per day and offers a last chance to fix your bike before heading south. (☎ 755 8662. Open M-F 8:30am-6pm, Sa 9am-12:30pm.) Tranquil weather often calls for an equally calming activity such as a paddle boat cruise from **Scenic Waterways** into the picturesque Lake Mahinapua. (☎ 755 7239. 1½hr., $20.)

The **West Coast Historical Museum,** at the corner of Tancred and Hamilton St. next to the Visitors Center, will dole out leaflets for a Hokitika heritage walk. (☎ 755 6898. Open daily 8:30am-6pm; in winter M-F 9am-5pm, Sa-Su 10am-3:30pm.) The **National Kiwi House** displays endangered kiwis and sundry aquatic creatures. A screening of audio-visual "Who Killed the Kiwi" is included with admission. (☎ 755 8904. Open daily 9am-6pm. $7, children $3.) Visitors for the weekend of March 8, 2003 have a chance to sample possum, whitebait, snail, venison, and even kangaroo at the **Wild Foods Festival.**

OKARITO ☎ 03

On the edge of the 3240-hectare Okarito Lagoon, this tiny seaside community offers serenity and scenery matchless along the coast. Certainly not known for its tourism or size (pop. 20), Okarito is famous instead as a habitat for a vast diversity of bird species. Some travelers use the town—just 28km north of Franz Josef Glacier and 13km off SH6—as a retreat from the over-touristed glaciers.

Okarito's treasure is its lagoon and the wildlife that goes with it—the best way to experience these is by getting out on the water. **Okarito Nature Tours** can supply kayaks, a map, and even a bird book to explore their well-marked routes. (☎ 753 4014; okarito@hotmail.com. Half-day $40, full-day $50; guided trips from $60.) Okarito also has several beautiful hikes. The **Okarito Trig Trail** (return 1hr.) leads uphill through kahikatea and rimu rainforest to a viewpoint. The **Coastal Walk** (return 3hr.) wanders through the bush above the shoreline.

Coaches stop (by request) at the turn-off to Okarito on SH6; it's a common place to hitch (not recommended by *Let's Go*) or a long walk into town. Alternatively, **The Royal Okarito (BBH) ❸** will pick up guests from the turn-off or even from Franz Josef for stays of two nights or more. This generosity typifies the Royal's atmosphere—hot water bottles warm the beds and laundry is free for longer-term guests. (☎ 753 4080; fax 753 4180; royalokarito@hotmail.com. Free breakfast. Occasional potluck dinners. 2-bed dorms $22; doubles $44; self-contained units $60.) **Okarito Hostel (YHA) ❷** sleeps guests in an 1870s schoolhouse.

Most of the ten beds share the same room as the kitchen and lounge. (☎753 4124. Showers at the campground. Dorms $18.) The **Okarito Campground ❶** only has unpowered sites. (Contact Tony and Rose-Ann Gray at The Royal Okarito ☎753 4080. Tent sites $5, children $1.) There are **no shops** in town, so bring food, insect repellent, and other necessities with you.

FRANZ JOSEF AND FOX GLACIERS

Finding yourself face-to-face with several billion cubic meters of rapidly moving (for a glacier) solid blue ice is typical when visiting Fox and Franz Josef. In fact, that's precisely why tourists flock to these gargantuan glaciers. The twins are extraordinary not only because of their size and speed of advance (or retreat), but also because they descend almost into the rainforest, terminating only 12km from the Tasman Sea. The glaciers' unique location, sandwiched between the sea and the Southern Alps in a temperate rainforest region, accounts for the massive 20 to 45m of snowfall that bury the top of the glaciers each year.

Fox and Franz Josef Glaciers are part of the 117,547-hectare **Westland National Park,** which contains a feast of hikes and bushwalks highlighting native biota. There are many ways to explore the glaciers: a hands-on hike on the glacier itself or a birds-eye helicopter tour are the most popular. Pressed for time, the hurried and harried traveler must often choose between Fox and Franz Josef Glaciers. Franz Josef Glacier, although smaller, may be more impressive than its icy neighbor, and therefore more popular. However, the town of Fox Glacier is slightly less commercial than its twin and refreshes with more bucolic views and relaxed locals. Both glaciers offer a range of options for exploration, including helicopter rides, hikes on the glaciers, ice climbing, and skiing.

FRANZ JOSEF GLACIER ☎03

Lying 140km south of Hokitika and 27km north of Fox Glacier, Franz Josef Village exists thanks to its massive glacier. With large Lake Mapourika nearby and more tourist outfitters than Fox, Franz is the destination of most tour groups and backpacker buses. To escape the crowds, slip down to the river for a picnic or a moonlight walk beneath the glacier's eerie glow.

▐ TRANSPORTATION

The **Glacier Shop** in the Alpine Adventure Building is the local agent for **InterCity** (☎752 0131). Daily buses head north to: **Nelson** (10hr., 9:30am, $81) via **Hokitika** (3hr., $33), **Greymouth** (4hr., $41), and **Westport** (6½hr., $52). There is also a daily southbound bus to **Queenstown** (8hr., 8am, $54) via **Fox Glacier** (45min., $8), the **Copland Track** (1hr., $13), and **Wanaka** (5hr., $65). **Atomic Shuttles** (☎752 0738), which books from Glowworm Cottages, provides northbound service to **Greymouth** (3hr., $30) via **Hokitika** (2hr., $20) and southbound to **Queenstown** (6hr., 10:15am, $50) via **Fox Glacier** (30min., $10), **Haast** (2hr., $30) and **Wanaka** (4hr., $40). The pick-up for both shuttle companies is at the coach stop on Main Rd. near the Cheeky Kea Cafe. For **bike rental,** visit **Glowworm Cottages.** (See below. Half-day $13, full-day $20.)

ORIENTATION AND PRACTICAL INFORMATION

Running through the center of town, **SH6,** known as **Main Road,** is the location of most of the town's services—backpackers are located on parallel **Cron Street,** also known as **Back Street.** The **Franz Josef Visitor Information Centre** and **DOC office,** on the south edge of town on SH6, have displays on glacial dynamics. (☎752 0796; fax

342 ■ FRANZ JOSEF AND FOX GLACIERS

FRANZ JOSEF GLACIER ■ 343

752 0797. Open daily 8:30am-6pm; in winter 8:30am-noon and 1-5pm.) There are **no banks or ATMs** in town; the **Mobil Station,** near the center of town on SH6, will cash traveler's checks and advance cash on credit cards in summer and pending cash in winter. It is also the **post office.** (☎ 752 0725. Open daily 8am-9pm; in winter 8am-6pm.) Cheap **Internet access** is available at **Icebridge Internet,** in the big red bus on Cron St. (☎ 752 0230. $5 per hr. Open daily 9am-9pm.)

ACCOMMODATIONS AND FOOD

Look for the roof-scaling mountaineers atop cozy **Chateau Franz (BBH/VIP) ❷,** 8 Cron St., where you can grab a round of pool ($1) or relax in the free spa. (☎ 752 0738 or 0800 728 372; fax 752 0743. Internet. Reception 8am-8pm. Dorms $18; twins $40; doubles $45; tent sites $10.) Slightly smaller, **Glowworm Cottages (BBH) ❷,** 27 Cron St., offers self-contained motel units in addition to standard backpacker digs. (☎ 752 0172 or 0800 151 027; fax 752 0173; glowwormcottages@hotmail.com. Dorms $18-20; doubles $45; motel units $85.) At the **Franz Josef YHA ❸,** 2-4 Cron St., a pool table, a sauna, and a video collection make for a pleasant end to a glacier-filled day. (☎ 752 0754; fax 752 0080; yhafzjo@yha.org.nz. Reception 8-10am, 4:30-6:30pm, and 8-9pm; extended hours in summer. Dorms $21-23; twins and doubles $47-50, with bath $55-62.) The clean and spacious **Montrose (BBH) ❷,** 9 Cron St., has vastly expanded its facilities and now hides a spa. (☎ 752 0188. Reception 8am-1pm and 4:30-7pm. Dorms $18; twins $40; doubles $44.) Join Kiwi Experiencers at the **Black Sheep Lodge (VIP) ❷.** Although it's a fair walk from the center of town, this mischievous ewe has a big TV with a collection of Hollywood's finest. (☎ 752 0007 or 0800 435 6733; fax 752 0023. Internet. Reception 7:30am-8pm. Dorms $19; twins and doubles $46.) Tent sites at the **Franz Josef Holiday Park ❶** are beside the Black Sheep. (☎ 752 0766 or 0800 435 6733; www.franzjosef.co.nz. Cottages $59-99 for 2, extra person $15; tent sites $9, powered $9.50.)

In a swinging locale just up from the petrol station, **The Blue Ice Cafe ❸** attracts crowds with a pizza-and-pint special for $15-19. (☎ 752 0707. Open daily 11am-late.) **Beeches ❷,** in the center of town, serves up a high-quality lunch menu (burgers $4 until 5:30pm). Happy Hour (4-6pm) makes for $3 beer-guzzling. (☎ 752 0721. Open daily 7:30am-late.) **The Cheeky Kea Cafe ❸,** next door, pleases budgeteers with a Saturday evening all-you-can-eat feast for $17.50. (☎ 752 0139. Open daily 7am-8pm.) **Fern Grove Food Centre,** on Main Rd., has a limited range of pricey groceries. (☎ 752 0731. Open daily 7:30am-10pm; in winter 7:30am-8:30pm.)

NIGHTLIFE

Although most ice trekkers don't have the energy to hit the town, a few Franz Josef pubs satiate the urge for a frosty brew. The **Blue Ice Cafe** (see **Food,** above) draws a loyal following of locals to its free pool table. The blazing fire at the **Franz Josef Glacier Hotel,** at the north edge of town, is guaranteed to warm all the limbs that you haven't already lost to frostbite. (☎ 752 0729. Open daily 2pm-late; in winter 3-10pm.) **Batson's Tavern,** at the far end of Cron St., has both a bar and a bottle shop for takeaway quaffing. (☎ 752 0740. Open daily 4pm-late.)

ACTIVITIES

ON THE GLACIER
The best way to appreciate the size and majesty of the glacier is up close and personal. The following companies run a variety of trips to Franz Josef.

THE BIG SPLURGE

HELI-HIKING THE GLACIERS

There's no doubt that hiking up to the face of an enormous glacier is exciting. You may tire of watching the back of the fellow plodding in front of you, but at least you'll spend some time on the majestic ice. Glacier walks are a fun, if mellow, way to see Fox and Franz Josef.

But what if fun and mellow aren't enough for your fiery blood? What if you yearn for the thrumming sound of a rotor and the truly dangerous crevasses and seracs? You'll have to pay $240 for the chance but heli-hiking the glaciers is the answer. Combining the scenic and speedy thrill of a helicopter flight with the indescribable beauty of a pristine glacier, heli-hiking offers those with cash to burn a less-trafficked taste of icy blue wonder. Heli-hikes plop you and a few friends down amidst delicate pinnacles, steep valley walls, and sparkling lakes inaccessible on a day walk from the terminus. It may be a lot of dough, but travelers concur that it's well spent.

Three companies based in Fox and Franz Josef Villages compete for the heli-hike market. All three whisk passengers high onto the glacier, allow them to explore in the company of a guide for two hours, and pick them up for a return flight to civilization. Trips depend on the often fickle weather, so if you're heart-set on a heli-hiking adventure, be prepared to hang around town a few days.

Alpine Guides Fox Glacier (p. 347), Franz Josef Glacier Guides (p. 344), and The Guiding Company (p. 344) all run heli-hikes. See individual listings for more details.

THE GUIDING COMPANY. This young but well respected operation leads both half- and full-day walks on the glacier. If you can handle up to five or six hours on the ice, pack a lunch and opt for the full-day trip. As the guides lead the way, chipping steps with an ice-axe, sure-footed hikers explore narrow crevasses, cavernous tunnels, and gorgeous glacial pools. The company also runs a fantastic full day of **ice-climbing** on the glacier, suitable for beginners and experienced climbers alike. (☎752 0047 or 0800 800 102; www.nzguides.com. Book ahead in summer as trip size is limited; report 30min. in advance. Half-day hike 3½hr., daily 9:15am and 2pm, $45. Full-day hike 7-8hr., daily 9:15am, $90. YHA 10% off on hikes. Ice climbing 9:15am, $175.)

FRANZ JOSEF GLACIER GUIDES. This older company serves a young backpacker bus crowd, making for lively interaction on the glacier. They also provide a specially-designed crampon/boot combination that offers excellent grip on the ice but forces visitors to relinquish their own comfy boots. (☎752 0763 or 0800 484 337; www.franzjosefglacier.com. Except for ice climbing, similar trips and prices to The Guiding Company. Book ahead in summer.)

HELI-HIKING. This high-flying adventure is a unique way to explore the glacier. Significantly more expensive than day hikes, a heli-hike deposits visitors atop the glacier, eliminating the trek to the terminal face, but provides less ice time to explore and gain confidence. Both guiding companies run trips. (3hr., around $230.)

SCENIC FLIGHTS

SKYDIVING. Professional and friendly, **Skydive New Zealand—Fox and Franz Josef Glaciers** is a small operation that provides a pre-jump scenic flight with views of Mt. Cook, Mt. Tasman, and the Tasman Sea. Lost in the magnificence of the Southern Alps, you'll almost forget your original reason for climbing to 12,000 ft.—almost. Bring a small camera for some unbeatable shots as you fall. (☎768 4777 or 0800 751 0080; skydivenz@yahoo.com. 9000 ft. $225, 12,000 ft. $265.)

HELICOPTER. Four different helicopter companies operate from Franz Josef. It pays to book ahead, especially in peak season from Jan.-Mar. All operators offer similar prices (and essentially the same tried-and-true routes) except for **Mountain Helicopters,** who provide a cheaper option as they are not licensed to land on the glacier. (☎0800 369 423. From $90.) **Fox and Franz Josef Heliservices** (☎752 0793 or 0800 800 793; www.newzealand.nz.co.nz/helicopters), **Glacier Southern Lakes Helicopters** (☎752 0755 or 0800 800 732;

www.heliflights.co.nz), and the **Helicopter Line** (☎ 752 0767 or 0800 807 767; *www.helicopter.co.nz*) have offices on the Main Rd. *(Tours of the Franz Josef Glacier, Fox Glacier, Tasman Glacier, and Mt. Cook range from $135-300.)*

PLANE. Air Safaris offers a "Grand Traverse" airplane tour. It does not include a snow landing, but it covers a greater area than the helicopter flights. *(☎ 752 0716 or 0800 723 274; www.airsafaris.co.nz. 50min. $230.)* **Aoraki Aero Company Ltd.** is the only plane permitted to land on the glaciers, although it also runs flights without landings. *(☎ 752 0714; www.aorakiaero.co.nz. $210-270.)*

LESS SLIPPERY WALKS

Make sure to check on the status of walks with DOC. Some walks will lose their views of the glacier in the course of a year depending on whether the glacier is advancing or receding. The tracks often get washed out as well.

GLACIER VALLEY WALK. This stroll leads right to the terminal face of the glacier and approaches the gargantuan ice cube without paying the hefty guided price tag. From there it's a hike along the Waiho River Bed (return 2hr. if you include a switchback trip up Sentinel Rock); observe markings and be careful. *(From the Visitors Center, turn right, cross the bridge, and follow the signs. Allow an hour to walk to the end of the access road, or drive the 4km.)*

ALEX KNOB WALK. On a clear day, this tramp—accessible when it's not snowed under—leads to breathtaking views from the ridge. This walk is best attempted before lunch as clouds usually roll in each afternoon. *(Return 8hr.)*

CANAVAN'S KNOB. Another walk to take on a clear day, the high points along the way rise above the rainforest to deliver views of both the glacier and the coast. *(Off SH6, 2km south of town. Return 40min.)*

ST. JAMES ANGLICAN CHURCH. The glacier view from the altar window of this church is so beautiful that it was put on a 1946 peace stamp that was issued to celebrate the end of World War II. *(A pleasant jaunt down SH6; turn onto the path at the right before the bridge; the church is through the brush at the end of the path.)*

GUIDED BUSHWALKS. Kamahi Tours leads guided trips in the Franz Josef and Okarito area. If you wish to approach the glacier, but not scale it, Kamahi runs a 2hr. tour to the base of the glacier with commentary about the area's history and geology. *(☎ 752 0699 or 752 0793. Trips range from 1hr. to full-day. 2½hr. $30.)*

OTHER ACTIVITIES

ALPINE ADVENTURE CENTRE. "Flowing West," a 20min. movie shown daily, catapults the viewer across rivers, through rainforest, over the Southern Alps, and finally out onto the glaciers. Much cheaper than a helicopter flight, this is a fine wet weather alternative well worth the price. *(☎ 752 0793. Up to 4 per day, guaranteed to show daily at 5pm. $10, children $5.)*

WHITE HERON SANCTUARY TOUR. This eco-tour brings a limited number of visitors to observe breeding pairs of white herons. Sacred to the Maori, these birds breed only in New Zealand. *(☎ 0800 523 456; www.whiteherontours.co.nz. Operates from Whataroa, a 30min. drive north of Franz Josef. Summer only for herons, but rainforest tour goes year-round. Book ahead. 2½hr. $89, children $40.)*

LAKE MAPOURIKA. The lake is stocked with brown trout and Quinnat salmon, and the nearby bush is rife with chamois and possums; fishermen and hunters can get licenses from DOC. For a guided trip, call **Chris Morris** (☎ 753 4177) or contact **Ferg's Kayaks** across from the Glowworm Cottages on Cron St. *(☎ 752 0230 or 0800 423 262. 3½hr. tour with digital photos of you on the lake $45.)*

FOX GLACIER ☎ 03

Twenty-seven kilometers south of Franz Josef on SH6, Fox Glacier is a diminutive village near a massive glacier. Normally visited only after a visit to Franz, Fox offers a refreshingly less commercial atmosphere, a profoundly serene environment, and quicksilver reflections of tranquil Lake Matheson (New Zealand's most photographed lake).

TRANSPORTATION

InterCity (☎ 751 0701) leaves from **Alpine Guides** and heads daily to: **Nelson** (11hr., 8:45am, $82) via **Franz Josef Glacier** (45min., $8), **Hokitika** (3½hr., $36), **Greymouth** (4½hr., $41), and **Westport** (7hr., $54); and **Queenstown** (7hr., 8:45am, $52) via the **Copland Track** (20min., $10) and **Wanaka** (5hr., $37). From Ivory Towers, **Atomic Shuttles** (☎ 768 5101) runs daily to: **Greymouth** (3½hr., 2pm, $30) via **Franz Josef Glacier** (1hr., $10) and **Hokitika** (3hr., $30); and **Queenstown** (7hr., 11am, $50) via **Haast** (3hr., $25) and **Wanaka** (5hr., $40). **Fox Glaciers Motors** is the last stop to fill up on **petrol** for 120km. (☎ 751 0823. Open from 8am-7:30pm; in winter 8am-6pm.) **Around Here Rentals** rents bikes. (☎ 751 0821. Half-day $10, full-day $15.)

ORIENTATION AND PRACTICAL INFORMATION

Running through the center of town, **SH6** is known as **Main Road**. It heads north over three arduous hills to Fox's comrade Franz Josef, south to the **Copland Track** trailhead, and then to **Haast** (121km). **Cook Flat Road** leads south from the center of town to wonderful views of the mountains over town. The famous reflecting **Lake Matheson** (6km) and seal-colonized **Gillespie's Beach** (20km) are located down Lake Matheson Rd., which is off Cook Flat Rd.

The **Fox Glacier Visitor Information Centre** and **DOC office** is located on SH6 north of the main village. (☎ 751 0807; fax 751 0858. Open daily 8:30am-5:30pm; in winter 9am-4:30pm.) In the center of everything, **Alpine Guides,** on Main Rd., is the headquarters for the glacier guides and serves as a **post office** and **currency exchange.** (☎ 751 0825. Open daily 8am-9pm; in winter 8:30am-5:30pm.) There are **no banks or ATMS;** Alpine Guides can do cash advances on your credit card for a fee. **Ivory Towers** has coin-operated **Internet** for $2 per 15min. (see **Accommodations,** below).

ACCOMMODATIONS AND FOOD

Without a doubt, the best part of **Ivory Towers (BBH)** ❷, on Sullivans Rd., is the company. A large dining room, TV lounge, garden, porch, and free spa pool promote mingling. (☎/fax 751 0838; ivorytowers@xtra.co.nz. Bike rental. Reception 8am-8:30pm. Dorms $20; singles $28-35; twins and doubles $48.) Next door, the **Fox Glacier Inn and Backpackers (VIP)** ❷ combines standard rooms and a kitchen with a popular local bar. (☎ 751 0022; fax 751 0024; foxglacierbackpackers@xtra.co.nz. Dorms $18; doubles $50; triples $66.) The **Fox Glacier Hotel** ❸, on Cook Flat Rd. just off Main Rd., offers privacy and beds that are softer than pudding. (☎ 751 0839. Reception 7am-10:30pm; in winter until 8pm. On-site bar and restaurant. No kitchen. Triples $126; hotel rooms $65-120.)

Eating options in town are slim but tasty. The **Cook Saddle Cafe and Saloon** ❹, on Main Rd., has American favorites like barbecued ribs ($18.75) to match its Western decor. (☎ 751 0700. Open daily 11am-late; in winter noon-late.) Just a few doors down, **Cafe Neve** ❺ serves fantastic meat dishes for a price. (☎ 751 0110. Open daily 9am-late; in winter noon-late.) On Main Rd. in the same building as Alpine Guides is **The Hobnail Cafe** ❶, a simpler dining option. Pack up lunch before your trip to the glacier (fritatta $5.50), or enjoy one of the light dishes after you get back. (☎ 751 0005. Open daily 7:30am-4pm; in winter 8am-3pm.) The only grocery is the small **Fox Glacier General Store.** (☎ 751 0829. Open daily 8am-9pm; in winter 8am-7:30pm.)

ACTIVITIES

ON THE GLACIER

ALPINE GUIDES. This is the only company that leads **guided walks** up Fox Glacier. The half-day trip begins with a steep and relatively lengthy ascent through the rainforest before stepping out onto the top of the glacier. If you can afford it, the **heli-hike** is a great way to avoid the rainforest trek and maximize ice time. (☎ 751 0825 or 0800 111 600; www.foxguides.co.nz. Half-day 4hr., 9:15am and 1:45pm, $45. Full-day 6hr., 9:15am, $75. Heli-hike 3hr., 9am and noon, $215. Ice-climbing trips 8am, $180. Chancellor trek $415, overnight in a hut on the glacier $665. Book ahead.)

SCENIC FLIGHTS

Fox Glacier offers aerial pursuits similar to those at Franz Josef. For information on specific **skydiving** and **helicopter flights**, see **Activities**, p. 344.

LESS SLIPPERY WALKS

GLACIER VIEWS. The **Chalet Lookout Walk** (1¼hr.; turn off onto Glacier View Rd. 2km south of town) yields a fantastic peek of the town's namesake, while the **Fox Glacier Valley Walk** (1hr.; take a left on the road to the glacier just south of town before the Fox River Bridge) follows the path taken by the guided glacier walks and leads directly to the terminal face itself.

LAKE MATHESON WALK. This walk offers unparalleled shots of Mt. Cook and Mt. Tasman in one of the most photographed reflecting lakes. Views are best in the morning and evening, when the water is undisturbed by wind; arrive 15-20min. before sunrise and walk to the nearest lookout point for some unadulterated New Zealand serenity. (6km out of town on Cook Flat Rd. Return 1½hr.)

SHORT JAUNTS. The **Minnehaha Walk** gives a sampling of Westland's rainforest as it wanders across bridges, over small trickling creeks, and through tall moss-covered trees surrounded by huge ferns and other primitive plants. (Return 20min.) Though not nearly as impressive as the display in Hokitika, there are indeed glowworms in Fox. (At the corner of Sullivans and Main Rd. Entrance through Fox Glacier Souvenirs. Glowworm viewing 7:30-9pm. $2.)

COPLAND TRACK. Connecting Westland National Park to Mt. Cook National Park, this 17km tramp should only be attempted by experienced hikers, though the first leg is manageable for hot pool lovers willing to overnight at the **Welcome Flat Hut Pools.** (Trailhead 26km south of Fox Glacier. InterCity and Atomic Shuttles make stops daily at 8:45 and 11:45am, respectively. See DOC office for track details and conditions.)

GILLESPIES BEACH. Travelers willing to venture out to the beach can stroll for some 2hr. along the shore of the Tasman. The **Seal Colony Walk,** at Gillespies Beach, leads to an endearing huddle of seals at Waikowhai Bluff. (20km from Fox Glacier. Transport available from Mac's Shuttle. Seal Colony Walk return 4hr.)

OTAGO

Otago thrives on the pioneer spirit that tamed its rocky coastlines and rugged hills. The region extends west from the seaside centers of Dunedin and Oamaru, through the arid slopes of Central Otago, and on to thrill-seeking Queenstown, placid Wanaka, and the spectacular Southern Alps that surround them. Rollicking Dunedin hops with student-packed pubs and the region's most vibrant cultural offerings, while playful Queenstown throngs with happy-go-lucky backpackers hankering after the latest adrenaline fix. Otago, with its formidable landscape and high-spirited residents, welcomes travelers with a warm and hardy Kiwi spirit.

OTAGO HIGHLIGHTS

RUSH Queenstown's adrenaline offerings—bungy jumping, skydiving, and skiing—by day (see p. 361), and **Dunedin's** marathon bar-hopping by night (see below).

SLOW DOWN by enjoying the **Otago Peninsula's** abundant wildlife (see p. 356) or relaxing lakeside in laid-back **Wanaka** (see p. 378).

SET A STEADY PACE in **Mt. Aspiring National Park** for some of the world's most glorious tramping (see p. 386).

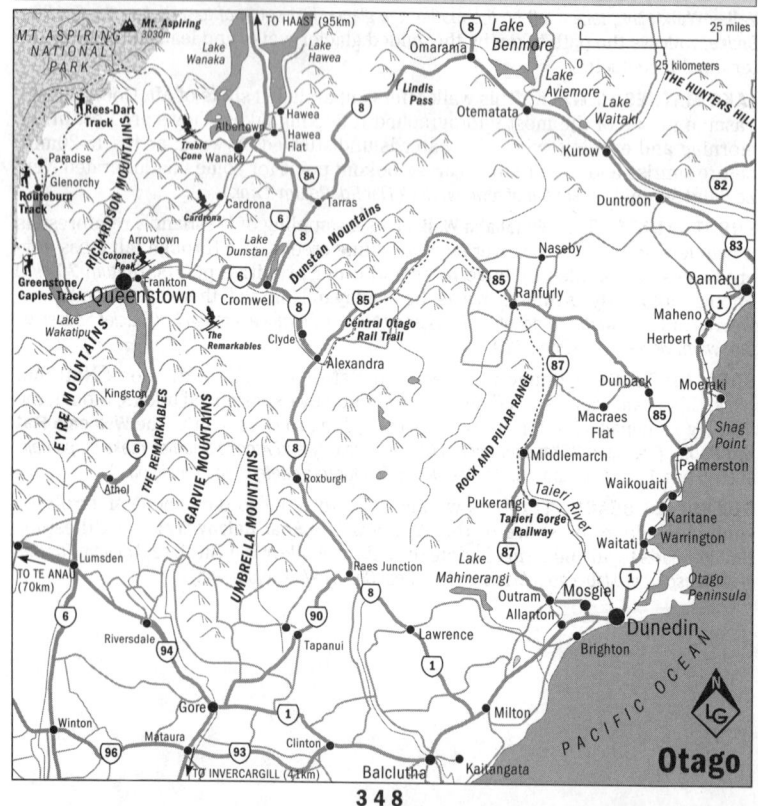

Otago

DUNEDIN ☎ 03

"The people here are Scots. They stopped here on their way home to heaven, thinking they had arrived."
—Mark Twain

Undoubtedly, the original Scottish settlers would be proud to see that Dunedin has maintained its grandeur and spirit. While statuesque whitestone buildings and galleries preserve the heritage of this harbor port, Dunedin's student population (peaking the town at 120,000) ensures that the Scottish pub culture continues to thrive. With its precipitous hills (Baldwin St. is the steepest street in the world) and magical harbor, Dunedin is deeply inscribed on Otago's historical and industrial heart.

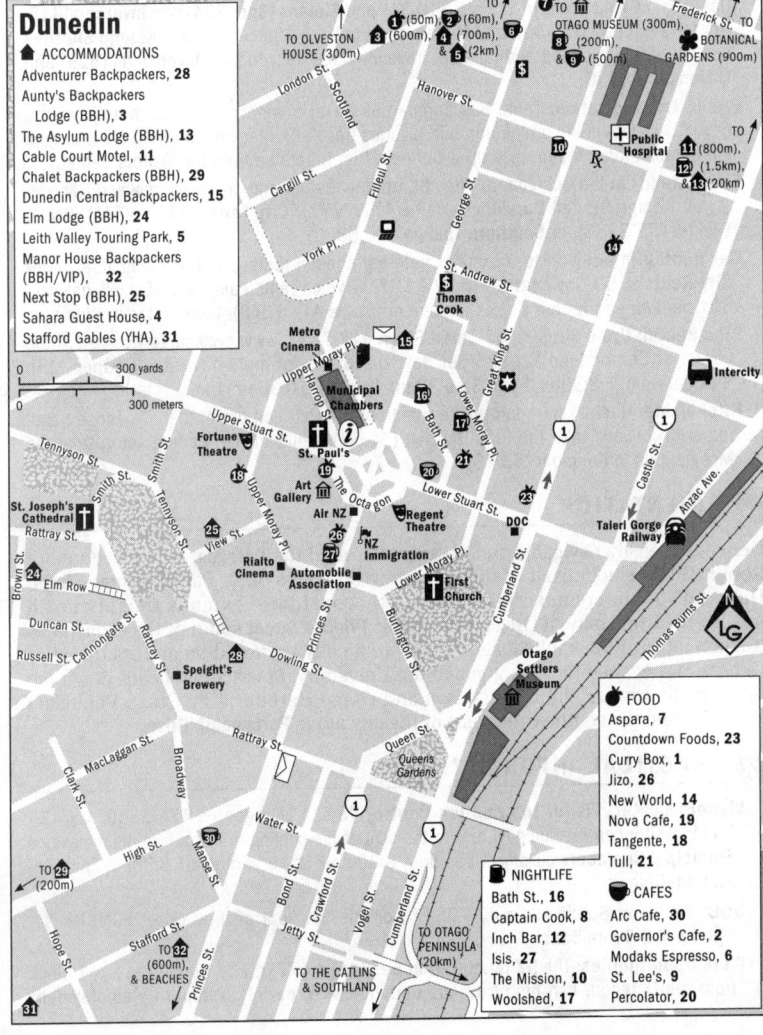

Dunedin

ACCOMMODATIONS
- Adventurer Backpackers, **28**
- Aunty's Backpackers Lodge (BBH), **3**
- The Asylum Lodge (BBH), **13**
- Cable Court Motel, **11**
- Chalet Backpackers (BBH), **29**
- Dunedin Central Backpackers, **15**
- Elm Lodge (BBH), **24**
- Leith Valley Touring Park, **5**
- Manor House Backpackers (BBH/VIP), **32**
- Next Stop (BBH), **25**
- Sahara Guest House, **4**
- Stafford Gables (YHA), **31**

FOOD
- Aspara, **7**
- Countdown Foods, **23**
- Curry Box, **1**
- Jizo, **26**
- New World, **14**
- Nova Cafe, **19**
- Tangente, **18**
- Tull, **21**

NIGHTLIFE
- Bath St., **16**
- Captain Cook, **8**
- Inch Bar, **12**
- Isis, **27**
- The Mission, **10**
- Woolshed, **17**

CAFES
- Arc Cafe, **30**
- Governor's Cafe, **2**
- Modaks Espresso, **6**
- St. Lee's, **9**
- Percolator, **20**

TRANSPORTATION

Flights: The **airport** is 30min. south on SH1. **Air New Zealand**, at the corner of Princes St. and the Octagon (☎479 6594 or 0800 737 000), flies one-way to **Auckland** (2¾hr., $268-475) and **Wellington** (2hr., $184-331), often via **Christchurch** (1hr., $96-236). Dunedin's taxi companies run scheduled airport shuttles for $15. An on-demand taxi will cost at least $50.

Trains: A scenic way to get to **Queenstown** is to make a bus connection in **Pukerangi** after taking the **Taieri Gorge Railway.** (☎477 4449; www.taieri.co.nz. About $110 one-way, standby $80.)

Buses: InterCity, 205 St. Andrew St. (☎474 9600), runs to **Christchurch** (6hr., 4-5 per day, $26-50) via **Oamaru** (1½hr., $10-24) and **Timaru** (3hr., $24-32); **Invercargill** (3-4hr., 1-2 per day, $20-40); and **Queenstown** (4¼hr., 1 per day, $29). **Atomic Shuttles** (☎322 8883) is cheap and reliable, traveling once daily to both Invercargill ($25) and Queenstown ($30).

Public Transportation: Three **bus** companies travel a variety of routes throughout the city ($1-4, depending on the number of zones traveled). Many depart from the Octagon. For detailed information, pick up a Dunedin Bus Timetable from the Visitors Center.

Taxis: Stands at the Octagon, on High St. off Princes St., and on St. Andrew and Hanover St. off George St. Call **Dunedin Taxis** (☎477 7777), **City Taxis** (☎477 1771), **Otago Taxi** (☎477 3333), or **Southern Taxi** (☎476 6300).

Car Rental: In addition to the major national chains, rental companies include: **Inner City Rentals,** 99 Crawford St. (☎477 3017), which rents cars from $50 per day and 50¢ per km; and **Jackie's,** 23 Cumberland St. (☎477 7848). Lower rates in winter.

Bike Rental: Cycle Surgery, 67 Stuart St. (☎477 7473; www.cyclesurgery.co.nz), at the corner of Cumberland St. $25 per day. Discounts for multi-day rentals. Open M-Th 8:30am-6pm, F 8:30am-9pm, Sa 9:30am-4pm, Su 10:30am-4pm.

Hitchhiking: Hitchhikers often take a bus from the Octagon out of the city. Those heading north usually take the Pine Hill bus ($1.50), while those heading south take the Mosgiel bus to Kenmont ($3.70).

ORIENTATION

Dunedin is easily navigable and organized around the **Octagon**, where a statue of Robert Burns sits in front of the gothic revival spires of St. Paul's. **George Street,** Dunedin's main commercial shopping thoroughfare, extends roughly north toward the University of Otago; it becomes **Princes Street** south of the Octagon as it nears most of the backpackers. Pubs are mostly scattered on and southeast of George St. between the Octagon and the University. **Stuart Street** heads down the hill directly toward the train station and Otago Harbour. The Otago Peninsula extends from the southeastern part of the city along **Portsmouth Drive.**

PRACTICAL INFORMATION

Visitors Center: Visitor Information Centre, 48 The Octagon (☎474 3300; fax 474 3311; visitor.centre@dcc.govt.nz), to the right of the soaring clock tower of the limestone **Municipal Chambers** building. Open daily 8:30am-6pm; in winter M-F 8:30am-5pm, Sa-Su 9am-5pm.

DOC: 77 Lower Stuart St. (☎477 0677), on the 1st floor of the Conservation House. Open M-F 8:30am-5pm.

Work Opportunities: The **NZ Immigration Service** (☎477 0820), on Princes St., 1 block from the Octagon, can help travelers obtain a **work permit. Temporary employment**

DUNEDIN ■ 351

agencies in Dunedin include: **Adecco Personnel Limited**, 10 George St. (☎477 4036); **Drake**, 83 Moray Pl. (☎474 5499); and **Student Job Search**, 640 Cumberland St. (☎474 0597). For information on **fruit-picking** jobs (usually available Jan.-May), call Alexandra at the Visitors Center (☎448 9515).

Budget Travel: STA Travel, 32 Albany St. (☎474 0146; fax 477 2741), a block down from George St. Open M-F 9am-5pm, Sa 10am-1pm.

Banks and Currency Exchange: Banks dot George and Princes St., most with **ATMs**. **Thomas Cook** (☎477 1532), 346 George St. Open M-F 8:30am-5pm, Sa 10am-2pm. The Visitors Center exchanges money outside these hours.

Police: 25 Great King St. (☎477 6011).

Medical Services: The **pharmacy** is at 95 Hanover St. (☎477 6344). Open M-F 6am-10pm, Sa-Su 10am-10pm. **Urgent Doctors** (☎479 2900) is next door. Open 24hr. **Dunedin Public Hospital** is at 201 Great King St. (☎474 0999).

Internet Access: Wayne's World, 20 St. Andrew St. (☎471 7172), connects to the web for $6 per hr. during the day and $4 per hr. at night. Min. charge $2. Open daily 9am-9pm. The **Arc Cafe** (see **Cafes**, p. 353) has 25min. of free access without purchase.

Post Office: (☎477 3517). At the corner of Princes and Rattray St. Poste Restante. Open M-F 8:30am-5:30pm.

ACCOMMODATIONS AND CAMPING

Edwardian hotels, former churches, and rambling homes converted into backpackers provide Dunedin with an impressive array of budget accommodations. Most are found within a 10min. walk of the Octagon. Book in advance when there's a big rugby game.

Chalet Backpackers (BBH), 296 High St. (☎479 2075). Take Princes St. to High St. and then go up the hill. Giant windows and plants add cheeriness to every room. They will wash and dry your laundry just like mom ($5). Reception 8am-10pm; in winter 9am-9pm. Dorms $16; singles $30; doubles $40. Cash only. ❷

Elm Lodge (BBH), 74 Elm Row (☎474 1872 or 0800 356-563; www.elmwildlifetours.co.nz/elm_lodge1.htm). Head up Rattray St. to Brown St., then uphill to Elm Row. Perched high above Dunedin, the Elm offers a homier atmosphere than most of the other backpackers in town. Free pick-up and drop-off. Key deposit $5. Laundry. Internet. Reception 8am-10pm. Dorms $17-18; doubles $40. ❷

The Asylum Lodge (BBH), 36 Russel Rd. (☎465 8123), in Seacliff, 25km north of Dunedin. Follow SH1 north from Dunedin and turn east on Coast Rd. at the signs for Seacliff and Warrington. Former asylum buildings and an extensive collection of unfinished classic cars may cause hesitation, but the art deco lodge is the coziest around. Activities include kayaking, surfing, horseback riding, fishing, and the chance to cruise the seashore in a '57 Chevy. Dorms $20; singles $24; doubles $44; tent sites $12. ❷

Manor House Backpackers (BBH/VIP), 28 Manor Pl. (☎477 0484 or 0800 477 0484; fax 477 8145; www.manorhousebackpackers.co.nz). Six blocks down Princes St. and to the right. Occupying 2 adjacent 1920s era houses, Manor House provides ample privacy. Free pick-up. Internet. Laundry. Reception 8:30am-10pm; in winter 8:30am-8pm. Dorms $17-18; twins and doubles $42; triples $60; tent sites $12. ❷

Stafford Gables (YHA), 71 Stafford St. (☎474 1919). Take Princes St. up several blocks to Stafford St. Intrepid guests navigate labyrinthine halls to discover a TV lounge and a rooftop with panoramic views. Internet. Laundry. Reception 8am-2pm and 4-9pm; in winter 8-10am and 7:30-10pm. Dorms $19; singles $31; doubles $46. ❷

Aunty's Backpackers Lodge (BBH), 3 Union St. (☎474 0708 or 0800 428 689; fax 474 0715; auntys@xtra.co.nz). Take George St. 5 blocks from the Octagon and turn left on Union St. Near the University, the public garden, and the pubs. The owner, an ex-Otago Highlander, takes guests to local rugby matches. Internet. Laundry. Reception 8:30am-8:30pm. Dorms $19; singles $30; twins and doubles $44. ❷

Next Stop (BBH), 2 View St. (☎477 0447; fax 477 0430; nextstop2@hotmail.com). From Princes St., go right on Moray Pl. and then left on View St. Recently renovated rooms with skylights (but no windows) surround a vast 2-story common space in this former church hall. Internet. Laundry. Reception 8:30am-10pm. Dorms $17-19; singles $30; twins and doubles $38. ❷

Adventurer Backpackers, 37 Dowling St. (☎/fax 477 7367 or 0800 422 257), 2 blocks from the Octagon down Princes St., then up Dowling St. Immense common area with pool table, fireside couches, and balcony crafts a social climate. Internet. Key deposit $10. Reception 8am-9pm. Dorms $16; singles $32; twins and doubles $40; triples and quads $34. ❷

Dunedin Central Backpackers, 243 Moray Pl. (☎0800 432 2322), a block from the Octagon in the heart of the city. A recent addition to Dunedin's budget accommodations, Central is a work in progress. The hostel comes with all the charms and disrepair of a multi-bachelor pad. Internet. Laundry. Reception 8:30am-9:30pm. Dorms $14; singles $16; twins $32; doubles $35. ❶

Sahara Guest House, 619 George St. (☎477 6662). Built on land purchased from the Queen in 1863, the latest reincarnation of this former house, hospital, and restaurant welcomes guests with a maroon hue of good karma. Single rooms with shared baths $55 (includes cooked breakfast); motel units from $70. ❹

Cable Court Motel, 833 Cumberland St. (☎0800 838 525), 7 blocks from downtown, near the University. Guests willing to tolerate mild street noise can lay claim to 4 well-equipped motel units at discount prices. Free laundry. Rooms from $92. ❺

Leith Valley Touring Park, 103 Malvern St. (☎467 9936), 2km from the city. Take George St., then turn left on Duke St. and continue up to Malvern St. A small, secluded park on Leith Stream with access to trails. Reception 9am-9pm. Caravan and tent sites $10 per person, min. charge $12; caravan doubles $30, $22 for 1; tourist flats $60 for 2, extra person $12. ❶

FOOD

Catering to budget-conscious students, Dunedin overflows with cheap quality eats. George St. between Albany and Andrew St. swarms with inexpensive Thai, Japanese, Korean, and Indian eateries. For a quick bite outdoors, look for the **Khmer Satay-Away** stand that appears around lunch time on the Octagon. Markets include **Countdown Foods,** 309 Cumberland St. (☎477 7283; open 24hr.) and **New World** on Cumberland St. between Andrew and Hanover St. (☎477 4677. Open M-F 8am-9pm, Sa-Su 8am-8pm.)

🌿 Tull, 29 Bath St. (☎477 5331), off Lower Stuart St. This hippie ode to Jethro Tull rates its 25 sinful triumphs according to decadence (desserts $7.50-15). The French bread sandwiches, called "flutes" in homage to Tull's Ian Anderson, are enormous and delicious ($6.50-8.50). Open M-F 11:30am-11pm, Sa 5:30-11pm. ❷

Jizo, 56 Princes St. (☎479 2692). Dark, stylized interior and slow jazz exude chic as business types and families enjoy quality Japanese food. The salmon sushi main ($14.50) defines fresh. Open M-Th 11:30am-9pm, F-Sa 11:30am-9:30pm. ❸

Aspara, 380 George St. (☎477 4499), opposite Albert Arms. The big Cambodian noodle soups (most $5) warm you from the inside out, and the curry veggies with coconut milk served over rice ($5) revitalize the taste buds. Open daily 11am-9pm. ❶

Curry Box, 442 George St. (☎ 477 4713), opposite Knox Church. Delectable Indian fare that's easy on your wallet. Enjoy the tastefully sparse decor or join the crowd and order carry-out. Mains $10-13. Open M-Sa 5-9:30pm; also M-F 11am-2:30pm. ❷

Tangente, 111 Moray Pl., (☎ 477 0232), left off Upper Stuart St., a block past the Octagon. Sip latte from a giant multi-colored goblet as you "celebrate our humanity" at this bright, family-friendly designer restaurant. Mains $12-20. Open M-Tu and Su 8am-3:30pm, W-Sa 8am-late. ❸

Nova Cafe (☎ 479 0808), in the Octagon adjoining the Public Gallery. An excellent all-purpose cafe and restaurant, choose mains ($12-18) from the eclectic menu or sample the all-day brekkie ($6-14). Open M-Th 7am-11pm, F 7am-midnight, Sa 9am-midnight, Su 9am-11pm. ❸

CAFES

Cafes are hot in Dunedin, speckling nearly every block (heck, McDonald's even has a McCafe). Some serve alcohol and figure in Dunedin's nightlife scene with live music or pulsing down-tempo beats, while others stay open late to revive sleepy students. Whether day or night, broody or bright, Dunedin has a cafe to suit any shade of mood.

■ **Arc,** 135 High St. (☎ 474 1135), a block up from Princes St. Bohemian cooperative and iconic Dunedin hangout, Arc serves coffee, wines and beers, baked snacks ($2-3), and veggie meals ($4-7). 25 min. of free Internet just for walking in the door. Frequent live music in the back room (often cover charge). Open M-Sa noon-late.

Modaks Espresso, 339 George St. (☎ 477 6563). Discuss last night's (and this morning's) Bath St. DJs at this local alternative establishment while sipping strong espresso to bring you to your senses. The narrow brick walls, dim lighting, and hypnotic beats could chill hot iron. Open daily 7:30am-7pm.

Percolater, 142 Lower Stuart St. (☎ 477 5462), just below the Octagon. With less self-consciously displayed character than many of the other cafes in town, Percolater makes its mark with excellent coffee ($3) and sandwiches ($7.50-9). Internet. Open M-Th and Su 9am-11pm, F-Sa 9am-late.

St. Lee's, 50 Dundas St. (☎ 477 9090). The simple and stylish interior of this former church breathes self-important comfort. Start a party night slowly with wines ($5-6) and bottled beers ($4-6), or sample from the extensive menu of pastas, salads, and gourmet burgers ($8.50-15.50). Open daily 11am-midnight.

Governor's Cafe, 438 George St. (☎ 477 6871). This is where U of Otago students go to procrastinate, refuel with cheap eats, and recharge with caffeine. Free 5min. Internet access upstairs. Open daily 8am-late.

ENTERTAINMENT

The Fortune Theatre Company, on upper Stuart St. and Moray Pl., puts on a number of professional shows throughout the year. (☎ 477 8323. Box office open M 10:30am-5pm, Tu 10:30am-6pm, W-F 10:30am-8:30pm, Sa 4:30-8:30pm. Tickets around $25, students $15.) The stately **Regent** in the Octagon, hosts an International Film Festival in July and August and several traveling shows throughout the year. (☎ 477 8597. Box office open M-F 8:30am-5pm, Sa 10:30am-1pm. Prices vary widely by performance.) The **Metro Cinema,** one block up Harrop St. from the Visitors Center, behind the Municipal Chambers, shows foreign and independent films. (☎ 474 3350; www.metrocinema.co.nz. $10, students $8.50, seniors $7; matinees before 5pm $7.) For a mix of big studio and independent films in an opulent theater, head to **Rialto,** 11 Moray Pl. (☎474 2200. $8-12; M-F $2 student discount.) Check the *Otago Daily Times* for screenings or pick up a copy of *Fink* at most cafes for entertainment listings.

NIGHTLIFE

As a university town, Dunedin has its fair share of banging-'til-6am standard student hangouts, but older and calmer travelers can find less frenetic options as well. The list below comprises a small sampling of Dunedin's variety; keep your eyes peeled for other nightlife venues.

- **Captain Cook** (☎474 1935), at the corner of Albany and Great King St. Even North Islanders have stories about this quintessential varsity pub with pool and a throbbing dance floor upstairs (W-Sa nights). Sports fans watch the big screens in the enclosed beer garden. $3 doubles, $2 beers W 8pm-midnight. Open daily 11am-late.

- **Inch Bar,** 8 Bank St. (☎473 6496), past the Botanical Gardens, NE Valley. It may be a long walk to dodge the student crowd in Dunedin, but this intimate, artsy venue is well worth the trip. Boutique beers ($5-10) are the specialty. Open daily 3pm-late.

- **The Woolshed,** 318 Moray Pl. (☎477 3246). Leave sobriety at the door before visiting this part Irish pub, part frontier saloon. Sloshed local mid-lifers drown their cares to classic feel-good tunes. Live Irish band every F and beer-for-a-song open mic nights on W. $6 meal-deals daily. Open daily 11am-late.

- **The Mission** (☎477 1637), at the corner of Great King and Hanover St. A dance floor throbs where pews used to stand and gyrating bodies flood the dais. The party mainly gets going on weekends around 1am. Open M-Sa 9pm-very late.

- **Bath St.,** 1 Bath St. (☎477 6750). Alternative types flock to the burgundy leather couches and laser-lit dance floor, as do some of the hottest DJs (W-Sa). Cover $3-5. The water gets hot around 1am. Open W-Sa from 10pm.

- **Isis** (☎477 8001), on Princes St., 1 block from the Octagon. The least expensive of Dunedin's chic new generation of cocktail bars, the plush leather seating, smooth piano music, and surrealist decoration put the lounge in lounge bar. Cocktails $8-12, during F night Happy Hours $5.50. Open daily 5pm-late.

SIGHTS

OTAGO MUSEUM. This extensive museum takes an in-depth look at the material culture and natural history of Otago. The recently opened Southern Lands Southern People gallery provides a beautifully modern and richly thorough introduction to the region. The museum's **Discovery World** has hands-on science exhibits that will enthrall children. *(Down the hill on Great King between Albany and Union St. ☎477 2372; www.otagomuseum.govt.nz. Open daily 10am-5pm. Recommended donation for museum $5. Discovery World admission $6, students $4, children $3. Daily tours 3:30pm, $10.)*

CHURCHES. The Gothic Revival churches established by early Scottish residents are worth a look, especially the **First Church of Otago,** with its rose window and vaulted wood ceiling. (Down Moray Pl. from Princes St.) **St. Paul's** in the Octagon has the only **stone-vaulted ceiling** in New Zealand, an organ with 3500 pipes, and the most impressive flying buttresses in the city. For those who can't get enough stone churches, **St. Joseph's Cathedral** (at the corner of Rattray and Smith St.) and **Knox Church** (at the corner of George and Pitt St.) are also worthwhile.

OLVESTON. Built in 1904, this perfectly preserved Edwardian mansion still feels lived-in. All the clocks still run, and even the 1926 Frigidaire continues to work.

The benefactor's will stipulated that anyone could tickle the ivories of the 1906 Steinway grand piano, so feel free to play. *(42 Royal Tce. Take George St. to Pitt St., then follow Royal Tce. until you see it on the right. ☎ 477 3320. Tours at 9:30, 10:45am, noon, 1:30, 2:45, and 4pm. $12, under 15 $4.)*

OTHER ARCHITECTURE. The Scottish Edwardian architecture of Dunedin's **railway station** is spectacular and is rivaled only by the black and white facade of the **University of Otago's main hall**, down Saint David St., which is spectacular at night.

OTAGO SETTLERS MUSEUM. A multi-cultural tribute to the hardy men and women who tamed New Zealand's frontier. Showcasing Maori, European, and Chinese settlers, the museum focuses on the social histories of Otago cultures. Be sure to try riding the gigantic penny farthing bicycle inside Dunedin's art deco former bus station, now adjoining the museum as the hall of transportation. *(31 Queens Garden, down Dowling St. ☎ 477 5052. Museum open daily 10am-5pm. $4, students and VIP/YHA members $3, children free.)*

DUNEDIN PUBLIC ART GALLERY. Well worth an afternoon, rain or shine, Dunedin's public gallery is a captivating artwork in itself. Galleries showcasing colonial and contemporary New Zealand art open onto a minimalist foyer. The gallery also houses a small collection of Renaissance and Japanese works, as well as an archive and viewing area for New Zealand films. *(In the Octagon. ☎ 474 3240. Open daily 10am-5pm. Regular exhibits free.)*

DUNEDIN HERITAGE TOUR. See the city in style, via a bright red double-decker bus. Tours depart from the Visitors Center daily at 10am, 12:45, and 3:30pm. The same company also provides transportation to Larnach Castle, leaving the Visitors Center daily at noon. *(Run by Citibus Newton, ☎ 477 5577; www.transportplace.co.nz. 1½hr. tours $20, children $10.)*

ACTIVITIES

SPEIGHT'S BREWERY HERITAGE TOUR AND MUSEUM. Judge the "Pride of the South" for yourself with free samples after the tour. A 1½hr. tour takes you through the history of beer-making from Egyptian beverages to modern microbrews. The building is built over a well, from which water for the beer is drawn. The water is the best in town, and thirsty post-rugby match locals line up at the outside tap to sip to their hearts' delight. *(From Princes St., turn right onto Rattray St.; you can't miss the protruding barrel. ☎ 477 7697. 4 tours per day F-Sa, with an additional 7pm tour M-Th. Bookings essential. $12, students $10.)*

DUNEDIN BEACHES. A favorite with locals, **St. Clair Beach** stuns with its striking collision of land and sea. The beach draws a steady stream of surfers, as do **Blackhead Beach** and **Warrington Point**. Among the best of local walks, the track to **Tunnel Beach** is only accessible at low tide. When it is above water, the hike leads through a century-old tunnel onto a secluded beach with sea caves carved into the walls. *(St. Clair Beach: Take the bus from the Octagon to St. Clair. Tunnel Beach: Take the Corstophine bus from the Octagon to Stenhope Crescent, then walk down Blackhead/Middleton Rd. By car, take Princes St., then make a right on King Edward St. Then turn right on Hillside Rd., which becomes Middleton Rd. Tunnel Beach is on the left on the far side of the hill. Walk 1hr. return from trailhead. Blackhead Beach is several km further down the road. Inaccessible Sept.-Oct.)*

TAIERI GORGE RAILWAY. If you're tired of being on your feet, ride on the train through the hinterlands of Dunedin's pioneer history. The railway flies precariously over spectacular gorges and into native forests, through tunnels and across viaducts en route to Pukerangi. (☎ 477 4449; www.taieri.co.nz. Departs from the railway station Oct.-Mar. 2:30pm; April-Sept. 12:30pm. $55, students $44.)

MT. CARGILL. A 4km track through a former tree-planting scheme brings a panoramic view of the harbor. Another 1hr. tramp will take you to the volcanic spires of the **Organ Pipes.** (Normanby bus to Norwood St.; walk to Bethunes Gully. Walk 3½hr. return.)

BOTANIC GARDENS. Established in 1863, Dunedin's gardens are arguably the best in the country. The annual **Rhododendron Festival** is world-renowned in botanic circles (late-Oct. 2003). The large aviary with native birds, including the kea, draws similar interest from ornithologists. Unprepared picnickers should grab a gourmet sandwich ($6.50-8) or a crêpe ($5-8) at **Croque-O-Dile Espresso ❷**, next to the information center and gift shop in the Gardens. (☎ 477 5455. Open daily 9:30am-late afternoon.) Continuing from the Botanic Gardens with a car, **Signal Hill** is a great place to admire the stars and the twinkling lights of the city below. (Gardens: Take any city bus from the Octagon down George St. or walk from the University on Leith St. Signal Hill: Accessible off Opoho Rd. on the northern side of the Botanic Gardens. Free.)

BIKING. A great **bike path** follows Thomas Burns St., which runs into Wharf St., toward the Otago Peninsula—look for blue and white signs. (To access the path, cross the foot bridge to the right of the train station.)

HORSEBACK RIDING. Explore the beaches to the south of Dunedin with a 2hr. ride from **Bums 'n' Saddles,** 8min. from the Octagon. (☎ 488 0097. $30. Transport $10.) **Hare Hill Horse Treks** also offers beach and hillside rides overlooking the harbor. (☎ 472 8496. Take the city bus from the Octagon to Port Chalmers for free pick-up. $25-50.)

OTAGO CENTRAL RAIL TRAIL. Stretching 150km between Middlemarch and Clyde, this historic trail offers striking vistas, small town pubs, precarious viaducts, and gentle gradients to attract walkers, bicyclists, and horse-riders. Following the course of the now defunct Otago Central Railway, the trail preserves the heritage of Otago's frontier and provides an excellent way to visit the historic towns of Otago's heartland. (The complete trail takes 3-5 days biking, 5-7 days walking, but it can be ridden for various lengths. Transport to trailheads is available from the Visitors Center in Dunedin. Call ☎ 448 9515 for details.)

OTAGO PENINSULA ☎ 03

Stretching over 20km from Dunedin, the serene Otago Peninsula has incomparable opportunities to experience an amazing ecology. Yellow-eyed penguins, fur seals, sea lions, and royal albatross claim the area's many weather-worn inlets, beaches, and promontories. The dramatic tip of the peninsula, **Taiaroa Head,** drops off onto seal-covered crags and great swaths of billowing kelp. The beaches teem with bird activity even before the penguins waddle ashore in the evening.

TRANSPORTATION. The best way to experience the peninsula is by car, although the flat terrain and harborside travel make for an excellent bicycle ride. **Portobello Road,** the sinuous coastal route along the bay, is full of treacherous curves—even the locals who know the road often don't drive it. If you decide to take a tour, there are many well-operated ones from which to choose. **Back to Nature Tours** has small, intimate tours with a very knowledgeable guide, Les. Free binoculars allow you to see nature in action. The tour ends at Sandfly Beach, where the yellow-eyes waddle up the cliff. (☎ 0800 477 0484; www.backtonature-tours.co.nz. 5hr., 1 per day; $50, backpackers $45. Free pick-up.) **Elm Wildlife Tours** also provides small (max. 10 people), in-depth walking wildlife excursions, going to a private beach that no other tour can visit. (☎ 0800 356 363; www.elmwildlifetours.co.nz. 6hr., 1 per day. About $43; free pick-up.) **Newton Tours** offers package tours to the sights. (☎ 477 5577. $20-35, plus entry fees to attractions.)

ACCOMMODATIONS AND FOOD. If you decide to stay over at the peninsula rather than daytrip from Dunedin, **homestays** are a possibility. Most cost about $50 per night per person; the Visitors Center in Dunedin will provide brochures, recommendations, and bookings. One farmstay that beats the cost curve is the **McFarmers Backpackers (BBH) ❷**, 774 Portobello Rd., a former pottery studio that provides stunning views of the harbor, as well as free boats and canoes, and bikes for hire. (☎ 478 0389 or 025 206 0650. Dorms $15; doubles $35; tent sites $10. Closed in June.) **Penguin Place ❷**, right next to the Yellow-eyed Penguin Reserve, has worn and sparsely furnished rooms with terrific views of the bay. (☎ 478 0286. Book ahead. $15 per person.) **Portobello Village Tourist Park ❷**, in Portobello, is a peaceful retreat midway between Dunedin and the albatross colony. Popular with tent campers, the park is a good starting point for exploring the peninsula by bike. (☎/fax 478 0359. Half-day bicycle rental $15, full-day $25. Reception 8am-10:30pm. Dorms $15-25; tent sites $9, powered $10; tourist flats $65.) Food options on the peninsula are limited, but one standout is the **1908 Cafe ❸**, 7 Harrington Point Rd., in sleepy Portobello. The cafe offers exquisite fine dining with the prices to match (lunch $7-25, dinner $24-35). Chef Ian will happily tailor menu items to your tastes, appetite, and budget. (☎ 478 0801. Open daily noon-2:30pm and 5pm-late. Bookings recommended. Winter hours are variable, but dinner is served nearly every night.) The **Portobello Store**, on Portobello Rd. at the junction with the road to the aquarium, stocks ice cream and limited groceries. (☎ 478 0555; open M-Th 7:30am-7pm, F 7:30am-7:30pm, Sa 8am-7:30pm, Su 8:30am-7pm.)

WILDLIFE. At the **Taiaroa Royal Albatross Colony** (☎ 478 0499), you'll learn that these massive birds, immortalized by poet Samuel Coleridge, are not merely seagulls with pituitary problems. Taiaroa is unique as the only mainland albatross colony on earth; these majestic wanderers fledge and rear their young here, then circumnavigate the globe without landing until they return. Entrance to the **Albatross Centre**, which houses extensive displays and live TV coverage of the birds' activities is by donation, but the educational tour and observatory viewing are rather costly. ($24, children $12; discounts in winter. Observing an albatross in flight is not guaranteed.) **Monarch Wildlife Cruises** runs a jolly skiff from Wellers Rock near the head, providing views of massive chimney roosts and rare cormorants. (☎ 477 4276. 2 per day. From the pier $27, children $13. Transport options from Dunedin $58-183.)

Rare yellow-eyed penguins *(hoiho)* have, with a little human assistance, recolonized Penguin Beach just beyond Taiaroa Head. Once as scarce as the Giant Panda, the penguins have begun a roaring comeback on the Peninsula, boosting the local eco-tourism industry with each new hatching. A wonder of nature themselves, the Reid family runs **Nature's Wonders** wildlife tours, a short drive past the Albatross Colony. Led by cheeky father Perry, the four Reid children whisk dazzled guests to remote wildlife sanctuaries on fully-amphibious, eight-wheel drive vehicles called ARGOs. This is nature at its most intimate—small groups of guests view wild birds, seals, and penguins at distances closer than in any zoo. (☎ 0800 246 446. Guided tours only, running daily every 15min., from 10am until dusk. $30, children $25.) At the **Yellow-eyed Penguin Conservation Reserve**, 40min. from Dunedin and 5min. before the Albatross Centre on Harrington Point Rd., a camouflaged trench system affords views of the sleek penguins from just a few meters away. (☎ 478 0286. 1½hr. tours run every 30min. Oct.-Apr. from 10am-7:45pm; May-Sept. 1 tour per day; $27, children $12. Book ahead in summer.)

◉ SIGHTS. To get up close and personal with Otago's rocky coastline, try sea kayaking with **Wild Earth Adventures Ltd.** (☎473 6535 or 0800 699 453; www.nzwildearth.com. Prices from $69.) One and a half kilometers up a dirt road from town in Portobello sits the **New Zealand Marine Studies Centre** run by the University of Otago. Doubling as a research center for budding marine scientists and as an educational mini-aquarium accessible to the public, the small display areas give a hands-on exposure to the local marine animals and ecosystems. (☎479 5826; www.otago.ac.nz/marinestudies. Open daily noon-4:30pm. $7, children $3, family pass $14.) For the historically inclined, **Larnach Castle** is a 43-room architectural marvel, though the story behind the castle may be even more interesting than the building itself. The virile Mr. Larnach (with six children by his first wife alone) eventually married his third wife when he was 57 (though she was 35). When she ran off with his second son, Larnach committed suicide in the Parliament building in Wellington. Take a self-guided tour through the inlaid mahogany, teak, and kauri foyer up the only hanging Georgian staircase in the Southern Hemisphere. The view of Dunedin and the entire peninsula from the battlements is incomparable. (☎476 1616. $12, children $4.50. Garden access $6, children $2.) To reach the purportedly haunted castle, take the Otago Road Services city bus from Stand 5 outside **New World** on Cumberland St. to the Company Bay stop ($2.50) and walk up the hill. **Citibus Newton** also provides transportation from the Dunedin Visitors Center to the castle. (☎477 5577. $30, children $15; castle admission included.) Halfway down the peninsula and 3km up the winding Castlewood Rd., the aptly named **High Cliff Road** is an alternate route with views of the south side of the peninsula. A mode of transport more befitting a stately visit, **Castle Discovery Horse Treks**, based in Broad Bay, embarks upon a 3hr. trip to Larnach Castle twice daily. (☎478 0796 or 0800 467 738. 9:30am and 1:15pm. $45, students $35, children $30; includes castle entrance fee.)

OAMARU ☎ 03

While the rest of the country must count sheep to fall asleep, the folks in Oamaru (pop. 12,400) picture the nightly return of their penguins. Although known primarily for its blue penguin colony (the smallest penguins in the world), visitors to this town can easily spend a day browsing antiques and collectables in the whitestone historic district. With ecological attractions and the nearby boulders at Moeraki, you'll find Oamaru a convenient and pleasant stop along the Otago coast.

▐ TRANSPORTATION. The cheapest and fastest bus on SH1, the **Atomic Shuttle** (☎322 8883) goes to **Christchurch** (3½hr., 1 per day, $25) and **Dunedin** (1¾hr., 1-2 per day, $15). **InterCity** also heads to **Christchurch** (4½hr., 2-3 per day, $26-32) and **Dunedin** (2¼hr., 2-3 per day, $10-25). The **Oamaru Mini-Coach** (☎439 4765) also services **Dunedin** (2hr., M-F 8am, $15-20). **Hitchhikers** report heading up Severn St. to the edge of town to catch a lift south. The upper end of Thames St. is reportedly the best place for a ride north, but it's a hard walk with a pack.

◪▨ ORIENTATION AND PRACTICAL INFORMATION. Coming from Timaru to the north, SH1 follows **Thames Street** into the heart of downtown Oamaru. From the Visitors Center, go left onto Itchen St. and then follow Tyne St. around to the right to reach the **historic precinct**. Continue on Tyne St. and make a left on Waterfront Rd. to get to the **Blue Penguin Colony**. The **Visitor Information Centre**, 1 Thames St., is on the left side of Thames St. just after the train tracks. By car, continue straight after SH1 veers right onto Severn St.; walking from the train station, go up one block, turn left onto Thames St., and continue 10min. The Visitors Center has maps and **DOC information**. (☎434 1656; fax 434 1657. Open M-F 9am-6pm, Sa-Su

10am-5pm; in winter M-F 9am-5pm, Sa-Su 10am-4pm.) The **BNZ**, 149 Thames St., one block left from the bus station, has an **ATM**. (Open M and Th-F 9am-4:30pm, Tu-W 9:30am-4:30pm.) Other services include: the **police station** (☎434 5198), off Severn St.; the **hospital**, on Devon St. (☎434 8770; follow Severn St. past the police station and turn right on Cross St.); the **post office** (☎434 7884; open M-F 8am-5:30pm), at Severn and Thames St.; and **Internet access** at the Visitors Center ($1.50 per 10min.) and **Small Bytes Computer**, 187 Thames St. (☎434 8490; $4 per 30min.; open M-F 8am-5pm, Sa 10am-12:30pm).

ACCOMMODATIONS AND CAMPING. Housed in a historic 1867 hotel, **Empire Backpackers (BBH)** ❷, 13 Thames St., combines a convenient location with Victorian charm. Be sure to ask about the penny farthing bicycles. (☎434 3446; empirehostel@hotmail.com. Dorms $17-19; twins and doubles $38.) Those who brave the uphill trek from the Visitors Center to **Swaggers Backpackers (BBH)** ❷, 25 Wansbeck St., will be rewarded with a cheery manager and the warmth of an 80-year-old home. (☎434 9999. Pick-up after 11am. Reception 8-10:30am and 5:30-10pm; self check-in during the day. Reservations recommended in summer. Dorms $15; singles $25; twins $34. Cash only.) The **Red Kettle Hostel (YHA)** ❷, at the corner of Cross and Reed St., is a simple, spotless, seasonal hostel with a large common area. (☎/fax 434 5008. Reception 8-10am and 5:30-10pm. Closed June-Aug., but call for specific dates. Dorms $18; twins and doubles $50.) The **Oamaru Gardens Top 10 Holiday Park** ❶, up Chelmer St., is a short walk from the center of town, with a bridge to the botanic gardens and a small grocery store next door. (☎434 7666 or 0800 280 202; fax 434 7662. Laundry. Reception 8am-10pm; in winter 8am-8pm. Cabins $22 for 1, $32 for 2; kitchen units $31/$44; self-contained units $39/$52; chalets $49/$62; tent sites $9.)

FOOD AND NIGHTLIFE. Eating in Oamaru tends to be a hearty sort of affair. Whether grabbing a greasy bar-snack from one of the town's old-style pubs or having a sit-down munch before penguin-viewing, be sure to bring your appetite. For a light meal, head to **Emma's Cafe** ❶, 30 Thames St., a bright and friendly eatery, where herbivorous delights like the seasonal vegetable quiche ($4.50) abound. (☎434 1165. Open Tu-Sa 9am-5:30pm, Su 10am-5pm.) Enjoy the "friendly food and delicious staff" at the **Star and Garter** ❸, 9 Itchen St., where dressed-up country mains in behemoth portions ($12-20) are served in a atmosphere steeped in homespun refinement. (☎434 5246. Open daily noon-2pm and 6pm-late.) **Woolworth's**, across from the BNZ on Thames St., fills all your grocery needs. (☎434 8127. Open M-F 7:30am-9:30pm, Sa-Su 7:30am-8pm.)

Although Oamaru isn't known for its nightlife, **Annie Flannagan's**, 84 Thames St., is a traditional Irish pub serving up $6 lunch specials, an ambitiously diverse menu of dinners (Calcutta beef curry $10), and drinks (pints $4). (☎434 8828. Live music F and Sa nights. Open M-Th 11:30am-10pm, F-Sa 11:30am-1:30am, Su noon-10pm.) The semi-secret music-lovers' hideout, **The Penguin Entertainers Club,** tucked away behind Harbour St. in the historic precinct, draws top blues, jazz, folk, and rock musicians who stop in for a night on their way to Dunedin. Friday night is club night. (☎437 1251. No food served. Call for semi-secret directions; semi-secret cover charge varies.)

SIGHTS AND ACTIVITIES. Let's be frank: you came to see penguins. And see penguins you shall. You can reach the **Oamaru Blue Penguin Colony** either by heading south from the center of town to Waterfront Rd. or via **Coastline Tours** (see below). Arrive well before dusk to secure a prime seat for the nightly penguin triathlon: swimming in the waves, climbing the rock wall, and scurrying to the breeding box. Flash cameras are not permitted, but bring warm clothes and binoculars. (☎433 1195. Viewing $8, students $6, under 15 free.)

In order to see the larger rare **yellow-eyed penguins** head to Bushey Beach. Only 400 breeding pairs remain on the mainland. You can drive down Bushey Beach Rd. or take a tour to both penguin colonies through **Coastline Tours.** (☎ 434 7744 or 021 118 8906. $15 includes free entrance to the penguin colony.)

While Oamaru's attractions center around its penguins, there's more than enough to fill a day in town. The **Historic Precinct,** with its mix of stately restored whitestone buildings and dilapidated facades, surrounds Harbour and Tyne St. where the **Sunday market** opens from 10am-4pm. You can view the work of local artists at the **North Otago Art Society Gallery** (☎ 477 9465; open F-Su 1:30-4pm), at the corner of Great King and Albany St. Browse for second-hand books at the **Slightly Foxed,** 11 Tyne St., a converted warehouse (open Tu-Sa 10am-5:30pm, Su-M 11am-3pm). **Vinbrox Bakery,** 4 Harbour St., has ambrosial sourdough bread (open Tu, Th, and Su 10am-4pm). The Visitors Center guides 1hr. **historic tours** of the precinct that peer inside the unrestored structures ($7.50, students $4, under 15 free).

Charming and well-kept, the **North Otago Museum,** 60 Thames St. (☎ 434 1652; open M-F 1-4:30pm, Sa 10am-1pm, Su 1-4:30pm; free) and the **Forrester Gallery,** 9 Thames St. (☎ 434 1653; open M-F 10:30am-4:30pm, Sa 10:30am-1pm, Su 1-4:30pm; free) make worthwhile rainy day activities. Great on sunny days, **Oamaru Gardens,** on Severn St., features rhododendron and rose gardens and the Summerhouse, a romantic spot that has been the site of many a marriage proposal.

AROUND OAMARU ☎ 03

For those endowed with personal transport, the area surrounding Oamaru offers a wealth of natural wonders, delicious eats, and pleasant accommodations. Head south of Dunedin on the Coast Rd. This scenic route, accessible by following Wharf St. to Kakanui Beach Rd., winds along the shore through sheep and cattle farms and meets SH1 about 30km south of Oamaru. Along the way, you can rest at **The Hall at Coastal Backpackers (BBH) ❷,** a couple of cozy bunkhouses on a family farm. Choose from bikes and bodyboards or take a short walk to the deserted beach to see Hector's dolphins. (☎ 439 5411; fax 439 5242; www.coastalbackpackers.co.nz. Dorms $18; doubles $40; tent sites $8. Cash only.) After returning to SH1, be sure to stop in the hilltop town of Hampden for the award winning "Big Fish, Big Chips" at **Andrew's Takeaways ❶,** on the highway. The locally-famous blue cod ($4.30 with chips) has won national and international renown as a fabulous flake of fried fish. (☎ 439 4744; open Tu-Th and Su 11am-8pm, F-Sa 11am-9pm.)

South of Hampden on SH1, the small hamlet of **Moeraki** and the nearby 60-million-year-old **Moeraki Boulders** lie about 40km from Oamaru (follow signs from SH1). One of the oldest European settlements in New Zealand, **Moeraki** itself is a sleepy fishing village just south of the boulders. Early European visitors to the famed site snatched up the smaller boulders for themselves; only 1-2m high giants remain for viewing, best done at low-tide. Scientifically known as **septarian concretions,** the 50-odd stones started out as bits of animal or plant matter on which successive layers of calcite grew, eventually forming the naturally spherical four-ton boulders. To reach the boulders, follow signs from SH1. **Coastline Tours** (see **Sights and Activities,** p. 359) runs tours to the boulders from Oamaru ($35). **Oamaru minicoaches** and **InterCity buses** will take you near the boulders or Moeraki (specify which you prefer), but often leave you with a 3km walk to town on SH1. The **Moeraki Motor Camp ❶,** a 45min. walk from the boulders, has a range of sites overlooking a peaceful cove as well as a playground, immaculate restrooms, a grocery with a wine and beer license, and petrol for your thirsty car. (☎ 439 4759. Tent sites $9.50; standard cabins $25 for 2; tourist flats $60-65 for 2; motel units $68 for 2.)

Taking Lighthouse Rd. south from Moeraki leads to the historic Moeraki lighthouse at **Kaitiki Point.** Follow trails from the lighthouse to catch an unobstructed peek at yellow and blue penguins. The point is also a popular fishing location, with anglers pulling in salmon from surf-cast lines. A final remote wildlife viewing opportunity is at **Shag Point**, a rocky promontory home to colonies of the New Zealand fur seal and the Stewart Island shag. To reach the point, follow the clearly-marked gravel road from SH1, about 11km south of the Moeraki Boulders.

THE SOUTHERN LAKES

The Southern Lakes region bellows through valleys and lakes deeply scoured by glaciers. The lure of its call seduces travelers to tempt fate in rash Queenstown or to unwind entirely in calmer Wanaka or in sleepy Glenorchy. Ripe with tremendous tramping, skiing, and adventure-sporting possibilities, the mountains surrounding Lakes Wakatipu and Wanaka allure growing streams of visitors to New Zealand's prime outdoor recreation destination.

QUEENSTOWN ☎ 03

Whether it's a bold daredevil diving off a local bungy, a drunken backpacker howling at the moon, or an awestruck tourist marveling at the sunset over Lake Wakatipu, there's always a faint scream in the air in Queenstown (pop. 14,000). Other Kiwis may denounce Queenstown's rampant consumerism, but the thousands of visitors who pack this outdoor mecca come for good reason—the arresting beauty of the lake and The Remarkables mountain range is undeniable. Linger long enough and the infectious excitement of other travelers will entice you to try the unimaginable, the outrageous, the insane, and, chances are, you'll leave glad for having done it.

TRANSPORTATION

Flights: The **airport** is 6km east of town in Frankton. Take **The Shopper Bus** (☎442 6647) from the McDonald's on Camp St. (every hr. from 7:15am, $3.50) or **Super Shuttle** (☎442 3639 or 0800 727 747; $10). Taxis to the airport are $15. **Air New Zealand** (☎441 1900 or 0800 737 000) has flights to: **Auckland** (3hr., 4-6 per day, from $337) via **Christchurch** (1hr., 4-6 per day, from $170); **Wellington** (2hr., 3-4 per day, from $249). Several airlines do scenic flights to **Milford Sound** (see p. 369).

Buses: InterCity (☎442 2800), departing from Camp St. beside the Visitors Center, **Atomic Shuttles** (☎442 8178), and **Southern Link** (☎358 8355) head to **Christchurch** (7-11hr., 4-5 per day, $45-50) and **Dunedin** (4hr., 4-5 per day, $29-30). **Topline Tours** (☎442 8178) heads to **Te Anau** (2hr.; 1-3 per day; $29, YHA $25) and **Southern Land Travel** (☎442 0099) to **Invercargill** (2¾hr., 8:30am, $38). Atomic Shuttles, InterCity, Southern Link, and **Wanaka Connexions** (☎443 9122) head to **Wanaka** (1¾hr., 4-5 per day, $20-25). Stop by one of Queenstown's many booking centers to compare current rates.

Regional Shuttles: The **Information & Track Centre,** 37 Shotover St. (☎442 9708; open daily 7am-9pm; in winter 7am-8pm), books trips through **Backpacker Express** (☎442 9939) to the **Routeburn** and **Greenstone and Caples Tracks** (1-2hr., 2 per day, $30). They will also book through various companies to **Milford Sound** (5hr., 2 per day, $139) via **Te Anau** (2-3hr., $25-33); and from the end of **Routeburn** to **Milford Sound** and back to **Queenstown** ($149). Open daily 7am-9pm. **Backpacker Express** (☎442 9939) runs shuttles from Queenstown to **Glenorchy** (in summer 8am, on demand in winter; $15).

Ski Shuttles: Ski Shuttle (☎442 8106) runs to: **Cardrona** (1½hr., 1 per day, return $35); **Coronet Peak** (45min., 3 per day, return $25); **The Remarkables** (45min., 3 per day, return

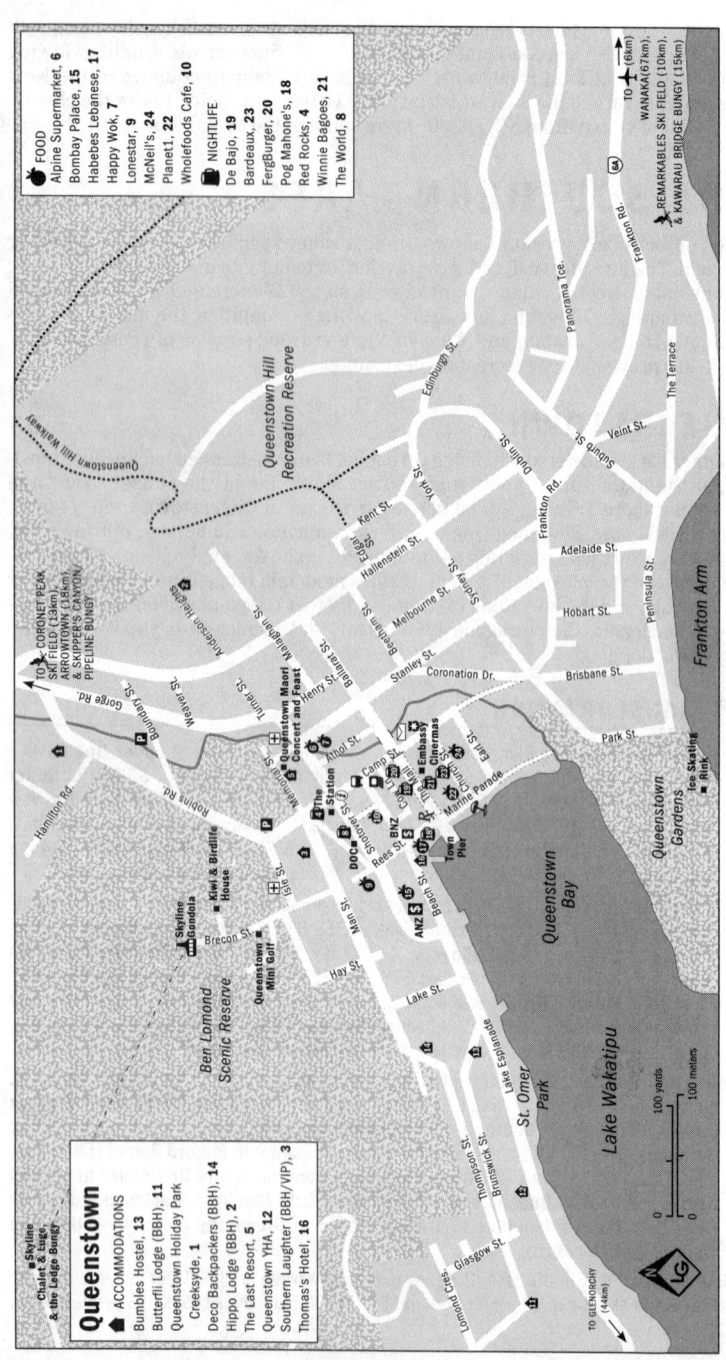

QUEENSTOWN ■ 363

$25); and **Treble Cone** (2hr., return $35). **Ski Link** (☎ 441 8395) offers the same service at comparable prices and is the only shuttle that goes to the night skiing. **AA Alpine Taxis** (☎ 442 6666) runs to Coronet Peak and the Remarkables for $18-25.

Local Buses: The **Shopper Bus** (☎ 442 6647) runs every hr. between most accommodations and the town center, and to **Frankton** and the **airport**. All destinations $3.50.

Taxis: Alpine Taxis (☎ 442 6666) and **Queenstown Taxis** (☎ 442 7788 or 0800 788 294) have **24hr.** service.

Car Rental: Pegasus Rental Cars (☎ 442 7176 or 0800 442 7176), at the top of The Mall, rents cars from $39 per day, with insurance and unlimited mileage for rentals of 4 days or more. Open M-F 9am-6pm, Sa 9am-9pm. **Network Car Rentals**, 34 Shotover St. (☎ 442 7055), has cars from $39 per day plus mileage. Open daily 8am-6pm. **Queenstown Car Rentals,** 26b Shotover St. (☎ 442 9220), has cars from $39 per day and unlimited mileage after 3 days. Open daily 8am-6:30pm. Must be 21 to rent.

Hitchhiking: Thumbers say getting to Glenorchy requires walking along the lake beyond the rotary at One Mile Creek. Hitching to Milford is an unlikely prospect; it involves taking the Shopper Bus to Frankton and walking past the airport along the road to Te Anau.

ORIENTATION

Queenstown's smaller satellite towns include **Glenorchy** (45min.) to the west and **Arrowtown** (30min.) to the northeast. Queenstown itself is very compact. Booking agencies, bars, and gear rental stores line **Shotover Street.** Shopping boutiques and restaurants are concentrated on **Beach Street** and **The Mall,** both of which run parallel to Shotover St. **Cow Lane,** an alleyway between Beach St. and The Mall is a well-kept local secret for nightlife venues. **Beach** and **Rees Streets** both lead to the lakefront. The spine of **The Remarkables** mountain range runs south down the east side of **Lake Wakatipu,** and **Coronet Peak** eyes the lake over the town's north shoulder.

PRACTICAL INFORMATION

Visitors Center: Nearly every shop in town vends its own spin on local information. The official source of info is the **Queenstown Visitor Information Network** (☎ 442 4100 or 0800 668 888; fax 442 8907; www.queenstown-nz.co.nz), at the Clocktower Centre. Open daily 7am-7pm; in winter 7am-6pm.

DOC: 37 Shotover St. (☎ 442 7935; fax 442 7934), has maps and information on local walks and the Great Walks. Open daily 9am-6pm; closed in mid-winter.

Work Opportunities: With extremely high turnovers, Queenstown's bars, restaurants, and accommodations are always looking for staff. Listen for the **Wakatipu Jobline** (☎ 442 7222) on local radio stations and watch for help-wanted ads lining shop windows. **Addstaff,** 22 The Mall (☎ 442 4307), is the local employment agency.

Banks and Currency Exchange: There are **ATMs** and **Bureaux de Changes** all over town. The **Station** (☎ 442 5252), at the corner of Camp and Shotover St., exchanges money at convenient hours. Open daily 10:30am-8:30pm. **BNZ** (☎ 442 5013), on Rees St., has good exchange rates. Its **Bureau de Change** is open M-F 9am-8pm, Sa-Su 10am-8pm. **ANZ Postbank** is on Beach St. near the waterfront. Open M-F 9am-4:30pm.

Ski and Snowboard Rental: Brown's, 39 Shotover St. (☎ 442 4003; www.brown-snz.com), has the best skis. Ski, boot, and pole hire $36 per day. Open May-Oct. daily 7:30am-9pm. **S & C,** 45 Camp St. (☎ 442 9330; www.snowboarder.co.nz), offers the best snowboards. Snowboard and boot hire $45 per day. Open daily 7:30am-9pm; shorter hours in summer. **Outside Sports & Doctor Bike** (☎ 442 8883; www.outside-sports.co.nz), at the top of the Mall, has a wide selection. Ski, boot, and pole hire $35 per day; snowboard and boot hire $45. Open daily 7am-10pm; in summer 8am-10pm.

Tramping Gear: Alpine Sports, 28 Shotover St. (☎442 7099; www.alpinesports.co.nz), rents the least expensive tramping gear in town. Tents $10 per day, packs $5 per day, sleeping bag with liner $5 per day. Open daily 10:30am-8:30pm. The **Information & Track Centre** rents packs and bags for $1 more but not tents (see **Regional Shuttles,** p. 361). **Outside Sports & Doctor Bike** (see **Ski and Snowboard Rental,** above) stocks an extensive selection of tramping gear for sale. They also rent mountain bikes (half-day $30, full-day $50). **Small Planet Sports,** 17 Shotover St. (☎442 6393), sells high-quality used tramping gear at bargain prices. Open daily 9am-6pm; in winter 7:30am-9pm.

Police: 11 Camp St. (☎442 7900).

Medical Services: Wilkinson's Pharmacy (☎442 7313), on Rees St., at the foot of The Mall. Open daily 8:30am-10pm; in winter daily 8:30am-9pm. The **Queenstown Medical Centre,** 9 Isle St. (☎441 0500).

Internet Access: Budget Communications, O'Connell's Mall, 2nd fl. (☎441 1562), for $5 per hr. Daily specials 9-11am and 9-11pm cost $3 per hr. Open daily 9am-11pm.

Post Office: (☎442 7670), at the corner of Camp and Ballarat St. Open M-F 8:30am-8pm, Sa 9am-8pm, Su 10am-6pm.

ACCOMMODATIONS AND CAMPING

Catering to honeymooners and broke ski bums alike, Queenstown has a staggering array of places to stay, with B&Bs and hostels springing up endlessly to meet the ever-expanding tourist demand. Backpackers in town fit neatly into two distinct categories: those that cater to the hard-partying, thrill-seeking crowd and those that seek to avoid it.

■ **Bumbles Hostel,** 2 Brunswick St. (☎442 6298 or 0800 428 625). From the Visitors Center, walk left down Beach St. to the lakeside; Bumbles faces the water at Brunswick St. and Lake Esplanade. Lake-view balconies, superb garden BBQ set-up, heated storage in winter, and mini-kitchens in each suite make this long-standing hostel an excellent choice. Laundry. Linen $1. Luggage storage $2. Reception 7:30am-8pm. Dorms $18; twin bunks $40; twins and doubles with linen $45. ❷

■ **Butterfli Lodge (BBH),** 67 Thompson St. (☎/fax 442 6367; jackiebutterfli@xtra.co.nz). This small lodge wows backpackers with fantastic lake-view doubles and actual beds in its dorm room. The modern showers and high-tech entertainment center ice the cake. Internet. Laundry. Dorms $20; twins and doubles $55. ❷

Deco Backpackers (BBH), 52 Man St. (☎442 7384; fax 442 6258; www.decobackpackers.co.nz). From the Visitors Center, walk left up Camp St., take a left on Man St. Spread between 2 buildings—one a 1950s Art Deco bungalow—this backpackers offers 2 kitchens, 2 TV lounges, and an excellent lake-view picnic area. Sturdy bunks with real mattresses soothe adrenaline-buzzed backpackers. Reception 8am-2pm and 4-8pm. Dorms $18; twins and doubles $44; tent sites (summer only) $12. ❷

Hippo Lodge (BBH), 4 Anderson Heights (☎442 5785; fax 442 5669; www.hippolodge.co.nz). A 15-20min. climb leads to this hilltop lodge, with the best view of any backpackers in Queenstown. Couples traveling by car should inquire about the **Hippo Hideaway,** a snug retreat at Arthur's Point. Internet. Laundry. Reception 8:30am-1pm and 3-8pm. Dorms $20; twins and doubles $50; tent sites (summer only) $13. ❷

Southern Laughter (BBH/VIP), 4 Isle St. (☎441 8828 or 0800 528 4483; fax 441 8834). Far Side cartoons and a collection of zany flotsam and jetsom bedeck the walls of this chuckle-inducing backpackers. Many of the dorm rooms are mini-suites with TVs and kitchenettes. Internet. Laundry. Pool table. Spa. Reception 8am-9pm. Dorms $19-22; doubles $46-48. ❷

Thomas's Hotel (VIP), 50 Beach St. (☎442 7180; fax 441 8417; www.thomashotel.co.nz). Go left down Shotover St., take the first left on Rees St., then the first right. This hotel is named after the gluttonous and aged tabby that seems to run the place. On-site cafe, TV in each immense dorm room. Kayak rental. Reception 6:30am-9:30pm. Dorms from $19; hotel singles $79; twins and doubles $70-109; triples $104. ❷

Pinewood Lodge, 48 Hamilton Rd. (☎442 8273 or 0800 746 396; fax 442 9470; www.pinewood.co.nz). From the Visitors Center, head left up Camp St., follow Robins Rd. around to the right, and then make a left on Hamilton. A separate village within Queenstown; up to 330 guests enjoy the expansive grounds. Spa, BBQ, trampoline, darts, 8-ball. Bike rental. Free pick-up. Laundry. Reception 6:30am-10pm. Dorms $18; twins and doubles $45-55; self-contained units from $90. Wheelchair accessible. ❷

Queenstown YHA, 88-90 Lake Esplanade (☎442 8413; fax 442 6561; yhaqutn@yha.org.nz), left down Shotover St. along the lakefront away from town. This flagship YHA is a 152-bed tourist-housing machine. The friendly staff will make adventure bookings with discounts. Internet. Laundry. Reception 6:30am-10pm. Reservations recommended. Dorms $23; twins and doubles $47-55; family rooms $63. ❸

The Last Resort, 6 Memorial St. (☎442 4320; fax 442 4330). From Beach St., walk one block up Camp St., past the Station, and turn right on Memorial St. Within stumbling distance of the bars, this small hostel has a warm feel and an extensive video collection for rainy days. Free towels and linens. Reception at staff's leisure. 4-bed dorms $20. ❷

Queenstown Holiday Park Creeksyde, 54 Robins Rd. (☎442 9447; fax 442 6621; www.camp.co.nz). Go up Camp St., and take a right on Robins Rd. Willows and a burbling brook surround grassy sites. Each unit showcases a different antique organ, a collecting passion of the owner. Internet. Laundry. Linen $5. Reception 7am-9:30pm; in winter 8am-8pm. Lodges $43-48 for 2; ensuite cabins $65-68, extra person $13; tent and powered sites $15. ❷

FOOD

Backpackers shouldn't have to look far to find a good crumb at a low price. Several of Queenstown's Japanese restaurants are engaged in a lunchtime sushi price-war: locals concur that the small stand, **Planet1** ❶, on Rees St. at the lakefront, has the freshest fish in town (8-piece maki $5; open daily M-F 11am-9pm, Sa noon-8pm). For dining out, stroll down to **The Mall, Beech Street,** or the waterfront. **Alpine Supermarket,** on upper Shotover St., is the most centrally located supermarket (☎442 8961; open M-F 8am-8pm, Sa-Su 9am-8pm), but **Fresh Choice,** on Gorge St., has a better selection (☎441 1252; open daily 8am-9pm).

Habebes Lebanese (☎442 9861), in the Wakatipu Arcade, accessible from both Beech and Rees St. Add your choice of tabouli and salads to the scrumptious lamb, chicken, or falafel pita ($5-10) and relish the tickle of the tahini trickling down your chin. The apricot orgasm ($2.50) delivers as promised. Open daily 11am-5:30pm. ❷

Happy Wok, 8 Shotover St. (☎442 4415), facing the parking lot of Alpine Supermarket. Pad Thai and curry dishes ($9.50-13) taste splendid with a BYO ($2 per person) wine from the supermarket. Check out the extra-terrestrial restroom. Open daily 5-10pm. ❷

Wholefoods Cafe (☎442 8991), in the Plaza Arcade connecting Shotover and Beach St. Veggie-friendly delights like refried bean enchiladas ($6.50) will please your hungry stomach and your nagging conscience. Used books for sale. Open daily 8am-5pm. ❷

McNeil's (☎442 9688), on Church St. Set in a historic 1890s home, this is the only place in town that brews its own beer. A full-bodied ale ($4.50) and a hearty pasta ($12-16) by the raging fire are the perfect cap to a long day on the slopes. Open daily 11am-2:30am. ❸

FROM THE ROAD

THE RITES OF LATEX

Queenstown is the bungy Mecca, the birthplace of the commercial bungy jump, and the site to which all adventure-seekers journey. As I stood peering down the 43m drop to the Kawarau River, I found myself an unlikely pilgrim. Not an adrenaline addict by any stretch of the imagination, I was just a journalist thrust into the role of bungy connoisseur. Growing up, my father feared riding the kiddy-gondola at the local amusement park—acrophobia is probably in my genes. Yet, somehow I'd been coaxed into a reckless bout of three bungy jumps in a single afternoon.

I hadn't planned on bungy jumping in Queenstown, figuring that press packs and accounts by fellow, braver travelers would suffice for research. The thought of testing the stretch of a length of latex with my own weight never really appealed to me—it seemed like a cheap thrill, an unearned rush. What's more, jumpers are generally tied around the ankles, cruelly converted into submissive penguins as they waddle up to the edge. A bit like walking the plank, and certainly not for me. Yes, I considered myself above the bungy. The marketing directors of the two Queenstown bungy rivals certainly didn't. Within moments of stepping into their offices to ask for press packs, I found myself signed up for every jump in town.

As I moved to the edge for my first jump, I was calm and composed. I'd just watched a timid crew of teenage Japanese girls do the jump, and I wasn't about to be fazed.

Lonestar, 14 Brecon St. (☎442 9995), offers a Kiwi take on the American West. The food comes in anatomically impossible helpings and the locals rave and rave. Ask for a ¾ portion—for $18.50, mains like Dixie Chicken and the Southwest Burrito are slightly more manageable. Open daily 5-11pm; bar open 4pm-2:30am. ❹

Bombay Palace, 66 Shotover St. (☎441 2886). A local favorite for cheap and tasty Indian food (mains $13-16), Bombay covers the basics with simple elegance. Early birds benefit from a $30 four-course meal for 2 (5-7pm). Open daily 5-10pm. ❸

🎵 🎭 ENTERTAINMENT& NIGHTLIFE

Queenstown's concentrated nightlife rocks with backpackers fresh off the slopes and bungy cords and activity operators who just can't get enough madness. For a quieter evening, **movies** are shown in the **Embassy Cinemas,** 11 The Mall. (Movieline ☎442 9990. $11, students $8; before 5pm $8.) An excellent start to any evening, the buffet dinner (with unlimited hokey pokey ice cream) and interactive performance at the 🎭**Queenstown Maori Concert and Feast,** on Memorial St., provide an enjoyable introduction to Maori traditions in food, culture, and unsurpassable hospitality. (☎442 8878. Dining 7-8:30pm, concert 8:30-9:30pm. $45, children $25.) Relieve the munchies late into the night at **Fergburger** ❷, on Cow Ln., a back-alley grill that serves burgers ($8-15) legendary for their behemoth size and their divine garlic mayonnaise. (☎441 1232. Open daily 5pm-5am).

🎭 **The World,** 27 Shotover St. (☎442 5714). Other bars have big nights but The World never stops spinning. Backpackers flock here for early drinks, cheap meals, and hard partying. Cut to the chase with one of their distinctive shakers ($15), all served in a teapot. DJs daily from 10:30pm. Arcade games and pool tables downstairs. Drink specials 5-8pm ($2 handles) and 10:30-11:30pm. Open daily 4pm-2:30am.

🎭 **Pog Mahone's,** 14 Rees St. (☎442 5382). A classy Irish pub where you can sit outside on the patio or the balcony for a view of Lake Wakatipu and the Eyre Mountains. If anyone asks you where you're going, just say "Kiss my ass!" (that's what Pog Mahone means in Irish). Live music most nights from 9:30pm. Open daily noon-2:30am.

De Bajo (☎442 6099), on Cow Ln. House beats rattle the liquor-rack Jesus figurine in this tapas lounge bar. The crowd comes in late and packs the leather sofas until sunrise. Cocktail hour 8-11pm. Th Havana night. Bottled beers $4-6. Open daily 5pm-5am.

Winnie Bagoes (☎442 8635), in the heart of The Mall. A balcony and a retractable roof cool off the steaming 20-something crowd. Happy Hour with $2 handles (6-7pm and 9-10pm). Open daily noon-2:30am.

Bardeaux (☎442 8284), just off The Mall. This upmarket lounge bar crafts an intimate scene with a blazing fire and plush leather sofas. Sink into wine (glasses from $8.50) and conversation with the après-ski crowd. Open daily 5pm-5am.

Red Rocks (☎442 6850), at the corner of Camp and Man St. Backpackers pre-party here before hitting The World, while grizzled outdoor operators share an after-work drink. As advertised, there's always free beer tomorrow, but today it'll cost you $4 for a handle. Happy Hour 7-8pm. Open daily noon-2:30am.

OUTDOOR ACTIVITIES

Queenstown is renowned for its heart-stopping thrills and breathtaking scenery; if you want to dive, ride, jump, saunter, float, dart, or glide through a spectacular setting, this is the place to be.

PLANNING

Budgeting for Queenstown activities requires either a magically expanding bank account or the mental resolve to watch your savings dwindle. For **cheaper activities**, we recommend frisbee golf at the **Queenstown Gardens** (maps and scorecards available at **Outside Sports**, at the top of The Mall, for $2), the luge, gold panning in Arrowtown, hiking the Ben Lomond or Queenstown Hill, ice skating, and a 4WD trip into Skippers Canyon. To maximize your money, consider buying a **pre-packaged** combo which can save you up to $100 on the more expensive activities. Combos comprise anywhere from two to five activities including helicopter flights, bungy jumps, jetboat rides, 4WD tours, and rafting trips. One of the best deals is the **Skippers Grand Slam** (see below).

There are many other combos available at booking agencies. **The Station,** at Shotover and Camp St., is gigantic; many activities depart from there. (☎442 5252. Open daily 7am-9pm; in winter 8am-8pm.) **The Information and Track Centre** is geared to backpackers and very well-informed about transport to local tracks and ski fields, tramping conditions and outfitting, and the major Queenstown activities. (See **Regional Shuttles,** p. 361.)

As far as numbers go, bungy ranks safer than flying in a plane, driving a car, or even crossing the street. I convinced myself that there was no real cause for concern. If I was going to bungy, I was going to do so with the sang-froid of a professional, no screaming or flailing limbs to betray my icy coolness.

And then, as instructed, I jumped like Superman, head first with arms and legs spread wide. For the few seconds of free-fall, I completely lost it: my arms swam desperately through the air and my vocal chords locked into a girlish squeal. No amount of self-mastery can control the body's reaction to the sensation of falling to death. I found it impossible to remember that I was attached to a bungy as I fell headlong towards the sparkling blue water below. The chord, however, didn't forget, and after rebounding first one, then two, and then three times, I settled into a still hang. Quickly taking inventory of my bodily functions, I realized that I had escaped the embarrassment of crapping on myself from fear (a fate that occasionally afflicts first-time jumpers). Whew, thank goodness for that. I may have lost my cool, but at least I was unsoiled.

Bungy jumping was a blast, a full-bodied, full-on rush unlike any other—height-fearing genes and journalistic composure be damned. As I was lowered onto the capture raft, I was pumped to jump again. And again. And again. Bring bungy on; this writer isn't afraid.

Really, I swear I'm not.

—Mark Kirby

BUNGY JUMPING

PIPELINE BUNGY. Opened in 1994 with the promise of the highest jump, Pipeline wooed a skeptical Queenstown with its 102m plunge from a restored pipeline bridge over Skippers Canyon. In a stunningly scenic and historic gold-mining locale on the Shotover River, Pipeline offers activities in and around the canyon. The ◾**Skippers Grand Slam** package includes jetboating, bungy jumping, 4W driving, and zipping over the canyon on the flying fox wire. *(27 Shotover St., next door to AJ Hackett.* ☎ *442 5455 or 0800 286 491; www.bungy.co.nz. Skippers Canyon $150, including 4WD transport along the road to the bridge and humorous commentary along the way. Grand Slam $255, including t-shirt.)*

AJ HACKETT. The original name in bungy now operates three Queenstown jump sites and sells its own line of thrill-seeker apparel. **The Ledge,** at the top of the gondola, may be the most unique jump—instead of being tied at the ankles, a waist-harness allows you to run and hurtle yourself over the 47m fall towards the twinkling lights of Queenstown. The 43m **Kawarau Bridge,** the world's first bungy bridge, can submerse you in the river below. The newest addition to Hackett's bungy madness is the ◾ **Nevis Highwire Bungy,** the country's highest at 134m. Operating from a mostly glass gondola suspended by wire cables between two mountains over a canyon, it's almost impossible to avoid looking down, so enjoy the sweet and anxious anticipation. Or, sample all three jumps with Hackett's **Bungy Thrillogy.** *(Office in the Station.* ☎ *442 7100 or 0800 286 492; www.ajhackett.com. The Ledge $125, including gondola ride and t-shirt. Open daily 3-9pm. Kawarau Bridge $125, including transport and t-shirt. Nevis Highwire $184, including transport and t-shirt. Thrillogy $249. Open daily 8am-8pm; in winter 8am-7pm.)*

JETBOATING

SKIPPERS CANYON JET. This trip combines history, breathtaking river scenery, and thrills as it cruises 16km past the precipitous walls of the old gold-mining canyon, under suspension bridges, and past abandoned pioneer settlements. Combo deals with a bungy jump are available. *(Run by Pipeline Bungy. $99, including transport from the Pipeline Bungy office on Shotover St., a guided tour of the museum, and gold-panning.)*

KAWARAU JET. The yellow-boat company initiated the jetboating craze in 1960, speeding eager vacationers down the Kawarau River. Their two-river trips last twice as long as other operators but are restricted to the lower reaches of the Shotover River and lack the narrow-canyon thrill. *(On the lakefront.* ☎ *442 6142 or 0800 527 292. Trips depart every hr. $69, children $39.)*

SHOTOVER JET. Less personal, Shotover is the most popular and the only company with the rights to what some would argue is the most daring stretch of canyon to boat. Skimming impossibly close to the rock walls and over waters as shallow as 10cm, the speedboats swivel and twist at 70kph. *(Pick-up from The Station every 30min.; otherwise, drive 15min. up the road toward Arrowtown to Arthur's Point.* ☎ *442 8570 or 0800 746 868; www.shotoverjet.co.nz. $79, children $39. YHA 10% discount. Combinations with scenic helicopter ride and skyline gondola, movie, and luge, $159.)* Shotover also runs ◾**Dart River Jet Safaris** *(*☎ *442 9992),* which offers more remote trips through the river valleys north of Glenorchy (see **Outdoor Activities,** p. 374).

RAFTING AND RIVER SPORTS

RAFTING. Although New Zealand is not known for world-class rapids, novice rafters will certainly be thrilled. The Shotover has more consistent Class 4 rapids and rides through the man-made 170m Oxenbridge Tunnel, but the Kawarau has a few wild sections (including the 400m Chinese Dog Leg, New Zealand's longest commercial whitewater segment). **Queenstown Rafting** *(*☎ *442 9792; www.raft-*

ing.co.nz), **Extreme Green Rafting** (☎ 442 8517; www.extremegreenrafting.com), and **Challenge Rafting** run half-day trips on the Shotover and Kawarau mornings and afternoons (☎ 442 7318; www.raft.co.nz; $109-129). For $119, **Serious Fun River Surfing** (☎ 442 5262 or 0800 737 4687) and **Mad Dog River Boarding** (☎ 442 7797) both lead audacious hydrophiles to boogie board the rapids on the Kawarau River. Advance instruction provides basic technique, but once you hit the rapids, you're on your own. Quality and availability of all trips depends on water levels in the rivers.

CANYONING. Routeburn Canyoning Ltd. and **Queenstown Canyoning** lead thrilling canyoning trips, which plunge into pools, rappel into ravines, and slide down chutes (not for those with fears of heights, water, or very hard rocks). The two companies share the same owners but run separately, leading two trips: a shorter, less expensive adventure at **12-Mile Delta** and a longer journey down scenic ■**Routeburn Canyon.** (☎ 442 3315 or 0800 222 696; www.xiimile.co.nz. *12-mile Delta $120, Routeburn Canyon $189. Min. age 16. Summer only.*)

SKYDIVING AND OTHER AERIAL ACTIVITIES

SKYDIVING. If the scenery looks beautiful from the waterfront, imagine what it looks like speeding towards you from 12,000ft. **NZONE** will pick you up, fly you to between 9000 and 15,000ft., drop you tandem until you reach your terminal velocity, and then let you float down between Lake Wakatipu and The Remarkables. (☎ 442 5867; www.skydivequeenstown.co.nz. *9000ft. $245, 12,000ft. $295, 15,000ft. $395.*)

SCENIC FLIGHTS. For slower aerial sightseeing, **Air Wakatipu** runs 20min. flights of the scenic and acrobatic varieties. (☎ 442 3148; www.flying.co.nz. *Scenic flight $59, acrobatic flight $104.*) **The Helicopter Line** has 20min. Remarkables trips. (☎ 442 3034 or 0800 500 575; www.new-zealand.com/thl. *$160, including a snow landing in winter.*) **Over The Top** has 20min. flights over The Remarkables, a longer 40min. flight with snow landing, and more expensive options to Milford or to remote rivers for fly fishing. (☎ 442 2233 or 0800 123 359; www.flynz.co.nz. *20min. from $99, 40min. $175.*) Several airlines do scenic flights to **Milford Sound** (*40min.; 2 per day; $215, standby $95, with cruise $245-279*), including **Air Fiordland** (☎ 442 3404; www.airfiordland.co.nz), **Milford Sound Scenic Flights** (☎ 442 3065; www.milfordflights.co.nz), and **Glenorchy Air** (☎ 442 2207; www.glenorchy.net.nz).

ZIPLINES. If you've ever imagined the thrills and perils of being strapped to a powerful engine, be sure to check out **Fly by Wire**, a missile-like personal craft equipped with a **60hp** light aircraft engine that hurtles its solo passenger to speeds topping 160kph. (☎ 442 2116 or 0800 359 299; www.flybywire.co.nz. *$145.*) If you're at Skippers Canyon and feel like a tame warm-up for your bungy jump, try the **Flying Fox,** a 250m zipline that reaches speeds of 70kph. (*Run by Pipeline Bungy; various packages are available. Flying Fox $75.*)

OTHER AERIAL ACTIVITIES. Aerophiles should try **paragliding:** a relaxing, exhilarating tandem ride from above the Skyline Gondola over Queenstown. Various companies at the top charge roughly $160 for about 10min. in the air. Try **Cloud Nine Tandem Paragliding,** a scenic glide from the top of the gondola above Queenstown, run by Tim, one of the owners of Deco Backpackers. (☎ 442 6289 or 025 326 732. *$170, including transport and a roll of film.*) For a faster, wilder ride, try **Sky Trek Tandem Hang Gliding,** a 15-25min. flight from Coronet Peak or The Remarkables (☎ 442 6311; *$155*), or ■**AntiGravity Hang Gliding** (☎ 441 8988 or 0800 426 445; www.antigravity.co.nz; *$160*), whose tandem fliers have set national records and won international flying competitions. **Paraflights** attaches you to a boat and lifts you to more than 300ft. as you cruise around Lake Wakatipu on a 10min. flight. (☎ 442 8507. *$75, tandem $65 per person.*)

ON THE SLOPES

From June to September, **skiing** and **snowboarding** take over Queenstown as enthusiasts flock to **Coronet Peak** and **The Remarkables**. Lift passes and transport are cheaper in town, particularly when part of a package. An ISIC card is not valid for student deals; another **student ID** is necessary. Roads to the mountains usually require chains; shuttles are a safer option. (See **Transportation,** p. 361) If you plan on skiing for a number of days or in a number of locations, you may wish to consider the **NZ Superpass** (see p. 317). If you're planning in advance to spend a ski season in Queenstown, consider purchasing a **Season Ski Pass** early—buying passes before April can save as much as $800. For more details, check www.nzski.com or stop by the ski desk in The Station.

CORONET PEAK. New Zealand's first commercial ski area (est. 1947), Coronet Peak (1650m; vertical rise 450m) is still popular today—in fact, the slopes are often uncomfortably crowded on weekends. Bigger and closer to Queenstown, Coronet has a longer season than the Remarkables, offers weekend night-skiing (a great budget deal), and contains two half-pipes and a terrain park with jumps and tabletops. Its slopes are suitable for all levels of skiers and boarders, particularly intermediate skiers. *(Office in The Station: ☎ 442 4620. Lift pass $70, students $58, children $36. Night-skiing lift pass valid F-Sa 4-10pm $36, children $25. Half-day rates available.)*

THE REMARKABLES. The Remarkables (1935m; vertical rise 360m) tries to resist the commercialized glitz of the Queenstown area but is still hugely popular. It usually has better snow conditions than Coronet, a wider beginner area, a greater range of off-piste extreme terrain, and more sun. Its slopes cater to skiers and snowboarders of all skill levels as well as to cross-country skiers. *(Office in The Station: ☎ 442 4615. Lift pass $68, students $50, children $34.)*

FARTHER AFIELD. Although Wanaka is more conveniently situated, skiers and snowboarders frequently stay in Queenstown and catch morning shuttles to **Cardrona** or make the longer drive to **Treble Cone**. (For more information on both ski fields, see **Wanaka: Outdoor Activities,** p. 383.)

HELISKIING. Heliskiing trips depart for the extreme, untouched powders of the Southern Alps, especially the chutes and bowls of the Harris Mountains, Mt. Aspiring, and Mt. Cook. **Southern Lakes Heliski** *(☎ 442 6222; www.southernlakesheliski.co.nz)*, **Over the Top** *(☎ 442 7733 or 0800 435 4754; www.flynz.co.nz)*, **Mt. Aspiring Guides** *(☎ 443 9422; www.mtaspiringguides.co.nz)*, and **Harris Mountains Heli-Ski** *(☎ 442 6722; www.heliski.co.nz)* have offices in Queenstown or Wanaka. All provide transport, experienced guides, powder ski rental, and mountain equipment. Prices range from $650-750 for three-run daytrips.

OFF-ROAD

4WD TOURS. The rock walls and precipitous road through **Skippers Canyon**, constructed during the gold-rush days, now attract 4WD tours that give the fantastic drive a historical perspective. **Skippers Grand Canyon Ltd.** will take you on the rugged, windy road into the canyon, stopping at historic sights and pausing for a stately tea. *(Run by Pipeline Bungy. 3-4hr., 3 per day, 4WD tours $59-199. Ask about various combos.)* **Nomad Safaris** guides morning and afternoon tours into Skippers Canyon and up to the mining settlements of Macetown and Seffertown. All tours include refreshments and gold panning. *(☎ 442 6699; www.outback.net.nz. Skippers Canyon 4hr.; $85, children $59. Macetown 4½hr.; $85, children $59.)*

BIKING. In the summer, **Gravity Action** runs half-day **mountain biking trips** to the canyon twice daily; they drive you (or helicopter you for $50 more) up to Skipper's saddle and Coronet Peak, let you coast down through creeks and over gravel, and give you a beer at the end. (☎441 1021; www.skitransport.com. $69; various Pipeline Bungy activities available for add-on.) Wild, off-road motorbike and ATV treks through the canyon and elsewhere are available through **Offroad Adventures**. (☎442 7858 or 442 9196; www.offroad.co.nz. 3hr. $199.) One especially good trip on your own is the 20km ride past Lake Hayes to Arrowtown, where you can stop to check out the historic Chinese settlement, pan for gold, or continue up the rugged 13km 4WD track to Macetown. (Rides start 12-15km out of Queenstown toward Glenorchy.)

ON THE LAKE

T.S.S. EARNSLAW. For decades, steamships were the sole form of transport across the lake to Glenorchy and to the area's various sheep stations. Today, only the revamped **T.S.S. Earnslaw** remains. While the lake traverse is tradition, the 10am, noon, 2, and 4pm ■**farm cruises to Walter Peak** with scrumptious afternoon tea are highlights. Once there, you can watch sheep shearing and a sheep dog demonstration, ride Duncan the Highland Bull, or enjoy a horse trek. The pricey dinner cruise involves a lamb and pavlova dinner followed by a rollicking farm show. (Cruises depart from the Steamer Wharf at the end of Shotover St. ☎442 7500 or 0800 656 503; www.fiordlandtravel.co.nz. Wakatipu cruise $34, children $15. Walter Peak cruise $52, children $15. Horse treks $49, only in summer. Dinner cruise 6pm; $88, children $44.)

OTHER ACTIVITIES. The lake comes alive in summer with **waterskiing, jetboating, fishing**, and **water taxis** to secluded picnic spots—just ask at any booking office.

WALKS AND HORSE TREKS

The DOC office and the Information and Track Centre next door sell a handy guide, *Wandering in the Wakatipu* ($6), which details walks in and around the Queenstown-Arrowtown-Glenorchy area. Shorter tracks on the way to Glenorchy offer less-trodden native forest experiences (some suitable for mountain biking or trail running). Trailheads are clearly marked along the road.

BEN LOMOND. One of the most difficult and rewarding treks is the climb to the top of ■**Ben Lomond**. Mt. Aspiring and an entire panorama of peaks can be seen from the steep summit on a clear day. (Check weather conditions with DOC before tramping. Return 6-8hr., just to saddle 3-4 hr.)

QUEENSTOWN HILL TIME WALK. A less arduous climb leads you through thick forest to the peak of Te Tapunui, where you can enjoy a breathtaking 360° view of The Remarkables, Cecil Peak, and Lake Wakatipu. (To get to the trailhead follow The Mall away from the Lake until you reach Hallenstein St., turn right, then left onto York St.; the trailhead is on the left side half a block past Kent St. Return 2-3hr.)

HORSE TREKS. A few stables operate in the valleys surrounding Queenstown and include trips through farmland, foothills, and mountain tracks. Full-day trips are by request and are only available in the summer. **Moonlight Stables** provides transportation and afternoon fishing. (☎442 1229; www.moonlightcountry.co.nz. 1½hr. $55, including transport.) **Shotover Stables** rides near Shotover canyon and books trips through the Information and Track Centre. (☎442 9708. 1¾hr. $55.)

OTHER SIGHTS AND ACTIVITIES

ABOVE QUEENSTOWN. The **Skyline Gondola** goes up to the Skyline restaurant ($36 for a fine-dining buffet splurge) and pricey bar for panoramic views of the lake and mountains. (☎441 0101; www.skyline.co.nz. Open daily 9am-9pm. $7, return $14.) Better yet, walk the **One Mile Creek Trail** (1hr. uphill), which starts along the lakefront toward Glenorchy, past the YHA, and passes through a canyon and pine forest to Skyline (where you can catch the gondola down). At the top, watch **Kiwi Magic**, a

30min. surround-sound visual experience about a bumbling American exploring New Zealand with a happy-go-lucky tour guide. *($8, students $6, children $4.)* By the top of the gondola, the **Skyline Luge** may look tame, but its sharp turns and steep straightaways are exciting when you're racing in a plastic cart. *($4.50 per ride; 5 rides $16, with return gondola $26. Open daylight hours in peak summer season.)*

KIWI AND BIRDLIFE PARK. The complex includes a nocturnal kiwi house, a range of native parakeets and ducks, and two of the world's rarest birds—the head-bobbing **black stilt** *(kaki)* and the **Campbell Island Teal.** Proceeds support captive breeding programs. *(At the base of the gondola. ☎ 442 8059; www.kiwibird.co.nz. Open daily 9am-7pm; in winter 9am-5pm. $12, children $4.50.)*

CLIMBING. Mountain Works runs introductory rock climbing courses in the summer, beginning ice-climbing in the winter, and multi-day guided ascents. *(17 Shotover St. ☎ 442 7329 or 0508 786 648; www.mountainworks.co.nz. Rock climbing from $195.)* **Independent Mountain Guides** also offers instruction in rock and ice climbing and can lead you on a full-day traverse of The Remarkables or snow-shoed climbs surrounding Queenstown. *(☎ 442 3381; www.independentmountainguides.co.nz. Rock climbing from $175, ice from $350.)* For a less intense but still personally challenging afternoon, try **Live Wire,** an adventure ropes course with a suspended climbing wall and a trapeze. *(☎ 0508 5483 9473; www.livewirenz.com. $80, including transport.)*

WINE TOURS. The dry mountainous terrain surrounding Queenstown produces some hearty varieties of grapes. A growing number of tour operators offer tours of local wineries as a sophisticated alternative to the standard adrenaline fix (although wine and jetboat and wine and bungy packages are available for the devoted combo-junkie). **It's Wine Time** guides small group tours of the area's wineries. *(☎ 0508 946 384; www.winetime.co.nz. $59, with lunch $89.)*

OTHER ACTIVITIES. At the end of the boardwalk, secluded views of the lake can be seen from the **Queenstown Gardens.** With a track looping out onto the peninsula, fitness stations scattered along the path, and an excellent frisbee golf course, the gardens will cure the adrenaline-induced turbidity in your soul and shrink the beer-born expansion in your gut. There's ice skating at the **Fun Centre,** inside the Gardens. *(☎ 441 8000. $12, children $7.50; skate rental $3.)* Within chirping distance of the birdpark, **Queenstown Mini Golf** is a good and affordable family activity. Play your best to vie for a spot on the chalkboard tally of top scores from different nations. *(28 Brecon St. ☎ 442 7652. Open daily 9:30am-late. $7, children $5.)*

ARROWTOWN

☎ 03

William Fox and a small band of miners pulled some 230 pounds of gold from the Arrow River in 1862, precipitating the development of Arrowtown and its satellite towns. Today, Arrowtown is a daytrip destination that continues in its gilded heritage with rows of classy cafes, upmarket restaurants, and pricey retailers lining its downtown thoroughfare, **Buckingham Street.** To access Arrowtown, the **Arrow Express** runs from outside the McCafe in **Queenstown** to outside the museum in Arrowtown. *(☎ 442 1900. 25min.; 5 per day; $10, return $18.)* **The Double Decker Bus** also runs 3hr. sightseeing trips from Queenstown via Lake Hayes and the Bungy Bridge to Arrowtown. *(☎ 442 6067. Departs 10am and 2pm, return $27.)* The **Lakes District Museum** has impressive exhibits and simultaneously serves as a **Visitors Center** for local information and bookings. Pick up explanatory brochures and local trail maps here. *(☎ 442 1824. Open daily 9am-5pm. Museum $5, children 50¢.)* For travelers staying in Arrowtown overnight, **Riverdown ❷,** on Bedford St., is a boutique backpackers set in a charming character home. *(☎ 409 8499. Dorms $20; doubles $50.)*

For a cultural diversion, **Dorothy Brown's Cinema**, on Buckingham St. behind Saffron restaurant, specializes in art house and foreign films, and serves food and drink during intermission. (☎ 442 1968; www.dorothybrowns.com. Reservations recommended. Open Th-Su. $15, students and seniors $10, children $5.) At the end of Buckingham St. is the historic **Chinese Settlement,** a series of mud-walled huts and signs that give a brief explanation of the former inhabitants and their lifestyle. A 9-ouncer and other special nuggets sit in a case at **The Gold Shop**, 29 Buckingham St. (☎ 442 1319. Open daily 8:30am-5:30pm.) If you've caught gold fever and don't want to leave Arrowtown without a little adventure and some gold to boot, you can join up with one of the **Golden Fox Tours**. These 1½hr. tours explain the history of the Chinese settlement, followed by some gold panning. (☎ 442 1432 or 025 416 083; http://goldenfox-tours.tripod.com. $40, children $20. Longer tours available; call ahead for reservations. Oct.-Apr. only.) Arrowtown comes to life in April with the brilliant colors of the changing trees and the annual **Autumn Festival** (last weekend of March), complete with a parade, live music, and street performers.

Several walking and mountain biking **tracks** depart from the settlement, though they can be very slippery in winter. (The museum/Visitors Center has information, though most tracks are sign-posted from the Macetown Rd. out of town.) **Arrowtown Lodge** leads guided historical and nature walks. (☎ 442 1101. $60-120.) **Macetown Road** is a rigorous 13km track upriver to another ghost town, along which many tracks begin and end. Ask for a map at the Visitors Center, or take a 4WD tour with **NOMAD Safaris**. (☎ 442 6699; www.outback.net.nz. $65-85. Summer only.)

GLENORCHY ☎ 03

Surrounded by frosty peaks reflected in the head of Lake Wakatipu's azure waters, Glenorchy (pop. 200) sits in a magical setting 48km north of Queenstown, where **Fiordland National Park** (see p. 406) and **Mt. Aspiring National Park** (see p. 386) meet. The area's majestic mountains and primordial forests became Middle Earth for several scenes in *Lord of the Rings* and locals are quick to boast of their roles as extras. The tiny pastoral community is encircled by sheep and cattle stations and summer hikers eager to undertake the **Routeburn Track** (see p. 375), **Greenstone and Caples Tracks** (see p. 377), the **Rees-Dart Track** (see p. 386), or one of the shorter, but celebrated, valley walks.

TRANSPORTATION. Backpacker Express (☎ 442 9939) has shuttles to and from Queenstown every few hours in summer and once daily in winter ($15). **Wakatipu Tours** (☎ 442 9986) runs the same tours at identical rates. **Dart River Jet Safaris** (☎ 442 9992) may give you a ride if there's room in the bus (2 per day, $14). The road is a winding 45min. drive along the side of Lake Wakatipu; some choose to hitch (not recommended by *Let's Go*), generally with good success in summer, although the road is sparsely traveled except for tourists.

PRACTICAL INFORMATION. The **Glenorchy Store**, at the Holiday Park on the way into town, is the **Visitors Center** and provides limited groceries (☎ 442 7171. Open daily 8:30am-7pm; in winter 8:30am-5pm.) The **DOC office**, at the end of Main Rd., has up-to-the-minute weather, hut, and trail condition reports as well as some basic camping supplies. (☎ 442 9937. Open daily 8:30am-4:30pm; in winter closed Sa-Su.) The **post office** in the Mobil station is at the end of town. (☎ 442 9913. Open daily 8am-6pm; in winter M-Sa 8am-5pm.)

ACCOMMODATIONS AND FOOD. The bucolic **Glenorchy Hotel ❷**, on Mull St., is run by a spunky crew of happy heartlanders. Beds in the bunkhouse abut an Oregon woodstove and canary-yellow kitchen; the hotel rooms are more comfortable. (☎ 442 9902 or 0800 453 667; fax 442 9912; relax@glenorchy.org.nz. Dorms

THE BIG SPLURGE

A TRAMPER'S TREAT: THE KINLOCH LODGE

A perfectly situated reward for several hard days on the Routeburn or Greenstone-Caples Tracks, the Kinloch Lodge continues more than a century's tradition of hospitality at the mouth of the Dart River. In the late 1800s, ferry passengers would travel up Lake Wakatipu from Queenstown to Kinloch for a retreat at the lake's headwaters. The views from the lodge-front dock have changed little in 100 years. Morning sunshine still illuminates mist over the lake with an ethereal glow.

Rooms in the Heritage wing (from $95 per person including 3-course dinner and breakfast) are surprisingly luxurious for the rustic setting. Enormous cast-iron tubs in the shared bathrooms allow guests to soak out tramping grime in a sea of soft bubbles. Hosts John and Toni take their hospitality seriously and offer guests their limitless knowledge of local activities. The in-house restaurant serves delectable mains (3 courses $32; 2 courses $25) and a flexible kitchen caters to individual tastes.

For travelers seeking a less-expensive splurge, the Lodge also contains several bunk-rooms (from $18), doubles ($55), and self-catering facilities. Even on a tight budget, sinful deserts like the Chocolate Truffle Rum Torte are impossible to resist after a few days of trail food.

Follow signs from Glenorchy for Kinloch or call the lodge for boat transport ($10) from Glenorchy. ☎ *442 4900; fax 442 9928; www.kinlochlodge.co.nz*

$16; motel units from $59.) The **Glenorchy Holiday Park** ❶ has an array of worn but cleanly options. (☎ 442 7171; fax 442 7172. Dorms $14; cabins $16 per person; tent sites $9, powered $10.) Classier rooms are available across the street from the Glenorchy Hotel at the **Glen-Royden Lodge** ❺. (☎ 442 9968. Doubles $90-110.)

▇**The Glenorchy Cafe** ❷, opposite the Mobil station, serves delectable pastries and light meals (chicken, brie, and mushroom panini $9). A vintage LP collection (great Tom Waites and Bob Dylan selection) and sunny porch invite itinerants to linger. (☎ 442 9958. Open daily 8am-late.) At the bar and restaurant of the **Glenorchy Hotel** ❷, the Kitchen Sink Burger ($10.50) comes with everything but the sink. A pricier list of stone-grilled mains ($17-25) indulge post-tramp cravings. (Open daily 8am-late.) At the **Glen-Royden Cafe-Restaurant** ❷, you can choose from assorted light meals ($3-8) or one of the larger pasta dishes ($10-15). (☎ 442 9968. Open daily 8am-9pm; bar open until late.)

◪ **OUTDOOR ACTIVITIES.** ▇**Dart River Jet Safaris** is a fast-paced foray up the Dart River, past Mt. Earnslaw and into the heart of Mt. Aspiring National Park. The trip enters the UNESCO South West New Zealand World Heritage Area, which contains flora and fauna descended from the creatures that once inhabited the ancient supercontinent of Gondwanaland. The jetboats spin, grind, and fly up the pebbled braids of the Dart River, stopping at scenic **Routeburn Valley**. A unique combination of speed and scenery, the 3hr. excursion cruises through exceptional scenery and might be worth the price to jetboat virgins. Also run by Dart River Safaris, **Fun Yaks** combines tranquil inflatable canoe rides downstream with jetboating upstream. Wetsuits are included and the personal crafts allow paddlers to explore an otherwise inaccessible gorge while still letting the river do most of the work. (☎ 442 9992 or 0800 327 8538; www.dartriverjet.co.nz. Jetboating runs daily 8:50am and 12:50pm; $145, children $72.50. Fun Yaks trips 6hr.; $195, children $146. Both trips depart 50min. earlier and costs $14 more from Queenstown.) The cheery staff at the **Glenorchy Store** also run **Dart Wilderness Adventures,** 3hr. jetboat trips on the Dart River. (☎ 442 7171. Departs 9:30am and noon; $135. Trips depart 1½hr. earlier and cost $10 more from Queenstown.) **High Country Horses** (☎ 442 9915) and **Dart Stables** (☎ 442 5688 or 0800 474 346; www.glenorchy.co.nz), on the road next to the motor park, offer guided tours ranging from casual saunters along the Wakatipu headlands to gallops through the breathtaking Rees and Dart Valleys. (Trip prices depend on duration; $50-750. High Country is cheaper for 2hr. rides; Dart is cheaper for daytrips.)

Free, self-guided walks around Glenorchy bring guests close to scenic paradise (or scenic Paradise, the filming location of the final battle in the *Lord of the Rings* movie trilogy). Many daytrippers hike the first leg of the **Routeburn Track** (see p. 375) for an afternoon glimpse of its legendary scenery. For a shorter walk, the **Invincible Gold Mine** walk (return 1½hr.) goes to an abandoned mine and affords arresting views of Mt. Earnslaw and the Rees Valley. The trail begins 10km north of town; follow Paradise Rd. north and continue straight when the road crosses the Rees River. The track to **Lake Sylvan** (return 2hr., also possible as a 3½hr. loop hike) is another popular day walk. Follow signs for Routeburn from Glenorchy to access the trail. The trailhead is about 5km north of the Dart River bridge.

ROUTEBURN TRACK

Lying half within Fiordland National Park (see p. 406) and half within Mt. Aspiring National Park (see p. 386), the Routeburn is the shortest of the Great Walks (34km) but among the most spectacular. The track climbs gently through the idyllic Routeburn Valley, passing the Harris Saddle and then ambling for several kilometers high above the treeline on the Serpentine Range. On clear days, the dramatic views approach the sublime: trampers gaze across the broad Hollyford Valley to the snow-capped peaks of the towering Darren Range. The map for the Routeburn Track is on p. 418.

Length: 32km, 2-4 days.

Trailheads: The Mt. Aspiring side of the track begins at **Routeburn Shelter,** 24km north of Glenorchy. The Fiordland side begins at **The Divide,** on the Milford Rd. 84km north of Te Anau. Trampers can walk the track in either direction, and many combine the track with either the **Caples** or **Greenstone** walks to create a loop.

Transportation: Both **Backpackers Express** (☎442 9939) and **Upper Lake Wakatipu Tours** (☎442 9986) run between **Routeburn Shelter** and **Glenorchy** (30min., $15) or **Queenstown** (1¼hr., $30) 2-3 times a day. **Tracknet** (☎249 7777 or 0800 483 2628) makes the most frequent trips to and from The Divide (to or from **Te Anau** 1½hr., $24; to or from **Milford Sound** 30min., $19). Although one should always consider the risks, patient **hitchhikers** report success getting to or from The Divide; those who've tried to hitch to or from Routeburn Shelter say it is quite difficult. Day hikers populate the lower stretches of the track in summer months; it's always wise to ask car-endowed fellow trampers for a ride out while on the track.

Seasonality: Year-round, however winter trips in the avalanche-prone Fiordland/Mt. Aspiring area are only for experienced and committed alpinists. May-Nov. are very dangerous. There is plentiful rainfall throughout the year.

Huts and Campsites: Late Oct.-late Apr., the 4 huts and 2 campsites operate on a **booking system.** Dec. and Jan. are busiest. In summer, all have gas cookers, taps, and flush toilets ($35 per night), and there's a 50% discount on a 3rd night's stay in either the Lake Howden or Routeburn Flats Hut. Camping is allowed only at the MacKenzie and the Routeburn Flats Huts. These campsites have toilets and cooking shelters but no stoves ($15). **Trampers must pick up their hut and campsite passes from a DOC office either the day before or by 2pm the day they start the track.** In winter (late Apr.-late Oct.), the gas is removed from the huts, hut fees revert to backcountry ticket system ($10 per night), and camping is free, but not recommended.

Bookings: The Routeburn fills up fast, almost as quickly as the Milford Track. Bookings are handled by the **Te Anau DOC Great Walks Booking Desk** (☎249 8514; fax 249 8515; greatwalksbooking@doc.govt.nz. See **Te Anau: Orientation and Practical Information, p. 408,** for location and hours.) **Applications** to walk the Routeburn are first-come, first-served, starting on the **July 1** for the following season (late Oct.-late Apr.; Dec. and Jan. fill up rapidly). If full, put your name on the **waiting list**—DOC will alert the freshly eligible by fax or email; couples and solo trampers have the best chances. Stopping by or calling the **Booking Desk** to inquire about cancellations can also sometimes yield a last-minute spot for those flexible with dates. **Guided Walks** of the Routeburn are also available for a hefty price (call **Ultimate Hikes**, ☎ 441 1138 or 0800 659 255; fax 441 1124; www.milfordtrack.co.nz).

Storage: Most accommodations will oblige free of charge. **Topline Tours** (☎ 249 7505 or 0508 832 628) transports **extra gear** between Te Anau and Queenstown ($5 per bag).

ROUTEBURN SHELTER TO ROUTEBURN FALLS HUT. *8.8km, 2-4hr.* From **Routeburn Shelter**, a gradual ascent through an ancient beech forest winds over and along various charging blue streams before reaching the turn-off (return 10min.) for **Routeburn Flats Hut** (20 bunks), which fronts a broad tussocked valley and the gentle Routeburn River. Fifteen-odd campsites lie secluded among tall grasses, well away from the hut. The **North Branch Routeburn** (return 4hr.), a flat-ish but barely marked valley sidetrip, begins across the river and explores the narrowing valley between Mt. Somnos and Mt. Erebus (Ask the Flats warden for directions). Back on the main track, gradually steepening now, the trail ascends through the ferned and forested flanks of the Routeburn Valley's southern side. The track crosses the scars of several slips while making the ascent, stony proof of the power of snow and rain to move mountains. Just at the edge of the treeline perches **Routeburn Falls Hut** (48 bunks), a wood-paneled palace with snazzy furniture, two separate bunkrooms, and a balcony overlooking the valley.

ROUTEBURN FALLS HUT TO LAKE MACKENZIE HUT AND CAMPSITE. *11.3km, 5-6hr.* This is the Routeburn's most awesome stretch and its most exposed and potentially hazardous; observe the advice of DOC staff. (It's also strewn with large, ankle-condemning rocks—though many are purple or pink, so watching where you walk isn't all boring.) Initially very steep, the track passes the neighboring guided walkers' hut and roaring **Routeburn Falls** before leveling out in a wide glacial bowl. It winds under craggy moss-encrusted peaks, then edges above **Lake Harris.** Just through the saddle from the lake, the **Harris Saddle Shelter** contains toilets, emergency equipment, and tasty-looking food for the guided walkers (hands off). From here, a steep and rewarding side trip leads to the top of **Conical Hill** (return 1½hr.), where on a clear day the 360° panorama encompasses crinkly ridges, unnamed glaciers, and the extent of the **Hollyford Valley's** stretch to the Tasman Sea. Meanwhile, the main track sidles along the mountainside above the **Hollyford Valley** traversing the treeless Serpentine Range and exposing greater views with every step. Once **Lake Mackenzie** comes into sight, the trail drops steeply to **Lake MacKenzie Hut** (48 bunks), another back-country grand hotel. Step outside to see up the lake to **Emily Peak** and take a limb-numbing, stench-masking dip for the benefit of your bunkmates. The **campground**—nine astroturf sites ringed by green trees—lies 100m farther along the trail.

LAKE MACKENZIE HUT AND CAMPSITE TO THE DIVIDE. *12km, 4-5½hr.* A steep ascent brings trampers to the bushline. Easing back down, the track weaves through the **Orchard,** a patch of pioneering ribbonwoods that deceive hungry trampers in their likeness to fruit-bearing trees. An hour later, the track passes the thundering 80m **Earland Falls. Lake Howden Hut** (28 bunks) sits on the shores of its namesake; the junction for the **Greenstone Track** is right outside. A 20min. hike along the Greenstone leads to the **free Greenstone Saddle Campsite,** which sports a pit toilet but no shelter or water. Back at the Lake Howden junction, the track ascends to the turn-off for **Key Summit** (return 1hr.), a popular day-hike for those cruising the Milford Rd., but a disappointment compared to the Routeburn's alpine views. A self-guided walk to the summit offers a rare chance to view three distinct river drainage systems simultaneously. The main

GLENORCHY ■ 377

track switchbacks down to **The Divide,** where there are toilets and shelter to freshen up and wait for a ride out.

GREENSTONE AND CAPLES TRACKS

A peaceful and pastoral pair, the Greenstone and Caples Tracks stretch around impressive mountain peaks and through cow-filled river valleys. While a tiny corner of the loop lies inside Mt. Aspiring National Park (see p. 386), most of it falls within the Wakatipu Recreational Hunting Area. Deer season is from April to September, though shooting is prohibited within 100m of tracks or on farmland. Black fallow deer are the most common animal on the track, although there are white fallow deer, chamois, and cattle who grace the grassy fields with their pies. The map for the Greenstone and Caples Tracks is on p. 418.

Length: 50km, 4-5 days.

Trailheads: The 2 tracks form a loop between Fiordland National Park and the Glenorchy area, which can be entered from the east via the **Greenstone Station** road-end (42km from Glenorchy) or from the west via **The Divide** (see p. 414), midway between Milford and Te Anau.

Transportation: Backpacker Express (☎ 442 9939) runs from the motor park in Glenorchy across Lake Wakatipu to this road-end. (30min.; departs Glenorchy Nov.-Apr. daily 10:30am and 1:30pm, departs trailhead 10am and 2pm; in winter runs on demand; $15.) They charge $15 to go between the Routeburn and the Greenstone and Caples within one day, and also travel to **Queenstown** ($15). **Upper Lake Wakatipu Tours** (☎ 442 9986 or 025 333 481) does the same.

Seasonality: Thick snow and a lack of hut wardens make the winter season more challenging than the summer, but the track is considered reasonably safe year-round.

Huts and Campsites: All of the huts (except for the tiny $5 Sly Burn) cost $10 per night year-round and provide coal stoves, water taps, outhouses, and a weather report; none offer cooking burners. **Mid Caples** and **Mid Greenstone Huts** have two bunkrooms flanking a small, central kitchen room; **Upper Caples** and **McKellar Huts** are identical one-room jobs. Camping is free and easy, permitted at least 50m away from huts or anywhere within the bush or bush edge but not on open flats (private land).

Special Gear: Chlorine or **Iodine tablets** or other **water purification** measures are crucial, since gut-wrenching giardia (see p. 21) has been detected on the track.

Storage: Most hostels will oblige. **Topline Tours** (☎ 249 8059 or 0508 832 628) will transport gear between Te Anau and Queenstown ($5 per bag).

ROAD-END TO MID CAPLES HUT. *7.5km. 2-3hr.* From the carpark at the end of the road, the track leads past the confluence of the Greenstone and Caples Rivers. Do not cross the river at the bridge for the Lake Rere track; keep to the downstream left bank, until you reach the swingbridge posted for the Greenstone track. The Caples Track branches off to the right alongside the river through beech forest until crossing a narrow gorge before **Mid Caples Hut** (12 bunks). This two-wing number has great views of fields, streams, and faraway peaks.

MID CAPLES HUT TO UPPER CAPLES HUT. *7.5km, 2-3hr.* The track weaves between beech forest and grassland replete with lovely mountain and river views before reaching the **Upper Caples Hut** (20 bunks; space for camping). The rugged **Steele Creek Route,** which essentially bisects the Greenstone and Caples loop, is accessible from the hut 20min. back up the track and is a highly unmarked, untrodden, and unforgiving path (8-10hr.) to **Mid Greenstone Hut** (see below).

UPPER CAPLES HUT TO LAKE MCKELLAR JUNCTION. *7.5km, 3-5hr.* Through moss and filmy ferns, the track ascends steeply but briefly before breaking onto the grasslands and misty mountain vistas of **McKellar Saddle**, conical Mt. Christina, and the Darron Mountains beckoning on the horizon. This root-entangled stretch is the steepest on the Greenstone and Caples; it's strenuous going up and slippery going down to the junction at **Lake McKellar**.

LAKE MCKELLAR JUNCTION TO THE DIVIDE. *6km, 1-2hr.* The northbound fork leads past the stream-fed, rocky, and free **Greenstone Saddle Campsite** (toilet, no tap) before joining the Routeburn Track at **Lake Howden Hut**. From here, you can head down to the **Milford Road** (see p. 414) or set off along the Routeburn.

LAKE MCKELLAR JUNCTION TO MCKELLAR HUT. *3km, 1-2hr.* From the junction, the track follows the lake past lichen-encrusted beeches and out of Fiordland National Park to **McKellar Hut** (20 bunks), a one-roomer in the shadow of McKellar Saddle.

MCKELLAR HUT TO MID GREENSTONE HUT. *13km, 4-6hr.* Through the forest, meadows, and cow herds, the track crosses a swingbridge over the Steele River, a half-hour shy of **Mid Greenstone Hut** (12 bunks). Besides its great valley view and forested tent sites, this hut boasts a genuine bovine skull on its commode.

MID GREENSTONE HUT TO ROAD-END. *14.5km, 3¾-5hr.* From the main track, a brief detour (10min.) leads across a stunning gorge to the tiny **Sly Burn Hut** (4 bunks) and a grassy field of potential tent sites. This is one end of the **Mavora-Greenstone Walkway** (51km, 4 days), which leads south to an unsealed offshoot of SH94. Back on the Greenstone, it's another rolling, blue-pooled riverside stretch back to the Caples junction and the carpark.

WANAKA ☎ 03

The jury's still out on whether or not Wanaka will become the dreaded "second Queenstown," but a tenacious cadre of anti-commercial locals will have to be evicted before it does. Wanaka manages to deliver an ample share of high adventure—climbing, jetboating, skiing, and skydiving—with a laid-back aplomb that shuns flashiness. Set against the majestic peaks of Mt. Aspiring and the fathomless expanse of Lake Wanaka, the town's outdoor-enthusiast spirit and relaxed atmosphere endear it to the ever-growing number of visitors.

TRANSPORTATION

Buses: Booking agencies all around town will eagerly arrange your transport business. Most buses and shuttles leave from **The Paper Place** on Upper Ardmore St., which also acts as a booking agent. **InterCity** runs to: **Christchurch** (9½hr., 8:10am, $50) via **Mt. Cook** (3½hr., $50); **Franz Josef Glacier** (5½hr., 9:50am, $40) via **Fox Glacier** (5hr., $37); and **Queenstown** (2hr., 2:40pm, $15). **Southern Link** goes to: **Christchurch** (6½hr., 10:40am, $50); **Dunedin** (4hr., 9am, $30); and **Queenstown** (2hr., 4:20pm, $15). **Wanaka Connexions** (☎ 443 9122) shuttles to **Queenstown** (1½hr.; 5 per day; $22-25, return $45). Also running 5 shuttles from **Queenstown** to **Wanaka** daily, they are your best bet for a daytrip. **Atomic Shuttles** goes just about anywhere you would want to go, including: **Christchurch** (7hr., 2pm, $45); **Dunedin** (5½hr., 2pm, $30); **Greymouth** (9hr., 9:15am, $80) via the **West Coast** (Fox and Franz Josef Glaciers and Hokitika); **Invercargill** (4½hr., 2pm, $30); and **Queenstown** (1½hr., 4:15pm, $15). Book InterCity and other shuttles at **Paper Place**, 84 Ardmore St. (☎ 443 7885; open daily 8am-5pm), or **Edgewater Adventures**, 59a Brownston St. (☎ 443 8422; open daily 8am-6pm; in winter 7:30am-7pm).

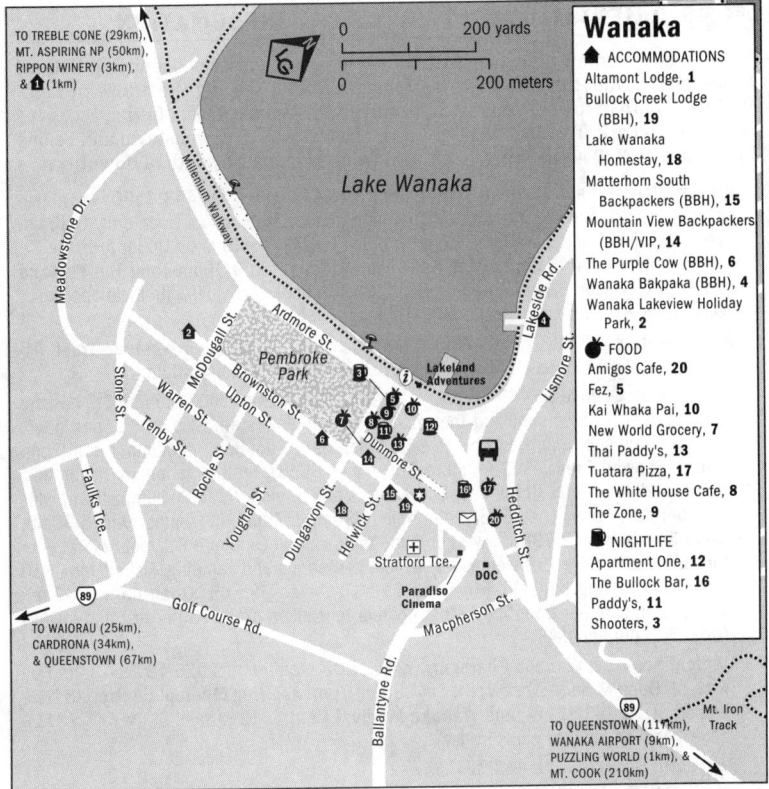

Shuttles: Shuttles run frequently from Wanaka to the ski slopes and to Mt. Aspiring trailheads. **Alpine Shuttles** (☎ 443 7966), **Mount Aspiring Express** (☎ 443 8422), and **Edgewater Adventure** (☎ 443 8422) make trailhead runs that cost anywhere from $5 to the Mt. Roy tramp to $25 to Raspberry Creek, the Mt. Aspiring National Park gateway. Book ahead to ski slopes with **Alpine Shuttles** (return $22) or **Edgewater Adventure** (return $22), both of which offer door-to-door pick-up and drop-off. **The Bus Company** (☎ 443 1855) runs to Cardrona only (return $20). The **Flying Bus** (☎ 443 9193) shuttles to Treble Cone only (return $18). **Wanaka Connexions** (☎ 443 8237) runs shuttles between Wanaka and **Queenstown,** via the airport.

Car Rental: Wanaka Rental Car (☎ 443 6641), at the corner of Ardmore and Brownston St., rents quality cars starting at $39 with unlimited mileage for rentals of 3 days or more. On-call 24hr.

Taxis: Wanaka Taxis (☎ 443 7999) operates late most nights. An airport run is $25.

Hitchhiking: Hitchhikers report finding rides easily out to the slopes, though shuttles are a reliable alternative and a must for Mt. Aspiring. At the west edge of town, the Cardrona/Queenstown-bound gather at the southwest corner of Pembroke Park (at Brownston and McDougall St.) and those going to Treble Cone at the northwest corner (at Ardmore and McDougall St.). Those heading up the coast wait past the DOC office on upper Ardmore St.

ORIENTATION AND PRACTICAL INFORMATION

Wanaka is extremely compact, with most shops and services occupying **Helwick Street**. **SH89** runs through town as **Ardmore Street**, tracing the shore of Lake Wanaka. South of town, Ardmore St. becomes **Mt. Aspiring Road**, offering access to the National Park. The **Cardrona Road** is the fastest way to Queenstown and begins in Wanaka as **McDougall Street**, a left turn from Ardmore St. south of downtown.

Visitors Center: Lake Wanaka Visitor Centre (☎ 443 1233; fax 443 1290; www.lakewanaka.co.nz) is in the waterfront log cabin on Lower Ardmore St. Open daily 8:30am-7pm; in winter daily 9am-5pm. The **DOC** office (☎ 443 7660) is on Upper Ardmore St. Open daily 8am-4:45pm; in winter M-F 8am-4:45pm, Sa 9:30am-4pm. The **Wanaka Adventure Centre**, 99 Ardmore St. (☎ 443 8174), books activities with local operators. Open daily 8:30am-7pm; closed Mar.-Apr.

Banks: National Bank (☎ 443 7521), on Upper Ardmore St., and **Westpac Trust**, 15 Helwick St. (☎ 443 7817), have **ATMs.** Open M-F 9 or 9:30am-4:30pm.

Gear Rental: **Base** (☎ 443 6699), at the corner of Helwick and Dunmore St., has the highest quality equipment and the most knowledgeable staff. Skis, boots, and pools $40 per day; snowboard and boots $48. Open daily 7am-8pm; in summer 9am-7pm. **Sun & Snowbusiness**, 103 Ardmore St. (☎ 443 8855), rents a variety of carver skis, boots, and poles for $30 per day. Snowboards and boots for $35. In summer waterskis $25 per day, fishing rods $15. Open daily 7:30am-8:30pm; in summer 9am-5:30pm. **Good Sports** (☎ 443 7966; www.good-sports.co.nz), on Dunmore St., rents winter gear for comparable prices, as well as a gear for other sports and camping. Fishing rods $10 per day, sleeping bags $7.50, tents $10-15, bikes $25-65. Open daily 7:30am-7:30pm; in summer 8am-5pm. Most hostels rent bikes (from $6 per hr.) and kayaks (from $25 per half-day).

Medical Services: Wanaka Pharmacy (☎ 443 8000, after hours 025 487 870), on Helwick St. Open M-Sa 8:30am-7pm, Su 4:30pm-7pm. **Aspiring Medical Centre**, 28 Dunvargon St. (☎ 443 1226), and **Wanaka Medical Centre**, 12 Russell St. (☎ 443 7811), have **24hr.** emergency call service.

Police: 28 Helwick St. (☎ 443 7272).

Internet Access: Budget Communications, 38 Helwick St. (☎ 443 4440). $6 per hr.; $5 per hr. noon-4pm. Open daily 9am-10pm.

Post Office: 39 Ardmore St. (☎ 443 8211). Open M-F 8:30am-5:30pm, Sa 9am-noon.

ACCOMMODATIONS AND CAMPING

In winter, the long-term ski and snowboard bunnies move in, often filling more than half of the hostel beds for weeks and months at a time; it is essential to book ahead. In summer, the excellent facilities are more sparsely graced by trampers escaping the Queenstown rush, but booking ahead is still advisable.

Matterhorn South Backpackers (BBH), 56 Brownston St. (☎ 443 1119; fax 443 8379; matterhorn@xtra.co.nz), at the corner of Helwick St. This winning backpackers offers plush seating around a wood-burning stove and private porches. Next door, the sparkling motel units share a modern kitchen and a quiet lounge. Internet. Laundry. Reception 8am-9pm; in winter 8am-8pm. Dorms $19-22; twins and doubles $42-70. ❷

Wanaka Bakpaka (BBH), 117 Lakeside Rd. (☎ 443 7837; wanakabakpaka@xtra.co.nz), perched on a hill 5min. from town. Small grassy patches and an herb garden provide relative seclusion. The dining area offers unparalleled lake views. Bike rental $20 per day. Internet. Key deposit $10. Laundry. Linen $3. Reception 8:30am-8:30pm; in winter 8am-8pm. Dorms $19-20; tiny single $18; twins $44; doubles $49. ❷

WANAKA ■ 381

The Purple Cow (BBH), 94 Brownston St. (☎443 1880 or 0800 772 277; fax 443 1870; www.purplecow.co.nz) has superb common spaces, a fireplace, a pool table, and nightly movie screenings on the big-screen TV. Bike and kayak rental. Internet. Linen $3. Reception 8am-9pm. Dorms $19; twins and doubles $52. ❷

Mountain View Backpackers (BBH/VIP), 71 Brownston St. (☎/fax 443 9010; mountainview@madmail.com), sits on an ideal slice of backpacker real estate (between the supermarket, an Internet cafe, and a laundromat). Friendly staff, clean facilities, and a cavernous TV lounge. Reception 9am-1pm and 4-8pm. Dorms $18; doubles $45. ❷

Bullock Creek Lodge (BBH), 50 Brownston St. (☎/fax 443 1265; bullockcreeklodge@clear.net.nz). The cinderblock motel dorms may seem cramped, but the modern kitchen and fireside lounge provide ample room for relaxation. All rooms have bath. Laundry. Linen $2.50. Dorms $20; doubles $50-60; triples $75. ❷

Altamont Lodge, 121 Mt. Aspiring Rd. (☎443 8864), more than 2km west out of town. Pine-paneled walls, free spa, ski-tuning room, and a welcoming hearth achieve a classic ski-lodge feel. An excellent choice for car-bound couples. Linen $5. Reception 8am-9pm. Singles $35; doubles $50; extra person $11. Book far in advance in winter. ❸

Lake Wanaka Homestay, 85 Warren St. (☎443 7995; fax 443 7945; www.wanakahomestay.co.nz), 5min. from town. This amiable and impeccable home with lake views is the best B&B bargain in town. Free breakfast. Twins and doubles $55, $90 for 2. ❹

Wanaka Lakeview Holiday Park, 212 Brownston St. (☎443 7883; fax 443 7883), past Pembroke Park. Built like a military installation, this motor camp is large, worn, and near town. 12-person dorms $13; cabins $35 for 2, extra person $14; newer tourist flats $62; tent and powered sites $10. ❶

FOOD

True-value budget ingredients abound at **New World**, on Dunmore St. (☎443 7168. Open daily 8am-8pm.) **Soul Food: Organic Oasis**, in the Pembroke Mall off Dunmore St., proffers organic produce and whole foods. (☎443 8297. Open daily 9am-6pm.)

Kai Whaka Pai (☎443 7795), at the corner of Ardmore and Helwick St., facing the lake. Decadence is an understatement in this small, earthy gourmet bake shop and cafe. Enormous and creative sandwiches on foccaccia bread ($5.50) and light meals are served all day ($7-23). Open daily 8am-midnight. ❷

The Zone (☎443 9220), in the Pembroke Mall off Dunmore St. Hang in the mall with Wanaka's climber crowd while sipping a smoothie from fresh-squeezed fruits ($5). The wholefoods menu complements the organic hairdos of the patrons. All-day brekkie ($8-14); paninis and eclectic wraps $7-8.50. Open daily 8am-late. ❷

The White House Cafe (☎443 9595), at the corner of Dunmore and Dungarvon St. Set in a 1933 Art Deco palace, meals here have an elegant, dinner-party aura. The vegetarian-friendly North African and Mediterranean dishes ($25) receive widespread acclaim. Open daily 11am-3pm and 6:30pm-late. ❺

Tuatara Pizza (☎443 8186), on Ardmore St. on the hill before the lake. Gourmet pizzas like spinach and sundried tomatoes ($15-25) nourish the ski-bum crowd for yet another day on the slopes. Open daily 6pm-late. ❸

Fez (☎443 7701), on Ardmore St. at the lakefront. With savory traditional Turkish kebabs ($7-9.50), Fez is *the* hot spot for late-night munchies. Open M-Th and Su 11am-11pm, F-Sa 11am-3am. ❷

Thai Paddy's, 21 Dunmore St. (☎443 7640), serves heaping portions of Thai specialties ($13-24), as well as a selection of New Zealand favorites (read: steak and potatoes $17-22). Steamed rice $2.50 extra. Open daily 11am-late. ❸

THE LOCAL STORY

LA DOLCE CINEMA

Calum MacLeod is the owner of Cinema Paradiso in Wanaka.

Q: What was the inspiration behind the funky place you have here?
A: Several years ago, while crammed into a theater in Christchurch [MacLeod is 6'4"], I was kicked out for putting my foot on the seat in front of me. I wanted a place with character, not one of those generic theatres that just grabs your cash and shoves you around. Here, folks can order a meal, a snack, or a glass of wine, whatever they like. They can relax knowing they have access to an armrest on both sides! We pass out tissues at intermission if it's a sad movie. We like to make it a special experience. If there's ever a contest for the best movie theatre in the world, I'd sure like to enter!

Q: What sorts of movies do you show?
A: Movies I like. Usually current films, but there's always at least one artsy film in the mix each week. Because it's my selection, I started introducing the films. Sometimes I'll crack a few jokes beforehand if it's a light film. People usually remember the tossy Scotsman along with the film.

Q: Why are their couches for seats?
A: In our old location, we only had hard plastic seats, which is fine if you're in for a short movie, but if you've got a *Braveheart* or a *Titanic*, well, we were practically massaging people's arses as they left. The hard seats were also why we started having an intermission. People just needed a break for their bums!

Amigos Cafe (☎443 7872), on Upper Ardmore St. The owner fries his own tortillas and makes and sells his own salsa in this Kiwi attempt at true Mexican fare. Combo platters from $15. Open daily 5:30-9pm. ❸

ENTERTAINMENT & NIGHTLIFE

Wanaka's bars pack with skiers seeking to warm tingling toes and climbers eager to discuss new routes. One staple of Wanaka nightlife, the legendary ☒**Paradiso Cinema,** 3 Ardmore St., is a quirky theater that doubles as a cafe, serving fresh-baked cookies during intermission, homemade ice cream, and an eclectic menu of pre- or mid-movie mains ($13-20). Watch a flick on the cushy sofas or snag a seat in the vintage car. (☎443 1505; www.paradiso.net.nz. Cafe open daily from 11am. $10, children $6.)

Shooters, 148 Ardmore St. (☎443 4345), consistently draws a young, party-hard crowd of travelers and skiers, eager to guzzle and mingle. Cheap beer is a big draw, with daily drink specials 5-6pm and 9-10pm. Nightly DJs in winter. Open daily 11am-late.

Apartment One, 99 Ardmore St. (☎443 4911). Go behind the Adventure Centre and head to the 2nd fl. The polished but not pretentious atmosphere is worth the price tag (beers from $4.50, wines from $6 per glass). Open daily 4pm-late.

Paddy's, 28 Dunmore St. (☎443 7640), behind Thai Paddy's. With Th and Sa "jam session" nights and the drum set always ready to go, a rousing round of rock anthems is never unexpected. Drink specials (5-6pm and 9-10pm). Open daily 4pm-late.

The Bullock Bar, 71 Ardmore St. (☎443 9258), is the *only* place to watch Rugby Union or veg out on pokey machines. Arrive early to talk fishing and politics with the locals; show up late to meet other ski-bums. Open daily 11am-late.

SIGHTS

Boggle your mind at **Puzzling World,** 3km out of town opposite Mt. Iron. Originally the humble project of a Wanaka man, this huge complex of illusions now draws a major crowd. With the world's first two-story **maze,** and a hall of chasing faces, you may get lost and never leave. (☎443 7489; www.puzzlingworld.co.nz. Open daily 8:30am-5:30pm. $6 for Puzzling World or the maze, children $4; both $9, children $6.)

The **Wanaka Beerworks** (☎443 1865; www.nzsouth.co.nz/wanakabeerworks) is a tiny micro-brewery that produced top prize winners (Brewski and Tall Black) at the 2000 New Zealand International Beer

Awards. The daily 2pm tour costs $5 and lasts about 5min., but the buzz from the brew keeps you happy much longer. Air-oriented activities are clustered around the brewery in the Sky Show Centre. The **New Zealand Fighter Pilots Museum** lauds the men and crafts that flew during the world wars. (☎ 443 7010; www.nzfpm.co.nz. Open daily 9am-4pm; late Dec.-Jan. 9am-6pm $8, children $4.) Transportation to the airport (including the Sky Show Centre and the Wanaka Transport Museum) is available through **Alpine Shuttles.** (☎ 443 7966. $7, return $12.) **Warbirds Over Wanaka** is a bi-annual flight show featuring WWII-era fighter planes and drawing as many as 100,000 visitors to the Wanaka area. The next show will occur Easter, 2004.

OUTDOOR ACTIVITIES

SKI FIELDS

Two major downhill ski fields are accessible from Wanaka, each with its own advantages—ask around to score some sweet deals on transport, tickets, and rentals. An ISIC card and another **student ID** are necessary for student deals. Serious ski-bums should buy season tickets as far in advance as possible for incredible savings. Conditions between the ski fields vary, and snow reports are posted in town and at accommodations in the morning. For information on **heliskiing,** see p. 370.

CARDRONA. Cardrona (1670m; vertical rise 390m) is a more family-oriented field, with wide, sunny slopes perfect for learning. They have predictably good, natural snow and varied terrain for all abilities. Three new half-pipes draw a large crowd of snowboarders. *(Ski field: 34km away on Cardrona Rd. ☎ 443 7341; www.cardrona.co.nz. Wanaka office: 18 Dunmore St., just west of Helwick. ☎ 443 7411. Open in season daily 8am-6pm, Sa 8am-noon. Lift pass $62, students $51, children $31.)*

TREBLE CONE. Treble Cone (2090m) has the longest vertical rise (660m) in the Southern Lakes and contains more skiable terrain than anywhere else on the South Island. Beautiful powdered chutes descend from lift-serviced areas and sweet off-piste extreme skiing and snowboarding await. Runs are generally steeper and more difficult than at Cardrona—beginner ski bums will have bruised bums. *(Ski field: 43km away. ☎ 443 7443; www.treblecone.co.nz. Wanaka office: on the waterfront, east of Helwick St. Open in season daily 7:45am-12:30pm and 3:30-6pm. Lift pass $63, students $51, children $32.)*

WAIORAU SNOW FARM. New Zealand's only cross-country ski area, the Snow Farm has an impressive venue (50km of trail) and breathtaking views of Cardrona Valley. Wide, well-groomed trails swoop across the hills and into the valleys, following ridgelines and rivers. Toyota and Subaru even use the legendary snows to test their tires. In late August, the Snow Farm plays host to international ski races and the famous "Merino Muster" community race. *(34km from Wanaka along the Cardrona Rd. ☎ 443 7542; www.snowfarmnz.com. Day pass $25, students $20, children $10.)*

SNOW PARK. Opened in 2002, this terrain park is already a favorite for both skiers and snowboarders. Three half-pipes, beginner and advanced terrain parks, and a Super Cross course cater to dare-devil tricksters. *(Off the Snow Farm access road. ☎ 443 9991; www.snowparknz.com. Day pass $45, university students $35, high school students $25; 5-day anytime pass $203.)*

ON THE WATER

Beautiful Lake Wanaka and the rivers that feed it are fished and played upon in all ways imaginable. Despite first impressions, not all watersports in Wanaka are adrenaline-powered. **Lakeland Adventures,** on the wharf, rents everything you need for a calm morning on the lake. (☎ 443 7495; www.lakelandadventures.co.nz. Kayaks $10-15 per hr.; dinghies $20 per hr., with motor $40; motorboats $30 per hr.)

CANYONING. ▨Deep Canyon Experience entices the bold to plunge from 25ft. into narrow pools, coaxes the timid to abseil slippery overhanging faces, and tempts thrill-seekers to slip down slick rock slides. After 3hr. of personal-limits-testing adventure, the canyon spits you out just in time for a proper picnic lunch. (☎ 443 7922 or 025 204 9296; www.deepcanyon.co.nz. Nov.-Mar. only. $175, including lunch.)

KAYAKING. Alpine River Guides runs whitewater and sea-kayak trips for both beginner and experienced paddlers on the lake and on many rivers in the area. Don't despair if your hips, the boat, and the river current can't find common ground—the constant dunking is refreshing. (☎ 443 9023; www.alpinekayaks.co.nz. Half-day $100; full-day $140, including gear and lunch.)

SLEDGING. Challenging the dominance of whitewater rafting and boogie-board river surfing, **Frogz Have More Fun** has a thrilling alternative. Careening through the rapids on your own, highly buoyant personal "sledge" (a cross between a personal raft and a kickboard) is literally the most in-your-face way to conquer the river thus far. (☎ 443 9130; www.frogz.co.nz. 4hr., Nov.-Apr. 2 per day, $109.)

JETBOATING. It wouldn't be the Southern Lakes region without a few opportunities to rip through water only a few centimeters deep. **Clutha River Jet** (☎ 443 7495) runs rides on Lake Wanaka and the Clutha River (1hr., $60). **Wanaka Jet** (☎ 0800 538 7746) shoots up the Clutha (1hr., $60) and the Matukituki River (2½hr., $95).

SAILING. For groups looking to sail to uninhabited islands on the lake, **Lake Wanaka Yacht Charters** lets you charter a boat for day. The rental is expensive for two, but more affordable for groups of five or six. (☎ 442 1369; www.sail-wanaka.co.nz. Half-day $160, full-day $240; with skipper additional $20 per hr.)

FISHING. Lakeland Adventures, conveniently located at the wharf, rents gear and sells licenses. (☎ 443 7495. Fishing rod hire $15 per day; one-day license $15.) Angling supplies are also available from **Good Sports,** on Dunmore St. (☎ 443 7966. Fishing rod $10 per day, including tackle; license $15-30.) If you're planning on fishing for multiple days, the multi-day licenses are the best deal. Inquire at the Visitors Center for a list of local trout and flyfishing guides, but be prepared to pay at least $250 for a half-day of fishing. Alternatively, try spinning some whopper fish-tales at the pub and see who takes you out the next morning.

WAKE BOARDING. The latest thrill on the lakefront is offered by **Wake Wanaka.** With an 80% success rate, their professional guides will have you up and wake boarding in an hour. (☎ 443 4350; www.wakewanaka.com. 1hr. $120 for several riders.)

ADVENTURE ACTIVITIES

SKYDIVING. If you're into breaking wind at 12000ft. with a jumpmaster strapped to your back, ▨**Tandem Skydive Wanaka** is more than happy to oblige. Their motto, "You call, we fall," is an apt description. The alpine views of Mt. Aspiring and Mt. Cook National Parks make Wanaka an excellent choice for a big fall. (☎ 443 7207; www.skydivenz.com. Includes 20min. scenic flight and pick-up. 9000ft. $245, 12,000ft. $295.)

PARAGLIDING. If you scoff at the word tandem, surrender yourself to **Wanaka Paragliding.** After you've mastered the basics during a full-day course on the grassy slopes of Mt. Iron, you are ready to fly solo. Once certified, it's just $15 to soar down any time you like. (☎ 443 9193; www.wanakaparagliding.co.nz. Full-day course $188.) **Lucky Montana's Flying Circus** (☎ 0800 247 287) also offers paragliding courses ($180) as well as tandem paragliding flights ($160).

MOUNTAIN BIKING. Alpine and Heli-Mountain Biking takes the uphill battle out of cycling by transporting riders to some of the country's highest terrain, either by van or helicopter, so they are well rested for the ride back down. (☎ 443 8943;

www.mountainbiking.co.nz. Van-transported rides from $95, heli-bike Treble Cone $235, heli-bike Mt. Alpha $215. Prices include bike hire.) For a more personal, individually-tailored day of riding, contact **Mountain Bike Wanaka** (☎ 443 7739; *3-4hr. trip $65*) or **Motatapu Adventures** (☎ 443 7377; *full-day $149*).

RALLY-CAR RIDING. Monster Mountain Rally offers the only opportunity in the world to ride along with professional drivers for all the dare-devil spinning and skidding found in an auto-racing video game. *(Track 25km from Wanaka along the Cardrona Rd., near the Snow Farm.* ☎ *443 6878 or 0800 872 559; www.mmrally.co.nz. $135.)*

OTHER ACTIVITIES

GOLF CROSS AND WINE TASTING. Unable to escape a vicious slice that's ruining your golf game? The rugby-ball shaped golf balls at the **Rippon Winery's Golf Cross** course fly truer than normal balls. What's more, wide goal-posts replace holes, a miracle for golf-neophytes. The winery itself is Central Otago's oldest and hosts **Rippon**, a bi-annual festival (early Feb., next festival 2004) of New Zealand music. *(On Mt. Aspiring Rd., 3km from Wanaka.* ☎ *443 8084; www.rippon.co.nz. Open daily 11am-5pm; in winter 1:30-4:30pm. Closed May-June. Golf cross $20, including wine tasting. Tasting only $3 for 5 wines.)*

HORSE TREKS. New Zealand Backcountry Saddle Expeditions (☎ 443 8151; www.ridenz.com/backcountry) runs daily 2hr. rides in the Cardrona Valley ($50, including transport) as well as overnight trips in the surrounding hills *(from $150).* **Lake Wanaka Horse Trekking** offers two 2hr. ride options. *(*☎ *443 7777. Lakeside ride $50; scenic ride to the top of Mt. Iron $45. Transport provided when available.)*

WALKS

Not just for the frugal, tramping abounds around Lake Wanaka and the surrounding mountains. Several walks begin right inside town tracing the scenic lake shore, although the more stunning tracks require either transport or very hardy legs. Most of the trails along the lake allow bikes. **Alpine Shuttles** (☎ 443 7966), in the morning, and **Mount Aspiring Express** (☎ 443 8422), run daily from October to May at 9:30am and 2:30pm. (Diamond Lake $10; Mt. Roy $5.) As always, the DOC office has up-to-the-minute information on track conditions.

SHORT HIKES. The **Diamond Lake Walk**, through glacially carved terrain, is one of the prettiest short hikes in New Zealand. The track is on private land (suggested donation $2) and can take anywhere between one and three hours depending on how high you climb: the best views are from atop Rocky Mountain. *(Trailhead is signposted from Mt. Aspiring Rd., 25min. out of Wanaka on Ardmore St. Bikes prohibited. Not recommended July-Sept.)* Beginning along the south side of the bay, the **Waterfall Creek Walk**, also known as the **Millennium Walkway**, is perfect for novice mountain bikers looking for quiet views of Lake Wanaka. *(Return 1½hr., with Millennium extension 4hr.)*

MOUNTAIN HIKES. The tramp up **Mt. Roy** delivers views of Mt. Aspiring National Park, including glimpses of the park's impressive namesake, also known as the Matterhorn of the South. *(The marked trailhead is off Mt. Aspiring Rd. about 6km from Wanaka. Return 5-6hr. Walkers only.)* A popular and challenging summertime route in the Wanaka area climbs from the end of Mt. Aspiring Rd. to a point near the ◼**Cascade Saddle**, one of the most acclaimed vantages in the Southern Alps. The route is a multi-day trip, with overnight options at the Aspiring and Dart Huts. It connects with the Rees-Dart Track (see below) on the far side of the saddle. Before attempting the climb, consult the Wanaka DOC office. In the other direction, a shorter hike ascends **Mt. Iron** and offers panoramic vistas of Lake Wanaka and the Clutha River valley. Cyclists are permitted on the west face of Mt. Iron but must turn around before descending the steeper east face. *(2km from Wanaka. Return 2hr.)*

MT. ASPIRING NATIONAL PARK   ☎ 03

The craggy, snow-covered peaks of Mt. Aspiring National Park are the center of the Te Wahipounamu South West New Zealand World Heritage Area. Of the park's 100-odd glaciers and 13 peaks over 2500m, Mt. Aspiring (3027m) is the perfectly pyramidal pinnacle. With the challenging Rees-Dart Track within reach of Glenorchy or Queenstown and walks up the breathtaking Matukituki Valley accessible from Wanaka, the park attracts a variety of trampers. The ancient and varied terrain in and around the park provided the Middle-Earthen template on which Frodo, Gandalf, and the gang performed several scenes in *Lord of the Rings*.

Most activities, hikes, and scenic flights are run out of the gateway towns of **Glenorchy** (see p. 373), **Queenstown** (see p. 361), and **Wanaka** (see p. 378). Even far-off **Te Anau** (see p. 406) takes part, as an access point for Fiordland's and Mt. Aspiring's shared **Routeburn Track** (see p. 375). Shorter tracks depart from both the **Glenorchy** and **Wanaka** areas, including the popular **Rob Roy Valley Track** (return 3hr.), which features dramatic views of the Rob Roy glacier.

AT A GLANCE	
AREA: 355,543 hectares.	**GATEWAYS:** Wanaka, Queenstown, Glenorchy, Te Anau.
CLIMATE: Pleasant, although occasionally very wet, climate in summer; dangerous conditions in winter.	**CAMPING:** Established camping areas, backcountry huts, and backcountry camping.
FEATURES: Haast River, Humbolt Mountains, and Red Hills "mineral belt."	**FEES & RESERVATIONS:** Hut Pass necessary for Routeburn Track, fees for other backcountry huts.
HIGHLIGHTS: Superb views and extreme terrain.	

WHEN TO GO The park is much safer in the summer months as the winter can get extremely cold in the high altitudes and tracks become more dangerous. Many trails lack hut wardens, and weather conditions such as thick snow and freezing wind can make trekking an experts-only activity.

REES-DART TRACK

As grandiose as any Great Walk (and likely to soon become one), the Rees-Dart Track forms a glorious loop through two river valleys, both lined with living glaciers. The track passes a great diversity of landscapes, including beech forests, subalpine herbfields, grassy flats, and man-made pastures. This is not an unduly easy walk, as many streams are unbridged and much of the path is invisible—poles and cairns make better friends than often misguided footprints. With two stunning daytrips beyond the main loop, including the jaw-dropping Cascade Saddle Route, the Rees-Dart richly rewards an increasing flow of trampers.

Length: 72km, 4-5 days.

Trailheads: Tracks begin at the road that ends north of **Glenorchy** and meet at **Dart Hut**. It is also possible to access the trail from Wanaka via the **Cascade Saddle**.

Transportation: Backpacker Express (☎ 442 9939) runs from **Glenorchy** (in summer daily 9:30am) to the **Rees Track trailhead** at Muddy Creek carpark (30min., $15). They also serve the **Dart Track trailhead** at Chinaman's Bluff (1hr., departs **Glenorchy** 12:30pm, $20), and will pick up at **Sandy Bluff** via jetboat ($80). **Upper Lake Wakatipu Tours** (☎ 442 9986 or 025 333 481) is similar. Both operators run between **Glenorchy** and **Queenstown** ($15).

MT. ASPIRING NATIONAL PARK ■ 387

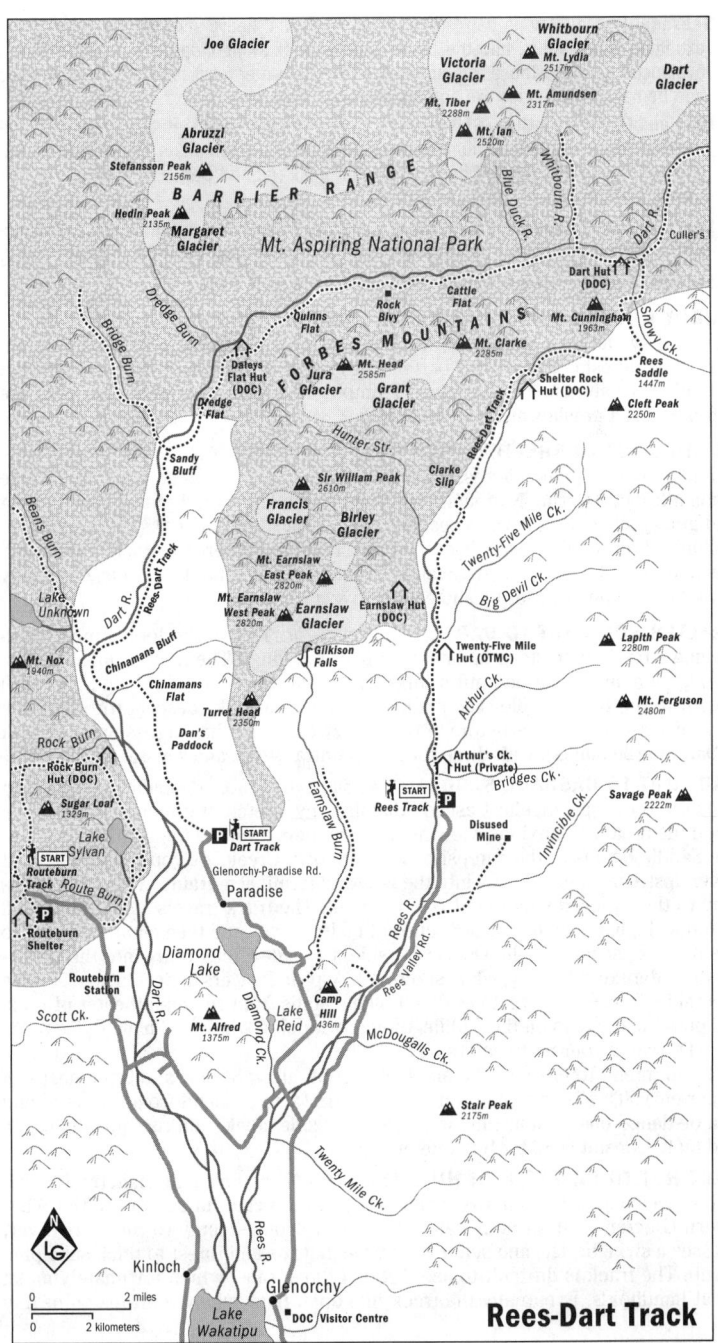

Seasonality: May-Nov. is dangerous. Avalanches and heavy snowfall make the going extremely treacherous, and the Upper Snowy Creek swingbridge is removed to avoid avalanche damage. Those attempting the track in winter must have alpine experience and be handy with an ice axe and crampons.

Huts and Campsites: Huts ($10 per night) except for the 25 Mile Hut ($3). Huts include heating, taps, and toilets; none have cooking stoves. Camping is free in forests and grassy flats but discouraged between Shelter Rock Hut and Dart Hut. There is trail-end camping at the Muddy Creek carpark.

Special Gear: Chlorine or **iodine tablets** or other **water purification** measures are crucial, since gut-wrenching giardia (see p. 21) has been detected on the track.

Storage: See **Greenstone and Caples Track: Storage, p. 377**.

MUDDY CREEK CARPARK TO 25 MILE HUT. *6km, 2-3hr.* This stretch of the Rees Valley can be a swampy walk along a lightly marked track. The mountain peaks are imposing but only get better. The grungy and character-laden **25 Mile Hut** (8 bunks) is maintained by the Otago Tramping and Mountaineering Club as a base camp for Mt. Earnslaw and a stone hearth.

25 MILE HUT TO SHELTER ROCK HUT. *10.5km, 4-5hr.* The Lovely Lennox Falls quickly come into view across the valley; about two hours later, a swingbridge leads into Mt. Aspiring National Park proper. Winding in and out of beech forest and grassy slip sites, the track reaches **Shelter Rock Hut** (20 bunks), a snazzy two-building abode on the east side of the river. Take care where the track crosses gullies above the bush; these are avalanche paths and can be dangerous, especially with the late snows in spring and early snows in summer.

SHELTER ROCK HUT TO DART HUT. *9km, 5-7hr.* This is the loop's most challenging stretch, with steep inclines and faint markings. The track climbs steadily through alpine vegetation until it hugs a bluff for the extremely steep (but brief) ascent to the Rees Saddle. The main track makes a tricky descent through even more diverse plant zones before hitting a cozy campsite. Just across Snowy Creek is **Dart Hut** (20 bunks), with three rooms, a central stove, and separate toilets.

DART HUT TO CASCADE SADDLE. *8km, 5hr.* Dart Hut is a popular base for day-trips up to the spectacular Cascade Saddle. Any stretch of crummy weather can flood the area with anxious, view-hungry trampers awaiting the sun. The track to the Saddle begins at the campsite across Snowy Creek. As you follow the Dart River upstream, it disappears into the gray and terminal moraine, which then gives way to the exposed ice of Dart Glacier itself. The track travels along the lateral moraine, high above the glacier's current melted level, and then climbs steadily to the prize: Cascade Saddle. On the far side, Cascade Creek roars into the beech-clothed Matukituki Valley, while snowy Mt. Aspiring towers in the distance; on the near side, Dart Glacier tumbles down blue icefalls from an amphitheater of rock. It's possible to camp on the Saddle, though whipping winds and naughty kea (see p. 64) threaten your tent's safety.

If you intend to cross to the **Mt. Aspiring Hut,** allow 8-10hr. and bring heaps of experience. This is an alpine route, is very tricky to descend from the west, and can be dangerous even in summer. The area's side creeks can rise quickly in rain and melt. Consult DOC for track details.

DART HUT TO DALEYS FLAT HUT. *15.5km, 8½-12½hr.* From the main track, a seldom-traveled spur leads across some difficult but beautiful country to the Whitbourn Glacier. Half an hour past Dart Hut it drops steeply to the Dart River, crosses a swingbridge, and scrambles through grass and forest to thick subalpine scrub. The track is difficult to see through the shrubs, which fortunately make great handholds. Eventually the track hits open flats, where a profusion of tiny plants spreads alongside the frothing Whitbourn River. Snowfields and waterfalls ring the lonely valley, which leads right up to the gritty snout of the Whitbourn Glacier itself, along the Whitbourn Track. Meanwhile, the main track becomes less strenuous across the wide Cattle Flat, where grassy terraces are framed by still more legions of glaciers. **Daleys Flat Hut** (20 bunks) is very spacious, with an idyllic riverside setting marred only by abundant sandflies.

DALEYS FLAT HUT TO CHINAMAN'S BLUFF. *14.5km, 4-6hr.* From the hut, it takes about an hour to reach some small, sandy bluffs that are *not* Sandy Bluff. The real McCoy is a walk away, by the signs for jetboat pick-up. From here, the jetboats zoom along the otherwise tranquil river, as the track runs up and over Chinaman's Bluff, beyond which lies the road to Paradise carpark.

SOUTHLAND

Southlanders ardently claim that the bottom of New Zealand should be at the top of any visitor's destination list. For what the region lacks in major tourist infrastructure and big-draw locales, it makes up for with a sincere peek into Kiwi life. The pastoral hospitality of the Catlins, the burgeoning cosmopolitanism of Invercargill, and the wild, untouched beauty of Stewart Island (New Zealand's newest National Park) deliver intriguing glimpses of off-the-beaten-track New Zealand.

SOUTHLAND HIGHLIGHTS

GET LOST in the quiet, rugged beauty of the **Catlins**, "New Zealand's best-kept secret" (see p. 394).

GET VOYEURISTIC Wandering amidst sleeping sea lions and squawking birds at **Surat Bay** (see p. 396).

GET NOWHERE on **Stewart Island**, remote even by Southland standards (see p. 400).

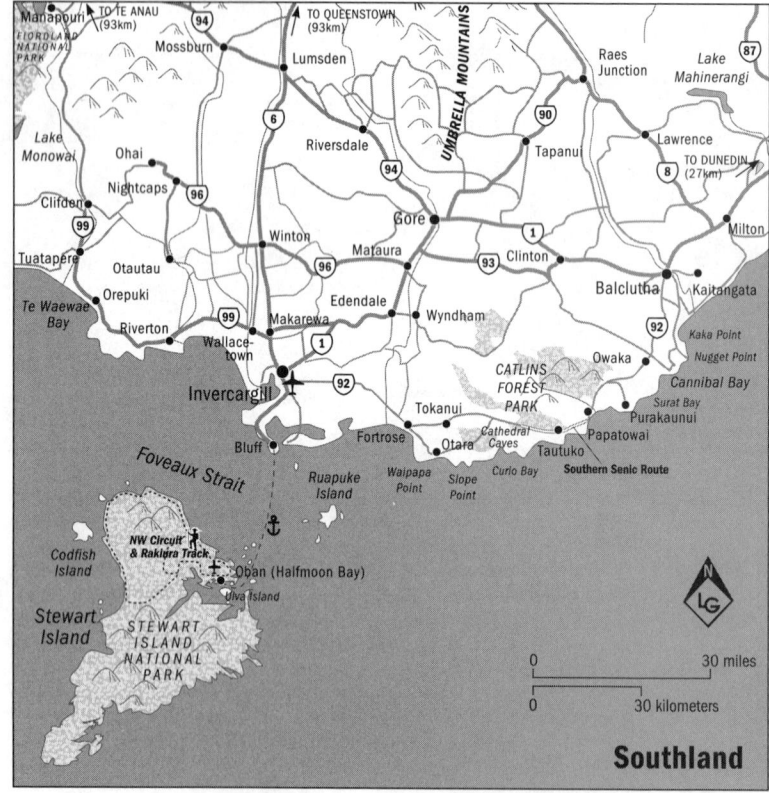

Southland

INVERCARGILL ☎ 03

Perpetually dumped on by its northern rivals, Christchurch and Dunedin, as well as by tactless international icon Mick Jagger, who, in 1967, called the area "the asshole of the earth," Invercargill (pop. 53,000) is now engaged in a fledgling renaissance. Students have been rushing here to enroll at the tuition-free Southern Institute of Technology and to enjoy the city's growing cafe scene and retail options. Yet, despite these improvements, nights on Dee St. are still best characterized by aimless local youth (called "bogans") revving up their hot-rods and drinking to a riotous fervor. There's change coming to Invercargill, but old habits die hard. Before darting off to destinations north or south, spend a night in Invercargill and check out this burgeoning urban center for yourself.

TRANSPORTATION

Flights: The **airport** is 2.5km west of the city. Take Dee St. south as it becomes Clyde St. and follow the signs on the roundabout to the airport. Or, take **Spitfire Shuttle** (☎ 214 1851; $5). A **taxi** to the airport costs $8. **Air New Zealand** flies frequently to **Auckland** (from $450 return; ISIC $316 one-way) and **Christchurch** (from $217 return; ISIC $125 one-way).

Invercargill

🏠 **ACCOMMODATIONS**
Backpackers Riverside Guesthouse, **2**
Invercargill Caravan Park and Camp, **1**
Tuatara Lodge (VIP/YHA), **7**
Southern Comfort Backpackers (BBH), **3**

🍴 **FOOD**
Fat Indian Curryhouse, **6**
Global Byte Cafe, **4**
New Zealand Natural Ice Cream Cafe, **9**
Tillerman's Cafe, **8**
Pak 'N Save, **13**
The Zookeepers Cafe, **11**

🍸 **NIGHTLIFE**
Embassy, **5**
Players, **10**
Sugar Shack, **12**

Buses: InterCity (☎214 0598) leaves the train station daily for **Christchurch** (9hr., 8:45am, $68-85) via **Dunedin** (3hr., $32-40). **Atomic Shuttles** (☎322 8883) has cheaper fares to **Christchurch** (2pm, $55) and **Dunedin** ($25). **Spitfire Shuttle Te Anau** (☎218 7381) runs to **Te Anau** (2½-3hr., 12:50pm, $34-39). **Southern Air Land Travel** (☎216 0717) goes daily to **Queenstown** (3hr., 1pm, $35-43), as does Atomic Shuttles ($35). Call for booking and pick-up. **Campbelltown Passenger Shuttles** (☎212 7404) runs to **Bluff** (5 per day, $13.50).

Public Transportation: (☎218 7108). Buses serve the suburbs M-F every hr. ($1.20). There's also a free bus for the downtown area. Most depart from near the library on Dee St.; the Visitors Center has schedules.

Taxis: Blue Star (☎218 6079) runs **24hr.**

Car Rental: Pegasus, 76 Clyde St. (☎214 3210 or 0800 803 580) has cheap rental cars from $35 per day, plus long-term rates. **First Choice Rent-a-car** (☎214 4820) and **Intercity Rentals** (☎214 5179) are both in budget range.

AA: 47-51 Gala St. (☎218 9033; fax 214 0246). Open M-F 9am-5pm.

Bike Rental: Wensley's Cycle Centre, 53 Tay St. (☎ 218 6206). Mountain bikes $12-20 per day. Open M-Th 8am-5:30pm, F 8am-8pm, Sa 9:30am-12:30pm.

Hitchhiking: Hitchers heading toward Queenstown are said to take the Waikiwi bus (#10) from the library up North Rd. as far as possible to Westlans Rd. For rides to Dunedin, hitchhikers take the Hawthornedale bus (#4), from Tay St. and Lithgow St., as far as it goes.

ORIENTATION AND PRACTICAL INFORMATION

From the train and bus station, cross **Leven Street** and pass through **Wachner Place** under the **clock tower** to enter downtown. **Dee Street,** Invercargill's main thoroughfare, runs to the south and east toward **Bluff** and the **Catlins,** and to the north toward **Queens Park** and **Queenstown.** North of the city, it becomes **North Road.** Across from the clock tower, **Esk Street** is the main shopping center. **SH1** from Dunedin cuts through the city via **Tay Street** and then turns south toward Bluff.

Visitors Center: The Invercargill Information Centre (☎214 6243; 218 4415; tourismandtravel.invercargill@thenet.net.nz) is on Victoria Ave., just off of Gala St., inside the massive white pyramid. From Wachner Pl., go left up Dee St., take a right at McDonald's onto Gala St., and the center is 2 blocks down on the left. They can handle transportation and accommodations bookings. Internet. Open M-F 9am-7pm, Sa-Su 10am-7pm; in winter until 5pm.

DOC: 33 Don St. (☎214 4589), State Insurance Bldg., 7th fl. Open M-F 8am-5pm.

Currency Exchange: Thomas Cook, 60 Tay St. (☎218 2008). Open M-F 9am-5:30pm.

Police: 117 Don St. (☎214 4039).

Pharmacy: Mills Pharmacy (☎214 4249), at the corner of Don and Kelvin St. Open M-Th 9am-5:30pm, F 9am-9pm, Sa 10am-1pm.

Medical Services: Urgent Doctor, 103 Don St. (☎218 8821). Open M-F 5-10pm; on call 24hr. Sa-Su and holidays. The **Southland Hospital** (☎214 5735) is on Kew Rd.

Internet Access: Clive Wilson Electronics, 31-33 Clyde St. Follow Dee St. south until it becomes Clyde for cheap rates ($5 per hr.) and fast computers. (☎214 4224. Open M-F 8:30am-5:30pm.) The **public library** (☎218 7025), on Dee St. near Wachner Pl., costs $2 per 15min. Open M-F 9am-8:30pm, Sa 10am-1pm.

Post Office: 51 Don St. (☎214 7700). Open M-F 8:30am-5pm, Sa 10am-12:30pm.

ACCOMMODATIONS AND CAMPING

Southern Comfort Backpackers (BBH), 30 Thomson St. (☎218 3838), treats you like only a fine bourbon could. From the Visitors Center, turn right down Victoria Ave., then take a right on Thomson St. The fire-warmed living room and the spotless, ultra-modern kitchen make you feel like a houseguest. Free bike use. Linen $2 per night. Reception 8am-10pm. Book ahead. Dorms $19; doubles $44. Cash only. ❷

Tuatara Lodge (VIP/YHA), 32 Dee St. (☎214 0954 or 0800 488 282; fax 214 0956), right downtown next to Wachner Pl. A new and modern backpackers with an institutionally hygienic feel. Guests enjoy a convenient location, a friendly staff, a spacious kitchen, and Sky TV. Internet. Laundry. Dorms $19; singles $25; twins and doubles $45; celebrity ensuites $65-70. ❷

Backpackers Riverside Guesthouse, 70 Filleul St. (☎218 9207 or 0800 736 323), just off Dee St., overlooking the Waihopai River. The carpark is at the end of the 1st driveway on the right behind the Asthma Society; the backpackers itself is the 2nd driveway. A friendly homestay, no frills. Dorms $15; cabins $10 per person; singles $32; doubles $39; B&B singles $40, doubles $55. Cash only. ❷

Invercargill Caravan Park and Camp, 20 Victoria St. (☎218 8787). Turn left off Dee St. just past McDonald's. Basic facilities on the asphalt and grass expanse of a former show ground. Far from nature, but the closest place to town to camp. Cabins $28-36; tent sites $7.50, powered $17 for 2. ❶

FOOD

Restaurants are scattered in the city (near Dee St.), and many double as bars. Additionally, a new cafe scene is on the rise. The **Pak 'N Save market** is at 95 Tay St. (☎214 4864. Open M-F 8:30am-10pm, Sa-Su 8:30am-8pm).

The Zookeepers Cafe, 50 Tay St. (☎218 3373). Graze with the cool-cat beasts at this chic cafe. Bottomless coffee goes for $2.50; several beers on tap are $3.50 for 12 oz. Snacks $6-8; light meals $12-14. Open daily 10am-late. ❷

Fat Indian Curryhouse (☎218 9933), on Piccadilly Ln., off 38 Dee St. Delicious Indian food served Prohibition-era style—in a back-alley hideaway with big band music and eager patrons crowding the space. Mains $9-14, sumptuous naan $2. Open daily noon-2pm and 4:30pm-late. ❷

Tillerman's Cafe, 16 Don St. (☎218 9240), has brick walls clad in classy modern art. Lunch is an affordable and healthy treat—the quiche, served with 2 salads, is only $8. The bar upstairs features a wide range of bands Th-Sa nights. Open M-F noon-2pm. Bar open Th-Sa 6pm-late. ❷

New Zealand Natural Ice Cream Cafe, 59 Esk St. (☎218 2863). Sorbets and fro-yo please waist-line watchers while flavorful ice creams and heaping kebabs ($4.50-6) greet the gluttonous. Open M-F 9:30am-5:30pm, Sa 10am-2pm. Cash only. ❶

Global Byte Cafe, 150 Dee St. (☎214 4724). Sparkling stainless steel and stylish iMacs craft the futurist feel at this Internet cafe. The coffee's rocket-fuel strong, the gourmet panini ($4-5) celestial, and the staff, well, they're local kids from Invercargill. Open daily 8am-5pm. ❶

ENTERTAINMENT AND NIGHTLIFE

Invercargill's up-and-coming cafe scene hops Thursday to Saturday and flops during the rest of the week while the students grind away. The cafe/bar **Tillerman's** (see **Food,** above) provides the local entertainment from Thursday to Saturday. *The Plot,* a weekly calendar posted at most venues, advertises DJs and live music. Once a theater, **Embassy,** on Dee St., now hosts national and local acts, heating up the techno scene with full audio-visual dance parties and three bars. (Call ☎ 214 0050 to check upcoming events or swing by any Th-Sa night.) **Players,** 25 Tay St., has pool tables for a quick game. (☎ 214 0206. Tables $8 per hr.; $5 per 30min.; students 20% off. Open M-W noon-11pm, Th-Sa noon-1am.) The **Sugar Shack,** 77 Don St., sets the mark for raucous Invercargill student partying with a cavernous interior mimicking a tropical village. (☎ 218 6125. Drink specials Th-F and DJs W-Sa. Open W-Sa 4pm-late.) The **Movieland 5 Theatre,** 29 Dee St., is the only place in 100km to catch a flick. (☎ 214 1110. $11; students $9 M-F after 5pm and weekends, $8 M-F before 5pm.)

SIGHTS

The **Southland Museum and Art Gallery,** at the city end of Queen's Park, is in the same gleaming white pyramid as the Visitors Center. The highlight is the tuatarium, a live exhibit of the nocturnal reptiles that once roamed all of New Zealand. The Roaring 40° gallery upstairs describes New Zealand's subantarctic islands and the megaherbs that thrive there, supremely adapted to the severe conditions. The dynamic slide show includes strobe lighting and may be as close as you can get to the restricted-access isles. Queen's Park itself is well worth a visit and boasts roses with names like "New Dawn" and "Madame de Port." On a clear, cool night, view the stars at the Observatory next to the Visitors Center. (☎ 218 9753. Museum open M-F 9am-5pm, Sa-Su 10am-5pm. By donation; slideshow $2, children 50¢. Observatory open Oct.-Apr. W 7-9pm. 50¢ admission includes slideshow.)

THE CATLINS ☎ 03

A coastline of untouched beaches, promontories, and ancient forests amid sheep paddocks and turnip patches—the Catlins region lives up to its reputation as the best-kept secret in New Zealand. Cliffs dotted with native bush drop into swirling Antarctic waters, while rare penguins waddle across stretches of white sand. With a bit of exploring, you may discover a private inlet shared only with sea lions. The area's remoteness is tempered by cordial coastal villages; there are few places in New Zealand where civilization can be so close and yet seem so distant.

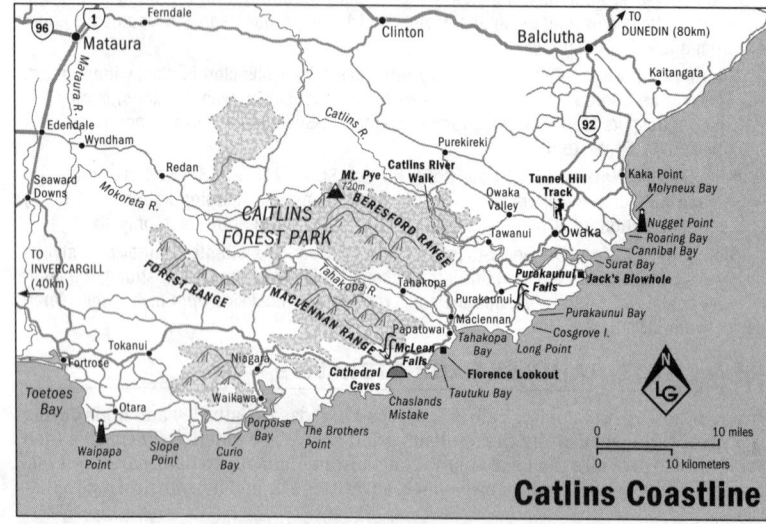

Catlins Coastline

TRANSPORTATION IN THE CATLINS

The **Southern Scenic Route** (**SH92**; see p. 424) runs 172km through the Catlins from Balclutha to Invercargill; anyone driving through the Catlins would do well to buy a detailed map. Twenty-three kilometers of the road between the Curio Bay cut-off and Papatowai are unsealed; allow 40min. to 1hr. to drive this portion of the road. A car or mountain bike (and strong lungs) is the best way to take in the coast at your own pace; bus tours demand a more programmed pace. **Kiwi Experience's Bottom Bus** departs from Dunedin on a 10hr. backpacker-oriented tour. The bus drops off in Riverton at the end of the day or in any of the towns along the way. (☎442 9708. Runs M, W, and F-Sa at 7:30-8am; fewer runs in winter. $85, free pick-up.) **Catlins Coaster** runs similar trips with experienced guiding staff and wildlife viewing licenses from Dunedin to Invercargill. (☎0800 304 333. In summer daily; in winter on demand. Min. 5 people. Departs Dunedin 8am. $120; ISIC, VIP, and YHA $10 discount on regular rates. $200 with arranged overnight farmstay.) Tours are also available from Queenstown or Te Anau ($135) with an option to include a return flight to Stewart Island ($265). **Catlins Mini Tours** allows you to choose your own destinations. (☎/fax 415 8686. Pick-up from Dunedin or Invercargill at 10am. Min. 2 people $60 each, $50 each for 4 or more.) Another option is **Catlins Natural Wonders**, which runs daytrips and overnights from Balclutha, Owaka, and Invercargill. (☎0800 353 941; $45-85. Transport from Dunedin available F and Su.) More comprehensive two-night tours are available through **Catlins Wildlife Trackers**, which runs from Balclutha. (☎415 8613 or 0800 228 546. M, W, and Sa 10am. $290.) Contact **Cycle-south** for information on vehicle-supported mountain bike day-tours of the Catlins. (☎0800 429 253. Oct.-May 2 tours per day. $79.) Although *Let's Go* does not recommend it, **hitchhiking** through the Catlins is said to be feasible in summer, but more difficult in winter when there's little traffic.

PRACTICAL INFORMATION

There are **no banks** between Balclutha and Invercargill. There are plenty of secluded **campsites**, but the comfort and coziness of the Catlins' top-mark backpackers should not be missed. Most of the region's budget accommodations have very few beds, creating an atmosphere ideal for relaxation and making advance booking essential.

BALCLUTHA ☎03

Balclutha (pop. 4100) is the "big city" of the Catlins, as it is the only convenient place between Dunedin and Invercargill to get groceries, withdraw money, or enjoy semi-urban conveniences. Located at the junction of SH1 and SH92, 30km from Owaka and 56km from Papatowai, Balclutha has accessible resources for Catlins-bound travelers, but little else of interest or attraction. The **Clutha Information Centre** is at 4 Clyde St. (☎418 0388; fax 418 1877; clutha.vin@cluthadc.govt.nz. Open M-F 8:30am-5pm, Sa-Su 9:30am-3pm.) Stock up on groceries at the **New World** down Lanark St. at the corner of Clyde St., a block before the bridge. (☎418 2850. Open M-F 8:30am-7pm, Sa-Su 9am-6pm.) Other Balclutha services include: **banks** with **ATMs** along Clyde St.; a **BP station** on Clyde St. (☎418 0034. Open M-F 7am-10pm, Sa-Su 7:30am-10pm); the **police**, 47 Renfrew St., two blocks down from Clyde St. (☎418 0203); and **Clutha Health First**, 3-7 Charlotte St., also accessible from Clyde St., which serves as the region's **hospital** (☎418 0500).

KAKA POINT, NUGGET POINT, AND ROARING BAY ☎03

The Catlins' claim to fame is its coastline, with fine sand beaches and jutting headlands where sea lions bask on the rocks with squawking colonies of birds. Start exploring at **Kaka Point,** 12km north of Owaka on a well-marked road off the Southern Scenic Route. Kaka Point is a tiny beach-retreat town, popular with surfers for the excellent swells that crash against its sandy shoreline. The beach at Kaka arcs toward **Nugget Point,** 8km south down a winding gravel road. The little lighthouse (the most southern in the world) is a 10min. jaunt along a rock ledge that towers over the blue-green sea, bending toward the fragmented islets that give the point its name. Fur seals, elephant seals, and hooker sea lions frolic on the waterlogged crags—the only place in New Zealand that these creatures coexist, but you'll need either superhuman vision or a good pair of binoculars to see them from the lighthouse. On the road to Nugget Point, **Roaring Bay** is home to yellow-eyed penguins that hop up the cliffs during the two hours before sunset. Their amiable socializing can be viewed from a hide-out above the beach. For more structured trips, **Nugget Point Ecotours** (run by the owners of Nugget View and Kaka Point Motels) run excursions to view local marine life. (☎412 8602. 2hr. trips from $50; other options include 5hr. fishing trips on the high seas among the albatrosses from $85.)

Kaka Point Stores has groceries, takeaways, a bar, and the **post office. The Point Cafe ❸,** in the same complex, affords the ocean views, pleasant ambience, and pricey meals (lunch $10-15, dinner $15-22) expected of a beach-resort bar. (☎412 8800. Open daily 8am-7pm; bar open late.) At **Nugget View and Kaka Point Motels ❹,** 11 Rata St., choose between luxury and budget rooms while enjoying the "southern hospitality" and impressive local knowledge of owners Jackie and Mike Coll. (☎412 8602 or 0800 525 278; fax 412 8623. Reception 24hr. Free laundry. Doubles $60-150.) A path through lush native bush leads to the tiny **Fernlea Backpackers (VIP) ❷,** off Moana St. directly beyond the store. Overlooking the bay, this bungalow feels like your granddad's well-worn vacation retreat. (☎412 8834. Reception 8am-10pm. Linen $2. Dorms $15; alcove doubles $30. Cash only.) **Kaka Point Camping Ground ❶** has two simple cabins, although you'll miss the ocean views. (☎412 8818. Self-registration. Singles $15; doubles $25, extra person $10; caravan sites $10, $15 for 2; tent sites $10/$15. Cash only.)

FROM KAKA POINT TO OWAKA ☎03

Beyond Kaka Point, follow the sign for **Tunnel Hill** on the main road to a 5min. walk through an abandoned railway tunnel. Turn off your flashlight for a spooky experience; the track is quite flat and smooth. Farther along the Southern Scenic Hwy., fur seals and sea lions congregate on the beach at **Cannibal Bay** or on the dunes at **Surat Bay** (see p. 397). Although human bones were once discovered at Cannibal Bay, it's more likely that the unlucky chap was killed in a battle rather than eaten by cannibals. Surat Bay is a shorter drive from the Southern Scenic Hwy., but you'll probably find human as well as sea lion company here.

OWAKA ☎03

Just 25km south of Balclutha, Owaka (o-WACK-a; pop. 400) is one of the few places that actually passes for a town in the Catlins. While here, stock up on petrol, supplies, and small-town hospitality.

🛈 PRACTICAL INFORMATION. The **Visitors Centre,** 20 Ryley St. (follow signs from the scenic route) offers area maps, accommodation listings, farmstay information and bookings, and displays on regional flora and fauna. (☎/fax 415 8371. Open M-F 9:30am-4:30pm, Sa-Su 10am-4pm.) **Helen's Dairy** has takeaways ($3.50) and operates a **post office** (☎ 415 8304; open M-Sa 7am-8pm), while **Niles Four Square** has provisions. (☎ 415 8201. Open M-Th 8:30am-5:30pm, F 8:30am-7:30pm, Sa 9am-5pm, Su 10am-2pm; in winter closes Sa at 1pm and closed Su.) Other services include: a **Shell petrol station** that is also an **AA service station** and the last cheap gas until Invercargill (☎ 415 8179; open M-Th 7:30am-6pm, F 7:30am-7pm, Sa 9am-1pm); the **police** at the west end of town (☎ 415 8056; after hours calls are directed to the Balclutha police); a **pharmacy**, 26 Waikowa Rd., opposite the police station (☎ 415 8109; open M-Th 8:45am-5:30pm, F 8:45am-7pm; also Th 7-9pm); the **Catlins Medical Centre**, 29 Main Rd. (24hr. ☎ 415 8006); and **Internet access** at the **Internet Cafe**, opposite the grocery, which has a connection faster than a diving albatross (☎ 415 8030; open M-F 9am-5pm, Sa 9am-noon; $2 per 15min).

ACCOMMODATIONS AND FOOD. 🎵**Catlins Retreat Guesthouse ❹**, 27 Main Rd., has brightly colored period rooms, friendly hosts, and a honeysuckle-ensconced spa out back that will coax even the weariest traveler into a delightful repose. (☎ 415 8830; catlinsbb@xtra.co.nz. Singles $45-55; doubles around $80. Breakfast included.) Across the street, 🎵**Blowhole Backpackers ❷**, 24 Main Rd., offers similar character-home comforts at budget prices. In season, harvest plums and veggies in the backyard. (☎/fax 415 8600. Dorms $17; doubles $45.) Follow the signs from Owaka to reach the sunny **Pounawea Motor Camp ❶**, by an estuary on the Catlins River. The Pounawea Bush Walk begins from the campground, and the trills of song birds will greet you in the morning. You can also rent canoes ($5) to explore the birdlife along the waterway. (☎/fax 415 8483. Reception 24hr. Cabins $15 per person; tent and caravan sites $8.) Across the bay from the motor camp, the **Surat Bay Lodge (BBH) ❷** is a low-key backpackers right on the water's edge, only a quick jaunt away from the ocean and a substantial sea lion colony. Follow the signs from Surat Bay Rd. (☎/fax 415 8099; www.suratbay.co.nz. Dorms $20; twins $44; doubles $47.)

The pub adjoining the **Owaka Inn ❷** has pool, darts, and lots of beer for little money. It's an authentic place to enjoy a hot meal or toss back a few cold ones with the old-timers. (Mains $10-20. Beer $5. Open daily 11am-late.) For a cold brew by a toasty fire, mosey on into the **Lumberjack Bar and Cafe ❸**. Lunches and items on the all-day "Woodcutter's" bar-food menu ($11.50-15) are the most affordable. (☎ 415 8747. Open daily noon-late.)

OUTDOOR ACTIVITIES. Ten minutes from town, **New Zealand sea lions** lounge, bray, and butt heads along the beach in **Surat Bay**. The sea lion colony, whose numbers swell to 40 in the winter, makes up a substantial percentage of a "mainland" population of 100; the rest are chilling in Antarctica. **Surat Bay Lodge** is positioned just a few hundred meters from the lions and will rent canoes to explore the surrounding estuary for $9.50 per hour. The Owaka region also has some of the best brown trout rivers for **fishing** in the country.

FROM OWAKA TO PURAKAUNUI ☎ 03

Just north of Owaka, signs point the way to **Jack's Blowhole**. More accurately called a slurp hole, the deep depression is connected to the ocean (200m away) by caves (walk the easy 30min. paddock track to reach it; visit at high tide for the most dramatic viewing). Once back on the highway, another side trip leads up the Owaka Valley through forests along the **Catlins River Gorge**. Get a ride to the top of the **Catlins River Track**, a well-maintained tramp through unspoiled beech forest and over three suspension bridges (one-way 5hr.). When the trout are biting, this is the place to catch 'em; you may even see the yellowhead or Mohua bird along the way. The track is accessible from a number of points, making it possible to vary the length of your hike. Both the **Surat Bay Lodge** (see **Accommodations and Food,** p. 397) and **Catlins Natural Wonders** (see **Transportation in the Catlins,** p. 395) provide transport to and from the trailheads (one-way $25, $50 if you don't have a car). There's no camping or facilities at the top of the track; the only four-walled toilets along the way are at the **Tawanui campsite** ($4 per person) near the track's base.

PURAKAUNUI BAY AND FALLS ☎ 03

Local beach cows munch kelp on the sand of **Purakaunui Bay** (a surfing beach for the brave-hearted). The mist from crashing waves creates a magical effervescence for the view from the popular **DOC campsite** ($4 per site; with toilets). To reach it, take the rough road south from the Scenic Route. Several well-marked routes south from SH92 (including the Purakaunui Bay turn) climb to **Purakaunui Falls.** The lush rainforest walk to the falls (10min. from the carpark) is as spectacular as the multi-tiered cascades themselves. On the road to the falls, stop for a night's rest at the **Falls Backpackers ❷.** Fresh eggs, comfy beds, electric blankets, and the warm tones of an antique valve radio greet travelers at this charming character farmhouse transported by truck to its hillside perch. (☎415 8724. Laundry. Dorms $20; twins $40; doubles $45.) Also on the same road, a little luxury is available at the **Greenwood Farmstay ❺,** a sophisticated B&B with meticulously gardened grounds. Call for pick-up from Owaka. Co-owner Alan will take you out farming with him if you ask. (☎415 8259. Dinner $30-35. Rooms $85. Cash only.)

PAPATOWAI ☎ 03

Papatowai Beach is gorgeous—crashing waves, mist rising off the sand, cliffs visible farther down the coast, and an estuary flowing through the dune forest. The town of Papatowai is well worth a stop, whether you intend to canoe or kayak in the estuary or simply want a scenic picnic. Clearly marked from SH92 and offering commanding views of the sea, the fabulous accommodations and enthusiastic hospitality at ◪**Hilltop Backpackers ❷** initiated the trend towards luxurious budget quarters that makes backpacking in the Catlins a five-star affair. The rugs, duvets, extravagant showers, glowing wood stove, lavish modern kitchen, and the pearly white tub all encourage instant relaxation. Canoes, bikes, surfboards, boogie boards, and wetsuits are all available for guests. (☎/fax 415 8028; hilltop@ihug.co.nz. Reception 24hr. Internet. Laundry. Dorms $20; doubles $45. Cash only.) Follow signs for Purakautiti from the Scenic Hwy. to get to the **Coastal View Backpackers ❷.** If you've ever dreamt of spending a night in a small hermit's cottage on a lonely seaside crag, then this rustic backpackers will be your fantasy come true. Perched on oceanside cliffs, the views are unparalleled. (☎415 8660. Dorms $15, private use of the entire unit $50.) In Papatowai proper, the **Southern Secret Motel ❺** has luxurious one-room apartments that share a view of the native bush and sheep-laden fields. (☎/fax 415 8600. Reception 24hr. Rooms $80; lower rates in winter.) The **Papatowai Motels and Store ❹** has gas, postal services, groceries, and spacious rooms behind the store. (☎/fax 415 8147. Reception and store open daily 8:30am-7pm; in winter M-Th and Su 9am-6pm, F-Sa 9am-7pm. Doubles $70; extra adult $12, extra child $8.) The **Papatowai Motor Park ❶** is behind the store in a bushy area filled with birds. (☎415 8565; fax 415 8503. Reception 8:30am-9:30pm. Dorms $12; cabins $20-30 for 2; tent sites $6; caravan sites $7.)

For travelers seeking to stroll the coast, the **Catlins Top Track** (☎0800 228 546) traces the shoreline on lonely beaches and towering cliffs over a two-day self-guided romp. The 10hr. track crosses private farmland and costs $25 for overnight or $10 for the day. South of Papatowai, the road becomes gravel and winds to **Florence Lookout** and a spectacular view of **Tautuku Beach.** Backed by olive and rusty hues of the native forest, Tautuku may be the best of the Catlins' remarkable beaches. Turn off for **Lake Wilkie** and its 20min. boardwalk a bit farther down the hill. Don't miss the **Cathedral Caves** turn-off, 16km from Tautuku, a highlight of the Catlins. The two 30m-tall mouths of the caves are only accessible at low tide; check a tide table at the Visitors Center or your accommodation before making the 30min. trek to **Waipati Beach** and the caves. (Gates open 2hr. either side of low-tide. $5 per car and 2 adults, extra person $1; walk-ins $2.) Just after the caves turn onto Rewcastle Rd. for the 30min. walk through the beech forest to **McLean Falls.**

WAIKAWA, CURIO BAY, AND SLOPE POINT ☎ 03

Continue towards **Invercargill** via **Tokanui** on the main road, or turn back toward **Waikawa** some 20km beyond the Cathedral Caves. Either way make sure to stop for a meal ($10-15), a snack, or an email check at the ⬛**Niagara Falls Cafe ❷**, about 1km towards Waikawa. This art gallery/cafe is an inviting and cosmopolitan oasis nestled in rural surrounds. (☎ 246 8577. Open daily 10am-7pm.) Once in Waikawa, the **Waikawa Dolphin Information Centre**, which acts as a **Visitors Center**, is located in a trim old church in the center of town and has displays on the area's marine mammals. Its small cafe serves snacks, and the center does bookings for daytime and twilight dolphin viewing tours. (☎ 246 8444 or 0800 377 581. Dolphin cruises daily 10am, 1, and 3pm for $50; twilight cruises 5:30pm. $75. Open Oct.-Apr. daily.) Across from the Visitors Center, **Waikawa Holiday Lodge (BBH) ❷** provides spartan rooms with metal frame bunks. (☎ 246 8552; fax 246 8877; greg.stephens@xtra.co.nz. Reception 24hr. Dorms $19; twins and doubles $44.)

Porpoise and **Curio Bays** are each a 10min. drive from Waikawa. Located about 1km before Curio Bay itself, ⬛**Curio Bay Backpackers ❷** is a remarkably and refreshingly modern flat, situated on a prime chunk of Porpoise Bay. You'll leave wishing your home was as nice. (☎ 246 8797. Dorms $18; doubles $50, with bath $120.) At the point of a craggy coastal peninsula, the **Curio Bay Campground ❶** has very basic facilities. (☎ 246 8897. Tent sites $5, powered $15 for 2.) On the other side of the point lie **Curio Bay** and a 180-million-year-old ⬛**petrified forest** visible on the rocky coast at low tide. Among pools of bead-like seaweed and unhinged bull kelp are the mineralized trunks of tall, ancient trees.

From the turn-off at Porpoise Bay, follow signs to **Slope Point,** the southernmost tip of the South Island. The lighthouse is a 10min. walk from the road markers; you'll pass **Slope Point Backpackers ❷** on the way. This sheep farm and friendly hostel sports gorgeous and colorful gardens. (☎/fax 246 8420. Reception 24hr. Reservations recommended. Dorms $15; doubles $35; tent sites $8. Cash only.) **Waipapa Point,** the site of the worst maritime disaster in New Zealand history (the wreck of the SS *Tararua* in 1881), is 20km from Slope Point past **Otara** toward **Invercargill.**

BLUFF ☎ 03

As the departure point for the ferry to Stewart Island, seaside Bluff (Invercargill's peninsular port town, 27km south of the city) also marks the beginning (or end) of SH1. Bluff is best known for it's world-famous **oysters.** If you're not a seafood fan, this industrial town has little to offer. The **Campbelltown Passenger Service** runs between Bluff and Invercargill. (☎ 212 7404. M-F 5 per day, Sa-Su 2 per day; $10. Bookings required.) At Bluff's **Visitors Center,** 74 Gore St., inside the gift shop, Yvonne and Jim will answer your queries. (☎ 212 8305. Open daily 9am-5pm.) With no bank, EFTPOS withdrawals at the **Service Centre** (open M-F 9am-4:30pm) on Gore St. are the only way to get cash; some backpackers, shops, and bars will also provide this service. Other services include: the **Medical Centre,** behind the camping ground (☎ 212 7337; open M-F 8:30am-5pm; after hours information available by phone) and the **post office,** next to the Visitors Center (☎ 212 8759; open M-F 9am-5pm, Sa 10am-7pm).

STEWART ISLAND

If you can't make it to Invercargill for the night, **Flynn Club's Hotel** ❷, 100 Gore St., is weathering in the tradition of the grandest European hotels. (☎212 8124. Reception in the adjacent bar. Budget rooms $15; singles $30; doubles $60.) **Bluff Backpackers and Hunting Lodge** ❶, 120 Gore St., is heavy on the hunting lodge, light on the backpackers. Be prepared to talk guns and game in this antiquated former post office. (☎025 207 7301. Reception 8am-6pm. Dorms $12-14.) Follow signs from Marine Pde. to the basic **Bluff Camping Ground** ❶. Pay by the honor system—there is no attendant. (Showers $2. Cabins $8 per person; tent sites $5.) **Groceries** are available at the **Four Square**. (Open M-W 8am-6pm, Th-Sa 8am-7pm, Su 9am-6pm.)

While waiting for the ferry, a handful of local sights will help you pass the time. The **Paua Shell House**, 258 Marine Pde., is a shrine to all things kitsch, most notably its collection of thousands of lacquered and colorful shells that adorns the interior. (☎212 8262. Open daily 9am-5pm.) The **Bluff Maritime Museum**, on the pier, is a good place to learn about the region's history. (☎212 7534. $2, students and seniors $1. Open M-F 10am-4:30pm, Sa-Su 1-5pm.) The only attraction in Bluff bordering on breathtaking is the lookout from **Bluff Hill**, an endless view extending to Stewart Island and over Invercargill to the southern corner of Fiordland National Park. To reach the lookout, follow the brown signs from Gore St. At the end of SH1, an **International Road Sign** marks the distances to such far-off locales as New York City and Tokyo.

STEWART ISLAND ☎03

Maori legend has it that when Maui fished up the North Island from his South Island canoe, Stewart Island was his anchor stone. Named *Rakiura* in Maori, "the place of glowing skies" sees fiery red sunsets and the eerie *aurora australis*. Muddy tracks and remote beaches retain the wild flavor of a land where kiwis still vastly outnumber Kiwis. Celebrating this untouched splendor, Stewart Island became New Zealand's newest national park in 2002. Bird life abounds, with wood pigeons noisily swooping through town, rarer birds thriving on rat-free Ulva Island, and droves of penguins and muttonbirds crowding beaches. The island's 390-odd (or 390 odd) residents cluster in the fishing village by Halfmoon Bay, gracefully weathering 290 days and 1580mm of rain per year. They insist, with good reason, that you haven't seen New Zealand until you've experienced their beech-free forests, pristine beaches, and relaxed lifestyle.

TRANSPORTATION

Flights: Stewart Island Flights (Invercargill for bookings ☎218 9129, Oban 219 1090) flies 9-seat prop planes to and from **Invercargill** (20min.; 3 per day and on demand; $80, return $145; standby $55, return $95). Only 15kg of baggage per person—extra gear must be flown over separately. Stewart Island Flights runs a free shuttle from their Stewart Island airstrip to **Halfmoon Bay. Spitfire Shuttle** (☎214 1851) goes between **Invercargill** and the **airport** (on demand; $6, $4 per person for 2-10 passengers). Standby flights to Stewart Island are much faster and almost as economical as taking the rough and rocky ferry ride.

Ferries: Foveaux Express (☎212 7660) runs a catamaran between Bluff and Halfmoon Bay (1hr.; 1-2 per day; $45, return $84, children half-price). Alternatively, the record for swimming the strait is 9hr. and 41min. **Campbelltown Passenger Service** (☎212 7404) provides connecting service between Bluff and Invercargill (30min., 5 per day, $10). Secure car-storage around the ferry terminal in Bluff costs $5 per night.

Shuttles and Rentals: Oban Tours and Shuttles (☎219 1456) hires **mopeds** (from $20 per hr.) and **cars** (half-day $50, full-day $70; includes mileage and petrol), and runs a **shuttle** service (on-call daily 7am-10pm).

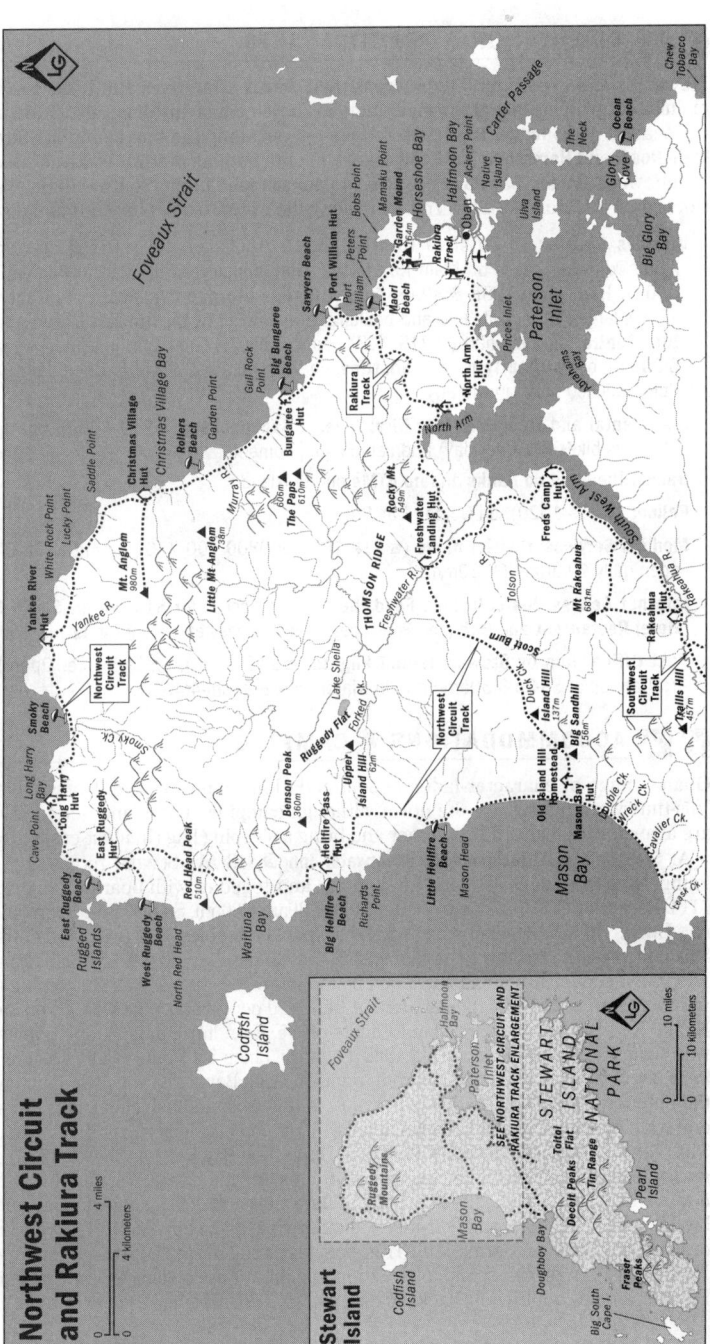

STEWART ISLAND

ORIENTATION & PRACTICAL INFO

Stewart Island lies about 35km across the **Foveaux Strait** from Bluff, the nearest mainland town. The island's primary human settlement is tiny **Oban,** also known by its location at **Halfmoon Bay.** **Elgin Terrace** curves along the bay, while **Ayr Street, Main Road,** and **Horseshoe Bay Road** branch inland; nothing in town is farther than a 15min. walk. **Golden Bay Road** crosses to **Paterson Inlet** in the South (10min.), and Horseshoe Bay Rd. and Elgin Tce. lead along the water to quiet beaches and coves.

Visitors Center: The **Visitor Centre** (☎219 0009; fax 219 1555; stewartislandfc@doc.govt.nz) is on Main Rd., in the same building as the **DOC office** (☎219 0002). Both open M-Sa 8:30am-7pm. **Luggage storage** available (small lockers $2.50, large $5). Activity info and bookings are handled by the **Stewart Island Adventure Centre,** on the wharf (☎219 1134; open daily 7:15am-7pm; in winter 7:15am-6:30pm), or by **Oban Tours and Shuttles,** on Main Rd. (☎219 1456. Open daily 9am-6pm; reduced hours in winter.)

Bike Rental and Tramping Gear Hire: Innes's Backpackers (☎219 1080), on Argyle St., rents bikes ($10 per day) and camping equipment.

Banks: There are **no banks** and **no ATMs** on the island.

Police: (☎219 1020), on Golden Bay Rd.

Medical Services: District nurse (☎219 1098 or 0800 100 776), on Argyle St. Clinic open daily 10:30am-12:30pm.

Internet Access: Justcafe (see **Food,** below) has access for $14 per hr. **South Sea Hotel Restaurant and Pub** (see **Food,** below) has access at the bar for $2 per 15min.

Post Office: Run by **Stewart Island Flights** (☎219 1090), on Elgin Tce. Open M-F 7:30am-6pm, Sa-Su 8:30am-5pm; in winter daily 8:30am-4:45pm.

ACCOMMODATIONS & CAMPING

Oban's range of character-laden accommodations is impressive. Homestays in '70s-time-warp houses are the norm, although camping, motel, and hotel options are available. Call ahead in summer and bring a sleeping bag (in most cases).

At **Stewart Island Backpackers/Shearwater Inn ❷,** 18 Ayr St., the rooms and the lounge with pool table, TV, and kitchen are knit together with boardwalks. (☎219 1114. Reception 7:30am-7pm; in winter M-Sa 7:30am-6:30pm, Su 8:30am-6:30pm. Internet. Dorms $18; backpacker singles $24; backpacker doubles $40 ; twins and doubles $60; tent sites $8.) **Michael's House Hostel ❷,** on Golden Bay Rd. off Ayr St., is run by Michael, a good-natured and garrulous fisherman whose home is as welcoming and weather-worn as the man himself. (☎219 1425. $20 per person.) **The View ❹,** up steep Nichol Rd., past the Stewart Island Flights office, is an intriguingly loopy homestay with fantastic harbor views. (☎219 1328. Laundry. Linen $5. Doubles $40. Cash only.) **Deep Bay Cabin ❹** is a 25min. trek from town, on Deep Bay. Call for a pick-up to enjoy the outdoor shower and ready-made aviary in this isolated bush-cabin, close to several walking tracks. (☎219 1219. No linen. $15 per person; sleeps up to 4, min. charge $40.) **Ferndale Campsite ❶** (☎219 1176), off Horseshoe Bay Rd., has showers ($2) and grassy tent sites ($8) with pine-hewn bathrooms, terrific bay views, and lovely hothouses. Next to Ferndale, the homestay at **Dave's Place ❷** has a sunny lounge with a big TV, video collection, and (surprise!) another view of the bay. (☎219 1427. No linen or advance bookings. Dorms $20.) Trampers preparing to rough it on the Rakiura or Northwest Passage can spend a transitional night at **Anne's Place ❶,** on Horseshoe Bay Rd., a rustic but friendly backpackers. (☎219 1065. No linen. $12 per person.)

FOOD

Dr. Britt's pottery-filled and earth-toned **Justcafe ❶**, on Main Rd., is a mellow and tasteful island-on-an-island, serving quality java ($3.50) and, contrary to its name, gourmet sandwiches ($4-5) and baked goods. (☎219 1422. Open daily 9am-6pm; closed June-July.) Mammoth wood-fired pizzas are the norm at Stewart Island's latest eatery, **The Lighthouse Pizzeria and Wine Bar ❹**, on Main Rd. The Big Glory, a concoction of salmon, mussels, avocado, capers, and dill smothering a doughy disk, goes for $25, but most large pizzas cost $20. (☎218 1208. Open Tu-Su 6:30pm-late; in winter Th-Su only.) Brass plates adorn the walls of the comfortable **South Sea Hotel Restaurant and Pub ❸**, at the corner of Main Rd. and Elgin Tce., where locals mingle to tell stories about (and drink like) fish. (☎219 1059. Mains from $14. Restaurant open daily 7-9:30am, noon-2pm, and 6-9pm; in winter 7-9:30am, noon-2pm, and 6-7:30pm. Pub open from 11am until "as late as necessary.") If in a rush, try elbowing your way to the counter at the **Kai Kart ❷**, on Ayr. St. Set in an old trailer, this greasy spoon has cheap takeaways (burgers $6) and sit-down diner-style meals (rumpsteak $15) in the evening. (Check window for hours.) The **Church Hill Cafe and Bar ❺**, 36 Kamahi Rd., sits beside the church at the top of the hill, behind the wharf. The food borders on dear (roast muttonbird $26), but the views and atmosphere are delightful. (☎219 1323. Open daily 10:30am-late; in winter W-Su 11:30am-late.) **Ship to Shore**, on Elgin Tce., sells a decent array of foodstuffs, with a slight strait-inspired price hike. (☎219 1069. Open daily 7:30am-7:30pm.)

OUTDOOR ACTIVITIES

Many easy day-walks start in Oban. **Observation Rock**, a 15min. walk up and beyond Ayr St., affords prime sunset views over Paterson Inlet. The 3hr. return walk to **Ackers Point**, east of town, is a great option for summer dusks, as muttonbirds fly here to nest. Quiet, sandy swimming beaches are close to town along any coastal road. Other day hikes include: the **Golden Bay/Deep Bay** walk (return 2hr.; follow Ayr Rd., then Golden Bay Rd. and look for track signs), which affords forest-framed views of the striking Paterson Inlet; the **Fern Gulley** walk (return 2hr.; take Main Rd. onto Kaipipi Rd. and follow track signs), which provides a brief glimpse of native bush and birds; and the **Garden Mound/Little River/Lee's Bay** walk (return 4-5hr.; walk along Horseshoe Bay Rd. for nearly 1hr., then turn left on Lee's Bay Rd. and look for track signs), which climbs to a lookout at Garden Mound and then emerges from the bush where the Little River meets the sea at Lee's Bay.

For more serious trampers, the challenging **North West Circuit Track**, which continues from the Rakiura Track (see below), rewards trampers with lots of mud, uncut forests, the well-named dunes of Ruggedy Beach, the option to scale the highest point on the island (Mt. Anglem, 980m), and best of all, a very strong chance of seeing kiwi along the wild west coast. The walk takes 10-12 days, not including a possible side-trip to the 3-4 day **Southern Circuit**, and is the best tramp to tackle if you have the time. The Southern Circuit branches from the Rakiura Track and provides a more direct route to the kiwi-viewing beaches of Mason Bay. **Mason Bay** is also accessible by taking a water taxi to Freshwater Landing and than tramping several hours to the bay. Backcountry huts ($5) along both the North West and Southern Circuits have running water and toilets but no cooking stoves; tenting is free.

Between December and February, DOC conducts its **Stewart Island Summer Visitor Programme**, including an evening slideshow ($3) and guided trips to the gloriously predator-free—and hence wildlife abundant—**Ulva Island** in Paterson Inlet. ($35, children $25; advance bookings essential.) Otherwise, **Seaview Water Taxi** (☎219 1014), **Stewart Island Watertaxi** (☎219 1394), **Rakiura Adventures** (☎219 1414

FROM THE ROAD

FEAR AND ITCHING ALONG THE RAKIURA TRACK

From cannibal legends to vampire myths to *Jaws*, the thought of becoming someone else's dinner is an enduring human nightmare. Though New Zealand lacks any indigenous predators lethal to man (the most dangerous pest is a mildly poisonous caterpillar), I came close to being eaten alive on the Rakiura Track. Camped on Maori Beach, New Zealand's most fearsome pests had somehow winnowed en masse into my sleeping bag, sucking my blood in hundreds of miniscule bites. Yes, I was being devoured by sandflies and mosquitoes. Most victims respond with swelling, itchy welts, and oozing wounds—and I was no exception.

Attempting to defeat the onslaught, I slapped them, I slathered on bug spray, I tightened the drawcord on my sleeping bag. When I realized that nothing would stop the bugs from invading my bag, I resigned myself to their feasting, consoled that my restless tossing and turning would squish them by the dozens.

After hours of fly-fearing insomnia, I gave up on sleeping around 4am. Even if it meant I'd be hiking in the dark, I decided that I'd be harder to eat as a moving target. When I emerged from my sleeping bag, my body was speckled with bright red welts and smeared with blood and mosquito carcasses.

It was a miserable night, perhaps my most uncomfortable ever. It's hard feeling so feeble, so hopeless, and so delicious when confronted with something so small. It ain't easy being someone else's dinner.

—Mark Kirby

or 219 1284), and **Seabuzzz** (☎ 219 1282) also make the bird-intensive trip (return $25, $20 per person for 2 or more; advance bookings essential). Seabuzzz leads glass-bottom boat trips to the salmon and mussel farm, as does **Talisker Charters** (☎ 219 1151). On alternate evenings, **Bravo Adventure Cruises** runs a cruise and bushwalk to see wild brown kiwi near the mouth of Paterson Inlet. With a 98% kiwi-spotting success rate, this is the surest way to behold the flightless icons without trekking the North West Circuit. (☎ 219 1144. 4hr. $60, max. 15 people; bookings essential.) **Ruggedy Range Expeditions** offers a variety of guided hikes, included two-day water-taxi/tramp trips to Mason Bay, the prime kiwi sighting site on the island. (☎ 219 1066. $265.)

Water activities in Stewart Island are as original as its residents; speak with booking agents to see what types of trips are running. **Completely Southern Sea Kayaks** (☎ 219 1275) rents boats ($40 per day) and runs guided paddles around Paterson Inlet and farther afield (from $65 per day). **Lo Loma** (☎ 219 1282), **Mareno Excursions** (☎ 219 1023), and **Talisker Charters** (☎ 219 1151) run fishing, sightseeing, and diving trips as well. **Oban Tours and Shuttles** (☎ 219 1456) rents two-tank scuba gear ($100 per day) and snorkeling sets ($40 per day); they also run daytime bus tours (1½hr.; $20, children $10) and sunset rides (Dec.-Feb.; 2½hr.; $30, children $15). Local naturalist and eccentric raconteur graybeard Sam teams up with his trusty vehicle as **Sam and Billy the Bus** to do an offbeat tour of Stewart Island's road-accessible sights. (☎ 219 1269. 1½hr. $20, children $10.) To flex your mental muscles after a day of touring, play **chess** on Oban's giant waterfront board.

THE RAKIURA TRACK

Cruising along a constantly undulating and occasionally monotonous boardwalk almost entirely below the bushline, the Rakiura Track lacks the spectacular flash boasted by more view-festooned Great Walks. There's plenty to delight the birdwatcher or botanist though, from numerous silver-throated tui to exquisite hanging orchids. The track is too close to the dogs and development of Halfmoon Bay to support many kiwi, but the beaches are clean and vital regardless.

Length: 36km, 2-3 days.

Trailheads: The DOC office is at the center. From the office, Main Rd. leads west about 2km to the **Kaipipi Road** trailhead. The other proper trailhead is at **Lee Bay,** about 5km from town; just across from the wharf, Horseshoe Bay Rd. runs north to Lee Bay Rd., which dead-ends at this trailhead.

TE ANAU ■ 407

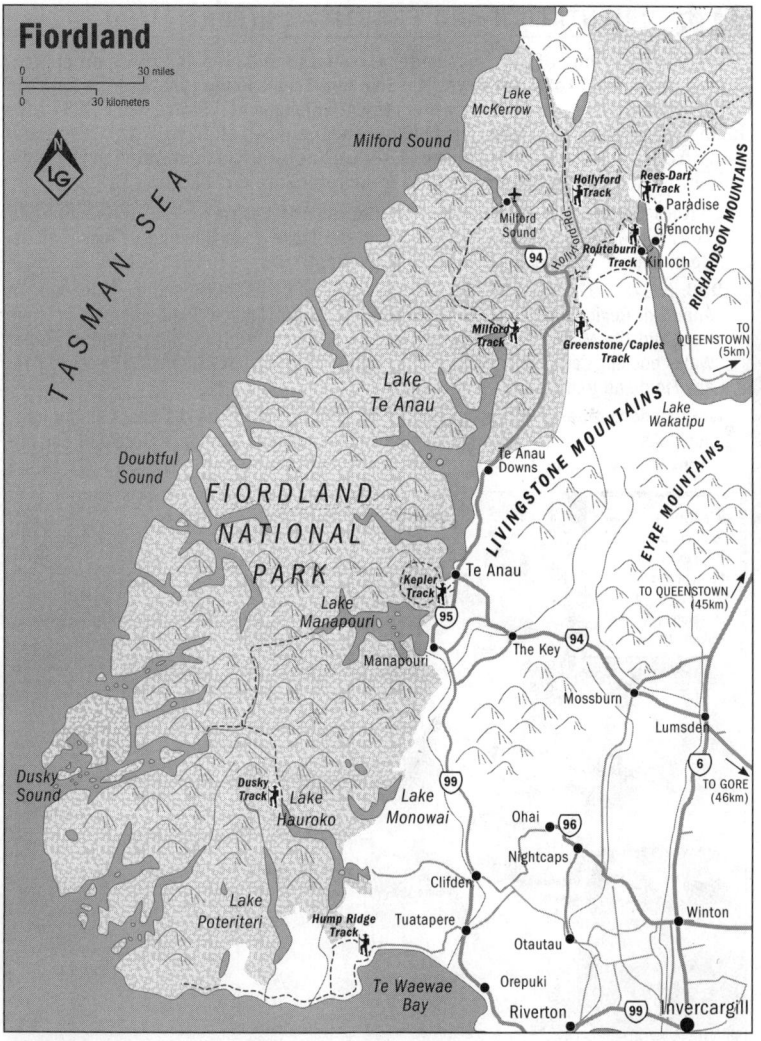

Fiordland

Boat Hire (☎ 249 8364), on the lake, rents kayaks ($10), canoes ($8), and dinghies ($5). All rates per 30min.

Hitchhiking: Though *Let's Go* does not recommend it, Milford hitchers generally walk out to the school at the north end of town. Hitching is nearly impossible in winter. Getting to Manapouri or Queenstown is also easy in summer and more difficult in winter; most thumbers walk to where the Southern Scenic Rte. splits from Lakefront Dr.

408 ■ FIORLAND

✈ ℹ ORIENTATION AND PRACTICAL INFORMATION

The short main drag of the town center is called **Town Centre** and runs perpendicular to the lake and **Lakefront Drive**. The **Southern Scenic Route** runs west beyond the DOC office (left as you face the water) toward **Manapouri** (20km), while **SH94** runs inland east toward **Mossburn**. The **Milford Road** branches off from Town Centre and away from the lake to **Milford Sound** (120km). Shops are concentrated in the town center, while booking agencies and tour operators are on Lakefront Dr.

Visitors Center: The **Te Anau Visitor Information Centre** (☎ 249 8900; fax 249 7022; vin@fiordlandtravel.co.nz), at **Fiordland Travel** (see **Booking Offices,** below). Open daily 8:30am-6pm; in winter 8:30am-5pm.

DOC: (☎ 249 7924; fax 249 7613), at the corner of Lakefront Dr. and the Manapouri-Te Anau Rd. Regional office for **Great Walks,** Fiordland National Park, tramping information, and the Milford Rd. Open daily 8:30am-6pm; in winter 8:30am-4:30pm; Great Walks booking desk closes at 5pm. They also sell **plastic pack liners** ($3), essential for any Fiordland tramping adventure.

Work Opportunities: Hostels, cafes, and big tour operators are the best bets for jobs; positions are scarce in the winter. The local employment agency is **Fiordland Employment Centre** (☎ 249 7754).

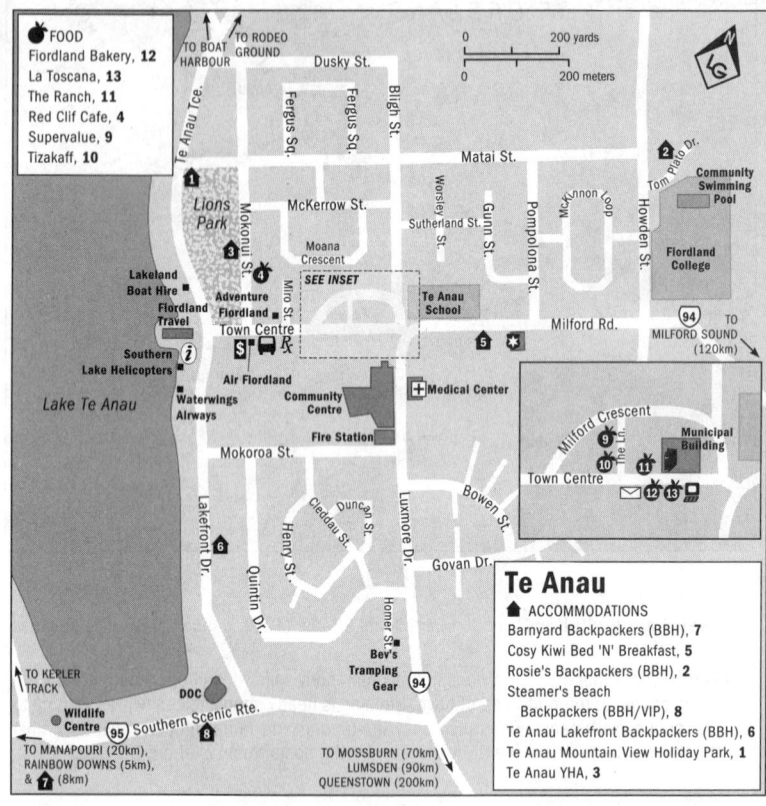

TE ANAU ■ 409

Booking Offices: Air Fiordland, 70 Town Ctr. (☎249 7505). Open daily 7:30am-8pm; in winter 8:30am-5:30pm. **Fiordland Travel** (☎249 7416), at the lakeside end of Town Ctr. Open daily 7:30am-9pm; in winter 8am-7pm. **Adventure Fiordland,** 69 Town Ctr. (☎249 8500), also arranges trips. Open daily 8am-9:30pm; in winter 11am-4pm. **T.A. Travel and Information Centre** (☎249 7516), on the lakefront next to the Moose Restaurant. Open daily 8am-7pm; in winter 9am-5pm.

Tramping Gear: Bev's Tramping Gear Hire, 16 Homer St. (☎249 7389; www.ubd.co.nz/bevs.hire), rents packs and sleeping bags for $20 each for 3-4 days and sells backcountry food. Her **Great Walks Package** (3-4 days, $80) includes everything—except boots—that an unprepared tramper could need. Open daily 9am-noon and 6-8pm. **Sports World,** in the town center (☎249 8195), also does rentals and has extensive outdoor retail. Open daily 9am-9pm; in winter 9am-6pm. **Mobil Station,** 80 Town Ctr. (☎249 7247), rents **PLBs (Personal Locator Beacons)** for $20 per week. Open daily 7am-8pm.

Banks: Westpac Trust (☎249 7824) and **BNZ** (☎249 7826), both in the town center, have **24 hr. ATMs.**

Police: 196 Town Ctr. (☎249 7600).

Medical Services: Te Anau Pharmacy, 60 Town Ctr. (☎249 7134). Open M-Sa 9:30am-7pm, Su 10am-1pm and 3:30-7pm; in winter closes at 6pm. There's also a **24hr. doctor** (☎249 7007).

Internet Access: Multi-task at **Wash 'N' Surf,** across from the Ranch on Town Ctr., a cyber-laundry stop with one of the best connections in town ($1 per 11min.). **Air Fiordland** costs $2 per 20min. (see **Booking Offices,** above).

Post Office: (☎249 7348), at **Paper Plus,** 102-104 Town Ctr. Open M-F 8:30am-8pm, Sa 9:30am-6pm.

ACCOMMODATIONS AND CAMPING

Rosie's Backpackers (BBH), 23 Tom Plato Dr. (☎249 8431; backpack@paradise.net.nz). Head up Milford Rd., turn left on Howden St., and right on Tom Plato Dr. A secluded home bordering sheep paddocks, Rosie's gives independent travelers a glimpse of family life. Free pick-up in town. Laundry. Reception 3-9pm. Book ahead as beds are few. Dorms $21; doubles $46. ❸

Barnyard Backpackers (BBH), 80 Mt. York Rd. (☎/fax 249 8006; rainbowdowns@xtra.co.nz), 8km from Te Anau toward Manapouri. Cozy ensuite cottages dot a broad hill with breathtaking views of Fiordland. Track shuttles to nearby walks make this an excellent staging stay. Discounts on horse treks and other excursions. Internet. Laundry. Reception 8:30am-8:30pm; on call 24hr. Dorms $19; twins and doubles $48. ❷

Steamer's Beach Backpackers (BBH/VIP), at the junction of Rte. 94 and 95 (☎249 7457 or 0800 483 2628; fax 249 7536; steamers@destinationnz.com). Check-in at Te Anau Lakeview Holiday Park, across from the DOC office. Modern and spacious kitchen and dining areas abut a welcoming fire-side TV lounge. Internet. Laundry. Reception 7:30am-9pm. Dorms $18; singles $46; doubles $48. ❷

Te Anau YHA, 29 Mokonui St. (☎249 7847; fax 249 7823; yhatanau@yha.org.nz). This clean and placid haven has powerful showers and a friendly staff that knows Te Anau from front to back. Reception 8am-9pm; in winter 4-8pm. Dorms $21-22; twins and doubles $44-46, with bath $56; self-contained cottage $75. ❸

Te Anau Lakefront Backpackers (BBH), 48 Lakefront Dr. (☎249 7974; fax 249 8319; www.teanaubackpackers.co.nz), is a 2-building affair. The backpackers on the right offers expansive common areas, a movie room, and a spa, while the building on the left affords a more private stay. Bike rental. Internet. Reception 7:30am-9:30pm; in winter 8:30am-7:30pm. Dorms $17-20; twins and doubles $42-60. ❷

Cosy Kiwi Bed 'N' Breakfast, 186 Milford Rd. (☎249 8471 or 0800 249 700; cosykiwi@teanau.co.nz). This new, slightly institutional house lures guests with professional hospitality, gourmet pancakes, and an outdoor spa. Singles $60-85; doubles $90-115; triples $115-135. ❹

Te Anau Mountain View Holiday Park (☎249 7462 or 0800 249 746; fax 249 7262; www.teanaumountainview.co.nz), on Te Anau Tce. From the town center, turn right along the waterfront. This is an award-winning holiday park. Bike rental. Spa. Internet. Laundry. Reception 7:30am-9pm. Standard cabins $46 for 2, with bath $75, extra person $14; tourist flats $85; motel units $98; tent and powered sites $12. ❶

FOOD AND NIGHTLIFE

If you're in need of groceries, **Supervalue,** 1 The Ln., in the town center, has the best selection, including heaps of expensive, freeze-dried tramping food. (☎249 9600. Open M-F 8am-8pm, Sa 8:30am-7pm, Su 10am-7pm.)

La Toscana, 108 Town Ctr. (☎249 7756). About as Italian as you can get in New Zealand. This is the perfect spot for a pre-tramp carbo-load or a post-tramp tiramisu indulgence. Cheesy thin-crust pizza ($8.50-17.50) and tantalizing desserts ($4-6.50). Free delivery. Open daily 5:30-10:30pm; in winter Tu-Su 5:30-9pm. ❷

Red Clif Cafe, 12 Mokonui St. (☎249 7431). This weathered cottage serves innovative takes on traditional New Zealand cuisine. The lamb rump steak is a remarkable leaning tower of mutton ($24.50). Locals congregate at the bar later. Open daily 5pm-late. ❹

Tizakaff, 9 The Ln. (☎249 9529), next to Supervalue. The newest of Te Anau's cafes serves eats, coffee, and mountain views. Breakfasts $8-11; toasted sandwiches $4; hearty vegetarian lasagna $7. Open daily 7am until 6pm-ish. ❷

Fiordland Bakery, 106 Town Ctr. (☎249 8899), is a great stop for an on-the-run lunch (sandwiches $3) or a creamy pastry. Breakfasts $7. Open daily 7am-5pm. ❶

The Ranch (☎249 8801), in the town center. This cowboy-themed pub has tacky frontier decor, "deals that helped tame the wild west," and meals that tame the wildest appetites. The $15 menu is a good feed, as are Su roasts ($10). Bands on weekends. Happy Hour with $1.50 drinks daily 8-9pm. Open M-F 4pm-late, Sa-Su 11am-late. ❷

OUTDOOR ACTIVITIES

As a starting point for three of New Zealand's **Great Walks** and a gateway to the Fiordland wilderness, Te Anau could entertain outdoor enthusiasts for months. Walk along the shore away from town (15min.) and past the DOC office to reach the **Wildlife Centre,** where you can commune with some of the earth's rarest birds: owls, parakeets, and kea reside in caged habitats. The perilously endangered takahe is an especially beautiful and sobering sight, especially with the Murchison Mountains, one of few remaining natural habitats for the birds, looming in the background across the lake. Continue around the lake about an hour (or grab a shuttle with **Tracknet** ☎249 7777; $5) to reach the **Mt. Luxmoore Track.** This tramp along a section of the **Kepler Track** (return 8-10hr.) offers fabulous lake and mountain views, and sore legs at day's end. **Sinbad Cruises** (☎249 7106) sails trampers to Brod Bay for a day walk up to Mt. Luxmoore. ($20; return $35. Departs 10:30am. Book in advance.) For more strolls in the hills around Te Anau pick up an infosheet on **Te Anau walks** at the DOC office.

Te Anau got its name from the **Te Ana-au Glowworm Caves** (some say it is Maori for "caves of rushing water"). Limestone walls worn away by 15,000 years of running waters have formed impressive caverns housing a spectacular glowworm grotto (see **Starry Night,** p. 158). Located across the lake, cave tours are run a few times daily by **Fiordland Travel.** (☎ 249 7416 or 0800 656 501. $44-51, children $15.) **Sinbad Cruises** takes aspiring sea dogs for a sail on **Lake Te Anau**, on board the hand-crafted and crimson-sailed gaff ketch *Little Ship Manuska*. (☎ 249 7106. $55.) **Rainbow Downs** runs **horse treks** through the bush from stables located between Te Anau and Manapouri. (☎ 249 8006. 1hr. $25, 2hr. $45. Pick-up $5 more. 15% discount for Barnyard Backpackers guests.) **High Ride** (☎ 0800 822 882; www.highride.co.nz) runs longer horse treks (3-3½hr., $60) and four-wheel ATV tours of the hills east of Te Anau (3hr., $98). For a cloud's view of the Fiordland area, call **Vertical Descent Skydiving.** (☎ 249 9116. 9000ft. $245; 12,000ft. $325.) Most charters on Lakes Te Anau and Manapouri run fishing trips, and plenty of locals lead guided **hunting** and **fishing excursions;** inquire at the Visitors Center.

Waterwings Airways, on the waterfront, runs a variety of floatplane flights. (☎ 249 7405. 10min. $55, children $35.) **Air Fiordland** (☎ 249 7505; www.airfiordland.co.nz) has a fantastic Doubtful Sound excursion (40min.; $180, children $110), while **Southern Lakes Helicopters** (☎ 249 7167 or 0508 249 7167; www.southernlakeshelicopters.co.nz), also on the lakefront, has a range of trips, some of which include snow landings (from $155). See **Milford Sound: Outdoor Activities,** p. 416, for information on flights from Te Anau to Milford Sound. Finally, Te Anau boasts access to the Kepler (see below), Routeburn (see p. 375), and Milford (see p. 417) Tracks.

KEPLER TRACK

Initially opened in 1988 to commemorate New Zealand's National Park's Centennial, the Kepler Track has become nearly as popular as its more historic neighbors, the Milford and Routeburn Tracks. Beginning along the sun-speckled shores of Lake Te Anau, the track climbs Mt. Luxmoore for an awe-inspiring ridge-walk before descending through ancient beech and podocarp forests to the shores of pristine Lake Manapouri. Although the track's popularity has spread rumors of a booking system, the Kepler remains the most accessible Great Walk, allowing independent trampers to set out on foot from Te Anau without transport costs or advance bookings and loop back several wondrous days later.

> **Length:** 67km, 3-4 days.
>
> **Trailheads:** The track forms a loop, beginning and ending at the **Control Gates** at the southern end of Lake Te Anau. The Control Gates can be reached from the DOC

IN RECENT NEWS

PESKY POSSUMS

Although New Zealand still lives up to its high sheep-to-people reputation, the fact is that there are now more possums than sheep. By some estimates, over 70 million of the marsupials now chew the tender leaves and damage the flowers of New Zealand's native trees. Possums carry disease, out-compete native birds for food, and are steadily consuming much of the country's remaining native bush.

As a result of their voracious appetites, possums have decimated native bird populations all over New Zealand and many of the nation's forests seem soberingly silent. In the rare areas of the country where possums have not struck, such as Great Barrier Island, the damage wreaked by the animals in the rest of the country becomes painfully apparent.

The Department of Conservation's response has ranged from poison-trapping to offering head bounties. Several New Zealand companies even market possum-fur garments. The latest, and most controversial, attack on the vermin is the use of aerial poison bombs. DOC has littered a supposedly natural, biodegradable toxin known as "1080" into many of the country's most rugged and intractable forests. DOC insists that studies overwhelmingly attest to 1080's safety, but environmentalists claim that the poison massacres the very birds it seeks to protect. Deer hunters also bemoan the use of 1080 because it devastates deer populations. Anything strong enough to kill a deer must be pretty potent, but 1080 might just be the bitter medicine needed to save New Zealand's forests and birds.

center via a 45min. walk through the Te Anau Wildlife Centre. Most walk the track in a counterclockwise direction, heading first towards Luxmore Hut.

Transportation: Although no transportation is needed beyond 2 functioning legs, some trampers choose to shorten the duration of their walk by shuttling to or from the Control Gates or Rainbow Reach. **Fiordland TrackNet** (☎ 249 7777) runs from **Steamer's Beach Backpackers/Te Anau Holiday Park** (see p. 409) to the **Control Gates** ($5) and to **Rainbow Reach** ($9). (10-15min. In summer 8:30, 9:30am, 2:45, and 4:45pm; in winter on demand. Pick-up from Rainbow Reach at 10am, 3, and 5pm.) **Sinbad Cruises** (☎ 249 7106 or 025 408 080) sails between Te Anau and Brod Bay, departing daily at 9 and 10:30am; **Lakeland Boat Hire** (☎ 249 8364) departs at 8:30 and 9:30am (both companies one-way $20, same-day return $35).

Seasonality: See **Routeburn Track: Seasonality,** p. 375.

Huts and Campsites: With gas cookers and live-in wardens during the summer ($20 per night, 3 nights $50); tent site quality varies as noted below ($9). In winter, when gas and wardens are removed, the huts revert to the backcountry system ($10 per night).

Storage: Most accommodations will oblige.

CONTROL GATES TO BROD BAY CAMPSITE. *5.6km, 1½hr.* From the Control Gates, which regulate the level of Lake Te Anau for the greater glory of hydroelectric power, the track eases motor-way broad into sandy and swim-worthy Dock

Bay. Farther along the lakeshore, the long beach of Brod Bay has a toilet, several sheltered campsites, unpurified lake water, and the opportunity to start day two by watching the sun rise over Lake Te Anau.

BROD BAY CAMPSITE TO MT. LUXMOORE HUT. *8.5km, 3½-4½hr.* The track steadily climbs a series of long, gradual switchbacks past great limestone bluffs, through a lichenologist's paradise of thick-trunked beech trees, and suddenly breaks out into golden alpine tussocks with views all around. A little farther, **Mt. Luxmoore Hut** (60 bunks) is a veritable mountain chalet with perhaps the best location of any hut in the Great Walks system. The South Fiord of Lake Te Anau and the Hidden Lakes sparkle far below, while in the distance hulk the Murchison Mountains, the last natural habitat of the fantastical takahe. Nearby are the spooky **Luxmoore Caves**, where at least two flashlights per person, an intrepid spirit, and a slim waist are wise bets. Mt. Luxmoore Hut is a fine day-hike destination and an ideal place for waiting when inclement weather bashes plans for the next stretch.

MT. LUXMOORE HUT TO IRIS BURN HUT. *18.6km, 5-6hr.* In this astounding alpine section, the track steeply ascends for about an hour until crossing the Luxmoore Saddle, just below the summit of **Mt. Luxmoore** (1472m). A 10min. scramble brings you to the top for a 360° panoramic view of the region, with sweeping glaciated terrain unfolding in every direction. The track then descends to **Forest Burn Shelter**, the first of two emergency-overnight-only shelters providing water and snack stops on days when lousy weather rages outside. The path to the second of these shelters, the **Hanging Valley Shelter**, is a prize in itself—the track follows the crest of several humped ridges, where fair weather brings awe-inducing mountain views and foul weather brings dangerously harsh winds. An extremely steep plunge back into the beeches follows a worthwhile lookout (return 5min.) over a full panorama of hanging valleys and green promontories. **Iris Burn Hut** (50 bunks) is somewhat cramped, with serviceable tent sites about 200m away. From the hut, a side trip leads to the 10m **Iris Burn Waterfall** (return 45min.).

IRIS BURN HUT TO MOTURAU HUT. *17.2km, 5-6hr.* The track briefly ascends past the hut, before opening into the **Big Slip**, a testament to erosive powers of water in this rainy land: the mountains are literally falling down. Here, in 1984, heavy rains sent a nice-sized chunk of mountain screaming down, obliterating the local tree population throughout a broad swath of the valley. Back in the intact forest, the track provides a reasonably level walk to **Moturau Hut** (40 bunks) by the shores of Lake Manapouri with a large communal area, a spiral staircase, and great sunsets. Trampers planning to complete the walk in three days often get an early start from Iris Burn and by-pass Moturau en route to the afternoon Tracknet Shuttle from Rainbow Reach.

MOTURAU HUT TO RAINBOW REACH. *6.2km, 1½-2hr.* Beyond Moturau Hut lies the turnoff to **Shallow Bay Hut** (6 bunks), a small and unserviced hut with a dunny (toilet) and a whole shore of free camping out back. Not part of the Great Walks system, this hut is cheap ($5). From the turn-off, the Kepler winds through bogland, crosses the Forest Burn River, and then reaches the swing bridge that leads to Rainbow Reach and its accompanying shuttles.

RAINBOW REACH TO THE CONTROL GATES. *10.9km, 2½-3½hr.* This less-traveled but beautiful stretch closes the loop back to the Control Gates. The track lies sandwiched between the Waiau River and Fiordland's forested border, promising a variety of views and a good chance to see parakeets or fish for trout.

THE MILFORD ROAD ☎ 03

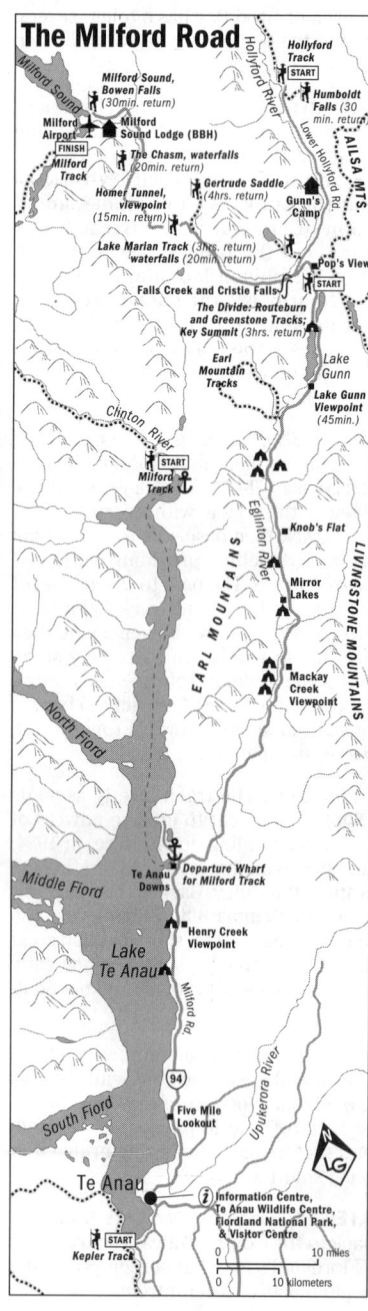

Getting there is half of the Milford Sound experience. From Te Anau to the Sound, the 119km (around 2hr. without stops and depending on bus traffic) Milford Rd. climbs through Fiordland National Park past staggeringly beautiful valleys, lakes, and creeks, so plan ahead for plenty of stops. Pick up a guide to the sights for $1 at the **DOC office.** Fiordland Travel and Red Boat Cruises have less extensive guides for free. In winter, make sure to stop at the DOC office in Te Anau to see if the road is passable or if tire chains are required (chains can be rented locally for about $25; when required, vehicles without them are subject to fines). After all, the stretch of road near the Homer Tunnel is one of the more avalanche-prone pieces of highway on earth—an average of one avalanche per day in winter keeps a full-time clearing crew stationed near the tunnel very busy. Te Anau provides the only reliable services for Milford Sound and the Milford Rd. There are no **gas stations** before Milford, and the price of gas at the sound will make you wish you'd left Te Anau with a full tank. Droves of tour-bus operators clog the length of the narrow road on their way to and from Milford Sound (see below for details). To avoid most of the tourist-bus traffic in the summer, try leaving Te Anau before 8am or after 11am. There are 12 handsome **DOC camping sites,** most with pit toilets, picnic tables, fire pits, and fresh water access, along the route ($5 per person, self-register).

From Te Anau, the road runs beside Lake Te Anau through sheep stations before entering the red-and-silver beech forest of Fiordland National Park. Traversing the broad U-shaped **Eglinton Valley,** the road runs through wide expanses of golden grassland beneath the backdrop of the Earl and Livingstone Ranges. Stop at **Mirror Lakes** to reflect on the tussocked swamp and teal ducks beyond the pools, or take a bathroom break in

Knob's Flat (where the toilet-to-inhabitant ratio is 35 to 1), with displays on avalanches and native bats (one of the only pre-human kiwi mammals). **Lake Gunn,** farther down the road, harbors a 45min., wheelchair-accessible walk through the moss-covered glory of the forest. Beaches and fishing spots abound.

A shelter at **The Divide** marks the starting point for the **Routeburn Track** (see p. 375) and the **Greenstone and Caples Tracks** (see p. 377). From here, the arresting valley views of the **Key Summit** (return 3hr.) make a great day-hike; a spot about 25min. along the track allows for views of both the road and a waterfall. Meanwhile, the road continues past **Pop's View,** a spectacular lookout named for a bulldozer operator killed in an avalanche, and over **Falls Creek,** where **Christie Falls** is visible from the roadside. Turn right onto **Lower Hollyford Road** to reach the track to **Lake Marian** (return 3hr.), which threads through lush rainforest and past waterfalls to an idyllic picnic spot in a hanging glacial valley. Farther down the Hollyford Rd. is the punishingly rugged **Hollyford Track** (56km, 4 days one-way), which penetrates lush lowland forest before reaching the sea at Martin's Bay. The route's low altitude makes it less scenic than other tracks, and the dense bush along the Demon Trail portion of the hike dissuades all but the most intrepid, but it is one of few hikes in Fiordland accessible year-round. **Fiordland Tracknet** (☎249 7777) runs on demand to the roadside trailhead from Te Anau ($37). **Huts** along the Hollyford cost $5 per night year-round; they have tank water and pit toilets but no cooking stoves.

Past the Lower Hollyford Rd. en route to Milford, the eerie **Homer Tunnel** is next; completed in 1953 after decades of work (but having the appearance of a dwarf's lair from a Tolkien novel), the rough-walled tunnel still has no internal lighting. Drivers must turn on headlights and take off sunglasses to navigate through its narrow 1km of darkness. After emerging on the other side of the mountain, hairpin turns down Milford Valley (pray not to get stuck behind a bus driving up this segment) lead to the **Chasm,** where a boardwalk (return 10min.) spans the **Cleddau River** and its surreal, water-hewn rock sculptures. Just beyond the Chasm lies the haunting Milford Sound itself.

MILFORD SOUND ☎03

Mystical and dramatic, Milford Sound (Piopiotahi) is the emblem of Fiordland National Park. In 1993, the Sound (actually a fjord) received designation as a marine reserve in recognition of its abundant sea-life, including unique waterline flora, bottlenose dolphins, fur seals, and the occasional Fiordland crested penguin. Sheer cliffs and snow-capped summits surround the Sound and its photogenic focal point, the rugged Mitre Peak. Waterfalls cascade from dizzying heights—at 146m, Stirling Falls is among the most spectacular—and grow and multiply after the frequent falls of heavy rain. Scarcely marred by a century of eager tourist eyes (commercial guided walks to the area began in the 1890s), Milford Sound retains its majesty despite the droning fleet of cruise ships and the buzzing swarm of scenic flights.

TRANSPORTATION

The variety of tour options to Milford Sound is staggering—in peak season, as many as 70 buses head up the Milford Rd. in the morning and back in the afternoon. Daytrips depart Queenstown or Te Anau early in the morning and don't return until evening; book well in advance and bring lunch with you—or prepare for high-priced mediocrity. Queenstown daytrips are long days, often 12hr. with 6hr. of driving; avoid this grueling haul by basing your tour in Te Anau. Daytrippers to Milford should try to get an early start as it sometimes clouds over on summer afternoons, while the morning fog in winter usually burns off by late morning. The following coach-cruise combos operate daily in the summer (Oct.-Apr.) and at least a few times a week during the rest of the year.

The friendly, tongue-in-cheek local guides from **Trips 'n' Tramps** run small (max. 12 people) tours from **Te Anau;** some of their trips allow several hours for tramping along the Milford and Routeburn Track. (☎ 249 7081; www.milfordtourswalks.co.nz. From $115, children from $60.) Another small option (max. 22 people), the **BBQ Bus,** based in Queenstown, stops its commentary for bushwalking and a barbecue lunch. (☎ 442 1045; www.milford.net.nz. $169, VIP/YHA members $139, children $95, 2 adult/2 child family package $433.) **Kiwi Experience** (☎ 442 9708) and Magic partner **Kiwi Discovery** (☎ 442 7340) offer comparable daytrips from **Queenstown** ($139) and one-way sector fares along the road (Kiwi Discovery's are a few dollars cheaper: **Queenstown** to **Te Anau** $30, **Te Anau** to **The Divide** $20, **The Divide** to **Milford Sound** $15). **Fiordland Travel** also offers large-scale excursions. (☎ 249 7416 or 0800 656 501. From Queenstown $170-185, children $85-$95; from Te Anau $100-120, children $51.50.) **InterCity's Milford Wilderness Explorer** offers similar service. (Air Fiordland, ☎ 249 7505, handles phone bookings in Te Anau. From Te Anau $109, children $72. Continuing tours to Queenstown $139.) Rosco's Sea Kayaks, Fiordland Wilderness Adventures, Tawaki Dive, and some of the scenic flight operators also offer packages that include transport to and from **Te Anau;** see **Outdoor Activities,** below, for more on these. Although *Let's Go* does not recommend it, **hitchhikers** report success getting to and from Milford Sound.

ACCOMMODATIONS AND FOOD

Milford Sound's hit-and-run style of tourism and DOC's control of real estate doesn't encourage an abundance of lodging and dining choices around the Sound, but the few options available are decent. The newly revamped **Milford Sound Lodge (BBH)** ❸ now offers clean rooms, new facilities, and a bistro-esque restaurant serving nouveau meals. The drying room, small grocery, and huge track map make the lodge an excellent layover for trampers. (☎ 249 8071; fax 249 8075; milford.sound.lodge@xtra.co.nz. Restaurant open daily 7:30-9am, noon-2pm, and 6-8:30pm; mains $11-17. Internet. Dorms $21; twins and doubles $52; tent sites $10, powered $12.) The **Mitre Peak Cafe** ❶, across from the boat terminal parking lot, has takeaways, sandwiches ($3-4), and steeply priced gasoline for those who forgot to fill up in Te Anau. (☎ 249 7931. Open daily 8am-5pm; in winter 9:30am-5pm.)

OUTDOOR ACTIVITIES

BY BOAT. Boat tours are the most popular way to see the Sound and the only way to view its entirety. Most trips last 1-3hr. Because of the Sound's widespread fame, prices tend to creep up every year; plan to spend a few dollars more than listed. **Fiordland Travel** sends out eight boats per day in the summer and at least three per day year-round. (☎ 249 7419 or 0800 656 501; www.fiordlandtravel.co.nz. $45-60, children $10.) Two of their summertime boats have a 10% YHA discount: the intimate, tugboat-esque *Friendship* and the *Milford Wanderer* sailboat. Both boats possess more character than many of the other vessels plowing the Sound; both also offer relaxed **overnight trips** that include a hearty dinner, breakfast, and kayaking ($155, children $77.50). **Red Boat Cruises** runs a fleet of modern, red-hulled cruise boats. (☎ 441 1137 or 0800 657 444; www.new-zealand.com/redboats. Oct.-Apr. 8 per day 9am-3pm; May-Sept. 5 per day 11am-1:30pm. $45-62, children $12-20, 10% YHA discount.) **Mitre Peak Cruises'** boats feature underwater portholes and a maximum capacity of 60 passengers. (☎ 249 8110 or 0800 744 633; www.mitrepeak.com. 3-4 trips daily 9:55am-4:50pm.

MILFORD SOUND ■ 417

$47-52, children $20, 10% YHA discount.) **Milford Deep**, the **underwater observatory** that floats more than 8m below the surface of the Sound, allows visitors a peek *($20, children $13)* at cool critters like black coral and snake stars, which grow close to the surface thanks to the light-repelling layer of fresh water that Fiordland's heavy rainfall deposits on the Sound. Most cruises can drop people off here—Red Boat Cruises offers the best price ($62) for those who want to combine a tour and an observatory visit. Milford Deep also runs its own shuttles from the boat terminal. *(☎ 249 9442 or 0800 326 969. Open daily 8am-5pm. $40, children $20.)*

BY KAYAK. Of course, **kayaking** may be the best way to comprehend the Milford Sound's vast scale, a vastness beyond the power of arms to see in a single day's paddle. **Rosco's Sea Kayaks** *(☎ 0800 476 726)* runs kayak tours early in the morning, late in the afternoon, and even after dark ($69-99), as well as daytrips ($115) that include transport to and from Te Anau. Operating out of Te Anau, **Fiordland Wilderness Experiences** offer coach-kayak-coach tours. *(☎ 249 7700 or 0800 200 434; www.fiordlandseakayak.co.nz. $110, from Milford Sound $90; not always available in winter.)* Meanwhile, **diving** in the Sound allows first-hand encounters with black coral and other creatures of the deep; **Tawaki Dive** runs great personalized excursions from Te Anau with a maximum of four people. *(☎ 249 9006; www.tawakidive.co.nz. 12hr. trip with a 4-5hr. cruise. $225, $185 from Milford Sound, $45 less without gear rental; winter trips on demand.)*

BY AIR. Breathtaking **helicopter** and **flightseeing** tours are dazzling but expensive. **Waterwing Airways** sends seaplanes from Te Anau on flights over the Sound *(☎ 249 7405; 1hr., $215)*, as does **Air Fiordland** *(☎ 249 7505 or 800 107 505; www.airfiordland.co.nz. 70min., $255)*. Air Fiordland also runs a posh flight-cruise-flight combo from Queenstown or Te Anau ($295-315). **Milford Sound Helicopters** *(☎ 249 7845)* take off straight from the Sound; trips range from a 10min. hover over the Sound ($120) to flights landing on the Tutoko Glacier ($170).

▶ MILFORD TRACK

New Zealand's Holy Grail of hikes, the astounding Milford Track opened in 1888 and soon became world famous. "The finest walk in the world!" gushed Victorian poet Blanche Baughan, who did the tramp with a walking stick, woolens, and an umbrella. Since then, over a century's worth of wide-eyed walkers has traversed the Milford's brief alpine pass and beech-lined, waterfall-laced valleys—a corner of Fiordland in pristine splendor. Today, DOC estimates that 12,000 people walk the track each year, and despite the high cost, tight regulation, occasional floods, and frequent view-spoiling but waterfall-enhancing downpours (the track has an average annual rainfall of 8m), it remains a singular experience for most trampers.

Length: <u>54km, 4 days.</u>

Trailheads: The track begins at Glade Wharf at the northern tip of Lake Te Anau and ends at Sandfly Point near Milford Sound. Both places are accessible only by boat.

Transportation: Tracknet (☎ 249 7777 or 0800 483 2628) runs from the DOC office in Te Anau to the boat launch at **Te Anau Downs** (25min.; 9:30am and 1:15pm; $12, under 14 $8), connecting to the boat run by **Fiordland Travel** (☎ 249 7416 or 0800 656 501) that heads across Lake Te Anau to **Glade Wharf** (1hr.; 10:30am, $38, under 14 $15; 2pm, $50, under 14 $15). From Sandfly Point, **Red Boat Cruises** (☎ 441 1137 or 0800 657 444) runs boats to **Milford Sound Launch Terminal** (20min.; 2:35 and 3:15pm; $22.50, under 14 $12.50), where you can catch Tracknet's 3 or 5:15pm bus to **Te Anau** (2hr.; $37, under 14 $26). The **Great Walks Booking Desk** (see **The Great Walks**, p. 71) can arrange these. From Sandfly Point, it's also possible to paddle into Milford Sound with **Rosco's Sea Kayaks** (☎ 0800 476 726; 2pm; $20, with bus

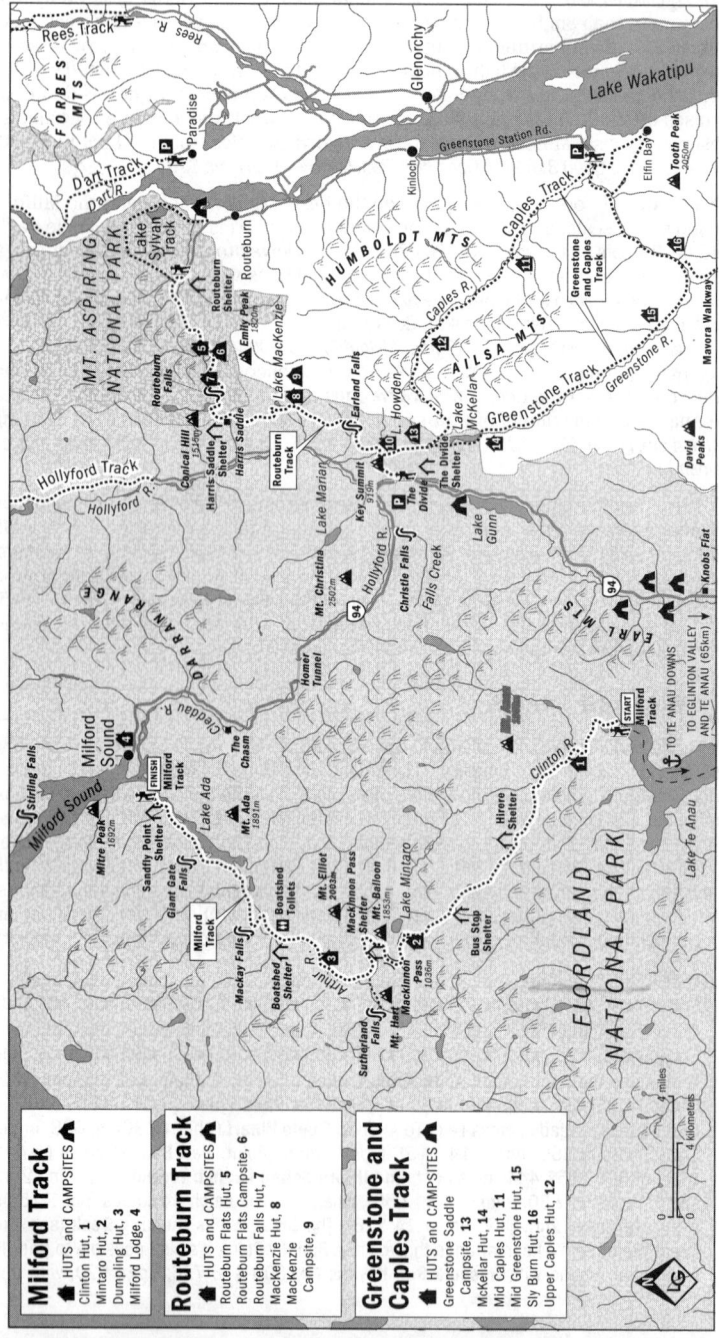

transport to Te Anau $49) or **Fiordland Wilderness Experiences** (☎ 249 7700 or 0800 200 434; 2:30pm; $49, including bus transport to Te Anau); kayaking takes 20-30min. **Sinbad Cruises** (☎ 249 7106) organizes a **sail-paddle-bus** round-trip from Te Anau ($110) and also runs a $60 sail shuttle from the lakefront in Te Anau to the Glade Wharf (departs daily 10:30am). Though *Let's Go* does not recommend it, **hitchers** set out very early or try to catch rides the day before in order to make the early boat the first morning of the tramp; returning to Te Anau, most summertime hitchers report success when hitching from near the exit to Milford Sound Lodge. Tracknet shuttles **extra gear** from Te Anau to Milford Sound ($5 per bag).

Seasonality: See **Routeburn Track: Seasonality,** p. 375.

Huts and Campsites: Six huts—3 for guided walkers and 3 for independent walkers. Huts are expensive—$105 total for 3 nights—with spacious common areas, flush toilet annexes, and rows of gas cookers (matches necessary but not provided). Each independent hut has its own DOC warden. Late Apr.-Oct. (the low season) has fuel for fires, pit loos, and fees revert to backcountry hut system ($10 per night). **Trampers must collect their hut passes from a DOC office either the day before or by 11am on the day they start the track. Camping on the Milford Track is not permitted.**

Bookings: Bookings are handled by the **Te Anau DOC Great Walks Booking Desk.** (☎ 249 8514; fax 249 8515; greatwalksbooking@doc.govt.nz. See **Te Anau Practical Information,** p. 408, for location and hours.) Unlike any other track in New Zealand, the Milford is entirely scripted: not only must you book in advance, but you **must stay in a designated hut each night.** This policy means that there's no waiting out the weather in hopes of better views. DOC allows 40 independent trampers to start the track each day. It's possible to do day hikes from Te Anau and Milford Sound, but you will not reach the best scenery in such a short time. **Ultimate Hikes** (☎ 441 1138 or 0800 659 255; fax 441 1124; www.milfordtrack.co.nz) charges $1300-1600 a head for the privilege of cooks and hot showers in upscale accommodations. **Applications** to walk the Milford independently are first-come, first-served, starting on **July 1** for the following season (late Oct.-Apr.; Dec. and Jan. fill up fast). If full, put your name on the **waiting list**—DOC will alert the freshly eligible by fax or email; couples and solo trampers have the best chances. Stopping by or calling the **Booking Desk** to inquire about cancellations can also sometimes yield a last-minute spot for those flexible on dates.

Storage: Most accommodations will oblige.

GLADE WHARF TO CLINTON HUT. *3.5km, 1hr.* The first day out is the shortest and the flattest, passing under tall, slender beech trees and the occasional totara. Just shy of the hut, the boardwalked **Wetlands Walk** (return 10min.) leads to carnivorous sundews, educational displays, and a great view out over the bog. **Clinton Hut** (40 bunks) is a corrugated outdoor mansion near the clear Clinton River. Those on the morning boat generally reach the hut very early in the afternoon and have time for a dip in some nearby frosty swimming holes.

CLINTON HUT TO MINTARO HUT. *16.5km, 5½hr.* Flat and slightly inclined tramping through beechy bush begins the second day's walk along the Clinton River. In dry conditions, the route fords various small streams; in wet conditions, the route fords various mid-sized rivers; in very, very wet conditions, this section of the track may well become a river carrying huts and trampers along with it. After several hours, the track begins to wind through open stretches allowing vantages of the stark rock walls encasing the valley. Massive cliff faces rise from either side of the valley, and a new view of a waterfall, mountaintop, or glacier awaits over every rise. A handmade sign points the way to the dramatic but carnivorous-eel-infested **Hidden Lake** (return 5min.); a safer and equally lovely swimming hole lies just a few minutes farther up the track. The way gets rougher and steeper just before passing the dank **Bus Stop** shelter and remains so as it approaches **Mintaro Hut** (40 bunks).

A cozy two-story affair, Mintaro couldn't occupy a more imposing location: step out of the front door, stare up at the 800m rock face that towers above **Lake Mintaro**, and get ready to climb tomorrow. Access to the lake is 100m past the hut turn-off on the main track.

MINTARO HUT TO DUMPLING HUT. *14km, 6hr.* Day three is the most taxing and the most incredible, given clear skies. Twenty minutes after departing Mintaro Hut, the track makes a switch-backed ascent (the Mile 15 marker indicates the halfway point) to **MacKinnon Pass**, where spectacular scenery makes tired legs an afterthought. Vast glacial valleys spread in either direction, while kea circle over the monument to Quintin MacKinnon, the Scotsman who discovered the pass and first guided people over it. Up and over another rise (20min.) waits the **MacKinnon Pass Shelter**, a cheerless but safe place sheltering gas cookers and a loo with a view. Heading back down, the track winds beneath a cliff topped by the **Jervois Glacier**, where wispy waterfalls dissolve into mist before they reach the ground. Once the trail enters the trees, a powerful series of waterfalls replaces the magnificent mountain scenery—behold the **Arthur River** beginning its tumultuous journey to the sea. At **Quintin Hut**, the next guided walkers' accommodation, independent trampers can stash their packs in the kea-proof day-shelter while they wander down the spur trail (return 1½hr.) that leads to the base of the three-tiered, 580m **Sutherland Falls**, the highest waterfall in New Zealand and the fifth highest in the world. The crash of water into water blows out enough mist to drench anyone within 10m, to say nothing of those who make the easy but slippery venture behind the torrent. One more hour leads down to **Dumpling Hut** (40 bunks); the boardwalked section just before this backcountry manor hosts hundreds of glowworms and an excellent swimming hole lies off a short track opposite the hut.

DUMPLING HUT TO SANDFLY POINT. *18km, 5hr.* The final day's flat tramping passes the guided walkers' **Boatshed Shelter** shortly before reaching **Mackay Falls** and resonant **Bell Rock** (keep a torch handy to check out the water-carved and insect-infested interior). The shelter near **Giant Gate Falls** is situated perfectly as a lunch stop, but the swarms of sandflies may demand tightening your belt until the enclosed shelter at the track's end. From the falls, the track traces the Arthur River, becoming rocky while navigating the shoreline of Lake Ada as it nears **Sandfly Point**. Here, a stout shelter protects trampers from the point's namesake as they await transport to Milford Sound. To get the boat from Sandfly Point to Milford Sound (see **Transportation**, p. 417), trampers should depart Dumpling Hut between 8 and 9am; those on the 2:30pm boat will reach the Sound in time for afternoon cruises and the 3pm bus to Te Anau.

MANAPOURI ☎ 03

The fog-shrouded peaks of the Hunter and Kepler mountain ranges preside with alpine majesty over the tiny, quiet town of Manapouri, nestled on the beech-clad banks of breathtaking Lake Manapouri. Lush rainforests and rugged, white-capped mountains reflect on the cool waters of this stunning "lake of the sorrowing heart," widely regarded as the most beautiful in New Zealand. Although tourist ventures are beginning to take hold, Manapouri remains a pristine gateway to the remote and serene Doubtful Sound.

TRANSPORTATION. Spitfire Shuttle Te Anau (☎ 218 7381) leaves for: **Invercargill** (2¼hr.; 2 per day, in winter M-F only; $35) via **Tuatapere** (1¼hr., $20) and **Riverton** (1¾hr., $30); and **Te Anau** (15min.; 2 per day, in winter M-F only; $10). Though *Let's Go* doesn't recommend it, **hitchhikers** report that getting a ride to Te Anau is easy, though buses are better for getting back to Manapouri again.

MANAPOURI ■ 421

ORIENTATION AND PRACTICAL INFORMATION. The town lies just west of the junction of the Southern Scenic Highway and SH95, 20km south of Te Anau (see p. 406), where you'll find the nearest **police station, doctor, bank,** and **DOC office**. **Visitor information** is provided by **Fiordland Travel** and **Adventure Charters** (see below). The **Beehive Cafe and Bar** (see below) has **Internet access** for $2 per 15min. The **post office** is inside the **Manapouri Store** (see below).

ACCOMMODATIONS AND FOOD. Freestone Backpackers (BBH) ❷, on the Southern Scenic Highway 2.5km south of Manapouri, is perfectly situated on a hill where locals used to collect rocks for building projects. The four hillside cabins enjoy delightful views and self-contained kitchens. (☎ 249 6893. Dorms $19; cabins $50 for 4. Closed June-Sept.) **The Lakeview Motor Inn ❷,** on the road to Te Anau, offers heaps of backpacker rooms with superb views and motel ambience. (☎ 249 6652. Dorms $20; full rooms $60-70.) Next door, the refreshingly quirky **Manapouri Lake View Motels and Motor Park ❷** has a vintage pinball machine in the game room and a rock from *Lord of the Rings* set in the reception room. (☎ 249 6624; fax 249 6699; manapouri@xtra.co.nz. Cabins $33 for 2; motel rooms $65-95; tent and powered sites $19-20 for 2.) For a snug retreat by a glowing hearth, try the **Cottage B&B ❹,** on Waiawa St. Two superb doubles with private gardens, meticulously attended grounds, and a sunny breakfast nook welcome guests. (☎ 249 6838; fax 249 6839; don.joymacduff@xtra.co.nz. Singles $65-70; doubles $90. Reservations recommended.)

The **Beehive Cafe and Bar ❷,** adjoining the Lakeview Motor Inn, is the only grog stop in town. (Meals from $10. Open M-Sa 11am-3am, Su noon-2pm; in winter M-Sa 2pm-3am, Su noon-10pm.) At the main crossroads, the **Manapouri Store** has two aisles of basic items; next door is the bright **Cathedral Cafe ❷,** with a lake view, assorted baked goods and cheap takeaways ($3), and tasty mains from $11. (☎ 249 6619. Store and cafe open daily 7am-8pm; reduced hours in winter.)

SIGHTS AND ACTIVITIES. Captain Cook was skeptical that there would be wind to return his ship to sea, so he skipped over ⚑**Doubtful Sound** in 1770, leaving only the name as his legacy. Rounded ranges carved by ancient glaciers mark the entrances to over 100km of waterways. Inaccessible by road, Doubtful Sound leaves its serenity to the pods of dolphins and Fiordland crested penguins that call it home. Boat tours of this pristine sound leave from Pearl Harbour in Manapouri, at the Waiau River outlet of the lake, crossing Lake Manapouri to the West Arm. From West Arm, land shuttles transport tourists over the Wilmot Pass Rd. (New Zealand's most expensive roadwork) to Deep Cove in Doubtful Sound.

All tour options that leave from Manapouri can also be booked from Te Anau. ⚑**Fiordland Wilderness Experience** offers acclaimed, two-day wilderness sea-kayaking excursions. The trips, conducted in sturdy two-person sea kayaks and led by experienced guides, explore a peaceful arm of the sound and include a night of camping deep in the Fiordland wilderness. (☎ 249 7700 or 0800 200 434; www.fiordlandseakayak.co.nz. $260, 3-day tours $355. Book ahead.) **Adventure Kayak and Cruise,** next to the Manapouri store, runs an 11hr. **cruise and kayak tour** of Doubtful Sound ($165, overnight $229), and cruises ($85 per hr.) and kayak rentals ($40 per day) on Lake Manapouri. Transport ($10) is available from Te Anau for the carless, but book ahead. (☎ 249 6626 or 0800 324 966; www.fiordlandadventure.co.nz. Open daily 8:30am-5:30pm. Closed June-Aug.)

Fiordland Travel (☎ 249 6602 or 0800 656 502; www.fiordlandtravel.co.nz), at the end of the road, offers extensive, full-day trips around Doubtful Sound, including a tour of the **Manapouri Power Station,** one of the world's most environmentally benign hydro-plants. Turbines at the end of a 2km tunnel beneath the earth's surface generate power from plummeting lake waters. After a lake cruise and an overland jaunt with knowledgeable ecological commentary, the tour heads through

FROM THE ROAD

DAUNTING THE DUSKY

"I didn't get where I am today by waiting out a Fiordland storm," reads a triumphant entry in the Lake Roe Hut book. After spending three days in that very same hut, waiting for the snow to stop, it was hard not to second-guess myself. I'd climbed quickly from Halfway Hut on Friday morning and reached Lake Roe by noon. Instead of pushing on to Loch Maree in the rain, I decided to stay at Lake Roe until the downpour stopped, hoping I would snag one of those supposedly splendid views of Dusky Sound from atop the Pleasant Range. By Saturday morning, the rain had turned to snow, but I continued to wait. Now it was late Monday morning, still snowing outside, and I'd just spent a restless and cold three days in the same cramped hut.

Fiordland is famous for its foul weather, but this Easter snowstorm was a bit too early to be so significant. An ominous mass of Antarctic air had taken up residence above a Tasman Sea anti-cyclone, blanketing the South Island in cold and pummeling the coast with precipitation. Where on Friday afternoon there had been rocks, alpine shrubs, and tussocks, now there was only an unending field of white.

The DOC credo on the Dusky Track is, "Prepare for the worst." In planning the trip, I'd heeded their advice beyond necessity and packed enough food and fuel to be in the woods for more than two weeks. With my ample supplies, there was no real urgency pushing me to leave the hut, save for a creeping cloud of cabin fever.

40km of Doubtful Sound to the **Tasman Sea** before returning to Manapouri. (Oct.-Apr. 3 tours per morning; May-Sept. 9:45am. $185, children $45; $35 discount for the 7:30am cruise. Overnight cruises from $340, including meals and kayaking.) There are also summer cruises to the power station only (12:30pm; $52, children $15). Bring your own lunch or pay the expensive penalty. For more intimate, less expensive trips (on a smaller boat), try **Fiordland Explorer Charters.** Their daily 8hr. journeys include 3hr. on Doubtful Sound. (☎ 0800 434 673. $150; max. 10.)

A variety of one- to three-day tracks in the area offer inexpensive—and relatively uncrowded—immersion in the grandeur of Fiordland. The **Circle Track** (return 3hr.) promises excellent lookouts of the Hope Arm of the lake, Mt. Titiroa, Manapouri, and Te Anau. Two huts ($5) are also available for longer hikes; pick up a pamphlet from Adventure Charters or the DOC office in Te Anau. **Adventure Charters** rents rowboats ($5 per person), which are necessary to cross the Waiau River from Pearl Harbor in Manapouri as all tracks begin on the far side.

DUSKY TRACK

The cardinal rule of walking the Dusky Track: unless some fortuitous Fiordland weather brings eight days of sunshine, it will take you longer than you think. The Dusky is legendary for stumbles along a gnarled root and mossy-rock footpath, wades through waist-deep mud, trudges across snow-covered alpine passes, and outright swims through flooded river backwaters. One of New Zealand's more brutal walks, the Dusky brings a weary but wide smile to intrepid trampers.

Length: 84km, 8-10+ days

Trailheads: Three access points serve the Dusky Track: Lake Hauroko (Tuatapere), Supper Cove (Dusky Sound), and Lake Manapouri (Manapouri). All 3 can be reached by boat, floatplane, or a murderous scramble through days of Fiordland bush.

Transportation: Lake Hauroko Tours (☎ 226 6681) offers service to the Lake Hauroko hut (M and Th $60, on demand for up to 10 people $350). **Fiordland Travel** (☎ 249 6602) services the West Arm of Lake Manapouri several times daily ($27; advanced booking required if beginning the track from the West Arm). From the drop-off, the track begins a 45min. walk down the Wilmot Pass Rd. **Fiordland Explorer Charters** (☎ 249 6616 or 0800 434 673) offers less expensive and less frequent service to the West Arm. They also provide shuttle service on Wilmot Pass Rd. to the track head ($25). **Waterwings Airways** (☎ 249 7405) flies floatplanes to Supper Cove ($183, min. 2 people;

weather dependent). **Spitfire Shuttle** (☎249 7505) runs between Te Anau, Manapouri, and Tuatapere ($15-25). **Parking** is available in Tuatapere and at the View St. lot in Manapouri. Though *Let's Go* doesn't recommend **hitchhiking,** trampers report success along the Southern Scenic Route.

Seasonality: Precipitation is always in the forecast. Winter months are dangerous as avalanche conditions on the track's alpine sections pose extreme risks.

Huts and Campsites: Eight **huts** service the Dusky Track ($5 per night). All huts have either fireplaces or pot-bellied stoves, with the exception of the tiny West Arm hut. With average tramping time exceeding 8 days, doing the Dusky makes an **Annual Hut Pass** an attractive option. Camping is permitted but strongly discouraged along the track. DOC recommends that all parties on the Dusky travel with **PLBs** or **mountain radios** (see **Camping and Tramping Equipment,** p. 69).

Storage: Accommodations in Tuatapere, Manapouri, and Te Anau will oblige.

WEST ARM TO UPPER SPEY HUT. *13km, 4½-6hr.*

Beginning at the DOC West Arm Visitors Center, the track follows the Wilmot Pass Rd. (New Zealand's most expensive piece of roadway) to a signpost indicating the start of the track. Descending to the Spey River, the track follows the river valley through beech forests. The first hour of the track is uncharacteristic; don't worry, the gravel runs out soon and there are plenty of muddy bogs ahead. The **West Arm Hut** (6 bunks) is a spare affair, with no heat source but plenty of screeching keas. **Upper Spey Hut** (16 bunks) sits in the middle of a swampy clearing. If your mate doesn't return from the loo, he may have disappeared into one of the abysmal mud pits.

UPPER SPEY HUT TO KINTAIL HUT. *6km, 5-7hr.*

After leaving the hut, the track climbs abruptly and then flattens to a gradual incline as it approaches the Warren Burn. Be sure to keep an eye out for the elusive orange markers along this section of the track. Climbing through tussocks of snowgrass, the track reaches Centre Pass affording arresting views of Tripod Hill, Gair Loch, and the distant Seaforth Valley. Don't pause for long because winds can be fierce; instead, follow the track along the ridge for more staggering views. The down-climb from the pass to the Kintail Burn is precipitous. **Kintail Hut** (16 bunks) lies sheltered against a hillside with a burbling stream out front.

KINTAIL HUT TO LOCH MAREE HUT. *9km, 6-8hr.*

Depending on the weather conditions, this section of the track can be one of the most demanding; when rain has been constant and heavy, the lower section

---

The hut began to feel smaller and smaller, colder and colder, constricting the horizon into a narrow view comprised of my sleeping bag, gas cooker, and endless packets of instant soup and mashed potatoes. Around 10:30am, I decided I'd had enough, packed my bag, struggled into my frozen socks and boots, and stumbled out into the storm, determined to make it to Loch Maree and give up on the fabled views of Dusky Sound.

It took only 1½hr. to realize that I needed to return to the hut or risk becoming lost and frozen. The drifts were chest-deep in places and the snow was poorly consolidated, making the speed of travel impossibly slow. What's more, if it had started snowing any harder, the bright orange snow-markers would have become invisible and the route over the Pleasant Range would have disappeared. I returned to the hut, resigned to give up my hopes of reaching Loch Maree.

I soon discovered that Fiordland occasionally rewards patience, and Tuesday morning brought brilliant sunshine. I made it to Loch Maree easily, enjoying snowcapped peaks and stunning views of Dusky Sound along the way. Looking at other hut-book entries, I realized that I had it pretty easy. Occasionally, trampers will get stuck for a week or more, run out of provisions, and have to be lifted out by helicopter. Moral: you can get where you need to go by waiting out a Fiordland storm. Just make sure you have an unlimited amount of time, a small library of books to fight the stir-craziness, and the entire stock of the local grocery store strapped to your back.

—Mark Kirby

of the track is impassable. Following the shores of Gair Loch, the track passes over rough terrain descending the gorge, and emerging near the head of an enormous slip. After crossing the Kenneth Burn walkwire, the track flattens out and passes easily underfoot for several kilometers, occasionally forcing trampers to wade across backwaters of the Seaforth River when it's been raining. The last several kilometers between the Deadwood Creek and Loch Maree are tricky underfoot and can be entirely flooded when the Seaforth is high. **Loch Maree Hut** (16 bunks; pot belly stove) provides a welcome respite to a long day of sludging through the muck.

LOCH MAREE HUT TO SUPPER COVE. *13km, 6-8hr.* Many trampers have spent a day, or two, or five, stranded at Loch Maree due to high flows of the Seaforth. The best indicators of whether or not the river's low enough to proceed are the tree trunks in the lake. When the trunks are completely submerged, sit it out or be prepared to swim for your life. The track to Supper Cove follows an old miners' road and can be easy going when not flooded. The last leg of the track after the Henry Burn can be rough, but trampers who have planned the tides right (there's a tide chart in Loch Maree Hut) can avoid this section by cutting across at low tide. **Supper Cove** (16 bunks) sits on the shores of the track's namesake, the Dusky Sound, and as the name of the cove implies, those who have lugged fishing line into the woods will be handsomely rewarded with fresh fish.

LOCH MAREE HUT TO LAKE ROE HUT. *8km, 5-7hr.* After leaving the hut, the track quickly approaches the most unpredictable obstacle on the Dusky Track, the three-wire crossing of the Seaforth. In foul weather, the entire far side of the crossing can be submerged by the engorged river, making it impossible to get across. There's a three-wall shelter on the far side above the flood level to harbor trampers coming from Lake Roe. Across the walkwire begins the steepest ascent on the Dusky, a 600m vertical scramble spread over only 1km of horizontal distance. The top rewards with exceptional views of Dusky Sound, the surrounding mountains, and the Tasman Sea. From here, the track traverses the Pleasant Range, achieving a series of alpine vistas as it travels to **Lake Roe Hut** (16 bunks; pot belly stove).

LAKE ROE HUT TO HALFWAY HUT. *7.5km, 3-5hr.* After about 45min. of tramping, the track dips below tree-line, following the Hauroko Burn as it descends rapidly. After crossing two walkwires, the track flattens a bit, following the burn through native beech forest. **Halfway Hut** (12 bunks) has an open fireplace.

HALFWAY HUT TO HAUROKO HUT. *9km, 4-6hr.* Similar to the previous day's tramping, the track winds through lush forests, occasionally offering scenic views of the Hauroko Burn. Once at **Hauroko Hut** (10 bunks), break out the bug spray and prepare to battle the sandflies as you wait for your boat out.

SOUTHERN SCENIC ROUTE

When heading to or from Te Anau and Invercargill consider taking the ⛰**Southern Scenic Route.** While the inland route passes through the service towns of Lumsden and Mossburn, the Southern Scenic Route takes an equally efficient but more enjoyable path, skirting ocean vistas and mountain panoramas before heading inland and upland to Te Anau. The stretch of road from Tuatapere to Riverton is dotted with small towns, a handful of motor parks and taverns, and innumerable bays and inlets with great surfing and paua shells.

The **Kiwi Experience Bottom Bus** runs from Invercargill to Te Anau with an overnight stay in Riverton. (☎442 9709. Daily 6pm; in winter M, W, and Sa only.) **Spitfire Shuttle Te Anau** runs in both directions. (☎218 7381. 2 per day; in winter M-F only; Invercargill to Te Anau $40, Te Anau to Tuatapere or Tuatapere to Invercargill $25.

Inquire about backpackers discounts. Book in advance.) Though *Let's Go* doesn't recommend it, **hitchhiking** along this stretch of the Southern Scenic Route is reportedly a good prospect in summer but uncertain in winter.

CLIFDEN ☎ 03

South of Manapouri and just 17km north of Tuatapere, the hamlet of Clifden is known for its **limestone caves,** located 1km up the road after the lime works on the route toward Winton. Prospective spelunkers should pick up a map in Tuatapere and bring a flashlight. The caves are cramped in places and sometimes flooded, so if you decide to go, be extremely careful. Take a moment to walk the historic **suspension bridge,** completed in 1902. Downstream, the protruding cliff face looks like the profile of a legendary Maori maiden whose broken heart drove her to leap off the precipice. From Clifden, the road heads through the Waiau River valley as the inaccessible Takitimu Mountains to the east and the distant heights of Fiordland to the west occasionally appear over the foothills.

TUATAPERE ☎ 03

Situated halfway between Invercargill and Te Anau, Tuatapere (tua-TAP-ery) has gone from a small logging town (pop. 700) to a destination in its own right thanks to the new Hump Ridge Track. When Tuatapere's logging industry shut down more than a decade ago, a group of local citizens formed a trust to create the track and to deliver the area from economic ruin. Finally opened in 2001, the project has been a huge success, drawing droves of Kiwi and international trampers.

TRANSPORTATION AND PRACTICAL INFORMATION. The **Spitfire Shuttle Te Anau** (☎218 7381) goes to **Invercargill** and **Te Anau** (2 per day, in winter M-F only; $25). Tuatapere's **Visitors Center & Bushman's Museum** is south of the bridge over the **Waiau River** and sells **hut passes** for DOC tramps. (☎226 6399. Open daily 9am-5pm; in winter 10am-3:30pm. Museum entrance by donation.) The **Hump Track Trust Office,** at the corner of Half Mile Rd. and Clifden Hwy., handles all Hump Track passes. (☎226 6739 or 0800 486 774. Open daily 7am-6pm; in winter M-F 8:30am-5pm.) **Tuatapere Health and Gift,** across from the Visitors Center, doubles as the **post office.** (☎226 6999. Open M-F 9:30am-5:30pm; also F 7-9pm.)

ACCOMMODATIONS AND FOOD. Tuatapere's beacon of "southern hospitality," the **Waiau Hotel ❹,** south of the town center, has pleasant, private rooms in a building dating from 1909. (☎226 6409. Breakfast $7-10. Singles $45, with bath $50; doubles $60, with bath $65.) A more budget-oriented lodge, **Five Mountains Holiday Park and Hump Track Backpackers ❶,** north of the bridge, has clean and crowded dorm rooms. They also run a 7am shuttle to the Hump Track trailhead for $10. (☎226 6418. Free laundry. Linen $5. 24hr. reception next door in the private residence. Dorms $10; cabins $30 for 2; tent sites $10; powered caravan sites $15.) Better camping sites can be found by the river past the Domain, though the cabins there are starkly basic (tent sites $6; cabins $12). Trampers planning to tackle the Hump Ridge Track will appreciate the hunting-lodge-style bunkrooms at the **Rarakau Homestay and Lodge ❷,** adjacent to the Hump Ridge carpark and trailhead. (☎226 8192. Dorms $15.) A warm home and fresh eggs welcome travelers at the **Kowhai Cottage B&B ❷,** 8 Grove Burn Rd. (☎226 6650. $20 per person. Breakfast included.) For the poshest digs in town, **The Highway 99 Cafe and Bar ❹,** 73 Main St., lets brand-new motel rooms. (☎226 6250. Singles $60; doubles $90.)

The **Waiau Hotel ❷** (see above) has full meals from $12.50, takeaways, and a cafe with delicious home cooking and baking. (Open daily 9am-late.) At **Dowling's Discounter's ❷,** 73 Main St., perennial takeaways generally start at $10. In the same building, **The Highway 99 Cafe and Bar ❷** (see above) serves country favorites ($10-

15) in a surprisingly modern setting. (Dowling's and Highway 99 open daily 8am-8:30pm; bar open until late.) Although Dowling's may have a better selection of **groceries**, the **Western Foodmarket,** north of the river, caters to trampers. (☎ 226 6292. Open M-Th 7am-7pm, F 7am-8:30pm, Sa 7am-5pm, Su 9am-4pm.)

SIGHTS AND ACTIVITIES. Though the **Tuatapere Scenic Reserve** no longer shelters ancient tuataras, it is now home to towering beeches. Grab an informative pamphlet from the Visitors Center and follow signs to the Domain for the **Tuatapere Walkway** (return 1½-2hr.). Mountain biking along the old logging roads to Lake Hauroko (roughly 40km west of Clifden) and down winding Borland Rd. to **Lake Monowai** is very popular. Tuatapere is also home to the annual **Wild Challenge** (☎ 226 6568), a 35km whitewater kayak, 30km run, and 32km bike race held the second Saturday in January. If you're only a minor masochist, the **Waiau Grunt** (13km kayak, 8km run, 20km bike) may be more appealing. Brimming with tourists in season and out, the **Giant Totara Tree Loop**, 30km northwest of Tuatapere on the edge of Dean Forest, has trees up to 1000 years old. To get there, take Clifden Lake-Hauroko Rd. via Motu Bush Rd.

Jetboat companies fly over **Lake Hauroko** and down the rapids of the **Wairaurahiri River.** The river drops more rapidly than any other jetboat-accessible river in New Zealand, making the high-speed rush here all the more intense. **Wairaurahiri Wilderness Jet** (☎ 225 8174 or 0800 270 556; www.wildernessjet.co.nz) and **Wairaurahiri Jet** (☎ 236 1137 or 0800 376 174) both run full-day trips (around $135; book ahead).

Tuatapere acts as a gateway to the rugged forests of Southern Fiordland. In addition to the new **Hump Ridge Track** (see below) and the daunting **Dusky Track** (see p. 422), the **South Coast Track** offers a path into the Fiordland wildlands. The track begins at **Bluecliffs Beach,** 28km south of town along Papatotara Rd., and follows the same coastal track as the Hump Ridge Track (in the opposite direction) to the **Percy Burn Viaduct,** the largest wooden viaduct in the world. Seeing this engineering marvel requires walking for three days and spending two nights at the DOC hut in Port Craig. The track continues west from the Viaduct but is extremely rough and challenging.

HUMP RIDGE TRACK

New Zealand's newest track, Hump Ridge is fast becoming one of the most popular. Some even claim that it rivals the Milford in splendor (shhh...don't tell DOC). The track traces its namesake, the Hump Ridge, along the untamed border of South Fiordland, returning to its starting point along a coastline walk over towering wooden viaducts and through historic sites. Unlike most New Zealand tracks, the Hump Ridge is not administered by DOC; a private trust based in Tuatapere built and now operates the route.

Length: 53km, 4 days.

Trailheads: The track is hiked as a loop, beginning and ending at Blue Cliffs Beach. The trailhead and carpark are about 30km southwest of Tuatapere, along Papatotara Rd.

Transportation: Brazier Motors (☎ 226 6715 or 226 6629) runs a shuttle Oct.-Apr. to the trailhead (pick-up from Tuatapere accommodations daily 7am, departs Tuatapere carpark daily 3pm; return $20). **Hump Heli Shuttle** (☎ 226 6535) provides helicopter lifts for hikers who don't want to make the climb with their pack ($100, pack to Okaka Hut $45, flight to Port Craig $80).

Seasonality: The entire track is open during the summer only. However, the South Coast Track to Port Craig Hut is open year-round.

Huts: The Hump Ridge Track Trust maintains 2 top-notch huts ($40, children $20) with live-in wardens, gas cookers, tables, and 4-bed dorms.

Bookings: Bookings are required, should be made far in advance, and are available from the **Hump Ridge Track Trust** (☎ 226 6739 or 0800 486 774; www.humpridge-track.co.nz), at the corner of Half Mile Rd. and Clifden Hwy., in Tuatapere. Pick up hut passes here. Open daily 7am-6pm.

Storage: Local accommodations are very track-friendly (the local economy depends on it) and will store gear for trampers.

BLUE CLIFFS BEACH TO FLAT CREEK. *10km, 2½-3½hr.* From the carpark, the track traces clifftops before descending a staircase to the beach. Trampers have the option of continuing along the beach for 3km or staying on firmer ground slightly inland by traveling along an old coastal road. Crossing several streams on swing bridges, the track reaches a junction, with the preferred right-hand route veering sharply inland just after Flat Creek. The left fork continues on to the **South Coast Track** (also the return route for the Hump Track).

FLAT CREEK TO OKAKA HUT. *8km, 4½-6hr.* After the junction at Flat Creek, the right fork begins a gradual, then increasingly steep, climb that will make you curse the misnomer "Flat." The track initially crosses three bridges, and trampers should be sure to have full water bottles after the last stream in preparation for the grueling slog onto the ridge. After passing Stag Point and reaching the ridge, another junction greets hikers. The much welcomed **Okaka Hut** (40 bunks) is along the right fork; the following day's tramping commences to the left.

OKAKA HUT TO LUNCHEON ROCK. *4km, 2½-3½hr.* The excellent facilities at Okaka rest on a perch often called the "Gateway to Heaven," which affords arresting views of both the tumultuous South Pacific and the southern corner of Fiordland National Park. Perhaps better situated along the trail for a mid-morning snack, Luncheon Rock has toilets, water, and views of the Percy Burn Viaduct.

LUNCHEON ROCK TO PERCY BURN VIADUCT. *7km, 3-4hr.* Past Luncheon Rock, the track begins a gradual descent. At the Edwin Burn Viaduct, the track splits, heading east (over the viaduct) toward the Port Craig Hut, and west toward the South Coast Track. Following the old railway line, the track soon reaches the Percy Burn Viaduct, the world's largest still-standing wooden viaduct.

PERCY BURN VIADUCT TO PORT CRAIG HUT. *7km, 1½-2½hr.* After crossing the valley on this historic walkway, the track crosses a third viaduct and changes from a promenade across soaring architectural wonders to a slog through the mud. Several hours of plodding later, the track enters the historic sawmill town of **Port Craig Hut** (40 bunks). Once home to over 200 people and New Zealand's largest sawmill, it is now a pit stop for weary backpackers.

PORT CRAIG HUT TO CARPARK. *17km, 5-7hr.* The hike out barely rises above sea level, mirroring the coast back to the starting point. On the way, keep an eye out for artifacts of 1920s settlement, Hector's dolphins, and, if the tides are right, several tidal blow holes. Parts of the track pass through uncut mixed podocarp forest, providing a close look at native flora and fauna.

OREPUKI ☎ 03

From Riverton, the Southern Scenic Route traverses open country past the Longwood Range to Tuatapere. **Colac Bay,** a former Maori settlement 10km beyond Riverton, is a popular surfing beach with a holiday park. Fifteen kilometers farther on, summer mist appears over **Te Wae Wae Bay,** where you can sometimes see whales or Hector's dolphins. Look out for windblown trees as you pass through **Orepuki** (pop. 150). Originally located at **Monkey Island** (or **Te Puka a Takatimu,** meaning "anchor stone of Tatuatea's great canoe"), this goldmining town was relocated three times to satisfy prospectors—follow signs from the highway when you reach the mouth of the Waiau River. Nearby at **Orepuki Beach** you can find tiny, low-grade gemstones amid the grains of sand; some hopefuls still pan for gold. The stretch of the Southern Scenic Highway between Orepuki and Tuatapere affords dramatic views of the Hump Ridge across the bay, suggestive of the rugged mountains farther up the road.

RIVERTON ☎ 03

One of New Zealand's oldest towns, Riverton (pop. 1850) is a seaside retreat. The main attraction, **Riverton Rocks,** over the bridge and a few kilometers along the coast, is a popular sheltered swimming beach with views of Invercargill and Stewart Island. Many short paths to beaches and unusual rock formations like the precarious Balancing Rock start at the **Aparima River Road** bridge. The **Maori Craft Centre,** 130 Palmerston St., is worth a look for unique mementos, with handwoven bulrush *(raupo)* and flax creations on display. (☎ 234 9965. Open M-Sa 9am-5pm, Su noon-6pm.) The **Visitors Center** is located in the **Wallace Early Settlers Museum,** 172 Palmerston St., opposite the Supervalue. (☎ 234 9991. Open Nov.-Apr. daily 10:30am-4pm; May-Oct. 2-4pm.) The museum displays an impressive collection of Riverton stock—a mint condition fire engine, Maori feather blankets, and a sled used by Sir Edmund Hillary during his exploration of Antarctica. (☎ 234 8520. Hours same as Visitors Center.)

Other services include: the **National Bank** (open M-F 9am-4:30pm); **Riverton Pharmacy,** 168 Palmerston St. (☎ 234 9999; open M-F 9am-5:30pm); a **medical center** (☎ 234 8290; open M-F 9am-12:30pm; also M, W, and F 2-5pm and Tu 4-7pm; on call after hours); and the **post office** in **Supervalue,** 163 Palmerston St. (☎ 234 8541; both open M-Th 7:45am-6:30pm, F 7:45am-8pm, Sa 9am-7pm, Su 9:30am-5pm).

At the stylishly refurbished **Riverton Rock Backpackers ❷,** 136 Palmerston St., you'll find a charming TV lounge with a wood stove right next to a modern kitchen. (☎ 234 8886; fax 234 8816; rivertonrockguesthouse@paradise.net.nz. Laundry. Linen $6. Dorms $19; twins and doubles $35-88.) **The Globe Backpackers (VIP) ❷,** 144 Palmerston St., is a fun-loving hostel, equipped with Sky TV, a pizzeria, and a bar. Reservations are essential in summer and advisable in winter since the Bottom Bus stops here. (☎/fax 234 8527 or 0800 843 456; globebackpackers@xtra.co.nz. Breakfast $3. Internet. Laundry. Linen $1. Reception 4pm-late at the bar. Dorms $17; twins and doubles $40; family units available.) The takeaway pies (all under $4) at **The Nostalgia Country Cafe ❸,** 108 Palmerston St., are a flavorful lunch-on-the-go bargain, while the nouveau dinners ($15-20) are served in a maritime setting. (☎ 234 9154. Open M-F 10:30am-3:30pm and 6pm-late.) The **Beach House Cafe and Bar ❸,** 126 Rocks Hwy., a 10min. drive from town on the way to the Rocks, is a popular cafe on the cliffside, offering lunches from $10 and dinners from $23. (☎ 234 8274. Internet. Open daily 10am-late; in winter closed M.)

FIJI (VITI)

HISTORY AND CURRENT EVENTS

VITIAN PRE-HISTORY

The Fijian archipelago was first settled c. 2000 BC by the **Lapita** people, who migrated to Fiji from somewhere in the area of Papua New Guinea. Migration to the Fijian Islands continued in waves over the next few thousand years, with the most recent inhabitants arriving from Melanesia c. AD 1000-1800.

Before the arrival of Europeans, the islanders called their home Viti. It was the Tongans who dubbed the island Fiji, a name that stuck with the European settlers.

CONTACT WITH EUROPEANS

Fiji was "discovered" by Europeans relatively late compared to other nearby archipelagos. While the Dutch explorer **Abel Tasman** was the first European to sight Fiji on his way to Australia and New Zealand in 1643, **Captain James Cook** first came ashore in 1774 after visiting Tonga. Having heard tales from the Tongans of the ferocious nature and cannibalistic tendencies of their western neighbors, a cautious Cook rowed ashore, glanced around, and quickly returned to the safety of the *Resolution*. His reports bolstered the only slightly exaggerated European image of Fiji as the "Cannibal Islands." The first accurate charting of Fiji was made by **Captain William Bligh** as he and 18 of his men (after being kicked off the *Bounty* in the infamous mutiny) sailed their dinghy through the islands in 1789 and returned later in 1792. Along with the European explorers came **missionaries,** who sought to convert the Fijians to Christianity and rid them of their cannibalistic ways.

Commercial interest in Fiji began in the early 1800s with the discovery of **sandalwood** and **bêche-de-mer** (sea cucumber). The

> ### THE *OTHER* OTHER WHITE MEAT
> During the 17th-19th centuries, fantastic stories of Fijian cannibalism abounded in impressionable Europe. Amazingly, most of these notions were highly accurate—the practice of eating enemies was commonplace in Fijian society by the time Europeans arrived. In a society rooted in ancestor worship, consuming a rival's flesh was the ultimate token of disrespect, dooming his soul for eternity. Often an arm or leg would be cut from a live victim, cooked, and eaten before his eyes—sometimes he would be forced to try a piece. Many powerful chiefs were infamous for their love of the "long pig." While cannibalism gradually died out as Christian missionaries (many of the early ones were eaten) won converts, the practice persisted through the early 1800s.

IMPORTANT EVENTS

c. 2000 BC
The Lapita people arrive in Fiji; over the next few thousand years they and their descendants populate ¼ of the globe's surface using only stone age technology—an achievement unrivalled in human history

1643
Dutch explorer Abel Tasman sights Nukubasaga and the peaks of Taveuni, becoming the first European explorer to see Fiji

1774
On his second voyage in the Pacific, English explorer James Cook sails from Tonga to Vatoa in the southern Lau Group; sights but never actually encounters any Fijians

1789
Captain William Bligh and 18 of his men sail through the "Cannibal Islands" en route to Jakarta, pursued by several canoes full of angry Fijians

1800
US schooner *Argo* is wrecked; surviving crew bring a devastating epidemic to Fiji, killing many indigenous inhabitants

1808
US ship *Eliza* sinks. Swedish sailor "Charles Savage" makes his way to Bau and becomes Fiji's most influential beachcomber

1813
Overharvesting finally depletes sandalwood supplies in Fiji. Beachcomber Charles Savage is killed in an ambush and his skull is made into a ceremonial kava cup

1820
Large-scale bêche-de-mer production under the principal direction of American merchant ships begins

1850
The final explosion of bêche-de-mer production comes to an end as sea cucumbers become increasingly hard to find

1870
"Blackbirding," the frequent kidnapping of other South Pacific peoples into forced labor in Fiji's sugar industry, is finally brought to an end

traders and beachcombers who descended upon the islands disrupted local Fijian life by introducing foreign diseases, which resulted in devastating epidemics, and modern weapons, which led to internal fighting. With the ensuing chaos, many chiefs became extremely concerned about losing control of Fiji. Eventually recognizing that foreign rule was inevitable, **Ratu Seru Cakobau**, the King of Fiji, elected to embrace what his government perceived as the lesser of the colonial evils. The chiefs officially ceded Fiji to Great Britain in 1874.

The first British governor of Fiji, **Sir Arthur Gordon**, tried to promote the development of his colony by importing **indentured laborers** from India to work the sugar plantations. Between 1879 and 1916, over 60,000 Indians were brought to Fiji under five-year contracts. These workers, known as **girmitiyas**, were often subject to gross human rights violations at the hands of supervisors. Yet, despite their horrendous conditions, most chose to stay after the completion of their terms. Gradually, public pressure mounted to put an end to the indentured servitude, and the practice was officially outlawed in 1919. The tide turned in the 20th century as Indo-Fijians became quite economically successful, controlling over 70% of the nation's wealth by the late '90s. This economic inequality sowed the seeds of the racial conflict that troubles the islands to this day.

In 1904, Fiji's first representative government was formed, composed of a Legislative Council with six Europeans and two Fijians. It wasn't until 1916 that the government appointed an Indian member to the council. In the years following World War II, Fiji found itself in a period of rapid democratization. In 1963 women and indigenous Fijians got the right to vote for the first time. However, despite these advancements, tension continued between indigenous Fijians and Indo-Fijians—the distribution of seats in Parliament was limited by racial quotas, and the main political parties were based on race, with the **Alliance Party** representing indigenous Fijians and the **National Federation Party (NFP)** chiefly supporting Indo-Fijian interests.

A gradual and peaceful transition to **independence** from Great Britain ended successfully on October 10, 1970, and was accompanied by a new constitution that preserved Fiji's racial segregation in politics. The first post-independence election was won by the Alliance, and **Ratu Sir Kamisese Mara (Ratu Mara)** became Prime Minister. He remained in power until 1987, winning every election in between.

POLITICAL UPHEAVAL: THE '80S, '90S, AND TODAY

In April 1987, a coalition of Indo-Fijian parties upset the faltering Alliance Party. Many indigenous Fijian leaders felt threatened due to the increase in elected Indo-Fijians, and extremist nationalists began a campaign of protest and destabilization. Indigenous Fijian army leader **Lieutenant Colonel Sitiveni Rabuka** stormed Parliament on May 14 in a bloodless coup that ousted the fledgling government. Claiming that he was acting in the interest of all indigenous Fijians, Rabuka suspended the constitution and proclaimed himself head of a military government. Although he was eventually convinced to step down in favor of an interim government, Rabuka remained in control of the army and police, and staged a second coup in September. This time, he dissolved the old constitution and declared Fiji a republic, renouncing its status as a member of the British Commonwealth. Rabuka appointed **Ratu Mara** as Prime Minister of the new interim government.

Rabuka officially made the move from the military to politics when he ran for Prime Minister in 1992, a position that he won and held until May 1999. The foundation upon which Rabuka built his government was shaky at best. The 1990 constitution was extremely racist and discriminatory towards Indo-Fijians, and many saw it as an institutionalized assurance of the political dominance of indigenous Fijians. From requiring an indigenous Fijian majority in the House of Representatives to imposing a Christian-based compulsory Sunday observance, the system accentuated the racially divided political system. Pressure for constitutional reform came to a head with the adoption of a vastly more democratic constitution in 1997.

In the May 1999 elections, a coalition of Labour and Indo-Fijian parties took the reigns from Rabuka. **Mahendra Chaudhry,** an Indo-Fijian, became Fiji's first non-indigenous Prime Minister. The country braced itself for the protests and chaos that had followed the 1987 election, but no violence erupted—until exactly one year later.

On May 19, 2000, the anniversary of Chaudhry's election, failed businessman and indigenous Fijian **George Speight** and a group of gunmen stormed the House of Parliament, taking Prime Minister Chaudhry and several other Ministers hostage and proclaiming a new all-indigenous government. Speight expected that popular anti-Indian sentiment would lead Fijians to support him, but after a 56-day standoff with the military, he returned the hostages and was later taken into custody.

The military restored order by placing an interim government into power under banker **Laisenia Qarase** on July 4, 2000. The country has experienced relatively little conflict since. The major exception was an attempted rebellion by Speight-supporting soldiers on November 2, 2000, in which eight soldiers died and ten were injured.

The government's legitimacy was shaken by a High Court ruling that Qarase's interim government is illegal—however, new (and legal) elections were held on August 28, 2001. All major parties contested in the election, including the new **Labour Unity Party (LUP),** which claims to be non-racial and interested in the good of all Fijians. The newly-elected Prime Minister was Qarase, who chose to defy the constitution by excluding Indo-Fijians from his cabinet. The **Soqosoqo Duavata ni Lewanivanua Party (SDL)** emerged with a majority of 31 seats (out of 71 contestable seats), while the **Fiji Labour Party (FLP)** won 27 seats. The LUP received only two seats in the government. Also elected to Parliament were former Prime Minister Mahendra Chaudry and George Speight's brother.

1871
Ratu Seru Cakobau, chief of Bau, declares himself the Tui Viti (King of Fiji)

Oct. 10, 1874
Fiji becomes a British colony. Virtually all chiefs signing the Deed of Cession are from the eastern parts of Fiji. An outbreak of measles claims the lives of 40,000 Fijians, over a third of the population

1877
The Fijian capital moves from Levuka, on the island of Ovalau, to Suva, in Viti Levu, where it remains to this day

1879
Indentured Indian laborers first brought in large numbers to work on the sugar plantations

1919
Indentured labor officially comes to an end. Most laborers voluntarily choose to remain in Fiji

Oct. 10, 1970
Fiji gains independence from Great Britain. Sir Ratu Sir Kamisese Mara appointed Prime Minister

Apr., 1987	Dr. Timoci Bavadra's Indo-Fijian Labour/National Federation Party defeats Ratu Mara's Alliance Party
May-Sept., 1987	Sitiveni L. Rabuka leads two military coups, declares himself ruler, and severs Fijian ties with the British Commonwealth
Dec., 1987	Ratu Mara appointed Prime Minister of interim government
June, 1992	Rabuka becomes Prime Minister
Sept. 30, 1997	Fiji re-enters the British Commonwealth
July, 1998	New Constitution supported by President Ratu Mara comes into effect
May 19, 1999	Mahendra Chaudhry becomes Fiji's first Indian Prime Minister
May 19, 2000	George Speight takes over the House of Parliament with armed supporters, taking PM Chaudhry and others hostage
May 20, 2000	Ratu Jope Seniloli sworn in by Speight and his men as "president"

In February 2002, Speight pleaded guilty to treason charges and was sentenced to death. However, his sentence was immediately commuted to life imprisonment by the high court, raising questions within the Fijian government about the legitimacy of capital punishment in Fiji (Speight was the first man to receive the death penalty). Speight and his collaborators now live on a guarded island off the coast of Suva.

FIJIAN CULTURE

THE PEOPLE

Fiji's population of 830,000 only inhabit 100 of the 320 islands that comprise the nation; 70% call Viti Levu home. Slightly more than half of the population are indigenous Fijians, while over forty percent are of Indian descent, many of whom are descendants of *girmitiyas* (see p. 430). Fijian, Hindi, and English are the principal languages.

Christianity, Hinduism, and Islam are the predominant religions. Coinciding largely with racial divisions, most indigenous Fijians are Christian (Methodism being the largest denomination), while most Indo-Fijians are Hindu. A smaller Muslim following (about 20%) is comprised mostly of Indo-Fijians.

FIJIAN TRADITIONS

Fijian tribes are based on a hierarchical system of several **mataqali** (clans). The importance of lineage is even reflected in architecture; the highest house within each village is traditionally the temple for worship of the *kalou vu* (ancestor-gods), with the chief living in the *valelevu*, the second tallest house. In contrast to the village-based culture of many Fijians, most Indo-Fijians live in the cane-growing areas, small towns, or in Suva. While Christianity has been strongly established, some villagers still retain animistic beliefs.

SPORTS. Fijians are sports fanatics. Rugby, soccer, and cricket are the most popular contests, and broadcasts of overseas tournaments are listened to religiously. At the time of publication, the Fiji National Rugby Team was ranked 10th in the world in international competition. Rugby is played only by Fijians, while soccer teams include both Fijians and Indo-Fijians. The most famous Fijian athlete today is golfer and Lautoka native **Vijay Singh**, winner of the 2000 Masters Tournament. He is currently ranked eighth in the world.

CLOTHING. Traditional Fijian dress consists of a *liku* (grass skirt) for women and a *malo* (loincloth) for men. Since the arrival of conservative Christianity, dress codes in villages have called for less exposed skin—long dresses or *sulus* (sarongs) are the norm for women, while men now commonly wear a sulu and a t-shirt. Indo-Fijian women tend to wear a long *sari*. In the more urban areas, Western-style clothing predominates.

GIFT GIVING. An important traditional Fijian concept is **sevusevu**. This is the practice of giving a gift in return for (and with full expectation of) some sort of favor—the recipient of the gift cannot refuse to perform the favor. While **yaqona** (kava) **root** is the most common item to give a Fijian, the greatest gift one can receive is the **tabua,** a sperm whale's tooth. Length and thickness determine the value of the present. It is doubtful visitors will see a *tabua* given; laws now prohibit whale-hunting.

FIJIAN VILLAGE ETIQUETTE. Correct and respectful entrance to a Fijian village is essential. Usually, visitors do not enter a village without a guide or permission; to wander in uninvited is very rude. **Dress conservatively;** do not wear shorts or a hat. A **sulu** (sarong) is always considered appropriate. Women should never bare their shoulders and should wear pants, below-the-knee skirts, or a sulu. Lone female travelers have had mixed experiences when visiting villages; if you are traveling solo, your best bet is to enter with a group.

Upon entering the village, be prepared to present the **Turaga ni Koro** (head of the village, chief) with a gift. **One kilogram of kava root** is both appropriate and common ($10-20). You will usually be brought to his home to present the gift. It will then be ground and you will be expected to take part in the kava ceremony. Be prepared to answer a lot of personal questions.

When invited into a **bure,** leave your shoes outside and stoop slightly upon entering; to stand upright inside is poor manners. If you are invited to spend the night indoors, stay. Pitching a tent outside indicates that you see that home as unfit for sleeping. When visiting with one family, do not accept invitations to eat or sleep with other families; politely decline explaining that you are a guest of another family. Remember to speak softly as loud voices are a sign of anger, and be sure not to touch a Fijian on the head, as this is an ultimate token of disrespect. Be cautious with compliments or praise for objects, as a Fijian may feel obligated to give you something as a gift even if they cannot afford to do so. Note that village water must be treated before drinking (see **Food- and Water-borne Diseases,** p. 21).

To show your appreciation for a family's hospitality if you spend the night, you may want to give each member of the family a useful gift of an appropriate value. If you would like to give more, ask the family what they might enjoy and purchase it; a bag of groceries **(powdered milk, flour, canned meat or fish, sugar, bread, tea)** is greatly appreciated by large families. Both children and many adults appreciate **sweets** (especially chocolates) and simple **school supplies** (pencils, rulers, erasers). Some villages, particularly those participating in ecotourism projects, charge a set fee (usually around $15) for staying with a family. It is often tempting to reward villagers with a **tip** after visiting. An understanding of the communal nature of a Fijian village, however, suggests that a personal reward, especially money, is not necessarily in keeping with custom. *Let's Go* recommends giving things that can be shared, like **books** or clothing (such as a **t-shirt**) to individual hosts or guides; it's even better to present the added gift during an appropriate time to the chief and the village as a whole, when both your gratitude and generosity can be shared with everyone.

July 4, 2000
Merchant banker Laisenia Qarase appointed Prime Minister of the interim government

July 13, 2000
After a 56-day standoff, Speight frees Chaudhry and the other hostages

July 26, 2000
Speight and his men arrested for treason

Nov. 2, 2000
Rebel army troops loyal to Speight briefly take over the main military barracks in Suva; 8 soldiers killed and 10 injured as Queen Elizabeth Barracks recaptured

Nov. 15, 2000
High Court rules that the 1997 Constitution is still in effect, therefore the interim government is illegal

Aug. 28, 2001
New election held with the assistance of foreign governments; SDL wins 31 of 71 seats. Qarase elected as Prime Minister

February, 2002
Speight convicted of treason and sentenced to death; sentence commuted to life imprisonment

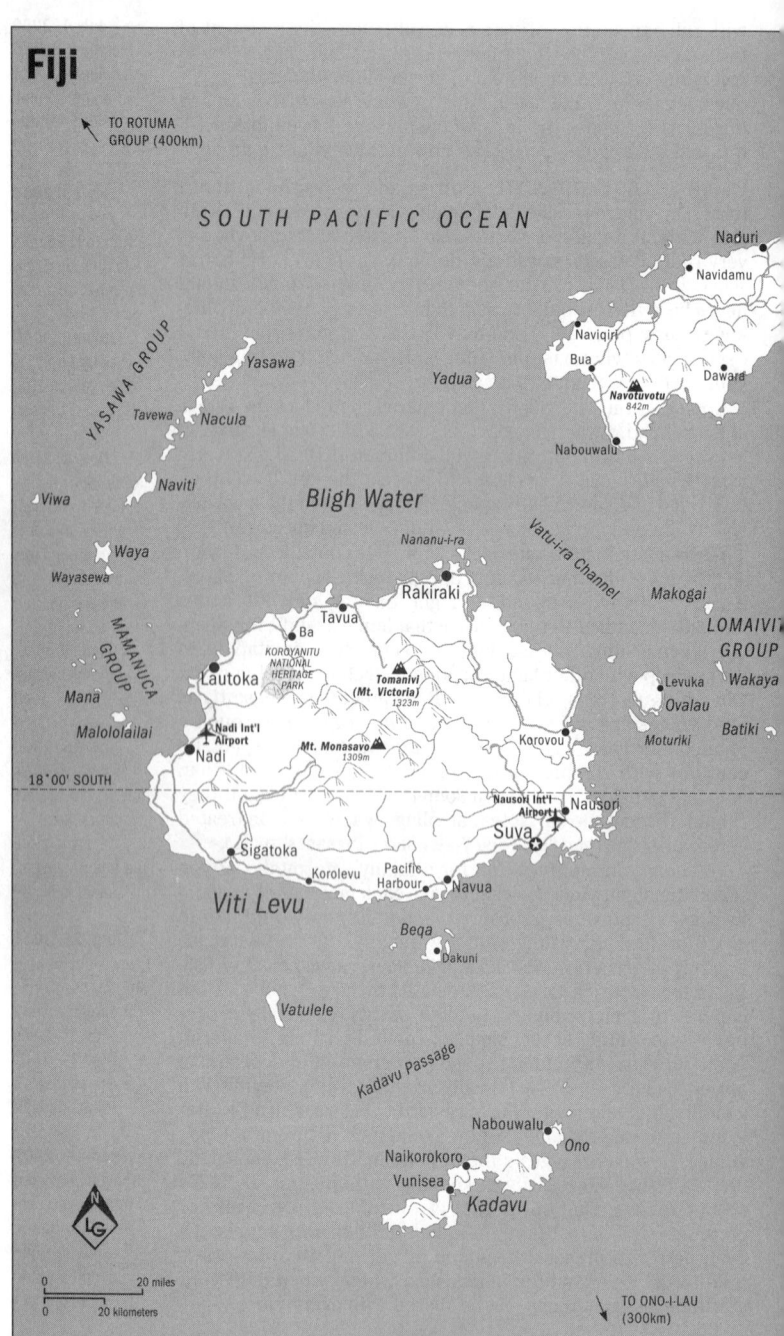

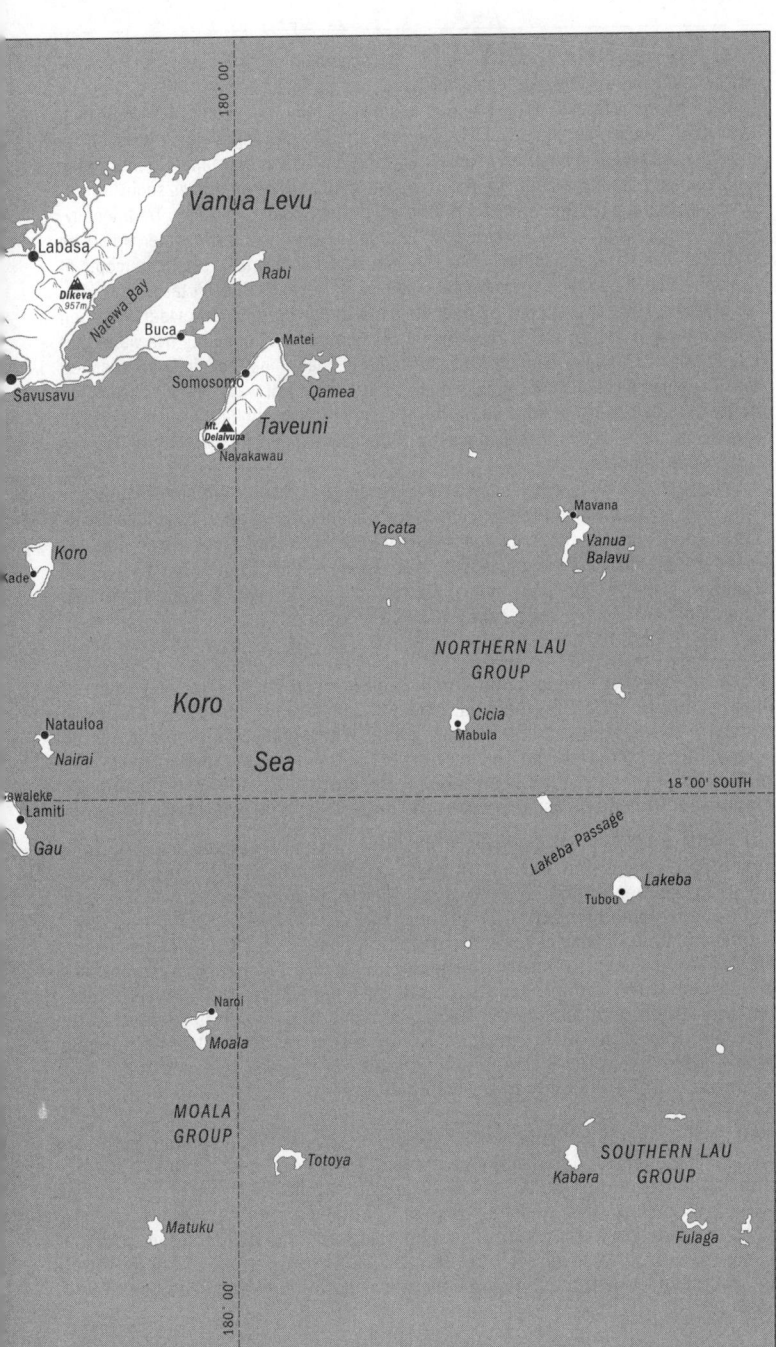

> **I CAN'T FEEL MY LIPS** According to legend, **yaqona** (yan-GO-nah) was created by the god Degei, who gave it to his sons to bring forth wisdom. His sons then gave it to their villages and in this way yaqona was shared with all Fijians. The national beverage, more commonly referred to by the Tongan name **kava** or the British term **"grog,"** remains an integral part of Fijian culture, consumed at welcoming ceremonies, funerals, weddings, major cricket matches, or any other social event. Kava root is the most appropriate gift for a chief when visiting a village. Traditionally, young women would chew on kava root and spit into a large bowl; water would be added to their collective spittle, which the men would consume. Western concepts of hygiene have altered this method slightly, although the result doesn't taste much better. Modern kava is prepared by pounding the dried root into a powder and then straining water through it. The resulting concoction resembles muddy riverwater and has the flavor of chalky earth with slight peppery tones—most definitely an acquired taste. The non-alcoholic brew affects drinkers in a variety of ways, the most common being a tingly feeling of **mild euphoria;** while excessive drinking over many years causes an unpleasant side-effect—scaling of the skin called *kanikani*—casual drinking is perfectly harmless.
>
> Participants in a yaqona ceremony should adhere to traditional protocol: **clap loudly once** with hands clasped together before receiving the *bilo* (coconut bowl), then drink the mixture without stopping. After returning the *bilo*, **clap three times** and say **"maca"** (MA-tha). After the first round the ceremony is officially over, but drinking will continue, sometimes for many hours. Asking for "high tide" will get you a full bowl, while "low-tide" will produce a more manageable amount.

Be sensitive when taking photographs, and never take pictures of a kava ceremony without explicit permission. Never wander around a village alone; only explore with an adult or child as your guide. While your experience in each village will differ, generally the further you get from cities, the greater the emphasis tradition will receive. Fijians greatly appreciate respect for their customs; the more respectful and pleasant you are, the more enjoyable your stay will be.

FOOD AND DRINK. Contemporary Fijian fare presents a mixed plate of indigenous Fijian, Polynesian, Indian, Chinese, and Western cuisine. Like most countries, Fiji has been infected by Western fast food, but this has yet to displace traditional cuisine in villages. Traditional Fijian food is typical of South Pacific islands and includes **tavioka** (cassava, tapioca), **dalo** (taro) roots, and seafood in **lolo** (coconut cream). **Mango, pineapple,** and **guava** are seasonal fresh fruits. Meat is also eaten with dalo roots after being fried and is often served in lolo. A delicious traditional dish called **kokoda** consists of raw fish marinated in lime juice and lolo. One of the stranger Fijian delicacies is the tail of the **balolo worm**—twice a year the worm fills its tail with sperm and releases it to float to the surface of the sea, only to be snatched up by the Fijians who hunt them on the surface.

An evening in a Fijian village will expose you to true Fijian cuisine. In the popular **lovo** banquet, food is wrapped in banana leaves and cooked over hot stones in an underground oven. A lovo is often accompanied by *meke* (see **Dance,** below). While tap water in some areas of Fiji may be potable, it is always safest to drink bottled water. Soft drinks and alcohol are also available; most alcohol is imported from Australia or New Zealand. Some drink the local beer, Fiji Bitter, but the most distinctive Fijian beverage is definitely **kava** (see **I Can't Feel My Lips,** above).

THE ARTS

HANDCRAFTS. Fijian women weave ceremonial **kuta mats** from the leaves of the pandanus tree. **Masi (tapa),** taken from the paper mulberry tree, is also a common material for mats. Many villages are famous for their **pottery,** both contemporary and ancient—some artifacts date from as early as 1290 BC. Fijian men have traditionally created **wood carvings,** ranging from clubs, spears, and cannibal forks to sophisticated outrigger canoes and intricately detailed *tanoa* (kava bowls). Some islands also feature crafts made of sanded and polished coconut shells.

FILM. Although Fiji has not produced many movie stars, it has been the site of many sets. Undoubtedly the most infamous films shot in Fiji are **Brooke Shields'** breakthrough performance in the 1979 classic *The Blue Lagoon* and its 1992 reprise *Return to the Blue Lagoon,* both of which take place on **Turtle Island** in the Yasawa Group. In 2000, **Tom Hanks** was stranded on Monuriki Island in the Mamanucas for the blockbuster hit *Cast Away.*

DANCE. The traditional dance of Fiji is called **meke.** Usually a narration of tales of ancestors and past wars, *meke* serves as the sole means of transmission for Fijian legends, and as such is crucial for the continuation of village identity. Each tribe has its own movements and dialect, all set to singing, chanting, and the beat of the **lali** (a type of drum hollowed from a tree trunk).

THE LAND AND ENVIRONMENT

PLANTS

Most of Fiji's plants and animals are Indo-Malayan. Europeans' first impression of Fiji was that it was covered by nothing but mangroves growing on salt mud flats, coconuts, lush rainforests, and bamboo. Today just over half of the islands are still covered with rainforest. However, this number is rapidly diminishing as forests are destroyed to make way for agriculture and development. Since 1960 over 15% of Fiji's forests have been cleared.

Fiji's islands are home to over 3000 identified plant species, of which 476 are indigenous to Fiji. Many are used as resources for food, medicine, and building materials. **Ota** are the ferns found in Fiji; some are edible, but are primarily used in the construction of *bures* (traditional Fijian houses). **Dakua** (Fijian kauri) and **yaka** are the most prevalent timber woods, although foreign pine planted for market export is becoming common. The most edible root crops are **tavioka, dalo,** and **yaqona.** The sap of **balabala** (tree fern) was once used by Fijians as a cure for headaches. In the late 1860s, **sugarcane** was introduced to Fiji and has since become an important national product.

ANIMALS

As an island nation, indigenous mammals in Fiji are few; only six species of bat and a small grey Polynesian rat are indigenous. Human immigrants from Polynesia introduced chickens, dogs, and pigs while all other mammals arrived within the last 200 years. Cattle and horses were brought by missionaries; settlers brought sheep. In an attempt to control Fijian pests, foreign pests were introduced. The Indian mongoose was imported in the 1880s to eat snakes and rats in the cane fields and is now a menace. In contrast, thousands of birds, over 100 species in all, are indigenous to Fiji, including a variety of parrots, honey-eaters, fantails, owls, ducks, rails, cuckoos, large swamp fowl, and kingfishers. The yellow-legged **Indian mynah** bird was introduced to Fiji in the early 20th century to control insects but has become a great pest, harming the trees it was supposed to protect.

Fiji has about 20 species of land reptiles, four species of turtle, and four species of sea snakes, mostly harmless. The most common snake is the **Pacific boa**, while the sole venomous terrestrial snake is the **bolo.** Coastal **seasnakes** are also poisonous, but rare. Reptiles and amphibians, including lizards, giant toads, and frogs, are a common sight. The crested iguana, thought to have floated over from South America on vegetation, is endangered and not often spotted.

Fiji's waters contain hundreds of species of coral, sea fans, sea urchins, and fish, all of which help to make diving in Fiji among the best in the world. Many marine mammals, including dolphins, pilot whales, and sperm whales, swim in the azure waters, and divers often report seeing sharks, mantas, and bill fish.

VITI LEVU

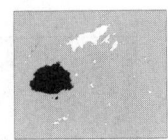

In the dart game of budget travel, you've hit the board with Viti Levu, Fiji's largest and most commercially important island. Getting a bull's-eye isn't the object of this game, however; most services, accommodations, and attractions lie along the Kings and Queens Roads, which encircle the perimeter of Viti Levu. The interior is mainly undeveloped and untouristed except for a few breathtakingly gorgeous highland villages. The western half of the island is home to Fiji's primary international airport and therefore sees the most tourist action. Also popular, the Coral Coast in the south offers exquisite beaches and easy transportation. The eastern half is home to the capital Suva, the largest city in all of Fiji.

VITI LEVU HIGHLIGHTS

LOOK OUT from the summit of Fiji's highest peak, Mt. Batilamu, in the heart of **Koroyanitu National Heritage Park** (see p. 459).

LOOK BACK thousands of years of Fijian tradition as you participate in a kava ceremony in **Navala Village** (see p. 457).

LOOK GOOD in your wetsuit as you windsurf the Bligh Waters north of **Nananu-i-ra** (see p. 451).

NADI

"Bula!" The band strumming guitars in the airport will sing it, the salesmen teeming the streets hawking swords and seashells will shout it, and almost every other local in Nadi (NAN-di) will undoubtedly announce, upon seeing a tourist, the spirited Fijian hello. As Fiji's major air traffic hub, Nadi (pop. 30,000) fits the phrase, welcoming, quite literally, most tourists to the islands. The friendliness may seem a bit purposeful, however, as it becomes clear that every taxi driver and resort representative vies for attention and business with their words. Most travelers move on quickly from this urban center to more idyllic destinations.

TRANSPORTATION

Flights: Almost all international flights to Fiji arrive at **Nadi International Airport**, 15min. by car outside Nadi on the Queens Road. Carriers include **Air New Zealand, Qantas Airways,** and **Air Pacific;** each runs multiple flights every week. Average flight times from the following hubs are: **Auckland** 3hr.; **Frankfurt** 22¼hr.; **Honolulu** 6½hr.; **L.A.** 10hr.; **London** 21½hr.; **Sydney** 3¾hr.; **Tokyo** 8½hr. Domestic carriers include **Sun Air** (☎ 672 3016; fax 672 0085; www.fiji.to), **Air Fiji Ltd.** (☎ 347 3155; fax 340 0479; www.airfiji.net), **Pacific Island Seaplanes** (☎ 672 5644; fax 672 5641; www.fijiseaplanes.com), **Turtle Airways** (☎ 672 1888; fax 672 0095; www.turtleairways.com), and **Island Hoppers** (☎ 672 0410; fax 672 0172).

Buses: Sunbeam Transport Ltd. (☎ 666 2822), **Sunset Express** (☎ 672 0266), and **Pacific Transport Ltd.** (☎ 670 0004) each go to: **Suva** (4hr., 2-14 per day) via **Sigatoka** (1¼hr.), **Korolevu** (2hr.), and **Pacific Harbour** (3hr.); **Lautoka** (45min., 3-14 per day); and **Ba** (1¾hr., 1 per day). All companies charge $2-11. The air-conditioned **Fiji Express** (contact United Touring Ltd. ☎ 672 2811) also goes to **Suva** with the same stops for $6-27. All buses leave from the **Nadi Airport** outside the Departures gate and

Viti Levu

from the **bus station** in Nadi proper, behind the market on Hospital Rd. **Van carriers** travel the same routes as buses and pick up passengers along the Queens Road.

Public Transportation: Within Nadi, local open-air buses are cheap and frequent (every 5-10 min. on the Queens Road), making them the primary means of transportation for most locals; they can even be waved down from the side of the road. Fare from the airport to Nadi proper is 65¢; the bus stop at the airport is immediately outside the gate and across the street on the Queens Road. Local buses do not adhere to a strict schedule.

Car Rentals: Avis, Budget, Hertz, Thrifty, and a slew of other car rental companies have offices in the Arrivals Concourse of the Nadi airport. Despite the competition, rentals are expensive; most economy-class cars start at more than $50 per day.

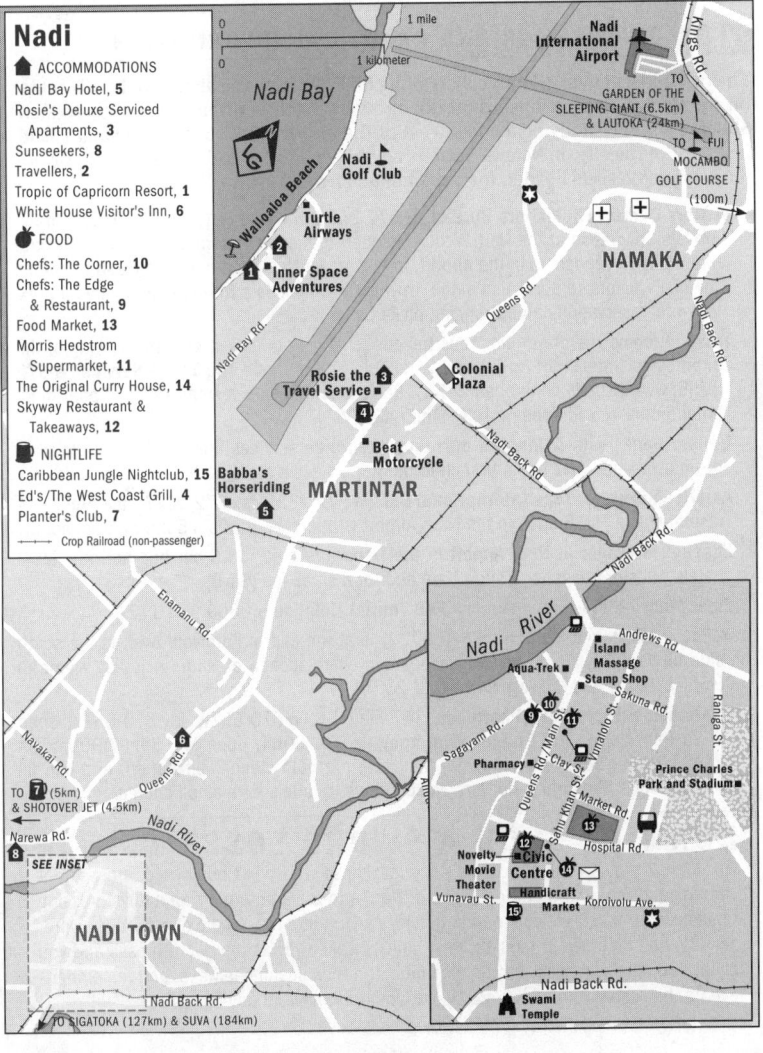

Taxis: While many **taxis** have meters, just as many do not and work on a **fixed price** system. Prices for tourists may vary wildly from prices for locals, however. Discussing a price before committing to the trip, and even haggling a bit, is common practice. It should cost no more than $10 to get from the airport to Nadi proper. Taxis coming back from a destination charge a **return fare,** the same as bus fare, and pick up as many passengers as possible; you've spotted one if it's half-full, honks at pedestrians walking along the road, and pulls over when you wave it down.

Scooter/Motorcycle Rentals: Beat Motorcycle & Rentals (☎/fax 672 1471 or 994 9383), halfway to the airport on the Queens Road near Ed's Bar, rents scooters and motorbikes from $10 per 2hr. or $33 per day. Insurance and helmet included. $200 deposit. Open M-F 8am-5pm, Sa 8am-1pm, Su by request.

ORIENTATION AND PRACTICAL INFORMATION

The city and its environs curve 9km along **Nadi Bay** from the **airport** to the **city center** on the **Queens Road,** whose final downtown stretch is often referred to as **Main Street.** The only sandy beach lies west of the airport, at **Wailoaloa. Denarau Island,** just west of the city on **Narewa Road,** is nestled in the Bay and serves as the port for most tourist vessels headed for the Mamanuca and Yasawa Groups.

Visitors Center: Fiji Visitors Bureau (☎ 672 2433 or 672 1721; fax 672 0141), in the Arrivals Concourse at the Nadi Airport, is open to meet all international flights. Beware that many travel agents in the airport, in downtown Nadi, and in hotels masquerade as "official" visitors centers. Also in the Arrivals Concourse is a **free phone,** handy for making hotel reservations and arranging pick-ups.

Travel Agency: There are numerous travel agents with offices in the arrivals wing of the airport and throughout Nadi town. A reliable one is **Rosie The Travel Service** (☎ 672 2755; www.rosiefiji.com; open **24hr.**). Rosie also manages a small series of apartment hotel rooms in Nadi (see p. 443). AmEx/MC/V.

Banks: Banks with **ATMs** and **currency exchange** services line the Queens Road in downtown Nadi. **ANZ** has a branch in the Airport. Most are closed Su and on holidays.

American Express: Tapa International Ltd. (☎ 672 2325; fax 672 1427), the AmEx representative in Fiji. Branch in the Nadi Airport is open M-F 8:30am-5pm, Sa 9am-noon.

Luggage Storage: At Nadi Airport in the Departure area. $3-6 per bag per day. Most hotels will store bags for a short time and for a small fee ($1-5).

Emergency: ☎ 911 throughout Fiji; **FVB Tourist Helpline** ☎ 0800 672 1721.

Police: Nadi Police Station (☎ 670 0222) is at the end of Koroivolu Ave. on the south side of Nadi City. There are police posts in every section of Nadi, including **Namaka** (☎ 672 2222) and the **Airport** (☎ 672 2355).

Pharmacies: Thakorlal's Pharmacy, 347 Main St. (☎ 670 5514; fax 670 5517; open M-Sa 8am-6pm), and **Budget Pharmacy** (☎ 670 0064; open M-F 8am-7:30pm, Sa 8am-3:30pm, Su 10am-noon), on Main St., are both clean, well-staffed, and can fill prescriptions. Thakorlal's delivers prescriptions to hotels for a small charge.

DON'T BE SUCH A SWORD LOSER Upon arriving in Fiji, tourists quickly fall into two categories: those who *don't* buy swords from street vendors and those who do and regret it. Nadi and Suva both teem with guys pressing to shake your hand, get your name, quickly carve it into the handle of a shoddy sword, sell it to you for loads of moolah, then quickly walk away as the sword breaks and you cry. It happens every day. Avoid these men and their scamming ways, and remember—even if they carve your name in a sword, you don't have to pay for it.

Medical Services: The best care in Fiji is found in Suva (see p. 462), at the **Lautoka Hospital** (see p. 446), or at a **private clinic**. The **Namaka Medical Centre** (☎672 2288, emergency 992 2288; fax 672 3926; open M-Sa 9am-10pm, Su 9:30am-5pm; AmEx/MC/V and most travel insurance accepted) and the **Shortlane Medical Centre** (☎672 5707, emergency 995 5151; fax 672 2888; open M-F 8am-5pm, Sa 8am-1pm; AmEx and some travel insurance accepted) are both on the Queens Road, near the MH Supermarket in Namaka.

Internet Access: The self-proclaimed **Fastest Internet in the West**, across the bridge in Nadi town (☎670 3562; 10¢ per min.; $5 per hr.; open daily 9am-7pm), has a slightly faster connection than its competitors. **CyberCafe** (☎670 2226; 10¢ per min.; $3 per hr.; open daily 8am-7pm) is in Sharma's Arcade on Main St.

Post Office: The **main** post office (☎330 2022) is in downtown Nadi behind the Civic Centre arcade, across from the bus terminal. Poste Restante. Open M-F 8am-4pm, Sa 8am-noon. There's also a roadside **stamp shop,** on Main St., next to Patel supermarket (open M-F 8am-1pm and 2-4pm, Sa 8am-noon).

ACCOMMODATIONS

Accommodations in Nadi run the gamut from dingy (in downtown) to resort-like (near the airport and the beach). All hotels listed have **24hr. reception, fans in rooms,** and **free airport pick-up.**

Tropic of Capricorn Resort, 11 Wasawasa Rd. (☎672 3089; fax 672 3050), off Wailoaloa Rd. Just a year old, the white tiles, metal-framed beds, and small maple kitchen still shine. Friendly staff, pool, and the best sunset views in Nadi. Free breakfast. Laundry. Dorms $15; quads $45; doubles $95. ❷

Nadi Bay Hotel (☎672 3599; fax 672 0092; nadibay@connect.com.fj), on Wailoaloa Rd. off the Queens Road halfway between the airport and Main St., packs blue pool, pink restaurant, and yellow sun into a prism of a place. Happy Hour 5-7pm at restaurant. Internet. Dorms $16.50; private dorms $20; singles $48, with bath $72; doubles $56/88. Stay 6 nights, 7th free. AmEx/MC/V. ❷

Sunseekers (☎670 0400; fax 670 2047), on Narewa Rd. Just a 2min. walk from town, Sunseekers is far enough removed to be quiet at night. Turn a blind eye to the green pool; instead, nestle into clean sheets and dream of the islands. Dorms $11, with YHA card $8.80; singles $33, with A/C $38.50; doubles $38.50/$44. ❶

Rosie's Deluxe Serviced Apartments (☎672 2935; fax 672 2607; res@rosie.com.fj), on the Queens Road, midway between the airport and downtown, has spacious apartments with balconies, full kitchens, comfy beds, and A/C. Studio (sleeps 4) $44; 1-bedroom (sleeps 5) $66; 2-bedroom (sleeps 7) $88. AmEx/MC/V. ❸

White House Visitor's Inn, 40 Kennedy Ave. (☎670 0022; fax 678 0468). Manager Joe will make you feel like one of his own. Your only chore: wash the dishes after eating free breakfast bread and jam. A/C $5. Dorms $11; singles $25; doubles $30. Cash only. ❶

Travellers (☎672 3322; fax 672 0026; beachvilla@connect.com.fj), at the end of Wasawasa Rd., off Wailoaloa Rd. Spacious lounge and smallish rooms with clean beds. Free Internet for 10min. after 6pm. Dorms $11; singles $40, with A/C $50; doubles $40/$55; triples $60. Stay 7 nights, 8th free. AmEx/MC/V. ❶

FOOD

Nadi's predominantly Indo-Fijian population guarantees that you'll find curries simmering at most eateries. The main supermarket, **Morris Hedstrom** (☎670 0033; open M-F 8am-6pm, Sa 7am-6pm, Su 8am-1pm), lies on the downtown stretch of Main St. A local **market** fills the area just off Hospital Rd. near the bus station.

Chefs (☎ 670 3131), off Sagayam Rd., runs 3 separate establishments in Nadi to cover all styles of dining. **Chefs: The Corner ❸**, at the corner of Main St., is like a New York diner with pink booths and mirrored walls, but with curry instead of kosher corned beef. Lamb with ginger ($9) and chicken stir-fry ($6) hit the spot. One of the speediest food options in town. Open M-Sa 8am-5pm; also Th-Sa 6-9pm. Across the street, **Chefs: The Edge ❹**, behind Jack's Handicrafts, is the bistro-style middle son. A complete menu of curries and continental fare ($9-25). Open M-Sa 9am-2pm and 6-9:30pm. **Chefs: The Restaurant ❺**, also behind Jack's Handicrafts, the suave eldest sibling, has had time to mature. Dishes like lobster bisque ($8) and crêpes suzette ($10) go well with an aged wine. Open M-Sa 11am-2pm and 6-10pm.

The Original Curry House (☎ 670 0798), at the corner of Main St. and Hospital Rd., dishes up *real* curries ($10-18) with enough zing to ensure you'll leave with smoke pouring from your ears. Open daily 7:30am-10pm. ❹

Skyway Restaurant & Takeaways (☎ 670 0204), in the Civic Centre on Main St., where the locals munch on Indian fast food. Veggie curry $3. Open M-Sa 7:30am-5pm. ❶

ENTERTAINMENT AND NIGHTLIFE

The **Sheraton at Port Denarau** presents **cultural shows**, including a firewalking demonstration, every Wednesday night at 8pm ($12). The **Novelty Movie Theatre**, in the Civic Centre on Main St., shows $2 movies from Hollywood and Bollywood.

Ed's/The West Coast Grill (☎ 672 4650), on the Queens Road just north of Wailoaloa Rd., is the bar at the top of everyone's list. A central location draws locals and tourists for music and beer ($3), while the grill feeds the bunch Thai mussels ($7.50) and burgers ($6). Ed's open daily 5pm-1am; West Coast open M-W 5-11pm, Th-Sa 5pm-1am.

Planter's Club (☎ 675 0777), in the Sheraton Fiji on Denarau Island at the end of Navewa Rd. The shroud of the Sheraton ensures a tidy and controlled atmosphere at this small bar. Buy a drink (beers $4.50) and swim in the posh pool for free. Wooden dance floor and DJ. Open daily 5pm-1am.

Caribbean Jungle Nightclub (☎ 667 0000), at the corner of Main St. and Koroivolu Ave. The best nightclub in Nadi, with occasional outbreaks of "hula fever" on the dance floor. Commonly referred to as "C.J.'s" or "the zoo" by locals. Beer $3. Open M-Sa 8pm-1am.

SIGHTS

GARDEN OF THE SLEEPING GIANT. Originally the collection of *Perry Mason* actor Raymond Burr, this rambling rainforest garden and nursery at the foot of the "Sleeping Giant" mountain provides a refuge from bustling Nadi. A 30min. walk through weaving paths will bring you partially up the hillside, past exotic birds, Asian orchids, sky-high bamboo, and lily pad fishponds. *(6.5km north of Nadi Airport on Wailoko Rd.; look for the small arrow sign. Taxi from airport $7-10. ☎ 672 2701. Open M-Sa 9am-5pm, Su 9am-noon. $9.50, children $5. Complimentary tropical drinks.)*

SWAMI TEMPLE. Sri Suva Subrahmanya Swami Devasthanam, known as the **Swami Temple**, shines at the south end of Main St. Bright pinks, blues, and greens dominate the ornate concrete sculpture of this Hindu temple, opened in 1994 after two years of labor by dozens of Indian *silpi* (craftsmen). Visitors must dress neatly and modestly, leave their shoes at the entrance, and refrain from eating any non-vegetarian food, smoking, or drinking alcohol on the day of the visit. *(☎ 670 0016. Open daily from dawn to dusk. Donations appreciated.)*

HANDICRAFT MARKET. Artisans beckon shoppers with shoes, shells, baskets, tapa cloths, skirts, wraps, kava, and wood carvings. Everything is cheaper here than in the stores on Main St. *(Off Koroivolu Ave. Most shops open M-Sa 8am-5:30pm.)*

ACTIVITIES

DIVING. Inner Space Adventures offers a range of dives in the Mamanucas. *(On Wasawasa Rd., at the end of Wailoaloa Rd. ☎/fax 672 3883. 1-tank $80, 2-tank $110, dive daily for $40 after $380-750 PADI course. Snorkeling trips $30. Hotel pick-up in the Nadi area and gear included.)* **Aqua-Trek** runs trips to Matamanoa, Beqa, and Mana. *(On Main St. ☎ 670 2413; www.aquatrek.com. 2 dives $160, night dive $96, gear hire $15 per dive. PADI course $440. 25% discount on the 2-tank dive for backpackers at the Beqa site.)*

GOLF. Nadi Golf Club, the first club in Nadi, has 150 members. *(At the end of Wailoaloa Rd. between the airport and the Bay. ☎ 672 2148. Open daily 7am-6pm for non-members. Buggy rental $3, clubs $20, greens fee $10.)* **Fiji Macambo Golf Course & Shop** is a modern, Western-style course on top of Namaca Hill. *(At the Fiji Macambo Hotel on Votualevu Rd., 2km east of the airport. ☎ 672 2000. Open daily sunrise to sunset. Buggy rental $5, clubs $11, greens fee $11.)*

HORSEBACK RIDING. Babba's Horseriding offers short jaunts along the beach or longer excursions through the Nausori Highlands. *(At Wailoaloa Beach. ☎ 672 4449. 1hr. $20, half-day $50; day of pig hunting with lunch $100. Includes hotel pick-up.)*

JETBOATING. Shotover Jet Fiji takes fast and wild 30min. rides around Denarau and up the Nadi River in 12-person jetboats. *(In Port Denarau. ☎ 675 0400; jetfiji@connect.com.fj. $75, children $35; includes hotel pick-up.)*

MASSAGES. Island Massage will start your tropical vacation off on the right note, correcting the damage your backpack has done. Relax in a bamboo booth as skilled hands knead your tired shoulders. *(Across the bridge from Main St. ☎ 670 0288. Open daily 9am-9pm. 30min. $15, 1hr. $25.)*

LAUTOKA

Lautoka looked lovely to the mutinied Captain Bligh of *HMS Bounty* fame when he spotted it from his dinghy in 1789. Today, the second largest city in Fiji plays host to a large fishing port, a distillery, a lumber and woodchip export plant, and the Colonial Refining Company.

TRANSPORTATION

Buses from **Sunbeam Transport Ltd.** (☎ 666 2822), **Sunset Express** (☎ 338 2811), and **Pacific Transport Ltd.** (☎ 666 0499) each go to: **Suva** (5hr., 2-14 per day) via **Nadi** (50min.), **Sigatoka** (70min.), **Korolevu** (3hr.), and **Pacific Harbour** (4hr.); and **Ba** (40min., 1 per day). All companies charge $2-11. Open-air **local buses** take longer, stopping at every bus shelter and village along the way, but come along main roads every 15min. during the week. During the morning, 12-person **vans** often travel between the bigger cities charging $20 a head from Suva to Lautoka. A private **taxi** from Nadi Airport takes 30min. ($20).

ORIENTATION AND PRACTICAL INFORMATION

Twenty-four kilometers north of Nadi Airport the **Queens Road** ends at the entrance to Lautoka, where it splits into **Navutu** and **Drasa Roads**. Navutu splits again before joining **Nadovu Road** and becoming **Vitogo Parade** in the city center. Vitogo Pde. runs parallel to **Naviti Street,** the four-block main drag. Drasa Rd.

446 ■ VITI LEVU

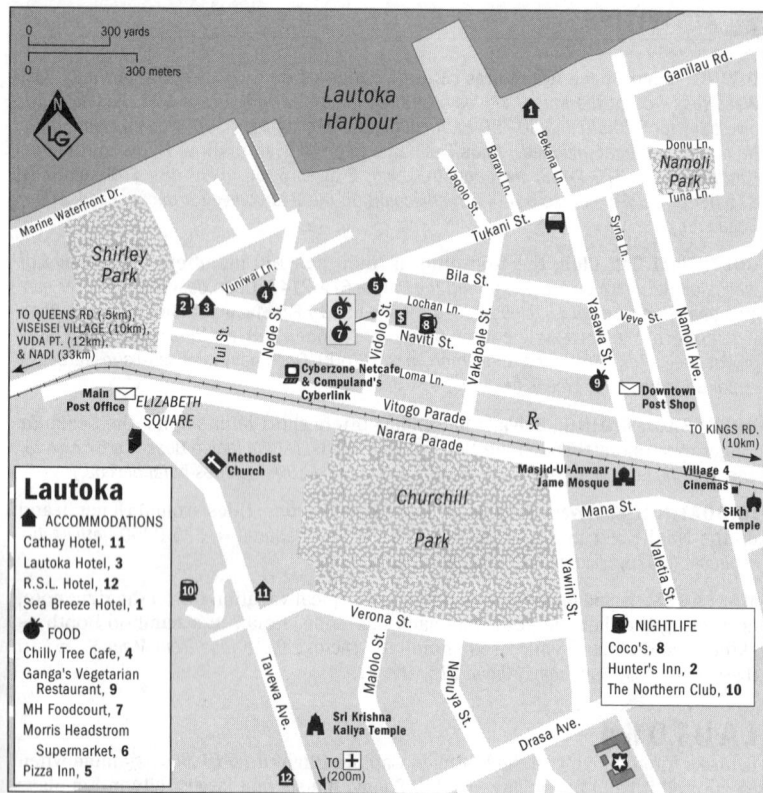

Lautoka

🏠 **ACCOMMODATIONS**
Cathay Hotel, **11**
Lautoka Hotel, **3**
R.S.L. Hotel, **12**
Sea Breeze Hotel, **1**

🍴 **FOOD**
Chilly Tree Cafe, **4**
Ganga's Vegetarian Restaurant, **9**
MH Foodcourt, **7**
Morris Headstrom Supermarket, **6**
Pizza Inn, **5**

🌙 **NIGHTLIFE**
Coco's, **8**
Hunter's Inn, **2**
The Northern Club, **10**

bypasses this central shopping district and spits north-bound vehicles onto the **Kings Road.**

Banks: All major banks with **ATMs,** including **ANZ** (open M-Th 9:30am-3pm, F 9:30am-4pm), lie along Naviti St.

Police: Lautoka Police Station (☎ 666 0222) is off Drasa Rd., across from Yawini St. just south of Churchill Park.

Medical Services: To reach the **ambulance,** call ☎ 666 0399. **Lautoka Hospital** (☎ 666 0399), at the end of Hospital Rd. off Thomson Crescent, or **private clinics** such as the **Bayly Clinic,** 5 Nede St. (☎ 666 5133 or 995 3197. Open M-F 8am-4:30pm, Sa 8am-1pm. Cash only). **Thakorlal's Pharmacy,** 103 Vitogo Pde. (☎ 666 4645 or 666 4044; fax 666 5946), right near the park. Thakorlal's window posts the location of that night's after hours service. Open M-F 8am-6pm, Sa 8am-1pm. As always, the best modern care is found in Suva (see p. 462).

Internet Access: Cyberzone Netcafe, 159 Vitogo Pde. (☎ 665 1675), set back from the street. 10¢ per min. $4 per hr., Sa-Su $3 per hr. Open M-Sa 8am-7pm, Su 9am-5pm.

Post Office: The main post office (☎ 666 0022; fax 666 4666), at the rotary at the end of Vitogo Pde., has Poste Restante. Open M-F 8am-4pm, Sa 8am-noon.

ACCOMMODATIONS

Lautoka's extremely affordable accommodations are outwardly attractive; however, many charge "hourly" room rates (read: prostitution). The **Mon Repo Backpackers** and the **Diamond Hotel** are actually brothels and should be avoided.

Lautoka Hotel, 2-12 Naviti St. (☎ 666 0388; fax 666 0201; itkhotel@connect.com.fj). The central location brings you closest to the fun—and the noise. Clean rooms share bathroom facilities. 8-bed dorms $15; singles $25; doubles $30. AmEx/MC/V. ❷

Cathay Hotel (☎ 666 0566; fax 666 0136), on Tavewa Rd. across from the Northern Club, has TV, a courtyard pool, and the best dorm deals in town. Dorms $12, with A/C $16; singles $35/$46; doubles $43.50/$53.25. AmEx/MC/V. ❶

Sea Breeze Hotel, 5 Bekana Ln. (☎ 666 0717; fax 666 6080). Feel ocean wind through the chain-link fence. The lush courtyard and pool help relieve the city tenement ambience. Clean private baths. Singles $33, with A/C $40; doubles $37/$45. Cash only. ❸

R.S.L. Hotel, 23 Tavewa Ave. (☎ 666 6546 or 995 5298; fax 665 1339). The 6 rooms are sparkling new, with A/C, 1 double and single bed each, big bathrooms, and glossy wood furniture. A great deal for a big group, as you can cram as many people as you'd like into one room at no extra charge. All rooms $55. ❹

FOOD

The **Lautoka Municipal Market,** in the arena on Naviti St. (open M-F 7am-5:30pm, Sa 5:30am-4pm), brings mountain-grown fruits and vegetables into town for fair (and marked) prices. Or, head to the jumbo supermarket **Morris Hedstrom,** on Naviti St. (☎ 666 2999; open M-Th 8am-6pm, F 8am-7pm, Sa 7:30am-4pm, Su 8:30am-12:30pm). The weekly **Hare Krishna vegetarian feast** (see **Sights and Activities: Local Places of Worship,** below) is not to be missed.

Chilly Tree Cafe (☎ 665 1824), at the corner of Nede and Naviti St. Browse through the extensive newspaper selection while you enjoy quiche ($3), deli sandwiches ($4-8), and gourmet coffee ($1-3). A/C. Open M-Sa 8am-6pm, Su 9am-noon. ❷

Pizza Inn, The Corner Cafe, and the **Sea View Restaurant,** 2 Naviti St. (☎ 666 4592), are all practically the same operation in the Lautoka Hotel. Partitions separate the more expensive Sea View from the others, which have lunch specials like chicken fried rice ($3) and club sandwiches ($4). Open daily 8am-9:30pm. ❷

MH Foodcourt (☎ 666 2999), in the back of the MH Supermarket at the corner of Vidilo St. Relax in a wicker chair with roast chicken and chips ($3.70) near Housewares in Aisle 3. Open M-F 8am-6pm, Sa 8am-4pm, Su 8:30am-12:30pm. ❷

Ganga's Vegetarian Restaurant (☎ 666 2990), at the corner of Yasawa and Naviti St. Tiny milk-and-sugar barfi (40¢) sooth after spicy samosas and chutney. Daily sampler $4.75. 3-scoop ice cream $1.80. Open M-F 9am-4:30pm, Sa 9am-1:30pm. ❶

NIGHTLIFE

Hunter's Inn (☎ 660 3881), at the corner of Tui and Naviti St. next to the Lautoka Hotel. Local youngbloods hunt this disco cave for a large mix of musical styles. Open M-W noon-midnight, Th-Sa noon-1:30am.

Coco's (☎ 666 8989), on Naviti St., is a dark disco playing popular music from reggae to techno. The owner's "Cruisers Band" plays on the top floor. $1.50 stubby during Happy Hour (6:30-8pm). Cover F-Sa from 9pm $5. Open W-Sa 6:30pm-1am.

FROM THE ROAD

THE KAVA HOP

Oh, kava. Magical kava. Fijian kava. Since day one in Fiji, I'd been intrigued, amused, mystified. "Kava" whispered around every corner, tailed every smiling "Bula," and lingered under every local's sweet breath. By day five, I was primed for a sip.

We took the boat to a nearby village, a nighttime ride under a surreal harvest moon. At the low-key ceremony, we sat, cross-legged on ebe-leaf mats in an open-air bure. A boom box played Fijian reggae. Smoke, giggles, claps, and reddened, turned-up eyes colored the scene. I was ready.

I asked for a "high tide," and one of the villagers filled my coconut bowl to the brim. I gulped it down, my lips set against the muddy water. When picking my poison, I tend to stick to wine and "girly drinks." But kava was another story. It tasted pretty good, like a medicinal Chinese tea. I waited for numbness and checked my skin for leathery scales, a symptom of over-indulgent kava drinking. But nothing of the sort. Lightweight Tamara felt alright.

A man tapped my elbow. "Excuse me," he said, wiggling. I interpreted it as, "Will you wiggle with me?" I wiggled. We wiggled. The crowd clapped for us and laughed at us. One woman cried, "Shake it, baby, shake it!" I shook, we shook, the kava shook in our bellies. I wiggled and shook and turned up that coconut bowl until the South Seas called for my return. On the boat ride back, soothing sleep capped off my long-awaited journey to the kava gods.

—Tamara Reichberg

The Northern Club (☎ 666 0184), on Yanduli Rd. off Tavewa Ave., is a members-only club (tourists welcome) with tennis facilities and a large lounge, bar, and pool. Stubbies $1.50. Open M-W and Sa 8am-10pm, Th 8am-11pm, F 8am-midnight, Su noon-8pm.

SIGHTS AND ACTIVITIES

Aside from the usual diversions of bargaining at the handicraft market and exploring the city, there is little to do inside Lautoka. The **Village 4 Cinemas** (☎ 666 3555) shows English and Hindi movies in constant rotation in its four modern theaters ($4, children $3.30), with late-night showings on Friday and Saturday.

LOCAL PLACES OF WORSHIP. The diverse city of Lautoka is home to the **Masjid-Ul-Anwaar Jame Mosque** *(at the end of Yasawa St.; trespassing prohibited);* the **Lautoka Methodist Church** *(on Tavewa St.);* the **Sikh Temple** *(on Vitogo Pde.;* ☎ *666 0685; open for prayers daily 5am-8pm; visitors must cover their heads with one of the provided cloths, dress conservatively, and bring no tobacco or alcohol inside the gate);* and the **Sri Krishna Kaliya Temple** *(on Tavewa Ave.;* ☎ *666 4112; open daily 4:30am-7pm).* The Krishna community hosts a free **vegetarian feast** every Sunday following the 11:30am recitation of the scriptures (the feast usually begins around 1pm). Tourists are welcome to join the more than 500 devotees in singing, dancing, and eating.

VISEISEI VILLAGE. Set on cut grass and banked by the sea, this well-groomed Fijian village was visited by Queen Elizabeth II, Princess Margaret, and Prince Charles in 1953. However, Viseisei's brushes with royalty don't stop there—the village's current chief, Ratu Joseph Iloilo, became President of Fiji after the coup in 2000, and is also the Tui (king) of three nearby villages. Every Sunday at 10am and Wednesday at 7pm, services are held at the Jone Wesele Methodist Church. *(At the foot of Vuda Point. Taxi fare from Lautoka $10, or take local bus to Nadi 85¢ and get off at the foot of the hill in Viseisei. Village tours with a local $2.)*

VUDA POINT. Vuda (VUN-da) Point is popularly considered the first landing spot of the Fijian people. Though fraught with significance, visitors here find neither hoopla nor monument; picnics by the marina are a nice alternative. *(Walk along the beach from Viseisei, or flag a taxi down in Lautoka. The local bus brings passengers along the Vuda Point access road 4 times daily for 40¢.)*

KINGS ROAD

Northern Viti Levu along the Kings Road is mostly agricultural and industrial land. Rolling hills and mountain backdrops stand in contrast to seaside vistas on the north coast, while on the east coast cow towns cluster together along the dirt stretch of the road. With fewer tourist services, visitors rarely receive as much attention as the cattle.

TRANSPORTATION ON THE KINGS ROAD

Buses are the cheapest transportation option along the Kings Road. **Sunbeam Transport Ltd.** (☎ 666 2822), **Sunset Express** (☎ 338 2811), and **Pacific Transport Ltd.** (☎ 670 0004) all go from **Nadi** and **Suva** to **Ba** (1 per day, $2-11). Only **Sunbeam** goes to **Rakiraki**. Local buses also run between **Lautoka, Ba, Tavua, Rakiraki, every eastern village, Korovou,** and **Nausori** before reaching **Suva** (5 transfers per day; about $3 per leg of the Lautoka-Rakiraki section). The dirt portion of the Kings Road between Dama and Korovou takes almost 2hr. by car and more than 2½hr. by bus ($5). **Carriers** and **mini-buses** are an alternative. Hiring private transport in the form of **taxi** or **rental car** is the easiest way to get around the Kings Road, especially for quick sightseeing; **taxis** are plentiful in most northern and eastern towns. A cab from Lautoka to Suva takes more than 4hr. and costs over $75; each leg of the Lautoka-Ba-Tavua-Rakiraki section takes about 30min. and costs $15-30. See **Interior Highlands,** p. 456, for information on treks to the interior of the island.

BA

Ba (pop. 13,000) serves as a base for interior village towns, including **Navala** (p. 457) and **Bukuya** (p. 458). The **bus station** is at the entrance to town across from the rotary and the Mobil station. For **ATMs**, try the **Exchange & Finance Fiji Ltd.** (☎ 667 0766; open M-F 8:30am-5pm, Sa 8:30am-1pm) or other banks on the main drag. Other services include: the **police station** (☎ 667 4222), at the corner of Koronubu and Kula St., east of the rotary just up the hill from the Ba Hotel; the **ambulance** (☎ 667 4108); **Dr. Mortel** at the **Ba Health Centre,** 50m past the police station (☎ 667 4108; open M-Th 8am-4:30pm, F 8am-4pm); the **Ba Mission Hospital** (☎ 667 4022), a 10min. drive past the bridge for after hours or weekend treatment; the **Western Pharmacy** (☎ 667 4561; fax 667 0158; open M-Sa 8am-6pm, Su 8am-noon); the **post office,** on Nareba St. across from the Civic Centre (☎ 667 4341; open M-F 8am-4pm, Sa 8am-noon); and **Internet access** at the **Downtown Internet Cafe,** between the bridge and the mosque on the third floor of the building with the yellow stairs. (☎ 667 1488. 8¢ per min.; $4.50 per hr. Open M-Sa 8am-8pm, Su 10am-3pm.) The **Town Square Cinema** (☎ 667 4048) only shows Hindi films (3-5 per day; $3, Tu $2).

The only accommodation is **Ba Hotel ❶,** on Banks St. near Varoka St., which offers 10 foam-mat beds in a tight dorm (the toilet is *in* the shower). Family rooms are nicer. All rooms surround the courtyard, with an open-air bar and pool. (☎ 667 4000; fax 667 0559. Dorms $10; singles $44; doubles $55; family rooms $66.) The hotel **restaurant ❷** is small (lemon chicken $5), while the bar hawks cheap beer. (Open daily 7:15-9am, noon-2pm, and 6-8pm.) **Chand's Restaurant ❷,** on Main St., has fast food downstairs and seated meals ($3-9) upstairs. (☎ 667 0822. Open M-Sa 8am-9pm.) **New World Supermarket** is behind the bus stand at the town entrance. (☎ 667 4600. Open M-Th 7:30am-6:30pm, F 7:30am-7pm, Sa 7am-7pm.)

TAVUA

An agricultural town, Tavua serves mainly as a launching pad for inland treks, although the villages are more easily accessed from Ba (see above). **Caboni**

(THAM-bo-nee) **Beach** provides a seaside respite 20min. farther along the Kings Road toward Rakiraki; ask local bus drivers for directions. Town services include: the **ANZ bank** with **ATM,** on Vatukoula St. (open M-Th 9:30am-3pm, F 9:30am-4pm); the **police station** on the hill (☎ 668 0222); the tiny **hospital** (☎ 668 0444 or 668 0347), past Hotel Tavua; the **Excel Pharmacy** (☎/fax 668 0108 or 991 2044, after hours 668 0229; open M-F 8:30am-5:30pm, Sa 8:30am-4pm, Su 9:30-11am); **Internet access** at a nameless Internet cafe on the Kings Road section of downtown (10¢ per min., $4.50 per hr.; open M-Sa 10am-5pm); and the **post office**, on Nasivi St. just west of the police station (☎ 668 0239; fax 668 1435; open M-F 8am-4pm, Sa 8am-noon).

The only place to stay in town is the **Tavua Hotel ❶**, at the top of the hill off Nabuna St. A grand 1930s Colonial building with a pool and a bar/nightclub, the dorm is tight but other options are spacious. (☎ 668 0522; fax 668 0522. Dorms $11; singles $44; doubles $55, with A/C $66.) The **restaurant ❷** serves decent food (breakfasts $2-3; dinners $6-8). **Lee's Hot Bread Takeaway & Restaurant ❶** is a cafeteria-style joint. Veggie curry costs $2.80. (☎ 668 1888. Restaurant open M-Sa 7:30am-5pm; takeaway open M-Sa 5am-7:30pm, Su 5-10am.) Outfit yourself at the **market**, at the edge of town across from the bus station on the Kings Road, or visit the **New World Supermarket,** around the corner on Vatukoula Rd. (open M-Sa 8am-7pm).

Midway between Tavua and Rakiraki, in the tiny town of **Yaqara** (YAN-ka-rah) sits the headquarters of Fiji's fastest growing export: **Fiji Water.** The new, ultra-modern bottling plant offers free 30min. tours through the viewing tunnels. (☎ 668 1364. Tours by appointment W-Th 7am-3pm.) The turn-off for the plant is 17km east of Tavua, in Yaqara; the plant itself is 2km from the Kings Road. A taxi from Tavua costs about $10, and from Rakiraki about $25.

RAKIRAKI

The northernmost town in Viti Levu, Rakiraki is most often used by budget travelers en route to Nananu-i-ra (see p. 451). While the town and the small surrounding region are referred to as Rakiraki, the miniature downtown area is properly called **Vaileka** and is reached by a 1km turnoff from the Kings Road at the rotary split and police post (the sign reads "Vaileka"). The downtown area is a small ring of shops surrounding the small local **market, bus station, police station** (☎ 669 4222), and **post office** (☎ 669 4060; open M-F 8am-4pm, Sa 8am-noon). The **water** in the area was deemed non-potable seven years ago after a major mainline contamination, and though locals now drink it, **visitors are still warned to avoid tap water.** Ironically, the major bottling plant for Fiji Water is just north of the city (see above). Other services include: the **Colonial Bank** with **ATM,** on the main drag across from the BP station (open M 9:30am-4pm, Tu-F 9am-4pm); and the **hospital** (☎ 669 4368).

The only budget accommodation option is the **Rakiraki Hotel ❸**, 3km east of Vaileka on the Kings Road. From "downtown" Vaileka, take a stage bus toward Korovou (50¢) or a taxi ($2.50). Rooms look onto a large bowling green and a bright pool. (☎ 669 4101; fax 669 4545; www.tanoahotels.com/rakiraki. Internet. Singles $37.50, with A/C $49.50; doubles $46/$66. AmEx/MC/V/traveler's checks.) The best chow in the area can be found at the restaurants at the **Rakiraki** (full meals from $11). There are also about a dozen **supermarkets** in the center of town.

Ellington Wharf, 9km east of Vaileka (taxi $10) and down a short access road, is where most boat transfers depart for Nananu-i-ra, as well as Vanua Levu and other islands. Aside from specific resort-run transfers to Nananu-i-ra, the **Safari Lodge** (☎ 669 3333; safarilodge@connect.com.fj) runs **licensed** and **safety-equipped boats** for transfer ($11 per person) and activity purposes (see **Activities,** p. 452) and runs a backpacker resort on Ellington (see **Accommodations,** p. 451). They stock a small store with basic foods on the Wharf.

The only tourist sight in town is **Udre Udre's Tomb,** the resting place of a former *Tui* (chief) from the 19th century. Located on the Kings Road 100m from the police post at the turn-off for Vaileka, the stories surrounding the tomb are more interesting than the site itself; each stone piled around his tomb represents the head of one of the more than 800 people Udre Udre killed and devoured before his own death. Udre Udre was drowned by the disapproving chiefs from other tribes but his legacy lives on—his great-grandson is the *Tui* of Rakiraki today.

DAYTRIP FROM RAKIRAKI: NAISERELAGI VILLAGE. About 25km south of Rakiraki along the Kings Road is **Naiserelagi Village** and its **Catholic Mission,** site of the famous **Black Christ** mural in the St. Francis Xavier Parish. The fresco, painted in 1962 by French artist Jean Charlotte and his son, Martin, at the request of then-caretaker Monsignor Franz Wagner (former singing tutor to the Von Trapp tots of *Sound of Music* fame), depicts the Christ story with racial diversity and traditional Fijian motifs. The church can be reached by taking a **stage bus** from Rakiraki (1hr., $1.85) to the Naiserelagi Mission Primary School. Then, follow the dirt road (lined by black crosses) to the top of the hill (500m). The church is open daily during daylight hours. VIsitors are welcome to the weekly Fijian mass (Sunday 8am).

NANANU-I-RA

Just off the northeastern shore of Viti Levu from Rakiraki, 870-acre Nananu-i-ra is patched with eight beaches, jostled by strong winds, and surrounded by coral-filled waters. Though primarily an activity-based destination, traces of ancient pottery and remnants of a Fijian fortress remind travelers of the island's rich history.

TRANSPORTATION. Most transfers leave from **Ellington Wharf** ($10 by water taxi from Rakiraki). In addition, each accommodation has its own boat that shuttles travelers for $9—just call from Rakiraki and they'll meet you at the wharf. The **Safari Lodge** (☎ 669 3333) also runs shuttle boats from Ellington Wharf ($11).

ORIENTATION AND PRACTICAL INFORMATION. Three of the four budget accommodations on Nananu-i-ra are clustered near the southern tip at a point between **Wainimolona** and **Lomanisue Bays.** North along **Lomanisue Beach** and up the hill is the **Mokusiga's Island Resort,** an upscale establishment that has claimed much of the central hill as private property. At the very north of the island is **One** (OH-knee) **Beach.** There is **no police, post office, emergency** medical facility, or **bank** on the island. There are **phones** at all hostels. The **Mokusiga Resort** may have the most resources to deal with an emergency, though any serious medical problems should be taken to **Suva.**

ACCOMMODATIONS. The three hostels grouped near the southern tip (Betham's, MacDonald's, and Charlie's) are similar in room style and meals. Reservations are recommended at each. **Betham's Beach Cottages ❷** has sparkling rooms framed in wood. Self-cater in the dorm's kitchenettes or savor the on-site restaurant's scrumptious dinners ($12-25; reserve meals by noon). (☎/fax 669 4132 or 0800 694 132; www.bethams.com.fj. Key deposit $10. 8-bed dorms $16.50, cottages $85. MC/V.) **MacDonald's Cottages ❷** is strikingly similar to Betham's but with tighter dorms. Dinner is usually curry or fish dishes for about $17; order before 4pm. (☎ 669 4633; fax 669 4302. Weekly lovo feast $20. 6-bed dorms $16.50; bures for 1 or 2 $71, extra person $9. MC/V/traveler's checks.) **Charlie's Place ❷** is the smallest hostel on the island but has the most breathing room in its three hilltop huts. (☎ 669 4676. Laundry. No food available. 7-bed dorms $16.50;

huts $66, extra person $8.) The **Safari Lodge ❷** has new accommodations on Ellington Wharf with outdoor showers, Internet, and direct transfers to their watersports activities. (☎ 669 3333; fax 669 3366; www.safarilodge.com.fj. Dorms $20; double bures $40.)

🍴🌙 FOOD AND NIGHTLIFE. The **Safari Lodge** stocks a small store with basic groceries on the Wharf, and both Betham's and McDonald's have their own minimarts. However, the food is cheaper and more varied in **Rakiraki**. The posh **Mokusiga's Island Resort** (☎ 669 4444) serves fresh specials from an ever-changing blackboard menu. Nightlife usually involves some sort of communal intoxication at **Mokusiga's Bar, Betham's,** or **McDonald's.** The **Safari Lodge** also has BBQ and lovo party nights twice a week at Ellington Wharf. ($15 includes food, entertainment, and return transport from Nananu-i-ra.)

🏖️ BEACHES AND ACTIVITIES. Of Nananu-i-ra's eight beaches, the nicest are **Lomanisue,** reached by the short path between Betham's and Charlie's, and **One Beach,** at the far northern shore.

Nananu-i-ra's accommodations offer competitively-priced activities: **snorkeling gear rental** ($10 per day); **snorkeling boat trips to One Beach** ($20); **sea kayaks** ($6 per hr.); and **fishing trips** (3hr., $20). Frequent strong winds make for some of the world's best **windsurfing.** While most windsurfers bring their own equipment, the **🏄Safari Lodge** hires top-quality boards (beginner gear $30 per hr., advanced gear $55 per hr.). Former pro-windsurfer Warren offers lessons (beginner $55 per hr., advanced $85 per hr.). The **Safari Lodge** also has boat cruises, sea-kayaking trips, and treks to Mt. Batilamu. **Ra Divers,** based on the island, is PADI-certified. (☎ 669 4511; www.radivers.com. Introductory course $140, successive dives $75; full package rental $25. Reservations essential.)

THE CORAL COAST

Traffic along the Queens Road between capital Suva and capitalistic Nadi is flanked to the north by fertile farmland and to the south by the region's namesake attraction—over 100km of fantastic soft coral. Though the Coast tends to be wetter than western parts of Viti Levu, the bevy of tourist spots, beautiful location, and quality surfing and diving are wonderful for resort-minded travelers.

🚌 TRANSPORTATION ON THE CORAL COAST

Buses from **Sunset Express** (Nadi ☎ 338 2811), **Fiji Express** (contact United Touring Ltd. ☎ 672 2811 or 672 2821), and **Pacific Transport Limited** (Nadi ☎ 670 0004) all serve the Queens Road and the Coral Coast. Buses go from **Nadi** and **Suva** to **Sigatoka, Korolevu,** and **Pacific Harbour.** Sunset and Pacific Transport charge $2-11 while Fiji Express charges $6-27. Open-air **public buses** come about every 15min., though they make many stops. Twelve-person **vans** and **taxis** often wait during the early morning for transfers to large towns and cities.

SIGATOKA AND SURROUNDS

Lying a third of the way between Nadi and Suva at the mouth of the Sigatoka River, Sigatoka (SING-uh-toke-ah) lives in the shadow of more idyllic places. However, with a handful of notable attractions and tourist resorts nearby, the town makes a convenient base for exploring the Coral Coast.

SIGATOKA AND SURROUNDS ■ 453

ORIENTATION AND PRACTICAL INFORMATION. Gas stations and a handful of **shops** line the stretch of the Queens Road east of the rotary and the bridge, where town-bound traffic splits off north onto **Sigatoka Valley Road.** **Market Road,** which circles the market and bus station, is the location of the majority of businesses, including the **banks** and **supermarkets.**

Four major **banks** in the immediate downtown area have **ATMs.** (Open M-Th 9:30am-3pm, F 9:30am-4pm.) The **police** (☎ 650 0222) are on Water Supply Rd.; reach the **ambulance** at ☎ 650 0264. **Medical emergencies** should be directed to the Suva Private Hospital (see p. 462) or the **Gerona Medical & Surgical Clinic,** on Valley Rd. (☎ 652 0128 or 997 5003. Open M-F 8:30am-4pm, Sa 8:30am-noon; night clinic open daily 6:30-8pm.) **Patel's Pharmacy,** in Market Sq., fills prescriptions. (☎ 650 0213. Open M-F 8am-7pm, Sa 8am-4pm; Su by appointment only.) The **post office** is across from the Shell station. (☎ 650 0321. Open M-F 8am-4pm, Sa 8am-noon.) **Le Café** has **Internet access** (see **Food,** below; 20¢ per min., $8 per hr.).

ACCOMMODATIONS. Club Masa ❸, down a 2km dirt road 1km west of Sigatoka near the sand dunes (look for signs off the Queens Road, take the thrice-daily Kulukulu bus from Sigatoka, or take a $4 taxi), attracts surfers, loungers, jokers, and tokers. Prices include breakfast and dinner. (☎ 651 1347. Board rentals $25. Horseback riding $20 per hr. 10-bed dorms $30; cabins $40; family rooms $60. Cash only.) The **Riverview Hotel ❷,** on the town side of the rotary, is a boarding house in classic small-town style. (☎ 652 0544; fax 652 0016. 3-bed dorms $15; singles $35; doubles $45, extra person $10; $5 more for A/C. Cash only.) The **Sigatoka Club ❷,** on the ocean side of the rotary, is primarily a bar but has rooms for rent and a large dorm. (☎ 650 0026. Dorms $19; singles $25; doubles $38. Cash only.)

FOOD AND NIGHTLIFE. Krispas Party Cake & Delicious Curry Shop ❶, halfway down Mission Rd., is a tiny local haunt that serves $3 curries and 60¢ fresh *roti* banana bread. (☎ 650 0445. Open M-Sa 8am-5pm.) **Lucky Corner ❶,** at the southwest corner of the market, seats hordes at lunchtime. Chinese and Indian foods are in full force, including 80¢ fried eggs and $2.50 chicken fried rice. (☎ 652 0275. Open M-Sa 8am-5pm.) For groceries, head to **Morris Hedstrom,** at the corner of Valley and Market Rd. (open M-Sa 9am-5pm). The **Sigatoka Club** draws locals with its beer and '50s-era feel. (☎ 650 0026. Open M-Sa 10am-10pm, Su 10am-9pm.)

SIGHTS. Enjoy views of the eastern mountains from the 650-hectare **Sigatoka Sand Dunes.** In 1989, archaeologists discovered skeletons from 5 BC in coral-mounded tombs along the dunes; soon after the Fijian government named the dunes the country's first national park. The park entrance and Visitors Center are clearly marked 5km west of Sigatoka. (☎ 652 0343. $5.) Frequent local buses headed to Nadi from Sigatoka make drops at the park for 40¢; taxis should cost about $6. **Natadola Beach,** 4km west of Sigatoka and an additional 8km down bumpy Natadola Rd., is one of the most beautiful beaches on Viti Levu. The **Natadola Beach Resort** (☎ 672 1001) has a **phone** in case of an emergency and a restaurant with $12 burgers. A local bus goes to the beach from Nadi via Sigatoka four times daily, dropping passengers 3km from the beach. If you are driving or biking, follow signs for the resort or for Robinson Crusoe Island, then take a left at the T about 6km further. Taxi fare from Sigatoka should be less than $10. The **Tavuni Hill Fort,** 4km north of Sigatoka near Naroro Village, is the ancient site of the first Tongan settlement in Fiji and is the only original "cannibal" village open to tourists. (☎ 924 8023. Open M-Sa 8am-5pm. $6, children $3. Carrier or taxi fare around $5; local bus 55¢.) The **Ka Levu Centre,** across from the Fijian Resort just west of Sigatoka, is a mock village and Fijian cultural museum introducing visitors to the basics of bure construction, pottery, and Fijian history. (☎ 652 0200. Open daily 10am-5pm. Standard Fijian tour $17; South Pacific tour $37.)

🏆 VILLAGE VISITS AND DAYTRIPS. The women in two villages just north of Sigatoka show visitors the process and products of their handiwork. **Lawai Village** is 2km from town down Valley Rd., clearly marked with a large sign, specializes in clay pottery. The 1hr. demonstration costs $5; visitors, welcome any time of day, should follow village rules and bring a *sevusevu*. The same applies for **Lakabuta Village**, 1km past Lawai, which specializes in both pottery and weaving. Demonstration costs $5. Cab fare to both villages should be $3-4.

To idle on **🏆Robinson Crusoe Island ❹** is to be in budget bliss. The resort is an all-inclusive grown-up version of summer camp, with cramped toilets, bucket showers, and an A-frame dorm. Hilarious activities fill the days, as island guests interrupt their sunbathing to participate in treasure hunts, hermit crab racing, and cannibal "attacks." Transfer to the island, including bus ride from Nadi or the Vatudradra police post (☎ 655 0222), just west of Sigatoka, and boat ride from the Natadola Road Jetty, costs $45 return; the jetty is 3km off the Queens Road west of Sigatoka. A **daytrip** to the island (Tu, Th, or Su) costs $79, including transfers from Nadi or the Coral Coast and an open bar at lunch. Once on the island, **dive** with Aqua-Trek (☎ 651 1500; www.aquatrek.com; 1 tank $80, 2 tank $120), **waterski** ($15 per 10min.), **windsurf** ($15 per hr., including lesson), or **cruise** on the catamaran. For overnighters, buffet-style meals, included in the room price, are very high quality. (☎/fax 651 0100; www.robinsoncrusoeislandfiji.com. Reservations recommended. Dorms $55; bure doubles $60; twin and double lodges $65. Cash only.)

KOROLEVU

Korolevu Town isn't much: it consists of a short strip of the Queens Road, lined by a **bus stop**, a **phone booth**, a couple of **petrol stations**, a **corner store** with a few groceries (☎ 653 0196; open M-Sa 6am-7:30pm, Su 8am-1pm), a **police** post (☎ 653 0122), the **Korolevu Health Centre** (☎ 653 0406; open M-F 8am-1pm, and 2-4:30pm; Sa 8am-noon), and a **post office** (☎ 653 0554; open M-F 8am-1pm and 2-4pm). Travelers on public transportation can stop here and call a ride to the one of the budget resorts.

Five kilometers east of Korolevu, the **🏆Beachouse ❷** is an enormously popular backpacker resort. Throngs of weary travelers rejuvenate in its crayon-box explosion of colors and the gently sloping beach. Kitchen facilities are available for those who can resist the excellent food at the Beachouse's **Coconut Cafe** (dinner $8). The resort also offers complimentary 4pm tea and free use of kayaks and bikes. (☎ 653 0500 or 0800 653 0530; www.fijibeachouse.com. Internet. Reservations recommended. Dorms $19-24; doubles $54; tent sites $12. MC/V.) At **Vilisite's Place ❹**, on the Queens Road just west of the Korolevu, bright billboards welcome travelers to a waterfront location. (☎/fax 653 0054. Doubles $55, extra person $11; family rooms $77.) The abutting **restaurant ❷** serves veggie curry for $4.40. Dinners are pricier. (Open daily 8am-9:30pm. MC/V.)

It's easy to stay well-fed with the resorts above, but for those in search of a temporary upgrade, the lux **Warwick Hotel** (☎ 653 0555), 3km west of the Beachouse, delivers: **Cafe Korolevu ❹** caters to the $12.50 burger crowd; **Sazanami ❺** serves spicy tuna sushi ($4) and teppanyaki dinner ($30); **Papagallo ❺** presents pizzas (margarita $18.50) and gourmet pastas; and **Wicked Walu's ❺** grills fresh seafood for around $25 on its own tiny island. Also at the Warwick, the **Sunset Lounge** toasts the colorful horizon, and the **Hibiscus Nightclub** (open daily 5pm-1am) rounds out the night with drinking and live bands.

The **Biasevu Falls** tour leaves from the Shell station in town. Just ask a truck carrier for a ride to the village (5min.), from which a guide will lead you on a 40min. walk to the falls. The truck, guide, and village fees cost $5. **Mike's Divers,** about 1km west of town, operates through a cooperative with nearby Votua Village—a percentage of all profits funds community projects. (☎653 0222; www.dive-fiji.com. 1 tank $75, 2 tanks $125, intro dive $85. Includes gear and hotel pick-up.)

PACIFIC HARBOUR

A product of wealthy developers and the booming '80s economy, Pacific Harbour in the town of **Deuba** (DOOM-ba) was supposed to be the all-in-one resort playground for Japanese, American, and Australasian tourists; financial (and political) fluctuations have left many of the upscale hotel rooms and stores empty. Still, quality accommodations and beckoning dive sites draw many guests.

ORIENTATION AND PRACTICAL INFORMATION. The town is a short strip of homes lining the Queens Road, with two central points—the **Cultural Centre** and the small **rotary** near the resorts at **Shell petrol station.** Frequent buses between Suva and Nadi stop at the **police** post, at the rotary (☎345 0156). The rotary leads to the Pacific Safari Club and Club Coral Coast (both with signs). One block east, next to the Cultural Centre, is the **post office.** (☎345 0602. Public phones available. Open M-F 8am-1pm and 2-4pm.) Inside the Cultural Centre complex is an **ANZ,** a **24hr. ATM, Internet access** at the **Oasis Restaurant** (see below; 40¢ per min. for the first 15min., then 25¢ per min.), and the **Pic n' Pac Supermarket and Cafe** (☎345 0200; open M-Sa 7am-6pm, Su 9am-6pm).

ACCOMMODATIONS AND CAMPING. Budgeteers will rejoice at the clean and homey **Deuba Inn ❶,** 1km west of Pacific Harbour on the Queens Road. Though the dorms are crunched for space, the roomy lounge has a piano, bar, restaurant, TV, and ping-pong. (☎345 0544 or 0800 345 0544; fax 345 0818; theislander@connect.com.fj. Internet. Kitchen. Laundry. Dorms $7; singles $16.50; doubles $26.40; self-contained apartments $50 for 4, extra person $10. MC/V.) **Club Coral Coast ❸** has tight budget quarters with small shared bathrooms and kitchenette-closets, but guests can use the gorgeous lounge, pool, grass tennis court, and weight room. (☎345 0421; fax 345 0900; clubcoralcoast@connect.com.fj. Free laundry. 1-2 bed dorms $25; deluxe self-contained apartments for 1-2 people $70, extra person $10. AmEx/MC/V.) It's service with a smile at the **Pacific Safari Club ❷.** With access to the Centra Resort's facilities across the street, backpackers enjoy an upgrade from the standard digs. Ask about their dive deals. (☎345 0498 or 0800 345 0498; fax 345 0499. Dorms $18; singles $40; twins and doubles $45. MC/V.) More rustic accommodations await in the A-frame villas at **Deuba SDA Camp ❷,** just across from the Cultural Centre. Fall asleep to the muted sounds of the surf on the camp's beach. (☎345 0402. Communal kitchen. Villas $20; tent sites $5. Cash only.)

FOOD. The **Oasis Restaurant ❸** delivers with darts, web access, and a small but busy bar (beer $3). Burgers and fish 'n' chips cost $7. (☎345 0617. Open M-Sa 9:30am-3pm and 6-11pm, Su 10am-3pm and 6-11pm.) **Kumaran's Restaurant & Milkbar ❷,** next to the Shell station, is a busy Indian eatery—especially at lunch, when $5 curries are served up fresh and hot. (☎345 0294. Open daily 8am-8:30pm.)

SIGHTS AND ACTIVITIES. Only a small section of the sprawling **Cultural Centre** has survived the '80s. Three days a week, cultural presentations portray traditional Fijian village life. (☎345 0095; www.pacific-harbour.com/cultural. Shows Tu 3pm, $18.50.) The **Centra Resort** (☎345 0022; centraresort@connect.com.fj) has a full range of activities open to non-guests, including **horseback riding** ($15 per hr.), **reef fishing** ($18), **sailing** ($10 per hr.), **windsurfing** ($20 per hr.), and **kayaking** ($10 per hr.). The highly-acclaimed ⚡**Jewel of Fiji** daytrip, based in nearby Navua, only 11km from Pacific Harbour, was recently awarded an international ecotourism award. (☎345 0180. Free hotel pick-up in Nadi, Suva, or along the Coral Coast. $70.) **Rivers Fiji**, based in the office at the entrance to Centra Resort, offers five adrenaline-packed adventures that combine sea-kayaking, whitewater rafting, snorkeling, and sailing in some of Fiji's most picturesque terrain. All meals and gear are included. (☎345 0147 or 999 2349; www.riversfiji.com. Trips $65-180.)

Most **dive** operators make the 1hr. boat ride to **Beqa** (m-BENG-gah) **Lagoon**, where the waters teem with soft coral, gorgonian fans, coral heads, and fish of all varieties. **Dive Connection** is the only operator to make the excursion a full-day affair. (☎345 0541 or 992 0541; www.pacific-harbor.com/diveconn. Intro dive $140; 2 tanks $130; equipment and lunch included.) **Aqua-Trek**, based at the **Centra Resort**, offers a backpackers special: $120 (including gear) for two dives a day. (☎345 0324; www.aquatrek.com. 2 dives $160; 4 dives $300; $15 gear per dive.) **Aquacadabra**, based at the Lagoon Resort, boasts the fastest dive boat and top-quality equipment. (☎345 0911 or 992 3483; www.aquacadabradiving.com. 2 tanks $130, intro dive $160.)

YANUCA ISLAND

Off the coast of Pacific Harbour, Yanuca (ya-NU-tha) Island draws divers with its proximity to the **Beqa Lagoon** (see above) and the legendary surf site at **Frigate Passage**, where consistent, fast, and hollow left-handed breaks beckon surfers from around the world. **Batiluvu Beach Resort** ❺ is a small surfing mecca situated on the island's best stretch of sand. For $100 per day, travelers get transport to Frigate Passage, deep sea fishing, gourmet meals, snorkeling, kayak use, and accommodation in the rustic open-air dorms. Free transport from Pacific Harbor, Nadi, Suva, or the Coral Coast. (☎/fax 345 1019 or 992 0019; www.batiluva.com. AmEx/MC/V.)

INTERIOR HIGHLANDS

Travelers circling Viti Levu's royal roads rarely decorate their plain vanilla itineraries with colorful journeys inland. The few who do find a cool, sweet treat: rocky roads dish out dollops of dewy rainforest, crunched by bits of thick grassland, and finish it all off with remote highland villages, where all-natural, no-frills experiences with local culture can be sweeter than a cherry on top.

TRANSPORTATION IN THE INTERIOR HIGHLANDS

Public **buses** visit all of the villages below (except Bukuya), though schedules often change. Buses are most frequent on Friday and Sunday evenings and during the day on Friday and Saturday. More dependable modes of transport are **carrier trucks.** For villages that do not have arrangements with specific carriers, find one in the access town.

Some rental car companies will not rent to drivers headed far into the highlands. **Budget** (Nadi Airport 24hr. ☎672 2735; fax 672 2053; www.budget.com.fj), with eight offices on Viti Levu, is the recommended company for renting a low-end (and less expensive) hard-top 4WD; taking a 2WD vehicle on many of the interior roads is a very bad idea, especially in the wet season. Ask carrier drivers or call the **Public Works Department** (☎670 0389) or **Forestry Department** (☎666 1085) for specific road conditions. Make sure to fill your car with a full tank as there are **no petrol stations** in the Highlands.

BURNT IN BEQA

Walking on hot rocks is painful, but for the people of Beqa Island, it's a soulful, sole-scorching tradition. According to legend, one day the great chief **Tui Qalita** accidentally captured **Tui Namoliwai**, leader of the *veli* band of lilliputian spirit gods who inhabit the Namoliwai River. The tiny *Tui* pleaded with the taller *Tui* for release, promising to magically make him the best fisherman, warrior, or wealthiest man in the village. Since the taller *Tui* was already a superstar, he chose instead to have power over fire. He tested the talent by *vilavilairevo* ("jumping into the oven"; placing one's feet on white hot coals). *Tui* Walita's descendents, the **Sawau** people, today serve as the *bete* (BAY-tay; priests) of the firewalkers. The *bete*, who abstain from sex and coconuts for a month before a ceremony, go to the same stream to prepare for a *vilavilairevo* ceremony by collecting the *drau ni balabala*, tree ferns used as firewalkers' anklets, and by calling to the *veli* and placing little twigs across streams and holes to allow the mini-men to follow to the village and watch over the hot feat. A pit is dug, stones are fired for half a day, and the *vilavilairevo* begins. Kitschy imitations of this amazing tradition can be seen in hotels throughout Fiji.

ORIENTATION AND PRACTICAL INFORMATION

There are **no police, postal,** or **emergency facilities** in any of the villages, although the **Visitors Center** in Abaca and the **guides** from Navilawa on the Mt. Batilamu Trek have **first-aid equipment.** There are temperamental **phones** in Navala and Bukuya, and **radio communication** is available in Abaca and Navilawa but only for emergency use. In all cases, the quickest way out if something goes wrong is by helicopter: call **Island Hoppers** (☎ 672 0410).

In all cases, follow village custom and dress requirements; bringing a *sevusevu* of kava (see **Village Etiquette,** p. 433) is also necessary, except for day trips to Abaca in the Koroyanitu Park. Visiting a village **unannounced on a Sunday** is a bad idea, though if it is necessary try to arrive early in the morning before Church services start (around 10am) or after they end (around noon).

NAVALA

In 1970, 100-year-old Romanu Nagate called a meeting of his fellow villagers in Navala, nestled deep within the Ba Highlands, and told them to save the village from encroaching modernization (though perhaps not in those words). True to his wishes, the members of this fascinating community continue to live only in traditional thatched-roof bures; not only does this make Navala unique, but it also makes this perhaps the most beautiful and picturesque village in all of Fiji.

TRANSPORTATION AND PRACTICAL INFORMATION. Navala is most easily accessed from the coastal town of **Ba** (see p. 449). Buses to the village depart from the bus station on some days, usually M-Sa around noon and 4pm. There is no specific carrier service for tourists to the village, so inquiring in Ba about the villagers' transport is a good idea. Alternatively, try calling the **single phone** in Navala (☎ 611 3214) or **Bulou's Lodge & Backpacker Hostel** (☎ 666 6644, wait for two beeps, then dial 2116) to see if arrangements can be made. A 4WD vehicle is necessary if driving; follow Rarawai Rd. from the central rotary in Ba around the bend near the sugar mill, and continue straight past several turn-offs until you reach the village 2hr. (26km) later. Have a strong heart; the road keeps going and going and going.

There is a one-time **entrance fee** of $15 to the village, which also pays for the privilege of taking photographs, and can be given to the host family or to the *Turaga-ni-koro* (elected chief), Karoalo Vaisewa. For visitors bringing their own vehicle, there's a $2 fee to open the gate.

458 ■ INTERIOR HIGHLANDS

ACCOMMODATIONS AND FOOD. There are two options for accommodations in Navala. The best is to **stay with a family** in the village itself and eat all meals with them. Visitors can be matched with a family by the chief (usually after the *sevusevu* ceremony), but more often are claimed by the first villager they meet upon arrival. Be prepared to sleep on the woven-mat covered ground and to eat mostly vegetables from the village farms. Outdoor toilets were installed just over a year ago. Though the bures are rustic, the experience of living with a family can be incredibly comfortable and comforting ($15 per person). The other option is at **Bulou's Lodge & Backpacker's Hostel ❹,** 1km past the village on the right when coming from Ba. (☎666 6644, wait for two beeps, then dial 2116.) Bulou sleeps eight guests in a house with real beds (meaning not just a floor), a connected bathroom (with new toilets and showers), and a kitchen, or four guests in a nearby one-room bure ($45 per person; all meals included). Bringing food as a gift for the owners is a good idea. Bulou also offers horseback riding ($20), *bilibili* raft building and riding ($20), and a 2½hr. mountain trek ($10).

ACTIVITIES. Activities beyond making the village a temporary home (helping to cook and farm) include treks to lookout points and a nearby waterfall (3km away). Finding a villager or a group of children willing to accompany you (sometimes for a fee, sometimes free) is easy. Of note in the village itself are the school (where visitors may be able to guest teach), the students' tiny fish pond, and the first school teacher's grave.

BUKUYA

Housing some 700 people in over 100 houses, Bukuya is one of the largest highland villages in Fiji. However, with mass comes a sprawling mess, meaning that all beauty of a picturesque type is found on a trek *away* in the surrounding hills, while the more sentimental kind of beauty can be found in one's heart after the enlightening experience of a long village stay. The village *tui* (chief) is also king of the ring, having won the Western Heavyweight Boxing Championship of Fiji in 1980 at the age of 24; the belts still line his walls. You won't have to see them by candlelight, because the village was recently given electricity.

The village is set at the intersection of two major highland roads, one coming 66km from southern Sigatoka and extending 36km to northern Ba, the other coming 41km from western Nadi. Most easily accessed from **Ba** by way of **Navala,** there is no specific truck **carrier** service for tourists to the village, so inquire at the market in Ba for the villagers' preferred transport. Alternatively, try finding **Peni** at the Civic Centre in Nadi to arrange return transport departing Nadi ($60, return $100). If driving from Ba, follow the directions to Navala but continue on the same road for 1hr. It's also possible to access the village driving from Nadi (1½hr.), but the road tends to be in worse condition and is often flooded in rain. Ask for road conditions and directions from local bus drivers, police, and the Public Works and Forestry Departments (see **Transportation in the Interior Highlands,** p. 456).

The village charges visitors anywhere from $50-150 for one night stays to $200 for five nights—the price may be entirely dependent on their whims and your bargaining skills. More consistently priced and much cheaper is **Peni's ❸,** just on the western edge of the village. Take the road to the left as you enter the village from Ba, the road straight as you come from Nadi. The four plain bures with thin floor foam pads, outdoor toilets, and concrete showers cost $30 for the first night and $20 for each night thereafter. Prices include three meals. Peni cooks traditional lovo feasts every Sunday, leads treks to the nearby smaller **Lolo Waterfall** (free for guests), and organizes activities like horseback riding ($15), wild-pig hunting ($20), and eel and prawn fishing ($10).

KOROYANITU NATIONAL HERITAGE PARK

Set in the hills above Nadi and the Western shores, the Koroyanitu Park is home to more than half of Fiji's native flora and fauna, including the immense dakua makadre and the rare Naivati falcon, of which there are only 100 pairs left. Only two years ago, the park was threatened by potential burning and logging; various international governments and their agencies banded together to establish a community-based ecotourism enterprise, which would at once support the villagers *and* protect the surrounding environment. Abaca and Navilawa's Mt. Batilamu Trek are the first fruits of their labor.

ABACA

In 1931, torrential rains drenched Viti Levu's highlands for two weeks, causing a great landslide that buried the village of Nagaga (meaning "cave," probably where everyone was hiding) and all but three of its villagers. Searching for a spot to establish a new village, the survivors came upon a rock etched with the letters A, B, and C (Abaca), which were interpreted to represent the words *ai vakatekivu* (beginning), *bulatawa mudu* (eternal life), and *cakacaka mana* (miracle work). Given a fresh start by government funds, self-sustaining Abaca (aum-BA-tha) now tells the world its story and provides visitors a Grade-A experience.

TRANSPORTATION AND PRACTICAL INFORMATION. Abaca is 16km from Lautoka. **Vijendra** provides carrier transport to the village. (☎666 6590 or 925 3014. 45min.; $10, return $18). The local **Tavakubu bus** leaves Lautoka and takes passengers as far as the Abaca junction, a 40min. walk from the village, twice daily for less than a dollar. **Drivers** and **cyclists** should get specific directions from Vijendra or the Visitors Center. **Entrance** to the park (and village) is $5.

The **Abaca Visitors Center** (☎666 6644, after two beeps, dial 1234) in the village arranges both daytrips and village or Nase stays. If the Visitors Center does not answer on the first try, try again after 10min.; it is the only phone in the village.

ACCOMMODATIONS AND FOOD. The modern **Nase Lodge ❸** has two spacious rooms and a central sitting room/dining and kitchen area with new wood furniture. (Call Abaca Visitors Center, above. Dorms $25; whole room for up to 6 people $80; whole lodge $150; tent sites $10, with use of lodge cooking facilities $15. Under 15 half-price. Village stays with a family $30, under 15 half-price; includes all meals. Reservations recommended. With a bit of warning the village women can prepare traditional **meals:** breakfast $5, lunch $7, dinner $10.)

OUTDOOR ACTIVITIES. There are two main treks: a 2hr. loop past the **Savuione Waterfall**, which ascends through primeval cloud forest and returns past yellow grassland and the roofed **Kokobula Scenic Viewpoint** ($5 with a village guide), and a 4hr. return trek over **Mt. Batilamu** ($15 with a village guide; overnight trip $30; accommodation at Batilamu $50). A 5min. walk from the village, a system of river rock pools flows past a lookout platform and over the **Verenu Falls.** Though the treks can be done with the map in the back of the **village guidebook** ($5), it's recommended to employ one of the villagers; they provide information and a safe trip, while you support their ecotourism plan. There are also **horse treks** (half-day $25, full-day $50) and **prawning trips** ($20, min. 5 people; best during new moons).

NAVILAWA

The Sleeping Giant's rocky repose casts a grand shadow over Navilawa, tucked in a pocket valley just west of the **Vatura Dam.** Lying at the geographic center of the area's volcanic activity, the village is bubbling with excitement after a successful start to its ecotourism enterprise. A town meeting hall has been built at the base of the village's giant boulder centerpiece (clay-oven kitchen, modern bath, and shower units alongside), while villagers have been trained as mountain guides and porters in preparation for the **Mt. Batilamu Trek,** a 2½-day guided jaunt from Navilawa over Mt. Batilamu and the Sleeping Giant to Abaca (see p. 459). While the cost of the trek is not exactly budget ($285 including all transportation, accommodation, meals, guides, kava for *sevusevu*, and park entry fees), it is personal (limited to 8 people) and one of the best ways to see the highlands. Pick-up in Nadi can be arranged with the trek booking office (see below). Trekkers sleep heavily on their first night in Navilawa after a full evening of kava-induced delirium and sleep lighter the second, way up near the summit of Mt Batilamu at a tent site; the route there is rough and steep in sections (with secured ropes aiding the way) and not as groomed as some Western-style trails but is still easily passable. The **Batilamu Trek Booking Office** (☎0800 672 0455), based at **Tourism Transport Fiji** (☎672 3311; fax 672 0184) in the Aerotown Mall next to the Nadi Airport, takes reservations. Alternatively, a day hike can be arranged from Abaca. It's a 2-3hr. hike from Abaca to the top of Mt. Batilamu then about 1½hr. down. A day hike guide is $20 and transportation from Lautoka to Abaca is $10 each way. The view from Mt. Batilamu's peak is spectacular, looking down on Nadi and long chains of Fiji's outer islands.

SUVA

When the British empire moved the capital of Fiji from Ovalau's Levuka to Suva (pop. 77,366) in 1882, they set the stage for what is now the most cosmopolitan city in the South Pacific. During the day, packed buses whiz by market stalls, trendy cafes, and weathered buildings while labyrinthine streets fill with sulu-cloaked Fijians, saree-covered Indians, and sun-burnt tourists. When night falls, neon lights and booming clubs take over in a subtle changing-of-the-guard. From sunrise to sunset, animated Suva is a non-stop haven for city-lovers, people-watchers, and vacationers suffering from beach resort overdose.

TRANSPORTATION

Flights: There is **no airport** within Suva; **Nausori Airport** (☎347 8344) handles the air traffic for the area. Most arriving flights are domestic, usually from Nadi, though **Air Pacific** (Nausori Airport office ☎347 8859) offers infrequent service from **Sydney** and **Auckland.** For information on flights from Suva to the **outer islands,** see the transportation sections for each island group. To get to the airport from Suva, take the bus to Nausori (40min., $1.50), then the bus heading to Bau/Waibokasi, and ask to be dropped off at the airport (20 min., 50¢).

Ferries: For information on ferries from Suva to the **outer islands,** see the transportation sections for each island group. All ferry services arrive and depart from **Bau Landing,** 24km north of Suva. Taxis to Bau Landing from Suva (45min.) cost $20. **Spirit of Fiji Islands (SOFI),** operated by **Consort Shipping** (☎330 2877, Savusavu 885 0279), has an office in the Dominion House Arcade on Thomson St. **Adi Savusavu,** operated by **Beachcomber Shipping** (☎330 7889, Savusavu 885 0266), is on Nina St.

Buses: Sunbeam Transport Ltd. (☎338 2122), **Sunset Express** (☎338 2811), and **Pacific Transport Ltd.** (☎330 4366) each go to: **Nadi** (4hr., 2-14 per day) via **Pacific Harbour** (1¼hr.), **Sigatoka** (3hr.), and **Korolevu** (2hr.). All companies charge

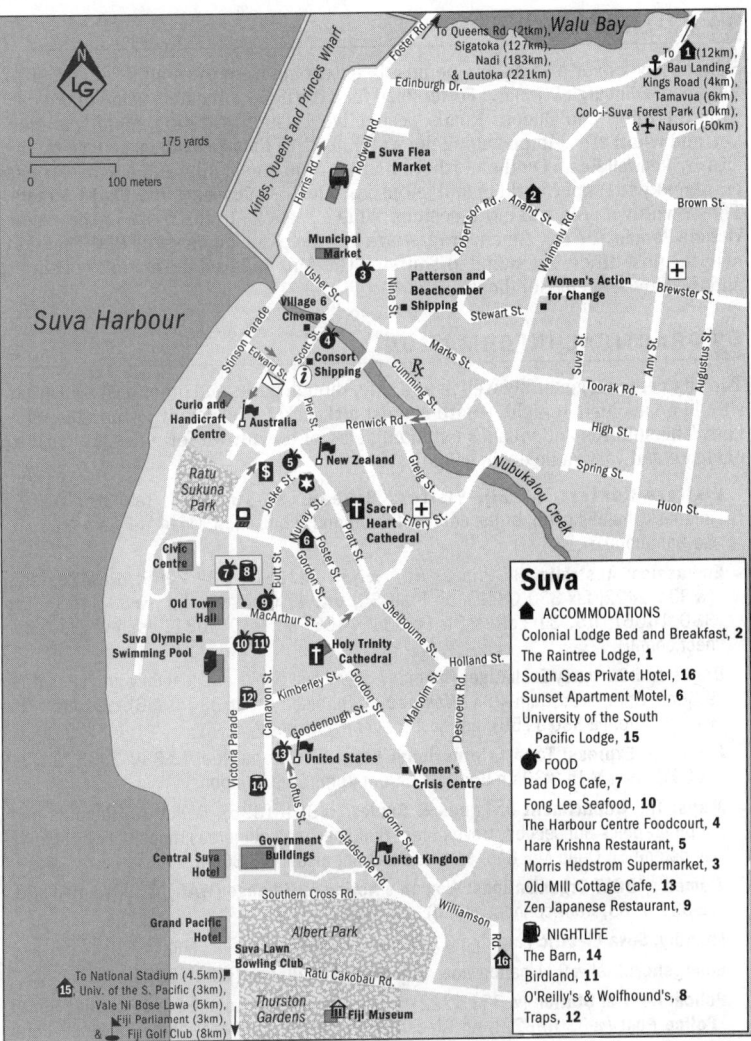

$2-11. **Fiji Express** (contact Coral Sun Fiji ☎ Suva 331 2287) also goes to **Nadi** with the same stops for $6-27. Sunbeam also goes to **Rakiraki** (4hr., 5-8 per day).

Taxis: Van carriers and taxis congregate near the bus station and behind the **MH Supermarket** in the early morning to take passengers west to Nadi and intermediary points ($15). **Regent Taxis** (☎ 331 2100) is one of many companies with 24hr. service.

Scooter and Motorbike Rental: Beat Motorcycle & Rentals (☎/fax 338 5355 or 991 2587), in Grantham Plaza off the Kings Road, hires scooters and motorbikes from $10 per 2hr. or $33 per day. Be cautious: Suva traffic can be fast and vicious and is **not recommended for beginner riders.**

SUVA

ORIENTATION

Suva sprawls over a 15 sq. km peninsula extending from the southeast corner of Viti Levu. **Edinburgh Drive** and **Foster Road** feed traffic into the north side of the city from the Kings and Queens Roads, respectively. The bus station, municipal market, and wharf are clumped along the water north of **Nubukalou Creek**, edged on the east by **Rodwell Road**. On the northern banks of the creek, hilly and narrow streets crammed with supermarkets and shops sprout from **Cumming** and **Marks Streets**. The downtown area and more cosmopolitan streets lie to the south of the creek. **Victoria Parade**, the city's main drag, starts its sweep one block south of the market near the post office, extending to Thurston Gardens and past the majority of shops and the Government Buildings.

PRACTICAL INFORMATION

The city center is generally well lit and safe, though parks and other deserted areas should be avoided at night. Guard against **pickpockets**, especially around the markets. The suburbs and villages extending east of downtown for miles are hard to navigate and vary radically in safety.

Visitors Center: The **Fiji Visitors Bureau** (☎330 2433; fax 330 0986; infodesk@bulafiji.com), at the corner of Scott and Thomson St. Open M-F 8am-4:30pm, Sa 8am-noon.

Embassies: Australia, 37 Princes Rd. (☎338 2211; fax 338 2065); **New Zealand** (☎331 1422; fax 330 0849), on Pratt St.; **UK,** 47 Gladstone Rd. (☎331 1033; fax 330 1406); **US,** 31 Loftus St. (☎331 4466; fax 330 0081; usembsuva@connect.com.fj).

Banks and Currency Exchange: The many downtown banks are generally are open M-Th 9:30am-3pm, F 9:30am-4pm. **Westpac,** 1 Thomson St. (☎330 0666), and **ANZ,** 25 Victoria Pde. (☎330 1755), are best for changing money.

American Express: Tapa International Ltd., 25 Victoria Pde. (☎330 2333 or 321 7689). Open M-Th 8:30am-5pm, F 8:30am-4pm, Sa 9am-noon.

Maps: The **Department of Lands & Survey** (☎321 1395), Room 10, Records and Reprographics Subsection, Government Buildings, has numerous maps of Fiji. Enter via Gladstone St. Open M-F 8am-1pm and 2-3pm; also F 3-3:30pm.

Women's/BGLT Organizations: Women's Action for Change (WAC), 333 Waimanu Rd. (☎331 4363; wac@connect.com.fj).

Laundry: Suva Electric Laundry, 31 Knollys St. (☎330 1442), charges $4.

Emergency: Dial ☎911 nationwide. **St. John's Ambulance** (☎330 2584).

Police: Central Station (☎331 1222), at the corner of Joske and Pratt St.; **Suva South Police Post** (☎330 9822), on Gladstone Rd. in the northeast corner of Albert Park; **Suva Point Police Post** (☎330 7057), at the bus station.

Crisis Lines: Fiji Women's Crisis Centre, 88 Gordon St. (☎331 3300), takes calls for any issue, though primarily domestic abuse. Open M-F 8:30am-4:30pm, Sa 9am-noon.

Pharmacy: The **Central Pharmacy,** 109 Cumming St. (☎330 1877; fax 330 3677), is open M-Th 8am-5:30pm, F 8am-6pm, Sa 8am-1pm. Second location in the Downtown Boulevard shopping center on Ellery St. (☎330 3770). The pharmacy at the **Suva Private Hospital** (☎331 3495) is open M-F 8am-8pm, Sa 8am-6pm, Su 11am-1pm.

Hospitals: Suva Private Hospital, 120 Amy St., east of downtown, has the best medical facilities in the country, including the **Amy Street Medical Centre** (open **24hr.**), a **helipad** for air transfers, and a **recompression chamber** for divers. (☎330 3404; fax 330

3456; healthcare@connect.com.fj. MC/V.) The **Downtown Boulevard Medical Centre**, 33 Ellery St. (☎ 331 3461, emergency 933 3616; fax 330 2423), in the shopping center, also offers quality care. Open M-F 8:30am-5pm, Sa 8:30-11:30am.

Recompression Chambers: The best option is the facility at the **Suva Private Hospital** (see above). The **Fiji Recompression Chamber** (emergency ☎ 999 5500, administrative 330 5154) is another good operation.

Internet Access: Alpha Computer Centre, 181 Victoria Pde. and in the Honson Arcade (☎ 330 0211), charges 15¢ per min. or $6 per hr. Open M-F 8am-7pm, Sa 8am-5pm, Su 10am-4pm. **Bav's Internet Service** (☎ 330 0917), on Victoria Pde., between Gordon and Macarthur St., charges 10¢ per min. or $6 per hr. Open M-Sa 7:30am-10pm, Su 9am-6pm.

Post Office: 10 Thomson St. (☎ 330 2022 or 0800 330 7966; fax 330 7819). Express mail service available. Poste Restante. Open M-F 7:30am-5pm, Sa 8am-noon.

ACCOMMODATIONS

The Raintree Lodge (☎ 332 0562; fax 332 0113; www.raintreelodge.com), opposite the police post in Colo-i-Suva, 12km from Suva on Princes Rd. Raintree's system of wooden lodges is a millionaire's dream. Kitchen. Laundry. Meals $6-25. Taxi from Suva $8; Sawani bus $1; minibus $1.50. Dorms $16.50; doubles $55; quads $96; tent sites $5. Children half-price. AmEx/MC/V/traveler's checks. ❷

Colonial Lodge Bed and Breakfast, 19 Anand St. (☎ 330 0655 or 331 3366). Suzie and Joe have a no-shoes-inside rule, hang laundry under the porch, and cook a $7 buffet dinner. New bathrooms and showers. Free hot breakfast. Internet. Dorms $17; twins $48; doubles $28; suites $66. ❷

South Seas Private Hotel, 6 Williamson Rd. (☎ 331 2296; fax 334 0236; southseas@fiji4less.com). Set on a hill, this bright white hotel has long hosted backpackers. Reception 7am-10pm. Dorms $11.50; shared singles $19; shared doubles $30; shared family rooms $35; singles and doubles with private bath $39.50. Cash only. ❶

Sunset Apartment Motel (☎ 330 1799; fax 330 3466), at the corner of Murray and Gordon St. While the dorm is dark and cramped, the tidy motel units with basic kitchenettes and private balconies have beautiful views. Dorms $9; singles $42; doubles $65. AmEx/MC/V/traveler's checks. ❶

University of the South Pacific Lodge (☎ 321 2614 or 321 2639; fax 331 4827; usplodges@usp.ac.fj), 200m after the main University entrance when coming from Suva on Laucala Bay Rd., is best suited for those seeking longer stays. The garden suites offer apartment-style comfort with immaculate baths and full kitchens. Take the Laucala Bay/Natadola Stadium bus from Suva (15min., 20¢). Breakfast $4-6. Singles $39-59; doubles $45-69; $475 per month, negotiable weekly rates. MC/V. ❸

FOOD

From market stalls piled high with *roti* sandwiches to sleek wine-and-dining, the streets in Suva present a wide variety of tasty eats. Stock up on groceries at the **Morris Hedstrom Supermarket,** across from the bus station. (☎ 331 1811. Open M-Th 7:30am-6pm, F 7:30am-7pm, Sa 7am-7pm.)

Old Mill Cottage Cafe, 49 Carnavon St. (☎ 331 2134). Neither a mill nor a cottage, the locals treat this old house as both, milling about the big porch like it's their second home. Home-cooked Fijian specialties ($1-6) only encourage the behavior. Open M-F 7am-6pm, Sa 7am-5pm. ❶

THE LOCAL STORY

FIJIAN POLITICS, OR, THE CULTURAL VIRTUES OF A HOT BREAKFAST

Emosi Yee Show is a Fijian hostel owner in Suva.

Q: What do Fijians think of George Speight?
A: A lot of Fijian villagers love Speight because when campaigning, he went for the Fijian people. He promised them the whole world. No matter what he does, the villagers will love him.

Q: What do the villagers hope will happen to him?
A: Well, the Fijian people are writing a big petition to try to get Speight out of jail. It would be very bad if they let him out because of all the damage he has done to the country. Thousands of people have no work now. He affected tourism, business, everything.

Q: What is the general consensus about Speight?
A: It's only at the village level that people approve of him. All the educated Fijian people don't like Speight.

Q: After the coup, how have the villagers continued to show their support?
A: Speight was going to stand [for election] again, but the law says he can't because he's in jail. So his brother stood. His brother won with flying colors.

Q: Do you think anyone with similar thoughts to Speight will attempt another coup?
A: A lot of big businesspeople were behind Speight. I don't think they'd fund another coup, though, because now the laws are much more strict.

Hare Krishna Restaurants (5 in the area) are determined to spread vegetarianism and the word of the Bagavad Gita. Potato, bean, pumpkin, or curd curry ($1.20) are 4 of the savory options. Try them at: the corner of Pratt and Joske St. (☎331 4154); in the FNPF Dolphin Foodcourt (☎330 4930); on Cumming St. (☎331 2295); at 82 Ratumara Rd. in the suburb of Samabula (☎338 6333); or on Laucala Bay Rd., across from USP (☎331 1683). Open M-F 9am-6pm, Sa 9am-3:30pm; near USP daily 8am-8pm. ❶

Fong Lee Seafood, 293 Victoria Pde. (☎330 4233). At first blush this pink 1-room restaurant would get average marks; however, give it an A+ for fresh fish and a friendly staff—this place is a palace, regarded by locals as serving the best seafood in town ($5-22). Open M-Sa 11am-2pm, daily 6-10pm. ❷

Bad Dog Cafe (☎331 2968), at the corner of Victoria Pde. and Macarthur St. Naughty puppies never had it so good: $7 bowls of pasta and meaty $8 burgers are more satisfying than any bone. Sa special on imported beers. Connects to Wolfhound and O'Reilly's Bar, listed below. Open M-W noon-10:30pm, Th-Sa noon-1am. ❷

Zen Japanese Restaurant (☎330 6314), at the corner of Macarthur and Butt St. Find tasty Zen on a futuristic, 2nd-fl. balcony while nibbling on mouth-watering sushi ($13), teriyaki chicken ($11), or a mean "zen omelette" from the lunch pack special ($7). Open M-Sa 11:30am-2:30pm; also M-F 6-9pm. ❹

The Harbour Centre Foodcourt (☎333 7811), on Scott St., across from Village 6 Cinemas. Bustling 2nd-fl. eateries overlook the fish market and Nubukalou Creek. **Govinda Vegetarian Restaurant** (☎330 0147) and **Harbour Garden Restaurant** (☎331 4723) are good options. Most open M-Sa 8am-9pm, Su 8am-5pm. ❷

The Republic of Cappuccino (☎330 0333), on Victoria Pde. in the FNPF Dolphin Foodcourt, is the favorite coffee spot for ex-pats, students, and posh locals; most check email, nosh on a slice of $4 cake, and down the requisite $2.50 cup-of-capp. Open M-Sa 8am-11pm, Su 9am-7pm. Also at 9 Renwick Rd. (☎330 0082). Open M-F 8am-9pm, Sa-Su 9am-7pm. ❷

NIGHTLIFE

Traps, 305 Victoria Pde. (☎331 2922). A cave-like labyrinth of red lights, drinks, and constant beats makes Traps the place for a solid nightclub fix. The after-work crowd fills up on $2 stubbies during Happy Hour 6-8pm weekdays, while a younger set takes over on weekends. Tu and Th live music. Open M-Sa 6pm-1am.

O'Reilly's and **Wolfhound's,** 5 McArthur St. (☎331 2884 or 331 2968), connected to the Bad Dog Cafe.

While a thick brogue may be out of place, a thick Guinness and some Irish pride are not. A huge dance floor, TV, pool tables, and shamrocks comfort in predictable pub fashion. Buy a beer and get a bargain $2.50 beef burger. Sa-Su 2-for-1 Lion Red. Open daily noon-1am.

Birdland, 112 Carnavon St. (☎330 3833), is a tiny, subterranean, poster-plastered 2-room bar devoted to jazz and its heroes. Live music Su 8pm-1am. Open M-W and Su 8pm-3am, Th-Sa 7pm-3am.

The Barn (☎330 7845 or 332 1845), on Carnavon St., across from the Government Buildings. Grab a cowboy hat for some country-western fun. Live music Tu-Sa starting at 9pm. Open M-Th 7pm-1am, F 6pm-1am, Sa 7:30pm-1am.

👁 SIGHTS

THE FIJI MUSEUM. When Sir William Allardyce presented his collection of Fijian artifacts to the Suva town board in 1904, he unwittingly started the Fiji Museum. The subsequent formation of the **Fijian Society,** along with donations from private and government sources, eventually led to the museum charter. Today, the museum has five galleries presenting different aspects of Fiji's culture and history, including: the **Taukei Gallery,** showcasing the culture of Native Fijians, and the **Art and Natural History Gallery,** highlighted by Belcher paintings of birds and orchids. Fijian potters extraordinaire, Diana Tugea and Taravini Wati, have clay demonstrations every Thursday and Friday. The reference library allows visitors to order reprints of any photo in their large historical collection. *(On the eastern edge of the gardens, past the Government Buildings on Victoria Pde. ☎331 5944; www.fijimuseum.org.fj. Museum open M-Th and Sa 9:30am-4pm, F 9:30am-3:30pm. Library open M-F 8am-4pm. $5.50, children $3.30.)*

SUVA MUNICIPAL MARKET. Purple eggplant piles, yellow banana mountains, pale root-crop bundles, and crowded, fish-bedded stands make up a brilliant rainbow at the market, forever changing in a kaleidoscope of crouching vendors and ambling buyers. The two **Handicraft Centres** around the corner cater almost exclusively to visitors, with heaps of woven mats and bags, wooden combs, printed masi, and other trinkets. Watch your belongings—pickpockets love the market as much as tourists. *(At the corner of Rodwell and Usher St., on the foreshore. The Handicraft Centres are both along Stinson Pde. Open M-Sa 8am-6pm.)*

THE OLD TOWN HALL. While the town hall used to host performing arts events, today it draws considerable and varied attention; upstairs Greenpeace lob-

---

Q: What do you think the outcome of the next election will be?
A: I think the Indian people are going to win it. The Indian people stick to each other. The Fijian people are too extreme in saying that they'll only support the Fijian people.

Q: What would the reaction be if Speight were set free?
A: Oh, very, very bad. I think the world would turn against Fiji.

Q: What can you say about racial relations between native Fijians and Indo-Fijians?
A: Inside, they're tense. Outside, everything is fine. Fijian people, we are often jealous because the Indian people are so hard-working and they own everything.

Q: What are the reasons for the differences?
A: I think it comes in the [Indian] culture. The Indian wives, they wake up at four in the morning and make lunch for their husband and children. See, Fijian people, we sleep. We drink grog and sleep, wake up at eight, no time to make breakfasts so we have to go restaurants to eat. That's why we can't save money. Also, the Fijian culture is responsible. Mainly, it's the *karekare*, which means borrowing. If I have no sugar in my house, I'll just go to you and say "Please can I have some sugar" and you have to give it. You can't say no in our culture. But the Indians don't do that. Now, Fijians just rely on friends for food and other things, so instead of saving, they spend their money on grog or beer. It's not good, you know.

bies for the environment of the Pacific, while downstairs three restaurants vie for tourist dollars. *(On Victoria Pde., just opposite Gordon St.)*

VALE NI BOSE LAWA. Based on a traditional chief's *vale* (house), the Fijian Parliament is set on elevated grounds, squeezed in by land and sea. The Parliament has recently stood out beyond its orange pyramid roof and distinctive *tapa* banners. In 2000, a gang of rebels held parliamentary members hostage during Fiji's infamous coup. *(5km from Suva on Battery Rd. in Veiuto. The Suva Bus Company's Naseisei bus goes by at least 5 times daily. ☎ 330 5811. Open M-F 8:30am-1pm and 2-4:30pm.)*

THE UNIVERSITY OF THE SOUTH PACIFIC. The USP was established in 1968 as the central institute for higher learning in the South Seas. Most of the students at the five schools (Agriculture, Education, Natural Resources, Social & Economic Development, and Humanities) are Fijian, though a large number come from the 11 other joint Pacific nations. The botanical gardens near the entrance make for a nice stroll. *(☎ 331 3900. For transport see **Accommodations: USP Lodge,** p. 463.)*

BEACHES. Nukumarorika-i, otherwise known as **Mosquito Island,** lies just offshore near **Raffle's Tradewinds Hotel** *(☎ 336 2450)* in Lami, 6km North of Suva on the Queens Road. Visitors can arrange for a short boat transfer (costing a few dollars) to the island from the hotel. Swimming across is also possible; follow the locals' lead and do it at low tide, when wading eases the full 10min. swim. The small, pretty beaches on the island have some sea snakes and sand flies but are much closer than **Deuba Beach,** 49km west and the only other option in the Suva area.

COLO-I-SUVA FOREST PARK. An anomaly in Fiji, Colo-i-Suva (THOLO-ee-suva) Forest Park is the only small, self-contained nature reserve with an official park staff and maintained hiking trails in the country. A misty, tropical rainforest only 10km from downtown Suva, the park's 16 different species of indigenous birds, including the Barking Pigeon, the Fiji Goshawk, and the Spotted Fantail, provide a natural soundtrack for the daily trekker. Well-suited for short day hikes, the 245-hectare park has 6.5km of trails, all starting from an entrance point and parking lot 2.5km down Kalabu Rd. from the main gate and Visitors Center. The **Waisila Creek** provides the biggest attractions, including three large swimming pools in the **upper pools** area (one with a rope swing), the **Waisila Falls** along the Falls Trail, and a system of small **lower pools** on the eastern edge of the park. Droptoilets, bure shelters, and BBQ grates dot the trails and pool areas. Iron cooking sheets for the fire grates are available from the Visitors Center. Camping is not allowed in the park, though officials may let campers pitch tent behind the gate near Princes Rd.; a better choice is to camp at the **Raintree Lodge** (see p. 463), 500m past the park across from the **police post.** *(10km northeast of Suva; follow Edinburgh Dr. from the north side of town to Princes Rd., then continue past the suburb of Tamavua; there are park signs. By bus, take the Tacirua Bus Company's Sawani bus for $1 from the Suva bus station, which runs M-F every 20min. and every hr. evenings and weekends. Visitors Center ☎ 332 0211; fax 332 0380. Open daily 8am-4pm. $5, teenagers $1, children 50¢.)*

⚑ ACTIVITIES

RECREATIONAL SPORTS. The **Suva Olympic Swimming Pool** is the place to masquerade as an international swimming champ. *(224 Victoria Pde. ☎ 331 3433, ext. 233. Swim for $1.40, children 70¢. Rent a changing cubicle for 22¢ with a $2 deposit. Open Apr.-Sept. M-F 10am-6pm, Sa-Su 8am-6pm; Oct.-Mar M-F 9am-7pm, Sa-Su 7am-7pm.)* Watch afternoon lawn bowling at the **Suva Lawn Bowling Club.** The bar overlooks three perfectly trimmed lawns and serves $3 beers and light $5 meals. *(Across from the western side of Thurston Gardens and diagonal to Albert Park. ☎ 330 2394. Open M-F 11am-10pm, Sa-Su 8am-*

10pm.) The **Natadola National Stadium** hosts rugby games most Saturdays from 8am-5pm and will host the 2003 South Pacific Games from June 20-July 29, 2003. *(At the corner of Queen Elizabeth Dr. and Laucala Bay Rd. Closed Dec.-Jan. $2-4.)* The **Fiji Golf Club** lets visitors strut their putting skills. *(15 Rifle Range Rd., in Vatuwaqa. ☎ 338 2872. 9-hole courses $15, 18-hole $20. Open to non-members M and W-F 6am-5pm.)*

Exercise your cinematic muscle at **Village 6 Cinemas,** which specializes in Hollywood and Bollywood flicks. *(On Scott St., next to Nubukalou Creek. ☎ 330 6006. $4.50, children $3.50. Open M-Th 8am-10pm, F-Sa 8am-midnight.)*

HIKING, RAFTING, AND SURFING. There are various hikes around Suva. To climb **Mt. Korobaba** (429m), take the Shore Bus to Lami/Wailakuta (15 min., 55¢) and get off at the Lami Cement Factory just past the Tradewinds Hotel. The trail starts beyond the factory on the right-hand side and forks after 45min. and again after a stream crossing. Keeping left at the first fork and right at the second is the way to summit splendor (one-way 1-2hr.). Climbing **Joske's Thumb** requires even more persistence. Take the Shore Bus heading towards Naboro and get off at Naikorokoro Rd. just outside Naikorokoro village (20min., 70¢). To get to the village, walk inland for 30min. and turn right across a bridge (ask permission for village entrance). The trail begins on the right and takes 3hr. one-way. For both trails, hiring a local guide might be a good idea. Also, it might be possible to tag along with members from the **Rucksack Club** *(☎ 332 0531 or 336 1361),* who meet in the downtown Government Buildings and occasionally run trips to the mountains. For other day hikes, see **Colo-i-Suva Forest Park,** p. 466.

Wilderness Ethnic Adventure Fiji rafts down the Navua River on full-day interior treks for $79, including BBQ lunch. *(☎ 331 5730 or 992 8731; www.wildernessfiji.com.fj. Tours run out of the University of the South Pacific. Departs Suva 9:30am, returns by 6:30pm.)*
Matthew Light picks up experienced surfers during high tide from the seawall on the eastern edge of Suva and takes them by boat to the reef breaks 10min. away. No rentals are available (yet) and this is not for beginners. *(☎ 999 8830. 4-6hr. $30.)*

OUTER ISLANDS

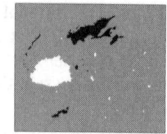

On a map of Fiji, Viti Levu might occupy most of the green and black ink, but the greatest pleasures of paradise lie scattered on the small dots surrounding it. These other islands, removed from the mainland frenzy, offer immersion into Fijian life and, better yet, a taste of lush and large living, Fijian-style. From the azure waters of the Blue Lagoon to the backpacker bacchanalia on Beachcomber to Taveuni's teeming rainforest reserves, the outer islands beckon travelers of all stripes.

OUTER ISLANDS HIGHLIGHTS

GET WET with well-oiled movie stars in the **Blue Lagoon**, the Yasawa Group's most frequently advertised secret (see p. 474).

GET DEEP in the Somosomo Strait and experience diving ecstasy at the world-renowned **Rainbow Reef** (see p. 489).

GET SCANDALOUS on **Beachcomber Island**, the craziest and most luxurious backpacker mecca in the Pacific (see p. 470).

THE MAMANUCA GROUP

While Nadi may be the gateway to Fiji, the Mamanucas (mah-mah-NUTH-uhs) are possibly its most popular destination. The 30-odd islands that make up the group rest securely along Viti Levu's Western shore, creating a 50km trail that tourists hop like frogs. The combination of established, relatively speedy transportation and the islands' proximity to the mainland attracts hordes of amphibian visitors eager to mix sand, surf, and semi-seclusion.

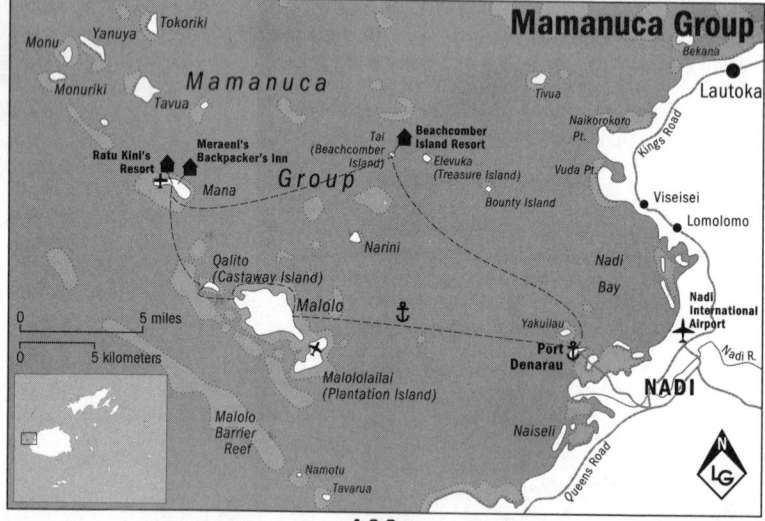

TRANSPORTATION

Flights: Island Hoppers offers speedy helicopter service from **Nadi** to the Mamanucas. (☎ 672 0410. 15min., 2-3 per day, $212.) **Turtle Airways** provides se aplane transfers from Nadi. (☎ 672 1888. 15min., $130-150.) **Sun Air** makes longer and less expensive flights. (☎ 672 3016. 70min., 5 per day, $99.)

Ferries: Port Denarau, at the end of Narewa Rd. near the Sheraton on Denarau Island in Nadi, is the departure point for most travelers headed to the Mamanucas. For transfers not docking directly on island jetties, water taxis from the islands provide the final leg, taking passengers from larger boats to the shore. Some boats also depart from **Lautoka Wharf** in downtown Lautoka off Waterfront Rd. To get to Mana Island, both Ratu Kini's and Mereani's (see **Mana Island: Accommodations and Food**, p. 469) organize transport for around $70 return; the two operators listed below have registered boats, life jackets, and other basic measures of safety and dependability. **South Sea Cruises** (☎ 675 0500) runs a variety of island transfer services. **Beachcomber** delivers guests to its own island resort (see p. 470) or **Treasure Island Resort** with courtesy transportation to the dock from area hotels. (☎ 666 1500. Departs **Denarau** or **Lautoka Wharf**. $40, return $70.)

MANA ISLAND

For travelers searching the high-priced seas of the Mamanucas for a low-cost alternative, Mana is like bread from heaven. Though slightly overshadowed by the island's luxurious Mana Resort, two hostels satiate budget-hunger with some of the cheapest options west of Nadi. In addition to the usual tourist fare, a small Fijian community has blossomed on Mana in the past three decades, growing from the resort's staff and family living quarters.

ORIENTATION AND PRACTICAL INFORMATION. Located only 30km west of Nadi, elbow-shaped Mana is home to the upscale, family-style **Mana Resort**, whose jetty and serenading staff greet disembarking passengers arriving with South Seas Cruises or Beachcomber Transport. While the resort is technically private property reserved for its own guests, the beach encircling the island is public. To the east lie the two budget accommodations and a ramshackle shanty-town village for resort workers; the north side of the island is home to spectacular **Dream Beach**. To the west of Mana Resort lies the romantic **Sunset Beach** and a short airstrip where **Island Hoppers** picks up passengers and persons in need of **emergency medical care**. Minor injuries may require boat transfer back to the mainland, for there is **no police, post, or medical presence** on the island. Bringing **cash** is recommended; there are **no banks or ATMs** on the island. There are **public phones** at Meraeni's and at the Mana Resort reception.

ACCOMMODATIONS AND FOOD. The two budget options are strikingly similar. The resemblance is fitting, considering they are run by two brothers who swear they've passed their competitive days and now work in cooperation. Both hostels have snacks and drinks for sale, safety deposit for valuables, **generators**, and **rain water** for drinking (don't drink from the tap). They also arrange bookings to and from Port Denarau on the high-speed ferries ($50, return $70), and provide transport on their own speed boats to Nadi Bay ($40). **All prices include three meals daily.** The larger of the two hostels, **Ratu Kini's Resort ❸**, lies 50m to the east of the wharf. (☎ 666 9143, airport office ☎ 672 1959; fax 672 0552; tkabu@connect.com.fj. Dorms $35; doubles $73, with bath $90; family room, bure, or deluxe double $120, extra person $20. MC/V/traveler's checks.) Next door, **Meraeni's Backpackers Inn ❸** has more modest rooms. (☎ 666 3099. Dorms $40; doubles $77; beachfront houses $85-120, extra person $35.)

ACTIVITIES. The beach near the hostels on the southern side of the island is nameless and rightly so; it is a pithy little stretch compared to beautiful **Sunset Beach** on the northern side, accessible by a short path through the Mana Resort from the jetty, left past the airstrip, or by a longer path directly through the hostel properties. **Snorkeling** close to shore yields a mix of pretty coral and bits of trash; both hostels rent equipment for $5-10. You can hire a boat for $15 to **Sand Bank Island**, a prime snorkeling spot 50m from shore. Those with deeper diving desires should check out the **Supermarket Reef** or visit batfish around the ominous three coral pinnacles in **Gotham City** with **Mana Pacific Divers**, just in front of the hostels (☎996 5741 or 993 2679; manapacific@yahoo.com. 1-tank $80, intro dive $100, PADI certification $400. Prices include gear rental.)

Trekking through the interior is a drier option. To reach the hills, walk east on the beach from the hostels to the first rocks and turn left on the path past the Sunday Church or take the longer path through the village; to reach the **lookout**, follow the signs through the resort. Thursday is **lovo night** at the hostels. Ratu Kini's offers **spear fishing** ($20; for an extra $2, you can have your daily catch cooked), **deep-sea fishing** ($25), and **kayak rental** ($5 per hr.) as well as **medicine and "legend" walks** (free). Both hostels offer **island-hopping** safaris to Plantation, Musket Cove, and Honeymoon Islands (full-day, $25).

BEACHCOMBER ISLAND

You don't need to search the sands with a fine-bristled brush to find this tiny 5-acre island completely covered by one resort. **Beachcomber ❺** (☎666 1500 or 672 3828; fax 666 4496; www.beachcomberfiji.com), just 17km northwest of Nadi, is popular, often packed, and precisely groomed like a pink poodle to be the ultimate resort and party spot for the backpacker (if not quite budget) set. In being so supremely organized with consistent, timely, and friendly service, the resort has also filtered out the idiosyncrasies of actual Fijian culture. Circling the round island (known in Fijian as Tai) takes 10min., meaning no one is ever far from the **main lodge**, where most of the action takes place. **Reception** is located here, as are the **phone** ($2.75 surcharge without Fijian phone card), expensive and slow **Internet access** ($6 for 15 min., $2 for each additional 5min.), the island **shop**, and **first aid** to deal with any minor injuries. Major emergencies are dealt with off the island (Beachcomber can arrange boat transfer; or see **Island Hoppers**, p. 469). Visitors can charge everything from activities to drinks to sunscreen to their room, meaning that **cash is not needed** (except for late-night *un*official kava parties). There is **no bank or ATM** on the island. The **Grand Bure Dorm** is a packed, clean, and 102-bed sprawl. Each guest receives a big **locker**. Other options include swank lodges with private bath, standard self-contained bures, and super-posh, budget-busting premium bures. **All prices include three meals daily.** (Dorms $75; lodges and bures $179-360. Laundry service available. AmEx/MC/V.)

Eating, lounging on the spacious cream-colored beach, and eating some more dominate the day scene, while drinking in the large sandy-floored bar is the favorite night pastime (**🖪lemon margaritas**); the house band entertains every evening with a wide repertoire, including the inescapable *Beachcomber* song, while weekly fire-warrior and hula-highlights pepper drinking games with a bit of variety. For those willing to actually get out of the jacuzzi, the resort offers jetskiing ($60 per 15min.), parasailing ($60 solo, $85 tandem), waterskiing ($28-32), windsurfing ($15; free lessons), and snorkeling (free with deposit). **Subsurface Fiji** offers dives to Namotu Passage, and the B-26 Bomber plane wreck, among the usual shark and fish sites. (☎666 6738; www.fijidiving.com. 1 dive $72, 3 for $204. Equipment rental $12 per dive. PADI courses available.)

The resort also offers a variety of mini cruises for exploring the surrounding Mamanucas. The **Seafari Cruise** (6¼hr., $45; buffet included) gives guests the standard morsel of Fijian culture, with stops at a Fijian village on Yanuya island, a meeting with schoolchildren and the chief, kava tasting, and snorkeling at Monuriki Island (site of the film *Cast Away*). The **Sunset Cruise** (2hr., $15) drifts lazily about the Mamanucas to the sound of cameras clicking and couples smooching. Make reservations for all cruises at the tour desk next to reception.

THE YASAWA GROUP

Palm trees fringing pristine white beaches, soft green mountains dipping into diamond blue waters, and tranquil lagoons teeming with dazzling aquatic life—the Yasawa Group (pop. 5000) has some of the most beautiful geography in all of Fiji. First charted by a US expedition in 1840, the Yasawas remained one of Fiji's most isolated regions well into the 20th century. Today, the 20 volcanic islands are a prime destination for budget-minded backpackers. Though the rise of tourism may threaten the group's exotic land and deep traditions, the Yasawas remain a slice of Fijian paradise.

TRANSPORTATION

Turtle Airways offers daily seaplane service between **Turtle Airways Base,** 20min. from Nadi airport on Viti Levu, and the waters off **Tavewa Island.** (☎672 1888. 30min. $99.) Alternately, **South Sea Cruises** operates the **Yasawa Flier** (a.k.a. the "Yellow Ferry"), a high-speed, air-conditioned 42-passenger boat that jets from Denarau Marina in Nadi to Tavewa and back. (☎675 0500; southsea@connect.com.fj. 2-4hr. $80.) Many resorts also do boat transfers to and from Viti Levu. Once in the Yasawa Group, travelers can hop around the major islands by arranging a ride on the Yasawa Flier. The Bula Pass ($240) allows for unlimited travel, ideal for three weeks of island hopping.

To island hop over smaller distances or within the same island, most resorts use their own transfer boats as **water taxis** ($5-40). Hiring boats from local villagers is another option. Be sure to check for life jackets when boarding smaller boats.

PRACTICAL INFORMATION

There are few amenities and services in the Yasawas. Aside from the village nurses and community shops stocked with minimal provisions, there are **no banks, post offices, hospitals, ATMs,** or **Internet access** on the islands. **Electricity** is available during limited hours at some budget resorts, and a majority of the resorts use radio phones. Most resorts provide boiled rainwater, although some sell bottled water. There are no independent restaurants, bars, or nightclubs; most resorts include a complete meal package in their prices and provide nightly entertainment for their guests in the form of string serenades, kava ceremonies, and dance performances. **Cooking is not allowed at most resorts,** but snacks are, so guests with big appetites may wish to stow some goodies in their bags.

WAYA AND WAYASEWA (WAYA LAILAI)

Winds blast across the razor-blade sharp peaks of Waya and Waya Lailai ("Little Waya"). While hikers drool over the dramatic islands, overgrown terrain might lead to dangerous, choose-your-own adventures—in 2000, one trekker died in the Waya mountains. The incident provoked government attention, and efforts have been made to improve trails. Meanwhile, like elsewhere in the Yasawas, snorkeling, diving, and worry-free beach-lounging compose a lackadaisical paradise.

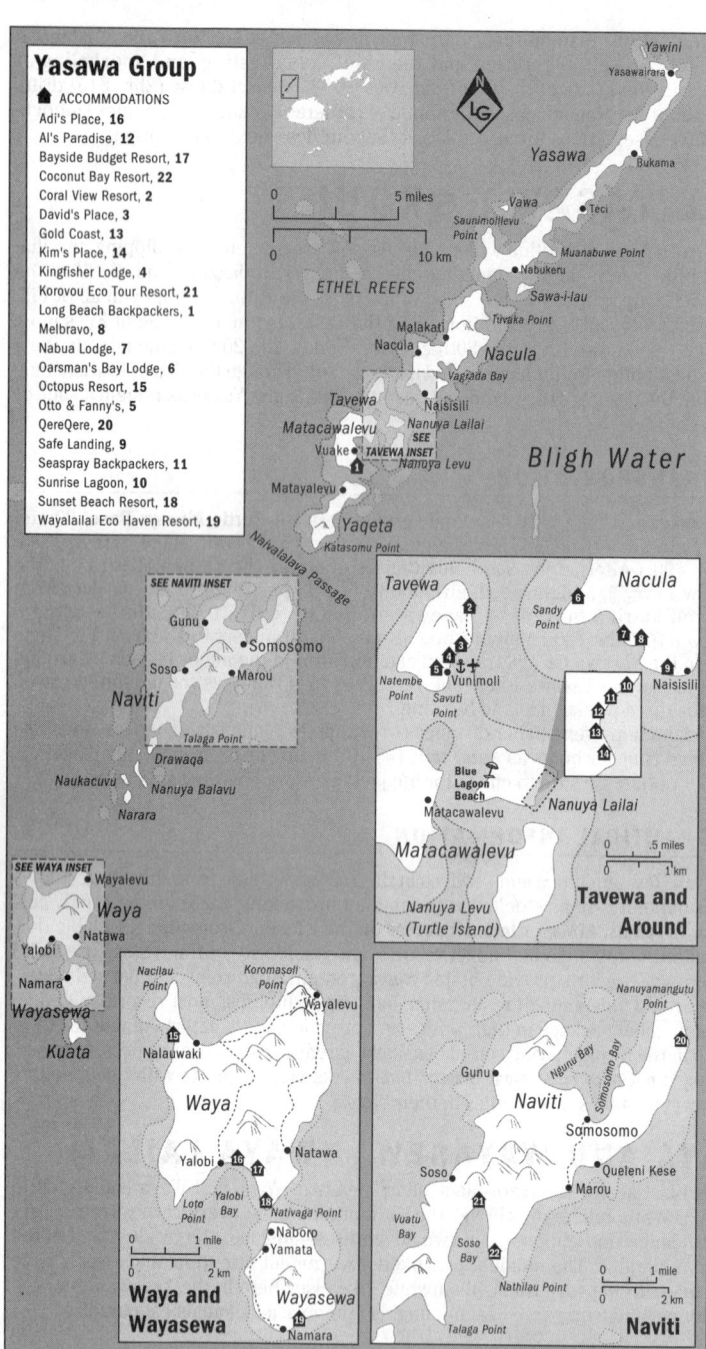

ACCOMMODATIONS AND CAMPING. Octopus Resort ❹, famed for its stellar snorkeling and slightly upscale suites, steals the Waya-bound crowd. The resort runs a daily boat service (licensed 14-passenger boat with life jackets) to and from Lautoka. (☎ 666 6337; fax 666 6210. Boat to Lautoka: 1hr., $60. Free beach shower. Laundry. Reservations strongly recommended. Prices include breakfast and dinner. Dorms $55; double bures $130-180; tent sites $40. MC/V/major currencies.) At **Bayside Budget Resort ❸**, a delicate garden trims hilltop rooms. Two pale blue, storybook huts twinkle on the picturesque summit. (☎ 611 3226. Prices include 3 meals per day and afternoon tea. 14-bed dorm $35; 2-room bures $35 per person; tent sites $25. Traveler's checks accepted.) On Wayasewa, **Wayalailai Eco Haven Resort ❸** is a village in itself. Bures and dorms span the length of three land tiers. On the third story grass-lot, serenaded guests dine on a balcony drenched in lime-green and electric-blue lights. (☎ 660 9725. Dive shop. Electricity after 6pm. Laundry. Prices include 3 meals and afternoon tea. Dorms $35; singles $40; twins and doubles $80; private 2-room bungalows $100-110; tent sites $25. MC/V/traveler's checks.) The panoramic **Sunset Beach Resort ❸** is linked to Wayalailai by a sandbar on which visitors can walk at low-tide. Unfortunately, sun sets quickly in the dark rooms. (☎ 672 4578. Laundry. Prices include 3 meals and afternoon tea. 10-person dorm $40; private double bures $140; tent sites $27.50. MC/V/traveler's checks.) Family-run, no-frills **Adi's Place ❸**, next to Yalobi Village, offers barn-like rooms dunked in peach paint. The resort also has a boat service to and from Lautoka. (Call the Cathay Hotel, Lautoka ☎ 666 0566. Boat shuttle to Lautoka: 1hr., $50. Prices include 3 meals per day and afternoon tea. Laundry. 12-bed dorms $35; 3-room bures $40 per person, max. 5 people; tent sites $25.)

ACTIVITIES. Octopus Resort operates its own PADI dive shop (1 tank $80; 2 tanks $150; $10-20 less with own gear.) The Dive Trek Shop at **Wayalailai** offers dives at similar prices. Octopus also offers its guests **guided village visits** ($10-20), **reef snorkeling** ($15), **night** or **daytime fishing** ($10-15), guided **mountain hiking** ($7-15), and **island hopping** ($25 including lunch). **Adi's Place, Bayside Budget Resort,** and **Sunset Beach Resort** offer horseback riding ($5-20).

NAVITI

Bulky Naviti reigns as king of the Yasawas, flexing a full 33km of sheer land mass. This muscle of resources serves as a hefty stronghold for a handful of villages and an impressive secondary boarding school. Naviti also has a gentle profile, beckoning backpackers with its soft sand and calm waves.

Coconut Bay Resort ❸ treats guests like royalty with Hibiscus-scented towels. A zesty dining-room overlooks Turtle Bay, a curve of beach crowned by a turtle-looking mountain. (☎ 666 6644, ext. 1300; www.coconutbayfiji.com. Electricity 6-11pm. Prices include 3 meals and afternoon tea. Dorms $27.50; double bures $90, with private indoor private facilities $100; tent sites $27.50-30.) Next-door, **Korovou Eco Tour Resort ❸** drips with cool pastels. Airy, bamboo-covered bures have cement patios, ideal for laid-back stooping when away from the beach or hammock. Korovou Dive Centre sits next door. (☎ 666 6644, ext. 2244 or 926 2762; korovoultk@connect.com.fj. Electricity after 6pm. Laundry. Phone service. Prices include 3 meals and afternoon tea. 13-bed dorms $40; double bures $100, with private indoor facilities $120.) **QereQere ❸** spoils the budget traveler with 2-bed dorms and loads of indoor facilities. A large, white-tiled dining room displays local Fijian artwork. (☎ 666 6644, ext. 6458. Free breakfast. Lunch $5; dinner $7. Electricity after 6pm. Laundry. Dorms $35; double bures $45; family bures $75.)

The **Korovou Resort Dive Centre** offers a spine-chilling dive to a crashed WWII aircraft. (☎ 666 6644, ext. 2244. 1 tank $60, 2 tanks $110.) All resorts have **snorkeling**

($10-15), **fishing** ($10), **village trips** ($15-20), and **hiking** (free). In addition, **QereQere** organizes **horse rides** ($5) and **Coconut Bay** has **cave trips** ($60).

NACULA TIKINA

A closely packed cluster of islands consisting of Nacula, Tavewa, Nanuya Lailai, Matacawalevu, Yaqeta, and Turtle Island (Nanuya Levu), this middle section of the Yasawas contains the world-famous ▨**Blue Lagoon** and is rapidly becoming the budget traveler's favored destination in Fiji.

NACULA

Nacula (NA-thu-la) radiates around the man in charge, the *Tui Drola* (high chief) Ratu Epeli Vuetibau, who lives in the direct center of this hilly island. Four villages sprawl around the spine of Nacula and four resorts border the outskirts.

All prices listed below include three meals daily. Splurge for paradise at ▨**Oarsman's Bay Lodge ❹,** set on pristine Nalova Bay, where sunsets melt over sparkling, crystal-blue waters and glistening white-sand beaches. The staff charms, especially on Fijian Nite Fridays, where kava, lovo, and song abound. Hot water, electricity, and ceiling fans are just some of the amenities. (Book through Turtle Airways ☎ 672 1888. Laundry. Reservations recommended. 13-bed dorms $63; double bures with bath $175; camping $57, with own tent $41. AmEx/MC/V/traveler's checks.) Resting on a silky beach at the southwestern tip of the island, **Safe Landing ❸** has a range of recently refurbished rooms. (Book through Turtle Airways ☎ 672 1888. 6-bed dorms $53; standard bures $101; deluxe bures $138-162; tent sites $36.) Also on the southwestern side, **Nabua Lodge ❸** has a beachfront collection of bures spaced over flat, grassy land. (Lautoka ☎ 666 9173. 6-bed dorms $44; standard bures $88, with private facilities $120; tent sites $33.) A mirror image of Nabua Lodge, neighbor **Melbravo ❸** offers similar accommodations. (Lautoka ☎ 665 0616. 8-bed dorms $35; double bures $77, with private facilities $100; camping $30 for 2, with own tent $25.)

All resorts on the island offer **snorkeling** at a modest rental fee ($2-5 per day), trips to Blue Lagoon for **sunbathing** and **fish-feeding** ($10-12 per person), **fishing trips** ($10-12), visits to nearby **limestone caves** ($25-30), and **village visits** ($2-12, usually including a kava ceremony and sometimes lunch). **Diving** is offered at **Tavewa Island Dive Centre** and **Coral View Resort** (see **Tavewa: Activities,** p. 475).

NANUYA LAILAI

While ritz glitters at Turtle Island and Tavewa crowds with backpackers, small Nanuya Lailai exudes rustic charm. Five budget resorts share the northern side of the island amidst rolling hills, mangroves, white sand, and lapping waves. At the southwestern corner of the island, the legendary ▨**Blue Lagoon Beach** steals both the Fijian and Hollywood spotlight. Luxurious cruise ships and yachts anchor here for sunbathing, snorkeling, diving, and barbecues.

When playing "name that resort," it might be hard to distinguish between the five budget accommodations on Nanuya Lailai's northern beach. Each offers a 10-30% *Let's Go* discount on bookings made directly and universal access to services (radio phone, boat rides for fishing, cave trips, snorkeling, etc.). **All prices include three meals daily.** Kick back at **Sunrise Lagoon ❸,** where owner Paosa dines with guests and organizes family kava ceremonies, card games, and volleyball. (Lautoka ☎ 995 1341. Electricity until 10pm. 8-bed dorms $35; double bures $77; family bures $105; tent sites $25.) The resort **Kim's Place ❸** snuggles into a small hill. Teas and cakes go fast at **Lo's,** the on-site, open-air tea house. (Nadi ☎ 772 3225. 5-bed dorms $35; double bures $77; tent sites $25. Lo's open daily 3:30-5:30pm.) **Gold Coast ❸** coughs up the only deluxe bure in town. (Lautoka ☎ 665 1580. Electricity until 10pm. 12-bed dorms $35; double bures $77; deluxe bures $120; tent sites $25.) At **Seaspray Backpackers ❸**, guests swing on hammocks under mangrove trees. (Lautoka ☎ 666 8962. 8-bed dorms $35; double bures $77; tent sites $27.) **Al's Paradise ❸** plunges Adam and Eve into backyard bure bliss including a child-like tree swing. (Lautoka ☎ 997 3800. 6-bed dorms $35; double bures $75; tent sites $25.)

Guests staying at the five resorts have access to any activities offered among them, such as: **trips to the Blue Lagoon** ($10), **village meke trips** ($10), **cave trips** ($25), **fishing trips** ($10), **Honeymoon Island trips** ($10), and **snorkeling gear rental** ($5 per day). **Diving** can be arranged with **Tavewa Island Dive Centre** or the dive shop at **Coral View Resort** on Tavewa Island (see p. 475).

TAVEWA

A mere 3km long by 1km wide, small, hilly Tavewa is the only island in the Yasawas not run by a high chief. Rather, Tavewa is home to one large, extended family, the Doughtys, who inherited the island as a dowry in the 19th century. Today, the European-Fijian family has built Tavewa up as one of the premier budget destinations in Fiji. Travelers who want to escape the resort frenzy should head to Savuti Point, a small strip of sand that kisses the Blue Lagoon.

ACCOMMODATIONS AND CAMPING. Prices at Tavewa's accommodations include three meals—though you may still be hungry. Reservations are recommended at all of the resorts. The largest resort, the Bruce family-run **Coral View Resort ❸**, teems with backpackers and runs its own ferry service to and from Nadi via Lautoka. (☎ 666 2648, Lautoka 666 9316, Nadi 672 4199; 6-7hr. M-Sa departs **Nadi** 9am, **Tavewa** 7am. $60, return $100. Equipped with life jackets.) With daily nighttime entertainment and its very own PADI shop, Coral View offers the "busiest" laid-back stay in Tavewa. (☎ 666 2648 or 992 9325; fax 666 9312; coral@connect.com.fj. Electricity. Laundry. Phone service. One free resort activity daily. Dorms $35; standard double bures $77; luxury double bures $88; tent sites $27.50.) Mellow **David's Place ❸**, run by David Doughty, has excellent lovo buffets every Thursday and barbecues on Saturday. Guests are welcome to attend Sunday services at the resort's—and the island's only—church. (Nadi ☎ 672 1820 or 995 0545. Electricity during limited hours. Laundry. Phone service. Dorms $40-45; double bures $95; tent sites $37.50. MC/V.)

Closest to Savuti Point, **Otto & Fanny's ❸** is a bit pricier, but Fanny dishes out the best grub on Tavewa. Blueprints for an official Otto and Fanny's bakery are in the works. (Lautoka ☎/fax 661 4621. Electricity in all buildings. Laundry. Phone. Reservations recommended. 8-bed dorms $70; double bures with bath $140. MC/V/traveler's checks.) Hidden rock-lights skirt the pathway to the upscale **Kingfisher Lodge ❺**, where three safari-style tents sit in a jungle garden. Honeymoon-oriented, the lodge feels slightly out of place on budget Tavewa. (Book through Turtle Airways ☎ 672 1888. Standard double bures $150. MC/V/traveler's checks.)

ACTIVITIES. All resorts offer **village trips** ($20 with lunch in the village), **cave trips** ($25), and **snorkeling gear** ($5 per day with $20 deposit). Or, you can hike for free up Tavewa's largest hill (return 1hr.). The best swimming (also free) is at Savuti Point. However, accessibility to PADI diving courses steals the activities spotlight. The well-established **Tavewa Island Dive Centre**, between Otto & Fanny's and David's Place, runs full-range PADI offerings for guests staying on Tavewa and nearby islands. (Call West Side Water Sports in Lautoka ☎ 666 1462 or 999 8862; 1 dive $88, 2 dives $145; 10 tanks $500, unlimited $600.) The **Coral View Resort PADI Dive Shop** offers similar dives at similar prices.

MATACAWALEVU AND YAQETA

The oval-shaped Matacawalevu (4km long) and Yaqeta have recently joined the Yasawa scene. Ripe for the budget traveler, **Long Beach Backpackers ❸** on Matacawalevu has planted the first seeds of tourism. Kind owners, Noah and Litia, care for the sand-lawns and whip up some mean Fijian cuisine. (☎666 644 3032; nacula@hotmail.com. Electricity after 6pm. Prices include 3 meals per day. 6-person dorms $35; double bures $75; tent sites $25. Discounts on longer stays.)

THE LOMAIVITI GROUP

The Lomaiviti ("central Fiji") Group surprises and allures lucky island-hoppers who accidently seem to trip over its less-touristed beaches. Located in the geographical heart of the Fijian archipelago, the Lomaiviti Group consists of seven large islands and a few smaller ones, with a total area of 400 square kilometers. Most of these posh sand strips are privately owned. However, thrifty travelers will find many sights to explore around Ovalau, the largest island in Lomaiviti.

PRACTICAL INFORMATION

The few budget accommodations in the Lomaiviti Group are mostly on Ovalau. Services such as **banks,** the **post office, grocery stores,** and **Internet access** are concentrated in **Levuka** on the eastern coast of Ovalau and are **not available on the smaller islands** such as Leleuvia and Caqelai. The budget resorts on Leleuvia and Caqelai offer **drinking water,** limited **electricity,** and regular **phone service.**

OVALAU

Lovely towns mushroom along the entire coast of Ovalau, surrounding a range of sun-kissed mountains. Set in a crater, the only interior village is Lovoni, guarded by Mt. Nadelaiovalau (620m) to the east. Farther east, Fiji's first capital, Levuka, oozes with historical pride. Though not as frequented as Lovoni or Levuka, other

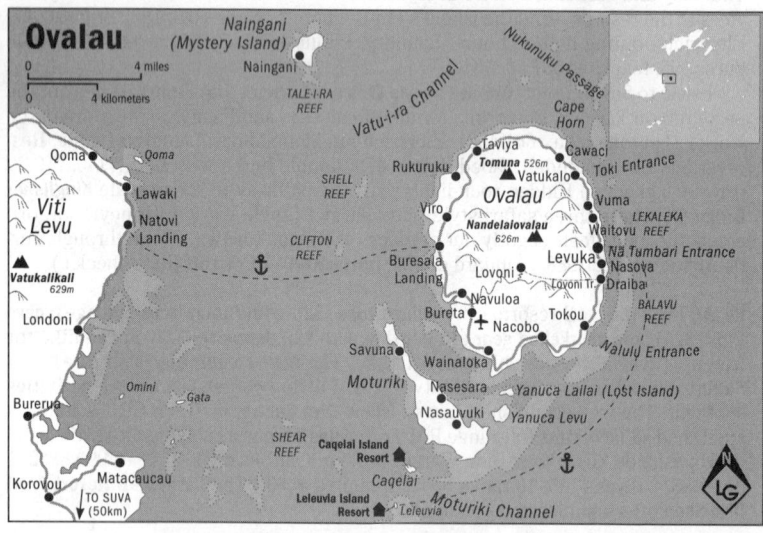

Ovalau towns are just as picturesque, touched by a midday glow and sprayed by waves that lap over sea-walls. Most travelers choose to dawdle on land before heading offshore to snorkel, dive, and kayak.

TRANSPORTATION

Air Fiji (☎344 0139) flies daily between **Suva** and **Levuka** (15min., $64). **Patterson Brothers Shipping** (☎344 0125), on Beach St. in Levuka, runs a ferry/bus service between **Suva** and **Levuka** (4½hr., M-Sa 1 per day, $22). **Leleuvia Island Resort** (☎330 1584) operates an on-demand boat-taxi service between **Suva** and **Levuka** via **Leleuvia** (80min., 1 per day, $100 Suva-Levuka return). **Carriers** within Ovalau (canopied open pickup trucks) depart when full, typically charging $1 within Levuka, and $3 between Levuka and Lovoni. **Minibuses** connect Bureta and Levuka (1hr., $3). **Taxis** charge up to $1.50 within Levuka and can be hired for $80 to go around the island. Call **Bob's Taxi** (☎344 0397) for hire. All land transport departs opposite the Sacred Heart Church. For a scenic way to explore the island, **Ovalau Watersports** (see **Orientation and Practical Information,** below) in Levuka rents out mountain bikes (1hr. $5, half-day $10, full-day $15).

LEVUKA

Historical Levuka (pop. 3000), the site of the first European settlement in Fiji, was a wild spot in the South Pacific during the 1840s. Whalers, beachcombers, runaway convicts, and speculators of all shades engaged in rowdy, drunken bouts that gave Levuka a notoriously bad name. Nevertheless, the British empire chose the city as the capital of Fiji in 1874 for its accessible port, central location between Viti Levu and Vanua Levu, and proximity to the important island of Bau. Today, hurricanes have ravished most of the hotels and bars that once lined Levuka's main thoroughfare, but an otherworldly colonial charm remains eerily untouched. Nominated by UNESCO as a World Heritage Site, Levuka lives in a time all its own.

ORIENTATION & PRACTICAL INFO

Levuka is located on a narrow coastal strip with the steep mountains as its backdrop and is easily explored on foot. Most shops and services are located along the waterfront on **Beach Street.** At the southern end of Beach St. sits the **Pacific Fishing Company (PAFCO),** the town's main employer and the lifeblood of its economy.

Visitors Center: The **Community Centre** (☎344 0356), in the Morris Hedstrom Bldg. Open M-F 9am-1pm and 2-4:30pm. **Ovalau Watersports** (☎344 0166), a few doors down on Beach St., also gives out information. Open M-F 8:30am-4pm, Sa 8:30am-1pm. The staff at the **Royal Hotel** (☎344 0024), on Langham St., are also helpful.

Banks: Both banks exchange currency and cash traveler's checks. **Colonial National Bank** (☎344 0300) is on Beach St. Open M 9:30am-4pm, Tu-F 9am-4pm. Also on Beach St., **Westpac Bank** (☎344 0346) gives Visa cash advances. Open M-Th 9:30am-12:30pm and 1:30-3pm, F 9:30am-4pm.

Police: (☎344 0222), at the corner of Garner Jones Rd. and Totogo Ln.

Pharmacy: Gulabdas & Sons (☎344 0015), on Beach St. Open M-Sa 7:30am-6pm.

Hospital: (☎344 0088), at the northern end of Beach St. Has an ambulance. Open M-F 8am-4pm; nurse on duty 24hr.

Internet Access: Ovalau Watersports (see above) charges 30¢ per min.

Post Office: (☎344 0141; fax 344 0633), at the southern end of Beach St. Has pay phones, Poste Restante mail, and Western Union. Open M-F 8am-4pm.

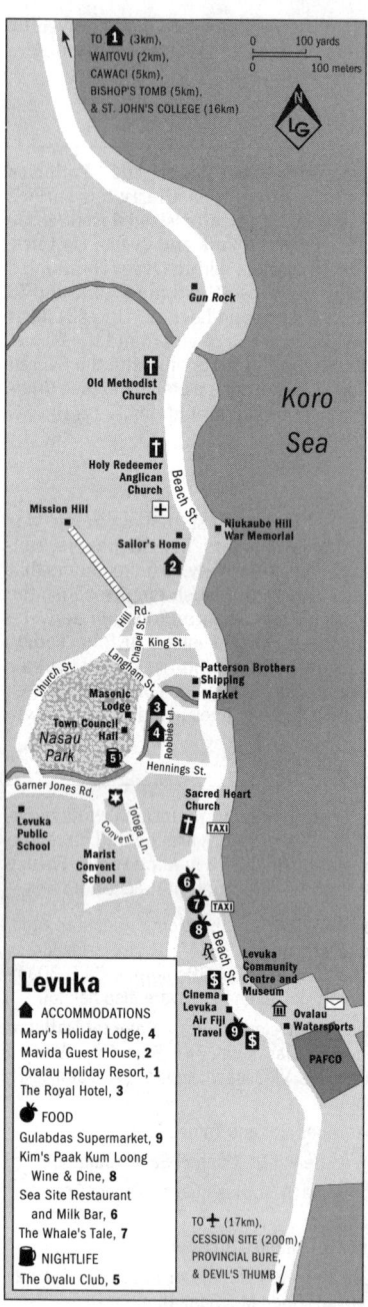

ACCOMMODATIONS

The Royal Hotel (☎ 344 0024; fax 344 0174; royal@connect.com.fj), on Langham St., close to Beach St., is the oldest continuously-operated hotel in the South Pacific. Relax amidst ceiling fans, historical photos, a century-old billiard table, and hibiscus flowers. Restaurant serves light meals ($2-8). Internet. Laundry. Dorms $10; singles $19; twins and doubles $27.50; triples $35; quads $48.40. Traveler's checks accepted. ❶

Mavida Guest House (☎ 344 0477; fax 330 1652), on Beach St., has a personal colonial flare. Family photos rest on dark furniture surrounded by perched-up gold plates. Free kayak rental. Breakfast included. Lunch and dinner each $6 per person. Kitchen use $2. Laundry. Dorms $10; doubles $40; private rooms $15 per person. ❶

Mary's Holiday Lodge (☎ 344 0023), on Beach St. Rooms branch off a dark-paneled hallway, bookended by an airy sitting room and a pink-themed lounge. Meals $4.50-7. Laundry. Dorms $8; singles $13; doubles $26.40; cottages $44. Cash only. ❶

Ovalau Holiday Resort (☎/fax 344 0329), a few km north of Levuka on a small bay, is hugged by quiet villages far from the downtown hussle. Free transport to and from Levuka. Restaurant $5.50-35. Snorkeling, reef fishing trips, and kayak rental available. 19-bed dorm $10.50; bungalows with bath $55-66; camping $5. 20% *Let's Go* discount. ❶

FOOD AND NIGHTLIFE

For groceries, head to **Gulabdas Supermarket,** at the southern end of Beach St. (☎ 334 0100. Open M-Sa 8am-7pm, Su 8am-1pm and 5-7pm.) There is also a market close to the Royal Hotel.

The Whale's Tale (☎ 344 0235), on Beach St., makes a savory splash over hungry tastebuds. Tourists pack the dimly-lit space for home-cooked burgers

($8), sandwiches with salad ($5), and 3-course dinner specials ($13). Open M-Sa 11am-3pm and 5-9pm. Traveler's checks accepted. ❷

Sea Site Restaurant and Milk Bar (☎344 0553), on Beach St. Join the locals for a hefty plate of curry ($4) or a bite of *roti* (50¢) from behind-the-counter warmers. Ice-cream tops it all off ($0.70-1.50). Open M-Sa 7am-9:30pm. ❶

Kim's Paak Kum Loong Wine & Dine (☎344 0059), on Beach St. The "long soup" ($4) is even longer than the restaurant's name—a never-ending bowl of wonton bliss. Tasty selection of Chinese, Fijian, and European dishes ($3-9). Su evening buffet $13. Open M-Sa 7am-3pm and 5-9pm, Su noon-2pm and 6-9pm. ❷

Cinema Levuka (☎344 0666), on Beach St. Tiger-striped chairs make this cinematic cafe the hippest place for a cup of tea (80¢), a sandwich (80¢), and a dose of music television. Open M-Tu 8am-5pm, W-Sa 8am to end of movie, Su 8am-3pm. ❶

The Ovalau Club (☎344 0507), next to Nasau Park and Town Council Hall, is the best bar in town. Established in 1904 and one of Fiji's oldest social clubs, Ovalau welcomes out-of-towners thirsty for a cold beer ($3) and a dash of history. Ask the bartender to show you the letter written by German sea raider Count Von Luckner during WWI. Open M-Th 4-10:30pm, F 2pm-midnight, Sa 10am-midnight, Su 10am-9pm.

SIGHTS AND ACTIVITIES

WALKING TOUR. A historical walking tour within and around Levuka makes for a pleasant afternoon. Starting at the **Cession Site Stones** in Nasova (10min. walk south of PAFCO), boulders commemorate the local signing of the Deed of Cession on October 10, 1874, Fiji's independence in 1970, and the centenary of the Deed of Cession in 1974. Across the street is the thatched-roof **Provincial Bure**, used by Prince Charles when he came to represent Queen Elizabeth during Fiji's transition to independence in 1970. Walking north past the PAFCO/Bumble Bee tuna cannery onto Beach St., the Oregon-timbered old **Morris Hedstrom Company Building** (1868) has survived many a hurricane since its early days as a merchant mecca. It now houses Levuka's Community Centre, library, and a modest museum displaying pictures, tools, weapons, tribal handicrafts, and shells. (Open M-F 8am-1pm and 2-4:30pm. $2 suggested donation.) Farther on, the town clock strikes twice each hour from the tower on the **Sacred Heart Roman Catholic Church** (1898), built in memory of Marist Father Breheret, the first Catholic priest to arrive in Levuka. Behind the church, on Totoga Ln., the pastel-blue **Marist Convent School** (1880) served as a temporary hospital in 1919, when a devastating influenza epidemic took approximately five lives per day. Today it functions as a coed primary school.

Northward on Totoga Ln. stands the police station compound and the wooden buildings of the **original police station** (1920; Fiji's first police station) and **former prison**. Across Totoga Creek are the **Ovalau Club** (1904), one of Fiji's oldest social clubs, and the adjacent **Town Council Hall,** erected in 1898 to celebrate Queen Victoria's silver jubilee. Next door lie the remains of the first **Masonic Lodge** in the South Pacific (1875), which was burned down in the wake of the May 2000 coup by villagers convinced of masonic devil worship.

Cross the creek again, turn right onto Garner Jones Rd., and **Levuka Public School,** founded in 1879 as Fiji's first public school, is on your left. At this point there is the option of a brief hike (return 20min.) up to **Freshwater Pool.** To get to this mini-waterfall and natural swimming pool, continue from the school towards the mountain following the stone path up the stairs and through a small village settlement. Sturdy shoes are needed to get down to the waterfall. For the more adventurous hiker, **Nadelaiovalau Peak** rises a steep 616m with a trail that begins to the left of the waterfall track, between the steel water tank and a fence. The trek

THE LOCAL STORY

HAIL TO THE CHIEF

Saiasi Rogoyawa is the chief of Lovoni Village.

Q: How long have you been chief of Lovoni?
A: For eight years now.

Q: How did you become chief?
A: My father was chief and I was the eldest son. When he died, I became chief of Lovoni.

Q: What is your main responsibility?
A: I make sure that there are no problems in the village. If there is a problem, members of different clans come to me and we try to solve it.

Q: What is a typical day like for you?
A: In the olden days, the chief would sit in his house and all his servants, the people of the village, would wait on him. These days, the chief must be self-sufficient and work for his own family, just like all the other families in the village. So, every day I go and work in my plantation.

Q: What are some Fijian traditions that apply to the chief?
A: When we drink kava, I have to sit before the kava bowl. When people come to visit me, they must present me with kava before wandering about the village. This comes more from tradition than anything else. In the olden days, when the chief didn't really work and mainly drank kava all the time, kava was an appropriate gift. Therefore, it is still a traditional gift and a sign of respect.

---

takes about 1½hr. one-way, with steep verticals in the beginning. A guide would be helpful. Back on Garner Jones Rd., turn left onto the bridge and go around Nasau Park on Church St. On the left are the 199 steps (the longest in Fiji) leading to **Mission Hill**, originally the site of the first mission school and now home to Delana Methodist School. Walk past the **Royal Hotel** (c. 1860) and turn left on Beach St. to reach seaside **Niukaube Hill**, site of the **First World War Memorial**, a white-washed monument in the form of an ionic stone column commemorating British Levuka residents who died in the war. King Cakobau's original Parliament House and Supreme Court once stood on this hill.

Farther north, the stained glass windows on the gray-faced **Holy Redeemer Anglican Church** (1904) remember a handful of early Levuka dwellers. King Cakobau personally worshipped in the simple **Old Methodist Church** (1866) about 200m down the road. Heading northward, **Gun Rock** juts out over Levuka village, scooped out along the base by a cannonball fired in 1849 by Captain J.E. Erskine, who meant to impress Cakobau with his mighty fleet. Two kilometers north of Levuka, picturesque **Waitovu Village** has a waterfall and swimming pool. Another 3km away, on the same road, the **Bishops' Tomb** (1922) is a burial ground for Roman Catholic bishops. The white tomb rests hill-top with a view of **St. John's College** (1894), where the sons of chiefs used to hit the books.

CINEMAS. Cinema Levuka shows Hollywood and Bollywood movies. *(On Beach St. ☎ 344 0666. Showtimes M-F 8pm; Sa 11am, 2, and 8pm; Su 2 and 8pm. $3, under 12 $1.50.)*

DIVING. Ovalau Watersports offers fine diving near Wakaya Island and around Ovalau, including several unexplored sites. *(In the Ovalau Tours and Transport building at the southern end of Beach St. ☎ 344 0166; dive@owlfiji.com. 2 tanks from $130; open-water course $460; reef snorkeling $30; snorkeling gear rental $10 per day.)*

DAYTRIPS. Ovalau Watersports is also the agent for transfer and daytrips to **Leleuvia Island Resort**. Daytrips to **Caqelai Island** can be booked at the **Royal Hotel**. Another great daytrip from Levuka is **Epi's Inland Tour** (also called Epi's Midland Tour) to Lovoni Village at the bottom of the central volcanic crater. You can ride on the village truck to Lovoni or hike over the mountains from Levuka (5hr.; hiking boots needed; carry plenty of water). If you travel by truck, Epi will take you to some waterfalls after lunch. During the hikes, Epi identifies various medicinal plants; he is most impressive when narrating the tragic history of his village. *(Book at the*

Royal Hotel. Leleuvia daytrip $35. Caqelai daytrip $30. Both trips include lunch. Epi's Tour starts from Levuka at 11am and returns by 7pm M-Sa on demand; $25, including lunch at Epi's home in Lovoni.)

CAQELAI AND LELEUVIA

The closest you may ever come to living out your tropical beach fantasy may be on Caqelai or Leleuvia. These tiny coral islands allure sunseekers and beach bums with every sort of temptation: luxurious golden sandy beaches, shallow azure water brimming with colorful fish, lush vegetation, and palm trees offering a cool reprieve from the sun. The area has some of the best fishing, snorkeling, and crab watching in Fiji. Caqelai is owned by the Methodist Church on nearby Moturiki Island, while Leleuvia belongs to the chiefs of Bau Island. No alcohol is sold on Caqelai, but guests may bring their own. Both resorts have boiled rainwater for drinking, phones, and snack shops. Caqelai runs its own boat service (canopied 15-passenger boat with life jackets) to Levuka (1hr.; departs Caqelai 8:30am, Levuka 10am; $15 one-way; book at the resort or at the Royal Hotel in Levuka—see p. 478) as does Leleuvia (for info on boat services to and from Leleuvia, see **Ovalau: Transportation**, p. 477). Caqelai also has service to Waindalice and Verata on Viti Levu (1hr.; departs Caqelai 8:30am, Waindalice 10am; $25). Either resort will transfer you to the other (5min., return $10).

On Leleuvia, **Leleuvia Island Resort** ❸ has yummy food, a knack for late-night partying (a.k.a kava by the bonfire), excellent snorkeling, and its own dive shop. (☎330 1584, Suva 330 1799. Electricity after 6pm. 12-bed dorm $30; bures $35; bungalows with bath $42; camping $24. Day trips to Honeymoon Island $5; snorkeling gear rental $10 per day; reef fishing $30 per hr.; Su village visits $4. Packages at the PADI dive shop include: 1 tank $75; 2 tanks $110; open-water course $390.) At **Caqelai Island Resort** ❸, on Caqelai, the handsome beach makes up for the roughing-it feel (bucket water for showers). During low tide, visitors can walk to nearby Snake Island. (☎343 0366. 12-bed dorm $28; bures $30; camping $24. Snorkeling gear rental $6 per day; reef fishing $5; village visits to Moturiki Island $10 per person; trips to nearby Honeymoon Island $5.) **Prices at both resorts include three meals per day.**

VANUA LEVU

Often dubbed "the friendly north," the irregularly-shaped Vanua Levu is Fiji's second largest island (5538 sq. km) and home to 20% of the Fijian popula-

Q: What changes would you most like to make in your village?
A: I would like to provide better education for the children in my village. For me, that is the most important thing.

Q: How is your village different from other villages?
A: My village is not different from any other villages. In our culture, it is important that each village is considered equal to one another. That way, we avoid conflict.

Q: If there was one message about Fiji you wanted to share with the rest of the world, what would it be?
A: I would want people to know that Fiji still has a strong devotion to our culture. For a large part, we have been Westernized. For example, my house has a TV. But Fiji still retains a culture that cannot be separated. My village and my people hold to that culture. We have a strong sense of tradition that has not faded and that will not fade.

Q: What is the best part of being chief?
A: There is no good part about being chief. It is very hard work. It is a headache, really. The only nice part is the respect. Here, the people have a lot of respect for the chief. We believe that each chief is protected by a spirit around him. Nobody can hurt the chief because of the spirit. If anybody says something or does something bad to the chief, that person will be cursed and the curse will not be taken off until an apology is made.

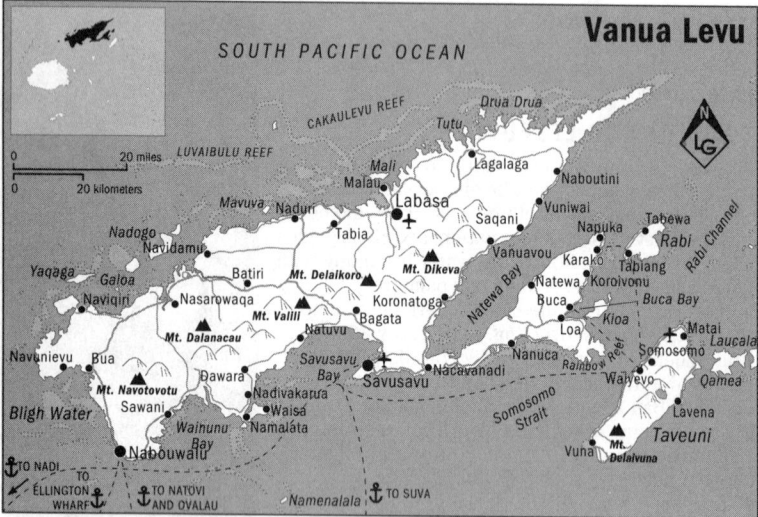

tion. A relative lack of sandy beaches and hiking trails has prevented tourism from supplanting the sugar and copra industries. However, the few travelers who do venture to Savusavu and Labasa are charmed by wide grassy fields and local farmers. More frequented is Vanua Levu's southeastern coast, renowned for its incredible diving, snorkeling, kayaking, and fishing.

SAVUSAVU

A popular port for yachts circling the globe, Savusavu (pop. 2000) is well-protected by a lovely harbor ringed by towering green mountains. A 19th-century European settlement that once bustled with whalers and sandalwood, gold, and copra traders, Savusavu is now a sleepy town that only dresses up for a biennial yacht race from New Zealand. Despite its calm and tranquil appearance, Savusavu sits atop a cauldron of geothermal activity—on a walk along the town's main road, visitors can sometimes see steam rising from a stream beside the sidewalk.

TRANSPORTATION

Flights: Air Fiji (☎885 0173), with an office in the Copra Shed Marina on the main road (open M-F 8:30am-4:30pm, Sa 8am-noon), flies twice daily from **Nadi** to Savusavu (1hr., $205), from **Suva** to Savusavu (1¾hr., $143), and from Savusavu to **Taveuni** (20min., $68). **Sun Air** (☎885 0141), whose office is next to Air Fiji (open M-F 8am-1pm and 2-5pm, Sa 8am-noon) flies twice daily from **Nadi** to Savusavu (1hr., $204) and to **Taveuni** (20min., $68). Taxis to the **Savusavu Airport** cost $2-3.

Ferries: Consort Shipping (☎885 0279), with an office on the main road west of the Planter's Club (open M-F 8am-4:30pm), goes from **Suva** to Savusavu (13hr., 2 per week, $40) and from Savusavu to **Taveuni** (5hr., 2 per week, $22). **Beachcomber Shipping** (☎885 0266), located next to Air Fiji (open M-F 8am-5pm, Sa 8am-1pm), goes from **Nadi** to Savusavu (5hr., 2 per week, $90) and from Savusavu to **Taveuni** (5hr., 3 per week, $22). **Grace Ferry** (Taveuni ☎888 0134 or 995 0775) offers a bus/ferry service to **Taveuni** via **Buca Bay** (5hr., 3 per week, $15). The trip between Buca Bay and Taveuni can be rough; don't get on the ferry if the weather looks threatening.

Buses: Buses run to: **Labasa** (3hr., 5 per day, $5.50); **Napuka** via **Buca Bay** (3hr., 2 per day, $5.50); and **Nakubalavu** towards **Lesiaceva Point** via **the Junction** (25min., 5 per day, $1.50). The bus stand is on the main road next to the market and police post.

Taxis: A **taxi** from Savusavu to Labasa costs about $60 and takes around 3hr. Savusavu is easily explored by foot, but a taxi ride anywhere in town costs only $1-1.50.

Car Rental: Budget (☎881 1999), at the Hot Spring Hotel. Open M-F 8am-4:30pm, Sa 8am-noon.

Bike Rental: Eco Divers-Tours (☎885 0122), inside Copra Shed Marina on the main road, rents mountain bikes (half-day $15, full-day $25).

ORIENTATION AND PRACTICAL INFORMATION

Most services in Savusavu are located on **Lesiaceva Road** (simply called the **main road**) along the waterfront. Behind this thin strip of flat coastal land rise the peaks of **Saqayaya** (878m) and **Macanabi** (800m).

Banks: ANZ, National, and **Westpac Banks** are all near the eastern end of town on the main road. ANZ and Westpac give cash advances on MC/V. All open approximately M-Th 9:30am-3pm, F 9:30am-4pm.

Laundry: The **Copra Shed Marina** washes and dries laundry for $7-10.

Police: Dial ☎911. On the main road 500m east of Savusavu (☎885 0222). There is also a police post on the main road in town next to the market (☎885 0120).

Pharmacy: There is no full pharmacy, but a couple of supermarkets have mini-pharmacy sections; try **J. Dayaram & Co.** (☎885 0247), diagonally across from the ANZ on the main road. Open M-F 8am-5pm, Sa 8am-1pm.

Medical Services: The **hospital** (☎885 0444) is several km east on the main road.

Internet Access: Plantation Real Estate (☎885 0801), across the main road from Copra Shed Marina charges 35¢ per min. Open M-Sa 8am-4pm.

Post Office: (☎885 0310; fax 885 0117), at the eastern end of town on the main road. Fax, telegram, pay phone, and Poste Restante. Open M-F 8am-4pm, Sa 8am-noon.

ACCOMMODATIONS

Hidden Paradise Guest House ❷, near the Morris Hedstrom Supermarket, has thin walls but spotless floors, subtle air-fresheners, and fake flowers that tug at the heart. With locks galore, friendly owner Vidya Chand is determined to keep guests safe. (☎885 0106. Cooking facilities. Fans in all rooms. Free hot breakfast. Singles $15; doubles $20.) **David's Budget Holiday Resort ❶,** behind Hidden Paradise, has hot, stuffy rooms that tend to fill up with divers. (☎885 0149. Cooking facilities. Free breakfast. 7-bed dorms $11; singles $20; doubles $25; family rooms $30.) The **Copra Shed Marina ❸,** on the main road, has two spacious self-catering apartment units offering great views of the harbor. (☎885 0457; fax 885 0989. Laundry. Reservations recommended. Studios $45; 2-room with bath $90. Discounts for longer stays.) If remoteness is on the agenda, **Vatukaluvi Holiday House ❹,** (a.k.a **Jeff Ray's**), lets you rent an entire two-story house 15min. away from Savusavu with killer views of Koro Sea. Catch the Nakubalavu bus (4 per day, 50¢) or a taxi ($4). (☎885 0143, Jeff at the Copra Marina ☎885 9561. Reservations recommended. 2-bedroom house for 6 with bath, kitchen, and deck $55.) For a funky stay, **Mumu's Traveler's Retreat ❷,** about 15km southeast of Savusavu on the coast, offers a hodge-podge cluster of basic mini-houses. Watch out for Mumu's pack of dogs. The bus from Savusavu (3-6 per day) is $1.30 and a taxi is $15. (☎885 0416; fax 885 0402. Breakfast or lunch $10; dinner $20. Cooking facilities. Laundry. Dorms $17; doubles $28-160. Traveler's checks accepted.)

🍴 FOOD AND NIGHTLIFE

Savusavu's cuisine options are edible evidence of Fiji's love for fast food. However, there are a few sit-down options. **Captain's Cafe ❷**, in the Copra Shed Marina, offers a bit of deck to munch on "the best pizza on Vanua Levu" ($3-15) and soak in harbor views. (☎885 0511. Open M-F 8:30am-8:30pm, Sa 9am-9pm, Su 11am-8:30pm.) **Bula Re Restaurant ❷**, a few doors west of the Westpac Bank on the main road, serves excellent cappuccino ($2.50) and makes a mean, though slow, Fijian lovo. (☎885 0307. A/C and fan. Open M-F 8am-10pm, Su 5-10pm.) **Vidya Chand's Seaview Restaurant ❶**, in front of Hidden Paradise Guest House, has the best curry ($2-4) in town. (☎885 0106. Open M-F 9am-4pm, Su 8am-6pm.) Locals praise **The New Tea Room ❷**, east of the market, for delicious fast-food ($3.50-5). (☎885 0108. Open M-Sa 7am-8pm.) For **groceries**, visit **Morris Hedstrom**, adjacent to the Shell station on the main road. (☎885 0030. Open M-F 8am-5pm, Sa 8am-1pm.) The town **market** is next to the police post on the main road. (Open M-F 7am-5pm, Sa 6am-3pm.)

The two watering holes in town are the **Savusavu Yacht Club**, inside Copra Shed Marina building (☎885 0685; beers $1.50-2.50; open daily 10am-11pm), and the **Planters Club,** in the weatherboard building behind the wooden fence along the main road, which has gaming tables, a TV, and lawn bowling (☎885 0233; beers $1-3; open M-Th 10am-10pm, F-Sa 10am-11pm, Su 10am-8pm).

🤿 ACTIVITIES

Diving around the peninsula takes place at moored sites such as **Shark Alley, Big Blue, Whales Tale,** and **Alice in Wonderland,** all notable for colorful soft corals and multitudes of fish. It is possible to access the dive sites of Rainbow Reef along the southeastern coast of Vanua Levu from the Savusavu area, but Rainbow Reef is best reached from Taveuni (see **Activities**, p. 489). The two dive shops in the Savusavu area are the upmarket outfit at **Jean-Michel Cousteau Fiji Islands Resort** (☎885 0188; jmcfir@aol.com) and **Eco Divers-Tours**, a well-established PADI operation located in the Waitui Marina building on the main road and run by Curly Carswell, president of the Fiji Dive Operators Association. (☎885 0122; www.ecodivers-tours.com. Open M-F 8am-5pm, Sa 8am-1pm. 2 tanks $130; open water course $495; Discover Scuba dive $126.) Eco Divers-Tours also offers **kayak rental** (single $15 per hr., double $20 per hr.), **snorkeling boat trips** ($25), **waterskiing/watersledding** ($50 per 30min.), tours of nearby **Naidi Village** (2-4hr., $25), **sailboat rental** (14ft. catamarans $15 per hr.), **bay cruises** ($40 per hr.), and **mountain and rainforest tours** (3-5hr., $40). The upscale **Hot Springs Hotel** (☎885 0195; hotspringshotel@is.com) offers **snorkeling** and **village visits** at similar prices and also runs trips to nearby **Waisale Rainforest,** which includes a **Copra Mill tour** (2-3hr., $35) as well as **sportfishing** trips (4 hr., $350; 8hr., $650).

LABASA

King of Fiji's sugar cane crop and the most populous town on Vanua Levu, Labasa (lam-BA-sa; pop. 25,000) bustles with industry. Rural gentility fill the dusty town while Indian farmers harvest the surrounding fields. Few tourists make the rocky three-hour drive from Savusavu to steaming Labasa, but those who do will be rewarded with warm hospitality and delicious food.

🚍 TRANSPORTATION

Flights: Sun Air, on Nasekula Rd. (☎881 1454; open M-F 8am-5pm, Sa 8am-noon), flies from **Nadi** to Labasa (2hr., 3 per day, $225), from **Suva** to Labasa (50min., 2 per day, $182) and from Labasa to **Taveuni** (35min., 2 per week, $71.50). **Air Fiji,** on Nasekula Rd. (☎881 1188; open M-F 8am-4:30pm, Sa 8am-noon) offers the same services as Sun Air with comparable prices. Buses to and from the airport run before and after flights (30min., 85¢).

Ferries: Patterson Brothers Shipping, on Nasekula Rd. (☎881 1454; open M-F 8:30am-1:30pm and 2:30-4:30pm, Sa 8:30am-noon), goes from **Nadi** to Labasa (12hr., 3 per week, $50) and from **Suva** to Labasa (10hr., 3 per week, $50). **Latchmen Ferry** (☎881 7981; fax 881 7980), on Nasekula Rd., in the Sharp Image store, makes bookings for the **Grace Ferry** and runs a ferry-bus service to **Taveuni** via **Savusavu** and **Buca Bay** (7hr., 3 per week, $20).

Buses: Buses run to **Savusavu** (3hr., 1-4 per day, $5.50) and **Nabouwalu** (6hr., 1-2 per day, $8). Other buses have frequent local routes that connect nearby suburbs.

Car Rental: Budget (☎881 1999; fax 881 3654), in the Vakamaisuasua complex. Open M-F 8am-4:30pm, Sa 8am-1pm.

ORIENTATION AND PRACTICAL INFORMATION

Nasekula Road, the busy main strip, runs roughly 600m and is cut by Labasa River to the east just past the bus station. The old cane railway runs parallel to downtown. The airport is southwest of the city and the sugar mill lies to the east.

Banks: ANZ, at the corner of Rosawa St. and Nasekula Rd., across from the bus station. Open M-Th 9:30am-3pm, F 9:30am-4pm. **Colonial National Bank,** on Nukusumi St., across from the bus station. Open M 9:30am-4pm, Tu-F 9am-4pm.

Police: (☎911 or 881 1222), on Nadawa St., a 3min. walk from town.

Pharmacy: My Chemist (☎881 4611), on Nasekula Rd. Open M-F 8am-6pm, Sa 8am-3pm.

Hospital: (☎881 1444), on Butinikama-Siberia Rd., a 5min. walk from town.

Post Office: (☎881 6022; fax 881 3666), on Nasekula Rd. across from the pharmacy, has Western Union and **Internet access.** Open M-F 7:30am-4pm, Sa 8am-noon.

ACCOMMODATIONS

Labasa Riverview Private Hotel ❷, on Nadawa St., a 5min. walk from town in the suburb of Namara, overlooks the Labasa River. Immaculate rooms and shiny-paneled dorms sparkle. (☎881 1367; fax 881 4337. Cooking facilities and bar. Dorms $15; singles $20, with shower $30; doubles $25/$40. AmEx/MC/V.) **Labasa Guest House ❷,** on Nanuku St., is a pink home with sagging beds. From the bus station, walk west down Nasekula Rd. and make the first right onto Nanuku St. (☎882 1551. Cooking facilities. Curfew 10pm. Singles and doubles $22, with fan $25; deluxe rooms $28.) Cross tiled floors to slip into crisp, white sheets at **Hotel Centerpoint ❸,** on Nasekula Rd. Rooms have tiny fridges, tea trays, and luggage holders. (☎881 1057; fax 881 5057. Restaurant and bar. Singles $38, with A/C $48; doubles $48/$58. Traveler's checks accepted.)

FOOD AND NIGHTLIFE

Joe's Restaurant ❷, on Nasekula Rd., is hands-down the best restaurant in town. Locals dash in for lip-smacking $2-9 Chinese food. (☎881 1766 or 881 1668. Open M-Sa 7:30am-10pm, Su 11am-2pm and 6-8:30pm.) For nicer ambience, **The Oriental Restaurant ❷,** on Rosawa St., goes beyond the Orient with curry and Fijian dishes ($4-20) amidst coconut husk ropes and red tablecloths. (☎881 7321. Open daily 6:30-10pm; also M-Sa 10am-3pm.) At **Eat Smart ❷,** on Nasekula Rd., colored lights add flare to fast-food curries ($2.50-8.50) as well as Chinese and Fijian eats. (☎881

6611. Open M-W 8am-6pm, Th-Sa 8:30am-10pm.) For **groceries**, go to **Morris Hedstrom**, on Nasekula Rd., (☎881 1211. Open M-W 8am-5pm, Th 8am-5:30pm, F 8am-7pm, Sa 8am-2pm.) The **market** is behind the bus station. (Open M-Sa 7:30am-5:30pm, Su 7:30am-1pm.)

When the hot sun sets, **The Bounty**, a disco-loving bar at Hotel Takia on Nasekula Rd., heats up. (☎881 3527. Bar open daily 9pm-1am; club Th-Sa only. Cover for club $4.) **The Labasa Club**, on Nanuku St., has snooker tables and a gate to keep rowdy folk from "snooking" in. (☎881 1304. Beer $3. Open daily 8am-10pm.)

SIGHTS

At the **Sugar Mill Factory**, 1.5km east of town, 600 workers churn out over 800,000 tons of sugar each year. (☎881 1511, ext. 3173. Tours Th-F with prior notification.) From the mill, check out the **Three Sisters Hill**. Legend has it that three sisters, running from marriage prospects, held hands and morphed into a triple-humped mountain. To get to the **Wasavulu Ceremonial Site**, in Wasavulu Village, 1.5km south of town, walk down Nakoroutari/Labasa Rd. or take the bus (5min., 40¢). A few stones mark a former slaughtering ground for ill-fated enemies. Locals claim the tallest monolith, which once served as a chopping block for enemy heads, grows daily. Hindus have their own magic rocks at **Snake Temple** (Naag Mandir), in Nagigi, 12km northeast of town. Built around a cobra-shaped stone, worshippers believe the serpent gets bigger by day. Taxi ($5-10) or bus to Nagigi (20 min., M-Sa, $1.30). The **Floating Island**, about 50km from Labasa between Nakelikoso and Nubu, curiously bobs on a lake. A walk across this grassy mat of palm trees is like stepping on a natural waterbed. To get there, take a taxi ($35-45) or a bus to Nubu (2hr., M-Sa 1pm, $3). For a birds-eye view of Labasa, head to the summit of **Mt. Delaikoro** (941m), 25km south on the Nakoroutari/Labasa Rd. The only catch: you need a 4WD for the chug up. A possible daytrip, **Nabouwalu** is a tiny government town displaying the windmills and solar panels that serve as an energy model for all of Fiji. To get there, take the bus from Labasa (2½-3hr., M-Sa 2-3 per day, $6-8).

TAVEUNI

Taveuni may have some of the wettest weather in Fiji, but nature lovers couldn't care less. Frequent downpours beget stunning waterfalls, virgin rainforests, and a fresh coat of sparkling green. Travelers flock to the "Garden Island" to check out relatively young volcanic formations, swim through the world-renowned Rainbow Reef, and sneak a peak at Fiji's unique national flower, the creeping tagimaucia. Unspoiled and undertouristed compared to Fiji's northwestern islands, travelers might soon spill the beans about Taveuni, the country's glistening Garden of Eden.

TRANSPORTATION

Taveuni is well connected to Viti Levu and Vanua Levu by sea and air. The **Coastal Road** runs along the island's perimeter, except for the portion between Lavena and Navakawau in the southeast. The road can be impassable after heavy rain; plan accordingly. Regularly scheduled bus services connect the **Naqara/Waiyevo** area with **Lavena** (via **Matei** in the north) and **Navakawau** (via **Vuna Point** in the south).

Flights: Air Fiji (☎888 0062) fly twice daily between Taveuni and **Nadi** (1½hr., $253) and between Taveuni and **Suva** (45min., $135). **Sun Air** (☎888 02186) flies between Taveuni and **Nadi** (1½hr., 3 per day, $253). For information on flights from **Savusavu** and **Labasa** to Taveuni, see p. 482 and p. 484.

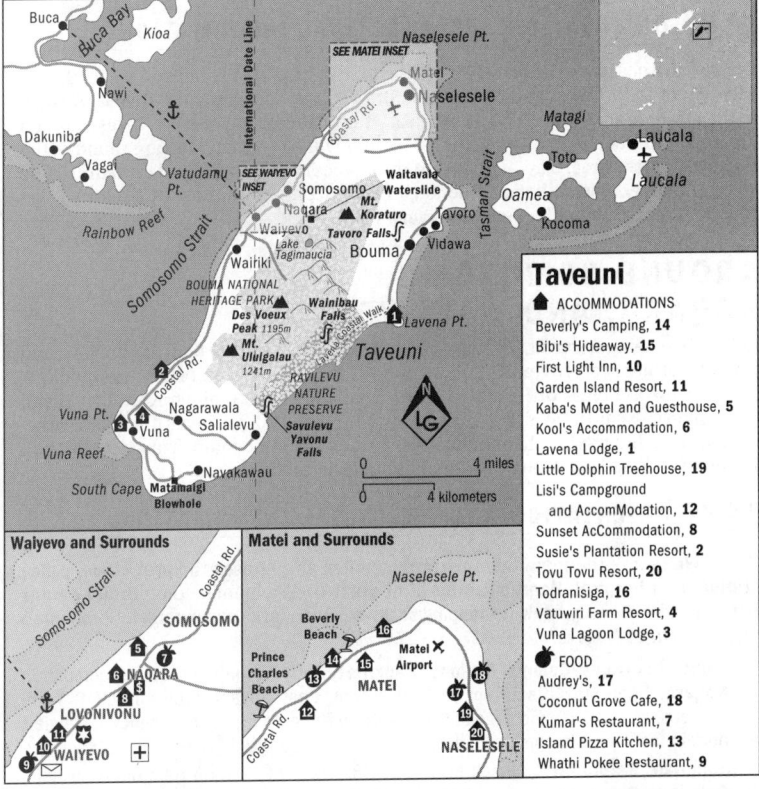

Taveuni

ACCOMMODATIONS
Beverly's Camping, 14
Bibi's Hideaway, 15
First Light Inn, 10
Garden Island Resort, 11
Kaba's Motel and Guesthouse, 5
Kool's Accommodation, 6
Lavena Lodge, 1
Little Dolphin Treehouse, 19
Lisi's Campground and AccomModation, 12
Sunset AcCommodation, 8
Susie's Plantation Resort, 2
Tovu Tovu Resort, 20
Todransiga, 16
Vatuwiri Farm Resort, 4
Vuna Lagoon Lodge, 3

FOOD
Audrey's, 17
Coconut Grove Cafe, 18
Island Pizza Kitchen, 13
Kumar's Restaurant, 7
Whathi Pokee Restaurant, 9

Ferries: Beachcomber Shipping (☎888 0261), in the fish market building across from Garden Island Resort, ferries between Taveuni and **Suva** (17hr., 3 per week, $64). **Consort Shipping** (☎888 0339), next to Garden Island Resort, does the same (20hr., 2 per week, $62). Both moor at the main government wharf in **Waiyevo** (the "Korean Wharf" just to the north is used for smaller boats). **Grace Ferry** (☎888 0134 or 995 0775) books across from Kaba's Supermarket in Naqara. For information on ferries from **Savusavu** and **Labasa** to Taveuni, see p. 482 and p. 484.

Buses: The **Pacific Bus Company** (☎888 0278) connects the **Waiyevo/Naqara** area with **Bouma** via **Matei**. (2hr. Departs Waiyevo M-Sa 9am, noon, and 4pm; Su 4pm; departs Bouma M-Sa 6:30, 11:30am, and 2:30pm). The same bus occasionally goes as far as **Lavena**. (2½hr. Departs Waiyevo M-Sa 4pm; also Tu and Th 9am; departs Lavena M-Sa 6am, Su 8am. Tickets $0.60-1.80.) Buses also run 3 times daily M-Sa (1 on Su) between **Naqara/Waiyevo** and **Navakawau** via **Vuna Point** (times depend on road conditions—inquire at Naqara bus station; Waiyevo-Vuna Point $2.55).

Taxis: Taxis from Matei Airport to all local destinations cost $2; from the **Naqara/Waiyevo** area to **Matei Airport** $15; to **Vuna Point** $25-30; to **Matei-Bouma** $15-20; to **Bouma-Lavena** $10. Though expensive, hiring taxis may be cheaper than renting a car if more than 2 people split the cost. Book ahead on Su.

Car Rental: Garden State Price Point (see **Groceries,** below) in Naqara is the local **Budget** agent. 4WDs available.

ORIENTATION AND PRACTICAL INFORMATION

On the northeastern corner of Fiji, Taveuni (435 sq. km) is hugged by the **Somosomo Strait** to the West and the **Tasman Strait** to the East. Offshore **Qamea, Matagi,** and **Laucala Islands** lie further northeast while Vanua Levu sits northwest. Within Taveuni, most services and amenities, including the ferry landing, are found in the **Waiyevo/Naqara area.** The airport and most accommodations and restaurants lie North in **Matei. Bouma National Heritage Park** encompasses most of Eastern Taveuni. Southern Taveuni loops around **Vuna Point.**

AROUND SOMOSOMO, NAQARA, AND WAIYEVO

Other than being a transit point for passengers on ferries that dock in Waiyevo and the site of most of Taveuni's shops and services, this area offers the quickest access to world-class diving at Rainbow Reef and sunbathing on Korolevu Island off Waiyevo. Near the Wairiki Catholic Mission (est. 1907), a beautiful stone cathedral set on a hill next to the mountains overlooking Somosomo Strait, are the trailheads for hiking Des Voeux Peak and Lake Tagimaucia.

ORIENTATION AND PRACTICAL INFORMATION

While **Waiyevo** is the main administrative center and houses the **post office, police station,** and **hospital, Naqara** (about 3km north) is Taveuni's commercial center with the island's only **bank,** a **shopping complex,** and a large **supermarket.** Somosomo is just north of Naqara.

Financial Services: Colonial National Bank (☎ 888 0433), in the shopping complex in **Naqara.** Open M 9:30am-4pm, Tu-F 9am-4pm. Cash advances on AmEx/MC/V are available with a 10% surcharge at **Garden State Price Point,** the mini-supermarket next door in the same shopping complex.

Groceries: Garden State Price Point (☎ 888 0291; open M-Sa 8am-6pm, Su 8am-1pm) and **Kaba's Supermarket** (☎ 888 0088; open M-F 8am-5:30pm, Sa 8am-1pm) in **Naqara.** All accept AmEx/MC/V.

Police: (☎ 888 0222), in **Waiyevo.**

Pharmacies: All of the grocery stores listed above maintain mini-pharmacy sections with antiseptic and basic first aid materials.

Hospital: (☎ 888 0444), near the police station in **Waiyevo.** Doctor on duty **24hr.**

Public Phones: Available at the post office and several other locations in the Naqara/Waiyevo/Wairiki area.

Post Office: (☎ 888 0027), in central **Waiyevo.** Fax, telegram, and Poste Restante. Open M-F 8am-1pm and 2-4pm.

ACCOMMODATIONS

First Light Inn (☎ 888 0339; firstlight@fj.com), between Garden Island Resort and the post office in central **Waiyevo,** has fantastic doubles with bath, fridge, TV, phones, coffee makers, and spacious interiors. Internet. Reception M-Sa 8am-5pm; see security after hours. Singles with fan $40; doubles with fan $50, with A/C $60. ❸

Kaba's Motel and Guesthouse (☎ 888 0233; fax 888 0202; kaba@connect.com.fj), across from the shopping center, is the best option in **Naqara.** 24hr. electricity. Laundry. All rooms have fans and phones. Motel rooms with bath and TV: singles $45; doubles

$55; twins $60. Guesthouse rooms with shared bath, kitchen, and lounge area: singles $25; doubles $35; twins $60. AmEx/MC/V/traveler's checks. ❸

Garden Island Resort (☎ 888 0286; fax 888 0288; garden@connect.com.fj), in **Waiyevo**, is a favorite for divers on package tours. All rooms have ocean-view balconies. Boats depart twice daily for the fine sandy beach on nearby Korolevu Island ($10, snorkeling gear rental $11 per day). Hiking and kayaking. Restaurant open daily 7-10am, 11:30am-3, and 7-9pm. 4-bed dorms with fan and bath $33; doubles with A/C and bath $146-184. AmEx/MC/V/traveler's checks. ❸

Kool's Accommodation (☎ 888 0395), a few doors opposite Kaba's Supermarket in **Naqara**. Mr. Singh cooks for guests ($3-5 per meal) at this rustic house with shared bath and kitchen. Free transfer to and from the wharf. Snorkeling gear $15 per day. 3-bed dorms $10; singles and doubles $30. ❶

Sunset Accommodation (☎ 888 0229), near the Korean Wharf between Waiyevo and Naqara, is the most humble option. The 3 tin-roofed houses share a kitchen and bath. Breakfast $4, dinner $6. Activities arranged locally. Singles $15; doubles $30. ❷

FOOD

Restaurants in Western Taveuni are few and far between, but a pair of fast-food picks hit the spot.

Kumar's Restaurant (☎ 888 0435), opposite Kaba's Motel and Guesthouse in **Naqara**. An electric blue hut shelters lime-green picnic tables. Hurried locals chomp on $3-4 Indian, Chinese, and Fijian chow. Open M-Sa 6:30am-5:30pm. ❶

Whathi Pokee Restaurant (☎ 888 0036), next to the post office in **Waiyevo**. Scents of fresh bread waft through the postered walls. Pick your lunch from the warmers, soda from the fridge, and ice cream from the cooler. Meals $3-5.50. Open M-F 7am-7pm. ❶

ACTIVITIES

IN THE WATER. The name ⬛**Rainbow Reef** is sacred to dive enthusiasts the world over. Though this 30km reef is actually near the southeastern corner of Vanua Levu, it is best accessed from Taveuni across the Somosomo Strait. Especially renowned is the **Great White Wall**, a dive site where a 12m underwater tunnel leads to a dramatic drop-off and a 40m wall resplendent with white soft coral. Other well-known sites include **Blue Ribbon Eel Reef** and **Annie's Bommie**. Because of the strong current, Rainbow Reef is best for experienced divers, but with the aid of a descent line, beginners can also experience the underwater wonders. The Reef is a 20min. boat ride from **Aqua-Trek Taveuni Dive Centre.** *(At Garden Island Resort. ☎ 888 0544; fax 888 0288; www.aquatrek.com; open daily 7am-4pm. 2-tank dive $165, open-water course $660, Discover Scuba course $148.)* This well-established PADI operation also offers **reef snorkeling trips** (snorkel gear not included) to Korolevu Island *(daily 10am and 2pm, $10)* and Rainbow Reef, where snorkelers explore a shallow protected reef separate from the dive sites *(2hr., daily 9am, $20)*. The Dive Centre also rents out **snorkeling gear** *($11 per day)* and **kayaks** *($11 per hr., $44 per day)*.

ON LAND. For hikers, the marked trail up to **Des Voeux Peak** (1195m) starts in Wairiki *(return 6-8hr.)*. **Lake Tagimaucia** is located just below and is visible from the peak. The challenging trail to the Lake starts in Naqara *(return 8-10hr.; a guide, sturdy shoes, plenty of water, warm clothes, and a packed lunch are recommended; leave before 6am)*. The highlands are home to Fiji's national blossom, the **tagimaucia**. A red- and white-flowered creeper linked to local legends involving a little girl's tears of blood, it grows only above 2000ft. and blooms between late September and late December.

Garden Island Resort organizes hikes to the lake (inquire at the reception). Naveen Singh, the owner/manager at **Kool's Accommodation** (☎ 888 0395) in Naqara, also organizes **hikes** to the peak *(half-day, $120 for 4WD rental)* and the lake *(usually $20)*.

OTHER ACTIVITIES. Local kids tummy-surf down the all-natural **Waitavala Waterslide**, a 25min. walk up the hill from Garden Island Resort. The slide is a series of smooth rocks and pools (the last large one at the bottom is swimmable). Good trousers make it easier on your butt, though heavy rainfall can do more than just bruise your bottom; exercise caution. Maps are available at Garden Island Resort. A 10min. walk south of Garden Island Resort leads to a shelter marking the **180° meridian line (International Date Line)**.

MATEI AND SURROUNDS

Situated on the northern tip of Taveuni, Matei is the island's prime destination for the budget traveler. Top-notch resorts, campgrounds, and restaurants sprinkle the countryside with an unobtrusive zest, and colorful entrepreneurs exude a down-to-earth warmth.

ORIENTATION AND PRACTICAL INFORMATION

It's a 45min. ride from Matei to both **Waiyevo** and **Bouma Falls** with an additional 20min. to the Lavena Coastal Walk. There is a **supermarket** in town (Bhula Bhai & Sons), a **police** post (☎ 888 0224) at the airport, and **pay phones** at the supermarket and airport. It takes 25min. to walk from the southwestern end of the area (near Lisi's Accommodation) to the southeastern end (near Tovutovu Resort).

ACCOMMODATIONS AND CAMPING

Matei's abundance of quality budget accommodations and campgrounds will please the Taveuni-bound budget traveler. Whether zipped up in a sleeping bag or tucked into a bed, you won't have to count sheep for a quiet night's rest.

- **Beverly's Camping** (☎ 888 0684), on Beverly Beach next to Aquaventure dive shop, comes with free fruits and bedding in a wooded, shady area. Happy campers stay for weeks. Communal bath and open-air kitchen meet your basic needs. Tent sites $10. ❶

- **Todranisiga** (☎ 888 0871), "a flaming ray of sun" in Fijian, is perched on a panoramic cliff located between Matei Point and Karin's Garden. Communal shower and sink. Camping in 4 large pre-set tents on the 5½-acre clifftop lawn. Mattress, sheets, and pillows provided. $15 per person. ❷

- **Tovu Tovu Resort** (☎ 888 0560; fax 888 0722; tovutovu@connect.com.fj), the farthest from the airport, southeast across from Viubani Island, is a 120-acre copra plantation. Attractive dorms are housed in a beautiful bure. Laundry. Reservations recommended. 8-bed dorms $15; bures $65, with kitchen $75. AmEx/MC/V/traveler's checks. ❷

- **Bibi's Hideaway** (☎ 888 0443), across from Karin's Garden. 20 beautifully landscaped acres shelter over 15 different species of birds. A 5min. walk to dive shops and beach. All accommodations come with bath and kitchen; meals available on arrangement. Electricity 6-9pm (afterwards lantern). Reservations recommended. Tent sites $25 for 2; singles $50; doubles $60; family cottages $80-100; honeymoon bures $80. ❸

- **Little Dolphin Treehouse** (☎ 888 0130), across from Bhula Bhai & Sons supermarket. This hideaway in the branches is a child's dream come true. A self-contained setup (downstairs kitchen, bath, fridge) and ocean-view balcony make it easy for adults. Free fruit from the garden in season. Electricity 6-10:30pm. Singles $80; studios $90. ❺

Lisi's Campground and Accommodation, farthest southwest, 200m from Beverly's, spreads along a stellar beach. Rooms are tight but campers can unwind in their own tents. Electricity 6-9:30pm. Singles $15; doubles $25; tent sites $8. ❶

FOOD

Coconut Grove Cafe (☎ 888 0328), at Coconut Grove Beachfront Cottage, 100m east of the airport, is the best restaurant in town. The international menu includes fruit shakes ($3-4) and homemade banana/papaya bread ($3.50). Weekly *lovo* and *meke* nights $19.50. Lunch $7.50-16; dinner $13.50-19.50. For dinner, order before 4pm. Backpackers 20% discount. Open daily 7:30am-5pm and 7-9pm. AmEx/MC/V. ❸

Tovu Tovu Restaurant (☎ 888 0560), at Tovu Tovu Resort. Once a cooking sensation in the US, the chef now cooks up Fijian and European dishes here in Matei. Enjoy delectable meals (breakfast $3-8, sandwiches $6-7, dinner $8-15) on the oceanview veranda. Open daily 8am-2pm and 5-9pm. AmEx/MC/V/traveler's checks. ❷

Island Pizza Kitchen, next to Aquaventure dive shop. This beachside hangout is perfect for viewing beer-in-hand sunsets and eating yummy—if not so budget—pizzas ($15-18). Open daily noon-9pm. ❺

Audrey's (☎ 888 0039), 200m east of the airport. Sip island-grown coffee and savor a slice of heavenly chocolate cake ($6) on Audrey's porch. Open daily 10am-6pm. ❷

ACTIVITIES

Diving is provided by **Aquaventure Taveuni** (☎/fax 888 0381; www.aquaventure.org. 2-tank with equipment US$76, open-water PADI course US$276) and **Swiss Fiji Divers** (☎ 888 0586; www.swissfijidivers.com; 2-tank without equipment US$95, open-water PADI course US$381, Discover Scuba dive US$130), which are located on either side of Beverly's Camping. The latter is a high-tech setup offering all sorts of groovy electronic equipment and instruction in German and French. Aquaventure also runs **reef snorkeling trips** ($10-40, snorkeling gear rental $12 per day), rents kayaks (double kayaks $10 per hr., $60 per day; singles $10 per hr., $35 per day), and does bookings for the **Waitabu Marine Park Tour** (half-day $25-50) and the **Vidawa Rainforest Hike** (full-day $40-60). Next door to Aquaventure is **Ringgold Reef Kayaking** (☎ 888 0083), whose owner/manager Keni is the local fishing trip guru—he also runs camping, kayaking, hiking, and horse treks, and rents kayaks.

SOUTHERN TAVEUNI

With wondrously fertile soil, southern Taveuni makes farmers giddy. Over a century ago, green-thumbed Europeans flocked here eager to plant. Today, the lush, remote countryside has no amenities other than a community grocery store, mellow vibes, and some of the best snorkeling in Fiji.

ACCOMMODATIONS AND FOOD. Under new German-Swiss management, **Susie's Plantation Resort** ❷, a former copra plantation, is set on a beautiful lawn overlooking a rocky deep-water coastline. (☎ 888 0125; susies@connect.com.fj. Snorkeling gear rental $10 per day. Electricity 6-9pm. Internet. Laundry. Breakfast $3.50-7, lunch $7.50, 3-course dinner $13. 8-bed dorms $15-30; doubles $30-50; bures with bath $75-80; tent sites $10. MC/V/traveler's checks.) The **Vatuwiri Farm Resort** ❺ was established in 1871 by James Valentine Tarte as a copra plantation; this 2000-acre estate now produces beef and copra and is one of the biggest farms in Fiji. Steeped in colonial history, the busy staff of 60 workers offer guests an intimate glimpse into Fiji's rural past. (☎888 0316; fax 888 0314. Laundry. Meal plan $35 per day. Cottage with double bed and bath or room in the owner's homestead $120. MC/V/traveler's checks.) **Vuna Lagoon Lodge** ❷ is located farthest south. Travelers rest weary feet under owner Adi's slow smiles. (☎888 0627. Electricity 6-10pm. Laundry. Outstanding kitchen; breakfast and dinner prepared on request $5-10. 4-bed dorms $15; singles $30; doubles with bath $50.)

ACTIVITIES. Dolphin Bay Retreat Divers (☎888 0125; 1-tank $85, 2-tank $130, shore dive $50, PADI open-water $550; instruction also in German), at Susie's Plantation, is the primary dive operator and also runs **reef snorkeling trips** ($15) and rents out **snorkeling gear** ($10 per day). **Susie's Plantation** organizes **horseback riding trips** to a nearby volcanic crater (half-day $35), **blowhole trips** (3-6hr., $30-40 cab fare), and trips covering just about any activity on the island. Guests at the plantation can follow **bush trails**, watching birds at leisure. **Vatuwiri Farm Resort** offers **fishing trips** ($15), **snorkeling** ($15), **guided horseback riding** ($35), and **guided hiking** to the volcanic crater (half-day $30). Finally, **Vuna Lagoon Lodge** also runs **horseback riding trips** ($35) and rents out **canoes** ($10 per half-day).

EASTERN TAVEUNI

Most of eastern Taveuni is included in **Bouma National Heritage Park** (15,000 hectares), which contains 80% of Taveuni's pristine rainforest, the three stunning Tavoro waterfalls, and the gorgeous Lavena Coastal Walk. A conservation success story, the park is the result of an agreement in the 1980s between the village communities of Waitabu, Vidawa, Korovou (Bouma), and Lavena, whereby the villagers rejected logging in favor of ecotourism as a means of generating income. Park entry fees go toward trail maintenance and to financing village projects and scholarships for children. Most tracks are on the coastal periphery except for the Vidawa Rainforest Hike, which leads into the heart of the forest.

A must-do while in Taveuni, the **Tavoro** (or **Bouma**) **Falls** offer walking, hiking, and swimming. From the Park Visitor Centre in Bouma, it's an easy 10min. walk to the first and tallest (30m) waterfall, which has the largest swimming pool. The second fall (a bit smaller, but good for swimming) is a relatively easy 40min. walk, which includes a stream crossing with the help of a rope. It takes an additional hour of more strenuous hiking along a less well-maintained track to reach the third fall, smaller than the first two. (Visitors Center ☎888 0390. Open daily 9am-4pm. Entry fee $5. Snacks and lunch available at the Center; order lunch in advance for $5. Don't go beyond the first fall after heavy rain.) Visiting the falls can be done as a daytrip by bus from either Matei or the Waiyevo/Naqara area (catch the first morning bus to Bouma; see **Taveuni: Transportation**, p. 486), or through an organized outing. **Kool's Accommodation** leads trips to **Bouma Falls** (full-day including Lavena Coastal Walk, $15 plus entry fees to Bouma, min. 4 persons) in his minivan. **Garden Island Resort** also organizes trips to the Falls and the Coastal Walk (park entry fee $5 at both Bouma and Lavena). For both operators, see **Accommodations**, p. 488.

The ▓**Lavena Coastal Walk,** along the coastal boundary of Bouma National Park, has remote sandy beaches (Taveuni's best), lush rainforest, stunning waterfalls, pristine streams, and some surf action off the beaches. The marked trail starts from the **Lavena Visitor Centre** (☎811 6801; open daily 9am-4pm; pay $5 entrance fee here) and continues along the coast past streams, two waterfalls, and over a suspension bridge before finally turning inland along **Wainibau Stream** and ending 50m downstream from the beautiful **Lower Wainibau Falls.** Only the bottom of the falls is visible from this point. Although *Let's Go* doesn't recommend it, to reach the falls you need to swim upstream, which can be very hazardous; don't swim if the water is murky—a sign of flooding—or if you can't see the rocks on the way upstream. The **Lavena Lodge ❷**, at the Visitors Center, has four simple rooms. Lunch ($10) can be ordered here in advance. (Electricity 6-11pm. Laundry. Breakfast $7. Dinner $10. 1 double and 3 triples with shared kitchen and bath $15 per person.) There is a village store nearby with the usual canned food and drinks, but it is wiser to bring food from Matei.

Wainibau Stream at the southern end of Lavena Coastal Walk is the southern boundary of Bouma National Heritage Park; on the other side is the 4000-hectare **Ravilevu Nature Reserve**, farther south of which is the village of **Salialevu**. Halfway down the coast from Wainibau Stream is the 20m **Savulevu Yavonu Falls**, which plunges into the ocean (accessible by boat only; inquire at Lavena Visitor Centre).

Not to be outdone by Korovou (Bouma) and Lavena, the villages of **Waitabu** and **Vidawa** (a bit north of Bouma) have also organized ecotourism projects such as the **Waitabu Marine Park** and the **Vidawa Rainforest Hike**. The Rainforest Hike is a challenging full-day hike. (Book with Bouma Visitor Centre ☎ 888 0390. $50-60, including transport to and from Matei, lunch, guide, and drinks.)

KADAVU

In Kadavu (pop. 12,000), hungry divers feast on the famous **Astrolabe Reef**, the third largest reef in the world. Carpeting the southern shores of the island, this 100km-long five-star underwater buffet whets any diver's appetite. On the menu: all-you-can-*see* rainbow-colored coral, virgin-blue waves, and otherworldly ocean critters. Although mainly underwater enthusiasts venture out to the undertouristed Kadavu, the island pleases surfers, birdwatchers (an absence of mongoose allows for a plethora of bird species), and sun-seekers alike.

TRANSPORTATION. Even though a bumpy landing and a dirt airstrip might suggest otherwise, the best way to get to Kadavu is by plane. **Air Fiji** (☎ 347 3155) flies daily between Kadavu and **Nadi** (45min., $144) and Kadavu and **Suva** (30min,

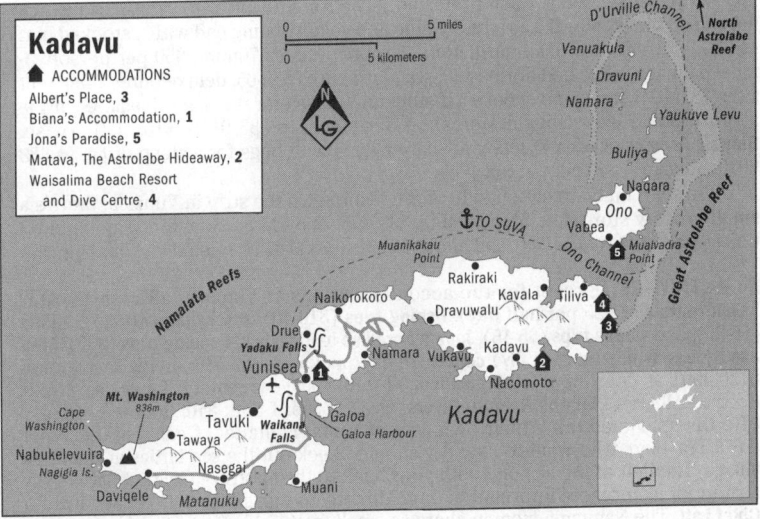

494 ■ KADAVU

$111). **Sun Air** (☎ 672 3016) flies twice daily between Kadavu and **Nadi** (45min., $144). For a long and often sea-sickening ride, **Kadavu Shipping** (☎ 331 2428) ferries between Kadavu and **Suva** (6hr., 1 per day, $45). On Kadavu, most transfer is done via boats owned by resorts and private operators.

◪🛈 ORIENTATION AND PRACTICAL INFORMATION.

Planes arrive at the **Namalata airstrip** (☎ 333 6042), across from Vunisea's Namalata Bay. A one-street strip of storefronts east of the airport, **Vunisea** rests on a narrow isthmus separating the eastern and western halves of the island. As Kadavu's administrative center, Vunisea provides some service for the isolated traveler. Just past the town's market, the road splits, and the path uphill leads to a **police station** (☎ 333 6007) and a **post office** that can **wire money** through Western Union (☎ 333 6001. Open M-F 8am-1pm and 2-4pm.) Since there are **no banks** on the island and few resorts take credit cards or checks, travelers should bring plenty of cash. A semi-rundown **hospital** (☎ 333 6008) is further along the uphill road.

🛏🍴 ACCOMMODATIONS AND FOOD.

All resorts drop off and pick up passengers from Namalata Bay in Vunisea. Arrangements should be made in advance. Melting into a rainforest backdrop, **Matava, The Astrolabe Hideaway ❷** offers superior access to all five Astrolabe passages as well as solar-powered comforts, cool spring water, and delicious meals on a wrap-around veranda. The eco-conscious owners can direct you to the beach, a quick paddle across the shore. (☎ 333 6098; matava@connect.com.fj. Airport transfer 1hr., $30 per person. Meal package $50. 4-bed dorm $18; double bures with shared facilities $55; private double bures $100-120.) At **Jona's Paradise ❹**, coral-floored bures sit next to Kadavu's finest beaches. (☎ 330 7058; fax 330 9676; jonasparadise@connect.com.fj. Airport transfer 80min., return $110. Electricity until 11pm. Internet. Prices include 3 meals per day. 3-bed dorms $60; standard bures $80; deluxe bures $100. MC/V/traveler's checks.) At **Albert's Place ❶**, wander amongst hammocks, coconuts, and chickens en route to dorms reminiscent of your teenage years. (☎ 333 6086. Airport transfer 90min., $55 per person for 1 or 2 people, $25 per person for 3 or more. Breakfast/lunch/dinner $6/10/13; $25 for a 3-meal pack. 2-bed dorms $12; double bures $30; tent sites $8. MC/V/traveler's checks. Cash preferred.) The Australian-owned **Waisalima Beach Resort and Dive Centre ❷** has a funky blue and yellow dining pad with a stocked bar. (☎ 333 6081; www.waisalimafiji.com. Airport transfer 70min., $50 per person. 3-meal package $47. 5-bed dorms $20; standard bures $50-65, deluxe bures $150; tent sites $8. MC/V/traveler's checks.) If stuck in Vunisea for the night, **Thema ❶**, at the airport kiosk, lets stragglers crash at her place. (☎ 333 0156. $10.) Otherwise, **Biana's Accommodation ❸** lets you share rooms with bugs for a steep price. (☎ 333 6010. Meals $5. $40 per person.)

There's not much to eat outside of the resorts. On the strip in Vunisea, there's a small grocery store, **One Stop Shop** (☎ 333 605; open M-Sa 6am-6pm), and a barebones **market ❶** that sells bread and $3 meals (☎ 333 6141; open daily 7am-4pm).

🏄 ACTIVITIES.

Except for the accommodations in Vunisea, all resorts offer **kayak rentals** ($5-25 per half-day), **fishing trips** ($10-40), **snorkeling** ($10-25), **hiking** ($5-35), and **village trips** ($5-15). **Jona's Paradise** leads **island-hopping trips** ($20). **Matava Hideaway** has its own **dive center** (diving packages $60-540; diving instruction $120-490), as does the PADI **Waisalima**. (1-tank $60; gear rental $25 per day.) Next door to Albert's Place is **Naiqoto Divers**. (☎ 333 6086. 1-tank $40; double boat dive $75. Divers should bring their own gear as rental is limited. Gear rental $20 per day.) Travelers who want to stay dry should check out the **sea turtles** at **Nanuama Village**, 1km left of the airport (with your back to the airstrip). Contact **Sevo** at the airport kiosk for more information or go directly to the village with some kava for **Chief Lati**. The Nanuama women charge a small fee ($5-10) for turtle viewing.

APPENDIX

GLOSSARY OF KIWI ENGLISH

abseil: rappel
Aotearoa: "land of the long white cloud," the Maori name for New Zealand
ANZAC: Australia New Zealand Army Corps (p. 52). Anzac Day is a national holiday (April 25th).
All Blacks: the national rugby team; never let on that you don't know what this is
Aussie ("Ozzie"): Australian
bach ("batch"): Small, often beachside holiday house; known as a "crib" on the South Island
backpackers: hostel
basin: bathroom sink;
bathroom: room with a bath; not necessarily a toilet
belt bag, bum bag: hip pack, fanny pack ("fanny" should not be used in New Zealand; it's a slang word referring to female genitalia)
big bikkies: big money, the big bucks
billy: backcountry cooking pot
bikkies: cookies, crackers
biscuit: cookie
bottle shop: liquor store; the only place to buy beer besides a bar/club
bloke: man
bloody: all purpose curse
bonnet: hood of car
boot: trunk of a car
brasserie: trendy cafe
brekkie: breakfast
bugger all: very little
bum: one's rear-end; arse
BYO: bring-your-own alcohol
capsicum: green, red, or yellow bell peppers
caravan: trailer, mobile home
carpark: parking lot
cashpoint: ATM
chat up: to hit on (eg. "I'm going to chat up that girl")
cheeky: rude, impertinent
cheers: goodbye; thanks; excuse me; and just about anything else you can think of
chemist: drugstore, pharmacy
chilly bin: portable cooler
chips: french fries
chocka, chockablock: packed, crowded, busy, full
choice: good, proper, sweet
chunder: vomit

coach: bus that travels long distances; not a local bus
college: secondary school
concessions: senior citizens
crib: South Island version of "bach," vacation home
crisps: potato chips
cruisy: mellow, no worries
cuppa: cup of tea or coffee
dag: good guy/joker
dairy: convenience store
dear: expensive
Devonshire tea: afternoon tea and scones, often with whipped cream; see p. 59
DOC ("dock"): Department of Conservation (see p. 68)
domain: public park
doughnut: cream- and jam-filled sweet dough roll
duvet: comforter, inch-thick feather blanket
entree: appetizer
Enzed: New Zealand ("NZ")
fair go: opportunity; a shot
feed: a meal
filled roll: sub sandwich
filter coffee: drip coffee
flash: snazzy, upscale, smart, trendy, glam
flat: apartment
flat white: coffee: a long black with a dollop of milk
footie: soccer
footpath: sidewalk
for donkey's years: for a long time
fortnight: two weeks
full-on: hardcore, intense
get on the piss: get drunk
Godzone: New Zealand (from "God's own")
good as gold: fine, sure, great
good on ya: good for you, good job
gridiron: American football
grotty: dirty, run-down
ground floor: an American first floor (and first floor is second floor, etc.)
gumboots: rubber boots
hard case: tough to get to know
hire: rent
hoe: to eat quickly
holiday: vacation
hokey pokey: NZ's favorite ice cream flavor; vanilla with round toffee-pieces
hoon: slob, jerk

hoover: to vacuum, or eat quickly
hottie: hot water bottle
hundreds and thousands: sprinkles
jandals: flip-flops
jersey, jumper: sweater
judder bar: speed bump
jugger: bloke, man
jumper: sweater
Kiwi: New Zealander; of or relating to New Zealand
kiwi: small flightless bird; the national symbol (never short for kiwifruit)
kiwifruit: a furry greenish-brown fruit
knickers: women's underwear
kumara: sweet potato
L&P: soda
lemonade: lemon-flavored carbonated soft drink
licensed: sells alcohol legally
lift: elevator
Lord of the Rings: NZ movie trilogy that everyone's talking about
local rag: local newspaper
long black: espresso with hot water; there's little filtered coffee in NZ
long drop: outhouse
loo: toilet
main: main course of a meal
Mainland: South Island
Maori: the indigenous peoples of New Zealand
Marmite: yeast spread
mate: friend, buddy, pal
metal road: gravel road
milk bar: convenience store
nappy: diaper
no joy: no luck
not a problem: you're welcome
note: currency bill
no worries: sure, fine
Oz, "Ozzie": technically "Aussie"; Australia, Australian
paddock: sheep pasture
Pakeha: person of European descent; foreigner
paper (university): class/course
petrol: gas
paua: abalone; a type of shellfish
pavlova: a creamy, fruity meringue dessert

pie: flaky pastry shell with a variety of fillings, usually with meat (mince)
pipi: clam-like shellfish
pissed: drunk
pissing down: raining hard
plate: potluck dinner
Pom: Englishman (often derogatory)
to post: to mail
pot plant: house plant
powerpoints: electrical hookups for tents or caravans
prawns: jumbo shrimp
push bike: bicycle
quai: "key"; a pier
queue: "Q"; a line of people
rag: local newspaper
rattle your dags: hurry up
ap-jumping: abseiling face-first down a building
return: round-trip
to have a row: to fight
ring: call
rubber: eraser
rubbish: garbage, trash
salad: usually cucumber, carrots, beetroot; "with salad" means that these items come on a sandwich or burger; not a separate side salad.
scroggin: trail mix, gorp
sealed road: paved road
serviette: napkin
shagging: having sex

shares: shared rooms at an accommodation
short black: coffee, flat white without the milk; between an espresso and a long black
Shortland Street: New Zealand soap opera; constant hostel entertainment
shout: to buy for someone (eg. "I'll shout you a drink")
skivvies: turtle-neck sweater
skull: to chug (as in beer)
Sky TV: satellite television
snog: kiss or make out
snooker: a game similar to pool
spinner: a jerk
strewth!: an exclamation; truly (from "God's truth")
stubby: small bottle of beer
sultanas: large raisins
suss out: to figure out
sweet as: great, cool
ta: thanks
TAB: shop to place bets without going to the tracks
take a sikkie: play hookey, pretend to be sick to skip work
takeaway: food to go, or a place that offers such
tariff: price
tea: hot drink; also refers to a full afternoon meal
that's all right, that's okay: you're welcome

tinny: lucky
togs: swimming suit
tomato sauce: ketchup; sold in small packets at restaurants
torch: flashlight
take the piss out of: to poke fun at someone
take the mickey out of: to ridicule
torch: flashlight
trainers: sneakers
transport: transportation;
tyre: tire
uni: university
ute: pick-up truck ("utility vehicle")
varsity: university
Vegemite: Australian yeast spread
wanker: jerk
wedges: large, thick slices of deep-fried potato; often served with sour cream
wellies: rubber boots
woolies: winter clothes; long underwear
Xena: "Xena, Warrior Princess" a TV show filmed in Northland
yob: see "hoon"
yonks: forever
zed: the letter "z"
zorb: to roll down a hill in a giant hamster ball

MAORI-ENGLISH DICTIONARY

(SEE ALSO **MAORI ARTS AND CULTURE, P. 55**)

ao: cloud
Aotearoa: Maori name for New Zealand
atua: gods or spirits
awa: river, valley
e noho ra: goodbye (said by the person leaving)
haere mai: welcome
haere ra: goodbye, farewell (said by the person staying)
haka: fierce war dance
hangi: underground Maori oven; also the meal
hapu: regional community
hau: wind
Hawaiki: mythical ancient homeland of the Maori
hoa: friend
hongi: Maori welcome expressed by the touching together of noses; literally, the "sharing of breath"
hui: meeting
ika: fish
iti: small
iwi: tribe, people, nation
ka pai: thank you; excellent

kai: food
kainga: village, town
karakia: chants, prayer
karanga: chant of welcome
kei te pehea koe: how are you? (one person)
kia ora: hello, health, luck
koe: you (singular)
korero: stories
koutou: you (plural)
kumara: sweet potato; a Maori food staple
mana: prestige, power
manaia: bird men
manga: river, stream
manuhiri: guest
Maoritanga: Maori culture
marae: a meeting place, sacred ground
maunga: mountain
mauri: essence of a natural state
mere: greenstone warclub
moana: sea, lake
moko: traditional facial tattoo
motu: island
namu: sandfly

noa: counterpart to tapu
nui: big, large
ngai, ngati: prefix indicating tribe, people, or clan
ngaru: wave
o: of
ora: life, alive, healthy, safe
pa: fortified Maori village, often on a hilltop
Pakeha: person of European descent; foreigner
patu: club (weapon)
pohatu: stone, rock
poi: a dance involving twirling balls on the ends of strings
pounamu: greenstone
powhiri: formal welcome ceremony
puna: spring (water)
rangi: the sky, the heavens
roto: lake
rua: two
takiwai: translucent greenstone
tane: man
tangata: humans, people

tangata whenua: local Maori people; "people of the land"
taniwha: water spirit, demon
taonga: highly treasured
taparahi: weaponless dances
tapu: taboo, holy, sacrosanct
te: the
teka: peace offering
tena-koe: hello (to one person)
tiki: small carved figurine of a human in wood, stone, or greenstone; when hung around the neck, a heitiki
tukutuku: woven reed panels frequently found in marae
tupuna: ancestors
umu: underground oven
wahi ngaro: lost aspects
wahine: woman
wai: water
waiata: traditional song, often of mourning or unrequited love; see p. 47
waka: canoe
wai: water
waiata: action songs
wero: challenge
whaikorero: welcome speech
whakama: ashamed or guilty
whanga: bay, body of water
whanau: family
whare: house
whenua: ground, land

FIJIAN-ENGLISH DICTIONARY

CONSONANTS
b = mb
d = nd
q = ng
g = ng
c = th

VOWELS
a = as in "watch"
e = as in "Che Guevara"
i = as in "knee"
o = as in "rope"
u = as in "Et tu, Brute?"

au vinakata ("aoo vina kahta"): I want
bele: a green, always boiled
bia ("bee-a"): beer
bilo: bowl for kava
bula ("mbula"): hello
bulumakau: cattle
bure/vale ("mburey/valey"): thatched house
ca ("tha"): bad
cakacaka ("thaka thaka"): work
dalo: taro (like potato)
Daru lako: Let's Go
dua ("ndua"): one
dua tale ("ndua ta lay"): one more
gone ("ngonay"): child
gunu ("goo noo"): drink
ika ("eekah"): fish
ilavo ("eelavo"): money
io ("ee-o"): yes
ivi: Fijian chestnut
jaina: banana
kakana: food
kana: eat
kanikani: scaly skin due to excessive kava
kauta mai ("ka ou tah my"): bring
koli: dog
koro: village
kumala: sweet potato
kuro: pot
kuwawa: guava
lailai ("lie lie"): small
lako mai ("la ko my"): come
lako tani ("la ko tanee"): go
levu ("layvu"): big, many
lilia ("leeah leeah"): stupid
lolo: coconut milk
maca ("matha"): thanks for kava
maleka: delicious
manumanu vuka: bird
maqo: mango
marama: lady
marau: happy
masese: matches
matai ("mahtye"): smart
meke: traditional Fijian dance
na cava oqo ("na thava on go"): what is this
nanoa: yesterday
ni mataka: tomorrow
ni sa bula ("nee sah mbula"): greetings/hello
ni sa moce ("ni sa moe-they"): goodbye
ni sa yadra ("ni sah yarn dra"): good morning
nikua: today
niu ("new"): coconut
puaka: pig
rua: two
sa moce ("sah more they"): goodbye
seqa ("senga"): no
sevusevu: gift
sitoa ("seetoah"): shop
sulu: sarong
tabua: tooth of sperm whale
tagane ("tahng-ahnay"): boy, male
tavako: tobacco
toa: chicken
totoka ("toe-toe-kah"): handsome, beautiful
tulou ("too low"): excuse me
ura: freshwater prawn
uto: breadfruit
uvi: yam
vaka lailai ("vaka lie lie"): little
vaka levu: plenty
vaka malua: slowly
vaka totolo: quickly
vale ni lotu ("valey nee lohtoo"): church
vale lailai ("valey lie lie"): toilet
vinaka ("vee naka"): thank you
vinaka vakalevu ("vee naka vakalevoo"): thank you very much
vivili: shellfish
vonu: turtle
wai: water
yalewa ("yah-lay-wah"): girl, female
yalo vinaka ("yarlo vee naka"): please
yavusa: extended family group derived from one original person

FIJIAN HINDI-ENGLISH DICTIONARY

aao: come
accha: good
baahut julum: very beautiful
chota: small (male)
choti: small (female)
dawai: medicine
dhanyabaadh: thank you
haan: yes
jao: go
kab: when
kahaan: where
kaise hai?: how are you?
khana: food
kitna?: how much?
kya: what
maaf kijye ga: excuse me
nahi: no
namaste: hello, goodbye
pani: water
rait: okay
roti: a flat Indian bread
sayit: maybe
yihaan: here

HOLIDAYS AND FESTIVALS

2003 DATE	HOLIDAY NAME	2003 DATE	HOLIDAY NAME
January 1-2	New Year	June 2	Ratu Sir Lala Sukuna Day (F)
February 6	Waitangi Day (NZ)	June 2	Queen's Birthday (NZ)
April 12	National Youth Day (F)	June 16	Queen's Birthday (F)
April 18	Good Friday	October 10	Fiji Day (F)
April 20	Easter	October 25	Diwali (F)
April 21	Easter Monday	October 27	Labour Day (NZ)
April 25	Anzac Day (NZ)	December 25	Christmas
May 12	Mohammed's Birthday (F)	December 26	Boxing Day

2003 DATE	FESTIVAL	LOCATION
January-February	Summer City Festival	Wellington (NZ)
February 14-23	Festival of Flowers	Christchurch (NZ)
February 10-25	HERO Gay and Lesbian Festival	Auckland (NZ)
February or March	Holi (Hindu Festival of Colours)	Fiji
March 8-9	Wild Foods Festival	Hokitika (NZ)
March or April	Ram Naumi (Hindu Birth of Lord Rama)	Fiji
April	Auckland-Suva Yacht Race	Auckland/Suva (NZ/F)
June 13-16	National Fieldays	Hamilton/Cambridge (NZ)
July	Bula Festival	Nadi (F)
July	International Film Festival	Auckland (NZ)
August	Winter Festival	Christchurch (NZ)
August	Hibiscus Festival	Suva (F)
August	Ritual Fire Walking (Hindu)	Suva (F)
September	Wearable Art Awards	Nelson (NZ)
September	Sugar Festival	Lautoka (F)
October 25	Diwali (Hindu Festival of Light)	Fiji

CLIMATE CHART

Av. Temp. lo/hi Precipitation	January			April			July			October		
	°C	°F	mm	°C	°F	mm	°C	°F	mm	°C	°F	mm
Auckland	16/23	61/73	79	13/19	55/66	97	8/13	46/55	145	11/17	52/63	102
Bay of Islands	14/25	57/77	12	17/26	89/95	12	15/19	47/59	12	25/30	58/99	12
Christchurch	12/21	54/70	56	7/17	45/63	482	2/10	36/50	69	7/17	45/63	56
Dunedin	10/19	50/66	86	7/15	45/59	71	3/9	37/48	79	6/15	43/59	89
Napier	14/24	57/75	74	10/19	50/66	76	5/13	41/55	102	9/19	48/66	56
Nelson	13/22	55/72	73	8/18	46/64	81	3/13	37/55	89	7/17	45/63	78
Queenstown	10/22	50/72	82	6/16	43/61	71	1/10	34/50	78	5/16	41/61	88
Rotorua	12/24	54/75	90	9/18	48/64	119	4/13	39/55	145	7/17	45/63	116
Wellington	13/21	55/70	81	11/17	52/63	97	6/12	43/54	137	9/16	48/61	102
Nadi (Fiji)	23/32	73/90	299	22/31	72/88	163	18/29	64/84	46	20/28	68/82	103
Suva (Fiji)	24/31	75/88	315	23/30	73/86	390	20/27	68/81	142	22/28	72/82	234

INDEX

A

Abaca 459
Abel Tasman Coastal Track 288
Abel Tasman National Park 285
Acacia Bay 203
Accident Compensation Corporation (ACC) 21, 29
accommodations
 bed and breakfasts (NZ) 38
 home exchanges and home rentals (NZ) 38
 homestays and farmstays (NZ) 38
 hostels (F) 43
 hostels (NZ) 35
 hotels (F) 43
 motor parks and camps 37
 resorts (F) 43
 village stays (F) 43
aerogrammes 39
Agrodome 167
Ahipara Gumfields 119
AIDS 21
Air New Zealand 30
air travel, domestic
 Fiji 42
 New Zealand 30
air travel, international 23
airfare 23
Akaroa 315
albatross 357
alcohol
 beer and wine 60
 safety 19
All Blacks 61
Alliance Party 430
America's Cup 55
American Express 16, 22, 25
amoebic meningitis 21
Anatoki eels 291
animals
 Fiji 64
 New Zealand 64
ANZAC 52
ANZUS Pact 53
Aoraki. See Mt. Cook National Park.
aquariums

National 195
aranaki 223
Aranui Cave 157
Arrowtown 372
art deco 194
Arthur's Pass 321
Arthur's Pass National Park 322
arts
 Fiji 437
 New Zealand 58
Astrolabe Reef 493
ATM cards 16
Auckland 76–98
 accommodations 85
 activities 96
 airport 76
 cafes 89
 daytrips 97
 entertainment 90
 Ferry Building 94
 food 87
 nightlife 91
  bars 91
  gay and lesbian nightlife 93
  nightclubs 92
 orientation 79
 practical information 83
 sights 93
 transportation 76, 82
Aupouri Peninsula 120
Australia and New Zealand Army Corps (ANZAC) 52
Automobile Association (AA) 35
Avon River 311

B

B&Bs 38
Ba 449
backpacker buses 31
backpackers (hostels) 35
backpacking. See tramping.
backpacks 69
Balclutha 395
banking 15
Banks Peninsula 315
Bau Landing 460
Baxter, James K. 58
Bay of Islands 109–119
Bay of Plenty 160–178

Baylys Beach 126
BBH 35
Beachcomber Island 470
bêche-de-mer 430
bed and breakfasts 38
Beehive 251
beer 60
Ben Lomond, Queenstown 371
Beqa 457
biking. See mountain biking.
bisexual travelers 27, 44
Black Christ mural 451
Black Magic 62
black stilt 64, 372
blackbirding 430
black-water rafting 157
Bledisloe Cup championship 61
Blenheim 271
Bligh, Captain William 429
blowholes 335
Blue Lagoon Beach 474
Blue Lagoon, The 437
Bluff 399
Bone People, The 58
Bouma National Heritage Park 492
Bouma Waterfalls. See Tavoro Waterfalls.
breweries
 DB, Timaru 324
 McCashin's, Nelson 283
 Miner's Brewery, Westport 334
 Monteith's, Greymouth 337
 Speight's, Dunedin 355
 Sunshine, Gisborne 184
 Wanaka Beerworks 382
Bridal Veil Falls 151
Broken River 318
Budget Backpacker Hostels 35
Bukuya 458
Buller River 333
Bunac 48
bungee rocket 172
bungy jump 72
 bridge of first 368
 Hanmer Springs 278

499

INDEX

Mt. Hutt 321
Queenstown 368
Rotorua 169
Taupo 204
Burns, Robert 350
bus travel
  Fiji 42
  New Zealand 31
Busby, James 51, 114
BYO 60

C

Cakobau, Ratu Seru 430
calling cards 25
Cambridge 147–148
campervans 37
camping 68
  environmentally responsible tourism 70
  equipment 69
  further reading and resources 75
  RVs and campers 37
camping in Fiji 43
Campion, Jane 59
Cannibal Bay 396
cannibalism in Fiji 429
canoeing
  Ohakune 217
  Punakaiki 335
  Stratford 227
  Whanganui River Journey 235
Canterbury 302–329
  skiing 316
Canterbury Museum 311
canyoning 72
  Auckland 97
  Queenstown 369
  Wanaka 384
Cape Foulwind 334
Cape Kidnappers 197
Cape Reinga 120
Caples Track. See Greenstone and Caples Track.
Caqelai 481
car travel
  Fiji 42
  New Zealand 33
    purchase in Auckland 83
caravans 37
Cardrona 383
Caroline Bay 324
carving
  Fiji 437
  New Zealand 57

Whitianga 137
Cascade Saddle 388
cash cards 16
casinos
  Auckland 91
  Christchurch 309
Cast Away 437
Castle Hill 323
Cathedral Caves 399
Cathedral Cove Marine Reserve 138
Catlins 394–399
Cave Stream Scenic Reserve 323
caves
  Arthur's Pass 323
  Greymouth 338
  Punakaiki 335
  Takaka 292
  Te Ana-au 410
  Waitomo 156
  Westport 333
Centers for Disease Control (CDC) 21
Centre of New Zealand Walk 283
Chalmers Track 313
Chateau 214
Chaudhry, Mahendra 431
children and travel 27
Christ Church Cathedral 311
Christchurch 302–314
  accommodations 306
  activities 313
  airport 302
  cafes 309
  daytrips 313
  entertainment 309
  food 308
  museums 311
  nightlife 310
  orientation 305
  practical information 306
  sights 311
  transportation 302, 305
  Wizard of 310
Church of the Good Shepherd 326
Cirrus 17
Clapham Clock Museum 108
Clark, Helen 54
Cleddau River 415
Clifden 425
climate 498
climbing 72
  Auckland 97
  Queenstown 372

Takaka 292
  Wharepapa South 154
clothing 23
Colac Bay 427
Collingwood 293
Colo-i-Suva Forest Park 466
Colville 135
condoms 23
conservation 65
Constitution Act (1852) 52
consulates
  in Fiji 41
  in New Zealand 28
consulates abroad
  Fiji 9
  New Zealand 9
Cook, Captain James 51, 429
Copland Track 347
Coral Coast 452–456
Coromandel (town) 132–135
Coromandel Forest Park 132
Coromandel Peninsula 127–141
Coromandel Walkway 135
Coronet Peak 370
Council Exchanges 48
Council Travel 24
Cousteau, Jacques 109
Craigieburn Forest Park 322
Craigieburn Valley 318
Crater Lake 165
Crater Rim Walkway 314
Craters of the Moon 202
credit cards 16
cricket 62
  Cambridge 148
  Wellington 250
Crowe, Russell 59
Curio Bay 399
currency
  Fiji Dollar 15
  New Zealand Dollar 15
current events. See New Zealand, current events or Fiji, current events.
Customs 15
cybercafes
  Fiji 44
  New Zealand 40
cycling. See mountain biking.

D

Dargaville 125–126

debit cards 17
dehydration 20
Denarau Island 442
Department of Conservation (DOC) 68
departure tax 18
Des Voeux Peak 489
designer waters
  Fiji water 450
Deuba 455
Deuba Beach 466
Devonport 97
dictionary. See glossary
dietary concerns 28
disabled travelers 27
  in Fiji 44
  in New Zealand 40
diseases
  amoebic meningitis 21
  giardia 21
  sexually transmitted 21
diving 73
  Astrolabe Reef (F) 493
  Beqa Lagoon (F) 456
  Mana Island (F) 470
  Marlborough Sounds (NZ) 269
  Milford Sound (NZ) 417
  Nadi (F) 445
  Ovalau (F) 480
  Paihia (NZ) 114
  Poor Knights Islands (NZ) 109
  Rainbow Reef (F) 489
  recompression chambers (F) 463
  Robinson Crusoe Island (F) 454
  Stewart Island (NZ) 404
  Tavewa (F) 475
  Vanua Levu (F) 484
dolphins. See swimming with dolphins.
Doubtful Sound 421
Doubtless Bay 119
drinking age 19
Driving Creek Railway 134
driving permit 32
drugs 19
drunk driving 29
Duff, Alan 58
dune surfing 75, 123
Dunedin 349–356
  accommodations 351
  activities 355
  cafes 353
  entertainment 353
  food 352
  nightlife 354
  orientation 350
  practical information 350
  sights 354
  transportation 350
Dusky Track 422
duty-free 15

E

East Cape 184–186
  camping 185
  lighthouse 186
East Coast 179–190
Eastern Taveuni 492
Edwin Fox 267
EFTPOS 29
Eglington Valley 414
Egmont National Park 223–226
Ellington Wharf 450
email 26
  in Fiji 44
  in New Zealand 40
embassies. See consulates.
emergency number
  Fiji, dial 000
  New Zealand, dial 111
Endeavour 51
Endless Summer, The 149
environment
  Fiji 437–438
  New Zealand 63–65
environmentally responsible tourism 70

F

Fairy Pools 119
Farewell Spit 293
farmstays 38, 228
Federal Express 25
female travelers. See women travelers.
Fenian Track 295
ferries
  Fiji 43
  New Zealand 30
festivals 498
Fiji
  animals 437
  arts 437
  clothing 432
  culture 432–437
  current events 430
  firewalking 457
  food and drink 436
  gift giving 432
  history 429–432
  plants and animals 437
  sports 432
  village etiquette 433
Fiji Museum, the 465
Fiji Visitors Bureau (FVB) 11
Fiji Water 450
film 23
  Fiji 437
  New Zealand 59
Fiordland National Park 406–428
firewalking 457
first-aid kit 23
firsts
  brewery in NZ 51
  bungy jump site 368
  car in NZ 52
  Christian sermon on NZ soil 50
  edition of *Let's Go New Zealand* 55
  European discovery of NZ 50
  female Prime Minister of NZ 55
  game of rugby in NZ 278
  kiwifruit cultivated in NZ 52
  licensed FM radio in NZ 53
  Maori king 51
  Mt. Everest summit 53
  New Zealand settlers 50
  rugby World Cup 54
  sheep on NZ soil 262
  suffrage for women 52
  television broadcast in NZ 53
  visit to NZ from sitting US President 55
  welfare, universal social 53
  woman elected to NZ Parliament 52
  woman to sail solo around the world 53
fishing
  Lake Mapourika 345
  Paihia 113
  Rotorua 168
  Taupo 205
  Tauranga 172
  Turangi 206
  Wanaka 384
  Whitianga 137
Fletcher Bay 135
flights. See scenic flights.
Florence Lookout 398
Fly By Wire 75
  Queenstown 369
  Wellington 255
Forest Parks
  Catlins 394

Coromandel 132
Craigieburn 322
Kaimanawa 207
Pirongia 151
Tararua 258
Waipoua 124
Whakarewarewa 169
Whirinaki 190
Forestry Department, Viti Levu 456
Foveaux Strait 402
Fox Glacier
  glacier hikes 347
Fox Glacier 346
Frame, Janet 58
Franz Josef Glacier 341
  glacier hikes 343
French Secret Service 112
frostbite 20
fruit-picking
  Blenheim 272
  Hastings 196
  Motueka 290
  Northland 118
  Tauranga 170

G

gannet, Australasian 197
Garden of the Sleeping Giant 444
gasoline. See petrol.
gay travelers 27, 44
General Delivery 25
genetically engineered foods 146
getting around Fiji
  by bus 42
  by car 42
  by ferry 43
  by plane 42
  by taxi 42
  by thumb 43
getting around New Zealand
  buy-backs 33
  by bus 31
  by car 32
  by ferry 30
  by plane 30
  by thumb 35
  by train 30
giardia 21
Gillespies Beach 347
girmitiyas 430
Gisborne 179–184
glacier hikes
  Fox Glacier 347
  Franz Josef Glacier 343

glassblowing
  Hokitika 340
  Nelson 283
Glenorchy 373
glossary
  Fijian-English 497
  Hindi-English 497
  Kiwi English 495
  Maori-English 496
glowworms 64
  Hokitika 340
  Te Ana-au 410
  Waitomo 156
Godley Head 313
gold mining
  Arrowtown 373
  Coromandel 135
  Thames 131
Golden Bay 285–295
golf
  Nadi 445
  Suva 467
  Wanaka 385
Gondwanaland 63
Goods and Services Tax (GST) 18
Gordon, Sir Arthur 430
government. See New Zealand, government or Fiji, government.
Grace, Patricia 58
Great Barrier Island 102
Great Exhibition Bay 121
Great Walks 71
  Abel Tasman Coastal Track 288
  Heaphy Track 296
  Kepler Track 411
  Lake Waikaremoana 189
  Milford Track 417
  Rakiura Track 404
  Routeburn Track 375
  Tongariro Northern Circuit 210
  Whanganui River Journey 235
Greenpeace. See *Rainbow Warrior*.
Greenstone and Caples Tracks 377
Grey, Governor George 52
Greymouth 335–338
GST 18

H

Habitat for Humanity 49
Hahei 138

haka 57
Halberg, Murray 60
Halfmoon Bay 402
Hamilton 142–147
hang gliding 369
hangi 56
  Queenstown 366
  Rotorua 168
hangi
  Christchurch 312
Hanmer Springs 277
Hastings 195
Hauraki Gulf 99–104
Hawera 228
Hawke's Bay 190–197
health 20
  Fiji 41
  New Zealand 29
Heaphy Track 296
heat exhaustion 20
heatstroke 20
Heke, Hone 51, 116
heliskiing 74
  Canterbury 321
  Queenstown 370
  South Canterbury 329
Hell's Gate 165
Hereheretaura Point 138
Hika, Hongi 116
hiking. See tramping
Hillary, Sir Edmund 60
history. See New Zealand, history or Fiji, history.
hitchhiking
  Fiji 43
  New Zealand 35
HIV 21
Hobson, Captain William 51
Hodgkins, Frances 58
hokey pokey (ice cream) 60
Hokianga region 122–124
Hokitika 338
holiday parks 37
holidays 498
Hollyford Track 415
home exchanges 38
Homer Tunnel 415
homestays 38
Honeycomb Cave 294
Hooker Valley 328
horse breeding 148
horse racing 148
horse treks
  Farewell Spit 294
  Glenorchy 374
  Great Barrier Island 104
  Kaikoura 276

Mt. Cook 329
Nelson 282
Otago Peninsula 358
Paihia 114
Punakaiki 335
Queenstown 371
Tauranga 173
Te Anau 411
Tekapo 326
Waiheke Island 102
Wanaka 385
Whitianga 138
Hostelling International 37
hot air ballooning 313
hot springs
 Hanmer Springs 278
 Hot Water Beach 139
 Mt. Maunganui 174
 Raglan 151
 Rotorua 168
 Taupo 202
 Turangi 207
Hot Water Beach 139
Huka Falls 204
Hulme, Keri 58
Hump Ridge Track 426
hunting
 Raglan 151
 Stratford 227
 Te Anau 411
huts 68
hypothermia 20

I

identification 13
Ihimaera, Witi 58
immunizations 20
independence
 Fiji 430
 New Zealand 53
innoculations 20
insurance
 car 33
 medical, trip, property, etc. 21
InterCity Coachline 31
Interior Highlands 456–460
Interislander ferry 243, 262
International Antarctic Centre 312
international calls 25
International Date Line 490
International Driving Permit (IDP) 32
International Student Identity Card (ISIC) 13, 22
International Teacher Identity Card (ITIC) 13, 22
International Youth Discount Travel Card (IYTC) 13
Internet 26
 cybercafes (F) 44
 cybercafes (NZ) 40
Invercargill 391–394

J

Jackson, Peter 59
jade 340
jetboating 73
 Christchurch (NZ) 313
 Glenorchy (NZ) 374
 Hanmer Springs (NZ) 278
 Nadi (F) 445
 Queenstown (NZ) 368
 Rotorua (NZ) 169
 Taupo (NZ) 205
 Tuatapare (NZ) 426
 Waitomo (NZ) 159
 Wanaka (NZ) 384
Joske's Thumb 467

K

Ka Levu Centre 453
Kadavu 493
kahikatea 63
Kahurangi National Park 295–301
Kai Iwi Lakes 126
Kaikoura 273–277
Kaimanawa Forest Park 207
Kaitaia 119
Kaiteriteri Beach 291
Kaiwhakauka Track 234
Kaka Point 396
kakapo 64
Kapiti Coast 253
Kapiti Island 254
Karamea 294
Karikari Peninsula 119
Katiki Point 360
Kauaeranga Valley 132
kauri 63
 Ancient Kauri Kingdom, Ltd. 119
 logging 131
 museum 126
 Tane Mahuta 124
 Te Matua Ngahere 124
 Thames 131
 Waiau Kauri Grove 134
 Waipoua Forest Park 124

kava 436
kayaking 74
 Abel Tasman National Park (NZ) 287
 Akaroa (NZ) 316
 Doubtful Sound (NZ) 421
 Great Barrier Island (NZ) 104
 Hahei (NZ) 139
 Kaikoura (NZ) 276
 Lake Tekapo (NZ) 326
 Marlborough Sounds (NZ) 269
 Milford Sound (NZ) 417
 Mt. Cook (NZ) 329
 Okarito (NZ) 340
 Otago Peninsula (NZ) 358
 Paihia (NZ) 113
 Rotorua (NZ) 168
 Stewart Island (NZ) 404
 Taupo (NZ) 205
 Taveuni (F) 491
 Waiheke Island (NZ) 102
 Wanaka (NZ) 384
kea 64, 332
Kelly Tarlton's Museum of Shipwrecks 115
Kelly Tarlton's Underwater World 95
Kepler Track 411
kereru 64
Kerikeri 116
King Country 142–159
King Movement 52
Kings Road 449–452
kiwi (bird) 64
 National Kiwi House 340
 Otorohanga 153
 Queenstown 372
Kiwi Experience 31
Knob's Flat 415
Kohukohu 124
Kokobula Scenic Viewpoint 459
Korolevu 454
Koroyanitu National Heritage Park 459
kosher, keeping 28
kumara 59
Kupe 122

L

Labasa 484
Labour Party (NZ) 53
Labour Unity Party (F) 431
Lakabuta Village 454
Lake Brunner 338

INDEX

Lake Ellesmere 315
Lake Gunn 415
Lake Hauroko 426
Lake Kai Iwi 126
Lake Mapourika 345
Lake Matheson 347
Lake Monowai 426
Lake Pupuke 98
Lake Rotoiti 284
Lake Rotorua 168
Lake Tagimaucia 489
Lake Taharoa 126
Lake Taupo 204
Lake Te Anau 406
Lake Waikareiti 188
Lake Waikaremoana 189
Lake Waikere 126
Lake Wakatipu 371
Lake Wanaka 383
Lake Wilkie 399
Lapita people 429
Larnach Castle 358
Lautoka 445
Lavena Coastal Walk 492
Lawai Village 454
Lawless, Lucy 59
Leleuvia 481
lesbian travelers 27, 44
Levuka 477–481
libraries
  Auckland University Library 94
  National Library 251
  National Library, Wellington 251
literature 58
Lolo Waterfall 458
Lomaiviti Group 476–481
  Caqelai 481
  Leleuvia 481
  Ovalau 476
Lomanisue Beach 452
Lonely Bay 137
loos
  musical 123
  Superloo 203
  toilet capital 415
Lord of the Rings 59
Lovelock, Jack 60
lovo 436
Lovoni Village 480
Lower Wainibau Waterfalls 492
luge
  Queenstown 372
  Rotorua 169
luggage 22

Lye, Len 59
Lyttelton 313

M

Magic Bus 32
mail 25
  General Delivery 25
  Poste Restante 25
  sending mail home from Fiji 43
  sending mail home from New Zealand 39
Mamanuca Group 468–471
  Beachcomber Island 470
  Mana Island 469
Mana Island (F) 469
Mana Island (NZ) 254
Manapouri 420
Manganui Ski Field 227
Mangapurua Track 234
Mansfield, Katherine 58
  birthplace 250
Manu Bay 149
Maori
  28th Battalion 53
  arts and culture 55–58
  basic concepts 56
  film 59
  King Movement 52, 142
  land rights 54
  settlement 50
  sovereignty 51
  tribal structure 56
Maoritanga 55–58
  basic concepts 56
  carving 57
  dance 57
  marae 56
  moko 57
  song 57
  tribal structure 56
Mara, Sir Ratu Sir Kamisese 430
marae
  Gisborne 183
  National (Nga Hau E Wha) 312
  Rotorua 168
  Taumarunui 239
  Whanganui National Park 236
Marlborough 262–278
Marlborough Sounds 267–271
Marsh, Dame Ngaio 58
Martinborough 257
masa 437

Massey University 258
Masterton 257
Matacawalevu 476
matai 63
Matauri Bay 112
Matei 490
Maui 50
Mayor Island 173
maze
  Omapere 122
  Wanaka 382
McCahon, Colin 58
McLean Falls 399
Medic Alert 20
meke 437
Mercury Bay 137
Methven 319
Metro Cave 333
Michael Fowler Centre 251
Milford Road 414
Milford Sound 415
Milford Track 417
Mine Bay 203
minority travelers 27, 44
miro 63
Mirror Lakes 414
Mission Bay 95
moa 63
Moana 338
Model Mugging 18
Moeraki 360
moko 57
money 15
  costs 17
  credit cards 16
  currency and exchange rates 15
  EFTPOS 29
  Fiji Dollar 15
  getting money from home 17
  New Zealand Dollar 15
  taxes 18
  tipping and bargaining 17
  traveler's checks 16
Monkey Island 428
Monteith's Brewing Co. 337
Mosquito Island 466
motor parks and camps 37
Motueka 290
Motutapu Island 99
mountain biking 73
  Christchurch 313
  Coromandel 134
  Great Barrier Island 104
  Hanmer Springs 278
  Marlborough Sounds 269
  Ohakune 217

Paihia 114
Queenstown 370
Tongariro National Park 213
Wanaka 384
Wanganui 233
Whangamata 141
mountaineering 73
Mt. Cook 329
Mt. Arnaud 284
Mt. Aspiring National Park 386
Mt. Batilamu 460
Mt. Cargill 356
Mt. Cheeseman 318
Mt. Cook (village) 327
Mt. Cook National Park 327–329
Mt. Eden 93
Mt. Egmont (Taranaki) 223
Mt. Hobson (Hirakimata) 104
Mt. Hutt 319
Mt. Iron 385
Mt. John 326
Mt. Karioi 151
Mt. Korobaba 467
Mt. Lyford 318
Mt. Maunganui 173
Mt. Moehau 136
Mt. Nadelaiovalau 479
Mt. Ngauruhoe 207
Mt. Olympus 318
Mt. Pirongia 151
Mt. Ruapehu 207
Mt. Somers 321
Mt. Taranaki (Egmont) 223
Mt. Taranaki Round-the-Mountain Circuit 225
Mt. Tarawera 166
Mt. Tongariro 207
Mt. Victoria 251
music 58
muttonbird 64

N

Nacula 474
Nacula Tikina 474–476
  Matacawalevu 476
  Nacula 474
  Nanuya Lailai 474
  Tavewa 475
  Yaqeta 476
Nadi 439–445
  accommodations 443
  activities 445
  airport 439

  food 443
  nightlife 444
  orientation and practical information 442
  sights 444
  transportation 439
Naiserelagi Catholic Mission 451
Naiserelagi Village 451
Nananu-i-ra 451
Nanuya Lailai 474
Napier 190–195
Naqara 488
Natadola Beach 453
National Federation Party (NFP) 430
National Maritime Museum 94
National Park Village 212
National Parks
  Abel Tasman (NZ) 285
  Aoraki/Mt. Cook (NZ) 327
  Arthur's Pass (NZ) 322
  Bouma National Heritage Park (F) 492
  Egmont (NZ) 223
  Fiordland (NZ) 406
  Kahurangi (NZ) 295
  Koroyanitu National Heritage Park (F) 459
  Mt. Aspiring (NZ) 386
  Nelson Lakes (NZ) 283
  Paparoa (NZ) 334
  Rakiura (NZ) 400
  Te Urewera (NZ) 186
  Tongariro (NZ) 207
  Westland (NZ) 341
  Whanganui (NZ) 233
Native Lands Act
  1865 52
  1873 52
  1909 53
Nausori Highlands. See Interior Highlands.
Navala 457
Navilawa 459
Naviti 473
Neill, Sam 59
Nelson 278–283
Nelson Lakes National Park 283
New Plymouth 219–222
New Zealand
  animals 64
  arts 58
  culture 55
  current events 54
  film 59
  food and drink 59

  government 54
  government, early 52
  government, today 54
  history 50
  literature 58
  music 58
  plants 63
  religion 55
  sports 60
New Zealand Tourism Board (NZTB) 11
Ninety Mile Beach 120
North Cape 121
North Shore, Auckland 97
North West Circuit Track 403
Northern Tip 135
Northland 105–126
nuclear power 54
Nugget Point 396
Nukumarorika-i 466

O

Oakura 223
Oamaru 358
Oban 402
Ohakune 214
Ohinemutu 167
Ohope Beach 177
Okarito 340
Old Town Hall, Suva 465
older travelers 26, 40
Olveston 354
Omahuta Forest 119
omandel 132
Omapere 122
ommodations 216
Omorehu Waterfall 238
Once Were Warriors 58
One Beach 452
One Tree Hill 93
Oparara Basin 294
Opo 123
Opononi 123
Opotiki 177
Opoutere 139
Opunake 223
Orakei Basin 95
Orakei Korako 202
Orana Park Wildlife Reserve 312
Orchestra. See Philharmonic.
orchids 444
Orepuki 427
Otago (region) 348–389

Otago Peninsula 356
Otago University 355
Otaki Gorge Rd. 258
Otara 399
Otorohanga 152
Outer Islands 468–494
Ovalau 476–481
　Levuka 477
　Lovoni Village 480
Owaka 396
Owhanga 237

P

Pacific Harbour 455
packing 22
packs 69
Paekakariki 255
Paihia 109–114
Pakeha 55
Palmerston North 258–261
pancake rocks 335
Paparoa National Park 334
Papatowai 398
Paquin, Anna 59
Paradiso Cinema 382
paragliding 74
　Christchurch 313
　Napier 195
　Nelson 283
　Queenstown 369
　Sumner 314
　Takaka 292
　Wanaka 384
Paraparaumu 255
parasites 21
Parliament, Fijian (Vale Ni Bose Lawa) 466
Parliament, NZ 54, 251
passports 11
penguins 64
　blue 359
　yellow-eyed 357, 360, 396
Percy Burn Viaduct 427
Pereira, Fernando 112
personal locator beacon (PLB) 70
petrol 34
Philharmonic
　Auckland 90
　New Zealand 90
phone cards 25
phones 25
Piano, The 59, 98
picking fruit. See fruit-picking.
Picton 262

Pihanga 207
Pipriki 238
Pirongia Forest Park 151
placing international calls 25
planes. See air travel.
plants
　Fiji 437
　New Zealand 63
plants and animals. See environment.
PLB 70
pohutukawa 64
Polynesian Spa 168
Poor Knights Islands 109
population
　Fiji 432
　New Zealand 55
Porirua 254
Porpoise Bay 399
Porter Heights 318
possums 411
postal services. See mail.
Poste Restante 25
prescription drugs 19
psychedelic rocks 376
Public Works Department, Viti Levu 456
Pukenui 121
Puketi Forest 119
Punakaiki 334
Punakaiki 334
Pupu Springs 292
Purakaunui Bay and Falls 398
Puzzling World 382

Q

Qarase, Laisenia 431
Queen Charlotte Track 269
Queenstown 361–372
　accommodations 364
　activities 367
　bungy jump 368
　food 365
　jetboating 368
　nightlife 366
　orientation 363
　practical information 363
　rafting 368
　skiing 370
　transportation 361
　walks 371

R

Rabuka, Lt. Col. Sitiveni 430
radiophone 44
Raetihi 237
rafting 73
　Christchurch 313
　Greymouth 338
　Hanmer Springs 278
　Karamea 296
　Queenstown 368
　Rotorua 169
　Tauranga 172
　Turangi 207
　Waitomo 157
　Westport 333
Raglan 149–151
Rainbow Reef 489
Rainbow Springs 167
Rainbow Warrior 54, 112
rainfall 498
Rakiraki 450
Rakiura National Park 400–405
Rakiura Track 404
Rangipo Desert 207
Rangitoto Island 99
rata 64
Raurimu Spiral 239
Ravilevu Nature Reserve 493
Rawene 123
Rawhiti Caves 292
recompression chambers 463
recreational vehicles 37
Red Rocks 252
Red Tarns 328
Rees-Dart Track 386
religion
　Fiji 432
　New Zealand 55
Remarkables, The 370
Return to the Blue Lagoon 437
rimu 63
River Road, the (Whanganui) 237
Riverton 428
Roaring Bay 396
rock climbing. See climbing.
Rotorua 161–169
　accommodations 163
　activities 168
　hangi 168
　hot springs 168

INDEX ■ 507

museums 167
sights 164
skydiving 169
zorbing 169
Round-the-Mountain Track (Tongariro) 209
round-the-world tickets 24
Routeburn Track 375
Routeburn Valley 374
Royal Ballet 90
rugby 61
  Bledisloe Cup 61
  league 62
  New Zealand Rugby Museum 261
  Super 12 league 61
  Suva 467
  Tri-Nations Games 61
  union 61
Russell 115
Rutherford, Ernest 312
RVs 37

S

safety and security 18
  accommodations and transportation 19
  drugs and alcohol 19
  financial security 19
  in Fiji 41
  in New Zealand 29
  personal safety 18
  prescription drugs 19
  self defense 18
  valuables, protecting 19
sailing
  America's Cup 62
  Auckland 97
  Paihia 113
  Taupo 203
  Te Anau 411
  Wanaka 384
sandflies 64
Savuione Waterfall 459
Savulevu Yavonu Falls 493
Savusavu 482
scenic flights
  Franz Josef and Fox Glaciers 344
  Milford Sound 417
  Mt. Cook 329
  Paihia 113
  Queenstown 369
  Te Anau 411
scuba diving. See diving.
sea kayaking. See kayaking.

security. See safety and security.
self-defense 18
senior travelers. See older travelers.
sexually transmitted diseases (STDs) 21
Shag Point 361
Shakespeare Lookout 137
Shantytown 338
Shearing Shed 159
Shipley, Jenny 54
shuttle buses 32
Sigatoka 452
  sand dunes 453
Sign of the Takahe 313
Singh, Vijay 432
skiing 74
  Canterbury 316
  Cardrona 383
  Coronet Peak 370
  Mt. Hutt 319
  Mt. Lyford 277
  Mt. Taranaki (Egmont) 227
  Nelson Lakes 284
  Queenstown 370
  Snow Park 383
  South Canterbury 327
  Southern Alps 316
  The Remarkables 370
  Tongariro National Park 210
  Treble Cone 383
  Turoa 210
  Waiorau Snow Farm 383
  Whakapapa 210
Sky City 78
skydiving 74
  Auckland 97
  cheapest 204
  Franz Josef and Fox Glaciers 344
  Napier 195
  Nelson 283
  Paihia 114
  Queenstown 369
  Rotorua 169
  Taupo 204
  Tauranga 172
  Te Anau 411
  Wanaka 384
Skyline Gondola 371
sledging 74
  Rotorua 169
  Wanaka 384
sleeping bag 69
Slope Point 399
slurp hole 397
Snell, Peter 60, 233
Snow Park 383

snowboarding. See skiing.
solo travel 26
Somosomo 488
South Canterbury 323–329
Southern Lakes 361–389
Southern Scenic Route 424–428
Southern Taveuni 491
Southland 391–405
special program visas 46
specific concerns
  bisexual, gay, and lesbian travelers 27, 44
  children and travel 27
  dietary concerns 28
  disabled travelers 27, 40, 44
  minority travelers 27, 44
  older travelers 40
  solo travel 26
  women travelers 26, 44
Speight, George 431
Speight's 355
spelunking. See caves.
Spirits Bay 121
sports
  cricket 62
  in Fiji 432
  in New Zealand 60
  rugby 61
  sailing 62
St. Arnaud 283
St. Francis Xavier Parish 451
St. Helier's Bay 95
STA Travel 24
State Department, US 17
STDs 21
Stewart Island 400–405
Stratford 226
student ID. See identification.
student visas 46
study abroad 46
Sugar Mill Factory 486
Sumner 314
sunburn 20
Super 12 league 61
Surat Bay 396
surfing 75
  dune surfing (NZ) 123
  Hot Water Beach (NZ) 139
  Manu Bay (NZ) 150
  Raglan (NZ) 150
  Suva (F) 467
  Tauranga Bay (NZ) 334
  Wanganui (NZ) 233
  Wellington (NZ) 253
  Whangamata (NZ) 141

508 ■ INDEX

Yanuca Island (F) 456
Sutherland Falls 420
Suva 460–467
  accommodations 463
  activities 466
  food 463
  nightlife 464
  orientation 462
  practical information 462
  sights 465
  transportation 460
Suva Municipal Market 465
Suva Old Town Hall 465
Suva Private Hospital 462
Swami Temple 444
swimming with dolphins 73
  Akaroa 316
  Auckland 97
  Greymouth 338
  Kaikoura 275
  Paihia 113
  Tauranga 172
  Whakatane 176

T

tagimaucia flower 489
Tahunanui Beach 283
Tai Island. See
  Beachcomber Island
Taiaroa Head 356
Taieri Gorge 355
takahe 64
Takaka 291
Takapuna Beach 98
Tane Mahuta 124
Taniwha Caves 338
tapa. See *masi.*
Tapotupotu Bay 121
Taranaki (region) 218–229
Tararua Forest Parks 258
Tasman, Abel 50, 429
Tattooed Rocks 151
Taumarunui 238
Taupo 198–205
  bungy jump 204
  fishing 205
  hot springs 202
  skydiving 204
Tauranga 170–173
Tauranga Bay 334
Tautuku Beach 398
Taveuni 486–493
  Eastern Taveuni 492
  Matei 490
  Naqara 488
  Somosomo 488
  Southern Taveuni 491

Wairiki 488
Waiyevo 488
Tavewa 475
Tavoro Waterfalls 492
Tavua 449
Tavuni Hill Fort 453
taxes
  departure tax (F) 18
  departure tax (NZ) 18
  Goods and Services Tax (NZ) 18
  Value Added Tax (F) 18
Taylor's Mistake 314
Te Ana-au Caves 410
Te Anau 406–411
Te Kanawa, Dame Kiri 59, 156
Te Matua Ngahere 124
Te Papa (Museum of New Zealand) 250
Te Urewera National Park 186–190
Te Waikoropupu Springs 292
Tekapo 325
telephones 25
  calling home from NZ and Fiji 25
  calling within Fiji 44
  calling within NZ 39
temperature 498
Temple Basin 318
tents 69
terrorism 19
Thames 129
thermal areas. See hot springs.
ticks 21
Timaru 323
tipping 17
toilets. See loos.
Tonga Island Marine Reserve 287
Tongariro National Park 207–212
Tongariro Northern Circuit 210
Tongariro River 206
Top 10 Holiday Parks 38
totara 63
tourism board. See New Zealand Tourism Board (NZTB) or Fiji Visitors Bureau (FVB).
trails. See tramping.
trains 30
tramping 68–72

Department of Conservation (DOC) 68
environmentally responsible tourism 70
equipment 69
Great Walks 71
huts and camping 68
wilderness safety 70
tramps
  Abel Tasman Coastal Track 288
  Dusky Track 422
  Greenstone and Caples Tracks 377
  Heaphy Track 296
  Hump Ridge Track 426
  Kepler Track 411
  Lake Waikaremoana 189
  Milford Track 417
  Queen Charlotte Track 269
  Rakiura Track 404
  Rees-Dart Track 386
  Routeburn Track 375
  Tongariro Northern Circuit 210
  Wangapeka Track 300
  Whanganui River Journey 235
transportation. See getting around New Zealand or Fiji
TranzAlpine 321, 335
TranzRail 30
TranzScenic 30
travel agencies 24
traveler's checks 16
traveling alone 26
Travers-Sabine Circuit 284
Treaty of Waitangi 51
Treaty of Waitangi Act (1975) 53
Treble Cone 383
trekking. See tramping.
Tri-Nations Games 61
Tuatapere 425
tuatara 64
Tunnel Beach 355
Tunnel Hill 396
Turangi 205
Turoa 210
Tutukaka 109

U

Udre Udre's Tomb 451
Ulva Island 400
universities
  Auckland 94
  Massey 258

INDEX ■ 509

Otago 355
  Waikato 142
University of the South Pacific (USP) 466
Urupukapuka Island 112
US State Department 17

V

vaccinations 20
Vaileka 450
Vale Ni Bose Lawa (Fijian Parliament) 466
valuables 19
Value Added Tax (VAT) 15, 18
Vanua Levu 481–486
  Labasa 484
  Savusavu 482
VAT 15, 18
Vatura Dam 459
vegetarians 28
Verenu Falls 459
Vidawa Rainforest Hike 491
vilavilairevo 457
village stays 43
village visits
  Abaca 459
  Bukuya 458
  Lakabuta Village 454
  Lawai Village 454
  Naidi Village 484
  Naiserelagi Village 451
  Navala 457
  Viseisei Village 448
vineyards. See wineries.
Visa 16
visas 13, 46
Viseisei Village 448
visitor permits 13
Visitor's Information Network (VIN) 28
visitors bureau. See New Zealand Tourism Board (NZTB) or Fiji Visitors Bureau (FVB).
Viti Levu 439–467
volcanoes
  Mt. Eden 93
  Mt. Maunganui 173
  Mt. Ngauruhoe 207
  Mt. Ruapehu 207
  Mt. Tarawera 166
  Mt. Tongariro 207
  White Island 176
volunteer abroad 49

Vuda Point 448
Vunisea 494

W

Waddell, Rob 61
Waiau Waterworks, the 134
Waiheke Island 99–102
Waikato 142–159
Waikato University 142
Waikawa 399
Waimangu Volcanic Valley 165
Waingaro Hot Springs 151
Wainibau Stream 492
Wainui Falls 291
Waiomu Kauri Grove 131
Waiorau Snow Farm 383
Wai-o-tapu 165
Waipapa Point 399
Waipoua 124
Waipoua Forest Park 124
Wairakei Park 203
Wairarapa 257
Wairaurahiri River 426
Wairiki 488
Waisila Creek and Falls 466
Waitabu Marine Park 491, 493
Waitakere Ranges 98
Waitangi 114
  Day Act (1960) 53
  National Reserve 114
  Treaty of 51
  Treaty of Waitangi Act (1975) 53
Waitavala Waterslide 490
Waitomo 154–159
  caving 156
Waiyevo 488
wake boarding 384
Wanaka 378–385
  accommodations 380
  activities 383
  food 381
  nightlife 382
  orientation and practical information 380
  sights 382
  skiing 383
  transportation 378
Wanganui 229–233
Wangapeka Track 300
wars
  Maori Wars 52
  Musket Wars 51

New Zealand Wars 52
World War I 52
World War II 53
water purification 69
Waya and Wayasewa (Waya Lailai) 471
weather 498
welfare, universal social 53
Wellington 240–253
  accommodations 245
  activities 252
  airport 240
  beaches 253
  cafes 247
  entertainment 248
  ferries 243
  food 246
  nightlife 249
    bars 249
    bars with dance floors 249
    clubs 250
  orientation 243
  Parliament 251
  practical information 244
  sights 250
  transportation 240
West Coast 330–347
Western Union 17
Westland National Park 341
Westport 330–334
weta 64
Whakapapa (ski field) 210
Whakapapa Village 214
Whakarewarewa Forest Park 169
Whakarewarewa Thermal Reserve 165
Whakatane 175
whale watching 276
Whangamata 140
Whanganui National Park 233–238
Whanganui River Journey 235
Whangaparaoa Peninsula 98
Whangarei 105–109
Whangaroa 120
Wharekawa Harbour Sandspit Wildlife Reserve 140
Wharepapa South 153
Whirinaki Forest Park 190
Whitbourn Glacier 388
White Island 176
whitewater rafting. See rafting.

INDEX

Whitianga 136
wilderness safety 70
Williams, Yvette 60
Willing Workers on Organic Farms (WWOOF) 49
Willowbank Wildlife Reserve 312
windsurfing
   Nananu-i-ra (F) 452
   Whangamata (NZ) 141
wine 60
wineries
   Auckland 97
   Blenheim 272
   Gisborne 184
   Hahei 139
   Napier 194
   Queenstown 372
   Tauranga
   Waiheke Island 102
   Wanaka 385
Wizard of Christchurch 310
women travelers 26
   in Fiji 44
   in New Zealand 40
work abroad 47
work permits 46
work visas 46
World Wide Web (WWW) 45

Y

Yanuca Island 456
Yaqeta 476
yaqona. See kava.
Yasawa Group 471–476
   Nacula Tikina 474
   Naviti 473
   Waya and Wayasewa (Waya Lailai) 471
YHA 37
Young Nick's Head 183

Z

ziplines
   Queenstown 369
zoos
   Auckland 96
   Wellington 252
zorbing 75
   Paihia 114
   Rotorua 169

Stay in Touch While Traveling!

With the LET'S GO Phonecard

Powered by

The Global Phonecard with More!

- Save up to 85% on calls & receive messages wherever you go.
- Friends and Family can leave voice messages for FREE!
- Access to FREE internet services designed especially for travelers!

Activate your Let's Go Phonecard today!

Go to www.letsgo.ekit.com or call 1-800-706-1333 in the US. Receive 15 minutes FREE* when you charge $20 by quoting reference code LGMAG01.

*based on call UK to US using economy access numbers. All amounts in US$.

MAP INDEX

Abel Tasman National Park 286
Auckland 80-81
Auckland Overview 79
Bay of Plenty 160
Canterbury 303
Canterbury Ski Fields 317
Catlins Coastline 394
Christchurch 304
Coromandel Peninsula 128
Dunedin 349
East Cape 184
East Coast and Hawke's Bay 180
Fiji 434-435
Fiordland 407
Gisborne 181
Greymouth 336
Hamilton 144
Heaphy Track and Kahurangi National Park 297
Invercargill 391
Kadavu 493
Kaikoura 273
Kepler Track 412
Lake Rotorua 166
Lautoka 446
Levuka 478
Mamanuca Group 468
Marlborough and Nelson 264
Marlborough Sounds and Queen Charlotte Walkway 268
Milford, Routeburn, and Greenstone and Caples Track 418
Mt. Cook and Westland National Parks and Franz Josef and Fox Glaciers 342
Nadi 441
Napier 191
Nelson 279
New Plymouth 219
New Zealand 2
North Island 77
Northland 106
Northwest Circuit and Rakiura Track and Stewart Island 401
Otago 348
Outdoor New Zealand: North Island 66
Outdoor New Zealand: South Island 67
Ovalau 476
Paihia 111
Palmerston North 259
Picton 266
Ponsonby 86
Queenstown 362
Rees-Dart Track 387
Rotorua 161
South Island 263
Southland 390
Suva 461
Taranaki and Wanganui 218
Taupo 200
Taupo and Tongariro 198
Tauranga 171
Taveuni 487
Te Anau 408
Te Urewera National Park and Lake Waikare-Moana Track 187
The Milford Road 414
The Waikato and King Country 143
The West Coast 331
Tongariro Northern Circuit 208
Vanua Levu 482
Viti Levu 440
Waitomo 154
Wanaka 379
Wanganui 230
Wellington 242
Wellington and Around 241
Whanganui River Journey 235
Yasawa Group 472

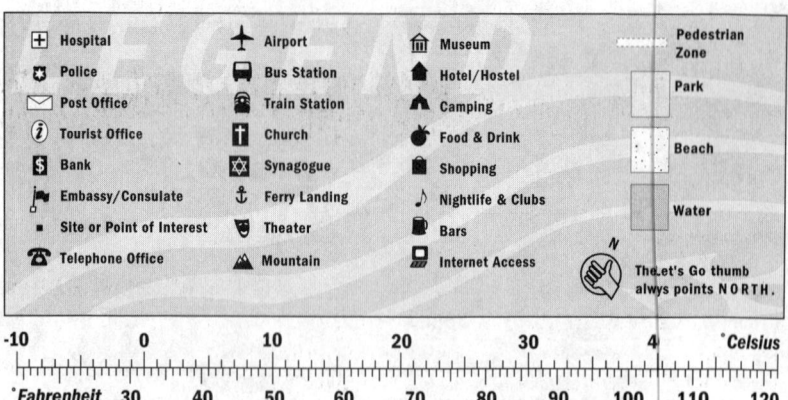